Contents

Preface

This twenty-second annual volume of the ***Index*** was produced with the cooperation of 287 participating periodicals from Canada, the United States, and the Caribbean. More than 7,100 entries for individual poets and translators are included, with some 20,000 entries for individual poems. A separate index provides access by title or first line.

The importance of the ***Index*** grows as its necessity becomes more apparent in circles of contemporary poetry research. The increasing demand for inclusion corroborates this fact. The ***Index*** constitutes an objective measure of poetry in North America, recording not only the publication of our own poets in Canada, the U.S., and the Caribbean, but also those from other lands and cultures and from other times. Of course, the ***Index***'s primary purpose is to show what poems have been published by particular poets, what poems have been translated by particular translators, and who wrote poems with particular titles or first lines. But taken together, the ***Index*** reveals trends and influences: the ebb and flow of particular poets, as well as the influence of cultures of other lands and times as represented by their poets published in North American journals.

James D. Anderson has made a major contribution to the ***Index*** by designing and refining computer programs that greatly facilitate the indexing process, proof-reading and error-checking, control of cross-references and consistency in names, sorting, formatting, and typesetting. To him also goes credit for managing relations with participating journals and for seeing that indexing gets done in a timely and accurate manner. Also, I want to express my sincere appreciation to Martha Park Sollberger, librarian *emerita*, for her valuable assistance.

Rafael Catalá
Co-Editor

Introduction

Scope

The ***Index of American Periodical Verse*** indexes poems published in a broad cross-section of poetry, literary, scholarly, popular, general, and "little" magazines, journals, and reviews published in the United States, Canada, and the Caribbean. These periodicals are listed in the "Periodicals Indexed" section, together with name of editor(s), address, issues indexed in this volume, and subscription information. Selection of periodicals to index is the responsibility of the editors, based on recommendations of poets, librarians, literary scholars, and publishers. Publishers participate by supplying copies of all issues to the editors. Criteria for inclusion include the quality of poems and their presentation and the status or reputation of poets. Within these very broad and subjective guidelines, the editors attempt to include a cross-section of periodicals by type of publisher and/or publication, place of publication, language, and type of poetry. Periodicals published outside of North America are included only if they have North American editors.

Compilation

Citation data are compiled using the WordStar word-processing program, version 4, on a 286 MS/DOS computer. "Shorthand" macro programs are used to repeat author headings for multiple poems by the same poet, create translator entries from author entries for translated poems, and transform complex author names into cross-reference entries. Sorting is done by "IOTA Big Sort," a fast program for sorting very large files written by Fred A. Rowley. Title entries are extracted from the original author entries. Sorted and formatted entries are transferred to a Macintosh computer with laser printer for typesetting and page formatting using Microsoft Word™ and PageMaker™ programs.

Persons interested in the precise details of compilation, including the computer programs used for error-checking, sorting, and formatting, should write to the editors at P.O. Box 38, New Brunswick, NJ 08903-0038. The ***Indexes*** for 1982 through 1992 are available from the editors on micro-computer disks.

Names and Cross-References

Because many poets have compound surnames and surnames containing various prefixes, we recognize the need for systematic provision of cross-references from alternative forms of surname to the form chosen for entry in the ***Index***. We have included cross-references whenever the form used for entry does not fall under the last part or element of the name. In addition, many poets publish under different forms of the same name, for example, with or without a middle initial. When poets are known to use different forms of the same name, alternative forms may be indicated using the format authorized by the *Anglo-American Cataloguing Rules*, Second Edition. For example:

WHEATLEY, Pat (Patience)

This heading indicates that this poet has poems published under two forms of name: Pat Wheatley and Patience Wheatley.

When two or more different names refer to the same poet, one name will be chosen, with "see" references to the chosen name from other names. When it is not possible to determine with assurance whether a single poet is using variant forms of name or different poets have similar names, both names will be used. In such cases, "see also" references may be added to headings to remind users to check the variant name forms that might possibly refer to the same poet.

Format and Arrangement of Entries

The basic format and style of the ***Index*** remain unchanged. Poets are arranged alphabetically first by surname, then by forenames. In creating this alphabetical sequence, we have adopted principles of alphanumeric arrangement adopted in 1980 by the American Library Association and the Library of Congress. Names are arranged on the basis of their spelling, rather than their pronunciation, so that, for example, names beginning with "Mac" and "Mc" are no longer interfiled. Similarly, the space consistently counts as a filing element, so that similar compound and prefixed surnames are often separated by some distance, as illustrated in the following examples. Note that "De BOLT" precedes "DeBEVOISE" by a considerable number of entries.

De ANGELIS
De BOLT
De GRAVELLES
De LOACH
De PALCHI
De RONSARD
De VAUL
DEAL
DeBEVOISE
DeFOE
DEGUY
Del VECCHIO
DeLISLE
DeMOTT
DENNISON
Der HOVANESSIAN
DESY
DeYOUNG

Van BRUNT
Van DUYN
Van HALTEREN
Van TOORN
Van TROYER
Van WERT
Van WINCKEL
VANCE
Vander DOES
VANDERBEEK
VanDEVENTER

Abbreviations are also arranged on the basis of spelling, rather than pronunciation, so that "ST. JOHN" is *not* filed as "SAINT JOHN," but as "S+T+

space+JOHN." Punctuation, signs, and symbols other than alphabetic letters and numerals are not considered; a hyphen is filed as if it were a space and apostrophes and accents are ignored for purposes of filing. In title entries, initial articles are also ignored. Numerals, including Roman numerals, are arranged in numerical order preceding alphabetical letters rather than as if they were spelled out.

Under each poet's name, poems are arranged alphanumerically by title or, if there is no title, by first line. Poems with only "Untitled" printed as if it were the title are entered as "Untitled" plus the first line of the poem. In the title index, two entries are provided, one under "Untitled" plus the first line, and one directly under the first line. Numbered poems are handled in the same way. Under poets, initial numbers are treated as the first part of titles, and they are so entered. In the title index, they are entered both under their initial numbers and under the part following the number, if any.

Poem titles and first lines are placed within quotation marks. All significant words of titles are capitalized, but in first lines, only the first word and proper nouns are capitalized. Incomplete excerpts from larger works are followed by the note "Excerpt" or "Excerpts," or, if they are presented as complete sections, by "Selection" or "Selections." The title, first line, or number of excerpts or selections may follow if given in the publication. For example:

WALCOTT, Derek
"Midsummer" (Selections: XXXIV-XXXVI). [Agni] (18) 83, p. 5-7.

WEBB, Phyllis
"The Vision Tree" (Selection: "I Daniel"). [PoetryCR] (5:2) Wint 83-84, p. 11.

WAINWRIGHT, Jeffrey
"Heart's Desire" (Excerpt: "Some Propositions and Part of a Narrative"). [Agni] (18) 83, p. 37.

WATTEN, Barret
"One Half" (Excerpts). [ParisR] (24:86) Wint 82, p. 112-113.

If an excerpt is treated as a complete "sub-work," it receives an independent entry, with reference to the larger work in a note. For example:

ANDERSON, Jack
"Magnets" (from "The Clouds of That Country"). [PoNow] (7:2, #38) 83, p. 23.

Notes about dedications, joint authors, translators, and sources follow the title, enclosed in parentheses. A poem with more than one author is entered under each author. Likewise, a translated poem is entered under each translator, as well as its author(s). Each entry includes the names of all authors and all translators. Multiple authors or translators are indicated by the abbreviation "w.," standing for "with." Translators are indicated by the abbreviation "tr. by," standing for "translated by," and original authors are indicated by the abbreviation "tr. of," standing for "translation of." For example:

AGGESTAM, Rolf
"Old Basho" (tr. by Erland Anderson and Lars Nordström). [NewRena] (16) Spr 83, p. 25.

ANDERSON, Erland
"Old Basho" (tr. of Rolf Aggestam, w. Lars Nordström). [NewRena] (16) Spr 83, p. 25.

NORDSTRÖM, Lars
"Old Basho" (tr. of Rolf Aggestam, w. Erland Anderson). [NewRena] (16) Spr 83, p. 25.

The periodical citation includes an abbreviation standing for the periodical title, followed by volume and issue numbers, date, and pages. The periodical abbreviation is enclosed in square brackets. An alphabetical list of these periodical abbreviations is included at the front of the volume, followed by the full periodical title, name of editor(s), address, the numbers of the issues indexed for this volume of the ***Index***, and subscription information. A separate list of indexed periodicals is arranged by full periodical title, with a reference to the abbreviated title. Volume and issue numbers are included within parentheses, e.g., (16:5) stands for volume 16, number 5; (21) refers to issue 21 for a periodical that does not use volume numbers. Dates are given using abbreviations for months and seasons. Year of publication is indicated by the last two digits of the year, e.g., 92. Please see the separate list of abbreviations at the front of the volume.

Compiling this year's ***Index*** has been an adventure into the wealth and variety of poetry published in U. S., Caribbean, and Canadian periodicals as well as the intricacies of bringing this richness together and organizing it into a consistent index. The world of poetry publication is a dynamic one, with new periodicals appearing, older periodicals declining, dying, reviving, and thriving. This year saw the loss of nine periodicals and the addition of ten new ones. Both deleted and newly added periodicals are listed at the front of the volume. Keeping up with these changes is a big job, and we solicit our readers' suggestions as to periodicals that should be included in future volumes of the ***Index***, and also, periodicals that could be dropped. Editors who would like their periodicals considered for inclusion in future volumes should send sample issues to:

Rafael Catalá, Editor
Index of American Periodical Verse
P.O. Box 38
New Brunswick, NJ 08903-0038

Although indexing is indispensable for the organization of any literature, so that particular works can be found when needed and scholarship and research facilitated, it is a tedious business. I know that we have made mistakes. We solicit your corrections and suggestions, which you may send to me at the above address.

James D. Anderson
Co-Editor

Abbreviations

dir., dirs.	director, directors
ed., eds.	editor, editors
(for.)	price for foreign countries
(ind.)	price for individuals
(inst.)	price for institutions
(lib.)	price for libraries
NS	new series
p.	page, pages
po. ed.	poetry editor
pub.	publisher
(stud.)	price for students
tr. by	translated by
tr. of	translation of
U.	University
w.	with

Months

Ja	January	Jl	July
F	February	Ag	August
Mr	March	S	September
Ap	April	O	October
My	May	N	November
Je	June	D	December

Seasons

Aut	Autumn	Spr	Spring
Wint	Winter	Sum	Summer

Years

87	1987	90	1990
88	1988	91	1991
89	1989	92	1992

Periodicals Added

Periodical acronyms are followed by titles. Full information may be found in the list of periodicals indexed.

Arion: ARION: A Journal of Humanities and the Classics

Art&Und: ART & UNDERSTANDING: The Journal of Literature and Art About AIDS

Conscience: CONSCIENCE: A Newsjournal of Prochoice Catholic Opinion

Epiphany: EPIPHANY: A Journal of Literature

Eyeball: EYEBALL

Light: LIGHT: A Quarterly of Humorous, Occasional, Ephemeral & Light Verse

Luz: LUZ: En Arte y Literatura

Noctiluca: NOCTILUCA: An International Magazine of Poetry

NoCarLR: NORTH CAROLINA LITERARY REVIEW

Sun: SUN: A Magazine of Ideas

Periodicals Deleted

ApalQ: APALACHEE QUARTERLY, Barbara Hamby, Pam Ball, Bruce Boehrer, Claudia Johnson, Paul McCall, eds., P.O. Box 20106, Tallahassee, FL 32316. No 1991 or 1992 issues received. Letters not answered.

BlueBldgs: BLUE BUILDINGS: An International Magazine of Poetry, Translations and Art, Guillaume Williams, ed., Dept. of English, Drake U., Des Moines, IA 50311. "Ceased publishing manuscripts in 1990" — letter, January 1993; last issue received was #12 (1990).

CuadP: CUADERNOS DE POÉTICA, Diógenes Céspedes, Director, Apartado Postal 1736, Santo Domingo, Dominican Republic; US Editors: Kate Nickel, 1111 Oldfather Hall, U. of Nebraska, Lincoln, NE 68588-0315, Rafael Catalá, P.O. Box 38, New Brunswick, NJ 08903. No 1991 or 1992 issues received. Letters not answered.

Imagine: IMAGINE: International Chicano Poetry Journal, Tino Villanueva, ed., 89 Mass. Ave., Suite 270, Boston, MA 02115. No 1991 or 1992 issues received. Letters not answered.

KanQ: KANSAS QUARTERLY, Harold Schneider, Ben Nyberg, W. R. Moses, John Rees, eds., Dept. of English, Denison Hall, Kansas State U., Manhattan, KS 66506-0703. No 1991 or 1992 issues received. Letters not answered.

LakeSR: THE LAKE STREET REVIEW, Kevin FitzPatrick, ed., Box 7188, Minneapolis, MN 55407. No. 25, indexed in the 1991 volume, was "the final issue."

PlumR: THE PLUM REVIEW, M. Hammer, Christina Daub, eds., 1654a Avon Pl. NW, Washington, DC 20007. No 1992 issues received. Letter returned, "moved, not forwardable."

SwampR: SWAMP ROOT, Al Masarik, ed., Route 2, Box 1098, Hiwassee One, Jacksboro, TN 37757. No 1992 issues received. Letter returned.

Timbuktu: TIMBUKTU, Molly Turner, ed., pub., RR 1, Box 758, Scottsville, VA 24590. No. 6 was "last issue"; No. 5 was not received.

Periodicals Indexed

Arranged by acronym, with names of editors, addresses, issues indexed, and subscription information. New titles added to the *Index* in 1992 are marked with an asterisk (*).

13thMoon: 13TH MOON : A Feminist Literary Magazine, Judith Emlyn Johnson, ed., Jill Hanifan, Judith Johnson, Mary Ann Murray, Sharon Stenson, po. eds., Dept. of English, State U. of NY, Albany, NY 12222. Issues indexed: (10:1/2). Subscriptions: $8/1 vol., $15/2 vols., $21.50/3 vols; Back issues: $6.50-$8/vol.

Abraxas: ABRAXAS, Ingrid Swanberg, ed., 2518 Gregory St., Madison, WI 53711. Issues indexed: No 1992 issues published -- No. 42 expected in Fall 93. Subscriptions: $12/4 issues; Single issue: $3; Double issues: $6.

Aerial: AERIAL, Rod Smith, ed., P.O. Box 25642, Washington, DC 20007. Issues indexed: No 1992 issues received. Subscriptions: $20/3 issues; Single issue: $7.50; Double issues: $15.

AfAmRev: AFRICAN AMERICAN REVIEW, Division on Black American Literature and Culture, Modern Language Association, Joe Weixlmann, ed., Dept. of English, Indiana State U., Terre Haute, IN 47809. Issues indexed: (26:1-4). Subscriptions: $20/yr. (ind.), $40/yr. (inst.), $27/yr. (for.), $47/yr. (for. inst.). Single issue: $10, $12 (for.).

Agni: AGNI, Askold Melnyczuk, ed., Creative Writing Program, Boston U., 236 Bay State Rd., Boston, MA 02115. Issues indexed: (35-36). Subscriptions: $12/yr., $23/2 yrs., $34/3 yrs.; $24/yr. (inst.); plus $4/yr. (for.); Single issue: $7.

Amelia: AMELIA, Frederick A. Raborg, Jr., ed., 329 "E" St., Bakersfield, CA 93304. Issues indexed: 19-20. Subscriptions: $25/yr. (4 issues), $48/2 yrs., $70/3 yrs.; $27/yr., $52/2 yrs., $76/3 yrs. (Canada, Mexico); $41/yr., $80/2 yrs., $88/3 yrs. (for. air mail); Single issue: $7.95, $8.50 (Canada & Mexico), $12 (for. air mail).

Americas: THE AMERICAS REVIEW, A Review of Hispanic Literature and Art of the USA, Julián Olivares, ed., U. of Houston, Houston, TX 77204-2090. Issues indexed: (19:2-3/4, 20:1-3/4). Subscriptions: $15/yr. (ind.), $20/yr. (inst.); Single and back issues: $5; Double issues. $10.

AmerPoR: THE AMERICAN POETRY REVIEW, Stephen Berg, David Bonanno, Arthur Vogelsang, eds., 1721 Walnut St., Philadelphia, PA 19103. Issues indexed: (21:1-6). Subscriptions: $14/yr., $25/2 yrs., $35/3 yrs.; $17/yr., $31/2 yrs., $44/3 yrs. (for.); classroom rate $7/yr. per student; Single issue: $3. PA residents add 6% periodical tax.

AmerS: THE AMERICAN SCHOLAR, Joseph Epstein, ed., The Phi Beta Kappa Society, 1811 Q St. NW, Washington, DC 20009. Issues indexed: (61:1-4). Subscriptions: $21/yr., $38/2 yrs., $57/3 yrs.; $25/yr., $46/2 yrs., $69/3 yrs. (inst.); plus $3/yr. (for.); Single issue: $5.75; $7 (inst.).

AmerV: THE AMERICAN VOICE, Frederick Smock, eds., The Kentucky Foundation for Women, Inc., 332 West Broadway, Suite 1215, Louisville, KY 40202. Issues indexed: (26-29). Subscriptions: $15/yr.; Back issues: $5; Single issue: $4.

AnotherCM: ANOTHER CHICAGO MAGAZINE, Barry Silesky, ed. & pub., 3709 N. Kenmore, Chicago, IL 60613. Issues indexed: 23-24. Subscriptions: $15/yr., $60/5 yrs., $199.95/lifetime; Single issue: $8.

Antaeus: ANTAEUS, Daniel Halpern, ed., The Ecco Press, 100 W. Broad St., Hopewell, NJ 08525. Issues indexed: (68-69). Subscriptions: $30/4 issues; Single issue: $10; Double issues: $15.

AnthNEW: THE ANTHOLOGY OF NEW ENGLAND WRITERS, Frank Anthony, ed., New England Writers/Vermont Poets Association, P.O. Box 483, Windsor, VT 05089. Issues indexed: (4).

AntigR: THE ANTIGONISH REVIEW, George Sanderson, ed., St. Francis Xavier U., Antigonish, Nova Scotia B2G 1C0 Canada. Issues indexed: (89-91). Subscriptions: $18/4 issues; Single issue: $5.

AntR: THE ANTIOCH REVIEW, Robert S. Fogarty, ed., David St. John, po. ed., P.O. Box 148, Yellow Springs, OH 45387. Issues indexed: (50:1/2-4). Subscriptions: $25/yr. (4 issues), $44/2 yrs., $62/3 yrs. (ind.); $36/yr., $66/2 yrs., $96/3 yrs. (inst.); $44/yr. (for.); Single issue: $5.50. Subscription address: P.O. Box 626, Dayton, OH 45459-0626.

Arc: ARC, John Barton, Nadine McInnis, eds., P.O. Box 7368, Ottawa, Ont. K1L 8E4 Canada. Issues indexed: (28-29). Subscriptions: $18/4 issues (2 years, USA and Canada); $22/yr. (for.); Single issue: $6 (USA and Canada), $7 (for.); Back issues: $2-$3.

Archae: ARCHAE, Alan Davis Drake, ed., 10 Troilus, Old Bridge, NJ 08857-2724. Issues indexed: (3-4). Subscriptions: $13/yr. (2 issues); $17/yr. (for.); Single issue: $7, $9 (for.).

Areíto: AREITO, Andrés Gómez, Director, P.O. Box 44-1803, Miami, FL 33144. Issues indexed: Segunda Epoca (3:10/11-12). Subscriptions: $12/yr. (ind.), $20/yr. (inst.), $18/yr. (for. ind.), $30/yr. (for. inst.).

*Arion: ARION: A Journal of Humanities and the Classics, Herbert Golder, ed., 745 Commonwealth Ave., Boston, MA 02215. Issues indexed: 3rd series (1:1-3, 2:1). Subscriptions: $19/yr. (3 issues, ind.), $35/yr. (inst.), $12/yr. (students), plus $3/yr. (for.); Subscription address: Arion, c/o Office of Scholarly Publications, Boston U., 985 Commonwealth Ave., Boston, MA 02215.

*Art&Und: ART & UNDERSTANDING: The Journal of Literature and Art About AIDS, David Waggoner, ed., Suite 205, 25 Monroe St., Albany, NY 12210. Issues indexed: (1:1-5). Subscriptions: $18/yr. (6 issues), $24/yr. (Canada), $36/yr. (elsewhere); Back issues: $5 plus $1 postage and handling; Single issue: $3.50, $4.50 (Canada).

ArtfulD: ARTFUL DODGE, Daniel Bourne, Karen Kovacik, eds., Dept. of English, College of Wooster, Wooster, OH 44691. Issues indexed: (23/23). Subscriptions: $10/2 double issues (ind.), $16/2 double issues (inst.); Single issue: $5.

Ascent: ASCENT, Audrey Curley, Mark Costello, Paul Friedman, Rocco Fumento, Philip Graham, Carol LeSeure, Jerry Mirskin, George Scouffas, Jean Thompson, Michael Van Walleghen, Kirsten Wasson, eds., P.O. Box 967, Urbana, IL 61801. Issues indexed: (16:3, 17:1). Subscriptions: $6/yr. (3 issues), $5.50/yr. (for.); Single issue: $2 (bookstore), $3 (mail).

Asylum: ASYLUM, Greg Boyd, ed., P.O. Box 6203, Santa Maria, CA 93456. Issues indexed: (7:3/4); vol. 7, no. 1 & 2 not received: "a special fiction issue that contained no verse." Subscriptions: $10/yr. (ind.), $15/yr. (inst.), plus $2/yr. (for.); Single issue: $5.

Atlantic: THE ATLANTIC, William Whitworth, ed., Peter Davison, po. ed., 745 Boylston St., Boston, MA 02116-2603. Issues indexed: (269:1-6, 270:1, 3-6). Subscriptions: $15.94/yr., $27.95/2 yrs., $39.95/3 yrs., plus $8/yr. (Canada), $12/yr. (for.); Single issue: $2.95. Subscription address: Atlantic Subscription Processing Center, Box 52661, Boulder, CO 80322.

Avec: AVEC: A Journal of Writing, Cydney Chadwick, ed., P.O. Box 1059, Penngrove, CA 94951. Issues indexed: (5:1). Subscriptions: $12/2 issues, $22/4 issues; $15/issue (inst.); Single issue: $7.50.

BambooR: BAMBOO RIDGE: The Hawaii Writers' Quarterly, Eric Chock, Darrell H. Y Lum, Holly Yamada, eds., P.O. Box 61781, Honolulu, HI 96839-1781. Issues indexed: (55/56). Subscriptions: $16/yr. (4 issues); Single issue, $4; Double issues: $8.

BellArk: BELLOWING ARK, Robert R. Ward, ed., P.O. Box 45637, Seattle, WA 98145. Issues indexed: (8:1-6). Subscriptions: $15/yr. (6 issues), $24/2 yrs.; Single issue: $3.

BellR: THE BELLINGHAM REVIEW, Susan E. Hilton, ed., 1007 Queen St., Bellingham, WA 98226. Issues indexed: (15:1-2, #31-32). Subscriptions: $5/yr. (2 issues), $9.50/2 yrs., $12.50/3 yrs.; plus $1/yr. (for.); through agencies, $6/yr.; Single issue: $2.50.

BelPoJ: THE BELOIT POETRY JOURNAL, Marion K. Stocking, ed., RR 2, Box 154, Ellsworth, ME 04605. Issues indexed: (42:3-4, 43:1-2). Subscriptions: $12/yr. (4 issues, ind.), $33/3 yrs.; $18/yr., $49.50/3 yrs. (inst.); plus $3.20/yr. (Canada), $3.70/yr. (for.); Single issue: $4.

BilingR: THE BILINGUAL REVIEW / LA REVISTA BILINGÜE, Gary D. Keller, ed., Hispanic Research Center, Arizona State U., Tempe, AZ 85287-2702. Issues indexed: (17:1-3). Subscriptions: $16/yr., $30/2 yrs., $42/3 yrs. (ind.); $28/yr. (inst.).

BlackALF: BLACK AMERICAN LITERATURE FORUM *see* AfAmRev: AFRICAN AMERICAN REVIEW (title change).

BlackBR: BLACK BEAR REVIEW, Ave Jeanne, po. ed., 1916 Lincoln St., Croydon, PA 19021. Issues indexed: (15-16). Subscriptions: $10/yr. (2 issues); Single issue: $5.

BlackWR: BLACK WARRIOR REVIEW, Glenn Mott, ed., James H. N. Martin, po. ed., U. of Alabama, P.O. Box 2936, Tuscaloosa, AL 35486-2936. Issues indexed: (18:2). Subscriptions: $9/yr. (ind.), $14/yr. (inst.); Single issue: $4.

Blueline: BLUELINE, Anthony O. Tyler, ed., Stephanie Coyne-DeGhett, Robert G. Foster, Jon Chatlos, Janice Londraville, Richard Londraville, Alan Steinberg, po. eds., English Dept., Potsdam College, SUNY, Potsdam, NY 13676. Issues indexed: (13). Single issue: $6.

Bogg: BOGG, John Elsberg, ed., 422 N. Cleveland St., Arlington, VA 22201. Issues indexed: (65). Subscriptions: $12/3 issues; Single issue: $4.50.

Bomb: BOMB MAGAZINE, Betsy Sussler, ed. & pub., Roland Legiardi-Laura, po. ed., New Art Publications, P.O. Box 2003, Canal Station, New York, NY 10013. Issues indexed: No 1992 issues received. Subscriptions: $16/yr., $30/2 yrs.; $26/yr. (for.); Single issue: $4.

BostonR: BOSTON REVIEW, Kim Cooper, managing ed., Sean Broderick, po. ed., 33 Harrison Ave., Boston, MA 02111. Issues indexed: (17:1-2, 3/4, 5-6). Subscriptions: $15/yr., $30/2 yrs. (ind.); $18/yr., $36/2 yrs. (inst.); plus $6/yr. (Canada, Mexico); plus $12/yr. (for.); Single issue: $4.

Boulevard: BOULEVARD, Richard Burgin, ed., Drexel U., P.O. Box 30386, Philadelphia, PA 19103. Issues indexed: (7:1, 7:2/3, #19, 20/21). Subscriptions: $12/3 issues, $20/6 issues, $25/9 issues; Single issue: $6; make checks payable to Opojaz, Inc.

BrooklynR: BROOKLYN REVIEW, Michael K. Franklin, Barbara Weisberg, po. eds., David Trinidad, faculty advisor, Dept. of English, Brooklyn College, Brooklyn, NY 11210. Issues indexed: (9). Subscriptions: $6/issue.

Caliban: CALIBAN, Lawrence R. Smith, ed., P.O. Box 561, Laguna Beach, CA 92652. Issues indexed: (11). Subscriptions: $10/yr. (2 issues), $18/2 yrs. (ind.); $17/yr. (inst.); plus $2/yr. (for.); Single issue: $6.

Callaloo: CALLALOO: A Journal of African-American and African Arts and Letters, Charles H. Rowell, ed., Dept. of English, Wilson Hall, U. of Virginia, Charlottesville, VA 22903. Issues indexed: (15:1-4). Subscriptions: $22/yr. (ind.), $47/yr. (inst.); plus $5.30 (Canada, Mexico); plus $17 (outside North America, airfreight); Subscription address: The Johns Hopkins University Press, Journals Publishing Division, 701 W. 40th St., Suite 275, Baltimore, MD 21211-2190.

CalQ: CALIFORNIA QUARTERLY, Jack Hicks, ed., Kristin Steege, po. ed., 159 Titus Hall, U. of California, Davis, CA 95616. Issues indexed: (37). Subscriptions: $14/yr. (4 issues); Single issue: $4.

Calyx: CALYX: A Journal of Art and Literature by Women, Margarita Donnelly, Managing ed., Catherine Holdorf, Susie Lisser, Barbara Rohde, Linda Varsell Smith, eds, P.O. Box B, Corvallis, OR 97339-0539. Issues indexed: (14:1-2). Subscriptions: $18/yr. (3 issues), $32/2 yrs., $42/3 yrs.; $22.50/yr. (inst.); $30/yr. (Canada); $36/yr. (for.); $15/yr. (low income ind.); Single issue: $8 plus $1.25 postage.

CanLit: CANADIAN LITERATURE, W. H. New, ed., U. of British Columbia, 2029 West Mall, Vancouver, B.C. V6T 1Z2 Canada. Issues indexed: (132-135). Subscriptions: $30/yr. (ind.), $45/yr. (inst.) plus $5/yr. outside Canada; Single issue: $15.

CapeR: THE CAPE ROCK, Harvey Hecht, ed., Southeast Missouri State U., Cape Girardeau, MO 63701. Issues indexed: (27:1-2). Subscriptions: $5/yr. (2 issues); Single issue: $3.

CapilR: THE CAPILANO REVIEW, Robert Sherrin, ed., Capilano College, 2055 Purcell Way, North Vancouver, B.C. V7J 3H5 Canada. Issues indexed: (Series 2:8-9). Subscriptions: $25/yr. (3 issues plus supplement), $45/2 yrs.; plus $5/yr. (USA, for.); Single issue: $9.

CarolQ: CAROLINA QUARTERLY, Amber Vogel, ed., Julia Stockton, po. ed., Greenlaw Hall CB#3520, U. of North Carolina, Chapel Hill, NC 27599-3520. Issues indexed: (44:2-3, 45:1). Subscriptions: $10/yr. (ind.), $12/yr. (3 issues) (inst.), $11/yr. (for.); Single issue: $5.

CentR: THE CENTENNIAL REVIEW, R. K. Meiners, ed., College of Arts and Letters, 312 Linton Hall, Michigan State U., East Lansing, MI 48824-1044. Issues indexed: (36:1-3). Subscriptions: $12/yr., $18/2 yrs., plus $4.50/yr. (for.); Single issue: $6.

CentralP: CENTRAL PARK, Stephen-Paul Martin, Eve Ensler, eds., Box 1446, New York, NY 10023. Issues indexed: (21). Subscriptions: $15/yr., 2 issues (ind.), $20/yr. (inst.); Single issue: $7.50 (ind), $9 (inst).

ChamLR: CHAMINADE LITERARY REVIEW, Loretta Petrie, ed., Chaminade U. of Honolulu, 3140 Waialae Ave., Honolulu, HI 96816. Issues indexed: (10/11). Subscriptions: $10/yr. (2 issues); $18/2 yrs.; plus $2 (for.).; Single issue: $5.

ChangingM: CHANGING MEN: Issues in Gender, Sex and Politics, Rick Cote, Michael Biernbaum, eds., 306 N. Brooks St., Madison, WI 53715; Bob Vance, po. ed., 1024 Emmet St., Petosky, MI 49770. Issues indexed: (24). Subscriptions: $24/4 issues, $40/4 issues (inst.); $16/4 issues (limited income); $27/4 issues (Canada & Mexico); $40/4 issues (for., air mail); Single issue: $6.

CharR: THE CHARITON REVIEW, Jim Barnes, ed., Northeast Missouri State U., Kirksville, MO 63501. Issues indexed: (18:1-2). Subscriptions: $9/4 issues; Single issue: $2.50.

ChatR: THE CHATTAHOOCHEE REVIEW: The DeKalb College Literary Quarterly, Lamar York, ed., Collie Owens, po. ed., 2101 Womack Road, Dunwoody, GA 30338-4497. Issues indexed: (12:2-4, 13:1). Subscriptions: $15/yr. (4 issues), $25/2 yrs.; Single issue: $4.

Chelsea: CHELSEA, Sonia Raiziss, ed., P.O. Box 5880, Grand Central Station, New York, NY 10163. Issues indexed: (53). Subscriptions: $11/yr. (2 issues or 1 double issue), $20/2 yrs.; $14/yr., $27/2 yrs. (for.); Single issue: $6, $7 (for.).

ChiR: CHICAGO REVIEW, David Nicholls, ed., Anne Myles, po. ed., 5801 South Kenwood, Chicago, IL 60637. Issues indexed: (37:4, 38:1/2-3). Subscriptions: $20/ yr. (ind.), $40/2 yrs., $60/3 yrs., plus $5/yr. (for.); $30/yr. (inst.); Single issue: $5.

ChironR: CHIRON REVIEW, Michael Hathaway, ed., Rt. 2 Box 111, St. John, KS 67576. Issues indexed: (11:1-4). Subscriptions: $8/yr. (4 issues); $16/yr. (for.); $20/yr. (inst.); Single issue: $2; $4. (for.).

ChrC: THE CHRISTIAN CENTURY, James M. Wall, ed., 407 S. Dearborn St., Chicago, IL 60605-1150. Issues indexed: (109:1-38). Subscriptions: $32/yr.; Single issue: $1.75.

CimR: CIMARRON REVIEW, Gordon Weaver, ed., Thomas Reiter, Randy Phillis, Sally Shigley, po. eds., 205 Morrill Hall, Oklahoma State U., Stillwater, OK 74078-0135. Issues indexed: (98-101). Subscriptions: $12/yr., $15 (Canada); $30/3 yrs., $40 (Canada); plus $2.50/yr. (for.); Single issue: $3.

CinPR: CINCINNATI POETRY REVIEW, Dallas Wiebe, ed., Dept. of English 069, U. of Cincinnati, Cincinnati, OH 45221. Issues indexed: (23). Subscriptions: $9/4 issues; Single issue: $3; Sample copies: $2.

CityLR: CITY LIGHTS REVIEW, Nancy J. Peters, ed., Lawrence Ferlinghetti, pub., City Lights Books, 261 Columbus Ave., San Francisco, CA 94133. Issues indexed: (5). Single issue: $11.95.

ClockR: CLOCKWATCH REVIEW: A Journal of the Arts, James Plath, ed., Dept. of English, Illinois Wesleyan Univ., Bloomington, IL 61702-2900. Issues indexed: No issues published in 1992. Subscriptions: $8/yr. (2 issues); Single issue: $4; Double issues: $8.

CoalC: COAL CITY REVIEW, Brian Daldorph, Sandra Tompson, eds., 1324 Connecticut, Lawrence, KS 66044. Issues indexed: (5). Subscriptions: $6/2 issues; Single issue: $4.

ColEng: COLLEGE ENGLISH, National Council of Teachers of English, Louise Z. Smith, ed., Helene Davis, Thomas Hurley, po. eds., Dept. of English, UMass-Boston, Boston, MA 02125. Issues indexed: (53:5-54:8). Subscriptions: $40/yr. (ind.), $50/yr. (inst.), plus $6/yr. (for.); Single issue: $6.25; NCTE, 1111 W. Kenyon Rd., Urbana, IL 61801-1096.

ColR: COLORADO REVIEW, David Milofsky, ed., Dept. of English, Colorado State U., 360 Eddy Bldg., Fort Collins, CO 80523. Issues indexed: (NS 19:1-2). Subscriptions: $15/yr. (2 issues), $25/2 yrs.; plus $4/yr. (for.); Single issue: $8. Subscription address: University Press of Colorado, P.O. Box 849, Niwot, CO 80544.

Colum: COLUMBIA: A Magazine of Poetry & Prose, Paul Gediman, David Elliott Kidd, eds., Richard Dock, Sarah Kennedy, po. eds., Graduate Writing Division, 404 Dodge Hall, Columbia Univ., New York, NY 10027. Issues indexed: No 1992 issues received. Subscriptions: $11/yr. (2 issues).

Comm: COMMONWEAL, Margaret O'Brien Steinfels, ed., Rosemary Deen, po. ed., 15 Dutch St., New York, NY 10038. Issues indexed: (119:1-22). Subscriptions: $36/yr., $39/yr. (Canada), $41/yr. (for.); $62/2 yrs., $66/2 yrs. (Canada), $72/2 yrs. (for.), ; Single issue: $2.

Confr: CONFRONTATION, Martin Tucker, ed., English Dept., C. W. Post Campus of Long Island U., Brookville, NY 11548. Issues indexed: (48/49, 50). Subscriptions: $10/yr., $20/2 yrs., $30/3 yrs.; plus $5/yr. (for.).; Single issue: $10.

Conjunc: CONJUNCTIONS: Bi-Annual Volumes of New Writing, Bard College, Bradford Morrow, ed., 33 W. 9th St., New York, NY 10011. Issues indexed: (18-19). Subscriptions: Bard College, Annandale-on-Hudson, NY 12504; $18/yr. (2 issues), $32/2 yrs. (ind.); $25/yr., $45/2 yrs. (inst., for.); Back and single issues: $10.

ConnPR: THE CONNECTICUT POETRY REVIEW, J. Claire White, Reginald A. Speers, eds., P.O. Box 3783, Amity Station, New Haven, CT 06525. Issues indexed: (11:1). Single issue: $3 (including postage).

*Conscience: CONSCIENCE: A Newsjournal of Prochoice Catholic Opinion, Maggie Hume, ed, Andrew Merton, po. ed., Catholics for a Free Choice, 1436 U St. NW, Washington, DC 20009-3997. Issues indexed: (13:1-4). Subscriptions: $10/yr.; Single issue: $3.50; Back issues: $1-3.

Contact: CONTACT II: A Poetry Review, Maurice Kenny, J. G. Gosciak, eds., P.O. Box 451, Bowling Green, New York, NY 10004. Issues indexed: (10:62/63/64). Subscriptions: $10/yr. (ind.); $16/yr. (inst.); Single issue: $6.

ContextS: CONTEXT SOUTH, David Breeden, po. ed., pub., Box 4504, Schreiner College, 2100 Memorial Blvd., Kerrville, TX 78028-5697. Issues indexed: No 1992 issues received. Subscriptions: $10/3 issues; Single issue: $3.

CrabCR: CRAB CREEK REVIEW, Linda Clifton, ed., 4462 Whitman Ave. N., Seattle WA 98103. Issues indexed: (8:1). Subscriptions: $8/volume (3 issues), $15/2 volumes; plus $5/volume (for.); Single issue: $3.

Crazy: CRAZYHORSE, Zabelle Stodola, managing ed., Ralph Burns, po. ed., Dept. of English, U. of Arkansas, 2801 S. University, Little Rock, AR 72204. Issues indexed: (42-43). Subscriptions: $10/yr. (2 issues), $18/2 yrs., $27/3 yrs. Single issue: $5.

CreamCR: CREAM CITY REVIEW, Sandra Nelson, eds., Aedan Hanley, Amy Minett, po. eds., English Dept., U. of Wisconsin, P.O. Box 413, Milwaukee, WI 53201. Issues indexed: (16:1-2). Subscriptions: $10/yr. (2 issues), $14/2 yrs.; Single issue: $6; Sample & back issues: $4.50.

CrossCur: CROSSCURRENTS, Linda Brown Michelson, ed., 2200 Glastonbury Road, Westlake Village, CA 91361. Issues indexed: (10:2). Subscriptions: $18/yr. (4 issues), $25/2 yrs., $30/3 yrs.; Single issue: $6.

Crucible: CRUCIBLE, Terrence L. Grimes, ed., Barton College, College Station, Wilson, NC 27893. Issues indexed: (28). Subscriptions: $5/yr. (1 issue), $10/2 yrs; Back issues: $4.

CumbPR: CUMBERLAND POETRY REVIEW, Ingram Bloch, Bob Darrell, Sherry Bevins Darrell, Malcolm Glass, Jeanne Gore, Thomas Heine, Laurence Lerner, Alison Touster-Reed, Eva Touster, eds., Poetics, Inc., P.O. Box 120128, Acklen Station, Nashville, TN 37212. Issues indexed: (11:2, 12:1). Subscriptions: $14/yr, $26/2 yrs. (ind.); $17/yr., $31/2 yrs. (inst.); $23/yr., $37/2 yrs. (for.); Single issue: $7; $10 (for.).

CutB: CUTBANK, Peter Fong, Dennis Held, ed., Joel Friederich, po. ed., Jocelyn Siler, faculty advisor, Dept. of English, U. of Montana, Missoula, MT 59812. Issues indexed: (37-38). Subscriptions: $12/yr., $22/2 yrs.; Single issue: $6.95; Sample copies: $4.

Dandel: DANDELION, Chris Horgan, managing ed., Deborah Miller, Allan Serafino, po eds., Alexandra Centre, 922 - 9th Ave., S.E., Calgary, Alberta T2G 0S4 Canada. Issues indexed: (19:1-3). Subscriptions: $10/yr. (2 issues), $18/2 yrs.; $15/yr. (inst.); Single issue: $6.

DenQ: DENVER QUARTERLY, Donald Revell, ed., U. of Denver, Denver, CO 80208. Issues indexed: (26:3-4, 27:1-2). Subscriptions: $15/yr., $18/yr. (inst.); $28/2 yrs.; plus $1/yr. (for.); Single issue: $5.

Descant: DESCANT, Karen Mulhallen, ed., P.O. Box 314, Station P, Toronto, Ontario M5S 2S8 Canada. Issues indexed: (23:1/2, 3, 23:4/24:1, #76/77, 78, 79/80). Subscriptions: $22.47/yr., $40.66/2 yrs., $58.85/3 yrs. (ind.); $31.03/yr., $62.06/2 yrs., $88.81/3 yrs. (inst.); plus $6/yr. (for.); Single issue: $14.95.

DogRR: DOG RIVER REVIEW, Laurence F. Hawkins, Jr., Allove DeVito, eds., Trout Creek Press, 5976 Billings Road, Parkdale, OR 97041-9610. Issues indexed: (11:1-2, #21-22). Subscriptions: $7/yr. (2 issues); Single issue: $3.50; Sample copy: $3.

DustyD: DUSTY DOG, John Pierce, ed. & pub., 1904-A Gladden, Gallup, NM 87301. Issues indexed: Chapbooks 3-5. Subscriptions: $8/yr. (3 chapbooks); Single chapbook: $3-5.95.

Elf: ELF: Eclectic Literary Forum, C. K. Erbes, ed., P. O. Box 392, Tonawanda, NY 14150. Issues indexed: (2:1-4). Subscriptions: $12/yr. (4 issues), $24/yr. (inst.), plus $8/yr. (for.); Single issue: $4.50.

EmeraldCR: EMERALD COAST REVIEW: West Florida Authors and Artists, Ellen G. Peppler, Charmaine Wellington, eds., West Florida Literary Federation, P.O. Box 1644, Pensacola, FL 32597-1644. Issues indexed: No 1992 issues received. Single issue: $9.95.

EngJ: ENGLISH JOURNAL, National Council of Teachers of English, Ben F. Nelms, ed., 200 Norman Hall, U. of Florida, Gainesville, FL 32611; Paul Janeczko, po. ed., P.O. Box 1079, Gray, ME 04039. Issues indexed: (80:5-8, 81:1-8). Subscriptions: $40/yr. (inst.), $35/yr. (ind.), plus $4/yr. (for.); Single issue: $5; Subscription address: 1111 Kenyon Rd., Urbana, IL 61801.

*Epiphany: EPIPHANY: A Journal of Literature, Gordon Grice, Bob Zordani, eds., P.O. Box 2699, University of Arkansas, Fayetteville, AR 72701. Issues indexed: (3:1-3). Subscriptions: $12/yr.; Single Copies: $4. Orders to Epiphany Publications, Inc., 408 E. Tulsa, Siloam Springs, AR 72761.

Epoch: EPOCH, Michael Koch, ed., 251 Goldwin Smith Hall, Cornell U., Ithaca, NY 14853-3201. Issues indexed: (41:1-3). Subscriptions: $11/yr.; $15/yr. (for).; Single issue: $5

Event: EVENT: The Douglas College Review, Dale Zieroth, ed., Gillian Harding-Russell, po. ed., Douglas College, P.O. Box 2503, New Westminster, B.C. V3L 5B2 Canada. Issues indexed: (20:1-3). Subscriptions: $15/yr. + $1.05 GST, $25/2 yrs. + $1.75 GST; Single issue: $6.

EvergreenC: THE EVERGREEN CHRONICLES: A Journal of Gay and Lesbian Literature, Jim Berg, Greta Gaard, M. Kiesow Moore, Mark Reschke, Betsy Rivers, eds., P.O. Box 8939, Minneapolis, MN 55408-0936. Issues indexed: (7:1-2). Subscriptions: $15/yr. (2 issues), $28/2 yrs.; $18/yr. (for.); $20/yr. (inst.); Single issue: $7.95.

*Eyeball: EYEBALL, Jabari Asim, ed., First Civilizations Inc, P.O. Box 8135, St. Louis, MO 63108. Issues indexed: (1). Subscriptions: $7/yr. (2 issues), $14/2 yrs., $21/3 yrs; $28/yr., $56/2 yrs., $82/3 yrs. (for.); Single issue: $3.50.

Farm: FARMER'S MARKET, Jean C. Lee, John E. Hughes, Jim McCurry, Lisa Ress, Tracey Rose, eds., Midwest Farmer's Market, Inc., P.O. Box 1272, Galesburg, IL 61402. Issues indexed: (9:1-2). Subscriptions: $8/yr. (2 issues); Single issue: $4.50.

Field: FIELD: Contemporary Poetry and Poetics, Stuart Friebert, David Young, eds., Rice Hall, Oberlin College, Oberlin, OH 44074. Issues indexed: (46-47). Subscriptions: $12/yr., $20/2 yrs.; Single issue: $6; Back issues: $12.

FloridaR: THE FLORIDA REVIEW, Russell Kesler, ed., Dept. of English, U. of Central Florida, Orlando, FL 32816. Issues indexed: (18:1-2). Subscriptions: $7/yr., $11/2 yrs.; Single issue: $4.50.

Footwork: FOOTWORK: The Paterson Literary Review, Maria Mazziotti Gillan, ed., Passaic County Community College, 1 College Boulevard, Paterson, NJ 07505-1179. Issues indexed: (1992). Subscriptions: $5/issue + $1.50 for postage and handling.

FourQ: FOUR QUARTERS, John J. Keenan, ed., La Salle U., 1900 W. Olney, Philadelphia, PA 19141. Issues indexed: (6:1-2). Subscriptions: $8/yr. (2 issues), $13/2 yrs.; Single issue: $4.

FreeL: FREE LUNCH: A Poetry Journal, Free Lunch Arts Alliance, Ron Offen, ed., P.O. Box 7647, Laguna Niguel, CA 92607-7647. Issues indexed: (9-10). Subscriptions: Free to all serious poets in the U.S.A.; $10/3 issues; $13/3 issues (for.); Single issue: $5, $6 (for.).

GeoR: GEORGIA REVIEW, Stanley W. Lindberg, ed., U. of Georgia, Athens, GA 30602. Issues indexed: (46:1-4). Subscriptions: $18/ yr., $30/2 yrs., plus $5/yr. (for.); Single issue: $7; Back issues: $7.

GettyR: GETTYSBURG REVIEW, Peter Stitt, ed., Gettysburg College, Gettysburg, PA 17325-1491. Issues indexed: (5:1-4). Subscriptions: $15/yr., $27/2 yrs., $36/3 yrs., plus $5/yr. (for.); Single issue: $6.

GrahamHR: GRAHAM HOUSE REVIEW, Peter Balakian, Bruce Smith, eds., Colgate U. Press, Box 5000, Colgate U., Hamilton, NY 13346; Issues indexed: (16). Subscriptions: $15/2 yrs. (2 issues); Single issue: $7.50.

Grain: GRAIN, Saskatchewan Writers Guild, Geoffrey Ursell, ed., Elizabeth Philips, po. ed., Box 1154, Regina, Saskatchewan S4P 3B4 Canada. Issues indexed: (20:1-4). Subscriptions: $15+$1.05 GST/yr., $28+$1.96 GST/2 yrs., plus $4/yr. (U.S.), plus $6/yr. (for.); Single issue: $5.

GrandS: GRAND STREET, Jean Stein, ed., Erik Rieselbach, po. ed., 131 Varick St. #906, New York, NY 10013. Issues indexed: (11:1-3, #41-43). Subscriptions: $24/yr. (4 issues), $34/yr. (for.); Single issue: $8.50; Subscription address: Dept. GRS, PO Box 3000, Denville, NJ 07834..

GreenMR: GREEN MOUNTAINS REVIEW, Neil Shepard, po. ed., Kate Riley, managing ed., Box A58, Johnson State College, Johnson, VT 05656. Issues indexed: (NS 5:2). Single issue: $4.

GreensboroR: THE GREENSBORO REVIEW, Jim Clark, ed., Melissa Brannon, po. ed., Dept. of English, U. of North Carolina, Greensboro, NC 27412. Issues indexed: (52-53). Subscriptions: $8/yr. (2 issues), $20/3 yrs.; Single issue: $4.

Gypsy: GYPSY, Belinda Subraman, S. Ramnath, eds, 10708 Gay Brewer Dr., El Paso, TX 79935. Issues indexed: (18-19); No. 18 published as "The Gulf War: Many Perspectives," ed. by Belinda Subraman (El Paso, TX: Vergin Press, 1992, 164 p.). Subscriptions: $14/yr. (2 issues); Single issue: $7.

HampSPR: THE HAMPDEN-SYDNEY POETRY REVIEW, Tom O'Grady, ed., P.O. Box 126, Hampden-Sydney, VA 23943. Issues indexed: Wint 1992. Subscriptions: $5/single issue; 1990 Anthology, $12.95.

HangL: HANGING LOOSE, Robert Hershon, Dick Lourie, Mark Pawlak, Ron Schreiber, eds., 231 Wyckoff St., Brooklyn, NY 11217. Issues indexed: (60-61). Subscriptions: $12.50/3 issues, $24/6 issues, $35/9 issues (ind.); $15/3 issues, $30/6 issues, $45/9 issues (inst.); $22/3 issues, $42/6 issues, $62/9 issues (for.); Sample issues: $5 plus $1.50 postage and handling.

Harp: HARPER'S MAGAZINE, Lewis H. Lapham, ed., 666 Broadway, New York, NY 10012. Issues indexed: (284:1700-1705, 285:1706-1711). Subscriptions: $18/yr., plus $2/yr. (USA possessions, Canada), plus $20/yr. (for.); Single issue: $2.95; Subscription address: P.O. Box 7511, Red Oak, IA 51591-0511.

HarvardA: THE HARVARD ADVOCATE, Kristen Ankiewicz, Managing ed., Stephen Burt, po. ed., 21 South St., Cambridge, MA 02138. Issues indexed: (126:2-4, 127:1, 125th anniversary issue); 126:4 (Sum 92) appears to be incorrectly numbered 127:4; 125th Anniversary Issue (F 92) is unnumbered. Subscriptions: $15/yr. (ind.), $17/yr. (inst.), $20/yr. (for.); Single issue: $4.

HawaiiR: HAWAI'I REVIEW, Jeanne K. Tsutsui, ed., Kathy Banggo, Jacqueline Chun, po. eds., Dept. of English, U. of Hawai'i, 1733 Donaghho Rd., Honolulu, HI 96822. Issues indexed: (16:2, #35). Subscriptions: $15/yr. (3 issues), $25/2 yrs.; Single issue: $5.

HayF: HAYDEN'S FERRY REVIEW, Salima Keegan, Managing ed., Jeffrey Coleman, Julius Sokenu, po. eds., Matthews Center, Arizona State U., Tempe, AZ 85287-1502. Issues indexed: (10-11). Subscriptions: $10/yr. (2 issues), $18/2 yrs.; $13/yr., $26/2 yrs. (inst.); Single issue: $5 plus $1 postage.

HeavenB: HEAVEN BONE, Steven Hirsch, ed., pub., P.O. Box 486, Chester, NY 10918. Issues indexed: None; No. 9 was indexed in 1991 vol; No. 10 will be indexed in 1993 volume. Subscriptions: $14.95/4 issues; Single issue: $5.

Hellas: HELLAS: A Journal of Poetry and the Humanities, Gerald Harnett, ed., The Aldine Press, Ltd., 304 S. Tyson Ave., Glenside, PA 19038. Issues indexed: (3:1-2). Subscriptions: $14/yr. (2 issues), $24/2 yrs.; plus $4/yr. (for.); Single issue: $7.50.

HighP: HIGH PLAINS LITERARY REVIEW, Robert O. Greer, Jr., ed., Joy Harjo, po. ed., 180 Adams St., Suite 250, Denver, CO 80206. Issues indexed: (7:1-3). Subscriptions: $20/yr. (3 issues), $38/2 yrs., plus $5/yr. (for.); Single issue: $7.

HiramPoR: HIRAM POETRY REVIEW, English Dept., Hiram College, Hale Chatfield & Carol Donley, eds., P.O. Box 162, Hiram, OH 44234. Issues indexed: (51/52). Subscriptions: $8/yr. (2 issues); $20/3 yrs. (ind.); Single issue: $4.

HolCrit: THE HOLLINS CRITIC, John Rees Moore, ed., Hollins College, VA 24020. Issues indexed: (29:1-5). Subscriptions: $6/yr., $10/2 yrs., $14/3 yrs.; $7.50/yr., $11.50/2 yrs., $15.50/3 yrs. (for.).

HopewellR: HOPEWELL REVIEW (formerly: Arts Indiana Literary Supplement), Alison Jester, ed., Arts Indiana, Inc., 47 S. Pennsylvania St., Suite 701, Indianapolis, IN 46204-3622. Issues indexed: (4). Subscriptions: $4.95/issue incl. postage, handling and tax.

Hudson: THE HUDSON REVIEW, Paula Deitz, Frederick Morgan, eds., 684 Park Ave., New York, NY 10021. Issues indexed: (44:4, 45:1-3). Subscriptions: $20/yr., $38/2 yrs., $56/3 yrs., plus $4/yr. (for.); Single issue: $6.

IndR: INDIANA REVIEW, Dorian Gossy, ed., Talvi Ansel, Bret Flournoy, Richard Seehuus, po. eds., 316 N. Jordan Ave., Bloomington, IN 47405. Issues indexed: (15:1-2). Subscriptions: $12/2 issues, $15/2 issues (inst.); $22/4 issues (ind.), $25/4 issues (inst.); plus $5/2 issues (for.). Single issue: $5.

Interim: INTERIM, A. Wilber Stevens, ed., Dept. of English, U. of Nevada, 4505 Maryland Parkway, Las Vegas, NV 89154-5011. Issues indexed: (11:1-2). Subscriptions: $8/yr. (2 issues), $13/2 yrs., $16/3 yrs. (ind.); $14/yr. (lib.), $16/yr. (for.); Single issue: $5, $8 (for.).

InterPR: INTERNATIONAL POETRY REVIEW, Mark Smith-Soto, ed., Dept. of Romance Languages, U. of North Carolina, Greensboro, NC 27412-5001. Issues indexed: (18:1-2). Subscriptions: $10/yr. (2 issues, ind.), $15/yr. (inst.); Plus $2/yr. (for.); Single issue: $5.

Inti: INTI, Revista de Literatura Hispánica, Roger B. Carmosino, ed., Dept. of Modern Languages, Providence College, Providence, RI 02918. Issues indexed: (36). Subscriptions: $25/yr. (2 issues, ind.), $40/yr. (inst.); Single issue: $20, $35 (double issues).

Iowa: IOWA REVIEW, David Hamilton, ed., 308 EPB, U. of Iowa, Iowa City, IA 52242. Issues indexed: (22:1-3). Subscriptions: $18/yr. (3 issues, ind.), $20/yr. (inst.), plus $3/yr. (for.); Single issue: $6.95.

Jacaranda: THE JACARANDA REVIEW, Bruce Kijewski, Katherine Swiggart, eds., Gregory Castle, po. ed., Dept. of English, U. of California, Los Angeles, CA 90024. Issues indexed: (6:1/2); issues between 4:1 and 6:1/2 not received. Subscriptions: $10/yr. (2 issues, ind.), $14/yr. (inst.); Sample issues: $6.

JamesWR: THE JAMES WHITE REVIEW, A Gay Men's Literary Journal, Phil Willkie, ed., Clif Mayhood, po. ed., P.O. Box 3356, Butler Quarter Station, Minneapolis, MN 55403. Issues indexed: (9:2-4, 10:1). Subscriptions: $12/yr., $20/2 yrs.; $14/yr. (Canada); $17/yr. (other for.); Single issue: $3; Back issues: $1 (for minimum order of $10).

JlNJPo: THE JOURNAL OF NEW JERSEY POETS, Sander Zulauf, ed., Center for Teaching Excellence, County College of Morris, 214 Center Grove Rd., Randolph, NJ 07869-2086. Issues indexed: (14:1-2). Subscriptions: $7/yr. (2 issues), $12/2 yrs.; Single issue: $4.

Journal: THE JOURNAL, Kathy Fagan, po. ed., The Ohio State U., Dept. of English, 164 W. 17th Ave., Columbus, OH 43210. Issues indexed: (16:1-2); 14:1 never received. Subscriptions: $8/yr. (2 issues), $16/2 yrs., $24/3 yrs.; Single issue: $5.

Kaleid: KALEIDOSCOPE, International Magazine of Literature, Fine Arts, and Disability, Darshan Perusek, ed., Chris Hewitt, po. ed. (51 W. 86th ST., #404, New York, NY 10024), United Cerebral Palsy and Services for the Handicapped, 326 Locust St., Akron, OH 44302. Issues indexed: (24-25). Subscriptions: $9/yr. (2 issues, ind.), $14/yr. (inst.), plus $5/yr. (Canada); plus $8/yr. (other for.); Single issue: $4.50, $7 (for.); Sample issue: $3. Also available on audio cassette.

Kalliope: KALLIOPE: A Journal of Women's Art, Mary Sue Koeppel, ed., Florida Community College at Jacksonville, 3939 Roosevelt Blvd., Jacksonville, FL 32205. Issues indexed: (14:1-3, 15:1). Subscriptions: $10.50/1 yr. (3 issues), $20/2 yrs. (ind.); $18/yr. (inst.); plus $6/yr. (for.); free to women in prison; Single issue: $7, plus $2 (for.), $3 (for., double issue); Back issues: $4-8.

KenR: KENYON REVIEW, Marilyn Hacker, ed., David Baker, po. ed., Kenyon College, Gambier, OH 43022. Issues indexed: (NS 14:1-4). Subscriptions: Kenyon Review, P.O. Box 8062, Syracuse, NY 13217; $22/yr., $40/2 yrs., $60/3 yrs. (ind.); $24/yr. (inst.); plus $8 (for.); Single issue: $7, including postage; Back issues: $10.

Lactuca: LACTUCA, Mike Selender, ed., P.O. Box 621, Suffern, NY 10901. Issues indexed: (15-16). Subscriptions: $10/3 issues, $13/3 issues (for.), $17/6 issues, $23/6 issues (for.); Single issue: $4, plus $2 (for.).

LaurelR: LAUREL REVIEW, Craig Goad, David Slater, William Trowbridge, eds., GreenTower Press, Dept. of English, Northwest Missouri State U., Maryville, MO 64468. Issues indexed: (26:1-2). Subscriptions: $8/yr. (2 issues), $14/2 yrs.; $11/yr., $20/2 yrs. (for.); Single issue: $5; Back issues: $4.50.

*Light: LIGHT: A Quarterly of Humorous, Occasional, Ephemeral & Light Verse, John Mella, ed., Box 7500, Chicago, IL 60680. Issues indexed: (1-4). Subscriptions: $12/yr. (4 issues); $18/yr. (for.); Single issue: $4.

LindLM: LINDEN LANE MAGAZINE, Belkis Cuza Malé, ed., P.O. Box 2384, Princeton, NJ 08543-2384. Issues indexed: (11:1-4). Subscriptions: $12/yr. (ind.), $22/yr. (inst.), $22/yr. (Latin America, Europe); Single issue: $2.

LitR: THE LITERARY REVIEW: An International Journal of Contemporary Writing, Walter Cummins, ed., Fairleigh Dickinson U., 285 Madison Ave., Madison, NJ 07940. Issues indexed: (35:2-4, 36:1). Subscriptions: $18/yr., $21/yr. (for.); $30/2 yrs., $36/2 yrs. (for.); Single issue: $5, $6 (for.).

LouisL : LOUISIANA LITERATURE: A Review of Literature and Humanities, David C. Hanson, ed., Dept. of English, Southeastern Louisiana Univ., Box 792, Hammond, LA 70402. Issues indexed: (9:1-2). Subscriptions: $10/yr. (2 issues, ind.); $12.50/yr. (inst.); plus $5/yr. (Canada), plus $10/yr. (other for.).

LullwaterR: LULLWATER REVIEW, Daniel A. Atkins, ed., Box 22036, Emory Univ., Atlanta, GA 30322. Issues indexed: (3:2-3, 4:1). Subscriptions: $10/yr. (2 issues), plus $3 (for.); Single issue: $5.

*Luz: LUZ: En Arte y Literatura, Verónica Miranda, Directora, Luz Bilingual Publishing, P.O. Box 571062, Tarzana, CA 91357. Issues indexed: (1-2). Subscriptions: $25/yr. (3 issues); $35/yr. (for.); Single issue: $10.50, $12 (for.).

MalR: THE MALAHAT REVIEW, Derk Wynand, ed., P.O. Box 1700, Victoria, BC, Canada V8W 2Y2. Issues indexed: (98-101). Subscriptions: $15 plus $1.05 GST/yr. (4 issues), $40 plus $2.80/3 yrs., (ind., USA, Canada); $25 plus $1.75 GST/yr. (inst., USA, Canada); Single issue: $6-8.

ManhatPR: MANHATTAN POETRY REVIEW, Elaine Reiman-Fenton, ed., P.O. Box 8207, New York, NY 10150-1917. Issues indexed: (14). Single issues: $7.50, plus $5 per item (for.).

ManhatR: THE MANHATTAN REVIEW, Philip Fried, ed., 440 Riverside Dr., #45, New York, NY 10027. (6:2). Subscriptions: $10/2 issues (ind.), $14/2 issues (inst.), plus $3/issue (outside USA & Canada); Back issues: $5 (ind.), $7 (inst); include 6" x 9" envelope and $1.25 for postage.

Manoa: MANOA: A Pacific Journal of International Writing, Robert Shapard, Frank Stewart, eds., Frank Stewart, po. ed., English Dept., U. of Hawaii, Honolulu, HI 96822. Issues indexed: (4:1-2). Subscriptions: $18/yr. (2 issues), $32/2 yrs. (ind.); $22/yr., $40/2 yrs. (inst.); $21/yr., $38/2 yrs. (for. ind.); $26/yr., $47/2 yrs. (for. inst.); plus $12/yr. (for. airmail); subscription address: Univ. of Hawaii Press, 2840 Kolowalu St., Honolulu, HI 96822.

MassR: THE MASSACHUSETTS REVIEW, Jules Chametzky, Mary Heath, Paul Jenkins, eds., Anne Halley, Paul Jenkins, po. eds., Memorial Hall, U. of Massachusetts, Amherst, MA 01003. Issues indexed: (33:1-3); 33:4 not received. Subscriptions: $15/yr. (4 issues, ind.), $20/yr. (lib.), $25/yr. (for.); Single issue: $5.

Mester: MESTER, Jacqueline Cruz, ed., Dept. of Spanish and Portuguese, U. of California, Los Angeles, CA 90024-1532. Issues indexed: (21:1-2). Subscriptions: $18/yr. (2 issues, ind.), $30/yr. (inst.), $12/yr. (stud.), $24/yr. (Latin America), plus $5/yr. outside U.S., Canada, Mexico.

MichQR: MICHIGAN QUARTERLY REVIEW, Laurence Goldstein, ed., 3032 Rackham Bldg., U. of Michigan, Ann Arbor, MI 48109. Issues indexed: (31:1-4). Subscriptions: $18/yr., $36/2 yrs. (ind.), $20/yr. (inst.); Single issue: $7; Back issues: $2.50.

MidAR: MID-AMERICAN REVIEW, Robert Early, George Looney, eds., Edward A. Dougherty, po. ed., 106 Hanna Hall, Dept. of English, Bowling Green State U., Bowling Green, OH 43403. Issues indexed: (12:2. 13:1-2). Subscriptions: $8/yr. (2 issues), $15/2 yrs., $20/3 yrs; Single issue: $5; Sample issue: $4.

MidwQ: THE MIDWEST QUARTERLY: A Journal of Contemporary Thought, James B. M. Schick, ed., Stephen E. Meats, po. ed., Pittsburg State U., Pittsburg, KS 66762-5889. Issues indexed: (33:2-4, 34:1). Subscriptions: $10/yr. plus $3 (for.); Single issue: $3.

Mildred: MILDRED, Ellen Biss, Kathryn Poppino, eds., 961 Birchwood Lane, Schenectady, NY 12309. Issues indexed: No 1992 issues received. Subscriptions: $12/yr. (2 issues), $20/2 yrs., $28/3 yrs.; $14/yr., $24/2 yrs., $30/3 yrs. (inst.); Single issue: $6; Double issues: $8.

MinnR: THE MINNESOTA REVIEW, Jeffrey Williams, ed, MaryJo Mahoney, po. ed., Dept. of English, East Carolina Univ., Greenville, NC 27858-4353. Issues Indexed: (NS 38-39). Subscriptions: $1-/yr. (2 issues); $20/yr. (inst. & for.), plus $5 for airmail; Single issue: $6.

MissouriR: THE MISSOURI REVIEW, Speer Morgan, ed., College of Arts & Science, 1507 Hillcrest Hall, U. of Missouri, Columbia, MO 65211. Issues indexed: (15:1-3). Subscriptions: $15/yr. (3 issues), $27/2 yrs., $36/3 yrs.; Single issue: $6.

MissR: MISSISSIPPI REVIEW, Frederick Barthelme, ed., The Center for Writers, U. of Southern Mississippi, Southern Station, Box 5144, Hattiesburg, MS 39406-5144. Issues indexed: (20:3). Subscriptions: $15/yr. (2 issues), $28/2 yrs., $40/3 yrs., plus $2/yr. (for.); Single issue: usually $8; double issues: $12.

MoodySI: MOODY STREET IRREGULARS: A Jack Kerouac Newsletter, Joy Walsh, Nan Pine eds., P.O. Box 157, Clarence Center, NY 14032. Issues indexed: (27). Subscriptions: $10/4 single, 2 double issues (ind.), $15/4 single, 2 double issues (lib.); Single issue: $3, double issues: $5.

Nat: THE NATION, Richard Lingeman, ed., Grace Schulman, po. ed., 72 Fifth Ave., New York, NY 10011. Issues indexed: (254:1-25, 255:1-22). Subscriptions: $44/yr., $75/2 yrs., plus $18/yr. (for.); Single issue: $2.25, $2.75 (Canada); Back issues: $4, $5 (for.). Send subscription correspondence to: P.O. Box 10763, Des Moines, IA 50340-0763.

NegC: NEGATIVE CAPABILITY, Sue Walker, ed., 62 Ridgelawn Dr. East, Mobile, AL 36608. Issues indexed: (12:1/2-3). Subscriptions: $15/yr. (3 issues, ind.), $20/yr. (inst., for.); Single issue: $5.

NewAW: NEW AMERICAN WRITING, Maxine Chernoff, Paul Hoover, eds., OINK! Press, 2920 West Pratt, Chicago, IL 60645. Issues indexed: (10). Subscriptions: $12/yr. (2 issues); $16/yr. (lib.).; $18/yr. (for.); Single issue: $6.

NewDeltaR: NEW DELTA REVIEW, Janet Wondra, ed., Ethan Gilsdorf, po. ed., James Gordon Bennett, faculty advisor, Creative Writing Program, English Dept., Louisiana State U., Baton Rouge, LA 70803-5001. Issues indexed: (8:1-2, 9:1-2). Subscriptions: $7/yr. (2 issues); Single issue: $4.

NewEngR: NEW ENGLAND REVIEW, Middlebury Series, T. R. Hummer, ed, Middlebury College, Middlebury, VT 05753. Issues indexed: (14:2-4). Subscriptions: $20/yr. (4 issues), $37/2 yrs., $55/3 yrs. (ind.); $35/yr., $65/2 yrs., $96/3 yrs. (lib., inst.); plus $10/yr. (for. surface) or $20/yr. (for. airmail); Single issue: $7, $9 (for. surface), $10 (for. airmail); subscription address: University Press of New England, 17 1/2 Lebanon St., Hanover, NH 03755.

NewL: NEW LETTERS, James McKinley, ed., U. of Missouri-Kansas City, 5100 Rockhill Rd., Kansas City, MO 64110. Issues indexed: (58:2-4, 59:1). Subscriptions: $17/yr. (4 issues), $28/2 yrs., $55/5 yrs. (ind.); $20/yr., $34/2 yrs., $65/5 yrs. (lib.); Single issue: $5.

NewMyths: NEW MYTHS, Robert Mooney, ed., State U. of New York, P.O. Box 6000, Binghamton, NY 13902-6000. Issues indexed: (1:2/2:1). Subscriptions: $12/yr. (2 issues), $20/2 yrs. (ind.); $15/yr., $25/2 yrs. (libs.); Single issue: $7.

NewOR: NEW ORLEANS REVIEW, John Biguenet, John Mosier, eds., Box 195, Loyola U., New Orleans, LA 70118. Issues indexed: (19:1-3/4); "The New Orleans Review will be on sabbatical during the 1993 calendar year." Subscriptions: $25/yr. (ind.), $30/yr. (inst.), $35/yr. (for.); Single issue: $9.

NewRena: THE NEW RENAISSANCE, Louise T. Reynolds, ed., James E. A. Woodbury, po. ed., 9 Heath Road, Arlington, MA 02174. Issues indexed: None published in 1992. Subscriptions: $19.50/3 issues, $37.50/6 issues; $21/3 issues, $39/3 issues (Canada); 23/3 issues, $41/6 issues (other for.); Single issue: $9, $9.50 (for.).

NewRep: THE NEW REPUBLIC, Andrew Sullivan, ed., Richard Howard, po. ed., 1220 19th St. NW, Washington, DC 20036. Issues indexed: (205:28/29-30 [sic, i.e., 206: 1/2-3?], 206:4-26, 207:2-27); there was no 207:1. The June 29 issue was numbered 206:26; the July 6 issue was number 207:2. Subscriptions: $69.97/yr., $84.97/yr. (Canada), $99.97/yr. (elsewhere). Back issues: $3.50. Single issue: $2.95. Subscription Service Dept., The New Republic, P.O. Box 56515, Boulder, CO 80322.

NewYorker: THE NEW YORKER, Pamela Maffei McCarthy, managing ed., 20 W. 43rd St., New York, NY 10036. Issues indexed: (67:46-52, 68:1-45). Subscriptions: $32/yr., $52/2 yrs.; $65.27/yr. (Canada); $76/yr. (other for.); Single issue: $1.95; Subscription correspondence to: Box 56447, Boulder, CO 80322.

NewYorkQ: THE NEW YORK QUARTERLY, William Packard, ed., P.O. Box 693, Old Chelsea Station, New York, NY 10113. Issues indexed: (47-49). Subscriptions: $15/yr., $30/2 yrs., $45/3 yrs.; $25/yr. (lib.); plus $5/yr. (for.); Single issue: $6; subscription address: 302 Neville Hall, U. of Maine, Orono, ME 04469.

NewYRB: THE NEW YORK REVIEW OF BOOKS, Robert B. Silvers, Barbara Epstein, eds., 250 W. 57th St., New York, NY 10107. Issues indexed: (39:1/2-21). Subscriptions: $45/yr.; Single issue: $2.95, $3.75 (Canada); NY Review of Books, P.O. Box 420384, Palm Coast, FL 32142-0384.

Nimrod: NIMROD, Francine Ringold, ed., Manly Johnson, po. ed., Arts and Humanities Council of Tulsa, 2210 S. Main St., Tulsa, OK 74114. Issues indexed: (35:2, 36:1). Subscriptions: $11.50/yr. (2 issues), $21/2 yrs., $30/3 yrs.; plus $3/yr. (for.); Single issue: $6.95.

*Noctiluca: NOCTILUCA: An International Magazine of Poetry, Judy Katz-Levine, ed., 10 Hillshire Ln., Norwood, MA 02062-3009. Issues indexed: (1:1-2). Subscriptions: $10/3 issues.

NoAmR: THE NORTH AMERICAN REVIEW, Robley Wilson, ed., Peter Cooley, po. ed., U. of Northern Iowa, Cedar Falls, IA 50614-0516. Issues indexed: (277:1-4). Subscriptions: $18/yr., $22/yr. (Canada, Latin America), $24/yr. (elsewhere); Single issue: $4, $5 (Canada).

*NoCarLR: NORTH CAROLINA LITERARY REVIEW, Alex Albright, ed., English Dept., East Carolina U., Greenville, NC 27858-4353. Issues indexed: (1:1). Subscriptions: $15/yr. (2 issues), $28/2 yrs.; plus $5/yr. (for.); Single issues: $8.50.

NoDaQ: NORTH DAKOTA QUARTERLY, Robert W. Lewis, ed., Jay Meek, po. ed., U. of North Dakota, Grand Forks, ND 58202-7209. Issues indexed: (60:1-4). Subscriptions: $15/yr., $20/yr. (inst.); $23/yr. (for. ind.), $28/yr. (for. inst.); Single issue: $5 (ind.), $7 (for.); Special issues: $10, $12 (for.).

Northeast: NORTHEAST, John Judson, ed., Juniper Press, 1310 Shorewood Dr., La Crosse, WI 54601. Issues indexed: (Ser. 5:6-7). Subscriptions: $33 (2 issues, ind.), $38 (inst.), includes two chapbooks and a minimum of two other books, in addition to NORTHEAST; Single issue: $4.

NorthStoneR: THE NORTH STONE REVIEW, James Naiden, ed., D Station, Box 14098, Minneapolis, MN 55414. Issues indexed: None; No. 11 published in 1993. Subscriptions: $15/yr. (2 issues); Single issue: $8.

Notus: NOTUS: New Writing, Pat Smith, ed., 2420 Walter Dr., Ann Arbor, MI 48103. Issues indexed: No 1992 issues received. Subscriptions: $12/yr. (2 issues, U.S. & Canada, ind.), $15/yr. (elsewhere), $15/yr. (inst.).

NowestR: NORTHWEST REVIEW, John Witte, ed. & po. ed., 369 PLC, U. of Oregon, Eugene, OR 97403. Issues indexed: (30:1-3). Subscriptions: $14/yr. (3 issues), $26/2 yrs., $35/3 yrs.; $12/yr., $22/2 yrs. (stud.); plus $2/yr. (for.); Single issue: $5.

Nuez: LA NUEZ: Revista Internacional de Arte y Literatura, Rafael Bordao, ed., P.O. Box 1655, Cooper Station, New York, NY 10276. Issues indexed: (:10/11-12). Subscriptions: $12/yr. (ind.), $15/yr. (inst.), $18/yr. (for.).

Obs: OBSIDIAN II: Black Literature in Review, Gerald Barrax, ed. & po. ed., Dept. of English, Box 8105, North Carolina State U., Raleigh, NC 27695-8105. Issues indexed: (7:1/2). Subscriptions: $12/yr. (2 issues), $20/2 yrs.; $13/yr. (Canada), $15/yr. (other for.); Single issue: $5; Double issues: $10.

OhioR: THE OHIO REVIEW, Wayne Dodd, ed., Ellis Hall, Ohio U., Athens, OH 45701-2979. Issues indexed: (48). Subscriptions: $16/yr. (3 issues), $40/3 yrs.; Single issue: $6.

Ometeca: OMETECA: Ciencia y Literatura, Science & Literature, Ciência e literatura, Rafael Catalá, ed., P.O. Box 38, New Brunswick, NJ 08903-0038. Issues Indexed: (2:2). Subscriptions: $20/yr. (2 issues) (ind.), $35/yr. (inst.) (USA, Canada, Mexico); $33/yr. (elsewhere).

OnTheBus: ONTHEBUS: A New Literary Magazine, Jack Grapes, ed., Bombshelter Press, 6421-1/2 Orange St., Los Angeles, CA 90048. Issues indexed: (4:2/5:1, #10/11). Subscriptions: $24/3 issues (ind.), $27/3 issues (inst.); Single issue: $9, plus $1 postage; Double issue: $13.50 plus $1.50 postage.

OntR: ONTARIO REVIEW, Raymond J. Smith, ed., 9 Honey Brook Dr., Princeton, NJ 08540. Issues indexed: (36-37). Subscriptions: $10/yr. (2 issues), $18/2 yrs., $24/3 yrs., plus $2/yr. (for.); Single issue: $4.95.

Os: OSIRIS, Andrea Moorhead, ed., P.O. Box 297, Deerfield, MA 01342. Issues indexed: (34-35). Subscriptions: $8/2 issues (ind.), $10/2 issues (inst.). Single issue: $5.

Outbr: OUTERBRIDGE, Charlotte Alexander, ed., English Dept. (A324), College of Staten Island, 715 Ocean Terrace, Staten Island, NY 10301. Issues indexed: (23). Subscriptions: $5/yr. (1 issue).

OxfordM: OXFORD MAGAZINE, Constance Pierce, editorial advisor, Dept. of English, Bachelor Hall, Miami U., Oxford, OH 45056. Issues indexed: (6:2, 7:1, 8:1-2); Vol. 7, No. 2 was indexed in the 1991 volume, but was not listed under "Periodicals Indexed". Single issue: $5.

PacificR: THE PACIFIC REVIEW: A Magazine of Poetry and Prose, Judith Hawkins, ed., James Brown, faculty ed., Derek McKown, po. ed., Dept. of English, California State U., 5500 University Parkway, San Bernardino, CA 92407-2397. Issues indexed: (11). Subscriptions: $6.50/yr. (1 issue), $12/2 yrs.; Back issues: $2.50.

Paint: PAINTBRUSH: A Journal of Poetry, Translations, and Letters, Ben Bennani, ed., Northeast Missouri State U., Kirksville, MO 63501. Issues indexed: (19:37). Subscriptions: $9/yr. (2 issues, ind.), $12/yr. (inst.); Single & back issues: $7.

PaintedB: PAINTED BRIDE QUARTERLY, Teresa Leo, ed., Painted Bride Arts Center, 230 Vine St., Philadelphia, PA 19106. Issues indexed: (45-48); No. 44 was indexed in the 1991 volume, but was not listed under "Periodicals Indexed." Subscriptions: $16/yr. (4 issues), $28/2 yrs., $20/yr. (lib, inst.); Single issue: $5. Distributed free to inmates.

PaintedHR: PAINTED HILLS REVIEW, Michael Ishii, Kara D. Kosmatka, eds., P.O. Box 494, Davis, CA 95617-0494. Issues indexed: (5-7). Subscriptions: $10/yr. (3 issues); $12/yr. (inst., Canada); $14/yr. (other for.); Single issue: $3.50.

ParisR: THE PARIS REVIEW, George A. Plimpton, Peter Matthiessen, Donald Hall, Robert B. Silvers, Blair Fuller, Maxine Groffsky, eds., Richard Howard, po. ed., Box S, 541 East 72nd St., New York, NY 10021. Issues indexed: (34:122-125). Subscriptions: $24/4 issues, $48/8 issues, $1000/life, plus $7/4 issues (for.); Single issue: $7; Subscription address: 45-39 171st Place, Flushing, NY 11358.

Parting: PARTING GIFTS, Robert Bixby, ed. & pub., March Street Press, 3413 Wilshire Dr., Greensboro, NC 27408-2923. Issues indexed: (5:1-2). Subscriptions: $5/yr. (2 issues), $9/2 yrs., $13/3 yrs.; Single issue: $3.

PartR: PARTISAN REVIEW, William Phillips, ed., Boston U., 236 Bay State Rd., Boston, MA 02215. Issues indexed: (59:1-4). Subscriptions: $18/yr. (4 issues), $33/2 yrs., $47/3 yrs.; $21/yr., $36/2 yrs. (for.); $28/yr. (inst.); Single issue: $5 plus $1.50 per issue postage and handling.

PassN: PASSAGES NORTH, Michael Barrett, ed., Mark Cox, po. ed., Kalamazoo College, 1200 Academy St., Kalamazoo, MI 49007. Issues indexed: (13:1-2). Subscriptions: $10/yr., $18/2 yrs; Single issue: $5.

Pearl: PEARL, Joan Jobe Smith, Marilyn Johnson, Barbara Hauk, eds., 3030 E. 2nd St., Long Beach, CA 90803. Issues indexed: (15-16). Subscriptions: $12/yr. (ind.); $20/yr. (lib.); $25/yr. (patrons); Single issue: $5.

Pembroke: PEMBROKE MAGAZINE, Shelby Stephenson, ed., Box 60, Pembroke State U., Pembroke, NC 28372. Issues indexed: (24). Subscriptions: $5/issue (USA, Canada, Mexico), $5.50/issue (other for.).

PennR: THE PENNSYLVANIA REVIEW, Ed Ochester, executive ed., Deborah Pursifull, Lori Jakiela, eds., Leasa Burton, Jan Beatty, po. eds., 526 Cathedral of Learning, U. of Pittsburgh, Pittsburgh, PA 15260. Issues indexed: No 1992 issues received. Subscriptions: $10/yr. (2 issues), $18/2 yrs.; Single issue: $5.

Pequod: PEQUOD, Mark Rudman, ed., Dept. of English, Room 200, New York U., 19 University Place, New York, NY 10003. Issues indexed: (33-34). Subscriptions: $12/yr. (2 issues), $20/2 yrs. (ind.); $18/yr., $34/2 yrs. (inst).; plus $3/yr. (for.); Single issue: $10.

Pig: PIG IRON, Jim Villani, Naton Leslie, eds., Pig Iron Press, P.O. Box 237, Youngstown, OH 44501. Issues indexed: No 1992 issues received. Single issue: $9.95.

PikeF: THE PIKESTAFF FORUM, Robert D. Sutherland, James R. Scrimgeour, eds./pubs., P.O. Box 127, Normal, IL 61761. Issues indexed: No 1992 issues received. Subscriptions: $10/6 issues; Single issue: $2.

Plain: PLAINSONGS, Dwight Marsh, ed., Dept. of English, Hastings College, Hastings, NE 68902. Issues indexed: (12:3, 13:1). Subscriptions: $9/yr. (3 issues).

Ploughs: PLOUGHSHARES, DeWitt Henry, executive director, David Daniel, Joyce Peseroff, po. eds., Emerson College, 100 Beacon St., Boston, MA 02116-1596. Issues indexed: (18:1, 2/3, 4). Subscriptions: $19/yr. (ind.), $24/yr. (for. ind.); $22/yr. (inst.), $27/yr. (for. inst.). Single issue: $8.95.

Poem: POEM, Huntsville Literary Association, Nancy Frey Dillard, ed., c/o English Dept., U. of Alabama, Huntsville, AL 35899. Issues indexed: (67-68). Subscriptions: $10/yr.; Back issues: $5; subscription address: Huntsville Literary Association, P.O. Box 919, Huntsville, AL 35804.

PoetC: POET AND CRITIC, Neal Bowers, ed., 203 Ross Hall, Iowa State U., Ames, IA 50011. Issues indexed: (23:2-3, 23:1). Subscriptions: Iowa State U. Press, South State St., Ames, IA 50010, $18/yr. (3 issues), $21/yr. (for.); $46/3 yrs, $55/3 yrs. (for.); Single issue: $8.

PoetL: POET LORE, Philip K. Jason, Barbara Goldberg, executive eds., The Writer's Center, 4508 Walsh St., Bethesda, MD 20815. Issues Indexed: (87:1-4). Subscriptions: $10/yr. (Writer's Center members); $15/yr. (ind.); $24/yr. (inst.), plus $5/yr. (for.); Single issue: $4.50, plus $1 postage and handling; Samples: $4.

Poetry: POETRY, Joseph Parisi, ed., 60 W. Walton St., Chicago, IL 60610. Issues indexed: (159:4-6, 160:1-6, 161:1-3). Subscriptions: $25/yr. (ind.); $31/yr. (for.); $27/yr. (inst.); $33/yr. (for. inst.); Single issue: $2.50 plus $1 postage; Back issues: $3 plus $1 postage.

PoetryC: POETRY CANADA, Barry Dempster, po. ed., P.O. Box 1061, Kingston, Ont. K7L 4Y5 Canada. Issues indexed: (12:2, 12:3/4, 13:1). Subscriptions: $17.12/4 issues (ind.); $34.24/4 issues (inst.); Back issues: $5; Single issue: $4.55, Double issues: $7.95.

PoetryE: POETRY EAST, Richard Jones, ed., Dept. of English, 802 W. Belden Ave., DePaul Univ., Chicago, IL 60614. Issues indexed: (33-34). Subscriptions: $12/yr.; Single issue: $7.

PoetryNW: POETRY NORTHWEST, David Wagoner, ed., U. of Washington, 4045 Brooklyn Ave. NE, Seattle, WA 98105. Issues indexed: (33:1-4). Subscriptions: $10/yr., $12/yr. (for.); Single issue: $3, $3.50 (for.).

PoetryUSA: POETRY USA, Jack Foley, ed., 2569 Maxwell Ave., Oakland, CA 94601. Issues indexed: (24). Subscriptions: $10/4 issues; Single issue: $1.

PottPort: THE POTTERSFIELD PORTFOLIO, Shari Andrews, Joe Blades, Jo-Anne Elder, Raymond Fraser, Carlos Gomes, Margaret McLeod, eds., Wild East Publishing Co-operative Ltd., 151 Ryan Court, Fredericton, NB, Canada E3A 2Y9. Issues indexed: (14:1-2). Subscriptions: $12/yr. (2 issues, ind.), $15/yr. (inst.); $9/yr. (students), $15/yr. (USA, for.); Single issue: $6.

PraF: PRAIRIE FIRE: A Canadian Magazine of New Writing, Andris Taskans, managing ed., Katharine Bitney, po. ed., 423-100 Arthur St., Winnipeg, Manitoba R3B 1H3 Canada. Issues indexed: (13:1-4, #58-61). Subscriptions: $24/yr., $44/2 yrs. (ind.); $32/yr. (inst.), plus $4 (USA), plus $6 (for.); Single issue: $7.95-12.95.

PraS: PRAIRIE SCHOONER, Hilda Raz, ed., 201 Andrews Hall, U. of Nebraska, Lincoln, NE 68588-0334. Issues indexed: (66:1-4). Subscriptions: $20/yr., $35/2 yrs., $46/3 yrs. (ind.); $22/yr. (lib.); Single issue: $6.45

Prima: PRIMAVERA, Lisa Grayson, Elizabeth Harter, Ruth Young, eds., 700 E. 61st St, Box 37-7547, Chicago, IL 60637. Issues indexed: No 1992 issues received. Single issue: $7; Back issues: $5-6.

Quarry: QUARRY, Steven Heighton, ed., P.O. Box 1061, Kingston, Ontario K7L 4Y5 Canada. Issues indexed: (41:1-4). Subscriptions: $20.33/yr. (4 issues), $36.38/2 yrs. (8 issues); Single issue: $5.95.

QRL: QUARTERLY REVIEW OF LITERATURE, T. & R. Weiss, eds., 26 Haslet Ave., Princeton, NJ 08540. Issues indexed: (Poetry series 11, vol. 31). Subscriptions: $20/2 volumes (paper), $20/volume (cloth, inst.).

QW: QUARTERLY WEST, Jeffrey Vasseur, M. L. Williams, eds., Janet Bianchi, Sally Thomas, po. eds., 317 Olpin Union, U. of Utah, Salt Lake City, UT 84112. Issues indexed: (34-36). Subscriptions: $11/yr. (2 issues), $20/2 yrs.; $14/yr., $26/2 yrs. (for.); Single issue: $5.

RagMag: RAG MAG, Beverly Voldseth, ed. & pub., Black Hat Press, Box 12, Goodhue, MN 55027. Issues indexed: (10:1-2). Subscriptions: $10/yr. (2 issues), $15/yr. (inst.); Single issue: $5.50 plus $1 postage.

Raritan: RARITAN: A Quarterly Review, Richard Poirier, ed., Rutgers U., 31 Mine St., New Brunswick, NJ 08903. Issues indexed: (11:3-4, 12:1-2). Subscriptions: $16/yr., $26/2 yrs. (ind.); $20/yr., $30/2 yrs. (inst.); plus $5.50/yr (for.); Single issue: $5; Back issues: $6.

RedBass: RED BASS, Jay Murphy, ed., 105 W. 28th St., New York, NY 10001-6102. Issues indexed: No 1992 issues published; No. 16 published in 1993. Subscriptions: $20/2 issues (ind.), $35 (inst., for.); Single issue: $8.50; Back issues: $5.

RiverC: RIVER CITY, Sharon Bryan, ed., Dept. of English, Memphis State U., Memphis, TN 38152. Issues indexed: (12:2). Subscriptions: $9/yr. (ind., 2 issues), $10/yr. (inst).; Single issue: $5.

RiverS: RIVER STYX, Lee Fournier, ed., 14 South Euclid, St. Louis, MO 63108. Issues indexed: (36). Subscriptions: $20/yr. (3 issues, $38/2 yrs.; Single issue: $7.

Rohwedder: ROHWEDDER: International Journal of Literature & Art, Nancy Antell, Angela Dawn Baldanado, Robert Dassanowsky-Harris, Hans Jurgen Schacht, eds., P.O. Box 29490, Los Angeles, CA 90029. Issues indexed: (7). Subscriptions: $12/4 issues (USA, Canada, Mexico, ind.); $18/4 issues (inst.); $16/4 issues (other for., surface mail, plus $1/copy airmail); Single issue: $4.

Salm: SALMAGUNDI: A Quarterly of the Humanities and Social Sciences, Robert Boyers, ed., Skidmore College, Saratoga Springs, NY 12866. Issues indexed: (93 94/95, 96). Subscriptions: $15/yr., $25/2 yrs. (ind.); $22/yr., $37/2 yrs. (inst.); plus $10/yr. (for.); Sample issues: $6; Single issue: $6.

SenR: SENECA REVIEW, Deborah Tall, ed., Hobart and William Smith Colleges, Geneva, NY 14456. Issues indexed: (21:2, 22:1-2). Subscriptions: $8/yr. (2 issues), $15/2 yrs.; Single issue: $5.

Sequoia: SEQUOIA: The Stanford Literary Journal, Marion Rust, managing ed., Annie Finch, Carlos Rodriguez, po. eds., Storke Publications Building, Stanford U., Stanford, CA 94305. Issues indexed: No 1992 issues received. Subscriptions: $10/yr. (2 issues), $11/yr. (for.), $15/yr. (inst.); Single issue: $5.

SewanR: THE SEWANEE REVIEW, George Core, ed., U. of the South, Sewanee, TN 37375. Issues indexed: (100:1-4). Subscriptions: $16/yr., $28/2 yrs., $40/3 yrs. (ind.); $20/yr., $38/2 yrs., $55/3 yrs. (inst.); plus $5/yr. (for.); Single issue: $5.75; Back issues: $7-10.

ShadowP: SHADOW PLAY, Jan Bender, ed., 99 Reynolds Rd., Grand Isle, VT 05458. Issues indexed: (3). Single issue: $3.

Shen: SHENANDOAH, Dabney Stuart, ed., Washington and Lee U., Box 722, Lexington, VA 24450. Issues indexed: (42:1-4). Subscriptions: $11/yr., $18/2 yrs., $25/3 yrs.; $14/yr., $24/2 yrs., $33/3 yrs. (for.); Single issue: $3.50; Back issues: $6.

Shiny: SHINY: The Magazine of the Future, Michael Friedman, ed. & pub., 39 E. 12th St., Suite 603, New York, NY 10003. Manuscripts to Kim Rosenfield, associate ed., 52 MacDougal St., Apt. 1C, New York, NY 10012. Issues indexed: (7/8). Subscriptions: $28/4 issues; Single issue: $5, double issue: $10.

Sidewalks: SIDEWALKS: An Anthology of Poetry, Short Prose, & Art, Tom Heie, ed., P.O. Box 321, Champlin, MN 55316. Issues indexed: No 1992 issues received. Subscriptions: $8/yr. (2 issues), $12/yr. (inst.); Single issue: $5.

SilverFR: SILVERFISH REVIEW, Rodger Moody, ed., P.O. Box 3541, Eugene, OR 97403. Issues indexed: (22-23). Subscriptions: $12/3 issues (ind.), $15/3 issues (inst.), Single issue: $4-5.

SingHM: SING HEAVENLY MUSE!: Women's Poetry and Prose, Ruth Berman, Joline Gitis, Karen Karsten, Carol Masters, Sue Ann Martinson, Corinna Nelson, Rafael Tilton, Linda Webster, eds, P.O. Box 13320, Minneapolis, MN 55414. Issues indexed: (20). Subscriptions: $14/2 issues, $19/3 issues, $36/6 issues (ind.); $21/3 issues, $40/6 issues (inst.); $16/3 issues (low income); Single issue: $7 plus $2 postage and handling.

SinW: SINISTER WISDOM: A Journal for the Lesbian Imagination in the Arts and Politics, Elana Dykewomon, ed. & pub., P.O. Box 3252, Berkeley, CA 94703. Issues indexed: (46-48). Subscriptions: $17/yr. (4 issues), $30/2 yrs. (ind.); $30/yr. (inst.); $22/yr. (for.); $8-15/yr. (hardship); Free on request to women in prisons and mental institutions; Single issue: $5.

SlipS: SLIPSTREAM, Robert Borgatti, Livio Farallo, Dan Sicoli, eds., P.O. Box 2071, Niagara Falls, NY 14301. Issues indexed: (12). Subscriptions: $8.50/2 issues; Single issue: $5.

SmPd: THE SMALL POND MAGAZINE OF LITERATURE, Napoleon St. Cyr, ed., pub., P.O. Box 664, Stratford, CT 06497. Issues indexed: (29:1-3, #84-86). Subscriptions: $8/yr. (3 issues), $15/2 yrs., $22/3 yrs., plus $1.50/yr. (for.); Single issue: $3; Random back issues, $2.50.

SnailPR: THE SNAIL'S PACE REVIEW: A Biannual Little Magazine of Contemporary Poetry, Ken Denberg, Darby Penney, eds., RR 2 Box 363 Brownell Rd., Cambridge, NY 12816. Issues indexed: (2:1-2). Subscriptions: $7/yr. (ind.), $12/yr. (inst.); Single issue: $4.

Sonora: SONORA REVIEW, Joan Marcus, Tony Brown, eds, Jennifer Rocco, Sue Collard, po. eds., Dept. of English, U. of Arizona, Tucson, AZ 85721. Issues indexed: (22/23). Subscriptions: $10/yr. (2 issues); Single issue: $5.

SoCaR: SOUTH CAROLINA REVIEW, Richard J. Calhoun, executive ed., Dept. of English, Clemson U., Strode Tower, Box 341503, Clemson, SC 29634-1503. Issues indexed: (24:2, 25:1). Subscriptions: $7/yr., $13/2 yrs. (USA, Canada, Mexico); $8.75/yr., $16.25/2 yrs. (inst.); plus $1.50/yr. (other for.); Back issues: $5.

SoCoast: SOUTH COAST POETRY JOURNAL, John J. Brugaletta, ed., English Dept., California State U., Fullerton, CA 92634. Issues indexed: (12-13); No. 13, received 6/25/92, is mistakenly labeled June 1993 and c1993. Subscriptions: $9/yr. (2 issues), $17/2 yrs. (ind.); $10/yr. (inst.); Single issue: $5.

SoDakR: SOUTH DAKOTA REVIEW, John R. Milton, ed., Dept. of English, U. of South Dakota, Box 111, U. Exchange, Vermillion, SD 57069. Issues indexed: (30:1-4). Subscriptions: $15/yr., $25/2 yrs. (USA, Canada); plus $1/yr. elsewhere; Single issue: $5.

SouthernHR: SOUTHERN HUMANITIES REVIEW, Dan R. Latimer, R. T. Smith, eds., 9088 Haley Center, Auburn U., AL 36849. Issues indexed: (26:1-4). Subscriptions: $15/yr.; Single issue: $5.

SouthernPR: SOUTHERN POETRY REVIEW, Lucinda Grey, Ken McLaurin, eds., English Dept., U. of North Carolina, Charlotte, NC 28223. Issues indexed: (32:1-2). Subscriptions: $8 yr.

SouthernR: SOUTHERN REVIEW, James Olney, Dave Smith, eds., Louisiana State U., 43 Allen Hall, Baton Rouge, LA 70803-5005. Issues indexed: (28:1-4). Subscriptions: $15/yr., $27/2 yrs., $38/3 yrs.; $30/yr., $52/2 yrs., $75/3 yrs. (inst.); Single issue: $5, $10 (inst.).

SouthwR: SOUTHWEST REVIEW, Willard Spiegelman, ed., Southern Methodist U., Dallas, TX 75275. Issues indexed: (77:1-4). Subscriptions: $20/yr., $40/2 yrs., $50/3 yrs. (ind.); $25/yr. (inst.); Single issue: $5.

Sparrow: SPARROW: A Politically Incorrect Verse Magazine, Felix Stefanile, ed., 103 Waldron St., West Lafayette, IN 47906. Issues indexed: (59). Single issue: $5.

Spirit: THE SPIRIT THAT MOVES US, Morty Sklar, ed., pub., P.O. Box 820, Jackson Heights, NY 11372. Issues indexed: No 1992 issues published; #12 expected in 1994.

SpiritSH: SPIRIT: A Magazine of Poetry, David Rogers, ed., Dept. of English, Seton Hall U., South Orange, NJ 07079. Issues indexed: (57). Subscriptions: $4/2 issues; Single issue: $2.

Spitball: SPITBALL: The Literary Baseball Magazine, Mike Shannon, pub. & ed., Charles Virgil Smith, po. ed., 6224 Collegevue Pl., Cincinnati, OH 45224. Issues indexed: (40-42); No. 40 was indexed by the editor. Subscriptions: $12/yr. (4 issues); $16/yr. (Canada, U.S. funds); Single issue: $4.

SpoonRQ: THE SPOON RIVER QUARTERLY, Lucia Cordell Getsi, ed., English Dept., Illinois State U., Normal, IL 61761. Issues indexed: (17:1/2-3/4). Subscriptions: $12/yr. (2 double issues); $15/yr. (inst.); Single issue: $6.

Stand: STAND MAGAZINE, Jessie Emerson, U.S.A. ed., P.O. Box 2812, Huntsville, AL 35804. Issues indexed: (33:2-4, 34:1). Subscriptions: $22/yr., $40/2 yrs.; $18/yr. (students, unwaged); Single issue: $6.50; U.S.A. distributor: Anton J. Mikovsky, 57 West 84th St., #1-C, New York, NY 10024.

Sulfur: SULFUR: A Literary Bi-Annual of the Whole Art, Clayton Eshleman, ed., English Dept., Eastern Michigan U., Ypsilanti, MI 48197. Issues indexed: (12:1-2, #30-31). Subscriptions: $13/2 issues (ind.), $19/2 issues (inst.), plus $4 (for.) or $10 (for. airmail postage); Single issue: $8.

*Sun: SUN: A Magazine of Ideas, Sy Safransky, ed., 107 N. Roberson St., Chapel Hill, NC 27516. Issues indexed: (194-204). Subscriptions: $30/yr., $50/2 yrs., $125/5 yrs., $250/10 yrs., $1,000 lifetime, plus $10/yr. (for.). The Sun, Subscription Service, P.O. Box 6706, Syracuse, NY 13217.

SycamoreR: SYCAMORE REVIEW, Linda Haynes, Michael Kiser, eds., Helene Barker, po. ed., Dept. of English, Heavilon Hall, Purdue U., West Lafayette, IN 47907. Issues indexed: (4:1-2). Subscriptions: $9/yr., $18/2 yrs.; Single issue: $5.

Talisman: TALISMAN: A Journal of Contemporary Poetry and Poetics, Edward Foster, ed., Box 1117, Hoboken, NJ 07030. Issues indexed: (8-9). Subscriptions: $9/yr. (2 issues); $13/yr. (inst.); plus $2/yr. (for.); Single issue: $5.

TampaR: TAMPA REVIEW: Literary Journal of the University of Tampa, Richard Mathews, ed., Donald Morrill, Kathryn Van Spanckeren, po. eds., Box 19F, U. of Tampa, 401 W. Kennedy Blvd., Tampa, FL 33606-1490. Issues indexed: (5); No. 4 was indexed in the 1991 volume, but was not listed in the "Periodicals Indexed" entry. Subscriptions: $10/yr. (1 issue); plus $4/yr. (for.); Single issue: $5.95.

TarRP: TAR RIVER POETRY, Peter Makuck, ed., Dept. of English, General Classroom Bldg., East Carolina U., Greenville, NC 27858-4353. Issues indexed: (30:2, 31:2, 32:1); the listing in the 1991 volume is wrong. It should have read: (31:1). Subscriptions: $8/yr (2 issues), $14/2 yrs.; Single issue: $4.50.

TexasR: TEXAS REVIEW, Paul Ruffin, ed., Division of English and Foreign Languages, Sam Houston State U., Huntsville, TX 77341. Issues indexed: (13:1/2-3/4). Subscriptions: $10/yr., $18/2 yrs., $26/3 yrs.; $10.50/yr. (Canada), $11/yr. (for.); Single issue: $5.

Thirteenth Moon: *See* 13thMoon *at beginning of file.*

ThRiPo: THREE RIVERS POETRY JOURNAL, Gerald Costanzo, Jim Daniels, ed., Three Rivers Press, P.O. Box 21, Carnegie-Mellon U., Pittsburgh, PA 15213. Issues indexed: (39/40) -- "the final issue," publised as "The Carnegie Mellon Anthology of Poetry."

Thrpny: THE THREEPENNY REVIEW, Wendy Lesser, ed., pub., P.O. Box 9131, Berkeley, CA 94709. Issues indexed: (48-51); Nos. 44-47 were indexed in the 1991 volume, not 44-45 as listed. Subscriptions: $12/yr., $20/2 yrs., $24/yr. (for.); Single issue: $3.

TickleAce: TICKLEACE, Pamela Hodgson, Lawrence Mathews, Bruce Porter, Michael Winter, eds., P.O. Box 5353, St. John's, Nfld. A1C 5W2 Canada. Issues indexed: No 1992 issues received. Subscriptions: $9/yr. (2 issues), $11/yr. (inst.), plus $3/yr. (for.); Single issue: $4.95.

Trans: TRANSLATION, The Journal of Literary Translation, Frank MacShane, Lori M. Carlson, eds., The Translation Center, 412 Dodge Hall, Columbia U., New York, NY 10027. Issues indexed: (26). Subscriptions: $18/yr. (2 issues), $34/2 yrs.; Single issue: $9.

Tribe: TRIBE: An American Gay Journal, Bernard Rabb, ed., Columbia Publishing Co., 234 E. 25th St., Baltimore, MD 21218. Issues indexed: No 1992 issues received. Subscriptions: $22/yr. (4 issues), $40/2 yrs., $58/3 yrs.; $26/yr., $48/2 yrs., $70/3 yrs. (for.); Single issue: $6 plus $1.50 postage and handling, $2.50 (for.).

TriQ: TRIQUARTERLY, Reginald Gibbons, ed., Northwestern U., 2020 Ridge Ave., Evanston, IL 60208. Issues indexed: (84-86). Subscriptions: $20/yr. (3 issues), $36/2 yrs., $500/life (ind.); $26/yr., $44/2 yrs., $300/life (inst.), plus $4/yr. (for.); Single issue: cost varies; Sample copies: $4.

Turnstile: TURNSTILE, Jill Benz, Lindsey Crittenden, Ann Biester Deane, Twisne Fan, Sara Gordonson, Mitchell Nauffts, Paolo Pepe, George Witte, eds., 175 Fifth Avenue, Suite 2348, New York, NY 10010. Issues indexed: (3:2). Subscriptions: $12/2 issues, $22/4 issues; Single issue: $6.50.

US1: US 1 WORKSHEETS, Willis, Irene, coordinating ed., Lois Marie Harrod, Ross Leckie, Virginia Lockwood, po eds., US 1 Poets' Cooperative, P.O. Box 1, Ringoes, NJ 08551. Issues indexed: (26/27). Subscriptions: $8/2 double issues; Single issue: $5.

Verse: VERSE, Henry Hart, U. S. ed., Dept. of English, College of William and Mary, Williamsburg, VA 23185. Issues indexed: (8:3/9:1, 9:2-3). Subscriptions: $15/yr. (3 issues), $21/yr. (libraries); Single issue: $5.

VirQR: THE VIRGINIA QUARTERLY REVIEW: A National Journal of Literature and Discussion, Staige D. Blackford, ed., Gregory Orr, po. consultant, One West Range, Charlottesville, VA 22903. Issues indexed: (68:1-4). Subscriptions: $15/yr., $22/2 yrs., $30/3 yrs. (ind.); $22/yr., $30/2 yrs., $50/3 yrs. (inst.); plus $3/yr. (for.); Single issue: $5.

Vis: VISIONS INTERNATIONAL, Bradley R. Strahan, po. ed., pub., Black Buzzard Press, 1110 Seaton Lane, Falls Church, VA 22046. Issues indexed: (38-40). Subscriptions: $14/yr. (3 issues), $27/2 yrs. (ind.); $42/3 yrs. (lib).; Single issue: $5.

WashR: WASHINGTON REVIEW, Clarissa K. Wittenberg, ed., P.O. Box 50132, Washington, DC 20091. Issues indexed: (17:5-6; 18:1-4). Subscriptions: $12/yr. (6 issues), $20/2 yrs.; Single issue: $3.

WeberS: WEBER STUDIES: An Interdisciplinary Humanities Journal, Neila C. Seshachari, ed., Weber State College, Ogden, UT 84408-1214. Issues indexed: (9:1-3). Subscriptions: $10/yr. (3 issues), $20/yr. (inst.); plus actual extra postage costs per year (for.); Back issues: $7; Single issue: $4.

WebR: WEBSTER REVIEW, Nancy Schapiro, Jason Sommer, Robert Boyd, Greg Marshall, eds., Webster U., 470 E. Lockwood, Webster Groves, MO 63119. Issues indexed: (16). Subscriptions: $5/yr. (1 issue).

WestB: WEST BRANCH, Karl Patten, Robert Taylor, eds., Bucknell Hall, Bucknell U., Lewisburg, PA 17837. Issues indexed: (30). Subscriptions: $7/yr. (2 issues), $11/2 yrs.; Single issue: $4.

WestCL: WEST COAST LINE: A Journal of Contemporary Writing and Criticism, Roy Miki, ed., English Dept., Simon Fraser U., Burnaby, B.C. V5A 1S6 Canada. Issues indexed: (25:3, 26:1-3, #6-9); Nos. 4-5, not Nos. 5-6 were indexed in the 1991 volume. Subscriptions: $20/yr. (ind., 3 issues), $26/yr. (inst.); Single issue: $10.

WestHR: WESTERN HUMANITIES REVIEW, Barry Weller, ed., Richard Howard, po. ed., U. of Utah, Salt Lake City, UT 84112. Issues indexed: (46:1-4); No. 4 is labeled No. 3 in error; all issues have a 1991 copyright date, also probably in error. Subscriptions: $18/yr. (4 issues, ind.), $24/yr. (inst.); Single issue: $5.

WilliamMR: THE WILLIAM AND MARY REVIEW, Alexandra Nemecek, ed., Adrien Ardoin, Bonnie Powell, po. eds., College of William and Mary, P.O. 8795, Williamsburg, VA 23187. Issues indexed: (30). Subscriptions: $4.50/single issue, plus $1.50 (for.); Single issue: $5.

WillowR: WILLOW REVIEW, Paulette Roeske, Sheila Norton, eds., College of Lake County, 19351 W. Washington St., Grayslake, IL 60030. Issues indexed: (19). Subscriptions: $10/3 issues, $16/5 issues; Single issue: $4.

WillowS: WILLOW SPRINGS, Nance Van Winckel, ed., Barbara Richardson, po. ed., Eastern Washington U., MS-1, Cheney, WA 99004. Issues Indexed: (29-30). Subscriptions: $8/yr. (2 issues), $15/2 yrs.; Single issue: $4.50.

Wind: WIND, Quentin R. Howard, ed., RFD Route 1, Box 809K, Pikeville, KY 41501. Issues indexed: (22:71); Nos. 68-70 not received. Subscriptions: $7/2 issues (ind.), $8/2 issues (inst.), $12/2 issues (for.); Single issue: $2.50; $5 (for.).

WindO: THE WINDLESS ORCHARD, Robert Novak, ed., English Dept., Indiana-Purdue U., Fort Wayne, IN 46805. Issues indexed: (56). Subscriptions: $10/3 issues; Single issue: $4.

Witness: WITNESS, Peter Stine, ed., Oakland Community College, Orchard Ridge Campus, 27055 Orchard Lake Road, Farmington Hills, MI 48334. Issues indexed: (5:1-2, 6:1-2); volume 4 consisted of only one number. Subscriptions: $12/yr. (2 issues), $22/2 yrs.; $18/yr., $34/2 yrs. (inst.); plus $4/yr. (for.); Single copies: $7.

WorldL: WORLD LETTER, Jon Cone, ed., 2726 E. Court St., Iowa City, IA 52245. Issues indexed: (3). Subscriptions: $9/2 issues (U.S.), $12/2 issues (Canada); Single issue: $5 (U.S.), $7 (Canada).

WorldO: WORLD ORDER, Firuz Kazemzadeh, Betty J. Fisher, Howard Garey, Robert H. Stockman, James D. Stokes, eds., National Spiritual Assembly of the Bahá'ís of the United States, 415 Linden Ave., Wilmette, IL 60091. Issues indexed: No 1992 issues published; 25:1 published Fall 1993. Subscriptions: $10/yr., $18/2 yrs. (USA, Canada, Mexico); $15/yr., $28/2 yrs. (elsewhere); $20/yr., $38/2 yrs. (for. airmail); Single issue: $3.

WormR: THE WORMWOOD REVIEW, Marvin Malone, ed., P.O. Box 4698, Stockton, CA 95204-0698. Issues indexed: (32:1-4; #125-128). Subscriptions: $8/4 issues (ind.), $10/4 issues (inst.); Single issue: $4.

Writ: WRIT, Roger Greenwald, ed., Innis College, U. of Toronto, 2 Sussex Ave., Toronto, Canada M5S 1J5. Issues indexed: No issues received in 1992; Nos. 23/24 (1991-1992) was indexed in the 1991 volume. Subscriptions: $15/2 issues (ind.), $18/2 issues (inst.); same amount in U.S. funds outside Canada; Back issues: $7.50-15.

Writer: THE WRITER, Sylvia K. Burack, ed., pub., 120 Boylston St., Boston, MA 02116-4615. Issues indexed: (105:1-12). Subscriptions: $27/yr., $50/2 yrs., $74/3 yrs.; plus $8/yr. (for.); $10/5 issues for new subscribers; Single issue: $2.25.

WritersF: WRITERS' FORUM, Alexander Blackburn, ed., Victoria McCabe, po ed., P.O. Box 7150, U. of Colorado, Colorado Springs, CO 80933-7150. Issues indexed: (18). Subscriptions: $8.95/yr. (1 issue) plus $1.05 postage and handling; Back issue sample: $5.95 plus $1.05 postage and handling.

YaleR: THE YALE REVIEW, J. D. McClatchy, ed., P.O. Box 1902A, Yale Station, New Haven, CT 06520. Issues indexed: (80:1/2-4). Subscriptions: $20/yr., $36/2 yrs., $54/3 yrs.; $30/yr., $54/2 yrs., $81/3 yrs. (for.); $40/yr. (inst.), $45/yr. (for. inst.); Single issues: $6.50, $12.00 (inst.).

YellowS: YELLOW SILK, Journal of Erotic Arts, Lily Pond, ed., pub., P.O. Box 6374, Albany, CA 94706. Issues indexed: (39-41); No. 40 is numbered as "Ten Years" rather than 40. Subscriptions: $30/yr. (ind.), $38/yr. (lib., inst.), plus $6/yr. (for. surface) or $20/yr. (for. air). Single issue: $6.

Zyzzyva: ZYZZYVA: The Last Word, West Coast Writers & Artists, Howard Junker, ed, 41 Sutter St., Suite 1400, San Francisco, CA 94104. Issues indexed: (8:1-4, #29-32). Subscriptions: $20/yr. (4 issues), $32/2 yrs. (ind.); $28/yr. (inst.); $30/yr. (for.); Single copies: $8 post paid.

Alphabetical List of Journals Indexed, with Acronyms

13th Moon: A Feminist Literary Magazine : 13th Moon

Abraxas : Abraxas
Aerial : Aerial
African American Review : AfAmRev
Agni : Agni
Amelia : Amelia
The American Poetry Review : AmerPoR
The American Scholar : AmerS
The American Voice : AmerV
The Americas Review: A Review of Hispanic Literature and Art of the USA : Americas
Another Chicago Magazine : AnotherCM
Antaeus : Antaeus
The Anthology of New England Writers : AnthNEW
The Antigonish Review : AntigR
The Antioch Review : AntR
Arc : Arc
Archae : Archae
Areíto : Areíto
Arion: A Journal of Humanities and the Classics : Arion
Art & Understanding: The Journal of Literature and Art About AIDS : Art&Und
Artful Dodge : ArtfulD
Arts Indiana Literary Supplement *see* Hopewell Review
Ascent : Ascent
Asylum : Asylum
The Atlantic : Atlantic
Avec : Avec

Bamboo Ridge: The Hawaii Writers' Quarterly : BambooR
The Bellingham Review : BellR
Bellowing Ark : BellArk
The Beloit Poetry Journal : BelPoJ
The Bilingual Review/La Revista Bilingüe : BilingR
Black American Literature Forum : BlackALF
Black Bear Review : BlackBR
Black Warrior Review : BlackWR
Blueline : Blueline
Bogg : Bogg
Bomb Magazine : Bomb
Boston Review : BostonR
Boulevard : Boulevard
Brooklyn Review : BrooklynR

Caliban : Caliban
California Quarterly : CalQ
Callaloo: A Journal of African-American and African Arts and Letters : Callaloo
Calyx: A Journal of Art and Literature by Women : Calyx
Canadian Literature : CanLit
The Cape Rock : CapeR
The Capilano Review : CapilR
Carolina Quarterly : CarolQ

The Centennial Review : CentR
Central Park : CentralP
Chaminade Literary Review : ChamLR
Changing Men: Issues in Gender, Sex and Politics : ChangingM
The Chariton Review : CharR
The Chattahoochee Review: The DeKalb College Literary Quarterly : ChatR
Chelsea : Chelsea
Chicago Review : ChiR
Chiron Review : ChironR
The Christian Century : ChrC
Cimarron Review : CimR
Cincinnati Poetry Review : CinPR
City Lights Review : CityLR
Clockwatch Review: A Journal of the Arts : ClockR
Coal City Review : CoalC
College English : ColEng
Colorado Review : ColR
Columbia: A Magazine of Poetry & Prose : Colum
Commonweal : Comm
Confrontation : Confr
Conjunctions : Conjunc
The Connecticut Poetry Review : ConnPR
Conscience: A Newsjournal of Prochoice Catholic Opinion : Conscience
Contact II : Contact
Context South : ContextS
Crab Creek Review : CrabCR
Crazyhorse : Crazy
Cream City Review : CreamCR
Crosscurrents : CrossCur
Crucible : Crucible
Cumberland Poetry Review : CumbPR
Cutbank : CutB

Dandelion : Dandel
Denver Quarterly : DenQ
Descant : Descant
Dog River Review : DogRR
Dusty Dog : DustyD

Elf: Eclectic Literary Forum : Elf
Emerald Coast Review : EmeraldCR
English Journal : EngJ
Epiphany: A Journal of Literature : Epiphany:
Epoch : Epoch
Event: The Douglas College Review : Event
The Evergreen Chronicles: A Journal of Gay & Lesbian Literature : EvergreenC
Eyeball

Farmer's Market : Farm
Field: Contemporary Poetry and Poetics : Field
The Florida Review : FloridaR
Footwork: The Paterson Literary Review : Footwork
Four Quarters : FourQ
Free Lunch : FreeL

Georgia Review : GeoR
Gettysburg Review : GettyR
Graham House Review : GrahamHR
Grain : Grain
Grand Street : GrandS
Green Mountains Review : GreenMR
The Greensboro Review : GreensboroR
Gypsy : Gypsy

The Hampden-Sydney Poetry Review : HampSPR
Hanging Loose : HangL

Harper's Magazine : Harp
The Harvard Advocate : HarvardA
Hawaii Review : HawaiiR
Hayden's Ferry Review : HayF
Heaven Bone : HeavenB
Hellas: A Journal of Poetry and the Humanities : Hellas
High Plains Literary Review : HighP
Hiram Poetry Review : HiramPoR
The Hollins Critic : HolCrit
Hopewell Review (*formerly* Arts Indiana Literary Supplement) : HopewellR
The Hudson Review : Hudson

Indiana Review : IndR
Interim : Interim
International Poetry Review : InterPR
Inti: Revista de Literatura Hispánica : Inti
Iowa Review : Iowa

The Jacaranda Review : Jacaranda
The James White Review: A Gay Men's Literary Journal : JamesWR
The Journal : Journal
The Journal of New Jersey Poets : JlNJPo

Kaleidoscope: International Magazine of Literature, Fine Arts, and Disability : Kaleid
Kalliope: A Journal of Women's Art : Kalliope
Kenyon Review : KenR

Lactuca : Lactuca
Laurel Review : LaurelR
Light: A Quarterly of Humorous, Occasional, Ephemeral & Light Verse : Light
Linden Lane Magazine : LindLM
The Literary Review: An International Journal of contemporary Writing : LitR
Louisiana Literature: A Review of Literature and the Humanities : LouisL
Lullwater Review : LullwaterR
Luz: En Arte y Literatura : Luz

The Malahat Review : MalR
Manhattan Poetry Review : ManhatPR
The Manhattan Review : ManhatR
Manoa: A Pacific Journal of International Writing : Manoa
The Massachusetts Review : MassR
Memphis State Review : *Name changed to* River City : RiverC
Mester : Mester
Michigan Quarterly Review : MichQR
Mid-American Review : MidAR
The Midwest Quarterly: A Journal of Contemporary Thought : MidwQ
Mildred : Mildred
The Minnesota Review : MinnR
Mississippi Review : MissR
The Missouri Review : MissouriR
Moody Street Irregulars : MoodySI
Mss : *superseded by* New Myths

The Nation : Nat
Negative Capability : NegC
New American Writing : NewAW
New Delta Review : NewDeltaR
New England Review : NewEngR
New Letters : NewL
New Myths : NewMyths
New Orleans Review : NewOR
The New Renaissance : NewRena
The New Republic : NewRep
The New York Quarterly : NewYorkQ

The New York Review of Books : NewYRB
The New Yorker : NewYorker
Nimrod : Nimrod
Noctiluca: An International Magazine of Poetry : Noctiluca
The North American Review : NoAmR
North Carolina Literary Review : NoCarLR
North Dakota Quarterly : NoDaQ
The North Stone Review : NorthStoneR
Northeast : Northeast
Northwest Review : NowestR
Notus: New Writing : Notus
La Nuez: Revista Internacional de Arte y Literatura : Nuez

Obsidian II: Black Literature in Review : Obs
The Ohio Review : OhioR
Ometeca: Ciencia y Literatura, Science & Literature : Ometeca
Ontario Review : OntR
OnTheBus: A New Literary Magazine : OnTheBus
Osiris : Os
Outerbridge : Outbr
Oxford Magazine : OxfordM

Pacific Review: A Magazine of Poetry and Prose : PacificR
Paintbrush: A Journal of Poetry, Translations, and Letters : Paint
Painted Bride Quarterly : PaintedB
Painted Hills Review : PaintedHR
The Paris Review : ParisR
Parting Gifts : Parting
Partisan Review : PartR
Passages North : PassN
Pearl : Pearl
Pembroke Magazine : Pembroke
The Pennsylvania Review : PennR
Pequod : Pequod
Pig Iron : Pig
The Pikestaff Forum : PikeF
Plainsongs : Plain
Ploughshares : Ploughs
Poem : Poem
Poet And Critic : PoetC
Poet Lore : PoetL
Poetry : Poetry
Poetry Canada : PoetryC
Poetry East : PoetryE
Poetry Northwest : PoetryNW
Poetry USA : PoetryUSA
The Pottersfield Portfolio : PottPort
Prairie Fire: A Canadian Magazine of New Writing : PraF
Prairie Schooner : PraS
Primavera : Prima

Quarry : Quarry
Quarterly Review of Literature : QRL
Quarterly West : QW

Rag Mag : RagMag
Raritan: A Quarterly Review : Raritan
Red Bass : RedBass
River City : RiverC
River Styx : RiverS
Rohwedder: International Journal of Literature & Art : Rohwedder

Salmagundi: A Quarterly of the Humanities and Social Sciences : Salm
Seneca Review : SenR
Sequoia: The Stanford Literary Journal : Sequoia

The Sewanee Review : SewanR
Shadow Play : ShadowP
Shenandoah : Shen
Shiny: The Magazine of the Future : Shiny
Sidewalks: An Anthology of Poetry, Short Prose, & Art : Sidewalks
Silverfish Review : SilverFR
Sing Heavenly Muse!: Women's Poetry and Prose : SingHM
Sinister Wisdom: A Journal for the Lesbian Imagination in the Arts and Politics : SinW
Slipstream : SlipS
The Small Pond Magazine of Literature : SmPd
The Snail's Pace Review: A Biannual Little Magazine of Contemporary Poetry : SnailPR
Sonora Review : Sonora
South Carolina Review : SoCaR
South Coast Poetry Journal : SoCoast
South Dakota Review : SoDakR
Southern Humanities Review : SouthernHR
Southern Poetry Review : SouthernPR
Southern Review : SouthernR
Southwest Review : SouthwR
Sparrow: A Politically Incorrect Verse Magazine : Sparrow
Spirit : SpiritSH
The Spirit That Moves Us : Spirit
Spitball: The Literary Baseball Magazine : Spitball
The Spoon River Quarterly : SpoonRQ
Stand Magazine : Stand
Sulfur: A Literary Bi-annual of the Whole Art : Sulfur
Sun: A Magazine of Ideas : Sun
Sycamore Review : SycamoreR

Talisman: A Journal of Contemporary Poetry & Poetics : Talisman
Tampa Review: Literary Review of the University of Tampa : TampaR
Tar River Poetry : TarRP
Texas Review : TexasR
Thirteenth Moon: *See* 13th Moon *at beginning of file*
Three Rivers Poetry Journal : ThRiPo
The Threepenny Review : Thrpny
TickleAce : TickleAce
Translation: The Journal of Literary Translation : Translation
Tribe: An American Gay Journal : Tribe
Triquarterly : TriQ
Turnstile : Turnstile

US 1 Worksheets : US1

Verse : Verse
The Virginia Quarterly Review: A National Journal of Literature and Discussion : VirQR
Visions International : Vis

Washington Review : Wash
Weber Studies: An Interdisciplinary Humanities Journal : WeberS
Webster Review : WebR
West Branch : WestB
West Coast Line: A Journal of Contemporary Writing and Criticism (*formerly* West Coast Review) : WestCL
Western Humanities Review : WestHR
The William and Mary Review : WilliamMR
Willow Review : WillowR
Willow Springs : WillowS
Wind : Wind
The Windless Orchard : WindO
Witness : Witness
World Letter : WorldL

World Order : WorldO
The Wormwood Review : WormR
Writ : Writ
The Writer : Writer
Writers' Forum : WritersF

The Yale Review : YaleR
Yellow Silk: Journal of Erotic Arts : YellowS

Zyzzyva: The Last Word, West Coast Writers and Artists : Zyzzyva

The Author Index

AAL, Katharyn Machan
See MACHAN, Katharyn Howd
1. AALFS, Janet
"Lesbian Metaphysics." [SinW] (46) Spr 92, p. 7.
2. AARON, Jonathan
"From the 1929 Edition of the Encyclopedia Britannica" (for Adam Zagajewski). [PartR] (59:1) Wint 92, p. 101-102.
3. ABAGYEH, Benjamin I.
"Ask Them." [HayF] (11) Fall-Wint 92, p. 72.
4. ABBE, Kate
"The Flood around Her." [LaurelR] (26:1) Wint 92, p. 95.
"From a Chinese Landscape." [GreenMR] (NS 5:2) Spr-Sum 92, p. 83.
5. ABBOTT, Anthony (Anthony S.)
"Coming Out." [Interim] (11:1) Spr-Sum 92, p. 5.
"Fathers" (For Cathy Smith Bowers). [Crucible] (28) Fall 92, p. 16-17.
"The Legendary Stillness of Herons" (for Emily Abbott Nordfeldt, 1900-1989). [LullwaterR] (3:2) Spr 92, p. 42-45.
"Remembrance." [Pembroke] (24) 92, p. 21.
"Unburdening." [Crucible] (28) Fall 92, p. 14-15.
6. ABBOTT, Keith
"Stupid Face Renku" (w. Pat Nolan and Michael Sowl). [HangL] (60) 92, p. 6-11.
7. ABELL, M. J.
"Close to the Ground" (For my father). [HiramPoR] (51/52) Fall 91-Sum 92, p. 9-10.
"First Poem for Curtis, August 1990." [US1] (26/27) 92, p. 21.
8. ABERG, William
"Note Left on the Bed." [Contact] (10:62/63/64) Fall 91-Spr 92, p. 52.
"Your Lap." [Sun] (194) Ja 92, p. 37.
9. ABERJHANI
"Blackman Sitting on a Rock." [AfAmRev] (26:2) Sum 92, p. 224.
10. ABERNETHY, Hugh, Jr.
"Hangover Politics." [MinnR] (38) Spr-Sum 92, p. 31-33.
11. ABRAHAM, Susan
"Dear God." [Poetry] (160:2) My 92, p. 92.
"Miniatures." [ParisR] (34:125) Wint 92, p. 118.
"Quick, Before the Wind." [ParisR] (34:125) Wint 92, p. 119.
12. ABRAMS, David
"Adam Sneaks Back into the Garden." [ChrC] (109:33) 11 N 92, p. 1030.
13. ABRAMS-MORLEY, Liz
"Night Watch at Forty" (for Steve). [Poem] (68) N 92, p. 32-33.
"Still Life with Football and Beach Grass." [Poem] (68) N 92, p. 30-31.
14. ABSE, Dannie
"Between 3 and 4 A.M." [Poetry] (161:2) N 92, p. 70-72.
"A Doctor's Register." [Poetry] (161:2) N 92, p. 76.
"How I Won the Raffle." [Poetry] (161:2) N 92, p. 74-75.
"Shmelke" (For A.B.). [Poetry] (161:2) N 92, p. 73.
15. ABU-SABA, Elias
"The Song of Ibn el Farihd." [InterPR] (18:1) Spr 92, p. 52-55.
16. ACEVES, Raúl
"Where the conch of yucatán" (tr. by Reginald Gibbons). [TriQ] (85) Fall 92, p. 162.
17. ACHTERBERG, Gerrit
"Skin" (tr. by James S Holmes). [Trans] (26) Spr 92, p. 114.
18. ACKERMAN, Diane
"Complaint on Her Cat." [Conjunc] (18) 92, p. 121.
19. ACKLEY, Daryl
"Where Does Paper Lead?" [DogRR] (11:1) Spr-Sum 92, p. 38.
20. ADAIR, Gilbert
"A Silhouette Can Cast a Shadow." [Avec] (5:1) 92, p. 73-79.

21. ADAMO, Ralph
"New Orleans." [SouthernR] (28:4) Aut, O 92, p. 812.
"Renting." [SouthernR] (28:4) Aut, O 92, p. 812.
22. ADAMS, Anna
"At Mauthausen Camp." [Stand] (33:4) Aut 92, p. 20-21.
"The Drunk." [NewYorkQ] (48) 92, p. 55-56.
23. ADAMS, Barbara
"Anachronism" (for Anacreon). [ChironR] (11:3) Aut 92, p. 29.
24. ADAMS, Jefferson,
"These Waters." [MissR] (20:3) Spr 92, p. 23.
25. ADAMS, Mary
"Child Reading." [WestHR] (46:2) Sum 92, p. 158-159.
"Some Lights." [WestHR] (46:2) Sum 92, p. 160.
26. ADAMS, Monica
"Dishes." [CreamCR] (16:1) Spr 92, p. 121.
"New Year's Day." [LitR] (35:3) Spr 92, p. 309.
ADAMS, Rebecca Hood
See HOOD-ADAMS, Rebecca
27. ADAMS, Stephen
"Blowfish." [AntigR] (90) Sum 92, p. 51-53.
28. ADAMSON, Eve
"Pig Facing East." [QW] (34) Wint-Spr 92, p. 86.
29. ADAMSON, Robert
"The Tomb of Language." [Stand] (33:2) Spr 92, p. 97.
30. ADCOCK, Betty
"Threshold." [Shen] (42:2) Sum 92, p. 100-101.
31. ADCOCK, Fleur
"Darwinism" (from "Niagara de Plumb," tr. of Daniela Crasnaru). [13thMoon] (10:1/2) 92, p. 11.
"Fear of Drifting" (tr. of Ioana Craciunescu). [13thMoon] (10:1/2) 92, p. 13.
"Grey Landscape" (tr. of Ioana Craciunescu). [13thMoon] (10:1/2) 92, p. 14.
"A Haunting." [Stand] (33:2) Spr 92, p. 105.
"Herbstmanöver" (from "Zoná de Protectie," tr. of Liliana Ursu). [13thMoon] (10:1/2) 92, p. 8.
"The Last Day of Pompeii" (from "Niagara de Plumb," tr. of Daniela Crasnaru). [13thMoon] (10:1/2) 92, p. 10.
"Naive Paintings" (tr. of Ioana Craciunescu). [13thMoon] (10:1/2) 92, p. 14.
"Orphic" (from "Niagara de Plumb," tr. of Daniela Crasnaru). [13thMoon] (10:1/2) 92, p. 9.
"Victory" (from "Niagara de Plumb," tr. of Daniela Crasnaru). [13thMoon] (10:1/2) 92, p. 12.
"Vieux Jeu" (from "Piata Aurarilor," tr. of Liliana Ursu). [13thMoon] (10:1/2) 92, p. 7.
32. ADDIEGO, John
"The Skate Palace." [NowestR] (30:1) 92, p. 33.
33. ADDINGTON, Rosa Lea
"There Were Neighborhoods." [ChatR] (12:2) Wint 92, p. 95-96.
34. ADDISON, Elizabeth
"Late Child." [ColEng] (54:6) O 92, p. 715-716.
35. ADDONIZIO, Kim
"Words Written During Your Operation." [NewMyths] (1:2/2:1) 92, p. 15.
36. ADKINS, Kieth Joseph
"Travels." [ChangingM] (24) Sum-Fall 92, p. 64.
37. ADLARD, John
"Oh, why is that young man looking so deathly?" [Verse] (8:3/9:1) Wint-Spr 92, p. 108.
38. ADLER, Cori
"Building a Cold Frame by Moonlight." [PoetryNW] (33:3) Aut 92, p. 19-20.
"Fugue." [PoetryNW] (33:3) Aut 92, p. 18-19.
39. ADONIS
"The Transformations of the Lover" (3 selections, tr. by Kamal Boullata and Susan Einbinder). [MichQR] (31:4) Fall 92, p. 619-623.
ADORNO, Pedro López
See LOPEZ ADORNO, Pedro
40. ADSIT, Kristin K.
"How Was School Today?" [Writer] (105:3) Mr 92, p. 22.

41. AFTEL, Andrew
"Jesus Visits My Uncle's Office." [PoetryE] (33) Spr 92, p. 7.

AGHA SHAHID ALI
See ALI, Agha Shahid

42. AGOOS, Julie
"Intensive." [YaleR] (80:4) O 92, p. 78.
"Persephone." [AmerV] (26) Spr 92, p. 38-39.

43. AGOSIN, Marjorie
"Buenos Aires" (tr. by Celeste Kostopulos-Cooperman). [Harp] (284:1703) Ap 92, p. 34.
"Evenings" (tr. by Cola Franzen). [13thMoon] (10:1/2) 92, p. 17.
"Homeland" (tr. by Cola Franzen). [13thMoon] (10:1/2) 92, p. 15-16.
"La Patria." [13thMoon] (10:1/2) 92, p. 15.
"To Jose Daniel" (tr. by C. Kostopulos-Cooperman). [AmerV] (26) Spr 92, p. 210-22.
"Visperas." [13thMoon] (10:1/2) 92, p. 17.

44. AGOSTINO, Paul
"Botany and Bricklaying." [SlipS] (12) 92, p. 30-31.
"The Emperor's New Clothes." [ChironR] (11:1) Spr 92, p. 7.
"Engagements and Disengagements." [ChironR] (11:1) Spr 92, p. 7.
"First Thought — Best Thought." [AnotherCM] (23) Spr 92, p. 5-6.
"The Left Ventricle, the Right Ventricle, and the Aorta." [Lactuca] (15) Mr 92, p. 55 - 56.
"Refuse Affirmations." [SlipS] (12) 92, p. 31.
"There's Money to Be Made in Reproduction." [ChironR] (11:1) Spr 92, p. 7.
"Violence, the Subconscious, and the Unconscious." [ChironR] (11:1) Spr 92, p. 7.
"Wrestling with Democracy." [ChironR] (11:3) Aut 92, p. 30.

45. AGUAYO-DELGADO, Deborah M.
"Stoop Summers." [SinW] (47) Sum-Fall 92, p. 39-40.

46. AGUERO, Kathleen
"Captain Colette." [Poetry] (160:2) My 92, p. 78.

47. AGÜEROS, Jack
"Sonnet for Miss Beausoleil." [Callaloo] (15:4) Fall 92, p. 946.

AGUIAR, Fred d'
See D'AGUIAR, Fred

48. AGUILAR, Luis Miguel
"Chetumal Bay Anthology" (5 selections, tr. from the Spanish). [Manoa] (4:2) Fall 92, p. 191-193.
"The Huapango" (tr. by Reginald Gibbons). [TriQ] (85) Fall 92, p. 90-91.

49. AHERN, Tom
"Vienna." [Avec] (5:1) 92, p. 28.
"A Wanderer's Phrase Buch" (tr. for German travelers by Rosmarie Waldrop). [Avec] (5:1) 92, p. 25-27.

50. AHLSCHWEDE, Margrethe
"24 December." [WeberS] (9:2) Spr-Sum 92, p. 85-86.
"Life After." [WeberS] (9:2) Spr-Sum 92, p. 83-84.
"Living History." [WeberS] (9:2) Spr-Sum 92, p. 84-85.
"Watching Water." [WeberS] (9:2) Spr-Sum 92, p. 82.

51. AHLSTROMER, David
"Words Said, Words Unsaid." [OxfordM] (8:1) Spr-Sum 92, p. 14.

52. AHO, Margaret
"Blood and Milk." [13thMoon] (10:1/2) 92, p. 19.
"From the Kore." [13thMoon] (10:1/2) 92, p. 18.

53. AI
"The Director: Hoover, Edgar J." [Agni] (35) 92, p. 37-40.
"Knockout" (For Desiree Washington & Mike Tyson). [Callaloo] (15:4) Fall 92, p. 880-881.
"Motherhood." [OnTheBus] (4:2/5:1, #10/11) 92, p. 50-52.
"Oswald Incognito & Astral Travels." [SnailPR] (2:2) Fall-Wint 92, p. 22-27.
"Party Line." [SnailPR] (2:2) Fall-Wint 92, p. 16-21.
"Self-Defense" (for Marion Barry). [Agni] (36) 92, p. 38-40.
"Self Defense" (For Marion Barry). [Callaloo] (15:4) Fall 92, p. 877-879.
"Self Defense" (For Marion Barry). [OnTheBus] (4:2/5:1, #10/11) 92, p. 47-48.
"Zero Velocity." [OnTheBus] (4:2/5:1, #10/11) 92, p. 49-50.

54. AI, Qing
"To the Soul of Danuska" (tr. by Eugene Chen Eoyang). [Trans] (26) Spr 92, p. 33-35.

55. AIKEN, Chris
"A Way to Believe in God." [HangL] (61) 92, p. 90.
56. AIKEN, William
"Myth." [Bogg] (65) 92, p. 37.
57. AISENBERG, Nadya
"Justice in Mexico City." [Agni] (35) 92, p. 229.
58. AIZENBERG, Susan
"Anniversary." [PassN] (13:1) Sum 92, p. 11.
59. AJANIKU, Imani P.
"For Cora Helen Smith Hadden." [SinW] (47) Sum-Fall 92, p. 91-92.
60. AJAY, Stephen
"Daybreak on Asi Ghat." [HolCrit] (29:1) F 92, p. 16-17.
AKEMI, Tomioka
See TOMIOKA, Akemi
61. AKERMAN, Darren J.
"Mid-Morning Breakdown at the Main Street Mill." [NewMyths] (1:2/2:1) 92, p. 77 - 86.
62. AKERS, Ellery
"Night: Volcano, California." [ThRiPo] (39/40) 92-93, p. 3-4.
63. AKHMADULINA, Bella
"Another" (tr. by Diana Senechal). [Trans] (26) Spr 92, p. 106.
"Don't Devote Much Time to Me" (tr. by Diana Senechal). [Trans] (26) Spr 92, p. 105.
"A New Notebook" (tr. by Diana Senechal). [Trans] (26) Spr 92, p. 107.
"Who Knows If I May Roam the Earth" (tr. by Diana Senechal). [Trans] (26) Spr 92, p. 106.
64. AKHMATOVA, Anna
"Requiem 1935-1940" (tr. by David Helwig). [Quarry] (41:1) Wint 92, p. 7-15.
65. AKITSU, Ei
"Ah, women" (tr. by Akemi Tomioka and Leza Lowitz). [Harp] (285:1706) Jl 92, p. 26.
"A ball of flesh" (tr. by Akemi Tomioka and Leza Lowitz). [Harp] (285:1706) Jl 92, p. 26.
"Leaving my house" (tr. by Akemi Tomioka and Leza Lowitz). [Harp] (285:1706) Jl 92, p. 26.
"Sorting out" (tr. by Akemi Tomioka and Leza Lowitz). [Harp] (285:1706) Jl 92, p. 26.
"Why was I given breasts" (tr. by Akemi Tomioka and Leza Lowitz). [Harp] (285:1706) Jl 92, p. 26.
66. AKMAKJIAN, Alan P.
"America's Cup." [BlackBR] (15) Spr-Sum 92, p. 37.
"Election Year Promises." [BlackBR] (16) Wint-Spr 92-93, p. 26.
"M.A.D.D. 1991." [BlackBR] (16) Wint-Spr 92-93, p. 21-22.
"Under the Influence, Boston." [BlackBR] (16) Wint-Spr 92-93, p. 26.
67. Al-QASSIM, Samih
"Conversation Between an Ear of Corn and a Jerusalem Rose Thorn" (tr. by Abdullah al-Udhari). [Paint] (19:37) Spr 92, p. 35.
"Sons of War" (tr. by Abdullah al-Udhari). [Paint] (19:37) Spr 92, p. 38.
"The Story of a City" (tr. by Abdullah al-Udhari). [Paint] (19:37) Spr 92, p. 36.
"Travel Tickets" (tr. by Abdullah al-Udhari). [Paint] (19:37) Spr 92, p. 37.
68. Al-UDHARI, Abdullah
"Conversation Between an Ear of Corn and a Jerusalem Rose Thorn" (tr. of Samih al - Qassim). [Paint] (19:37) Spr 92, p. 35.
"Sons of War" (tr. of Samih al-Qassim). [Paint] (19:37) Spr 92, p. 38.
"The Story of a City" (tr. of Samih al-Qassim). [Paint] (19:37) Spr 92, p. 36.
"Travel Tickets" (tr. of Samih al-Qassim). [Paint] (19:37) Spr 92, p. 37.
69. ALARCON, Francisco X.
" *Chicome-Coatl* / Seven Snake." [Americas] (19:3/4) Wint 91, p. 36.
"Cutting Wood." [Americas] (19:3/4) Wint 91, p. 34.
"For Planting *Camotes*" (Ruiz de Alarcón III:7). [Americas] (19:3/4) Wint 91, p. 37.
"Herbs." [HighP] (7:2) Fall 92, p. 65-66.
"Seer." [BrooklynR] (9) 92, p. 98.
"To Earthworms Before Fishing with a Hook" (Ruiz de Alarcón II:15). [Americas] (19:3/4) Wint 91, p. 35.
"To Undo Sleep Spell" (Ruiz de Alarcón II:2). [Americas] (19:3/4) Wint 91, p. 38.
70. ALBERT, Alan
"The Janitor's Life." [AmerPoR] (21:6) N-D 92, p. 20.

71. ALBERTS, Mick
"Jet Black Eyes." [PoetryNW] (33:3) Aut 92, p. 10.
"Spontaneous Human Combustion." [PoetryNW] (33:3) Aut 92, p. 9-10.
72. ALBO, Mike
"Driving Sex" (Selections: 4 poems). [WashR] (18:3) O-N 92, p. 27.
73. ALBON, George
"Dust." [Avec] (5:1) 92, p. 80.
"The Evening Call" (Excerpt). [Avec] (5:1) 92, p. 81-82.
"Lands and Peoples" (Selections: 3-4). [Caliban] (11) 92, p. 94-95.
74. ALBRECHT, Abigail
"Time and Roses." [SoCoast] (12) Ja 92, p. 49.
75. ALBRECHT, Laura
"On a Red Afternoon." [CimR] (100) Jl 92, p. 106-107.
"Some Love." [CapeR] (27:2) Fall 92, p. 30.
"Twelve Stories." [CapeR] (27:2) Fall 92, p. 31.
76. ALCALA, Carlos
"The Six-Pachyderms." [Light] (4) Wint 92-93, p. 11.
77. ALCALAY, Ammiel
"Axiom"" (tr. of Yehuda Halevi). [Paint] (19:37) Spr 92, p. 39.
"The Cairo Notebooks." [CityLR] (5) 92, p. 172-181.
"Checkmate in the Garden" (tr. of Shelley Elkayam). [Paint] (19:37) Spr 92, p. 41.
"Embroidered Rag: Poem on Umm Kulthum" (tr. of Roni Someck). [Paint] (19:37) Spr 92, p. 44.
"Jasmine: Poem on Sandpaper" (tr. of Roni Someck). [Paint] (19:37) Spr 92, p. 43.
"Love Poems"" (tr. of Yehuda Halevi). [Paint] (19:37) Spr 92, p. 40.
"Purim Sequence" (tr. of Tikva Levi). [PaintedB] (47) 92, p. 16-25.
"Seven Stanzas to an Indian Chief" (tr. of Shelley Elkayam). [Paint] (19:37) Spr 92, p. 42.
78. ALCMAN
"A Garland from Alcman" (tr. by Rosanna Warren). [Arion] 3d series (1:1) Wint 90, p. 179.
79. ALDER, David
"No Sign of Spring." [Quarry] (41:4) Fall 92, p. 46.
"Wintering." [Quarry] (41:4) Fall 92, p. 46.
80. ALESHIRE, Joan
"Body of Earth." [CreamCR] (16:2) Fall 92, p. 22.
"World's End." [CreamCR] (16:2) Fall 92, p. 23.
ALESSANDRO, Patricia D'
See De ALESSANDRO, Patricia
81. ALEXANDER, Elizabeth
"Apollo." [Poetry] (160:1) Ap 92, p. 19.
"Cough Medicine." [Poetry] (160:1) Ap 92, p. 20.
"Stravinsky in L.A." [Poetry] (160:1) Ap 92, p. 18.
82. ALEXANDER, Floyce
"Blood Rivers." [YellowS] (41) Fall-Wint 92-93, p. 18.
"Endsong." [YellowS] (41) Fall-Wint 92-93, p. 19.
"Song." [YellowS] (41) Fall-Wint 92-93, p. 19.
83. ALEXANDER, Marlene
"For My Cousin." [OnTheBus] (4:2/5:1, #10/11) 92, p. 53-55.
"Smoke Signals." [OnTheBus] (4:2/5:1, #10/11) 92, p. 55.
84. ALEXANDER, Meena
"Asylum." [MichQR] (31:4) Fall 92, p. 617-618.
"Desert Rose." [ChiR] (38:1/2) 92, p. 11.
"Estrangement Becomes the Mark of the Eagle." [ChiR] (38:1/2) 92, p. 12-13.
"Skin Song." [RiverS] (36) 92, p. 51-55.
85. ALEXANDER, Pamela
"Mt. Pinatubo, the Philippines" (an alphabet poem). [NewRep] (207:22) 23 N 92, p. 42.
86. ALEXANDER, Will
"Return Stroke" (Part III, from "Lightning"). [Sulfur] (12:1, #30) Spr 92, p. 11-18.
87. ALEXIE, Sherman
"Breakaway Bar #5." [Lactuca] (16) Ag 92, p. 19.
"Breakaway Bar #8." [Lactuca] (16) Ag 92, p. 20.
"Breakaway Bar #9." [Lactuca] (16) Ag 92, p. 20.
"Citizen Kane." [KenR] (NS 14:3) Sum 92, p. 47.
"Crazy Horse Dreams." [Lactuca] (16) Ag 92, p. 21-22.

"The Ditch Digger." [BlackBR] (16) Wint-Spr 92-93, p. 24-25.
"Fire Storm." [BelPoJ] (42:4) Sum 92, p. 5-14.
"How to Obtain Eagle Feathers for Religious Use" (for G. S.). [NewYorkQ] (48) 92, p. 87-88.
"The Last Indian Bar in Spokane." [KenR] (NS 14:3) Sum 92, p. 44.
"The Native American Broadcasting System." [HangL] (61) 92, p. 7-11.
"The Reservation Cab Driver." [ChironR] (11:1) Spr 92, p. 26.
"Reservation Drive-In." [HangL] (61) 92, p. 5-6.
"Seattle, 1987." [Jacaranda] (6:1/2) Wint-Spr 92, p. 58.
"Some Assembly Required." [SlipS] (12) 92, p. 25.
"Split Decisions." [NewYorkQ] (49) 92, p. 87-89.
"The Texas Chainsaw Massacre." [KenR] (NS 14:3) Sum 92, p. 45-46.
"Vision (1)." [HangL] (61) 92, p. 12-13.

88. ALI, Agha Shahid
"Clipper Class Travel." [GrahamHR] (16) Fall 92, p. 21.
"Ghazal: The pure pain with which he recognizes angels." [ChiR] (38:1/2) 92, p. 108 - 109.
"The Last Saffron." [SenR] (22:2) Fall 92, p. 8-10.

89. ALICE, M. S.
"A leaf." [DogRR] (11:2, #22) Fall-Wint 92, p. 17.
"Plastic." [DogRR] (11:2, #22) Fall-Wint 92, p. 17.

ALIGHIERI, Dante
See DANTE ALIGHIERI

90. ALKALAY-GUT, Karen
"At an Israeli Rock Concert" (for Sharon Moldavi). [Gypsy] (19) 92, p. 12-13.
"Love Soup." [PraS] (66:2) Sum 92, p. 66-71.
"Reader Response." [Gypsy] (19) 92, p. 13.
"Stop Talking." [Amelia] (6:4, #19) 92, p. 132.

91. ALLAN, Rob
"Alistair Cook." [Vis] (40) 92, p. 51.
"Cocteau." [Vis] (40) 92, p. 51.

92. ALLARDT, Linda
"The Quarry." [CinPR] (23) Wint 91-92, p. 31.

93. ALLBERY, Debra
"New Flower Rules." [SouthernR] (28:1) Wint, Ja 92, p. 60-61.

94. ALLEN, Barbara
"Lies." [Ploughs] (18:1) Spr 92, p. 73-74.
"Still Life." [Ploughs] (18:1) Spr 92, p. 75.

95. ALLEN, Beverly
"Idiom (Idioma)" (8 selections, tr. of Andrea Zanzotto). [Sulfur] (12:2, #31) Fall 92, p. 220-228.

96. ALLEN, Blair H.
"An Equal Opportunity Employer." [Gypsy] (18) 92, p. 33-35.

97. ALLEN, Dick
"Daytime Moon." [SilverFR] (23) Wint 92, p. 22.
"Outside Elements." [Poetry] (160:1) Ap 92, p. 15.
"The Parents." [SilverFR] (23) Wint 92, p. 23.
"The Same River, Twice." [Poetry] (160:1) Ap 92, p. 16.
"Still Waters." [Poetry] (160:1) Ap 92, p. 17.

98. ALLEN, Gilbert
"The Accountant." [LullwaterR] (3:3) Sum 92, p. 38-39.
"The Author." [CumbPR] (11:2) Spr 92, p. 1-2.
"God in the Hands of the Angry Sinners." [PoetC] (23:3) Spr 92, p. 32.
"Monday." [ManhatPR] (14) [92?], p. 54.
"One More." [LullwaterR] (3:2) Spr 92, p. 28-29.
"Sitting Next to the Telephone in the Kitchen." [HiramPoR] (51/52) Fall 91-Sum 92, p. 11.
"Spring at Once." [SouthernR] (28:3) Sum, Jl 92, p. 638.
"Variations Upon a Statement by Arnold Schwarzenegger." [PoetC] (23:3) Spr 92, p. 33-34.
"Violets." [CumbPR] (12:1) Fall 92, p. 45-46.
"A Voice from the Machine." [CumbPR] (12:1) Fall 92, p. 43-44.

99. ALLEN, Jed
"Chaos Never Wears Shoes." [SpoonRQ] (17:1/2) Wint-Spr 92, p. 104.
"His Flute Was Packed with Dead Hummingbirds." [SpoonRQ] (17:1/2) Wint-Spr 92, p. 105.

"The King, Borborygmus, Prays at Winter Solstice." [SpoonRQ] (17:1/2) Wint-Spr 92, p. 102.
"Letter from Champs-Pourri." [SpoonRQ] (17:1/2) Wint-Spr 92, p. 103.
"Outcry" (From "Letters to Doctor Soledad"). [Asylum] (7:3/4) 92, p. 60-61.

100. ALLEN, Jeffery Renard
"Dues for Two." [HangL] (60) 92, p. 15.
"Ewe." [HangL] (60) 92, p. 14.
"The Other" (for Sylvester, in memory, after his death from AIDS). [HangL] (60) 92, p. 12-13.
"Rails Under My Back." [Obs] (7:1/2) Spr-Sum 92, p. 59-67.

101. ALLEN, Laura
"If locked in a cell." [Amelia] (6:4, #19) 92, p. 116.
"Phobia." [Amelia] (6:4, #19) 92, p. 114-115.
"Shooting Up." [Amelia] (6:4, #19) 92, p. 115-116.
"When They Drop the Bomb." [Amelia] (6:4, #19) 92, p. 114.

102. ALLEN, Paul
"This Year." [ColEng] (54:1) Ja 92, p. 34.
"An Ugly Retirement." [CharR] (18:2) Fall 92, p. 76-78.

103. ALLEN, Paula Gunn
"Something Fragile, Broken." [Jacaranda] (6:1/2) Wint-Spr 92, p. 56-57.

104. ALLEY, Rick
"Airfield." [ColEng] (54:3) Mr 92, p. 292.
"The Man Who Hugs the Ground." [ColEng] (54:3) Mr 92, p. 291.
"The Mayor of Harmony." [ColEng] (54:3) Mr 92, p. 294.
"The Museum of Contemporary Envy." [ColEng] (54:3) Mr 92, p. 293.

ALLFREY, Phyllis Shand
See SHAND-ALLFREY, Phyllis

105. ALLIN, Louise
"The Fly." [SmPd] (29:1, #84) Wint 92, p. 23.
"Whales." [SmPd] (29:1, #84) Wint 92, p. 23.

106. ALLISON, John
"Tane in the City." [Vis] (40) 92, p. 40.

107. ALLMAN, John
"Wilma's House Burns Down." [MassR] (23:2) Sum 92, p. 217-218.

ALLYN, Adeline Lynn
See LYNN-ALLYN, Adeline

108. ALMON, Bert
"Blockbuster." [TexasR] (13:1/2) Spr-Sum 92, p. 84.
"Charleston" (Firle, East Sussex). [WebR] (16) Fall 92, p. 69.
"Water of Life." [Light] (3) Aut 92, p. 11-12.

109. ALMON, Margaret
"Woman Poet" (1992 AWP Intro Award Winner). [IndR] (15:2) Fall 92, p. 147.

110. ALONSO, Dámaso
"Insomniac" (tr. by Janet Ruth Heller). [ArtfulD] (22/23) 92, p. 31.

111. ALPAUGH, David
"Hunger Artists." [PoetC] (23:3) Spr 92, p. 23-24.
"Rollfast." [Wind] (22:71) 92, p. 1-2.

112. ALSBERG, Fred
"Waiting for That Day." [GreensboroR] (52) Sum 92, p. 67.

113. ALTHAUS, Keith
"Childhood." [Ploughs] (18:4) Wint 92-93, p. 100.
"For Ellery." [Agni] (35) 92, p. 192-193.
"From Memory" (for Greg Orr). [Agni] (35) 92, p. 194-196.
"I-81." [VirQR] (68:1) Wint 92, p. 75-76.
"Near Christmas." [Ploughs] (18:4) Wint 92-93, p. 98-99.
"An Old Story." [Ploughs] (18:4) Wint 92-93, p. 101-102.
"Piero Manzoni." [VirQR] (68:1) Wint 92, p. 74-75.
"Poem: Remembered backwards." [SenR] (22:1) Spr 92, p. 19.
"Something About the Stars." [SenR] (22:1) Spr 92, p. 20.

114. ALTIOK, Metin
"Avalanche" (tr. by Nermin Menemencioglu). [Trans] (26) Spr 92, p. 89.

ALVAREZ, Juan Carlos García
See GARCIA ALVAREZ, Juan Carlos

ALVAREZ, Pansy Maurer
See MAURER-ALVAREZ, Pansy

115. ALVAREZ-KOKI, Francisco
"Meditation" (tr. by Angela McEwan). [Luz] (1) My 92, p. 17, 19.
"Sombra de Luna" (4 selections). [Luz] (1) My 92, p. 13-18.
116. AMABILE, George
"Star Chant Against Extinction" (for Mike Olito). [Grain] (20:1) Spr 92, p. 274.
AMARAL, José Vázquez
See VAZQUEZ-AMARAL, José
117. AMAROWICZ, Eva
"Waiting." Sparks! Writing by High School Students (1:1), a supplement to [PraF] (13:4, #61) Wint 92-93, p. 3-4.
118. AMATO, Joe
"Poaching a Myth" (2nd Prize, 6th Annual Contest). [SoCoast] (12) Ja 92, p. 15.
119. AMBLER, Sam
"Fritz" (For Fritz Kirk, 1944-1991). [Art&Und] (1:1) Fall 91, p. 20.
"Night/Light." [JamesWR] (9:2) Wint 92, p. 8.
120. AMICHAI, Yehuda
"Human Bodies" (tr. by Barbara and Benjamin Harshav). [ParisR] (34:122) Spr 92, p. 208.
"Late Wedding" (tr. by Barbara and Benjamin Harshav). [ParisR] (34:122) Spr 92, p. 211.
"North of Beer Sheva" (tr. by Barbara and Benjamin Harshav). [ParisR] (34:122) Spr 92, p. 210.
"Sandals" (tr. by Barbara and Benjamin Harshav). [ParisR] (34:122) Spr 92, p. 209.
121. AMICO, Santa Helena
"Brothers." [Footwork] 92, p. 83.
"Public School Grade 3." [Footwork] 92, p. 83.
122. AMIDON, Richard
"Afterlife." [SlipS] (12) 92, p. 79.
123. AMIRTHANAYAGAM, Indran
"204 Messages to K." [GrandS] (11:1, #41) 92, p. 127-128.
"The Blood Abroad." [KenR] (NS 14:3) Sum 92, p. 119-120.
"You Must Love." [KenR] (NS 14:3) Sum 92, p. 118.
124. AMMONS, A. R.
"Broad Brush." [NoCarLR] (1:1) Sum 92, p. 7.
"Garbage." [AmerPoR] (21:2) Mr-Ap 92, p. 36-41.
"Middling Seasons." [YaleR] (80:4) O 92, p. 37.
"Small Song." [BelPoJ] (42:4) Sum 92, p. 43.
"Spike-Tooth Harrows." [YaleR] (80:4) O 92, p. 39.
"Tape for the Turn of the Year" (Originally written on a roll of adding machine tape in the form of a journal covering the period 6 Dec. 1963 to 10 Jan. 1964. Selections). [NoCarLR] (1:1) Sum 92, p. 47-57.
"Whitewater." [YaleR] (80:4) O 92, p. 38.
"Wiring." [BelPoJ] (42:4) Sum 92, p. 43.
125. ANDERS, Shirley
"Winter Sparrows Observed in Late Fall." [SouthernR] (28:4) Aut, O 92, p. 813-814.
126. ANDERSEN, Delphine D.
"Maggie." [HayF] (11) Fall-Wint 92, p. 75-77.
127. ANDERSON, Carmen Hayes
"Enactment." [ChrC] (109:37) 16 D 92, p. 1162.
128. ANDERSON, Chuck
"The Rooster." [HiramPoR] (51/52) Fall 91-Sum 92, p. 12-15.
129. ANDERSON, Curt
"Good Morning America." [Caliban] (11) 92, p. 147.
130. ANDERSON, Daniel
"The Burning Bush." [SouthernR] (28:3) Sum, Jl 92, p. 647-648.
"Dontophobic." [SouthernR] (28:3) Sum, Jl 92, p. 648-649.
"To Charcot: A Letter Never Posted, Sigmund Freud, October, 1886." [SouthernR] (28:3) Sum, Jl 92, p. 649-651.
131. ANDERSON, Doug
"Doc." [Ploughs] (18:4) Wint 92-93, p. 199.
"Itinerary." [MassR] (23:2) Sum 92, p. 219-220.
"Monsoon." [PoetC] (24:1) Fall 92, p. 33.
"Rain." [Ploughs] (18:4) Wint 92-93, p. 201.
"Recovery." [Ploughs] (18:4) Wint 92-93, p. 200.
132. ANDERSON, Gary
"Lo-Fi." [Elf] (2:2) Sum 92, p. 26.

"Zachary." [ChironR] (11:1) Spr 92, p. 21.

133. ANDERSON, Jack
"Things Coming and Going." [Caliban] (11) 92, p. 83.
"Who Are the Rich and Where Do They Live?" [PoetryE] (33) Spr 92, p. 8.

134. ANDERSON, James C. (James Clark)
"Coal Scuttle." [Confr] (48/49) Spr-Sum 92, p. 206.
"Touching the Horse." [TarRP] (30:2) Spr 91, p. 5.

135. ANDERSON, Kath M.
"Hauling Water." [QW] (36) Wint 92-93, p. 121.

136. ANDERSON, Ken
"The Dead Cyclist." [LullwaterR] (3:2) Spr 92, p. 40.
"The Visit." [LullwaterR] (3:2) Spr 92, p. 69-71.

137. ANDERSON, Maggie
"Epistemological." [AmerPoR] (21:1) Ja-F 92, p. 21.
"Imperative." [AmerPoR] (21:1) Ja-F 92, p. 21.

138. ANDERSON, Mia
"The Shambles" (12 selections). [MalR] (100) Fall 92, p. 233-263.

139. ANDERSON, Robert R.
"Nude." [KenR] (NS 14:2) Spr 92, p. 37.

140. ANDERSON, Sascha
"Nicolaus Löwenthal" (2 selections, tr. by John Epstein). [Shiny] (7/8) 92, p. 147.

141. ANDERSON, Stephanie
"Village Song" (tr. of Blanca Varela). [Field] (47) Fall 92, p. 70-71.

142. ANDERSON, Teresa
"The Transients" (2 selections, tr. of Myriam Moscona). [Manoa] (4:2) Fall 92, p. 21 - 22.

143. ANDRADE, Eugénio de
"Animals" (tr. by Alexis Levitin). [Trans] (26) Spr 92, p. 90.
"Another Madrigal" (tr. by Alexis Levitin). [Os] (34) Spr 92, p. 5.
"Arima" (tr. by Alexis Levitin). [TexasR] (13:3/4) Fall-Wint 92, p. 72.
"Canção." [InterPR] (18:2) Fall 92, p. 14.
"Do Not Ask" (tr. by Alexis Levitin). [Os] (34) Spr 92, p. 7.
"Home" (tr. by Alexis Levitin). [Trans] (26) Spr 92, p. 22.
"Litania com o Teu Rosto." [InterPR] (18:2) Fall 92, p. 16.
"Litany with Your Face" (tr. by Alexis Levitin). [InterPR] (18:2) Fall 92, p. 17.
"Madrigal" (in Portuguese). [Os] (34) Spr 92, p. 4.
"Madrigal" (tr. by Alexis Levitin). [Os] (34) Spr 92, p. 5.
"Não Perguntes." [Os] (34) Spr 92, p. 6.
"Outro Madrigal." [Os] (34) Spr 92, p. 4.
"Peaches" (tr. by Alexis Levitin). [Trans] (26) Spr 92, p. 23.
"Solar Matter" (Selections: 28, 37, tr. by Alexis Levitin). [SnailPR] (2:1) Spr-Sum 92, p. 20-21.
"Song" (tr. by Alexis Levitin). [InterPR] (18:2) Fall 92, p. 15.
"Song Written in the Sands of Laga" (tr. by Alexis Levitin). [TexasR] (13:3/4) Fall - Wint 92, p. 73.
"Still on Purity" (tr. by Alexis Levitin). [Trans] (26) Spr 92, p. 23.
"To Follow Still Those Signs" (tr. by Alexis Levitin). [Trans] (26) Spr 92, p. 22.
"To My Enemies" (tr. by Alexis Levitin). [GrahamHR] (16) Fall 92, p. 75.
"Where To" (tr. by Alexis Levitin). [GrahamHR] (16) Fall 92, p. 76.

ANDRADE, Héctor Manuel Enríquez
See ENRIQUEZ ANDRADE, Héctor Manuel

144. ANDRE, Jean
"A Message for Baby Doe's Mother." [Elf] (2:2) Sum 92, p. 35.

145. ANDRES, Cira
"Danger Zone" (tr. by Betty Wilson). [LitR] (35:4) Sum 92, p. 449.
"Zona de Peligro." [LitR] (35:4) Sum 92, p. 590.

146. ANDREWS, A. Douglas
"Lambchops." [PoetryUSA] (24) 92, p. 26.

147. ANDREWS, Bruce
"Definition" (Selection: "C"). [Avec] (5:1) 92, p. 71-72.
"Divestiture-C" (Excerpt). [Talisman] (9) Fall 92, p. 106-109.
"Moebius" (4 selections). [WestCL] (26:2, #8) Fall 92, p. 36-39.
"Tizzy Boost" (Selections: 5, 7, 8, 11). [Avec] (5:1) 92, p. 66-70.
"Tizzy Boost" (Selections: 34-35, 43-44, 47). [NewAW] (10) Fall 92, p. 43-46.
"Verbal Sallies." [Shiny] (7/8) 92, p. 73-79.

148. ANDREWS, Claudia Emerson
"Bait." [Shen] (42:3) Fall 92, p. 23.
"Barn Cat." [Crazy] (43) Wint 92, p. 19.
"Cleaning the Graves." [Crazy] (43) Wint 92, p. 21.
"The Drowning" (for Dr. Betty). [CumbPR] (12:1) Fall 92, p. 42.
"House Call." [Crazy] (43) Wint 92, p. 20.
"Looking for Grandmother's Grave." [SouthernR] (28:4) Aut, O 92, p. 815-816.
"The Milk Cow Speaks of Winter." [Shen] (42:3) Fall 92, p. 21.
"The Monkey's Tale." [CumbPR] (12:1) Fall 92, p. 40-41.
"One Hand on the Wheel." [SouthernR] (28:4) Aut, O 92, p. 817-818.
"Plagues." [Shen] (42:3) Fall 92, p. 22-23.
"Skin Deep." [SouthernR] (28:4) Aut, O 92, p. 816-817.
"Stoic." [Crazy] (43) Wint 92, p. 18.
149. ANDREWS, Linda
"Embrace." [PoetryNW] (33:2) Sum 92, p. 24.
"Two Hearted River." [PoetryNW] (33:2) Sum 92, p. 25.
150. ANDREWS, Michael
"Co Trinh Wathes [i.e., Watches] from the Trees." [OnTheBus] (4:2/5:1, #10/11) 92, p. 56-57.
"Daedalus and Icarus." [OnTheBus] (4:2/5:1, #10/11) 92, p. 59-60.
"Flag Decal." [OnTheBus] (4:2/5:1, #10/11) 92, p. 61-65.
"I Lost It." [OnTheBus] (4:2/5:1, #10/11) 92, p. 57-58.
151. ANDREWS, Nin
"The Life of Nin Andrews." [DenQ] (26:4) Spr 92, p. 7.
"Red Blossoms." [ParisR]] (34:124) Fall 92, p. 133.
152. ANDREWS, Shari
"Open Our Veins in Canada." [Event] (21:3) Fall 92, p. 72.
"When Field Stones Are Shifted." [Event] (21:3) Fall 92, p. 73.
153. ANDREWS, Tom
"Praying with George Herbert in Late Winter." [Poetry] (161:3) D 92, p. 149-150.
"Reading the *Dao Te Ching* in the Hospital." [Poetry] (161:3) D 92, p. 148.
154. ANDROLA, Ron
"Driving a Sludge Truck." [SlipS] (12) 92, p. 81.
"Expecting Bukowski." [Bogg] (65) 92, p. 18.
"Facing the Day." [SlipS] (12) 92, p. 81.
"Sunday Morning, Dying." [SlipS] (12) 92, p. 82.
155. ANEIRIN
"Gododdin" (Excerpt, tr. by W. S. Merwin). [GrandS] (11:2, #42) 92, p. 174-181.
156. ANGEL, Ralph
"Months Later." [AmerV] (26) Spr 92, p. 20.
157. ANGELAKI-ROOKE, Katerina
"The Scar." [Stand] (33:4) Aut 92, p. 97.
"Withered Lips." [Stand] (33:4) Aut 92, p. 96.
ANGHELAKI-ROOKE, Katerina
See ANGELAKI-ROOKE, Katerina
158. ANGIOLIERI, Cecco
"You, Ciampol, taking long looks at that crone" ("Two Views of Courtly Love," tr. by Felix Stefanile). [Sparrow] (59) S 92, p. 15.
159. ANGLETON, Cicely
"Erosions." [PoetL] (87:4) Wint 92-93, p. 31-32.
160. ANGUITA, Eduardo
"Mester de Clerecia en Memoria de Vicente Huidobro" (Por encargo de Gonzalo de Berceo). [Inti] (36) Otoño 92, p. 130-131.
"Misa Breve" (Fragmento inicial). [Inti] (36) Otoño 92, p. 137-138.
"La Muerte Es la Suma de Muchas Vidas." [Inti] (36) Otoño 92, p. 131.
"Resumen." [Inti] (36) Otoño 92, p. 132-133.
"Sensacion de Lo Que Podria Llamarse Origen del Conocimiento." [Inti] (36) Otoño 92, p. 132.
"Unica Razon de la Pasion de N.S.J.C." [Inti] (36) Otoño 92, p. 136.
"Venus en el Pudridero" (Fragmento). [Inti] (36) Otoño 92, p. 135.
"El Verdadero Momento." [Inti] (36) Otoño 92, p. 133-134.
161. ANIAKOR, Chike C.
"Lesson From a Hibiscus Flower." [Obs] (7:1/2) Spr-Sum 92, p. 68.
"Noises in the Market Place." [Obs] (7:1/2) Spr-Sum 92, p. 69-70.
"Questions for the Mystical Bird." [Obs] (7:1/2) Spr-Sum 92, p. 70-71.

162. ANNUCCI, Marilyn
"Butter." [CreamCR] (16:2) Fall 92, p. 21.
"Clorox." [ArtfulD] (22/23) 92, p. 135.
"Windex." [ArtfulD] (22/23) 92, p. 134.

163. ANONYMOUS
"Agüeynaba." [Areíto] (3:10/11) Abril 92, p. 72.
"From the Gilgamesh Epic: The Death of Enkidu" (Tablets VII-IX, tr. by David Ferry). [Raritan] (11:4) Spr 92, p. 24-37.
"Hatuey." [Areíto] (3:10/11) Abril 92, p. 72.
"Ishtar & Gilgamesh" (from Tablet VI of *The Gilgamesh Epic,* based on the literal tr. by E. A. Speiser, version by David Ferry). [PartR] (59:2) Spr 92, p. 260-263.
"El Profeta" (El Libro de Libros de Chilam Balam). [Areíto] (3:10/11) Abril 92, p. 72.
"There was a young woman from Paris." [Elf] (2:1) Spr 92, p. 53.
"Thirty days has Septober." [Elf] (2:1) Spr 92, p. 53.

164. ANONYMOUS (Azteca)
"Testimonio Azteca." [Areíto] (3:10/11) Abril 92, p. 74.

165. ANONYMOUS (Babylonian)
"Gilgamesh: Tables X and XI" (tr. by David Ferry based mainly on the literal tr. by E. A. Speiser). [Arion] 3d series (1:3) Fall 91, p. 92-116.
"Prayer to the Gods of the Night" (tr. by David Ferry based on the literal tr. by William L. Moran). [Arion] 3d series (1:1) Wint 90, p. 186.

166. ANONYMOUS (Maya)
"Testimonio Maya." [Areíto] (3:10/11) Abril 92, p. 74.

167. ANONYMOUS (Náhuatl)
"Canto a la Madre de los Dioses" (Himno sagrado náhuatl, del apéndice del Libro II del Códice Florentino). [Areíto] (3:10/11) Abril 92, p. 67.
"Icnocuícatl, el Canto de Angustia" (De los Anales de Tlatelolco, Siglo XVI). [Areíto] (3:10/11) Abril 92, p. 73.

168. ANONYMOUS (Old Scottish Ballad)
"Mary Hamilton." [Elf] (2:2) Sum 92, p. 52.

169. ANONYMOUS (Popul vuh)
"El Fuego." [Areíto] (3:10/11) Abril 92, p. 68.

170. ANONYMOUS (Tradición cashinahua)
"El Amor." [Areíto] (3:10/11) Abril 92, p. 70.
"La Noche." [Areíto] (3:10/11) Abril 92, p. 69.
"El Poder." [Areíto] (3:10/11) Abril 92, p. 71.

171. ANONYMOUS (Tradición huarochirí)
"La Resurrección." [Areíto] (3:10/11) Abril 92, p. 69.

172. ANONYMOUS (Tradición inca)
"La Ciudad Sagrada." [Areíto] (3:10/11) Abril 92, p. 71.

173. ANONYMOUS (Tradición makiritare)
"La Creación." [Areíto] (3:10/11) Abril 92, p. 68.

174. ANONYMOUS (Tradición onas)
"La Autoridad." [Areíto] (3:10/11) Abril 92, p. 70.

175. ANSANO, Richinel
"Appeal from a Mother" (tr. of Jeanne Henriquez, w. Joceline Clemencia). [LitR] (35:4) Sum 92, p. 575.
"Gossip" (tr. of Arnela Ten Meer, w. Joceline Clemencia). [LitR] (35:4) Sum 92, p. 582.
"On My Shoulders" (tr. of Micky Hart, w. Joceline Clemencia). [LitR] (35:4) Sum 92, p. 574.
"Sit 'n See" (tr. of Reyna Joe, w. Joceline Clemencia). [LitR] (35:4) Sum 92, p. 576.
"Three Mirrors" (tr. of Joceline Clemencia, w. the author). [LitR] (35:4) Sum 92, p. 571.

176. ANSAY, A. Manette
"Dialogue with Angels as Your Mother Calls You Home." [Plain] (12:3) Spr 92, p. 32.
"Insomnis." [SouthernPR] (32:2) Fall 92, p. 68-69.
"Nails." [CapeR] (27:1) Spr 92, p. 48.

177. ANSEL, Talvikki
"In Fragments, in Streams" (Excerpts from a larger sonnet sequence growing out of her experiences working in the Brazilian rain forest. Tom McAfee Discovery Feature). [MissouriR] (15:2) 92, p. 151-160.

178. ANTIN, David
"Determination Suspension Diversion Digression Destruction." [Conjunc] (19) 92, p. 51-78.
179. ANTLER
"Anthem." [Sun] (197) Ap 92, p. 7.
"Atheist Conches." [Sun] (194) Ja 92, p. 19.
"Babyteeth Necklace." [Confr] (50) Fall 92, p. 257.
"Babyteeth Necklace." [Lactuca] (16) Ag 92, p. 49.
"Bedrock Mortar Full Moon Illumination." [Sun] (195) F 92, p. 38.
"Blowjob Education Advance: How Cocksuckers, Blowjobs and Come Grow in Stature and Wisdom and Favor in the Boyhood Mind." [JamesWR] (10:1) Fall 92, p. 13.
"Blowjobscope." [ChironR] (11:4) Wint 92, p. 7.
"Dachau Stone." [NewYorkQ] (49) 92, p. 39-40.
"Everything Is Different Now." [ChironR] (11:1) Spr 92, p. 21.
"Everything Is Different Now." [Lactuca] (16) Ag 92, p. 47.
"The Gift." [Lactuca] (16) Ag 92, p. 45-47.
"Giraffologist Field Notes." [Lactuca] (16) Ag 92, p. 51.
"Hot Summernight Cloudburst Rendezvous." [Lactuca] (16) Ag 92, p. 48-49.
"Looking Through Baby Footprints." [Noctiluca] (1:2) Wint 92 [on cover: Wint 93], p. 12.
"On Learning on the Clearest Night Only 6000 Stars Are Visible to the Naked Eye." [Lactuca] (16) Ag 92, p. 40.
"Paying Lipservice to Blowjob." [ChironR] (11:4) Wint 92, p. 7.
"Pussysmell Candlelight." [ChironR] (11:3) Aut 92, p. 17.
"Pussysmell Candlelight." [NewYorkQ] (47) 92, p. 32.
"Shitwombreality and Beejackofftime." [NewYorkQ] (48) 92, p. 53.
"Snowflakes." [Lactuca] (16) Ag 92, p. 51.
"Somewhere Along the Line." [Sun] (198) My 92, p. 15.
"Star-Struck Utopias of 2000." [Elf] (2:3) Fall 92, p. 41.
"Tagteam Blowjob." [ChironR] (11:4) Wint 92, p. 7.
"The Word Boy." [ChironR] (11:4) Wint 92, p. 7.
"Zero-Hour Day Zero-Day Workweek." [Sun] (204) D 92, p. 12-13.
180. ANTRIM, Kathie
"Increments" (w. Richard Kostelanetz). [ChironR] (11:2) Sum 92, p. 11.
181. ANUSAVICE, Sandi
"Grandmother Organizes a Hog-killing." [Kalliope] (14:2) 92, p. 30.
182. AOYAMA, Miyuki
"Haiku" (3 poems, tr. of Sonoko Nakamura, w. Leza Lowitz). [Noctiluca] (1:2) Wint 92 [on cover: Wint 93], p. 3.
183. APOLLONIUS of Rhodes
"The Clashing Rocks" (The Argonautica, Book II, lines 536-610, tr. by Peter Green). [SouthernHR] (26:1) Wint 92, p. 9-10.
184. APPLEFIELD, David
"Oran." [CimR] (100) Jl 92, p. 47.
185. APPLEWHITE, James
"After *Winslow Homer's Images of Blacks*." [SouthernR] (28:4) Aut, O 92, p. 821-822.
"Almon and Jane." [SouthernR] (28:4) Aut, O 92, p. 819-820.
"A Change of Sky." [Shen] (42:3) Fall 92, p. 86-87.
"Echoes of Origin." [SouthernR] (28:4) Aut, O 92, p. 824.
"Going for a Late Hike." [Verse] (9:2) Sum 92, p. 67.
"A Grave in the Forest." [Verse] (9:2) Sum 92, p. 65.
"Home Team." [SouthernR] (28:4) Aut, O 92, p. 823-824.
"Riverwalk with *Owl*, After the Funeral." [Writer] (105:9) S 92, p. 25.
"Time at Seven Springs." [Verse] (9:2) Sum 92, p. 65-66.
186. AQUINO, Jennifer
"The Taste of Us." [ChironR] (11:1) Spr 92, p. 25.
187. AQUINO, Norma
"A Ciencia Cierta." [LindLM] (11:4) D 92, p. 9.
"Cuando veo a Jesús." [LindLM] (11:4) D 92, p. 9.
"Sobreviviente." [LindLM] (11:4) D 92, p. 9.
"Yo, Descansada." [LindLM] (11:4) D 92, p. 9.
188. ARABOV, Yuri"
"Thoughts on Formal Logic" (tr. by Forrest Gander and Sara Dickinson). [Agni] (35) 92, p. 264-265.

189. ARAM, Sholom
"Two Poems on the Theme of Incest." [ChangingM] (24) Sum-Fall 92, p. 16-17.
190. ARANDA, José Antonio
"Sextina." [Nuez] (4:10/11) 92, p. 8.
191. ARCHER, Anne
"The Mary Poems." [AntigR] (89) Spr 92, p. 21-22.
"Nights of Adrenalin" (Selections: xxv-xxvi, tr. of Carmen Ollé). [AnotherCM] (23) Spr 92, p. 149-153.
192. ARCHER, Nuala
"From a Mobile Home: See You in Electra." [AmerPoR] (21:5) S-O 92, p. 8-10.
"A Story That Preceded My First Hearing of the Word Orgasm." [AmerPoR] (21:5) S-O 92, p. 8.
193. ARCHIBALD, Andy
"Objects in Mirror Are Closer Than They Appear." [JamesWR] (9:3) Spr 92, p. 7.
194. ARCHIBALD, William
"Us Clowning, Four Different Poses." [PacificR] (11) 92-93, p. 44-47.
ARELANO NOLLA, Olga Ramirez de
See NOLLA, Olga Ramirez de Arelano
195. ARENAS, Marion
"The Closed Family Explains." [JlNJPo] (14:2) Aut 92, p. 44.
"The Common Moon." [ManhatPR] (14) [92?], p. 21.
"Family Reunion." [WestB] (30) 92, p. 106-107.
"Miss Newno, Second Grade Teacher, Has Such Perfect Yellow Waves Around Her Head." [NewYorkQ] (49) 92, p. 90.
"The View from the AIDS Ward, Christ Hospital, Jersey City." [JlNJPo] (14:2) Aut 92, p. 43.
"The Woman at Our Lady of Sorrows Cemetery." [ManhatPR] (14) [92?], p. 21.
196. ARENAS, Reinaldo
"Autoepitafio" (Nueva York, 1989). [Nuez] (4:12) 92, p. 2.
197. ARENAS, Rosa Maria
"What I Can't Tell You." [RiverS] (36) 92, p. 65-66.
198. ARGÜELLES, Ivan
"Disorientation" (section from liber primus partis secondae "Pantograph," for Jack Foley). [PoetryUSA] (24) 92, p. 19.
"For Diotima." [Talisman] (8) Spr 92, p. 175.
"If I Serve One I Must Lack the Other." [YellowS] (Ten Years [i.e. 40]) Sum-Fall 92, p. 6-7.
"Let them all die" (from "Pantograph: Suplemento IV — Trono de los Dioses). [PoetryUSA] (24) 92, p. 19.
"(RAD)" (Excerpt from "Translation," for Rosebud Abigail Denovo — RAD). [PoetryUSA] (24) 92, p. 38.
"Une Vie Perdue." [SilverFR] (23) Wint 92, p. 26-28.
199. ARGÜELLES, Juan Domingo
"Casa Paterna." [LindLM] (11:2) Je 92, p. 12.
"Estanque." [LindLM] (11:2) Je 92, p. 12.
"Justicia." [LindLM] (11:2) Je 92, p. 12.
"Lluvia." [LindLM] (11:2) Je 92, p. 12.
200. ARGUELLO, Alberto Ordonez
"Canción de Neztahualcoyotl 1." [NewYorkQ] (49) 92, p. 100.
"Song of Neztahualcoyotl 1" (tr. by Joel Zeltzer). [NewYorkQ] (49) 92, p. 101.
201. ARGYROS, Alex
"Letter from Spyridon Messimeris to His Sister, My Mother, Mosha Messimeris." [Confr] (48/49) Spr-Sum 92, p. 220-221.
"Popper's Three Worlds in a Coffee House" (after George Herbert). [CumbPR] (11:2) Spr 92, p. 28.
"Postmortem." [CumbPR] (11:2) Spr 92, p. 29.
202. ARIDJIS, Ana
"Carta a Marina Tsvietaieva." [Nuez] (4:10/11) 92, p. 6.
203. ARIDJIS, Homero
"Angry the Old People" (tr. by Jessie Kuhn). [AmerPoR] (21:6) N-D 92, p. 36.
"Rain in the Night" (tr. by Jessie Kuhn). [AmerPoR] (21:6) N-D 92, p. 36.
"Teotihuacán" (tr. by Jessie Kuhn). [AmerPoR] (21:6) N-D 92, p. 36.
"Words Don't Tell" (tr. by Jessie Kuhn). [AmerPoR] (21:6) N-D 92, p. 36.
204. ARMANTROUT, Rae
"The Known." [Avec] (5:1) 92, p. 9.
"One Remove." [Avec] (5:1) 92, p. 9.

"A Pulse." [GrandS] (11:1, #41) 92, p. 54-55.
"Relations." [Avec] (5:1) 92, p. 10.
"Sets." [Shiny] (7/8) 92, p. 65.
"Taking Steps." [Shiny] (7/8) 92, p. 66.
"Visibility." [Avec] (5:1) 92, p. 11.

205. ARMENGOL, Alejandro A.
"Romancero." [LindLM] (11:2) Je 92, p. 8.
"Romancero (II)." [LindLM] (11:2) Je 92, p. 8.
"Romancero (III)." [LindLM] (11:2) Je 92, p. 8.

206. ARMER, Sondra Audin
"Blood and Circuses." [WestHR] (46:3) Fall 92 [i.e. (46:4) Wint 92], p. 427.
"Bridgework." [WestHR] (46:3) Fall 92 [i.e. (46:4) Wint 92], p. 428.
"I Dream of Finding My Father Among Street People." [WestHR] (46:3) Fall 92 [i.e. (46:4) Wint 92], p. 426.
"To Spring: A Toast." [WestHR] (46:3) Fall 92 [i.e. (46:4) Wint 92], p. 429.

207. ARMITAGE, Barri
"Bedding Down." [PraS] (66:3) Fall 92, p. 84-85.
"Funeral Pilgrimage" (For Great-aunt Anna, 1876-1978). [PoetL] (87:1) Spr 92, p. 23-24.
"Journal: Outliving Our Firstborn." [PraS] (66:3) Fall 92, p. 83-84.

208. ARMITAGE, Simon
"Book of Matches" (Excerpt). [Verse] (9:3) Wint 92, p. 97-101.

209. ARMSTRONG, Gene
"First Rain on Slick Streets." [BellArk] (8:1) Ja-F 92, p. 27.
"June." [BellArk] (8:1) Ja-F 92, p. 7.
"Promise." [BellArk] (8:1) Ja-F 92, p. 27.
"Seeking the Wisdom of Artists." [BellArk] (8:1) Ja-F 92, p. 23.

210. ARMSTRONG, Glen
"Brown Shoes." [BlackBR] (15) Spr-Sum 92, p. 23, repeated on p. 34.
"Milk Babies." [FreeL] (9) Wint 92, p. 25.

211. ARMSTRONG, Lisa
"Freeway Living." [OnTheBus] (4:2/5:1, #10/11) 92, p. 67.
"Mother." [OnTheBus] (4:2/5:1, #10/11) 92, p. 66.
"Sunday Morning." [OnTheBus] (4:2/5:1, #10/11) 92, p. 67-68.
"Webs." [OnTheBus] (4:2/5:1, #10/11) 92, p. 68.

212. ARMSTRONG, Patricia Mees
"Seduction." [Writer] (105:6) Je 92, p. 26.

213. ARMSTRONG, Tom
"So Maybe I'm Not the Cat's Meow." [Light] (1) Spr 92, p. 9.

214. ARNETT, Harold
"Sunday Shirts." [WindO] (56) Fall-Wint 92, p. 27.

215. ARNOLD, Anita
"Eat Your Heart Out, Barbara Cartland." [EngJ] (81:5) S 92, p. 103.

216. ARNOTT, Joanne
"Enchantment & Freedom." [PoetryC] (13:1) N 92, p. 4.

217. ARONSON, Trudy
"As the Crow Flies." [Light] (4) Wint 92-93, p. 10.

ARPINO, Tony d'
See D'ARPINO, Tony

218. ARRIETA, Marcia
"Evidence of Passage." [RagMag] (10:2) 92, p. 13.
"In My Grandfather's Garage." [SmPd] (29:2, #85) Spr 92, p. 13.
"In the Land of Sun." [Elf] (2:4) Wint 92, p. 33.
"North Fork of the Merced." [RagMag] (10:2) 92, p. 12.
"Send Some Biographical Information." [Wind] (22:71) 92, p. 3.
"Shall We Speak of Failure or Success?" [RagMag] (10:2) 92, p. 14.
"Stepping into Trees." [MidwQ] (33:3) Spr 92, p. 305.
"Survival." [RagMag] (10:2) 92, p. 15.

219. ARRILLAGA, María
"I Have Just Died" (tr. of Angela Maria Davila). [LitR] (35:4) Sum 92, p. 514.
"I Want for My Name" (tr. of Angela Maria Davila). [LitR] (35:4) Sum 92, p. 515.
"To Julia de Burgos" (tr. of Julia de Burgos). [LitR] (35:4) Sum 92, p. 516.

220. ARROWSMITH, William
"After a Flight" (tr. of Eugenio Montale). [AmerPoR] (21:3) My-Je 92, p. 33-34.
"All Souls' Day" (from the "Quaderno di quattro anni," tr. of Eugenio Montale). [AmerPoR] (21:3) My-Je 92, p. 35.

"Aspasia" (tr. of Eugenio Montale). [ParisR] (34:122) Spr 92, p. 98.
"The Chiming Pendulum Clock" (tr. of Eugenio Montale). [Boulevard] (7:2/3, #20/21) Fall 92, p. 123.
"The Dead" (tr. of Eugenio Montale). [PartR] (59:2) Spr 92, p. 259-260.
"El Desdichado" (tr. of Eugenio Montale). [WestHR] (46:3) Fall 92, p. 228.
"Early or Late" (tr. of Eugenio Montale). [AmerPoR] (21:3) My-Je 92, p. 35.
"L'Élan Vital" (tr. of Eugenio Montale). [WestHR] (46:3) Fall 92, p. 229.
"Eugenio Montale's 'Xenia II'." [Agni] (35) 92, p. 13-26.
"Fanfare" (tr. of Eugenio Montale). [Pequod] (33) 92, p. 160-162.
"Intermezzo" (tr. of Eugenio Montale). [Trans] (26) Spr 92, p. 29.
"Lac D'Annecy" (tr. of Eugenio Montale). [Boulevard] (7:2/3, #20/21) Fall 92, p. 124.
"The Lemon Trees" (tr. of Eugenio Montale). [AmerPoR] (21:3) My-Je 92, p. 35.
"The Lord of the Revels" (tr. of Eugenio Montale). [WestHR] (46:3) Fall 92, p. 230.
"Piròpo, in Conclusion" (tr. of Eugenio Montale). [AmerPoR] (21:3) My-Je 92, p. 34.
"Reading Cavafy" (tr. of Eugenio Montale). [ParisR] (34:122) Spr 92, p. 97.
"Sorapis, Forty Years Ago" (tr. of Eugenio Montale). [ParisR] (34:122) Spr 92, p. 94.
"To Pio Rajna" (tr. of Eugenio Montale). [ParisR] (34:122) Spr 92, p. 95.
"Transvestisms" (tr. of Eugenio Montale). [ParisR] (34:122) Spr 92, p. 96.

221. ARROYO, Rane
"Angel." [Americas] (20:2) Sum 92, p. 64-66.
"Blonde as a Bat." [Americas] (20:3/4) Fall-Wint 92, p. 248-250.
"Caribe Poems." [Americas] (20:2) Sum 92, p. 67-68.
"Columbus's Children." [Americas] (20:3/4) Fall-Wint 92, p. 251-252.
"Crimes of Capitalism" (for Brecht). [OxfordM] (8:1) Spr-Sum 92, p. 35.
"Dante's Darling." [Epiphany] (3:2) Ap (Spr) 92, p. 96.
"Hola, Hollywood!" [Nimrod] (36:1) Fall-Wint 92, p. 75.
"The Poet's Life." [Epiphany] (3:2) Ap (Spr) 92, p. 95.
"Puerto Rico, 1493." [Nimrod] (36:1) Fall-Wint 92, p. 74.
"Returning to Scenes of My Crimes in Salt Lake City." [ChironR] (11:4) Wint 92, p. 21.
"Secrets in Pockets." [ChironR] (11:4) Wint 92, p. 21.
"Southern Exposures." [Epiphany] (3:2) Ap (Spr) 92, p. 97.
"Strip Jeopardy." [JamesWR] (10:1) Fall 92, p. 16.
"Tenderness." [ChironR] (11:4) Wint 92, p. 21.
"Two New World Meditations." [OxfordM] (8:1) Spr-Sum 92, p. 34.
"Wedding Gift." [Epiphany] (3:2) Ap (Spr) 92, p. 97.
"Why I Didn't Write This Poem." [EvergreenC] (7:1) Wint-Spr 92, p. 12.

ARSDALE, Sarah van
See Van ARSDALE, Sarah

222. ARSENEAU, Marc
"Générique." [PottPort] (14:2) Fall-Wint 92, p. 74.
"Instinct." [PottPort] (14:2) Fall-Wint 92, p. 73.

223. ARTHUR, Chris
"Dinosaurs." [SouthernR] (28:2) Spr, Ap 92, p. 258-259.
"May Who Walks Upon This Rug of Lies Be Cursed." [Event] (21:2) Sum 92, p. 44-45.
"Swifts." [SouthernR] (28:2) Spr, Ap 92, p. 259-260.
"Verbum." [Event] (21:2) Sum 92, p. 43.

224. ASAPH, Philip (R. Philip)
"Century's End." [ChatR] (13:1) Fall 92, p. 1-3.
"Saying Grace." [SlipS] (12) 92, p. 33.

225. ASEKOFF, L. S.
"Casa Blanca." [AmerPoR] (21:3) My-Je 92, p. 4-6.
"Iceboats." [Field] (47) Fall 92, p. 72.
"Invisible Hand." [AmerPoR] (21:3) My-Je 92, p. 7.
"Island." [AmerPoR] (21:3) My-Je 92, p. 6.
"The Premonition." [AmerPoR] (21:3) My-Je 92, p. 3.
"The Punished Net." [Field] (47) Fall 92, p. 74.
"The Shoes Are Death." [Field] (47) Fall 92, p. 73.
"Sirocco." [AmerPoR] (21:3) My-Je 92, p. 7.
"Writing in the Rain." [AmerPoR] (21:3) My-Je 92, p. 3.

226. ASHBAUGH, Gwendolyn
"Namesake" (honorable mention, Eve of Saint Agnes Contest). [NegC] (12:3) 92, p. 6-7.

227. ASHBERY, John
"As Oft It Chanceth." [NewYRB] (39:14) 13 Ag 92, p. 6.
"Baked Alaska." [NewYorker] (68:19) 29 Je 92, p. 40-41.
"A Call for Papers." [YaleR] (80:1/2) Apr 92, p. 44-45.
"Fruit and Tea." [NewYRB] (39:14) 13 Ag 92, p. 6.
"The Garden of False Civility." [NewYorker] (68:32) 28 S 92, p. 36.
"The Great Bridge Game of Life." [PaintedB] (46) 92, p. 5.
"A Hole in Your Sock." [HarvardA] (125th Anniversary Issue) F 92, p. 7.
"Irresolutions on a Theme of La Rochefoucauld." [MichQR] (31:3) Sum 92, p. 321 - 322.
"It Must Be Sophisticated." [Conjunc] (19) 92, p. 209-212.
"The Large Studio." [NewYorker] (68:12) 11 My 92, p. 42-43.
"Light Turnouts." [Art&Und] (1:5) S-O 92, p. 12.
"Mixed Feelings" (from "Self-Portrait in a Convex Mirror"). [NewEngR] (14:4) Fall 92, p. 222-223.
"Musica Reservata." [ParisR] (34:123) Sum 92, p. 74-75.
"Oeuvres Complètes." [NewAW] (10) Fall 92, p. 15-16.
"The Phantom Agents." [NewYorker] (67:50) 3 F 92, p. 30.
"Quartet." [Shiny] (7/8) 92, p. 37-39.
"Withered Compliments." [NewYorker] (68:6) 30 Mr 92, p. 44.
"The Youth's Magic Horn." [ParisR] (34:123) Sum 92, p. 76-77.
228. ASHBURY, Susan
"Tumor." [Kalliope] (14:2) 92, p. 20-21.
229. ASHEAR, Linda
"Ernestine Little and the Elf at the Ocean." [Light] (1) Spr 92, p. 28.
"Since Propitious Time May Never Come." [SoCoast] (13) Je 93 [i.e. 92], p. 56-57.
230. ASHLEY, Renée (Renée A.)
"Entertaining the Angel." [WestHR] (46:3) Fall 92, p. 310.
"For Brigit in Illinois." [KenR] (NS 14:2) Spr 92, p. 1-2.
"How Much I Love My Life." [Footwork] 92, p. 33.
"Knife." [Footwork] 92, p. 33.
"Missing You." [Poetry] (159:5) F 92, p. 253.
"Pressing the Body On." [Poetry] (159:6) Mr 92, p. 319.
"Taking Off." [Footwork] 92, p. 33.
231. ASHTON, Jennifer
"Angel Hidden in a Landscape." [ChiR] (38:3) 92, p. 54-55.
232. ASIAIN, Aurelio
"After Everything" (tr. by Reginald Gibbons). [TriQ] (85) Fall 92, p. 271.
"Life" (tr. by Reginald Gibbons). [TriQ] (85) Fall 92, p. 272.
233. ASKEW, Ana Y.
"Stonewall Jackson Worshipped Here: Sunday Sermon, 20 Minutes to Go." [HolCrit] (29:4) O 92, p. 17.
234. ASPENBERG, Gary
"The Way to Our House." [Lactuca] (16) Ag 92, p. 25.
235. ASPINWALL, Dorothy
"Situation" (tr. of Roger Aralamon Hazoumé). [WebR] (16) Fall 92, p. 30.
"Tablet of Wisdom" (tr. of Victor Segalen). [WebR] (16) Fall 92, p. 31.
236. ATALLA, S. V.
"Rock Cakes." [PaintedB] (47) 92, p. 13-14.
"Story." [PaintedB] (47) 92, p. 15.
237. ATENCIA, María Victoria
"Cave Canem" (in Spanish and English, tr. by Mark Smith-Soto). [InterPR] (18:1) Spr 92, p. 18-19.
"La Frontera." [InterPR] (18:1) Spr 92, p. 16.
"The Frontier" (tr. by Mark Smith-Soto). [InterPR] (18:1) Spr 92, p. 17.
238. ATHANASES, Steven Z.
"Letter from the Farm." [EngJ] (80:7) N 91, p. 99.
239. ATHANASOURELIS, John
"Distinguishing Categories of Rain." [NewDeltaR] (9:1) Fall 91-Wint 92, p. 17.
240. ATKINS, Cynthia
"Candid." [PraS] (66:2) Sum 92, p. 122-123.
"Itinerant Mice." [Confr] (50) Fall 92, p. 265.
241. ATKINS, Harry
"Galatas." [LullwaterR] (4:1) Fall 92, p. 9.
242. ATKINSON, Alan
"As Usual." [ChironR] (11:4) Wint 92, p. 43.

"Passion." [ChironR] (11:4) Wint 92, p. 46.
243. ATKINSON, Jennifer
"And Sweetness Out of the Strong." [Thrpny] (48) Wint 92, p. 27.
244. ATKINSON, Michael
"American Son." [PraS] (66:3) Fall 92, p. 57-58.
"Callisto Alone." [PaintedB] (45) 92, p. 8-9.
"Candles." [PraS] (66:3) Fall 92, p. 59-60.
"Faith." [SpoonRQ] (17:1/2) Wint-Spr 92, p. 50-51.
"Life after Death." [Crazy] (43) Wint 92, p. 41-42.
"Love Poem." [Confr] (48/49) Spr-Sum 92, p. 200.
"Mysteries." [SycamoreR] (4:1) Wint 92, p. 42-44.
"One Hundred Children Waiting for a Train." [PraS] (66:3) Fall 92, p. 61-64.
"Overnight Tank." [OntR] (36) Spr-Sum 92, p. 102.
"Rain Forest." [SpoonRQ] (17:1/2) Wint-Spr 92, p. 48-49.
"Rosie O'Grady." [ChiR] (38:3) 92, p. 24-26.
"The Same Troubles with Beauty You've Always Had." [OntR] (36) Spr-Sum 92, p. 100-101.
"The Sea Robin." [CentR] (36:1) Wint 92, p. 135-136.
"With Lupe Velez on North Rodeo Drive." [HiramPoR] (51/52) Fall 91-Sum 92, p. 16-18.
245. ATWOOD, Margaret
"Three-Eyes" (after the Brothers Grimm). [WestCL] (25:3, #6) Wint 91-92, p. 142 - 143.
246. AUDEN, W. H.
"Atlantis." [CumbPR] (11:2) Spr 92, p. 53-55.
247. AUGUSTINE, Jane
"Metaphysics of the Interior" (2 selections). [Archae] (4) late 92-early 93, p. 24-28.
248. AUSLANDER, Bonnie
"Miller's Pond." [WilliamMR] (30) 92, p. 83.
"My Half-Sister's Older Now." [LullwaterR] (3:2) Spr 92, p. 51.
"On Not Learning Danish Outside Copenhagen." [CreamCR] (16:1) Spr 92, p. 116 - 118.
249. AUSTIN, Annemarie
"So." [Verse] (9:2) Sum 92, p. 64.
250. AUSTIN, Jerry
"Animis Opibusque Parati." [BellArk] (8:1) Ja-F 92, p. 22.
"Mosque." [BellArk] (8:2) Mr-Ap 92, p. 24.
"Ocean Shores." [BellArk] (8:1) Ja-F 92, p. 22.
"Running Wind-Sprints at Twenty-Eight." [BellArk] (8:4) Jl-Ag 92, p. 25.
"Two Stones." [BellArk] (8:6) N-D 92, p. 14.
251. AUTRAN, Christina
"Em Verde-Amarelo." [InterPR] (18:2) Fall 92, p. 42.
"In Yellow and Green" (colors of the Brazilian flag, tr. by the author). [InterPR] (18:2) Fall 92, p. 43.
"Melancholing" (tr. by the author). [InterPR] (18:2) Fall 92, p. 47.
"Melancolando." [InterPR] (18:2) Fall 92, p. 46.
"Reminiscences" (in Portuguese and English, tr. by the author). [InterPR] (18:2) Fall 92, p. 44-45.
252. AUTREY, Ken
"Altar." [SoCarR] (25:1) Fall 92, p. 96.
"Dry Season in Ghana." [TexasR] (13:3/4) Fall-Wint 92, p. 74.
"Hard Bargain." [Sun] (201) S 92, p. 7.
"National Geographic." [TexasR] (13:3/4) Fall-Wint 92, p. 75.
AUTRY, Ken
See AUTREY, Ken
253. AVALOS, Daniel O.
"At Norman's Coffee Comes with Scream and Sweet." [Amelia] (7:1, #20) 92, p. 123.
254. AVENA, Thomas
"Fable." [NowestR] (30:1) 92, p. 118.
"False Arabia." [Lactuca] (15) Mr 92, p. 34.
"Land's End" (San Francisco, 1985). [NowestR] (30:1) 92, p. 115-117.
255. AVERILL, Diane
"Bad for You." [ThRiPo] (39/40) 92-93, p. 4-5.
"Letter to Dembrow from Beside a Crystal Vase." [Kalliope] (14:2) 92, p. 11.
"Renewal" (for Joel). [ThRiPo] (39/40) 92-93, p. 5-6.
"Taking Time." [Calyx] (14:1) Sum 92, p. 5.

256. AVERY, Brian C.
"In Bed with the Watchmaker's Widow." [QW] (36) Wint 92-93, p. 127.
257. AVERY, Patricia Klos
"Origins." [PraS] (66:2) Sum 92, p. 73-74.
"Poland." [PraS] (66:2) Sum 92, p. 71-73.
258. AVILES, Paul
"Guanajuato." [IndR] (15:2) Fall 92, p. 83-84.
259. AVISON, Margaret
"ASAP, etc." [PoetryC] (12:3/4) Jl 92, p. 4.
"Family Members." [PoetryC] (12:3/4) Jl 92, p. 4.
"The Implosive Reality" (after I Cor. 25: 20-28). [PoetryC] (12:3/4) Jl 92, p. 5.
"A Novel's Coda." [PoetryC] (12:3/4) Jl 92, p. 5.
"To Two Who Know." [PoetryC] (12:3/4) Jl 92, p. 5.
260. AWAD, Joseph
"Piazza di Spagna 26, Roma." [NegC] (12:1/2) 92, p. 217.
261. AXINN, Donald Everett
"Byrd, Richard Evelyn, Rear Admiral, U.S.N." [Antaeus] (69) Aut 92, p. 139-142.
262. AYALA, Naomi
"Lawns," [Callaloo] (15:4) Fall 92, p. 949.
"Wild Animals on the Moon" (for Ivor Delve). [Callaloo] (15:4) Fall 92, p. 947-948.
263. AYER, David
"The Golden Egg." [Dandel] (19:1) 92, p. 12.
264. AYRE, David
"Struggle." [CapilR] (2:9) Fall 92, p. 29-35.
265. AZNAR, Pilar
"A la noche." [Nuez] (4:12) 92, p. 19.
266. AZRAEL, Mary
"A Tale for Pigs." [PoetL] (87:2) Sum 92, p. 40.
267. BAATZ, Ronald
"Between Dreams." [WormR] (32:1, #125) 92, p. 10.
"Chinese Take-Out." [WormR] (32:1, #125) 92, p. 11.
"Except for August." [YellowS] (41) Fall-Wint 92-93, p. 28.
"Fires." [Archae] (4) late 92-early 93, p. 32-33.
"More Tomatoes from My Father's Garden." [WormR] (32:1, #125) 92, p. 10-11.
"Of Late." [Archae] (4) late 92-early 93, p. 29.
"Oranges and Roses." [YellowS] (Ten Years [i.e. 40]) Sum-Fall 92, p. 16.
"A Poem About Moving to the Desert When I Am an Old Man." [Archae] (4) late 92 - early 93, p. 30-31.
"Summer." [Archae] (4) late 92-early 93, p. 34.
"An Undiscovered Lake." [SmPd] (29:1, #84) Wint 92, p. 19.
"Voices." [WormR] (32:1, #125) 92, p. 12.
"Women's Magazines." [WormR] (32:1, #125) 92, p. 9.
BACA, Jimmy Santiago
See SANTIAGO-BACA, Jimmy
268. BACHARACH, Deborah
"Americans." [BellArk] (8:4) Jl-Ag 92, p. 24.
"At Thirteen." [SoCoast] (12) Ja 92, p. 52.
269. BACHE-SNYDER, Kaye
"A Concert in Aspen's Tent" (honorable mention, Eve of Saint Agnes Contest). [NegC] (12:3) 92, p. 8.
270. BACHMANN, Ingeborg
"Advertisement" (tr. by Steven Frattali). [WebR] (16) Fall 92, p. 10.
"After This Flood" (tr. by Thomas Dorsett). [InterPR] (18:2) Fall 92, p. 35.
"Dem Abend Gesagt." [InterPR] (18:2) Fall 92, p. 36.
"Every Day" (tr. by Thomas Dorsett). [SnailPR] (2:2) Fall-Wint 92, p. 1.
"Exile" (tr. by Steven Frattali). [GrahamHR] (16) Fall 92, p. 104.
"Fall ab, Herz." [InterPR] (18:2) Fall 92, p. 32.
"Fall Away, Heart" (tr. by Thomas Dorsett). [InterPR] (18:2) Fall 92, p. 33.
"Hotel de la Paix" (tr. by Steven Frattali). [WebR] (16) Fall 92, p. 10.
"In Apulia" (tr. by Steven Frattali). [GrahamHR] (16) Fall 92, p. 103.
"Nach Dieser Sintflut." [InterPR] (18:2) Fall 92, p. 34.
"Told to Evening" (tr. by Thomas Dorsett). [InterPR] (18:2) Fall 92, p. 37.
271. BACK, Rachel Tzvia
"East Elements (1)." [AmerPoR] (21:2) Mr-Ap 92, p. 24.
272. BADEN, Ruth Kramer
"Telephone Calls." [PraS] (66:3) Fall 92, p. 81-83.

273. BAER, Tom
"$2.39." [RagMag] (10:2) 92, p. 76.
274. BAGG, Robert
"The Hour Exam." [Paint] (19:37) Spr 92, p. 25-28.
275. BAGGETT, Rebecca
"An American Primitive: *Before the Fall*." [13thMoon] (10:1/2) 92, p. 20.
"Art of the Amish" (A Quilt Exhibition: 3 selections). [Calyx] (14:1) Sum 92, p. 12 - 14.
"Injustice." [Calyx] (14:2) Wint 92-93, p. 51.
"Last Day of June, First Rain." [MidAR] (13:2) 92, p. 157.
"Sisters-In-Law." [Calyx] (14:2) Wint 92-93, p. 52-53.
"Sleepwalker." [BostonR] (17:2) Mr-Ap 92, p. 22.
276. BAHLER, Beth
"After Surgery." [Footwork] 92, p. 88.
277. BAHORSKY, Russell
"Memorial." [VirQR] (68:2) Spr 92, p. 307-308.
"Revival Sunday." [TarRP] (31:2) Spr 92, p. 5.
278. BAILEY, Clay
"Truth in Advertising." [ChironR] (11:2) Sum 92, p. 13.
279. BAILEY, Jan
"Joint Custody." [GreensboroR] (52) Sum 92, p. 21.
"Rite of Passage." [GreensboroR] (52) Sum 92, p. 19.
"Separation." [PraS] (66:1) Spr 92, p. 120.
"The Writing Student." [GreensboroR] (52) Sum 92, p. 20.
280. BAIN, Gordon Orville
"Except, Keep This." [PraF] (13:4, #61) Wint 92-93, p. 13.
"The Road Winds Far Away Among Mountains." [PraF] (13:4, #61) Wint 92-93, p. 14.
281. BAKER, Alison
"New Happiness." [Nimrod] (36:1) Fall-Wint 92, p. 124.
282. BAKER, David
"Along the Storm Front." [SewanR] (100:2) Spr 92, p. 266-267.
"Charming." [Poetry] (159:6) Mr 92, p. 323.
"Dogwood Mist." [Crazy] (42) Spr 92, p. 37.
"The Extinction of the Dinosaurs." [Poetry] (159:6) Mr 92, p. 324.
"Labor." [Crazy] (42) Spr 92, p. 38.
"Murder" (for Barry Weller). [Pequod] (33) 92, p. 172-175.
"Petit Mal." [MissR] (20:3) Spr 92, p. 24.
"Phases of the Moon." [SewanR] (100:2) Spr 92, p. 267.
"The Politics of Lyric." [TriQ] (84) Spr-Sum 92, p. 105-107.
"Salvation." [Crazy] (42) Spr 92, p. 39.
"Snow Fall." [NewRep] (206:26 [sic, i.e. 207:1]) 29 Je 92, p. 40.
"Space / Time." [TriQ] (84) Spr-Sum 92, p. 103-104.
"The Story." [MissR] (20:3) Spr 92, p. 25.
"Trees in the Night." [Nat] (254:7) 24 F 92, p. 241.
283. BAKER, Devreaux
"The Jungle Speaks to Livingstone." [AmerV] (27) 92, p. 13.
"Welcoming the New Year." [PacificR] (11) 92-93, p. 97-99.
284. BAKER, Donald W.
"A Florist." [Interim] (11:1) Spr-Sum 92, p. 19.
285. BAKER, Houston A., Jr.
"The Elm." [OxfordM] (7:1) Spr-Sum 91, p. 38-39.
286. BAKER, June Frankland
"Coquinas" (butterfly-shell clams). [Comm] (119:14) 14 Ag 92, p. 27.
"New Year's." [OxfordM] (7:1) Spr-Sum 91, p. 99.
"Please Send." [PoetryNW] (33:1) Spr 92, p. 19-20.
"Putting Up the Tree." [OxfordM] (7:1) Spr-Sum 91, p. 98.
"Their Woods." [Blueline] (13) 92, p. 30.
287. BAKER, Lois
"Tracers." [Poetry] (160:6) S 92, p. 337.
"What Climbers Know." [Poetry] (160:6) S 92, p. 336.
288. BAKER, S. D.
"Salton Sea Elegy." [Caliban] (11) 92, p. 160-161.
"Your Aversion to the Color Red" (for Wayne). [Caliban] (11) 92, p. 162.
289. BAKER, Winona
"Snowflakes fill." [Amelia] (7:1, #20) 92, p. 43.

290. BAKOWSKI, Peter
"The Arsonist." [WormR] (32:3, #127) 92, p. 104.
"Bath Plug." [WormR] (32:4 #128) 92, p. 137.
"Bondi Afternoons" (for Yusuke Keida). [MoodySI] (27) Spr 92, p. 18.
"A Book by Conrad." [WormR] (32:3, #127) 92, p. 104.
"La Brea Tar Pits of the Mind." [WormR] (32:4 #128) 92, p. 137.
"The Father Bends." [WormR] (32:3, #127) 92, p. 103.
"Fire, Fire, in the Mouth of Many Things." [Quarry] (41:1) Wint 92, p. 41.
"The Hotel of Secrets" (Paris, 1978). [FreeL] (10) Sum 92, p. 27.
"The Masters." [WormR] (32:4 #128) 92, p. 138.
"Monetary Haiku." [WormR] (32:3, #127) 92, p. 103.
"My Sometimes Disenchantment with the West." [Amelia] (7:1, #20) 92, p. 153.
"Observation, Number Three." [WormR] (32:4 #128) 92, p. 137.
"Of Trains and Hearts and Students of the Dream." [Vis] (40) 92, p. 10-13.
"One for Charles Bukowski." [Bogg] (65) 92, p. 26-28.
"One Theory." [WormR] (32:4 #128) 92, p. 138.
"Outside Night Window." [WormR] (32:3, #127) 92, p. 103.
"Outside Night Window." [WormR] (32:4 #128) 92, p. 138.
"Poetry." [WormR] (32:3, #127) 92, p. 104.
"Poetry or Murder." [WormR] (32:3, #127) 92, p. 103.
"Self-Portrait As Giraffe Poem and Cafe Habitue." [WormR] (32:3, #127) 92, p. 104.
"Self-Portrait with Paul Klee Watching Over My Shoulder" (for Natalie Davey). [Amelia] (7:1, #20) 92, p. 154.
"Some Friends of Ruth and Ellis Get Married" (For Dan Lenihan). [WormR] (32:4 #128) 92, p. 136-137.
"This Transient Kingdom." [Vis] (40) 92, p. 14.
291. BALABAN, Camille
"A Morning Like This." [EngJ] (81:1) Ja 92, p. 97.
292. BALABAN, John
"Viewing the New World Order." [Witness] (6:1) 92, p. 9-11.
293. BALAKIAN, Peter
"Out of School." [SouthernR] (28:1) Wint, Ja 92, p. 103-104.
"Some Notes Before Quitting." [Antaeus] (69) Aut 92, p. 143-145.
294. BALAN, Jars
"Genesis" (from the forthcoming collection, "Alter-ego," tr. of Victor Neborak). [PraF] (13:3, #60) Aut 92, p. 142-144.
"Supper" (from the forthcoming collection, "Alter-ego," tr. of Victor Neborak). [PraF] (13:3, #60) Aut 92, p. 146.
"There are mirrors and doors" (from the forthcoming collection, "Alter-ego," tr. of Victor Neborak). [PraF] (13:3, #60) Aut 92, p. 145.
"Visual Poems" (from the series "Poems in a Plain Style Script"). [PraF] (13:3, #60) Aut 92, p. 24-30.
"What kind of a beast" (from the forthcoming collection, "Alter-ego," tr. of Victor Neborak). [PraF] (13:3, #60) Aut 92, p. 144.
295. BALAZ, Joe
"Half Marathon." [ChamLR] (10/11) Spr-Fall 92, p. 85-88.
"Like Waves Against Rocks." [ChamLR] (10/11) Spr-Fall 92, p. 84.
296. BALAZS, Mary
"Potato-Digging." [Poem] (67) My 92, p. 38.
297. BALBO, Ned
"Carnival." [HiramPoR] (51/52) Fall 91-Sum 92, p. 20.
"Legacy" (After Herrick). [FourQ] (6:1) Spr 92, p. 9.
"The Stairway Down to the Sea" (For M.W., Father's Day, 1987). [FourQ] (6:1) Spr 92, p. 10-11.
"A View from the Tower." [HiramPoR] (51/52) Fall 91-Sum 92, p. 19.
298. BALDASTY, Richard
"Cameo." [Poem] (67) My 92, p. 33.
"Pyre." [Poem] (67) My 92, p. 32.
299. BALDONADO, Angela Dawn
"Hunting the Goddess." [Rohwedder] (7) Spr-Sum 92, p. 41.
300. BALK, Christianne
"Dusk Choir." [BellR] (15:2) Fall 92, p. 6.
"Separation." [CutB] (37) Wint 92, p. 61-62.
"Steheken Light." [CutB] (37) Wint 92, p. 59-60.
301. BALL, Angela
"Adjustments." [LitR] (25:2) Wint 92, p. 272.

"Lofty Cities." [AmerV] (26) Spr 92, p. 115-116.
"Nancy Cunard." [MalR] (100) Fall 92, p. 204-217.
"Sylvia Beach" (for Noel Riley Fitch, author of *Sylvia Beach and the Lost Generation*). [NegC] (12:3) 92, p. 45-54.
"Trace." [YellowS] (41) Fall-Wint 92-93, p. 20.

302. BALL, Candice
"Men Love Women Love Men." [Grain] (20:1) Spr 92, p. 237.

303. BALL, Joseph (Joseph H.)
"As the Heart Grows Older." [DogRR] (11:2, #22) Fall-Wint 92, p. 14.
"Bike Ride." [EngJ] (81:5) S 92, p. 102.
"Born in the Century of the Movies." [SouthernPR] (32:2) Fall 92, p. 55.
"Jenny Says." [EngJ] (81:5) S 92, p. 102.
"South Hampton Summer." [SoDakR] (30:4) Wint 92, p. 115.

304. BALL, Roger A.
"Dry Dream." [CoalC] (5) My 92, p. 5.

305. BALL, Sally
"One Story of Conversion." [Thrpny] (50) Sum 92, p. 32.

306. BALLARD, Charles
"Time Was the Trail Went Deep." [Jacaranda] (6:1/2) Wint-Spr 92, p. 59.

307. BALOIAN
"For the Moment." [MidwQ] (33:3) Spr 92, p. 306.

308. BALTAG, Cezar
"Blind Above the Words" (tr. by Adam J. Sorkin w. the poet). [PoetL] (87:4) Wint 92-93, p. 38.
"The Gray Squirrel" (tr. by Adam J. Sorkin w. the poet). [PoetL] (87:4) Wint 92-93, p. 38.

309. BALTATZI, Adamantia (Amanda)
"Damp your sandals" (tr. of Yannis Ritsos, w. Jose Garcia). [Vis] (39) 92, p. 39.
"Third Series" (Selections: 10, 23, 27, 42, 48, tr. of Yannis Ritsos, w. José García). [PaintedHR] (5) Wint 92, p. 5.

310. BAMBER, Linda
"Homage to Frank O'Hara." [KenR] (NS 14:4) Fall 92, p. 65-68.

311. BAMFORTH, Iain
"Calvinist Geography." [Verse] (9:2) Sum 92, p. 88-89.
"Mandate for Mending." [Verse] (9:2) Sum 92, p. 87.

312. BANAS, Kathy
"Hands Filled with Figs." [BellArk] (8:4) Jl-Ag 92, p. 21.

313. BANDEROB, Randy
"Codeine Hums a Little Ditty." [PraF] (13:2, #59) Sum 92, p. 83.
"Hopefully My Last Nasty Poem." [PraF] (13:2, #59) Sum 92, p. 83.

314. BANERJEE, Paramita
"About My Little Sister" (tr. of Anuradha Mahapatra, w. Carolyne Wright). [KenR] (NS 14:2) Spr 92, p. 75.
"Along the Railroad Track" (tr. of Kanchan Kuntala Mukherjee, w. Arlene Zide). [ChiR] (38:1/2) 92, p. 122-123.
"Cow and Grandmother" (tr. of Anuradha Mahapatra, w. Carolyne Wright). [KenR] (NS 14:2) Spr 92, p. 75-76.
"A Little Folktale" (tr. of Anuradha Mahapatra, w. Carolyne Wright). [KenR] (NS 14:2) Spr 92, p. 74.
"The Ritual of *Sati*" (tr. of Gita Chattopadhyay, w. Carolyne Wright). [ChiR] (38:1/2) 92, p. 93.

315. BANERJEE, Ron D. K.
"The Naked Solitary Hand" (tr. of Jibanananda Das). [Trans] (26) Spr 92, p. 116-118.
"The Runaway Streetcar" (tr. of Nikolai Gumilev). [Trans] (26) Spr 92, p. 46-48.

316. BANGAI, Siah Salma
"Maternity." [AfAmRev] (26:2) Sum 92, p. 278.

317. BANKAY, AnneMaria
"Imperfect Poem" (tr. of Dulce Maria Loynaz). [LitR] (35:4) Sum 92, p. 452.
"Like a Strange Bird from the South" (tr. of Reina Maria Rodriguez). [LitR] (35:4) Sum 92, p. 465.
"Poem in Which I Celebrate" (tr. of Chely Lima). [LitR] (35:4) Sum 92, p. 451.
"Room vs. Room" (tr. of Raisa White). [LitR] (35:4) Sum 92, p. 467.
"Train Dreams" (tr. of Reina Maria Rodriguez). [LitR] (35:4) Sum 92, p. 466.

318. BANKS, Kenneth
"Le Tombeau de Paul Celan (1920-1970)." [AntigR] (91) Fall 92, p. 8-10.

319. BANNER, Vera
"For All the Children." [Gypsy] (18) 92, p. 108-109.
320. BAÑUELOS, Raúl
"A Life" (tr. by Reginald Gibbons). [TriQ] (85) Fall 92, p. 348-349.
321. BANUS, Maria
"Don't Be Surprised" (tr. by Mary Mattfield). [PoetryE] (33) Spr 92, p. 164.
"Monstril / Monsters" (in Romanian and English, tr. by Mary Mattfield). [Nimrod] (35:2) Spr-Sum 92, p. 41.
322. BARAKA, Amiri
"Art." [WorldL] (3) 92, p. 4-7.
"Wise I." [Sulfur] (12:1, #30) Spr 92, p. 182.
323. BARANCZAK, Stanislaw
"Maybe All This" (tr. of Wislawa Szymborska, w. Clare Cavanagh). [NewYorker] (68:43) 14 D 92, p. 94.
"One Version of Events" (tr. of Wislawa Szymborska, w. Clare Cavanagh). [ManhatR] (6:2) Fall 92, p. 43-46.
324. BARANOW, Joan
"Bruised Rib." [US1] (26/27) 92, p. 23.
325. BARANSZKY, László
"On Liberty" (tr. of Péter Kantor). [Agni] (35) 92, p. 270-271.
326. BARAS, Alejandro
"Carta" (tr. by Rigas Kappatos and Carlos Montemayor). [Nuez] (4:12) 92, p. 24.
"Pasan los Asiáticos" (tr. by Rigas Kappatos and Carlos Montemayor). [Nuez] (4:12) 92, p. 24.
327. BARATTA, Edward
"Credo." [LitR] (25:2) Wint 92, p. 261.
"Sometimes Gray." [LitR] (25:2) Wint 92, p. 260.
328. BARBARESE, J. T.
"Labor Day: Tall Trees' Creaking" (for Almitra David). [SouthernR] (28:3) Sum, Jl 92, p. 641-642.
329. BARBER, Connie
"The Propinquity of Species." [Vis] (40) 92, p. 32.
"A Short Time." [Vis] (40) 92, p. 33.
330. BARBER, David
"The Favor." [Poetry] (159:5) F 92, p. 255-256.
"Ladies of the Necropolis." [Agni] (35) 92, p. 117-119.
"Memo on the Hereafter." [Agni] (35) 92, p. 122-123.
"My Quarrel with Queen Anne's Lace." [Agni] (35) 92, p. 120-121.
331. BARBER, Ellen
"Red Pepper with White China." [Jacaranda] (6:1/2) Wint-Spr 92, p. 38.
332. BARBER, Jennifer (Jenny)
"181st Street." [Pequod] (33) 92, p. 46-47.
"The Courtesan." [Noctiluca] (1:1) Spr 92, p. 1.
"History of Love." [Pequod] (33) 92, p. 45.
"Homeland, 1946" (for R.). [Noctiluca] (1:1) Spr 92, p. 2.
"Two Women." [Noctiluca] (1:2) Wint 92 [on cover: Wint 93], p. 26-27.
"The Unpaid." [Pequod] (33) 92, p. 43.
"The White Rooster." [Pequod] (33) 92, p. 44.
333. BARBER, Joanne
"Late Saturday Afternoon." [Footwork] 92, p. 127.
"The Morning After." [Footwork] 92, p. 128.
"Sons." [Footwork] 92, p. 127.
"Tonight." [Footwork] 92, p. 127.
"Winter." [Footwork] 92, p. 128.
334. BARBOUR, Douglas
"Breath Ghazal 15." [Descant] (23:3, #78) Fall 92, p. 7.
"Breath Ghazal 21." [PraF] (13:4, #61) Wint 92-93, p. 15.
"Breath Ghazal 26" (for Chet Baker, playing Edmonton, 1982). [Descant] (23:3, #78) Fall 92, p. 8.
"Breath Ghazal 29." [PraF] (13:4, #61) Wint 92-93, p. 16.
"Breath Ghazal 30." [PraF] (13:4, #61) Wint 92-93, p. 17.
335. BARDON, James
"To a Child Who Died Last Night." [Crucible] (28) Fall 92, p. 50.
336. BAREA, Michael
"Floral" (tr. of Gabriel Ferrater). [Nimrod] (35:2) Spr-Sum 92, p. 13.

337. BARGEN, Walter
"95." [CapeR] (27:1) Spr 92, p. 28.
"Act One." [NewL] (58:3) Spr 92, p. 93.
"Friendly Fire." [SpoonRQ] (17:3/4) Sum-Fall 92, p. 94-95.
"Headache." [SenR] (22:2) Fall 92, p. 20.
"Moment of Reflection." [SpoonRQ] (17:3/4) Sum-Fall 92, p. 96.
"Or Worse." [Farm] (9:2) Fall-Wint 92-93, p. 13-14.
"Queen Anne's Lace." [NewL] (58:3) Spr 92, p. 94-95.
"Rates." [Farm] (9:2) Fall-Wint 92-93, p. 15-16.
"Stress Test." [CapeR] (27:1) Spr 92, p. 29.
"Ultimate Beliefs." [SpoonRQ] (17:3/4) Sum-Fall 92, p. 92-93.
"When the Cows Come Home." [CharR] (18:2) Fall 92, p. 99-100.
338. BARGOWSKI, John D.
"Mission Girl." [JlNJPo] (14:2) Aut 92, p. 19-21.
339. BARI, Károly
"Forgotten Fires" (from "Elfelejtett Tüzek," tr. by Judit Molnár). [PoetryC] (12:2) Ap 92, p. 24.
"Gypsy-Row" (from "Elfelejtett Tüzek," tr. by Judit Molnár). [PoetryC] (12:2) Ap 92, p. 24.
"Pvt. János Vajda's Confession in Front of Sándor Petöfi's Immortal Soul" (tr. by Judit Molnár). [PoetryC] (12:2) Ap 92, p. 24.
"Suffering Set Me on the Road" (from "Holtak arca fölé," tr. by Endre Farkas). [PoetryC] (12:2) Ap 92, p. 25.
"Wandering Gypsies" (from "Holtak arca fölé," tr. by Endre Farkas). [PoetryC] (12:2) Ap 92, p. 25.
340. BARKAN, Stanley H.
"Daughters & Parents." [Footwork] 92, p. 52.
"For Sal Sanjamino" (on his retirement). [Footwork] 92, p. 51.
"In the Back of the Grocery Store." [Footwork] 92, p. 51.
"The Thing Left Out." [Footwork] 92, p. 52.
"Two Poets by an Open Window" (for Menke Katz and Yussel Greenspan). [NewOR] (19:3/4) Fall-Wint 92, p. 144-145.
"Under the Williamsburg Bridge" (for Menke Katz and Yussel Greenspan). [NewOR] (19:3/4) Fall-Wint 92, p. 37.
341. BARKER, Helene
"Demokleides, Son of Demetrios" (high classical stele, Athens Archeological Museum). [CapeR] (27:2) Fall 92, p. 33.
"The Light Fantastic." [CapeR] (27:2) Fall 92, p. 34-35.
342. BARKER, Wendy
"In Venice the Travellers." [AntR] (50:4) Fall 92, p. 710-711.
"On the Bottom." [TarRP] (32:1) Fall 92, p. 38.
"Reason of Lace." [Poetry] (159:5) F 92, p. 264-265.
343. BARLOW, John
"I wrote my father and asked him." [PraF] (13:4, #61) Wint 92-93, p. 34.
"Like Watching Civilization." [PraF] (13:4, #61) Wint 92-93, p. 33-34.
344. BARNES, Dick
"A Clarification." [Light] (1) Spr 92, p. 9.
"Doomsday" (tr. of Jorge Luis Borges). [ArtfulD] (22/23) 92, p. 26.
"Everness" (tr. of Jorge Luis Borges, w. Robert Mezey). [SoCoast] (12) Ja 92, p. 37.
"Ewigkeit" (tr. of Jorge Luis Borges, w. Robert Mezey). [SoCoast] (12) Ja 92, p. 35.
"A Fable for Also-Rans." [Light] (3) Aut 92, p. 17.
"Fourteen-Syllable Lines" (tr. of Jorge Luis Borges, w. Robert Mezey). [ArtfulD] (22/23) 92, p. 27.
"Granite Intrusive." [ArtfulD] (22/23) 92, p. 21.
"The Inquisitor" (tr. of Jorge Luis Borges, w. Robert Mezey). [ParisR] (34:125) Wint 92, p. 233.
"Last Evening" (tr. of Jorge Luis Borges, w. Robert Mezey). [ParisR] (34:125) Wint 92, p. 229.
"Looking for You." [ArtfulD] (22/23) 92, p. 22.
"María Kodama." [ParisR] (34:125) Wint 92, p. 234-235.
"Milonga of the Stranger" (tr. of Jorge Luis Borges, w. Robert Mezey). [ParisR] (34:125) Wint 92, p. 229-230.
"The Moon" (tr. of Jorge Luis Borges, w. Robert Mezey). [ParisR] (34:125) Wint 92, p. 232.
"The Thing I Am" (tr. of Jorge Luis Borges, w. Robert Mezey). [ParisR] (34:125) Wint 92, p. 231-232.

345. BARNES, Jane
"Hot Nights / Atlanta, 1963." [BrooklynR] (9) 92, p. 63.
346. BARNES, Jim
"After the Parade" (14.vii.91). [SoDakR] (30:4) Wint 92, p. 122-124.
"At the Coupole." [SoDakR] (30:4) Wint 92, p. 121.
"At the Festival de Poésie." [ArtfulD] (22/23) 92, p. 11.
"At Zimmer's." [IndR] (15:2) Fall 92, p. 69.
"By the Seine, a Promise." [IndR] (15:2) Fall 92, p. 70-71.
"Captives among the stalks" (tr. of Claire-Sara Roux). [ArtfulD] (22/23) 92, p. 14.
"Le Colisée, des Champs Élysées." [SoDakR] (30:4) Wint 92, p. 126-127.
"Down the Colonnade." [Paint] (19:37) Spr 92, p. 7.
"Fireworks Over Parc Monceau." [Paint] (19:37) Spr 92, p. 10.
"Flushing the Game" (tr. of Dagmar Nick). [ArtfulD] (22/23) 92, p. 15.
"From the Balcony: Hotel Plaza Haussmann." [Paint] (19:37) Spr 92, p. 9.
"From the Pantheon." [Paint] (19:37) Spr 92, p. 5-6.
"Looking for Hemingway's Ghost at the Crillon." [SoDakR] (30:4) Wint 92, p. 125.
"Meeting Susan S. at Musée de l'Orangerie." [ArtfulD] (22/23) 92, p. 12.
"Near Proust's Apartment." [Paint] (19:37) Spr 92, p. 8.
"The song is choked" (tr. of Claire-Sara Roux). [ArtfulD] (22/23) 92, p. 13.
"Tracking Rabbits: Night." [Jacaranda] (6:1/2) Wint-Spr 92, p. 62.
"Twilight" (tr. of Dagmar Nick). [Trans] (26) Spr 92, p. 80.
347. BARNES, Kim
"Hanging the Swing" (for Bob and Jordan). [Shen] (42:2) Sum 92, p. 102.
"The Regular." [Shen] (42:2) Sum 92, p. 103.
348. BARNES, Richard
"Clouds" (tr. of Jorge Luis Borges, w. Robert Mezey). [Iowa] (22:3) Fall 92, p. 72.
"General Quiroga Rides to His Death in a Carriage" (tr. of Jorge Luis Borges, w. Robert Mezey). [Iowa] (22:3) Fall 92, p. 71-72.
"The Nightmare" (tr. of Jorge Luis Borges, w. Robert Mezey). [GrandS] (11:3 #43) 92, p. 185.
349. BARNES, Tim
"Academic Reason." [PaintedHR] (6) Spr 92, p. 24.
350. BARNETT, Cathy
"Rachel's Gift." [BellR] (15:2) Fall 92, p. 30.
351. BARNETT, Pamela E.
"Circle." [SoCoast] (13) Je 93 [i.e. 92], p. 6-7.
"Eugenia, The Baroness Munster" (Heroine of *The Europeans* by Henry James). [NegC] (12:1/2) 92, p. 9.
352. BARNETT, Ruth Anderson
"Abiding Flower." [FloridaR] (18:1) Spr-Sum 92, p. 29.
"The Breakdown." [FloridaR] (18:1) Spr-Sum 92, p. 28.
353. BARNEY, William D.
"The Buss as a Form of Elizabethan Transport." [Light] (4) Wint 92-93, p. 16.
"Clerihew: 'I wonder,' said Noah." [Light] (4) Wint 92-93, p. 11.
354. BARNSTONE, Tony
"Deep South Mountain" (tr. of Wang Wei, w. Willis Barnstone and Xu Haixin). [LitR] (25:2) Wint 92, p. 220.
"The Dump." [Nimrod] (36:1) Fall-Wint 92, p. 42-43.
"Errand in the Wilderness" (Lumber and Toxins: Three Poems. Honorable Mention, The Pablo Neruda Prize for Poetry). [Nimrod] (36:1) Fall-Wint 92, p. 41.
"For Someone Far Away" (tr. of Wang Wei, w. Willis Barnstone and Xu Haixin). [LitR] (25:2) Wint 92, p. 220.
"In the Mountains" (tr. of Wang Wei, w. Willis Barnstone and Xu Haixin). [LitR] (25:2) Wint 92, p. 221.
"Lakeside Pavilion" (tr. of Wang Wei, w. Willis Barnstone and Xu Haixin). [LitR] (25:2) Wint 92, p. 221.
"Mountain Stream Spilling from a Dream" (From "The Wild Moon" series, tr. of Tang Yaping, w. Newton Liu). [LitR] (35:3) Spr 92, p. 384.
"Night Over the Huai River" (tr. of Wang Wei, w. Willis Barnstone and Xu Haixin). [LitR] (25:2) Wint 92, p. 220.
"Winter Night, Writing About My Emotion" (tr. of Wang Wei, w. Willis Barnstone and Xu Haixin). [LitR] (25:2) Wint 92, p. 221.
355. BARNSTONE, Willis
"Deep South Mountain" (tr. of Wang Wei, w. Tony Barnstone and Xu Haixin). [LitR] (25:2) Wint 92, p. 220.

"For Someone Far Away" (tr. of Wang Wei, w. Tony Barnstone and Xu Haixin). [LitR] (25:2) Wint 92, p. 220.
"In the Mountains" (tr. of Wang Wei, w. Tony Barnstone and Xu Haixin). [LitR] (25:2) Wint 92, p. 221.
"Lakeside Pavilion" (tr. of Wang Wei, w. Tony Barnstone and Xu Haixin). [LitR] (25:2) Wint 92, p. 221.
"Night Over the Huai River" (tr. of Wang Wei, w. Tony Barnstone and Xu Haixin). [LitR] (25:2) Wint 92, p. 220.
"When the Marble Dark Comes, Ink Will Boil into a Dawn of Time." [LitR] (25:2) Wint 92, p. 259.
"Winter Night, Writing About My Emotion" (tr. of Wang Wei, w. Tony Barnstone and Xu Haixin). [LitR] (25:2) Wint 92, p. 221.

356. BARON, Todd
"Intending a Raft" (for Margy Sloan). [Talisman] (9) Fall 92, p. 98-105.
"Measure" (dedication). [Avec] (5:1) 92, p. 125-128.

357. BARONE, Patricia
"Palimpsest." [Vis] (39) 92, p. 23-24.

358. BARR, Burlin
"Cul de Sac." [GrandS] (11:2, #42) 92, p. 132-133.

359. BARR, Charlotte
"The Death of Cousins." [CumbPR] (11:2) Spr 92, p. 5.

360. BARR, John
"There's Nae Place Like Otago Yet." [Verse] (9:3) Wint 92, p. 118.

361. BARR, Tina
"Magician's Tricks." [Pequod] (33) 92, p. 40-42.

362. BARRAX, Gerald
"Counting the Ways." [SouthernR] (28:4) Aut, O 92, p. 825.

363. BARRESI, Dorothy
"Mother Hunger and Her Seatbelt." [Agni] (36) 92, p. 100-103.
"Skirts & Skins." [SycamoreR] (4:2) Sum 92, p. 34-38.

364. BARRETT, Allan
"Don't Pray for the Dead." [AntigR] (89) Spr 92, p. 82.

365. BARRETT, Carol
"Christmas Card." [OxfordM] (6:2) Fall-Wint 90, p. 16-17.

366. BARRETT, Ed
"All the While Knowing." [PaintedB] (48) 92, p. 42-43.
"Looking for Halley's Comet with Liz" (for Joe and Gay Halderman). [PaintedB] (46) 92, p. 11-13.
"Odeon." [Agni] (36) 92, p. 92.
"The Same Song They Whistle in the Future." [PaintedB] (46) 92, p. 15.
"Six Trilogies for Annie." [PaintedB] (46) 92, p. 16-17.
"Your Next Interview." [PaintedB] (46) 92, p. 14.

367. BARRETT, Kevin
"The Ballad of Alfred Jarry." [JlNJPo] (14:1) Spr 92, p. 54-56.

368. BARRIENTOS, Raúl
"And What Did They Do to the Strike?" (tr. by Ben Heller). [InterPR] (18:2) Fall 92, p. 51, 53.
"Domingo." [InterPR] (18:2) Fall 92, p. 54, 56, 58.
"It Would Be Better, Really, If They Devoured Everything and We Ended This" (— César Vallejo, tr. by Ben Heller). [InterPR] (18:2) Fall 92, p. 61, 63.
"Más Valdría, en Verdad, Que Se Lo Coman Todo y Acabemos" (— César Vallejo). [InterPR] (18:2) Fall 92, p. 60, 62.
"Sunday" (tr. by Ben Heller). [InterPR] (18:2) Fall 92, p. 55, 57, 59.
"¿Y Qué Hicieron con la Huelga?" [InterPR] (18:2) Fall 92, p. 50, 52.

369. BARRIER, Don
"Blind Hearted Man." [Vis] (40) 92, p. 54.

370. BARRINGTON, Judith
"The Age of the Sea" (tr. of Cristina Peri Rossi). [Trans] (26) Spr 92, p. 28.
"Bad News Pantoum." [13thMoon] (10:1/2) 92, p. 23.
"Dream" (for Ursula). [13thMoon] (10:1/2) 92, p. 24.
"The Dyke with No Name Thinks About Landscape." [AmerV] (27) 92, p. 72-78.
"Falling." [13thMoon] (10:1/2) 92, p. 25.
"Grace." [13thMoon] (10:1/2) 92, p. 21.
"Layers of Sound." [BlackBR] (16) Wint-Spr 92-93, p. 13-14.
"Oil." [BlackBR] (16) Wint-Spr 92-93, p. 15.

"Sounds Like Motion" (for Debbie Gilbert and Tish Lilly). [13thMoon] (10:1/2) 92, p. 22.

371. BARROWS, Anita
"The Road Past the View" (for Nora and Viva and in memory of Mary Oppen). [QRL] (Poetry Series 11: vol. 31) 92, 66 p.

372. BART, Jill
"Big Betty." [PoetL] (87:1) Spr 92, p. 38.
"On Losing My Head." [NegC] (12:3) 92, p. 55.

373. BART, Nigel
"Into My Hands." Sparks! Writing by High School Students (1:1), a supplement to [PraF] (13:4, #61) Wint 92-93, p. 7.

374. BARTH, Bob
"Historical Irony." [Light] (1) Spr 92, p. 18.
"The New Cavalier Lyric." [Light] (3) Aut 92, p. 19.
"The Way It Is." [Light] (1) Spr 92, p. 29.

375. BARTH, Pam
"Thoughts." [PaintedB] (48) 92, p. 74.

376. BARTHELME, Steven
"Father." [SouthernR] (28:1) Wint, Ja 92, p. 62.

377. BARTLETT, Brian
"Long Distance and Bleach." [Event] (21:2) Sum 92, p. 40-41.

378. BARTOLOMÉ, Efraín
"Monkey House" (tr. by Reginald Gibbons). [TriQ] (85) Fall 92, p. 380-381.

379. BARTON, Fred
"Field Trip." [HiramPoR] (51/52) Fall 91-Sum 92, p. 21.

380. BARTON, John
"Artificial Intelligence." [MalR] (99) Sum 92, p. 85-86.
"C-Level Cirque." [PoetryC] (13:1) N 92, p. 10.
"Field Guide." [Dandel] (19:1) 92, p. 13-14.
"Interior Design." [JamesWR] (9:2) Wint 92, p. 10-11.
"Lake Louise." [Dandel] (19:1) 92, p. 15.
"The Man from Grande Prairie." [EvergreenC] (7:2) Sum-Fall 92, p. 25-26.
"Ripening." [EvergreenC] (7:2) Sum-Fall 92, p. 27-28.
"Ripper." [ChironR] (11:4) Wint 92, p. 45.
"Ripper." [PoetryC] (13:1) N 92, p. 11.
"Stains." [PoetryC] (13:1) N 92, p. 10.

381. BARTOSOVA, Madga
"And That Is Why." [PraS] (66:4) Wint 92, p. 46.

382. BARTOW, Stuart
"Apple Spell." [Poem] (68) N 92, p. 38.
"Drawn by Far Lights." [SnailPR] (2:1) Spr-Sum 92, p. 6.
"Of Sleep and Snowy Fields." [JlNJPo] (14:2) Aut 92, p. 38.
"Sulphurs." [Poem] (68) N 92, p. 36.
"Veined Whites." [Poem] (68) N 92, p. 37.

383. BARYLANKA, Jola
"Dance" (for Maria Kuncewiczowa, tr. by Reuel K. Wilson). [Trans] (26) Spr 92, p. 102.

384. BASINSKI, Michael
"0." [SlipS] (12) 92, p. 16.
"Camel's Ledge." [SlipS] (12) 92, p. 14.
"Rats." [SlipS] (12) 92, p. 15.
"Shootin' the Shit" (a.k.a. Shop Floor Haiku). [SlipS] (12) 92, p. 16-17.
"Steel sleep." [PoetryUSA] (24) 92, p. 22.

385. BASKETT, Franz K.
"The Antique." [SouthernR] (28:4) Aut, O 92, p. 827.
"The Book Reflects on Style and Time." [CapeR] (27:2) Fall 92, p. 10.
"Bridge." [CapeR] (27:2) Fall 92, p. 9.
"The Jains." [Epiphany] (3:4) O (Fall) 92, p. 229.
"Letting the Dog Off." [SouthernR] (28:4) Aut, O 92, p. 826.
"Lying Down in Snow." [Epiphany] (3:4) O (Fall) 92, p. 230-231.

386. BASNEY, Lionel
"After Love." [SewanR] (100:2) Spr 92, p. 264.

387. BASS, Emily
"Crewcut." [HangL] (60) 92, p. 71.
"It So Happens." [HangL] (60) 92, p. 68.
"Shy is a spontaneous pregnancy." [HangL] (60) 92, p. 69.

"The Truth." [HangL] (60) 92, p. 70.

388. BASSO, Eric
"The Hand." [CentralP] (21) Spr 92, p. 165-166.

389. BASU, Ram
"A Strange Man" (tr. by Chitra Divakaruni). [ChiR] (38:1/2) 92, p. 134-135.

390. BAT-YISRAEL, Shulamith
"Simultaneous Transmission" (Jerusalem, August 26, 1990). [Gypsy] (18) 92, p. 65 - 68.

391. BATEMAN, Claire
"Character." [KenR] (NS 14:4) Fall 92, p. 166-167.
"Gloves." [PassN] (13:2) Wint 92, p. 24.
"It Happened Again." [SoCarR] (24:2) Spr 92, p. 138.
"Milk." [KenR] (NS 14:4) Fall 92, p. 168.
"On the True Use of Musick." [SouthernR] (28:1) Wint, Ja 92, p. 30-31.
"Waiting for Red." [SouthernR] (28:1) Wint, Ja 92, p. 29-30.

392. BATES, Scott
"History Lesson." [Light] (2) Sum 92, p. 16.
"Letters from the North Pole — II" (from the Toy Factory). [Light] (4) Wint 92-93, p. 19.
"Nude Man Disrupts Administration Dinner." [Light] (2) Sum 92, p. 11.

393. BATHANTI, Joseph
"At the Bay of Albemarle." [PaintedB] (47) 92, p. 45.
"Daria." [LouisL] (9:1) Spr 92, p. 63-64.

394. BATTRAM, Michael R.
"Taking a Powder." [MoodySI] (27) Spr 92, p. 42.

395. BAUER, Grace
"Christmas Day at County Prison." [NegC] (12:1/2) 92, p. 13-14.
"For My Mother at the New Year." [NegC] (12:1/2) 92, p. 12.
"A Letter to William Hathaway on His Letter to William Wordsworth." [NegC] (12:1/2) 92, p. 11.
"Nana, Baking." [NegC] (12:1/2) 92, p. 10.
"Where You're Seen Her Before" [sic] (after Cindy Sherman). [SouthernPR] (32:1) Spr 92, p. 25-27.

396. BAUER, Steven
"Dried Arrangement with Old Woman." [HopewellR] (4) 92, p. 8.
"Olive Trees." [HopewellR] (4) 92, p. 16.

397. BAUER, Tricia
"Sauna." [Kalliope] (14:1) 92, p. 68.

398. BAUGH, Edward
"It Was the Singing." [CinPR] (23) Wint 91-92, p. 36-37.
"Journey" (to the memory of Edna Manley, sculptor). [CinPR] (23) Wint 91-92, p. 40.
"Nigger Sweat." [CinPR] (23) Wint 91-92, p. 38-39.

399. BAUGHN, Marianna
"Box-Camera Snapshot." [JINJPo] (14:2) Aut 92, p. 6.

400. BAUMGAERTNER, Jill P.
"Compulsive's Confession." [ChrC] (109:32) 4 N 92, p. 999.
"Gardening: The Professor" (For Rolland Hein). [CentR] (36:3) Fall 92, p. 538-539.
"The Private World of Women." [CentR] (36:3) Fall 92, p. 540.

401. BAUMGARTNER, William
"Arach-My-Brain." [EngJ] (81:6) O 92, p. 93.

402. BAUSCH, Robert
"From the Novel, *Almighty Me*." [HampSPR] Wint 92, p. 56.

403. BAWER, Bruce
"Art and Worship." [AmerS] (61:1) Wint 92, p. 122-123.
"August." [SouthwR] (77:1) Wint 92, p. 71.

404. BAXTER, Meg
"Misguided Tulips." [NegC] (12:1/2) 92, p. 15.

405. BAYER, Deanne
"In the Path of the Comet." [Elf] (2:2) Sum 92, p. 38.

406. BAZZET, Mike
"Angst Poem." [Pearl] (16) Fall 92, p. 27.
"Barnyard Connection." [Pearl] (15) Spr-Sum 92, p. 61.

407. BEACH, E. L.
"American Display." [JamesWR] (10:1) Fall 92, p. 16.

408. BEALE, Richard A.
"An Obligation of Trees." [BlackBR] (16) Wint-Spr 92-93, p. 5.
BEAR, Ray Young (Ray A. Young)
See YOUNG BEAR, Ray (Ray A.)
409. BEARD, David
"Crisis." [Sun] (200) Ag 92, p. 7.
BÉARN, Roger du
See Du BÉARN, Roger
410. BEASLEY, Bruce
"Eve, Learning to Speak." [ParisR]] (34:124) Fall 92, p. 170-172.
"On Easter." [SouthernR] (28:4) Aut, O 92, p. 829.
"Summer." [SouthernR] (28:4) Aut, O 92, p. 828.
"Utter." [Agni] (35) 92, p. 227-228.
"Vesper." [SouthwR] (77:4) Aut 92, p. 560-561.
411. BEASLEY, Sherry
"My Mother Remembers the War." [CapeR] (27:2) Fall 92, p. 16.
412. BEATTY, Jan
"Ghost Orchid." [SouthernPR] (32:1) Spr 92, p. 22.
"Ravenous Blue." [SouthernPR] (32:2) Fall 92, p. 59-60.
413. BEATTY, Paul
"No Tag Backs." [Eyeball] (1) 92, p. 15-18.
"Two Pink Dots? You Positive?" [WestCL] (26:2, #8) Fall 92, p. 40-45.
414. BEAUMONT, Jeanne
"Aspidistra" (after Orwell). [RiverC] (12:2) Spr 92, p. 29.
"Barometrics." [Poetry] (160:5) Ag 92, p. 269.
"Childhood of the Invisible Woman." [RiverC] (12:2) Spr 92, p. 32-33.
"First and Last Chances." [CreamCR] (16:1) Spr 92, p. 125.
"The Greening of the Fire Escape." [Nat] (255:5) 17-24 Ag 92, p. 182.
"Metal and Bone." [LaurelR] (26:2) Sum 92, p. 83.
"Mr. Ripley Writes a Preface." [GettyR] (5:2) Spr 92, p. 355-356.
"Mrs. Ripley Gets It Off Her Chest." [GettyR] (5:2) Spr 92, p. 357-358.
"Nature Morte." [RiverC] (12:2) Spr 92, p. 30-31.
"A Night at the Ripleys." [Harp] (285:1707) Ag 92, p. 34.
"Pattern." [Boulevard] (7:1, #19) Spr 92, p. 131-132.
"Visual Field Test." [NewAW] (10) Fall 92, p. 98-99.
415. BECK, Art
"Dream Politics." [FreeL] (9) Wint 92, p. 3.
416. BECK, Julian
"His nipples" (from "living in volkswagen buses and other Songs of the Revolution"). [PoetryUSA] (24) 92, p. 18.
"It's my time. as if a lamp were to raise its paws in anger" (from "living in volkswagen buses and other Songs of the Revolution"). [PoetryUSA] (24) 92, p. 22.
417. BECKER, Kristin
"Bad Luck" (for J.M.). [PaintedHR] (5) Wint 92, p. 26.
418. BECKER, Robin
"Contra-Dancing in Nelson, N.H." (for Leslie). [KenR] (NS 14:1) Wint 92, p. 26-27.
"The Crypto-Jews." [LitR] (36:1) Fall 92, p. 30.
"The Elimination of First Thoughts." [Agni] (35) 92, p. 189.
"Haircut on Via di Mezzo." [Agni] (35) 92, p. 190-191.
"In Pietrasanta." [AmerPoR] (21:3) My-Je 92, p. 18.
"Port-Au-Prince, 1960." [AmerPoR] (21:3) My-Je 92, p. 18.
419. BECKER, Therese
"Saving the Animals." [Witness] (6:1) 92, p. 54-55.
420. BECKER, Tracy
"Speak." [SinW] (48) Wint 92-93, p. 111.
421. BECKER, Uli
"The God-like Flash" (tr. by Charles Paul). [ParisR] (34:123) Sum 92, p. 41-42.
422. BECKETT, Larry
"The mooring poles, in colors, all faded." [WilliamMR] (30) 92, p. 64.
423. BECKETT, Tom
"Luscious surface" (for barbara). [Talisman] (9) Fall 92, p. 214.
424. BECKMAN, Paul
"Vows." [Parting] (5:1) Sum 92, p. 17.
425. BEDARD, Brian
"Tribal News: The Sixth Quartet" (4 poems). [CharR] (18:2) Fall 92, p. 106-108.

426. BEDDOES, Thomas Lovell
"Lord Alcohol." [Light] (4) Wint 92-93, p. 30.

427. BEDELL, Jack B.
"A Fair Share of Morning" (for Lee and Kelly). [LouisL] (9:1) Spr 92, p. 71.

428. BEDFORD, William
"Shelling Peas" (For my mother). [Verse] (9:2) Sum 92, p. 90.

429. BEDIENT, Calvin
"The Shepherd Leading His Flock to the Rainbow." [NewAW] (10) Fall 92, p. 86.

430. BEEBE, Brent
"The Hoopers' Index." [CalQ] (37) 92, p. 29-39.

431. BEECHHOLD, Henry F.
"Reflection." [US1] (26/27) 92, p. 23.

432. BEECHY, Leonard
"John the Baptist." [ChrC] (109:19) 3-10 Je 92, p. 574.

BEEK, Edith van
See Van BEEK, Edith

433. BEGGS, Marck (Marck L.)
"This Lesson." [DenQ] (26:3) Wint 92, p. 6.
"Under Hopkins, Falling." [GreensboroR] (53) Wint 92-93, p. 95.

BEGGS-UEMA, Marck (Marck L.)
See BEGGS, Marck (Marck L.)

434. BEHL, Aditya
"One After Another After Another" (tr. of Teji Grover). [ChiR] (38:1/2) 92, p. 104 - 105.

435. BEHLING, Matthew
"A Class Act." [MoodySI] (27) Spr 92, p. 28.

436. BEHN, Robin
"The Bassoonist." [Iowa] (22:2) Spr-Sum 92, p. 44-46.
"The Experiment." [Crazy] (42) Spr 92, p. 30-33.
"French Horn." [Iowa] (22:2) Spr-Sum 92, p. 41-43.
"Grackles." [Field] (47) Fall 92, p. 81-82.
"On Giving My Father a Book About Roses." [Field] (47) Fall 92, p. 78-80.
"The One Girl on the Soccer Team." [Crazy] (42) Spr 92, p. 34.
"The Paperweight" (for my mother's mother). [SpoonRQ] (17:3/4) Sum-Fall 92, p. 51-52.
"The Saving Grace of Mozart." [Iowa] (22:2) Spr-Sum 92, p. 47-48.
"Those Unitarian Sundays." [AmerV] (26) Spr 92, p. 110-111.
"The Year He Tried Business." [SenR] (22:2) Fall 92, p. 84-85.

437. BEHRENDT, Stephen C.
"Writer's Block." [PacificR] (11) 92-93, p. 86-87.

438. BEI, Dao
"Absence" (tr. by Donald Finkel and Xueliang Chen). [ManhatR] (6:2) Fall 92, p. 15.
"Eventful Autumn" (tr. by Donald Finkel and Xueliang Chen). [ManhatR] (6:2) Fall 92, p. 18.
"Midnight Singer" (tr. by Donald Finkel and Xueliang Chen). [ManhatR] (6:2) Fall 92, p. 17.
"Outside" (tr. by Donald Finkel and Xueliang Chen). [ManhatR] (6:2) Fall 92, p. 19.
"Summer's Brass" (tr. by Donald Finkel and Xueliang Chen). [ManhatR] (6:2) Fall 92, p. 16.
"Year's End" (tr. by Donald Finkel and Xueliang Chen). [ManhatR] (6:2) Fall 92, p. 14.

439. BEINING, Guy R.
"Stoma 1929." [NewDeltaR] (8:1) Fall 90-Wint 91, p. 95.

440. BEISCH, June
"The Dentist." [Epiphany] (3:4) O (Fall) 92, p. 293.
"The Painters." [Epiphany] (3:4) O (Fall) 92, p. 292.

441. BEITTEL, Charles R., Jr.
"Tekel." [Hellas] (3:2) Fall 92, p. 53.

442. BÉLANCE, Réne
"Clameur." [Callaloo] (15:3) Sum 92, p. 608.
"Clamor" (tr. by Carrol F. Coates). [Callaloo] (15:3) Sum 92, p. 607.
"Comfort" (tr. by Carrol F. Coates). [Callaloo] (15:3) Sum 92, p. 605.
"Confort." [Callaloo] (15:3) Sum 92, p. 606.
"Fetiche." [Callaloo] (15:3) Sum 92, p. 604.
"Fetish" (tr. by Carrol F. Coates). [Callaloo] (15:3) Sum 92, p. 603.
"Nerve" (tr. by Carrol F. Coates). [Callaloo] (15:3) Sum 92, p. 609.

"Nervure." [Callaloo] (15:3) Sum 92, p. 610.

443. BELCHER, Charles
"Candlelight." [Obs] (7:1/2) Spr-Sum 92, p. 72-73.
"Minimum Wage." [Obs] (7:1/2) Spr-Sum 92, p. 72.

444. BELDING, Patricia
"Sic Semper Tyrannis" (Winner, Annual Free Verse Contest, 1991). [AnthNEW] (4) 92, p. 21.

445. BELEV, Georgi
"And When the Winter Wind" (tr. of Georgi Borisov, w. Lisa Sapinkopf). [CrabCR] (8:1) Sum-Fall 92, p. 17.
"Between Two Shopfronts" (tr. by the author and Lisa Sapinkopf). [Vis] (39) 92, p. 19-20.
"A Cry" (tr. by Lisa Sapinkopf). [MidAR] (13:2) 92, p. 78.
"Dove" (tr. by Lisa Sapinkopf, w. the author). [WebR] (16) Fall 92, p. 13.
"Garden of Questions" (tr. of Ivan Metodiev, w. Lisa Sapinkopf). [CrabCR] (8:1) Sum-Fall 92, p. 15.
"Give the snow a good interrogation!" (tr. by Lisa Sapinkopf, w. the author). [Confr] (50) Fall 92, p. 299.
"Love" (tr. by Lisa Sapinkopf, w. the author). [HolCrit] (29:2) Ap 92, p. 16.
"Memory" (A cycle of fifteen poems. Selection: II, tr. of Marin Georgiev, w. Lisa Sapinkopf). [Agni] (36) 92, p. 164-165.
"Miracle" (tr. of Nikolai Kantchev, w. Lisa Sapinkopf). [Vis] (39) 92, p. 20.
"Monastery" (tr. of Ivan Davidkov, w. Lisa Sapinkopf). [Nimrod] (35:2) Spr-Sum 92, p. 25.
"Moth" (tr. by Lisa Sapinkopf). [Nimrod] (35:2) Spr-Sum 92, p. 27.
"Night Storm" (tr. by Lisa Sapinkopf, w. the author). [ArtfulD] (22/23) 92, p. 38.
"The Old City" (tr. of Ivan Teofilov, w. Lisa Sapinkopf). [Nimrod] (35:2) Spr-Sum 92, p. 24.
"Rock on the Seashore" (tr. by Lisa Sapinkopf). [Boulevard] (7:1, #19) Spr 92, p. 210.
"Romance" (in Bulgarian and English, tr. by Lisa Sapinkopf). [Nimrod] (35:2) Spr - Sum 92, p. 26.
"A Scene" (tr. of Ani Ilkov, w. Lisa Sapinkopf). [Agni] (36) 92, p. 162-163.
"Sealed Garden" (tr. by Lisa Sapinkopf). [PartR] (59:2) Spr 92, p. 270.
"A Sign from Heaven" (tr. of Boris Hristov, w. Lisa Sapinkopf). [CrabCR] (8:1) Sum-Fall 92, p. 16.
"Spaces" (tr. by Lisa Sapinkopf). [PartR] (59:2) Spr 92, p. 270-271.
"Untitled: Should you wish someone dead" (tr. by Lisa Sapinkopf). [Boulevard] (7:1, #19) Spr 92, p. 211-212.

446. BELL, Jacqueline
"Eggs." [Dandel] (19:1) 92, p. 32-33.
"Nature of the Crime." [Dandel] (19:1) 92, p. 31.

447. BELL, Marvin
"The Book of the Dead Man" (Selections: I-II). [GettyR] (5:3) Sum 92, p. 528-529.
"Cryptic Version of Ecstasy." [Stand] (33:2) Spr 92, p. 18.
"Florida." [Verse] (8:3/9:1) Wint-Spr 92, p. 35.
"Gemwood" (to Nathan and Jason, our sons). [ThRiPo] (39/40) 92-93, p. 8-9.
"March." [Stand] (33:2) Spr 92, p. 17.
"The Mystery of Emily Dickinson." [ThRiPo] (39/40) 92-93, p. 7.
"Stars Which See, Stars Which Do Not See." [ThRiPo] (39/40) 92-93, p. 6-7.
"The Uniform." [Stand] (33:2) Spr 92, p. 18.
"Whitman's Grass." [MassR] (23:1) Spr 92, p. 70-71.

448. BELL, Patrick
"Mario Mercado and His Grandmother." [PaintedHR] (6) Spr 92, p. 22-23.

449. BELLEN, Martine
"A/Z/." [Talisman] (9) Fall 92, p. 193.
"The Tale of Murasaki." [GrandS] (11:3 #43) 92, p. 85-91.

450. BELLEROSE, Sally
"Mama Was Not." [ChironR] (11:4) Wint 92, p. 42.

451. BELMONT, Cynthia
"Another Version of the Dinner." [CreamCR] (16:2) Fall 92, p. 88-89.
"Poem for Olivia." [CreamCR] (16:2) Fall 92, p. 87.
"Speaks the Masochist, on a Pleasure." [CreamCR] (16:2) Fall 92, p. 86.

452. BELOIT/FUDAN TRANSLATION WORKSHOP
"Fish" (tr. of Yu Jian). [ManhatR] (6:2) Fall 92, p. 20-21.

453. BELROSE-HUYGHUES, Allix
"Le Lambi." [LitR] (35:4) Sum 92, p. 609.
"The Lambi Shell." [LitR] (35:4) Sum 92, p. 525.
"Qui Etre." [LitR] (35:4) Sum 92, p. 609.
"Who to Be." [LitR] (35:4) Sum 92, p. 526.
454. BEN-LEV, Dina
"Curse on the Man Who Tried to Burglarize My Apartment While I Was Sleeping." [PoetryNW] (33:4) Wint 92-93, p. 37.
"What a Trappist Monk on the Plane to Paris told Me." [SoCoast] (13) Je 93 [i.e. 92], p. 36-37.
"What My Father Said About the Fifties." [PoetryNW] (33:4) Wint 92-93, p. 35-36.
"What the Landlord Did Not Say" (For Ralph Gertz). [SoCoast] (13) Je 93 [i.e. 92], p. 54.
455. BENDALL, Molly
"After Estrangement." [Ploughs] (18:1) Spr 92, p. 137-138.
"Belated Palms and Orchids." [AmerV] (26) Spr 92, p. 8-10.
"Breastplate" (tr. of Joyce Mansour). [Field] (46) Spr 92, p. 46.
"Light as a Shuttle Desire" (tr. of Joyce Mansour). [Field] (46) Spr 92, p. 47-48.
"Spring Sale at Bendel's" (for Florine Stettheimer, 1871-1944). [ParisR] (34:125) Wint 92, p. 249-251.
456. BENDER, Kristy
"Obituary." [ArtfulD] (22/23) 92, p. 150.
457. BENDER, Margo
"Creation" (tr. of Manuel Antonio Serna-Maytorena). [InterPR] (18:1) Spr 92, p. 27.
"Echos" (tr. of Manuel Antonio Serna-Maytorena). [InterPR] (18:1) Spr 92, p. 29.
"The Eraser" (tr. of Manuel Antonio Serna-Maytorena). [InterPR] (18:1) Spr 92, p. 25.
"It is the witches' hour" (tr. of Silvia Tomasa Rivera). [InterPR] (18:1) Spr 92, p. 47.
"Offering" (tr. of Manuel Antonio Serna-Maytorena). [InterPR] (18:1) Spr 92, p. 33, 35.
"Prelude" (tr. of Manuel Antonio Serna-Maytorena). [InterPR] (18:1) Spr 92, p. 31, 33.
458. BENEDETTI, Mario
"Choosing My Landscape" (tr. by Harry Morales). [Nimrod] (36:1) Fall-Wint 92, p. 79.
"However" (from "Only in the Meantime: Poems 1948-1950," tr. by Harry Morales). [Nimrod] (36:1) Fall-Wint 92, p. 78.
"Nocturnal" (tr. by Harry Morales). [InterPR] (18:2) Fall 92, p. 29, 31.
"Nocturno." [InterPR] (18:2) Fall 92, p. 28, 30.
"Typist" (tr. by Harry Morales). [AmerV] (26) Spr 92, p. 91-92.
459. BENEDIKT, Michael
"Of Debauchery." [MinnR] (39) Fall-Wint 92-93, p. 23-26.
"Of Living Alone But Not Brooding Too Much About It." [Agni] (35) 92, p. 130-131.
"Of Panty-Lines That Show." [NewYorkQ] (48) 92, p. 64-65.
"Of People Who Attempt to Relate by Demanding What Psychologists Term 'Negative Reinforcement'." [Agni] (35) 92, p. 138-139.
"Of Sexual Style." [PoetryE] (33) Spr 92, p. 9-10.
"The Slumming-Place" (tr. of Chen Yuan). [Light] (2) Sum 92, p. 18.
"The Social Life of Sally's Cute and Generously-Endowed Little Teen-Aged Daughter." [NoDaQ] (60:3) Sum 92, p. 163.
"Time Is a Toy, or, Of Being Overly Busy, As of Course All of Us Too Often Are." [NewYorkQ] (49) 92, p. 41-43.
"Veins." [NoDaQ] (60:3) Sum 92, p. 164.
460. BENÉT, Stephen Vincent
"American Names." [FreeL] (10) Sum 92, p. 32.
"There Was a Girl I Used to Go With." [FreeL] (10) Sum 92, p. 31.
461. BENEVENTO, Joe
"Her First Bill Fish." [Pearl] (16) Fall 92, p. 53.
"Your New Boyfriend." [Pearl] (15) Spr-Sum 92, p. 16.
462. BENIS, Allison
"The Woman Inside." [OnTheBus] (4:2/5:1, #10/11) 92, p. 69.
463. BENITEZ, Luis
"En el Manso Universo de la Abeja." [Nuez] (4:10/11) 92, p. 39.
"Herederos de la Carne y de la Sombra." [Nuez] (4:10/11) 92, p. 39.
"Luz de la Calle." [Nuez] (4:10/11) 92, p. 39.

BENITO, Juan Luis Pla
See PLA BENITO, Juan Luis
464. BENJAMIN, Jerry
"It Was Really" (for Andy Warhol). [ChironR] (11:3) Aut 92, p. 32.
"Landscape." [DogRR] (11:2, #22) Fall-Wint 92, p. 26.
465. BENNETT, Bruce
"According to Stone." [Light] (3) Aut 92, p. 19.
"Animal Myths Debunked" (from an article in the "International Herald Tribune"). [Light] (1) Spr 92, p. 12.
"Aside." [Light] (1) Spr 92, p. 7.
"A Buddy of Housman's." [Light] (1) Spr 92, p. 20.
"E.P.A." (after Robert Frost). [Light] (2) Sum 92, p. 15.
"A Live Politician." [Light] (1) Spr 92, p. 22.
"Understanding." [Pearl] (15) Spr-Sum 92, p. 63.
466. BENNETT, John M.
"Annointing the Holes." [Asylum] (7:3/4) 92, p. 37.
467. BENNETT, Martin
"Woodcarver." [Stand] (33:3) Sum 92, p. 71.
468. BENNETT, Sally
"Chiron." [HampSPR] Wint 92, p. 46.
"Two Pinches of Yellow" (for my mother). [SycamoreR] (4:2) Sum 92, p. 23.
469. BENNETT, Stefanie
"Rosa Alba and the Volatile Principle." [Footwork] 92, p. 141.
470. BENSE, Robert
"Cross Point." [Poem] (67) My 92, p. 8.
"Fly in Amber." [Poem] (67) My 92, p. 4.
"Giving Back." [Poem] (67) My 92, p. 5.
"Last Post" (St. Germain-en-Laye). [Poem] (67) My 92, p. 6-7.
471. BENSEN, Robert
"Night Crossing, the Irish Sea." [WebR] (16) Fall 92, p. 76.
"Scriptures of Venus." [WebR] (16) Fall 92, p. 75.
"The Truth about Everything." [ParisR] (34:122) Spr 92, p. 197-200.
"What the Static Said." [WebR] (16) Fall 92, p. 77.
472. BENTLEY, Beth
"Archaic Couple." [GettyR] (5:1) Wint 92, p. 144-145.
"Discovery." [TarRP] (31:2) Spr 92, p. 25.
473. BENTLEY, Roy
"Notwithstanding a Love of the Truth Instilled in Her by Her Father." [Journal] (16:2) Fall-Wint 92, p. 89.
474. BENTLEY, Sean
"Le Chateau des Pyrenees" (after Magritte). [CinPR] (23) Wint 91-92, p. 32-33.
"Razor Edge." [PaintedB] (47) 92, p. 4.
475. BENTTINEN, Ted
"At the Moment We Leave." [CharR] (18:2) Fall 92, p. 89.
"The Robes of El Greco." [Confr] (50) Fall 92, p. 260.
"Winter Eeling." [BostonR] (17:3/4) My-Jl 92, p. 31.
"Winter Flowers." [Confr] (50) Fall 92, p. 259.
476. BERG, Catherine
"On the Other Side" (tr. of Pierre Reverdy, w. Brent Duffin). [Vis] (38) 92, p. 19.
477. BERG, Stephen
"Cold Cash" (for Helen, at 60). [KenR] (NS 14:3) Sum 92, p. 115-117.
478. BERGAMINO, Gina
"As I Write This Poem." [Footwork] 92, p. 76.
"Autumn Sky." [ChironR] (11:1) Spr 92, p. 13.
"Blue Hotel." [ChironR] (11:1) Spr 92, p. 13.
"Christo Diablo Fixing Straight Perfect Blankets." [NewYorkQ] (48) 92, p. 89.
"Christo Diablo Making Me Promise I'll Write 1,000 Poems in His Name." [NewYorkQ] (48) 92, p. 89.
"Christo Diablo Pushing White Carnations Up My Pussy." [NewYorkQ] (49) 92, p. 80.
"Christo Diablo Sliding an Ice Cube Up My Cunt." [NewYorkQ] (49) 92, p. 80.
"Christo Diablo Wanting My Cunt Stretched Bigger Than the Grand Canyon." [NewYorkQ] (48) 92, p. 89.
"Christo Diablo with a Two-Hour Hard-On." [NewYorkQ] (49) 92, p. 80.
"Feet." [ChironR] (11:1) Spr 92, p. 13.
"Hallelujah." [Footwork] 92, p. 76.

"If I Could." [ChironR] (11:1) Spr 92, p. 13.
"In the Bible." [ChrC] (109:18) 20-27 My 92, p. 552.
"Limited Sight." [Footwork] 92, p. 76.
"The Next Thing I Know." [ChironR] (11:1) Spr 92, p. 13.
"Voices." [Footwork] 92, p. 76.
"When You Read This You'll Know Who You Are." [ChironR] (11:1) Spr 92, p. 13.
"White Horse Cafe." [Footwork] 92, p. 76.
"Wings." [ChironR] (11:1) Spr 92, p. 13.

479. BERGER, Bruce
"Across, Down." [Poetry] (160:3) Je 92, p. 149.
"Astrophysicists." [Light] (2) Sum 92, p. 16.
"Dining Late." [Light] (1) Spr 92, p. 10.
"Kitsch." [Light] (1) Spr 92, p. 7.
"Omissions." [Light] (4) Wint 92-93, p. 25.
"Science." [Poetry] (160:3) Je 92, p. 148.
"Sheep Shots." [Light] (1) Spr 92, p. 19.

480. BERGER, Margi
"Rumor." [Poetry] (160:4) Jl 92, p. 190.
"You'd Think You'd Hear the Sky." [Poetry] (160:4) Jl 92, p. 191.

481. BERGMAN, David
"The Care and Treatment of Pain" (In memory of Allen Barnett). [Art&Und] (1:1) Fall 91, p. 8.
"Days of the 1970s." [Art&Und] (1:4) Jl-Ag 92, p. 8.
"Heroic Measures." [KenR] (NS 14:1) Wint 92, p. 30-32.
"The Witness to the Arrest" (Mark 14:50-52). [Art&Und] (1:4) Jl-Ag 92, p. 8.
"A World of Difference." [KenR] (NS 14:1) Wint 92, p. 28-30.

482. BERGMAN, Denise
"Anna in Hudson, N.Y." [Kalliope] (15:1) 92, p. 35-36.

483. BERKE, Judith
"Jane Goodall." [PraS] (66:3) Fall 92, p. 64-65.
"Not Eden" (Chapbook: 7 poems). [OhioR] (48) 92, p. 57-66.
"The Strangler Fig." [SenR] (22:1) Spr 92, p. 74.
"Zoo Fable." [PraS] (66:3) Fall 92, p. 65.

484. BERKLEY, Faye H.
"Wake." [AfAmRev] (26:2) Sum 92, p. 279.

485. BERLAND, Dinah
"The Casting Lesson." [Iowa] (22:1) Wint 92, p. 121-122.
"Indian Girl." [SoCoast] (12) Ja 92, p. 10-11.
"Portrait, Age Seven." [Ploughs] (18:1) Spr 92, p. 103-104.

486. BERLIND, Bruce
"Afterwards You Came Out" (tr. of Imre Oravecz). [Sonora] (22/23) Spr 92, p. 127.
"The Angel of Traffic" (Los Angeles, tr. of Ottó Orbán, w. Mária Körösy). [KenR] (NS 14:1) Wint 92, p. 83.
"As You Recall" (tr. of Imre Oravecz). [Sonora] (22/23) Spr 92, p. 129.
"At First It Was Easy" (tr. of Imre Oravecz). [PoetL] (87:4) Wint 92-93, p. 43.
"The Dazzling Disparity in Size" (Minnesota Public Radio, metro area traffic report, tr. of Ottó Orbán, w. Mária Körösy). [KenR] (NS 14:1) Wint 92, p. 84.
"The Dream of H. Bosch" (tr. of Imre Oravecz, w. Maria Körösy). [PoetryE] (33) Spr 92, p. 167.
"The End of Adventures" (A KSTP TV Publication: "AIDS — What to know about It?", tr. of Ottó Orbán, w. Mária Körösy). [Nimrod] (35:2) Spr-Sum 92, p. 35.
"Epitaph." [Light] (3) Aut 92, p. 24.
"The Four-Wheeled Man" (tr. of Ottó Orbán, w. Mária Körösy). [KenR] (NS 14:1) Wint 92, p. 82.
"From a Philosopher's Insights" (tr. of Gyula Illyé, w. Mária Körösy). [SilverFR] (23) Wint 92, p. 33.
"I Confess, I'm Still" (tr. of Imre Oravecz). [GrahamHR] (16) Fall 92, p. 14.
"I Loved Someone Before You" (tr. of Imre Oravecz). [GrahamHR] (16) Fall 92, p. 13.
"In a Blacksmith's House on the Puszta" (tr. of Gyula Illyés, w. Maria Körösy). [TexasR] (13:3/4) Fall-Wint 92, p. 87-88.
"The Journey of Barbarus" (tr. of Ottó Orbán, w. Maria Körösy). [ParisR] (34:123) Sum 92, p. 134.
"Last Night" (tr. of Imre Oravecz). [Sonora] (22/23) Spr 92, p. 128.
"Marble Arch Blues." [Light] (1) Spr 92, p. 14.

"Mr. E. Veryman, President of Whatever Works Works" (tr. of Ottó Orbán, w. Mária Körösy). [Nimrod] (35:2) Spr-Sum 92, p. 36.
"A Nest for Seasons in the Concrete Jungle" (tr. of Gyula Illyé, w. Mária Körösy). [SilverFR] (23) Wint 92, p. 29.
"Oklahoma Summer" (tr. of Ottó Orbán, w. Mária Körösy). [Nimrod] (35:2) Spr-Sum 92, p. 37.
"Old Fiddlers' Picnic" (tr. of Ottó Orbán, w. Mária Körösy). [Nimrod] (35:2) Spr - Sum 92, p. 35.
"Once Again" (tr. of Imre Oravecz, w. Mária Körösy). [LitR] (25:2) Wint 92, p. 176.
"Phoenix" (tr. of Gyula Illyés, w. Maria Körösy). [TexasR] (13:3/4) Fall-Wint 92, p. 89-91.
"Sappho, Her Absences." [Poetry] (160:2) My 92, p. 73.
"The Sun Is Shining" (tr. of Imre Oravecz, w. Mária Körösy). [LitR] (25:2) Wint 92, p. 177.
"Supper" (tr. of Imre Oravecz, w. Mária Körösy). [ArtfulD] (22/23) 92, p. 33.
"Then I Picked Up That Woman" (tr. of Imre Oravecz). [GrahamHR] (16) Fall 92, p. 16.
"Tonight, Around Eleven" (tr. of Imre Oravecz). [GrahamHR] (16) Fall 92, p. 15.
"Uncle Gábor" (tr. of Imre Oravecz, w. Mária Korösy). [WebR] (16) Fall 92, p. 33 - 34.
"Unsteadily." [Light] (2) Sum 92, p. 7.
"Water" (tr. of Imré Oravecz, w. Mária Körösy). [PartR] (59:2) Spr 92, p. 266-267.
"Why Wouldn't I Live in America?" (tr. of Ottó Orbán, w. Mária Körösy). [LitR] (25:2) Wint 92, p. 173-175.
"With a Stranger" (tr. of Gyula Illyé, w. Mária Körösy). [SilverFR] (23) Wint 92, p. 31.
"World-Order" (tr. of Gyula Illyé, w. Mária Körösy). [SilverFR] (23) Wint 92, p. 30.
"You Ask" (tr. of Imre Oravecz). [PoetL] (87:4) Wint 92-93, p. 41.
"You Could Have Spotted Me" (tr. of Gyula Illyé, w. Mária Körösy). [SilverFR] (23) Wint 92, p. 32.
"You Don't Love Me Anymore" (tr. of Imre Oravecz). [PoetL] (87:4) Wint 92-93, p. 42.

487. BERNARD, Artis
"Mount Saint Helens Guidebook and Photograph." [WestHR] (46:1) Spr 92, p. 88-89.

488. BERNARD, Betty
"For Dolores Haze." [Pearl] (16) Fall 92, p. 13.

489. BERNARD, Nejc
"To Kill Poets" (Excerpt, tr. of Miroslav Djurovic). [Nimrod] (35:2) Spr-Sum 92, p. 64-66.

490. BERNHARD, Jim
"Slim." [BellArk] (8:3) My-Je 92, p. 14.

491. BERNHARD, Thomas
"This Year Is Like the Year a Thousand Years Ago" (tr. by L. D. Davidson and Chris Hewitt). [Salm] (94/95) Spr-Sum 92, p. 136.
"The year is like a year a thousand years ago" (from "Under the Iron of the Moon," tr. by James Reidel). [ArtfulD] (22/23) 92, p. 30.

492. BERNSTEIN, Carole
"Cure." [Poetry] (161:2) N 92, p. 77-78.
"Mah-Jongg, 1967." [Poetry] (160:1) Ap 92, p. 22-23.
"Profaning the Dead." [HangL] (61) 92, p. 16.
"When My Grandmother Said 'Pussy'." [HangL] (61) 92, p. 15-16.

493. BERNSTEIN, Charles
"Sunset Sail." [Talisman] (8) Spr 92, p. 171.

494. BERNSTEIN, J. B.
"Half-Dead Roses." [Gypsy] (19) 92, p. 26-27.

495. BEROTTI, Kathleen
"Joe." [AntR] (50:4) Fall 92, p. 734-735.

496. BERROUËT-ORIOL, Robert
"Dissidence, I" (tr. by Carrol F. Coates). [Callaloo] (15:2) Spr 92, p. 506-508.
"Dissidence, Je." [Callaloo] (15:2) Spr 92, p. 509-511.
"Incunable." [Callaloo] (15:2) Spr 92, p. 515-517.
"Incunabulum" (tr. by Carrol F. Coates). [Callaloo] (15:2) Spr 92, p. 512-514.

497. BERRY, D. C.
"Cigar" (for the Krewe of Bovine). [SoCarR] (24:2) Spr 92, p. 107.
"Gulfport Lover's Confusion." [Poetry] (160:4) Jl 92, p. 192.

498. BERRY, Jake
"IG 9." [PoetryUSA] (24) 92, p. 16.
"IG 10." [PoetryUSA] (24) 92, p. 16.
499. BERRY, Roger
"Four Days from Leaving Your Husband." [CimR] (98) Ja 92, p. 82.
"Turning in the Surf: Seaside, Oregon." [DogRR] (11:2, #22) Fall-Wint 92, p. 23.
"Voyeurs." [SmPd] (29:2, #85) Spr 92, p. 14.
500. BERRY, Wendell
"Sabbaths 1989." [SewanR] (100:4) Fall 92, p. 509-515.
501. BERSSENBRUGGE, Mei-mei
"Daughter." [Conjunc] (18) 92, p. 332.
502. BERTOLDI, Elizabeth
"Unsung Tyrant." [Arc] (29) Aut 92, p. 49-50.
503. BERTOLINO, James
"The Coons." [ThRiPo] (39/40) 92-93, p. 9-10.
"The Landscape." [ThRiPo] (39/40) 92-93, p. 11.
"On a Line by John Ashbery." [ThRiPo] (39/40) 92-93, p. 10-11.
504. BERTON, M.
"Summer Camp." [AntR] (50:3) Sum 92, p. 522-523.
505. BESENTHAL, Kirby
"Meditation at the Continent's Edge." [Amelia] (7:1, #20) 92, p. 25.
506. BESKIN, Lisa
"At the Bookstore in Seattle." [ChironR] (11:4) Wint 92, p. 10.
"At the Bookstore in Seattle." [NewYorkQ] (49) 92, p. 85.
"Massage" (for Karen and Elizabeth). [ChironR] (11:4) Wint 92, p. 10.
"Sex with Evan." [ChironR] (11:4) Wint 92, p. 10.
507. BESLER, Carol M.
"Awakening." [LaurelR] (26:1) Wint 92, p. 87.
508. BESS, Robert
"Quality Inn: Binghamton." [Light] (4) Wint 92-93, p. 23.
509. BETTARINI, Mariella
"Obsessed Objects / Spiritualized Matter" (tr. by Corrado Federici). [PoetryC] (13:1) N 92, p. 22.
510. BETTENCOURT, Michael
"Cat." [Amelia] (6:4, #19) 92, p. 123-124.
BEUKEL, Karlien van den
See Van den BEUKEL, Karlien
511. BEUM, Robert
"A Lost Lady." [SewanR] (100:3) Sum 92, p. 366.
512. BEUS, David
"Exposed to Sun" (tr. of Edouard Maunick, w. Brian Evenson). [CentralP] (21) Spr 92, p. 134-138.
513. BEVAN, J. Thomas
"It Is Not Easy." [ArtfulD] (22/23) 92, p. 67.
"Theater of War." [ArtfulD] (22/23) 92, p. 68.
"A Walk." [Boulevard] (7:2/3, #20/21) Fall 92, p. 242-243.
514. BEVERIDGE, Robert P.
"For Leslie." [NewYorkQ] (48) 92, p. 97.
515. BEYNON, B. W.
"His Ghost on a Hill." [NegC] (12:1/2) 92, p. 16.
516. BEZAYIFF, David A.
"October Ritual." [Spitball] (40) Spr 92, p. 50.
517. BHAPKAR, Anjali
"Weird Harmony: Billions of Cells Collide" (Inside My Sister). [Kalliope] (14:1) 92, p. 35.
518. BHARATHAN, Vipin
"On Arranging the Funeral of a Loved One." [Footwork] 92, p. 36.
"To the Puma." [Footwork] 92, p. 36.
519. BHARTRIHARI
"Dug into earth's crust" (tr. by Andrew Schelling). [Sulfur] (12:1, #30) Spr 92, p. 160.
"Grieve, brother" (tr. by Andrew Schelling). [Sulfur] (12:1, #30) Spr 92, p. 160-161.
520. BHAVANI, V. Indira
"Avatars" (tr. by Martha Ann Selby and K. Paramasivam). [ChiR] (38:1/2) 92, p. 189-191.

521. BIBBINS, Julia O.
"Naturaleza Muerta Resuscitando" (The last painting of Remedios Varo 1908-1963). [Noctiluca] (1:1) Spr 92, p. 10.
522. BIDLAKE, S. P.
"The Post Game (or, Teaching a Square Roundball)." [Salm] (94/95) Spr-Sum 92, p. 140-141.
523. BIENEK, Horst
"The Alphabet" (tr. by Paul Morris — for Nelly Sachs). [Trans] (26) Spr 92, p. 79.
"Gathering" (tr. by Michael Bullock). [Stand] (33:4) Aut 92, p. 69.
"King Oedipus" (tr. by Michael Bullock). [Stand] (33:4) Aut 92, p. 70.
524. BIENVENU, Roberta
"The Dredge." [NewEngR] (14:3) Sum 92, p. 110-112.
"Emerson's Umbrella." [NewEngR] (14:3) Sum 92, p. 112-113.
525. BIERDS, Linda
"Flood." [NewYorker] (68:42) 7 D 92, p. 110.
526. BIESPIEL, David
"Bascom Hill." [ChatR] (12:3) Spr 92, p. 24.
"Before the First Light." [RiverC] (12:2) Spr 92, p. 65.
"Lilacs" (Allston, Massachusetts, 1985). [AntR] (50:3) Sum 92, p. 526-527.
527. BIGEAGLE, Duane
"Pull." [Zyzzyva] (8:3) Fall 92, p. 119-120.
528. BIGGINS, Michael
"At the Bottom" (tr. of Ales Debeljak). [Verse] (9:3) Wint 92, p. 43.
"The Cantina in Queretaro" (tr. of Tomaz Salamun). [Descant] (23:3, #78) Fall 92, p. 83.
"Hear me out" (tr. of Tomaz Salamun). [AmerPoR] (21:4) Jl-Ag 92, p. 42.
"The Hunter" (tr. of Tomaz Salamun). [ParisR] (34:122) Spr 92, p. 89.
"I Love You" (tr. of Tomaz Salamun). [Descant] (23:3, #78) Fall 92, p. 84-85.
"In Central Europe" (tr. of Tomaz Salamun). [AmerPoR] (21:4) Jl-Ag 92, p. 41.
"The Light in Winter" (tr. of Ales Debeljak). [Verse] (9:3) Wint 92, p. 43.
"Man and Boy" (tr. of Tomaz Salamun). [AmerPoR] (21:4) Jl-Ag 92, p. 42.
"Persons" (tr. of Jure Potokar). [GrandS] (11:3 #43) 92, p. 186.
"To Read: To Love" (tr. of Tomaz Salamun). [AmerPoR] (21:4) Jl-Ag 92, p. 42.
"Touching" (tr. of Jure Potokar). [GrandS] (11:3 #43) 92, p. 187.
529. BIGUENET, John
"His Unemployment." [Thrpny] (51) Fall 92, p. 32.
"Nine Nudes." [Boulevard] (7:1, #19) Spr 92, p. 95-96.
BILBAO, Manuel López
See LOPEZ BILBAO, Manuel
530. BILGERE, George
"Grove Boys." [TarRP] (32:1) Fall 92, p. 21.
"Midnight." [TarRP] (32:1) Fall 92, p. 20.
"Sleepless." [LitR] (35:3) Spr 92, p. 343.
"A Visiting Professor." [ChatR] (12:2) Wint 92, p. 67-68.
531. BILLINGTON, David
"Kissing the Mirror." [Bogg] (65) 92, p. 54.
532. BILYEU, Jody
"On Sundays, My Extended Family Got Together." [LaurelR] (26:2) Sum 92, p. 64 - 65.
533. BIRDSEY, Tal
"We Rode the Engine's Heat." [SouthernPR] (32:2) Fall 92, p. 39-40.
534. BISHOP, Bonnie
"After Viewing Chinese Porcelain at the Museum of Fine Arts." [CumbPR] (12:1) Fall 92, p. 36.
535. BISHOP, Elizabeth
"The Buck in the Snow." [GettyR] (5:1) Wint 92, p. 19.
"Dead." [GettyR] (5:1) Wint 92, p. 15.
"A Drunkard." [GeoR] (46:4) Wint 92, p. 608-609.
"Manners" (For a child of 1918). [AntigR] (91) Fall 92, p. 57.
"Salem Willows." [GeoR] (46:4) Wint 92, p. 609-610.
"Suicide of a Moderate Dictator" (for Carlos Lacerda). [GeoR] (46:4) Wint 92, p. 611.
536. BISHOP, Wendy
"Buttons: A Photograph." [PraS] (66:1) Spr 92, p. 30-31.
"Crow Time." [PraS] (66:1) Spr 92, p. 31-32.
"The Cultivation of Mind." [PraS] (66:1) Spr 92, p. 29-30.

"Farm Wife." [PraS] (66:1) Spr 92, p. 32.
"The Man and the Broncos." [NewDeltaR] (9:2) Spr-Sum 92, p. 21.
"Wife Beating." [LitR] (35:3) Spr 92, p. 374.
"Your Letter Comes." [LullwaterR] (3:2) Spr 92, p. 73.

537. BISSETT, Bill
"Deep Image in Winnipeg" (for patrick carol marijke n niko). [PraF] (13:1, #58) Spr 92, p. 41.
"Eye Went in 2 See Earle Birney." [PottPort] (14:2) Fall-Wint 92, p. 75-79.
"For Beautee." [PottPort] (14:2) Fall-Wint 92, p. 80.
"Inkorrect Thots." [PottPort] (14:2) Fall-Wint 92, p. 81-82.
"Mor Inkorrect Thots." [PottPort] (14:2) Fall-Wint 92, p. 83.

538. BITA, Lili
"The Howling" (in Greek and English, tr. by Robert Zaller). [InterPR] (18:2) Fall 92, p. 4-7.

539. BITNEY, Katharine
"The Wedding." [Grain] (20:2) Sum 92, p. 45.
"Woman / Bone Flute / The Theory of Music." [Grain] (20:2) Sum 92, p. 44.

540. BJÖRLING, Gunnar
"Least of all somebody wants to read what your write" (tr. by Lennart and Sonja Bruce). [CityLR] (5) 92, p. 68.
"There was a poem, a confined picture, it is no more" (tr. by Lennart and Sonja Bruce). [CityLR] (5) 92, p. 68.

541. BLACK, David
"Dry Weather." [BellArk] (8:6) N-D 92, p. 21.
"Grandpa M. Birdwatches." [DogRR] (11:1) Spr-Sum 92, p. 40.
"Tracks." [TarRP] (30:2) Spr 91, p. 33.
"Winter Game." [DogRR] (11:1) Spr-Sum 92, p. 40.

542. BLACK, Ralph (Ralph W.)
"The Muses of Farewell." [GettyR] (5:4) Aut 92, p. 723-724.
"October Migration." [MidAR] (13:2) 92, p. 75.

543. BLACK, Sophie Cabot
"After Longing." [Ploughs] (18:4) Wint 92-93, p. 19.
"By Lamplight." [Agni] (35) 92, p. 127.
"Daughter." [AmerV] (26) Spr 92, p. 127-128.
"If Only for a Little While." [Ploughs] (18:4) Wint 92-93, p. 17.
"Interrogation." [Agni] (35) 92, p. 126.
"Tearing It Up and Starting Over." [AmerV] (26) Spr 92, p. 129.
"What I Want." [Ploughs] (18:4) Wint 92-93, p. 18.

544. BLACK, Star
"Sepia." [Confr] (50) Fall 92, p. 278.

545. BLAIR, Peter
"Coke Man." [Crazy] (42) Spr 92, p. 66-67.
"Track Boss." [Crazy] (42) Spr 92, p. 68-69.
"Wing Damage" (or the assembled wreckage, bird-shaped on the hangar floor — for Steve). [RiverC] (12:2) Spr 92, p. 68-70.

546. BLAKE, Jonathan
"Opening My First Gift: Four Tang Poets: Wang Wei, Li Po, Tu Fu, Li Ho." [Blueline] (13) 92, p. 63.

BLANC, René Le
See LeBLANC, René

547. BLANCHARD, Len
"Video Madonna." [Outbr] (23) 92, p. 67.
"Wisdom." [GreensboroR] (53) Wint 92-93, p. 30-31.

548. BLANCHARD, Margaret
"Dormant." [SinW] (46) Spr 92, p. 79-80.

549. BLANCHARD, Sarah
"By the Rippowam." [Conscience] (13:2) Sum 92, p. 10.

550. BLANCO, Alberto
"Paper Roads" (tr. by Reginald Gibbons). [TriQ] (85) Fall 92, p. 397-398.
"Settling Accounts" (tr. by Reginald Gibbons). [TriQ] (85) Fall 92, p. 397-398.

551. BLAND, James
"The Archaic Torso of Apollo" (After Rilke). [WindO] (56) Fall-Wint 92, p. 29.
"Billie Holiday in Tokyo." [KenR] (NS 14:3) Sum 92, p. 23.
"Menage a Trois." [WindO] (56) Fall-Wint 92, p. 31.
"The Revival Meeting." [WindO] (56) Fall-Wint 92, p. 32.

552. BLANDIANA, Ana
"Amber" (tr. by Marguerite Dorian and Elliott Urdang). [MidAR] (13:2) 92, p. 9.
"Mother" (tr. by Marguerite Dorian and Elliott Urdang). [MidAR] (13:2) 92, p. 10.
"Piéta" (tr. by Marguerite Dorian and Elliott Urdang). [MidAR] (13:2) 92, p. 11-12.
553. BLANK, Myles K.
"Question Mark." [PraF] (13:4, #61) Wint 92-93, p. 35.
"Wordblind." [PraF] (13:4, #61) Wint 92-93, p. 36.
554. BLASING, Randy
"Chambers of the Heart." [Poetry] (161:2) N 92, p. 95.
"Faded Kodachrome." [Nat] (254:17) 4 My 92, p. 604.
"Mother Tongue." [Poetry] (159:4) Ja 92, p. 200.
555. BLASKI, Steven
"Letter to a Retarded Boy." [Confr] (48/49) Spr-Sum 92, p. 212.
"The Tale of the Man Who Loves Too Much." [CreamCR] (16:1) Spr 92, p. 95.
556. BLATNER, Barbara
"Dark Night." [Noctiluca] (1:2) Wint 92 [on cover: Wint 93], p. 25.
"A Long Mirage." [Noctiluca] (1:2) Wint 92 [on cover: Wint 93], p. 24.
557. BLAUNER, Laurie
"At the Scene of the Crime." [KenR] (NS 14:2) Spr 92, p. 117.
"Dinosaurs." [KenR] (NS 14:2) Spr 92, p. 118.
"The Metempsychosis of Strangers." [AmerPoR] (21:1) Ja-F 92, p. 36.
"On Being Fat." [Sonora] (22/23) Spr 92, p. 1.
"Theories of Failure." [MidAR] (12:2) 92, p. 1.
"What the Fish Say." [QW] (34) Wint-Spr 92, p. 83.
558. BLAUSTONE, Jeff
"Sawtooth Ridge." [Epiphany] (3:4) O (Fall) 92, p. 232.
"The Wheat." [Epiphany] (3:4) O (Fall) 92, p. 233.
559. BLAZEKOVA, Daniela
"Sun Sutra." [PraS] (66:4) Wint 92, p. 73-74.
560. BLED, Roman
"Lacio Drom" (tr. by Dino Tebaldi, w. Marta Knobloch). [Vis] (38) 92, p. 16.
561. BLEHERT, Dean
"Aged by the ticking." [Bogg] (65) 92, p. 63.
"Asking for who the bell tolls." [Bogg] (65) 92, p. 63.
"Fishing." [Bogg] (65) 92, p. 64.
"Funeral: much adieu about nothing." [Bogg] (65) 92, p. 63.
"Hunters wear bright colors lest they be." [Bogg] (65) 92, p. 63.
"I am a man of principle: when money talks." [Bogg] (65) 92, p. 63.
"Just as I reach out to touch you." [Bogg] (65) 92, p. 62.
"A lady of exceedingly whole sum parts." [Bogg] (65) 92, p. 63.
"Loneliness is no big deal." [Bogg] (65) 92, p. 63.
"Manhattan autumn." [Bogg] (65) 92, p. 62.
"People trying to find themselves rarely." [Bogg] (65) 92, p. 63.
"Then there's the dyslexic poet whose." [Bogg] (65) 92, p. 63.
"This poem is bio-degradable." [Bogg] (65) 92, p. 63.
"We are such fools as worlds are made by." [Bogg] (65) 92, p. 64.
"When a tool is worn out, it is thrown away." [Bogg] (65) 92, p. 64.
"The world is too much with it." [Bogg] (65) 92, p. 63.
562. BLESSINGTON, Francis
"Self-Portrait as a Bored Boy." [CumbPR] (11:2) Spr 92, p. 3.
563. BLEVINS-CHURCH, Adrian
"What the Body Knows." [SpiritSH] (57) Spr-Sum 92, p. 49.
564. BLOCH, Chana
"Alone on the Mountain" (on my birthday). [Ploughs] (18:1) Spr 92, p. 42.
"Deaths I Come Back To." [Ploughs] (18:1) Spr 92, p. 43.
"The Ghost Worm Monster." [Poetry] (159:5) F 92, p. 276-277.
"Inside." [Poetry] (159:5) F 92, p. 278.
"The Secret Life." [Poetry] (159:5) F 92, p. 275.
"Tuesday." [Poetry] (159:5) F 92, p. 278.
565. BLOK, Alexander
"All That Is Done, Done, Done Forever" (tr. by R. H. Morrison). [LitR] (35:3) Spr 92, p. 383.
566. BLOMAIN, Karen
"Blood at Solstice." [Sun] (201) S 92, p. 33.
567. BLOMQUIST, Eric
"Father Wiley's Christian Retreat." [Pembroke] (24) 92, p. 150.

568. BLONSTEIN, Anne
"Sibyl." [Kalliope] (14:1) 92, p. 48.
569. BLOOMFIELD, Maureen
"Street Songs." [KenR] (NS 14:3) Sum 92, p. 29-30.
570. BLOSSOM, Lavina
"A Still Life Rearranged." [BellR] (15:1) Spr 92, p. 6-7.
571. BLUE CLOUD, Peter
"Coyote, Coyote, Please Tell Me." [Jacaranda] (6:1/2) Wint-Spr 92, p. 60-61.
572. BLUESTONE, Stephen
"In a Cemetery of the Bialystok District." [SouthernPR] (32:2) Fall 92, p. 60-61.
573. BLUGER, Marianne
"Levertov." [Arc] (28) Spr 92, p. 27-28.
574. BLUMENSTEIN, Ruth Ann
"Mother." [JlNJPo] (14:2) Aut 92, p. 22.
575. BLUMENTHAL, Jay A.
"Going Overboard." [NowestR] (30:2) 92, p. 82.
"Observing Emily." [LitR] (35:3) Spr 92, p. 323.
"Parallel Universe." [SoCarR] (24:2) Spr 92, p. 84.
576. BLUMENTHAL, Michael (*See also* BLUMENTHAL, Michael C.)
"Blue." [ThRiPo] (39/40) 92-93, p. 12.
"Emilio Roma Is Dead" (in memoriam, Emilio Roma, III, Professor of Philosophy). [Agni] (35) 92, p. 47-48.
"I Remember Toscanini." [Agni] (35) 92, p. 49-50.
"In a Cemetery in Keene, New Hampshire, September 1986." [SouthwR] (77:2/3) Spr-Sum 92, p. 207.
"Juliek's Violin." [ThRiPo] (39/40) 92-93, p. 13-14.
577. BLUMENTHAL, Michael C. (*See also* BLUMENTHAL, Michael)
"I Do Not Care Where Goodness Comes From." [Nat] (254:24) 22 Je 92, p. 871.
578. BLUMER, Dana
"Pared Down." [Writer] (105:12) D 92, p. 18.
579. BLY, Robert
"Sitting with My Mother and Father." [Antaeus] (69) Aut 92, p. 66-68.
"The Slate Junco." [NewL] (58:3) Spr 92, p. 73.
580. BLYTHE, Randy
"Coyote As Houseguest." [PoetL] (87:2) Sum 92, p. 31.
BOARDMAN, Paul Harris
See HARRIS-BOARDMAN, Paul
581. BOBRICK, James
"Another Nineties, New Bedford." [Lactuca] (16) Ag 92, p. 9.
"Life's a Beach." [Lactuca] (16) Ag 92, p. 8-9.
"Swain School of Design 1881-1988." [Lactuca] (16) Ag 92, p. 8.
582. BOCK, D.
"Judson." [SlipS] (12) 92, p. 47-48.
583. BOCK, Lee
"I Don't Get It." [RagMag] (10:1) 92, p. 74.
584. BOCKES, Zan
"My Father, Towing Me." [TarRP] (30:2) Spr 91, p. 16-17.
585. BODEEN, Jim
"The Gulf War from Yakima." [CrabCR] (8:1) Sum-Fall 92, p. 23-28.
586. BOE, Marilyn J.
"Sleeping with Grandma." [PoetL] (87:2) Sum 92, p. 6.
587. BOES, Don
"Introduction to Bioacoustics." [MidwQ] (33:2) Wint 92, p. 193.
"Lost at Sea." [MidwQ] (34:1) Aut 92, p. 57.
588. BOGEN, Don
"The Nudes." [Salm] (94/95) Spr-Sum 92, p. 80-81.
"Snowfall." [Journal] (16:2) Fall-Wint 92, p. 92.
589. BOGEN, Laurel Ann
"Caught in the Crossfire." [Rohwedder] (7) Spr-Sum 92, p. 6.
590. BOHANAN, Audrey
"Having a Taste of It." [Verse] (9:3) Wint 92, p. 133.
"In for the Evening." [AntR] (50:4) Fall 92, p. 727.
"In Which You Leave It Behind." [Shen] (42:3) Fall 92, p. 26.
"Inalterable." [Verse] (9:3) Wint 92, p. 131-132.
"Jerry Seals His Fate." [HampSPR] Wint 92, p. 33.
"A Little Kindling at a Time." [Verse] (9:3) Wint 92, p. 132-133.

"Particular Days." [SenR] (22:1) Spr 92, p. 80.

591. BOIRE, Jennifer
"Hoc Est Corpus Meum." [PoetryC] (12:2) Ap 92, p. 17.
"In Italy, They." [PoetryC] (12:2) Ap 92, p. 17.
"Naming Adam." [PoetryC] (12:2) Ap 92, p. 17.
"Song for the Heart." [PoetryC] (12:2) Ap 92, p. 17.
"Taboo." [PoetryC] (12:2) Ap 92, p. 17.

592. BOISCLAIR, Joan
"Who Is Eating at Your House?" [NewDeltaR] (9:1) Fall 91-Wint 92, p. 34-35.

593. BOISSEAU, Michelle
"Chalk Lineament." [SouthernR] (28:1) Wint, Ja 92, p. 58-59.
"Pink Swing." [NoAmR] (277:2) Mr-Ap 92, p. 26.

594. BÖK, Christian
"A Fractal." [Descant] (23:4/24:1, #78/79) Wint-Spr 92-93, p. 127.
"Fractal Geometry." [Descant] (23:4/24:1, #78/79) Wint-Spr 92-93, p. 129-133.
"Fractal(s)." [Descant] (23:4/24:1, #78/79) Wint-Spr 92-93, p. 128.
"Krystalloneiros." [Descant] (23:4/24:1, #78/79) Wint-Spr 92-93, p. 134.

595. BOLAND, Eavan
"The Dolls' Museum in Dublin." [NewYorker] (68:36) 26 O 92, p. 56.

596. BOLDT, Christine H.
"Undertakings." [ChrC] (109:11) 1 Ap 92, p. 334.

597. BOLLS, Imogene
"Osteology." [TexasR] (13:3/4) Fall-Wint 92, p. 76-77.
"Reading the Bones." [TexasR] (13:1/2) Spr-Sum 92, p. 85.

598. BOLSTRIDGE, Alice
"Delicate Consistency." [Outbr] (23) 92, p. 17-18.
"Echo to Narcissus." [CimR] (101) O 92, p. 21-22.

599. BOLTON, Joe
"Everything" (Fragment, tr. of Julio Flórez). [NewOR] (19:2) Sum 92, p. 51.
"Yes" (tr. of Pedro Salinas). [NewOR] (19:3/4) Fall-Wint 92, p. 161.

600. BONAFFINI, Luigi
"Perhaps You Want Me" (tr. of Albino Pierro). [Vis] (39) 92, p. 39.
"That Year" (tr. of Achille Serrao). [Vis] (39) 92, p. 22.
"Yesterday" (tr. of Albino Pierro). [Vis] (39) 92, p. 39.

601. BOND, Bruce
"Bach's Idiot Son." [Quarry] (41:4) Fall 92, p. 67-68.
"Caravaggio: The Supper at Emmaus." [SouthernR] (28:3) Sum, Jl 92, p. 635-636.
"Elegiac Stanzas." [SouthernR] (28:3) Sum, Jl 92, p. 636-637.
"Infidelity" (Second Prize, Cincinnati Poetry Review Competition). [CinPR] (23) Wint 91-92, p. 28-29.
"Invisible Man." [SouthwR] (77:1) Wint 92, p. 136-137.
"Margin of Need." [WestHR] (46:3) Fall 92, p. 309.
"Messiaen." [Quarry] (41:4) Fall 92, p. 68.
"New York Movie, 1939." [QW] (36) Wint 92-93, p. 118-119.
"Robin's Voice." [WebR] (16) Fall 92, p. 68.

602. BOND, David
"Inheritance." [SpoonRQ] (17:1/2) Wint-Spr 92, p. 19.

603. BONDS, Diane (Diane S.)
"1945." [SouthernPR] (32:2) Fall 92, p. 24.
"Honeymoon, Mountain Resort." [PoetL] (87:2) Sum 92, p. 9.
"Late Portrait in a Boat." [PoetL] (87:2) Sum 92, p. 8.
"Orion." [SouthernPR] (32:2) Fall 92, p. 22-23.
"Saving the Trees." [SoCarR] (25:1) Fall 92, p. 115.

604. BONILLA, Yolanda
"You're in Texas." [Lactuca] (15) Mr 92, p. 27.

605. BONNEFOY, Yves
"The All, the Nothing" (From "Beginning and End of Snow," 1991, tr. by Lisa Sapinkopf). [Confr] (50) Fall 92, p. 296-297.
"Beginning and End of Snow" (tr. by Lisa Sapinkopf). [QRL] (Poetry Series 11: vol. 31) 92, 37 p.
"The Curved Mirror" (From "Ce qui fut sans lumière" (1987), tr. by Lisa Sapinkopf). [Verse] (9:3) Wint 92, p. 51.
"Debut en Fin de la Neige" (Excerpt, tr. by Lisa Sapinkopf). [QW] (35) Sum-Fall 92, p. 117.
"The Dream's Restlessness" (tr. by Lisa Sapinkopf). [Agni] (35) 92, p. 58-62.
"Hopkins Forest" (tr. by Lisa Sapinkopf). [Pequod] (34) 92, p. 110-111.

"On Snow-Laden Branches" (tr. by Lisa Sapinkopf). [NewOR] (19:3/4) Fall-Wint 92, p. 82-83.
"The Only Rose" (tr. by Lisa Sapinkopf). [SpoonRQ] (17:3/4) Sum-Fall 92, p. 46-48.
"Passing the Fire" (tr. by Lisa Sapinkopf). [Salm] (96) Fall 92, p. 170-171.
"The Sparrow Hawk" (tr. by Lisa Sapinkopf). [Stand] (33:4) Aut 92, p. 46.
"A Stone" (tr. by Lisa Sapinkopf). [Stand] (33:4) Aut 92, p. 45.
"The Trees" (From "Ce qui fut sans lumière" (1987), tr. by Lisa Sapinkopf). [Verse] (9:3) Wint 92, p. 52.
"The Voice Resumed" (tr. by Lisa Sapinkopf). [NewOR] (19:3/4) Fall-Wint 92, p. 81.

606. BONNETT, Jo-Ann
"Monument to the Five Greatest Words in English Literature" (Concrete Poem, w. brian j(o(h)n)ston). [WestCL] (26:3, #9) Wint 92-93, p. 74.

BONTÉ, Karen la
See LaBONTÉ, Karen

607. BOOK, M. K.
"Words move more than wheels." [WormR] (32:1, #125) 92, p. 6.

608. BOOKER, Stephen (Stephen Todd)
"In the Interest of Anthropology." [RiverS] (36) 92, p. 21-22.
"Spartacus in Metus." [NewDeltaR] (8:2) Spr-Sum 91, p. 73-74.

609. BOOTH, Philip
"Chances." [GeoR] (46:2) Sum 92, p. 354.
"Guide." [OntR] (36) Spr-Sum 92, p. 83.
"Hope." [NewEngR] (14:3) Sum 92, p. 193.
"Long Story." [OntR] (36) Spr-Sum 92, p. 83.
"Navigation." [NoDaQ] (60:1) Wint 92, p. 44.
"Requiescat: Western Union." [NewYorker] (68:11) 4 My 92, p. 60.
"Seasons." [BelPoJ] (43:1) Fall 92, p. 24-25.
"Terms." [NewEngR] (14:3) Sum 92, p. 192.

BORDA, Juan Gustavo Cobo
See COBO BORDA, Juan Gustavo

610. BORDAO, Rafael
"Inaplazable Fugitivo" (2 de enero, 1991, Manhattan, N.Y.). [Nuez] (4:12) 92, p. 3.

611. BORGES, Jorge Luis
"1929" (tr. by Robert Mezey). [WestHR] (46:2) Sum 92, p. 122-123.
"A Mi Padre." [SoCoast] (12) Ja 92, p. 38.
"Alexandria, 641 A.D." (tr. by Robert Mezey). [Iowa] (22:3) Fall 92, p. 70-71.
"Another Version of Proteus" (tr. by Robert Mezey). [Iowa] (22:3) Fall 92, p. 69-70.
"Ash" (tr. by Robert Mezey). [Iowa] (22:3) Fall 92, p. 73.
"Caesar" (tr. by Robert Mezey). [Raritan] (12:2) Fall 92, p. 22.
"Camden, 1892" (tr. by Robert Mezey). [NewYRB] (39:10) 28 My 92, p. 5.
"Chess" (tr. by Robert Mezey). [Raritan] (12:2) Fall 92, p. 26-27.
"The Clepsydra" (tr. by Robert Mezey). [Raritan] (12:2) Fall 92, p. 24.
"Clouds" (tr. by Richard Barnes and Robert Mezey). [Iowa] (22:3) Fall 92, p. 72.
"El Desterrado" (1977). [SoCoast] (12) Ja 92, p. 32.
"Doomsday" (tr. by Dick Barnes). [ArtfulD] (22/23) 92, p. 26.
"Everness" (in Spanish). [SoCoast] (12) Ja 92, p. 36.
"Everness" (tr. by Robert Mezey and Dick Barnes). [SoCoast] (12) Ja 92, p. 37.
"Ewigkeit" (in Spanish). [SoCoast] (12) Ja 92, p. 34.
"Ewigkeit" (tr. by Robert Mezey and Dick Barnes). [SoCoast] (12) Ja 92, p. 35.
"The Exile" (1977, tr. by Robert Mezey). [SoCoast] (12) Ja 92, p. 33.
"Fifteen Coins" (tr. by Robert Mezey). [WestHR] (46:2) Sum 92, p. 124-126.
"For a Version of the I Ching" (tr. by Robert Mezey). [NewYRB] (39:11) 11 Je 92, p. 25.
"Fourteen-Syllable Lines" (tr. by Robert Mezey and Dick Barnes). [ArtfulD] (22/23) 92, p. 27.
"General Quiroga Rides to His Death in a Carriage" (tr. by Richard Barnes and Robert Mezey). [Iowa] (22:3) Fall 92, p. 71-72.
"Heraclitus" (East Lansing, 1976, tr. by Robert Mezey). [Raritan] (12:2) Fall 92, p. 25.
"Heraclitus" (tr. by Thomas Frick). [Agni] (36) 92, p. 247.
"In Praise of Darkness" (tr. by Robert Mezey). [Poetry] (161:1) O 92, p. 11-12.
"The Inquisitor" (tr. by Robert Mezey and Dick Barnes). [ParisR] (34:125) Wint 92, p. 233.
"June 1968" (tr. by Thomas Frick). [Agni] (36) 92, p. 248.
"Last Evening" (tr. by Robert Mezey and Dick Barnes). [ParisR] (34:125) Wint 92, p. 229.

"Lines I Might Have Written and Lost Around 1922" (tr. by Robert Mezey). [ArtfulD] (22/23) 92, p. 29.
"The Lost" (tr. by Robert Mezey). [ArtfulD] (22/23) 92, p. 28.
"Manuel Peyrou" (tr. by Robert Mezey). [Field] (47) Fall 92, p. 103.
"Manuscript Found in a Conrad Novel" (tr. by Robert Mezey). [Field] (47) Fall 92, p. 102.
"May 20, 1928" (tr. by Robert Mezey). [Poetry] (161:1) O 92, p. 10.
"Milonga of the Stranger" (tr. by Robert Mezey and Dick Barnes). [ParisR] (34:125) Wint 92, p. 229-230.
"The Moon" (tr. by Robert Mezey and Dick Barnes). [ParisR] (34:125) Wint 92, p. 232.
"Music Box" (tr. by Robert Mezey). [GrandS] (11:3 #43) 92, p. 184.
"My Books" (tr. by Robert Mezey). [Harp] (284:1700) Ja 92, p. 42.
"The Nightmare" (tr. by Robert Mezey and Richard Barnes). [GrandS] (11:3 #43) 92, p. 185.
"Proteus" (tr. by Robert Mezey). [Iowa] (22:3) Fall 92, p. 69.
"The Thing I Am" (tr. by Robert Mezey and Dick Barnes). [ParisR] (34:125) Wint 92, p. 231-232.
"The Things" (tr. by Robert Mezey). [Raritan] (12:2) Fall 92, p. 23.
"To a Minor Poet of 1899" (tr. by Robert Mezey). [Raritan] (12:2) Fall 92, p. 23.
"To My Father" (tr. by Robert Mezey). [SoCoast] (12) Ja 92, p. 39.
"A Wolf" (tr. by Robert Mezey). [Poetry] (161:1) O 92, p. 9.

612. BORISOV, Georgi
"And When the Winter Wind" (tr. by Lisa Sapinkopf, w. Georgi Belev). [CrabCR] (8:1) Sum-Fall 92, p. 17.

613. BORKHUIS, Charles
"Proximity (Stolen Arrows)." [Avec] (5:1) 92, p. 106-108.
"The Solitary Speaker" (for Liz Diamond and Robert Pinget). [NewAW] (10) Fall 92, p. 117-118.

614. BORN, Anne
"China Observed through Greek Rain in Turkish Coffee" (tr. of Henrik Nordbrandt). [Stand] (33:4) Aut 92, p. 7-8.
"Our Love Is Like Byzantium" (tr. of Henrik Nordbrandt). [Stand] (33:4) Aut 92, p. 6-7.
"The Water Mirror" (tr. of Henrik Nordbrandt). [Stand] (33:4) Aut 92, p. 8.

615. BORUCH, Marianne
"The Boy Ghost." [Field] (46) Spr 92, p. 70-71.
"Distance." [AmerPoR] (21:5) S-O 92, p. 42.
"The Going Out of Business Greenhouse." [NowestR] (30:2) 92, p. 83.
"In Summer." [SenR] (22:2) Fall 92, p. 70.
"Spring." [SenR] (22:2) Fall 92, p. 69.
"The Stairway." [Iowa] (22:1) Wint 92, p. 29-35.
"Up in Air." [Field] (46) Spr 92, p. 72-73.

616. BORUN, Katarzyna
"German Gothic" (tr. by Karen Kovacik). [GrahamHR] (16) Fall 92, p. 50.
"Her" (tr. by Karen Kovacik). [GrahamHR] (16) Fall 92, p. 48.
"Penelomedea" (tr. by Karen Kovacik). [GrahamHR] (16) Fall 92, p. 49.

617. BOSLEY, Keith
"The Goat" (tr. of Umberto Saba). [Stand] (33:4) Aut 92, p. 105.
"May" (tr. of Ieuan Jones Talsarnau). [Stand] (33:4) Aut 92, p. 153.
"Remembering Borsieri" (tr. of Franco Fortini). [Stand] (33:4) Aut 92, p. 109.

618. BOSS, Laura
"Growing Up in the Fifties." [Footwork] 92, p. 32.
"My Lover Says I Don't Pay Enough Attention to Him." [Footwork] 92, p. 32.

619. BOSS, Todd
"Blackberries" (for Beth). [RagMag] (10:1) 92, p. 28.
"A Fish-Belly White" (To my father). [RagMag] (10:1) 92, p. 27.
"Summer Walls." [RagMag] (10:1) 92, p. 26-27.

620. BOSSELAAR, Laure-Anne
"Amen." [HayF] (11) Fall-Wint 92, p. 57-58.
"An Illegal Affair." [HayF] (11) Fall-Wint 92, p. 55-56.
"The Radiator." [HayF] (11) Fall-Wint 92, p. 59.

621. BOSTIAN, Barbara S.
"Refurbishing." [Kalliope] (14:3) 92, p. 42.

622. BOSWELL, Parley Ann
"Driving Me Home." [Epiphany] (3:4) O (Fall) 92, p. 285.

623. BOSWELL, Robin
"My Dreams Are So Many Sheep." [MassR] (23:2) Sum 92, p. 286-293.
624. BOTKIN, Nancy
"Letter to the Water Dept." [PoetryE] (33) Spr 92, p. 11.
625. BOTTOMS, David
"Elegy for a Trapper." [SouthernR] (28:4) Aut, O 92, p. 830-831.
"Hard Easter, Northwest Montana." [ParisR]] (34:124) Fall 92, p. 132.
"In the Massachusetts Wilderness." [Poetry] (161:3) D 92, p. 138-139.
"Steve Belew Plays the National Steel." [Poetry] (160:3) Je 92, p. 134-135.
626. BOUCHERON, Robert
"Horace Ode 1, 22 *Integer Vitae*." [Hellas] (3:1) Spr 92, p. 20.
627. BOULETTE, Linda
"Medieval Lullabies" (For Joey). [Art&Und] (1:1) Fall 91, p. 17.
628. BOULLATA, Kamal
"The Transformations of the Lover" (3 selections, tr. of Adonis, w. Susan Einbinder). [MichQR] (31:4) Fall 92, p. 619-623.
"Visions from the Journey of Jonah." [PaintedB] (47) 92, p. 11-12.
629. BOULLOSA, Carmen
"Letter to the Wolf" (tr. by Cynthia Steele). [TriQ] (85) Fall 92, p. 84-86.
630. BOULTER, Doug
"Sunday Service." [AmerS] (61:3) Sum 92, p. 350-351.
631. BOURKE, Lawrence
"Canberra." [Vis] (39) 92, p. 6-10.
"In the Sunroom." [Vis] (40) 92, p. 30-31.
"Passing Through." [Footwork] 92, p. 139-140.
632. BOURNE, Daniel
"At Night" (tr. of Bronislav Maj). [Salm] (93) Wint 92, p. 187.
"Generals Mean Well" (tr. of Ryszard Holzer). [CharR] (18:1) Spr 92, p. 100.
"I the Rat" (tr. of Stanislaw Esden-Tempski). [AnotherCM] (23) Spr 92, p. 71.
"Martial Law Primer # 1" (tr. of Ryszard Holzer). [CharR] (18:1) Spr 92, p. 99.
"Martial Law Primer # 2" (tr. of Ryszard Holzer). [CharR] (18:1) Spr 92, p. 99.
"No one will ever claim the age we live in" (tr. of Bronislaw Maj). [GrahamHR] (16) Fall 92, p. 81.
"Probably he can only see" (tr. of Bronislaw Maj). [GrahamHR] (16) Fall 92, p. 80.
"The Recycling of My Body" (tr. of Stanislaw Esden-Tempski). [AnotherCM] (23) Spr 92, p. 73.
"Rust" (tr. of Stanislaw Esden-Tempski). [AnotherCM] (23) Spr 92, p. 72.
"Still Life." [NewOR] (19:3/4) Fall-Wint 92, p. 17.
"Untitled: There are places we most likely will never get to see" (tr. of Ryszard Holzer). [CharR] (18:1) Spr 92, p. 100.
633. BOURNE, Lesley-Anne
"The Helmet Maker's Beautiful Wife" (6 selections). [MalR] (98) Spr 92, p. 85-90.
"The Virus." [Event] (21:1) Spr 92, p. 54.
634. BOURNE, Louis
"Among Trees" (tr. of José Hierro). [AmerPoR] (21:6) N-D 92, p. 48.
"The Fatal" (tr. of Blas de Otero). [AmerPoR] (21:6) N-D 92, p. 46.
"I Asked the Rocks" (tr. of José Hierro). [AmerPoR] (21:6) N-D 92, p. 50.
"I Between Poplars and Rivers?" (tr. of Blas de Otero). [AmerPoR] (21:6) N-D 92, p. 48.
"Man in Disgrace" (tr. of Blas de Otero). [AmerPoR] (21:6) N-D 92, p. 47.
"The Mirror" (tr. of Carlos Murciano). [Stand] (33:4) Aut 92, p. 148-149.
"Mortal and Alive" (tr. of Blas de Otero). [AmerPoR] (21:6) N-D 92, p. 46.
"Portrait in a Concert" (Homage to J.S. Bach, tr. of José Hierro). [AmerPoR] (21:6) N-D 92, p. 49-50.
"Return" (tr. of José Hierro). [AmerPoR] (21:6) N-D 92, p. 49.
"Sun Round Alone" (tr. of Blas de Otero). [AmerPoR] (21:6) N-D 92, p. 47.
"Then and Moreover" (tr. of Blas de Otero). [AmerPoR] (21:6) N-D 92, p. 47.
635. BOURQUE, Darrell
"Holy Water." [LouisL] (9:2) Fall 92, p. 17-21.
636. BOUVARD, Marguerite (Marguerite Guzman)
"Father Sky, Mother Earth." [MidwQ] (34:1) Aut 92, p. 57-58.
"A White Shawl." [PraS] (66:2) Sum 92, p. 85.
"Younger Sister." [PraS] (66:2) Sum 92, p. 86.
637. BOWDAN, Scott
"Wolf-Boy." [JamesWR] (10:1) Fall 92, p. 1.

638. BOWEN, Janene
"After Tequila." [WeberS] (9:1) Wint 92, p. 83.
"Chador." [WeberS] (9:1) Wint 92, p. 81.
"Hating Black Boys." [WeberS] (9:1) Wint 92, p. 84-85.
"Le's Dragon." [WeberS] (9:1) Wint 92, p. 82.
"Walter Helps Aunt Betsy Unplug the Drain." [WeberS] (9:1) Wint 92, p. 85.
639. BOWEN, Kevin
"The Arts of Love and Hydrology as Practiced in Hanoi" (for Thuy). [PraS] (66:3) Fall 92, p. 30-31.
"Chung's House: The Liberation of Hanoi." [SilverFR] (23) Wint 92, p. 10.
"Made in Hanoi" (for the disabled workers of An Duong). [SilverFR] (23) Wint 92, p. 13.
"Midnight, the Cuu Long." [SilverFR] (23) Wint 92, p. 11.
"Missing." [PoetL] (87:3) Fall 92, p. 43-44.
"Nhat Da Trach: One Night Swamp." [OhioR] (48) 92, p. 56.
"Snail Gatherers of Co Loa Thanh." [AmerPoR] (21:6) N-D 92, p. 22.
"A Soldier's Home" (for Ivor Gurney). [PoetL] (87:3) Fall 92, p. 41-42.
"The Temple of Literature" (Hanoi, 1987). [SilverFR] (23) Wint 92, p. 12.
640. BOWEN, Lindsey Martin
"Waiting for Glory in Winchell's." [BlackBR] (16) Wint-Spr 92-93, p. 16.
641. BOWERING, George
"Tango." [WestCL] (25:3, #6) Wint 91-92, p. 145.
"Winter 1981, Venice." [WestCL] (25:3, #6) Wint 91-92, p. 144.
642. BOWERING, Marilyn
"Letter from Portugal." [MalR] (100) Fall 92, p. 42-43.
643. BOWERS, Cathy Smith
"A Southern Rhetoric." [Poetry] (160:2) My 92, p. 80.
644. BOWERS, Edgar
"Breaths." [SewanR] (100:4) Fall 92, p. 536.
"Grasses." [SewanR] (100:4) Fall 92, p. 537.
"Numbers." [SewanR] (100:4) Fall 92, p. 538.
"Spaces." [SewanR] (100:4) Fall 92, p. 539.
645. BOWERS, Neal
"Addie's Story" (Addie Darnell Bowers, 1891-1981). [TarRP] (31:2) Spr 92, p. 31.
"Art Thief." [Poetry] (159:4) Ja 92, p. 221.
"Auditing the Crash." [Shen] (42:1) Spr 92, p. 107.
"Communications." [Poetry] (160:2) My 92, p. 81.
"Divining Love" (For Nancy). [Poetry] (160:4) Jl 92, p. 197.
"Driving Lessons." [Shen] (42:2) Sum 92, p. 42-43.
"Dropping Off." [AmerS] (61:2) Spr 92, p. 222.
"Family Matters." [Poetry] (160:4) Jl 92, p. 196.
"Forced Flowers." [Poetry] (160:4) Jl 92, p. 195.
"The Future" (Detroit, 1950). [Shen] (42:2) Sum 92, p. 40-42.
"The Game." [TarRP] (31:2) Spr 92, p. 43-44.
"The Half Life." [Poetry] (159:5) F 92, p. 262.
"Iowa." [TarRP] (31:2) Spr 92, p. 32.
"Our Neighbor's Other Life." [HighP] (7:3) Wint 92, p. 26-27.
"The Principal." [SewanR] (100:4) Fall 92, p. 540-541.
"Repairs" (For Nancy). [Poetry] (159:5) F 92, p. 263.
"The Secret Place." [HighP] (7:3) Wint 92, p. 25.
"Sharing a Dream Before Sleep." [TarRP] (31:2) Spr 92, p. 30.
"A Short History of Graves." [SewanR] (100:4) Fall 92, p. 541-542.
"Signs and Wonders." [SewanR] (100:2) Spr 92, p. 265.
"Two Men Under a Car." [Shen] (42:1) Spr 92, p. 106.
"A Visit from the Blues." [HighP] (7:3) Wint 92, p. 23-24.
646. BOWLES, Ka
"The Barbican." [BellR] (15:1) Spr 92, p. 41.
"Glass Slippers." [BellR] (15:1) Spr 92, p. 40.
"Keep Out." [BellR] (15:1) Spr 92, p. 42.
647. BOWLING, Tim
"Chinese Take-Away." [Grain] (20:2) Sum 92, p. 154-155.
"Crosswalk." [CapilR] (2:9) Fall 92, p. 81-82.
"The Last Sockeye" (for my brother). [CapilR] (2:9) Fall 92, p. 79-80.
"Your Faithful & Obedient Servant." [Grain] (20:2) Sum 92, p. 153-154.
648. BOWMAN, Catherine
"Demographics." [TriQ] (86) Wint 92-93, p. 25-26.

649. BOWMAN, Jim
"To Joycey Glassman." [MoodySI] (27) Spr 92, p. 16.
650. BOYCE, Robert C.
"From the Racetrack." [Bogg] (65) 92, p. 29.
651. BOYCE, Scott
"Cups Filled by God and by Man." [Quarry] (41:2) Spr 92, p. 20.
"A Guest! a Guest!" [Quarry] (41:2) Spr 92, p. 19.
"In This Green House." [Quarry] (41:2) Spr 92, p. 21.
"Snowshoes." [Quarry] (41:2) Spr 92, p. 22.
652. BOYCHUK, Bohdan
"God Is With Us" (tr. by Askold Melnyczuk). [PartR] (59:2) Spr 92, p. 272.
"The Grapes of Generation" (tr. by Askold Melnyczuk). [PartR] (59:2) Spr 92, p. 273-274.
"Open My Lips" (tr. by Askold Melnyczuk). [PartR] (59:2) Spr 92, p. 273.
"Spring Rainstorm" (tr. of Boris Pasternak, w. Mark Rudman). [NewYRB] (39:21) 17 D 92, p. 10.
"Your Plenitude" (tr. by Askold Melnyczuk). [PartR] (59:2) Spr 92, p. 271-272.
653. BOYD, G.
"The Ladies at Cards, Unawares." [US1] (26/27) 92, p. 8.
654. BOYD, Greg
"Carnival Aptitude" (Selections). [Noctiluca] (1:1) Spr 92, p. 8-10.
655. BOYD, Robert
"In the Orchard." [CharR] (18:1) Spr 92, p. 84.
"Snapshots from My Family Album." [WebR] (16) Fall 92, p. 107-108.
656. BOYD, William L.
"Poetic Penguins" (Selections: 10 poems). [Pembroke] (24) 92, p. 10-19.
657. BOYE, Karin
"Ja Visst Gör Det Ont." [NewYorkQ] (49) 92, p. 74.
"Oh Yes, It Hurts" (tr. by Claes Lilja). [NewYorkQ] (49) 92, p. 75.
658. BOYER, Dale W.
"The Disease." [ChironR] (11:4) Wint 92, p. 46.
659. BOYER, Patsy
"For Ellen" (tr. of Luz María Umpierre). [Americas] (19:3/4) Wint 91, p. 44.
"To a Beautiful Illusion, Fleeting" (tr. of Luz María Umpierre). [Americas] (19:3/4) Wint 91, p. 41-42.
660. BOYLE, Kevin
"Beyond the Pleasure Principle." [NowestR] (30:1) 92, p. 34-35.
"Catechize." [DenQ] (26:4) Spr 92, p. 8-9.
"I Didn't Do It." [CutB] (37) Wint 92, p. 20-21.
661. BOZANIC, Nick
"The Calm." [Manoa] (4:1) Spr 92, p. 134-135.
"The Children's Hour." [Manoa] (4:1) Spr 92, p. 133.
"Early Out on Lake Ann Road." [Manoa] (4:1) Spr 92, p. 134.
"Lions in Winter." [YellowS] (Ten Years [i.e. 40]) Sum-Fall 92, p. 38.
"Luxe, Calme et Volupté." [YellowS] (41) Fall-Wint 92-93, p. 22.
"Overture." [Manoa] (4:1) Spr 92, p. 135-136.
"The Rain." [YellowS] (41) Fall-Wint 92-93, p. 22.
662. BOZDECHOVA, Ivana
"Open Letter" (tr. by Ewald Osers). [PraS] (66:4) Wint 92, p. 35.
663. BRACHO, Coral
"In This Warm Dark Mosque" (tr. by Suzanne Jill Levine). [TriQ] (85) Fall 92, p. 382-384.
"Refracted in Your Life Like an Enigma" (tr. by Suzanne Jill Levine). [TriQ] (85) Fall 92, p. 385-386.
664. BRACKENRIDGE, Valery
"Amateur Paleontology." [Footwork] 92, p. 111.
"Mother and Daughter." [Footwork] 92, p. 111.
"Relativity." [Footwork] 92, p. 111.
665. BRACKER, Jonathan
"Loneliness." [JamesWR] (9:4) Sum 92, p. 12.
"Starling." [Light] (4) Wint 92-93, p. 9.
666. B'RACZ, Emoke
"Caught" (tr. of Gyula Illyés, w. David Zucker). [WebR] (16) Fall 92, p. 31.
667. BRADLEY, John
"From the Faraway Nearby." [OxfordM] (6:2) Fall-Wint 90, p. 73.
"Why I Am Not a Tire Iron." [NewDeltaR] (8:1) Fall 90-Wint 91, p. 109.

668. BRADLEY, Lawrence
"The Carriers." [SenR] (22:1) Spr 92, p. 61.
BRADLEY, Martha Carlson
See CARLSON-BRADLEY, Martha
669. BRADLEY, Peter
"Spring / Summer / Autumn / Winter." [JamesWR] (9:3) Spr 92, p. 5.
670. BRADSTOCK, Margaret
"The Homecoming." [Vis] (40) 92, p. 22.
671. BRADY, Philip
"The Birds of Ireland." [NewMyths] (1:2/2:1) 92, p. 39-45.
"Flying West from Belfast" (for Anne Davey Orr). [GrahamHR] (16) Fall 92, p. 64 - 65.
"In *Pére* Paul's Room." [NewMyths] (1:2/2:1) 92, p. 49-52.
"Two Bathrooms." [HiramPoR] (51/52) Fall 91-Sum 92, p. 22-23.
"Wiretap." [NewMyths] (1:2/2:1) 92, p. 46-48.
672. BRAID, Kate
"Falsework." [SingHM] (20) 92, p. 5-6.
673. BRAMBACH, Rainer
"The Stranger" (tr. by Sammy McLean). [Vis] (39) 92, p. 34.
674. BRAND, Alice (Alice G.)
"About My Son." [Confr] (50) Fall 92, p. 263.
"Elasticity." [Rohwedder] (7) Spr-Sum 92, p. 16.
"The Treatment of Space." [NewDeltaR] (8:1) Fall 90-Wint 91, p. 106.
675. BRAND, Dionne
"Out There." [MalR] (100) Fall 92, p. 115-119.
676. BRAND, Ian
"The Crows." [HawaiiR] (16:2, #35) Spr 92, p. 107.
"Holiday Crows." [Blueline] (13) 92, p. 20.
"The Maps." [HawaiiR] (16:2, #35) Spr 92, p. 106.
677. BRANDEL, Christine
"Sleep Among the Reeds." [OxfordM] (7:1) Spr-Sum 91, p. 37.
"To Find the Perfect Circle." [OxfordM] (7:1) Spr-Sum 91, p. 36.
678. BRANDON, Sherry
"AngelCake." [BellArk] (8:1) Ja-F 92, p. 1.
"The Big Steal." [BellArk] (8:1) Ja-F 92, p. 1.
"Cats' Eyes." [BellArk] (8:1) Ja-F 92, p. 1.
"I Remember When There Wasn't None of That Here." [BellArk] (8:6) N-D 92, p. 12.
"A Moment, a Monet." [BellArk] (8:6) N-D 92, p. 12.
679. BRANDT, Di
"Jerusalem Poems" (Excerpts). [Arc] (29) Aut 92, p. 12-18.
"(Not wanting to leave Winnipeg in May, the incredible." [PraF] (13:3, #60) Aut 92, p. 43.
"Three women are sitting at a table in a cottage by the sea." [PraF] (13:3, #60) Aut 92, p. 42.
"Why you keep on doing it, getting up in the morning." [PraF] (13:3, #60) Aut 92, p. 43.
680. BRANDT, Tim
"Pat's Muscle, Pat's Beach" (poem for a picture of a poet). [PraF] (13:1, #58) Spr 92, p. 68.
681. BRASCHI, Giannina
"The Empire of Dreams" (3 excerpts, tr. by Tess O'Dwyer and José Vázquez - Amaral). [Luz] (1) My 92, p. 20-26.
"El Imperio de los Sueños" (3 excerpts). [Luz] (1) My 92, p. 20-26.
"Pastoral" (Excerpt, tr. by Tess O'Dwyer). [Sonora] (22/23) Spr 92, p. 116.
682. BRASFIELD, James
"Night Tram" (tr. of Oksana Zabuzhko). [InterPR] (18:2) Fall 92, p. 11.
"Sweetness of words" (tr. of Oksana Zabuzhko). [InterPR] (18:2) Fall 92, p. 13.
"Throw on a flagrant cape" (tr. of Oksana Zabuzhko). [InterPR] (18:2) Fall 92, p. 9.
683. BRASON, Maris
"Fieldscape." [QW] (36) Wint 92-93, p. 106-107.
684. BRATRSOVSKA, Zdena
"The Swans of Prague" (tr. by Dominika Winterová and Richard Katrovas). [NewOR] (19:3/4) Fall-Wint 92, p. 26.
685. BRAUN, Mónica
"Biografía." [Nuez] (4:10/11) 92, p. 9.

686. BRAVERMAN, Kate
"Desperate Hallucinations." [OnTheBus] (4:2/5:1, #10/11) 92, p. 71-72.
"Postcard from Aspen." [OnTheBus] (4:2/5:1, #10/11) 92, p. 70-71.
687. BRECKENRIDGE, Jill
"Winter Sun at Ragdale." [WillowR] (19) Spr 92, p. 32-33.
688. BREGER, Miranda
"Old Digs." [Vis] (38) 92, p. 20.
"Porch, July 4." [Vis] (39) 92, p. 36.
689. BREHM, John
"What I Would Wish For." [NewOR] (19:1) Spr 92, p. 70-71.
690. BREMER, Kate
"Children of the Earth." [Noctiluca] (1:2) Wint 92 [on cover: Wint 93], p. 39.
"Shrine." [Noctiluca] (1:2) Wint 92 [on cover: Wint 93], p. 40.
691. BRENNAN, Matthew
"Dirty." [TarRP] (30:2) Spr 91, p. 22.
"John Huston's *The Dead*." [CapeR] (27:1) Spr 92, p. 13.
692. BRENT, Barry
"Frog in Cave Creek." [CimR] (99) Ap 92, p. 50-51.
693. BRESLIN, Julia Galligan
"Andromache." [Boulevard] (7:1, #19) Spr 92, p. 187.
"Hakiu [i.e. Haiku] for the Morning Moon." [Boulevard] (7:1, #19) Spr 92, p. 186.
694. BRETON, André
"I Hear the Beaches There Are Black" (tr. by C. Mulrooney). [PacificR] (11) 92-93, p. 43.
695. BRETT, Peter
"Ballerinas." [DogRR] (11:1) Spr-Sum 92, p. 21.
"Exhaust." [Lactuca] (16) Ag 92, p. 26.
"Fiesta." [Lactuca] (16) Ag 92, p. 26.
"Letter from Tecate." [Lactuca] (16) Ag 92, p. 27.
696. BREWER, Kenneth W.
"Another Accident Brings the Poet to the Brink of Happiness." [Interim] (11:1) Spr - Sum 92, p. 8-9.
697. BREYTENBACH, Breyten
"Death in the Poem." [NewL] (58:4) 92, p. 56-57.
"Poem on Toilet Paper." [NewL] (58:4) 92, p. 54-55.
698. BRICCETTI, Lee Ellen
"The Renaissance Happening at Once." [RiverS] (36) 92, p. 91.
"Speaking Italian." [RiverS] (36) 92, p. 90.
699. BRICKHOUSE, Robert
"Three to Watch For." [ChatR] (12:4) Sum 92, p. 43.
700. BRIDGES, William
"The Idea of Dominion." [PoetL] (87:1) Spr 92, p. 43-44.
"Night Song." [HiramPoR] (51/52) Fall 91-Sum 92, p. 24.
701. BRIDGFORD, Kim
"And Now" (For Pete). [LitR] (25:2) Wint 92, p. 267.
"Bells." [Outbr] (23) 92, p. 22-23.
"Betrayal." [LaurelR] (26:2) Sum 92, p. 85.
"Dust." [LaurelR] (26:1) Wint 92, p. 28.
"Excess." [Outbr] (23) 92, p. 21.
"Hobbies." [MidwQ] (33:4) Sum 92, p. 404.
"In This Place." [MidwQ] (34:1) Aut 92, p. 58-59.
"The Kiss." [SoCoast] (13) Je 93 [i.e. 92], p. 30.
"Salt." [MidwQ] (33:4) Sum 92, p. 403.
702. BRIERRE, Jean
"Black Soul" (Fragment, in French). [Callaloo] (15:3) Sum 92, p. 577-580.
"Black Soul" (Fragment, tr. by Carrol F. Coates). [Callaloo] (15:3) Sum 92, p. 573 - 576.
"Here I Am Again, Harlem" (tr. by Carrol F. Coates). [Callaloo] (15:3) Sum 92, p. 581-582.
"Me Revoici, Harlem" (Au souvenir des lynchés de Géorgie, victimes du fachisme blanc). [Callaloo] (15:3) Sum 92, p. 583-584.
703. BRILLIANT, Alan D.
"Living Simply." [Sun] (199) Je-Jl 92, p. 11.
704. BRINT, Armand
"Girls Gather Around the Coffee Machine." [Lactuca] (15) Mr 92, p. 47.

705. BRISBANE, Marianne
"In the cool mall." [Amelia] (6:4, #19) 92, p. 11.
706. BRITT, Alan
"All Day Long I Don't Know If I'm Coming or Going." [MidwQ] (33:3) Spr 92, p. 307.
"The Optimist." [MidwQ] (33:3) Spr 92, p. 308.
707. BRITT, Terry L.
"Contact Hitter." [Spitball] (40) Spr 92, p. 35.
708. BRITTLE, Angela
"Watching." [Amelia] (6:4, #19) 92, p. 74.
709. BRIXIUS, Liz
"The Floating World." [WillowS] (30) Sum 92, p. 76.
"Insofar as a Man Will Howl." [DenQ] (26:4) Spr 92, p. 10.
"Labor Day Dusk at the Fairgrounds, Minnesota." [PoetryE] (33) Spr 92, p. 13.
"The Morning Raymond Dean Nearly Got Away with It." [PoetryE] (33) Spr 92, p. 16.
"Romeo, Romeo." [WillowS] (30) Sum 92, p. 77.
"Toward Mercy." [PoetryE] (33) Spr 92, p. 14-15.
710. BROADHURST, Nicole
"Song of Miami" (for Jimi Hendrix). [KenR] (NS 14:3) Sum 92, p. 25-28.
711. BROADWAY, Robert
"Confirmation." [DogRR] (11:2, #22) Fall-Wint 92, p. 10.
"Elegy." [Elf] (2:1) Spr 92, p. 43.
"A Farewell to My Friend." [CapeR] (27:1) Spr 92, p. 19.
"A Farewell to My Friend." [Elf] (2:2) Sum 92, p. 34.
"Jubilee Beach." [DogRR] (11:2, #22) Fall-Wint 92, p. 8-9.
"Limerick." [Elf] (2:1) Spr 92, p. 43.
"Limerick." [Elf] (2:2) Sum 92, p. 34.
712. BROBST, Richard
"Milkblood." [CumbPR] (12:1) Fall 92, p. 32-35.
713. BROCK, Randall
"I Am." [Wind] (22:71) 92, p. 35.
714. BROCK-BROIDO, Lucie
"Black Arcadia." [AmerV] (26) Spr 92, p. 26-33.
715. BROCKI, A. C.
"Composers." [SmPd] (29:1, #84) Wint 92, p. 33.
"Imploding." [CapeR] (27:2) Fall 92, p. 42.
"Luncheon." [WritersF] (18) 92, p. 50.
716. BROCKWAY, James
"Little Litany for the Third World" (tr. of Peter Verstegen). [Stand] (33:4) Aut 92, p. 116.
"Sometimes" (tr. of Hans Warren). [Stand] (33:4) Aut 92, p. 115.
"Still-Life with Sunflowers" (tr. of Rutger Kopland). [Stand] (33:4) Aut 92, p. 115.
"Their Boheme" (tr. of Jan Deloof). [Stand] (33:4) Aut 92, p. .117.
"When Shall I Have the Courage" (tr. of Hans Lodeizen). [Stand] (33:4) Aut 92, p. 114.
717. BROCKWELL, Stephen
"Constructive Geometry." [Descant] (23:4/24:1, #78/79) Wint-Spr 92-93, p. 7.
"Cube." [Descant] (23:4/24:1, #78/79) Wint-Spr 92-93, p. 11.
"Sphere." [Descant] (23:4/24:1, #78/79) Wint-Spr 92-93, p. 10.
"Torus." [Descant] (23:4/24:1, #78/79) Wint-Spr 92-93, p. 8.
"Wormhole." [Descant] (23:4/24:1, #78/79) Wint-Spr 92-93, p. 9.
718. BRODSKY, Joseph
"Lines for the Winter Recess" (Washington, D.C.). [NewYorker] (68:11) 4 My 92, p. 34.
"Transatlantic." [NewYorker] (68:24) 3 Ag 92, p. 32.
719. BRODSKY, Louis Daniel
"The Cosmic Clock." [ChamLR] (10/11) Spr-Fall 92, p. 152.
"Hapless Ever After" (For Ann Bohman). [FourQ] (6:1) Spr 92, p. 32.
"Just Jazz" (The Horizon Group — Bobby Watson. For Edie and Austin Tashma). [ChamLR] (10/11) Spr-Fall 92, p. 148-150.
"The Key Master of Gozer: Data Processor, Purina." [ChamLR] (10/11) Spr-Fall 92, p. 151.
"Lovers' Last Evening in the Warsaw Ghetto." [NewYorkQ] (48) 92, p. 90.
"Sewing Friendship Robes" (For my best friend, Jane). [ChamLR] (10/11) Spr-Fall 92, p. 153.

"The Trysting Place." [SoCarR] (25:1) Fall 92, p. 111-112.
720. BRODY, Deborah
"Peach Preserves." [GreensboroR] (52) Sum 92, p. 116.
721. BRODY, Polly
"Satori of the Leaves." [SpoonRQ] (17:1/2) Wint-Spr 92, p. 97.
722. BROGAN, Jacque Vaught
"The Bond" (Winner, Annual Free Verse Contest, 1991). [AnthNEW] (4) 92, p. 26.
BROIDO, Lucie Brock
See BROCK-BROIDO, Lucie
723. BROMIGE, David
"Irony" (Long After Aragon). [Avec] (5:1) 92, p. 46.
"Like Unity." [Avec] (5:1) 92, p. 45.
"Logic." [Avec] (5:1) 92, p. 44.
"Unfootnote." [Avec] (5:1) 92, p. 44.
"Unparenthetic." [Avec] (5:1) 92, p. 43.
724. BROMLEY, Anne C.
"My Mother's Face Never Moved." [ThRiPo] (39/40) 92-93, p. 15-16.
"Slow Men Working in Trees." [ThRiPo] (39/40) 92-93, p. 14-15.
"Teel St. Trailer Court." [ThRiPo] (39/40) 92-93, p. 16.
725. BRONDY, Michele
"Au Jeu" (Excerpt, tr. of Philippe Remy). [Vis] (39) 92, p. 18.
"In Stain" (tr. of Philippe Remy). [Vis] (38) 92, p. 39.
BROOK, Kimball MacKay
See MacKAY-BROOK, Kimball
726. BROOKS, Gwendolyn
"A Welcome Song for Laini Nzinga." [Art&Und] (1:5) S-O 92, p. 10.
727. BROSMAN, Catharine Savage
"At Lake Ganado" (From a Southwestern Suite). [SewanR] (100:4) Fall 92, p. 546.
"By Alexander's Tent." [SewanR] (100:1) Wint 92, p. 53-54.
"Ocotillo" (From a Southwestern Suite). [SewanR] (100:4) Fall 92, p. 543-544.
"Shiprock" (From a Southwestern Suite). [SewanR] (100:4) Fall 92, p. 545.
728. BROUGHTON, James
"Defective Wiring." [NewYorkQ] (47) 92, p. 33.
"For the Young Departed." [ChironR] (11:4) Wint 92, p. 42.
729. BROUGHTON, T. Alan
"Beyond the Picturesque." [LitR] (25:2) Wint 92, p. 250.
"Hold, Hold." [ThRiPo] (39/40) 92-93, p. 18-19.
"I Make This Leap for You" (for Nancy Willard). [Poem] (67) My 92, p. 45.
"The Limits of Translation." [NewOR] (19:3/4) Fall-Wint 92, p. 136.
"Lyric." [ThRiPo] (39/40) 92-93, p. 17.
"Recognitions." [NewOR] (19:3/4) Fall-Wint 92, p. 182.
"Riding the Thermals." [LitR] (25:2) Wint 92, p. 251.
"Serenade for Winds." [ThRiPo] (39/40) 92-93, p. 19-20.
730. BROUMAS, Olga
"The Contemplation." [AmerPoR] (21:6) N-D 92, p. 31.
"The Continuo." [AmerPoR] (21:6) N-D 92, p. 31.
"Grace." [AmerPoR] (21:6) N-D 92, p. 31.
731. BROWN, Alan (*See also* BROWN, Alan C.)
"A Small Dead Girl" (tr. of Anne Hébert). [Trans] (26) Spr 92, p. 52.
732. BROWN, Alan C. (*See also* BROWN, Alan)
"Birchwood Mother." [Stand] (33:2) Spr 92, p. 133-134.
"Legend." [Stand] (33:2) Spr 92, p. 134.
"Siberia." [Stand] (33:2) Spr 92, p. 133.
733. BROWN, Bill
"Confession." [Pearl] (15) Spr-Sum 92, p. 20.
"Out the Window." [PaintedB] (45) 92, p. 6.
734. BROWN, Charles
"The Nightingale's Own Ode." [NewYorkQ] (49) 92, p. 70.
735. BROWN, Chris
"Manhattan: West 14th Street." [NewYorkQ] (48) 92, p. 70.
736. BROWN, Cory
"Answering." [ChatR] (12:4) Sum 92, p. 33.
"Corkscrew Hickory." [WestB] (30) 92, p. 18.
"Naming Hills." [WestB] (30) 92, p. 19.
"Occasional Poem." [Farm] (9:1) Spr-Sum 92, p. 34.

737. BROWN, Diane
"Ripe for the Eating." [Vis] (40) 92, p. 52.
738. BROWN, Dorothy Hanson
"Jacob, Plain and Sturdy." [Elf] (2:4) Wint 92, p. 39.
"View-point." [Elf] (2:4) Wint 92, p. 38-39.
739. BROWN, Glen
"Birth of an Angel." [CapeR] (27:2) Fall 92, p. 19.
"The Checkup" (or Symphony for the Dental Hygienist). [SpoonRQ] (17:1/2) Wint-Spr 92, p. 83-84.
"Maybe." [Poetry] (161:2) N 92, p. 98.
"Munditia, Patron Saint of Lonely Women" (for M.K.). [WillowR] (19) Spr 92, p. 8.
740. BROWN, Heather
"Change of Heart." [Bogg] (65) 92, p. 56.
741. BROWN, James
"Lemons." [PoetL] (87:2) Sum 92, p. 16.
742. BROWN, Kurt
"Exodus." [MassR] (23:3) Fall 92, p. 400.
743. BROWN, Lee Ann
"Pregnant C." [Epoch] (41:3) 92, p. 395.
744. BROWN, Mary M.
"Eve's Regret." [ChrC] (109:32) 4 N 92, p. 1006.
745. BROWN, Peter
"Women of Hospice." [Noctiluca] (1:1) Spr 92, p. 3.
746. BROWN, Robert
"Black Lily in Clouded Moonlight." [Poem] (67) My 92, p. 58.
"The Carving of a Star." [Poem] (67) My 92, p. 56.
"The Eye of the Storm." [CharR] (18:2) Fall 92, p. 87.
"Having Followed Neither Destiny Nor Duty." [CapeR] (27:1) Spr 92, p. 44.
"Soul of Lead." [Poem] (67) My 92, p. 57.
"The Walks." [Elf] (2:2) Sum 92, p. 40.
747. BROWN, Ronnie R.
"States of Matter." [Arc] (28) Spr 92, p. 11-14.
748. BROWN, Sean Brendan
"An Irish Nun at Ypres, 1917" (for Les Dames Irlandaises of the Royal Benedictine Abbey). [Vis] (38) 92, p. 33.
749. BROWN, Stephanie
"Chapter One." [AmerPoR] (21:4) Jl-Ag 92, p. 32.
"Kitsch." [AmerPoR] (21:4) Jl-Ag 92, p. 33.
"No Longer a Girl." [AmerPoR] (21:4) Jl-Ag 92, p. 33.
"Reading True Crime Stories." [AmerPoR] (21:4) Jl-Ag 92, p. 32.
750. BROWN, Steven Ford
"Birthday Poem" (tr. of Ana Maria Fagundo, w. Moira Perez). [SenR] (22:1) Spr 92, p. 49.
"Counter-Order (Poetics That I Announce on Certain Days)" (tr. of Angel Gonzalez, w. Gutierrez Revuelta). [SenR] (22:1) Spr 92, p. 53.
"Dawn in the Monastery of the Olive Trees" (for Julia Gonzalez, tr. of Ana Maria Fagundo, w. Moira Perez). [SenR] (22:1) Spr 92, p. 51-52.
"The Day Has Gone" (tr. of Angel Gonzalez, w. Gutierrez Revuelta). [SenR] (22:1) Spr 92, p. 56.
"Here, Madrid, 1954" (tr. of Angel Gonzalez, w. Gutierrez Revuelta). [SenR] (22:1) Spr 92, p. 57.
"The Sower" (tr. of Ana Maria Fagundo, w. Moira Perez). [SenR] (22:1) Spr 92, p. 50.
"Zero City" (tr. of Angel Gonzalez, w. Gutierrez Revuelta). [SenR] (22:1) Spr 92, p. 54-55.
751. BROWN, Susan M.
"The Keeper of Sheep" (Excerpt, tr. of Fernando Pessoa (Alberto Caeiro), w. Edwin Honig). [Trans] (26) Spr 92, p. 14-15.
752. BROWN, Toni P.
"The Swimmers." [SinW] (47) Sum-Fall 92, p. 7.
753. BROWN-DAVIDSON, Terri
"Block Bébé." [TriQ] (86) Wint 92-93, p. 62-63.
"The Bright Clay Forest." [BelPoJ] (43:2) Wint 92-93, p. 20-21.
"The Photos of the Funeral." [ChamLR] (10/11) Spr-Fall 92, p. 38.
"The Sexual Jackson Pollock." [NewYorkQ] (48) 92, p. 92-93.
"Shadow Twin, Play." [BelPoJ] (43:1) Fall 92, p. 18-22.

754. BROWNE, Andrew
"She." [Vis] (40) 92, p. 8.
755. BROWNE, Laynie
"Definitions of Space with Correspondences to a Story." [WestCL] (26:2, #8) Fall 92, p. 48-49.
"Means to Send" (Part 2 from "Sending the Lake": excerpts). [WestCL] (26:2, #8) Fall 92, p. 46-47.
"One Constellation" (Excerpts). [WestCL] (26:2, #8) Fall 92, p. 48.
"Sending the Lake" (Excerpts). [PaintedB] (47) 92, p. 8-9.
756. BROWNE, Michael Dennis
"Basswood Leaf Falling." [WillowS] (30) Sum 92, p. 7.
"Epithalamion / Wedding Dawn" (for Nicholas & Elena). [ThRiPo] (39/40) 92-93, p. 25-27.
"Talk to Me, Baby." [ThRiPo] (39/40) 92-93, p. 20-25.
757. BROWNING, Deborah
"Visiting Her in the Home." [TarRP] (31:2) Spr 92, p. 39.
758. BROWNING, Robert
"Garden Fancies (II)." [Light] (2) Sum 92, p. 30.
759. BROWNSBERGER, Sarah M.
"Chandler's Pond, December." [Hudson] (44:4) Wint 92, p. 620.
"For Posterity" (Chandler's Pond, August). [Hudson] (44:4) Wint 92, p. 619.
760. BROWNSTEIN, Michael
"Neighbors Next Door." [FreeL] (9) Wint 92, p. 24.
761. BRUCE, Debra
"Two Couples." [KenR] (NS 14:2) Spr 92, p. 154.
"A Valediction in the Waiting Room." [AmerV] (26) Spr 92, p. 18-19.
"What Wind Will Do." [KenR] (NS 14:2) Spr 92, p. 155-156.
762. BRUCE, Lennart
"Least of all somebody wants to read what your write" (tr. of Gunnar Björling, w. Sonja Bruce). [CityLR] (5) 92, p. 68.
"There was a poem, a confined picture, it is no more" (tr. of Gunnar Björling, w. Sonja Bruce). [CityLR] (5) 92, p. 68.
763. BRUCE, Sonja
"Least of all somebody wants to read what your write" (tr. of Gunnar Björling, w. Lennart Bruce). [CityLR] (5) 92, p. 68.
"There was a poem, a confined picture, it is no more" (tr. of Gunnar Björling, w. Lennart Bruce). [CityLR] (5) 92, p. 68.
764. BRUCHAC, Joseph
"Exchange." [Contact] (10:62/63/64) Fall 91-Spr 92, p. 48.
"Lava Flow at Kalapana." [Contact] (10:62/63/64) Fall 91-Spr 92, p. 49.
"Sweat Lodge by Bell Brook." [Contact] (10:62/63/64) Fall 91-Spr 92, p. 48.
765. BRUCHANSKI, Rhonda
"The Antidyke II." [PraF] (13:3, #60) Aut 92, p. 46-47.
"Cows are my favorite." [PraF] (13:3, #60) Aut 92, p. 44.
"Psalm of Sodom." [PraF] (13:3, #60) Aut 92, p. 45.
766. BRUCK, Julie
"Kampuchea by the Weekend." [MalR] (100) Fall 92, p. 177.
"Reprints" (for Duane Michals). [MalR] (100) Fall 92, p. 173.
"Snakes & Wrenches." [MalR] (100) Fall 92, p. 176.
"Stone's Throw." [MalR] (100) Fall 92, p. 174-175.
"Timing Your Run" (Philippe Laheurte, 1957-1991). [MalR] (100) Fall 92, p. 178.
767. BRUGALETTA, John
"Demolition." [NegC] (12:1/2) 92, p. 182.
"The Poor Little Poems." [NegC] (12:1/2) 92, p. 178.
"Twelve Ways." [NegC] (12:1/2) 92, p. 179.
"With This Poem, All Things Are Possible." [NegC] (12:1/2) 92, p. 180-181.
768. BRUGALETTA, John J.
"Biography of White." [TarRP] (30:2) Spr 91, p. 36.
"The Most Beautiful Thing" (after Sappho). [Hellas] (3:1) Spr 92, p. 22.
"A Pillar of the Community." [Light] (1) Spr 92, p. 27.
769. BRUINING, Mi Ok
"Not Just Another One of Those Identity Poems" (For Lanuola). [SinW] (47) Sum - Fall 92, p. 118-120.
770. BRUNK, Juanita
"Anniversary." [PassN] (13:2) Wint 92, p. 8.
"On This Earth." [PassN] (13:2) Wint 92, p. 8.

BRUNO, Carmen Michael la
See LaBRUNO, Michael (Carmen Michael)
BRUNO, Michael la (Michael C. la)
See LaBRUNO, Michael (Carmen Michael)
BRUNT, Lloyd van
See Van BRUNT, Lloyd
771. BRUSH, Thomas
"In the Waiting Room." [Poetry] (161:2) N 92, p. 81.
772. BRUTUS, Dennis
"Haiku: South Africa." [Nimrod] (35:2) Spr-Sum 92, p. 114.
773. BRYAN, Sharon
"-Esque." [Atlantic] (269:1) Ja 92, p. 89.
"Ultrasound." [GettyR] (5:2) Spr 92, p. 283.
"What Biology Is All About." [GettyR] (5:2) Spr 92, p. 284-285.
"Wish You Were Here." [Nat] (254:15) 20 Ap 92, p. 535.
774. BRYAN, Tom
"Legacy." [Verse] (9:2) Sum 92, p. 64.
775. BRYANT, Tisa
"The Fling." [Eyeball] (1) 92, p. 5.
776. BRYNER, Jeanne
"Homesick." [LullwaterR] (3:3) Sum 92, p. 37.
"Sunday Morning." [HiramPoR] (51/52) Fall 91-Sum 92, p. 25-26.
777. BUCHANAN, Carl
"The Haunted." [Poem] (68) N 92, p. 57-58.
"I, Julius." [Poem] (68) N 92, p. 59.
"The Line." [MidwQ] (34:1) Aut 92, p. 59.
"Six Victims" (to Diane). [ParisR] (34:125) Wint 92, p. 48-53.
778. BUCHANAN, Stephanie
"After Triumph." [HolCrit] (29:2) Ap 92, p. 15.
779. BUCK, Paula Closson
"The Acquiescent Villa." [AntR] (50:3) Sum 92, p. 502-503.
"From a Porthole." [WillowS] (29) Wint 92, p. 27-28.
"The Man at Pensione Marta Looks at His Eye." [WillowS] (29) Wint 92, p. 26.
"Off-Season." [DenQ] (26:4) Spr 92, p. 11.
780. BUCKHOLTS, Claudia
"Clearing the Field." [PraS] (66:2) Sum 92, p. 88.
"Managua." [MinnR] (38) Spr-Sum 92, p. 10-12.
"A Medieval Story." [MinnR] (38) Spr-Sum 92, p. 10.
"My Father, in the War." [ConnPR] (11:1) 92, p. 3-4.
"Waiting for the Messiah." [PraS] (66:2) Sum 92, p. 87.
781. BUCKINGHAM, Polly
"Hotel Florida." [Kalliope] (14:2) 92, p. 13.
782. BUCKLEY, B. J.
"Logging." [CumbPR] (12:1) Fall 92, p. 13-15.
"Mad Alyce in February / II" (Honorable Mention, Robert Penn Warren Poetry Prize). [CumbPR] (12:1) Fall 92, p. 10-12.
783. BUCKLEY, Christopher
"Art & Science, 1961." [NewEngR] (14:3) Sum 92, p. 147-148.
"Day After Christmas: The the West Coast." [SewanR] (100:4) Fall 92, p. 549.
"Eschatology." [Poetry] (160:6) S 92, p. 345-346.
"Evening in Cortona" (for Nadya). [QW] (36) Wint 92-93, p. 110-111.
"The Last Days of Rome" (Third Place, The Paintbrush Award, Poetry). [PaintedHR] (7) Fall 92, p. 12-13.
"Leaving the West Coast — Santa Barbara 1987" (after Cavafy). [SewanR] (100:4) Fall 92, p. 547-548.
"The Moroccans" (after Matisse, 1916 — for Sherod Santos). [PoetL] (87:2) Sum 92, p. 35-37.
"Old Love." [QW] (36) Wint 92-93, p. 112.
"Pange Lingua." [SenR] (22:1) Spr 92, p. 13-15.
"Prima Facie." [PoetL] (87:2) Sum 92, p. 38-39.
"Seasonal: For Ernesto Trejo." [NewEngR] (14:3) Sum 92, p. 148-149.
"Star Journal." [PassN] (13:1) Sum 92, p. 28.
"Still Life with Grenadines" (after Matisse, 1947). [DenQ] (26:3) Wint 92, p. 7.
"Sycamore Canyon Nocturne." [Poetry] (160:6) S 92, p. 343-345.
784. BUDAN, John A.
"On Reading Poetry in a Dentist's Office." [MoodySI] (27) Spr 92, p. 33.

785. BUDBILL, David
"Bugs in a Bowl." [Sun] (200) Ag 92, p. 31.
"Raymond and Ann." [Sun] (196) Mr 92, p. 24-27.
786. BUDDE, Charles
"7/9/91." [Eyeball] (1) 92, p. 10.
787. BUDDINGH, Mary E.
"Coyote calling." [Amelia] (7:1, #20) 92, p. 15.
788. BUDY, Andrea Hollander
"Black." [GeoR] (46:2) Sum 92, p. 240.
"Gray." [NewEngR] (14:3) Sum 92, p. 120.
"What You Find." [NewEngR] (14:3) Sum 92, p. 121.
789. BUEHLER, Stephanie Pershing
"Schubert on the Powder" (for Jane, a Wyoming poem). [HighP] (7:1) Spr 92, p. 75.
790. BUFFALOE, Julie
"Don't Write a Poem about Rape" (For the editor who told me rape is not a fresh subject — he knows who he is). [Calyx] (14:1) Sum 92, p. 50-53.
"Miss Eula's Garden" (Eula Jessamine Williams, 1896-1976). [Grain] (20:3) Fall 92, p. 54-56.
791. BUFFAM, Suzanne
"Grandmother." [CapilR] (2:9) Fall 92, p. 48.
792. BUGEJA, Michael (Michael J.)
"Amenities." [ChamLR] (10/11) Spr-Fall 92, p. 122.
"Blue." [TarRP] (31:2) Spr 92, p. 17.
"Coccinella 7-Punctata." [PoetC] (24:1) Fall 92, p. 13.
"Cops, Rainbows, The Light the Children See." [JlNJPo] (14:2) Aut 92, p. 25-26.
"Energy." [PoetryE] (33) Spr 92, p. 12.
"Environmental." [CinPR] (23) Wint 91-92, p. 18-19.
"Evangelists, Environmentalists." [PoetC] (24:1) Fall 92, p. 14.
"Hitler's Hypothermia" (for Bob Stewart). [PoetC] (23:2) Wint 92, p. 3-5.
"Second Fiddle, Philharmonic, Our Lives Going to the Pits." [CimR] (101) O 92, p. 24-26.
"Trakl & Grete." [PraS] (66:1) Spr 92, p. 68-75.
"Trakl's Cellmate." [Amelia] (6:4, #19) 92, p. 72.
"The Unification of Love." [CimR] (101) O 92, p. 23-24.
793. BUHROW, B. J.
"At Dairy Queen." [SpoonRQ] (17:3/4) Sum-Fall 92, p. 56.
"Pearl Lake." [SpoonRQ] (17:3/4) Sum-Fall 92, p. 55.
"Rural Madness." [SpoonRQ] (17:3/4) Sum-Fall 92, p. 53-54.
"White Trash." [SpoonRQ] (17:3/4) Sum-Fall 92, p. 57.
794. BUKOWSKI, Charles
"After Reading a Certain Poet." [MidwQ] (33:4) Sum 92, p. 405.
"Agnostic's Prayer." [WorldL] (3) 92, p. 15-16.
"Ah." [WillowS] (29) Wint 92, p. 84.
"As the Poems Go." [OnTheBus] (4:2/5:1, #10/11) 92, p. 28.
"Bach, Come Back." [Antaeus] (69) Aut 92, p. 70-71.
"A Banner of Snake Eyes and Faulty Screams." [NewYorkQ] (49) 92, p. 32-33.
"Bar Stool." [ChironR] (11:1) Spr 92, p. 5.
"Black." [CharR] (18:1) Spr 92, p. 94.
"A Cat Is a Cat Is a Cat Is a Cat." [WormR] (32:4 #128) 92, p. 173-174.
"City Boy." [NewYorkQ] (48) 92, p. 42-44.
"Clipboard." [ChironR] (11:3) Aut 92, p. 10.
"A covering letter." [NewYorkQ] (47) 92, p. 30.
"The Crowd." [MidwQ] (34:1) Aut 92, p. 60-61.
"The Death of an Era." [PaintedB] (48) 92, p. 22-24.
"Eating Out." [OnTheBus] (4:2/5:1, #10/11) 92, p. 39-44.
"Everywhere, Everywhere." [MidwQ] (33:4) Sum 92, p. 406.
"Finis." [Bogg] (65) 92, p. 22.-24.
"Funeraless." [NewYorkQ] (49) 92, p. 30.
"The Girls." [OnTheBus] (4:2/5:1, #10/11) 92, p. 30-31.
"Giving Thanks." [Pearl] (15) Spr-Sum 92, p. 6-7.
"Hands." [NewYorkQ] (48) 92, p. 48.
"Hell Is Always Now." [NewYorkQ] (48) 92, p. 45-47.
"Hello Wm Packard." [NewYorkQ] (49) 92, p. 34-35.
"I'm a Failure." [WormR] (32:1, #125) 92, p. 38-39.
"Just Trying to Do a Good Deed." [PaintedB] (48) 92, p. 17-18.
"Large and Small and None at All." [ChironR] (11:3) Aut 92, p. 10.

"Last Call." [OnTheBus] (4:2/5:1, #10/11) 92, p. 36-37.
"Late Payment." [OnTheBus] (4:2/5:1, #10/11) 92, p. 28.
"Laugh a Minute." [WorldL] (3) 92, p. 13-14.
"London Bridges." [WormR] (32:4 #128) 92, p. 173.
"The Misanthrope." [Asylum] (7:3/4) 92, p. 68-70.
"The Modern Life." [Antaeus] (69) Aut 92, p. 69.
"Murder." [NewYorkQ] (47) 92, p. 31.
"No More, No More, No More." [NewYorkQ] (49) 92, p. 31.
"Old Man Dead in a Room." [PoetryE] (34) Fall 92, p. 21-22.
"One to Lead the Way." [PaintedB] (48) 92, p. 19, 21.
"The Parade." [WorldL] (3) 92, p. 16-17.
"Pershing Square, Los Angeles, 1939." [CreamCR] (16:2) Fall 92, p. 48-50.
"Prescience." [NewYorkQ] (49) 92, p. 30.
"Problems." [WormR] (32:4 #128) 92, p. 172-173.
"Problems in the Checkout Line." [WormR] (32:1, #125) 92, p. 37-38.
"The Puking Lady." [Pearl] (16) Fall 92, p. 6-7.
"Rift." [WormR] (32:4 #128) 92, p. 174.
"Room 106." [NewYorkQ] (48) 92, p. 49.
"The Shape of the Star." [Bogg] (65) 92, p. 20-22.
"Short Muck Poem." [PaintedB] (48) 92, p. 25.
"The Sickness." [WormR] (32:4 #128) 92, p. 171.
"The Similarity." [OnTheBus] (4:2/5:1, #10/11) 92, p. 32-33.
"Small Cafe." [Lactuca] (15) Mr 92, p. 5-7.
"Small Conversation in the Afternoon." [NewYorkQ] (49) 92, p. 29.
"A Social Call." [Bogg] (65) 92, p. 19-20.
"Somewhere in Texas." [WorldL] (3) 92, p. 14-15.
"The Stages." [OnTheBus] (4:2/5:1, #10/11) 92, p. 33-36.
"The Star." [WormR] (32:4 #128) 92, p. 172.
"Thoughts on Being 71." [CreamCR] (16:2) Fall 92, p. 46-47.
"Three Oranges." [OnTheBus] (4:2/5:1, #10/11) 92, p. 38.
"To Hell and Back in a Buggy Carriage." [OnTheBus] (4:2/5:1, #10/11) 92, p. 29-30.
"Tragedy?" [NewYorkQ] (49) 92, p. 33.
"Training for Kid Aztec." [WormR] (32:3, #127) 92, p. 123-126.
"The Trash Can." [LitR] (35:3) Spr 92, p. 310.
"Trollius and Trellises." [BostonR] (17:6) N-D 92, p. 26-27.
"We Don't Read." [NewYorkQ] (48) 92, p. 38-41.
"Writing." [OnTheBus] (4:2/5:1, #10/11) 92, p. 31-32.
"Zero." [WormR] (32:3, #127) 92, p. 126.

795. BULL, Arthur
"Borduas." [Arc] (28) Spr 92, p. 26.

796. BULLOCK, Marnie
"Bone Deep." [LaurelR] (26:2) Sum 92, p. 48.
"Godly Woman Go-Go." [CutB] (38) Sum 92, p. 7-8.
"Independence Day." [CutB] (38) Sum 92, p. 9-10.

797. BULLOCK, Michael
"Gathering" (tr. of Horst Bienek). [Stand] (33:4) Aut 92, p. 69.
"King Oedipus" (tr. of Horst Bienek). [Stand] (33:4) Aut 92, p. 70.

798. BUMSTEAD, Leslie
"Woman on Cross." [PaintedB] (47) 92, p. 5.

799. BUNCH, Richard Alan
"A Foggy Morning." [ChamLR] (10/11) Spr-Fall 92, p. 171.

800. BUNDY, Erik
"Boatwoman's Brunch." [CimR] (100) Jl 92, p. 55.
"The Magic Fountain." [CimR] (100) Jl 92, p. 56.

801. BUNDY, Gary
"Black Weeds." [NewDeltaR] (8:1) Fall 90-Wint 91, p. 91-93.

802. BURCH, Sauda
"And so it was that Grace found Sarah" (from "Excerpt from a Novel-in-Progress"). [SinW] (48) Wint 92-93, p. 44-45.

803. BURDEN, Jean
"For Hildegarde Who Received for Christmas a Moon-Window in a Wall." [PoetC] (23:3) Spr 92, p. 45.
"Free Association" (for Hildegarde). [PoetC] (23:2) Wint 92, p. 23-24.

BUREN, David van
See Van BUREN, David

804. BURGESS, Lynne
"Root Woman Comes." [Northeast] (5:6) Spr 92, p. 21-22.
805. BURGIN, Richard
"Necessary Night." [PaintedB] (48) 92, p. 30-31.
806. BURGOS, Julia de
"A Julia de Burgos." [LitR] (35:4) Sum 92, p. 604.
"Call Out My Number" (tr. by Julio Marzán). [LitR] (35:4) Sum 92, p. 518.
"Dadme Mi Número." [LitR] (35:4) Sum 92, p. 605.
"Poem with the Final Tune" (tr. by Julio Marzán). [LitR] (35:4) Sum 92, p. 517.
"Poema con la Tonada Ultima." [LitR] (35:4) Sum 92, p. 605.
"To Julia de Burgos" (tr. by María Arrillaga). [LitR] (35:4) Sum 92, p. 516.
807. BURIANOVA, Svetlana
"If I could" (tr. by Dominika Winterová and Richard Katrovas). [NewOR] (19:3/4) Fall-Wint 92, p. 25.
808. BURK, David
"Outing." [EngJ] (81:3) Mr 92, p. 92.
809. BURK, Ronnie
"Elegy" (for my brothers . . .). [Caliban] (11) 92, p. 33-36.
810. BURKARD, Michael
"Another Infinity." [GettyR] (5:4) Aut 92, p. 590-591.
"The Boy Who Had No Shadow." [AmerV] (28) 92, p. 38-39.
811. BURKE, Brian
"How Things Change." [Dandel] (19:2) 92, p. 20.
"Zen Snow." [CanLit] (135) Wint 92, p. 14.
812. BURKE, Daniel
"Shadow." [FourQ] (6:2) Fall 92, p. 48.
"Spell." [FourQ] (6:2) Fall 92, p. 48.
"Wedlock." [FourQ] (6:2) Fall 92, p. 47.
813. BURKE, Liam
"Ghostweight: The Anniversary." [CimR] (100) Jl 92, p. 48-50.
"X." [CimR] (100) Jl 92, p. 51-52.
814. BURKE, Marianne
"At the Palace of Fine Arts in San Francisco." [Thrpny] (48) Wint 92, p. 27.
"Little Whaley, Pawling, N.Y." [NewYorker] (68:26) 17 Ag 92, p. 30.
"Shirts." [NewYorker] (68:15) 1 Je 92, p. 46.
815. BURLINGAME, Robert
"Words for Wild Cherries." [SoDakR] (30:2) Sum 92, p. 112.
816. BURNABY, Frank
"I Hate to Baby Sit." [OnTheBus] (4:2/5:1, #10/11) 92, p. 73-74.
817. BURNETT, David
"To Posterity." [Stand] (33:2) Spr 92, p. 148.
818. BURNHAM, Deborah
"Perfect Game." [WestB] (30) 92, p. 105.
819. BURNS, Gerald
"Easy As Pie." [Talisman] (9) Fall 92, p. 194-195.
"The Maritime Graveyard" (tr. of Paul Valéry). [AnotherCM] (23) Spr 92, p. 173 - 175.
820. BURNS, Jim
"Poem for Booksellers." [Verse] (9:3) Wint 92, p. 151.
821. BURNS, Michael
"Cooking Breakfast After Reading Robert Penn Warren." [Poetry] (160:5) Ag 92, p. 281.
822. BURNS, Suzanne
"Eclipse." [GrahamHR] (16) Fall 92, p. 42.
"Finding the Bluefish." [GrahamHR] (16) Fall 92, p. 43.
823. BURNSIDE, John
"Another Loneliness" (Excerpt). [Verse] (9:2) Sum 92, p. 83-84.
824. BURR, Gray
"The Damned." [Sparrow] (59) S 92, p. 26.
"The Eye." [Sparrow] (59) S 92, p. 26.
825. BURR, Lonnie
"Cinema." [Pearl] (15) Spr-Sum 92, p. 18.
"Nuance." [Pearl] (15) Spr-Sum 92, p. 18.
826. BURRIS, Sidney
"An Anti-Pastoral for Friends Moving to the Country." [SouthernR] (28:4) Aut, O 92, p. 832-834.

"King of Seasons." [SouthernR] (28:4) Aut, O 92, p. 835.
"To a Friend in HMP Maze, 1989." [SouthernR] (28:4) Aut, O 92, p. 834.
"To a Reader of Mysteries." [SouthernR] (28:4) Aut, O 92, p. 835-837.

827. BURROWAY, Janet
"This Hammock Is for Peter." [ChatR] (12:4) Sum 92, p. 16-17.

828. BURROWS, E. G.
"Lepidoptera." [Ascent] (16:3) Spr 92, p. 68.
"Pioneer." [CreamCR] (16:2) Fall 92, p. 13.

829. BURRS, Mick
"Approaching Zero, Leaving Melville." [Grain] (20:1) Spr 92, p. 276.
"Dymaxion." [AntigR] (89) Spr 92, p. 10.
"Solo." [Grain] (20:1) Spr 92, p. 275.

830. BURSK, Christopher (Chris)
"Allegiances." [MassR] (23:1) Spr 92, p. 141-147.
"Blood for Oil." [Sun] (200) Ag 92, p. 23.
"Foot Soldiers." [NoAmR] (277:5) S-O 92, p. 15.
"Home Care." [NoAmR] (277:2) Mr-Ap 92, p. 25.
"Incontinent." [Sun] (202) O 92, p. 32.
"Leverage." [ManhatR] (6:2) Fall 92, p. 38.
"My Savior Jesus." [Sun] (201) S 92, p. 19.

831. BURSKY, Rick
"I Can Prove It With Photographs." [Plain] (13:1) Fall 92, p. 31.

832. BURT, Stephen
"Spanish Sonnet." [HarvardA] (126:2) Wint 92, p. 22.

833. BURTON, John
"Hunger." [WebR] (16) Fall 92, p. 103.
"Parole." [WebR] (16) Fall 92, p. 103.

834. BURTON, Scott
"Blue Moon." [RagMag] (10:2) 92, p. 38-39.
"It's Me." [RagMag] (10:2) 92, p. 40.

835. BURTON, Sue D.
"Home Movie." [Calyx] (14:2) Wint 92-93, p. 50.
"Placenta Accreta." [WestB] (30) 92, p. 83.

836. BURWELL, M. S.
"16." [Lactuca] (15) Mr 92, p. 46.
"Q." [Lactuca] (15) Mr 92, p. 46.

837. BUSAILAH, Reja-e
"The Last Phase of Chanticleer." [OxfordM] (8:1) Spr-Sum 92, p. 58-59.
"Matchless." [OxfordM] (8:1) Spr-Sum 92, p. 57.
"Migrants." [OxfordM] (8:1) Spr-Sum 92, p. 56.

838. BUSCH, Trent
"Back Road to Florida." [FloridaR] (18:2) Fall-Wint 92, p. 112-113.

839. BUSH, Barney
"My Horse." [Jacaranda] (6:1/2) Wint-Spr 92, p. 63.

840. BUSHKOWKSY, Aaron
"Dawn of Time." [Arc] (28) Spr 92, p. 15.
"Diamonds in the Sky." [Arc] (28) Spr 92, p. 16.

BUSTILLO, Camilo Pérez
See PÉREZ-BUSTILLO, Camilo

841. BUTCHER, Grace
"Chase Burcher." [GettyR] (5:1) Wint 92, p. 80.
"If Death Hovers Anywhere." [GreenMR] (NS 5:2) Spr-Sum 92, p. 32.
"Leaving the House." [NegC] (12:1/2) 92, p. 17.
"Q: What Are You Afraid Of?" [TarRP] (30:2) Spr 91, p. 37.

842. BUTLER, Lynne Burris
"Nothing to Fear." [Ascent] (16:3) Spr 92, p. 23.

843. BUTSCHER, Edward
"Eros Descending" (In memory of Amy Elisabeth Rothholz for always and a day). [DustyD] (Chapbook Series #3) 92, 24 p.

844. BUTSON, Barry
"Poems Can Break Your Arm If They Want." [EngJ] (81:6) O 92, p. 93.
"Spirals." [Descant] (23:4/24:1, #78/79) Wint-Spr 92-93, p. 45-46.

845. BUTSON, Denver
"Dear Prophets." [Caliban] (11) 92, p. 84.
"From His Bed." [ChatR] (12:3) Spr 92, p. 44-45.
"Seven Analogies." [Caliban] (11) 92, p. 85.

846. BUTTERWORTH, D. S.
"Anniversary." [PoetL] (87:4) Wint 92-93, p. 33-34.
847. BUTTS, W. E.
"The Children's Poetry" (for Richard Martin). [Wind] (22:71) 92, p. 4-5.
848. BYARD, Olivia
"Girls on the Gower 1955." [Quarry] (41:1) Wint 92, p. 20.
849. BYER, Kathryn Stripling
"Before Dawn." [GreensboroR] (53) Wint 92-93, p. 32-33.
"Night Shade." [GeoR] (46:4) Wint 92, p. 763.
850. BYNNER, Witter
"The Summer Palace" (tr. of Chen Yuan). [Light] (2) Sum 92, p. 18.
851. BYRD, Joel
"Fenceposts." [GreensboroR] (52) Sum 92, p. 170.
852. BYRD, Sigman
"Bigfoot Happy Hour." [Ploughs] (18:4) Wint 92-93, p. 77.
"Diorama of the End of the Century I." [Ploughs] (18:4) Wint 92-93, p. 75.
"Diorama of the End of the Century II." [Ploughs] (18:4) Wint 92-93, p. 76.
853. BYRNE, Donald E., Jr.
"Peripheral Vision." [NegC] (12:3) 92, p. 56-57.
854. BYRNE, Edward
"Wisconsin Evening." [SycamoreR] (4:1) Wint 92, p. 41.
855. BYRON, Catherine
"Calling on Annie at Holly Hill." [MalR] (98) Spr 92, p. 64.
"Let-Down" (for Medbh McGuckian). [MalR] (98) Spr 92, p. 65.
856. CABACUNGAN, Darryl Keola
"Boys' Day Triptych." [ChamLR] (10/11) Spr-Fall 92, p. 49-50.
CABALLERO, José Molina
See MOLINA CABALLERO, José
857. CABALQUINTO, Luis
"Alignment." [Manoa] (4:1) Spr 92, p. 17.
858. CABLE, Gerald
"The Road to Cantwell." [AnotherCM] (23) Spr 92, p. 30-31.
CABRAL de MELO NETO, João
See NETO, João Cabral de Melo
859. CACCAVARI, Peter
"His Chest." [Elf] (2:1) Spr 92, p. 38.
860. CADDEL, Richard
"Charms & Curses." [WestCL] (26:1, #7) Spr 92, p. 30-31.
861. CADDY, David
"On the Deaths of Leigh and Adlem." [ChironR] (11:1) Spr 92, p. 14.
"Tonight I Want Diana and the Moon." [ChironR] (11:1) Spr 92, p. 14.
862. CADNUM, Michael
"Abundance." [MidwQ] (33:3) Spr 92, p. 309.
"Acacias." [MidwQ] (33:3) Spr 92, p. 310.
"The Army Has Taken Over the Airport" (Istanbul). [PacificR] (11) 92-93, p. 60-61.
"Cocktails by the River." [NewDeltaR] (8:1) Fall 90-Wint 91, p. 25.
"Controlled Burn." [Interim] (11:2) Fall-Wint 92-93, p. 14.
"Does at Sunset." [Footwork] 92, p. 97.
"The First Man to Live a Thousand Years." [WillowS] (30) Sum 92, p. 56-57.
"Flight." [PoetryNW] (33:4) Wint 92-93, p. 32.
"Lake George." [Wind] (22:71) 92, p. 6.
"Letter to a Ghost." [PoetryNW] (33:4) Wint 92-93, p. 31.
"The Lost." [PoetryNW] (33:4) Wint 92-93, p. 33.
"The Prodigal Son Among the Swine." [Interim] (11:2) Fall-Wint 92-93, p. 13.
"The Starling." [Wind] (22:71) 92, p. 6-7.
"The Two-Hundred Year-Old Foetus in the Rue Jacob." [WritersF] (18) 92, p. 146.
"Vigil" ("Fourteen-Year-Old Dancer" by Edgar Degas). [PoetryNW] (33:4) Wint 92 - 93, p. 30.
863. CADY, Barbara
"English Department Meeting" (Winner, Annual Free Verse Contest, 1991). [AnthNEW] (4) 92, p. 23.
CAEIRO, Alberto
See PESSOA, Fernando
864. CAFAGNA, Marcus
"Dybbuks." [Poetry] (160:1) Ap 92, p. 26-27.

865. CAGAN, Penny
"Temple Emanu-el." [BlackBR] (15) Spr-Sum 92, p. 11-12.
866. CAIRNS, Scott
"Dead Sea Bathers." [NewRep] (206:17) 27 Ap 92, p. 39.
"The Death of Penelope." [NewRep] (206:12) 23 Mr 92, p. 38.
"The Recovered Midrashim of Rabbi Sab" (Selections: 1-3). [CharR] (18:2) Fall 92, p. 81-82.
867. CAKS, Aleksandrs
"Young Woman with a Dog" (tr. by Inara Cedrins). [Trans] (26) Spr 92, p. 49-50.
868. CALABRESE, Lynda
"Richard Speaks from Buddha's Garden." [Crucible] (28) Fall 92, p. 55.
869. CALBERT, Cathleen
"Lunatic Snow." [PoetryE] (33) Spr 92, p. 17-18.
"School-yard." [Nat] (254:5) 10 F 92, p. 174.
870. CALDARA, Anna Maria
"To a Young Man Killed at Murfreesboro" (a town in Tennessee and the site of a Civil War battle in 1862). [NewYorkQ] (47) 92, p. 64.
871. CALDWELL, Lynn
"Dial-a-Prayer." [AntigR] (91) Fall 92, p. 36.
872. CALHOUN, Colleen
"Caught There." [ChironR] (11:4) Wint 92, p. 43.
"The Unicorn." [ChironR] (11:4) Wint 92, p. 45.
873. CALISCH, Richard
"The Songs of My Childhood." [Elf] (2:4) Wint 92, p. 29.
874. CALL, Jennifer
"Apocrypha." [WestHR] (46:1) Spr 92, p. 90-91.
"How Agassiz Taught Shaler." [WestHR] (46:1) Spr 92, p. 92.
875. CALL, Nancy
"To Julie: More Than Ten Years Later" (Winner, Annual Free Verse Contest, 1991). [AnthNEW] (4) 92, p. 16.
876. CALLEN, P. M.
"To the Little Brown Snake I Encountered in the Driveway of United Jersey Bank in the Meadowlands." [Outbr] (23) 92, p. 3-4.
877. CALVIN, T. (a pseudonym, 12 years old, submitted by Wm. A. Newman)
"---365--- -365-(6)Lea --365-." [PoetryUSA] (24) 92, p. 30-31.
878. CAM, Heather
"Je Ne Sais Pas." [Footwork] 92, p. 135.
"The Other Side." [Footwork] 92, p. 135.
879. CAMERON, Mary
"Correspondence." [PoetryC] (12:3/4) Jl 92, p. 27.
"Deer." [PoetryC] (12:3/4) Jl 92, p. 27.
"Flight." [PoetryC] (12:3/4) Jl 92, p. 27.
"Hunter." [PoetryC] (12:3/4) Jl 92, p. 27.
"Kaleidoscopes." [Dandel] (19:1) 92, p. 21.
"Katie." [Dandel] (19:1) 92, p. 20.
"Nineteen." [PoetryC] (12:3/4) Jl 92, p. 27.
"Search." [PoetryC] (12:3/4) Jl 92, p. 27.
"Wind Chimes." [Dandel] (19:1) 92, p. 22.
880. CAMILLO, Victor
"Bar Mitzvah in Iowa." [Vis] (38) 92, p. 11.
"Spring Comes to Iowa." [Footwork] 92, p. 85-86.
"The Waking Man of Spring." [Farm] (9:1) Spr-Sum 92, p. 16.
881. CAMMIADE, Denise
"Light Year." [MalR] (98) Spr 92, p. 84.
882. CAMPBELL, Barbara
"The Love Object." [SpoonRQ] (17:3/4) Sum-Fall 92, p. 63-65.
883. CAMPBELL, John (*See also* CAMPBELL, John R.)
"Delusion." [NowestR] (30:2) 92, p. 57.
"John O' the Woods." [NowestR] (30:2) 92, p. 56.
"Misreading Anna Akhmatova." [NowestR] (30:2) 92, p. 58.
"Notes Toward a Wild Domesticity." [NowestR] (30:2) 92, p. 53-55.
884. CAMPBELL, John R. (*See also* CAMPBELL, John)
"Prince Charles Lectures the Public on Architectural Character." [PoetryE] (33) Spr 92, p. 20.
"Sulphur." [PoetryE] (33) Spr 92, p. 19.

885. CAMPBELL, Mary Belle
"The Myth of Marsyus — an Old, Old Story." [Pembroke] (24) 92, p. 147-148.
886. CAMPION, Dan
"The Ballad of the 'Chez Mouquin'" (After the 1905 painting by Glackens in the Art Institute of Chicago). [Light] (3) Aut 92, p. 21.
"Home Remedy." [Light] (1) Spr 92, p. 25.
"Indoor Sports." [Light] (4) Wint 92-93, p. 11.
"Saccade." [Light] (1) Spr 92, p. 18.
"Still Life." [Light] (2) Sum 92, p. 13.
887. CAMPO, Rafael
"A Dying Art" (for Eve). [KenR] (NS 14:4) Fall 92, p. 1-2.
"He Interprets the Dream." [KenR] (NS 14:4) Fall 92, p. 3.
"A Medical Student Learns Love and Death." [KenR] (NS 14:4) Fall 92, p. 4.
"Our Country of Origin." [KenR] (NS 14:4) Fall 92, p. 3.
"Towards Curing AIDS." [KenR] (NS 14:4) Fall 92, p. 5.
"Translation." [KenR] (NS 14:4) Fall 92, p. 4.
"When Rafael Met Jorge." [KenR] (NS 14:4) Fall 92, p. 2.
888. CANELO, Pureza
"November" (tr. by Mark Smith-Soto). [InterPR] (18:1) Spr 92, p. 21, 23.
"Noviembre." [InterPR] (18:1) Spr 92, p. 20, 22.
889. CANNER, Niko
"Auguries." [HarvardA] (127:1) Fall 92, p. 10.
"The Emperor's Son." [HarvardA] (127:4 [i.e. 126:4?]) Sum 92, p. 17.
"Lines for a Witness." [HarvardA] (127:1) Fall 92, p. 10.
"Wittgenstein on Certainty, 1951." [HarvardA] (127:4 [i.e. 126:4?]) Sum 92, p. 27.
890. CANNON, Maureen
"Plant Chant." [Light] (1) Spr 92, p. 12.
"Quip Slip." [Light] (2) Sum 92, p. 11.
CANNON, Particia
See CANNON, Patricia
891. CANNON, Patricia
"Cow's Skull on Red" (Painting by Georgia O'Keefe [sic], 1931-36). [Kalliope] (14:3) 92, p. 74.
892. CANSEVER, Edip
"Table" (tr. by Richard Tillinghast). [Atlantic] (270:6) D 92, p. 81.
893. CANTALUPO, Charles
"Cathedral" (an excerpt from "WO/MAN"). [Talisman] (8) Spr 92, p. 133-134.
"Convergence." [Paint] (19:37) Spr 92, p. 18-19.
"An Unoccupied Graveyard." [Talisman] (9) Fall 92, p. 210-211.
894. CANTIRAKANTI
"Wanted: A Broom" (tr. by Martha Ann Selby and K. Paramasivam). [ChiR] (38:1/2) 92, p. 31.
895. CANTON y CANTON, Juan José
"Abandono de la Poesía." [Nuez] (4:12) 92, p. 27.
"Paréntesis." [Nuez] (4:12) 92, p. 27.
896. CANTOR, Ellen
"The Jazz Workshop, Boston, 1967" (for John Coltrane, 1926-1967). [GeoR] (46:4) Wint 92, p. 681-682.
897. CANTRELL, Charles
"Mythologies." [WillowR] (19) Spr 92, p. 18.
"Out In It" (Finalist, The Pablo Neruda Prize for Poetry). [Nimrod] (36:1) Fall-Wint 92, p. 53.
898. CANTWELL, Kevin
"Decolletage." [CimR] (99) Ap 92, p. 44-45.
"Southside City Cemetery." [AntR] (50:3) Sum 92, p. 512-514.
899. CAPES, Andrew
"A Civil Marriage." [Verse] (9:3) Wint 92, p. 146.
"Civilian Twilight." [Verse] (9:3) Wint 92, p. 146.
"The Courthouse Windows." [Verse] (9:3) Wint 92, p. 145.
"So Much a Stem." [Verse] (9:3) Wint 92, p. 145.
900. CAPONE, Janet / Giovanna
"Rape and Empowerment: Three Pictures." [SinW] (48) Wint 92-93, p. 117-118.
901. CAPPELLO, Rosemary
"For My Sister Bea." [Pearl] (15) Spr-Sum 92, p. 27.
902. CAPPELUTI, Jo-Anne
"Direction." [NewYorkQ] (48) 92, p. 106.

"Profession" (to Ruth, a fellow traveler). [NegC] (12:1/2) 92, p. 183.
903. CARDENAL, Ernesto
"Prayer for Marilyn Monroe" (tr. by John Samuel Tieman). [RiverS] (36) 92, p. 67 - 68.
904. CARDENAS, Georgina Herrera
"Reflections" (tr. by Betty Wilson). [LitR] (35:4) Sum 92, p. 450.
"Reflexiones." [LitR] (35:4) Sum 92, p. 590-591.
905. CARDENAS, Rene F.
"The Borrachon Tree of Antioquia." [SycamoreR] (4:2) Sum 92, p. 45-46.
906. CARDILLO, Joe
"Antidote." [RagMag] (10:1) 92, p. 19.
"Passing the Reservoir." [RagMag] (10:1) 92, p. 18.
907. CAREY, Barbara
"A Bird in the Hand." [PoetryC] (12:2) Ap 92, p. 4.
"Bread on the Water." [PoetryC] (12:2) Ap 92, p. 4.
"The Reach of the Heart." [PoetryC] (12:2) Ap 92, p. 4.
"When Did the Gods Begin to Fail Us." [PoetryC] (12:2) Ap 92, p. 4.
908. CAREY, Michael
"Burning Barrel." [OnTheBus] (4:2/5:1, #10/11) 92, p. 75.
"A Different Slant of Light." [US1] (26/27) 92, p. 24.
"Early Crime in Fremont County" (found poem). [Plain] (12:3) Spr 92, p. 7.
"In Saecula Saeculorum." [Plain] (13:1) Fall 92, p. 26-27.
"The Reason for Poetry." [OnTheBus] (4:2/5:1, #10/11) 92, p. 75-76.
909. CAREY, Tom
"Parliaments." [Shiny] (7/8) 92, p. 114.
"Plain air" (For James Schuyler). [Shiny] (7/8) 92, p. 113.
910. CARIELLO, Matthew
"Alphabet." [ArtfulD] (22/23) 92, p. 137.
911. CARLILE, Henry
"For a Fisherman" (Raymond Carver, 1938-1988). [Crazy] (42) Spr 92, p. 50-55.
"Mercy." [Crazy] (42) Spr 92, p. 47-49.
912. CARLIN, Mike
"Exiled." [BlackBR] (16) Wint-Spr 92-93, p. 32.
"Racing." [BlackBR] (16) Wint-Spr 92-93, p. 31.
913. CARLIN, Vuyelwa
"Ash." [GettyR] (5:2) Spr 92, p. 329.
"The Blindness." [GettyR] (5:2) Spr 92, p. 330.
"Crazy Girl Candy." [Poetry] (160:1) Ap 92, p. 21.
"The Lepers of Languedoc." [Stand] (33:3) Sum 92, p. 28.
914. CARLISLE, S. E.
"Nocturnal on the Winter Solstice." [Agni] (35) 92, p. 180.
915. CARLISLE, Thomas John
"Missed the Most." [ChrC] (109:20) 17-24 Je 92, p. 618.
916. CARLSEN, Ioanna
"Love's Interest." [Poetry] (160:4) Jl 92, p. 200.
"Weeping." [ManhatPR] (14) [92?], p. 48.
917. CARLSON, Barbara (Barbara Siegel)
"Net of Jewels." [PassN] (13:2) Wint 92, p. 20.
"Rosh Hashanah." [SpoonRQ] (17:3/4) Sum-Fall 92, p. 36-37.
"Self-Love" (After Chagall). [MidAR] (13:2) 92, p. 33-35.
"Suburban Education." [Agni] (35) 92, p. 242-244.
918. CARLSON, Burton L.
"The Reverend J. W. Burton's Wife." [CapeR] (27:2) Fall 92, p. 4.
919. CARLSON, Michael
"Another Country." [ShadowP] (3) 92, p. 43.
"Crystals in Their Hearts." [ShadowP] (3) 92, p. 39.
"Dawn, Belsize Park." [ShadowP] (3) 92, p. 42.
"Forgetfulness." [ShadowP] (3) 92, p. 40.
"Wave." [ShadowP] (3) 92, p. 41.
"Winter on the Lake." [ShadowP] (3) 92, p. 38.
920. CARLSON, R. S.
"Clear Cut." [PoetL] (87:1) Spr 92, p. 41-42.
"Creche." [CapeR] (27:1) Spr 92, p. 18.
"In the Distance." [HolCrit] (29:4) O 92, p. 15.
"Indian Bride Lake." [CapeR] (27:1) Spr 92, p. 16-17.
"Shelf Life." [BlackBR] (16) Wint-Spr 92-93, p. 39.

921. CARLSON, Thomas C.
"Letter to My Mother" (tr. of Mircea Dinescu). [Chelsea] (53) 92, p. 80.
"Rusting" (tr. of Mircea Dinescu). [Chelsea] (53) 92, p. 80.
"The Transfiguration" (tr. of Mircea Dinescu). [Chelsea] (53) 92, p. 81.

922. CARLSON-BRADLEY, Martha
"What the Dead Man Wants." [CarolQ] (45:1) Fall 92, p. 50.

CARMEN, Aisha Eshe
See ESHE, Aisha

CARMEN, Marilyn Elain
See ESHE, Aisha

923. CARNERO, Guillermo
"Oscar Wilde in Paris" (tr. by Michael L. Johnson). [WebR] (16) Fall 92, p. 14.

924. CARNEVALE, Robert
"Patsy Morrocco." [Footwork] 92, p. 97.

925. CARNEY, Gene
"Country." [Spitball] (41) Sum 92, p. 23-24.
"Horsehide." [Spitball] (40) Spr 92, p. 43.
"The Lip." [Spitball] (42) Fall 92, p. 42-43.
"Rajah." [Spitball] (41) Sum 92, p. 22-23.

926. CARNEY, Jeanne
"Soul Salad." [SingHM] (20) 92, p. 47.

927. CARNEY, Rob
"Strange Meadowlark / Man, Like Wiggsville, You Really Grooved Me with Those Nutty Changes." [BellArk] (8:2) Mr-Ap 92, p. 3.

928. CARPENTER, Bogdana
"About Mr. Cogito's Two Legs" (tr. of Zbigniew Herbert, w. John Carpenter). [ParisR]] (34:124) Fall 92, p. 221-222.
"An Answer" (tr. of Zbigniew Herbert, w. John Carpenter). [NewYRB] (39:1/2) 16 Ja 92, p. 17.
"Balconies" (tr. of Zbigniew Herbert, w. John Carpenter). [Salm] (93) Wint 92, p. 130-131.
"Farewell to the City" (tr. of Zbigniew Herbert, w. John Carpenter). [NewYorker] (68:13) 18 My 92, p. 64.
"How We Were Introduced" (for perfidious protectors, tr. of Zbigniew Herbert, w. John Carpenter). [Salm] (93) Wint 92, p. 139-140.
"In a Studio" (tr. of Zbigniew Herbert, w. John Carpenter). [Salm] (93) Wint 92, p. 132-133.
"A Journey" (tr. of Zbigniew Herbert, w. John Carpenter). [Salm] (93) Wint 92, p. 126-127.
"Late Autumnal Poem of Mr. Cogito Destined for Women's Magazines" (tr. of Zbigniew Herbert, w. John Carpenter). [ParisR]] (34:124) Fall 92, p. 220.
"Mr. Cogito and a Poet of a Certain Age" (tr. of Zbigniew Herbert, w. John Carpenter). [NewYorker] (67:51) 10 F 92, p. 38.
"Mr. Cogito and Pure Thought" (tr. of Zbigniew Herbert, w. John Carpenter). [ParisR]] (34:124) Fall 92, p. 219-220.
"Mr. Cogito and the Pearl" (tr. of Zbigniew Herbert, w. John Carpenter). [ParisR]] (34:124) Fall 92, p. 222.
"Mr. Cogito Encounters a Statuette of the Great Mother in the Louvre" (tr. of Zbigniew Herbert, w. John Carpenter). [ParisR]] (34:124) Fall 92, p. 223.
"Mr. Cogito Looks at His Face in the Mirror" (tr. of Zbigniew Herbert, w. John Carpenter). [ParisR]] (34:124) Fall 92, p. 224-225.
"My City" (tr. of Zbigniew Herbert, w. John Carpenter). [Salm] (93) Wint 92, p. 129 - 130.
"Old Prometheus" (tr. of Zbigniew Herbert, w. John Carpenter). [ParisR]] (34:124) Fall 92, p. 216.
"Prayer of the Old Men" (tr. of Zbigniew Herbert, w. John Carpenter). [NewYorker] (68:40) 23 N 92, p. 68.
"Request" (tr. of Zbigniew Herbert, w. John Carpenter). [Salm] (93) Wint 92, p. 141 - 142.
"A Small Bird" (tr. of Zbigniew Herbert, w. John Carpenter). [Salm] (93) Wint 92, p. 134-135.
"Song of the Drum" (tr. of Zbigniew Herbert, w. John Carpenter). [Salm] (93) Wint 92, p. 136-137.
"Speculations on the Subject of Barabbas" (tr. of Zbigniew Herbert, w. John Carpenter). [ParisR]] (34:124) Fall 92, p. 215-216.

"Thorns and Roses" (tr. of Zbigniew Herbert, w. John Carpenter). [Salm] (93) Wint 92, p. 128.
"Those Who Lost" (tr. of Zbigniew Herbert, w. John Carpenter). [ParisR]] (34:124) Fall 92, p. 217.
"The Troubles of a Little Creator" (tr. of Zbigniew Herbert, w. John Carpenter). [Salm] (93) Wint 92, p. 137-139.
"Wagon" (tr. of Zbigniew Herbert, w. John Carpenter). [NewYorker] (68:32) 28 S 92, p. 42.
"We Fall Asleep on Words" (tr. of Zbigniew Herbert, w. John Carpenter). [NewYRB] (39:1/2) 16 Ja 92, p. 17.
"Wit Stwosz: Madonna Falling Asleep" (tr. of Zbigniew Herbert, w. John Carpenter). [ParisR]] (34:124) Fall 92, p. 218.

929. CARPENTER, Carol
"The Cats." [Plain] (13:1) Fall 92, p. 35.
"Diary of a Night Watchman." [QW] (35) Sum-Fall 92, p. 116.
"To My Daughter on a Fine Fall Day." [Elf] (2:3) Fall 92, p. 34.

930. CARPENTER, J. D.
"Shakespearean Garden." [CanLit] (135) Wint 92, p. 79.
"Window Display" (Thuna Herbalist, Toronto). [CanLit] (135) Wint 92, p. 48-49.

931. CARPENTER, John
"About Mr. Cogito's Two Legs" (tr. of Zbigniew Herbert, w. Bogdana Carpenter). [ParisR]] (34:124) Fall 92, p. 221-222.
"An Answer" (tr. of Zbigniew Herbert, w. Bogdana Carpenter). [NewYRB] (39:1/2) 16 Ja 92, p. 17.
"Balconies" (tr. of Zbigniew Herbert, w. Bogdana Carpenter). [Salm] (93) Wint 92, p. 130-131.
"Farewell to the City" (tr. of Zbigniew Herbert, w. Bogdana Carpenter). [NewYorker] (68:13) 18 My 92, p. 64.
"How We Were Introduced" (for perfidious protectors, tr. of Zbigniew Herbert, w. Bogdana Carpenter). [Salm] (93) Wint 92, p. 139-140.
"In a Studio" (tr. of Zbigniew Herbert, w. Bogdana Carpenter). [Salm] (93) Wint 92, p. 132-133.
"A Journey" (tr. of Zbigniew Herbert, w. Bogdana Carpenter). [Salm] (93) Wint 92, p. 126-127.
"Late Autumnal Poem of Mr. Cogito Destined for Women's Magazines" (tr. of Zbigniew Herbert, w. Bogdana Carpenter). [ParisR]] (34:124) Fall 92, p. 220.
"Mr. Cogito and a Poet of a Certain Age" (tr. of Zbigniew Herbert, w. Bogdana Carpenter). [NewYorker] (67:51) 10 F 92, p. 38.
"Mr. Cogito and Pure Thought" (tr. of Zbigniew Herbert, w. Bogdana Carpenter). [ParisR]] (34:124) Fall 92, p. 219-220.
"Mr. Cogito and the Pearl" (tr. of Zbigniew Herbert, w. Bogdana Carpenter). [ParisR]] (34:124) Fall 92, p. 222.
"Mr. Cogito Encounters a Statuette of the Great Mother in the Louvre" (tr. of Zbigniew Herbert, w. Bogdana Carpenter). [ParisR]] (34:124) Fall 92, p. 223.
"Mr. Cogito Looks at His Face in the Mirror" (tr. of Zbigniew Herbert, w. Bogdana Carpenter). [ParisR]] (34:124) Fall 92, p. 224-225.
"My City" (tr. of Zbigniew Herbert, w. Bogdana Carpenter). [Salm] (93) Wint 92, p. 129-130.
"Old Prometheus" (tr. of Zbigniew Herbert, w. Bogdana Carpenter). [ParisR]] (34:124) Fall 92, p. 216.
"Prayer of the Old Men" (tr. of Zbigniew Herbert, w. Bogdana Carpenter). [NewYorker] (68:40) 23 N 92, p. 68.
"Request" (tr. of Zbigniew Herbert, w. Bogdana Carpenter). [Salm] (93) Wint 92, p. 141-142.
"A Small Bird" (tr. of Zbigniew Herbert, w. Bogdana Carpenter). [Salm] (93) Wint 92, p. 134-135.
"Song of the Drum" (tr. of Zbigniew Herbert, w. Bogdana Carpenter). [Salm] (93) Wint 92, p. 136-137.
"Speculations on the Subject of Barabbas" (tr. of Zbigniew Herbert, w. Bogdana Carpenter). [ParisR]] (34:124) Fall 92, p. 215-216.
"Thorns and Roses" (tr. of Zbigniew Herbert, w. Bogdana Carpenter). [Salm] (93) Wint 92, p. 128.
"Those Who Lost" (tr. of Zbigniew Herbert, w. Bogdana Carpenter). [ParisR]] (34:124) Fall 92, p. 217.
"The Troubles of a Little Creator" (tr. of Zbigniew Herbert, w. Bogdana Carpenter). [Salm] (93) Wint 92, p. 137-139.

"Wagon" (tr. of Zbigniew Herbert, w. Bogdana Carpenter). [NewYorker] (68:32) 28 S 92, p. 42.
"We Fall Asleep on Words" (tr. of Zbigniew Herbert, w. Bogdana Carpenter). [NewYRB] (39:1/2) 16 Ja 92, p. 17.
"Wit Stwosz: Madonna Falling Asleep" (tr. of Zbigniew Herbert, w. Bogdana Carpenter). [ParisR]] (34:124) Fall 92, p. 218.

932. CARPENTER, Linda
"Morgue." [Event] (21:2) Sum 92, p. 59.
"Suicide Note." [Event] (21:2) Sum 92, p. 58.

933. CARPENTER, Lucas
"Anonymous Poet on the Nature of Belief." [ChatR] (12:3) Spr 92, p. 13-14.
"Ethnic Brain Dance." [LullwaterR] (3:3) Sum 92, p. 47-49.

934. CARPENTER, Sandra
"Break-up at Daybreak." [Writer] (105:12) D 92, p. 20.

935. CARPENTER, Tom
"The Grass Fire." [WritersF] (18) 92, p. 145.

936. CARPENTER, William
"A Boy with His Final Dinosaur" (to a picture by Robert Shetterly). [BelPoJ] (42:3) Spr 92, p. 33.
"Cabin Fever" (to a picture by Robert Shetterly). [BelPoJ] (42:3) Spr 92, p. 15.
"A Homeless Person's Halloween Costume" (to a picture by Robert Shetterly). [BelPoJ] (42:3) Spr 92, p. 19.
"Leaving Home" (to a picture by Robert Shetterly). [BelPoJ] (42:3) Spr 92, p. 16.
"The Man Who Wants More" (to a picture by Robert Shetterly). [BelPoJ] (42:3) Spr 92, p. 30.
"Metamorphosis" (to a picture by Robert Shetterly). [BelPoJ] (42:3) Spr 92, p. 25.
"The Necessity of Faith" (to a picture by Robert Shetterly). [BelPoJ] (42:3) Spr 92, p. 35.
"Power of Concentration" (to a picture by Robert Shetterly). [BelPoJ] (42:3) Spr 92, p. 21.
"Reasoning with the Tree" (to a picture by Robert Shetterly). [BelPoJ] (42:3) Spr 92, p. 22-23.
"Setting It Right" (to a picture by Robert Shetterly). [BelPoJ] (42:3) Spr 92, p. 29.
"Song of Childhood" (to a picture by Robert Shetterly). [BelPoJ] (42:3) Spr 92, p. 36.
"Speaking Fire at Stones" (poems to pictures by Robert Shetterly). [BelPoJ] (42:3) Spr 92, p. 9-36.
"Spring" (to a picture by Robert Shetterly). [BelPoJ] (42:3) Spr 92, p. 13.
"Still" (to a picture by Robert Shetterly). [BelPoJ] (42:3) Spr 92, p. 27.
"There's This Poet Going Round, Speaking Fire at Stones" (to a picture by Robert Shetterly). [BelPoJ] (42:3) Spr 92, p. 11.

937. CARPENTER, Yvonne
"The Parcel." [Grain] (20:3) Fall 92, p. 76.
"White October." [Grain] (20:3) Fall 92, p. 77.

938. CARPER, Thomas
"Creation." [Sparrow] (59) S 92, p. 10.
"Doing Dishes." [Sparrow] (59) S 92, p. 12.
"The Dump Man." [Sparrow] (59) S 92, p. 11.
"Kollam." [Poetry] (160:5) Ag 92, p. 282.
"The Liberation of Birds." [Sparrow] (59) S 92, p. 14.
"A Picture of the Reverend's Family with the Child of One." [Sparrow] (59) S 92, p. 11.
"Posthumous Sonnet." [Sparrow] (59) S 92, p. 13.
"Regrets: Sonnet XXXI." [Sparrow] (59) S 92, p. 12.
"A Sonnet for Hélène." [Sparrow] (59) S 92, p. 13.

939. CARR, Dan
"I Have Been a Wave of the Sea" (The tidal rip). [ConnPR] (11:1) 92, p. 29-30.

940. CARR, Peggy
"Macho Man." [LitR] (35:4) Sum 92, p. 545.
"When He Went Away." [LitR] (35:4) Sum 92, p. 546-547.

941. CARR, Richard
"Escape." [Contact] (10:62/63/64) Fall 91-Spr 92, p. 61.
"The Mothers of Civilization." [Plain] (13:1) Fall 92, p. 24.

942. CARRADICE, Phil
"An Ode for Billy Joe." [Bogg] (65) 92, p. 15.

943. CARREL, Ann
"Catching." [ThRiPo] (39/40) 92-93, p. 27.

"The Treacherous Death of Jesse James." [ThRiPo] (39/40) 92-93, p. 28.
944. CARRETO, Héctor
"The House at 5 Allende Street" (tr. by Reginald Gibbons). [TriQ] (85) Fall 92, p. 273-274.
945. CARRIER, Warren
"To Robert Orth, Burma, 1944." [Northeast] (5:6) Spr 92, p. 12.
"View from the Top." [Northeast] (5:6) Spr 92, p. 11.
946. CARRILLO, Albino
"Clenched by the Gospel of Wind." [Caliban] (11) 92, p. 119.
"Weather Map." [Caliban] (11) 92, p. 120.
947. CARRINO, Michael
"Corvette." [HayF] (11) Fall-Wint 92, p. 99-100.
"Cugeens." [PassN] (13:1) Sum 92, p. 4.
948. CARROLL, Anthony
"10:30, Sunday A.M." [NewYorkQ] (49) 92, p. 79.
949. CARROLL, Rhoda
"Those Christmas Lights, That Trompe L'Oeil Ridge" (corrected reprint of second stanza from Sum-Fall 91). [GreenMR] (NS 5:2) Spr-Sum 92, p. 114.
950. CARRUTH, Hayden
"Bennington Poem." [SouthernHR] (26:4) Fall 92, p. 349.
CARRUTH, J. McLaughlin
See McLAUGHLIN-CARRUTH, J.
951. CARRUTH, Joe-Anne
"Gall." [PoetryE] (33) Spr 92, p. 22.
"In the Heat of Things." [PoetryE] (33) Spr 92, p. 21.
952. CARSON, Anne
"The Brainsex Paintings" (tr. of Mimnermos). [Raritan] (11:3) Wint 92, p. 3-5.
"Carmina" (Selections: 15 poems, tr. of Gaius Valerius Catullus). [AmerPoR] (21:1) Ja-F 92, p. 15-16.
953. CARSON, Jo Ellen
"To a Great Aunt." [Lactuca] (16) Ag 92, p. 12.
954. CARTER, Jared
"Cipher." [Vis] (38) 92, p. 27.
"Panorama." [NewL] (58:3) Spr 92, p. 5-7.
"Reminiscence" (A Suite for piano & voice). [PaintedB] (45) 92, p. 48-55.
"Stars in Daylight." [Vis] (39) 92, p. 25-27.
"Summit" (for Don Miller). [MidwQ] (33:4) Sum 92, p. 407-408.
955. CARTER, Jimmy
"Always a Reckoning." [NoDaQ] (60:1) Wint 92, p. 30.
"Life on a Killer Submarine." [NoDaQ] (60:1) Wint 92, p. 28.
"Of My Father's Cancer and His Dreams." [NoDaQ] (60:1) Wint 92, p. 31.
"The Pasture Gate: To A.D. and Johnny." [NoDaQ] (60:1) Wint 92, p. 29.
"Rachel." [NewL] (58:4) 92, p. 51-53.
"Some Things I Love." [NewL] (58:4) 92, p. 50.
"With Words We Learn to Hate." [NewL] (58:4) 92, p. 49.
956. CARTER, John
"Africa." [Lactuca] (16) Ag 92, p. 5-7.
"Ode on the Death of Night." [Lactuca] (16) Ag 92, p. 4.
"Stranger in Town." [Lactuca] (16) Ag 92, p. 2-3.
957. CARTER, Kim
"Chewing Gum." [Quarry] (41:2) Spr 92, p. 17-18.
"Walking Alone at Night." [Quarry] (41:2) Spr 92, p. 18.
958. CARTER, Michael
"Eric." [BrooklynR] (9) 92, p. 69.
CARTER, Roberta Rennert
See RENNERT-CARTER, Roberta
CARTERET, Mark de
See DeCARTERET, Mark
959. CARTWRIGHT, Keith
"Brer Bouki Builds a Banjo." [Shen] (42:2) Sum 92, p. 44-45.
960. CARVER, Raymond
"Colibrí" (para Tess, tr. by Harry Morales). [Nuez] (4:10/11) 92, p. 24.
961. CASEBEER, Edwin F.
"Way to Go." [HopewellR] (4) 92, p. 31.
962. CASEY, Philip
"Starling." [Stand] (33:2) Spr 92, p. 101.

963. CASSELLS, Cyrus
"The Hurricane" (Culebra Island, Puerto Rico, 1989). [Agni] (35) 92, p. 245-246.
964. CASSELMAN, Barry
"Certain Aromas." [AnotherCM] (23) Spr 92, p. 32.
965. CASSIAN, Nina
"Horizon" (tr. by Eva Feiler). [Trans] (26) Spr 92, p. 76.
"It Can't Be Otherwise" (tr. by Eva Feiler). [Trans] (26) Spr 92, p. 75.
"Point of View" (tr. by Eva Feiler). [Trans] (26) Spr 92, p. 75.
966. CASSITY, Turner
"At the Palace of Fine Arts." [Poetry] (159:4) Ja 92, p. 211.
"Meaner Than a Junkyard Dog, or, Turner's Evil Twin." [Poetry] (159:4) Ja 92, p. 212.
"Monumental Is More Than a Question of Scale." [Poetry] (159:4) Ja 92, p. 209-210.
967. CASTANON, Ana
"Deep-Seated Comfort." [SinW] (47) Sum-Fall 92, p. 77.
968. CASTEDO, Elena
"Did Franco Die?" [NewL] (58:4) 92, p. 143-145.
969. CASTERA, Georges
"Mise en Demeure." [Callaloo] (15:2) Spr 92, p. 532.
"Notice" (tr. by Carrol F. Coates). [Callaloo] (15:2) Spr 92, p. 531.
970. CASTILLA, Leopoldo
"La Araña." [Ometeca] (2:2) 91 [published 92], p. 25.
"Ecuación." [Ometeca] (2:2) 91 [published 92], p. 27.
"El Mutante." [Ometeca] (2:2) 91 [published 92], p. 26.
971. CASTILLO, Arnulfo
"A la Virgen de Guadalupe: Declamación." [BilingR] (17:2) My-Ag 92, p. 122-123.
"Al Sagrado Misterio: Declamación." [BilingR] (17:2) My-Ag 92, p. 116-117.
"El Arbol Frondoso: Alabado" (Salutación al amanecer). [BilingR] (17:2) My-Ag 92, p. 124.
"Arrullamiento del Niño Dios: Arrullo." [BilingR] (17:2) My-Ag 92, p. 117-118.
"Declamación a María y Nacimiento del Divino Verbo: Alabado." [BilingR] (17:2) My-Ag 92, p. 118.
"Levantamiento del Niño Dios: Alabado." [BilingR] (17:2) My-Ag 92, p. 113.
"Mi Abogada: Alabado." [BilingR] (17:2) My-Ag 92, p. 124-125.
"El Paraíso Terrenal: Declamación" (Coloquio). [BilingR] (17:2) My-Ag 92, p. 113 - 114.
"Recitación a Mi Madrecita: Alabado" (Salutación al amanecer). [BilingR] (17:2) My-Ag 92, p. 122.
"Recitación de Noche Buena al Niño Dios: Alabado." [BilingR] (17:2) My-Ag 92, p. 115-116.
"Santa Navidad: Religious Canción." [BilingR] (17:2) My-Ag 92, p. 121.
"La Venida del Angel con los Pastores: Declamación." [BilingR] (17:2) My-Ag 92, p. 115.
"Virgen Soberana: Alabado." [BilingR] (17:2) My-Ag 92, p. 123.
"Virgencita de Mi Barrio: Imploración." [BilingR] (17:2) My-Ag 92, p. 119-120.
"Virgencita de San Juan: Imploración." [BilingR] (17:2) My-Ag 92, p. 118-119.
"La Visita de los Tres Reyes Magos al Redentor: Declamación" (coloquio). [BilingR] (17:2) My-Ag 92, p. 120-121.
972. CASTILLO, Jeanette
"My Contribution." [SingHM] (20) 92, p. 77-78.
973. CASTILLO, Ricardo
"Ode to Feeling Like It" (tr. by Reginald Gibbons). [TriQ] (85) Fall 92, p. 376-377.
974. CASTLE, Luanne
"Hemmed In." [13thMoon] (10:1/2) 92, p. 26.
"Pearl Diving off Mikura Jima." [13thMoon] (10:1/2) 92, p. 27.
975. CASTLEMAN, David
"Whose Hand Maintains America the Beautiful?" [Gypsy] (18) 92, p. 121-122.
CASTRO, Tania Diaz
See DIAZ CASTRO, Tania
976. CASWELL, Donald
"Discouraging Words." [SoCoast] (13) Je 93 [i.e. 92], p. 4-5.
977. CATALANO, Gary
"The Behaviour of Trucks." [Footwork] 92, p. 99.
"The Desertion." [Footwork] 92, p. 99.
"Silver and Gold." [Footwork] 92, p. 99.

978. CATES, Ed
"Masters of Balance." [Noctiluca] (1:1) Spr 92, p. 35.
979. CATHERINE, Barbara
"Billy Brackee." [Bogg] (65) 92, p. 48-49.
980. CATHERS, Ken
"Childhood." [Arc] (29) Aut 92, p. 40.
"A First Time." [Arc] (29) Aut 92, p. 38-39.
981. CATHERWOOD, Michael R.
"The Clean Game." [Plain] (12:3) Spr 92, p. 10.
"The Crap Game." [Plain] (12:3) Spr 92, p. 11.
982. CATINA, Ray
"Shooting the Breeze." [Parting] (5:1) Sum 92, p. 33.
"Tour of Duty." [Parting] (5:1) Sum 92, p. 39.
983. CATLIN, Alan
"Chappie's." [SlipS] (12) 92, p. 32.
"Closing Time." [SlipS] (12) 92, p. 32-33.
"Contacts." [WormR] (32:1, #125) 92, p. 17-18.
"A Double Vodka Martian." [Lactuca] (15) Mr 92, p. 64.
"I Go Out Alot." [MoodySI] (27) Spr 92, p. 27.
"I Was Watching Gabby." [WormR] (32:1, #125) 92, p. 20.
"Poster Child from Hell." [WormR] (32:1, #125) 92, p. 17.
"She Looked As If Starring." [WormR] (32:1, #125) 92, p. 19.
"The Spring of Rickey Henderson's Discontent." [WormR] (32:1, #125) 92, p. 20.
"Sub Shop Kama Sutra." [WormR] (32:1, #125) 92, p. 18-19.
"Working Hard on 10 to 15." [WormR] (32:1, #125) 92, p. 19.
984. CATTAFI, Bartolo
"Fibre" (tr. by Ruth Feldman and Brian Swann). [Stand] (33:4) Aut 92, p. 111.
985. CATULLUS, Gaius Valerius
"Carmina" (Selections: 15 poems, tr. by Anne Carson). [AmerPoR] (21:1) Ja-F 92, p. 15-16.
986. CAUDILL, Carla
"Angels' Abode" (clue from a crossword puzzle). [HopewellR] (4) 92, p. 16.
987. CAUFIELD, Tom
"Just the Right Speed." [WormR] (32:1, #125) 92, p. 13-14.
"Today Is." [WormR] (32:1, #125) 92, p. 13.
"Tough Bitch." [ChironR] (11:2) Sum 92, p. 29.
"Waiting on the Goddamn Bus." [WormR] (32:1, #125) 92, p. 14.
988. CAULFIELD, Carlota
"Angel Dust" (2 selections, tr. by Carol Maier). [Luz] (2) S 92, p. 20-24.
"Polvo de Angel / Angel Dust" (2 selections). [Luz] (2) S 92, p. 20-24.
989. CAULFIELD, Edward
"The Saintly Cigar." [Light] (2) Sum 92, p. 13.
990. CAVAFY, Constantine (Constantine P.)
"Ithaca" (tr. by Rae Dalven). [CumbPR] (11:2) Spr 92, p. 58-59.
991. CAVALCANTI, Guido
"You, who through my eyes reached to my heart" ("Two Views of Courtly Love," tr. by Felix Stefanile). [Sparrow] (59) S 92, p. 15.
992. CAVALIERI, Grace
"End of an Age." [PoetL] (87:4) Wint 92-93, p. 40.
"The Lavender Night." [US1] (26/27) 92, p. 21.
993. CAVANAGH, Clare
"Maybe All This" (tr. of Wislawa Szymborska, w. Stanislaw Baranczak). [NewYorker] (68:43) 14 D 92, p. 94.
"One Version of Events" (tr. of Wislawa Szymborska, w. Stanislaw Baranczak). [ManhatR] (6:2) Fall 92, p. 43-46.
994. CAVANAUGH, William
"Kisses." [HopewellR] (4) 92, p. 32.
995. CAVIS, Ella
"Bag Lady." [ManhatPR] (14) [92?], p. 7.
"Cedar Key, Florida." [SmPd] (29:3, #86) Fall 92, p. 33.
"Letter to Emily Dickinson." [ManhatPR] (14) [92?], p. 7.
996. CAWS, Ian
"Stepney Morning." [Stand] (33:2) Spr 92, p. 145.
"The Vigil." [SoCoast] (13) Je 93 [i.e. 92], p. 21.
997. CAWS, Mary Ann
"Frequency" (tr. of Rene Char, w. Patricia Terry). [Pequod] (34) 92, p. 183.

"In Love" (tr. of Rene Char, w. Patricia Terry). [Pequod] (34) 92, p. 182.
"With a Free Scythe" (tr. of Rene Char, w. Patricia Terry). [Pequod] (34) 92, p. 184.

998. CAY, Marilyn
"Hog's Head." [Grain] (20:3) Fall 92, p. 63.
"Seeding Time." [Grain] (20:3) Fall 92, p. 69.

999. CAYLE
"The Ax of Love." [NegC] (12:3) 92, p. 58.

1000. CAYLOR, Duane K.
"Lovers' Leap, Vernon County, Wisconsin." [MidwQ] (34:1) Aut 92, p. 61-62.

1001. CEASER, R. Lance
"Guilt." [PraF] (13:4, #61) Wint 92-93, p. 47.
"Spring-Loaded Dog." [PraF] (13:4, #61) Wint 92-93, p. 46.

1002. CECIL, Richard
"Allegory Detour." [Crazy] (42) Spr 92, p. 7-9.
"Bay Cruise." [SouthernR] (28:2) Spr, Ap 92, p. 285-287.
"The Exstasie." [Crazy] (42) Spr 92, p. 13-15.
"The Fall." [NoDaQ] (60:1) Wint 92, p. 66-68.
"Family Romance." [Crazy] (42) Spr 92, p. 18.
"Life Is Like a Mountain Railway." [Crazy] (42) Spr 92, p. 16-17.
"Night Walk in Time of War." [SouthernR] (28:2) Spr, Ap 92, p. 287-288.
"Second Honeymoon." [HopewellR] (4) 92, p. 24.
"The Tao of Winter." [HopewellR] (4) 92, p. 17.
"Thanatopsis." [Crazy] (42) Spr 92, p. 10-12.

1003. CEDERING, Siv
"Country Music." [GeoR] (46:4) Wint 92, p. 692-693.

1004. CEDRINS, Inara
"Young Woman with a Dog" (tr. of Aleksandrs Caks). [Trans] (26) Spr 92, p. 49-50.

1005. CELAC, Sergiu
"Cats of the Vatican" (tr. of Mircea Dinescu, w. Adam J. Sorkin). [ArtfulD] (22/23) 92, p. 39.

1006. CELAN, Paul
"At the white phylacteries" (tr. by Luitgard N. Wundheiler). [PartR] (59:2) Spr 92, p. 265.
"Corroded by the undreamed" (tr. by Luitgard N. Wundheiler). [PartR] (59:2) Spr 92, p. 264.
"Flower" (tr. by Luitgard N. Wundheiler). [PartR] (59:2) Spr 92, p. 263.
"In the Air" (tr. by Michael Hamburger). [Stand] (33:4) Aut 92, p. 86.
"Pale filaments of suns" (tr. by Luitgard N. Wundheiler). [PartR] (59:2) Spr 92, p. 264.
"Threadsuns" (Selections: 18 poems, being the complete fourth cycle, tr. by Pierre Joris). [Sulfur] (12:1, #30) Spr 92, p. 36-45.
"With their masts singing earthwards" (tr. by Luitgard N. Wundheiler). [PartR] (59:2) Spr 92, p. 264.

1007. CELAYA, Gabriel
"Porque vivimos a golpe" (tr. by Paco Ibañez). [Areíto] (3:10/11) Abril 92, p. 78.

1008. CELESTINE, Alfred
"The Letters and Numbers of Straw." [JamesWR] (9:3) Spr 92, p. 3.

1009. CERNUDA, Luis
"Impression of Exile" (tr. by Hardie St. Martin). [Trans] (26) Spr 92, p. 43-44.

1010. CERULLI, Francette B.
"Kinds of Murder." [NegC] (12:3) 92, p. 59-60.

1011. CERVANTES, Lorna Dee
"Blue Full Moon in Witch." [Americas] (20:3/4) Fall-Wint 92, p. 234.
"The Captive's Verses" (after Neruda). [Americas] (20:3/4) Fall-Wint 92, p. 237.
"From the Cables of Genocide." [Americas] (20:3/4) Fall-Wint 92, p. 235.
"On Love and Hunger." [Americas] (20:3/4) Fall-Wint 92, p. 236.
"The Poet Is Served Her Papers." [Americas] (20:3/4) Fall-Wint 92, p. 233.

1012. CERVENCIKOVA, Silvia
"For Emily Dickinson" (tr. of Margita Dobrovicová). [PraS] (66:4) Wint 92, p. 24.
"I Am Allowed" (tr. of Margita Dobrovicová). [PraS] (66:4) Wint 92, p. 21.
"The Nights" (tr. of Margita Dobrovicová). [PraS] (66:4) Wint 92, p. 20.
"X X X: Eve was whispering" (tr. of Margita Dobrovicová). [PraS] (66:4) Wint 92, p. 22-23.
"X X X: The cyclist was quick in taking off" (tr. of Margita Dobrovicová). [PraS] (66:4) Wint 92, p. 21.

"X X X: The deep stars, the empty strings" (tr. of Margita Dobrovicová). [PraS] (66:4) Wint 92, p. 22.
"X X X: The station loudspeaker did not work" (tr. of Margita Dobrovicová). [PraS] (66:4) Wint 92, p. 23.

1013. CERVO, Nathan
"Death Everlasting." [SpiritSH] (57) Spr-Sum 92, p. 13.
"The Eternal Bushwhacker." [SpiritSH] (57) Spr-Sum 92, p. 16-17.
"Goblin Market Revisited." [SpiritSH] (57) Spr-Sum 92, p. 15.
"Golgotha." [SpiritSH] (57) Spr-Sum 92, p. 14.
"On Powerbridge Road." [SpiritSH] (57) Spr-Sum 92, p. 13.
"The River." [SpiritSH] (57) Spr-Sum 92, p. 17.
"Sunyatta." [SpiritSH] (57) Spr-Sum 92, p. 10-12.

1014. CESARINY, Mário
"Breyten Breytenbach" (tr. by Jean R. Longland). [Stand] (33:4) Aut 92, p. 136-140.

1015. CÉSPEDES, Jorge Enrique de
"Nocturno." [Nuez] (4:10/11) 92, p. 21.

1016. CETRANO, Sal
"Always." [NegC] (12:1/2) 92, p. 18.

1017. CHADWICK, Cydney
"Illustrations" (Excerpt). [Asylum] (7:3/4) 92, p. 32.
"Photo Booth." [Asylum] (7:3/4) 92, p. 32.
"Shrub." [CentralP] (21) Spr 92, p. 168.

1018. CHALLENDER, Craig
"At My Father-in-Law's: Summer, 1986." [TarRP] (31:2) Spr 92, p. 14-15.

1019. CHALLIS, Chris
"Jack Kerouac in St. Ives." [MoodySI] (27) Spr 92, p. 13-15.

1020. CHALMER, Judith
"The Archivist." [PraS] (66:3) Fall 92, p. 24.
"At a Party in Heaven." [Poem] (68) N 92, p. 54-55.
"Folk Art." [Poem] (68) N 92, p. 56.
" *Ketubah*, A Marriage Contract." [Poem] (68) N 92, p. 52-53.
"On Eli's 5th Birthday." [PraS] (66:3) Fall 92, p. 25.
"On Our Behalf." [Kalliope] (14:2) 92, p. 26.
"Pink." [SpoonRQ] (17:3/4) Sum-Fall 92, p. 9-11.
"Refuge on Hunger Mountain." [GreenMR] (NS 5:2) Spr-Sum 92, p. 15.
"Rhapsody." [SpoonRQ] (17:3/4) Sum-Fall 92, p. 8.
"Rising." [Poem] (68) N 92, p. 51.
" *Schmatzing* on My Father's Food." [PoetL] (87:3) Fall 92, p. 15-16.
"Sharpshooter." [BelPoJ] (42:3) Spr 92, p. 2-3.
"Sons and Daughters." [GreenMR] (NS 5:2) Spr-Sum 92, p. 17-18.
"The Surface of the Water." [GreenMR] (NS 5:2) Spr-Sum 92, p. 16.
"To Dream a Tongue Loose." [SpoonRQ] (17:3/4) Sum-Fall 92, p. 7.

1021. CHAMBERLAIN, Cara
"The Field Behind My Office." [HiramPoR] (51/52) Fall 91-Sum 92, p. 27.
"October on the Highline Canal Trail." [HiramPoR] (51/52) Fall 91-Sum 92, p. 28.
"Osprey." [GreensboroR] (52) Sum 92, p. 115.

1022. CHAMBERS, Carole
"Maid No More." [YellowS] (41) Fall-Wint 92-93, p. 5.

1023. CHAMPAGNE, John
"At Thirty." [KenR] (NS 14:2) Spr 92, p. 36.

1024. CHANDLER, Tom
"The Ants." [PoetryE] (33) Spr 92, p. 26.
"At the William Stafford Reading." [PoetryE] (33) Spr 92, p. 23.
"The Bear Roast." [Interim] (11:2) Fall-Wint 92-93, p. 3.
"Churchill, Manitoba." [Interim] (11:2) Fall-Wint 92-93, p. 5.
"A Current Affair." [Interim] (11:2) Fall-Wint 92-93, p. 4.
"Downproofing." [PoetryE] (33) Spr 92, p. 24.
"Little Tiny Ironies." [Interim] (11:2) Fall-Wint 92-93, p. 6.
"The Trees." [PoetryE] (33) Spr 92, p. 25.

1025. CHANDRA, G. S. Sharat
"Exile." [WeberS] (9:3) Fall 92, p. 91.
"Screws & Hinges." [LaurelR] (26:1) Wint 92, p. 67.
"Sraddha." [WeberS] (9:3) Fall 92, p. 89.
"Valley of the Crows, India." [WeberS] (9:3) Fall 92, p. 90-91.

1026. CHANG, Diana
"En Plein Air." [Footwork] 92, p. 16.

"The Estranging." [Footwork] 92, p. 17.
"A Harvest." [Footwork] 92, p. 16.
"Real Time." [Contact] (10:62/63/64) Fall 91-Spr 92, p. 64.
"The Time Being January 1991." [Contact] (10:62/63/64) Fall 91-Spr 92, p. 64.
"Time Stands Still Near the Ponte Vecchio." [Footwork] 92, p. 17.
"Where We Are Now." [Contact] (10:62/63/64) Fall 91-Spr 92, p. 64.

1027. CHANG, Lisbeth
"Nighthawks at the Coupe de Ville." [HarvardA] (126:2) Wint 92, p. 14-15.

CHANG, Soo Ko
See KO, Chang Soo

1028. CHANG, Victoria
"The Day My Aunt Married a White Man." [CreamCR] (16:2) Fall 92, p. 12.

1029. CHAPMAN, Robin S.
"Algorithms of Loss" (For A.T.). [Nimrod] (36:1) Fall-Wint 92, p. 123.
"Field Trip." [Ascent] (17:1) Fall 92, p. 28.
"G-Spot." [BelPoJ] (42:3) Spr 92, p. 43.
"Menopause." [BelPoJ] (42:3) Spr 92, p. 42.
"Prairie Dock." [Ascent] (17:1) Fall 92, p. 28.
"The Way In." [Hudson] (45:3) Aut 92, p. 441-442.

1030. CHAR, Rene
"The Epte Woods" (tr. by Mark Hutchinson). [Pequod] (34) 92, p. 195.
"Frequency" (tr. by Mary Ann Caws and Patricia Terry). [Pequod] (34) 92, p. 183.
"In Love" (tr. by Mary Ann Caws and Patricia Terry). [Pequod] (34) 92, p. 182.
"The Inventors" (tr. by Mark Hutchinson). [Pequod] (34) 92, p. 196-197.
"The Latitudes of Alsace" (tr. by Mark Hutchinson). [Pequod] (34) 92, p. 194.
"The Sorgue" (Song for Yvonne, tr. by Mark Rudman). [Pequod] (34) 92, p. 185.
"With a Free Scythe" (tr. by Mary Ann Caws and Patricia Terry). [Pequod] (34) 92, p. 184.

1031. CHARACH, Ron
"Colonoscopy." [Descant] (23:4/24:1, #78/79) Wint-Spr 92-93, p. 25-27.
"Remembering: The First Round." [Descant] (23:1/2, #76/77) Spr-Sum 92, p. 165.
"There Is a Familiarity." [Descant] (23:4/24:1, #78/79) Wint-Spr 92-93, p. 28-29.

1032. CHARENTZ, Yeghisheh
"I Love the Sun-Baked Taste of Armenian Words" (tr. by Diana Der-Hovanessian). [Trans] (26) Spr 92, p. 99.

1033. CHARLTON, Elizabeth
"Ministrations for Recovery." [Kalliope] (14:2) 92, p. 31.

1034. CHARLTON, George
"Greensleeves in the Fifties." [Verse] (9:2) Sum 92, p. 5.

CHARME, Barbara Dellner du
See DuCHARME, Barbara Dellner

1035. CHARNEY, Morris B.
"Flames couple with flames." [Amelia] (6:4, #19) 92, p. 6.

1036. CHASE, Alfonso
"Entre el Ojo y la Noche" (3 selections: 3, 9, 11). [Luz] (1) My 92, p. 52-55.

1037. CHASE, C. D.
"Earth Words." [BlackBR] (16) Wint-Spr 92-93, p. 28.
"Sioux Circles." [BlackBR] (15) Spr-Sum 92, p. 40.

1038. CHASE, Jeanne
"Expected As a Unicorn." [WillowR] (19) Spr 92, p. 19.

1039. CHATTOPADHYAY, Gita
"The Ritual of *Sati*" (tr. by Paramita Banerjee and Carolyne Wright). [ChiR] (38:1/2) 92, p. 93.

1040. CHEN, Shi-Zheng
"City of the Dead Poets" (tr. of Lian Yang, w. Heather S. J. Steliga). [GrahamHR] (16) Fall 92, p. 100.
"Games of Lies" (tr. of Lian Yang, w. Heather S. J. Steliga). [GrahamHR] (16) Fall 92, p. 98-99.
"War Museum" (tr. of Lian Yang, w. Heather S. J. Steliga). [GrahamHR] (16) Fall 92, p. 101-102.
"Winter Garden" (tr. of Lian Yang, w. Heather S. J. Steliga). [GrahamHR] (16) Fall 92, p. 95-97.

1041. CHEN, Xueliang
"Absence" (tr. of Bei Dao, w. Donald Finkel). [ManhatR] (6:2) Fall 92, p. 15.
"Eventful Autumn" (tr. of Bei Dao, w. Donald Finkel). [ManhatR] (6:2) Fall 92, p. 18.

"Midnight Singer" (tr. of Bei Dao, w. Donald Finkel). [ManhatR] (6:2) Fall 92, p. 17.
"Outside" (tr. of Bei Dao, w. Donald Finkel). [ManhatR] (6:2) Fall 92, p. 19.
"Summer's Brass" (tr. of Bei Dao, w. Donald Finkel). [ManhatR] (6:2) Fall 92, p. 16.
"Year's End" (tr. of Bei Dao, w. Donald Finkel). [ManhatR] (6:2) Fall 92, p. 14.

CHEN, Yuan
See YUAN, Chen

1042. CHEN EOYANG, Eugene
"To the Soul of Danuska" (tr. of Ai Qing). [Trans] (26) Spr 92, p. 33-35.

CHENG, Gu
See GU, Cheng

1043. CHENOWETH, Okey Canfield
"All Night the Guns." [Footwork] 92, p. 42.
"Don't Waste the Day." [Footwork] 92, p. 41.
"The Loonies." [Footwork] 92, p. 41.
"A Military Funeral for My Student." [Footwork] 92, p. 41.
"My Darling, Take Off Your Clothes." [Footwork] 92, p. 42.

1044. CHERKOVSKI, Neeli
"Chapultepec." [AnotherCM] (24) Fall 92, p. 27-30.
"Eyes" (For Rufino Tamayo). [AnotherCM] (24) Fall 92, p. 31-33.
"Hunter." [OnTheBus] (4:2/5:1, #10/11) 92, p. 77.
"Mis Manos." [PoetryUSA] (24) 92, p. 17.

1045. CHERNOFF, Maxine
"Nature Morte." [Sulfur] (12:2, #31) Fall 92, p. 192.
"The North Sea." [Sulfur] (12:2, #31) Fall 92, p. 193.
"Not." [Sulfur] (12:2, #31) Fall 92, p. 193-194.

1046. CHERNOW, Ann
"Utopia." [NewYorkQ] (48) 92, p. 103.

1047. CHERRY, Kelly
"Going Down on America." [ThRiPo] (39/40) 92-93, p. 28-29.
"Grammaire Générale: A Review" (for J.F.). [RiverS] (36) 92, p. 82-83.
"History." [Hellas] (3:2) Fall 92, p. 92.
"Lepidopterology: A Lecture." [ArtfulD] (22/23) 92, p. 94.
"Moses on the Way Down." [CreamCR] (16:1) Spr 92, p. 133.
"On Watching a Young Man Play Tennis." [Witness] (6:2) 92, p. 28-29.

1048. CHESLEY, Stephen
"The sun goes to dream." [Amelia] (6:4, #19) 92, p. 34.

1049. CHESMORE, Matt
"The Garden." [HangL] (60) 92, p. 72-73.
"Tinky" (for Raymond Thomas Griffin). [HangL] (60) 92, p. 76-77.

1050. CHESS, Richard
"At the Rabbi's Study Group." [Poetry] (160:1) Ap 92, p. 24.
"The Cello I Love" (for Eugene Friesen). [RiverC] (12:2) Spr 92, p. 42.
"Growing Up in a Jewish Neighborhood." [Poetry] (160:1) Ap 92, p. 25.

1051. CHETCUTI, Vincent
"Visions of Kerouac." [MoodySI] (27) Spr 92, p. 21.

1052. CHEVAKO, M. R.
"On the Turtle's Back." [AntR] (50:3) Sum 92, p. 515.

1053. CHIDESTER, E. Leon
"Columbus (Postils on Documents of Doubt)" (6 poems). [WeberS] (9:3) Fall 92, p. 45-48.

1054. CHIGAS, George
"Kerouac." [MoodySI] (27) Spr 92, p. 19-21.

1055. CHIKHLADZE, David
"* * *" (visual poem, in Georgian?). [Archae] (3) early 92, p. 25.

1056. CHILDERS, David C.
"Report." [SouthernHR] (26:3) Sum 92, p. 230.

1057. CHILDRESS, Jess
"They're having a heyday. The cotton's high." [PoetryUSA] (24) 92, p. 28.

1058. CHIN, Marilyn
"A Portrait of the Self As Nation, 1990-1991." [Zyzzyva] (8:2) Sum 92, p. 112-117.

CHIN, Woon Ping
See PING, Chin Woon

1059. CHING, Jennifer
"To My Grandmother." [Footwork] 92, p. 92.

1060. CHIOLES, John
"The Birth of Aphrodite" (tr. of Nasos Vayenas). [Trans] (26) Spr 92, p. 96.
1061. CHIPASULA, Frank M.
"The Raging Silence." [Stand] (33:3) Sum 92, p. 25.
"The Water Talks" (about the phenomenon called "Accidentalization"). [Stand] (33:3) Sum 92, p. 26.
1062. CHITWOOD, Michael
"The Buoys." [Thrpny] (48) Wint 92, p. 5.
"Hosanna." [PoetC] (23:3) Spr 92, p. 19-20.
"Six Month Old." [CutB] (38) Sum 92, p. 130.
"Trophy." [Pembroke] (24) 92, p. 96.
"Whet." [Thrpny] (50) Sum 92, p. 16.
1063. CHMIELARZ, Sharon
"The Lightplant Keeper During Thunderstorms." [SlipS] (12) 92, p. 39.
1064. CHOE, Wolhee
"All Right Then" (tr. of Munhyang, w. Constantine Contogenis). [Pequod] (34) 92, p. 115.
"Between the Cold Pine Arbor's Moon" (tr. of Hongjang, w. Constantine Contogenis). [Pequod] (34) 92, p. 113.
"Blue stream, don't show off your speed" (a Kisang Poem, tr. of Hwang Jini, w. Constantine Contogenis). [GrandS] (11:3 #43) 92, p. 174.
"Do They Say" (tr. of Okson, w. Constantine Contogenis). [Pequod] (34) 92, p. 118.
"Don't Tell Me the Face" (tr. of Myongok, w. Constantine Contogenis). [Pequod] (34) 92, p. 116.
"Has the Silver River above risen further" (a Kisang Poem, tr. of Songi, w. Constantine Contogenis). [GrandS] (11:3 #43) 92, p. 174.
"My Thoughts of Him" (tr. of Maehwa, w. Constantine Contogenis). [Pequod] (34) 92, p. 117.
"An Urban Butterfly" (tr. of Songdaechun, w. Constantine Contogenis). [Pequod] (34) 92, p. 114.
1065. CHOI, Janet
"What I'm Wild For." [GrahamHR] (16) Fall 92, p. 84-85.
1066. CHOI, Kathleen T.
"Lab Notes." [HawaiiR] (16:2, #35) Spr 92, p. 48.
1067. CHOPPA, Danielle
"The Turn-Around Tree." [BellArk] (8:5) S-O 92, p. 14.
1068. CHORLTON, David
"An Alien Left to Find His Way." [Parting] (5:1) Sum 92, p. 21.
"A Colonial Lesson." [InterPR] (18:1) Spr 92, p. 62.
"The Convalescent." [OxfordM] (7:1) Spr-Sum 91, p. 64.
"Cortez Dreams." [InterPR] (18:1) Spr 92, p. 61-62.
"Early Frost." [Parting] (5:1) Sum 92, p. 19.
"The Gates." [WebR] (16) Fall 92, p. 47.
"Gifts for Father Kino." [DogRR] (11:2, #22) Fall-Wint 92, p. 46.
"Gifts for Father Kino." [InterPR] (18:1) Spr 92, p. 60.
"Shostakovich." [WebR] (16) Fall 92, p. 46-47.
"The Snails." [OxfordM] (7:1) Spr-Sum 91, p. 65.
"Snowflight." [Parting] (5:1) Sum 92, p. 22.
"Station to Station." [InterPR] (18:1) Spr 92, p. 63-64.
"Vukovar." [DogRR] (11:2, #22) Fall-Wint 92, p. 7.
CHOSHOSHI, Kinoshita
See KINOSHITA, Choshoshi
1069. CHOU, Ping
"Ways of Looking at a Poet." [CentR] (36:1) Wint 92, p. 211-212.
1070. CHOULIARAS, Yiorgos
"The Body of Anaxagoras" (tr. by David Mason and the author). [NoDaQ] (60:4) Fall 92, p. 12.
"The Day Arrives" (tr. by David Mason w. the poet). [PoetL] (87:4) Wint 92-93, p. 47.
"The Dream of Phernazes" (tr. by David Mason and the author). [GrandS] (11:2, #42) 92, p. 147-149.
"The Family of Greeks" (tr. by David Mason and the author). [GrandS] (11:2, #42) 92, p. 150.
"Thus" (tr. by David Mason w. the poet). [PoetL] (87:4) Wint 92-93, p. 46.
1071. CHOW, Edmond
"For Evelyn Lau." [Grain] (20:4) Wint 92, p. 98.

"Photograph" (for T.K.F., 1989). [Grain] (20:4) Wint 92, p. 97.

1072. CHRISTENSEN, Donna
"Birth Poem." [BrooklynR] (9) 92, p. 55.

1073. CHRISTENSEN, Peter A.
"The Stripling." [Amelia] (6:4, #19) 92, p. 17.

1074. CHRISTIANSON, Kiel
"Catnap." [CapeR] (27:1) Spr 92, p. 45.

1075. CHRISTIE, A. V.
"Evermay-on-the-Delaware." [PoetryNW] (33:4) Wint 92-93, p. 10.
"Passage." [MassR] (23:2) Sum 92, p. 167-170.

1076. CHRISTINA, Martha
"Lately I've Had So Little to Say." [PassN] (13:2) Wint 92, p. 25.
"Like Castanets." [TarRP] (32:1) Fall 92, p. 37-38.

1077. CHRISTOPHER, G. B.
"Nude Self-Portrait: Eightieth Birthday" (for Alice Neal). [Kalliope] (14:3) 92, p. 14.

1078. CHRISTOPHER, Nicholas
"Angel's Bakery." [NewRep] (206:21) 25 My 92, p. 42.
"Hibiscus Tea." [NewRep] (207:27) 28 D 92, p. 41.
"Notes Towards a History of Imperialism." [LitR] (36:1) Fall 92, p. 13-14.
"The Skeleton of a Trout in Shallow Water." [NewYorker] (68:8) 13 Ap 92, p. 54.

CHRISTY-PINE, Ana
See PINE/CHRISTY, Ana

CHUONG, Doan
See DOAN, Chuong

CHURCH, Adrian Blevins
See BLEVINS-CHURCH, Adrian

1079. CHURCHILL, Charlotte
"Order." [Elf] (2:3) Fall 92, p. 36-37.

1080. CHUTE, Robert M.
"Confusing Fall Warblers." [Ascent] (17:1) Fall 92, p. 29.
"Initiate: Marking Time." [HiramPoR] (51/52) Fall 91-Sum 92, p. 29.
"The Sea Shell." [CapeR] (27:2) Fall 92, p. 23.
"The Southern Continent: Discovered But Unknown" (from the maps of Queiros). [SmPd] (29:1, #84) Wint 92, p. 14.

1081. CIARDI, John
"Call It a Day." [JlNJPo] (14:2) Aut 92, p. 1.
"Food Notes." [JlNJPo] (14:2) Aut 92, p. 2.
"This Morning." [JlNJPo] (14:2) Aut 92, p. 3.

1082. CIHLAR, Jim
"To Execute." [Plain] (13:1) Fall 92, p. 36.

1083. CINELLI, Joan Eheart
"Circle." [ChrC] (109:22) 15-22 Jl 92, p. 686.

1084. CINTI, Renata
"Federico Garcia Lorca" (Rosita stays single or the language of flowers — in different gardens, tr. of Friederike Zelesko). [Vis] (38) 92, p. 18.

1085. CIOFALO, J. F.
"De Sorore." [NegC] (12:1/2) 92, p. 19.

1086. CIRINO, Leonard
"The Host." [Asylum] (7:3/4) 92, p. 46.

1087. CIRJANIC, Gordana
"Artificial Limb" (tr. by Nina Zivancevic). [Talisman] (8) Spr 92, p. 144.

1088. CITINO, David
"An Argument Against the Aluminum Bat." [EngJ] (81:2) F 92, p. 97.
"Beating the Olive Trees." [LaurelR] (26:1) Wint 92, p. 29.
"Charms Against Writer's Block." [CentR] (36:3) Fall 92, p. 531-532.
"Eating the Placenta." [LaurelR] (26:1) Wint 92, p. 30-31.
"Illustration." [NewL] (58:3) Spr 92, p. 66-67.
"Magnetic Resonating Imager, University Hospitals." [PraS] (66:2) Sum 92, p. 41-43.
"The Newlywed Game." [LitR] (25:2) Wint 92, p. 256.
"Reading the Graves." [PraS] (66:2) Sum 92, p. 43-45.
"The Sorrow of What Flies." [CentR] (36:3) Fall 92, p. 532-533.
"Teenage Mutant Ninja Turtles." [DenQ] (26:4) Spr 92, p. 12-13.

1089. CLAMAN, Elizabeth
"Snow." [SilverFR] (23) Wint 92, p. 24.

"Yo-Yos." [RiverS] (36) 92, p. 20.

1090. CLAMPITT, Amy

"Brought from Beyond." [NewYorker] (68:45) 28 D 92-4 Ja 93, p. 116.

"A Cadenza." [NewYorker] (68:8) 13 Ap 92, p. 34.

"Homeland." [SouthwR] (77:2/3) Spr-Sum 92, p. 151-152.

"In Umbria: A Snapshot." [NewYorker] (68:25) 10 Ag 92, p. 50.

"Matrix" (Villa Serbelloni, Lake Como, for Karen Chase). [ParisR]] (34:124) Fall 92, p. 34-38.

"Nondescript." [WilliamMR] (30) 92, p. 51.

"Seed." [ParisR]] (34:124) Fall 92, p. 31-33.

1091. CLANCY, Joseph P.

"The Resurrection of the Words." [Comm] (119:22) 18 D 92, p. 15.

1092. CLAPS, Robert

"Chore." [GreenMR] (NS 5:2) Spr-Sum 92, p. 26.

1093. CLARE, Elizabeth

"At Seneca Army Depot." [SinW] (46) Spr 92, p. 39-40.

"Graffiti in Four Voices." [EvergreenC] (7:2) Sum-Fall 92, p. 8-9.

"Left with the Ocean" (for Adrianne). [EvergreenC] (7:2) Sum-Fall 92, p. 7.

1094. CLARK, Elizabeth B.

"Lights" (tr. of Mario Rivero). [Pequod] (34) 92, p. 181.

"Smooth" (tr. of Mario Rivero). [Pequod] (34) 92, p. 180.

1095. CLARK, Gary

"Breaking in Dying Light." [CarolQ] (44:2) Wint 92, p. 87.

1096. CLARK, J. Wesley

"In the Kentucky Club" (Juarez, Chihuahua — 1958). [Amelia] (6:4, #19) 92, p. 73.

1097. CLARK, Kevin

"Dependents." [AntR] (50:4) Fall 92, p. 726.

"Plume." [CharR] (18:2) Fall 92, p. 88.

1098. CLARK, Naomi

"The Single Eye" (for my family: Burnie, Diane and Ray, David and Pirjo, Joel and Sue). [QRL] (Poetry Series 11: vol. 31) 92, 76 p.

"The Song of Polyphemus." [LitR] (25:2) Wint 92, p. 268-269.

"The Witch's Tit." [LaurelR] (26:2) Sum 92, p. 51.

1099. CLARK, Patricia

"Betrayal." [Poetry] (160:3) Je 92, p. 153.

1100. CLARK, Suzanne Underwood

"Sparklers." [Shen] (42:1) Spr 92, p. 29.

1101. CLARK, Thomas A.

"Through White Villages" (Andalucia, Winter 1988). [Verse] (9:2) Sum 92, p. 68 - 73.

1102. CLARK, Tom

"40 Days." [CityLR] (5) 92, p. 69-70.

"As the Human Village Prepares for Its Fate." [AmerPoR] (21:1) Ja-F 92, p. 23.

"Bathed." [AmerPoR] (21:1) Ja-F 92, p. 23.

"Before Dawn." [AmerPoR] (21:1) Ja-F 92, p. 23.

"Calling Infinity." [AmerPoR] (21:1) Ja-F 92, p. 24.

"The Domestic Life of Ghosts." [Shiny] (7/8) 92, p. 96.

"Energy of the Pre-World As a Bungee Cable Jumper." [AmerPoR] (21:1) Ja-F 92, p. 24.

"First Cold Winter Twilights." [BrooklynR] (9) 92, p. 96.

"In the Bond Scandals." [AmerPoR] (21:1) Ja-F 92, p. 26.

"In the Dark Mountains, Brilliant." [Shiny] (7/8) 92, p. 95.

"The Lyric." [Conjunc] (19) 92, p. 281.

"My Hypertrophic Devotion." [AmerPoR] (21:1) Ja-F 92, p. 25.

"Narcissism." [AmerPoR] (21:1) Ja-F 92, p. 25.

"Nodding." [AmerPoR] (21:1) Ja-F 92, p. 24.

"On Marine Silence Street." [Shiny] (7/8) 92, p. 93.

"Out of Darkness I Came." [Conjunc] (19) 92, p. 282.

"Personal Angel Glimpsed." [AmerPoR] (21:1) Ja-F 92, p. 25.

"Poem for Jack Kerouac in California" (Feb. 15, 1982). [MoodySI] (27) Spr 92, p. 2.

"A Point Is Fixed." [Conjunc] (19) 92, p. 282.

"Retro." [AmerPoR] (21:1) Ja-F 92, p. 25.

"Sedge." [AmerPoR] (21:1) Ja-F 92, p. 23.

"The Silence of Lambs." [AmerPoR] (21:1) Ja-F 92, p. 26.

"Sleepwalker." [CityLR] (5) 92, p. 72.

"Sleepwalker's Fate." [CityLR] (5) 92, p. 71.

"Sleepwalker's Way." [AmerPoR] (21:1) Ja-F 92, p. 24.
"Somnambulism." [AmerPoR] (21:1) Ja-F 92, p. 24.
"Statue." [AmerPoR] (21:1) Ja-F 92, p. 23.
"A Theory of the Universe." [Shiny] (7/8) 92, p. 94.
"Time." [AmerPoR] (21:1) Ja-F 92, p. 25.
"Withdrawal." [AmerPoR] (21:1) Ja-F 92, p. 25.

1103. CLARKE, Cheryl
"Rondeau." [Hellas] (3:2) Fall 92, p. 91.

1104. CLARKE, John
"Telephone Booth." [TarRP] (31:2) Spr 92, p. 38.
"Winterwatch." [TarRP] (31:2) Spr 92, p. 38.

1105. CLARY, Killarney
"I am annoyed as she repeats herself, her excuses for some action which." [YaleR] (80:4) O 92, p. 73-74.
"I set the letter I might send him on the shelf near the atlas outlining." [YaleR] (80:4) O 92, p. 73.
"Water echoes under the bridge, dark slap against the pilings." [YaleR] (80:4) O 92, p. 74.

1106. CLAUSEN, Jan
"Ahora, Ahorita." [13thMoon] (10:1/2) 92, p. 30-31.
"The Observable Moment When Things Turn into Their Opposites." [13thMoon] (10:1/2) 92, p. 29.
"Other." [13thMoon] (10:1/2) 92, p. 28.
"Other." [Contact] (10:62/63/64) Fall 91-Spr 92, p. 55.
"Prospect Park Shocker, Polar Bear Rips B'klyn Boy." [13thMoon] (10:1/2) 92, p. 32.

1107. CLAWSON, Scott
"Landing." [US1] (26/27) 92, p. 20.

CLAYTON, Nancy Gall
See GALL-CLAYTON, Nancy

1108. CLEAR, Edeltraud Harzer
"With Her Vermeer" (for Patricia Ver Ellen). [BellArk] (8:2) Mr-Ap 92, p. 6.

1109. CLEAR, T.
"Death by Nasturtium." [BellR] (15:2) Fall 92, p. 19.

1110. CLEARY, Brendan
"Beer & Sympanth." [NewEngR] (14:2) Spr 92, p. 48-49.
"Down South." [NewEngR] (14:2) Spr 92, p. 46-47.
"Graveside." [NewEngR] (14:2) Spr 92, p. 49-50.
"Wedding in Omagh." [NewEngR] (14:2) Spr 92, p. 45-46.

1111. CLEARY, Suzanne
"Birdsall Street." [SouthernPR] (32:2) Fall 92, p. 6-7.
"The Horse Latitudes." [PoetryNW] (33:1) Spr 92, p. 36.
"In My Favorite Recent Dream." [PoetryNW] (33:1) Spr 92, p. 35.
"There Is No Such Thing as Moonlight" (after a photograph of Frida Kahlo and Diego Rivera — Guy Owen Poetry Prize Winner, James Tate, Judge). [SouthernPR] (32:2) Fall 92, p. 5-6.
"This Poem Is a Brick Through Your Window" (for J.L.). [NewMyths] (1:2/2:1) 92, p. 184-185.
"Waiting." [MissR] (20:3) Spr 92, p. 26.

1112. CLEMENCIA, Joceline
"Appeal from a Mother" (tr. of Jeanne Henriquez, w. Richinel Ansano). [LitR] (35:4) Sum 92, p. 575.
"Gossip" (tr. of Arnela Ten Meer, w. Richinel Ansano). [LitR] (35:4) Sum 92, p. 582.
"Nan Tres." [LitR] (35:4) Sum 92, p. 612.
"On My Shoulders" (tr. of Micky Hart, w. Richinel Ansano). [LitR] (35:4) Sum 92, p. 574.
"Sit 'n See" (tr. of Reyna Joe, w. Richinel Ansano). [LitR] (35:4) Sum 92, p. 576.
"Three Mirrors" (tr. by Richinel Ansano and the author). [LitR] (35:4) Sum 92, p. 571.

1113. CLEMENTS, Arthur
"A Good Word." [Footwork] 92, p. 82.
"Sestina for My Father." [Footwork] 92, p. 82.

1114. CLEMENTS, Susan
"Birthday." [Footwork] 92, p. 156.
"Lost Luggage." [NewMyths] (1:2/2:1) 92, p. 135-136.

"Night Bombing of Baghdad." [MidAR] (13:2) 92, p. 29-30.
"Plum Creek." [MidAR] (13:2) 92, p. 27-28.
"Prisms." [Footwork] 92, p. 155.
"The River." [Footwork] 92, p. 156.
"Wild Horses." [Footwork] 92, p. 157.

1115. CLEVE, Emerald
"Lost Kingdom." [SpiritSH] (57) Spr-Sum 92, p. 25.
"New Year's Day." [SpiritSH] (57) Spr-Sum 92, p. 24.
"The Swans." [SpiritSH] (57) Spr-Sum 92, p. 26.
"Watching You." [SpiritSH] (57) Spr-Sum 92, p. 24.
"Winter Journey." [SpiritSH] (57) Spr-Sum 92, p. 23.

1116. CLEVER, Bertolt
"Trees." [ChangingM] (24) Sum-Fall 92, p. 35.

1117. CLEVERDON, Mary
"Nesting" (Eve of Saint Agnes Contest winner). [NegC] (12:3) 92, p. 3-4.

1118. CLEWELL, David
"America's Bed-and-Breakfasts" (For G. Barnes, who really did try to book me into something a little more my style). [Poetry] (160:5) Ag 92, p. 277-280.
"Carnival Heaven." [OntR] (36) Spr-Sum 92, p. 103-105.
"The Final Meeting of the Pessimists Club." [CharR] (18:2) Fall 92, p. 83-85.
"I Can't Believe the Face on Mars" (For D.). [Poetry] (160:5) Ag 92, p. 272-277.
"If the Wisdom Holds." [Boulevard] (7:2/3, #20/21) Fall 92, p. 136-137.

1119. CLIFF, Michelle
"And What Would It Be Like." [AmerV] (29) 92, p. 19-23.

CLIFF DWELLER
See DWELLER, Cliff

1120. CLIFTON, Harry
"Eclogue." [Stand] (33:4) Aut 92, p. 14-15.
"Exiles." [Verse] (8:3/9:1) Wint-Spr 92, p. 128.
"Letter from the South." [Stand] (33:4) Aut 92, p. 16.

1121. CLIFTON, Lucille
"A Song of Mary." [NewEngR] (14:4) Fall 92, p. 224.

1122. CLINTON, Michelle T.
"Blood." [OnTheBus] (4:2/5:1, #10/11) 92, p. 78.
"The Girl Hero." [Rohwedder] (7) Spr-Sum 92, p. 5.

1123. CLINTON, Robert
"Modulation." [Ploughs] (18:4) Wint 92-93, p. 44.
"The Sleeping Beauty." [Ploughs] (18:4) Wint 92-93, p. 45.

1124. CLIPMAN, William
"Jokes in a Hard Climate, Love in a Dry Land." [SouthernPR] (32:2) Fall 92, p. 30 - 33.

CLOUD, Peter Blue
See BLUE CLOUD, Peter

1125. CLOVER, Joshua
"1/16/91." [Iowa] (22:2) Spr-Sum 92, p. 79-80.
"1/20/91." [Iowa] (22:2) Spr-Sum 92, p. 81.
"The Nevada Glassworks, 4cc." [Iowa] (22:2) Spr-Sum 92, p. 78-79.
"There Is the Body Lying in State." [Agni] (36) 92, p. 166-167.

1126. CLOVES, Jeff
"The Night Visitor." [MoodySI] (27) Spr 92, p. 29.

1127. CLUFF, Russell M.
"The Memory of Silver" (tr. of Carlos Montemayor, w. L. Howard Quackenbush). [TriQ] (85) Fall 92, p. 203-204.

1128. COATES, Carole
"Cruising." [ChironR] (11:2) Sum 92, p. 12.

1129. COATES, Carrol F.
"Anacaona" (tr. of Davertige (Denis Villard)). [Callaloo] (15:3) Sum 92, p. 637.
"The Austerity of Your Body" (tr. of Joël Des Rosiers). [Callaloo] (15:2) Spr 92, p. 407-410.
"Black Orchid" (Excerpt, tr. of Anthony Phelps). [Callaloo] (15:2) Spr 92, p. 371 - 375.
"Black Soul" (Fragment, tr. of Jean Brierre). [Callaloo] (15:3) Sum 92, p. 573-576.
"Carib Father" (To Franck Fouché, tr. of Anthony Phelps). [Callaloo] (15:2) Spr 92, p. 347-351.
"The Charm of the Bitter Dream" (tr. of St-Valentin Kauss). [Callaloo] (15:3) Sum 92, p. 699.

"Clamor" (tr. of Réne Bélance). [Callaloo] (15:3) Sum 92, p. 607.
"A Collage for Servant Children" (tr. of René Philoctète, w. Cheryl Thomas). [Callaloo] (15:3) Sum 92, p. 619-620.
"Comfort" (tr. of Réne Bélance). [Callaloo] (15:3) Sum 92, p. 605.
"Dissidence, I" (tr. of Robert Berrouët-Oriol). [Callaloo] (15:2) Spr 92, p. 506-508.
"Dyakout 1, 2, 3, 4" (Selections, tr. of Félix Morisseau-Leroy). [Callaloo] (15:3) Sum 92, p. 671-677.
"Fetish" (tr. of Réne Bélance). [Callaloo] (15:3) Sum 92, p. 603.
"Here I Am Again, Harlem" (In memory of those lynched in Georgia, victims of white fascism, tr. of Jean Brierre). [Callaloo] (15:3) Sum 92, p. 581-582.
"I Understood, But Too Late" (tr. of Erma Saint-Grégoire). [Callaloo] (15:2) Spr 92, p. 476.
"Idem" (tr. of Davertige (Denis Villard)). [Callaloo] (15:3) Sum 92, p. 633-634.
"Incunabulum" (tr. of Robert Berrouët-Oriol). [Callaloo] (15:2) Spr 92, p. 512-514.
"Misery by Sunlight" (tr. of René Philoctète, w. Cheryl Thomas). [Callaloo] (15:3) Sum 92, p. 617.
"My Wife with the Brocade Eyes" (excerpts, for Guedlie Lafayette, tr. of St-John Kauss). [Callaloo] (15:3) Sum 92, p. 701-702.
"Native Natal" (Excerpt from "Ex-Ile," tr. of Gary Klang). [Callaloo] (15:3) Sum 92, p. 595.
"Nerve" (tr. of Réne Bélance). [Callaloo] (15:3) Sum 92, p. 609.
"Notice" (tr. of Georges Castera). [Callaloo] (15:2) Spr 92, p. 531.
"Oh in the Absence of All Fear" (tr. of St-Valentin Kauss). [Callaloo] (15:3) Sum 92, p. 695.
"Oh Mother of the Seven Sorrows" (Excerpt from "Ex-Ile," tr. of Gary Klang). [Callaloo] (15:3) Sum 92, p. 599.
"Orphan of My Island" (Excerpt from "Ex-Ile," tr. of Gary Klang). [Callaloo] (15:3) Sum 92, p. 597.
"Poemes de Reconnaissance" (Excerpts, tr. of Roland Morisseau). [Callaloo] (15:3) Sum 92, p. 647-648.
"Prologue" (tr. of Davertige (Denis Villard)). [Callaloo] (15:3) Sum 92, p. 629-630.
"La Promeneuse au Jardin" (Excerpts, tr. of Roland Morisseau). [Callaloo] (15:3) Sum 92, p. 651-656.
"Serene, in Situ . . . for the Dead" (tr. of Erma Saint-Grégoire). [Callaloo] (15:2) Spr 92, p. 472-473.
"She Had Come from Faraway Dawns" (for Marie, tr. of Erma Saint-Grégoire). [Callaloo] (15:2) Spr 92, p. 468.
"Songs from Roland" (Excerpts, tr. of Roland Morisseau). [Callaloo] (15:3) Sum 92, p. 643-644.
"Urinary" (excerpt, tr. of Serge Legagneur). [Callaloo] (15:3) Sum 92, p. 705-707.
"Where the Cinders Are Imprinted" (tr. of Erma Saint-Grégoire). [Callaloo] (15:2) Spr 92, p. 470.
"White Woman of the Pure Exterior" (tr. of Joël Des Rosiers). [Callaloo] (15:2) Spr 92, p. 415-420.

1130. COATES, Chris
"War Poster." [FreeL] (9) Wint 92, p. 5.

1131. COBO BORDA, Juan Gustavo
"Made by Everyone: Poetry" (tr. by Margarita Nieto). [OnTheBus] (4:2/5:1, #10/11) 92, p. 271.
"Portraits" (tr. by Margarita Nieto). [OnTheBus] (4:2/5:1, #10/11) 92, p. 270.

1132. COCHRAN, Jo Whitehorse
"Cante Ista: Heart's Eye." [PoetryE] (33) Spr 92, p. 27.

1133. COCHRAN, Leonard
"By Return Mail." [SpiritSH] (57) Spr-Sum 92, p. 22.
"Cautionary Tale." [SpiritSH] (57) Spr-Sum 92, p. 21.
"Cousins Travelling." [SpiritSH] (57) Spr-Sum 92, p. 21.
"An Onion." [SpiritSH] (57) Spr-Sum 92, p. 23.
"A Sentence." [SpiritSH] (57) Spr-Sum 92, p. 22.

1134. COCHRANE, Mark
"The Adventures of Kid Bean II." [Arc] (28) Spr 92, p. 20-21.
"Circulation." [Arc] (28) Spr 92, p. 19.
"Fireworks over the Ottawa River." [CanLit] (135) Wint 92, p. 67.
"Icarus of Montreal." [CanLit] (135) Wint 92, p. 111.
"A Parcel for Naomi." [CapilR] (2:9) Fall 92, p. 101-102.
"Tonguage: 28th & Main." [CapilR] (2:9) Fall 92, p. 97-100.
"(T)rial Separation." [CanLit] (135) Wint 92, p. 110-111.

1135. COCHRANE, Shirley G.
"The Place Where You Died." [CapeR] (27:2) Fall 92, p. 22.
1136. COCHRON, Leonard
"The Vintner" (Luke 5:39). [ChrC] (109:5) 5-12 F 92, p. 151.
1137. COELHO, Art
"Something Dark to Remind Me." [Grain] (20:1) Spr 92, p. 259.
"Wheatland Basin." [Grain] (20:1) Spr 92, p. 258.
1138. COFER, Judith Ortiz
"The Changeling." [PraS] (66:3) Fall 92, p. 28-29.
"La Fe." [Americas] (20:3/4) Fall-Wint 92, p. 153.
"Hostages to Fortune." [PraS] (66:3) Fall 92, p. 27-28.
"The Latin Deli." [Americas] (20:3/4) Fall-Wint 92, p. 156-157.
"Letter from My Mother in Spanish." [PraS] (66:3) Fall 92, p. 26-27.
"My Grandfather's Hat" (in memory of Basiliso Morot Cordero). [BilingR] (17:2) My-Ag 92, p. 161.
"El Olvido" (según las madres). [Americas] (20:3/4) Fall-Wint 92, p. 154.
"So Much for Mañana." [Americas] (20:3/4) Fall-Wint 92, p. 155.
"To a Daughter I Cannot Console." [SouthernPR] (32:1) Spr 92, p. 10-11.
1139. COFFEL, Scott
"Curly Throws a Cream Pie at Larry Only to Hit Moe." [NewMyths] (1:2/2:1) 92, p. 88.
"Tsingtao." [NewMyths] (1:2/2:1) 92, p. 89.
1140. COFFEY, Kathy
"Summer under Glass." [EngJ] (81:4) Ap 92, p. 95.
1141. COFFMAN, Lisa
"In Frazier's Mills." [CinPR] (23) Wint 91-92, p. 12.
1142. COGSWELL, Kelly Jean
"Sonnets for God." [SinW] (48) Wint 92-93, p. 119-122.
1143. COHEE, Marcia
"Amphibian." [Calyx] (14:1) Sum 92, p. 54-55.
"Hecate's Feast." [Elf] (2:4) Wint 92, p. 36-37.
"Survival." [FreeL] (9) Wint 92, p. 21.
1144. COHEN, Andrea
"Roll Call: Between the Coups." [CumbPR] (12:1) Fall 92, p. 23-24.
1145. COHEN, Bruce
"Bed Stew." [PaintedHR] (6) Spr 92, p. 6.
"Brunch." [PaintedHR] (6) Spr 92, p. 7.
"Reclusive X." [PassN] (13:1) Sum 92, p. 13.
1146. COHEN, Elizabeth (*See also* COHEN, Elizabeth Krajeck)
"The Oldest Cowgirl in the World." [Footwork] 92, p. 98.
"Vanishing Boundaries." [ManhatPR] (14) [92?], p. 46.
1147. COHEN, Elizabeth Krajeck (*See also* COHEN, Elizabeth)
"Reunion." [HopewellR] (4) 92, p. 23.
1148. COHEN, Jed A.
"Naiad." [SoCoast] (12) Ja 92, p. 12.
1149. COHEN, Marc
"Poem: Decapitated carnation stems." [AnotherCM] (23) Spr 92, p. 42.
"Rattlesnake Song." [BrooklynR] (9) 92, p. 73-74.
"Their Prudent Key." [DenQ] (26:4) Spr 92, p. 14-15.
"The Way Station." [NewAW] (10) Fall 92, p. 87-88.
1150. COHEN, S. B.
"River Oaths." [BellArk] (8:4) Jl-Ag 92, p. 24.
COHN, Maggie Hunt
See HUNT-COHN, Maggie
1151. COKINOS, Christopher
"Killing Seasons." [CreamCR] (16:2) Fall 92, p. 91-102.
"This." [MidwQ] (33:2) Wint 92, p. 194.
1152. COLANDER, Valerie Nieman
"Mirabilia" (Reflections on Leslie Fiedler's "Freaks". Honorable Mention, New Letters Poetry Award). [NewL] (58:2) Wint 92, p. 75-77.
"Police at the Scene." [WestB] (30) 92, p. 84-85.
1153. COLBURN, Don
"De Kooning in Court at 85." [PoetL] (87:2) Sum 92, p. 43.
"Emerson and I Stare at the Sunset." [Iowa] (22:1) Wint 92, p. 118.
"Etheridge." [Iowa] (22:1) Wint 92, p. 117.
"Fall Migration at Brigantine." [Iowa] (22:1) Wint 92, p. 115.

"On the Eighteenth Day of Bombing, I Go for a Hike." [Ploughs] (18:4) Wint 92-93, p. 16.
"There." [Ploughs] (18:4) Wint 92-93, p. 14.
"To a Condemned Man Now Dead." [Ploughs] (18:4) Wint 92-93, p. 15.
"To Bill Buckner on His Release by the Boston Red Sox" (July 24, 1987). [Iowa] (22:1) Wint 92, p. 116-117.
"To Lee Atwater on His Fortieth Birthday." [PoetL] (87:2) Sum 92, p. 44.

1154. COLE, Douglas
"The Cloud Splitter." [BellR] (15:2) Fall 92, p. 36-37.
"Holy Woman." [BellR] (15:2) Fall 92, p. 35.

1155. COLE, Henri
"100 B.C." [Nat] (254:17) 4 My 92, p. 606.
"Ex-Voto." [Thrpny] (51) Fall 92, p. 25.
"The Gondolas." [SouthwR] (77:2/3) Spr-Sum 92, p. 166.
"Marius, Son of Sarkis, Named for the Roman Consul, Savior from the Barbarians, Putative Husband of Mary Magdalene." [ParisR] (34:122) Spr 92, p. 168.
"The New Life." [Boulevard] (7:1, #19) Spr 92, p. 162-163.
"The Pink and the Black." [NewRep] (207:2) 6 Jl 92, p. 40.
"Une Lettre á New York." [ParisR] (34:122) Spr 92, p. 166-167.

1156. COLE, Michael
"Still Life with Pears." [OhioR] (48) 92, p. 78.

1157. COLE, Norma
"Mercury." [Talisman] (8) Spr 92, p. 67-74.

1158. COLE, Peter (*See also* COLE, Peter J.)
"Gazing Through the Night" (after the Hebrew of Samuel Hanagid, 993-1056 C.E.). [Agni] (35) 92, p. 96-97.
"On Flkeeing His City" (after the Hebrew of Samuel Hanagid, 993-1056 C.E.). [Agni] (35) 92, p. 98-99.

1159. COLE, Peter J. (*See also* COLE, Peter)
"A Poem for My Father." [Grain] (20:1) Spr 92, p. 38-42.

1160. COLE, Richard
"You Must Change Your Life." [AmerV] (26) Spr 92, p. 126.

1161. COLE, Robert
"Cangrejo (Zipolite)" (for Suzie). [Interim] (11:2) Fall-Wint 92-93, p. 24.
"In Place of the Coyote" (Leon Trotsky Museum — Mexico City). [Interim] (11:2) Fall-Wint 92-93, p. 22.
"Santo Domingo, San Cristobal, Mexico." [Interim] (11:2) Fall-Wint 92-93, p. 23.
"Sweatshop" (Runwell Asylum). [Stand] (33:2) Spr 92, p. 60.

1162. COLE, William Rossa
"Drifting on the wide Potomac." [Light] (3) Aut 92, p. 29.
"In my battered barque, on the Biafran Bight." [Light] (2) Sum 92, p. 29.
"River Rhymes." [Light] (1) Spr 92, p. 32.
"Wandering by the Williwaw." [Light] (4) Wint 92-93, p. 29.

1163. COLEMAN, Hildy
"Thirteen Ways of Looking at a Cat in the Rain." [Confr] (48/49) Spr-Sum 92, p. 237-239.

1164. COLEMAN, John
"Folding Dresses." [ColEng] (54:8) D 92, p. 939.
"Grace." [PoetL] (87:1) Spr 92, p. 50.

1165. COLEMAN, Wanda
"American Sonnet (10)." [Obs] (7:1/2) Spr-Sum 92, p. 78.
"Buttah." [Contact] (10:62/63/64) Fall 91-Spr 92, p. 54.
"Casting Call (2)." [Obs] (7:1/2) Spr-Sum 92, p. 74-75.
"Chair Affair." [AnotherCM] (23) Spr 92, p. 44.
"Essay on Language." [KenR] (NS 14:4) Fall 92, p. 122-123.
"Ethnographs." [AfAmRev] (26:2) Sum 92, p. 223.
"Hollywood Zen." [OnTheBus] (4:2/5:1, #10/11) 92, p. 79.
"Message from Xanadu (2)." [AnotherCM] (23) Spr 92, p. 43.
"A Nigger's Voice Feels Curiously Cool" (line from e.e. cummings). [Obs] (7:1/2) Spr-Sum 92, p. 77-78.
"No Malice in Movieland." [Obs] (7:1/2) Spr-Sum 92, p. 75.
"Notes of a Cultural Terrorist." [CityLR] (5) 92, p. 111-112.
"Of Apes and Men." [Obs] (7:1/2) Spr-Sum 92, p. 75-77.
"Sex and Politics in Fairyland." [AfAmRev] (26:2) Sum 92, p. 221.
"Soul Eyes" (after Coltrane). [Obs] (7:1/2) Spr-Sum 92, p. 78-79.
"The Tao of Unemployment." [AfAmRev] (26:2) Sum 92, p. 222.

"Violences." [AfAmRev] (26:2) Sum 92, p. 222.

1166. COLIMON, Marie-Therese
"Encounter" (tr. by Betty Wilson). [LitR] (35:4) Sum 92, p. 509.
"Rencontre." [LitR] (35:4) Sum 92, p. 600.

1167. COLINA, Nicolás
"Cortés y La Malinche en el Pabellón de los Condenados" (for Ana Castillo). [Americas] (20:2) Sum 92, p. 55-56.
"Escuadrón de las Venganzas." [Americas] (20:2) Sum 92, p. 58-59.
"La Máquina." [Americas] (20:2) Sum 92, p. 57.
"El Pueblo Vive por Amor." [Americas] (20:2) Sum 92, p. 53-54.

1168. COLLIER, Michael
"Breughel." [Poetry] (161:2) N 92, p. 92-93.

1169. COLLIER, Phyllis
"The Last Bus to Ephesus." [Nimrod] (35:2) Spr-Sum 92, p. 84.

1170. COLLINGS, Susan
"The Nest in the Rigging." [GreensboroR] (53) Wint 92-93, p. 109.

1171. COLLINS, Andrea (Andrea V.)
"Blue Milk." [SouthernR] (28:2) Spr, Ap 92, p. 326-328.
"Inferno * Purgatorio * Paradiso." [Agni] (36) 92, p. 96.
"Tell Them You Are Innocent." [ColEng] (54:1) Ja 92, p. 37.
"To the Crossing Guard, with Her Back to the Traffic." [ColEng] (54:1) Ja 92, p. 36.

1172. COLLINS, Billy
"Lolita in New Mexico." [FreeL] (10) Sum 92, p. 24.
"Paperwork." [Poetry] (159:4) Ja 92, p. 189-190.
"Piano Lessons." [OnTheBus] (4:2/5:1, #10/11) 92, p. 80-81.
"Refrigerator Light." [FreeL] (10) Sum 92, p. 24.
"Rooming House." [FreeL] (10) Sum 92, p. 23.
"Solo." [OnTheBus] (4:2/5:1, #10/11) 92, p. 80.
"Thelonious Monk." [FreeL] (10) Sum 92, p. 23.
"Tuesday, June 4th, 1991." [Poetry] (160:4) Jl 92, p. 215-217.
"Wedding Anniversary." [OnTheBus] (4:2/5:1, #10/11) 92, p. 80.

1173. COLLINS, Floyd
"Lizard." [TarRP] (30:2) Spr 91, p. 32.

1174. COLLINS, June
"I Dreamed About You." [NewYorkQ] (48) 92, p. 105.

1175. COLLINS, Loretta
"El Día de los Muertos" (Hornitos, California, for Kevin. Tom McAfee Discovery Feature). [MissouriR] (15:3) 92, p. 162-164.
"Love at Seventeen" (Tom McAfee Discovery Feature). [MissouriR] (15:3) 92, p. 165-167.
"Photo, Fable, Fieldtrip" (Tom McAfee Discovery Feature). [MissouriR] (15:3) 92, p. 170-171.
"Soup" (Tom McAfee Discovery Feature). [MissouriR] (15:3) 92, p. 168-169.

1176. COLLINS, Martha
"Last Portrait" (tr. of Richard Exner, w. the author). [Agni] (35) 92, p. 182.
"Love Lettuce." [Field] (47) Fall 92, p. 87-88.
"Mystery Rides." [WestB] (30) 92, p. 34-35.
"Pietà Rondanini" (tr. of Richard Exner). [Agni] (35) 92, p. 181.
"Remember the Trains?" [SnailPR] (2:2) Fall-Wint 92, p. 2-3.
"The Scribe, Distracted from Her Labors." [AmerV] (26) Spr 92, p. 93-94.
"Verticals." [SnailPR] (2:2) Fall-Wint 92, p. 4.

1177. COLLINS, Richard
"Poetry Is Legal, Tender." [NegC] (12:1/2) 92, p. 20.

1178. COLLINS, Terry
"Reading Al Purdy." [AntigR] (91) Fall 92, p. 7.

1179. COLM-HOGAN, Patrick
"After the Deputy Prime Minister of Iraq Announced That in Less Than Four Weeks 20,000 Iraqis Have Died from Allied Fire." [MinnR] (38) Spr-Sum 92, p. 7-9.

1180. COLONNESE, Michael
"Stations of the Cross." [PaintedB] (47) 92, p. 7.
"Where My Father Used to Work." [Pembroke] (24) 92, p. 80.

1181. COLUMBUS, Claudette
"Quichua." [SenR] (22:2) Fall 92, p. 93.
"Silence." [SenR] (22:2) Fall 92, p. 94.

1182. COLWELL, Anne (Anne A.)
"Christina River." [SouthernPR] (32:1) Spr 92, p. 63.

"Processional." [MidwQ] (33:2) Wint 92, p. 195.
1183. COMANESCU, Denisa
"Sports Poem" (tr. by Adam Sorkin and Angela Jianu). [Vis] (38) 92, p. 34.
1184. COMANN, Brad
"Dolls" (for Carmen and Kelly). [GreensboroR] (52) Sum 92, p. 135-137.
1185. COMBELLICK, Henry
"Two Sounds." [PraS] (66:3) Fall 92, p. 56.
COMPTE, Kendall Le
See LeCOMPTE, Kendall
1186. COMPTON, Cathy
"Letter from a Mining Town, 1839." [Ploughs] (18:1) Spr 92, p. 168.
"Sailing for California: Panamanian Market, 1850." [Ploughs] (18:1) Spr 92, p. 169.
"Words from Buffalo Bill's Wife." [Ploughs] (18:1) Spr 92, p. 167.
1187. COMPTON, Diane
"They Came to Explore." [ChamLR] (10/11) Spr-Fall 92, p. 134.
1188. CONANT, Jeff
"Concrete Remains" (Excerpts). [Talisman] (9) Fall 92, p. 207.
1189. CONAWAY, Frank
"On a Bus." [CumbPR] (12:1) Fall 92, p. 31.
"On a Bus." [WestB] (30) 92, p. 107.
"Works in Progress." [CumbPR] (12:1) Fall 92, p. 30.
1190. CONDINI, Ned (Ned E.)
"Mother and Son" (tr. of Mario Luzi). [Trans] (26) Spr 92, p. 65.
"Nighttime Washes the Mind" (tr. of Mario Luzi). [MidAR] (12:2) 92, p. 23.
"Saul Bellow at the Confessinal." [NegC] (12:3) 92, p. 61-63.
1191. CONDON, Helen
"Signora." [WillowR] (19) Spr 92, p. 21.
1192. CONE, Jon
"I have been dragging this pig's skull." [WorldL] (3) 92, p. 43.
1193. CONKLE, D. Steven
"Mémère." [MoodySI] (27) Spr 92, p. 18.
1194. CONKLING, Helen
"What If You Wanted to Write a Poem." [GeoR] (46:4) Wint 92, p. 707-708.
1195. CONLEY, Toni
"Science Project." [EngJ] (81:3) Mr 92, p. 93.
1196. CONN, Jan
"Composition with Yellow at the Epicentre." [MalR] (98) Spr 92, p. 53.
"The Dead." [MalR] (98) Spr 92, p. 54.
"Woken at Night by Rain, Falling" (for Andy Brower and Jackie Brown). [MalR] (98) Spr 92, p. 55.
1197. CONN, Stewart
"Boat Trip." [Verse] (9:2) Sum 92, p. 6.
1198. CONNELLAN, Leo
"Finally, Day of the Femme." [NewYorkQ] (48) 92, p. 56.
"Sloughter Poet." [NewYorkQ] (47) 92, p. 34.
1199. CONNELLY, Karen
"An Evening Wake, Its Prayer." [PoetryC] (12:3/4) Jl 92, p. 37.
"Isadora and the Basque Photographer." [PoetryC] (12:3/4) Jl 92, p. 36.
"There Are Charms for Every Kind of Journey." [Arc] (28) Spr 92, p. 5-6.
"These Doors So Open." [PoetryC] (12:3/4) Jl 92, p. 36.
"The Word Is Absurd." [MidwQ] (33:3) Spr 92, p. 311-312.
1200. CONNELLY, Patricia
"The Interview." [Amelia] (6:4, #19) 92, p. 55.
1201. CONNOLLY, Geraldine
"The Future." [HayF] (10) Spr-Sum 92, p. 49.
1202. CONNOLLY, M. J.
"Tornado Alley." [LullwaterR] (4:1) Fall 92, p. 24.
1203. CONNORS, Colleen
"In Potter's Field" (Selections: VI-VII). [DenQ] (26:4) Spr 92, p. 16-17.
1204. CONOLEY, Gillian
"Back Alley." [NewAW] (10) Fall 92, p. 97.
"Elsewhere." [MissouriR] (15:1) 92, p. 178.
"Fearsome." [MissouriR] (15:1) 92, p. 171-173.
"Hidden Drive." [MissouriR] (15:1) 92, p. 174-175.
"I'd Like a Little Love in the Wine-red Afternoon." [ThRiPo] (39/40) 92-93, p. 30-31.

"My Sister's Hand in Mine." [AmerPoR] (21:3) My-Je 92, p. 9.
"Some Gangster Pain." [ThRiPo] (39/40) 92-93, p. 29-30.
"The Ten Commandments." [DenQ] (26:4) Spr 92, p. 18.
"Unchained Melody." [ThRiPo] (39/40) 92-93, p. 31-32.
"We Don't Have to Share a Fate." [MissouriR] (15:1) 92, p. 176-177.

1205. CONOVER, Carl
"After the Annunciation." [CumbPR] (11:2) Spr 92, p. 19.
"Drought." [SoCarR] (25:1) Fall 92, p. 64.
"Hadrian and Antinous." [PoetL] (87:1) Spr 92, p. 49.

1206. CONQUEST, Robert
"Through Persepolis." [Hellas] (3:1) Spr 92, p. 49.

1207. CONRAD, C. A.
"The Poem I've Spent My Life Trying Not to Write." [PaintedB] (48) 92, p. 64-65.

1208. CONSTANTINO, Anthony O.
"The Watchers." [EngJ] (80:8) D 91, p. 98.

1209. CONTI, Edmund
"Badge of Honor." [NegC] (12:1/2) 92, p. 21.
"Breakdown." [Light] (3) Aut 92, p. 14.
"Frostfree." [Light] (2) Sum 92, p. 9.
"Jogging Memory." [Light] (1) Spr 92, p. 30.
"Monday the Rabbi Wrote Poems." [Light] (4) Wint 92-93, p. 26.
"Sailing on the Naragansett." [Light] (2) Sum 92, p. 29.
"Sailing on the Sea of Tranquility." [Light] (3) Aut 92, p. 29.
"Sleeping on the River Styx." [Light] (4) Wint 92-93, p. 29.
"Speaking of Ostrich Eggs." [Light] (3) Aut 92, p. 7.
"Split Decision." [Light] (2) Sum 92, p. 7.
"Suspense." [Light] (1) Spr 92, p. 28.

1210. CONTOGENIS, Constantine
"All Right Then" (tr. of Munhyang, w. Wolhee Choe). [Pequod] (34) 92, p. 115.
"Between the Cold Pine Arbor's Moon" (tr. of Hongjang, w. Wolhee Choe). [Pequod] (34) 92, p. 113.
"Blue stream, don't show off your speed" (a Kisang Poem, tr. of Hwang Jini, w. Wolhee Choe). [GrandS] (11:3 #43) 92, p. 174.
"Do They Say" (tr. of Okson, w. Wolhee Choe). [Pequod] (34) 92, p. 118.
"Don't Tell Me the Face" (tr. of Myongok, w. Wolhee Choe). [Pequod] (34) 92, p. 116.
"Has the Silver River above risen further" (a Kisang Poem, tr. of Songi, w. Wolhee Choe). [GrandS] (11:3 #43) 92, p. 174.
"My Thoughts of Him" (tr. of Maehwa, w. Wolhee Choe). [Pequod] (34) 92, p. 117.
"An Urban Butterfly" (tr. of Songdaechun, w. Wolhee Choe). [Pequod] (34) 92, p. 114.

1211. COOGAN, Irene Prieto
"Luna." [Nuez] (4:10/11) 92, p. 34.
"Vuelta hacia el poniente" (A O. Paz). [Nuez] (4:10/11) 92, p. 34.

1212. COOK, Albert
"Motets, No. 2." [Hellas] (3:2) Fall 92, p. 31.
"Motets, No. 14." [Hellas] (3:2) Fall 92, p. 31.

1213. COOK, Méira
"Crazy Woman." [PraF] (13:4, #61) Wint 92-93, p. 50.
"Dodge '72." [Dandel] (19:1) 92, p. 6-7.
"The Earth My Body This Tree." [PraF] (13:4, #61) Wint 92-93, p. 48.
"Icarus II." [PraF] (13:4, #61) Wint 92-93, p. 49.
"The Last Grand Picture Show." [WestCL] (26:3, #9) Wint 92-93, p. 15-17.

1214. COOK, R. L.
"Epitaph." [NegC] (12:1/2) 92, p. 22.
"The Seed of Light." [DogRR] (11:2, #22) Fall-Wint 92, p. 27.

1215. COOK-LYNN, Elizabeth
"The Remembered Earth." [Jacaranda] (6:1/2) Wint-Spr 92, p. 66.

1216. COOLEY, Nicole
"For My Sister." [PoetryNW] (33:4) Wint 92-93, p. 34-35.

1217. COOLEY, Peter
"Ararat." [ThRiPo] (39/40) 92-93, p. 32-33.
"Dusk." [IndR] (15:2) Fall 92, p. 50.
"The Elect." [ThRiPo] (39/40) 92-93, p. 33-34.
"Let Me Tell You About Happiness." [NewOR] (19:3/4) Fall-Wint 92, p. 67.
"The Loom." [ThRiPo] (39/40) 92-93, p. 34.

"The Other." [ThRiPo] (39/40) 92-93, p. 35.
"Poem on My Birthday." [IndR] (15:2) Fall 92, p. 51.

1218. COOLIDGE, Clark
"For Ted." [Talisman] (8) Spr 92, p. 170.
"To the Cold Heart" (After Han Shan). [Sulfur] (12:2, #31) Fall 92, p. 204-209.
"The Zihua Blues." [Shiny] (7/8) 92, p. 85-89.

1219. COONEY, Ellen
"Advice to a Boy." [Bogg] (65) 92, p. 16.

1220. COOPER, Courtney
"The Day Before Burial." [LouisL] (9:1) Spr 92, p. 76-77.

1221. COOPER, David
"Dis Dance" (apologies to Monk). [PaintedB] (45) 92, p. 7.
"From the Memoirs of Rabbi Eliezer Ben Hyrcanus." [MassR] (23:2) Sum 92, p. 171-173.
"Reading *Midrash Proverbs*." [PassN] (13:2) Wint 92, p. 16.

1222. COOPER, Jane (*See also* COOPER, Jane Todd)
"For a Birthday." [AmerV] (28) 92, p. 3.
"Vocation: A Life Suite Based on Four Words from Willa Cather." [KenR] (NS 14:1) Wint 92, p. 67-76.

1223. COOPER, Jane Todd (*See also* COOPER, Jane)
"Angela and the Host." [Footwork] 92, p. 94.
"Cold War." [Footwork] 92, p. 93.
"Hide 'n Seek." [Footwork] 92, p. 94.
"Imagining August, 1945." [Footwork] 92, p. 93.

1224. COOPER, M. Truman (Marsha Truman)
"At the Dutch Gardens Restaurant." [Lactuca] (15) Mr 92, p. 48.
"An Industry on Both Sides of the Ocean." [LitR] (35:3) Spr 92, p. 396.
"True Ferns." [Kalliope] (14:1) 92, p. 41.

1225. COOPER, Wyn
"Junkyard." [QW] (36) Wint 92-93, p. 108-109.
"The Sound of Her Life." [PassN] (13:1) Sum 92, p. 32.
"Stories" (for Holly). [GreenMR] (NS 5:2) Spr-Sum 92, p. 66.

1226. COOPERAMN, Robert
"Marie-Elisabeth Menetre, 1802." [Asylum] (7:3/4) 92, p. 14.

COOPERMAN, Celeste Kostopulus
See KOSTOPULUS-COOPERMAN, C. (Celeste)

1227. COOPERMAN, Matthew
"Obsidian." [HighP] (7:2) Fall 92, p. 15.

1228. COOPERMAN, Robert
"Aboard the *Maria Crowther*, Bay of Naples, 1820, Keats Seals a Letter to Mrs. Frances Brawne, Mother of His Ex-Fiancee." [NegC] (12:1/2) 92, p. 218-219.
"At the Crown Inn, Liverpool, Keats Says Good-bye to His Brother George." [Poem] (67) My 92, p. 10.
"At the Physical Therapist's." [WebR] (16) Fall 92, p. 49.
"The Attic." [Confr] (50) Fall 92, p. 274.
"A Community of Voices." [Dandel] (19:1) 92, p. 30.
"Dr. Edward Terhune Bennett Writes to His Sister-in-Law, Agatha Starling Lawson, from London, 20 June 1876." [Bogg] (65) 92, p. 45-46.
"An Exchange." [CoalC] (5) My 92, p. 1.
"Generations." [BellR] (15:2) Fall 92, p. 28.
"The Gold Cross Found on a Spanish Galleon Sunk Off Key West." [Plain] (13:1) Fall 92, p. 37.
"Jewish Partisans, Vilna, 1943." [ChatR] (12:4) Sum 92, p. 56-57.
"John Keats Lies Awake in His Rented Room at Margate, Summer, 1816." [WebR] (16) Fall 92, p. 48-49.
"Keats Arrives in the Campagna with Severn, 7 November 1820." [Parting] (5:1) Sum 92, p. 25-26.
"Lester Scrit, Vietnam Veteran, Confesses to the Murder of Jimmy Ray Seagraves." [NewYorkQ] (48) 92, p. 100.
"Letter, Richard Lovell, Colorado Territory, to Sophia Starling-Bennett, London, on the Death of John Sprockett, 1876." [Bogg] (65) 92, p. 44-45.
"Mary Lafrance, Prostitute, Gold Creek, Colorado Territory, 1874." [Bogg] (65) 92, p. 43-44.
"Mary Shelley, on the Night *Frankenstein* Was Born." [SoCarR] (25:1) Fall 92, p. 110-111.
"Mount Unzen Erupts: Japan, June 3, 1991." [SoDakR] (30:2) Sum 92, p. 104.

"My Father's Millinery Factory." [NewDeltaR] (8:1) Fall 90-Wint 91, p. 44-45.
"Nine Months After His Murder, Sprockett Widows Come Forward" (Article in the *The Denver Ledger*, December 13, 1876). [AntigR] (90) Sum 92, p. 86-87.
"Roland of Nantes Sets Out in the Army of Louis VII, for the Second Crusade, 29 June 1147." [Poem] (67) My 92, p. 9.
"Rubble." [DogRR] (11:1) Spr-Sum 92, p. 35.
"Sissy Kelly Remembers the Orphan Trains, 1871." [SoCoast] (12) Ja 92, p. 50-51.
"Visiting Rights." [LullwaterR] (3:2) Spr 92, p. 32.
"War Insurance." [SnailPR] (2:2) Fall-Wint 92, p. 10.

1229. COPE, Wendy
"An Attempt at Unrhymed Verse." [Light] (3) Aut 92, p. 7.
"Let Me Tell You." [Light] (2) Sum 92, p. 20.

1230. CORA, María
"To Provoke a Change." [SinW] (47) Sum-Fall 92, p. 130-131.

1231. CORBEN, Beverly
"Lines for J. Alfred from the Bayou." [TexasR] (13:1/2) Spr-Sum 92, p. 86.

1232. CORBETT, William
"Dead of Winter." [Agni] (35) 92, p. 202.
"Last Words." [Conjunc] (19) 92, p. 318-319.
"Song." [BrooklynR] (9) 92, p. 90.

1233. CORBUS, Patricia
"Late-Summer Cassandra." [CreamCR] (16:2) Fall 92, p. 14.
"Lovers: Stillness, Burning." [CreamCR] (16:2) Fall 92, p. 15.

1234. CORDING, Robert
"For Rex Brasher, Painter of Birds." [NewEngR] (14:3) Sum 92, p. 98-102.
"A History." [SouthwR] (77:2/3) Spr-Sum 92, p. 288.
"In the Hummingbird Aviary, Sonora Desert Museum, Tucson, Arizona." [SouthernR] (28:2) Spr, Ap 92, p. 280-282.
"Zuni Fetish." [TarRP] (31:2) Spr 92, p. 36.

1235. COREY, Chet
"Revelation." [Plain] (12:3) Spr 92, p. 12.

1236. COREY, Stephen
"Halves of Houses." [SouthernPR] (32:1) Spr 92, p. 42-44.
"Li Po Enters New York City" (from a sequence titled "Li Po and Tu Fu in America"). [PoetC] (23:2) Wint 92, p. 10.
"Past, Present, Future." [LaurelR] (26:2) Sum 92, p. 45.
"Poppy Field Near Giverny." [YellowS] (39) Spr-Sum 92, p. 18-19.
"Prayer for Offering Prayer" (from a sequence in which the poet transplants the classical Chinese poets Li Po and Tu Fu from 8th c. China to 20th c. United States). [LaurelR] (26:2) Sum 92, p. 46.
"Travels in Two Worlds" (from a sequence titled "Li Po and Tu Fu in America"). [PoetC] (23:2) Wint 92, p. 9.
"Writer." [LaurelR] (26:2) Sum 92, p. 44-45.

1237. CORKERY, Christopher Jane
"As in the Days of the Prophets." [Atlantic] (269:6) Je 92, p. 76.

1238. CORLEY, Wm. J.
"Midnight Woman." [PoetryUSA] (24) 92, p. 27.

1239. CORMAN, Cid
"3 Poems." [Noctiluca] (1:1) Spr 92, p. 38-39.
"I won't tell on you." [Conjunc] (19) 92, p. 293.
"Since the ether cone." [WorldL] (3) 92, p. 42.
"To come out of a life." [Conjunc] (19) 92, p. 293.

CORMIER-SHEKERJIAN, Regina de
See DeCORMIER-SHEKERJIAN, Regina

1240. CORN, Alfred
"1990." [Antaeus] (69) Aut 92, p. 136-137.
"1992" (3 selections). [KenR] (NS 14:3) Sum 92, p. 48-56.
"1992" (Selection: 8). [PartR] (59:3) Sum 92, p. 479-482.
"1992" (Selections: "1949," "1977," "1990"). [ParisR] (34:122) Spr 92, p. 252-265.
"Right and Left Hand." [SouthwR] (77:1) Wint 92, p. 74.

1241. CORNISH, Sam
"Have You Heard the Little Presbyterian Children Sing." [KenR] (NS 14:3) Sum 92, p. 79-80.
"The Talented 90%." [KenR] (NS 14:3) Sum 92, p. 79.

1242. CORNISH, Steven Patrick
"Desire in Vermont!" [WebR] (16) Fall 92, p. 101.

1243. CORNWELL, Margery
"Pieces from an African Landscape, Revisited." [Outbr] (23) 92, p. 7-9.
1244. CORONEL RIVERA, Juan
"Tundra." [Nuez] (4:10/11) 92, p. 6.
1245. CORPI, Lucha
"Canción de Invierno" (A Magdalena Mora, 1952-1981). [Americas] (20:3/4) Fall - Wint 92, p. 212.
"Fuga." [Americas] (20:3/4) Fall-Wint 92, p. 210-211.
"Invernario." [Americas] (20:3/4) Fall-Wint 92, p. 209.
1246. CORREA DIAZ, Luis
"Rosario de Actos de Habla" (Fragmentos). [Inti] (36) Otoño 92, p. 139-142.
1247. CORRETJER, Juan Antonio
"Now I Take My Leave" (tr. by Camilo Pérez-Bustillo and Martín Espada). [Callaloo] (15:4) Fall 92, p. 951.
CORRETJER, Zoe Jimenez
See JIMENEZ CORRETJER, Zoe
1248. CORRIE, Daniel
"New York Debut." [LullwaterR] (4:1) Fall 92, p. 25.
"Their World." [SouthernHR] (26:4) Fall 92, p. 348.
"Unpromised." [SoCarR] (25:1) Fall 92, p. 135.
1249. CORSI, Wendy
"M & M." [Amelia] (7:1, #20) 92, p. 71.
1250. CORTEZ, Jayne
"It Came." [Sulfur] (12:2, #31) Fall 92, p. 34-35.
"Lynch Fragment I." [Sulfur] (12:2, #31) Fall 92, p. 33.
"Ogun's Friend." [Sulfur] (12:2, #31) Fall 92, p. 35-37.
1251. CORTEZ, Sarah
"Her." [ChironR] (11:4) Wint 92, p. 45.
1252. CORY, Jim
"Darling." [BrooklynR] (9) 92, p. 68.
"Feet." [ChironR] (11:4) Wint 92, p. 41.
1253. CORYELL, Sabrina
"Lilith in the Garden." [Noctiluca] (1:2) Wint 92 [on cover: Wint 93], p. 42.
"The Magnetics of Desire." [Noctiluca] (1:2) Wint 92 [on cover: Wint 93], p. 43.
1254. COSBY, Allison
"India ink spill." [Amelia] (7:1, #20) 92, p. 31.
1255. COSERI, Gary
"An Amaranth for Chico." [CityLR] (5) 92, p. 246-247.
1256. COSIER, Tony
"The Corn Mask." [CanLit] (134) Aut 92, p. 73-74.
"On a Grey Day Like Today." [CanLit] (134) Aut 92, p. 200.
1257. COSTANZO, Mike
"Seen from a Bus Window." [JlNJPo] (14:1) Spr 92, p. 40.
1258. COSTEA, Luciana
"Creation" (tr. of Marin Sorescu, w. W. D. Snograss and Dona Rosu). [Poetry] (159:4) Ja 92, p. 191.
"I Bound Up the Trees' Eyes" (tr. of Marin Sorescu, w. W. D. Snograss and Dona Rosu). [Poetry] (159:4) Ja 92, p. 194.
"Solemnly" (tr. of Marin Sorescu, w. W. D. Snograss and Dona Rosu). [Poetry] (159:4) Ja 92, p. 192.
"Thieves" (tr. of Marin Sorescu, w. W. D. Snograss and Dona Rosu). [Poetry] (159:4) Ja 92, p. 193.
1259. COSTIGAN, Marguerite
"September: Open-Heart Surgery." [Asylum] (7:3/4) 92, p. 53.
1260. COSTOPOULOS, Olga
"A Sunday Curse." [Light] (4) Wint 92-93, p. 22.
1261. COTTER, Craig
"My Hands He Said." [BrooklynR] (9) 92, p. 58.
1262. COULEHAN, Jack
"My Poetry Teacher Sells Used Cars." [HiramPoR] (51/52) Fall 91-Sum 92, p. 30 - 31.
"The Worm" (Elderslie Clinic, Jamaica). [SnailPR] (2:2) Fall-Wint 92, p. 12-13.
1263. COULETTE, Henri
"The Renaissance in England." [KenR] (NS 14:1) Wint 92, p. 139.
"Tea Dance at the Nautilus Hotel (1925)" (On a painting by Donald Justice). [Verse] (8:3/9:1) Wint-Spr 92, p. 33.

1264. COULOMBE, Gerard
"Cat Owl." [PoetL] (87:1) Spr 92, p. 39-40.
"Great Lives from the Ordinary." [OxfordM] (6:2) Fall-Wint 90, p. 15.
"The Kitchen." [CapeR] (27:2) Fall 92, p. 21.
COURCY, Lynne H. de
See DeCOURCY, Lynne H.
1265. COURSEN, H. R.
"Fast Pitch, 1963." [SmPd] (29:1, #84) Wint 92, p. 12.
1266. COURSEN, Herbert
"6 July, '91: For M.H.C., 1901-1991." [LitR] (35:3) Spr 92, p. 314.
"A Note to Leigh." [LitR] (35:3) Spr 92, p. 314.
1267. COUTURIER, John
"The Good Life." [BrooklynR] (9) 92, p. 56.
"One-Armed Sailor." [NewYorkQ] (47) 92, p. 63.
1268. COVEY, Patricia
"The Gardener of Bedlam." [NewYorkQ] (48) 92, p. 99.
"Southern Gothic." [WillowR] (19) Spr 92, p. 15-16.
"This Is a Poem." [NewYorkQ] (49) 92, p. 84.
1269. COVICH, Susan
"Facing the Butterfly." [Vis] (40) 92, p. 35.
1270. COWEE, Bill
"A Prophet Finds Himself in the River." [Interim] (11:1) Spr-Sum 92, p. 3.
1271. COX, Andrew
"Ben's Sneakers." [RiverS] (36) 92, p. 63-64.
"Spring Cleaning." [RiverS] (36) 92, p. 62.
1272. COX, Ed
"Passenger" (from "Part Of"). [WashR] (18:4) D 92-Ja 93, p. 16.
1273. COX, M. J.
"Creative Writing at the University of Iowa." [PoetL] (87:4) Wint 92-93, p. 48.
1274. COX, Mark
"Canning." [QW] (35) Sum-Fall 92, p. 108-109.
"The Hand." [PoetryE] (33) Spr 92, p. 28.
"The Knives." [PoetryE] (33) Spr 92, p. 29.
"Levitation." [Pequod] (34) 92, p. 54-55.
"Or Else." [PoetryE] (33) Spr 92, p. 30-31.
"The Rest." [NewEngR] (14:4) Fall 92, p. 169-170.
"Sleep Apnea." [NewEngR] (14:4) Fall 92, p. 170-171.
"The Wasps." [Pequod] (34) 92, p. 53.
1275. COX, Nathan H.
"The Double." [ChiR] (38:3) 92, p. 37-44.
1276. COX, Wayne
"II. There is also the housewife in seventeen" (tr. of Miquel Martí i Pol, w. Lourdes Manyé i Martí). [Stand] (33:4) Aut 92, p. 145.
"III. The leaves and also the rustle of the leaves" (tr. of Miquel Martí i Pol, w. Lourdes Manyé i Martí). [Stand] (33:4) Aut 92, p. 145.
"IV. There are dull afternoons and exciting afternoons" (tr. of Miquel Martí i Pol, w. Lourdes Manyé i Martí). [Stand] (33:4) Aut 92, p. 146.
"V. I bid you good-bye with leaves. I will return next year." (tr. of Miquel Martí i Pol, w. Lourdes Manyé i Martí). [Stand] (33:4) Aut 92, p. 147.
"Afterwards." [SouthernHR] (26:3) Sum 92, p. 276.
"The Dark Drum" (tr. of Miquel Martí i Pol, w. Lourdes Manyé i Martí). [Chelsea] (53) 92, p. 78-79.
"Not to Cry" (tr. of Miquel Martí i Pol, w. Lourdes Manyé i Martí). [Chelsea] (53) 92, p. 77.
"A Second Letter." [CharR] (18:2) Fall 92, p. 86.
"Water Wheel" (tr. of Miquel Martí i Pol, w. Lourdes Manyé i Martí). [Chelsea] (53) 92, p. 76.
1277. COYLE, Bill
"Ancestors." [SouthernPR] (32:1) Spr 92, p. 38.
1278. COYNE, Kevin
"Not So Final Rest." [MoodySI] (27) Spr 92, p. 9.
CRABBE, Chris Wallace
See WALLACE-CRABBE, Chris
1279. CRACIUNESCU, Ioana
"Fear of Drifting" (tr. by Fleur Adcock). [13thMoon] (10:1/2) 92, p. 13.
"Grey Landscape" (tr. by Fleur Adcock). [13thMoon] (10:1/2) 92, p. 14.

"Naive Paintings" (tr. by Fleur Adcock). [13thMoon] (10:1/2) 92, p. 14.

1280. CRAIG, Christine
"Florida Blues" (for Diedre and Marsha). [LitR] (35:4) Sum 92, p. 471.
"Part III, Lithographs." [LitR] (35:4) Sum 92, p. 472-473.
"Poems for Two Daughters" (I. for Rachael, II. for Rebecca). [LitR] (35:4) Sum 92, p. 470-471.

1281. CRAIG, Richard
"84 Days." [FreeL] (9) Wint 92, p. 10-11.

1282. CRAIN, Joyce
"The Watch." [ChrC] (109:25) 26 Ag-2 S 92, p. 778.

1283. CRAIN, Rachel Channon
"In Plato's Cave: Death of a Black Widow." [PoetL] (87:1) Spr 92, p. 37.
"Job Again: Andrew Jones." [PoetL] (87:1) Spr 92, p. 36.

1284. CRAM, David
"Coming to Order." [Light] (4) Wint 92-93, p. 24.

1285. CRAMER, Barbara
"Ripening." [NewYorkQ] (49) 92, p. 86.

1286. CRAMER, Steven
"After Bypass" (for my mother). [PartR] (59:3) Sum 92, p. 477-478.
"The Black Minus." [NoAmR] (277:2) Mr-Ap 92, p. 22.
"The Feeder." [Boulevard] (7:2/3, #20/21) Fall 92, p. 87-88.
"His Wish." [Boulevard] (7:2/3, #20/21) Fall 92, p. 86.
"The Storyline." [NewRep] (206:6) 10 F 92, p. 35.

1287. CRANDALL, Jeff
"Conversation Over Dinner." [ChironR] (11:4) Wint 92, p. 46.

1288. CRANE, George
"Remains." [Archae] (4) late 92-early 93, p. 23.
"A Toy to Touch." [Archae] (4) late 92-early 93, p. 21.
"Winter Whispers." [Archae] (4) late 92-early 93, p. 22.

1289. CRANE, T.
"Love Pome # 9360." [CapilR] (2:9) Fall 92, p. 57.
"My smoking harbourlite pistol tells no lies." [CapilR] (2:9) Fall 92, p. 55-56.

1290. CRANFIELD, Steve
"Give Me Back My Man" (in memoriam Ricky Wilson). [Art&Und] (1:5) S-O 92, p. 12.

1291. CRAPSEY, Adelaide
"I make my shroud, but no one knows." [PoetryUSA] (24) 92, p. 18.

CRARY, Jim Mc
See Mc CRARY, Jim

1292. CRASNARU, Daniela
"Darwinism" (from "Niagara de Plumb," tr. by Fleur Adcock). [13thMoon] (10:1/2) 92, p. 11.
"The Last Day of Pompeii" (from "Niagara de Plumb," tr. by Fleur Adcock). [13thMoon] (10:1/2) 92, p. 10.
"Orphic" (from "Niagara de Plumb," tr. by Fleur Adcock). [13thMoon] (10:1/2) 92, p. 9.
"Victory" (from "Niagara de Plumb," tr. by Fleur Adcock). [13thMoon] (10:1/2) 92, p. 12.

1293. CRATE, Joan
"Dreams of My Father." [Grain] (20:1) Spr 92, p. 36.

1294. CRAVEN, Grey
"My Father's Car." [GreensboroR] (52) Sum 92, p. 39.
"On the State of Future Collections at a Small-Town Library." [GreensboroR] (52) Sum 92, p. 40.

1295. CRAVER, Mark
"Amy Reads Anne Sexton Over My Body." [WilliamMR] (30) 92, p. 40.

1296. CRAWFORD, David
"A. C. T." [HangL] (60) 92, p. 78.
"Teen Love." [HangL] (60) 92, p. 80.
"Uprooted." [HangL] (60) 92, p. 79.

1297. CRAWFORD, John W.
"Sorghum Making Time." [Elf] (2:1) Spr 92, p. 33.

1298. CRAWFORD, Tom
"The Heart." [PoetryE] (33) Spr 92, p. 34.
"Snow." [PoetryE] (33) Spr 92, p. 32.
"Washing." [PoetryE] (33) Spr 92, p. 33.

1299. CREASY-FONTAINE, Paula
"Karate Pants Cover a Good Hard-On (or Men in Love)." [WormR] (32:3, #127) 92, p. 102.
"Next Time I'll Keep My Mouth Shut." [WormR] (32:3, #127) 92, p. 102.
"Seeing My Name in Print Is Emotional." [WormR] (32:3, #127) 92, p. 102.
"Sexisms." [ChironR] (11:1) Spr 92, p. 26.
"There Can't Be a Connection But." [WormR] (32:3, #127) 92, p. 102.
1300. CREEDON, Carolyn
"Litany." [AmerPoR] (21:5) S-O 92, p. 48.
1301. CREELEY, Robert
"Faint Faces." [GrandS] (11:3 #43) 92, p. 28.
"Heaven." [GrandS] (11:3 #43) 92, p. 29.
"Here." [WashR] (18:4) D 92-Ja 93, p. 28.
"Loop." [WashR] (18:4) D 92-Ja 93, p. 28.
"One Way." [GrandS] (11:3 #43) 92, p. 29-30.
"Star." [WashR] (18:4) D 92-Ja 93, p. 28.
"A Testament." [AntR] (50:1/2) Wint-Spr 92, p. 190-191.
"The Window." [Talisman] (8) Spr 92, p. 44.
1302. CREW, Louie (*See also* LI, Min Hua)
"The Mist in the Valley Below." [EvergreenC] (7:2) Sum-Fall 92, p. 56-57.
1303. CREW, Louis
"Mark this pimple." [Contact] (10:62/63/64) Fall 91-Spr 92, p. 47.
1304. CREWS, Judson
"I Was Out-Mannoeuvred from the Start." [ChironR] (11:1) Spr 92, p. 2.
"It Seems the Besetting Cause of Generic Man's." [ChironR] (11:1) Spr 92, p. 2.
"My Old Typewriter Is Dead. It Is." [ChironR] (11:1) Spr 92, p. 2.
"My Studio, As I Call It — Where I Live. That." [ChironR] (11:1) Spr 92, p. 2.
"The Poisoned Springs of My Unction — How." [ChironR] (11:1) Spr 92, p. 2.
1305. CREWS, Richard
"The Interview." [SoCoast] (12) Ja 92, p. 56-57.
1306. CRILL, Hildred
"Elsewhere Condition." [Poetry] (160:1) Ap 92, p. 1.
1307. CRINNIN, Gerry
"Matins." [SpiritSH] (57) Spr-Sum 92, p. 59.
1308. CRISICK, Maureen Micus
"Coffee with Ivan." [Kalliope] (14:2) 92, p. 19.
1309. CRNJANSKI, Milos
"Parting at Kalemegdan" (tr. by David Sanders and Dubravka Juraga). [NewOR] (19:3/4) Fall-Wint 92, p. 108.
1310. CROCKETT, Mary
"Syncopation." [SouthernPR] (32:2) Fall 92, p. 35-36.
1311. CROLL, Su
"Lune de Miel." [PraF] (13:2, #59) Sum 92, p. 16.
"A Mild Milking and Its Cheeses Then a Bleeding." [Grain] (20:3) Fall 92, p. 57 - 58.
"Pigs and Pearls." [PraF] (13:2, #59) Sum 92, p. 17.
1312. CROOKER, Barbara
"At the Château." [PoetC] (24:1) Fall 92, p. 28-29.
"Coal." [WestB] (30) 92, p. 77.
"Grating Parmesan." [Kaleid] (25) Sum-Fall 92, p. 44.
"Vegetable Love." [WestB] (30) 92, p. 76-77.
"The World According to Maleska" (Eugene Maleska, editor of the *New York Times* Crossword Puzzle). [PoetL] (87:1) Spr 92, p. 35.
1313. CROSS, Elsa
"The Cenote at Zac-quí" (tr. by Cynthia Steele). [TriQ] (85) Fall 92, p. 248-250.
1314. CROW, Mary
"The Deaths" (tr. of Olga Orozco). [InterPR] (18:2) Fall 92, p. 25.
"Eleventh IV.20" (for Eduardo Acevedo, tr. of Roberto Ruarroz). [Pequod] (34) 92, p. 52.
"The Foreigner" (tr. of Olga Orozco). [InterPR] (18:2) Fall 92, p. 23.
"Olga Orozco" (tr. of Olga Orozco). [InterPR] (18:2) Fall 92, p. 19, 21.
"Westering." [MidwQ] (34:1) Aut 92, p. 62-63.
"Winter Poem" (tr. of Jorge Teillier). [InterPR] (18:2) Fall 92, p. 27.
1315. CROW, Steve
"Dream Tree House." [PraS] (66:2) Sum 92, p. 22-23.
"Para Manuelito." [PraS] (66:2) Sum 92, p. 20-21.

"Windless Midnight." [PraS] (66:2) Sum 92, p. 24.
1316. CROYDON, Steven
"Young Man with a Dancer's Walk." [Amelia] (6:4, #19) 92, p. 125-126.
1317. CROYSTON, John
"Early Photographs" (NSW Library Exhibition). [Footwork] 92, p. 136.
"Mrs Hughes." [Footwork] 92, p. 136.
1318. CROZIER, Lorna
"The Brain" (using the first stanza of Charles Simic's "Harsh Climate" as the first two lines). [Descant] (23:4/24:1, #78/79) Wint-Spr 92-93, p. 16-17.
"A Brief History of the Horse." [SouthernR] (28:2) Spr, Ap 92, p. 220-222.
"Cleaning Fish." [MalR] (98) Spr 92, p. 47-48.
"Dividing by Seven." [MalR] (98) Spr 92, p. 49-50.
"Faces Shaped Like Hearts." [MalR] (98) Spr 92, p. 45-46.
"Gardens." [CanLit] (133) Sum 92, p. 52-53.
"Inventing the Hawk." [SouthernR] (28:2) Spr, Ap 92, p. 216-217.
"The Memorial Wall." [SouthernR] (28:2) Spr, Ap 92, p. 219-220.
"Paper Boy." [SouthernR] (28:2) Spr, Ap 92, p. 217-218.
"Sturgeon." [MalR] (98) Spr 92, p. 51-52.
"Ways of Seeing" (for E.C., d. 1990). [Descant] (23:4/24:1, #78/79) Wint-Spr 92 - 93, p. 15.
1319. CRUMMEY, Michael
"Michelangelo." [AntigR] (91) Fall 92, p. 18-19.
"Silk Road 1." [Grain] (20:4) Wint 92, p. 108.
1320. CRUSER, Patricia
"The Wall." [Amelia] (7:1, #20) 92, p. 93.
1321. CRUSZ, Rienzi
"Bouquet to My Colonial Masters." [CanLit] (132) Spr 92, p. 15.
"Why I Can Talk of the Angelic Qualities of the Raven." [CanLit] (132) Spr 92, p. 42-43.
CRUZ, Victor Hernández
See HERNANDEZ-CRUZ, Victor
1322. CSAMER, Mary Ellen
"A Resignation." [Event] (21:2) Sum 92, p. 70-71.
1323. CSIFFARY, Sylva
"Forróság / Torrid Heat" (tr. of Béla Markó). [Nimrod] (35:2) Spr-Sum 92, p. 40.
1324. CSOORI, Sándor
"A Close Friend of Words" (tr. by Nicholas Kolumban). [AntigR] (90) Sum 92, p. 55.
"The Dog from Next Door Still Comes Over" (tr. by William Jay Smith). [Trans] (26) Spr 92, p. 104.
"I Wanted to Arrange" (tr. by Len Roberts). [IndR] (15:2) Fall 92, p. 72.
"Igy Lásson, Aki Látni Akar." [AntigR] (90) Sum 92, p. 54.
"Letter to the American Poet Gregory Corso" (tr. by Len Roberts and László Vértes). [Agni] (36) 92, p. 253-255.
"No Kin of Yours, Just a Friend" (tr. by Len Roberts and Laszlo Vertes). [KenR] (NS 14:1) Wint 92, p. 86-87.
"Returning Home from the Flight After the War" (tr. by Len Roberts). [Field] (46) Spr 92, p. 22.
"Somebody Consoles Me with a Poem" (tr. by Len Roberts and Laszlo Vertes). [KenR] (NS 14:1) Wint 92, p. 85-86.
"The Time Has Come" (tr. by Len Roberts). [PoetryE] (33) Spr 92, p. 163.
1325. CUADRA, Angel
"The Affairs of Disaster" (Translation Chapbook Series, No. 20, in Spanish and English, tr. by Silvia Curbelo and Dionisio D. Martínez). [MidAR] (13:2) 92, p. 43-67.
1326. CUADRA, Pablo Antonio
"About the Poet" (tr. by Florinda Mintz and Paul Vangelisti). [OnTheBus] (4:2/5:1, #10/11) 92, p. 272.
"Exiles" (Dedicated to Stefan Baciu, tr. by Florinda Mintz and Paul Vangelisti). [OnTheBus] (4:2/5:1, #10/11) 92, p. 273.
1327. CUDDIHY, Michael
"The Pendulum." [ThRiPo] (39/40) 92-93, p. 36-37.
"Steps" (for Andy Meyer). [ThRiPo] (39/40) 92-93, p. 35-36.
"This Body." [ThRiPo] (39/40) 92-93, p. 37.
1328. CUDDY, Dan
"On the Death of a Cousin." [Epiphany] (3:1) Ja (Wint) 92, p. 21.

"The Story of the Laughing Cavalier." [Epiphany] (3:1) Ja (Wint) 92, p. 22-23.

1329. CULHANE, Brian
"Ars Poetica." [WestHR] (46:1) Spr 92, p. 20.

1330. CULLEN-DuPONT, Kathryn
"Behind Convent Walls." [NewYorkQ] (48) 92, p. 102.

1331. CULLINAN, Patrick
"Etruscan Girl." [Stand] (33:3) Sum 92, p. 8-9.

1332. CULLY, Barbara
"My Involuntary Creation." [FreeL] (9) Wint 92, p. 19-20.
"Repressed Theme." [FreeL] (9) Wint 92, p. 18-19.

1333. CUMBERLAND, Sharon
"Madame Tussaud Remembers: Marie Gersholtz Forgets." [BelPoJ] (43:2) Wint 92 - 93, p. 12-15.

1334. CUMMINS, James
"Reading Hemingway." [KenR] (NS 14:3) Sum 92, p. 83-84.
"White Rose." [KenR] (NS 14:3) Sum 92, p. 83.

1335. CUMMINS, Richard
"'Biology!' Says Tina." [Amelia] (7:1, #20) 92, p. 116-117.
"Quick Fixics." [Epiphany] (3:3) Jl (Sum) 92, p. 187-188.
"Stuffed Animals" (for Bodi). [Epiphany] (3:3) Jl (Sum) 92, p. 189-190.
"Summer & Flute." [Epiphany] (3:3) Jl (Sum) 92, p. 188-189.
"Welcome to the World." [Epiphany] (3:3) Jl (Sum) 92, p. 191.

1336. CUNNINGHAM, Brent
"Elegies for Zooey." [QW] (36) Wint 92-93, p. 103-105.

1337. CUNNINGHAM, Eleanor L.
"Catgut." [PoetL] (87:1) Spr 92, p. 34.

1338. CUNNINGHAM, Mark
"Ineradicable Events." [Asylum] (7:3/4) 92, p. 21.
"The Melancholy of the Hands." [Asylum] (7:3/4) 92, p. 20.
"Mondrian." [NewDeltaR] (8:2) Spr-Sum 91, p. 72.
"Peace." [LitR] (35:3) Spr 92, p. 328.
"The Table of Silences." [Asylum] (7:3/4) 92, p. 20-21.
"Trees at Night." [LitR] (35:3) Spr 92, p. 328.

1339. CURBELO, Silvia
"The Affairs of Disaster" (Translation Chapbook Series, No. 20, tr. of Angel Cuadra, w. Dionisio D. Martínez). [MidAR] (13:2) 92, p. 43-67.
"Witness." [PassN] (13:2) Wint 92, p. 24.

1340. CURREY, Richard
"Winter: Ordinary, West Virginia." [HighP] (7:1) Spr 92, p. 74.

1341. CURRY, Elizabeth R.
"Filaments." [OxfordM] (6:2) Fall-Wint 90, p. 91.
"The Furies." [OxfordM] (6:2) Fall-Wint 90, p. 90.

1342. CURTIS, Dana
"The Hand I Wrote With." [SingHM] (20) 92, p. 93.
"How to Impregnate a Man." [SingHM] (20) 92, p. 94.

1343. CURTIS, Gregory
"Zhou En-lai." [NegC] (12:3) 92, p. 64-66.

1344. CURTIS, Tony
"The Pew." [TarRP] (32:1) Fall 92, p. 44.
"A Sloping House." [TarRP] (32:1) Fall 92, p. 43.

1345. CURZEN, Leo M.
"Define." [DogRR] (11:1) Spr-Sum 92, p. 37.

1346. CUSHING, James
"Come Day, Go Day" (honorable mention, Eve of Saint Agnes Contest). [NegC] (12:3) 92, p. 9.
"More Than You Know." [NegC] (12:1/2) 92, p. 185.
"Some of These Days." [NegC] (12:1/2) 92, p. 184.
"We'll Be Together Again." [AntR] (50:4) Fall 92, p. 720.
"Where Is Love?" [ArtfulD] (22/23) 92, p. 95.
"You Are Too Beautiful." [HawaiiR] (16:2, #35) Spr 92, p. 28.

1347. CUSHING JAMES
"A Sleepin' Bee." [OnTheBus] (4:2/5:1, #10/11) 92, p. 82.

1348. CUSTIS, Keith
"One of the Watchers." [CreamCR] (16:2) Fall 92, p. 64.
"Words from an Ex-Miner's Handbook." [PoetL] (87:1) Spr 92, p. 25-26.

1349. DABASI, Roseann
"About Beets." [EvergreenC] (7:1) Wint-Spr 92, p. 19-20.
1350. DABNEY, Janice
"The Stroke: Past and Present." [NegC] (12:3) 92, p. 67-68.
1351. DABROCK, Martha
"Who Will Listen to My Song?" [NegC] (12:1/2) 92, p. 23.
1352. DABYDEEN, Cyril
"Acorn's Third World." [CanLit] (132) Spr 92, p. 58-59.
"The Cida Poet Writes of Guyana." [CanLit] (132) Spr 92, p. 124-125.
1353. DACEY, Philip
"After Editing" (for David Jauss, upon his resignation as editor of Crazy Horse). [TarRP] (31:2) Spr 92, p. 1-2.
"Bachspeed." [RiverC] (12:2) Spr 92, p. 7-8.
"Death and Television." [NewEngR] (14:3) Sum 92, p. 144-146.
"The Deathbed Playboy" (for Terry Bernhardt). [Hudson] (44:4) Wint 92, p. 607 - 610.
"Difficult Corners." [Shen] (42:1) Spr 92, p. 31-33.
"How I Escaped from the Labyrinth." [ThRiPo] (39/40) 92-93, p. 40.
"Looking at Models in the Sears Catalogue." [ThRiPo] (39/40) 92-93, p. 39-40.
"The Neighbors." [PoetryNW] (33:1) Spr 92, p. 9-10.
"Not About Pie Thieves." [TarRP] (31:2) Spr 92, p. 2-3.
"Perennials." [LaurelR] (26:2) Sum 92, p. 37.
"Porno Love" (for Darlene and Mae). [ThRiPo] (39/40) 92-93, p. 38.
"The President." [Shen] (42:1) Spr 92, p. 33-34.
"Rat" (Florence to Parthenope Nightingale, 22 April 1856). [GeoR] (46:4) Wint 92, p. 727-728.
"Recorded Message." [BelPoJ] (43:1) Fall 92, p. 6-7.
"Small Dark Song." [ThRiPo] (39/40) 92-93, p. 37.
"Study" (for the painter Edward Evans). [MidwQ] (33:2) Wint 92, p. 196-197.
"Why Jesus Was Crucified." [NewEngR] (14:3) Sum 92, p. 143-144.
"The Wound" (for Leo Dangel). [PoetryNW] (33:1) Spr 92, p. 10-11.
1354. DAGAMA, Steven
"A Midsummer Night's Vigil." [YellowS] (Ten Years [i.e. 40]) Sum-Fall 92, p. 17.
1355. D'AGUIAR, Fred
"1492." [Verse] (9:2) Sum 92, p. 29-47.
"At the Grave of the Unknown African, Henbury Parish Church." [Callaloo] (15:4) Fall 92, p. 894-898.
1356. DAHAKE, Vasant Abaji
"Deciphering a Stone Inscription" (tr. by Vilas Sarang). [ChiR] (38:1/2) 92, p. 97.
1357. DAIGON, Ruth
"It Is Enough." [Poem] (67) My 92, p. 46.
"Messages." [InterPR] (18:1) Spr 92, p. 57.
"Messages." [Poem] (67) My 92, p. 47.
"Ordinary Things." [Vis] (38) 92, p. 15.
"Stung." [Pearl] (15) Spr-Sum 92, p. 46.
"The Void." [NegC] (12:1/2) 92, p. 186.
1358. DAILEY, Joel
"Impossumibilities" (for Everette Maddox). [ColEng] (53:8) D 91, p. 910.
"Tu Fu: A Question." [ColEng] (53:8) D 91, p. 909.
1359. DAJENYA
"Born black and white." [SinW] (47) Sum-Fall 92, p. 56.
1360. DALDORPH, Brian
"The Economic Police." [FreeL] (9) Wint 92, p. 27.
1361. DALGON, Ruth
"Bloodline." [CoalC] (5) My 92, p. 4.
"Reasons." [CoalC] (5) My 92, p. 3.
"Still Life." [CoalC] (5) My 92, p. 3.
1362. DALISAY, Jose, Jr.
"Homecoming." [Manoa] (4:1) Spr 92, p. 39.
1363. DALVEN, Rae
"Ithaca" (tr. of Constantine (Constantine P.) Cavafy). [CumbPR] (11:2) Spr 92, p. 58-59.
1364. DALY, Chris
"Kilo Note Address." [ChironR] (11:3) Aut 92, p. 29.
1365. DALY, Daniel
"Leafing Toward Light." [Epiphany] (3:4) O (Fall) 92, p. 255.

"Spin." [Epiphany] (3:4) O (Fall) 92, p. 254.
"Time-Out Arcade." [Epiphany] (3:4) O (Fall) 92, p. 256.

1366. DALY, Frederica Y.
"River Rock." [Elf] (2:1) Spr 92, p. 29.

1367. DALY, M. A.
"The Mississippi River and Prairie du Chien, Wisconsin." [CutB] (38) Sum 92, p. 128-129.

1368. DAME, Enid
"Ethel Rosenberg Revisited." [NewYorkQ] (48) 92, p. 59-61.

1369. DAMERON, Chip
"South Texas Boxcar Blues." [TarRP] (30:2) Spr 91, p. 9.

1370. DAMIAN, Mark
"In Another Life." [OnTheBus] (4:2/5:1, #10/11) 92, p. 83.

1371. DANA, Robert
"At Bridget's Well." [Iowa] (22:3) Fall 92, p. 139-140.
"For Sister Mary Apolline." [Iowa] (22:3) Fall 92, p. 135-137.
"Now." [Iowa] (22:3) Fall 92, p. 137-139.

1372. DANGEL, Leo
"The End of the Drought." [NoDaQ] (60:4) Fall 92, p. 120.

1373. DANIEL, Hal J., III
"Emment." [DogRR] (11:2, #22) Fall-Wint 92, p. 36.
"He Keeps It Under the Jelly Worms." [DogRR] (11:2, #22) Fall-Wint 92, p. 37-38.
"Why I Dream of Green Fish." [HiramPoR] (51/52) Fall 91-Sum 92, p. 32-33.

1374. DANIELS, Barbara
"Just Looking." [FourQ] (6:1) Spr 92, p. 21.
"Losing the Farm" (Recipient, The Richard E. Lautz Poetry Award). [FourQ] (6:2) Fall 92, p. 33.
"The Ordinary Destination." [FourQ] (6:1) Spr 92, p. 22.

1375. DANIELS, Carl M.
"A Sweet Story." [ChironR] (11:4) Wint 92, p. 26.

1376. DANIELS, Jim
"Afternoons." [TampaR] (5) Fall 92, p. 22-23.
"Banking the Fire." [OhioR] (48) 92, p. 94-97.
"A Day of Sainthood." [PassN] (13:1) Sum 92, p. 5.
"Donuts, the Color of." [TampaR] (5) Fall 92, p. 21.
"Driving Factory Row, 1989." [NegC] (12:1/2) 92, p. 24.
"Everydude, on Planet Detroit." [CinPR] (23) Wint 91-92, p. 60-61.
"I Used to Be Alive with Death." [ColR] (9:1) Spr-Sum 92, p. 156-158.
"It." [OxfordM] (8:1) Spr-Sum 92, p. 24.
"Sin Sandwich." [ColR] (9:1) Spr-Sum 92, p. 152-155.
"Strong Arm." [BellR] (15:2) Fall 92, p. 12.

1377. DANIELS, Peter
"Blessings." [JamesWR] (9:3) Spr 92, p. 13.
"Curiosities." [JamesWR] (9:3) Spr 92, p. 13.
"Hunger." [JamesWR] (9:4) Sum 92, p. 12.

1378. DANKLEFF, Richard
"Into a Choppy Sea." [NowestR] (30:3) 92, p. 42.
"On the Beach at Beira." [NowestR] (30:3) 92, p. 43.

1379. DANTE ALIGHIERI
"Al Poco Giorno" (tr. by John Paul Russo). [HarvardA] (125th Anniversary Issue) F 92, p. 9.
"Inferno" (Selection: Canto XXV, tr. by Richard Wilbur). [Antaeus] (69) Aut 92, p. 21-28.
"Inferno: Canto XXVIII" (tr. by Robert Pinsky). [ParisR] (34:123) Sum 92, p. 110 - 115.

DAO, Bei
See BEI, Dao

1380. DARIO, Rubén
"La Victoria de Samotracia." [YaleR] (80:3) Jl 92, p. 116.
"The Victory of Samothrace." [YaleR] (80:3) Jl 92, p. 116.

1381. DARNIELLE, John
"The Eagle Has Landed." [SpoonRQ] (17:1/2) Wint-Spr 92, p. 100.
"Ninonolyonotza" (Aztec word meaning "I address myself to my heart"). [SpoonRQ] (17:1/2) Wint-Spr 92, p. 101.
"An Unrecorded Vision of Jesus." [SpoonRQ] (17:1/2) Wint-Spr 92, p. 98-99.

1382. D'ARPINO, Tony
"Railroad Tennis." [Parting] (5:2) Wint 92-93, p. 4.
1383. DARRAGH, Simon
"Profession: Writer." [Amelia] (6:4, #19) 92, p. 128.
"Situation Wanted." [Hellas] (3:2) Fall 92, p. 45.
1384. DARRAGH, Tina
"She mouthed "He won't remember that he threw you out of the house" without a sound." [Talisman] (8) Spr 92, p. 82-83.
1385. DAS, B. K.
"Winter Morning, Mist" (tr. of Sitakanta Mahapatra). [ChiR] (38:1/2) 92, p. 73.
1386. DAS, J. P.
"The Tryst" (tr. of Sunanda Tripathy, w. Arlene Zide). [ChiR] (38:1/2) 92, p. 211.
1387. DAS, Jibanananda
"The Naked Solitary Hand" (tr. by Ron D. K. Banerjee). [Trans] (26) Spr 92, p. 116 - 118.
1388. DAS, Mahadai
"God and the Cat under the Tub." [LitR] (35:4) Sum 92, p. 585.
"Hummingbird." [LitR] (35:4) Sum 92, p. 584.
"Learner." [LitR] (35:4) Sum 92, p. 583.
"Lucky." [LitR] (35:4) Sum 92, p. 584.
1389. DASSANOWSKY-HARRIS, Robert
"At This Age." [Os] (35) Fall 92, p. 6.
"For the Man Who Knows He Is Romania and Will Not Be Named Here." [OnTheBus] (4:2/5:1, #10/11) 92, p. 84.
"Prelude to a Revolution." [OnTheBus] (4:2/5:1, #10/11) 92, p. 84.
"Upon Seeing the Panels of Pierre Puvis de Chavannes (1824-1898)." [Lactuca] (16) Ag 92, p. 24.
1390. DATTA, Jyotirmoy
"Household Snake" (tr. of Anuradha Mahapatra, w. Carolyne Wright). [KenR] (NS 14:2) Spr 92, p. 76-77.
1391. DAUENHAUER, William
"For Mark Twain in Purgatory." [NewYorkQ] (47) 92, p. 63.
1392. DAUER, Lesley
"Harold Is Sad Today." [ColEng] (54:5) S 92, p. 589.
"On the 24th Story." [ColEng] (54:5) S 92, p. 588-589.
"The Woman in the Film." [ColEng] (54:5) S 92, p. 590.
1393. DAUNT, Jonathan
"Crossing." [MalR] (98) Spr 92, p. 56-57.
"Flight 7." [CarolQ] (44:2) Wint 92, p. 80-82.
"Volcanoes" (First Prize, Cincinnati Poetry Review Competition). [CinPR] (23) Wint 91-92, p. 15-17.
1394. DAVERTIGE (Denis Villard)
"Anacaona" (in French). [Callaloo] (15:3) Sum 92, p. 638.
"Anacaona" (tr. by Carrol F. Coates). [Callaloo] (15:3) Sum 92, p. 637.
"Idem" (in French). [Callaloo] (15:3) Sum 92, p. 635-636.
"Idem" (tr. by Carrol F. Coates). [Callaloo] (15:3) Sum 92, p. 633-634.
"Prologue" (in French). [Callaloo] (15:3) Sum 92, p. 631-632.
"Prologue" (tr. by Carrol F. Coates). [Callaloo] (15:3) Sum 92, p. 629-630.
1395. DAVID, Don
"The Occulation." [BlackWR] (18:2) Spr-Sum 92, p. 103.
"The Source." [BlackWR] (18:2) Spr-Sum 92, p. 102.
1396. DAVIDKOV, Ivan
"Monastery" (tr. by Lisa Sapinkopf, w. Georgi Belev). [Nimrod] (35:2) Spr-Sum 92, p. 25.
1397. DAVIDSON, Ann
"In the Hot Tub." [Kalliope] (14:3) 92, p. 10.
1398. DAVIDSON, Catherine (*See also* DAVIDSON, Catherine Temma)
"Thanksgiving in the Country." [Plain] (12:3) Spr 92, p. 23.
1399. DAVIDSON, Catherine Temma (*See also* DAVIDSON, Catherine)
"Across the Water." [Kalliope] (15:1) 92, p. 30.
1400. DAVIDSON, Daniel
"An Account." [WashR] (18:1) Je-Jl 92, p. 6.
1401. DAVIDSON, L. D.
"At the Fringe" (tr. of Georg Trakl, w. Christopher Hewitt). [PassN] (13:1) Sum 92, p. 31.

"This Year Is Like the Year a Thousand Years Ago" (tr. of Thomas Bernhard, w. Chris Hewitt). [Salm] (94/95) Spr-Sum 92, p. 136.

1402. DAVIDSON, Michael
"Aubade." [Avec] (5:1) 92, p. 1-2.
"Screens" (Selections). [Avec] (5:1) 92, p. 2-5.

1403. DAVIDSON, Phebe
"Applefall." [Amelia] (7:1, #20) 92, p. 151.
"Cruciform." [Amelia] (6:4, #19) 92, p. 75.
"The House As Vortex." [JlNJPo] (14:2) Aut 92, p. 30-31.
"How Mountains Crumble." [JlNJPo] (14:2) Aut 92, p. 29.
"Signs of the Times." [JlNJPo] (14:2) Aut 92, p. 27-28.
"To the Toltec Priest at Spring Sacrifice." [Amelia] (7:1, #20) 92, p. 152.
"Wave Rider." [Amelia] (7:1, #20) 92, p. 151-152.

DAVIDSON, Terri Brown
See BROWN-DAVIDSON, Terri

1404. DAVIES, Alan
"Sei Shonagon." [WestCL] (26:2, #8) Fall 92, p. 50-53.

1405. DAVIGNON, Richard
"Bacon Double Cheeseburgers." [SoCoast] (13) Je 93 [i.e. 92], p. 12.
"Bag Lady Alice Answers the Big One." [SoCoast] (13) Je 93 [i.e. 92], p. 13.
"Humpty's Wake." [Asylum] (7:3/4) 92, p. 54.
"Norman the Mormon & Me." [Elf] (2:4) Wint 92, p. 37.

1406. DAVILA, Angela Maria
"Acabo de Morir." [LitR] (35:4) Sum 92, p. 603.
"I Have Just Died" (tr. by María Arrillaga). [LitR] (35:4) Sum 92, p. 514.
"I Want for My Name" (tr. by María Arrillaga). [LitR] (35:4) Sum 92, p. 515.
"Para Mi Nombre Quiero." [LitR] (35:4) Sum 92, p. 603-604.

1407. DAVIS, Angela J.
"Salvador / December 1980." [OnTheBus] (4:2/5:1, #10/11) 92, p. 85.

1408. DAVIS, Caroline
"A Day in Bali." [Journal] (16:2) Fall-Wint 92, p. 81-82.

1409. DAVIS, Christopher
"A Babel Scraping His Blue Eye." [AmerV] (26) Spr 92, p. 119-120.
"God's Cut-Off TV Screen's Vanishing Mirror Seems an Unshared Point." [AmerV] (26) Spr 92, p. 121-122.

1410. DAVIS, Cortney
"To the Mother of the Burned Child." [Kaleid] (25) Sum-Fall 92, p. 50.

1411. DAVIS, Joann
"My Toenails Are a Rich Shade of Mauve." [Pearl] (15) Spr-Sum 92, p. 24.

1412. DAVIS, John (*See also* DAVIS, Jon)
"Chucker at the Yard Sale." [LaurelR] (26:1) Wint 92, p. 51.
"Chucker Helps Jim Move." [LaurelR] (26:1) Wint 92, p. 48.
"Chucker's Crowded Bus Ride Home." [LaurelR] (26:1) Wint 92, p. 48-49.
"Chucker's Four Tons." [LaurelR] (26:1) Wint 92, p. 50-51.
"Chucker's Wide World of Sports." [LaurelR] (26:1) Wint 92, p. 49-50.
"Eighth Grader." [OxfordM] (8:1) Spr-Sum 92, p. 78.
"Hold All of Us." [PoetryNW] (33:3) Aut 92, p. 17.
"Prayer." [CreamCR] (16:1) Spr 92, p. 110.
"Saturday Night Overtime." [CutB] (37) Wint 92, p. 18-19.

1413. DAVIS, Jon (*See also* DAVIS, John)
"Faster and Faster the Word of the Lord." [CutB] (38) Sum 92, p. 45-53.
"Local Color: The Local Yard Dog Takes a Break" (Cape Cod). [TexasR] (13:3/4) Fall-Wint 92, p. 78.
"The Rebel Makes His Stand Before Leaving" (for Tim Kelly). [OntR] (36) Spr - Sum 92, p. 81-82.

1414. DAVIS, Melody
"Pretext for Being Human." [SingHM] (20) 92, p. 91-92.
"Sinks." [WestB] (30) 92, p. 112.
"To the Cockroach That Lives in My Message Machine." [Chelsea] (53) 92, p. 44.
"Tools." [Chelsea] (53) 92, p. 45.

1415. DAVIS, Richard
"Kaposi's Sarcoma in White Male Adult, Age 29" (Taken from The Singing Bridge: A National AIDS Poetry Archive). [Art&Und] (1:5) S-O 92, p. 8.

1416. DAVIS, Ted
"Slaughterhouse Floor" (A Plainsongs Award Poem). [Plain] (12:3) Spr 92, p. 36 - 37.

1417. DAVIS, Tim
"Dance" (for Henri Matisse). [YellowS] (39) Spr-Sum 92, p. 15.
"Love Poem #2." [YellowS] (41) Fall-Wint 92-93, p. 25.
1418. DAVIS, William Virgil
"Another Room." [WestHR] (46:3) Fall 92, p. 284.
"Changes." [TarRP] (30:2) Spr 91, p. 20.
"Night in Venice." [TexasR] (13:3/4) Fall-Wint 92, p. 79.
"Night Train." [PoetC] (24:1) Fall 92, p. 16-17.
"On Lookout" (Guadalupe River Ranch). [SouthwR] (77:2/3) Spr-Sum 92, p. 307.
"The Scar." [Agni] (36) 92, p. 54.
"Soliloquy from the Other Side." [GreenMR] (NS 5:2) Spr-Sum 92, p. 67.
"Stave Church" (Bygdøy, Oslo). [WestHR] (46:3) Fall 92, p. 314.
"A Walk Around the Lake." [Agni] (36) 92, p. 55.
1419. DAVISON, Scott
"Alter Ego" (tr. of Cesare Pavese). [CharR] (18:1) Spr 92, p. 97.
"Awakening" (tr. of Cesare Pavese). [CimR] (100) Jl 92, p. 102.
"The Boy Who Was in Me" (tr. of Cesare Pavese). [CimR] (100) Jl 92, p. 101-102.
"Creation" (tr. of Cesare Pavese). [CimR] (100) Jl 92, p. 105.
"Earth and Death" (tr. of Cesare Pavese). [Paint] (19:37) Spr 92, p. 48-53.
"End of the Fantasy" (tr. of Cesare Pavese). [CharR] (18:1) Spr 92, p. 98.
"The Friend Who Sleeps" (tr. of Cesare Pavese). [CimR] (100) Jl 92, p. 104.
"Habits" (tr. of Cesare Pavese). [CimR] (100) Jl 92, p. 103.
"The House" (tr. of Cesare Pavese). [ChiR] (38:3) 92, p. 69.
"I Will Pass Through Piazza di Spagna" (tr. of Cesare Pavese). [ChiR] (38:3) 92, p. 75.
"Indifference" (tr. of Cesare Pavese). [CimR] (100) Jl 92, p. 104-105.
"Landlords" (tr. of Cesare Pavese). [ChiR] (38:3) 92, p. 72-73.
"The Peace That Reigns" (tr. of Cesare Pavese). [Poetry] (161:1) O 92, p. 13-14.
"Sad Wine" (tr. of Cesare Pavese). [QW] (35) Sum-Fall 92, p. 118.
"Song" (tr. of Cesare Pavese). [CharR] (18:1) Spr 92, p. 96.
"Street Song" (tr. of Cesare Pavese). [Poetry] (161:1) O 92, p. 14-15.
1420. DAVISON, Steven Dale
"Turning Forty." [US1] (26/27) 92, p. 8.
1421. DAWE, Gerald
"Heart of Hearts." [Verse] (9:3) Wint 92, p. 8.
1422. DAWSON, Hester
"Mrs. Tarradiddle Takes Up Poetry." [JlNJPo] (14:1) Spr 92, p. 37-39.
1423. DAWSON, Mark
"The Bright Hues of the Sistine Chapel." [AntR] (50:3) Sum 92, p. 525.
"Dog Sledding to the North Pole, 1888." [PoetC] (23:3) Spr 92, p. 5-6.
"Individual Claims." [NoAmR] (277:2) Mr-Ap 92, p. 23.
1424. DAWSON, Royal
"New York Manifesto." [FreeL] (9) Wint 92, p. 26.
1425. DAY, Jean
"The Irrational." [Avec] (5:1) 92, p. 35-38.
1426. DAY, Lucille
"Bomb Threat." [Hudson] (45:3) Aut 92, p. 442-443.
1427. DAY, Meara
"Love Poem with Dental Instruments." [LullwaterR] (4:1) Fall 92, p. 43.
"Love Poem with Exotic Animals." [LullwaterR] (4:1) Fall 92, p. 42.
De . . .
See also names beginning with "De" without the following space, filed below in their alphabetic positions, e.g., DeFOE.
1428. De ALESSANDRO, Patricia
"Grief Encounter." [Epiphany] (3:2) Ap (Spr) 92, p. 98-99.
"Zia Sabbatini." [Epiphany] (3:2) Ap (Spr) 92, p. 99-100.
De ANDRADE, Eugénio
See ANDRADE, Eugénio de
De ARELANO NOLLA, Olga Ramirez
See NOLLA, Olga Ramirez de Arelano
De BURGOS, Julia
See BURGOS, Julia de
De CÉSPEDES, Jorge Enrique
See CÉSPEDES, Jorge Enrique de

1429. De DIOS, Mary Joyce
"Her, She." Sparks! Writing by High School Students (1:1), a supplement to [PraF] (13:4, #61) Wint 92-93, p. 6.

1430. De FILIPPO, Vira J.
"Lancaster, One Sunday Morning." [Blueline] (13) 92, p. 75.

1431. De GEUS, Cynthia
"Ode to the Body Bountiful." [HawaiiR] (16:2, #35) Spr 92, p. 77.

De GIOVANNINI, Juan José
See GIOVANNINI, Juan José de

De GRAZIA, Emilio
See DeGRAZIA, Emilio

De HOYOS, Angela
See HOYOS, Angela de

De IZAGUIRRE, Ester
See IZAGUIRRE, Ester de

1432. De JONG, Daphne
"Thyme." [Vis] (40) 92, p. 47.
"Waiheke Weather" (Waiheke Is., Hauraki Gulf, Feb. 1991). [Vis] (40) 92, p. 47-48.

De LESCOËT, Henri
See LESCOËT, Henri de

De LISLE, Charles-René Marie Leconte
See LECONTE de LISLE, Charles-René Marie

1433. De MATTIA, Sally
"At a Deeper Level" (for Gianluca Galasso). [BellArk] (8:3) My-Je 92, p. 6-7.
"Beyond That Line (In Honor of New Beginnings)" (for Stefania Schiavone). [BellArk] (8:1) Ja-F 92, p. 14.
"In the Realm of the Waking World: A Suite of Visions and Signals" (Selection: Part one, "Stefania's Poem: Silencing the Dragon"). [BellArk] (8:4) Jl-Ag 92, p. 20.
"In the Realm of the Waking World: A Suite of Visions and Signals" (Selections: Part Two, "Celia's Poem: Walking in a Real Dream"). [BellArk] (8:5) S-O 92, p. 22-23.
"In the Realm of the Waking World: A Suite of Visions and Signals" (Selections: Part Two, Nunzia's Poem, Salvatore's Poem). [BellArk] (8:6) N-D 92, p. 22-24.
"The Transformation Trilogy." [BellArk] (8:2) Mr-Ap 92, p. 12-13.
"The Transformation Trilogy" (corrected reprint). [BellArk] (8:3) My-Je 92, p. 4.

De MELO NETO, João Cabral
See NETO, João Cabral de Melo

1434. De NICOLA, Deborah
"Matisse in Nice, 1917-1930." [AntR] (50:4) Fall 92, p. 712-713.

De NIORD, Chard
See DeNIORD, Chard

De OLIVEIRA, Carlos
See OLIVEIRA, Carlos de

De OTERO, Blas
See OTERO, Blas de

1435. De STEFANO, John
"Epithalamium." [NowestR] (30:2) 92, p. 42-43.
"Ode on a Markov Chain." [NowestR] (30:2) 92, p. 44.

De TORRES, Juan Ruiz
See RUIZ DE TORRES, Juan

De UNGRIA, Ricardo M.
See UNGRIA, Ricardo M. de

1436. De VITO, E. B.
"Make No Mistake." [Comm] (119:19) 6 N 92, p. 17.

1437. De WIT, Johan
"The George IV." [Avec] (5:1) 92, p. 118.
"Prince of Whales." [Avec] (5:1) 92, p. 119.
"The Telegraph." [Avec] (5:1) 92, p. 120.

1438. DEAGON, Andrea Webb
"The Dream of the Mortal Sun." [Poem] (68) N 92, p. 13.

1439. DEAKIN, Douglas
"Shoreline and Ritual Sight." [PoetL] (87:3) Fall 92, p. 9-10.

1440. DEAN, Debi Kang
"Wild Horse Island" (for Lee). [TarRP] (31:2) Spr 92, p. 26.

"With My Mother and Aunts in the Kitchen" (for Auntie Alice). [TarRP] (31:2) Spr 92, p. 27.

1441. DEAN-MORRISON, C.
"Back Home Stories." [Grain] (20:1) Spr 92, p. 257.

1442. DEANOVICH, Connie
"History as Bourgeois Construct." [Sulfur] (12:2, #31) Fall 92, p. 196-198.
"I've Just Returned from an Athletic Competition." [NewAW] (10) Fall 92, p. 63.
"Silver Nakedness in Calumet City." [Sulfur] (12:2, #31) Fall 92, p. 198-199.
"Virtue Is Not Photogenic." [NewAW] (10) Fall 92, p. 66-67.
"Watusi *Titanic*." [Sulfur] (12:2, #31) Fall 92, p. 195-196.
"What's the Best Way to Live Here?" [NewAW] (10) Fall 92, p. 64-65.

1443. DEAVEL, Christine
"Each Day on the Verge." [AmerPoR] (21:4) Jl-Ag 92, p. 13.
"French Lesson." [PoetryE] (33) Spr 92, p. 35.
"The Other, Like Coral." [AmerPoR] (21:4) Jl-Ag 92, p. 13.
"Water." [AmerPoR] (21:4) Jl-Ag 92, p. 13.

1444. DEBELJAK, Ales
"At Home in Exile" (tr. by the author). [SpoonRQ] (17:3/4) Sum-Fall 92, p. 39.
"At the Bottom" (tr. by Michael Biggins). [Verse] (9:3) Wint 92, p. 43.
"Biography of Dreamtime" (Selections: 1, 5-6, tr. by Sonja Kravanja). [Nimrod] (35:2) Spr-Sum 92, p. 58-59.
"By the Open Window in the Alps" (tr. by the author). [SpoonRQ] (17:3/4) Sum - Fall 92, p. 41.
"Daybreak" (tr. by the author). [MidAR] (12:2) 92, p. 5.
"For You, Maybe" (tr. by the author). [SpoonRQ] (17:3/4) Sum-Fall 92, p. 40.
"Gradations of Despair." [Pequod] (34) 92, p. 65.
"The House in Darkness" (for Malcolm Lowry, tr. by the author). [IndR] (15:1) Spr 92, p. 78.
"In Response to a Long-Distance Call." [Pequod] (34) 92, p. 64.
"The Light in Winter" (tr. by Michael Biggins). [Verse] (9:3) Wint 92, p. 43.
"The Messenger" (tr. by the author). [IndR] (15:1) Spr 92, p. 79.
"Standing By" (tr. by the author). [DenQ] (26:4) Spr 92, p. 19.
"Unmailed Letter." [Pequod] (34) 92, p. 66.
"Winter Pilgrimage." [GreensboroR] (53) Wint 92-93, p. 38.
"Winter Pilgrimage." [Pequod] (34) 92, p. 67.
"Winter Pilgrimage" (tr. by the author). [SpoonRQ] (17:3/4) Sum-Fall 92, p. 38.
"Without Anesthesia" (Selections: 1, 3, 7, tr. by Sonja Kravanja). [Nimrod] (35:2) Spr-Sum 92, p. 60-61.
"Without Anesthesia VI" (tr. by Sonja Kravanja). [Vis] (39) 92, p. 32.

1445. DeCARTERET, Mark
"The Location of the Soul." [Sonora] (22/23) Spr 92, p. 15.

1446. DECKER, Diana P.
"Babel Bárbara" (for Federica, tr. of Cristina Peri Rossi). [QRL] (Poetry Series 11: vol. 31) 92, 52 p.

1447. DeCORMIER-SHEKERJIAN, Regina
"The Bellringer's Wife's Journal" (Selections: 1-2). [Nimrod] (36:1) Fall-Wint 92, p. 105-106.
"Flowers." [Nimrod] (36:1) Fall-Wint 92, p. 109.
"Lamentation for Sunday." [AmerPoR] (21:2) Mr-Ap 92, p. 49.
"Lupe." [Nimrod] (36:1) Fall-Wint 92, p. 107-108.
"Testimony." [AmerPoR] (21:2) Mr-Ap 92, p. 49.

1448. DeCOURCY, Lynne H.
"The Fire at the Rim." [MidAR] (12:2) 92, p. 25-26.
"In Our Room." [TarRP] (30:2) Spr 91, p. 17.
"Independence Day." [CinPR] (23) Wint 91-92, p. 10.

DeDIOS, Mary Joyce
See De DIOS, Mary Joyce

DeFILIPPO, Vira J.
See De FILIPPO, Vira J.

1449. DeFOE, Mark
"In the Painting of the Newly Painted Porch." [Sparrow] (59) S 92, p. 19.
"Little Old Man." [SouthernHR] (26:2) Spr 92, p. 143.
"Money." [ChatR] (12:4) Sum 92, p. 32.
"Remembering Mr. Mayes, Little League Coach." [Witness] (6:2) 92, p. 66.
"Table Setting." [SoCoast] (13) Je 93 [i.e. 92], p. 10-11.

1450. DeFREES, Madeline
"Apartment Complex Dialogue in the Laundry Center." [Ploughs] (18:1) Spr 92, p. 227.
"Cortège for My Sister's Husband." [Ploughs] (18:1) Spr 92, p. 226.
DeGEUS, Cynthia
See De GEUS, Cynthia
1451. DeGRAZIA, Emilio
"Reading Between the Lines." [BlackBR] (15) Spr-Sum 92, p. 27.
1452. DeGROOTE, Judith
"Blackberries." [Vis] (38) 92, p. 13.
Del PINO, José Manuel
See PINO, José Manuel del
1453. DELANO, Page Dougherty
"Battle Woman." [DenQ] (26:4) Spr 92, p. 20-21.
"The Boys Who Go Easily." [MinnR] (38) Spr-Sum 92, p. 13-14.
"Common Rain." [PraS] (66:3) Fall 92, p. 33-34.
"Learn by Anatomy." [PoetL] (87:2) Sum 92, p. 25-26.
"Living by the Train Yards." [PraS] (66:3) Fall 92, p. 32-33.
"Naming the Body." [GettyR] (5:3) Sum 92, p. 406-409.
"Radical Forgetting." [Agni] (36) 92, p. 89-91.
"Selling the Paper at K-Mart." [PoetL] (87:2) Sum 92, p. 27.
"Town Living." [MinnR] (38) Spr-Sum 92, p. 14-15.
1454. DELANTY, Greg
"Corc's Golden Vessel." [NewMyths] (1:2/2:1) 92, p. 28-29.
"The Rising" (for Terence Brown). [NewMyths] (1:2/2:1) 92, p. 27.
1455. DELAVEAU, Philippe
"XIX. The trees remember more clearly than us" (tr. by Anthony Rudolf). [Stand] (33:4) Aut 92, p. 47.
"Ars Poetica" (tr. by Claire Nicholas White). [Footwork] 92, p. 90.
"Eucharis" (tr. by Claire Nicholas White). [Footwork] 92, p. 90.
DELGADO, Deborah M. Aguayo
See AGUAYO-DELGADO, Deborah M.
1456. DELGADO, Juan
"Loosening Braids." [ConnPR] (11:1) 92, p. 17-18.
"Sagging Lines." [ConnPR] (11:1) 92, p. 14.
1457. DELGUERCIO, Margaret
"The End from Saint-Lazare, Her Prison Cell." [JlNJPo] (14:1) Spr 92, p. 36.
"Shredded Pork and Stir-Fried Vegetables for Charlie Jones." [JlNJPo] (14:2) Aut 92, p. 34.
"Still Life at Christmas." [JlNJPo] (14:2) Aut 92, p. 35.
"Time Warp." [JlNJPo] (14:2) Aut 92, p. 32-33.
1458. D'ELIA, Gregory S.
"Stuttering to Rainer, in Darkness" (tr. of Balázs Mezei). [Agni] (35) 92, p. 257-258.
1459. DELIGIORGIS, Stavros
"Unpleasant Poem" (tr. of Tassos Denegris). [Stand] (33:4) Aut 92, p. 102.
1460. DELISLE, Greg
"Training the Bees." [ChatR] (12:3) Spr 92, p. 25.
1461. DELLABOUGH, Robin
"In December." [NegC] (12:1/2) 92, p. 25.
1462. DELOOF, Jan
"Their Boheme" (tr. by James Brockway). [Stand] (33:4) Aut 92, p. .117.
1463. DeLOTTO, Jeffrey
"Smelling Salt in an On-Shore Breeze." [ColEng] (54:2) F 92, p. 159.
"Ted Renner — at Jerry's Restaurant." [ColEng] (54:2) F 92, p. 160.
1464. DELTORO, Antonio
"Sunken Landscapes" (tr. by Reginald Gibbons). [TriQ] (85) Fall 92, p. 282.
"Thursday" (tr. by Reginald Gibbons). [TriQ] (85) Fall 92, p. 280-281.
1465. DeMARS, Douglas
"To My Mother, Drinking." [PoetL] (87:4) Wint 92-93, p. 44.
1466. DeMARTINO, Marjorie
"The Bone White Hollow of Shoulder." [SoDakR] (30:2) Sum 92, p. 103.
"Eskimo Children." [SoDakR] (30:2) Sum 92, p. 100.
"Mannerisms of the Dead." [SoDakR] (30:2) Sum 92, p. 99.
"The Story Okshena Told." [SoDakR] (30:2) Sum 92, p. 101-102.

1467. DEMBO, L. S.
"Counting Down" (From "Vanishing Points"). [Northeast] (5:7) Wint 92-93, p. 23 - 26.
1468. DEMCAK, Andrew
"The Beautiful House." [ChironR] (11:2) Sum 92, p. 14.
"Indifference: A Trio" (for Gavin Cato). [ChironR] (11:1) Spr 92, p. 22.
"Moth Knowledge." [ChironR] (11:4) Wint 92, p. 22.
"To the Man Who Kissed Me Twice at the Poetry Reading." [ChironR] (11:4) Wint 92, p. 22.
"Waiting for Noah." [Pearl] (15) Spr-Sum 92, p. 46.
"Wanting to Die." [ChironR] (11:4) Wint 92, p. 22.
1469. DEMERS, D. A.
"Thursday Night" (tr. of Éva Tóth). [Trans] (26) Spr 92, p. 87.
1470. DEMETRICK, Mary
"I Study Italian." [Footwork] 92, p. 47.
"Mountain Ash." [Footwork] 92, p. 47.
1471. DEMING, Kay
"Confluence: A Poem in Two Voices." [RagMag] (10:2) 92, p. 42.
"I Miss Being Kissed." [RagMag] (10:2) 92, p. 43.
"I've Been Gone Too Long" (for Jim). [RagMag] (10:2) 92, p. 41.
1472. DeMOTT, Robert
"Easter Diary: Hospital Visit" (for J.D.). [TexasR] (13:3/4) Fall-Wint 92, p. 80-81.
"Heat of Georgia." [TexasR] (13:3/4) Fall-Wint 92, p. 82.
1473. DEMPSTER, Barry
"Books Are" (from "Letters from a Long Illness with the World, the D. H. Lawrence Poems"). [CanLit] (133) Sum 92, p. 23.
"The Christmas Eve Abyss. Florence 1927." [Arc] (28) Spr 92, p. 25.
"Eastwood 1906" (from "Letters from a Long Illness with the World, the D. H. Lawrence Poems"). [CanLit] (133) Sum 92, p. 21.
"Green as the Vein in a Young Man's Desire. Eastwood 1906." [Arc] (28) Spr 92, p. 23-24.
"Omens . . . Cornwall 1916" (from "Letters from a Long Illness with the World, the D. H. Lawrence Poems"). [CanLit] (133) Sum 92, p. 21-23.
1474. DENBERG, Ken
"Blueberry Pie." [Agni] (36) 92, p. 95.
"Wet." [CinPR] (23) Wint 91-92, p. 57.
"Winter Hawks." [SouthernPR] (32:1) Spr 92, p. 29.
"Winter, Sometimes, and the Gilded Carp." [ManhatPR] (14) [92?], p. 43.
1475. DENEGRIS, Tassos
"Impressions of a Poetry Reading in Japanese" (tr. by Gail Holst-Warhaft). [Stand] (33:4) Aut 92, p. 103.
"Unpleasant Poem" (tr. by Stavros Deligiorgis). [Stand] (33:4) Aut 92, p. 102.
DeNICOLA, Deborah
See De NICOLA, Deborah
1476. DeNIORD, Chard
"Acheron." [DenQ] (26:3) Wint 92, p. 37-38.
"Burnt Offering." [GrahamHR] (16) Fall 92, p. 24-25.
"The Flashing Zone." [MissR] (20:3) Spr 92, p. 53.
"Midway." [MissR] (20:3) Spr 92, p. 54-55.
"Transubstantiation" (for Marie Howe). [GrahamHR] (16) Fall 92, p. 22-23.
"With Adultery in My Heart." [DenQ] (26:3) Wint 92, p. 36.
"With Lips Made New" (For A.R.S.). [GrahamHR] (16) Fall 92, p. 26-27.
1477. DENNIS, Carl
"Art News." [AmerPoR] (21:5) S-O 92, p. 15.
"Bimini Queen." [Poetry] (160:5) Ag 92, p. 266-268.
"Bivouac Near Trenton." [Atlantic] (270:5) N 92, p. 109.
"Grace." [NewRep] (207:16) 12 O 92, p. 44.
"Help from the Audience." [Poetry] (160:5) Ag 92, p. 264-265.
"Holy Brethren." [Poetry] (160:5) Ag 92, p. 265-266.
"Local Government." [Shen] (42:1) Spr 92, p. 56.
"The Miracle." [ThRiPo] (39/40) 92-93, p. 40-41.
"Nuts and Raisins." [ThRiPo] (39/40) 92-93, p. 41-42.
"Spring." [GeoR] (46:1) Spr 92, p. 94-95.
"The Window in Spring." [Shen] (42:1) Spr 92, p. 54-55.
1478. DENNISON, Julie
"Digging Out My Name." [PottPort] (14:1) Spr-Sum 92, p. 58-59.

"Draw from Life" (for all the men who teach me). [PottPort] (14:1) Spr-Sum 92, p. 60-61.
"It Isn't Always Physical." [PottPort] (14:1) Spr-Sum 92, p. 56-57.
"Saying Salt." [PottPort] (14:1) Spr-Sum 92, p. 54-55.

1479. DENNISON, Matt
"The Attic." [Outbr] (23) 92, p. 78-80.
"Something Actual." [ChironR] (11:2) Sum 92, p. 29.
"Sunday Brunch Musings at the Outdoor Cafe." [ChironR] (11:1) Spr 92, p. 24.

1480. DENNISON, Michael
"The King of Barbary." [NewDeltaR] (9:1) Fall 91-Wint 92, p. 1-5.

1481. DENNY, Alma
"Black Track." [Light] (1) Spr 92, p. 26.
"Hail, Ginger Ale!" [Light] (1) Spr 92, p. 16.

1482. DENNY, Evelyn C. B.
"The Jovial Christian." [ChrC] (109:12) 8 Ap 92, p. 364.

DeNORD, Chard
See DeNIORD, Chard

1483. DENSON, Carol
"The Baby's Eyes." [HawaiiR] (16:2, #35) Spr 92, p. 50.
"Gentle Knuckles." [HawaiiR] (16:2, #35) Spr 92, p. 49.

1484. DENT, Peter
"Reach." [Os] (35) Fall 92, p. 3.

1485. DENT, Tory
"How Can I Go Forward If I Don't Know Which Way I'm Facing?" [AntR] (50:3) Sum 92, p. 517.
"What Silence Equals" (for André Françoise Villon). [Talisman] (9) Fall 92, p. 170 - 171.

DePONT, Kathryn Cullen
See CULLEN-DuPONT, Kathryn

1486. DEPTA, Victor M.
"Fix the Bike." [SoCarR] (24:2) Spr 92, p. 64.
"The Foyer." [BelPoJ] (43:1) Fall 92, p. 23.
"Good Old Boy." [GrahamHR] (16) Fall 92, p. 30.
"The Hound and the Moon." [NegC] (12:3) 92, p. 69.

1487. DER-HOVANESSIAN, Diana
"Charm Against Inertia." [GrahamHR] (16) Fall 92, p. 56-57.
"Evening Star" (tr. of Sappho). [13thMoon] (10:1/2) 92, p. 36.
"Finding Words." [Agni] (35) 92, p. 254.
"I Love the Sun-Baked Taste of Armenian Words" (tr. of Yeghisheh Charentz). [Trans] (26) Spr 92, p. 99.
"I Loved You Athis" (tr. of Sappho). [13thMoon] (10:1/2) 92, p. 36.
"Men Want Us Thin." [13thMoon] (10:1/2) 92, p. 34.
"Mother, I Cannot Weave" (tr. of Sappho). [13thMoon] (10:1/2) 92, p. 35.
"Muse." [GrahamHR] (16) Fall 92, p. 58.
"My Mother" (tr. of Sappho). [13thMoon] (10:1/2) 92, p. 36.
"No Maestro" (Composition without title or conductor by John Cage). [Agni] (35) 92, p. 255-256.
"Recycling Today." [AmerS] (61:2) Spr 92, p. 254-255.
"To Aphrodite" (tr. of Sappho). [13thMoon] (10:1/2) 92, p. 35.
"What Promethea Said." [13thMoon] (10:1/2) 92, p. 33.
"Yearning" (tr. of Sappho). [13thMoon] (10:1/2) 92, p. 35.

1488. DeRATOLLO, A.
"Midnight Melody Played in a Minor Key." [PoetryUSA] (24) 92, p. 27.

1489. DERKSEN, Jeff
"Lap Top" (for Erin O'Brien). [Avec] (5:1) 92, p. 12-15.

1490. DERRICK, Curtis
"How the Garden Roots Inside Us." [WillowS] (29) Wint 92, p. 50.

1491. DERRICKSON, Deborah
"Confession." [Conscience] (13:4) Wint 92-93, p. 11.

1492. DERRICOTTE, Toi
"Bird." [ParisR]] (34:124) Fall 92, p. 43.
"Color Line." [13thMoon] (10:1/2) 92, p. 39.
"Peripheral." [ParisR]] (34:124) Fall 92, p. 43.
"Soul" (For Tony). [13thMoon] (10:1/2) 92, p. 37-38.
"The Touch." [13thMoon] (10:1/2) 92, p. 40.

1493. DERRINGER, Sally
"Stocking Up." [NewYorkQ] (48) 92, p. 111.
1494. DERRY, Alice
"Not as You Once Imagined." [RiverC] (12:2) Spr 92, p. 26-28.
1495. DES ROSIERS, Joël
"L'Austerite de Ton Corps." [Callaloo] (15:2) Spr 92, p. 411-414.
"The Austerity of Your Body" (tr. by Carrol F. Coates). [Callaloo] (15:2) Spr 92, p. 407-410.
"Femme Blanche au Pur Dehors." [Callaloo] (15:2) Spr 92, p. 421-426.
"White Woman of the Pure Exterior" (tr. by Carrol F. Coates). [Callaloo] (15:2) Spr 92, p. 415-420.
1496. DESAI, Ravi
"The Mapmaker's Salvation" (after Gerardus Mercator). [WestHR] (46:2) Sum 92, p. 148-149.
DeSENA, Laura Hennessey
See HENNESSEY-DeSENA, Laura
1497. DESILETS, E. Michael
"Knee Reliquary Triptych." [ChatR] (12:3) Spr 92, p. 26-27.
"Susan at the Stop." [HiramPoR] (51/52) Fall 91-Sum 92, p. 34.
1498. DeSTEFANO, Darin
"Cateclipsis." [WashR] (18:4) D 92-Ja 93, p. 14-15.
1499. DESY, Peter
"Buckeye Lake, Ohio, July." [Lactuca] (16) Ag 92, p. 11.
"The End of Something." [SnailPR] (2:1) Spr-Sum 92, back cover.
"Following Directions." [LitR] (35:3) Spr 92, p. 327.
"The Heart of It All." [QW] (34) Wint-Spr 92, p. 79.
"Junkyard at Dusk." [Lactuca] (16) Ag 92, p. 10.
"Losing It." [QW] (34) Wint-Spr 92, p. 80.
"Love in the 50's." [WestB] (30) 92, p. 37.
"Mother Dying." [WritersF] (18) 92, p. 134.
"My Father's Colostomy." [NewYorkQ] (48) 92, p. 85.
"A Short History of Psychoanalysis." [ChironR] (11:1) Spr 92, p. 25.
"Sometimes We Like the Inside, Sometimes the Out, But Not Always Together." [Ascent] (17:1) Fall 92, p. 17.
"Telephone Wire." [Lactuca] (16) Ag 92, p. 10.
1500. DeTAL, Vicki Clark
"Night Fevers." [Kalliope] (15:1) 92, p. 34.
1501. DEUTCH, Richard
"Floating the Woman" (For Theodore Weiss). [Vis] (40) 92, p. 38.
1502. DEUTSCH, Laynie Tzena
"Charms for the Insomniac." [Sonora] (22/23) Spr 92, p. 147-148.
1503. DEV SEN, Nabaneeta
"Another Country" (tr. by Sunil B. Ray and Carolyne Wright, w. the author). [Agni] (36) 92, p. 214.
"Room" (tr. by Sunil B. Ray and Carolyne Wright). [ChiR] (38:1/2) 92, p. 17.
"So Many Crazy Blue Hills" (tr. by Sunil B. Ray and Carolyne Wright). [ChiR] (38:1/2) 92, p. 18-19.
1504. DEVENISH, Alan
"Letter to Gretel." [ColEng] (54:2) F 92, p. 164.
"Postcard." [ColEng] (54:2) F 92, p. 163.
DeVITO, E. B.
See De VITO, E. B.
1505. DeVOSS, Dale
"Time Traveller." [MoodySI] (27) Spr 92, p. 39-40.
1506. DeWEESE, Jeanne
"In the beginning" (tr. of Tadeusz Rózewicz). [Descant] (23:3, #78) Fall 92, p. 144.
"In the beginning" (tr. of Tadeusz Rócewicz). [NowestR] (30:3) 92, p. 47.
"It's high time" (to the memory of Konstanty Puzyna, tr. of Tadeusz Rózewicz). [Descant] (23:3, #78) Fall 92, p. 147.
"It's high time" (to the memory of Konstanty Puzyna, tr. of Tadeusz Rócewicz). [NowestR] (30:3) 92, p. 48.
"Poetry not always takes the shape of verse" (tr. of Tadeusz Rózewicz). [Descant] (23:3, #78) Fall 92, p. 148.
"Something Like That" (tr. of Tadeusz Rózewicz). [Descant] (23:3, #78) Fall 92, p. 149.

"'Success' and Requests" (tr. of Tadeusz Rózewicz). [Descant] (23:3, #78) Fall 92, p. 145-146.

DeWIT, Johan
See De WIT, Johan

1507. DeWITT, Jim
"Bring a Big Bag of Oranges." [US1] (26/27) 92, p. 11.
"The Foghorning's Warning." [Elf] (2:1) Spr 92, p. 42.
"How It All Began: A Legend." [ChamLR] (10/11) Spr-Fall 92, p. 189.
"Plain Girl." [Plain] (13:1) Fall 92, p. 6-7.

DeWITT, Susan Kelly
See KELLY-DeWITT, Susan

1508. DHARMARAJ, Ramola
"Andromeda, Cassiopeia, Perseus." [GreenMR] (NS 5:2) Spr-Sum 92, p. 11.
"Daybreak at Kanya Kumari." [GreenMR] (NS 5:2) Spr-Sum 92, p. 12.
"In the Hour of Healing." [GreenMR] (NS 5:2) Spr-Sum 92, p. 8-9.
"The Incidence of Light." [GreenMR] (NS 5:2) Spr-Sum 92, p. 10.

1509. DHARWADKER, Aparna
"Preparations of War" (tr. of Kunwar Narayan, w. Vinay Dharwadker). [ChiR] (38:1/2) 92, p. 149.

1510. DHARWADKER, Vinay
"Blank Page" (tr. of Kedarnath Singh). [ChiR] (38:1/2) 92, p. 46-47.
"Fear" (tr. of Raghuvir Sahay). [ChiR] (38:1/2) 92, p. 148.
"Himayoga" (A Meditation on Snow, Chicago, 1967-68, tr. of Vinda Karandikar). [ChiR] (38:1/2) 92, p. 212-217.
"Language of Communication" (tr. of Kedarnath Singh). [ChiR] (38:1/2) 92, p. 45.
"Preparations of War" (tr. of Kunwar Narayan, w. Aparna Dharwadker). [ChiR] (38:1/2) 92, p. 149.
"Questions" (tr. of P. S. Rege). [ChiR] (38:1/2) 92, p. 42-43.
"Snapshot" (tr. of Arun Kolatkar). [ChiR] (38:1/2) 92, p. 44.

1511. DHERE, Aruna
"Night has come to an end, the woman starts her grinding" (tr. by Asha Mundlay and Arlene Zide). [ChiR] (38:1/2) 92, p. 103.

1512. DHURJATI
"For the Lord of the Animals" (Excerpt, tr. by Hank Heifetz and Velcheru Narayana Rao). [Trans] (26) Spr 92, p. 119-120.

Di . . .
See also names beginning with "Di" without the following space, filed below in their alphabetic positions, e.g., DiPALMA

Di PALMA, Ray
See DiPALMA, Ray

1513. Di PASQUALE, Emanuel
"Extended Memory." [AmerPoR] (21:4) Jl-Ag 92, p. 33.

1514. Di PIERO, W. S.
"On a Picture by Cézanne." [Poetry] (159:4) Ja 92, p. 218.

1515. Di PINTO, John
"Babies Without Anuses." [PraF] (13:2, #59) Sum 92, p. 77.

1516. Di SUVERO, Victor
"Beyond Poetry" (tr. of Agostinho Neto). [Nimrod] (36:1) Fall-Wint 92, p. 92.
"Letter to Agostinho Neto." [Nimrod] (36:1) Fall-Wint 92, p. 89.
"Macchu Picchu." [Nimrod] (36:1) Fall-Wint 92, p. 93.
"Night" (tr. of Agostinho Neto). [Nimrod] (36:1) Fall-Wint 92, p. 91.
"Pause" (tr. of Agostinho Neto). [Nimrod] (36:1) Fall-Wint 92, p. 90.

1517. DIAMOND, Ann
"Cruel Restraint." [PoetryC] (12:3/4) Jl 92, p. 21.
"Inmate." [PoetryC] (12:3/4) Jl 92, p. 21.
"The Messiah." [PoetryC] (12:3/4) Jl 92, p. 21.
"Romantic Exiles." [PoetryC] (12:3/4) Jl 92, p. 21.

1518. DIAZ, Leonardo
"(Díaz) de Cemento." [Nuez] (4:10/11) 92, p. 4.

DIAZ, Luis Correa
See CORREA DIAZ, Luis

1519. DIAZ CASTRO, Tania
"Everyone Will Have to Listen" (tr. by Carolina Hospital and Pablo Medina). [AmerV] (29) 92, p. 18.

1520. DIAZ ENCISO, Adriana
"Tendida en el suelo." [Nuez] (4:10/11) 92, p. 9.

1521. DIAZ MARTINEZ, Manuel
"El Imaginero de Cadiz" (a Nadia y Fernando Quiñones). [LindLM] (11:1) Mr 92, p. 12.
"Posible Epitafio para Antonio Machado." [LindLM] (11:1) Mr 92, p. 12.
"La Rosa Otra" (Homenaje a Mariano Brull). [LindLM] (11:1) Mr 92, p. 12.
"La Visita." [LindLM] (11:1) Mr 92, p. 12.
1522. DICKEY, R. P.
"Chimney Sweepers Are What *We* Called Them." [Light] (3) Aut 92, p. 16.
"Clumsiness." [Light] (4) Wint 92-93, p. 13.
1523. DICKEY, Stephen M.
"Elegy for Parenthood." [SoCoast] (13) Je 93 [i.e. 92], p. 31.
"Im Mainzer Dom." [SoCoast] (13) Je 93 [i.e. 92], p. 35.
1524. DICKEY, William
"Those Who Have Burned." [AntR] (50:1/2) Wint-Spr 92, p. 155.
1525. DICKINSON, Sara
"On the Removal of Troops from Afghanistan" (tr. of Aleksandr Eremenko, w. Forrest Gander). [Agni] (35) 92, p. 268-269.
"Thoughts on Formal Logic" (tr. of Yuri" Arabov, w. Forrest Gander). [Agni] (35) 92, p. 264-265.
1526. DICKINSON, Stephanie
"Fallout." [NewYorkQ] (47) 92, p. 95-96.
"On a July Night." [NewYorkQ] (48) 92, p. 108.
"Whore." [NewYorkQ] (49) 92, p. 81.
1527. DICKSON, John
"The Apartment." [WillowR] (19) Spr 92, p. 12-13.
"Fast Food Restaurant." [Poetry] (160:1) Ap 92, p. 11-12.
"The Funeral." [Elf] (2:2) Sum 92, p. 21.
"Rarely, If Ever, Is Flame Obsessed." [Elf] (2:2) Sum 92, p. 20.
"Second Chance." [Poetry] (160:1) Ap 92, p. 10-11.
"Sunday Dinner." [SpoonRQ] (17:1/2) Wint-Spr 92, p. 81-82.
"Thomas Wolfe." [AmerS] (61:1) Wint 92, p. 81-82.
"The Wild Blue Yonder." [PoetL] (87:3) Fall 92, p. 17-18.
1528. DIDSBURY, Peter
"Pokerwork." [ChironR] (11:2) Sum 92, p. 12.
1529. DIEHL-JONES, Charlene
"M/utterings." [WestCL] (26:3, #9) Wint 92-93, p. 18-21.
1530. DIEMER, Gretchen
"Keeping the Family Faith." [PoetryNW] (33:3) Aut 92, p. 24.
1531. DIESENDORF, Margaret
"The Swan" (After Rainer Maria Rilke). [Bogg] (65) 92, p. 38.
1532. DIETZ, Sheila
"Clara Haskil" (Mozart Pianoconcert in A-major, tr. of Ida Gerhardt). [Vis] (39) 92, p. 35.
"The Moon's Eye." [AntR] (50:4) Fall 92, p. 723.
"My Mother's Ghost." [Crazy] (43) Wint 92, p. 43-45.
1533. DIGGES, Deborah
"For the Lost Adolescent." [NewYorker] (68:40) 23 N 92, p. 86.
1534. DILLARD, Gavin
"Geeks and Peeks." [ChironR] (11:4) Wint 92, p. 9.
"Smoke Rings." [ChironR] (11:4) Wint 92, p. 9.
"Socks and Shorts." [ChironR] (11:4) Wint 92, p. 9.
"Taylor." [ChironR] (11:4) Wint 92, p. 9.
1535. DILLON, Andrew
"At Dinner." [Poem] (67) My 92, p. 48.
"My Daughter." [CumbPR] (12:1) Fall 92, p. 22.
"Towns That Won't Die." [InterPR] (18:1) Spr 92, p. 58.
"Translating the Oedipus Rex" (for Constantine Santas). [PoetC] (24:1) Fall 92, p. 19.
"Trashing a Flyer for a Book of Poems." [CumbPR] (12:1) Fall 92, p. 21.
"Writing Every Day." [InterPR] (18:1) Spr 92, p. 59.
1536. DILSAVER, Paul
"Alignment." [WritersF] (18) 92, p. 53.
"Cosmic Shit Poem." [Pearl] (15) Spr-Sum 92, p. 44.
"Metastasis." [WritersF] (18) 92, p. 52.
1537. DIMAGGIO, Jill
"Fireplaces." [Gypsy] (19) 92, p. 41.

1538. DIMITROVA, Blaga
"Amnesia in Reverse" (tr. by Ludmilla Popova-Wightman). [LitR] (25:2) Wint 92, p. 180.
"Forbidden Sea" (in Russian and English, tr. by Ludmilla Popova-Wightman and Elizabeth Anne Socolow). [US1] (26/27) 92, p. 26.
"Nightlight: Eye of the Owl" (tr. by Heather McHugh and Nikolai Popov). [Trans] (26) Spr 92, p. 53-54.
"The Shadows of the Trees" (tr. by Ludmilla Popova-Wightman). [LitR] (25:2) Wint 92, p. 179-180.
1539. DINE, Carol
"At Sea." [Kalliope] (14:1) 92, p. 52-53.
1540. DINESCU, Mircea
"Cats of the Vatican" (tr. by Adam J. Sorkin and Sergiu Celac). [ArtfulD] (22/23) 92, p. 39.
"Letter to My Mother" (tr. by Thomas C. Carlson). [Chelsea] (53) 92, p. 80.
"Rusting" (tr. by Thomas C. Carlson). [Chelsea] (53) 92, p. 80.
"The Transfiguration" (tr. by Thomas C. Carlson). [Chelsea] (53) 92, p. 81.
DiNIORD, Chard
See DeNIORD, Chard
DiNORD, Chard
See DeNIORD, Chard
DIOS, Mary Joyce de
See De DIOS, Mary Joyce
1541. DiPALMA, Ray
"21 Down." [NewAW] (10) Fall 92, p. 40.
"All Right I Mean of Course." [WashR] (17:5) F-Mr 92, p. 15.
"Atlantic Stripe." [CentralP] (21) Spr 92, p. 87.
"Burning Bricks." [Shiny] (7/8) 92, p. 112.
"Commotion" (for Betsi). [NewAW] (10) Fall 92, p. 41.
"Four Part Invention." [WashR] (17:5) F-Mr 92, p. 15.
"However Apollo." [Avec] (5:1) 92, p. 137.
"Lines for E." [Avec] (5:1) 92, p. 138.
"Post Hoc." [NewAW] (10) Fall 92, p. 42.
"The Prerogative of Lieder." [GrandS] (11:2, #42) 92, p. 189.
"Qwat." [Avec] (5:1) 92, p. 139.
"Rebus Balconies." [Shiny] (7/8) 92, p. 111.
"Said Looking." [Talisman] (9) Fall 92, p. 215.
"Small Elegy." [Talisman] (9) Fall 92, p. 215.
"Watching the Mountain Burn." [WashR] (17:5) F-Mr 92, p. 15.
"White City." [WashR] (17:5) F-Mr 92, p. 15.
DiPASQUALE, Emanuel di
See Di PASQUALE, Emanuel
DiPIERO, W. S.
See Di PIERO, W. S.
1542. DISCH, Tom
"After Duchamp." [Light] (1) Spr 92, p. 4.
"The Beautiful Salt Shakers." [Light] (1) Spr 92, p. 6.
"A Benevolent Villanelle." [Light] (1) Spr 92, p. 5.
"Birdsong Interpreted." [Light] (1) Spr 92, p. 3.
"The Exigent Poet" (for Rogerio Santiago). [Light] (1) Spr 92, p. 6.
"An Expression of Faith." [Verse] (8:3/9:1) Wint-Spr 92, p. 36.
"Imperfect Love" (for Nelson Denoon). [Light] (1) Spr 92, p. 3.
"Jerusalem Recaptured." [WestHR] (46:1) Spr 92, p. 3-6.
"L.A. Freeway." [Light] (1) Spr 92, p. 4.
"The Last Time I Saw Paris." [AmerS] (61:3) Sum 92, p. 352.
"Love Is." [Light] (1) Spr 92, p. 5.
"On Returning to *The Golden Treasury*" (for Celia). [Light] (1) Spr 92, p. 4.
"Pervigilium Veneris 1991." [Boulevard] (7:1, #19) Spr 92, p. 98.
"The Pet Shop After Dark." [Light] (1) Spr 92, p. 5.
"Red Tulips in 1947." [Poetry] (159:4) Ja 92, p. 197.
"Rejection Letter." [Light] (1) Spr 92, p. 5.
"Remarks Concerning the Fitness of All Things." [Poetry] (159:4) Ja 92, p. 198.
"September." [Boulevard] (7:1, #19) Spr 92, p. 97.
"September." [Harp] (286:1708) S 92, p. 34.
"Springtime in Tokyo." [Light] (1) Spr 92, p. 4.

"Sylvan Marriage" (a Rustic Epithalamion for Glen and Lynn). [Light] (1) Spr 92, p. 5.
"Three People and Their Feelings." [Poetry] (159:4) Ja 92, p. 195-196.
"Uncanny England." [Light] (1) Spr 92, p. 6.
"Villanelle for Charles Olson." [Poetry] (159:4) Ja 92, p. 199.
"A Vision of Christ" (in memoriam Terence Cardinal Cooke). [Light] (1) Spr 92, p. 4.
"We Are Divided Everywhere in Two Parts." [SouthwR] (77:4) Aut 92, p. 500-502.

1543. DISCHELL, Stuart
"Buddies." [Agni] (36) 92, p. 123-124.
"The Retirement of the Troubadour." [PartR] (59:3) Sum 92, p. 478-479.
"Sand." [Agni] (35) 92, p. 51-57.

1544. DITSKY, John
"An Argument for God's Existence." [LullwaterR] (3:2) Spr 92, p. 25.

1545. DITTA, Joseph M.
"But the Earth Abideth Forever." [MissouriR] (15:2) 92, p. 180-185.
"Drought." [MissouriR] (15:2) 92, p. 186-187.

1546. DITTBERNER-JAX, Norita
"Why Boys Don't Have to Iron." [SingHM] (20) 92, p. 24-25.

1547. DIVAKARUNI, Chitra
"The Alley of Flowers." [Calyx] (14:2) Wint 92-93, p. 12-13.
"Bengal Night." [Amelia] (6:4, #19) 92, p. 110-111.
"Childhood." [LitR] (25:2) Wint 92, p. 270.
"Deaf Boy at Seashore." [Amelia] (6:4, #19) 92, p. 111-112.
"Leroy at the Zoo." [LitR] (25:2) Wint 92, p. 270-271.
"The Return." [Amelia] (6:4, #19) 92, p. 111.
"A Strange Man" (tr. of Ram Basu). [ChiR] (38:1/2) 92, p. 134-135.
"Tiger Mask Ritual" (after a photograph by Raghubir Singh). [ChiR] (38:1/2) 92, p. 94-95.
"The Widow at Dawn." [Calyx] (14:2) Wint 92-93, p. 10-11.

1548. DIXON, K. Reynolds
"All Clear." [Thrpny] (50) Sum 92, p. 20.

1549. DJANIKIAN, Gregory
"About Distance." [AmerS] (61:3) Sum 92, p. 444-445.
"Agami Beach" (Alexandria, 1955). [ThRiPo] (39/40) 92-93, p. 42-43.
"Dark Quarrel." [Boulevard] (7:1, #19) Spr 92, p. 160-161.
"How I Learned English." [ThRiPo] (39/40) 92-93, p. 44-45.
"When I First Saw Snow" (Tarrytown, N.Y.). [ThRiPo] (39/40) 92-93, p. 43-44.

1550. DJURDJIC, Liljana
"European Show" (tr. by Nina Zivancevic). [Talisman] (8) Spr 92, p. 144.

1551. DJUROVIC, Miroslav
"To Kill Poets" (Excerpt, tr. by Nejc Bernard). [Nimrod] (35:2) Spr-Sum 92, p. 64 - 66.

1552. DLUGI-KING, Julie
"La Llorona." [QW] (34) Wint-Spr 92, p. 63.
"Nightfall in El Paso." [QW] (34) Wint-Spr 92, p. 63.

1553. DLUGOS, Tim
"All Souls Day." [Art&Und] (1:1) Fall 91, p. 5.
"As Alive." [Art&Und] (1:1) Fall 91, p. 5.
"Erosion." [Art&Und] (1:3) Spr 92, p. 13.
"Healing the World from Battery Park." [HangL] (60) 92, p. 19-21.
"LIT." [HangL] (60) 92, p. 17.
"The Nineteenth Century Is 183 Years Old" (for Keith Milow). [HangL] (60) 92, p. 16.
"Psalm." [BrooklynR] (9) 92, p. 29.
"Signs of Madness." [Art&Und] (1:1) Fall 91, p. 6.
"Spinner." [BrooklynR] (9) 92, p. 30.
"Summer, South Brooklyn." [HangL] (60) 92, p. 18.

1554. DMBASO, Carloa
"Dunk dat Skunk." [Archae] (3) early 92, p. 55.

1555. DOAN, Chuong
"Initiation Rites." [HangL] (60) 92, p. 80.

1556. DOBBIE, Joan
"About Blocking Highway I-5 in the Light of the 400 Iraqi Civilians Who Were Also in the Wrong Place at the Wrong Time." [Gypsy] (18) 92, p. 17-20.

1557. DOBLER, Patricia
"1920 Photo." [ThRiPo] (39/40) 92-93, p. 46-47.
"His Depression." [ThRiPo] (39/40) 92-93, p. 46.
1558. DOBROVICOVA, Margita
"For Emily Dickinson" (tr. by Silvia Cervencíková). [PraS] (66:4) Wint 92, p. 24.
"I Am Allowed" (tr. by Silvia Cervencíková). [PraS] (66:4) Wint 92, p. 21.
"The Nights" (tr. by Silvia Cervencíková). [PraS] (66:4) Wint 92, p. 20.
"X X X: Eve was whispering" (tr. by Silvia Cervencíková). [PraS] (66:4) Wint 92, p. 22-23.
"X X X: The cyclist was quick in taking off" (tr. by Silvia Cervencíková). [PraS] (66:4) Wint 92, p. 21.
"X X X: The deep stars, the empty strings" (tr. by Silvia Cervencíková). [PraS] (66:4) Wint 92, p. 22.
"X X X: The station loudspeaker did not work" (tr. by Silvia Cervencíková). [PraS] (66:4) Wint 92, p. 23.
1559. DOBYNS, Stephen
"Bad Luck Fence." [CreamCR] (16:2) Fall 92, p. 51-53.
"Black Dog, Red Dog." [ThRiPo] (39/40) 92-93, p. 47-48.
"Fatal Kisses." [ParisR]] (34:124) Fall 92, p. 41-42.
"Favorite Iraqi Soldier." [ParisR]] (34:124) Fall 92, p. 39-40.
"General Matthei Drives Home Through Santiago." [ThRiPo] (39/40) 92-93, p. 52 - 53.
"The Gun." [ThRiPo] (39/40) 92-93, p. 50-51.
"Hidden Within the Sleeves of Those Dark Robes." [Salm] (94/95) Spr-Sum 92, p. 78-79.
"Syracuse Nights." [Salm] (94/95) Spr-Sum 92, p. 75-76.
"Topless." [Salm] (94/95) Spr-Sum 92, p. 77-78.
"What You Have Come to Expect." [ThRiPo] (39/40) 92-93, p. 48-49.
1560. DODD, Elizabeth
"Business As Usual." [SycamoreR] (4:2) Sum 92, p. 40-41.
"Easter Island, 1500 A.D." [SycamoreR] (4:2) Sum 92, p. 42.
"Hickory Ridge." [PoetC] (23:3) Spr 92, p. 28-29.
"Petroglyphs" (Chaco Canyon, New Mexico). [TarRP] (31:2) Spr 92, p. 28-29.
"Tsankawi." [HighP] (7:2) Fall 92, p. 31-33.
1561. DODD, Wayne
"Letter." [ThRiPo] (39/40) 92-93, p. 54.
"Like Deer Our Bodies." [ThRiPo] (39/40) 92-93, p. 55.
"Luxe, Calme, et Volupté." [GeoR] (46:3) Fall 92, p. 438-439.
"Ouside My Cabin." [ThRiPo] (39/40) 92-93, p. 53-54.
"Sestet for Many Voices." [GeoR] (46:2) Sum 92, p. 207-212.
"We Look and We Look, Oh We Keep Looking." [Journal] (16:2) Fall-Wint 92, p. 14-15.
1562. DODDS, Charles
"Born Human: I Traded Innocence for a Shadow." [PoetryUSA] (24) 92, p. 26.
1563. DODGE, Robert K.
"My Song." [Interim] (11:2) Fall-Wint 92-93, p. 21.
1564. DODIC, N. J.
"Ode to Mary Magdalene." [Dandel] (19:2) 92, p. 32.
"The Things He Made." [AntigR] (90) Sum 92, p. 78.
1565. DODSON, Keith A.
"Dating the School Janitor." [SlipS] (12) 92, p. 54.
"Did You See Something?" [SlipS] (12) 92, p. 53-54.
"Nothing Like a." [FreeL] (9) Wint 92, p. 8.
"The Razor." [Pearl] (15) Spr-Sum 92, p. 16.
"Used to Get Together." [Pearl] (15) Spr-Sum 92, p. 16.
"You'll Like It Better If It's Wet." [ChironR] (11:1) Spr 92, p. 20.
"Got This Friend." [ChironR] (11:2) Sum 92, p. 13.
1566. DOERING, Steven
"Intro to Sociology." [ChironR] (11:1) Spr 92, p. 15.
"Slithering thru the Mail." [ChironR] (11:1) Spr 92, p. 15.
"Ten Years Gone." [ChironR] (11:1) Spr 92, p. 15.
"Yes, the System Doesn't Work." [ChironR] (11:1) Spr 92, p. 15.
1567. DOERR, Uta
"Silent" (tr. of Marie Luise Kaschnitz, w. Colin O'Connell). [AntigR] (90) Sum 92, p. 89.

1568. DOLAN, Kathleen Hunt
"Still-Life with Dream, Dogs, Child, etc." [NegC] (12:1/2) 92, p. 26-27.
"Still-Life with Dream, Dogs, Child, etc." [NegC] (12:3) 92, p. 70-71.
1569. DOLE, X.
"Clenched fists and tears." [Amelia] (7:1, #20) 92, p. 47.
1570. DOLGIN, Steve
"Dancer Road." [CoalC] (5) My 92, p. 10.
1571. DOLGORUKOV, Florence
"Mary to Her Mother." [NegC] (12:3) 92, p. 72-73.
1572. DOLTON, Alexia Lyn
"The Garden." [Pearl] (15) Spr-Sum 92, p. 45.
1573. DOMANSKI, Don
"Mare Serenitatis." [Event] (21:3) Fall 92, p. 58.
"Transmigrational Poems." [Event] (21:3) Fall 92, p. 54-55.
"Ursa Major." [Event] (21:3) Fall 92, p. 56-57.
"The Vertebrate Body." [Event] (21:3) Fall 92, p. 52-53.
1574. DOMINA, Lynn
"Eulogy for a Suicide." [WillowS] (29) Wint 92, p. 25.
"The Museum of Childhood." [OxfordM] (7:1) Spr-Sum 91, p. 15-19.
1575. DONAGHY, Michael
"The Commission." [Verse] (9:3) Wint 92, p. 34-36.
"A Reprieve." [Poetry] (160:3) Je 92, p. 133.
1576. DONAHUE, Joseph
"Christ Enters Manhattan (III)." [Talisman] (8) Spr 92, p. 105-106.
1577. DONALD, Andrew
"From the Sequence *Kore* Poems." [Footwork] 92, p. 129.
"I Visit My Mentor." [Footwork] 92, p. 129.
"The Prophet Speaks" (for Terry Falla). [Footwork] 92, p. 129.
DONG-PO, Su
See SU, Dong-Po
1578. DONLAN, John
"Fly or Dig" (for Don Hunkin). [Event] (21:1) Spr 92, p. 17.
"For John Clare." [AntigR] (90) Sum 92, p. 48.
"Halloween." [Event] (21:1) Spr 92, p. 19.
"Higher Power." [MalR] (98) Spr 92, p. 62.
"Purkinje Shift." [AntigR] (90) Sum 92, p. 50.
"Shield." [Event] (21:1) Spr 92, p. 18.
"Unqualified Good Time." [MalR] (98) Spr 92, p. 63.
"Wild London." [AntigR] (90) Sum 92, p. 49.
1579. DONNELL, David
"Tobacco Heaven." [MalR] (99) Sum 92, p. 98-99.
1580. DONNELLY, J. R.
"Drinking Coffee Late One Night." [Epiphany] (3:1) Ja (Wint) 92, p. 13.
"Ice Picks." [Epiphany] (3:1) Ja (Wint) 92, p. 12.
"The Last Time." [Epiphany] (3:1) Ja (Wint) 92, p. 14.
"To a Friend in Beijing." [Epiphany] (3:1) Ja (Wint) 92, p. 11.
1581. DONNELLY, P. N. W.
"Rarewa-Fatality." [Vis] (40) 92, p. 46.
"Wednesday." [Vis] (40) 92, p. 46.
1582. D'ONOFRIO, Lisa
"Blowing Out the Candle to St. Jack." [MoodySI] (27) Spr 92, p. 7.
1583. DONOHUE, Angelin Moran
"Pantoum I — Workshop." [PoetL] (87:2) Sum 92, p. 47-48.
1584. DONOVAN, Daria
"He Wants Me." [OnTheBus] (4:2/5:1, #10/11) 92, p. 86.
"Let It Go." [OnTheBus] (4:2/5:1, #10/11) 92, p. 87.
1585. DONOVAN, Gerard
"Columbus Rides Again." [Shen] (42:4) Wint 92, p. 94-96.
"New Irises." [MidAR] (12:2) 92, p. 155.
"Sleep Jewelry." [MidAR] (12:2) 92, p. 156.
1586. DONOVAN, Gregory
"Buddy Bolden, Buddy Bartley: Calling His Children Home." [SouthernR] (28:4) Aut, O 92, p. 838-841.
"The Grandfather in the Rafters." [SoCoast] (12) Ja 92, p. 16-17.
"Homing" (in memory of my grandfather, C.E. Friederich, Sr.). [CutB] (37) Wint 92, p. 38-43.

"Men's Room." [HayF] (11) Fall-Wint 92, p. 49-51.
"Penelope in Brazil" (for Betsy Blue). [HayF] (11) Fall-Wint 92, p. 47-48.
"Ragman, 1958." [NewEngR] (14:2) Spr 92, p. 51-52.
"Runes" (Winner, Annual Free Verse Contest, 1991). [AnthNEW] (4) 92, p. 9.
"Satchel Mouth." [NewEngR] (14:2) Spr 92, p. 53.

1587. DONOVAN, Karen
"Brief History of Peacetime." [ColEng] (53:7) N 91, p. 792.
"Dissipative Structures." [ColEng] (53:7) N 91, p. 790-791.
"Walking the Ouachita." [SouthernPR] (32:2) Fall 92, p. 36-38.

1588. DONOVAN, Laurence
"Advice from Further Up." [SpiritSH] (57) Spr-Sum 92, p. 5-6.
"Dog Island." [SpiritSH] (57) Spr-Sum 92, p. 2.
"Having Come This Way" (Washington, D.C., 1945, 1962). [SpiritSH] (57) Spr - Sum 92, p. 1.
"A Poem for Borges." [SpiritSH] (57) Spr-Sum 92, p. 7-9.
"Transcriptions." [SpiritSH] (57) Spr-Sum 92, p. 3-4.

1589. DONOVAN, Stewart
"The Gulf of Maine." [AntigR] (90) Sum 92, p. 22-25.
"Partridge Island, Saint John" (for Danny Britt). [AntigR] (91) Fall 92, p. 125-127.
"The Resurrection at the Beaverbrook Gallery" (after Stanley Spencer). [AntigR] (89) Spr 92, p. 96.
"Tar Ponds." [AntigR] (90) Sum 92, p. 26.

1590. DOOLEY, Maura
"Does It Go Like This?" [SouthernR] (28:2) Spr, Ap 92, p. 247-248.
"Ice." [SouthernR] (28:2) Spr, Ap 92, p. 248.
"KLM 468 / Dep. Rotterdam 10:45, Arr. London 10:45." [SouthernR] (28:2) Spr, Ap 92, p. 250.
"Niagara." [Verse] (9:3) Wint 92, p. 34.
"Up on the Roof." [SouthernR] (28:2) Spr, Ap 92, p. 248-249.

1591. DOOLEY, Tim
"Preparing to Meet the Day." [Verse] (8:3/9:1) Wint-Spr 92, p. 131.

1592. DOR, Moshe
"Coalman" (tr. by Barbara Goldberg). [Trans] (26) Spr 92, p. 91.

1593. DORESKI, William
"Autumn Infarctions." [SenR] (22:2) Fall 92, p. 32-33.
"Batik Flannel Dress." [CimR] (99) Ap 92, p. 59-60.
"Boston Fog." [Agni] (35) 92, p. 259-260.
"Mid-May Thunderstorm in Fitzwilliam." [CapeR] (27:1) Spr 92, p. 33.
"Necro-Aesthetica." [BellR] (15:1) Spr 92, p. 46-47.
"Neither Scholar Nor Spy." [Agni] (35) 92, p. 262.
"Post-Structuralism in Cambridge." [CapeR] (27:1) Spr 92, p. 32.
"Radon." [Agni] (35) 92, p. 261.
"Sacred Turtle." [CimR] (99) Ap 92, p. 60-61.
"Sappho." [OxfordM] (6:2) Fall-Wint 90, p. 88-89.
"Under the Volcano." [OxfordM] (6:2) Fall-Wint 90, p. 87.
"When the War Began." [BellR] (15:1) Spr 92, p. 44-45.

1594. DORF, Marilyn
"Manda's Father." [Plain] (12:3) Spr 92, p. 15.

1595. DORIAN, Marguerite
"Amber" (tr. of Ana Blandiana, w. Elliott Urdang). [MidAR] (13:2) 92, p. 9.
"Mother" (tr. of Ana Blandiana, w. Elliott Urdang). [MidAR] (13:2) 92, p. 10.
"Piéta" (tr. of Ana Blandiana, w. Elliott Urdang). [MidAR] (13:2) 92, p. 11-12.

1596. DORION, Hélène
"I Don't Know Yet" (tr. by Yann Levelock). [Stand] (33:2) Spr 92, p. 136-139.

1597. DORIS, Stacy
"The Frogs" (Excerpts). [Talisman] (9) Fall 92, p. 125-127.

1598. DORN, Alfred
"Masseuse" (a somonka). [Amelia] (7:1, #20) 92, p. 48.

1599. DORPH, Doug
"Two Pictures of My Father." [BellR] (15:1) Spr 92, p. 5.

1600. DORSETT, Thomas
"After This Flood" (tr. of Ingeborg Bachmann). [InterPR] (18:2) Fall 92, p. 35.
"The Emperor's New Sonnet." [Light] (2) Sum 92, p. 8.
"Every Day" (tr. of Ingeborg Bachmann). [SnailPR] (2:2) Fall-Wint 92, p. 1.
"Fall Away, Heart" (tr. of Ingeborg Bachmann). [InterPR] (18:2) Fall 92, p. 33.
"The Potato." [Confr] (50) Fall 92, p. 276.

"A Question from an Advaitin." [Hellas] (3:1) Spr 92, p. 22.
"Told to Evening" (tr. of Ingeborg Bachmann). [InterPR] (18:2) Fall 92, p. 37.

1601. DOTY, Catherine
"Daddy." [Footwork] 92, p. 37.
"French Coke." [Footwork] 92, p. 37.
"Peril." [Footwork] 92, p. 37.

1602. DOTY, Mark
"Almost Blue" (Chet Baker, 1929-1988). [PassN] (13:2) Wint 92, p. 4.
"Beach Roses." [Art&Und] (1:5) S-O 92, p. 10.
"Brilliance." [AmerV] (26) Spr 92, p. 15-17.
"Broadway" (for Jean Valentine). [AmerV] (26) Spr 92, p. 12-14.
"A Letter from the Coast." [PassN] (13:2) Wint 92, p. 3.
"With Animals." [Boulevard] (7:1, #19) Spr 92, p. 55-58.

1603. DOUGHERTY, Edward A.
"R5: The Paoli Local." [Wind] (22:71) 92, p. 8.

1604. DOUGHERTY, Justine
"Apartment 201." [CimR] (100) Jl 92, p. 116.
"A Visit." [TarRP] (31:2) Spr 92, p. 16.

1605. DOUGHERTY, Mary Ellen
"Alzheimer's Unit." [ChrC] (109:24) 12-19 Ag 92, p. 744.

1606. DOUGLAS, Ann
"Visit from B." [Nimrod] (35:2) Spr-Sum 92, p. 92.
"Waiting to Know." [Nimrod] (35:2) Spr-Sum 92, p. 88-91.

1607. DOULIS, Thomas
"The Speech of Hands" (tr. of Nikiphoros Vrettakos). [Nimrod] (35:2) Spr-Sum 92, p. 72.

1608. DOUSKEY, Franz
"A Brief Layman's Guide to the Catholic Fuck." [NewYorkQ] (49) 92, p. 44.
"Dog Days and Delta Nights." [YellowS] (41) Fall-Wint 92-93, p. 24.
"Fourteen Reasons Why Sportsmen Need Assault Weapons." [NewYorkQ] (48) 92, p. 62-63.

1609. DOVE, Rita
"The Bird Frau." [ThRiPo] (39/40) 92-93, p. 60-61.
"Demeter's Prayer to Hades." [Poetry] (161:1) O 92, p. 23.
"The Event." [ThRiPo] (39/40) 92-93, p. 57-58.
"Geometry." [ThRiPo] (39/40) 92-93, p. 61.
"Parsley." [ThRiPo] (39/40) 92-93, p. 58-60.
"Protection." [Poetry] (161:1) O 92, p. 24.
"Sonnet: Nothing can console me. You may bring silk." [Poetry] (161:1) O 92, p. 24.
"The Venus of Willendorf." [Poetry] (161:1) O 92, p. 25-27.
"Weathering Out." [ThRiPo] (39/40) 92-93, p. 56-57.

1610. DOW, Leslie Smith
"The Wildcat Forest." [Bogg] (65) 92, p. 52.

1611. DOWDEN, Kaviraj George
"Master Wordslinger, Great Beat Historian and Story Teller" (Jack Kerouac's Birthday '81). [MoodySI] (27) Spr 92, p. 31-33.

1612. DOWNING, Ben
"Nora Considers the Book" (Zürich, June 16, 1942). [LullwaterR] (3:3) Sum 92, p. 50-51.

1613. DOWNS, Buck
"The Sonnets" (Excerpt). [WashR] (17:6) Ap-My 92, p. 13.

1614. DOXEY, W. S.
"The Good Ol' Boy." [Amelia] (6:4, #19) 92, p. 86.

1615. DOYLE, Gary
"On Keokuk Street." [CapeR] (27:2) Fall 92, p. 25.
"Souvenirs." [CapeR] (27:2) Fall 92, p. 26-27.

1616. DOYLE, James
"Purgatory." [LitR] (25:2) Wint 92, p. 262.

1617. DOYLE, Lynn
"From Proverbs." [PoetryE] (33) Spr 92, p. 36-38.
"Life, Imposing." [OhioR] (48) 92, p. 84-85.
"Natural Selection." [OhioR] (48) 92, p. 83.

1618. DOYLE, R. Erica
"Yanki Vini." [SinW] (47) Sum-Fall 92, p. 136-137.

1619. DRAKE, Alan
"Te Moana" (Excerpt). [Archae] (4) late 92-early 93, p. 76-82.
1620. DRAKE, Jeannette
"Palette." [SouthernR] (28:4) Aut, O 92, p. 842-843.
1621. DRAKE, Jennifer
"Convergence, or Seven to the Sixth." [Caliban] (11) 92, p. 168-169.
1622. DRAZAN, Karel
"Dance of Death" (Excerpt, tr. of Karel Siktanc, w. Daniela Drazanová). [PraS] (66:4) Wint 92, p. 171-172.
1623. DRAZANOVA, Daniela
"Dance of Death" (Excerpt, tr. of Karel Siktanc, w. Karel Drazan). [PraS] (66:4) Wint 92, p. 171-172.
1624. DREHER, Dorothy
"Dorothy Parker Update." [Light] (4) Wint 92-93, p. 18.
DRESSAY, Anne Le
See Le DRESSAY, Anne
1625. DREW, George
"The Czar's Petition Box." [PoetryNW] (33:3) Aut 92, p. 32-33.
"Leaving Little Newell Out." [TexasR] (13:1/2) Spr-Sum 92, p. 87-88.
"Let Us Consider the Tiger." [PoetryNW] (33:3) Aut 92, p. 33-34.
"The Lord Might Be a Shepherd." [SnailPR] (2:1) Spr-Sum 92, p. 24-25.
1626. DREXEL, John
"Correspondences." [SouthernR] (28:3) Sum, Jl 92, p. 640.
"Et in Arcadia Ego." [SouthernR] (28:3) Sum, Jl 92, p. 639.
"Foreign Service." [CumbPR] (12:1) Fall 92, p. 38.
"Homecomings (II)." [CumbPR] (12:1) Fall 92, p. 37.
1627. DROMEY, John
"Last Straw." [Light] (2) Sum 92, p. 23.
1628. DRUCKER, Bruce (*See also* DUCKER, Bruce)
"The Frying Pan in Winter." [Comm] (119:3) 14 F 92, p. 18.
1629. DRUMMEY, Jennifer
"Tattoo Baby." [HiramPoR] (51/52) Fall 91-Sum 92, p. 35.
1630. DRURY, John
"Apartment Building Corridors." [HighP] (7:3) Wint 92, p. 28-29.
"Learning Cursive." [WestHR] (46:3) Fall 92 [i.e. (46:4) Wint 92], p. 409.
"On Location." [HighP] (7:3) Wint 92, p. 30-31.
"Stadium." [NewRep] (206:18) 4 My 92, p. 34.
1631. DRYANSKY, Amy
"Bow Season." [NegC] (12:1/2) 92, p. 29-30.
1632. DSIDA, Jenö
"Far" (tr. by Nicholas Kolumban). [CharR] (18:2) Fall 92, p. 115.
"On the Porch" (tr. by Nicholas Kolumban). [ArtfulD] (22/23) 92, p. 37.
"Residents of the Mountain" (tr. by Nicholas Kolumban). [ArtfulD] (22/23) 92, p. 36.
Du . . .
See also names beginning with "Du" without the following space, filed below in their alphabetic positions, e.g., DuPLESSIS.
1633. Du BÉARN, Roger
"Clerihews for the Clerisy, or: A Quick Fix for Cultural Illiteracy." [AmerS] (61:3) Sum 92, p. 399-401.
1634. Du PASSAGE, Mary
"The Pig." [HolCrit] (29:4) O 92, p. 15.
1635. DUARTE, Mario
"The Garden." [AmerPoR] (21:6) N-D 92, p. 26.
"Hat." [CarolQ] (45:1) Fall 92, p. 32.
"Over the Mississippi River." [AmerPoR] (21:6) N-D 92, p. 26.
1636. DUBAROVA, Petya
"Spring" (tr. by Don D. Wilson). [SenR] (22:2) Fall 92, p. 57.
"Summer has run off, like singing water" (tr. by Don D. Wilson). [SenR] (22:2) Fall 92, p. 58.
"There in the clouds, somewhere in crazy vines" (tr. by Don D. Wilson). [SenR] (22:2) Fall 92, p. 59-60.
"To Fifteen-Year-Olds" (tr. by Don D. Wilson). [SenR] (22:2) Fall 92, p. 56.
DuBÉARN, Roger
See Du BÉARN, Roger

1637. DUBIE, Norman
"Revelation, 20:11-15" (for Tito). [OnTheBus] (4:2/5:1, #10/11) 92, p. 88.
1638. DuCHARME, Barbara Dellner
"Cabbages." [Wind] (22:71) 92, p. 10-11.
"The Shepherdess's Almanac." [Wind] (22:71) 92, p. 9-10.
"Tribute." [Wind] (22:71) 92, p. 10.
1639. DUCKER, Bruce (*See also* DRUCKER, Bruce)
"Fragment." [Comm] (119:4) 28 F 92, p. 22.
"Picnic." [Poetry] (160:5) Ag 92, p. 255.
1640. DUDIS, Ellen Kirvin
"Bats." [ManhatPR] (14) [92?], p. 3.
1641. DUDLEY, Ellen
"The Hunters." [RiverC] (12:2) Spr 92, p. 6.
1642. DUDOIT, Darlaine M. M.
"The Stick Figures at Ban-Pu." [HawaiiR] (16:2, #35) Spr 92, p. 26-27.
1643. DUEHR, Gary
"Paradise Condition." [NewDeltaR] (8:1) Fall 90-Wint 91, p. 9-10.
"Room." [LitR] (25:2) Wint 92, p. 274-275.
"Table, Ghost, Shelf." [NewDeltaR] (8:1) Fall 90-Wint 91, p. 7.
1644. DUEMER, Joseph
"Pine." [NoDaQ] (60:1) Wint 92, p. 281-282.
"What We Thought We Knew." [NoDaQ] (60:1) Wint 92, p. 279-280.
1645. DUFF, S. K.
"Image That Haunts." [JamesWR] (9:3) Spr 92, p. 20.
"The Six A.M. Signing Off." [JamesWR] (9:2) Wint 92, p. 10.
1646. DUFFIN, Brent
"Meter Maid." [Light] (2) Sum 92, p. 22.
"On the Other Side" (tr. of Pierre Reverdy, w. Catherine Berg). [Vis] (38) 92, p. 19.
"Plaint at Forty." [Light] (1) Spr 92, p. 30.
"Sigh in a Popular Bookstore." [Light] (1) Spr 92, p. 20.
1647. DUFFY, Carol Ann
"The Grammar of Light." [AmerS] (61:3) Sum 92, p. 374.
1648. DUFFY, Patricia (Patty)
"Pimp-sly eyes gleaming." [Amelia] (7:1, #20) 92, p. 11.
"Second Wind." [Amelia] (7:1, #20) 92, p. 50.
"There was a young man with broad hips." [Amelia] (7:1, #20) 92, p. 33.
1649. DUGUID, Sandra R.
"Davenport." [JlNJPo] (14:2) Aut 92, p. 9.
1650. DUHAMEL, Denise
"Assumptions" (for Pat Vega). [Pequod] (33) 92, p. 187-191.
"Bulimia." [PoetL] (87:4) Wint 92-93, p. 23-25.
"Ecofeminism in the Year 2000" (w. Maureen Seaton). [MidAR] (13:2) 92, p. 125 - 129.
"Feminism." [HangL] (61) 92, p. 28-29.
"Jung Says the Soul Is Round" (Tompkins Square Park). [WestB] (30) 92, p. 17.
"Literary Barbie." [PoetL] (87:4) Wint 92-93, p. 5.
"New York Heroine." [PaintedB] (48) 92, p. 50-51.
1651. DUKE, Lee
"Billboards." [FreeL] (9) Wint 92, p. 25.
1652. DUKES, Thomas
"Snow in Ohio" (For Mary Oliver). [Poetry] (161:3) D 92, p. 143.
1653. DUMAINE, Christine
"The Heron" (for my brother). [LouisL] (9:1) Spr 92, p. 74-75.
1654. DUMARS, Denise
"Charles & Di." [Pearl] (15) Spr-Sum 92, p. 63.
"Dinner at Mel's" (w. Todd Mecklem). [Pearl] (15) Spr-Sum 92, p. 62.
"Sun Pork." [Pearl] (16) Fall 92, p. 51.
1655. DUMDUM, Simeon, Jr.
"Communion." [Manoa] (4:1) Spr 92, p. 68.
"Some Are Smarter Than Others." [Manoa] (4:1) Spr 92, p. 67.
"Variation on a Note from Yena." [Manoa] (4:1) Spr 92, p. 67.
1656. DUNATOV, Anne Marie
"Moonie." [NewYorkQ] (49) 92, p. 83.
1657. DUNCAN, Ginny
"Walk in the Woods." [BellArk] (8:2) Mr-Ap 92, p. 7.

1658. DUNCAN, Graham
"The Closet." [Poem] (68) N 92, p. 50.
"High-Tech Casualty" (suggested by Ken Jarecke's photograph of a dead Iraqi soldier). [Poem] (68) N 92, p. 48.
"The Silence We Cannot Imagine." [SouthernPR] (32:1) Spr 92, p. 32-33.
"Waiting for an Angel" (for Carol Frost). [Poem] (68) N 92, p. 47.
"Wayward Thought." [Poem] (68) N 92, p. 49.
1659. DUNCAN, Peter
"Stopover at Omaha Beach." [JlNJPo] (14:2) Aut 92, p. 36.
1660. DUNETZ, Lora
"My Father, the Weatherman." [WindO] (56) Fall-Wint 92, p. 11.
1661. DUNGAN, S. L.
"You Can't Fuck a Pizza." [OnTheBus] (4:2/5:1, #10/11) 92, p. 89.
1662. DUNKERLEY, Hugh
"Mouthpiece." [Stand] (33:2) Spr 92, p. 148.
1663. DUNN, Carolyn
"Sleeping with the Enemy." [Jacaranda] (6:1/2) Wint-Spr 92, p. 64-65.
1664. DUNN, Kathryn
"And What, Anyway, Is Political?" [MinnR] (39) Fall-Wint 92-93, p. 1.
1665. DUNN, Stephen
"Desire." [ThRiPo] (39/40) 92-93, p. 66.
"Essay on the Personal." [ThRiPo] (39/40) 92-93, p. 64-65.
"A Good Life." [ParisR]] (34:124) Fall 92, p. 138-140.
"Honesty." [GrahamHR] (16) Fall 92, p. 7-8.
"Let's See If I Have It Right." [ThRiPo] (39/40) 92-93, p. 61-62.
"Night Truths." [GrahamHR] (16) Fall 92, p. 9.
"The Observer." [GeoR] (46:4) Wint 92, p. 743-744.
"A Petty Thing." [SouthernR] (28:2) Spr, Ap 92, p. 244-245.
"Radical." [MidAR] (13:2) 92, p. 5-6.
"The Resurrection." [SouthernR] (28:2) Spr, Ap 92, p. 245-246.
"The Routine Things Around the House." [ThRiPo] (39/40) 92-93, p. 62-64.
"The Snowmass Cycle" (For Laure-Anne Bosselaar and Kurt Brown). [Poetry] (160:6) S 92, p. 327-334.
"Truck Stop: Minnesota." [ThRiPo] (39/40) 92-93, p. 65.
"The Vanishings." [ParisR]] (34:124) Fall 92, p. 136-138.
1666. DUNWOODY, Michael
"The Brahms Suite" (Selections: 1-3, 6, 9, 13). [AntigR] (89) Spr 92, p. 49-51.
1667. DUODUO
"I'm Reading" (tr. by Gregory B. Lee). [ManhatR] (6:2) Fall 92, p. 9.
"I've Always Delighted in a Shaft of Light in the Depth of Night" (tr. by Gregory B. Lee). [ManhatR] (6:2) Fall 92, p. 8.
"Morning" (tr. by Gregory B. Lee). [ManhatR] (6:2) Fall 92, p. 11-12.
"The Rivers of Amsterdam" (tr. by Gregory B. Lee). [ManhatR] (6:2) Fall 92, p. 5.
"There Is No" (tr. by Gregory B. Lee). [ManhatR] (6:2) Fall 92, p. 10.
"Watching the Sea" (tr. by Gregory B. Lee). [ManhatR] (6:2) Fall 92, p. 6-7.
"Windmill" (tr. by Gregory B. Lee). [ManhatR] (6:2) Fall 92, p. 4.
1668. DuPRIEST, Travis
"Sunday Afternoon." [ChrC] (109:10) 18-25 Mr 92, p. 302.
1669. DURAN, Luis Horacio
"Pájaro de Silencio." [Nuez] (4:10/11) 92, p. 32.
1670. DURDAG, Kerem
"Catching the Ceiling." [BlackBR] (15) Spr-Sum 92, p. 36.
"Over the River, Under the Bridge." [Gypsy] (19) 92, p. 33.
1671. DURHAM, Tina Quinn
"After the Birth of Our First Child." [BostonR] (17:6) N-D 92, p. 31.
1672. DUSEK, Barbara
"No Blades on Our Feet." [FreeL] (10) Sum 92, p. 10.
DUYN, Mona van
See Van DUYN, Mona
1673. DWELLER, Cliff
"Taking a Powder." [MoodySI] (27) Spr 92, p. 42.
1674. DWORKIN, Joy
"Gannet." [ParisR] (34:123) Sum 92, p. 84-85.
"The Tigers Win the Pennant, October 4, 1987. 1-0." [EngJ] (81:2) F 92, p. 96.
1675. DWYER, Tamarina
"Temper of Change." [RagMag] (10:1) 92, p. 60.

1677. DYBEK, Stuart
"Dusk, Ravenswood El." [Witness] (6:1) 92, p. 74.
"The Egg Beater." [Light] (2) Sum 92, p. 14.
"Fish Camp." [Witness] (6:2) 92, p. 81.
"House." [Light] (4) Wint 92-93, p. 9.
"Jasmine." [RiverS] (36) 92, p. 103.
"Jump." [RiverS] (36) 92, p. 103.
"Nylon." [Witness] (6:1) 92, p. 75.
1678. DYER, Kevin
"San Francisco, Roots, and Tree Trunks." [DenQ] (27:1) Sum 92, p. 112-113.
1679. DYJAK-GLECKMAN, Pat
"I Will Do This, I Will Not Do This." [PassN] (13:2) Wint 92, p. 10.
1680. DYKEWOMON, Elana
"Oakland: February 1991, 1 AM." [SinW] (46) Spr 92, p. 37-38.
1681. DYSON, Ketaki Kushari
"After the Rain Has Ended" (tr. by Leslie Minot and Satadru Sen). [ChiR] (38:1/2) 92, p. 188.
1682. EADY, Cornelius
"All God's Dangers." [SenR] (22:2) Fall 92, p. 27.
"Empty Choice Blues." [SenR] (22:2) Fall 92, p. 23-24.
"The Killing Floor." [SenR] (22:2) Fall 92, p. 22.
"My Mother's Blues About the Numbers." [SenR] (22:2) Fall 92, p. 25-26.
"Sherbet." [ThRiPo] (39/40) 92-93, p. 68-70.
"The Supremes." [ThRiPo] (39/40) 92-93, p. 67.
"Thrift." [ThRiPo] (39/40) 92-93, p. 70-71.
"Young Elvis." [ThRiPo] (39/40) 92-93, p. 68.
1683. EARL, James W.
"Coma." [Hellas] (3:2) Fall 92, p. 55.
1684. EARL, Martin
"Pasternak." [Conjunc] (19) 92, p. 191.
"Portrait of a Watchtower." [Conjunc] (19) 92, p. 192.
1685. EASTMAN, Jon
"Cherry Picking — Villa Fumanelli." [CharR] (18:2) Fall 92, p. 92.
"Reunion in a Formal Garden." [CharR] (18:2) Fall 92, p. 93.
1686. EATON, Charles Edward
"Calipers." [CharR] (18:2) Fall 92, p. 62.
"The Great Train Robbery." [Sonora] (22/23) Spr 92, p. 114-115.
"The River Boat." [CharR] (18:1) Spr 92, p. 77-78.
"The Shoot-Out." [CharR] (18:2) Fall 92, p. 63.
"Split Decisions." [Hellas] (3:1) Spr 92, p. 94.
"Strings." [InterPR] (18:1) Spr 92, p. 70.
"The Swan at Sunset." [Hellas] (3:1) Spr 92, p. 93.
"The Tent." [CharR] (18:1) Spr 92, p. 79.
"Tweezers." [SouthernPR] (32:1) Spr 92, p. 31-32.
"Undine." [CharR] (18:2) Fall 92, p. 61.
"Up Close and Person." [LaurelR] (26:2) Sum 92, p. 18.
"The Vigneron." [Agni] (35) 92, p. 239.
1687. EATON, Mae
"And a hard man is good to find." [WormR] (32:1, #125) 92, p. 20.
1688. EATON, Tom
"Ten Fingers, Ten Toes." [Gypsy] (19) 92, p. 6.
1689. EBERLY, David
"People Places and Things." [Art&Und] (1:4) Jl-Ag 92, p. 10.
1690. ECHERRI, Vicente
"Autorretrato de Durero" (A Manuel Santayana). [LindLM] (11:3) S 92, p. 12.
"Beaux Arts." [LindLM] (11:3) S 92, p. 12.
"Dans la Conciergerie." [LindLM] (11:3) S 92, p. 12.
"La Tour de M. Gustave Eiffel" (Para Angel Luis Fernández). [LindLM] (11:3) S 92, p. 12.
1691. ECHOLS, Elvira
"Take." [NegC] (12:1/2) 92, p. 221.
1692. ECURY, Nydia
"Habai." [LitR] (35:4) Sum 92, p. 613-614.
"Kantika Pa Mama Tera." [LitR] (35:4) Sum 92, p. 612-613.
"Old Lady." [LitR] (35:4) Sum 92, p. 573.
"Song for Mother Earth." [LitR] (35:4) Sum 92, p. 572.

1693. EDDY, Elizabeth
"Auricula." [Light] (3) Aut 92, p. 9.
"Borborygmata." [Light] (1) Spr 92, p. 24.
"Dispatch." [Light] (1) Spr 92, p. 26.
"Friends." [Light] (3) Aut 92, p. 22.
"Glory." [Light] (1) Spr 92, p. 30.
"Good News." [Light] (4) Wint 92-93, p. 19.
"Late 20th Century." [Light] (4) Wint 92-93, p. 12.
1694. EDELMANN, Carolyn Foote
"Removals." [US1] (26/27) 92, p. 34.
1695. EDFELT, Johannes
"Chalcidice" (tr. by Stephen Klass). [Hellas] (3:1) Spr 92, p. 44.
1696. EDITH, Patricia
"On Television." [Parting] (5:2) Wint 92-93, p. 14.
"Stampede." [MinnR] (38) Spr-Sum 92, p. 38-39.
"Your Assignment." [MinnR] (38) Spr-Sum 92, p. 39.
1697. EDKINS, Anthony
"Cnut's Day Out." [SpiritSH] (57) Spr-Sum 92, p. 44-45.
"Flood Warning." [SpiritSH] (57) Spr-Sum 92, p. 45.
"Revisiting Luarca." [SpiritSH] (57) Spr-Sum 92, p. 46.
"Trick or Treat." [SpiritSH] (57) Spr-Sum 92, p. 42-43.
1698. EDMONDSON, Dorothea
"After the Flood." [LitR] (35:4) Sum 92, p. 476.
"Disposables." [LitR] (35:4) Sum 92, p. 477.
"Rasta-Catholic." [LitR] (35:4) Sum 92, p. 474.
"She Shall Have Music." [LitR] (35:4) Sum 92, p. 475.
1699. EDSON, Russell
"The Babies." [CreamCR] (16:1) Spr 92, p. 102.
"The Time Bank." [Field] (46) Spr 92, p. 19.
"Winter Fever." [Field] (46) Spr 92, p. 18.
1700. EDWARDS, Elizabeth
"Sunset at Frick Park: The Dream of a Curve Ball." [Witness] (6:2) 92, p. 71.
1701. EDWARDS, Nancy
"Pre-Nuptial." [Amelia] (7:1, #20) 92, p. 163.
1702. EDWARDS, Robert
"At Cliff's House." [ChatR] (12:3) Spr 92, p. 46.
"Breath." [HampSPR] Wint 92, p. 36-37.
"Forestville State Park." [Vis] (39) 92, p. 11-12.
"Wild Apples." [DogRR] (11:2, #22) Fall-Wint 92, p. 24-25.
1703. EDWARDS, Thomas S.
"Advance Guard Here" (tr. of Reiner Kunze). [NewOR] (19:2) Sum 92, p. 69.
"Fleeing the Literary Business" (tr. of Reiner Kunze). [NewOR] (19:2) Sum 92, p. 70.
"In the Provence" (tr. of Reiner Kunze). [NewOR] (19:2) Sum 92, p. 74.
"Night Journey" (tr. of Reiner Kunze). [NewOR] (19:2) Sum 92, p. 71.
"Plea at Your Feet" (tr. of Reiner Kunze). [NewOR] (19:2) Sum 92, p. 72.
"Under Dying Trees" (tr. of Reiner Kunze). [NewOR] (19:2) Sum 92, p. 73.
1704. EGAN, Elisabeth
"Rattle in the Kitchen." [HangL] (60) 92, p. 83.
1705. EGAN, Matthew
"Thanksgiving Psalm" (for St. Matthew's Lutheran Church, Renton, Washington). [BellArk] (8:2) Mr-Ap 92, p. 7.
1706. EGAN, Moira
"Vespers" (For Michael Egan, 1939-1992). [HampSPR] Wint 92, p. 55.
1707. EGLINTON, Edna
"Remission." [SoCoast] (12) Ja 92, p. 22.
"An Uncertain Starter." [SoCoast] (12) Ja 92, p. 23.
1708. EGUIA-LIS PONCE, Gabriela
"Camellos para Guillotinar." [Nuez] (4:10/11) 92, p. 4.
1709. EHRHART, W. D.
"After the Latest Victory." [Gypsy] (18) 92, p. 57-58.
"After the Latest Victory." [VirQR] (68:2) Spr 92, p. 309-310.
"The Cradle of Civilization." [Gypsy] (18) 92, p. 21.
"Finding My Old Battalion." [VirQR] (68:2) Spr 92, p. 308-309.
"Love in an Evil Time" (for Diana Bedell). [AmerPoR] (21:3) My-Je 92, p. 30.
"What We're Buying." [AmerPoR] (21:3) My-Je 92, p. 30.

1710. EHRLICH, Linda C.
"The Gulf." [InterPR] (18:1) Spr 92, p. 67.
1711. EHRLICH, P. S.
"Acting Out Actaeon." [SoCoast] (13) Je 93 [i.e. 92], p. 51.
EI, Akitsu
See AKITSU, Ei
1712. EIBEL, Deborah
"Adagio Cantabile." [CanLit] (135) Wint 92, p. 94-95.
"The Family Goldminer." [CanLit] (135) Wint 92, p. 93-94.
1713. EICH, Günter
"A Moment in June" (tr. by Francis Golffing). [Trans] (26) Spr 92, p. 112-113.
1714. EIGNER, Janet B.
"Old Time Religion." [Vis] (39) 92, p. 30.
1715. EIGNER, Larry
"Corner stop-sign STOP WAR." [Sulfur] (12:1, #30) Spr 92, p. 115.
"Getting It Together: a Film on Larry Eigner Poet (1973)" (Transcript: poetry by Larry Eigner, read by Allen Ginsberg). [PoetryUSA] (24) 92, p. 2-5.
"June 23-Jly 15 90, 1687 — Jly 26f 90, 1690." [ShadowP] (3) 92, p. 8-14.
"No clouds cross the sky." [Sulfur] (12:1, #30) Spr 92, p. 116.
"A rider pedaling." [Sulfur] (12:1, #30) Spr 92, p. 115.
"Rvrbrance" (for JF and JM). [Sulfur] (12:1, #30) Spr 92, p. 111-114.
"Spectra." [Sulfur] (12:1, #30) Spr 92, p. 114.
"You don't know how much (little)." [Sulfur] (12:1, #30) Spr 92, p. 116.
1716. EIMERS, Nancy
"Born Worrier." [Crazy] (43) Wint 92, p. 32-34.
"In the New Year" (for Lynda Schraufnagel, in memory). [PoetryNW] (33:2) Sum 92, p. 14-15.
"Lakes." [Crazy] (43) Wint 92, p. 35-37.
"Live Oaks." [Crazy] (43) Wint 92, p. 38-40.
"Of the Constellation Perseus." [PoetryNW] (33:2) Sum 92, p. 16.
1717. EINBINDER, Susan
"The Transformations of the Lover" (3 selections, tr. of Adonis, w. Kamal Boullata). [MichQR] (31:4) Fall 92, p. 619-623.
1718. EINZIG, Barbara
"The Sight of a Lion That Appeared to Me and Seemed to Be Coming at Me" (— Dante). [Conjunc] (19) 92, p. 294-295.
1719. EISELE, Thomas
"The phone rang and I picked it up." [NewYorkQ] (48) 92, p. 113.
1720. EISEN, Christine
"Feeling Alive." [BellArk] (8:2) Mr-Ap 92, p. 6.
"Feeling Alive" (corrected reprint). [BellArk] (8:3) My-Je 92, p. 7.
"Necessity." [BellArk] (8:2) Mr-Ap 92, p. 7.
"Necessity." [BellArk] (8:3) My-Je 92, p. 5.
"A Perfect Lie." [BellArk] (8:6) N-D 92, p. 7.
"Silences." [BellArk] (8:5) S-O 92, p. 20.
"Sun in Water." [BellArk] (8:6) N-D 92, p. 6.
"Who Has Been Sitting in My Chair?" (to M). [BellArk] (8:6) N-D 92, p. 7.
1721. EISENBERG, Susan
"Force Equals Distance Times Weight" (for the pipe fitter apprentice at the Hynes). [SlipS] (12) 92, p. 94.
"Partner #5." [SingHM] (20) 92, p. 52.
"Partner #6." [SingHM] (20) 92, p. 54.
"Work Fantasy, with Apologies to the Anti-Nuclear Movement." [SingHM] (20) 92, p. 53.
1722. EISENZIMMER, Mark
"Mythology of Love." [Grain] (20:2) Sum 92, p. 32.
1723. EISIMINGER, Skip
"Absolute Freedom." [Light] (1) Spr 92, p. 23.
"American Symbols." [Light] (2) Sum 92, p. 19.
"A Pinch of Peril." [Light] (3) Aut 92, p. 10.
"Reflections on the Bustle." [Light] (1) Spr 92, p. 16.
1724. EISMAN, G. D.
"White Elephant Sale." [AnotherCM] (24) Fall 92, p. 36.
1725. EKLUND, George
"The Blue Rock." [PoetryNW] (33:2) Sum 92, p. 35.
"The Ghost." [NegC] (12:3) 92, p. 74.

"Market Street." [WillowS] (30) Sum 92, p. 52.
"Morgan's Pockets." [WillowS] (30) Sum 92, p. 53.
"Señor Prado." [NewYorkQ] (48) 92, p. 112.

1726. El-ETR, Fouad
"Tonight the Stars Are in Tatters" (tr. by Edouard Roditi). [Caliban] (11) 92, p. 37.

1727. El GUINDI, Yussef
"The Housing Authority." [BlackBR] (16) Wint-Spr 92-93, p. 38.
"Keep." [BlackBR] (16) Wint-Spr 92-93, p. 38.
"Traveling." [BlackBR] (16) Wint-Spr 92-93, p. 38.

1728. El RAMEY, Debra
"All That Is Left." [Pembroke] (24) 92, p. 78-79.

1729. ELANA, Myrna
"Air over Breath." [ChironR] (11:4) Wint 92, p. 13.
"Sleep Over." [ChironR] (11:4) Wint 92, p. 13.

1730. ELDER, Karl
"Dream: Accountability." [SlipS] (12) 92, p. 99.

1731. ELDER, Mary
"Inheritance" (for Marion Hines Furey, 1903-1981). [GreensboroR] (52) Sum 92, p. 65.
"Watchmaker." [GreensboroR] (52) Sum 92, p. 66.

1732. ELGORRIAGO, José
"Autumn Begins" (tr. of Antonio Machado, w. Philip Levine). [NewEngR] (14:4) Fall 92, p. 43.
"Fields of Soria" (tr. of Antonio Machado, w. Philip Levine). [NewEngR] (14:4) Fall 92, p. 39-42.
"The House So Dear" (tr. of Antonio Machado, w. Philip Levine). [NewEngR] (14:4) Fall 92, p. 43.
"I Go on Dreaming" (tr. of Antonio Machado, w. Philip Levine). [NewEngR] (14:4) Fall 92, p. 44.
"In the Center of the Square" (tr. of Antonio Machado, w. Philip Levine). [NewEngR] (14:4) Fall 92, p. 45.

1733. ELIZABETH, Martha
"The Ending." [MidAR] (13:2) 92, p. 170.
"Manon Considers When to Leave Her Lover." [PoetL] (87:3) Fall 92, p. 21.
"Manon Remembers What She First Noticed About Her Lover." [PoetL] (87:3) Fall 92, p. 22.

1734. ELKAYAM, Shelley
"Checkmate in the Garden" (tr. by Ammiel Alcalay). [Paint] (19:37) Spr 92, p. 41.
"Seven Stanzas to an Indian Chief" (tr. by Ammiel Alcalay). [Paint] (19:37) Spr 92, p. 42.

1735. ELKIND, Sue Saniel
"Everyday Is Hers." [Wind] (22:71) 92, p. 13.
"Fifty-Seventh High School Reunion." [Wind] (22:71) 92, p. 12-13.
"Grandmother." [Wind] (22:71) 92, p. 12.
"Light from the Shtetle." [Interim] (11:1) Spr-Sum 92, p. 20.

1736. ELLEDGE, Jim
"Slasher." [LaurelR] (26:2) Sum 92, p. 71.

1737. ELLEFSON, J. C.
"The Available Supporting Female Roles" (From the Modern Latin Theatre). [VirQR] (68:1) Wint 92, p. 79-80.
"Circling the House and Grounds of Henrique Bernardo." [MalR] (101) Wint92, p. 90.
"For Pete's Sake." [ColEng] (54:3) Mr 92, p. 290.
"In Dreams Eduarda Maria Is in Love and Living in Paris." [HampSPR] Wint 92, p. 23.
"Kramer Now Reports on Angst." [ColEng] (54:3) Mr 92, p. 289.
"Lilly Going Down the Big Road." [VirQR] (68:1) Wint 92, p. 80-81.
"Postcard from the Cobblestone City." [MalR] (101) Wint92, p. 91.
"What It Looks Like and How to Mean It." [HampSPR] Wint 92, p. 22-23.

1738. ELLEN
"I Didn't Even Know I Had a Hole." [SlipS] (12) 92, p. 66.

1739. ELLENBOGEN, George
"Morning Gothic." [PraF] (13:2, #59) Sum 92, p. 32-33.

1740. ELLIOT, Alistair
"Cornelia." [Arion] 3d series (1:2) Spr 91, p. 129-130.

"A Journey to Brindisi in 37 B.C." (Satire 1.5, tr. of Horace). [Arion] 3d series (1:1) Wint 90, p. 180-183.
"Seeing Things." [NoDaQ] (60:3) Sum 92, p. 1-2.
"Talking to Ronnie Tylecote." [Verse] (8:3/9:1) Wint-Spr 92, p. 129-131.

ELLIOT, William P. Haynes
See HAYNES/ELLIOT, William P.

1741. ELLIS, Gregg
"Hands That Pray" (tr. of Philippe Soupault). [PoetryE] (33) Spr 92, p. 161-162.

1742. ELLIS, Pamela
"Nula." [NegC] (12:1/2) 92, p. 30-31.

1743. ELLIS, Stephen
"6 AM morning star bright in cedar." [Talisman] (8) Spr 92, p. 114.
"Sonnet After, and For, Jack Spicer." [Talisman] (8) Spr 92, p. 114.

1744. ELLIS, Thomas Sayers
"A Baptist Beat." [Agni] (36) 92, p. 34.
"Being There" (Kennedy Playground, Washington, D.C.). [Ploughs] (18:4) Wint 92 - 93, p. 68.
"Glory." [GrahamHR] (16) Fall 92, p. 54.
"Hush Yo Mouf" (for Bob Kaufman). [Agni] (35) 92, p. 162-163.
"The Man in the Dark Room." [Agni] (35) 92, p. 164.
"A Shaved and Uncombed Universe." [Agni] (35) 92, p. 160-161.
"Slow Fade to Black" (for Thomas Cripps). [Ploughs] (18:4) Wint 92-93, p. 69.
"Spellbound" (The Brattle Theatre, Cambridge, Massachusetts). [GrahamHR] (16) Fall 92, p. 55.
"Zapruder." [Ploughs] (18:4) Wint 92-93, p. 67.

1745. ELLISON, Julie
"Nightly." [MinnR] (38) Spr-Sum 92, p. 21.

1746. ELLISON, Mary
"Trafalgar Square." [PoetryUSA] (24) 92, p. 15.

1747. ELLMAN, Kitsey
"The Red Blouse" (after a painting by Matisse). [NewMyths] (1:2/2:1) 92, p. 181 - 183.

1748. ELLSWORTH, Anne
"The Commitment." [Amelia] (6:4, #19) 92, p. 43.

1749. ELLSWORTH, Priscilla
"Late Celebration." [Confr] (48/49) Spr-Sum 92, p. 235.

1750. ELMUSA, Sharif S.
"Just a Few Things." [PoetryE] (33) Spr 92, p. 39.

1751. ELOVIC, Barbara
"Anxiety." [Confr] (50) Fall 92, p. 289.
"Departure." [NewMyths] (1:2/2:1) 92, p. 13.
"Snowmen." [OxfordM] (7:1) Spr-Sum 91, p. 110.

1752. ELSBERG, John
"The Formality of a Logical Approach." [Wind] (22:71) 92, p. 14.

1753. ELSON, Rebecca A. W.
"The Last Animists." [Poetry] (161:3) D 92, p. 131.
"Like Eels to the Sargasso Sea." [US1] (26/27) 92, p. 21.

1754. ELUARD, Paul
"Woman in Love" (tr. by Cyntha Hendershot). [Asylum] (7:3/4) 92, p. 8.

1755. ELVRIDGE-THOMAS, Roxana
"Partes Mi sombra." [Nuez] (4:10/11) 92, p. 6.

1756. EMANUEL, James A.
"Breakaway Haiku." [AfAmRev] (26:2) Sum 92, p. 276.
"The Downhill Blues." [AfAmRev] (26:2) Sum 92, p. 274.
"The Knockout Blues." [AfAmRev] (26:2) Sum 92, p. 275.
"The Poor Man Blues." [AfAmRev] (26:2) Sum 92, p. 277.

1757. EMANUEL, Lynn
"Homage to Dickinson." [TriQ] (84) Spr-Sum 92, p. 123.
"Patient." [ThRiPo] (39/40) 92-93, p. 71-72.
"The Poet in Heaven." [TriQ] (84) Spr-Sum 92, p. 126-127.
"Self-Portrait at Eighteen." [ThRiPo] (39/40) 92-93, p. 73-74.
"What Did You Expect?" [TriQ] (84) Spr-Sum 92, p. 125.
"What Dying Was Like." [TriQ] (84) Spr-Sum 92, p. 124.
"What Grieving Was Like." [ThRiPo] (39/40) 92-93, p. 72-73.

1758. EMAZ, Antoine
"Poème, Ça Passe." [Os] (35) Fall 92, p. 32.

1759. EMERY, Thomas
"At the Center." [Light] (3) Aut 92, p. 8.
"My Mother's Shirt." [HopewellR] (4) 92, p. 27.
"Red-Wheeled Chevy." [HopewellR] (4) 92, p. 17.

ENCISO, Adriana Díaz
See DIAZ ENCISO, Adriana

1760. ENDREZZE, Anita
"The Medicine Woman's Daughter." [YellowS] (Ten Years [i.e. 40]) Sum-Fall 92, p. 17.
"Return of the Wolves." [Jacaranda] (6:1/2) Wint-Spr 92, p. 67.

1761. ENGELHARDT, Hardin
"Math Teachers." [LullwaterR] (3:3) Sum 92, p. 52-53.

1762. ENGELS, John
"In a Side Aisle of Kennedy Bros. Antiques Mall." [NewEngR] (14:2) Spr 92, p. 108.
"Locked Out." [NewEngR] (14:2) Spr 92, p. 106-107.
"A Reading." [Nat] (255:1) 6 Jl 92, p. 31.
"Waking from Nightmare." [NewEngR] (14:2) Spr 92, p. 109.
"Watching for Animals." [NewEngR] (14:2) Spr 92, p. 110-111.

1763. ENGLE, Diane
"Sunset Over Saratoga." [Elf] (2:3) Fall 92, p. 33.

1764. ENGLE, John D., Jr.
"Divine Secret of Success." [Light] (1) Spr 92, p. 31.
"Fall from Graces." [Light] (4) Wint 92-93, p. 23.
"To the Cape Cod Gull That Dumped on Me." [Light] (3) Aut 92, p. 14.

1765. ENGLER, Robert Klein
"St. Augustine." [Conscience] (13:2) Sum 92, p. 33.

1766. ENGMAN, John
"Chlorine." [PoetryE] (33) Spr 92, p. 40-41.
"The Window in the Cow." [GreenMR] (NS 5:2) Spr-Sum 92, p. 90.

1767. ENNS, Victor Jerrett
"A Poem of Pears." [Grain] (20:1) Spr 92, p. 84-90.

1768. ENRIQUEZ ANDRADE, Héctor Manuel
"El Frío Muerde los Pulgares." [Nuez] (4:10/11) 92, p. 8.

1769. ENSING, Riemke
"The Artist in His Studio" (black and white photograph, Leiden, 1976, after reading Ian Wedde on Leon van den Eijkel in *Art New Zealand* 58). [Descant] (23:3, #78) Fall 92, p. 137-138.
"In Camera" (for Frank Hofmann, photographer, 1916-1989). [Descant] (23:3, #78) Fall 92, p. 134-136.
"Kirikau" (Poems for Bill). [Descant] (23:4/24:1, #78/79) Wint-Spr 92-93, p. 195 - 208.

1770. ENSLER, Eve
"A Terrorist Angel" (For Richard). [Art&Und] (1:4) Jl-Ag 92, p. 11.

1771. ENTREKIN, Gail Rudd
"At Dawn He Takes My Hand." [NegC] (12:3) 92, p. 75-76.

1772. ENZENSBERGER, Hans Magnus
"Appearances" (tr. by Michael Hamburger). [Stand] (33:4) Aut 92, p. 82.
"April" (tr. by Reinhold Grimm). [Pembroke] (24) 92, p. 30.
"The Blank Sheet" (tr. by Michael Hamburger). [Stand] (33:4) Aut 92, p. 81.
"Candide" (tr. by Reinhold Grimm). [Pembroke] (24) 92, p. 31.
"Carceri d'Invenzione" (tr. by Reinhold Grimm). [Pembroke] (24) 92, p. 38.
"A Cherry Orchard in the Snow" (tr. by Reinhold Grimm). [Pembroke] (24) 92, p. 39.
"Consistency" (tr. by Michael Hamburger). [Stand] (33:4) Aut 92, p. 81.
"A Didactic Poem on Murder" (tr. by Reinhold Grimm). [Pembroke] (24) 92, p. 35.
"Glass Architecture" (tr. by Reinhold Grimm). [Pembroke] (24) 92, p. 42.
"Grand Tour" (tr. by Reinhold Grimm). [Pembroke] (24) 92, p. 32.
"Grasp of the Wind" (tr. by Reinhold Grimm). [Pembroke] (24) 92, p. 40.
"The Great Inventions" (tr. by Reinhold Grimm). [Pembroke] (24) 92, p. 36.
"Indulgence" (tr. by Reinhold Grimm). [Pembroke] (24) 92, p. 43.
"An Option for Real Estate" (tr. by Reinhold Grimm). [Pembroke] (24) 92, p. 34.
"Same Old Story" (tr. by Reinhold Grimm). [Pembroke] (24) 92, p. 41.
"Taking Leave of a Wednesday" (tr. by Reinhold Grimm). [Pembroke] (24) 92, p. 33.
"This Is the Dog" (tr. by Reinhold Grimm). [Pembroke] (24) 92, p. 37.

"This Number Has Been Disconnected" (tr. by Reinhold Grimm). [Pembroke] (24) 92, p. 44.

EOYANG, Eugene Chen
See CHEN EOYANG, Eugene

1773. EPSTEIN, John
"Early Dawn" (tr. of Uwe Kolbe). [Shiny] (7/8) 92, p. 141.
"Nicolaus Löwenthal" (2 selections, tr. of Sascha Anderson). [Shiny] (7/8) 92, p. 147.
"Philomela" (2 selections). [Shiny] (7/8) 92, p. 138-139.
"To Live" (tr. of Uwe Kolbe). [Shiny] (7/8) 92, p. 140.

1774. EQUI, Elaine
"After Bacon." [NewAW] (10) Fall 92, p. 60.
"Flutter." [Epoch] (41:1) 92, p. 124.
"For Ad Reinhardt." [Epoch] (41:1) 92, p. 126.
"Moonlight on Lobster." [Epoch] (41:1) 92, p. 122.
"Permission." [Epoch] (41:1) 92, p. 123.
"Poem: Like a window open in winter." [Conjunc] (19) 92, p. 118.
"Reading Akhmatova." [AmerV] (26) Spr 92, p. 124-125.
"Sarcophagus." [NewAW] (10) Fall 92, p. 61-62.
"This Is Not a Poem." [Conjunc] (19) 92, p. 117.
"Years Later." [Epoch] (41:1) 92, p. 125.

1775. ERDRICH, Louise
"Dear John Wayne." [Jacaranda] (6:1/2) Wint-Spr 92, p. 68-69.

1776. EREMENKO, Aleksandr
"On the Removal of Troops from Afghanistan" (tr. by Forrest Gander and Sara Dickinson). [Agni] (35) 92, p. 268-269.

1777. ERHARDT, Jean
"Kings Island." [ChironR] (11:4) Wint 92, p. 47.
"Later That Same Year." [ChironR] (11:4) Wint 92, p. 46.

1778. ERIANNE, John C.
"Tarot." [Asylum] (7:3/4) 92, p. 59.

1779. ERICHSEN, Per-Otto
"The Season of the Lion." [FourQ] (6:1) Spr 92, p. 13.

1780. ERMINI, Flavio
"Delosea." [Os] (34) Spr 92, p. 17.
"Kleist." [Os] (35) Fall 92, p. 2.
"Segnitz." [Os] (34) Spr 92, p. 16.

1781. ERNST, Myron
"The Abravayas, the Levys and Hattems" (for the Quincentennial of the Edict of Expulsion, 1492). [MidwQ] (34:1) Aut 92, p. 63.
"Florida, How the Very Old Do Move About." [PoetryE] (33) Spr 92, p. 43.
"Florida, Two Old Sisters." [PoetryE] (33) Spr 92, p. 42.

1782. ERON, Don
"The Shooter." [GrahamHR] (16) Fall 92, p. 77-79.

1783. ERSHAD, H. M.
"Blooming Happily Again." [NegC] (12:1/2) 92, p. 175.
"A Day to Live." [NegC] (12:1/2) 92, p. 176.

1784. ESCOBAR GALINDO, David
"De Rerum Natura" (tr. by Florinda Mintz and Paul Vangelisti). [OnTheBus] (4:2/5:1, #10/11) 92, p. 274.
"Letter with Roses" (tr. by Florinda Mintz and Paul Vangelisti). [OnTheBus] (4:2/5:1, #10/11) 92, p. 275.

1785. ESCOFFERY, Gloria
"Bullet Wood." [LitR] (35:4) Sum 92, p. 480.
"Communication." [LitR] (35:4) Sum 92, p. 479.
"Drive Carefully." [LitR] (35:4) Sum 92, p. 480.
"Letter from Gilbert." [LitR] (35:4) Sum 92, p. 481.
"Serenade: No Woman, No Cry." [LitR] (35:4) Sum 92, p. 478.
"Sharing a Joke." [LitR] (35:4) Sum 92, p. 479.
"Spaced In." [LitR] (35:4) Sum 92, p. 479.

1786. ESCUDERO, Ernesto
"Cántico" (A Reinaldo Arenas). [Nuez] (4:12) 92, p. 10.

1787. ESDEN-TEMPSKI, Stanislaw
"I the Rat" (tr. by Daniel Bourne). [AnotherCM] (23) Spr 92, p. 71.
"The Recycling of My Body" (tr. by Daniel Bourne). [AnotherCM] (23) Spr 92, p. 73.

"Rust" (tr. by Daniel Bourne). [AnotherCM] (23) Spr 92, p. 72.

1788. ESH, Sylvan
"Downturn." [Farm] (9:2) Fall-Wint 92-93, p. 74-75.

1789. ESHE, Aisha (Marilyn Elain Carmen)
"Sunday Afternoon Shopping." [Footwork] 92, p. 89.

1790. ESHLEMAN, Clayton
"Carrion Gossip." [DenQ] (27:1) Sum 92, p. 84-86.
"Hardball" (from "Under World Arrest"). [Sulfur] (12:2, #31) Fall 92, p. 14-15.
"Rhapsody on a Theme by Vallejo." [Sulfur] (12:1, #30) Spr 92, p. 108-110.
"Trilce" (Selections: XXXII, XXXVI, XXXVIII, tr. of César Vallejo, w. Julio Ortega). [GrandS] (11:1, #41) 92, p. 57-61.
"Trilce" (Selections: LXXI-LXXIII, tr. of César Vallejo, w. Julio Ortega). [WorldL] (3) 92, p. 1-3.
"Under World Arrest, Section III." [RiverS] (36) 92, p. 1-2.

1791. ESPADA, Martín
"The Broken Window of Rosa Ramos" (Chelsea, Massachusetts 1991). [Callaloo] (15:4) Fall 92, p. 958.
"Cockroaches of Liberation" (for Víctor Rivera, Puerto Rico). [DenQ] (27:1) Sum 92, p. 87-88.
"Colibrí" (for Katherine, one year later). [Americas] (20:3/4) Fall-Wint 92, p. 178 - 179.
"Cuando los Cantos Se Vuelven Agua" (para *Diario Latino*, El Salvador, 1991, tr. by Camilo Pérez-Bustillo). [PaintedB] (48) 92, p. 10-11.
"David Leaves the Saints for Paterson." [Americas] (20:3/4) Fall-Wint 92, p. 177.
"The Hidalgo's Hat and a Hawk's Bell of Gold." [BostonR] (17:5) S-O 92, p. 4.
"Now I Take My Leave" (tr. of Juan Antonio Corretjer, w. Camilo Pérez-Bustillo). [Callaloo] (15:4) Fall 92, p. 951.
"Shaking Hands with Mongo" (For Mongo Santamaría). [Americas] (20:3/4) Fall - Wint 92, p. 181.
"The Toolmaker Unemployed" (Connecticut River Valley, 1992). [DenQ] (27:1) Sum 92, p. 89.
"When Songs Become Water" (for *Diario Latino*, El Salvador, 1991). [PaintedB] (48) 92, p. 8-9.
"The Words of the Mute Are Like Silver Dollars" (Prince George's County, Maryland, 1976). [Americas] (20:3/4) Fall-Wint 92, p. 180.
"The Year I Was Diagnosed with a Sacrilegious Heart." [DenQ] (27:1) Sum 92, p. 90-91.

1792. ESPAILLAT, Rhina P.
"Cat Scan." [Sparrow] (59) S 92, p. 25.
"Circling the Jellyfish." [Amelia] (7:1, #20) 92, p. 84-85.
"The Waking." [Sparrow] (59) S 92, p. 25.

1793. ESPINA, Eduardo
"Decir de Dudas del Filantropo." [Inti] (36) Otoño 92, p. 146.
"Mas Felices Que en Vietnam." [Inti] (36) Otoño 92, p. 144-146.
"La Novia de Hitler." [Inti] (36) Otoño 92, p. 143-144.

1794. ESPINOSA, Resurrección
"Aloe." [BilingR] (17:3) S-D 92, p. 265.
"Easy, Man." [BilingR] (17:3) S-D 92, p. 266-267.
"Hibiscus." [BilingR] (17:3) S-D 92, p. 265-266.
"Mother" (for my mother). [BilingR] (17:3) S-D 92, p. 264-265.

1795. ESPOSITO, Nancy
"Supposing That Truth Is a Woman — What Then?" [PoetL] (87:2) Sum 92, p. 29 - 30.

1796. ESPRIU, Salvador
"Cemetery of Sinera" (Selections: I-V, tr. by James Kirkup). [Stand] (33:4) Aut 92, p. 151-152.
"Easy Prey" (tr. by James Kirkup). [Stand] (33:4) Aut 92, p. 151.
"For a Canticle in the Temple" (tr. by James Kirkup). [Stand] (33:4) Aut 92, p. 151.
"For My People of Sépharad" (tr. by James Kirkup). [Stand] (33:4) Aut 92, p. 150.
"Prometheus" (tr. by James Kirkup). [Stand] (33:4) Aut 92, p. 150.

1797. ESQUINCA, Jorge
"Alliance of the Kingdoms" (Selections from Part II. Flocks: 1-2, 5-6, tr. by Tino Villanueva). [Manoa] (4:2) Fall 92, p. 128-130.
"Episode in Al-Qayrawan" (tr. by Reginald Gibbons). [TriQ] (85) Fall 92, p. 87-89.

1798. ESSEX, David
"Epistemology 1." [WilliamMR] (30) 92, p. 35-38.

1799. ESSINGER, Cathryn
"Growing Accustomed to Green." [Poetry] (160:5) Ag 92, p. 262.
"You Are Right." [Poetry] (160:5) Ag 92, p. 263.
1800. ESTABROOK, Michael
"After the Meeting." [Amelia] (7:1, #20) 92, p. 80.
"Bastard." [RagMag] (10:2) 92, p. 95.
"Dented Shiny Shovels." [DogRR] (11:2, #22) Fall-Wint 92, p. 46-47.
"Drunk All the Time" (for Charles Bukowski). [ChironR] (11:3) Aut 92, p. 28.
"Each Other." [RagMag] (10:2) 92, p. 94.
"He Was Staring at Something." [Lactuca] (16) Ag 92, p. 29.
"Paper-Thin Pink Morning Glories." [Parting] (5:2) Wint 92-93, p. 5.
"Right in Frong of Us." [NegC] (12:1/2) 92, p. 32.
1801. ESTABROOK, Susan
"Railroad Tracks." [OnTheBus] (4:2/5:1, #10/11) 92, p. 90-91.
1802. ESTES, Angie
"After Darwin." [SouthernPR] (32:2) Fall 92, p. 44.
"The Classical Tradition." [AntR] (50:4) Fall 92, p. 722.
1803. ESTESS, Sybil
"Native on Land." [WestHR] (46:1) Spr 92, p. 84-85.
1804. ESTEVE, Jean
"Big Moon." [CarolQ] (45:1) Fall 92, p. 26.
"First Grandchild." [FloridaR] (18:1) Spr-Sum 92, p. 90.
1805. ESTEVES, Sandra María
"Amor Negro." [Americas] (20:3/4) Fall-Wint 92, p. 144.
"Portraits for Shamsul Alam." [Americas] (20:3/4) Fall-Wint 92, p. 145-146.
"Transference." [Americas] (20:3/4) Fall-Wint 92, p. 147-148.
1806. ESTRIN, Jerry
"Rome, a Mobile Home" (Excerpts). [Talisman] (8) Spr 92, p. 97-99.
1807. ETTARI, Gary
"Internal Combustion." [TarRP] (31:2) Spr 92, p. 15.
1808. ETTER, Carrie
"Five Years After Placing My Son for Adoption." [Pearl] (15) Spr-Sum 92, p. 25.
1809. EUBANKS, Georgann
"The Median." [SouthernR] (28:1) Wint, Ja 92, p. 43-44.
"White Cat." [NegC] (12:1/2) 92, p. 33-34.
1810. EUBANKS, L. Terry
"Did We, Either of Us, Mean to Get the Other?" [BellArk] (8:5) S-O 92, p. 5.
"Then Return." [BellArk] (8:5) S-O 92, p. 5.
1811. EVANS, David Allan
"The Game." [Epiphany] (3:4) O (Fall) 92, p. 302-304.
"The Kiss." [Epiphany] (3:4) O (Fall) 92, p. 301.
1812. EVANS, Kevin
"Loving the World." [LouisL] (9:1) Spr 92, p. 72.
1813. EVANS, M. Jerome
"Cleaning the Fish" (for Alysia, with her first catch). [Amelia] (7:1, #20) 92, p. 162.
"Dance at Bougival." [Amelia] (6:4, #19) 92, p. 122.
1814. EVANS, Michael
"At the Edge of the Continent." [GreensboroR] (53) Wint 92-93, p. 107-108.
"Capital Reef, Utah." [TexasR] (13:3/4) Fall-Wint 92, p. 83.
"Cutting the Apple Tree." [MidAR] (12:2) 92, p. 3-4.
"Driving Past the Battlefield at Cross Keys, Virginia." [Poem] (68) N 92, p. 16.
"The Miner Outside His Tent" (Photograph, Circa 1912). [TexasR] (13:3/4) Fall - Wint 92, p. 84-85.
"Salvaging." [Poem] (68) N 92, p. 14.
"Snakeskin." [Poem] (68) N 92, p. 15.
1815. EVENSON, Brian
"Exposed to Sun" (tr. of Edouard Maunick, w. David Beus). [CentralP] (21) Spr 92, p. 134-138.
1816. EVERDING, Kelly
"Sebastian." [DenQ] (26:3) Wint 92, p. 8-9.
1817. EVERETT, Graham
"Near Thanksgiving." [Contact] (10:62/63/64) Fall 91-Spr 92, p. 55.
1818. EVERWINE, Peter
"A Story." [QW] (36) Wint 92-93, p. 4.
1819. EWART, Gavin
"Advice to Wendy Cope on Touring the USA." [Light] (2) Sum 92, p. 6.

"Beginning of a Ballad: At the Literary Party" (from "Eight Little Ones"). [Light] (2) Sum 92, p. 5.
"Cats and Owls." [Light] (2) Sum 92, p. 4.
"Cats and Women." [Light] (2) Sum 92, p. 4.
"Haiku of a Japanese Surgeon." [Light] (2) Sum 92, p. 4.
"I'm Drunk As I Live Boys Drunk." [Light] (1) Spr 92, p. 3.
"Instructions for London Transport Passengers." [Light] (1) Spr 92, p. 27.
"The Irritation of Life." [Light] (2) Sum 92, p. 3.
"A Little Larkinish Lyric." [Light] (2) Sum 92, p. 5.
"Lucky Jim's Sonnet on Putney Bridge." [Light] (2) Sum 92, p. 4.
"The Marvellous Writer." [Light] (2) Sum 92, p. 6.
"My Beard." [Light] (2) Sum 92, p. 3.
"A Skull in Chain Mail." [Light] (2) Sum 92, p. 5.
"T.R.O.T.N.*" (* *The Return of the Native* by Thomas Hardy). [Light] (4) Wint 92-93, p. 15.
"Talking to Women." [Light] (2) Sum 92, p. 5.
"Two Advertising Triolets" ("Grape-Nuts" and "Watney's Red Barrel"). [Light] (2) Sum 92, p. 4.
"War Generations" (A Loaded Lyric). [Light] (2) Sum 92, p. 6.

1820. EWING, Blair
"Capital Haiku." [WashR] (17:6) Ap-My 92, p. 15.

1821. EWING, Jim
"Glasgow Tram." [TexasR] (13:3/4) Fall-Wint 92, p. 86.

1822. EXNER, Richard
"Last Portrait" (tr. by the author and Martha Collins). [Agni] (35) 92, p. 182.
"Pietà Rondanini" (tr. by Martha Collins). [Agni] (35) 92, p. 181.

EYNDEN, Keith Vanden
See Vanden EYNDEN, Keith

1823. FABILLI, Mary
"Aurora Bligh" (Excerpt). [Talisman] (8) Spr 92, p. 176.

1824. FAGLES, Robert
"After Robert Capa" (For Bernard Knox. Cordoba, c. September 6, 1936). [SewanR] (100:1) Wint 92, p. 59.
"Crazy Horse" (after Mari Sandoz). [SewanR] (100:1) Wint 92, p. 55-58.

1825. FAGUNDO, Ana Maria
"Birthday Poem" (tr. by Steven Ford Brown and Moira Perez). [SenR] (22:1) Spr 92, p. 49.
"Dawn in the Monastery of the Olive Trees" (for Julia Gonzalez, tr. by Steven Ford Brown and Moira Perez). [SenR] (22:1) Spr 92, p. 51-52.
"The Sower" (tr. by Steven Ford Brown and Moira Perez). [SenR] (22:1) Spr 92, p. 50.

1826. FAHEY, W. A.
"After Celan." [Confr] (50) Fall 92, p. 282.

1827. FAINLIGHT, Ruth
"The Coptic Wedding." [NewYorker] (67:50) 3 F 92, p. 38.
"The Cranes." [SouthwR] (77:4) Aut 92, p. 535.
"The Future." [ThRiPo] (39/40) 92-93, p. 76-77.
"On the Coast Road." [Thrpny] (49) Spr 92, p. 26.
"Spring in the City." [ThRiPo] (39/40) 92-93, p. 75-76.
"Stubborn." [ThRiPo] (39/40) 92-93, p. 74-75.

1828. FAITH, Sam
"13 — Line Invention." [Epiphany] (3:2) Ap (Spr) 92, p. 90.
"Aubade." [LullwaterR] (4:1) Fall 92, p. 7.
"Love (Beauty)." [Epiphany] (3:2) Ap (Spr) 92, p. 90.
"National Convention: High School Model U.N." [LullwaterR] (3:2) Spr 92, p. 54.
"One Example." [LullwaterR] (4:1) Fall 92, p. 59.
"Postcard." [Epiphany] (3:2) Ap (Spr) 92, p. 88.
"Prelude to 'Hello'." [Epiphany] (3:2) Ap (Spr) 92, p. 89.
"Santorini 1988" (Pantoum, Descending). [Vis] (38) 92, p. 17.
"Tropical." [ChatR] (13:1) Fall 92, p. 45.
"Unrhymed." [Epiphany] (3:2) Ap (Spr) 92, p. 88.

1829. FAIZ, Faiz Ahmed (Faiz Ahmad)
"Dedication" (tr. by Daud Kamal). [Vis] (38) 92, p. 47.
"An Apology" (tr. by Andrew McCord). [Agni] (36) 92, p. 20.
"Last Days" (tr. by Andrew McCord). [Agni] (35) 92, p. 234.
"Love's Captives" (tr. by Naomi Lazard). [Trans] (26) Spr 92, p. 95.

"Prison Meeting" (tr. by Naomi Lazard). [Trans] (26) Spr 92, p. 39-40.
"When Autumn Came" (tr. by Naomi Lazard). [Trans] (26) Spr 92, p. 5.

1830. FAJARDO, Ana Bantigue
"Island Dream." [SinW] (47) Sum-Fall 92, p. 41-42.

1831. FALCO, Edward
"Casting Out." [WestHR] (46:3) Fall 92, p. 308.
"Night Drives." [CarolQ] (44:2) Wint 92, p. 83.

1832. FALK, Pat
"Vietnam, 1967." [BlackBR] (15) Spr-Sum 92, p. 13.

1833. FALKENBERG, Betty
"Hagar and Ishmael" (tr. of Else Lasker-Schüler). [Boulevard] (7:2/3, #20/21) Fall 92, p. 240.
"Jacob and Esau" (tr. of Else Lasker-Schüler). [Boulevard] (7:2/3, #20/21) Fall 92, p. 241.

1834. FALLA, Jonathan
"Clara." [Verse] (9:2) Sum 92, p. 92.

1835. FALLER, Francis
"Dispatches from the Forest." [Stand] (33:3) Sum 92, p. 10-11.

1836. FALLON, Teresa
"Christmas Mandala." [PoetC] (24:1) Fall 92, p. 32.
"Cocoa." [PoetC] (24:1) Fall 92, p. 30-31.

1837. FANDEL, John
"Pentecost" (corrected reprint). [Comm] (119:8) 24 Ap 92, p. 26.
"Pentecost" (incomplete). [Comm] (119:5) 13 Mr 92, p. 31.

1838. FANELLI, Michael
"Mackeral Sun." [Wind] (22:71) 92, p. 29.
"You Go First." [NewYorkQ] (47) 92, p. 70.

1839. FANNING, Roger
"Dance Manias During the Plague." [AmerPoR] (21:6) N-D 92, p. 55.
"Puddle of Catsup, Parsley Sprig." [AmerPoR] (21:6) N-D 92, p. 55.
"Tadpoles." [AmerPoR] (21:6) N-D 92, p. 55.

1840. FANTHORPE, U. A.
"Costa Geriatrica." [13thMoon] (10:1/2) 92, p. 41.
"The Moment (19-20 August, 1932)" (for Rosie). [13thMoon] (10:1/2) 92, p. 42-43.

1841. FARALLO, Livio
"No Car, No Brains." [SlipS] (12) 92, p. 96.

1842. FAREWELL, Patricia
"Unfinished Business." [NewYorkQ] (48) 92, p. 71.

1843. FARGAS, Laura
"Cross-casting, for Beginners." [GeoR] (46:1) Spr 92, p. 73.
"If There Is A." [ParisR]] (34:124) Fall 92, p. 144.
"Psyche." [PoetL] (87:1) Spr 92, p. 48.
"Reflecting What Light We Can't Absorb." [ParisR]] (34:124) Fall 92, p. 144.
"Speaking" (for Li-Young Lee). [PoetL] (87:1) Spr 92, p. 48.

1844. FARGNOLI, Patricia
"Christmas Eve, Our Father." [CapeR] (27:2) Fall 92, p. 13.
"Sagg Beach in Winter" (for Maureen). [CapeR] (27:2) Fall 92, p. 12.

1845. FARHI, Moris
"Three Songs from Istanbul." [Confr] (48/49) Spr-Sum 92, p. 214-215.

1846. FARKAS, Endre
"Suffering Set Me on the Road" (from "Holtak arca fölé," tr. of Károly Bari). [PoetryC] (12:2) Ap 92, p. 25.
"Wandering Gypsies" (from "Holtak arca fölé," tr. of Károly Bari). [PoetryC] (12:2) Ap 92, p. 25.

1847. FARLEY, Joseph
"Yet Another." [Pearl] (15) Spr-Sum 92, p. 17.

1848. FARMER, David
"The Writer." [Epiphany] (3:1) Ja (Wint) 92, p. 1.

1849. FARMER, Harold
"Drums." [Nimrod] (35:2) Spr-Sum 92, p. 118.
"Gomo" (Hill). [Nimrod] (35:2) Spr-Sum 92, p. 120.
"Locusts." [Stand] (33:3) Sum 92, p. 13.
"Ngesi." [Nimrod] (35:2) Spr-Sum 92, p. 119.

1850. FARMER, Rod
"Berries." [DogRR] (11:2, #22) Fall-Wint 92, p. 4.
"Deities." [DogRR] (11:2, #22) Fall-Wint 92, p. 4.

"Despite." [HampSPR] Wint 92, p. 32.
"Maine Winter." [Elf] (2:3) Fall 92, p. 35.
"This Moment Now." [HampSPR] Wint 92, p. 32.

1851. FARMER, Ruth
"Subway Scenes." [SinW] (47) Sum-Fall 92, p. 128-129.

1852. FARNSWORTH, Jared D.
"Caressing My Wife." [YellowS] (41) Fall-Wint 92-93, p. 32.

1853. FARNSWORTH, Robert
"The Owl" (for Nate). [SenR] (22:1) Spr 92, p. 76-78.
"Patrimony." [SenR] (22:1) Spr 92, p. 79.
"Realistic Satisfactions, or, Upon Westminster Bridge." [BlackWR] (18:2) Spr-Sum 92, p. 105-106.
"Unforgivable Landscape." [NewEngR] (14:4) Fall 92, p. 95.
"Why I've Never Bought You Fishnet Stockings." [PoetryE] (33) Spr 92, p. 44-45.
"Why Then" (for Tom). [WestHR] (46:3) Fall 92, p. 246-247.

1854. FARQUHAR, Dion
"Figure This." [AfAmRev] (26:2) Sum 92, p. 286-287.

1855. FARR, Robert
"Circe." [Lactuca] (16) Ag 92, p. 30.

1856. FARR, Sheila
"Translation of an Old English Riddle." [BellR] (15:1) Spr 92, p. 39.

1857. FARRAH, David
"Waiting to Be Filled" (Chapbook: 5 poems). [OhioR] (48) 92, p. 37-46.

1858. FARRINGTON, Margot
"The Snakes." [Outbr] (23) 92, p. 71.

1859. FARRIS, Nettie
"You Know Me Better." [HawaiiR] (16:2, #35) Spr 92, p. 29.

1860. FARUQI, Moeen
"Partition." [Verse] (9:2) Sum 92, p. 28.

1861. FASEL, Ida
"Bell." [ChrC] (109:25) 26 Ag-2 S 92, p. 768.
"A Holy Place." [CapeR] (27:1) Spr 92, p. 11.
"Outlook for Spring." [ChrC] (109:13) 15 Ap 92, p. 389.
"Reflections on Unclean Spirits." [ChrC] (109:31) 28 O 92, p. 977.

1862. FAUST, Clive
"Carrying On." [Footwork] 92, p. 138.

1863. FAWCETT, Susan
"Black Water Diving." [Poetry] (160:5) Ag 92, p. 257-258.
"Dark Blue Bee." [Ploughs] (18:4) Wint 92-93, p. 11-12.
"Retablos." [Ploughs] (18:4) Wint 92-93, p. 13.

1864. FAY, Julie
"Provençal Laundry." [Hellas] (3:2) Fall 92, p. 93-94.
"Witches at St. Guilhem-le-Desert." [LaurelR] (26:2) Sum 92, p. 38-39.

1865. FEATHERSTON, Dan
"Pomegranate." [Sulfur] (12:2, #31) Fall 92, p. 67-69.

1866. FEATHERSTONE, Charles
"Bird" (from "Fenced Passions," San Quentin, 1991). [PoetryUSA] (24) 92, p. 27.
"Coltrane" (from "Fenced Passions," San Quentin, 1991). [PoetryUSA] (24) 92, p. 27.
"Miles" (from "Fenced Passions," San Quentin, 1991). [PoetryUSA] (24) 92, p. 27.

1867. FEAVER, Jane
"The Last Woman." [Verse] (8:3/9:1) Wint-Spr 92, p. 108.

1868. FECTEAU, Janette
"Mathematics." [PottPort] (14:1) Spr-Sum 92, p. 35-40.

1869. FEDERICI, Corrado
"Arranged" (tr. of Amelia Rosselli). [PoetryC] (13:1) N 92, p. 23.
"The Cancer of Civilization" (tr. of Maria Luisa Spaziani). [PoetryC] (13:1) N 92, p. 22.
"The End of the Year 1975 for Andrea Zanzotto" (tr. of Franco Fortini). [PoetryC] (13:1) N 92, p. 20.
"Far" (tr. of Dacia Maraini). [PoetryC] (13:1) N 92, p. 23.
"Horizons" (tr. of Andrea Zanzotto). [PoetryC] (13:1) N 92, p. 21.
"Hypothesis on What Is Ours" (tr. of Elio Pagliarani). [PoetryC] (13:1) N 92, p. 21.
"In the Beginning Was Calculation" (tr. of Edoardo Sanguineti). [PoetryC] (13:1) N 92, p. 20.

"Infinite Forms of Entertainment" (tr. of Lamberto Pignotti). [PoetryC] (13:1) N 92, p. 21.
"The Knife Thrower" (tr. of Margherita Guidacci). [PoetryC] (13:1) N 92, p. 23.
"Obsessed Objects / Spiritualized Matter" (tr. of Mariella Bettarini). [PoetryC] (13:1) N 92, p. 22.
"Syntactic and Verbal" (tr. of Guilia Niccolai). [PoetryC] (13:1) N 92, p. 23.
"The Uranoscopus" (tr. of Biancamaria Frabotta). [PoetryC] (13:1) N 92, p. 21.

1870. FEDERMAN, Raymond
"Morning Rain." [Os] (35) Fall 92, p. 33.

1871. FEHLER, Gene
"A Butterfly's Feat." [Light] (4) Wint 92-93, p. 11.

1872. FEILER, Eva
"Horizon" (tr. of Nina Cassian). [Trans] (26) Spr 92, p. 76.
"It Can't Be Otherwise" (tr. of Nina Cassian). [Trans] (26) Spr 92, p. 75.
"Point of View" (tr. of Nina Cassian). [Trans] (26) Spr 92, p. 75.

1873. FEINFELD, D. A.
"For Catherine Block" (Killed in a car crash in August, 1965). [Elf] (2:2) Sum 92, p. 30-31.

1874. FEINSTEIN, Robert N.
"Big Ben's Bong!" [Amelia] (7:1, #20) 92, p. 51.
"Crustaceans." [Light] (3) Aut 92, p. 10.
"Plea of a Verbophile." [HolCrit] (29:2) Ap 92, p. 19.
"The Soused Cow." [Light] (4) Wint 92-93, p. 24.
"To a Fast-Food Server." [Light] (1) Spr 92, p. 10.

1875. FELDMAN, Irving
"The Affair." [Nat] (254:12) 30 Mr 92, p. 423.
"How Wonderful." [Nat] (254:11) 23 Mr 92, p. 391.
"The Knot." [Nat] (255:15) 9 N 92, p. 552.
"Small Talk for a Sage." [Confr] (50) Fall 92, p. 258.
"Story." [Nat] (254:3) 27 Ja 92, p. 100.

1876. FELDMAN, Laura
"Cable Car Turnaround" (taken from a photograph). [NowestR] (30:1) 92, p. 108 - 112.
"Hudson Pier 12/10/90." [NowestR] (30:1) 92, p. 113-114.
"Moving Carrier" (Selections). [Avec] (5:1) 92, p. 100-102.
"Sierra Marsh Marigold" (excerpted from "Flammulated Owlet with Moth Oak and Moon?"). [BlackWR] (18:2) Spr-Sum 92, p. 72.
"Walking the Embarcadero Freeway from Foot of Broadway Entrance to Embarcadero Exit at Night. 8/19/90." [BlackWR] (18:2) Spr-Sum 92, p. 73-74.

1877. FELDMAN, Rebecca
"Poem for the Day My Mother Was Born." [HangL] (60) 92, p. 84-85.

1878. FELDMAN, Ruth
"Colette Was Right." [Agni] (35) 92, p. 240-241.
"Fibre" (tr. of Bartolo Cattafi, w. Brian Swann). [Stand] (33:4) Aut 92, p. 111.
"Like This, My Papa in America" (tr. of Rocco Scotellaro, w. Brian Swann). [Stand] (33:4) Aut 92, p. 108.

1879. FELL, Mary
"Craft." [HopewellR] (4) 92, p. 18.
"Traveler's Advisory." [HopewellR] (4) 92, p. 23.

1880. FELTGES, Ken
"Working Stiff." [SlipS] (12) 92, p. 108-109.

FEMINA, Gerry La
See LaFEMINA, Gerry

1881. FENG, Anita
"Among Things Not Known." [SpoonRQ] (17:1/2) Wint-Spr 92, p. 79.
"By the Jade Steps" (originally published in Nimrod as "On the Guilded Staircase"). [SpoonRQ] (17:1/2) Wint-Spr 92, p. 64-65.
"Coming Through." [SpoonRQ] (17:1/2) Wint-Spr 92, p. 59.
"Concerning Children." [SpoonRQ] (17:1/2) Wint-Spr 92, p. 75.
"The Fish Are at Home." [SpoonRQ] (17:1/2) Wint-Spr 92, p. 60.
"For the Softened Lungs of Birds." [SpoonRQ] (17:1/2) Wint-Spr 92, p. 74.
"Fountain in the Courtyard of the Public Library." [SpoonRQ] (17:1/2) Wint-Spr 92, p. 78.
"Ghost Marriage." [SpoonRQ] (17:1/2) Wint-Spr 92, p. 57.
"How Capable." [SpoonRQ] (17:1/2) Wint-Spr 92, p. 63.

"A Letter to Beijing." [SpoonRQ] (17:1/2) Wint-Spr 92, p. 76.
"Momentum." [SpoonRQ] (17:1/2) Wint-Spr 92, p. 70.
"Not to Be Apprehended." [SpoonRQ] (17:1/2) Wint-Spr 92, p. 77.
"Prosperous with Birds." [SpoonRQ] (17:1/2) Wint-Spr 92, p. 73.
"Sailing from the Future to the Past" (parts originally published under different titles in Nimrod). [SpoonRQ] (17:1/2) Wint-Spr 92, p. 61-62.
"Seed." [SpoonRQ] (17:1/2) Wint-Spr 92, p. 67.
"Softness." [SpoonRQ] (17:1/2) Wint-Spr 92, p. 71.
"Spring Cosmology." [SpoonRQ] (17:1/2) Wint-Spr 92, p. 69.
"Two Green Hands Open Wide." [SpoonRQ] (17:1/2) Wint-Spr 92, p. 58.
"Verging." [SpoonRQ] (17:1/2) Wint-Spr 92, p. 68.
"The Visa Papers Expire Soon." [SpoonRQ] (17:1/2) Wint-Spr 92, p. 72.
"The Waltz Itself." [SpoonRQ] (17:1/2) Wint-Spr 92, p. 66.
"What Stays, What Goes." [SpoonRQ] (17:1/2) Wint-Spr 92, p. 80.

1882. FENSTERMAKER, Vesle
"Option." [HopewellR] (4) 92, p. 12.

1883. FENTON, James
"Cut-throat Christ, or The New Ballad of the Dosi Pares." [NewYRB] (39:17) 22 O 92, p. 10-11.

1884. FERGAR, Feyyaz
"Mystery" (tr. of Hilmi Yavuz). [Trans] (26) Spr 92, p. 16-17.

1885. FERGUSON, Penny L.
"Sometimes." [AntigR] (91) Fall 92, p. 20.

FERNANDEZ, Alberto López
See LOPEZ FERNANDEZ, Alberto

1886. FERNANDEZ RETAMAR, Roberto
"Duerme, Sueña, Haz." [Inti] (36) Otoño 92, p. 147-148.

1887. FERRARI, Mary
"Cairo — January, '91" (for Amo and Priscilla). [HangL] (61) 92, p. 35-36.
"The Eleventh Night" (for Catherine Murray, d. 1/10/90). [HangL] (61) 92, p. 30.
"Holy Thursday Flying North." [HangL] (61) 92, p. 33-34.
"Rules" (for Frank). [HangL] (61) 92, p. 31-32.

1888. FERRATER, Gabriel
"Floral" (in Catalan). [Nimrod] (35:2) Spr-Sum 92, p. 12.
"Floral" (tr. by Michael Barea). [Nimrod] (35:2) Spr-Sum 92, p. 13.
"Helena." [Verse] (9:3) Wint 92, p. 140.

1889. FERRO, Jeanpaul
"Fuchsia Lighting." [DogRR] (11:1) Spr-Sum 92, p. 4.
"Plant Shuffling In and Out." [DogRR] (11:1) Spr-Sum 92, p. 5.

1890. FERRY, David
"From the Gilgamesh Epic: The Death of Enkidu" (tr. of Tablets VII-IX). [Raritan] (11:4) Spr 92, p. 24-37.
"Gilgamesh: Tables X and XI" (tr. of the Babylonian epic based mainly on the literal tr. by E. A. Speiser). [Arion] 3d series (1:3) Fall 91, p. 92-116.
"Ishtar & Gilgamesh" (from Tablet VI of *The Gilgamesh Epic,* based on the literal tr. of E. A. Speiser). [PartR] (59:2) Spr 92, p. 260-263.
"Mary in Old Age." [Raritan] (12:2) Fall 92, p. 16-21.
"Prayer to the Gods of the Night" (tr.of an Old Babylonian poem based on the literal tr. by William L. Moran). [Arion] 3d series (1:1) Wint 90, p. 186.

1891. FETTERS, Clifford Paul
"When the Whistle Blows." [Interim] (11:1) Spr-Sum 92, p. 11.

1892. FICKERT, Kurt
"Antique Sewing Machine for Sale." [Elf] (2:2) Sum 92, p. 27.
"An Encounter: T. S. Eliot and Ezra Pound." [NewYorkQ] (47) 92, p. 66.

1893. FIELD, Edward
"Anthropologist" (For Tobias Schneebaum). [ChironR] (11:2) Sum 92, p. 32.
"Dirty Old Man." [ChironR] (11:1) Spr 92, p. 21.
"From *The Booke of Shyting*." [ChironR] (11:3) Aut 92, p. 16.
"The Guide." [Nat] (255:14) 2 N 92, p. 519.
"One More for the Quilt" (for Seth Allen). [ChironR] (11:4) Wint 92, p. 27.
"The Reprieve." [Pearl] (16) Fall 92, p. 24.
"The Romance of Extinct Birds: The Carrier Pigeon." [Nat] (255:11) 12 O 92, p. 400.
"Self Portrait in the Bathroom Mirror." [Pearl] (15) Spr-Sum 92, p. 21.

1894. FIELD, M. W.
"Velvet Cairn." [CanLit] (134) Aut 92, p. 40.

1895. FIELDS, Leslie Leyland
"Fairy Shrimp." [Kalliope] (15:1) 92, p. 23.
"Note to a Poet in the Yukon." [Kalliope] (15:1) 92, p. 25.
"Notes to a Poet in the Yukon." [Elf] (2:4) Wint 92, p. 35.
"Photograph." [BlackBR] (16) Wint-Spr 92-93, p. 7.
"Reasons Not to Die." [Kalliope] (15:1) 92, p. 24.
"What the Salmon Know." [SoCoast] (12) Ja 92, p. 13.
1896. FIFER, Ken
"A Mower Against Gardens." [US1] (26/27) 92, p. 8.
1897. FIGGIS, Jean
"Now Lucy's Gone." [ChironR] (11:2) Sum 92, p. 12.
1898. FIGMAN, Elliot
"Great Lake." [AmerV] (26) Spr 92, p. 50-51.
"Night and Day." [Poetry] (159:5) F 92, p. 273.
1899. FIKE, Darrell
"I-10 Semiotics." [NewDeltaR] (9:1) Fall 91-Wint 92, p. 33.
FILIPPO, Vira J. de
See De FILIPPO, Vira J.
1900. FILKINS, Peter
"The Roar" (for Jan & Jamie). [Journal] (16:2) Fall-Wint 92, p. 16.
1901. FINCH, Annie
"Dickinson." [Os] (34) Spr 92, p. 2.
1902. FINCH, Casey
"Problem with Narrative" (A Birthday Poem for Tory Dent). [DenQ] (27:1) Sum 92, p. 114-115.
1903. FINCH, Robert
"Bird Market." [BelPoJ] (43:2) Wint 92-93, p. 11.
1904. FINCH, Roger
"Seen Through the Window of a Car." [LitR] (35:3) Spr 92, p. 321.
1905. FINCKE, Gary
"The A Capella Rehab." [PoetC] (23:3) Spr 92, p. 21-22.
"Booths." [MissouriR] (15:2) 92, p. 37-39.
"Class A, Salem, the Rookie League." [GettyR] (5:3) Sum 92, p. 498-499.
"The Day of the Dead." [LaurelR] (26:1) Wint 92, p. 14.
"The Elephant Paintings." [Poetry] (159:4) Ja 92, p. 219-220.
"Forecasting the Dragon." [MissouriR] (15:2) 92, p. 40-41.
"The Fuhrer Weekend." [PoetL] (87:1) Spr 92, p. 30.
"The Habits of Eating." [BelPoJ] (42:4) Sum 92, p. 35-41.
"Hurricane Fringe." [Amelia] (6:4, #19) 92, p. 105-106.
"Inventing Angels." [Harp] (284:1702) Mr 92, p. 35.
"Rounds." [MissouriR] (15:2) 92, p. 42-43.
"Squaring the Twins." [MissouriR] (15:2) 92, p. 44-45.
"Watching the Tied Boy." [LitR] (35:3) Spr 92, p. 326-327.
1906. FINDLAY, Barbara
"Ancient History" (from "Pièces de résistance"). [SinW] (48) Wint 92-93, p. 65-66.
"Twenty Years Gone: The Conversation Poem for Sheila" (w. Sheila Gilhooly. From "Pièces de résistance"). [SinW] (48) Wint 92-93, p. 63-64.
1907. FINK, Robert A.
"After Athens, Paul Refuses to Use the Devices of Greek Philosophy." [GrahamHR] (16) Fall 92, p. 60.
"Nearing the End of His Journey, Paul Considers What Comfort He Has Brought His Friends." [GrahamHR] (16) Fall 92, p. 59.
"Procreation." [EngJ] (81:2) F 92, p. 96.
1908. FINK, Thomas
"Patience." [ManhatPR] (14) [92?], p. 45.
"Samson Renewed." [ManhatPR] (14) [92?], p. 45.
1909. FINKEL, Donald
"Absence" (tr. of Bei Dao, w. Xueliang Chen). [ManhatR] (6:2) Fall 92, p. 15.
"Eventful Autumn" (tr. of Bei Dao, w. Xueliang Chen). [ManhatR] (6:2) Fall 92, p. 18.
"Getting the Message." [Antaeus] (69) Aut 92, p. 138.
"The Matter at Hand." [DenQ] (26:4) Spr 92, p. 23.
"Midnight Singer" (tr. of Bei Dao, w. Xueliang Chen). [ManhatR] (6:2) Fall 92, p. 17.
"Outside" (tr. of Bei Dao, w. Xueliang Chen). [ManhatR] (6:2) Fall 92, p. 19.

"Summer's Brass" (tr. of Bei Dao, w. Xueliang Chen). [ManhatR] (6:2) Fall 92, p. 16.
"Three Standard Stoppages" (Marcel Duchamp). [ChiR] (37:4) 92, p. 77-79.
"What To Do with Your New Goya." [DenQ] (26:4) Spr 92, p. 22.
"Year's End" (tr. of Bei Dao, w. Xueliang Chen). [ManhatR] (6:2) Fall 92, p. 14.

1910. FINKELSTEIN, Caroline
"Anger." [BostonR] (17:2) Mr-Ap 92, p. 20.
"The Brave Little Tailleurs of 1935." [BostonR] (17:2) Mr-Ap 92, p. 20.
"Exhaustion." [Witness] (6:1) 92, p. 117.
"The Firefighter." [BostonR] (17:2) Mr-Ap 92, p. 20.
"Honesty" (after a painting by Lucian Freud). [BostonR] (17:2) Mr-Ap 92, p. 20.
"Not Responsible." [BostonR] (17:2) Mr-Ap 92, p. 20.
"Our Tale from Hoffman." [Witness] (6:1) 92, p. 117.
"Shabby Private Club." [Witness] (6:1) 92, p. 116.
"The Soul in the Bowl." [BostonR] (17:2) Mr-Ap 92, p. 20.
"With Fox Eyes." [BostonR] (17:2) Mr-Ap 92, p. 20.

1911. FINKELSTEIN, Norman
"A Poem for Vixen Sharp-Ears." [Salm] (96) Fall 92, p. 174-175.

1912. FINLEY, Jeanne
"The Mothers and the Fathers." [NewMyths] (1:2/2:1) 92, p. 163-164.

1913. FINLEY, Karen
"The War at Home." [CityLR] (5) 92, p. 85-89.

1914. FINLEY, Michael
"The Clarinet Is a Difficult Instrument." [Light] (1) Spr 92, p. 25.

1915. FINN, Morgan
"On the Way to Pump Iron at Tully's." [Kalliope] (15:1) 92, p. 40.

1916. FINNEGAN, James
"That Day I Died." [WebR] (16) Fall 92, p. 41.

1917. FINNELL, Dennis
"Bonfire's Story" (In memory of Crystal Field). [NewL] (58:3) Spr 92, p. 64-65.
"Fame and Fortune." [CharR] (18:1) Spr 92, p. 92.
"Hanging Bridge." [Pequod] (34) 92, p. 168.
"Hannibal, Revisited." [NewL] (58:3) Spr 92, p. 62-63.
"Kiss." [Pequod] (34) 92, p. 169-170.
"Letter to Wang Wei, Envoy to the Barbarian Pass." [MassR] (23:2) Sum 92, p. 174.

1918. FIORILLA, Steve
"The Daddy Beats." [MoodySI] (27) Spr 92, p. 1.

1919. FIREBAUGH, Anita J.
"Apteryx." [Amelia] (6:4, #19) 92, p. 104.

1920. FIRER, Susan
"The Head-Carriers." [SouthernPR] (32:2) Fall 92, p. 58-59.
"In Blowzy Quarks of Love." [SmPd] (29:3, #86) Fall 92, p. 31.
"The Lives of the Saints." [CreamCR] (16:2) Fall 92, p. 78.
"On the Fairway of Dreams: Nights' Hobos." [CreamCR] (16:1) Spr 92, p. 86-87.
"Saint Christina the Astonishing, 1224." [CreamCR] (16:2) Fall 92, p. 76-77.

FIRMAT, Gustavo Pérez
See PÉREZ FIRMAT, Gustavo

1921. FIRTH, A. Lee
"Hitchhiker." [Bogg] (65) 92, p. 38.

1922. FISCHER, Aaron
"Dead Weight." [WillowS] (30) Sum 92, p. 78-80.

1923. FISCHER, Neil
"For Betty, Moon-Loved Machinist." [Ploughs] (18:4) Wint 92-93, p. 129.
"To the Man." [BelPoJ] (43:2) Wint 92-93, p. 18-19.
"The Wish." [Ploughs] (18:4) Wint 92-93, p. 128.

1924. FISCHEROVA, Sylva
"And They Come, the Guests Awaiting Liquor" (tr. by James Naughton). [PraS] (66:4) Wint 92, p. 110-111.
"Black Tiger" (tr. by James Naughton). [PraS] (66:4) Wint 92, p. 109-110.
"Drinking Coffee" (tr. by James Naughton). [PraS] (66:4) Wint 92, p. 103.
"The Garden" (tr. by James Naughton). [PraS] (66:4) Wint 92, p. 104-106.
"Lazarus, White Holly Berries" (tr. by Vera Orac and Stuart Friebert, w. the author). [PraS] (66:4) Wint 92, p. 89-90.
"Lovers in the Sand" (tr. by James Naughton). [PraS] (66:4) Wint 92, p. 104.
"Moravia" (tr. by Vera Orac and Stuart Friebert, w. the author). [PraS] (66:4) Wint 92, p. 86-87.

"Necessary" (tr. by James Naughton). [PraS] (66:4) Wint 92, p. 106-108.
"Pax Vobiscum" (tr. by Vera Orac and Stuart Friebert, w. the author). [PraS] (66:4) Wint 92, p. 87-88.
"The Stones Speak Czech" (tr. by James Naughton). [PraS] (66:4) Wint 92, p. 108.
"Who Knows Something about Women?" (tr. by Vera Orac and Stuart Friebert, w. the author). [PraS] (66:4) Wint 92, p. 85-86.
"X X X: and what remained, a desire for destiny" (tr. by Vera Orac and Stuart Friebert, w. the author). [PraS] (66:4) Wint 92, p. 84-85.
"X X X: Give me ashes, earth, and my dead" (tr. by Vera Orac and Stuart Friebert, w. the author). [PraS] (66:4) Wint 92, p. 88-89.

1925. FISER, Karen
"Ontological Relativity." [GreenMR] (NS 5:2) Spr-Sum 92, p. 14.
"The Problem of Personal Identity." [AmerV] (27) 92, p. 61-62.
"The Visitant." [GreenMR] (NS 5:2) Spr-Sum 92, p. 13.
"What Keeps Me Here." [Kaleid] (24) Wint-Spr 92, p. 24.
"Wheelchair Dreams." [Kaleid] (24) Wint-Spr 92, p. 37.

1926. FISH, Karen
"The Beginning." [DenQ] (26:4) Spr 92, p. 24.
"Letter from the Modern World" (for JoEllen Kwiatek). [AmerPoR] (21:5) S-O 92, p. 30-31.
"Paradise." [AmerPoR] (21:5) S-O 92, p. 30.

1927. FISHER, Adam D.
"Husband and Wife." [Footwork] 92, p. 49.

1928. FISHER, David Lincoln
"An Attempt to Imitate the General Paralysis of Airport Fiction." [FreeL] (10) Sum 92, p. 15.
"My Sons Are Like Books." [FreeL] (10) Sum 92, p. 14-15.

1929. FISHER, Janet
"A Question of Age." [Verse] (9:3) Wint 92, p. 107.

1930. FISHER, Lori M.
"Diary Page 75" (Karlsbad, Thomayer Sanitarium, tr. of Reiner Kunze). [Trans] (26) Spr 92, p. 41.

1931. FISHER, Roy
"Talking to Cameras" (part of a text commissioned for the film "Birmingham's What I Think With"). [Stand] (33:2) Spr 92, p. 10-13.

1932. FISHER, Steve
"Frenching Spanish for Cherry Jean." [Pearl] (16) Fall 92, p. 51.

1933. FISHMAN, Charles
"Broich's Boat." [Grain] (20:2) Sum 92, p. 124.
"Far into Vermont" (For Leonard and Shirley Rose). [HawaiiR] (16:2, #35) Spr 92, p. 119.
"Listening to Brahms." [HawaiiR] (16:2, #35) Spr 92, p. 120.
"A Shade from 'Glory'" (Charlottesville, 1990). [BelPoJ] (43:2) Wint 92-93, p. 31.

1934. FISTER, Mary
"On the Question of Starfish." [Ascent] (16:3) Spr 92, p. 61.
"The Physics of Pure Moment." [Ascent] (16:3) Spr 92, p. 60.

1935. FITTERMAN, Robert
"Heaven & East Houston" (Excerpts). [Shiny] (7/8) 92, p. 81-83.
"Now" (Excerpts). [Talisman] (8) Spr 92, p. 100-101.

1936. FITZGERALD, Judith
"Indigo." [PoetryC] (13:1) N 92, p. 8-9.

1937. FITZSIMMONS, Janet B.
"Eden: The Misunderstanding." [Dandel] (19:2) 92, p. 23.

1938. FITZSIMMONS, Thomas
"Normandy: (The Summer Beaches)." [Vis] (39) 92, p. 14.

1939. FIX, Charlene (Charlene Cohen)
"I Resist Haircuts with the Feeling of One Descended." [PaintedB] (45) 92, p. 11.
"Persephone's Cry." [NegC] (12:1/2) 92, p. 35-36.

1940. FIXEL, Lawrence
"Something That the Name Gathers." [Talisman] (8) Spr 92, p. 123-124.

1941. FLANAGAN, Bob
"Balladeer." [Shiny] (7/8) 92, p. 67-69.
"Handcuffs." [BrooklynR] (9) 92, p. 35.

1942. FLANDERS, Jane
"Digging Up Soldiers." [WestHR] (46:2) Sum 92, p. 162.
"The Hard Way." [Poetry] (161:2) N 92, p. 90-91.

"The Nest." [WestHR] (46:2) Sum 92, p. 163.
1943. FLECK, Richard
"On the Edge of Charleston." [Paint] (19:37) Spr 92, p. 20.
1944. FLECKENSTEIN, Mark
"If Despair." [PassN] (13:1) Sum 92, p. 29.
1945. FLEMING, Anne
"North Toronto." [PoetryC] (12:3/4) Jl 92, p. 28.
"Pumpkin Patch, Highway 7." [PoetryC] (12:3/4) Jl 92, p. 28.
1946. FLEMING, Thomas
"Epiphany." [Confr] (50) Fall 92, p. 256.
"Fantasy on Sutton Place." [Confr] (50) Fall 92, p. 255.
1947. FLETCHER, Greg
"Father and Son." [Vis] (40) 92, p. 50.
"Ne Sus Minervam." [Vis] (40) 92, p. 49-50.
1948. FLINT, Roland
"Austere." [SouthernR] (28:1) Wint, Ja 92, p. 24.
"Comforts." [PaintedHR] (6) Spr 92, p. 20.
"Fleas." [SouthernR] (28:1) Wint, Ja 92, p. 25-26.
"Land of Cotton." [SouthernR] (28:1) Wint, Ja 92, p. 23-24.
"Little Men Who Come Blindly." [SouthernR] (28:1) Wint, Ja 92, p. 21-22.
"Married." [PaintedHR] (6) Spr 92, p. 21.
"Singapore." [SouthernR] (28:1) Wint, Ja 92, p. 28.
"Strawberries Like Raspberries." [SouthernR] (28:1) Wint, Ja 92, p. 26-27.
1949. FLOCK, Miriam
"His New Life." [CumbPR] (12:1) Fall 92, p. 66.
"Proprioception." [CumbPR] (12:1) Fall 92, p. 64-65.
"The Scientist's Wife." [CumbPR] (12:1) Fall 92, p. 62-63.
1950. FLOREA, Ted
"In Spring (For a Friend, Dying of Cancer)." [Plain] (13:1) Fall 92, p. 8.
1951. FLOREZ, Julio
"Everything" (Fragment, tr. by Joe Bolton). [NewOR] (19:2) Sum 92, p. 51.
1952. FLOWERS, Charles
"Shaving My Father." [IndR] (15:1) Spr 92, p. 66-67.
"Wanting." [IndR] (15:1) Spr 92, p. 69.
"Will." [IndR] (15:1) Spr 92, p. 68.
1953. FLOYD, Marguerite
"Bridges." [Wind] (22:71) 92, p. 17.
1954. FLYNN, David
"In a Good Mood, Let It Slip." [ChamLR] (10/11) Spr-Fall 92, p. 147.
1955. FLYNN, Nick
"Alan Dugan Telling Me I Have a Problem With Time." [Ploughs] (18:4) Wint 92 - 93, p. 7-8.
"Emptying Town." [Ploughs] (18:4) Wint 92-93, p. 9-10.
"Even Now She Is Turning, Saying Everything I Always Wanted Her to Say." [Ploughs] (18:4) Wint 92-93, p. 6.
1956. FLYNN, Sharon
"Grandpa's Faith" (Winner, Annual Free Verse Contest, 1991). [AnthNEW] (4) 92, p. 28.
FOE, Mark de
See DeFOE, Mark
1957. FOERSTER, Richard
"Atmospherics." [Poetry] (161:1) O 92, p. 32.
"Fishing Charter." [SouthwR] (77:2/3) Spr-Sum 92, p. 230.
"The Hours." [Poetry] (159:6) Mr 92, p. 313-317.
1958. FOGDALL, Kristin
"My Name Is Legion" (Mark 5:1-20). [NewRep] (207:11/12) 7-14 S 92, p. 49.
1959. FOGDEN, Barry
"The Afternoon Session." [Elf] (2:2) Sum 92, p. 23.
"Allegiances." [Elf] (2:2) Sum 92, p. 22.
"Machu Picchu." [Elf] (2:2) Sum 92, p. 25.
"Part-Objects." [Verse] (9:3) Wint 92, p. 130.
"Wu-wei." [Elf] (2:2) Sum 92, p. 24-25.
1960. FOGEL, Alice (Alice B.)
"Lullaby." [BostonR] (17:3/4) My-Jl 92, p. 36.
"The Necessity." [BostonR] (17:3/4) My-Jl 92, p. 36.
"The Particulars." [BostonR] (17:3/4) My-Jl 92, p. 36.

"Still Life with Woman." [BostonR] (17:3/4) My-Jl 92, p. 36.
"This Afternoon." [BostonR] (17:3/4) My-Jl 92, p. 36.
"Unfinished Poem" (After the Michelangelo sculptures, each called "The Captive," often referred to as "The Unfinished Sculptures"). [Conscience] (13:1) Spr 92, p. 26.
"The White and Frozen Place" (With thanks to Howard Norman). [BostonR] (17:3/4) My-Jl 92, p. 36.

1961. FOGELMAN, Betsy
"Manmade Waterfall in Turtle Bay Park." [SenR] (22:2) Fall 92, p. 74-75.

1962. FOGG, Karen
"Opening" (1st prize, Grain Prose Poem contest). [Grain] (20:4) Wint 92, p. 9.

1963. FOLEY, Adelle
"Alternative Haikus" (In Memoriam, Pat Lewis, 1940-1992). [PoetryUSA] (24) 92, p. 17.

1964. FOLEY, Jack
"Fifty." [Talisman] (8) Spr 92, p. 152-162.
"For Lou Harrison's 75th Birthday, May 14, 1992." [PoetryUSA] (24) 92, p. 22.

1965. FOLKART, Barbara
"Micro-event: May." [Arc] (28) Spr 92, p. 35.
"Wind and Water Poems." [Arc] (28) Spr 92, p. 33-34.

1966. FOLLETT, C. B.
"And Freddie Was My Darling." [SoCoast] (13) Je 93 [i.e. 92], p. 40-41.
"Where Are You, John Muir?" [BlackBR] (16) Wint-Spr 92-93, p. 36.

FOLLY, Dennis
See PRAHLAD, Sw. Anand (Dennis Folly)

1967. FOLSOM, Eric
"Desperate Manners." [Quarry] (41:1) Wint 92, p. 56.
"On Embracing." [Quarry] (41:1) Wint 92, p. 58.
"White Diva." [Quarry] (41:1) Wint 92, p. 57.

1968. FONDANE, Benjamin
"Hertza" (tr. by Franz Hodjak and Edouard Roditi). [Pequod] (34) 92, p. 76-77.
"Poet and Shadow" (tr. by Leonard Schwartz). [Pequod] (34) 92, p. 96.
"Sometimes" (tr. by Anthony Rudolf). [Stand] (33:4) Aut 92, p. 39.
"Ulysses" (Excerpt, tr. by Leonard Schwartz). [Pequod] (34) 92, p. 97-98.

1969. FONSECA, Harry
"Coyote." [Jacaranda] (6:1/2) Wint-Spr 92, p. 70-71.

FONTAINE, Paula Creasy
See CREASY-FONTAINE, Paula

1970. FONTENOT, Ken
"Man at Ninety" (tr. of Heinz Piontek). [NewOR] (19:1) Spr 92, p. 23.

1971. FOOTE, Robert S.
"Reunion" (At Carnton). [LullwaterR] (3:2) Spr 92, p. 74-77.

1972. FORBES, Linzy
"Morning Song." [Vis] (40) 92, p. 44.

1973. FORCE, Kathy
"Going to Market with a Cotton Bag." [RagMag] (10:2) 92, p. 36.
"When Our Husbands Come to Us." [RagMag] (10:2) 92, p. 37.

1974. FORD, Adrian Robert
"Radio Tower." [ChrC] (109:35) 2 D 92, p. 1093.

1975. FORD, Cathy
"Loon, la Lune" (for my brother). [PoetryC] (12:2) Ap 92, p. 18-19.

1976. FORD, Deborah
"Fragile Days." [ChamLR] (10/11) Spr-Fall 92, p. 21.

1977. FORD, Michael C.
"Dennis Hopper Hopes, Once More, to Replace the Blue Velvet Vaudeville (or Something Like It)." [AntR] (50:4) Fall 92, p. 719.
"A Little Girl Under a Tree in 1948." [OnTheBus] (4:2/5:1, #10/11) 92, p. 92.

1978. FORD, Robert Archibald
"SASE." [Light] (4) Wint 92-93, p. 15.

1979. FORD, William
"Thanksgiving." [PoetC] (23:3) Spr 92, p. 11.

1980. FORHAN, Chris
"The Body at Night." [TarRP] (30:2) Spr 91, p. 23.
"Cracking Open." [PraS] (66:3) Fall 92, p. 38.
"Etta Mae Crumpler, 1891-1962." [GreensboroR] (52) Sum 92, p. 152.
"Night Construction." [TarRP] (30:2) Spr 91, p. 22.

"A Test of Character." [WebR] (16) Fall 92, p. 67.
"A Visit to the Country." [CreamCR] (16:1) Spr 92, p. 128.
"The Woman Who Could Not Wear a Hat." [PraS] (66:3) Fall 92, p. 39.

1981. FORMENTO, Dennis
"In Memory of James Black" (For all the jazz musicians). [AnotherCM] (24) Fall 92, p. 37-38.

FORONDA, Carolyn Gomez
See GOMEZ-FORONDA, Carolyn

FORONDA, Carolyn Kreiter
See KREITER-FORONDA, Carolyn

1982. FORSTER, Stephen
"Dreamtime." [Noctiluca] (1:1) Spr 92, p. 45.
"Mishima Variations." [Noctiluca] (1:1) Spr 92, p. 46.

1983. FORT, Charles
"How Old Are the People of the World." [ThRiPo] (39/40) 92-93, p. 78-79.
"The Town Clock Burning." [ThRiPo] (39/40) 92-93, p. 79.
"The Worker (We Own Two Houses)." [ThRiPo] (39/40) 92-93, p. 77-78.

1984. FORTINI, Franco
"The End of the Year 1975 for Andrea Zanzotto" (tr. by Corrado Federici). [PoetryC] (13:1) N 92, p. 20.
"Remembering Borsieri" (tr. by Keith Bosley). [Stand] (33:4) Aut 92, p. 109.

1985. FORTUNATO, Peter
"Hotel Anonymous." [YellowS] (Ten Years [i.e. 40]) Sum-Fall 92, p. 8.

1986. FOSS, Phillip
"Capricci 25." [DenQ] (26:3) Wint 92, p. 10-12.
"Purgatory." [DenQ] (26:3) Wint 92, p. 13-16.

1987. FOSTER, Leslie (Leslie D.)
"A Friend Stops By." [ChrC] (109:36) 9 D 92, p. 1140.
"Mortal Flowers." [ChrC] (109:18) 20-27 My 92, p. 542.
"Song for Monday." [Lactuca] (16) Ag 92, p. 54.

1988. FOSTER, Linda Nemec
"Copper Harbor, Michigan: Early October." [ChironR] (11:3) Aut 92, p. 8.
"Housework." [OnTheBus] (4:2/5:1, #10/11) 92, p. 93.
"In the Vicinity of Orion's Arm." [HiramPoR] (51/52) Fall 91-Sum 92, p. 36-37.
"Nature of the Beast" (3rd place winner, Chiron Review 1992 Poetry Contest). [ChironR] (11:3) Aut 92, p. 14.
"Nightmare." [GeoR] (46:1) Spr 92, p. 113.
"That Wild Boy." [ChironR] (11:3) Aut 92, p. 8.
"Untangling the Knot." [ChironR] (11:3) Aut 92, p. 8.

1989. FOSTER, Sesshu
"I awoke and it was already midday." [SnailPR] (2:2) Fall-Wint 92, p. 15.
"In 1911 I came from Veracruz and was erased by measles." [SnailPR] (2:2) Fall-Wint 92, p. 14.

1990. FOTHE, Lawrence C.
"Glimpse." [Pearl] (15) Spr-Sum 92, p. 50.

1991. FOURTOUNI, Eleni
"The Voice of the Watchman" (tr. of Victoria Theodorou). [PoetryC] (12:3/4) Jl 92, p. 32.

1992. FOUST, Graham
"Erosion in a Stolen Country." [MidAR] (13:2) 92, p. 164-165.

1993. FOWLER, Allan
"Ruminations Re Ruminants." [Light] (4) Wint 92-93, p. 10.

1994. FOWLER, Anne Carroll
"Sandra." [OxfordM] (7:1) Spr-Sum 91, p. 108.
"The Sorrow of the King." [LitR] (25:2) Wint 92, p. 273.
"The Trick Is, Getting It Right." [OxfordM] (7:1) Spr-Sum 91, p. 109.
"Western Passage." [CumbPR] (11:2) Spr 92, p. 49.
"What the camera." [CumbPR] (11:2) Spr 92, p. 47-48.

1995. FOWLER, James
"Cultivation." [Hellas] (3:1) Spr 92, p. 45.

1996. FOX, Charles
"The Effects of Time on Space." [LullwaterR] (4:1) Fall 92, p. 38.

1997. FOX, Hugh
"Carlo Saraceni — Paradise." [Pearl] (16) Fall 92, p. 53.
"Christmas Day." [ChironR] (11:1) Spr 92, p. 8.
"Jamais Vu" (for Harry Smith). [Pearl] (16) Fall 92, p. 53.

"Reincarnation." [ChironR] (11:1) Spr 92, p. 8.
"The Rilke Message." [SmPd] (29:2, #85) Spr 92, p. 24.
"You can die here too." [BlackBR] (15) Spr-Sum 92, p. 19.

1998. FOX, Joan
"Trilogy: The Bride, Her Child and Her Animals." [WritersF] (18) 92, p. 72-73.

1999. FOX, Kent
"Home." [PassN] (13:2) Wint 92, p. 23.

2000. FOX, Lucía
"Spaceport." [Nuez] (4:12) 92, p. 20.

2001. FOX, Valerie
"I Will Support the Government After All." [PaintedB] (48) 92, p. 54.

2002. FRABOTTA, Biancamaria
"The Uranoscopus" (tr. by Corrado Federici). [PoetryC] (13:1) N 92, p. 21.

2003. FRACH, Shannon
"Old." [ChironR] (11:1) Spr 92, p. 23.

2004. FRAGOS, Emily
"Hotel Hanover." [Parting] (5:1) Sum 92, p. 18.
"Il Maestro del Violino." [AmerV] (28) 92, p. 86-88.

2005. FRANCE, Linda
"Bluebell and Father Are Different Words." [Stand] (33:2) Spr 92, p. 49.

2006. FRANCIS, Scott
"Fox Dreams (#3)." [DogRR] (11:1) Spr-Sum 92, p. 39.

2007. FRANCIS, Sean
"An Air." [Light] (2) Sum 92, p. 9.

2008. FRANCISCO, Nia
"Roots of Blue Bells." [Jacaranda] (6:1/2) Wint-Spr 92, p. 72.

2009. FRANCO, Georgina
"Mandrágora Viviente." [Nuez] (4:10/11) 92, p. 5.

2010. FRANCO, Michael
"Turning Toward an Old Form" (Two poems for Katharine Killion who asked if I weren't nostalgic). [Agni] (36) 92, p. 310-316.

2011. FRANETA, Sonja
"Untitled: What was your pink nipple" (tr. of Olga Krause). [SinW] (46) Spr 92, p. 18.

2012. FRANKLIN, Jeffrey
"Florida." [Hudson] (45:2) Sum 92, p. 277-278.

2013. FRANKLIN, Walt
"Mike's Truck." [Grain] (20:3) Fall 92, p. 152.

2014. FRANZEN, Cola
"Cockcrow from Afar" (tr. of Saúl Yurkievich). [WorldL] (3) 92, p. 9.
"Evenings" (tr. of Marjorie Agosin). [13thMoon] (10:1/2) 92, p. 17.
"Homeland" (tr. of Marjorie Agosin). [13thMoon] (10:1/2) 92, p. 15-16.
"The park shrunk to its wintry marrow" (tr. of Saúl Yurkievich). [WorldL] (3) 92, p. 8.
"Quiet" (tr. of Saúl Yurkievich). [NewOR] (19:3/4) Fall-Wint 92, p. 125.
"Winnowing" (tr. of Saúl Yurkievich). [WorldL] (3) 92, p. 10-12.

2015. FRASER, Caroline
"The Fragility of Heavy Machinery." [NewYorker] (68:10) 27 Ap 92, p. 36.
"Passes." [NewYorker] (68:20) 6 Jl 92, p. 38.

2016. FRASER, Diane
"Boylston Street." [SinW] (46) Spr 92, p. 61.

2017. FRASER, Greg
"Blood Work." [WestHR] (46:3) Fall 92 [i.e. (46:4) Wint 92], p. 410.

2018. FRASER, Kathleen
"In That Purely Phonetic City" (for S.G.). [Talisman] (9) Fall 92, p. 150-151.

2019. FRATTALI, Steven
"Advertisement" (tr. of Ingeborg Bachmann). [WebR] (16) Fall 92, p. 10.
"Exile" (tr. of Ingeborg Bachmann). [GrahamHR] (16) Fall 92, p. 104.
"Hotel de la Paix" (tr. of Ingeborg Bachmann). [WebR] (16) Fall 92, p. 10.
"In Apulia" (tr. of Ingeborg Bachmann). [GrahamHR] (16) Fall 92, p. 103.
"Nightmares." [Blueline] (13) 92, p. 81.
"Summer" (tr. of Georg Trakl). [WebR] (16) Fall 92, p. 11.
"Wax on Snow." [Blueline] (13) 92, p. 41.

2020. FRAZEE, James E.
"Firebreather." [SenR] (22:2) Fall 92, p. 28-29.
"Veronica." [SenR] (22:2) Fall 92, p. 30-31.

2021. FRAZIER, Jan
"The First Cool Mother." [MinnR] (38) Spr-Sum 92, p. 22-23.
2022. FRAZIER, Robert
"Maurits Cornelis Escher: Unfolding a New Physics." [Ometeca] (2:2) 91 [published 92], p. 17-19.
2023. FREED, Ray
"This ain't no Philharmonic Jack." [MoodySI] (27) Spr 92, p. 8.
2024. FREEDMAN, Robert
"Errata Slips." [WestB] (30) 92, p. 80-81.
"Yiddish." [PoetL] (87:2) Sum 92, p. 24.
2025. FREEDMAN, William
"The Cat and the Moon." [AmerPoR] (21:4) Jl-Ag 92, p. 16.
2026. FREEMAN, Glenn
"The Word." [Outbr] (23) 92, p. 62-63.
2027. FREEMAN, Jan
"Green Trap." [AmerPoR] (21:2) Mr-Ap 92, p. 50.
"Her Oddity." [AmerV] (26) Spr 92, p. 7.
2028. FREEMAN, Jessica
"Turf Battle." [PacificR] (11) 92-93, p. 63.
2029. FREEMAN, Keller Cushing
"At My Cousin's Wedding." [CarolQ] (45:1) Fall 92, p. 54.
"Compare / Contrast." [Kalliope] (14:1) 92, p. 7.
FREES, Madeline de
See DeFREES, Madeline
2030. FREESPIRIT, Judy
"Persimmon." [SinW] (46) Spr 92, p. 73.
2031. FREITAS, Jackie
"As We Know It." [Art&Und] (1:2) Wint 92, p. 9.
2032. FRENCH, Catherine
"Alphabet." [Nat] (254:12) 30 Mr 92, p. 422.
2033. FRETWELL, Kathy
"Hooked on Advice with Egg on Our Face." [Dandel] (19:1) 92, p. 35.
"In the Spirit." [Dandel] (19:1) 92, p. 34.
2034. FRICK, Thomas
"Heraclitus" (tr. of Jorge Luis Borges). [Agni] (36) 92, p. 247.
"June 1968" (tr. of Jorge Luis Borges). [Agni] (36) 92, p. 248.
2035. FRIEBERT, Stuart
"1. Again and again, never mind we know love's landscape" (tr. of Rainer Maria Rilke). [CentR] (36:3) Fall 92, p. 534.
"2. I want to speak up, no more the worried" (tr. of Rainer Maria Rilke). [CentR] (36:3) Fall 92, p. 534.
"Artist" (tr. of Karl Krolow). [TarRP] (32:1) Fall 92, p. 29.
"Blacknose Shark" (tr. of Rainer Maria Rilke). [CentR] (36:3) Fall 92, p. 535.
"Calliope." [Shen] (42:1) Spr 92, p. 76.
"Daring" (tr. of Karl Krolow). [Field] (46) Spr 92, p. 53.
"Doctor Bird." [NoDaQ] (60:3) Sum 92, p. 161.
"Dog Eye." [OnTheBus] (4:2/5:1, #10/11) 92, p. 94.
"Donkey Ball." [NoDaQ] (60:3) Sum 92, p. 160.
"Dutchman's Anchor." [Wind] (22:71) 92, p. 15.
"Earlier" (tr. of Karl Krolow). [Field] (46) Spr 92, p. 52.
"Eleanor." [SnailPR] (2:1) Spr-Sum 92, p. 8-9.
"Fatty Arbuckle." [GreensboroR] (53) Wint 92-93, p. 97.
"A Feeble Affair" (tr. of Karl Krolow). [ChamLR] (10/11) Spr-Fall 92, p. 165.
"Ferry Wheel." [SnailPR] (2:1) Spr-Sum 92, p. 10.
"Fifty-O." [OnTheBus] (4:2/5:1, #10/11) 92, p. 94-95.
"Fool Hen." [Wind] (22:71) 92, p. 16.
"Four Thieves Vinegar." [Parting] (5:2) Wint 92-93, p. 1.
"Fried Shirt." [ManhatPR] (14) [92?], p. 24.
"Gyascutus." [Ascent] (17:1) Fall 92, p. 52.
"Hark From the Tomb." [Wind] (22:71) 92, p. 15-16.
"The Hobs of Hell." [Ascent] (17:1) Fall 92, p. 53.
"The Landscape Where Illusion Begins" (Translation Chapbook Series, No. 18, tr. of Karl Krolow). [MidAR] (12:2) 92, p. 59-87.
"Lazarus, White Holly Berries" (tr. of Sylva Fischerová, w. Vera Orac and the author). [PraS] (66:4) Wint 92, p. 89-90.
"Mooneye." [NegC] (12:1/2) 92, p. 37.

"Moravia" (tr. of Sylva Fischerová, w. Vera Orac and the author). [PraS] (66:4) Wint 92, p. 86-87.
"Nice" (tr. of Karl Krolow). [Field] (46) Spr 92, p. 54.
"On Thirst." [DogRR] (11:2, #22) Fall-Wint 92, p. 6.
"Orpheus and Eurydice" (tr. of Judith Vaiciunaite, w. Viktoria Skrupskelis). [Confr] (50) Fall 92, p. 300-303.
"Pastorals" (tr. of Judita Vaiciunaite, w. Viktoria Skrupskelis). [HayF] (10) Spr-Sum 92, p. 51.
"Pax Vobiscum" (tr. of Sylva Fischerová, w. Vera Orac and the author). [PraS] (66:4) Wint 92, p. 87-88.
"Pomological Poems" (7 poems, tr. of Karl Krolow). [WebR] (16) Fall 92, p. 5-9.
"The Rebel" (tr. of Judita Vaiciunaite, w. Viktoria Skrupskelis). [HayF] (10) Spr - Sum 92, p. 50.
"Shared Spring" (tr. of Karl Krolow). [TarRP] (32:1) Fall 92, p. 31.
"Supper" (tr. of Karl Krolow). [ChamLR] (10/11) Spr-Fall 92, p. 166.
"Waking Dream" (tr. of Karl Krolow). [Field] (46) Spr 92, p. 55.
"Way Down" (tr. of Karl Krolow). [ArtfulD] (22/23) 92, p. 32.
"When It Was Time" (tr. of Karl Krolow). [ChamLR] (10/11) Spr-Fall 92, p. 164.
"Who Knows Something about Women?" (tr. of Sylva Fischerová, w. Vera Orac and the author). [PraS] (66:4) Wint 92, p. 85-86.
"X X X: and what remained, a desire for destiny" (tr. of Sylva Fischerová, w. Vera Orac and the author). [PraS] (66:4) Wint 92, p. 84-85.
"X X X: Give me ashes, earth, and my dead" (tr. of Sylva Fischerová, w. Vera Orac and the author). [PraS] (66:4) Wint 92, p. 88-89.

2036. FRIED, Elliot
"I Wrote This Poem." [ChironR] (11:2) Sum 92, p. 5.
"Near Afton Canyon." [ChironR] (11:2) Sum 92, p. 5.
"Please Recycle This." [ChironR] (11:2) Sum 92, p. 5.

2037. FRIED, Michael
"Japan." [AmerPoR] (21:5) S-O 92, p. 16.
"Somewhere a Seed." [AmerPoR] (21:5) S-O 92, p. 16.
"The Wild Irises." [ParisR] (34:123) Sum 92, p. 98.

2038. FRIED, Philip
"Right Hand." [BelPoJ] (43:1) Fall 92, p. 17.

2039. FRIEDENBERG, Anita
"Sunbreaks." [BellArk] (8:1) Ja-F 92, p. 13.

2040. FRIEDERICH, Joel
"Evagrios the Solitary Mistakes Texans for a Band of Demons." [CreamCR] (16:2) Fall 92, p. 66-67.

2041. FRIEDMAN, Alan H.
"Round Robin." [AnotherCM] (24) Fall 92, p. 51.

2042. FRIEDMAN, Anne Laura
"Breakthrough." [Ploughs] (18:4) Wint 92-93, p. 80.
"Surveyors." [Ploughs] (18:4) Wint 92-93, p. 78-79.

2043. FRIEDMAN, Ed
"Casual Tones." [Shiny] (7/8) 92, p. 71.
"Floating Sonnet (My Type)." [HangL] (60) 92, p. 25.
"Floating Sonnet (Sanction Currency)." [HangL] (60) 92, p. 25.
"Fuckin' Banshees." [Shiny] (7/8) 92, p. 72.
"Rapture." [HangL] (60) 92, p. 23-24.

2044. FRIEDMAN, Jeff
"The Customers in Dogtown" (Selling Fuller Brush in the summer of my 16th year). [Turnstile] (3:2) 92, p. 85-86.
"The Cutters" (Martha Manning Dress Factory). [AmerPoR] (21:2) Mr-Ap 92, p. 22.
"Face Off." [AmerPoR] (21:2) Mr-Ap 92, p. 22-23.

2045. FRIEDMAN, Lisa Berdann
"The Natural History of Litter." [BellArk] (8:6) N-D 92, p. 25.

2046. FRIEDMAN, Michael
"Dream." [Shiny] (7/8) 92, p. 100.
"Earth." [PaintedB] (47) 92, p. 6.
"Moon." [Shiny] (7/8) 92, p. 97.
"Rain." [Shiny] (7/8) 92, p. 99.
"Water." [Shiny] (7/8) 92, p. 98.

2047. FRIEDMAN, Stan
"Assume That Memory Is a Glass Sheet." [Sulfur] (12:1, #30) Spr 92, p. 117-118.
"Land of the Giants." [Sulfur] (12:1, #30) Spr 92, p. 118-119.

"Tangle." [Sulfur] (12:1, #30) Spr 92, p. 120-121.
"Unwanted Light." [Sulfur] (12:1, #30) Spr 92, p. 119-120.

2048. FRIEND, Robert
"Oh Where Is Little Ciso?" [Light] (1) Spr 92, p. 25.

2049. FRIES, Kenny
"Saturn Return." [Confr] (48/49) Spr-Sum 92, p. 190.
"Surgery." [Confr] (48/49) Spr-Sum 92, p. 191.

2050. FRIESEN, Patrick
"Anna First Dance" (Excerpt). [PraF] (13:1, #58) Spr 92, p. 177.
"Anna Second Dance" (Excerpt). [PraF] (13:1, #58) Spr 92, p. 181.
"At 2 a.m." [PraF] (13:1, #58) Spr 92, p. 43.
"An Audience with the Dalai Lama or, the Old-Fashioned Pas de Deux." [PraF] (13:1, #58) Spr 92, p. 148-150.
"Black Umbrella" (2 poems). [PoetryC] (12:3/4) Jl 92, p. 12-13.
"Bluebottle." [PraF] (13:1, #58) Spr 92, p. 114.
"A Dream of Mothers." [PoetryC] (12:3/4) Jl 92, p. 12.
"Fatherless Again." [PraF] (13:1, #58) Spr 92, p. 140-141.
"Fathers Die: for J.K." [PraF] (13:1, #58) Spr 92, p. 30-31.
"Flicker and Hawk." [PraF] (13:1, #58) Spr 92, p. 146-147.
"The Forge (the Man Who Licked Stones)." [PraF] (13:1, #58) Spr 92, p. 10.
"His mother thought it was the second coming one taken one left." [PraF] (13:1, #58) Spr 92, p. 32.
"The Impossibility of Love." [PraF] (13:1, #58) Spr 92, p. 142-143.
"Living in another world." [PraF] (13:1, #58) Spr 92, p. 33.
"Lost Boys." [PoetryC] (12:3/4) Jl 92, p. 13.
"Starry Night." [PraF] (13:1, #58) Spr 92, p. 186-187.
"Sunday Afternoon." [PraF] (13:1, #58) Spr 92, p. 144-145.
"Thursday afternoon thunder." [PraF] (13:1, #58) Spr 92, p. 42.
"Trying Hard to Die." [PraF] (13:1, #58) Spr 92, p. 124-125.
"You say you've read about Simons." [PraF] (13:1, #58) Spr 92, p. 44.

2051. FRIMAN, Alice
"Journal Entry for Late October." [Chelsea] (53) 92, p. 82-83.
"The Last Soirée." [HawaiiR] (16:2, #35) Spr 92, p. 103.
"Letting It Go." [CreamCR] (16:2) Fall 92, p. 10.
"Rubber Band." [TarRP] (31:2) Spr 92, p. 10.
"Shadow." [SouthernPR] (32:1) Spr 92, p. 22-23.
"Shame" (March 1991). [HopewellR] (4) 92, p. 12.
"Sunflowers" (France 1990). [HopewellR] (4) 92, p. 23.
"Watching Trees at Steepletop." [Chelsea] (53) 92, p. 84.

2052. FRITZ, Walter Helmut
"At Fifty" (tr. by Reinhold Grimm). [Pembroke] (24) 92, p. 57.
"Atlantis" (tr. by Reinhold Grimm). [Pembroke] (24) 92, p. 54.
"The Burial of the Writer Hans Juergen Froehlich" (tr. by Reinhold Grimm). [Pembroke] (24) 92, p. 71.
"But Then?" (tr. by Reinhold Grimm). [Pembroke] (24) 92, p. 62.
"The Density of Mobile Bodies" (I, VII, tr. by Reinhold Grimm). [Pembroke] (24) 92, p. 67.
"The Earth in a Photo" (tr. by Reinhold Grimm). [Pembroke] (24) 92, p. 50.
"Encounter" (tr. by Reinhold Grimm). [Pembroke] (24) 92, p. 65.
"Here Our Longing Rhymes with the Moment" (I-III, V, tr. by Reinhold Grimm). [Pembroke] (24) 92, p. 60-61.
"I Won't Forget" (tr. by Reinhold Grimm). [Pembroke] (24) 92, p. 69.
"Insoluble" (tr. by Reinhold Grimm). [Pembroke] (24) 92, p. 64.
"Lest Our Words Go Blind" (tr. by Reinhold Grimm). [Pembroke] (24) 92, p. 63.
"The Losers" (tr. by Reinhold Grimm). [Pembroke] (24) 92, p. 59.
"Mandelstam" (tr. by Reinhold Grimm). [Pembroke] (24) 92, p. 72.
"My Friend, the American Indian, Says" (tr. by Reinhold Grimm). [Pembroke] (24) 92, p. 56.
"Nearly Everything Remains to Be Done" (tr. by Reinhold Grimm). [Pembroke] (24) 92, p. 68.
"Often" (tr. by Reinhold Grimm). [Pembroke] (24) 92, p. 70.
"The Old Woman" (tr. by Reinhold Grimm). [Pembroke] (24) 92, p. 52.
"Script and Counterscript" (tr. by Reinhold Grimm). [Pembroke] (24) 92, p. 72.
"So as Not to Perish" (tr. by Reinhold Grimm). [Pembroke] (24) 92, p. 58.
"Those Who Die Are the Others" (tr. by Reinhold Grimm). [Pembroke] (24) 92, p. 51.

"Thus We Ask and Keep on Asking" (tr. by Reinhold Grimm). [Pembroke] (24) 92, p. 55.
"To Heck with It" (III, VI, tr. by Reinhold Grimm). [Pembroke] (24) 92, p. 66.
"Window" (tr. by Reinhold Grimm). [Pembroke] (24) 92, p. 53.

2053. FROLICK, Gloria Kupchenko
"Glory of the Heart" (For Flying Officer William Osadchy, perished on a bombing raid over Hamburg, Germany, July 1944). [PraF] (13:3, #60) Aut 92, p. 56-58.

2054. FROME, Carol
"Flying." [SouthernPR] (32:2) Fall 92, p. 48-49.
"Into Winter." [PoetC] (23:3) Spr 92, p. 7.
"Intruder" (winner of Discovery — The Nation '92). [Nat] (254:19) 18 My 92, p. 671.
"Palmistry." [Vis] (38) 92, p. 30.
"Some Nights." [SouthernPR] (32:2) Fall 92, p. 49.

2055. FROST, Carol
"American Primitives." [PraS] (66:3) Fall 92, p. 75-76.
"Away." [NewEngR] (14:3) Sum 92, p. 90-91.
"Concert for Dead Composers." [NewEngR] (14:3) Sum 92, p. 92.
"Garden of Earthly Delights." [LitR] (35:3) Spr 92, p. 311.
"Harm." [TriQ] (86) Wint 92-93, p. 66.
"Love." [NoAmR] (277:5) S-O 92, p. 21.
"Mind." [NoAmR] (277:5) S-O 92, p. 21.
"Old." [NoAmR] (277:5) S-O 92, p. 21.
"Pure." [TriQ] (86) Wint 92-93, p. 67.

2056. FROST, Celestine
"Epic." [Epoch] (41:2) 92, p. 261.
"An Imagined Experience Over the Entrance." [DustyD] (Chapbook Series #5) 92, 55 p.
"Redefining Balance." [Talisman] (9) Fall 92, p. 128-129.

2057. FROST, Kenneth
"Piercing the Electron's Veil." [ManhatPR] (14) [92?], p. 14-17.
"This Ought to Prove." [ManhatPR] (14) [92?], p. 14.
"Where." [ManhatPR] (14) [92?], p. 17-18.

2058. FROST, Linda A.
"The Bakery Ladies" (to Marilyn and Dorothy). [SingHM] (20) 92, p. 70-71.

2059. FROST, Richard
"Reunion." [MissR] (20:3) Spr 92, p. 56.

2060. FRUTKIN, Mark
"Burning Horse." [Arc] (29) Aut 92, p. 75.

2061. FRY, Jane Gilliat
"Birdshot." [Light] (4) Wint 92-93, p. 11.

2062. FRY, Phil
"Wildfire." [PoetryUSA] (24) 92, p. 26.

2063. FRYE, Nancy
"The World Contained." [Archae] (4) late 92-early 93, p. 40-42.

2064. FUHRMAN, Joanna
"Comouflage." [HangL] (61) 92, p. 93.
"Maltwood, New York." [HangL] (61) 92, p. 91.
"Rousseau." [HangL] (61) 92, p. 92.
"Scene." [HangL] (61) 92, p. 94.

2065. FUJIWARA no SEKIO
"Frost one thread" (Kokinshu 291, in Japanese and English, tr. by Emily Nguyen). [Archae] (4) late 92-early 93, p. 15.

2066. FULKER, Tina
"Glamour This." [Bogg] (65) 92, p. 51.

2067. FULLER, Kate
"After Dinner." [BellArk] (8:2) Mr-Ap 92, p. 13.
"Sandhill Cranes." [BellArk] (8:2) Mr-Ap 92, p. 1.

2068. FULTON, Alice
"A.M.: The Hopeful Monster" (For John H. Holland). [AmerV] (26) Spr 92, p. 57 - 58.
"Slate" (For Robert Weisbuch). [AmerV] (26) Spr 92, p. 55-56.

2069. FULTON, Robin
"Refuge Behind Refuge" (for Peter Huchel, tr. of Reiner Kunze). [Stand] (33:4) Aut 92, p. 71.

2070. FUNGE, Robert
"First of April" (for Geri Ulik). [Pearl] (15) Spr-Sum 92, p. 66.
"A Tenpenny Poem." [HolCrit] (29:1) F 92, p. 17-18.
2071. FUNK, Allison
"August: A Lunar Eclipse." [PoetryNW] (33:1) Spr 92, p. 25.
"The Moons of Uranus." [PoetryNW] (33:1) Spr 92, p. 24.
"Turning Forty." [Poetry] (161:1) O 92, p. 33.
2072. FUNKHOUSER, Erica
"Owl Pellet." [Atlantic] (270:5) N 92, p. 124.
2073. FUQUA, Christopher S.
"1963." [Lactuca] (15) Mr 92, p. 22.
"At This Distance." [Lactuca] (15) Mr 92, p. 21.
"The Iron Bed." [Lactuca] (15) Mr 92, p. 22.
"Metallic Wisdom." [Lactuca] (15) Mr 92, p. 21.
2074. FURBUSH, Matthew
"A Piece of the Wall" (A Poem Ending in Now). [Agni] (35) 92, p. 285.
2075. FURTH, Robin
"Beware." [BelPoJ] (43:1) Fall 92, p. 34-35.
FUSAE, Kaibara
See KAIBARA, Fusae
2076. FUSCO, Peter
"Happy Birthday, Steve." [Light] (1) Spr 92, p. 29.
2077. FUSEK, Serena
"Butchering." [SlipS] (12) 92, p. 49.
"Dismal Swamp Blues." [Amelia] (6:4, #19) 92, p. 87.
"Night Shift in the Mine." [SlipS] (12) 92, p. 50.
"Tip." [SlipS] (12) 92, p. 50-51.
2078. FUSHIMI, Emperor (1265-1317)
"Lightning" (tr. by Graeme Wilson). [Jacaranda] (6:1/2) Wint-Spr 92, p. 151.
2079. FUSSELMAN, Amy
"The Bugs." [MinnR] (38) Spr-Sum 92, p. 40-41.
"Impotence." [NewYorkQ] (47) 92, p. 62.
2080. GABBARD, G. N.
"Apologia." [Light] (2) Sum 92, p. 12.
"Clerihew: John Ruskin proclaimed a new era." [Light] (4) Wint 92-93, p. 15.
"Poultry." [Light] (1) Spr 92, p. 21.
2081. GADANYI, Joli
"Muteness" (tr. by Elizabeth Molnar Rajec). [Confr] (48/49) Spr-Sum 92, p. 219.
2082. GADD, Bernard
"Olduvaian." [Vis] (40) 92, p. 53.
"Wallace Stevens and I Try 'Oh Susannah'." [Bogg] (65) 92, p. 5.
2083. GADE, Lisa
"Imaginary Prisons." [SouthernPR] (32:2) Fall 92, p. 27-30.
2084. GAGNON, Madeleine
"Ils sont frileux sous terre et nous tissons des sarcophages." [Os] (35) Fall 92, p. 35.
"Les morts enterrées nos balbutiements." [Os] (35) Fall 92, p. 34.
2085. GAISER, Carolyn
"Endings." [Nat] (255:10) 5 O 92, p. 372.
2086. GAJDA, Michael J.
"A Drunk I Met." [Elf] (2:1) Spr 92, p. 34-35.
2087. GAJUS, Greg
"Untitled: Black hair and blood lips." [JamesWR] (9:2) Wint 92, p. 8.
2088. GALASSI, Jonathan
"Flâneur." [NewRep] (207:24) 7 D 92, p. 44.
"Motets" (tr. of Eugenio Montale). [GrandS] (11:1, #41) 92, p. 24-33.
2089. GALBRAITH, Iain
"Truce." [Stand] (33:2) Spr 92, p. 100.
"The Wanderer" (for Luigi Nono). [Stand] (33:2) Spr 92, p. 99-100.
2090. GALEF, David
"Foreign Articles." [Light] (1) Spr 92, p. 8.
"In Our Time." [Light] (2) Sum 92, p. 7.
"Possessions." [Light] (1) Spr 92, p. 18.
2091. GALICH, A.
"Clouds" (tr. by Mark Halperin). [SenR] (22:1) Spr 92, p. 24-25.
"In Memory of B. L. Pasternak" (tr. by Mark Halperin). [SenR] (22:1) Spr 92, p. 30 - 32.

"Legend of Some Smokes" (tr. by Mark Halperin). [SenR] (22:1) Spr 92, p. 27-30.
"Nothing on Time" (tr. by Mark Halperin). [SenR] (22:1) Spr 92, p. 26-27.
"Without a Name" (tr. by Mark Halperin). [SenR] (22:1) Spr 92, p. 23.

GALINDO, David Escobar
See ESCOBAR GALINDO, David

2092. GALL-CLAYTON, Nancy
"Sense." [Wind] (22:71) 92, p. 17.

2093. GALLAGHER, E. J.
"Pentecost." [ChrC] (109:30) 21 O 92, p. 940.

2094. GALLAGHER, Richard
"Scratching the Post." [Amelia] (6:4, #19) 92, p. 104.

2095. GALLAGHER, Tess
"After the Chinese." [AmerPoR] (21:1) Ja-F 92, p. 33.
"Anatomy of a Kiss." [CreamCR] (16:2) Fall 92, p. 8-9.
"Androgynous Kiss." [AmerV] (26) Spr 92, p. 89-90.
"Before." [AmerPoR] (21:1) Ja-F 92, p. 34.
"Birthmark." [Witness] (6:2) 92, p. 100-101.
"Breeze." [AmerPoR] (21:1) Ja-F 92, p. 35.
"Canned Salmon." [Witness] (6:2) 92, p. 102.
"Cherry Blossoms." [CimR] (98) Ja 92, p. 88.
"Essentials." [Witness] (6:2) 92, p. 98-99.
"Fable of a Kiss." [MichQR] (31:3) Sum 92, p. 363-364.
"Fathomless." [AmerPoR] (21:1) Ja-F 92, p. 35.
"Fresh Stain." [AmerPoR] (21:1) Ja-F 92, p. 34.
"Glow." [AmerPoR] (21:1) Ja-F 92, p. 33.
"The Kiss of the Voyeur." [TampaR] (5) Fall 92, p. 38.
"Kiss Without a Body." [OntR] (36) Spr-Sum 92, p. 30.
"Kissing the Blindman." [CreamCR] (16:2) Fall 92, p. 5.
"Last Look." [AmerPoR] (21:1) Ja-F 92, p. 34.
"Like the Sigh of Women's Hair." [OntR] (36) Spr-Sum 92, p. 29.
"Liliana" (for Liliana Ursu, Madrid, June 14, 1990). [PassN] (13:2) Wint 92, p. 12.
"No Fingertips." [MichQR] (31:3) Sum 92, p. 364.
"Paradise." [AmerPoR] (21:1) Ja-F 92, p. 33.
"Port Angeles" (tr. of Liliana Ursu, w. the author). [PassN] (13:2) Wint 92, p. 12.
"Two Locked Shadows." [CimR] (98) Ja 92, p. 87.
"Two of Anything." [AmerPoR] (21:1) Ja-F 92, p. 34.
"White Kiss." [Zyzzyva] (8:1) Spr 92, p. 134-135.
"Why I Am the Silent One." [TampaR] (5) Fall 92, p. 39.
"Your Hands, Which I Love to Kiss." [CreamCR] (16:2) Fall 92, p. 6-7.

2096. GALLAGHER, Timothy
"To the Lighthouse." [JamesWR] (9:3) Spr 92, p. 6.

2097. GALLAS, John
"At the Funeral of a Nationalist." [Stand] (33:4) Aut 92, p. 31.
"Woolwich Arsenal." [Stand] (33:4) Aut 92, p. 30.

2098. GALLER, David
"The Children." [TriQ] (86) Wint 92-93, p. 81-83.
"The Mirage." [SouthwR] (77:4) Aut 92, p. 573-574.

2099. GALLIK, Daniel
"At Seventeen." [WindO] (56) Fall-Wint 92, p. 28.
"A Time in the Past The Distance Between Galaxies Must Have Been Zero." [HiramPoR] (51/52) Fall 91-Sum 92, p. 38.

2100. GALVIN, Brendan
"At the Duncan Ban MacIntyre Memorial" (1724-1812). [TarRP] (32:1) Fall 92, p. 47-48.
"Chickadee." [ThRiPo] (39/40) 92-93, p. 81-82.
"A Cold Bell Ringing in the East." [TarRP] (32:1) Fall 92, p. 48-49.
"Listening to September." [ThRiPo] (39/40) 92-93, p. 83-84.
"Seals in the Inner Harbor." [ThRiPo] (39/40) 92-93, p. 82-83.
"St. Brendan Discovers an Iceberg" (Irish, 6th century). [CimR] (98) Ja 92, p. 69-76.
"Town Pier Parking Lot." [ThRiPo] (39/40) 92-93, p. 84-85.
"Willow, Wishbone, Warblers." [ThRiPo] (39/40) 92-93, p. 80-81.

2101. GALVIN, James
"Real Wonder." [Atlantic] (269:3) Mr 92, p. 81.
"Western Civilization" (Winner, 1991-92 Richard Hugo Memorial Poetry Award). [CutB] (38) Sum 92, p. 84-89.
"Winter Road." [CutB] (38) Sum 92, p. 90-91.

2102. GALVIN, Martin
"Steak and Kidney Pie." [Bogg] (65) 92, p. 42.
2103. GANASSI, Ian
"The Business." [Pequod] (33) 92, p. 37-39.
"Civilization and Its Discontents." [ParisR] (34:123) Sum 92, p. 94-95.
2104. GANDER, Forrest
"The Faculty for Hearing the Silence of Jesus." [Conjunc] (19) 92, p. 229-238.
"Isn't She Not a Bird" (tr. of Nina Iskrenko, w. Mala Kotamraju). [Agni] (35) 92, p. 166-167.
"On the Removal of Troops from Afghanistan" (tr. of Aleksandr Eremenko, w. Sara Dickinson). [Agni] (35) 92, p. 268-269.
"Thoughts on Formal Logic" (tr. of Yuri" Arabov, w. Sara Dickinson). [Agni] (35) 92, p. 264-265.
2105. GANGEMI, Kenneth
"The Time Machine." [Pequod] (33) 92, p. 184-186.
2106. GANICK, Peter
"Cafe Unreal" (Excerpt). [Talisman] (9) Fall 92, p. 205-206.
"Remove a Concept." [BlackWR] (18:2) Spr-Sum 92, p. Selections: *4004, *4019, *4030, *4037). [BlackWR] (18:2) Spr-Sum 92, p. 26-28.
2107. GANNON, Mary
"Beyond the Mouth of Plenty's Horn." [HayF] (10) Spr-Sum 92, p. 90.
2108. GANZ, David
"In His Cloister, Close to Easter." [CarolQ] (45:1) Fall 92, p. 30.
2109. GARANIS, Myrna
"Raspberry Rules." [Grain] (20:1) Spr 92, p. 83.
"Solar Storms." [PraF] (13:4, #61) Wint 92-93, p. 51.
2110. GARBETT, Ann Davison
"Before Mother's Parade." [ChamLR] (10/11) Spr-Fall 92, p. 37.
"Driving Across Iowa Again." [ChamLR] (10/11) Spr-Fall 92, p. 36.
"Leftovers." [ChrC] (109:23) 29 Jl-5 Ag 92, p. 700.
2111. GARCIA, Carlos
"Para Siempre de Puntillas" (tr. of James Reams). [Nuez] (4:10/11) 92, p. 25.
2112. GARCIA, José
"Damp your sandals" (tr. of Yannis Ritsos, w. Amanda Baltatzi). [Vis] (39) 92, p. 39.
"The Terror." [Gypsy] (18) 92, p. 69-70.
"Third Series" (Selections: 10, 23, 27, 42, 48, tr. of Yannis Ritsos, w. Adamantia Baltatzi). [PaintedHR] (5) Wint 92, p. 5.
2113. GARCIA, Richard
"In the Eye of the Storm." [YellowS] (Ten Years [i.e. 40]) Sum-Fall 92, p. 31.
"In the Year 1946." [Ploughs] (18:1) Spr 92, p. 8.
"Like a Chicken About to Cross a Road." [Pearl] (16) Fall 92, p. 52.
"Why I Left the Church." [Ploughs] (18:1) Spr 92, p. 6-7.
2114. GARCIA ALVAREZ, Juan Carlos
"Portero sin Suerte." [Nuez] (4:10/11) 92, p. 5.
2115. GARCIA LASCURAIN, Ignacio
"Regreso de selvosos." [Nuez] (4:10/11) 92, p. 10.
2116. GARCIA LORCA, Federico
"1910" (an interlude, new york, august 1929, tr. by Joel Zeltzer). [NewYorkQ] (47) 92, p. 97.
"1910" (intermedio, nueva york, agosto 1929). [NewYorkQ] (47) 92, p. 97.
"Death" (tr. by Joel Zeltzer). [ChironR] (11:2) Sum 92, p. 4.
"Gypsy Nun" (tr. by Joel Zeltzer). [ChironR] (11:2) Sum 92, p. 4.
"Lament for Ignacio Sanchez Majias" (Excerpt, tr. by Robin Skelton). [Arc] (28) Spr 92, p. 63.
"Silly Song" (tr. by Robin Skelton). [Arc] (28) Spr 92, p. 60.
"Street of the Mutes" (tr. by Robin Skelton). [Arc] (28) Spr 92, p. 60.
"Tree, Tree" (tr. by Robin Skelton). [Arc] (28) Spr 92, p. 64-65.
GARDEUR, Lili le
See LeGARDEUR, Lili
2117. GARDINIER, Suzanne
"Museum of the American Indian." [TriQ] (84) Spr-Sum 92, p. 113-115.
"Where Blind Sorrow Is Taught to See." [AmerV] (27) 92, p. 22-23.
2118. GARDNER, Delbert R.
"Casey Bats Again (Post-1981)." [HolCrit] (29:4) O 92, p. 18-19.

2119. GARDNER, Drew
"Clown." [Talisman] (8) Spr 92, p. 173.
"Commander in Chief of the Barbarians." [Talisman] (8) Spr 92, p. 173.
2120. GARDNER, Eric
"Rope." [WillowR] (19) Spr 92, p. 17.
2121. GARDNER, Geoffrey
"Forty-Six." [InterPR] (18:1) Spr 92, p. 76-78.
"Without Walls" (tr. of Jules Supervielle). [PartR] (59:1) Wint 92, p. 106-107.
2122. GARDNER, Isabella
"Convalescence in Summer 1949." [Contact] (10:62/63/64) Fall 91-Spr 92, p. 87.
"Your Fearful Symmetries" (for Alice Neel). [Contact] (10:62/63/64) Fall 91-Spr 92, p. 87.
2123. GARDNER, Joann
"Killing Day." [TampaR] (5) Fall 92, p. 65.
2124. GARDNER, Stephen
"Directions for Finding the Best Way Out." [CimR] (101) O 92, p. 64.
"Home Voyager." [CimR] (101) O 92, p. 63.
2125. GARGANO, Elizabeth
"How the Leaves Spoke to Me." [Poem] (67) My 92, p. 44.
"Second Sight" (for Joseph and Peter). [Poem] (67) My 92, p. 43.
2126. GARMON, John Frederic
"Biscuits and Gravy at Ma Black's." [Ploughs] (18:1) Spr 92, p. 228-229.
2127. GARREN, Christine
"The Enamel Bird." [Shen] (42:3) Fall 92, p. 105.
"From Another Country." [Shen] (42:3) Fall 92, p. 106.
"On Suffering." [Shen] (42:3) Fall 92, p. 106.
"Saying What Needs to Be Said." [Shen] (42:3) Fall 92, p. 107.
2128. GARRETT, Evvy
"A Beautiful Sunrise, Summer Early." [Pearl] (15) Spr-Sum 92, p. 25.
2129. GARRETT, George
"Bennington College (1979)." [Witness] (5:2) 91, p. 137.
"Gadfly." [Witness] (5:2) 91, p. 116-117.
"Or Death and December." [Witness] (5:2) 91, p. 133.
"Professor of Belles Lettres." [Witness] (5:2) 91, p. 134.
"Wonderful Pen (A Snapshot)." [Witness] (5:2) 91, p. 136-137.
2130. GARRIGUE, Jean
"The Brook." [AmerPoR] (21:2) Mr-Ap 92, p. 15.
"Cracked Looking Glass." [AmerPoR] (21:2) Mr-Ap 92, p. 16.
"A Figure for J. V. Meer." [AmerPoR] (21:2) Mr-Ap 92, p. 15.
2131. GARRIOTT, Maria
"The Poet's Daughter at Eight." [ChrC] (109:22) 15-22 Jl 92, p. 669.
2132. GARRISON, David
"Numbers" (tr. of Pedro Salinas). [ColR] (9:1) Spr-Sum 92, p. 113.
2133. GARRISON, Deborah
"The Firemen." [NewYorker] (68:22) 20 Jl 92, p. 54.
"You Prune Your List in Summer." [NewYorker] (68:36) 26 O 92, p. 78.
2134. GARRISON, Jay
"Captive Audience." [Plain] (13:1) Fall 92, p. 9.
2135. GARRISON, Peggy
"The Bay of Martigues." [LitR] (36:1) Fall 92, p. 48.
2136. GARTEN, Bill
"Looking Eye to Eye." [Epiphany] (3:2) Ap (Spr) 92, p. 101.
"Recognition # 11." [Epiphany] (3:2) Ap (Spr) 92, p. 102.
"Recognition # 12." [Epiphany] (3:2) Ap (Spr) 92, p. 102.
"Recognition # 13." [Epiphany] (3:2) Ap (Spr) 92, p. 102.
2137. GARTHE, Karen
"Miss America." [NewAW] (10) Fall 92, p. 89.
"Rogue Winter" (Chavez County, NM, 1933). [NewAW] (10) Fall 92, p. 90.
2138. GARZA, Rosa
"Picking Cherries in the Springtime." [Amelia] (6:4, #19) 92, p. 112.
2139. GASH, Sondra
"Remnants, Paterson, N. J., 1946." [US1] (26/27) 92, p. 48.
2140. GASPAR, Frank
"Angels." [PraS] (66:2) Sum 92, p. 74-76.
"Boston." [DenQ] (26:4) Spr 92, p. 25-26.
"Chronicle." [AntR] (50:4) Fall 92, p. 724-725.

"Underwood." [GeoR] (46:1) Spr 92, p. 96.
"Walking Out in Fog." [PraS] (66:2) Sum 92, p. 76-77.

2141. GASSLER, Marta M.
"Archeology." [PraF] (13:4, #61) Wint 92-93, p. 53.
"Night Shapes." [PraF] (13:4, #61) Wint 92-93, p. 52.

2142. GASTIGER, Joseph
"Found in Supposedly Empty Equipment." [SycamoreR] (4:2) Sum 92, p. 29-30.
"Half an Hour Before the War." [TriQ] (86) Wint 92-93, p. 59-61.
"January Thaw." [SycamoreR] (4:2) Sum 92, p. 27-28.
"Speed." [ColEng] (54:8) D 92, p. 943-944.
"Words We Love More Than the Things Themselves." [NewDeltaR] (9:2) Spr-Sum 92, p. 23.

2143. GASTON, Elaine
"The Whole Spectrum." [Verse] (9:3) Wint 92, p. 10.

2144. GATES, Edward
"Ghazal." [AntigR] (90) Sum 92, p. 47.
"Two Ghazals." [Event] (21:2) Sum 92, p. 46-47.

2145. GAUTHIER, Marcel
"Elegy." [GreensboroR] (52) Sum 92, p. 55-57.

2146. GAVARRE, Benjamín
"Fiesta para Peces Desnudos." [Nuez] (4:10/11) 92, p. 4.

2147. GAVIN, Tim
"Broken Angel." [NegC] (12:1/2) 92, p. 38-40.
"I could make my bed." [Wind] (22:71) 92, p. 18.
"On I-95." [BlackBR] (16) Wint-Spr 92-93, p. 33.
"Redemption." [Wind] (22:71) 92, p. 18-19.

2148. GAVRONSKY, Serge
"Fragmented Circle" (Selections: 11-20). [Talisman] (9) Fall 92, p. 139-141.

2149. GAZDAG, Judith
"Anisette Toast" (in memory of my Italian grandmother). [Footwork] 92, p. 100.

2150. GEAUVREAU, Cherie
"The Shadow of the Crow." [AmerV] (27) 92, p. 24-26.

2151. GEBHARD, Christine
"The Promise of Hope Against Hope." [PoetryNW] (33:4) Wint 92-93, p. 25.

2152. GEDDES, Gary
"Super Latex." [WestCL] (25:3, #6) Wint 91-92, p. 146.

GEERMAN, Lydia Marchena
See MARCHENA-GEERMAN, Lydia

2153. GEIGER, Timothy
"The Catechism of Light." [CapeR] (27:1) Spr 92, p. 34.
"Eclipses" (for Chris Buckley). [LullwaterR] (3:2) Spr 92, p. 41.
"Faith During the Dry Summer of 1975." [PoetL] (87:1) Spr 92, p. 33.
"With No Name." [PassN] (13:2) Wint 92, p. 22.

2154. GELETA, Greg
"A Tiger Speaks" (tr. of Silvina Ocampo). [Asylum] (7:3/4) 92, p. 38-39.

2155. GELLAND, Carolyn
"Acropolis Grotesque." [NegC] (12:1/2) 92, p. 43.
"Presentation of the Mask." [ManhatPR] (14) [92?], p. 19.
"To a Twentieth-Century Princess." [NegC] (12:1/2) 92, p. 41-42.
"Transformations." [NegC] (12:1/2) 92, p. 44-45.

2156. GELMAN, Juan
"History" (tr. by John Lindgren). [Vis] (39) 92, p. 14.
"The Way It Happens" (tr. by John Lindgren). [Vis] (39) 92, p. 14.

2157. GELSANLITER, David
"House Guest." [NewYorkQ] (47) 92, p. 74.
"New Woman." [NewYorkQ] (48) 92, p. 116.

2158. GEMIL, Henok
"Sound." Sparks! Writing by High School Students (1:1), a supplement to [PraF] (13:4, #61) Wint 92-93, p. 7.

2159. GENEGA, Paul
"That Winter." [LitR] (35:3) Spr 92, p. 372.

2160. GENEVA, Andrew J.
"Harvest Sequence." [Amelia] (6:4, #19) 92, p. 67.

2161. GENSLER, Kinereth
"Writing Poetry" (After William Stafford). [Poetry] (160:2) My 92, p. 72.

2162. GENT, Andrew
"The Ancient Philosophers." [PoetryE] (33) Spr 92, p. 46.
2163. GENTRY, Bruce
"Kindergarten Dropout." [HopewellR] (4) 92, p. 31.
2164. GEORGE, Ann (*See also* GEORGE, Anne)
"For Earl Who Got a Haircut from a Barber Named Butch with Tattoos." [Light] (1) Spr 92, p. 28.
2165. GEORGE, Anne (*See also* GEORGE, Ann)
"Crabapple Branches." [NegC] (12:1/2) 92, p. 123.
"Davidsohn's Wife." [NegC] (12:1/2) 92, p. 124.
"For My Friend Who Would Prove Divinity with Numbers." [NegC] (12:1/2) 92, p. 122.
"Hang Gliders at Highlands." [NegC] (12:1/2) 92, p. 126.
"Mary, Third from the Left." [NegC] (12:1/2) 92, p. 121.
"October Ferry." [NegC] (12:1/2) 92, p. 125.
"Rocking McKenzie to Sleep." [NegC] (12:1/2) 92, p. 127.
"Sagittarius." [NegC] (12:1/2) 92, p. 120.
2166. GEORGE, Emery
"Four-Liner" (tr. of János Pilinszky). [SouthernHR] (26:1) Wint 92, p. 26.
"Fragment" (tr. of Miklós Radnóti). [Nimrod] (35:2) Spr-Sum 92, p. 30.
"The Henchman's Room" (tr. of János Pilinszky). [SouthernHR] (26:1) Wint 92, p. 25.
"Holy Thief" (for Mari Töröcsik, tr. of János Pilinszky). [PartR] (59:2) Spr 92, p. 268.
"I Cannot Know" (tr. of Miklós Radnóti). [Nimrod] (35:2) Spr-Sum 92, p. 29.
"Meetings" (for Júlia Szilágyi, tr. of Janos Pilinsky). [Nimrod] (35:2) Spr-Sum 92, p. 31.
"Perpetuum Mobile" (tr. of János Pilinszky). [SouthernHR] (26:1) Wint 92, p. 24.
2167. GEORGE, Faye
"A Cry of Bells." [Interim] (11:1) Spr-Sum 92, p. 13.
"Like Anne Shirley's House." [Poetry] (160:4) Jl 92, p. 213.
"No One Plays the Piano." [Poetry] (160:4) Jl 92, p. 214.
"Witch." [Interim] (11:1) Spr-Sum 92, p. 12.
2168. GEORGE, Gerald
"Bahasa Berirama." [CumbPR] (11:2) Spr 92, p. 16.
"Epilogue." [CumbPR] (11:2) Spr 92, p. 18.
"Garuda." [CumbPR] (11:2) Spr 92, p. 14-15.
" *Sjair*: Wise Man and Holy." [CumbPR] (11:2) Spr 92, p. 17.
"Three *Pantun* Poems." [CumbPR] (11:2) Spr 92, p. 13.
2169. GEORGE, Terrence
"Prosopography." [DenQ] (26:4) Spr 92, p. 27.
2170. GEORGIEV, Marin
"Memory" (A cycle of fifteen poems. Selection: II, tr. by Lisa Sapinkopf, w. Georgi Belev). [Agni] (36) 92, p. 164-165.
2171. GERARD, Mary Ann
"The Bear." [Jacaranda] (6:1/2) Wint-Spr 92, p. 73.
2172. GERBER, Natalie Ellen
"Mutes." [Agni] (35) 92, p. 100-102.
2173. GERHARDT, Ida
"Clara Haskil" (Mozart Pianoconcert in A-major, tr. by Sheila Dietz). [Vis] (39) 92, p. 35.
2174. GERLACH, Lee
"Molior to His First Wife." [Agni] (35) 92, p. 183-184.
"The West Window." [Verse] (9:2) Sum 92, p. 85.
2175. GERSTLE, Val
"The End of the World." [BellR] (15:2) Fall 92, p. 15.
"The Visiting Poet from England." [BellR] (15:2) Fall 92, p. 14.
2176. GERSTLER, Amy
"Dear Mom." [Witness] (5:1) 91, p. 29.
"Dust." [IndR] (15:2) Fall 92, p. 171-172.
"Ether." [Witness] (5:1) 91, p. 28.
"On Wanting to Grow Horns." [Witness] (5:1) 91, p. 26-27.
2177. GERTLER, Pesha
"Apologia: For the Society of Orthodox Jewish Women." [Calyx] (14:2) Wint 92 - 93, p. 16.
"Late Gift." [CutB] (37) Wint 92, p. 44.

GERVEN, Claudia van
See Van GERVEN, Claudia
2178. GERVIN, Charles A.
"That's What I Want for Christmas" (after Jane Cortez, for Kevin Ziegler). [JamesWR] (9:4) Sum 92, p. 12.
2179. GESIN, Julie
"On New Year's Day" (tr. of Ivan Zhdanov, w. John High). [Avec] (5:1) 92, p. 124.
"Untitled: ('Stone')" (tr. of Ivan Zhdanov, w. John High). [Avec] (5:1) 92, p. 124.
2180. GETSI, Lucia C. (Lucia Cordell)
"And Then There Was One." [GreenMR] (NS 5:2) Spr-Sum 92, p. 19.
"Inside the Light, the Figure That Holds Us." [SouthernR] (28:2) Spr, Ap 92, p. 296 - 297.
"Outswimming." [SouthernR] (28:2) Spr, Ap 92, p. 298-299.
"Reading the Graves." [Epiphany] (3:4) O (Fall) 92, p. 310-311.
"Shells." [GreenMR] (NS 5:2) Spr-Sum 92, p. 20.
"Shells." [SouthernR] (28:2) Spr, Ap 92, p. 297-298.
"What I Can Say to You Now You Are Leaving." [SouthernR] (28:2) Spr, Ap 92, p. 299-300.
"Wings." [Epiphany] (3:4) O (Fall) 92, p. 308-309.
2181. GETTLER, Andrew
"Kill the Messenger, Wait for Better News." [HawaiiR] (16:2, #35) Spr 92, p. 11-12.
2182. GETTY, Sarah
"Corn." [ParisR] (34:125) Wint 92, p. 152-155.
"Mother, May I." [ParisR] (34:125) Wint 92, p. 148-149.
"The Wash." [ParisR] (34:125) Wint 92, p. 150-152.
GEUS, Cynthia de
See De GEUS, Cynthia
2183. GEWANTER, David
"Conduct of Our Loves." [Ploughs] (18:4) Wint 92-93, p. 130-131.
"In the Belly." [Ploughs] (18:4) Wint 92-93, p. 132.
"Leopard Man." [Agni] (36) 92, p. 97-99.
2184. GEYER, William
"Disputed Meaning." [WritersF] (18) 92, p. 133-134.
2185. GHAI, Gail
"Mounting the Yellow Crane Tower" (tr. of Li Po, w. Tracy Xie). [Epiphany] (3:1) Ja (Wint) 92, p. 28.
"Parched Grasses" (tr. of Li Po, w. Tracy Xie). [Epiphany] (3:1) Ja (Wint) 92, p. 29.
"Quiet Night Thoughts" (tr. of Li Po, w. Tracy Xie). [Epiphany] (3:1) Ja (Wint) 92, p. 30.
GHATA, Vénus Khoury
See KHOURY-GHATA, Vénus
2186. GHIGNA, Charles
"The Adoration of Eve." [PoetL] (87:3) Fall 92, p. 8.
"Mother Knows Best." [Light] (4) Wint 92-93, p. 13.
2187. GHOLSON, Christien
"Hold still." [Bogg] (65) 92, p. 53.
2188. GIANNINI, David
"10 A.M. / 21 July 1990" (for Brian & Joan). [ShadowP] (3) 92, p. 32.
"Anniversary." [ShadowP] (3) 92, p. 26.
"Carl." [ShadowP] (3) 92, p. 25.
"The Circle." [ShadowP] (3) 92, p. 28.
"Coyote." [ShadowP] (3) 92, p. 31.
"Flock." [ShadowP] (3) 92, p. 23.
"From a Letter to Geneva." [ShadowP] (3) 92, p. 30.
"Journal — Monument Mountain" (for Pamela). [ShadowP] (3) 92, p. 34-37.
"Lumber Stacked Indoors." [ShadowP] (3) 92, p. 33.
"Paul." [ShadowP] (3) 92, p. 24.
"Shiplap" (Excerpt). [Talisman] (8) Spr 92, p. 113.
"Stream of Lives." [ShadowP] (3) 92, p. 27.
"Wellfleet — Audubon Sanctuary" (for Ted Enslin). [ShadowP] (3) 92, p. 29.
2189. GIANNINI, Laura
"Aunt Jenny." [Noctiluca] (1:2) Wint 92 [on cover: Wint 93], p. 20.
"Blue Moon." [US1] (26/27) 92, p. 24.
2190. GIBB, Robert
"Fugue for a Late Snow." [PraS] (66:3) Fall 92, p. 90-95.
"Japanese." [Field] (46) Spr 92, p. 62.

"Ohio." [CinPR] (23) Wint 91-92, p. 61.
"Rogation Days." [QW] (34) Wint-Spr 92, p. 65-66.
"Salting the Slugs." [Field] (46) Spr 92, p. 63.

2191. GIBBONS, Reginald
"After Everything" (tr. of Aurelio Asiain). [TriQ] (85) Fall 92, p. 271.
"Discoveries" (tr. of Eduardo Langagne). [TriQ] (85) Fall 92, p. 218.
"Dogs" (tr. of Roberto Vallarino). [TriQ] (85) Fall 92, p. 206.
"Episode in Al-Qayrawan" (tr. of Jorge Esquinca). [TriQ] (85) Fall 92, p. 87-89.
"The House at 5 Allende Street" (tr. of Héctor Carreto). [TriQ] (85) Fall 92, p. 273 - 274.
"How Robert Schumann Was Defeated by Demons" (Excerpt, tr. of Francisco Hernández). [TriQ] (85) Fall 92, p. 278-279.
"The Huapango" (tr. of Luis Miguel Aguilar). [TriQ] (85) Fall 92, p. 90-91.
"The Last of the Tribe" (tr. of Fabio Morábito). [TriQ] (85) Fall 92, p. 92-95.
"Life" (tr. of Aurelio Asiain). [TriQ] (85) Fall 92, p. 272.
"A Life" (tr. of Raúl Bañuelos). [TriQ] (85) Fall 92, p. 348-349.
"Like the Ocean" (tr. of Víctor Manuel Mendiola). [TriQ] (85) Fall 92, p. 202.
"Monkey House" (tr. of Efraín Bartolomé). [TriQ] (85) Fall 92, p. 380-381.
"Ode to Feeling Like It" (tr. of Ricardo Castillo). [TriQ] (85) Fall 92, p. 376-377.
"Paper Roads" (tr. of Alberto Blanco). [TriQ] (85) Fall 92, p. 397-398.
"Poets Don't Go to Paris Anymore" (for José Peguero, tr. of Rubén Medina). [TriQ] (85) Fall 92, p. 166-167.
"Popocatépetl" (tr. of Verónica Volkow). [TriQ] (85) Fall 92, p. 345.
"Priam" (tr. of Rubén Medina). [TriQ] (85) Fall 92, p. 163-165.
"Quito" (tr. of Verónica Volkow). [TriQ] (85) Fall 92, p. 346.
"The Room" (tr. of Víctor Manuel Mendiola). [TriQ] (85) Fall 92, p. 201.
"A Season of Paradise" (tr. of José Luis Rivas). [TriQ] (85) Fall 92, p. 407-412.
"Settling Accounts" (tr. of Alberto Blanco). [TriQ] (85) Fall 92, p. 397-398.
"The Stone at the Bottom" (tr. of Manuel Ulacia). [TriQ] (85) Fall 92, p. 78-83.
"The street doesn't understand what I say" (tr. of Mónica Mansour). [TriQ] (85) Fall 92, p. 118.
"Sunken Landscapes" (tr. of Antonio Deltoro). [TriQ] (85) Fall 92, p. 282.
"Tea Blues" (tr. of David Huerta). [TriQ] (85) Fall 92, p. 341.
"There are lovers who appear" (tr. of Mónica Mansour). [TriQ] (85) Fall 92, p. 118 - 119.
"Thursday" (tr. of Antonio Deltoro). [TriQ] (85) Fall 92, p. 280-281.
"Virgins" (tr. of Lucía Manríquez Montoya). [TriQ] (85) Fall 92, p. 169.
"Where the conch of yucatán" (tr. of Raúl Aceves). [TriQ] (85) Fall 92, p. 162.
"A Woman and a Man" (tr. of Vicente Quirarte). [TriQ] (85) Fall 92, p. 160-161.
"Women — for example, three women" (tr. of Mónica Mansour). [TriQ] (85) Fall 92, p. 119.

2192. GIBBS, Robert
"Earth Aches." [PoetryC] (12:2) Ap 92, p. 22.
"This Catching of Breath at the Top." [PoetryC] (12:2) Ap 92, p. 22.
"When My Mother Played and Sang Spiritual Songs." [PoetryC] (12:2) Ap 92, p. 22.

2193. GIBSON, Amy
"An Absence of Light." [PoetryNW] (33:2) Sum 92, p. 20-21.
"Snapshot." [PoetryNW] (33:2) Sum 92, p. 22.

2194. GIBSON, Grace Loving
"The Blowhole" (Sam Ragan Prize, 1992 Literary Contest). [Crucible] (28) Fall 92, p. 4.

2195. GIBSON, Margaret
"Kate." [SouthernR] (28:4) Aut, O 92, p. 844-848.
"Lila" (one of the "voices" from the forthcoming book, "The Vigil"). [TarRP] (32:1) Fall 92, p. 16-19.
"Lila's Dream." [SouthernR] (28:4) Aut, O 92, p. 848-851.
"The Vigil" (Selections). [IndR] (15:1) Spr 92, p. 88-96.

2196. GIBSON, Morgan
"In the Dark Window." [Confr] (50) Fall 92, p. 283.

2197. GIBSON, Stephen (*See also* GIBSON, Stephen R.)
"Woman with Chrysanthemums" (Degas). [Poetry] (159:4) Ja 92, p. 217.

2198. GIBSON, Stephen R. (Stephen Robert) (*See also* GIBSON, Stephen)
"As We Light Out for New Orleans to Be Rescued by Aliens We Pause and Wish You Would Have Joined Us." [PoetryNW] (33:3) Aut 92, p. 35.
"Rain." [Ploughs] (18:4) Wint 92-93, p. 153.
"Systems Engage Under November Skies." [Ploughs] (18:4) Wint 92-93, p. 154.

2200. GIESECKE, Lee
"Dandelion." [NewYorkQ] (49) 92, p. 93.
2201. GIGUERE, Roland
"Landscape Estranged" (tr. by F. R. Scott). [Trans] (26) Spr 92, p. 27.
2202. GILBERT, Celia
"Absence." [Poetry] (160:4) Jl 92, p. 193.
"Cinders of Eve." [SouthwR] (77:1) Wint 92, p. 72-73.
"Naked Seed." [NewYorker] (67:48) 20 Ja 92, p. 66.
2203. GILBERT, Cheryl
"Themis and Lyric." [Caliban] (11) 92, p. 82.
"Themis Is Not Related to Zeus. She's Just a Bird with a Funny Name." [Caliban] (11) 92, p. 80.
"There Are Five Senses But No One Has Told Themis." [Caliban] (11) 92, p. 81.
2204. GILBERT, Christopher
"Blues / The Blue Case Against the Lack of." [WilliamMR] (30) 92, p. 53-54.
2205. GILBERT, Gerry
"Friends." [WestCL] (26:3, #9) Wint 92-93, p. 43-54.
2206. GILBERT, Margaret
"In the blue room of my epilepsy." [NewYorkQ] (47) 92, p. 98-102.
2207. GILBERT, Sandra M.
"Notes on Masada." [OntR] (37) Fall-Wint 92-93, p. 5-13.
2208. GILCHRIST, Ellen
"Passion." [PraS] (66:2) Sum 92, p. 19.
"Third Poem." [PraS] (66:2) Sum 92, p. 18-19.
2209. GILDNER, Gary
"Cabbage in Polish." [ThRiPo] (39/40) 92-93, p. 85.
"Epithalamion." [CreamCR] (16:2) Fall 92, p. 54-46.
"Primarily We Miss Ourselves As Children" (a Warsaw student, overheard). [ThRiPo] (39/40) 92-93, p. 87-88.
"String." [ThRiPo] (39/40) 92-93, p. 85-87.
2210. GILDROY, Doreen
"Industrial Landscape." [Jacaranda] (6:1/2) Wint-Spr 92, p. 124-127.
"Work." [Jacaranda] (6:1/2) Wint-Spr 92, p. 128.
"Worker." [Jacaranda] (6:1/2) Wint-Spr 92, p. 123.
2211. GILES, B. L.
"My Oedipus." [LullwaterR] (3:2) Spr 92, p. 52.
2212. GILGUN, John
"Clyde Steps In." [Elf] (2:1) Spr 92, p. 37.
"Cremation." [ChironR] (11:4) Wint 92, p. 20.
"In Which Niki Is Observed Sleeping" (Selection from "The Singing Bridge: A National AIDS Poetry Archive"). [Art&Und] (1:2) Wint 92, p. 16.
"Right From Wrong." [ChironR] (11:4) Wint 92, p. 20.
"Who Was That Masked Man?" [Elf] (2:1) Spr 92, p. 37.
2213. GILHOOLY, Sheila (*See also* GILLOOLY, Sheila)
"Twenty Years Gone: The Conversation Poem for Sheila" (w. Barbara Findlay. From "Pièces de résistance"). [SinW] (48) Wint 92-93, p. 63-64.
2214. GILL, Charmaine
"Paul." [LitR] (35:4) Sum 92, p. 549.
"Why." [LitR] (35:4) Sum 92, p. 548.
2215. GILL, Evalyn Pierpoint
"Renaissance Doorway." [Crucible] (28) Fall 92, p. 12-13.
2216. GILL, Gagan
"The Girl's Desire Moves among the Bangles" (tr. by Mrinal Pande and Arlene Zide). [ChiR] (38:1/2) 92, p. 106-107.
2217. GILL, James Vladimir
"Dans un Miroir en Guise d'Adieu." [CimR] (100) Jl 92, p. 57.
"Hatchards, Sunday Night, 1984." [CimR] (100) Jl 92, p. 58.
2218. GILL, Margaret
"Bridge." [LitR] (35:4) Sum 92, p. 550.
2219. GILL-LONERGAN, Janet
"First Date." [BellArk] (8:1) Ja-F 92, p. 6.
"From My Window." [BellArk] (8:2) Mr-Ap 92, p. 1.
"Reincarnate." [BellArk] (8:2) Mr-Ap 92, p. 1.
"Snow." [BellArk] (8:1) Ja-F 92, p. 3.
"Song." [BellArk] (8:1) Ja-F 92, p. 3.

2220. GILLESPIE, Elizabeth
"The Gas Station" (Winner, Annual Free Verse Contest, 1991). [AnthNEW] (4) 92, p. 15.
2221. GILLETT, Mary Jo Firth
"Two Lanes, Up North, Michigan Way." [BellArk] (8:3) My-Je 92, p. 23.
2222. GILLILAND, Mary
"Blessed Events" (tr. of Jenny Mastoraki, w. Helen Kolias). [Nimrod] (35:2) Spr - Sum 92, p. 68-69.
"Classics Illustrated" (tr. of Jenny Mastoraki, w. Helen Kolias). [Nimrod] (35:2) Spr-Sum 92, p. 70-71.
2223. GILLIS, David Michael
"Boys' Town." [CapilR] (2:8) Spr 92, p. 44-45.
"Dead." [CapilR] (2:8) Spr 92, p. 46.
"On Little Town of Drainagebrook." [CapilR] (2:8) Spr 92, p. 42-43.
2224. GILLIS, Margie
"Pat Friesen." [PraF] (13:1, #58) Spr 92, p. 113.
2225. GILLISON, Kate S.
"The Roads Not Taken" (by Roberta Mist — Apologies to Robert Frost). [EngJ] (80:6) O 91, p. 103.
2226. GILLMAN, Richard
"By Way of a Eulogy" (for Martin Robbins). [SewanR] (100:3) Sum 92, p. 367-369.
"Nothing Blossomed Like My Bedroom." [SewanR] (100:3) Sum 92, p. 370-371.
2227. GILLOOLY, Sheila (*See also* GILHOOLY, Sheila)
"Water Moccasin." [Amelia] (6:4, #19) 92, p. 60.
2228. GILMORE, Barry
"My Mother's Sickness." [CumbPR] (11:2) Spr 92, p. 7.
2229. GILSDORF, Ethan
"D NER." [CutB] (38) Sum 92, p. 40-43.
"Ethan." [LouisL] (9:1) Spr 92, p. 66.
"Grammar Lesson." [NewYorkQ] (47) 92, p. 42.
"Words to Use in Future Poems." [NewYorkQ] (48) 92, p. 96.
2230. GILSON, Barbara
"Amor de la Calle." [NewYorkQ] (49) 92, p. 82.
2231. GILSON, William
"For My Mother." [SmPd] (29:1, #84) Wint 92, p. 18.
2232. GINSBERG, Allen
"After the Big Parade." [CityLR] (5) 92, p. 119.
"G.S. Reading Poesy at Princeton." [AntR] (50:1/2) Wint-Spr 92, p. 192.
"I Love Old Whitman So" (Baoding, China, Novmeber 20, 1984, from "White Shroud"). [MassR] (23:1) Spr 92, p. 77.
"Just Say Yes Calypso." [CityLR] (5) 92, p. 120-121.
"Transformation of Bai's 'A Night in Xingyang'" (Part VII from "Reading Bai Juyi," White Shroud Poems 1980-1985). [Footwork] 92, p. 12.
2233. GIOIA, Dana
"Alley Cat Serenade." [Light] (2) Sum 92, p. 8.
"Hercules in Frenzy" (Selection: Chorus, Act One, tr. of Seneca). [Sparrow] (59) S 92, p. 32-34.
2234. GIONET, Renee
"A Road Trip Down the Columbia Gorge." [PaintedHR] (5) Wint 92, p. 9.
2235. GIORDANO, Gay
"Annunciation." [LullwaterR] (3:2) Spr 92, p. 7.
2236. GIOSEFFI, Daniela
"American Sonnets for My Father." [Footwork] 92, p. 20.
"The Blind Soprano Sings" (for Cheryl Taylor). [Footwork] 92, p. 20.
"Lady Godiva's Horse." [Footwork] 92, p. 21.
"Unfinished Aleotropic Autobiography" (for Carolyn Forché, October 7, 1990). [Footwork] 92, p. 21-22.
2237. GIOVANNINI, Juan José de
"En esta cascada la nave." [Nuez] (4:10/11) 92, p. 5.
2238. GIRR, Catherine
"At Putah Creek." [NewYorkQ] (47) 92, p. 72.
2239. GITZEN, Julian
"Climbing with the Wren." [OxfordM] (8:1) Spr-Sum 92, p. 55.
2240. GIZZI, Peter
"Asserted Abundance" (for Bernadette Mayer). [PaintedB] (48) 92, p. 55.
"Dear Jack." [Talisman] (8) Spr 92, p. 115.

"Hard As Ash." [NewAW] (10) Fall 92, p. 51-56.
"Periplum." [Avec] (5:1) 92, p. 30-34.

2241. GLADDING, Jody
"Footwork." [PoetryNW] (33:1) Spr 92, p. 29.
"Here, a Shark's Eye." [PoetryNW] (33:1) Spr 92, p. 27-28.
"Undercurrent." [PoetryNW] (33:1) Spr 92, p. 29.

2242. GLADE, Jon Forrest
"Bitter Springs." [Pearl] (16) Fall 92, p. 35.
"Missing." [NewYorkQ] (49) 92, p. 95.

2243. GLADHART, Amalia
"Gathering Figs." [Iowa] (22:2) Spr-Sum 92, p. 132-133.
"Hopital Girl." [Iowa] (22:2) Spr-Sum 92, p. 133.
"Remote, Named Places." [SouthernPR] (32:1) Spr 92, p. 13-14.
"What If I Told You He Had Died." [SenR] (22:2) Fall 92, p. 73.

2244. GLANCY, Diane
"Buffalo Medicine." [MichQR] (31:1) Wint 92, p. 37.
"Christopher." [NewL] (58:4) 92, p. 19.
"Furniture." [SenR] (22:1) Spr 92, p. 7-12.
"Meatloaf." [MichQR] (31:1) Wint 92, p. 36.

2245. GLANCY, Gabrielle
"What I See I Am." [Agni] (36) 92, p. 126-127.
"The World Before Me." [NewAW] (10) Fall 92, p. 79-80.

2246. GLASER, Elton
"Anecdotal Evidence." [PoetryNW] (33:3) Aut 92, p. 45.
"Astral Tangents." [LaurelR] (26:1) Wint 92, p. 53.
"At Rivendell Farm." [Journal] (16:2) Fall-Wint 92, p. 31.
"Beyond Repair." [CinPR] (23) Wint 91-92, p. 21.
"Grand Isle." [SouthernHR] (26:1) Wint 92, p. 35.
"Poem in Two Movements." [LaurelR] (26:1) Wint 92, p. 52.
"Refusing October." [SouthernHR] (26:1) Wint 92, p. 36.
"Sharp Practices." [Plain] (13:1) Fall 92, p. 10-11.
"Spring Offensive." [Journal] (16:2) Fall-Wint 92, p. 32-33.

2247. GLASER, Michael S.
"Loss" (for Eva). [ChrC] (109:21) 1-8 Jl 92, p. 651.
"Old Enough." [ChrC] (109:17) 13 My 92, p. 520.

2248. GLASS, Malcolm
"To the Beach." [ChatR] (12:2) Wint 92, p. 69-70.

2249. GLATT, Lisa
"Itch." [WormR] (32:3, #127) 92, p. 92.
"Real Writer." [WormR] (32:3, #127) 92, p. 92.
"Sweet." [WormR] (32:3, #127) 92, p. 92-93.
"Woman Without Skin" (15 poems). [Pearl] (16) Fall 92, p. 36-50.

2250. GLAZE, Andrew
"Most You." [NewYorkQ] (48) 92, p. 57.
"Thoreau Again." [NegC] (12:1/2) 92, p. 47.
"Yeats and Berryman Have Tea." [NegC] (12:1/2) 92, p. 46.

2251. GLAZER, Michele
"Her Eyes." [ColEng] (54:4) Ap 92, p. 422.

2252. GLAZIER, Loss Pequeño
"Mexico Primera" (Selection: 10). [Os] (34) Spr 92, p. 26.

2253. GLAZIER, Lyle
"Searching for Amy, V." [ShadowP] (3) 92, p. 44-52.

2254. GLAZNER, Greg
"Concentrating on Photographs: The Vatican." [CutB] (38) Sum 92, p. 34-35.
"In Praise of Motivated Blindness." [Pequod] (34) 92, p. 164-165.
"A Later Hour." [Pequod] (34) 92, p. 166-167.

2255. GLEASON, Marian
"Tree Family." [ChrC] (109:22) 15-22 Jl 92, p. 679.

2256. GLEASURE, James
"Claustrophobia" (tr. of Seán O Ríordáin). [Trans] (26) Spr 92, p. 63.

GLECKMAN, Pat Dyjak
See DYJAK-GLECKMAN, Pat

2257. GLENDAY, John
"A Nest of Boxes." [Verse] (8:3/9:1) Wint-Spr 92, p. 102.

2258. GLENN, Ann
"Portrait." [AntR] (50:3) Sum 92, p. 519.

"The Wasp" (to Jean Paul Sartre and Simone de Beauvoir, tr. of Francis Ponge). [AmerPoR] (21:6) N-D 92, p. 43-44.
2259. GLENN, Helen Trubek
"Inside the Mountain" (for my father). [SpoonRQ] (17:3/4) Sum-Fall 92, p. 30.
2260. GLENN, Laura
"All Winter I Watch the Ice River." [Ascent] (16:3) Spr 92, p. 45.
"Driving by the Water's Edge." [Ascent] (16:3) Spr 92, p. 44.
2261. GLICKMAN, Susan
"The Lost Child." [CanLit] (133) Sum 92, p. 39.
2262. GLOEGGLER, Tony
"Blue Collar." [NewYorkQ] (49) 92, p. 98.
"Children's Ward." [Lactuca] (16) Ag 92, p. 32.
"Cripple." [NewYorkQ] (47) 92, p. 73.
"Latch Keys." [Lactuca] (16) Ag 92, p. 33.
"Victims." [NewYorkQ] (49) 92, p. 97.
2263. GLORIA, Eugene
"Before the Angels Dance." [OxfordM] (8:2) Fall-Wint 92, p. 8.
"For the Dead and What's Inside Us." [GreensboroR] (53) Wint 92-93, p. 88-89.
"My Small Happiness." [OxfordM] (8:2) Fall-Wint 92, p. 9.
2264. GLOVER, Jon
"And So the Blue Sky Again." [Stand] (33:2) Spr 92, p. 104.
"Angry Birdsong." [Stand] (33:2) Spr 92, p. 104.
"Fairground." [Stand] (33:2) Spr 92, p. 103.
2265. GLOWACKI, Richard
"Extremities." [Farm] (9:1) Spr-Sum 92, p. 56.
2266. GLÜCK, Louise
"Clear Morning." [AmerPoR] (21:2) Mr-Ap 92, p. 30.
"End of Summer." [AmerPoR] (21:2) Mr-Ap 92, p. 33.
"Field Flowers." [NewYorker] (68:1) 24 F 92, p. 42.
"Gold Lily." [NewYorker] (68:6) 30 Mr 92, p. 36.
"The Hawthorn Tree." [AmerPoR] (21:2) Mr-Ap 92, p. 30.
"Heaven and Earth." [AmerPoR] (21:2) Mr-Ap 92, p. 31.
"Lamium." [YaleR] (80:1/2) Apr 92, p. 46.
"Lullaby." [AmerPoR] (21:2) Mr-Ap 92, p. 33.
"Matins: The sun shines, by the mailbox, leaves." [AmerPoR] (21:2) Mr-Ap 92, p. 29.
"Matins: Unreachable father, when we were first exiled from heaven." [AmerPoR] (21:2) Mr-Ap 92, p. 29.
"Midsummer." [AmerPoR] (21:2) Mr-Ap 92, p. 32.
"The Red Poppy." [Thrpny] (49) Spr 92, p. 19.
"Retreating Wind." [AmerPoR] (21:2) Mr-Ap 92, p. 30.
"Scilla." [AmerPoR] (21:2) Mr-Ap 92, p. 31.
"September Twilight." [YaleR] (80:1/2) Apr 92, p. 47.
"Trillium." [Thrpny] (49) Spr 92, p. 19.
"Vespers." [YaleR] (80:1/2) Apr 92, p. 48.
"Vespers: Even as you appeared to Moses." [AmerPoR] (21:2) Mr-Ap 92, p. 32.
"Vespers: Once I believed in you, I planted a fig tree." [AmerPoR] (21:2) Mr-Ap 92, p. 32.
"Vespers: You thought we didn't know." [AmerPoR] (21:2) Mr-Ap 92, p. 33.
"The White Lilies." [AmerPoR] (21:2) Mr-Ap 92, p. 33.
"The White Rose." [AmerPoR] (21:2) Mr-Ap 92, p. 29.
"Witchgrass." [AmerPoR] (21:2) Mr-Ap 92, p. 31.
2267. GNUP-KRUIP, Valentina
"Rare Spices." [BellArk] (8:4) Jl-Ag 92, p. 21.
2268. GODIN, Deborah
"Long Weekend." [PoetryC] (12:3/4) Jl 92, p. 41.
"Midnight, Mid-August." [PoetryC] (12:3/4) Jl 92, p. 41.
"Second Law." [PoetryC] (12:3/4) Jl 92, p. 41.
2269. GODING, Cecile
"After the Shootout at June & 6th, Joe's Heart Speaks." [SouthernPR] (32:2) Fall 92, p. 56-58.
"Conversation with Lyla." [PoetryNW] (33:1) Spr 92, p. 38-40.
"Enough." [PoetryNW] (33:4) Wint 92-93, p. 45-47.
"Field Trip." [PoetryNW] (33:4) Wint 92-93, p. 43-45.
"The March of the Dung Beetle." [CharR] (18:1) Spr 92, p. 89.
"Waling Glass." [GreensboroR] (53) Wint 92-93, p. 85-87.

"Watching Backwards." [PoetryNW] (33:1) Spr 92, p. 40-41.
"Yankee Doodle." [GeoR] (46:2) Sum 92, p. 236-237.

2270. GODOY, Iliana
"Andamiaje del Viento" (a la danza mexica). [InterPR] (18:2) Fall 92, p. 48.
"Lente Púrpura." [Nuez] (4:10/11) 92, p. 36.
"Ratas." [Nuez] (4:10/11) 92, p. 36.
"Scaffolding of Wind" (to Mexican dance, tr. by Mark Smith-Soto). [InterPR] (18:2) Fall 92, p. 49.

2271. GODREJ, Dinyar
"A Strange Music." [JamesWR] (9:3) Spr 92, p. 12.
"Untitled: Anyone could succumb to those eyes." [JamesWR] (9:3) Spr 92, p. 12.

2272. GOEDICKE, Patricia
"The Arm of Accident." [RiverC] (12:2) Spr 92, p. 43-45.
"Coin of the Realm." [ThRiPo] (39/40) 92-93, p. 89-91.
"Dead Baby." [PraS] (66:2) Sum 92, p. 38-41.
"Occasionally Yes." [CharR] (18:2) Fall 92, p. 64-66.
"On the Porch." [CreamCR] (16:2) Fall 92, p. 62-63.
"One More Time." [ThRiPo] (39/40) 92-93, p. 88-89.
"The Only Mirror." [CharR] (18:2) Fall 92, p. 67-69.
"Tabu." [SenR] (22:1) Spr 92, p. 16-18.
"We." [WestB] (30) 92, p. 22-23.
"Whatever Happens." [PraS] (66:2) Sum 92, p. 36-38.
"When Sheryl Reads Her Poetry." [HampSPR] Wint 92, p. 4-6.
"Where there's a Roadblock." [WillowS] (29) Wint 92, p. 7-9.

2273. GOETT, Lise
"Lemanjá." [PassN] (13:1) Sum 92, p. 14.
"Ode to a Pair of White Gloves." [PassN] (13:1) Sum 92, p. 14.

2274. GOGINS, Michael (Michael K.)
"The Bread Dreams." [Asylum] (7:3/4) 92, p. 25.
"Los Angeles Sequence." [Pearl] (15) Spr-Sum 92, p. 47-48.

2275. GOHORRY, John
"The Anatomist" (From "Amber"). [AntigR] (91) Fall 92, p. 86.
"The Arranger" (From "Amber"). [AntigR] (91) Fall 92, p. 88.
"The Inheritance" (From "Amber"). [AntigR] (91) Fall 92, p. 87.

2276. GOLDBARTH, Albert
"1563." [IndR] (15:1) Spr 92, p. 85-87.
"1954: The Chandelier." [AnotherCM] (24) Fall 92, p. 72-73.
"Alveoli." [Poetry] (161:2) N 92, p. 63-64.
"The Amounts." [Poetry] (161:2) N 92, p. 67-69.
"Architectural." [PoetryE] (33) Spr 92, p. 48.
"Armadillo." [Light] (3) Aut 92, p. 16.
"The Armies of Ignorance Poem." [PoetryNW] (33:4) Wint 92-93, p. 17.
"At 5306." [LaurelR] (26:1) Wint 92, p. 98.
"Believing a Resonant Chord Exists Between His Work and the World, Pieter Bruegel Attempts to Help Banish the Tarantella." [WestHR] (46:3) Fall 92, p. 220-223.
"Bilingual." [Boulevard] (7:1, #19) Spr 92, p. 44-45.
"Blips, Berg, Etc." [AnotherCM] (24) Fall 92, p. 60-61.
"The Book of Speedy." [TriQ] (84) Spr-Sum 92, p. 128-143.
"Change." [PoetryE] (33) Spr 92, p. 47.
"Cholent." [Light] (2) Sum 92, p. 14.
"A Comb in My Hands." [OnTheBus] (4:2/5:1, #10/11) 92, p. 96-97.
"Correlative 101." [NoDaQ] (60:1) Wint 92, p. 53.
"The Counterfeit Earth!" [NewEngR] (14:3) Sum 92, p. 32-34.
"Crystal / Window / Gem." [VirQR] (68:2) Spr 92, p. 304.
"From Out of Another Year's Chaos." [Boulevard] (7:1, #19) Spr 92, p. 48-50.
"From the Committee's Grant Report." [AnotherCM] (24) Fall 92, p. 74.
"G.U.T. and The Other Question." [AnotherCM] (24) Fall 92, p. 62-69.
"Gallery." [OntR] (36) Spr-Sum 92, p. 13-14.
"Is Diss a System!" [NoDaQ] (60:1) Wint 92, p. 54-55.
"The Jewish Poets of Arabic Spain (10th to 13th Centuries), with Chinese Poets Piping Out of Clouds (and Once an Irishman)." [DenQ] (26:3) Wint 92, p. 17-26.
"Life Is Happy." [Boulevard] (7:1, #19) Spr 92, p. 46-47.
"Malokhim." [IndR] (15:1) Spr 92, p. 83-84.
"Melville, in a Letter to Hawthorne." [Light] (4) Wint 92-93, p. 15.

"The Mysteries." [NewEngR] (14:3) Sum 92, p. 29-31.
"Mythic." [AnotherCM] (24) Fall 92, p. 52-54.
"No More Trivia, Please." [PoetryE] (33) Spr 92, p. 49-50.
"Pass It On: An Essay." [Shen] (42:2) Sum 92, p. 25-26.
"The Planets." [AnotherCM] (24) Fall 92, p. 58-59.
"Poem with One Hand on the Bible." [NoDaQ] (60:1) Wint 92, p. 56-58.
"The Point." [OnTheBus] (4:2/5:1, #10/11) 92, p. 97-98.
"Saving the World." [AnotherCM] (24) Fall 92, p. 55-57.
"Seriema Song." [PoetryNW] (33:4) Wint 92-93, p. 15-16.
"Sill Ritual: A Survey." [LaurelR] (26:1) Wint 92, p. 99-101.
"A Slightly Shuffled History of Western Civilization, with Three Moons." [LaurelR] (26:1) Wint 92, p. 96-97.
"Sonnet: 'In true sexual reproduction, . . .'" (for Sarah in her 9th month). [AnotherCM] (24) Fall 92, p. 70-71.
"Stories." [VirQR] (68:2) Spr 92, p. 301-303.
"The Story of Dorsett." [GettyR] (5:4) Aut 92, p. 682-684.
"Substance." [Shen] (42:2) Sum 92, p. 24.
"The Systems." [NewYorker] (68:44) 21 D 92, p. 118.
"Three Degrees of It." [AnotherCM] (24) Fall 92, p. 75-76.
"Time." [PoetryE] (33) Spr 92, p. 51.
"The Tortes." [LaurelR] (26:1) Wint 92, p. 101-102.
"What Photographs Are." [LaurelR] (26:1) Wint 92, p. 102-103.
"When Wild Beasts Charge." [Poetry] (161:2) N 92, p. 65-67.
"Why / Slinky Marie's / Nor / & Why." [Shen] (42:2) Sum 92, p. 22-24.
"The Winds." [PoetryNW] (33:2) Sum 92, p. 8.
"A World Above Suffering." [OntR] (36) Spr-Sum 92, p. 15-19.
"Wrestling With Each Other." [Witness] (6:1) 92, p. 176-179.

2277. GOLDBERG, Barbara
"Coalman" (tr. of Moshe Dor). [Trans] (26) Spr 92, p. 91.
"Fun with Dick." [Light] (1) Spr 92, p. 15.
"A Matter of Choice." [NewEngR] (14:4) Fall 92, p. 207.
"Riddle." [Light] (2) Sum 92, p. 7.

2278. GOLDBERG, Beckian Fritz
"A Day Passes Through the Medium of Identity." [AmerPoR] (21:6) N-D 92, p. 42.
"The Dead Are Faithful." [PoetryNW] (33:2) Sum 92, p. 45-46.
"The Future." [PoetryNW] (33:2) Sum 92, p. 44-45.
"The Gulf." [AmerPoR] (21:6) N-D 92, p. 42.
"Letter to My Twilight." [PoetryNW] (33:2) Sum 92, p. 42-43.
"My Sister Fear." [PoetryNW] (33:2) Sum 92, p. 47.
"One Eye." [PoetryNW] (33:2) Sum 92, p. 43-44.

GOLDBERG, Caryn Mirriam
See MIRRIAM-GOLDBERG, Caryn

2279. GOLDBLATT, Eli
"Folk Tales." [AnotherCM] (23) Spr 92, p. 77.
"On Pornography." [AnotherCM] (23) Spr 92, p. 78-79.

2280. GOLDEMBERG, Isaac
"The Angel of Jealousy" (tr. by David Unger). [RiverS] (36) 92, p. 73.
"La Vida al Contado" (Selection: "Resucitar un Muerto"). [Luz] (2) S 92, p. 29-30.

2281. GOLDENSOHN, Barry
"Dance Music" (Excerpt). [Salm] (94/95) Spr-Sum 92, p. 138-139.
"Lute and Virginal Outdoors." [SouthernR] (28:2) Spr, Ap 92, p. 251.

2282. GOLDFARB, David
"A Tree." [CarolQ] (44:3) Spr-Sum 92, p. 57.

2283. GOLDFARB, Rebecca
"Bezazel Street, Orthodox Quarter." [HangL] (61) 92, p. 95.

2284. GOLDIE, Matthew
"Pinned Up for the Nose." [BrooklynR] (9) 92, p. 91.

2285. GOLDMAN, Judy
"Bob." [QW] (34) Wint-Spr 92, p. 75.
"Passover." [PoetC] (23:2) Wint 92, p. 16-18.

2286. GOLDMAN, Kathleen Zeisler
"May." [OnTheBus] (4:2/5:1, #10/11) 92, p. 99.

2287. GOLDSBERRY, Tripp
"I Have This to Say." [QW] (34) Wint-Spr 92, p. 77.
"The Order of Infirmity." [QW] (34) Wint-Spr 92, p. 78.

2288. GOLDSMITH, Ellen
"Bone Scan." [Footwork] 92, p. 106.
"Daily Life." [Footwork] 92, p. 106.
"Summer Fruit." [SmPd] (29:1, #84) Wint 92, p. 11.
"Well Water." [SmPd] (29:1, #84) Wint 92, p. 11.
"The Year I Lived with My Grandmother." [Footwork] 92, p. 106.
2289. GOLDSTEIN, Dana Leslie
"Tuna Canning Plant in Long Beach, Long Island." [NewEngR] (14:2) Spr 92, p. 149.
2290. GOLDSTEIN, Laurence
"Cold Reading." [TexasR] (13:1/2) Spr-Sum 92, p. 89-92.
"Conceptual Art." [OnTheBus] (4:2/5:1, #10/11) 92, p. 100.
"Preschool Visitation." [Iowa] (22:1) Wint 92, p. 78-80.
2291. GOLFFING, Francis
"A Moment in June" (tr. of Günter Eich). [Trans] (26) Spr 92, p. 112-113.
2292. GOMEZ, Magdalena
"Mami." [Callaloo] (15:4) Fall 92, p. 959-960.
2293. GOMEZ-FORONDA, Carolyn
"You Don't Need Binoculars to Be a Bird Watcher." [PoetL] (87:1) Spr 92, p. 20.
2294. GOMEZ ROSA, Alexis
"Billboard" (tr. by Elizabeth Macklin). [Nimrod] (36:1) Fall-Wint 92, p. 76.
"Great Distance Between Two Walls" (tr. by Elizabeth Macklin). [Nimrod] (36:1) Fall-Wint 92, p. 77.
2295. GONÇALVES, Egito
"Dedikation #5" (tr. by Alexis Levitin). [Agni] (36) 92, p. 132.
2296. GONNELLO, Larry
"No Armor Protection." [HangL] (60) 92, p. 85.
2297. GONTAREK, Leonard
"The Existence of God." [PaintedB] (45) 92, p. 30-31.
"The Pillow Book of Leonard Gontarek." [PaintedB] (45) 92, p. 32-37.
"The Possible." [PaintedB] (48) 92, p. 32.
2298. GONZALEZ, Angel
"Counter-Order (Poetics That I Announce on Certain Days)" (tr. by Steven Ford Brown and Gutierrez Revuelta). [SenR] (22:1) Spr 92, p. 53.
"The Day Has Gone" (tr. by Steven Ford Brown and Gutierrez Revuelta). [SenR] (22:1) Spr 92, p. 56.
"Here, Madrid, 1954" (tr. by Steven Ford Brown and Gutierrez Revuelta). [SenR] (22:1) Spr 92, p. 57.
"Zero City" (tr. by Steven Ford Brown and Gutierrez Revuelta). [SenR] (22:1) Spr 92, p. 54-55.
2299. GONZALEZ, Miguel
"Primera Elegia para Ofelia." [LindLM] (11:4) D 92, p. 4.
2300. GONZALEZ, Ray
"Black Wasp." [Ploughs] (18:1) Spr 92, p. 196.
"Two Wolf Poems." [Americas] (20:3/4) Fall-Wint 92, p. 201-202.
"Walk" (for John Brandi). [Americas] (20:3/4) Fall-Wint 92, p. 200.
2301. GONZALEZ, Sara
"Girón, La Victoria!" [Areíto] (3:10/11) Abril 92, p. 79.
2302. GONZALEZ-T., César A.
"Calvary Cemetery, East Los." [BilingR] (17:1) Ja-Ap 92, p. 80.
"Of Thee I Sing." [BilingR] (17:1) Ja-Ap 92, p. 79.
"The Way of the Rose." [BilingR] (17:1) Ja-Ap 92, p. 80.
2303. GOOBIE, Beth
"Behind the Bible Face." [Grain] (20:1) Spr 92, p. 143.
"My Father's World." [Event] (21:3) Fall 92, p. 51.
2304. GOOCH, Amy Alley
"Cemetery." [PoetryUSA] (24) 92, p. 30.
"Comrades." [PoetryUSA] (24) 92, p. 31.
"Enemy." [PoetryUSA] (24) 92, p. 32.
"Fragile." [PoetryUSA] (24) 92, p. 30.
"Frantic." [PoetryUSA] (24) 92, p. 32.
2305. GOODELL, Larry
"For Robert Duncan." [Contact] (10:62/63/64) Fall 91-Spr 92, p. 81.
2306. GOODIN, Thom
"The Oaxaca Lies." [Poem] (68) N 92, p. 44-45.

2307. GOODISON, Lorna
"Birth Stone." [LitR] (35:4) Sum 92, p. 483.
"Bun Down Cross Roads." [LitR] (35:4) Sum 92, p. 482.
"In the Mountains of the Moon Uganda." [LitR] (35:4) Sum 92, p. 484.
"Love Song of Cane in Three Parts." [Nimrod] (36:1) Fall-Wint 92, p. 69.
"On Becoming a Tiger." [LitR] (35:4) Sum 92, p. 484-485.
"Sometimes on a Day Such as This." [Nimrod] (36:1) Fall-Wint 92, p. 67-68.
"Thyme" (from "The Garden of the Women Once Fallen"). [Nimrod] (36:1) Fall - Wint 92, p. 70.
"White Birds." [LitR] (35:4) Sum 92, p. 483-484.
2308. GOODMAN, Loren
"This Business." [NewYorkQ] (48) 92, p. 69.
2309. GOODMAN, Michael
"The Bulldog." [OnTheBus] (4:2/5:1, #10/11) 92, p. 101.
2310. GOODMAN, Miriam
"Incentives / Sales Meeting." [SingHM] (20) 92, p. 76.
"Losing the Words." [Poetry] (160:2) My 92, p. 71.
2311. GOODWIN, June
"Beside Herself." [Pearl] (16) Fall 92, p. 33.
"Once Upon a Floor." [ColEng] (54:2) F 92, p. 163.
2312. GOODWIN, Rufus
"Night Is Witness." [Noctiluca] (1:2) Wint 92 [on cover: Wint 93], p. 24.
2313. GORBANEVSKAYA, Natalya
"And only the non-Russian name is not yet strewn" (tr. by Lara Shapiro). [GrahamHR] (16) Fall 92, p. 10.
"In the far away long ago far" (tr. by Lara Shapiro). [GrahamHR] (16) Fall 92, p. 11.
"In the far away long ago far" (tr. by Lara Shapiro). [Vis] (38) 92, p. 29.
"The soul of this love no longer even breathes" (tr. by Lara Shapiro). [GrahamHR] (16) Fall 92, p. 12.
2314. GORCZYNSKI, Renata
"Incorporeal Ruler" (tr. of Adam Zagajewski, w. Benjamin Ivry and C. K. Williams). [Thrpny] (48) Wint 92, p. 4.
2315. GORDON, Charlotte
"Weight Watchers." [Kalliope] (14:3) 92, p. 63.
2316. GORDON, Kevin
"I'm Telling You." [DenQ] (26:3) Wint 92, p. 27.
2317. GORDON, Kirpal
"Dueños Means Dreams in Spanish." [BlackBR] (15) Spr-Sum 92, p. 6-9.
"Enrich Your Vocabulary Now." [SlipS] (12) 92, p. 83-84.
2318. GORDON, Myles
"Inspiration without Revision." [BlackBR] (15) Spr-Sum 92, p. 48-49.
2319. GORDON, Robert M.
"Edges." [SoDakR] (30:4) Wint 92, p. 50.
"Fiddler Crab." [SoDakR] (30:4) Wint 92, p. 51.
2320. GORDON, Sarah
"Traveling Light: In Pursuit of the Serial Killer." [NegC] (12:1/2) 92, p. 48-50.
2321. GORDON, Stephanie Boehmer
"Stars." [Crucible] (28) Fall 92, p. 57-58.
2322. GORENBERG, Gershom
"The Random Dictionary" (Section II). [NewYorkQ] (47) 92, p. 65.
"The Random Dictionary: Last Words." [NewYorkQ] (49) 92, p. 92.
2323. GOREY, E. W.
"Sick Joke." [Light] (3) Aut 92, p. 25.
2324. GORHAM, Sarah
"Bisecting a Water Lily." [AmerV] (26) Spr 92, p. 59.
"Cautionary Tale, 3 A.M." [MissouriR] (15:3) 92, p. 52.
"Chinese Ideogram" (after Fenollosa — from "The Dragon's Lullaby," a sequence of 50 sonnets tracing the rise and fall of the last empress of China). [Sparrow] (59) S 92, p. 17.
"Clear Air Turbulence." [MissouriR] (15:3) 92, p. 46.
"Concubine of the Lowest Rank." [KenR] (NS 14:1) Wint 92, p. 35.
"The Dying Empress" (from "The Dragon's Lullaby," a sequence of 50 sonnets tracing the rise and fall of the last empress of China). [Sparrow] (59) S 92, p. 16.

"The Empress Receives the Head of a Taiping Rebel" (from "The Dragon's Lullaby," a sequence of 50 sonnets tracing the rise and fall of the last empress of China). [Sparrow] (59) S 92, p. 17.
"Hot Water." [MissouriR] (15:3) 92, p. 48.
"National Enquirer." [OhioR] (48) 92, p. 23.
"Princess Parade" (from "The Dragon's Lullaby," a sequence of 50 sonnets tracing the rise and fall of the last empress of China). [Sparrow] (59) S 92, p. 16.
"Still Life: Sarasota, Florida." [MissouriR] (15:3) 92, p. 47.
"The Tension Zone." [MissouriR] (15:3) 92, p. 45.
"Tiptoe." [MissouriR] (15:3) 92, p. 49.
"Visit from the Footbinder." [KenR] (NS 14:1) Wint 92, p. 35.
"Water House, Shakertown." [MissouriR] (15:3) 92, p. 50-51.

2325. GORMAN, John
"Memory, Middle Age." [SpoonRQ] (17:3/4) Sum-Fall 92, p. 72.
"Wild Mustard." [SpoonRQ] (17:3/4) Sum-Fall 92, p. 71.

2326. GORMAN, LeRoy
"Devotionals" (3 selections). [Quarry] (41:2) Spr 92, p. 61-62.

2327. GORRELL, Nancy
"The First Time." [EngJ] (81:8) D 92, p. 85.

2328. GOSNELL, W. C.
"Flash Fire in the Grass." [NegC] (12:1/2) 92, p. 51.

GOTIN, Renee Maurin
See MAURIN-GOTIN, Renee

2329. GOTTESMAN, Carl A.
"The Meran Defense." [Salm] (93) Wint 92, p. 165-177.

2330. GOTTLIEB, Michael
"The Gray Review" (Selections: iii, v-vi, xi, xiii). [CentralP] (21) Spr 92, p. 161 - 162.

2331. GOULBOURNE, Jean
"Dilemma." [LitR] (35:4) Sum 92, p. 486.
"Preservation." [LitR] (35:4) Sum 92, p. 487.

2332. GOULD, Janice
"Beneath My Heart." [Jacaranda] (6:1/2) Wint-Spr 92, p. 74.

2333. GOULD, Roberta
"Entre Silencios." [Nuez] (4:10/11) 92, p. 25.

2334. GOURLAY, Elizabeth
"The Lack." [CanLit] (134) Aut 92, p. 75-76.

2335. GOVE, Jim
"Eskimos Love You." [WormR] (32:1, #125) 92, p. 1.
"Moto Magic." [WormR] (32:1, #125) 92, p. 2-3.

2336. GOWLAND, Mary Lee
"Kisses." [RagMag] (10:2) 92, p. 78.
"Lester's Widow." [RagMag] (10:2) 92, p. 79.

2337. GOYER, Eric
"Against the wind." [Amelia] (7:1, #20) 92, p. 8.

2338. GRABILL, James
"On the Beach in Heavy Wind at the Edge of a Grain of Sand." [SoDakR] (30:4) Wint 92, p. 54-55.

2339. GRABINER, Gene
"Non-Controversial Lunch." [Elf] (2:1) Spr 92, p. 39.

2340. GRACE, Susan Andrews
"Overwhelming Gratitude" (honourable mention, Grain Prose Poem contest). [Grain] (20:4) Wint 92, p. 16.

2341. GRADY, Carolyn Kieber
"North Fork of the Ausable River." [Blueline] (13) 92, p. 56.

2342. GRADY, James
"Suicide Sale." [Confr] (48/49) Spr-Sum 92, p. 209.

2343. GRADY, John
"Jack and Bill Go Sailing." [MoodySI] (27) Spr 92, p. 23-26.

2344. GRADY, Ross
"Cop." [CarolQ] (44:3) Spr-Sum 92, p. 103.

2345. GRAF, Nico
"The Gloves from the Camp" (tr. by W. Martin). [Stand] (33:4) Aut 92, p. 113.

2346. GRAFÉ, Robert
"Ravels" (tr. by Yann Lovelock). [Stand] (33:4) Aut 92, p. 5.

2347. GRAFF, Herman
"In Río de Janeiro." [Lactuca] (15) Mr 92, p. 26.
"The Last Stop." [Lactuca] (15) Mr 92, p. 26-27.
"Protocol in Romania." [Lactuca] (15) Mr 92, p. 25-26.
"Thicket Objects." [Lactuca] (15) Mr 92, p. 24-25.
2348. GRAFTON, Grace
"Castle Rock." [BellArk] (8:3) My-Je 92, p. 23.
"To Touch That Water." [BellArk] (8:3) My-Je 92, p. 23.
"Turning Gold." [BellArk] (8:3) My-Je 92, p. 23.
"Watching the Pond, Ideas Take Their Proper Place." [BellArk] (8:3) My-Je 92, p. 23.
2349. GRAHAM, David
"A Lecture on Whitman." [Caliban] (11) 92, p. 153-154.
2350. GRAHAM, Desmond
"Kristallnacht." [MalR] (99) Sum 92, p. 56.
"She Is Making a Word." [MalR] (99) Sum 92, p. 55.
"Small Things" (tr. of Anna Kamienska, w. Tomasz P. Krzeszowski). [Verse] (8:3/9:1) Wint-Spr 92, p. 110.
2351. GRAHAM, Jorie
"Event Horizon" (For Bei Dao, June 1989). [YaleR] (80:3) Jl 92, p. 53-57.
"History." [AntR] (50:1/2) Wint-Spr 92, p. 444-445.
"Manifest Destiny" (For Diana Michener). [GrandS] (11:2, #42) 92, p. 65-78.
"Notes on the Reality of the Self." [NewYorker] (68:27) 24 Ag 92, p. 28.
"The Right to Life." [Thrpny] (50) Sum 92, p. 24-25.
"What the Instant Contains" (Lyle Van Waning, 1922-1988). [Epoch] (41:2) 92, p. 254-259.
2352. GRAHAM, Matthew
"Snapshots from the Southeast." [IndR] (15:2) Fall 92, p. 143-144.
2353. GRAHAM, Neile
"Fool's Gold on the Snow." [Grain] (20:2) Sum 92, p. 102-103.
"Tuppence in Pocket." [Grain] (20:2) Sum 92, p. 104.
"White Lies" (for Christine). [CanLit] (133) Sum 92, p. 37-38.
2354. GRAHAM, Taylor
"Anita at 12." [OxfordM] (6:2) Fall-Wint 90, p. 61.
"December 3 AM." [PaintedHR] (6) Spr 92, p. 8.
"Like a Prayer" (Mexico City earthquake). [Amelia] (7:1, #20) 92, p. 144.
"The Mother of Baby Elise." [OxfordM] (8:2) Fall-Wint 92, p. 13.
"Mushrooms in Drought." [OxfordM] (6:2) Fall-Wint 90, p. 62.
"On the Gulf." [Contact] (10:62/63/64) Fall 91-Spr 92, p. 53.
"Out of the Desert: Platoon Minus One" (for a Marine Missing on Maneuvers). [Amelia] (7:1, #20) 92, p. 144-146.
"Pickin's" (Independent Hill, Va). [Sonora] (22/23) Spr 92, p. 32.
"Roadkill Collection." [TarRP] (30:2) Spr 91, p. 27.
"Seeing Bighorn." [Parting] (5:2) Wint 92-93, p. 31.
"Tomaseño." [Contact] (10:62/63/64) Fall 91-Spr 92, p. 53.
"Top of the News." [CoalC] (5) My 92, p. 18.
2355. GRAHAM, Valerie
"Behind Glass" (Winner, Annual Free Verse Contest, 1991). [AnthNEW] (4) 92, p. 24.
2356. GRAHAM, Vicki
"Cape Blanco." [Poetry] (160:6) S 92, p. 316.
"Positions." [Poetry] (160:6) S 92, p. 313-315.
2357. GRANATO, Carol
"In the Stout Face of Winter." [Epiphany] (3:1) Ja (Wint) 92, p. 16.
"Seaside Geometry." [Epiphany] (3:1) Ja (Wint) 92, p. 16.
"Sun & Moon." [Epiphany] (3:1) Ja (Wint) 92, p. 15.
"To Begin Again." [Epiphany] (3:1) Ja (Wint) 92, p. 15.
2358. GRANT, Frances
"Great Mother." [Pembroke] (24) 92, p. 126.
"Head of a Bodhissatva." [Pembroke] (24) 92, p. 122.
"Home Thoughts to Abiquiu." [Pembroke] (24) 92, p. 125.
"Instant in Eternity." [Pembroke] (24) 92, p. 131.
"The Lizard." [Pembroke] (24) 92, p. 133.
"Opus." [Pembroke] (24) 92, p. 134.
"Pampas in Autumn." [Pembroke] (24) 92, p. 124.
"Passage by Night." [Pembroke] (24) 92, p. 132.

"Rain Forest." [Pembroke] (24) 92, p. 123.
"Rain in the Night." [Pembroke] (24) 92, p. 127.
"The Seasons." [Pembroke] (24) 92, p. 130.
"Sinai." [Pembroke] (24) 92, p. 129.
"Sonnet: Say who I am, if I am not my heart." [Pembroke] (24) 92, p. 128.
"Thoughts in Assisi." [Pembroke] (24) 92, p. 121.

2359. GRANT, Paul
"Betrayal." [NegC] (12:3) 92, p. 77-78.
"Courtesy." [GeoR] (46:1) Spr 92, p. 140-141.
"Joshua." [SewanR] (100:1) Wint 92, p. 60.
"Milenburg Joys." [NewDeltaR] (8:1) Fall 90-Wint 91, p. 27-28.
"Once Upon a Time." [SewanR] (100:2) Spr 92, p. 268-269.
"Over Your Shoulder." [GreensboroR] (52) Sum 92, p. 41.
"The People Upstairs." [SewanR] (100:2) Spr 92, p. 270.

2360. GRANT, Steven M.
"Search for Comparison." [Writer] (105:12) D 92, p. 19.

2361. GRASSETTI, Nelida
"Presencia en Mi." [Luz] (1) My 92, p. 31.
"Sobre un grito primario, huracanado." [Luz] (1) My 92, p. 30.

2362. GRAVES, Michael P.
"Job the Rhetor." [ChrC] (109:15) 29 Ap 92, p. 455.

2363. GRAVES, Paul
"As Catullus Wrote" (from "Apollo in the Snow," tr. of Aleksandr Kushner, w. Carol Ueland). [Arion] 3d series (1:2) Spr 91, p. 128.
"A Party on Women's Day" (tr. of Olesia Nikolaeva, w. Carol Ueland). [KenR] (NS 14:4) Fall 92, p. 117-118.
"Seven Beginnings" (tr. of Olesia Nikolaeva, w. Carol Ueland). [KenR] (NS 14:4) Fall 92, p. 115-116.
"Untitled: Here, everything gets eaten: drippings, marinade" (tr. of Olesia Nikolaeva, w. Carol Ueland). [KenR] (NS 14:4) Fall 92, p. 117.

2364. GRAVES, Steven
"Concessions in the Garden." [WestHR] (46:3) Fall 92 [i.e. (46:4) Wint 92], p. 425.
"Concessions to Love." [WestHR] (46:3) Fall 92 [i.e. (46:4) Wint 92], p. 424.
"New Years Eve in Mazatlan." [WebR] (16) Fall 92, p. 100.
"Recessional." [ParisR] (34:125) Wint 92, p. 127.
"A Run Along the Blackened Rhine." [ParisR] (34:125) Wint 92, p. 124-125.
"Sandbar on the Colorado." [ParisR] (34:125) Wint 92, p. 125-126.

2365. GRAY, Cecile
"Cutting the Strings." [SpiritSH] (57) Spr-Sum 92, p. 50.
"An Easter Fire." [SpiritSH] (57) Spr-Sum 92, p. 51.
"The Resurrection." [SpiritSH] (57) Spr-Sum 92, p. 52.
"The Return." [SpiritSH] (57) Spr-Sum 92, p. 53.
"Trees Behind Wrought-Iron Fences." [SouthernR] (28:4) Aut, O 92, p. 852-853.

2366. GRAY, Douglas
"Baby Born with Tattoo Dated 1817" ("National Enquirer" series). [RagMag] (10:1) 92, p. 62-63.
"Circus Hippo Swallows Dwarf" (from the "National Enquirer" series). [SpoonRQ] (17:3/4) Sum-Fall 92, p. 112-113.
"Mother's Ghost Saves Doomed Skydiver" (tabloid headline). [FloridaR] (18:1) Spr - Sum 92, p. 30-31.
"Piranha Kill Fifteen at Outdoor Baptism" (from the "National Enquirer" series). [SpoonRQ] (17:3/4) Sum-Fall 92, p. 110-111.
"Twelve Singers Seduced by Choir Director" (from the "National Enquirer" series). [SpoonRQ] (17:3/4) Sum-Fall 92, p. 114.

2367. GRAY, Libba Moore
"The Uncovered Dish." [Agni] (36) 92, p. 57-62.

2368. GRAY, Martin
"Death of Villeneuve" (8 May 1982). [Event] (21:2) Sum 92, p. 63-66.

2369. GRAY, Mary
"Tomatoes." [WilliamMR] (30) 92, p. 93.

2370. GRAY, P. W. (*See also* GRAY, Patrick Worth)
"Foreclosure." [OxfordM] (8:1) Spr-Sum 92, p. 12.

2371. GRAY, Patrick Worth (*See also* GRAY, P. W.)
"1948." [ChrC] (109:4) 29 Ja 92, p. 96.
"Nebraska." [MidwQ] (34:1) Aut 92, p. 64.
"Traffic Incident." [ColEng] (53:7) N 91, p. 793.

"Wade in the Water." [WebR] (16) Fall 92, p. 106.
"Where the Light Shivers." [CapeR] (27:1) Spr 92, p. 12.
2372. GRAYHURST, Allison
"Crow." [AntigR] (89) Spr 92, p. 52.
GRAZIA, Emilio de
See DeGRAZIA, Emilio
2373. GREALY, Lucy
"Shame." [Ploughs] (18:4) Wint 92-93, p. 151-152.
"When It Happens." [Ploughs] (18:4) Wint 92-93, p. 149.
"X Marks the Spot." [Ploughs] (18:4) Wint 92-93, p. 150.
2374. GREEN, Benjamin
"January: New Year's Bike Ride." [BellArk] (8:6) N-D 92, p. 13.
"March: Tree Planting." [BellArk] (8:6) N-D 92, p. 13.
2375. GREEN, Daniel
"Albatross" (Hood Island Galapagos). [Outbr] (23) 92, p. 65.
2376. GREEN, David H.
"While sailing on the Tappan Zee." [Light] (2) Sum 92, p. 29.
2377. GREEN, Jaki Shelton
"Clinton Used to Sing." [Crucible] (28) Fall 92, p. 60-61.
2378. GREEN, Jim
"Dear Mac." [Grain] (20:3) Fall 92, p. 30-31.
"Mountain Likker." [Grain] (20:3) Fall 92, p. 32.
2379. GREEN, Joseph
"My Neighbor's New Mercury Vapor Lamp Washes Out the Stars." [DogRR] (11:1) Spr-Sum 92, p. 9.
2380. GREEN, Kelly
"Billy Was the Babysitter." [Lactuca] (16) Ag 92, p. 34-35.
"Church in Chester Creek." [Lactuca] (16) Ag 92, p. 35.
"Fun." [Pearl] (15) Spr-Sum 92, p. 62.
2381. GREEN, Loweda B.
"Three Dresses." [Crucible] (28) Fall 92, p. 8.
2382. GREEN, Paul
"Green" (Selections: 5-6). [Os] (34) Spr 92, p. 12.
2383. GREEN, Peter
"The Clashing Rocks" (The Argonautica, Book II, lines 536-610, tr. of Apollonius of Rhodes). [SouthernHR] (26:1) Wint 92, p. 9-10.
2384. GREEN, Sherry
"Defiance." [PacificR] (11) 92-93, p. 84.
2385. GREEN, W. H.
"Sufficiency." [CumbPR] (11:2) Spr 92, p. 36.
2386. GREENBAUM, Jessica
"Back at the Cemetery." [PraS] (66:1) Spr 92, p. 56-57.
"Blown-Away-Roof." [KenR] (NS 14:2) Spr 92, p. 27-29.
"Early Morning of an Argument, in Spring, about When to Have Children." [PraS] (66:1) Spr 92, p. 58.
2387. GREENBERG, Alvin
"Cigar-Store Indians." [GeoR] (46:1) Spr 92, p. 13.
"Crystal Night." [ColR] (9:1) Spr-Sum 92, p. 49.
"The Fastest Thing Alive." [GeoR] (46:1) Spr 92, p. 14.
"Hurry Back." [GettyR] (5:3) Sum 92, p. 513.
"In Those Crystalline Moments." [NoAmR] (277:6) N-D 92, p. 7.
"Last Things." [ColR] (9:1) Spr-Sum 92, p. 50.
"McGrath Bros. Funeral Home." [Witness] (6:2) 92, p. 123.
"Northern Lights." [Shen] (42:3) Fall 92, p. 108.
"Saturday Matinees." [GeoR] (46:1) Spr 92, p. 12-13.
"Shadows." [Shen] (42:3) Fall 92, p. 109.
"Starlight, Starbright." [OhioR] (48) 92, p. 22.
2388. GREENBLATT, Ray
"Immigrant." [MidwQ] (34:1) Aut 92, p. 64-65.
2389. GREENE, Janice R.
"Grace Notes." [Obs] (7:1/2) Spr-Sum 92, p. 81.
"Prayer." [Obs] (7:1/2) Spr-Sum 92, p. 80-81.
"Tithes to the Heart." [Kalliope] (15:1) 92, p. 26-27.
2390. GREENE, Jeffrey
"Arolla." [Poetry] (160:6) S 92, p. 335.
"Headlands." [ManhatPR] (14) [92?], p. 28.

"The Whitestone Bridge." [ManhatPR] (14) [92?], p. 28-29.

2391. GREENE, Renee
"Chamber Music." [CapeR] (27:2) Fall 92, p. 17.

2392. GREENE, Robin
"Dehorning the Bull." [CarolQ] (44:2) Wint 92, p. 74-75.

2393. GREENFIELD, Robert
"Perspicacious." [NewYorkQ] (47) 92, p. 71-72.

2394. GREENHAW, Wayne
"The Death Mask of Frida." [NegC] (12:1/2) 92, p. 52-53.

2395. GREENING, John
"A Fen Blow." [Verse] (9:3) Wint 92, p. 128.

2396. GREENLEY, Emily
"Now Begin Without." [HarvardA] (125th Anniversary Issue) F 92, p. 20.
"Two-Step." [HarvardA] (125th Anniversary Issue) F 92, p. 20.

2397. GREENWALD, Martha
"Beginning Ballroom Dance 101: Foxtrot to Rumba." [PoetL] (87:1) Spr 92, p. 45 - 47.

2398. GREENWALD, Roger
"Old Cities in Auvergne" (tr. of Rolf Jacobsen). [Trans] (26) Spr 92, p. 93.
"Sand" (tr. of Rolf Jacobsen). [Trans] (26) Spr 92, p. 92.

2399. GREENWAY, William
"Anniversary." [SouthernHR] (26:2) Spr 92, p. 129.
"A Blue Easterly." [CinPR] (23) Wint 91-92, p. 14.
"Bus Stations in August." [CapeR] (27:2) Fall 92, p. 11.
"Disserth." [SouthernR] (28:2) Spr, Ap 92, p. 254.
"Hardheads" (for Matt). [PoetryNW] (33:4) Wint 92-93, p. 11.
"History." [PoetC] (23:2) Wint 92, p. 32.
"How the Dead Bury the Dead." [AmerPoR] (21:1) Ja-F 92, p. 6.
"In the Old Neighborhood." [SouthernR] (28:2) Spr, Ap 92, p. 255.
"White Horse in Snow." [PoetC] (23:2) Wint 92, p. 31.

2400. GREER, Michael
"Disturbances." [Confr] (50) Fall 92, p. 290.

2401. GREGER, Debora
"The Garden." [Pequod] (33) 92, p. 30.
"The Hustler de Paris." [NewYorker] (68:39) 16 N 92, p. 104.
"Leaves of Asphalt" (illustrated by a "Construction," also by Debora Greger). [MassR] (23:1) Spr 92, p. 78-79.
"Miranda on the British Isles." [WestHR] (46:1) Spr 92, p. 82-83.
"Miranda's Drowned Book." [AmerV] (26) Spr 92, p. 44-46.
"Off-Season at the Edge of the World." [NewYorker] (68:5) 23 Mr 92, p. 36.
"The Right Whale in Iowa." [WestHR] (46:1) Spr 92, p. 81.
"The Sadness of the Subtropics." [KenR] (NS 14:4) Fall 92, p. 163-164.
"Tapestry." [SewanR] (100:3) Sum 92, p. 372-373.
"There Now." [Nat] (255:19) 7 D 92, p. 714.
"Three Graces" (after Canova). [Pequod] (33) 92, p. 29.
"Les Très Riches Heures de Florida." [Pequod] (33) 92, p. 31-33.
"Under Cancer." [SewanR] (100:3) Sum 92, p. 374.
"Wind Wrapped in Snow." [KenR] (NS 14:4) Fall 92, p. 164-165.

2402. GREGG, Linda
"Aphrodite and the Nature of Art." [Atlantic] (270:1) Jl 92, p. 52.
"Caught in Mortal Heat." [NewL] (58:4) 92, p. 141.
"The Ninth Dawn." [Antaeus] (69) Aut 92, p. 109.
"No More Marriages." [NewEngR] (14:4) Fall 92, p. 225.
"Nothing Strange." [NewL] (58:4) 92, p. 140.
"The Thing That Continues." [NewL] (58:4) 92, p. 142.

GRÉGOIRE, Erma Saint
See SAINT-GRÉGOIRE, Erma

2403. GREGOR, Arthur
"White" (Château de la Motte). [Nat] (254:5) 10 F 92, p. 172.

2404. GREGORIO, Louis
"And One Hand to Hold the Map." [Amelia] (7:1, #20) 92, p. 17.

2405. GREGORIO, Renée
"The End Is Lit." [Noctiluca] (1:2) Wint 92 [on cover: Wint 93], p. 44.

2406. GREGORY, Carolyn
"Beginnings" (for Thomas Miller). [Epiphany] (3:2) Ap (Spr) 92, p. 104-105.
"Dark Morning." [Epiphany] (3:2) Ap (Spr) 92, p. 104.

"Farm Woman at Dusk." [Epiphany] (3:2) Ap (Spr) 92, p. 105-106.
"Old Man on Porch" (after a photo by Bernice Abbot). [Epiphany] (3:2) Ap (Spr) 92, p. 103.
"Recovery." [Noctiluca] (1:1) Spr 92, p. 26-27.
"The Sea with No End." [Noctiluca] (1:1) Spr 92, p. 27-28.

2407. GREGORY, David
"The Morning After." [Bogg] (65) 92, p. 55.

2408. GREGORY, Eric
"This Poem." [BellR] (15:2) Fall 92, p. 43.

2409. GREGORY, Robert
"Thomas Jefferson's Garden of White Machines." [Caliban] (11) 92, p. 138-140.

2410. GREIG, Andrew
"The Heretical Buddha: Three Extracts." [Verse] (9:3) Wint 92, p. 66-74.

2411. GRELL, Terri Lee
"Purple Crayon." [CoalC] (5) My 92, p. 19.

2412. GRENIER, Arpine Konyalian
"Nothing Is Dirtier Than Virginity" (— Desnos). [ChironR] (11:3) Aut 92, p. 2.
"Orestes Weeps." [ChironR] (11:3) Aut 92, p. 2.
"Things In You We Wish Were Us." [ChironR] (11:3) Aut 92, p. 2.

2413. GRENNAN, Eamon
"Birthday." [NewYorker] (68:32) 28 S 92, p. 56.
"Bubbles." [NewYorker] (68:15) 1 Je 92, p. 36.
"Cuckoo." [Nat] (254:12) 30 Mr 92, p. 423.
"Day's Work." [NewYorker] (68:7) 6 Ap 92, p. 36.
"Journey." [Thrpny] (51) Fall 92, p. 11.
"Snails." [Nat] (255:2) 13 Jl 92, p. 67.
"Whistling in the Dark." [NewYorker] (68:43) 14 D 92, p. 86-87.

2414. GREY, John
"The Naturalist." [ChironR] (11:1) Spr 92, p. 23.
"On Tour." [Bogg] (65) 92, p. 14.
"Positioning Myself." [Plain] (13:1) Fall 92, p. 12.
"Visiting My Ex-Wife and Her New Husband." [ChironR] (11:2) Sum 92, p. 17.
"The Whitman Research." [ChamLR] (10/11) Spr-Fall 92, p. 197-198.
"The Wings of Extinction." [SmPd] (29:3, #86) Fall 92, p. 12.

2415. GREY, Lucinda
"Sábado de Gloria." [WillowS] (29) Wint 92, p. 20-21.

2416. GREY, Robert
"Guadalupé." [SycamoreR] (4:1) Wint 92, p. 26.

2417. GREY, Thomas C.
"Poor Villanelle." [NegC] (12:1/2) 92, p. 187.

2418. GRIBBLE, John
"From a Doorway at Angel's Gate" (for Miwako). [Pearl] (16) Fall 92, p. 58.

2419. GRICE, Gordon
"The Shadows." [LouisL] (9:2) Fall 92, p. 46.

2420. GRIFFIN, James
"Interstate." [MidwQ] (33:3) Spr 92, p. 313-314.

2421. GRIFFIN, Kate
"Flight." [LitR] (35:3) Spr 92, p. 373.

2422. GRIFFIN, Maureen Ryan
"Such Foolishness." [Kalliope] (14:3) 92, p. 11.
"When the Leaves Are in the Water." [Crucible] (28) Fall 92, p. 44-45.

2423. GRIFFIN, S. A.
"It." [MoodySI] (27) Spr 92, p. 48.
"There's Always Fear in All of Your Love Songs." [Pearl] (15) Spr-Sum 92, p. 13.

2424. GRIFFIN, Shaun T.
"Those People." [Grain] (20:2) Sum 92, p. 106.

2425. GRIFFIN, Susan
"In the Path of the Ideal." [CityLR] (5) 92, p. 77-78.

2426. GRIFFIN, Walter
"Clocks." [Plain] (12:3) Spr 92, p. 16.
"Clocks." [SouthernR] (28:3) Sum, Jl 92, p. 643.
"The Dark Eaters." [Nimrod] (35:2) Spr-Sum 92, p. 94.
"The Dark Eaters." [Plain] (13:1) Fall 92, p. 25.
"First Bath." [SouthernR] (28:3) Sum, Jl 92, p. 643-644.
"In This Suspect Light." [SouthernR] (28:3) Sum, Jl 92, p. 645-646.
"My Stepfather's Eyebrows." [PacificR] (11) 92-93, p. 109.

"Night Trains." [Asylum] (7:3/4) 92, p. 45.
"The Season of the Falling Face." [Nimrod] (35:2) Spr-Sum 92, p. 95.
"The Season of the Falling Face." [PacificR] (11) 92-93, p. 108.
"The Season of the Falling Face." [SouthernR] (28:3) Sum, Jl 92, p. 644-645.
"The Season of the Falling Face." [SycamoreR] (4:1) Wint 92, p. 37.
"The Secrets of Ballroom Dancing." [Nimrod] (35:2) Spr-Sum 92, p. 93.
"The Secrets of Ballroom Dancing." [NoDaQ] (60:4) Fall 92, p. 73.
"The Secrets of Ballroom Dancing." [Plain] (12:3) Spr 92, p. 16.

2427. GRIFFITH, D. Gregory
"Elegy for a Tabloid Cover Girl." [CinPR] (23) Wint 91-92, p. 64.

2428. GRIFFITH, Gail
"Dolce Spazio, Los Gatos, CA." [Vis] (39) 92, p. 41.

2429. GRIFFITH, Kevin
"Apology." [MidwQ] (33:2) Wint 92, p. 198.
"Dusk: Public Swimming Pool after Closing." [LullwaterR] (3:2) Spr 92, p. 27.
"Rain, Light, Architecture." [PoetC] (24:1) Fall 92, p. 15.
"The Shower" (Bejing, 1990). [MinnR] (39) Fall-Wint 92-93, p. 13.
"Sin." [MidwQ] (33:2) Wint 92, p. 199.
"Sleep Mining." [Ascent] (16:3) Spr 92, p. 14.
"Storm Guard #1005 Receives Orders to Liquidate Corpses and Destroy Evidence." [NewYorkQ] (49) 92, p. 96.
"Waking." [Ascent] (16:3) Spr 92, p. 15.

2430. GRIFFITHS, Sharon
"From These Fires." [Rohwedder] (7) Spr-Sum 92, p. 42.

2431. GRIGG, Phoebe
"Because You're Drunk." [Bogg] (65) 92, p. 18.

2432. GRIM, Jessica
"Diminishment Falls." [Talisman] (9) Fall 92, p. 216-218.

2433. GRIMES, Linda Sue
"Iron Robert." [DogRR] (11:2, #22) Fall-Wint 92, p. 41.

2434. GRIMM, Reinhold
"April" (tr. of Hans Magnus Enzensberger). [Pembroke] (24) 92, p. 30.
"At Fifty" (tr. of Walter Helmut Fritz). [Pembroke] (24) 92, p. 57.
"Atlantis" (tr. of Walter Helmut Fritz). [Pembroke] (24) 92, p. 54.
"The Burial of the Writer Hans Juergen Froehlich" (tr. of Walter Helmut Fritz). [Pembroke] (24) 92, p. 71.
"But Then?" (tr. of Walter Helmut Fritz). [Pembroke] (24) 92, p. 62.
"Candide" (tr. of Hans Magnus Enzensberger). [Pembroke] (24) 92, p. 31.
"Carceri d'Invenzione" (tr. of Hans Magnus Enzensberger). [Pembroke] (24) 92, p. 38.
"A Cherry Orchard in the Snow" (tr. of Hans Magnus Enzensberger). [Pembroke] (24) 92, p. 39.
"The Density of Mobile Bodies" (I, VII, tr. of Walter Helmut Fritz). [Pembroke] (24) 92, p. 67.
"A Didactic Poem on Murder" (tr. of Hans Magnus Enzensberger). [Pembroke] (24) 92, p. 35.
"The Earth in a Photo" (tr. of Walter Helmut Fritz). [Pembroke] (24) 92, p. 50.
"Encounter" (tr. of Walter Helmut Fritz). [Pembroke] (24) 92, p. 65.
"Garden at Breitenfelde" (tr. of Guenter Kunert). [Pembroke] (24) 92, p. 45.
"Glass Architecture" (tr. of Hans Magnus Enzensberger). [Pembroke] (24) 92, p. 42.
"Grand Tour" (tr. of Hans Magnus Enzensberger). [Pembroke] (24) 92, p. 32.
"Grasp of the Wind" (tr. of Hans Magnus Enzensberger). [Pembroke] (24) 92, p. 40.
"The Great Inventions" (tr. of Hans Magnus Enzensberger). [Pembroke] (24) 92, p. 36.
"Guests of Summer" (tr. of Guenter Kunert). [Pembroke] (24) 92, p. 48.
"Here Our Longing Rhymes with the Moment" (I-III, V, tr. of Walter Helmut Fritz). [Pembroke] (24) 92, p. 60-61.
"I Won't Forget" (tr. of Walter Helmut Fritz). [Pembroke] (24) 92, p. 69.
"Indulgence" (tr. of Hans Magnus Enzensberger). [Pembroke] (24) 92, p. 43.
"Insoluble" (tr. of Walter Helmut Fritz). [Pembroke] (24) 92, p. 64.
"Lest Our Words Go Blind" (tr. of Walter Helmut Fritz). [Pembroke] (24) 92, p. 63.
"The Losers" (tr. of Walter Helmut Fritz). [Pembroke] (24) 92, p. 59.
"Mandelstam" (tr. of Walter Helmut Fritz). [Pembroke] (24) 92, p. 72.
"My Friend, the American Indian, Says" (tr. of Walter Helmut Fritz). [Pembroke] (24) 92, p. 56.

"Nearly Everything Remains to Be Done" (tr. of Walter Helmut Fritz). [Pembroke] (24) 92, p. 68.
"Often" (tr. of Walter Helmut Fritz). [Pembroke] (24) 92, p. 70.
"The Old Woman" (tr. of Walter Helmut Fritz). [Pembroke] (24) 92, p. 52.
"An Option for Real Estate" (tr. of Hans Magnus Enzensberger). [Pembroke] (24) 92, p. 34.
"Perspective" (tr. of Guenter Kunert). [Pembroke] (24) 92, p. 49.
"Same Old Story" (tr. of Hans Magnus Enzensberger). [Pembroke] (24) 92, p. 41.
"Script and Counterscript" (tr. of Walter Helmut Fritz). [Pembroke] (24) 92, p. 72.
"So as Not to Perish" (tr. of Walter Helmut Fritz). [Pembroke] (24) 92, p. 58.
"Taking Leave" (tr. of Guenter Kunert). [Pembroke] (24) 92, p. 47.
"Taking Leave of a Wednesday" (tr. of Hans Magnus Enzensberger). [Pembroke] (24) 92, p. 33.
"This Is the Dog" (tr. of Hans Magnus Enzensberger). [Pembroke] (24) 92, p. 37.
"This Number Has Been Disconnected" (tr. of Hans Magnus Enzensberger). [Pembroke] (24) 92, p. 44.
"Those Who Die Are the Others" (tr. of Walter Helmut Fritz). [Pembroke] (24) 92, p. 51.
"Thus We Ask and Keep on Asking" (tr. of Walter Helmut Fritz). [Pembroke] (24) 92, p. 55.
"To Heck with It" (III, VI, tr. of Walter Helmut Fritz). [Pembroke] (24) 92, p. 66.
"The Transformation" (tr. of Guenter Kunert). [Pembroke] (24) 92, p. 46.
"Window" (tr. of Walter Helmut Fritz). [Pembroke] (24) 92, p. 53.

2435. GRIMM, Susan
"The Bowl of Dread." [PoetryNW] (33:3) Aut 92, p. 36-37.
"Past Tense." [CinPR] (23) Wint 91-92, p. 65.
"The Small House of Love." [PoetryNW] (33:3) Aut 92, p. 37.
"We Have Begun to Suspect That It Isn't True." [PoetryNW] (33:3) Aut 92, p. 38.

2436. GRINBERG, Ana
"De un tajo terminó agosto." [Nuez] (4:10/11) 92, p. 8.

2437. GRIOTTI, Graciela
"Una Luminosidad en la Piel" (2 selections). [Luz] (2) S 92, p. 25-27.

2438. GRIPPE, Kerry
"Testing, Testing." [Art&Und] (1:2) Wint 92, p. 8.

2439. GRISWOLD, Jay
"In Praise of Bones." [Plain] (12:3) Spr 92, p. 6.
"It Happens." [Gypsy] (19) 92, p. 46-47.
"Pablo." [InterPR] (18:1) Spr 92, p. 50-51.
"The Skin of the Invisible." [WritersF] (18) 92, p. 106.

2440. GROCH, Eric
"All Sun, from Light to Light." [PraS] (66:4) Wint 92, p. 127-128.
"Friend to Birds." [PraS] (66:4) Wint 92, p. 129.
"I'm Thinking of the Time that Must Come." [PraS] (66:4) Wint 92, p. 131.
"Indescribable Vision." [PraS] (66:4) Wint 92, p. 130.
"There Are Some Important." [PraS] (66:4) Wint 92, p. 132.
"X X X: A man walking down the staircase." [PraS] (66:4) Wint 92, p. 127.
"X X X: A white dove." [PraS] (66:4) Wint 92, p. 128.
"Yana Has Yozho, Mara Has Yan and I Have." [PraS] (66:4) Wint 92, p. 126.

2441. GROGG, Charles
"Fear." [Elf] (2:4) Wint 92, p. 43.
"Keepers." [Poem] (68) N 92, p. 9.
"Under an Old Woman Dancing." [Poem] (68) N 92, p. 8.

2442. GROOM, Kelle
"Burial" (for E.I. Halunen). [FloridaR] (18:2) Fall-Wint 92, p. 118.

GROOTE, Judith de
See DeGROOTE, Judith

2443. GROSHOLZ, Emily
"Autumn Sonata." [Hudson] (44:4) Wint 92, p. 611-612.
"The Pot of Basil." [Raritan] (12:1) Sum 92, p. 25-26.
"Rain or Shine." [Hudson] (44:4) Wint 92, p. 612-613.
"Symmetry." [Raritan] (12:1) Sum 92, p. 27-28.
"Two Passages from Colette." [PartR] (59:1) Wint 92, p. 107-108.

2444. GROSJEAN, Glen
"In the Laboratory" (tr. of Ok-Koo Kang Grosjean, w. the author). [PoetryUSA] (24) 92, p. 17.

"Presence" (tr. of Ok-Koo Kang Grosjean, w. the author). [PoetryUSA] (24) 92, p. 18.

2445. GROSJEAN, Ok-Koo Kang
"In the Laboratory" (tr. by the author and Glen Grosjean). [PoetryUSA] (24) 92, p. 17.
"Presence" (tr. by the author and Glen Grosjean). [PoetryUSA] (24) 92, p. 18.

2446. GROSS, Pamela
"Bowline." [Comm] (119:11) 5 Je 92, p. 15.
"Cow Hitch / Lark's Head." [Comm] (119:11) 5 Je 92, p. 20.
"The Crows Give Chase at Dusk." [OhioR] (48) 92, p. 70.
"The Hive." [Poetry] (160:5) Ag 92, p. 261.
"Res Ipsa." [SouthernR] (28:3) Sum, Jl 92, p. 607.
"Some Uses of Moonlight." [SouthernR] (28:3) Sum, Jl 92, p. 606.
"Swarm." [PoetryNW] (33:3) Aut 92, p. 40.
"The Webs of the Orb Weavers." [SouthernR] (28:3) Sum, Jl 92, p. 605.

2447. GROSS, Philip
"Beyonders." [Stand] (33:2) Spr 92, p. 55-56.

2448. GROSSMAN, Edith
"Rest in Peace" (tr. of Nicanor Parra). [Trans] (26) Spr 92, p. 55-56.

2449. GROSSMAN, Rebekah
"The Cave of the Sleeping Sharks." [BelPoJ] (42:3) Spr 92, p. 4-5.

2450. GROVE, C. L.
"The Amazon flows on and on." [Light] (4) Wint 92-93, p. 29.
"If a Scot goes forth from the Firth of Forth." [Light] (2) Sum 92, p. 29.

2451. GROVE, Garry
"Pome to Jack." [MoodySI] (27) Spr 92, p. 1.

2452. GROVER, Teji
"One After Another After Another" (tr. by Aditya Behl). [ChiR] (38:1/2) 92, p. 104 - 105.

2453. GROW, Mary E.
"Two Pasts and a Present." [NegC] (12:1/2) 92, p. 54.

2454. GROWNEY, Jo Anne
"Boston Aunt." [FourQ] (6:1) Spr 92, p. 38.
"Paradoxes." [FourQ] (6:1) Spr 92, p. 37.

2455. GRUBBS, Gerald R.
"At the Library." [ChatR] (12:2) Wint 92, p. 23.

2456. GRUPO MONCADA
"Elegía." [Areíto] (3:10/11) Abril 92, p. 82.

2457. GRUWEZ, Luuk
"Aesthetics" (tr. by Ria Leigh-Loohuizen). [SouthernR] (28:2) Spr, Ap 92, p. 331.
"Fat People" (tr. by Ria Leigh-Loohuizen). [SouthernR] (28:2) Spr, Ap 92, p. 330 - 331.
"Hell under a Skirt" (tr. by Ria Leigh-Loohuizen). [SouthernR] (28:2) Spr, Ap 92, p. 329.
"Years Later" (tr. by Ria Leigh-Loohuizen). [SouthernR] (28:2) Spr, Ap 92, p. 332.

2458. GU, Cheng
"After the Air-Raid" (tr. by Ginny MacKenzie and Wei Guo). [ArtfulD] (22/23) 92, p. 20.
"Dream Garden" (tr. by Ginny MacKenzie and Wei Guo). [ArtfulD] (22/23) 92, p. 19.
"The Green Window" (tr. by Ginny MacKenzie and Wei Guo). [ArtfulD] (22/23) 92, p. 18.
"Undercover" (tr. by Ginny MacKenzie and Wei Guo). [Pequod] (34) 92, p. 124.

2459. GUBMAN, G. D.
"Connections." [US1] (26/27) 92, p. 8.

2460. GUDAS, Eric
"Silence." [PassN] (13:1) Sum 92, p. 30.

2461. GUENTHER, Charles
"Three Sisters." [WebR] (16) Fall 92, p. 39-40.

2462. GUEREÑA, Jacinto-Luis
"Lumière Marine." [Os] (34) Spr 92, p. 29.
"Tant de rythmes." [Os] (34) Spr 92, p. 30-37.

2463. GUERIN, Christopher (Christopher D.)
"Discovery." [MidwQ] (34:1) Aut 92, p. 66.
"Our Winter." [HopewellR] (4) 92, p. 33.

2464. GUERNSEY, Bruce
"At the Grave of Thomas Lincoln" (January 31, 1861). [SpoonRQ] (17:3/4) Sum - Fall 92, p. 77-78.
"Crosshairs." [Epiphany] (3:4) O (Fall) 92, p. 284.
"The Lost Brigade." [SpoonRQ] (17:3/4) Sum-Fall 92, p. 86-87.
"Once Upon a Time." [SpoonRQ] (17:3/4) Sum-Fall 92, p. 83-84.
"Pasquaney." [SpoonRQ] (17:3/4) Sum-Fall 92, p. 88-89.
"The Passing." [Epiphany] (3:4) O (Fall) 92, p. 283.
"The Porchlight." [SpoonRQ] (17:3/4) Sum-Fall 92, p. 85.
"Stations of the Cross." [SpoonRQ] (17:3/4) Sum-Fall 92, p. 80-82.
"Waking in a Child's Room." [SpoonRQ] (17:3/4) Sum-Fall 92, p. 90-91.
"The Wall." [SpoonRQ] (17:3/4) Sum-Fall 92, p. 79.
2465. GUEST, Barbara
"Above Rio and Above." [WestCL] (26:2, #8) Fall 92, p. 54.
"The Advance of the Grizzly." [AmerPoR] (21:4) Jl-Ag 92, p. 21.
"Broken Blossoms." [WestCL] (26:2, #8) Fall 92, p. 56.
"Earrings." [AmerPoR] (21:4) Jl-Ag 92, p. 21.
"The Glass Mountain" (in memory of J.S.). [Conjunc] (19) 92, p. 201-204.
"Greenish Marble." [WestCL] (26:2, #8) Fall 92, p. 55.
"Gwen John." [WestCL] (26:2, #8) Fall 92, p. 57.
"Ink Poem." [WestCL] (26:2, #8) Fall 92, p. 55.
"The Japanese Sandman." [WestCL] (26:2, #8) Fall 92, p. 57.
"Like Queen Eleanor." [AmerPoR] (21:4) Jl-Ag 92, p. 22.
"Red Dye." [AmerPoR] (21:4) Jl-Ag 92, p. 22.
"Restlessness." [NewAW] (10) Fall 92, p. 1-3.
"The Surface As Object." [Sulfur] (12:2, #31) Fall 92, p. 80-81.
"The Tent." [AmerPoR] (21:4) Jl-Ag 92, p. 22.
"You Can Discover." [AmerPoR] (21:4) Jl-Ag 92, p. 22.
2466. GUIDACCI, Margherita
"Dark Sorrow" (tr. by James Kirkup). [Stand] (33:4) Aut 92, p. 106-107.
"The Knife Thrower" (tr. by Corrado Federici). [PoetryC] (13:1) N 92, p. 23.
2467. GUIDE, James
"Thanks, Nighthawk." [Footwork] 92, p. 103.
2468. GUIDO, Margarita
"Cuando los Perros No Ladraron." [Americas] (20:2) Sum 92, p. 69-70.
"Poema 17." [Americas] (20:2) Sum 92, p. 71.
2469. GUILBERT, Naomi
"Curse Poem." [SinW] (48) Wint 92-93, p. 36.
2470. GUILLORY, Stella Jeng
"My Voyage to Mecca." [MidAR] (13:2) 92, p. 166-167.
GUIN, Ursula K. le
See Le GUIN, Ursula K.
GUINDI, Yussef el
See El GUINDI, Yussef
2471. GUISTA, Michael Blaine
"Radio." [ColEng] (53:8) D 91, p. 911.
2472. GUITART, Jorge
"The Dismantling of Bourgeois Discourse Proceeds Imperfectly." [SnailPR] (2:1) Spr-Sum 92, p. 1.
"The Encounter." [LindLM] (11:4) D 92, p. 32.
"Fragments of a Chronicle." [LindLM] (11:4) D 92, p. 32.
"I Was Talking to the Others." [SnailPR] (2:1) Spr-Sum 92, p. 2.
"Memory." [LindLM] (11:4) D 92, p. 32.
"This Is to Say." [LindLM] (11:4) D 92, p. 32.
2473. GUMILEV, Nikolai
"The Runaway Streetcar" (tr. by Ron D. K. Banerjee). [Trans] (26) Spr 92, p. 46-48.
GUNDY, Douglas van
See Van GUNDY, Douglas
2474. GUNDY, Jeff
"Knowing the Father." [LaurelR] (26:1) Wint 92, p. 27.
"Seams." [ArtfulD] (22/23) 92, p. 69-70.
2475. GUNN, Lisa S.
"A Doctor Explains the Virus." [Boulevard] (7:2/3, #20/21) Fall 92, p. 277.
2476. GUNN, Thom
"The Butcher's Son." [NewYorker] (67:51) 10 F 92, p. 32.
"The Gas-Poker." [Thrpny] (49) Spr 92, p. 10.

"Herculaneum" (specifics derived from "Herculaneum," by Joseph Jay Deiss). [Conjunc] (19) 92, p. 139-141.
"In the Post Office." [Thrpny] (50) Sum 92, p. 35.
"Meat" (Two versions). [Agni] (36) 92, p. 300-302.
"Rapallo." [NewYorker] (67:46) 6 Ja 92, p. 38.

2477. GUNNELL, Bryn
"The Nettle-Tree." [Stand] (33:2) Spr 92, p. 149.

2478. GUO, Wei
"After the Air-Raid" (tr. of Gu Cheng, w. Ginny MacKenzie). [ArtfulD] (22/23) 92, p. 20.
"Dream Garden" (tr. of Gu Cheng, w. Ginny MacKenzie). [ArtfulD] (22/23) 92, p. 19.
"The Green Window" (tr. of Gu Cheng, w. Ginny MacKenzie). [ArtfulD] (22/23) 92, p. 18.
"Undercover" (tr. of Gu Cheng, w. Ginny MacKenzie). [Pequod] (34) 92, p. 124.
"What Is There" (tr. of Shu Ting, w. Ginny MacKenzie). [Pequod] (34) 92, p. 122-123.

2479. GURAN, Holly
"Forest Trail." [Noctiluca] (1:1) Spr 92, p. 18.
"Four AM." [Noctiluca] (1:1) Spr 92, p. 19.
"Soon." [Noctiluca] (1:1) Spr 92, p. 17.

2480. GURKIN, Kathryn Bright
"Recluse." [Crucible] (28) Fall 92, p. 29.

2481. GURKIN, Worth W., Jr.
"Letter from an Educated Woman to Her Husband at War (1863)." [Crucible] (28) Fall 92, p. 26-27.

2482. GURLEY, James
"In a Yup'ik village on the Johnson River, Southwest Alaska" (for Bain). [NegC] (12:1/2) 92, p. 55-57.

2483. GURRY-ZENTNER, Robert
"As for Him." [YellowS] (39) Spr-Sum 92, p. 25.
"Now and Then." [YellowS] (39) Spr-Sum 92, p. 25.
"Two of Them." [YellowS] (39) Spr-Sum 92, p. 25.
"Zamboanga." [YellowS] (39) Spr-Sum 92, p. 24.

2484. GUSSLER, Phyllis Sanchez
"Lacuna." [NewOR] (19:3/4) Fall-Wint 92, p. 48-49.
"Younger Brother, Age Thirteen." [LullwaterR] (3:3) Sum 92, p. 36.

2485. GUSTAFSON, Ralph
"20th Configuration." [PoetryC] (13:1) N 92, p. 18.
"29th Configuration." [PoetryC] (13:1) N 92, p. 19.
"Amsterdam." [PoetryC] (13:1) N 92, p. 19.
"Funeral Music." [PoetryC] (13:1) N 92, p. 19.

2486. GUSTAFSSON, Lars
"Austin, Texas" (tr. by Yvonne L. Sandstroem). [NewYorker] (68:27) 24 Ag 92, p. 36.
"Itemized Expenses" (August Strindberg, 1849-1912, tr. by Yvonne L. Sandstroem). [NewYorker] (68:7) 6 Ap 92, p. 30.

GUT, Karen Alkalay
See ALKALAY-GUT, Karen

2487. GUTHRIE, Hamish
"A Song for Jack Kerouac." [MoodySI] (27) Spr 92, p. 1.

GUTIERREZ, Amparo Pérez
See PÉREZ GUTIERREZ, Amparo

2488. GUTIERREZ REVUELTA, Pedro
"Counter-Order (Poetics That I Announce on Certain Days)" (tr. of Angel Gonzalez, w. Steven Ford Brown). [SenR] (22:1) Spr 92, p. 53.
"The Day Has Gone" (tr. of Angel Gonzalez, w. Steven Ford Brown). [SenR] (22:1) Spr 92, p. 56.
"Here, Madrid, 1954" (tr. of Angel Gonzalez, w. Steven Ford Brown). [SenR] (22:1) Spr 92, p. 57.
"Zero City" (tr. of Angel Gonzalez, w. Steven Ford Brown). [SenR] (22:1) Spr 92, p. 54-55.

2489. GUTIERREZ VIDAL, Carlos Adolfo
"Sonreir." [Luz] (2) S 92, p. 28.
"To Smile." [Luz] (2) S 92, p. 28.

2490. GUTTMAN, Melinda Jo
"Susan Rising." [ManhatPR] (14) [92?], p. 4-5.
2491. GUZLOWSKI, John
"Pigeons." [SpoonRQ] (17:1/2) Wint-Spr 92, p. 111.
2492. GUZMAN, Catherine
"My House" (tr. of Jeanette Miller). [LitR] (35:4) Sum 92, p. 512.
"Woman" (tr. of Jeanette Miller). [LitR] (35:4) Sum 92, p. 513.
GUZMAN, Esteban Torres
See TORRES-GUZMAN, Esteban
2493. GUZZARDI, Anne
"The Kiss." [TriQ] (86) Wint 92-93, p. 47.
"Wake" (for M.H., 1914-1989). [TriQ] (86) Wint 92-93, p. 48-49.
2494. GWYNN, R. S.
"The Easiest Room in Hell." [Sparrow] (59) S 92, p. 4.
"The Great Fear." [Epiphany] (3:4) O (Fall) 92, p. 267.
"Sonnet Against the *Phaedra* of Racine (1677)." [Sparrow] (59) S 92, p. 5.
HA, Jin
See JIN, Ha
2495. HAAREN, Michael
"Makeup is to the truth of age." [Light] (1) Spr 92, p. 24.
2496. HABER, Leo
"About Pablo Casals." [NegC] (12:3) 92, p. 79-80.
2497. HABOVA, Dana
"About the Brain" (tr. of Miroslav Holub, w. David Young). [GrahamHR] (16) Fall 92, p. 38-39.
"Imagination" (tr. of Miroslav Holub, w. David Young). [GrahamHR] (16) Fall 92, p. 36-37.
"My Mother Learns Spanish" (tr. of Miroslav Holub, w. David Young). [Field] (47) Fall 92, p. 76-77.
"Spinal Cord" (tr. of Miroslav Holub, w. David Young). [Field] (47) Fall 92, p. 75.
"The Third Language" (tr. of Miroslav Holub, w. David Young). [GrahamHR] (16) Fall 92, p. 40-41.
2498. HABRA, Hedy
"That Day in Heliopolis." [NegC] (12:3) 92, p. 81.
2499. HACKER, Marilyn
"Against Elegies." [AmerV] (28) 92, p. 71-75.
"Ballad of Ladies Lost and Found." [Hellas] (3:2) Fall 92, p. 97-100.
"Chiliastic Sapphics." [NewEngR] (14:2) Spr 92, p. 140-141.
"Dusk: July." [ParisR]] (34:124) Fall 92, p. 212-214.
"For K.J., Between Anniversaries." [NewEngR] (14:2) Spr 92, p. 142-143.
"Street Scenes II." [ParisR]] (34:124) Fall 92, p. 211-212.
2500. HADAS, Rachel
"The Bath." [HarvardA] (125th Anniversary Issue) F 92, p. 18.
"The Bees of the Invisible" (In memory of Dan Conner). [ParisR]] (34:124) Fall 92, p. 48-49.
"Birthday: Aubade and Argument." [KenR] (NS 14:2) Spr 92, p. 30-31.
"A Copy of Ariel." [Raritan] (12:1) Sum 92, p. 23-24.
"In the Mirror." [KenR] (NS 14:2) Spr 92, p. 31-32.
"Into the Wind." [ParisR]] (34:124) Fall 92, p. 47-48.
"Learning to Talk." [SouthwR] (77:4) Aut 92, p. 503.
"Lunch the Day After Thanksgiving." [SouthwR] (77:4) Aut 92, p. 504-505.
"On Dreams." [YaleR] (80:3) Jl 92, p. 127-131.
"The Red Coat." [AmerV] (26) Spr 92, p. 34.-35.
"Red House." [NewYorker] (67:49) 27 Ja 92, p. 34.
"The Second Death." [Hellas] (3:1) Spr 92, p. 54-55.
"Thank You and Goodbye" (in memory of David Kalstone). [Thrpny] (49) Spr 92, p. 20.
"Three from Tibullus" (1.2, 1.6, 1.10, tr. of Tibullus). [Arion] 3d series (2:1) Wint 92, p. 148-156.
"War and Love." [CreamCR] (16:2) Fall 92, p. 24-28.
2501. HADDAWAY, J. L.
"Finite Math." [DogRR] (11:2, #22) Fall-Wint 92, p. 12-13.
"Traveling" (for M.). [HawaiiR] (16:2, #35) Spr 92, p. 92.
2502. HADEN, Amy Clark
"Underground Writing." [HayF] (11) Fall-Wint 92, p. 111.

2503. HADFIELD, Charles
"Cartographies." [Os] (35) Fall 92, p. 8-12.
2504. HAENEL, Paul R.
"Garden of Eden." [Parting] (5:2) Wint 92-93, p. 20.
"Recollection in a False Spring." [PoetC] (23:2) Wint 92, p. 25-26.
2505. HAGEDORN, Curt
"The Dinner Parties" (for Greg Campora). [JamesWR] (9:3) Spr 92, p. 17.
"Mid-Iowa" (for Caroline Palmer). [JamesWR] (9:2) Wint 92, p. 4.
"Thanksgiving" (for Greg Campora). [JamesWR] (9:3) Spr 92, p. 17.
"Valentine's Day." [JamesWR] (9:2) Wint 92, p. 4.
2506. HAGER, Stephanie
"Telling Tomorrow to Be Kind." [OnTheBus] (4:2/5:1, #10/11) 92, p. 102-103.
2507. HAHN, Elizabeth
"In Chinese" (To the memory of Ernest Fenollosa). [WebR] (16) Fall 92, p. 38.
"Pageant." [ChrC] (109:37) 16 D 92, p. 1162.
2508. HAHN, Lauren
"The End of Art" (tr. of Michael Krüger). [WebR] (16) Fall 92, p. 12.
"On Hope" (tr. of Michael Krüger). [WebR] (16) Fall 92, p. 12.
2509. HAHN, Robert
"Five Views of This and the Other World." [CentR] (36:1) Wint 92, p. 133-134.
"The Rainbow Over Lake Buttermere." [CentR] (36:1) Wint 92, p. 130-132.
"Sundown at Santa Cruz." [SouthwR] (77:1) Wint 92, p. 57-58.
2510. HAHN, Susan
"Calendar." [Poetry] (159:4) Ja 92, p. 206.
"Devices for Torture." [Pequod] (33) 92, p. 220.
"Dialysis." [PoetryE] (33) Spr 92, p. 52.
"Directions to Where I Live." [PoetryE] (33) Spr 92, p. 53.
"The Hemlock Society." [Poetry] (160:2) My 92, p. 85-86.
"The Hope." [Pequod] (33) 92, p. 217.
"Hysterectomy As Metaphor." [Shen] (42:4) Wint 92, p. 77.
"Jealousy." [Boulevard] (7:1, #19) Spr 92, p. 128.
"Obsession." [Boulevard] (7:1, #19) Spr 92, p. 129-130.
"Rejection." [Pequod] (33) 92, p. 219.
"Rib." [Pequod] (33) 92, p. 218.
"The Shape of Happiness." [Pequod] (33) 92, p. 221.
2511. HAI-JEW, Shalin
"Artificial Day, Nanchang, Jiangxi Province, P.R.C." [Kalliope] (14:2) 92, p. 51-52.
"Comfort for a Muse." [Contact] (10:62/63/64) Fall 91-Spr 92, p. 51.
"The Farewell Party" (from a mixed media piece titled "Witness," by Harold Tovish, 1985). [Contact] (10:62/63/64) Fall 91-Spr 92, p. 50.
HAI-PENG, Huang
See HUANG, Hai-Peng
2512. HAIGHT, Robert
"Balony." [SoCoast] (12) Ja 92, p. 53.
"The Desire to Farm." [SoCoast] (12) Ja 92, p. 18.
2513. HAINES, Anne
"Let X Equal." [NowestR] (30:3) 92, p. 36.
2514. HAINES, John
"A Guide to the Asian Museums." [Hudson] (45:3) Aut 92, p. 402-403.
"In the Sleep of Reason." [Hudson] (45:3) Aut 92, p. 400-402.
"The Poem without Meaning." [Hudson] (45:3) Aut 92, p. 403-406.
"To the Wall." [Atlantic] (270:5) N 92, p. 109.
HAIXIN, Xu
See XU, Haixin
2515. HALEVI, Yehuda
"Axiom"" (tr. by Ammiel Alcalay). [Paint] (19:37) Spr 92, p. 39.
"Love Poems"" (tr. by Ammiel Alcalay). [Paint] (19:37) Spr 92, p. 40.
2516. HALEY, Vanessa
"For My Cousin, Found in a Ravine." [HampSPR] Wint 92, p. 42-43.
"Last Day on the Chickahominy." [HampSPR] Wint 92, p. 44-45.
2517. HALL, Barry
"Losing Faith." [Vis] (39) 92, p. 36.
"Still" (For Christine). [Vis] (39) 92, p. 36.
2518. HALL, Daniel
"Son." [NewRep] (207:8/9) 17-24 Ag 92, p. 48.

2519. HALL, Donald
"Another Elegy" (in Memory of William Trout). [Iowa] (22:3) Fall 92, p. 43-49.
"Baseball" (Selection: "The Seventh Inning"). [Boulevard] (7:2/3, #20/21) Fall 92, p. 83-85.
"Baseball" (Selection: "The Sixth Inning"). [Boulevard] (7:1, #19) Spr 92, p. 22-24.
"Baseball" (Selections: 1st & 2nd Innings). [NewAW] (10) Fall 92, p. 30-34.
"The Eighth Inning." [GettyR] (5:3) Sum 92, p. 430-432.
"Extra Innings." [NewEngR] (14:4) Fall 92, p. 159-168.
"The Fifth Inning." [GettyR] (5:3) Sum 92, p. 427-429.
"The Fourth Inning." [GettyR] (5:3) Sum 92, p. 424-426.
"Lines in Furtherance of a Jumprope Rhyme" (collected by E.A. Botkin in "A Treasury of New England Folklore"). [NewRep] (206:22) 1 Je 92, p. 48.
"Meditating Virtues." [NewRep] (207:10) 31 Ag 92, p. 40.
"The Museum of Clear Ideas, or Say: Horsecollar's Odes." [ParisR] (34:123) Sum 92, p. 189-213.
"The Ninth Inning." [Agni] (36) 92, p. 11-13.
"Pluvia." [Nat] (254:12) 30 Mr 92, p. 424.
"The Thought." [Light] (1) Spr 92, p. 31.
2520. HALL, Earl N.
"So scared that this would be my last breath." [PoetryUSA] (24) 92, p. 29.
2521. HALL, Gregory
"Even the Sun Is Naked" (Selections: II-III, tr. of Anthony Phelps). [Callaloo] (15:2) Spr 92, p. 357-363.
2522. HALL, Jim
"The Figure a Poem Makes." [ThRiPo] (39/40) 92-93, p. 93-94.
"Maybe Dats Your Pwoblem Too." [ThRiPo] (39/40) 92-93, p. 94-95.
"The Reel World." [ThRiPo] (39/40) 92-93, p. 92-93.
"Reign of Terror." [ThRiPo] (39/40) 92-93, p. 92.
2523. HALL, Judith
"In an Empty Garden." [KenR] (NS 14:1) Wint 92, p. 33-34.
"Love Poem for the Declaration of Independence." [WestHR] (46:2) Sum 92, p. 119.
"Song of Many Pauses." [Boulevard] (7:1, #19) Spr 92, p. 195-196.
2524. HALL, Kathryn
"Sunday." [PoetL] (87:3) Fall 92, p. 19-20.
2525. HALL, Michael L.
"Dona Minervae." [SewanR] (100:1) Wint 92, p. 61-62.
2526. HALL, Phil
"A Mandelstam in Guthrie Clothing." [Event] (21:1) Spr 92, p. 13-14.
2527. HALL, Sidney L., Jr.
"Clock." [ChatR] (13:1) Fall 92, p. 28.
2528. HALLAWELL, Susan (Susan W.)
"Against Monogamy." [LullwaterR] (3:3) Sum 92, p. 21.
"For Anoujka Odette Mead (1976-1989), After Reading Her Poems." [SouthernPR] (32:1) Spr 92, p. 23-24.
"Impotence." [NoAmR] (277:6) N-D 92, p. 18-19.
"Sheets." [TarRP] (31:2) Spr 92, p. 40-41.
2529. HALLIDAY, Mark
"Ketchup and Heaven." [Poetry] (160:1) Ap 92, p. 32-33.
"My Plan." [VirQR] (68:2) Spr 92, p. 312-313.
"Personal Details." [VirQR] (68:2) Spr 92, p. 313-314.
"There" (For Keats). [Poetry] (160:1) Ap 92, p. 33.
"Vegetable Wisdom." [VirQR] (68:2) Spr 92, p. 310-312.
"Why the HG is Holy." [YaleR] (80:1/2) Apr 92, p. 239.
"Years Ago." [ParisR] (34:123) Sum 92, p. 39-40.
2530. HALMAN, Talat Sait
"Those Women" (tr. of Özcan Yalim). [Trans] (26) Spr 92, p. 88.
"War and Peace" (tr. of Onat Kutlar). [Trans] (26) Spr 92, p. 38.
2531. HALME, Kathleen
"Mary Magdalene's Ideal Christmas." [SoCarR] (25:1) Fall 92, p. 108-110.
2532. HALPERIN, Joan
"If You Want to Know." [Confr] (48/49) Spr-Sum 92, p. 229-230.
2533. HALPERIN, Mark
"Anarchist." [CrabCR] (8:1) Sum-Fall 92, p. 13.
"Clouds" (tr. of A. Galich). [SenR] (22:1) Spr 92, p. 24-25.
"In Memory of B. L. Pasternak" (tr. of A. Galich). [SenR] (22:1) Spr 92, p. 30-32.

"A Legend of Moses." [Shen] (42:4) Wint 92, p. 30-31.
"Legend of Some Smokes" (tr. of A. Galich). [SenR] (22:1) Spr 92, p. 27-30.
"Nothing on Time" (tr. of A. Galich). [SenR] (22:1) Spr 92, p. 26-27.
"Webs (I)." [SouthernPR] (32:1) Spr 92, p. 34.
"Without a Name" (tr. of A. Galich). [SenR] (22:1) Spr 92, p. 23.

2534. HALPERN, Daniel
"The Last Day." [NewYorker] (68:37) 2 N 92, p. 81.
"Our Boys: The Eighth Pillar." [NewRep] (206:16) 20 Ap 92, p. 44.
"Postcard." [NewEngR] (14:3) Sum 92, p. 189.

2535. HAM, Judy F.
"Exposure." [BelPoJ] (43:2) Wint 92-93, p. 34-35.

2536. HAMBERGER, Robert
"Spaces." [Verse] (9:2) Sum 92, p. 86.

2537. HAMBLIN, Robert
"For Dal, on the Fourth of July." [Spitball] (42) Fall 92, p. 44-45.

2538. HAMBURGER, Michael
"Apparition." [Stand] (33:2) Spr 92, p. 57.
"Appearances" (tr. of Hans Magnus Enzensberger). [Stand] (33:4) Aut 92, p. 82.
"The Blank Sheet" (tr. of Hans Magnus Enzensberger). [Stand] (33:4) Aut 92, p. 81.
"Consistency" (tr. of Hans Magnus Enzensberger). [Stand] (33:4) Aut 92, p. 81.
"A Garden for Keith Jarrett" (tr. of Michael Krüger). [Stand] (33:4) Aut 92, p. 66 - 67.
"In the Air" (tr. of Paul Celan). [Stand] (33:4) Aut 92, p. 86.

2539. HAMBY, Barbara
"The Language of Bees." [AnotherCM] (23) Spr 92, p. 87-88.
"My Sin." [AnotherCM] (23) Spr 92, p. 89.

2540. HAMILL, Sam
"Translations from the 10th century Japanese *Kokinshu*." [AnotherCM] (23) Spr 92, p. 90-92.

2541. HAMILTON, Alfred Starr
"Ancient City." [WormR] (32:3, #127) 92, p. 98-99.
"Foliage." [WormR] (32:3, #127) 92, p. 98.
"Funny." [WormR] (32:3, #127) 92, p. 97.
"Glass and Sand." [WormR] (32:3, #127) 92, p. 99-100.
"Law and Azure." [WormR] (32:3, #127) 92, p. 99.
"The Law of the Jungle." [JlNJPo] (14:1) Spr 92, p. 31.
"Men and Steeples and Stars." [JlNJPo] (14:2) Aut 92, p. 39.
"Moon and Stars." [WormR] (32:3, #127) 92, p. 99.
"Othello and Paul." [JlNJPo] (14:1) Spr 92, p. 32.
"A Painter." [JlNJPo] (14:1) Spr 92, p. 33.
"Pavements." [WormR] (32:3, #127) 92, p. 98.
"Prisms." [JlNJPo] (14:1) Spr 92, p. 35.
"A Socialist." [WormR] (32:3, #127) 92, p. 97.
"Sun and Stars." [JlNJPo] (14:1) Spr 92, p. 34.

2542. HAMILTON, Carol (*See also* HAMILTON, Carol V.)
"Pony Legs." [NewYorkQ] (47) 92, p. 75.
"Resurrections." [MidwQ] (33:4) Sum 92, p. 409.

2543. HAMILTON, Carol V. (*See also* HAMILTON, Carol)
"Music for Thunderstorm and Pianoforte." [PassN] (13:1) Sum 92, p. 11.

2544. HAMILTON, Fritz
"The Alliance." [NewYorkQ] (47) 92, p. 54.
"American Ladder!" [SmPd] (29:1, #84) Wint 92, p. 35-36.
"Cow's Bones!" [MidwQ] (33:3) Spr 92, p. 315.
"Getting It Right." [SmPd] (29:1, #84) Wint 92, p. 7.
"Not Growing!" [SmPd] (29:1, #84) Wint 92, p. 35.
"Reaction Formation" (for Tom). [SmPd] (29:1, #84) Wint 92, p. 7.

2545. HAMILTON, J. A.
"February 14." [MalR] (99) Sum 92, p. 76.
"Home Birth." [MalR] (99) Sum 92, p. 71-75.
"The Proposal." [MalR] (99) Sum 92, p. 77.

2546. HAMILTON, Jeff
"Loyalties." [WebR] (16) Fall 92, p. 104.

2547. HAMILTON, Judith
"The Birth." [LitR] (35:4) Sum 92, p. 490-491.
"Cat." [LitR] (35:4) Sum 92, p. 488.
"Epitaph." [LitR] (35:4) Sum 92, p. 491.

"Farmer's Prayer." [LitR] (35:4) Sum 92, p. 489.
"Moonstruck." [LitR] (35:4) Sum 92, p. 489.
"Peanut Seller." [LitR] (35:4) Sum 92, p. 490.
"Rain Carvers." [LitR] (35:4) Sum 92, p. 491.

2548. HAMILTON, Kitty
"The Gift." [AmerPoR] (21:4) Jl-Ag 92, p. 42.

2549. HAMILTON, Saskia
"Early April Tuesday." [NewEngR] (14:4) Fall 92, p. 96-97.
"Reading." [NewEngR] (14:4) Fall 92, p. 97.

2550. HAMMER, Alice
"Recognizing Richard Hugo." [CrabCR] (8:1) Sum-Fall 92, p. 7.

2551. HAMMER, Mark
"Working for Yourself." [TexasR] (13:1/2) Spr-Sum 92, p. 93.

2552. HAMMIAL, Phillip
"A Message." [Footwork] 92, p. 102.
"Three Short Stories." [Footwork] 92, p. 102.

2553. HAMMOND, Catherine
"The Bluebeard Room." [Jacaranda] (6:1/2) Wint-Spr 92, p. 132.
"Castalia." [MissR] (20:3) Spr 92, p. 57-59.
"A Dock in Cozumel." [NoAmR] (277:3) My-Je 92, p. 13.

2554. HAMMOND, Lucia Capria
"Scherzo." [PoetryUSA] (24) 92, p. 11.

2555. HAMMOND, Mary Stewart
"Cosmetcis." [Field] (46) Spr 92, p. 89.
"Open Season" (Postmark: Peterborough, NH, Oct. 25, 198_). [Field] (46) Spr 92, p. 95-99.
"Saving Memory." [Field] (46) Spr 92, p. 88.

2556. HAMPTON, Robert Tudor
"Shakespeare's Room." [Northeast] (5:7) Wint 92-93, p. 10-11.

2557. HAN, Yong-Woon
"The Artist" (tr. by Bruce Taylor). [Trans] (26) Spr 92, p. 110.
"Cinnamon Moon" (tr. by Bruce Taylor). [Trans] (26) Spr 92, p. 111.

2558. HANCOCK, Hugh
"August." [Amelia] (6:4, #19) 92, p. 113.
"Finding Someone." [Amelia] (7:1, #20) 92, p. 133.
"Man Out of Time (5:27)." [Amelia] (7:1, #20) 92, p. 161.
"On the road to Arvin." [Amelia] (7:1, #20) 92, p. 160.
"Windows." [Amelia] (7:1, #20) 92, p. 160-161.

2559. HANCOCK, Ken
"The Blues." [ChironR] (11:3) Aut 92, p. 5.
"Cooking Pancakes." [PoetL] (87:2) Sum 92, p. 22-23.
"The Edge." [PoetL] (87:2) Sum 92, p. 21.
"Epitaphs." [ChironR] (11:3) Aut 92, p. 5.
"The Obsession." [ChironR] (11:3) Aut 92, p. 5.

2560. HANDLER, Joan Cusack
"Before Anesthesia." [US1] (26/27) 92, p. 11.
"The Only God" (honorable mention, Eve of Saint Agnes Contest). [NegC] (12:3) 92, p. 10-11.

2561. HANDLEY, Don
"My Intentions." [Gypsy] (18) 92, p. 133-134.

2562. HANDLIN, Jim
"A Goodbye." [Footwork] 92, p. 40.
"Hunting in the Andes." [Footwork] 92, p. 40.
"In Vitro: A Prayer." [Footwork] 92, p. 40.
"Puppetry." [Footwork] 92, p. 40.

2563. HANDY, Nixeon (Nixeon Civille)
"Anima: Dream Sequence II." [NewYorkQ] (49) 92, p. 102.
"Motherless Covered Wagon." [BellArk] (8:1) Ja-F 92, p. 11.

2564. HANEBURY, Derek
"Ceremonial Unearthing" (dedicated to Carolyn Pruyser, missing since May 17, 1984). [Event] (21:1) Spr 92, p. 46.
"Rain" (dedicated to Carolyn Pruyser, missing since May 17, 1984). [Event] (21:1) Spr 92, p. 47.
"Too Much Water" (dedicated to Carolyn Pruyser, missing since May 17, 1984). [Event] (21:1) Spr 92, p. 45.

2565. HANIFAN, Jill
"Four Stone Horses." [SnailPR] (2:1) Spr-Sum 92, p. 3.
2566. HANKS, D. Trinidad
"I Been Fractured." [AfAmRev] (26:2) Sum 92, p. 235.
2567. HANLEN, Jim
"Goodbye Creek." [EngJ] (81:7) N 92, p. 98.
2568. HANNON, Theresa
"Waymire's Lawn Ornament Sales." [QW] (34) Wint-Spr 92, p. 85.
2569. HANSBURY, Gia
"Walking 14th Street Home." [NewYorkQ] (47) 92, p. 80-81.
2570. HANSE, Buffa
"Blind Date." [Epiphany] (3:3) Jl (Sum) 92, p. 183.
"Invitation for One." [Epiphany] (3:3) Jl (Sum) 92, p. 183.
"Signs." [Epiphany] (3:3) Jl (Sum) 92, p. 181-182.
2571. HANSEN, J. Vincent
"Reflections from Main Street." [RagMag] (10:1) 92, p. 21.
"Weather Vane." [RagMag] (10:1) 92, p. 20.
2572. HANSEN, Tom
"At the Library." [WebR] (16) Fall 92, p. 37.
"East-River Dakota." [Amelia] (6:4, #19) 92, p. 50.
"Poem Beginning with Two Lines by Gabriela Mistral." [PoetryNW] (33:3) Aut 92, p. 25.
"A Scholar of Summer." [CapeR] (27:2) Fall 92, p. 45.
2573. HANSEN, Twyla
"Dream of Fields." [PraS] (66:1) Spr 92, p. 33-34.
2574. HANSON, Julie Jordan
"Consignment Shop." [TarRP] (30:2) Spr 91, p. 19.
2575. HANZLICEK, C. G.
"C. G. Hanzlicek" (after Atilla Jozsef). [ThRiPo] (39/40) 92-93, p. 97-98.
"In the Dark Again." [ThRiPo] (39/40) 92-93, p. 96-97.
"Room for Doubt." [ThRiPo] (39/40) 92-93, p. 95-96.
2576. HARAD, Alyssa
"Piéta." [HarvardA] (126:2) Wint 92, p. 11.
2577. HARDENBROOK, Yvonne
"Fact of Life." [Amelia] (7:1, #20) 92, p. 115.
"Haiku: ground fog." [Amelia] (7:1, #20) 92, p. 12.
"Senryu: in the dimness." [Amelia] (7:1, #20) 92, p. 12.
2578. HARDIN, Jeff
"Blanket." [CharR] (18:1) Spr 92, p. 90.
"Foolishness." [PoetC] (24:1) Fall 92, p. 18.
2579. HARDY, Catherine
"The Country for Which There Is No Map." [MidAR] (13:2) 92, p. 77.
2580. HARER, Katharine
"Hazards." [OnTheBus] (4:2/5:1, #10/11) 92, p. 104.
"Ice Cream." [HangL] (61) 92, p. 42.
"Leo Is Talking About Death." [HangL] (61) 92, p. 44.
"The Mammogram." [HangL] (61) 92, p. 43.
"The Silver Moon." [OnTheBus] (4:2/5:1, #10/11) 92, p. 105-106.
"Sunday Morning Sinatra." [HangL] (61) 92, p. 41.
2581. HARGRAVES, Joseph
"Phyllis." [NewYorkQ] (49) 92, p. 104.
2582. HARJO, Joy
"Eagle Poem." [Jacaranda] (6:1/2) Wint-Spr 92, p. 75.
2583. HARLEY, John
"2 O'Clock Meeting." [MalR] (101) Wint92, p. 23-24.
2584. HARLOW, Renee
"Dreams are victories for the sleeper." [GrahamHR] (16) Fall 92, p. 67.
"Everything." [GrahamHR] (16) Fall 92, p. 66.
"Hiding." [MinnR] (38) Spr-Sum 92, p. 30.
2585. HARMON, Geoff W.
"The Land of Bach and Frankenstein." [ChironR] (11:4) Wint 92, p. 43.
"Piano Lessons." [ChironR] (11:4) Wint 92, p. 43.
2586. HARMON, William
"A Bearing." [SewanR] (100:4) Fall 92, p. 550-552.
"Gymnosophistry" (Saussurean Villanelle). [CarolQ] (45:1) Fall 92, p. 28.
"Identity" (Saussurean Villanelle). [CarolQ] (45:1) Fall 92, p. 29.

"Jonath-Elem-Rechokim." [FreeL] (10) Sum 92, p. 26-27.
"(Love Theme from) Bloodsucking Freaks." [CarolQ] (45:1) Fall 92, p. 27.

2587. HARMS, James
"Breakfast on the Patio." [ThRiPo] (39/40) 92-93, p. 98-99.
"Close Your Eyes and Go to Heaven." [SouthernPR] (32:1) Spr 92, p. 36-37.
"Epithalamium." [AntR] (50:4) Fall 92, p. 729.
"Explaining the Evening News to Corbyn" (after Ben Watt). [ThRiPo] (39/40) 92 - 93, p. 99-101.
"Fin de Siecle." [AmerV] (26) Spr 92, p. 43.
"The Joy Addict." [PoetryE] (33) Spr 92, p. 54-55.
"My Androgynous Years." [ThRiPo] (39/40) 92-93, p. 101-102.
"Sky." [AntR] (50:4) Fall 92, p. 730.
"The Tables on the Plaza." [AmerV] (26) Spr 92, p. 40-42.
"Tomorrow, We'll Dance in America." [DenQ] (26:4) Spr 92, p. 28-29.

2588. HARNACK, Curtis
"Union Square Market." [Nat] (254:15) 20 Ap 92, p. 534.

2589. HARP, Jerry
"The Grammarian at the End of the Day." [Light] (2) Sum 92, p. 9.
"Lyric Artist." [Light] (1) Spr 92, p. 15.

2590. HARPER, Elizabeth
"Georgia & Howe." [CanLit] (135) Wint 92, p. 66-67.
"Huts" (for Earle Birney 1979). [CanLit] (135) Wint 92, p. 63-64.
"Pin Setter: Point Grey." [CanLit] (135) Wint 92, p. 65-66.

2591. HARPER, Lynn
"Aloha Dreams." [ChamLR] (10/11) Spr-Fall 92, p. 73.

2592. HARPER, Michael S.
"Manna" (For Roger B. Henkle, in memoriam, 1935-1991). [GrahamHR] (16) Fall 92, p. 44-47.

2593. HARPER, Sue
"Hippo Lady" (For Ann Butler). [Crucible] (28) Fall 92, p. 30.
"Poem for My Cousin Clayton." [AntigR] (91) Fall 92, p. 134.

2594. HARPER, Thomas J.
"In Praise of Shadows" (tr. of Junichiro Tanizaki, w. Edward G. Seidensticker). [Trans] (26) Spr 92, p. 66.

2595. HARPOOTIAN, Alysia K.
"Nothing Better Comes After This." [Parting] (5:1) Sum 92, p. 24.
"We Had a Problem with This from the Start." [PoetryE] (33) Spr 92, p. 56.
"When Stella Cut Too Much Off My Hair." [Parting] (5:1) Sum 92, p. 16.

2596. HARRINGTON, Ed
"Clinkers in the Grate." [OnTheBus] (4:2/5:1, #10/11) 92, p. 109.
"Dyslexia." [OnTheBus] (4:2/5:1, #10/11) 92, p. 108-19.
"Loose Change." [OnTheBus] (4:2/5:1, #10/11) 92, p. 107-108.

2597. HARRINGTON, Jeanne
"Haiku" (two poems). [Amelia] (7:1, #20) 92, p. 85.

2598. HARRINGTON, Jonathan
"Corn." [EngJ] (81:7) N 92, p. 99.
"The Far South." [EngJ] (80:7) N 91, p. 98.
"Traffic." [EngJ] (81:5) S 92, p. 103.

2599. HARRIS, Craig G.
"No Private Matter." [Art&Und] (1:2) Wint 92, p. 5.
"Patrimony." [BrooklynR] (9) 92, p. 39.
"State of Grace" (For Lawrence Washington). [Art&Und] (1:3) Spr 92, p. 9.

2600. HARRIS, James (*See also* HARRIS, Jim)
"Aspens." [SouthernR] (28:2) Spr, Ap 92, p. 225.
"The Body." [Manoa] (4:2) Fall 92, p. 108.
"Evening Exercise." [SouthernR] (28:2) Spr, Ap 92, p. 223.
"New Mexico Dog." [SouthernR] (28:2) Spr, Ap 92, p. 224.
"Open Secrets." [Manoa] (4:2) Fall 92, p. 107-108.
"Taking Down the Frame." [PoetryE] (33) Spr 92, p. 58.
"Warbler." [Manoa] (4:2) Fall 92, p. 109.
"Well Well Well." [PoetryE] (33) Spr 92, p. 57.

2601. HARRIS, Jana
"Avalanche, Rattlesnake Canyon, February 1888." [OntR] (36) Spr-Sum 92, p. 64 - 66.
"Dialogue." [13thMoon] (10:1/2) 92, p. 44-46.
"Slippage" (for Cheri Fein). [OntR] (36) Spr-Sum 92, p. 61-63.

2602. HARRIS, Jim (*See also* HARRIS, James)
"The Berlin Wall Falls." [BlackBR] (15) Spr-Sum 92, p. 26-27.
"Rainbow Family." [NewYorkQ] (49) 92, p. 99.
2603. HARRIS, Joseph
"On the Value of Critics." [Light] (4) Wint 92-93, p. 16.
"This Poem." [AmerS] (61:3) Sum 92, p. 349.
2604. HARRIS, Judith
"My Husband Dreaming." [HiramPoR] (51/52) Fall 91-Sum 92, p. 39-40.
"My Mother's Keepsake Drawer." [WestB] (30) 92, p. 82.
2605. HARRIS, Lynn Farmer
"Two Feet From the End of the Fork." [LullwaterR] (3:2) Spr 92, p. 78-79.
2606. HARRIS, MacDonald
"The Old Man." [Pearl] (16) Fall 92, p. 60.
2607. HARRIS, Maureen
"Occasional Letters" (for Rhea Tregebov). [Event] (21:1) Spr 92, p. 55-58.
2608. HARRIS, Peter
"Breakfast." [HiramPoR] (51/52) Fall 91-Sum 92, p. 41.
"Intimations in Waterville." [CutB] (38) Sum 92, p. 94-95.
HARRIS, Robert Dassanowsky
See DASSANOWSKY-HARRIS, Robert
2609. HARRIS, Skip
"Who Will Save the Children?" [Gypsy] (18) 92, p. 135-136.
2610. HARRIS-BOARDMAN, Paul
"Ballad of the Aging Shingler." [Amelia] (7:1, #20) 92, p. 86-87.
2611. HARRISON, DeSales
"In Our Moment." [AntR] (50:4) Fall 92, p. 733.
2612. HARRISON, Devin
"Night-Light." [Lactuca] (16) Ag 92, p. 42.
"The Road to Zipolite." [Lactuca] (16) Ag 92, p. 41.
"The Summer Cottage" (Val David, 1947). [Lactuca] (16) Ag 92, p. 40-41.
2613. HARRISON, Jack
"Writers' Tea." [EngJ] (80:8) D 91, p. 99.
2614. HARRISON, James
"Disdain." [MalR] (101) Wint92, p. 110.
2615. HARRISON, Jeffrey
"Adirondack Moosehead." [Poetry] (160:6) S 92, p. 347.
"Arrival in Kathmandu." [DenQ] (26:4) Spr 92, p. 30.
"Child Reading an Almanac" (tr. of Francis Jammes). [SenR] (22:1) Spr 92, p. 40.
"Letter from the Golden Triangle." [Boulevard] (7:2/3, #20/21) Fall 92, p. 134-135.
"Like an insect, the mowing machine" (tr. of Francis Jammes). [SenR] (22:1) Spr 92, p. 41.
"The Omniscience of Snow." [SouthernR] (28:2) Spr, Ap 92, p. 257.
"Parable of the Fish and Heart." [SouthernR] (28:2) Spr, Ap 92, p. 256.
"A Shave by the Ganges." [NewYorker] (68:28) 31 Ag 92, p. 36.
"Swifts at Evening." [Poetry] (160:6) S 92, p. 348.
"There Were Carafes of clear water" (tr. of Francis Jammes). [SenR] (22:1) Spr 92, p. 42.
"The Village at Noon" (tr. of Francis Jammes). [SenR] (22:1) Spr 92, p. 43.
"Vines." [NewEngR] (14:3) Sum 92, p. 88-89.
2616. HARRISON, Joseph
"Orpheus." [WestHR] (46:3) Fall 92, p. 176-177.
2617. HARRISON, Pamela
"Field in Snow." [Poetry] (161:3) D 92, p. 140.
"Unhinged." [GreenMR] (NS 5:2) Spr-Sum 92, p. 113.
2618. HARRISON, Richard
"Because They Make Decisions." [PoetryC] (12:3/4) Jl 92, p. 19.
"Defense Mechanisms." [PoetryC] (12:3/4) Jl 92, p. 19.
"Face-Off." [PoetryC] (12:3/4) Jl 92, p. 19.
"The Praise of Men." [PoetryC] (12:3/4) Jl 92, p. 19.
"The Use of Force" (New York Rangers at Montreal, February 10, 1991). [PoetryC] (12:3/4) Jl 92, p. 19.
"Using the Body." [PoetryC] (12:3/4) Jl 92, p. 19.
2619. HARRISON, T. J.
"Lesson in Watercolors" (For my Grandmother). [SouthernPR] (32:1) Spr 92, p. 66 - 67.

2620. HARROD, Lois Marie
"Doctor Sweetheart." [PoetL] (87:3) Fall 92, p. 24-25.
"Fragments from the Gulf War." [Vis] (38) 92, p. 31.
"Listening to God." [Kalliope] (15:1) 92, p. 13-15.
"Poster from a Photography Exhibition." [JlNJPo] (14:2) Aut 92, p. 5.
"Rescue." [LitR] (25:2) Wint 92, p. 253.
"Talking About Important Things" (a letter to my sister). [JlNJPo] (14:2) Aut 92, p. 4.
"Three Windows." [PoetL] (87:3) Fall 92, p. 23.
"The Tower of Babel." [CarolQ] (44:3) Spr-Sum 92, p. 7.
"The Walrus with Her Luminous Whiskers." [US1] (26/27) 92, p. 11.
"Wind." [Vis] (39) 92, p. 29.
2621. HARROLD, William
"Supreme Morning" (after Edward Hopper's *Gas*, 1940). [CreamCR] (16:1) Spr 92, p. 112-113.
2622. HARSHAV, Barbara
"Human Bodies" (tr. of Yehuda Amichai, w. Benjamin Harshav). [ParisR] (34:122) Spr 92, p. 208.
"Late Wedding" (tr. of Yehuda Amichai, w. Benjamin Harshav). [ParisR] (34:122) Spr 92, p. 211.
"North of Beer Sheva" (tr. of Yehuda Amichai, w. Benjamin Harshav). [ParisR] (34:122) Spr 92, p. 210.
"Sandals" (tr. of Yehuda Amichai, w. Benjamin Harshav). [ParisR] (34:122) Spr 92, p. 209.
2623. HARSHAV, Benjamin
"Human Bodies" (tr. of Yehuda Amichai, w. Barbara Harshav). [ParisR] (34:122) Spr 92, p. 208.
"Late Wedding" (tr. of Yehuda Amichai, w. Barbara Harshav). [ParisR] (34:122) Spr 92, p. 211.
"North of Beer Sheva" (tr. of Yehuda Amichai, w. Barbara Harshav). [ParisR] (34:122) Spr 92, p. 210.
"Sandals" (tr. of Yehuda Amichai, w. Barbara Harshav). [ParisR] (34:122) Spr 92, p. 209.
2624. HARSHMAN, Marc
"Miracle." [SycamoreR] (4:2) Sum 92, p. 47-48.
2625. HART, Henry
"Byrd in Antarctica." [SouthernR] (28:1) Wint, Ja 92, p. 101-102.
2626. HART, Jack
"The House of the Murdered Man." [Pearl] (15) Spr-Sum 92, p. 14.
"A Thought for the Season." [Pearl] (15) Spr-Sum 92, p. 14.
"World Enough and Time." [Elf] (2:3) Fall 92, p. 38.
2627. HART, John W.
"Love Poem." [Pearl] (15) Spr-Sum 92, p. 18.
2628. HART, Micky
"On My Shoulders" (tr. by Richinel Ansano and Joceline Clemencia). [LitR] (35:4) Sum 92, p. 574.
"Riba Mi Skouder." [LitR] (35:4) Sum 92, p. 614.
2629. HARTEIS, Richard
"Genetics" (for Audrey Garbisch). [ThRiPo] (39/40) 92-93, p. 105-106.
"The Hermit's Curse." [ThRiPo] (39/40) 92-93, p. 103-104.
"Mirage" (In Memoriam, Katharine Meredith Goldenberg). [ThRiPo] (39/40) 92-93, p. 104-105.
"Stellar, on Your Anniversary." [AmerV] (26) Spr 92, p. 69.
2630. HARTOG, Diana
"The Black Bull." [MalR] (100) Fall 92, p. 44.
"Courtesy of Texaco." [Trans] (26) Spr 92, p. 59-60.
"Cruelty to Animals." [MalR] (100) Fall 92, p. 46.
"Spider Web." [MalR] (100) Fall 92, p. 45.
2631. HARTSELL, Lynn
"Lullaby." [Writer] (105:3) Mr 92, p. 21.
2632. HARVEY, Andrew
"Priam to Achilles." [NewYorkQ] (47) 92, p. 74.
2633. HARVEY, Gayle Elen
"The Darkness Gone and the Darkness Still to Come." [PaintedHR] (5) Wint 92, p. 8.
"A Daughter's Recital" (for Linda). [LullwaterR] (4:1) Fall 92, p. 58.

"Sculptor" (for Jim). [SnailPR] (2:1) Spr-Sum 92, p. 12.
"Thief of the Miniature Orchid." [SnailPR] (2:1) Spr-Sum 92, p. 13.
"Without a Sound" (for David). [LullwaterR] (4:1) Fall 92, p. 27.

2634. HARVEY, John
"On Not Translating Paul Valéry." [NewRep] (206:13) 30 Mr 92, p. 36.

2635. HARVEY, Philip
"The Daily Adult." [Vis] (38) 92, p. 27.
"The Passport German." [Vis] (40) 92, p. 6.

2636. HARVEY, Richard
"Inner City." [NewYorkQ] (47) 92, p. 75.

2637. HARVEY, Suzanne
"In the Shadow of Lassen Volcano." [BlackBR] (15) Spr-Sum 92, p. 35.
"Off Limits." [BlackBR] (15) Spr-Sum 92, p. 35.

2638. HARVOR, Elisabeth
"Always the Noise the Nights I Am Alone." [Quarry] (41:4) Fall 92, p. 7-9.
"The Death of the Nurse." [NewYorker] (68:13) 18 My 92, p. 40.
"Do You Live Alone?" [Arc] (28) Spr 92, p. 7-10.
"Fortress of Chairs." [Event] (21:1) Spr 92, p. 25-27.
"The Gender of the Hands of Whoever Comes Walking." [PottPort] (14:1) Spr-Sum 92, p. 5-7.
"I Don't Ask for Real Happiness." [PottPort] (14:1) Spr-Sum 92, p. 8-11.

2639. HARVOR, Richard
"Seagulls." [Arc] (28) Spr 92, p. 31-32.

2640. HARWOOD, Lee
"Homage to Albert Ryder and Bill Corbett, 1990." [JamesWR] (9:3) Spr 92, p. 6.

2641. HASCALL, Nancy (Nancy B.)
"Fox Squirrel." [EngJ] (81:8) D 92, p. 84.
"Illusion." [EngJ] (81:7) N 92, p. 98.

2642. HASHMI, Alamgir
"World's Garden: The First Stage" (Our Time Speaks with the Time to Come. The first section of the long poem, "Bagh-i Dunya/World's Garden," 1987, tr. of Gilani Kamran). [Elf] (2:2) Sum 92, p. 32-33.

2643. HASKINS, Lola
"Chewing the Soup." [PraS] (66:2) Sum 92, p. 10.
"The Cow." [ArtfulD] (22/23) 92, p. 63.
"Emergency" (for the minister's son). [CreamCR] (16:2) Fall 92, p. 43.
"The Field." [ArtfulD] (22/23) 92, p. 62.
"First Person Singular." [FreeL] (10) Sum 92, p. 26.
"El Gran Eclipse de Mexico." [ArtfulD] (22/23) 92, p. 61.
"Home School, Idaho." [FloridaR] (18:1) Spr-Sum 92, p. 110.
"How I Learned" (for my daughter). [SouthernR] (28:4) Aut, O 92, p. 854.
"Keys." [SouthernR] (28:4) Aut, O 92, p. 855.
"The Landscape of the Piano." [GeoR] (46:4) Wint 92, p. 662.
"The Rim-Benders." [PraS] (66:2) Sum 92, p. 11.
"Salvation in a Catholic Country." [TampaR] (5) Fall 92, p. 11.
"Second Variation on a Text by Vallejo." [ArtfulD] (22/23) 92, p. 58.
"Table Decorations for a Children's Party" (from "An Encyclopedia for Women," 1906). [FreeL] (10) Sum 92, p. 29.
"Wait for Us." [ArtfulD] (22/23) 92, p. 60.
"What the Recruiter Said." [ArtfulD] (22/23) 92, p. 59.

2644. HASS, Robert (*See also* HASS, Robert Bernard)
"Capri" (tr. of Czeslaw Milosz, w. the author). [NewYorker] (68:41) 30 N 92, p. 157.
"A Lecture" (tr. of Czeslaw Milosz, w. the author). [NewYorker] (68:18) 22 Je 92, p. 32.
"Why?" (tr. of Czeslaw Milosz, w. the author). [NewRep] (206:24) 15 Je 92, p. 44.

2645. HASS, Robert Bernard (*See also* HASS, Robert)
"Rite of Spring." [PoetL] (87:3) Fall 92, p. 27.
"Under the Influence." [PoetL] (87:3) Fall 92, p. 26.

2646. HASTINGS, Nancy Peters
"Father to Son." [NegC] (12:1/2) 92, p. 58.

2647. HATHAWAY, Michael
"As If I Didn't Have Enough Poets Crawling Out of the Woodwork." [Pearl] (15) Spr-Sum 92, p. 60.
"A Secret." [DogRR] (11:2, #22) Fall-Wint 92, p. 11.

2648. HATHAWAY, William
"How Gail's Love Defeats the Domination of Night." [PoetL] (87:4) Wint 92-93, p. 15.
"How the Existence of Gail Disproves Andreas Cappellanus' Thesis That Love Is a Form of Sickness." [PoetL] (87:4) Wint 92-93, p. 14.
"Morning Mists." [ColEng] (54:2) F 92, p. 161-162.
"Urban Animals" (for Marsha). [GreenMR] (NS 5:2) Spr-Sum 92, p. 91-95.
"Woe to Weal" (an elegy for John Logan). [CimR] (99) Ap 92, p. 35-36.
2649. HATTERSLEY, Geoff
"Eye, Lips, Miss." [Verse] (9:3) Wint 92, p. 105.
"Remembering Dennis's Eyes." [Verse] (9:3) Wint 92, p. 104.
"Tea Boy." [Verse] (9:3) Wint 92, p. 105.
2650. HAUG, James
"Homesickness" (for Mike Linden). [ColEng] (53:5) S 91, p. 536.
"Poverty Mountain." [ColEng] (53:5) S 91, p. 534.
"Some Information." [ColEng] (53:5) S 91, p. 535-536.
2651. HAUGHT, Kaylin
"Delicious Words." [OnTheBus] (4:2/5:1, #10/11) 92, p. 110.
"What I Learned in Two Marriages." [OnTheBus] (4:2/5:1, #10/11) 92, p. 110-111.
2652. HAUSER, Alisa
"Leba." [PoetryUSA] (24) 92, p. 31.
2653. HAVIARAS, Stratis
"Farm Woman" (tr. of Yannis Ritsos). [Trans] (26) Spr 92, p. 77-78.
HAWK, Red
See RED HAWK
2654. HAWKER, Heather
"Señor Castenago's Vision at the Guatemala Marketplace, June 1985." [CreamCR] (16:1) Spr 92, p. 96-97.
2655. HAWKES, Robert
"From a City Council Report." [PottPort] (14:1) Spr-Sum 92, p. 53.
"Interdict." [PottPort] (14:1) Spr-Sum 92, p. 52.
"Rehearsal: Medieval Priest." [PottPort] (14:1) Spr-Sum 92, p. 51-52.
2656. HAWKHEAD, John
"The Interferer." [SoCoast] (13) Je 93 [i.e. 92], p. 3.
"The Problem with Sharing." [SoCoast] (13) Je 93 [i.e. 92], p. 50.
2657. HAWKINS, Hunt
"The Invisible Hand Meets the Dead Hand High Above Washington D.C." [MinnR] (38) Spr-Sum 92, p. 44.
"Wallet." [FloridaR] (18:1) Spr-Sum 92, p. 32.
2658. HAWKINS, Tom
"Every Animal a Philosophy." [Crucible] (28) Fall 92, p. 19.
2659. HAWLEY, Beatrice
"Temporary Incarceration." [AmerPoR] (21:3) My-Je 92, p. 32.
2660. HAWLEY, Mary Kathleen
"Hands of God" (for jacquee). [SpoonRQ] (17:3/4) Sum-Fall 92, p. 58-60.
"Innocences" (for k.). [SpoonRQ] (17:3/4) Sum-Fall 92, p. 61-62.
2661. HAWLEY-MEIGS, James
"Late May" (for David Craig Austin). [Iowa] (22:3) Fall 92, p. 178-179.
"Malay Melee." [Iowa] (22:3) Fall 92, p. 177-178.
"The Yald-Swevyn Galimaufry of His Lives." [Iowa] (22:3) Fall 92, p. 177.
2662. HAWTHORNE, Susan
"First Breath" (from "the Language in My Tongue — A sequence of 23 poems on epilepsy). [SinW] (46) Spr 92, p. 20.
"New Tongue" (from "the Language in My Tongue — A sequence of 23 poems on epilepsy). [SinW] (46) Spr 92, p. 21.
2663. HAXTON, Brooks
"1969." [NewEngR] (14:4) Fall 92, p. 112-115.
"Auspice." [ThRiPo] (39/40) 92-93, p. 106-108.
"Her Parents Brought Suit, But Since She Was Incoherent and Profane." [VirQR] (68:3) Sum 92, p. 490-493.
"Horologe." [ParisR] (34:123) Sum 92, p. 93.
"The Sun at Night." [Atlantic] (270:6) D 92, p. 124.
"Traveling Company." [ThRiPo] (39/40) 92-93, p. 108-109.
2664. HAYDEN, Frances
"The Wonders of the Night." [OnTheBus] (4:2/5:1, #10/11) 92, p. 112.

2665. HAYDEN, Robert
"(American Journal)." [Field] (47) Fall 92, p. 52-55.
"Entrances and Tableaux for Josephine Baker" (an unfinished draft). [MichQR] (31:3) Sum 92, p. 318-320.
"Free Fantasia: Tiger Flowers" (For Michael). [Field] (47) Fall 92, p. 10-11.
"Middle Passage." [Field] (47) Fall 92, p. 14-19.
"Monet's Waterlilies." [Field] (47) Fall 92, p. 47.
"Runagate Runagate." [Field] (47) Fall 92, p. 31-33.
"Those Winter Sundays." [Field] (47) Fall 92, p. 8.
2666. HAYDON, Rich
"Grist." [CapeR] (27:2) Fall 92, p. 15.
2667. HAYES, Ann
"Much Ado About Nothing, Thanksgiving, 1972." [ThRiPo] (39/40) 92-93, p. 110-112.
"Pietá." [ThRiPo] (39/40) 92-93, p. 109-110.
2668. HAYES, N. D.
"Transfiguration." [MidAR] (13:2) 92, p. 79.
2669. HAYES, Noreen
"Garden Madonna." [ChrC] (109:21) 1-8 Jl 92, p. 653.
2670. HAYMAN, Dick
"Anglophile." [Light] (4) Wint 92-93, p. 10.
"Grand Canyon." [Light] (3) Aut 92, p. 12.
"No Mousetaking It." [Light] (3) Aut 92, p. 16.
2671. HAYMAN, Gina Sangster
"The Boys in the Morning." [SlipS] (12) 92, p. 57.
2672. HAYMON, Ava Leavell
"Catechism: Om Mani Padme Um" (for Ming Mah). [NowestR] (30:3) 92, p. 38.
"The Way Down Is Steep As the Way Up." [NowestR] (30:3) 92, p. 37.
2673. HAYNES/ELLIOT, William P.
"Kerouac's Blues" (a X-mas song). [MoodySI] (27) Spr 92, p. 35.
2674. HAYWARD, Camille
"And Not Even Bacchus." [BellArk] (8:3) My-Je 92, p. 5.
"The Bee Goes Looking About." [BellArk] (8:6) N-D 92, p. 28.
2675. HAYWARD, Steve
"Christmas, My Brother Home from the Nuthouse." [PoetL] (87:3) Fall 92, p. 29-30.
"What I've Learned from My Father's War Trophies." [PoetL] (87:3) Fall 92, p. 28.
2676. HAZNERS, Dainis
"Against Winter." [SouthernPR] (32:1) Spr 92, p. 27-28.
"In My Dream I Meet God, Hunting." [SouthernPR] (32:2) Fall 92, p. 47-48.
2677. HAZO, Samuel
"En Route." [FourQ] (6:2) Fall 92, p. 18-19.
2678. HAZOUMÉ, Roger Aralamon
"Situation" (tr. by Dorothy Aspinwall). [WebR] (16) Fall 92, p. 30.
HE, Li
See LI, He
2679. HEAD, Gwen
"Barbarossa." [SouthernR] (28:1) Wint, Ja 92, p. 36-37.
"Bruise." [SouthernR] (28:1) Wint, Ja 92, p. 39.
"Clumsy Ghazal." [SouthernR] (28:1) Wint, Ja 92, p. 40-41.
"Popcorn, Cotton." [SouthernR] (28:1) Wint, Ja 92, p. 37-38.
"The Tower." [SouthernR] (28:1) Wint, Ja 92, p. 41-42.
2680. HEAD, Robert
"Everytime I see her I start dissolving." [WormR] (32:3, #127) 92, p. 100.
"Hwy [i.e. Why?] is it always the same dream." [WormR] (32:3, #127) 92, p. 101-102.
"I think of Elizabeth and hear the ringing." [WormR] (32:3, #127) 92, p. 101.
"The thing to do is like Norman Vincent Peale said." [WormR] (32:3, #127) 92, p. 100.
"Well I've askt 2 women for a date." [WormR] (32:3, #127) 92, p. 101.
2681. HEADLEY, Robert
"Miscarried." [WritersF] (18) 92, p. 97.
2682. HEANEY, Seamus
"The Cure at Troy" (Choruses, from "Philoctetes," tr. of Sophocles). [Arion] 3d series (1:2) Spr 91, p. 131-138.
"Keeping Going." [NewYorker] (68:34) 12 O 92, p. 76-77.
"A Sofa in the Forties." [Verse] (9:3) Wint 92, p. 6-7.

2683. HEARD, George
"Alexandria." [EngJ] (80:7) N 91, p. 98.
2684. HEARLE, Kevin
"One Day." [QW] (34) Wint-Spr 92, p. 76.
2685. HEATH-STUBBS, John
"The Three Venturers." [Interim] (11:1) Spr-Sum 92, p. 14-15.
2686. HÉBERT, Anne
"A Small Dead Girl" (tr. by Alan Brown). [Trans] (26) Spr 92, p. 52.
2687. HECHT, Susan
"What My Hands Know." [Calyx] (14:2) Wint 92-93, p. 48-49.
2688. HEDIN, Robert
"The Age of the Great Liners" (after Jacobsen). [PoetryE] (33) Spr 92, p. 59.
"Just Delicate Needles" (tr. of Rolf Jacobsen). [LitR] (35:3) Spr 92, p. 324.
"The Streetlamp" (tr. of Rolf Jacobsen). [LitR] (35:3) Spr 92, p. 343.
"Wash & Dry Co" (tr. of Rolf Jacobsen). [LitR] (35:3) Spr 92, p. 342.
2689. HEFER, Haim
"Israel's American Hostages" (from "Hostages"). [Harp] (284:1700) Ja 92, p. 22.
2690. HEFFERNAN, Michael
"Angelology." [Iowa] (22:2) Spr-Sum 92, p. 134.
"Badia Fiesolana." [GettyR] (5:4) Aut 92, p. 697.
"Cafe Paradiso." [WillowS] (30) Sum 92, p. 8.
"Lawn Mower." [Iowa] (22:2) Spr-Sum 92, p. 135.
"A Temptation in the Wilderness." [WillowS] (30) Sum 92, p. 9.
2691. HEGI, Ursula
"One Katarina." [HighP] (7:1) Spr 92, p. 98-99.
2692. HEGLAND, Jean
"Abandonment." [Kalliope] (14:1) 92, p. 54-55.
2693. HEIDEMAN, Kathleen
"She Used to Have Some Cows" (for joy harjo and her horses). [Northeast] (5:7) Wint 92-93, p. 17-20.
2694. HEIFETZ, Hank
"For the Lord of the Animals" (Excerpt, tr. of Dhurjati, w. Velcheru Narayana Rao). [Trans] (26) Spr 92, p. 119-120.
2695. HEIGHTON, Steven
"Icarus." [Agni] (35) 92, p. 286-287.
2696. HEIKKINEN, Jim
"Roadside Passion." [InterPR] (18:2) Fall 92, p. 79.
2697. HEIM, Scott
"Brian Bloodynose." [ChironR] (11:4) Wint 92, p. 25.
"The Collector." [ChironR] (11:3) Aut 92, p. 3.
"I Crawl Inside Your Skin." [BrooklynR] (9) 92, p. 70.
"Killing Sam." [ChironR] (11:3) Aut 92, p. 3.
2698. HEINLEIN, D. A.
"Sunday Noon." [US1] (26/27) 92, p. 33.
2699. HEINRICH, Peggy
"Kitchen Riddles." [Elf] (2:3) Fall 92, p. 40.
"Triangles." [Elf] (2:3) Fall 92, p. 40.
2700. HEINZ, Susanne
"Calgary: 9:23am." [Dandel] (19:2) 92, p. 5.
2701. HEITHAUS, Joe
"Butcher's Son." [AntR] (50:4) Fall 92, p. 732.
2702. HEITZMAN, Judy Page
"March." [ThRiPo] (39/40) 92-93, p. 113.
"Spaces." [ThRiPo] (39/40) 92-93, p. 112-113.
2703. HEJINIAN, Lyn
"Sleeps" (Poetry Chapbook). [BlackWR] (18:2) Spr-Sum 92, p. 29-42.
"Untitled: A man comes in, his suit is crumpled" (tr. of Sergei Timofeyev, w. Irina Osadchaya). [Avec] (5:1) 92, p. 39.
"White Heart" (tr. of Sergei Timofeyev, w. Irina Osadchaya). [Avec] (5:1) 92, p. 39.
2704. HELD, Dennis
"Reuben, Sunday Morning, 1967." [Poetry] (161:3) D 92, p. 144.
2705. HELDER, Herberto
"The Lover Transforms" (tr. by Richard Zenith). [Stand] (33:4) Aut 92, p. 130.
"Seated Theory — II" (tr. by Richard Zenith). [Stand] (33:4) Aut 92, p. 131.

2706. HELLER, Ben
"And What Did They Do to the Strike?" (tr. of Raúl Barrientos). [InterPR] (18:2) Fall 92, p. 51, 53.
"It Would Be Better, Really, If They Devoured Everything and We Ended This" (— César Vallejo, tr. of Raúl Barrientos). [InterPR] (18:2) Fall 92, p. 61, 63.
"Sunday" (tr. of Raúl Barrientos). [InterPR] (18:2) Fall 92, p. 55, 57, 59.
2707. HELLER, Chaia (Chaia Zblocki)
"The Erotic Manifesto." [Kalliope] (14:3) 92, p. 16-18.
"Gift." [Calyx] (14:1) Sum 92, p. 56.
"Israeli Dancing." [ChironR] (11:4) Wint 92, p. 48.
"Moths." [Calyx] (14:1) Sum 92, p. 57-59.
2708. HELLER, Dorothy
"Gift Rap." [Light] (1) Spr 92, p. 16.
2709. HELLER, Janet Ruth
"Insomniac" (tr. of Dámaso Alonso). [ArtfulD] (22/23) 92, p. 31.
2710. HELMUTH, Willard
"Dinner at the Red Lobster." [Kaleid] (24) Wint-Spr 92, p. 29.
2711. HELWIG, David
"Pisanello: St. George and the Princess." [Grain] (20:4) Wint 92, p. 51-55.
"Requiem 1935-1940" (tr. of Anna Akhmatova). [Quarry] (41:1) Wint 92, p. 7-15.
2712. HEMAN, Bob
"Fingers." [Caliban] (11) 92, p. 134.
"I." [Caliban] (11) 92, p. 135.
"Passage." [Caliban] (11) 92, p. 134.
"Sacrifice." [Caliban] (11) 92, p. 134.
"True or False?" [Caliban] (11) 92, p. 135.
2713. HEMMINGSON, Michael
"Retail." [SlipS] (12) 92, p. 72-73.
2714. HEMP, Christine
"Pulling Peter Back." [BostonR] (17:1) F 92, p. 28.
2715. HEMPEL, Wes
"I Try to Get Attention." [BrooklynR] (9) 92, p. 57.
2716. HENDERSHOT, Cynthia
"Twenty Shores." [Asylum] (7:3/4) 92, p. 4.
"Woman in Love" (tr. of Paul Eluard). [Asylum] (7:3/4) 92, p. 8.
"The Wooden Cage." [Asylum] (7:3/4) 92, p. 70.
"Your Fingers Grow Out of His Palms." [Asylum] (7:3/4) 92, p. 71.
2717. HENDERSON, Archibald
"Elephants." [NegC] (12:1/2) 92, p. 60.
"Skirting Utopia." [NegC] (12:1/2) 92, p. 59.
"The White Crane." [NegC] (12:1/2) 92, p. 61.
2718. HENDERSON, David
"The Mortality of Bees." [Arc] (29) Aut 92, p. 56-57.
"Woman with Suitcase." [Arc] (29) Aut 92, p. 55.
"Woodsinger." [Arc] (29) Aut 92, p. 58-59.
2719. HENDERSON, Lydia
"If." Sparks! Writing by High School Students (1:1), a supplement to [PraF] (13:4, #61) Wint 92-93, p. 8.
2720. HENDRYSON, Barbara
"The Lake of Unceasing Fire." [Vis] (38) 92, p. 29.
2721. HENLEY, Jim
"Amphibian." [ChamLR] (10/11) Spr-Fall 92, p. 79.
"Kapoho." [ChamLR] (10/11) Spr-Fall 92, p. 78.
2722. HENN, Mary Ann
"Can I Tame the Echo?" [Footwork] 92, p. 88.
"On the Night." [Footwork] 92, p. 88.
2723. HENNESSEY-DeSENA, Laura
"Returning." [JINJPo] (14:2) Aut 92, p. 17.
2724. HENRIQUEZ, Francisco
"Sin Hora." [Nuez] (4:12) 92, p. 21.
2725. HENRIQUEZ, Jeanne
"Appeal from a Mother" (tr. by Richinel Ansano and Joceline Clemencia). [LitR] (35:4) Sum 92, p. 575.
"Plegaria di un Mama." [LitR] (35:4) Sum 92, p. 614.
2726. HENRY, Daniel
"The Dead Metaphor File (for Donald Hall)." [EngJ] (81:6) O 92, p. 93.

"Thomasdancing." [EngJ] (81:3) Mr 92, p. 93.
2727. HENRY, Gerrit
"Alone at Last." [ParisR] (34:122) Spr 92, p. 191-193.
"Recession." [BrooklynR] (9) 92, p. 93-94.
2728. HENRY, Pamela C.
"Blue Fall." [RagMag] (10:1) 92, p. 68.
"Tracks." [RagMag] (10:1) 92, p. 69.
2729. HENSLEY, Becca
"Family Tree." [CapeR] (27:2) Fall 92, p. 5.
2730. HENSON, David
"Auditioning the Alternatives." [LullwaterR] (3:3) Sum 92, p. 7.
"The Marriage in a Demanding Mood." [Ascent] (17:1) Fall 92, p. 50.
"The Marriage Trying to Reverse the Hex." [Ascent] (17:1) Fall 92, p. 51.
"The Old Woman in Charge of Creating Stars." [LaurelR] (26:2) Sum 92, p. 23.
"The Orgy." [LullwaterR] (3:3) Sum 92, p. 58.
2731. HENSON, Lance
"Anniversary Poem for the Cheyennes Who Died at Sand Creek." [Jacaranda] (6:1/2) Wint-Spr 92, p. 76.
2732. HENSON, Reg
"The Burial." [Wind] (22:71) 92, p. 20.
"Passion." [AfAmRev] (26:2) Sum 92, p. 236.
"Riding Shotgun" (w/ Birdie). [AfAmRev] (26:2) Sum 92, p. 236.
"Solitaire." [AfAmRev] (26:2) Sum 92, p. 237.
2733. HENSON, Sandy Meek
"Dust to Dust." [MidAR] (13:2) 92, p. 17-18.
2734. HENTZ, Robert R.
"A Critique of Pure Kant." [SoCoast] (12) Ja 92, p. 40.
"A Matter of Motivation." [Hellas] (3:1) Spr 92, p. 24-25.
"No Swimming Allowed." [Hellas] (3:1) Spr 92, p. 24.
2735. HERBECK, Ernst
"The Dream" (tr. by Melissa Monroe). [GrandS] (11:1, #41) 92, p. 221.
"Das Eichkätzchen." [GrandS] (11:1, #41) 92, p. 222.
"Heimweh." [GrandS] (11:1, #41) 92, p. 218.
"Homesickness" (tr. by Melissa Monroe). [GrandS] (11:1, #41) 92, p. 219.
"Der Morgen." [GrandS] (11:1, #41) 92, p. 218.
"Morning" (tr. by Melissa Monroe). [GrandS] (11:1, #41) 92, p. 219.
"The Squirrel" (tr. by Melissa Monroe). [GrandS] (11:1, #41) 92, p. 223.
"Der Traum." [GrandS] (11:1, #41) 92, p. 220.
2736. HERBERT, W. N.
"Cinema Paradiso." [Verse] (9:2) Sum 92, p. 92.
"Pictish Whispers." [Verse] (9:2) Sum 92, p. 91.
2737. HERBERT, Zbigniew
"About Mr. Cogito's Two Legs" (tr. by John and Bogdana Carpenter). [ParisR]] (34:124) Fall 92, p. 221-222.
"An Answer" (tr. by John and Bogdana Carpenter). [NewYRB] (39:1/2) 16 Ja 92, p. 17.
"Balconies" (tr. by John and Bogdana Carpenter). [Salm] (93) Wint 92, p. 130-131.
"Farewell to the City" (tr. by John and Bogdana Carpenter). [NewYorker] (68:13) 18 My 92, p. 64.
"How We Were Introduced" (for perfidious protectors, tr. by John and Bogdana Carpenter). [Salm] (93) Wint 92, p. 139-140.
"In a Studio" (tr. by John and Bogdana Carpenter). [Salm] (93) Wint 92, p. 132-133.
"A Journey" (tr. by John and Bogdana Carpenter). [Salm] (93) Wint 92, p. 126-127.
"Late Autumnal Poem of Mr. Cogito Destined for Women's Magazines" (tr. by John and Bogdana Carpenter). [ParisR]] (34:124) Fall 92, p. 220.
"Mr. Cogito and a Poet of a Certain Age" (tr. by John and Bogdana Carpenter). [NewYorker] (67:51) 10 F 92, p. 38.
"Mr. Cogito and Pure Thought" (tr. by John and Bogdana Carpenter). [ParisR]] (34:124) Fall 92, p. 219-220.
"Mr. Cogito and the Pearl" (tr. by John and Bogdana Carpenter). [ParisR]] (34:124) Fall 92, p. 222.
"Mr. Cogito Encounters a Statuette of the Great Mother in the Louvre" (tr. by John and Bogdana Carpenter). [ParisR]] (34:124) Fall 92, p. 223.
"Mr. Cogito Looks at His Face in the Mirror" (tr. by John and Bogdana Carpenter). [ParisR]] (34:124) Fall 92, p. 224-225.
"My City" (tr. by John and Bogdana Carpenter). [Salm] (93) Wint 92, p. 129-130.

"Old Prometheus" (tr. by John and Bogdana Carpenter). [ParisR]] (34:124) Fall 92, p. 216.
"Prayer of the Old Men" (tr. by John and Bogdana Carpenter). [NewYorker] (68:40) 23 N 92, p. 68.
"Request" (tr. by John and Bogdana Carpenter). [Salm] (93) Wint 92, p. 141-142.
"Rovigo" (tr. by Charles S. Kraszewski). [Antaeus] (69) Aut 92, p. 61-62.
"A Small Bird" (tr. by John and Bogdana Carpenter). [Salm] (93) Wint 92, p. 134 - 135.
"Song of the Drum" (tr. by John and Bogdana Carpenter). [Salm] (93) Wint 92, p. 136-137.
"Speculations on the Subject of Barabbas" (tr. by John and Bogdana Carpenter). [ParisR]] (34:124) Fall 92, p. 215-216.
"Thorns and Roses" (tr. by John and Bogdana Carpenter). [Salm] (93) Wint 92, p. 128.
"Those Who Lost" (tr. by John and Bogdana Carpenter). [ParisR]] (34:124) Fall 92, p. 217.
"The Troubles of a Little Creator" (tr. by John and Bogdana Carpenter). [Salm] (93) Wint 92, p. 137-139.
"Wagon" (tr. by John and Bogdana Carpenter). [NewYorker] (68:32) 28 S 92, p. 42.
"We Fall Asleep on Words" (tr. by John and Bogdana Carpenter). [NewYRB] (39:1/2) 16 Ja 92, p. 17.
"Wit Stwosz: Madonna Falling Asleep" (tr. by John and Bogdana Carpenter). [ParisR]] (34:124) Fall 92, p. 218.

HERK, Aritha van
See Van HERK, Aritha

2738. HERMAN, Maja
"Under the Glass Bell" (tr. by the author and Mark Strand). [ParisR] (34:123) Sum 92, p. 34.

2739. HERMSEN, Terry
"Fable." [Journal] (16:2) Fall-Wint 92, p. 26-27.
"Rodan" (for Michael C. Perrie). [Outbr] (23) 92, p. 35-36.

2740. HERNANDEZ, David
"Florencia." [TriQ] (86) Wint 92-93, p. 64-65.

2741. HERNANDEZ, Francisco
"Deep Waters" (Selections: 7, 15-17, tr. by Martha B. Jordan). [Manoa] (4:2) Fall 92, p. 23-24.
"How Robert Schumann Was Defeated by Demons" (Excerpt, tr. by Reginald Gibbons). [TriQ] (85) Fall 92, p. 278-279.

2742. HERNANDEZ, Miguel
"Andaluces de Jaén." [Areíto] (3:12) Octubre 92, inside back cover.
"Elegía" (De: "El rayo que no cesa"). [Areíto] (3:12) Octubre 92, p. 42.
"Eterna Sombra" (De: "Poemas últimos"). [Areíto] (3:12) Octubre 92, p. 44.
"First Song" (tr. by Don Share). [Noctiluca] (1:2) Wint 92 [on cover: Wint 93], p. 14.
"In the Depths of Man" (tr. by Don Share). [Noctiluca] (1:2) Wint 92 [on cover: Wint 93], p. 13.
"Orillas de Tu Vientre" (De: "Poemas últimos"). [Areíto] (3:12) Octubre 92, p. 41.
"Por Desplumar Arcángeles Glaciales" (De: "El rayo que no cesa"). [Areíto] (3:12) Octubre 92, p. 43.
"Sentado sobre los Muertos" (De: "Viento del pueblo"). [Areíto] (3:12) Octubre 92, inside front cover.
"Tristes Guerras" (De: "Cancionero y romancero de ausencias"). [Areíto] (3:12) Octubre 92, p. 44.
"Yo No Quiero Más Luz Que Tu Cuerpo ante el Mío" (De: "Poemas últimos"). [Areíto] (3:12) Octubre 92, p. 43.

2743. HERNANDEZ-CRUZ, Victor
"White Table" (Excerpts). [Callaloo] (15:4) Fall 92, p. 952-957.

2744. HERRERA, Juan Felipe
"Alligator." [AmerPoR] (21:6) N-D 92, p. 45.
"Cimabue, Goya, Beginnings." [InterPR] (18:1) Spr 92, p. 72.
"Crescent Moon on a Cat's Collar" (for Alurista). [InterPR] (18:1) Spr 92, p. 73-74.
"Foreign Inhabitant." [InterPR] (18:1) Spr 92, p. 74-75.
"Glamorous Treacheries." [HighP] (7:1) Spr 92, p. 100-101.
"Inside the Jacket." [InterPR] (18:1) Spr 92, p. 71.
"Loss, Revival & Retributions (Neon Desert Collage)." [AmerPoR] (21:6) N-D 92, p. 45.

"Muscatine County Fair at West Liberty, Iowa" (for George Barlow). [RiverS] (36) 92, p. 3-8.
"On the Day of the Dead, Mr. Emptiness Sings of Love" (for Ernesto Padilla and Yolanda Luera). [NewEngR] (14:4) Fall 92, p. 216-217.
"Saudi Journal." [RiverS] (36) 92, p. 9-10.
"Shawashté." [NewEngR] (14:4) Fall 92, p. 218-220.

2745. HERRICK, Robert
"To Live Merrily, and to Trust to Good Verses." [Light] (3) Aut 92, p. 30.

2746. HERRSTROM, David
"One Act of Cat." [US1] (26/27) 92, p. 12.

2747. HERSCHBACH, Robert
"Legend." [CreamCR] (16:2) Fall 92, p. 82-83.

2748. HERSHON, Robert
"Doctor in the House." [BrooklynR] (9) 92, p. 54.
"Door Screen Door Storm Door." [PoetryNW] (33:2) Sum 92, p. 11.
"The Dream That You Work There Again." [Talisman] (8) Spr 92, p. 20.
"How It Ends." [PoetryNW] (33:2) Sum 92, p. 10.
"Late March in the Botanic Garden" (for Harvey Shapiro). [Talisman] (8) Spr 92, p. 20.
"Operation Welcome Home, Late That Day." [WilliamMR] (30) 92, p. 9.
"The Other Last Man at the Party Turns Out to Be a Bore." [PoetryNW] (33:2) Sum 92, p. 9.

2749. HERTZ, Dalia
"Workshop." [MichQR] (31:3) Sum 92, p. 390.

2750. HESS, Mary Barbara
"Grass Dance — Dakota Territory, 1888." [BellR] (15:1) Spr 92, p. 35.

2751. HESS, Sonya
"Rain Dance." [Noctiluca] (1:2) Wint 92 [on cover: Wint 93], p. 30.

2752. HESSE, Herman
"The Seducer" (tr. by William Packard). [NewYorkQ] (48) 92, p. 82.
"Verführer." [NewYorkQ] (48) 92, p. 82.

2753. HESTER, Alan
"Is Anyone Sitting There?" [SoCoast] (12) Ja 92, p. 48.

2754. HEWETT, Greg
"Father Installs Shower, ca. 1962." [PacificR] (11) 92-93, p. 82-83.
"Garbo Behind Black Screen." [Interim] (11:2) Fall-Wint 92-93, p. 9-12.
"SAID." [Art&Und] (1:4) Jl-Ag 92, p. 10.

2755. HEWITT, Bernard R.
"The Change." [Amelia] (6:4, #19) 92, p. 117.
"Higher." [Amelia] (6:4, #19) 92, p. 117.

2756. HEWITT, Christopher (Chris)
"At the Fringe" (tr. of Georg Trakl, w. L. D. Davidson). [PassN] (13:1) Sum 92, p. 31.
"Giving Way to Light" (In Memory of Bart G.). [Art&Und] (1:3) Spr 92, p. 11.
"The Granary Wall." [JamesWR] (9:4) Sum 92, p. 7.
"On Raggedstone Hill." [JamesWR] (9:3) Spr 92, p. 13.
"Recovery" (in memory of Troy Davis). [JamesWR] (9:3) Spr 92, p. 13.
"This Year Is Like the Year a Thousand Years Ago" (tr. of Thomas Bernhard, w. L. D. Davidson). [Salm] (94/95) Spr-Sum 92, p. 136.

2757. HEYEN, William
"Fulcrum: The New Poem." [AmerPoR] (21:2) Mr-Ap 92, p. 34.
"Fur." [SouthernR] (28:1) Wint, Ja 92, p. 55.
"The Gift." [AmerPoR] (21:2) Mr-Ap 92, p. 34.
"The Traffic." [SouthernR] (28:1) Wint, Ja 92, p. 56.
"Transcendentalism." [SouthernR] (28:1) Wint, Ja 92, p. 57.

2758. HEYMAN, Mark Steven
"Infink Skyward After Noon." [NowestR] (30:1) 92, p. 37.
"Infink Swims." [NowestR] (30:1) 92, p. 36.

2759. HEYNAN, Jim
"Bird Songs." [Zyzzyva] (8:1) Spr 92, p. 85.

2760. HIBBARD, Tom
"Edouard." [AnotherCM] (24) Fall 92, p. 89.
"Savings Account." [AnotherCM] (24) Fall 92, p. 88.
"Woollcott." [AnotherCM] (24) Fall 92, p. 90.

2761. HICOK, Bob
"85." [Iowa] (22:1) Wint 92, p. 184.

"530 Lakewood." [SycamoreR] (4:2) Sum 92, p. 49-50.
"AIDS." [Witness] (5:1) 91, p. 94-95.
"Alice Wakes at Two and Looks Out the Window." [Witness] (5:1) 91, p. 93.
"Alzheimer's." [SycamoreR] (4:2) Sum 92, p. 51.
"Bear This in Mind." [Iowa] (22:1) Wint 92, p. 185.
"Bedtime Story." [PoetryE] (33) Spr 92, p. 60.
"By the Hour." [TarRP] (31:2) Spr 92, p. 11-12.
"Instinct." [CreamCR] (16:2) Fall 92, p. 32-33.
"Ohmy." [RiverC] (12:2) Spr 92, p. 46.
"Totem." [CimR] (99) Ap 92, p. 56.
"The Twins." [RiverC] (12:2) Spr 92, p. 47.
"Waiting." [CreamCR] (16:2) Fall 92, p. 34.
"A Way Home." [MidAR] (12:2) 92, p. 44.

2762. HIERRO, José
"Among Trees" (tr. by Louis Bourne). [AmerPoR] (21:6) N-D 92, p. 48.
"I Asked the Rocks" (tr. by Louis Bourne). [AmerPoR] (21:6) N-D 92, p. 50.
"Portrait in a Concert" (Homage to J.S. Bach, tr. by Louis Bourne). [AmerPoR] (21:6) N-D 92, p. 49-50.
"Return" (tr. by Louis Bourne). [AmerPoR] (21:6) N-D 92, p. 49.

2763. HIGGINBOTHAM, Patricia
"The Art of Fiction." [Elf] (2:2) Sum 92, p. 29.

2764. HIGGINS, Andrew
"Francine Strength." [NewYorkQ] (49) 92, p. 78-79.

2765. HIGGINS, Mary Rising
"Acclimation." [DenQ] (27:1) Sum 92, p. 116.

2766. HIGH, John
"The Lives of Thomas" (5 selections). [Avec] (5:1) 92, p. 115-117.
"On New Year's Day" (tr. of Ivan Zhdanov, w. Julie Gesin). [Avec] (5:1) 92, p. 124.
"Untitled: ('Stone')" (tr. of Ivan Zhdanov, w. Julie Gesin). [Avec] (5:1) 92, p. 124.

2767. HIGHBERG, Nels P.
"After Dinner." [EvergreenC] (7:2) Sum-Fall 92, p. 42.

2768. HILBERRY, Jane
"Fireweed." [HighP] (7:2) Fall 92, p. 67.

2769. HILBERT, Donna
"Deep Red." [Pearl] (16) Fall 92, p. 56.
"Mr. Eliot." [Pearl] (15) Spr-Sum 92, p. 51.
"My Mother Tongue." [Pearl] (15) Spr-Sum 92, p. 51.
"Neighbors." [ChironR] (11:2) Sum 92, p. 7.
"Please Knock Softly." [ChironR] (11:2) Sum 92, p. 7.
"Ragtime." [Pearl] (16) Fall 92, p. 56.
"Test." [Pearl] (16) Fall 92, p. 56.
"Uncle Eugene." [ChironR] (11:2) Sum 92, p. 7.

2770. HILDEBIDLE, John
"For Omaira Sanchez: November, 1985." [CentR] (36:1) Wint 92, p. 137-138.

2771. HILL, Adam Craig
"My Neighbor." [PoetC] (24:1) Fall 92, p. 34-35.

2772. HILL, Henry F.
"No Appeal." [Light] (3) Aut 92, p. 24.

2773. HILL, Lindsay
"Ndjen Ferno." [Caliban] (11) 92, p. 113-116.

2774. HILL, Nick
"Un Altar for the Abuelitos." [BilingR] (17:3) S-D 92, p. 268-269.
"Mundane Rights of Redemption / Ritos de Rendencion Mundanos." [MinnR] (39) Fall-Wint 92-93, p. 6.
"A Papelaria." [MinnR] (39) Fall-Wint 92-93, p. 7-8.
"Transfer Points." [BilingR] (17:3) S-D 92, p. 270-272.

2775. HILL, Norah
"Dusting, Holding Her on My Palm." [Stand] (33:2) Spr 92, p. 52-54.

2776. HILL, Pamela Steed
"Addressing Dream." [PaintedB] (47) 92, p. 26.
"Addressing Dream." [PaintedHR] (6) Spr 92, p. 5.
"The Blueberry Man." [Poem] (68) N 92, p. 39.
"An Infinity of Leaps." [Nimrod] (35:2) Spr-Sum 92, p. 96-97.
"Invocation." [Poem] (68) N 92, p. 41.
"Renewal." [Poem] (68) N 92, p. 40.

2777. HILL, Steve (*See also* HILL, Steven)
"Battered Wife." [PoetryUSA] (24) 92, p. 30.
"Elder Skelter." [PoetryUSA] (24) 92, p. 32.
2778. HILL, Steven (*See also* HILL, Steve)
"Monopoly Capital Sexuality." [MinnR] (38) Spr-Sum 92, p. 42-43.
2779. HILLARD, Jeffrey
"Blennerhassett Island, 1811." [RiverS] (36) 92, p. 25.
"End to End, 1690." [RiverS] (36) 92, p. 23-24.
"The Rousters, 1850." [WestB] (30) 92, p. 63-64.
"Several Hundred Broadwings." [Farm] (9:2) Fall-Wint 92-93, p. 115-116.
2780. HILLES, Robert
"Apollo." [Event] (21:2) Sum 92, p. 67.
"Apples." [Quarry] (41:1) Wint 92, p. 22-23.
"Blue Mud." [Descant] (23:3, #78) Fall 92, p. 9-13.
"Deathness." [AntigR] (91) Fall 92, p. 128-130.
"Fools on Saturday." [Descant] (23:3, #78) Fall 92, p. 14-15.
"Love Suite" (for Rebecca). [CapilR] (2:8) Spr 92, p. 24-30.
"The Man inside Her." [Grain] (20:2) Sum 92, p. 47.
"Smallness." [Quarry] (41:1) Wint 92, p. 21-22.
"Stubbornness." [CanLit] (134) Aut 92, p. 60-61.
"Swan." [Grain] (20:2) Sum 92, p. 46.
"The Wind Inside." [WestCL] (26:1, #7) Spr 92, p. 71-72.
2781. HILLILA, Bernhard
"Springing." [Light] (1) Spr 92, p. 12.
2782. HILLMAN, Brenda
"Branch, Scraping." [Epoch] (41:2) 92, p. 265-267.
"A Dwelling." [AmerPoR] (21:6) N-D 92, p. 9.
"An Entity." [AmerPoR] (21:6) N-D 92, p. 9.
"Luminous Textures." [Epoch] (41:2) 92, p. 268-270.
"Much Hurrying." [AmerPoR] (21:6) N-D 92, p. 10.
"Near Jenner." [AmerPoR] (21:6) N-D 92, p. 9.
"Reverse Seeing." [AmerPoR] (21:6) N-D 92, p. 10.
"Spare World" (from "Bright Existence"). [Zyzzyva] (8:1) Spr 92, p. 69-71.
"Toll Collector." [Thrpny] (51) Fall 92, p. 9.
"Trapped Light." [Nat] (255:22) 28 D 92, p. 820.
"Why did you tremble when you came in here." [Epoch] (41:2) 92, p. 264.
"Yellow Tractate" (from "Death Tractates," a book about grief). [Zyzzyva] (8:1) Spr 92, p. 73-75.
2783. HILLMAN, Elizabeth
"The Pirate." [Confr] (48/49) Spr-Sum 92, p. 234.
2784. HILLMER, Timothy
"Hunger" (For Nancy). [ChironR] (11:1) Spr 92, p. 27.
"Sister Lenora." [ChironR] (11:2) Sum 92, p. 17.
2785. HILTON, Barbara
"Mama Danced." [ChironR] (11:1) Spr 92, p. 26.
2786. HILTON, David
"Mass at Rathmullen." [BelPoJ] (42:4) Sum 92, p. 42.
"Tips on the Burren." [Bogg] (65) 92, p. 8.
2787. HINDEN, Michael
"Butter My Toast" (After John Donne). [Light] (2) Sum 92, p. 10.
2788. HINDLEY, Chris
"A Letter to Mrs. Kawamura" (1992 AWP Intro Award Winner). [IndR] (15:2) Fall 92, p. 151.
2789. HINES, Debra
"Dominion." [Iowa] (22:1) Wint 92, p. 38-40.
"The Spoiled Woman." [Iowa] (22:1) Wint 92, p. 37-38.
"Trademark." [Iowa] (22:1) Wint 92, p. 36-37.
2790. HINMAN, Mimi Walter
"The Man of *Shibui* Voice." [HawaiiR] (16:2, #35) Spr 92, p. 73-74.
2791. HINRICHSEN, Dennis
"Perfect Pitch." [PoetryNW] (33:2) Sum 92, p. 12-13.
"Power Surge." [PoetryNW] (33:2) Sum 92, p. 12.
2792. HINSHELWOOD, Nigel
"Exquisite Sensibilities." [WashR] (17:6) Ap-My 92, p. 14.
"The Minimalist." [WashR] (17:6) Ap-My 92, p. 14.

2793. HINTON, David
"Wild Apples." [Sulfur] (12:1, #30) Spr 92, p. 67-68.
"Window." [Sulfur] (12:1, #30) Spr 92, p. 66.
2794. HIPPERT, Rebecca
"The Angel" (for Olivier Rebbot). [GreenMR] (NS 5:2) Spr-Sum 92, p. 28-29.
"Bohemian Glass." [GreenMR] (NS 5:2) Spr-Sum 92, p. 30-31.
2795. HIRANANDANI, Popati
"The Husband Speaks" (tr. by the author, with editing by Arlene Zide). [ChiR] (38:1/2) 92, p. 180-181.
2796. HIRSCH, Edward
"Apostrophe" (In Memory of Donald Barthelme, 1931-1989). [NewRep] (206:7) 17 F 92, p. 34.
"Away from Dogma." [ParisR] (34:125) Wint 92, p. 163-165.
"Blunt Morning." [NewYorker] (68:22) 20 Jl 92, p. 40.
"Devil's Night." [MichQR] (31:2) Spr 92, p. 194.
"Earthly Light" (Homage to the 17th-Century Dutch Painters). [NewEngR] (14:3) Sum 92, p. 223-228.
"In Memorium Paul Celan." [NewRep] (206:4) 27 Ja 92, p. 35.
"The Reader." [IndR] (15:1) Spr 92, p. 54.
"Scorched." [Nat] (254:12) 30 Mr 92, p. 422.
"Simone Weil: The Year of Factory Work (1934-35)." [NewYorker] (67:47) 13 Ja 92, p. 34-35.
"The Watcher" (Leopardi in Rome, 1823). [Antaeus] (69) Aut 92, p. 134-135.
2797. HIRSCH, Gene
"Maria Sabina" (Based partly on predictions of Maria Sabina, Mazatec healer, told by John Bierhorst). [HiramPoR] (51/52) Fall 91-Sum 92, p. 42.
2798. HIRSCHFIELD, Ted
"Cemetery to the American War Dead in Luxembourg." [CapeR] (27:1) Spr 92, p. 20.
"Cemetery to the German War Dead in Luxemburg." [CapeR] (27:1) Spr 92, p. 21.
2799. HIRSHFIELD, Jane
"The Heart As Origami." [ParisR]] (34:124) Fall 92, p. 177.
"In Yellow Grass." [YellowS] (Ten Years [i.e. 40]) Sum-Fall 92, p. 38.
"The Shadow." [Zyzzyva] (8:1) Spr 92, p. 64-65.
"A Sweetening All Around Me As It Falls." [Poetry] (160:5) Ag 92, p. 254.
"The Weighing." [ParisR]] (34:124) Fall 92, p. 176.
2800. HIRSHKOWITZ, Lois
"Advent with a Lower Case 'a'." [Epiphany] (3:4) O (Fall) 92, p. 257-258.
"Finale." [NewDeltaR] (8:2) Spr-Sum 91, p. 115-116.
"Power Out at the Pleasure Factory." [Epiphany] (3:4) O (Fall) 92, p. 259.
"Snow Flakes." [Epiphany] (3:4) O (Fall) 92, p. 260.
2801. HIRSHMAN, Jack
"Human Interlude" (for Terry Garvin). [PoetryE] (34) Fall 92, p. 94.
"The Jacket" (in memory of Leopoldo Fiorenzato, suicided 1987). [PoetryE] (34) Fall 92, p. 95-96.
"The Night" (for Cornelius Cardew, People's Composer). [PoetryE] (34) Fall 92, p. 113.
"Streetscene." [PoetryE] (34) Fall 92, p. 116-117.
"The Weeping." [PoetryE] (34) Fall 92, p. 115-116.
"A Woman Gives Food" (for Sarah Menefee). [PoetryE] (34) Fall 92, p. 114.
2802. HIX, Blacky
"Back Road to Beyond." [ChironR] (11:1) Spr 92, p. 4.
"Dogs." [ChironR] (11:1) Spr 92, p. 4.
"Lice." [ChironR] (11:1) Spr 92, p. 4.
"They Strapped Him." [ChironR] (11:1) Spr 92, p. 4.
"Wild Dog" (In memory of Terry Ray Hix). [ChironR] (11:3) Aut 92, p. 16.
2803. HIX, H. Edgar
"Back Before." [Writer] (105:12) D 92, p. 20.
"A Married Man." [Epiphany] (3:2) Ap (Spr) 92, p. 107.
"Peter Pan." [Epiphany] (3:2) Ap (Spr) 92, p. 108.
"Road." [Epiphany] (3:2) Ap (Spr) 92, p. 109.
2804. HIX, H. L.
"Don't Wait on Me, She Said. Patience Is a Virtue, and You Should." [NowestR] (30:3) 92, p. 30.
"A Grace It Had, Devouring." [BlackWR] (18:2) Spr-Sum 92, p. 45.
"Lament for the Blood." [ChatR] (12:2) Wint 92, p. 48.

"Lament for the Lungs." [ChatR] (12:2) Wint 92, p. 47.
"Lament for the Tongue." [ChatR] (12:2) Wint 92, p. 46.
"Necessity Breaks Iron" (— Feuerbach, "The Essence of Christianity"). [FourQ] (6:2) Fall 92, p. 20.
"One Is the Point, Two the Line, Three the Triangle, Four the Pyramid" (— Speusippus, on Pythagoras). [GeoR] (46:4) Wint 92, p. 644.
"This Particular Eden." [BlackWR] (18:2) Spr-Sum 92, p. 46-47.

2805. HNATIW, Chrystyna
"Only the crickets remind me." [PraF] (13:3, #60) Aut 92, p. 61.
"Tell me, did you not cry inside." [PraF] (13:3, #60) Aut 92, p. 59-60.

2806. HOAGLAND, Tony
"In the Land of Lotus Eaters." [GeoR] (46:2) Sum 92, p. 234-235.
"In the Land of Lotus Eaters." [Harp] (286:1710) N 92, p. 36.
"You're the Top." [GeoR] (46:3) Fall 92, p. 479-480.

2807. HOBBS, Blair
"Sister's Life." [GeoR] (46:3) Fall 92, p. 450-451.
"Yoshitoshi's Women" (For Ellen). [PraS] (66:2) Sum 92, p. 11-15.

2808. HOBSON, Geary
"Buffalo Poem #1" (or, On Hearing That a Small Herd of Buffalo has "Broken Loose" . . .). [Jacaranda] (6:1/2) Wint-Spr 92, p. 77.

2809. HOCHMAN, Benjamin
"Nine and How Many?" [Light] (4) Wint 92-93, p. 8.

2810. HODGE, Jan D.
"In Memory: John Bennett." [BelPoJ] (43:1) Fall 92, p. 42.

2811. HODGE, Lonnie
"Cathedral." [WindO] (56) Fall-Wint 92, p. 15.
"The Clearing." [WindO] (56) Fall-Wint 92, p. 16.

2812. HODGE, Margaret
"For William Stafford Reading from His Book for Children." [BellArk] (8:4) Jl-Ag 92, p. 19.
"A Ninth Memorial Day" (to Randy). [BellArk] (8:5) S-O 92, p. 21.

2813. HODGES, Lesley
"Another Face." [PacificR] (11) 92-93, p. 38-39.
"Catherine the Great." [PacificR] (11) 92-93, p. 40.

2814. HODJAK, Franz
"Hertza" (tr. of Benjamin Fondane, w. Edouard Roditi). [Pequod] (34) 92, p. 76-77.

2815. HODOR, Timothy
"The Meaning of the Meadow." [Comm] (119:20) 20 N 92, p. 18.
"The Narcissus Bone." [Comm] (119:6) 27 Mr 92, p. 19.

2816. HOEPPNER, Edward Haworth
"Furlough" (from "Opposite Keys"). [Nimrod] (35:2) Spr-Sum 92, p. 98-99.
"Piano." [Boulevard] (7:1, #19) Spr 92, p. 166.
"Willows." [FloridaR] (18:2) Fall-Wint 92, p. 33.

2817. HOEY, Allen
"The Heart Sutra." [OhioR] (48) 92, p. 91-93.
"Rose Moon." [Hudson] (44:4) Wint 92, p. 617-618.

2818. HOFFMAN, Daniel
"Called Back." [Hudson] (45:2) Sum 92, p. 219-220.
"Mean Street." [Hudson] (45:2) Sum 92, p. 218-219.

2819. HOFFMANN, Roald
"The Bering Bridge." [NewEngR] (14:4) Fall 92, p. 191.

2820. HOGAN, Judy
"Beaver Soul 11" (April 19, 1992). [Crucible] (28) Fall 92, p. 10-11.

2821. HOGAN, Linda
"Blessings." [Jacaranda] (6:1/2) Wint-Spr 92, p. 78-79.
"Other, Sister, Twin." [KenR] (NS 14:2) Spr 92, p. 3-4.

2822. HOGAN, Michael
"Dry Thoughts in a Rainy Season." [ColR] (9:1) Spr-Sum 92, p. 135.
"For a Student Tempted by Suicide." [OxfordM] (6:2) Fall-Wint 90, p. 76-77.
"Letter from Mother." [OxfordM] (6:2) Fall-Wint 90, p. 75.
"On Translating a Mexican Poet." [ColR] (9:1) Spr-Sum 92, p. 133-134.

HOGAN, Patrick Colm
See COLM-HOGAN, Patrick

2823. HOGAN, Wayne
"Colors in the Soviet Union." [SlipS] (12) 92, p. 70.
"A Sucker for Science." [Light] (1) Spr 92, p. 24.

"What's Light Verse." [Light] (1) Spr 92, p. 7.

2824. HOGGARD, James
"Convocation of Words" (tr. of Tino Villanueva). [TriQ] (86) Wint 92-93, p. 96-97.
"Promised Lands" (tr. of Tino Villanueva). [TriQ] (86) Wint 92-93, p. 93-95.
"You, If No One Else" (tr. of Tino Villanueva). [TriQ] (86) Wint 92-93, p. 91-92.

2825. HOGGE, Robert M.
"Searching for the City of Heaven — Bartolome de Las Casas's Abstract of Columbus's *Journal*." [WeberS] (9:3) Fall 92, p. 65.

2826. HOHN, Donovan
"The Man Wearing White Robes and a Strange Hat" (honorable mention, Eve of Saint Agnes Contest). [NegC] (12:3) 92, p. 12-13.

2827. HOLBO, Christine
"Gomorrah." [NewYorker] (67:49) 27 Ja 92, p. 30.

2828. HOLBROOK, Lisa
"Disguised under our skin" (tr. of Vénus Khoury-Ghata). [SpoonRQ] (17:3/4) Sum - Fall 92, p. 42.
"If there were not these men enslaved to the sun" (tr. of Vénus Khoury-Ghata). [SpoonRQ] (17:3/4) Sum-Fall 92, p. 43.
"Stained by prayers and fears" (tr. of Vénus Khoury-Ghata). [SpoonRQ] (17:3/4) Sum-Fall 92, p. 44.
"Through colors" (tr. of Nadia Tueni). [SpoonRQ] (17:3/4) Sum-Fall 92, p. 45.

2829. HOLBROOK, Susan
"Six Trans Poems to Federico García Lorca's *Poema del Cante Jondo*." [WestCL] (26:3, #9) Wint 92-93, p. 7-12.

2830. HOLCOMB, Jesse
"Last Year." [HangL] (60) 92, p. 88.
"Typing." [HangL] (60) 92, p. 89.

2831. HOLCOMBE, Emily G.
"Class's End." [ChrC] (109:13) 15 Ap 92, p. 398.

2832. HOLDEN, Jonathan
"Falling from Stardom" (for S.). [ThRiPo] (39/40) 92-93, p. 115-117.
"Gulf: January 17, 1991" (for Ana). [NewDeltaR] (9:2) Spr-Sum 92, p. 64-65.
"Liberace." [ThRiPo] (39/40) 92-93, p. 117.
"Losers." [ThRiPo] (39/40) 92-93, p. 114-115.
"Reading 'Snow White' to My Son, Age 7." [NewDeltaR] (9:2) Spr-Sum 92, p. 66.
"Spook House." [NewDeltaR] (9:2) Spr-Sum 92, p. 67-68.
"Western Meadowlark" (for A.). [NewDeltaR] (9:2) Spr-Sum 92, p. 69-70.

2833. HÖLDERLIN, Friedrich
"Columbus" (tr. by Richard Sieburth). [Conjunc] (19) 92, p. 37-43.

2834. HOLDT, David
"The Search." [Blueline] (13) 92, p. 28-29.
"Settling In." [Blueline] (13) 92, p. 82-83.

2835. HOLENDER, Barbara D.
"From His Coy Mistress." [Light] (3) Aut 92, p. 8.

2836. HOLIDAY, D. Alexander
"Not at Home." [Art&Und] (1:4) Jl-Ag 92, p. 10.

2837. HOLINGER, Richard
"Four Paintings in the Louvre." [Boulevard] (7:1, #19) Spr 92, p. 164-165.

2838. HOLLADAY, Hilary
"52 Mal Mae Court." [Pembroke] (24) 92, p. 82.
"Glowing." [Pembroke] (24) 92, p. 83.

2839. HOLLAHAN, Eugene
"Blue Girls of 1990." [WeberS] (9:1) Wint 92, p. 66.
"Neville Chamberlain Invents Snooker" (Ootacamund Club, India, 1875). [LullwaterR] (3:3) Sum 92, p. 33-35.
"Or, As R. J. E. Clausius Would Say, Entropy." [SnailPR] (2:2) Fall-Wint 92, p. 8.
"Palimpsest." [LullwaterR] (4:1) Fall 92, p. 10-11.
"Road Runner." [ChatR] (12:2) Wint 92, p. 27.
"Saving Your Grace" (The Hermitage, 15 January). [Verse] (9:2) Sum 92, p. 94.
"Searching for Pocahontas." [WeberS] (9:1) Wint 92, p. 66-67.

2840. HOLLAND, Barbara A.
"Above the Pond." [Contact] (10:62/63/64) Fall 91-Spr 92, p. 63.
"Mosquito Rites." [Contact] (10:62/63/64) Fall 91-Spr 92, p. 63.

2841. HOLLAND, Michelle
"Your Love." [US1] (26/27) 92, p. 12.

2842. HOLLAND, Walter
"Easter in Washington" (For B. Jones). [Art&Und] (1:5) S-O 92, p. 15.
"Journal of the Plague Years." [Art&Und] (1:5) S-O 92, p. 16.
"The NAMES Project, San Francisco, 1989" (For R.S.). [Art&Und] (1:5) S-O 92, p. 16.
"The Road to Emmaus." [Art&Und] (1:5) S-O 92, p. 15.
"Stephen's Illness." [Art&Und] (1:5) S-O 92, p. 15.
2843. HOLLANDER, Jean
"Comfort Me with Apples." [US1] (26/27) 92, p. 36.
"My Name Was Josephine." [Footwork] 92, p. 67.
"Snow, Gently Like a Bandaging." [Footwork] 92, p. 67.
"To Clotho, in Care of Sears." [Footwork] 92, p. 67.
2844. HOLLANDER, John
"At the Follies." [ParisR] (34:125) Wint 92, p. 39-40.
"Early Inscription." [ParisR] (34:125) Wint 92, p. 40-42.
"February Madrigal." [QW] (36) Wint 92-93, p. 134.
"Final Arrangements." [KenR] (NS 14:4) Fall 92, p. 171-172.
"On North Rock." [SouthwR] (77:2/3) Spr-Sum 92, p. 191-199.
"Variations on a Fragment by Trumbull Stickney." [ParisR] (34:125) Wint 92, p. 42 - 43.
2845. HOLLANDER, Martha
"Giorgione's *Tempest:* Another Story." [Poetry] (159:5) F 92, p. 272.
"The History of Art." [ParisR] (34:125) Wint 92, p. 145-146.
"Three Geographers." [ParisR] (34:125) Wint 92, p. 146-147.
"The Web." [Poetry] (160:6) S 92, p. 341-342.
2846. HOLLEY, Margaret
"Autumn by Anton Bruckner." [Boulevard] (7:2/3, #20/21) Fall 92, p. 275-276.
"Blueberries." [Verse] (9:3) Wint 92, p. 134.
"Coming to Kansas." [MidwQ] (34:1) Aut 92, p. 67-68.
"Eurydice in the Garden." [CumbPR] (11:2) Spr 92, p. 22-23.
"The Flower Bed." [SouthernPR] (32:1) Spr 92, p. 8-9.
"The Prayer Plant." [Nat] (254:16) 27 Ap 92, p. 571.
"Rabbit." [Poem] (67) My 92, p. 37.
"The Sea Urchin." [Poem] (67) My 92, p. 36.
"Spinoza's Gold." [KenR] (NS 14:2) Spr 92, p. 141-142.
"The Water of Life." [CumbPR] (11:2) Spr 92, p. 21.
"Weeping Cherries." [AmerS] (61:1) Wint 92, p. 47-48.
2847. HOLLO, Anselm
"All these are gifts" (tr. of Tomaz Salamun, w. the author). [AmerPoR] (21:4) Jl-Ag 92, p. 41.
"A Tribe" (tr. of Tomaz Salamun, w. the author). [AmerPoR] (21:4) Jl-Ag 92, p. 41.
2848. HOLLOWAY, Eachan
"I Saw the Face." [MassR] (23:3) Fall 92, p. 430.
"Recovery." [MassR] (23:3) Fall 92, p. 429.
2849. HOLLOWAY, Glenna
"Addie At Eighty" (3rd place winner, Chiron Review 1992 Poetry Contest). [ChironR] (11:3) Aut 92, p. 15.
"Dinner Flight." [Light] (4) Wint 92-93, p. 22.
"Moonwatch, Floodwatch." [LouisL] (9:2) Fall 92, p. 22-23.
2850. HOLLOWAY, John
"Reveille." [Hudson] (44:4) Wint 92, p. 614.
2851. HOLM, Bill
"Fortune Telling in Hanyang." [SenR] (22:2) Fall 92, p. 7.
"Official Talk in Wuhan, 1992." [SenR] (22:2) Fall 92, p. 5.
"Reading Su Dongpo on a Bleak Day in Wuhan." [SenR] (22:2) Fall 92, p. 6.
2852. HOLMAN, Bob
"Crying Stupidly in the Rain." [Talisman] (9) Fall 92, p. 185.
"The Death of Poetry." [Talisman] (9) Fall 92, p. 185-186.
2853. HOLMES, Darryl
"Circles" (for Malcolm X on the 66th anniversary of his birth). [Eyeball] (1) 92, p. 24-25.
"Fire." [AfAmRev] (26:2) Sum 92, p. 218-219.
"Havana Knows" (for Assata Shakur). [Eyeball] (1) 92, p. 25.
"Oil Spills." [AfAmRev] (26:2) Sum 92, p. 217-218.
"Out of the Soil." [AfAmRev] (26:2) Sum 92, p. 216-217.

2854. HOLMES, Elizabeth
"The Patience of the Cloud Photographer." [MichQR] (31:2) Spr 92, p. 192-193.
2855. HOLMES, James S
"Skin" (tr. of Gerrit Achterberg). [Trans] (26) Spr 92, p. 114.
2856. HOLMES, Michael
"Translating Neruda." [Quarry] (41:2) Spr 92, p. 9-10.
2857. HOLMES, Nancy
"The Decline of Irresponsibility." [Event] (21:3) Fall 92, p. 60-61.
"Sheet Lightning." [Event] (21:3) Fall 92, p. 59.
"The Various Contrivances by Which Orchids Are Fertilized by Insects." [Event] (21:3) Fall 92, p. 62-63.
2858. HOLST-WARHAFT, Gail
"Impressions of a Poetry Reading in Japanese" (tr. of Tassos Denegris). [Stand] (33:4) Aut 92, p. 103.
2859. HOLSTAD, Scott C.
"Address." [ChamLR] (10/11) Spr-Fall 92, p. 123-124.
"Be." [HawaiiR] (16:2, #35) Spr 92, p. 13.
"Phoenix." [MinnR] (39) Fall-Wint 92-93, p. 9-10.
2860. HOLSTEIN, Amara
"Reflections." [HangL] (61) 92, p. 96.
2861. HOLT, Beatrice G.
"Stillwater Minnesota." [RagMag] (10:1) 92, p. 22.
"Today." [RagMag] (10:1) 92, p. 23.
2862. HOLT, Gary
"The Frog's Fingerprint." [NegC] (12:1/2) 92, p. 62.
2863. HOLT, Rochelle (Rochelle Lynn)
"February House" (for Carson McCullers). [MoodySI] (27) Spr 92, p. 37-38.
"Ode to Flesh." [Kalliope] (14:3) 92, p. 26-27.
2864. HOLUB, Miroslav
"About the Brain" (tr. by Dana Hábová and David Young). [GrahamHR] (16) Fall 92, p. 38-39.
"Imagination" (tr. by Dana Hábová and David Young). [GrahamHR] (16) Fall 92, p. 36-37.
"My Mother Learns Spanish" (tr. by Dana Hábová and David Young). [Field] (47) Fall 92, p. 76-77.
"Spinal Cord" (tr. by Dana Hábová and David Young). [Field] (47) Fall 92, p. 75.
"The Third Language" (tr. by Dana Hábová and David Young). [GrahamHR] (16) Fall 92, p. 40-41.
2865. HOLZER, Ryszard
"Generals Mean Well" (tr. by Daniel Bourne). [CharR] (18:1) Spr 92, p. 100.
"Martial Law Primer # 1" (tr. by Daniel Bourne). [CharR] (18:1) Spr 92, p. 99.
"Martial Law Primer # 2" (tr. by Daniel Bourne). [CharR] (18:1) Spr 92, p. 99.
"Untitled: There are places we most likely will never get to see" (tr. by Daniel Bourne). [CharR] (18:1) Spr 92, p. 100.
2866. HOMER, Art
"Wedge-Tailed Eagles" (Great Dividing Range, Australia). [NoAmR] (277:2) Mr-Ap 92, p. 22.
2867. HONCHIN, Ron
"Mushroom." [Pearl] (15) Spr-Sum 92, p. 44.
2868. HONGJANG
"Between the Cold Pine Arbor's Moon" (tr. by Constantine Contogenis and Wolhee Choe). [Pequod] (34) 92, p. 113.
2869. HONIG, Edwin
"The Keeper of Sheep" (Excerpt, tr. of Fernando Pessoa (Alberto Caeiro), w. Susan M. Brown). [Trans] (26) Spr 92, p. 14-15.
2870. HONZA, Annabelle
"Are My World." [CreamCR] (16:2) Fall 92, p. 20.
"L'Otre Vie (Beyond Life)" (Excerpts, tr. of Marie Uguay). [GrahamHR] (16) Fall 92, p. 86-93.
2871. HOOD, David
"Reflection in a Lover's Eye." [Crucible] (28) Fall 92, p. 46.
2872. HOOD, Mary Winifred
"My Piano." [Hudson] (45:3) Aut 92, p. 437-438.
"Two Octopuses." [Hudson] (45:3) Aut 92, p. 439-440.
2873. HOOD-ADAMS, Rebecca
"Just Another Story." [MinnR] (38) Spr-Sum 92, p. 17.

"Lines for Mrs. Maude Collins on Her 100th Brithday." [MinnR] (38) Spr-Sum 92, p. 16-17.

2874. HOOGESTRAAT, Jane
"Days We Would Not Have Thought to Ask For." [Poem] (68) N 92, p. 70.
"Windows on Winter." [Poem] (68) N 92, p. 67-69.

2875. HOOGLAND, Cornelia
"The Elizabeth Smart Poems." [PoetryC] (12:3/4) Jl 92, p. 23.
"These Geese Are Having Fun" (Pender Harbor, B.C.). [PoetryC] (12:3/4) Jl 92, p. 23.
"A Woman's Strength." [Quarry] (41:1) Wint 92, p. 36-37.
"Writing." [PoetryC] (12:3/4) Jl 92, p. 23.

2876. HOOK, Catherine
"Wild Kingdom." [NewYorkQ] (47) 92, p. 76.

2877. HOOPER, Patricia
"Crossing." [PraS] (66:2) Sum 92, p. 15-16.

2878. HOOPER-TODD, Nita
"The Office of Unemployment (A Learning Center)." [Pearl] (16) Fall 92, p. 27.

2879. HOOVER, Paul
"Baseball." [AnotherCM] (24) Fall 92, p. 91-94.
"Baseball." [Witness] (6:2) 92, p. 178-181.

2880. HOPE, A. D.
"Hymn to Saint Barbara." [Raritan] (12:2) Fall 92, p. 44-45.
"Orpheus." [Raritan] (12:2) Fall 92, p. 46.
"Visitant." [Raritan] (12:2) Fall 92, p. 43.

2881. HOPE, Akua Lezli
"Hairdressers." [AfAmRev] (26:2) Sum 92, p. 225-227.

2882. HORACE
"A Journey to Brindisi in 37 B.C." (Satire 1.5, tr. by Alistair Elliot). [Arion] 3d series (1:1) Wint 90, p. 180-183.
"Ode 1, 22 *Integer Vitae*" (tr. by Robert Boucheron). [Hellas] (3:1) Spr 92, p. 20.
"Pyrrha" (Odes I.5, tr. by Diane Arnson Svarlien). [Arion] 3d series (1:1) Wint 90, p. 185.

2883. HORN, Bernard
"Our Daily Words." [MissR] (20:3) Spr 92, p. 60-61.

HORN, Stephanie van
See Van HORN, Stephanie

2884. HORNE, Lewis
"Rain in Mallorca." [BelPoJ] (43:2) Wint 92-93, p. 22-23.

2885. HORNER, Jan
"Waspish." [Grain] (20:1) Spr 92, p. 99.

2886. HORNIK, Jessica
"East Hill Road." [Nat] (254:7) 24 F 92, p. 245.
"Gratitude." [Atlantic] (269:6) Je 92, p. 86.

2887. HORNING, Ron
"The Vocalist" (Selection: 2, w. David Lehman). [DenQ] (26:3) Wint 92, p. 28-29.

2888. HORNOSTY, Cornelia C.
"Mummers." [CanLit] (134) Aut 92, p. 39.
"Ricochet." [Event] (21:3) Fall 92, p. 68-69.
"This Desperate Skulduggery." [Event] (21:2) Sum 92, p. 51.

2889. HOROWITZ, Mikhail
"Gnaws that stays gnaws." [YellowS] (Ten Years [i.e. 40]) Sum-Fall 92, p. 24.
"Horseshoe Crabs." [Archae] (4) late 92-early 93, p. 39.

2890. HOROWITZ, Rose
"Sweet Potato." [OnTheBus] (4:2/5:1, #10/11) 92, p. 113.

2891. HORSTING, Eric
"Courage." [Agni] (36) 92, p. 168.
"Credo." [Agni] (36) 92, p. 169.
"Damaged Goods." [GreensboroR] (53) Wint 92-93, p. 42.
"The Farm That Bore You." [Confr] (48/49) Spr-Sum 92, p. 196.
"Memory: Five A.M." [LitR] (35:3) Spr 92, p. 407.

2892. HORTON, Barbara
"Ponies Grazing." [Northeast] (5:6) Spr 92, p. 25.
"To Name the Stars." [Northeast] (5:6) Spr 92, p. 19.

2893. HORVATH, Brooke
"The Feminine Ending." [Light] (3) Aut 92, p. 9.
"The Green Flash." [NegC] (12:3) 92, p. 82-85.

"Where Shade Comes Down." [HiramPoR] (51/52) Fall 91-Sum 92, p. 43.
2894. HORVITZ, Lori
"Survival." [BrooklynR] (9) 92, p. 61.
2895. HOSPITAL, Carolina
"Blake in the Tropics." [LindLM] (11:2) Je 92, p. 17.
"Dear Tía." [Americas] (20:3/4) Fall-Wint 92, p. 223.
"Everyone Will Have to Listen" (tr. of Tania Diaz Castro, w. Pablo Medina). [AmerV] (29) 92, p. 18.
"Modern Faith." [LindLM] (11:2) Je 92, p. 17.
"Ocean Drive." [LindLM] (11:2) Je 92, p. 17.
"Papa." [Americas] (20:3/4) Fall-Wint 92, p. 224.
"Silhouettes of Women" (for Emma, Hedda, Edna, Sylvia, Graciela and Simone). [LindLM] (11:2) Je 92, p. 17.
"An Unexpected Conversion." [Confr] (48/49) Spr-Sum 92, p. 199.
HOSPITAL, Caroline
See HOSPITAL, Carolina
2896. HOSPODAR, Riq
"The Innocent One" (for Kimberley Bergalis, Florida woman apparently infected with HIV by her dentist). [ChironR] (11:4) Wint 92, p. 12.
"Queers in Space." [ChironR] (11:4) Wint 92, p. 12.
2897. HOSTOVSKY, Paul
"First Kiss." [Hellas] (3:2) Fall 92, p. 37.
"Flowers." [Hellas] (3:2) Fall 92, p. 37.
"Harmonicas." [JINJPo] (14:1) Spr 92, p. 30.
"Photograph." [Hellas] (3:2) Fall 92, p. 38.
"Stages." [Hellas] (3:2) Fall 92, p. 38.
2898. HOTHAM, Gary
"Awake or asleep." [DogRR] (11:1) Spr-Sum 92, p. 31.
"Low tide-." [DogRR] (11:1) Spr-Sum 92, p. 39.
"She picks up the seashell." [DogRR] (11:1) Spr-Sum 92, p. 39.
"Summer Morning." [DogRR] (11:1) Spr-Sum 92, p. 31.
"Their last sound." [DogRR] (11:1) Spr-Sum 92, p. 39.
2899. HOUCHIN, Ron
"What the Things Say." [CumbPR] (12:1) Fall 92, p. 27.
2900. HOUGHTON, Timothy
"The Old Place." [GreensboroR] (52) Sum 92, p. 113-114.
"Single in the New Apartment." [PoetL] (87:2) Sum 92, p. 15-16.
2901. HOUSE, Elizabeth
"Alter Ego." [Amelia] (7:1, #20) 92, p. 132.
2902. HOUSKEEPER, Margaret
"Sunday Drive" (Winner, Annual Free Verse Contest, 1991). [AnthNEW] (4) 92, p. 17.
2903. HOUSTON, Beth
"After Rain." [ChiR] (38:3) 92, p. 62-64.
"Earthquake and Aftershocks" (San Francisco, October 1989). [LitR] (25:2) Wint 92, p. 278-279.
"Epistemology." [MassR] (23:3) Fall 92, p. 427.
"Menstruation." [MassR] (23:3) Fall 92, p. 428.
2904. HOUSTON, Peyton
"Images of the Garden." [Hudson] (45:2) Sum 92, p. 272-273.
"Importance of the Unicorn." [Hudson] (45:2) Sum 92, p. 273-275.
HOVANESSIAN, Diana Der
See DER-HOVANESSIAN, Diana
2905. HOWARD, David
"Envoi." [Vis] (40) 92, p. 55.
"Or Not" (in memory of David Vogel 1891-?1944). [Vis] (40) 92, p. 48.
"Valentino" (after Guido Gozzano). [Vis] (40) 92, p. 49.
2906. HOWARD, Dorothy
"Going Up She Said Descending." [Arc] (28) Spr 92, p. 29.
2907. HOWARD, Jim
"Epithalamium for a Future Time." [FreeL] (10) Sum 92, p. 18.
"The Maelstrom." [FreeL] (10) Sum 92, p. 17-18.
"The Third Being." [FreeL] (10) Sum 92, p. 16-17.
2908. HOWARD, Julie Kate
"On the Anniversary of My Mother's Death" (for Betsy, who told me). [GreensboroR] (53) Wint 92-93, p. 39-41.

2909. HOWARD, Richard
"Lives of the Painters: Artists' Antidotes." [NewYorker] (68:24) 3 Ag 92, p. 38.
"Occupations." [KenR] (NS 14:4) Fall 92, p. 21-29.
"A Poem: Man Who Beat Up Homosexuals Reported to Have AIDS Virus" (New York Times : March 8, 1991). [Salm] (93) Wint 92, p. 51-60.
"Reading the Letters from Lisbon." [YaleR] (80:3) Jl 92, p. 58-59.
"To a Librettist at Liberty" (For J. D. McC.). [Poetry] (159:4) Ja 92, p. 201-202.
"Undertakings." [NewYorker] (68:28) 31 Ag 92, p. 42.
2910. HOWARD, Willie Abraham, Jr.
"Black Panther" (Requiem for Huey P. Newton). [AfAmRev] (26:2) Sum 92, p. 234.
"The Projects." [Obs] (7:1/2) Spr-Sum 92, p. 82.
2911. HOWART, Hank (Henry Lewis)
"Big City, Failing Citizens." [BostonR] (17:2) Mr-Ap 92, p. 4.
2912. HOWE, Fanny
"On Saving History." [Conjunc] (19) 92, p. 15-18.
2913. HOWE, Ken
"A Cider Bottle." [Grain] (20:4) Wint 92, p. 117.
"A Microwave Dish." [Grain] (20:4) Wint 92, p. 115.
"A Refrigerator." [Grain] (20:4) Wint 92, p. 116.
"A Window." [Grain] (20:4) Wint 92, p. 118.
2914. HOWE, Susan (*See also* HOWE, Susan Elizabeth)
"Melville's Marginalia" (Excerpts). [Avec] (5:1) 92, p. 140-149.
2915. HOWE, Susan Elizabeth (*See also* HOWE, Susan)
"Lessons of Erosion." [PraS] (66:3) Fall 92, p. 113.
"Sophia Whispers." [PraS] (66:3) Fall 92, p. 112.
2916. HOWELL, Abigail
"The Fates Write Their Memoirs of Janis." [QW] (36) Wint 92-93, p. 129-130.
2917. HOWELL, Christopher
"The Abomination of Fallen Things." [ColEng] (53:5) S 91, p. 539.
"Blessing's Precision." [PoetryNW] (33:4) Wint 92-93, p. 12-13.
"The Bride of Long Division." [WillowS] (29) Wint 92, p. 22.
"Event." [GettyR] (5:2) Spr 92, p. 252.
"The Hermit's Childhood." [WillowS] (29) Wint 92, p. 23-24.
"Letter from the Base Betrayer." [ColEng] (53:5) S 91, p. 538.
"The Pipes of Oblivion." [GettyR] (5:2) Spr 92, p. 251.
2918. HOWER, Mary
"Surfers in December." [Thrpny] (48) Wint 92, p. 13.
"Under the Raft." [VirQR] (68:1) Wint 92, p. 77-78.
2919. HOWES, Meghan
"Could You Use the Microphone While Reading as I Am Deaf in One Ear" (with thanks to Ira Sadoff). [ArtfulD] (22/23) 92, p. 97.
"Lesson." [ArtfulD] (22/23) 92, p. 96.
2920. HOWEY, Janet
"Still." [Art&Und] (1:3) Spr 92, p. 11.
2921. HOYOS, Angela de
"How to Eat Crow on a Cold Sunday Morning." [Americas] (20:3/4) Fall-Wint 92, p. 150.
"Ramillete para Elena Poniatowska." [Americas] (20:3/4) Fall-Wint 92, p. 151.
"Ten Dry Summers Ago." [Americas] (20:3/4) Fall-Wint 92, p. 149.
"When Conventinal Methods Fail." [Americas] (20:3/4) Fall-Wint 92, p. 152.
2922. HRISTIC, Jovan
"A Sentimental Voyage around My Room" (tr. by Charles Simic). [ParisR]] (34:124) Fall 92, p. 143.
"That Night They All Gathered on the Highest Tower" (tr. by Charles Simic). [ParisR]] (34:124) Fall 92, p. 143.
2923. HRISTOV, Boris
"At Night" (tr. by Lisa Sapinkopf). [ConnPR] (11:1) 92, p. 33.
"A Sign from Heaven" (tr. by Lisa Sapinkopf, w. Georgi Belev). [CrabCR] (8:1) Sum-Fall 92, p. 16.
HUA, Li Min
See LI, Min Hua
2924. HUANG, Hai-Peng
"Drinking Joy" (To the Tune of Rumengling, tr. of Qing-Zhao Li, w. Min Xiao - Hong and Gordon T. Osing). [CrabCR] (8:1) Sum-Fall 92, p. 18.
"In Praise of Lotus" (To the Tune of Yuanwangsun, tr. of Qing-Zhao Li, w. Min Xiao-Hong and Gordon T. Osing). [CrabCR] (8:1) Sum-Fall 92, p. 18.

2925. HUBBUCH, Christopher
"Sundial." [LullwaterR] (3:2) Spr 92, p. 10.
2926. HUDDLE, David
"Close" (for Ted Littwin and Lyn Mattoon). [AmerPoR] (21:2) Mr-Ap 92, p. 28.
"Rakes." [AmerPoR] (21:2) Mr-Ap 92, p. 28.
"The Spider, the Coffee, and the Computer: A Brief Essay on Quotidian Physics." [Light] (2) Sum 92, p. 15.
"Visit of the Hawk." [AmerPoR] (21:2) Mr-Ap 92, p. 28.
2927. HUDGINS, Andrew
"Acquired Taste." [Hudson] (45:1) Spr 92, p. 86-87.
"Biff Burger." [NewEngR] (14:4) Fall 92, p. 110.
"Fist." [ParisR] (34:125) Wint 92, p. 117.
"Gospel Villanelle." [Shen] (42:3) Fall 92, p. 40.
"Granny Pounds." [Hudson] (45:1) Spr 92, p. 87.
"Mother's Funeral." [ParisR] (34:125) Wint 92, p. 115-117.
"My Father's Rage." [Hudson] (45:1) Spr 92, p. 88.
"Patchwork." [Shen] (42:3) Fall 92, p. 43.
"Red Rover." [AmerV] (26) Spr 92, p. 36.
"The Roosting Tree." [Hudson] (45:1) Spr 92, p. 85.
"The Tell-Tale Heart." [Hudson] (45:1) Spr 92, p. 86.
"The Telling." [Shen] (42:3) Fall 92, p. 42.
"Transistor Radio." [Shen] (42:3) Fall 92, p. 41.
"Tricks of the Body." [NewEngR] (14:4) Fall 92, p. 109.
"Versification of a Passage from *Penthouse*." [WestHR] (46:3) Fall 92 [i.e. (46:4) Wint 92], p. 391.
"The Visible Man." [ParisR] (34:125) Wint 92, p. 114.
"Wisdom and Advice." [NewEngR] (14:4) Fall 92, p. 111.
2928. HUDSON, June
"Souvenir of First Retrieval from Timberlawn, or What You Get for Your Money." [LouisL] (9:1) Spr 92, p. 69-70.
2929. HUDZIK, Robert
"Imelda Chooses Her Shoes." [CinPR] (23) Wint 91-92, p. 70-71.
2930. HUERTA, David
"Tea Blues" (tr. by Reginald Gibbons). [TriQ] (85) Fall 92, p. 341.
2931. HUERTA, Efraín
"Alabama in Bloom" (for Paul Robeson, tr. by Jim Normington). [Talisman] (8) Spr 92, p. 143.
2932. HUERTA, Joel
"El Big Man." [Americas] (19:3/4) Wint 91, p. 60.
"Las Chrome Doors of Heaven." [Americas] (19:3/4) Wint 91, p. 61-62.
"La Smiley." [Americas] (19:3/4) Wint 91, p. 55-59.
2933. HUESGEN, Jan
"A Broad Gauge." [Farm] (9:2) Fall-Wint 92-93, p. 113-114.
"The Strength of the Prairie Flower." [Grain] (20:1) Spr 92, p. 100-101.
"Territorial Rites." [Grain] (20:1) Spr 92, p. 101.
2934. HUFF, Michael
"She Is Fair." [Interim] (11:1) Spr-Sum 92, p. 9.
2935. HUFFSTICKLER, Albert
"Butchery." [FreeL] (9) Wint 92, p. 12-13.
"Concerning Role Models,Sand Sharks and Time." [RagMag] (10:2) 92, p. 93.
"Deja Vu." [Lactuca] (15) Mr 92, p. 42.
"Edna." [Parting] (5:1) Sum 92, p. 27-28.
"Requiescat." [Lactuca] (15) Mr 92, p. 41.
"She Said" (Excerpt: "She said she didn't know if she wanted any more men"). [CoalC] (5) My 92, p. 19.
"She Said" (Excerpt: "She said she was going till she was too far away"). [CoalC] (5) My 92, p. 8.
"Short Order Waiter." [Parting] (5:1) Sum 92, p. 15-16.
"Stopped for the Night." [Lactuca] (15) Mr 92, p. 42.
2936. HUGGINS, Peter
"Crow on God." [Outbr] (23) 92, p. 5.
"Cutting Missionary Ridge." [ChatR] (12:2) Wint 92, p. 22.
"Gulliver in London." [NegC] (12:3) 92, p. 86-87.
"Zeno and the Garden." [Outbr] (23) 92, p. 6.
2937. HUGHES, Benedict
"Islands." [BrooklynR] (9) 92, p. 97.

2938. HUGHES, Charlie G.
"Nocturne." [HolCrit] (29:3) Je 92, p. 19.
2939. HUGHES, Henry J.
"New Year's with Christine." [TarRP] (30:2) Spr 91, p. 38.
2940. HUGHES, Jeremy
"The Bricklayer." [Verse] (8:3/9:1) Wint-Spr 92, p. 133.
2941. HUGHES, John Calvin
"Luck." [MissR] (20:3) Spr 92, p. 66.
2942. HUGHES, Langston
"Christ in Alabama." [NoCarLR] (1:1) Sum 92, p. 23.
2943. HUGHES, Mary Gray
"Plea-Bargaining." [Wind] (22:71) 92, p. 21-22.
2944. HUGHES, Sheila Hassell
"Compact." [LullwaterR] (4:1) Fall 92, p. 51.
"Sacramentalizing." [LullwaterR] (4:1) Fall 92, p. 44-45.
2945. HUGHES, Ted
"Opus 131." [NewYorker] (68:41) 30 N 92, p. 132.
HUIDOBRO, Matías Montes
See MONTES HUIDOBRO, Matías
HUIGANG, Tian
See TIAN, Huigang
2946. HUK, Romana
"Aubade." [Conscience] (13:4) Wint 92-93, p. 27.
2947. HULL, C. E.
"Winter Becoming." [Gypsy] (19) 92, p. 45.
2948. HULL, David M.
"Hamlet." [PoetL] (87:2) Sum 92, p. 20.
2949. HULL, Lynda
"Chiffon." [AmerV] (26) Spr 92, p. 60-62.
"Fiat Lux." [NewEngR] (14:4) Fall 92, p. 88-90.
"Frugal Repasts." [Pequod] (33) 92, p. 34-36.
"River Bridge." [DenQ] (26:4) Spr 92, p. 31-36.
"The Window." [NewEngR] (14:4) Fall 92, p. 85-88.
2950. HULL, Robert
"Rewind" (reprinted to correct error in the Spr 91 issue). [CumbPR] (11:2) Spr 92, p. 34-35.
2951. HUMES, Harry
"After a Sleepless Night I Walk into the Woods in the Rain." [LaurelR] (26:2) Sum 92, p. 49.
"Cramp." [SnailPR] (2:1) Spr-Sum 92, p. 14-15.
"The Deer." [PoetryNW] (33:2) Sum 92, p. 28-29.
"Dust." [PoetryNW] (33:2) Sum 92, p. 26-27.
"Fox." [PoetryNW] (33:2) Sum 92, p. 28.
"The Geek." [SnailPR] (2:1) Spr-Sum 92, p. 16-17.
"The Last Woods Bison." [Shen] (42:4) Wint 92, p. 76.
"Lee & Melissa, Always." [TarRP] (31:2) Spr 92, p. 9.
"My Mother Ate Hill Dirt." [PoetryNW] (33:2) Sum 92, p. 26.
"Showing a Friend My Town." [GeoR] (46:2) Sum 92, p. 233.
"Small Yellow Flowers." [Shen] (42:4) Wint 92, p. 74.
"The Swimming Pool." [Shen] (42:4) Wint 92, p. 75.
"Yonko." [QW] (34) Wint-Spr 92, p. 70-71.
2952. HUMMELL, Austin
"Aubade." [Poem] (67) My 92, p. 51.
"Cleaving and Rocking." [Poem] (67) My 92, p. 55.
"Manners of the Unreachable." [DenQ] (26:3) Wint 92, p. 30.
"No Lifeguard." [Poem] (67) My 92, p. 52-53.
"This Mute Pleading." [Poem] (67) My 92, p. 54.
2953. HUMMER, T. R.
"The Antichrist in Arkansas." [SouthernR] (28:4) Aut, O 92, p. 859-860.
"Friendly Fire." [ParisR] (34:125) Wint 92, p. 44.
"The Heavenly Doctor." [SouthernR] (28:4) Aut, O 92, p. 856-858.
"My Funny Valentine in Spanish" (for Philip Levine). [ParisR] (34:125) Wint 92, p. 46-47.
"Scrutiny." [ParisR] (34:125) Wint 92, p. 45.
"Two Angels Torturing a Soul." [Agni] (35) 92, p. 103-104.

2954. HUMPHREY, Paul
"Angel Face." [Light] (4) Wint 92-93, p. 16.
"Cold Shoulders." [Light] (3) Aut 92, p. 21.
"Light." [Light] (1) Spr 92, p. 14.
"Photogeneric." [Light] (2) Sum 92, p. 13.
"Roomoresque." [Light] (2) Sum 92, p. 20.
"Whereabouts!" [Light] (3) Aut 92, p. 14.
2955. HUMPHREYS, Helen
"Blurring." [MalR] (99) Sum 92, p. 80-81.
"The Perils of Geography." [MalR] (99) Sum 92, p. 78.
"Walking on Water." [MalR] (99) Sum 92, p. 79.
2956. HUNOLD, Rose Marie
"Lula Twisted, I Resisted." [Obs] (7:1/2) Spr-Sum 92, p. 83-84.
2957. HUNT, Anthony
"XIX. The witches are skirting the coastline" (tr. of Loreina Santos Silva). [Nimrod] (36:1) Fall-Wint 92, p. 73.
"Apocryphal Children" (from "Metalepsis," tr. of Loreina Santos Silva). [Nimrod] (36:1) Fall-Wint 92, p. 71-72.
2958. HUNT-COHN, Maggie
"Invitation." [Confr] (50) Fall 92, p. 295.
"Late Crop." [WindO] (56) Fall-Wint 92, p. 12.
2959. HUNTER, Donnell
"Keeping Their Place." [MalR] (101) Wint92, p. 22.
2960. HUNTER, Terrell
"Fur." [NewYorkQ] (49) 92, p. 73.
2961. HURLEY, Maureen
"Buddha Moon." [ChamLR] (10/11) Spr-Fall 92, p. 5-6.
"Dream Vessel #1: Mayim" (from a collage by Marsha Connell entitled "Mayim"). [ChamLR] (10/11) Spr-Fall 92, p. 8-9.
"Dream Vessel #5: Shards of Destruction" (from a collage by Marsha Connell). [ChamLR] (10/11) Spr-Fall 92, p. 10.
"Invisible Boundaries" (From an etching, "After the Flood" by April Gornik). [ChamLR] (10/11) Spr-Fall 92, p. 2-4.
"Umbra, City of Refuge, Hawaii, 7/11/91." [ChamLR] (10/11) Spr-Fall 92, p. 1.
2962. HURLOW, Marcia L.
"Nuclear Romance." [Poetry] (159:5) F 92, p. 274.
2963. HUTCHINSON, Mark
"The Epte Woods" (tr. of Rene Char). [Pequod] (34) 92, p. 195.
"The Inventors" (tr. of Rene Char). [Pequod] (34) 92, p. 196-197.
"The Latitudes of Alsace" (tr. of Rene Char). [Pequod] (34) 92, p. 194.
2964. HUTCHISON, Joseph
"This Day." [WritersF] (18) 92, p. 96.
2965. HUTCHISON, Scott Travis
"Man-Steel." [GeoR] (46:3) Fall 92, p. 501-502.
"Peeking in Windows." [SouthernPR] (32:1) Spr 92, p. 11-12.
"Reconciliation." [ChatR] (13:1) Fall 92, p. 61.
"Root Doctor." [Poem] (67) My 92, p. 1-2.
2966. HUTH, Geof
"Of that of the . . . inscriptions." [WorldL] (3) 92, p. 21.
"Protyle." [Archae] (3) early 92, p. 15-17.
"To draw this thing." [WorldL] (3) 92, p. 20.
HUYGHUES, Allix Belrose
See BELROSE HUYGHUES, Allix
2967. HUYLER, Frank
"In Vitro." [Poetry] (160:1) Ap 92, p. 7.
2968. HWANG, Jini
"Blue stream, don't show off your speed" (a Kisang Poem in Korean and English, tr. by Constantine Contogenis and Wolhee Choe). [GrandS] (11:3 #43) 92, p. 174-175.
2969. HYDE, Christine
"My Affair with a Poet" (A Published One). [Bogg] (65) 92, p. 36-37.
2970. HYETT, Barbara Helfgott
"American Crocodile" (Crocodylus acutus). [HampSPR] Wint 92, p. 21.
"Texas Blind Salamander." [SouthernPR] (32:2) Fall 92, p. 45.
2971. HYLAND, Gary
"Danica at the Goya Exhibition." [Grain] (20:1) Spr 92, p. 139-141.

"Rehearsals." [Grain] (20:1) Spr 92, p. 142.

2972. HYMANS, Don
"The Tin-Men" (In memory of Robert Motherwell). [DenQ] (26:4) Spr 92, p. 37.

2973. IDDINGS, Kathleen
"Matriarch." [SingHM] (20) 92, p. 7.

2974. IFOWODO, E. Ogaga
"For Otamowerai." [Stand] (33:3) Sum 92, p. 69.

2975. IGNATOW, David
"Absolutely." [Boulevard] (7:1, #19) Spr 92, p. 127.
"At the Pool." [FourQ] (6:1) Spr 92, p. 31.
"The Housewife." [NewMyths] (1:2/2:1) 92, p. 102.
"The Human Condition III." [NewMyths] (1:2/2:1) 92, p. 103.
"If We Knew." [BlackWR] (18:2) Spr-Sum 92, p. 17.
"Insight." [NewMyths] (1:2/2:1) 92, p. 101.
"Lives." [VirQR] (68:1) Wint 92, p. 83-84.
"Living." [Boulevard] (7:1, #19) Spr 92, p. 126.
"Love Poem." [BlackWR] (18:2) Spr-Sum 92, p. 18.
"Night Thoughts." [VirQR] (68:1) Wint 92, p. 85-86.
"Now." [BelPoJ] (42:4) Sum 92, p. 45-46.
"Resolution." [BlackWR] (18:2) Spr-Sum 92, p. 16.
"Sometimes." [NewMyths] (1:2/2:1) 92, p. 100.
"Suburbia I." [NewMyths] (1:2/2:1) 92, p. 99.
"What Next?" [VirQR] (68:1) Wint 92, p. 84-85.

2976. IKINS, Rachael
"The Tree Thieves" (Winner, Annual Free Verse Contest, 1991). [AnthNEW] (4) 92, p. 27.

2977. ILKOV, Ani
"A Scene" (tr. by Lisa Sapinkopf, w. Georgi Belev). [Agni] (36) 92, p. 162-163.

2978. ILLICK, Peter
"Celebrate." [Epiphany] (3:2) Ap (Spr) 92, p. 86.
"Charity." [Epiphany] (3:2) Ap (Spr) 92, p. 87.
"Rites." [SoCoast] (12) Ja 92, p. 14.
"Sunday Morning in November." [Epiphany] (3:2) Ap (Spr) 92, p. 84.
"Time & Tide." [Epiphany] (3:2) Ap (Spr) 92, p. 85.
"Vanishing." [Epiphany] (3:2) Ap (Spr) 92, p. 83.

2979. ILLYÉS, Gyula
"Caught" (tr. by Emoke B'racz and David Zucker). [WebR] (16) Fall 92, p. 31.
"From a Philosopher's Insights" (tr. by Bruce Berlind, w. Mária Körösy). [SilverFR] (23) Wint 92, p. 33.
"In a Blacksmith's House on the Puszta" (tr. by Bruce Berlind and Maria Körösy). [TexasR] (13:3/4) Fall-Wint 92, p. 87-88.
"A Nest for Seasons in the Concrete Jungle" (tr. by Bruce Berlind, w. Mária Körösy). [SilverFR] (23) Wint 92, p. 29.
"Phoenix" (tr. by Bruce Berlind and Maria Körösy). [TexasR] (13:3/4) Fall-Wint 92, p. 89-91.
"With a Stranger" (tr. by Bruce Berlind, w. Mária Körösy). [SilverFR] (23) Wint 92, p. 31.
"A World in Crystal" (tr. by William Jay Smith). [Trans] (26) Spr 92, p. 25-26.
"World-Order" (tr. by Bruce Berlind, w. Mária Körösy). [SilverFR] (23) Wint 92, p. 30.
"You Could Have Spotted Me" (tr. by Bruce Berlind, w. Mária Körösy). [SilverFR] (23) Wint 92, p. 32.

2980. IMSDAHL, Peter
"Tuesday Afternoon." [HayF] (11) Fall-Wint 92, p. 91.

2981. INEZ, Colette
"Day Visitor, Susquehanna University." [AmerV] (28) 92, p. 4.
"Dee's Migraines." [NewL] (58:3) Spr 92, p. 97.
"Instructions for the Erection of a Statue to Myself in Central Park." [ThRiPo] (39/40) 92-93, p. 120.
"Journey From Santa Cruz." [NewEngR] (14:4) Fall 92, p. 192.
"Mirror Story." [OhioR] (48) 92, p. 24.
"The Old Lady Across the Hall Has Gone to Live Behind the Door." [ThRiPo] (39/40) 92-93, p. 119.
"Slumnight." [ThRiPo] (39/40) 92-93, p. 120.
"Sylvia, Aloft" (for my mother-in-law). [BrooklynR] (9) 92, p. 64.

"The Woman Who Loved Worms" (from a Japanese Legend). [ThRiPo] (39/40) 92 - 93, p. 118-119.

2982. INFANTE, Judith
"Connestee Falls." [HighP] (7:1) Spr 92, p. 95-96.
"Retrato de Helen." [AmerPoR] (21:5) S-O 92, p. 29.
"Vacant Lots" (2 selections, tr. of Fabio Morábito). [Manoa] (4:2) Fall 92, p. 183 - 190.

2983. INGALLS, J. Peter
"The Romance of Robert Cohn." [NewDeltaR] (9:1) Fall 91-Wint 92, p. 18-19.

2984. INGEBRETSEN, Mark
"The Lesson." [NegC] (12:1/2) 92, p. 63-65.

2985. INGERSON, Martin I.
"As a Breeze Parts the Palanquin's Curtain." [BellArk] (8:1) Ja-F 92, p. 6.
"Epithalamium." [BellArk] (8:5) S-O 92, p. 13.
"Moonlight Sonatina." [BellArk] (8:1) Ja-F 92, p. 27.

2986. INMAN, Peter
"Likeness." [Talisman] (8) Spr 92, p. 80-81.

2987. INMAN, Will
"Black Night of My Thirst." [ChironR] (11:4) Wint 92, p. 2.
"Flora Jane." [ChamLR] (10/11) Spr-Fall 92, p. 192-193.
"Fractions for Wholeness." [ChironR] (11:4) Wint 92, p. 3.
"Her Soundings." [ChamLR] (10/11) Spr-Fall 92, p. 191.
"John Baptizes Jesus." [ChironR] (11:4) Wint 92, p. 3.
"Mechanics' Beach." [ChironR] (11:4) Wint 92, p. 3.
"Steep Limbs." [ChironR] (11:4) Wint 92, p. 2.
"Woke Strawberries." [ChironR] (11:4) Wint 92, p. 2.

IOANNA-VERONIKA
See WARWICK, Ioanna-Veronika

2988. IOANNOU, Susan
"Subtexts." [CanLit] (133) Sum 92, p. 76.

2989. IRBY, James
"Thoughts in Havana" (tr. of José Lezama Lima). [Sulfur] (12:2, #31) Fall 92, p. 70 - 79.

2990. IRIBARNE, Jeanne
"The Death of Silence." [Arc] (28) Spr 92, p. 30.

2991. IRIE, Kevin
"The Photo." [AntigR] (89) Spr 92, p. 29-32.

2992. IRION, Mary Jean
"The Bed Maker." [ChrC] (109:9) 11 Mr 92, p. 276.
"Hollows." [ChrC] (109:5) 5-12 F 92, p. 119.
"Lice in Church on a Steamy Sunday." [Light] (2) Sum 92, p. 24.

2993. IRWIN, Mark
"Elegy." [HayF] (11) Fall-Wint 92, p. 112.
"Heart." [Agni] (36) 92, p. 131.
"North." [Pequod] (34) 92, p. 171-173.
"Turbo-Descartes." [DenQ] (27:1) Sum 92, p. 51-65.

2994. ISAACSON, Bruce
"After Doing Too Much Schoolwork & Feeling a Little Depressed." [BrooklynR] (9) 92, p. 59.

2995. ISHII, Michael
"Arbuckle." [Amelia] (7:1, #20) 92, p. 78.
"December 29, Four Days After Christmas." [Amelia] (6:4, #19) 92, p. 61.
"Leaving Xian." [Amelia] (7:1, #20) 92, p. 79.

2996. ISKRENKO, Nina
"Isn't She Not a Bird" (tr. by Forrest Gander, w. Mala Kotamraju). [Agni] (35) 92, p. 166-167.

2997. ISMAIL, Jam
"Apchrlneeeio." [CanLit] (132) Spr 92, p. 79.
"Cheerio Plane." [CanLit] (132) Spr 92, p. 81.
"Herloined Letter." [CanLit] (132) Spr 92, p. 80.
"Lyrics" (to n. rimsky-korsakov, 'song of india,' op. 5, 'sadho'). [CanLit] (132) Spr 92, p. 81.

2998. ISON, John M.
"Lady in Satin." [EvergreenC] (7:1) Wint-Spr 92, p. 26.

2999. ISRAELI, Henry
"Fan." [CanLit] (135) Wint 92, p. 50.

3000. ISTVAN, Dárday
"Az Öröm Fája." [Os] (35) Fall 92, p. 16.
"The Tree of Pleasure" (tr. by Zsuzsanna Ozsváth and Martha Satz). [Os] (35) Fall 92, p. 17.
3001. ITO, Sally
"Al's Inside His Sax and Won't Come Out" (tr. of Kazuko Shiraishi). [WestCL] (26:3, #9) Wint 92-93, p. 83.
"The Ostrich Is Short Tempered Because" (tr. of Kazuko Shiraishi). [WestCL] (26:3, #9) Wint 92-93, p. 82.
"Penguin Cafe" (tr. of Kazuko Shiraishi). [WestCL] (26:3, #9) Wint 92-93, p. 80-82.
"The Way Birds Laugh" (tr. of Kazuko Shiraishi). [WestCL] (26:3, #9) Wint 92-93, p. 83.
3002. IUPPA, M. J.
"Making Resolutions." [Amelia] (6:4, #19) 92, p. 136.
3003. IVEREM, Esther
"Daddy's Friends." [AfAmRev] (26:2) Sum 92, p. 266.
"From North Philly." [Nat] (254:24) 22 Je 92, p. 870.
3004. IVERSEN, Linda
"Alone." [NewYorkQ] (48) 92, p. 114.
3005. IVES, Rich
"The Faith Healer's Secret Confession." [ColEng] (54:5) S 92, p. 585-586.
"A Late Afternoon View of Several Misplaced Objects." [ColEng] (54:5) S 92, p. 587.
3006. IVO, Lêdo
"The Crab" (tr. by Kerry Shawn Keys). [NowestR] (30:2) 92, p. 50.
"Santa Leopoldina Asylum" (tr. by Kerry Shawn Keys). [NowestR] (30:2) 92, p. 49.
"To the Gnawers" (tr. by Kerry Shawn Keys). [NowestR] (30:2) 92, p. 51-52.
3007. IVRY, Benjamin
"Incorporeal Ruler" (tr. of Adam Zagajewski, w. Renata Gorczynski and C. K. Williams). [Thrpny] (48) Wint 92, p. 4.
3008. IWANAGA, Ryan
"My Only Father." [NegC] (12:1/2) 92, p. 203-205.
3009. IZAGUIRRE, Ester de
"Si Preguntan por Alguien con Mi Nombre" (3 selections). [Luz] (1) My 92, p. 7-12.
"Tramp" (tr. by Angela McEwan). [Luz] (1) My 92, p. 11.
J-SON, Wooi-chin Ong
See WOOI-CHIN, J-son
3010. JABBOUR, Mick
"Cobwebs." [Paint] (19:37) Spr 92, p. 17.
"Crowded Bus in Cadiz." [Paint] (19:37) Spr 92, p. 16.
3011. JABÈS, Edmond
"Bell" (tr. by Anthony Rudolf). [Stand] (33:4) Aut 92, p. 38.
"Deep Waters" (tr. by Anthony Rudolf). [Stand] (33:4) Aut 92, p. 32-37.
"Dog" (tr. by Anthony Rudolf). [Stand] (33:4) Aut 92, p. 38.
"Mirror" (tr. by Anthony Rudolf). [Stand] (33:4) Aut 92, p. 38.
"Song for Three Dead Men, Astonished" (tr. by Anthony Rudolf). [Stand] (33:4) Aut 92, p. 37.
3012. JACK, Rodney T.
"My Mother's Image." [ChatR] (12:2) Wint 92, p. 97.
3013. JACKMAN, Vernon (Vernon L.)
"Eyes." [AfAmRev] (26:2) Sum 92, p. 288-289.
"Mornings." [Obs] (7:1/2) Spr-Sum 92, p. 86-87.
"Pa." [Obs] (7:1/2) Spr-Sum 92, p. 85-86.
"Rites." [AfAmRev] (26:2) Sum 92, p. 288.
"Shipwrecked." [Obs] (7:1/2) Spr-Sum 92, p. 87-88.
3014. JACKSON, Angela
"Faith." [Eyeball] (1) 92, p. 6.
"Koko" (For Mrs. Koko Taylor). [Eyeball] (1) 92, p. 6.
3015. JACKSON, Fleda (Fleda Brown)
"The Biographer Begins Writing the Multiple Lives of the Devil's Child." [Shen] (42:4) Wint 92, p. 51-57.
"Dumuzi, the Courtship." [PoetL] (87:2) Sum 92, p. 42.
"Inanna, Her Second Descent." [PoetL] (87:2) Sum 92, p. 41.
"Olga Knipper to Anton Chekhov, January 1902." [SouthernHR] (26:1) Wint 92, p. 67.

3016. JACKSON, Gale
"Elizabeth Freeman's Will, 1742-1829." [KenR] (NS 14:1) Wint 92, p. 4.
"Mary Prince, Bermuda. Turks Island. Antigua. 1787." [KenR] (NS 14:1) Wint 92, p. 6-8.
"She Lucy. 1849." [KenR] (NS 14:1) Wint 92, p. 4-5.
3017. JACKSON, Katherine
"Axe Music." [CumbPR] (12:1) Fall 92, p. 16.
"The Crossing." [CumbPR] (12:1) Fall 92, p. 20.
"The Frost Place" (Franconia, N. H.). [CumbPR] (12:1) Fall 92, p. 19.
"The Return." [CumbPR] (12:1) Fall 92, p. 18.
"Tidelines." [CumbPR] (12:1) Fall 92, p. 17.
3018. JACKSON, Lillian Rachel
"The 1 A.M. Sermon." [PacificR] (11) 92-93, p. 64.
3019. JACKSON, Mary Hale
"Hawaiian Names." [ChamLR] (10/11) Spr-Fall 92, p. 74.
"Mark Kadota's Rocks." [ChamLR] (10/11) Spr-Fall 92, p. 75.
3020. JACKSON, Reuben
"F Street Rush Hour." [WashR] (17:6) Ap-My 92, p. 15.
3021. JACKSON, Richard
"The Italian Phrase Book." [ColEng] (53:6) O 91, p. 661-663.
"Self Portrait of Rivard by Jackson." [MissR] (20:3) Spr 92, p. 62-63.
"Victor Hugo's Hunchback of Notre Dame." [MissR] (20:3) Spr 92, p. 64-65.
"While Dancing at the V.F.W., Seductive Melancholy Taps You on the Shoulder." [NewEngR] (14:3) Sum 92, p. 85-87.
3022. JACKSON, Sheila Cathryn
"A Rubber Ball." [CimR] (101) O 92, p. 106.
"Touched." [CimR] (101) O 92, p. 106.
3023. JACOB, Bob
"Waking the Dead." [US1] (26/27) 92, p. 43.
3024. JACOB, John
"Canso, Canza." [AnotherCM] (23) Spr 92, p. 93-102.
3025. JACOBIK, Gray
"The Banquet of Life." [Epiphany] (3:4) O (Fall) 92, p. 282.
"Cliff Waters and Mary Ann Whalen." [HampSPR] Wint 92, p. 12.
"July." [Epiphany] (3:4) O (Fall) 92, p. 281.
"Rappelling." [LouisL] (9:2) Fall 92, p. 73.
3026. JACOBOWITZ, Judah
"A February Florida." [Gypsy] (19) 92, p. 42.
"Marshmallows." [JINJPo] (14:2) Aut 92, p. 40.
"Omnibus Judgment." [JINJPo] (14:1) Spr 92, p. 29.
"Viola Quintet." [JINJPo] (14:1) Spr 92, p. 28.
3027. JACOBS, Kathryn
"The God Within." [Elf] (2:4) Wint 92, p. 27.
3028. JACOBSEN, Josephine
"Hourglass." [NewYorker] (68:28) 31 Ag 92, p. 54.
"Poetry Review." [Poetry] (160:2) My 92, p. 79.
3029. JACOBSEN, Rolf
"Just Delicate Needles" (tr. by Robert Hedin). [LitR] (35:3) Spr 92, p. 324.
"Old Cities in Auvergne" (tr. by Roger Greenwald). [Trans] (26) Spr 92, p. 93.
"Sand" (tr. by Roger Greenwald). [Trans] (26) Spr 92, p. 92.
"The Streetlamp" (tr. by Robert Hedin). [LitR] (35:3) Spr 92, p. 343.
"Wash & Dry Co." (tr. by Robert Hedin). [LitR] (35:3) Spr 92, p. 342.
3030. JACOBSEN, Steinbjorn
"I Am No Flower" (tr. by George Johnston). [Vis] (38) 92, p. 47.
3031. JACOBSON, Bonnie
"By the Sea, by the Sea." [Light] (3) Aut 92, p. 14.
"A Kindness." [Light] (4) Wint 92-93, p. 21.
"Miss Lochenmeyer Visits Hawaii." [Light] (3) Aut 92, p. 13.
"A Poor Example of Himself." [Light] (3) Aut 92, p. 16.
"Upon Visiting a Lady in Akron, Ohio." [Light] (2) Sum 92, p. 20.
"X's Letter to Y." [Light] (4) Wint 92-93, p. 13.
3032. JACOBSON, Dan
"A Month in the Country" (The Mary Elinore Smith Poetry Prize). [AmerS] (61:2) Spr 92, p. 223-240.
JACOME ROCA, Daniel
See ROCA, Daniel Jácome

JAE-CHUN, Park
See PARK, Jae-Chun
3033. JAEGER, Lowell
"Breakdown: Hitting the Wall" (Honorable Mention, 1992 Literary Awards). [GreensboroR] (53) Wint 92-93, p. 20-21.
"His Song." [GreensboroR] (53) Wint 92-93, p. 22-23.
"Letter to Everyone." [CharR] (18:2) Fall 92, p. 90-91.
"On Facing Miro's 'Tete'." [PoetryNW] (33:1) Spr 92, p. 11-12.
"On My Thirty-Ninth Birthday." [SoCoast] (13) Je 93 [i.e. 92], p. 25.
3034. JAFFE, Harold
"Slam Dance." [CityLR] (5) 92, p. 126-128.
3035. JAFFE, Maggie
"In a San Diego Sweat." [SingHM] (20) 92, p. 74.
"Information Explosion." [Gypsy] (19) 92, p. 11.
"The Old God of War." [Vis] (38) 92, p. 32.
"Poverty Sucks." [SlipS] (12) 92, p. 68-69.
3036. JAKIELA, Lori
"Believing We Could Learn to Love Each Other." [Calyx] (14:1) Sum 92, p. 7.
JAME, Adele Ne
See NeJAME, Adele
3037. JAMES, Clive
"What Happened to Auden." [NewYorker] (68:37) 2 N 92, p. 84.
3038. JAMES, Cynthia
"An Immigrant's Welcome (Temple at Orange Valley)." [LitR] (35:4) Sum 92, p. 558.
"Turtle Watching — 1." [LitR] (35:4) Sum 92, p. 559.
3039. JAMES, David
"The Blind Man Who Sells Brushes." [ThRiPo] (39/40) 92-93, p. 123-124.
"For the Sake of Grace in My Life." [Poem] (67) My 92, p. 3.
"Harvest." [ThRiPo] (39/40) 92-93, p. 121-122.
"The Love of Water Faucets." [ThRiPo] (39/40) 92-93, p. 122.
"The Process of Aging." [PoetryNW] (33:2) Sum 92, p. 22-23.
"Summer Vacation." [ChironR] (11:1) Spr 92, p. 21.
"Why Are Cows Milked from the Right Side?" [ChironR] (11:2) Sum 92, p. 16.
3040. JAMES, Kedrick
"Scavenger's Autopsy." [CapilR] (2:9) Fall 92, p. 66-77.
3041. JAMES, L. L.
"A Mouldering Crypt." [Vis] (40) 92, p. 9.
"Now Nijinsky." [Vis] (40) 92, p. 9.
3042. JAMES, Mike
"Broken Speakers." [TarRP] (31:2) Spr 92, p. 12.
3043. JAMES, Sibyl
"Bridal Thoughts." [AmerV] (28) 92, p. 76-77.
"Lamia's Confidences with Elizabeth." [AmerV] (28) 92, p. 78-79.
3044. JAMES, Syndey
"The Ghost of Absalom." [NegC] (12:3) 92, p. 88.
3045. JAMMES, Francis
"Child Reading an Almanac" (tr. by Jeffrey Harrison). [SenR] (22:1) Spr 92, p. 40.
"Like an insect, the mowing machine" (tr. by Jeffrey Harrison). [SenR] (22:1) Spr 92, p. 41.
"There Were Carafes of clear water" (tr. by Jeffrey Harrison). [SenR] (22:1) Spr 92, p. 42.
"The Village at Noon" (tr. by Jeffrey Harrison). [SenR] (22:1) Spr 92, p. 43.
3046. JANECZKO, Paul B.
"Stars" (for Emma, on her first birthday). [EngJ] (81:3) Mr 92, p. 93.
3047. JANÉS, Clara
"Estrella del ocaso entre los árboles." [InterPR] (18:1) Spr 92, p. 6.
"Mozart, Concerto No. 20" (tr. by Mark Smith-Soto). [InterPR] (18:1) Spr 92, p. 9.
"Mozart, Concierto No. 20." [InterPR] (18:1) Spr 92, p. 8.
"Star of twilight among the trees" (tr. by Mark Smith-Soto). [InterPR] (18:1) Spr 92, p. 7.
3048. JANOWITZ, Phyllis
"Chef's Dream." [Epoch] (41:3) 92, p. 286-289.
"Ha! Ha!" [Epoch] (41:3) 92, p. 390-391.
"Lenora, Later." [Epoch] (41:3) 92, p. 385.

3049. JANSMA, Esther
"Plaza Real, Barcelona" (for Casper le Fèvre, tr. by the author and Steve Orlen). [Agni] (35) 92, p. 173.
"Transportation" (tr. by the author and Steve Orlen). [Agni] (35) 92, p. 174.
3050. JANZEN, Jean
"Anna Rieger at the Blackboard." [CinPR] (23) Wint 91-92, p. 8.
"Dividing the Night." [GettyR] (5:4) Aut 92, p. 577.
"New Country." [CinPR] (23) Wint 91-92, p. 9.
"Summer in the Dark, 1944." [WestB] (30) 92, p. 60-61.
"Watermelon Pickles." [WestB] (30) 92, p. 59.
3051. JANZEN, Rhoda
"Doubt in Pale Gold." [SoDakR] (30:4) Wint 92, p. 53.
"North Dakota Sestina" (Ending with a line from Psalm 19). [ChrC] (109:31) 28 O 92, p. 966.
"The Rhythm of Irony." [SoDakR] (30:4) Wint 92, p. 52.
3052. JAQUISH, Karen I.
"Bits and Pieces." [Plain] (12:3) Spr 92, p. 34-35.
"Once in Prague" (for Vaçlac Havel). [HopewellR] (4) 92, p. 33.
"Twilight." [Plain] (13:1) Fall 92, p. 33.
3053. JARMAN, Mark
"A.M. Fog." [NewYorker] (68:3) 9 Mr 92, p. 36-37.
"California Pastoral." [PoetryNW] (33:1) Spr 92, p. 37-38.
"Cavafy in Redondo." [ThRiPo] (39/40) 92-93, p. 124-126.
"Creator." [PraS] (66:2) Sum 92, p. 17-18.
"Inside." [PraS] (66:2) Sum 92, p. 16.
"The Instant." [PoetryNW] (33:1) Spr 92, p. 37.
"The Mirror." [ThRiPo] (39/40) 92-93, p. 126-127.
"Outside." [PraS] (66:2) Sum 92, p. 16-17.
"Proverbs." [Boulevard] (7:2/3, #20/21) Fall 92, p. 130-131.
"Questions for Ecclesiastes." [NewEngR] (14:4) Fall 92, p. 80-82.
"A Song of Songs." [AmerV] (26) Spr 92, p. 65-66.
"The Supremes." [ThRiPo] (39/40) 92-93, p. 127-128.
3054. JARNAGIN, Bob
"Doll Story." [AntR] (50:3) Sum 92, p. 501.
"The Tattoo." [AntR] (50:3) Sum 92, p. 500.
3055. JARRARD, Kyle
"Perfume." [WormR] (32:3, #127) 92, p. 103.
"Saved." [WormR] (32:3, #127) 92, p. 103.
3056. JARRELL, Randall
"A Girl in a Library." [NoCarLR] (1:1) Sum 92, p. 14-15.
"The Mockingbird." [NoCarLR] (1:1) Sum 92, p. 15.
"Next Day." [NoCarLR] (1:1) Sum 92, p. 16.
"Pictures from an Institution" (Excerpt). [NoCarLR] (1:1) Sum 92, p. 10.
3057. JASON, Kathrine
"Small Navigations." [OxfordM] (6:2) Fall-Wint 90, p. 78-79.
3058. JASPER, Matt
"Moth Moon." [GrandS] (11:2, #42) 92, p. 101.
3059. JAUSS, David
"Black Orchid" (Miles Davis, New York, August 1950 — for Lynda Hull). [IndR] (15:2) Fall 92, p. 1-2.
"Never" (Norfork River, Arkansas). [Poetry] (160:5) Ag 92, p. 256.
"Portrait of the Artist as the God Libet." [ColR] (9:1) Spr-Sum 92, p. 136-137.
JAX, Norita Dittberner
See DITTBERNER-JAX, Norita
3060. JAY, Peter
"Discussion and Confession" (tr. of Éva Tóth). [Trans] (26) Spr 92, p. 85-86.
"Genesis" (tr. of Éva Tóth). [Trans] (26) Spr 92, p. 115.
3061. JENKIN, Ann Timoney
"A Quadrina for the First Day of Winter." [Footwork] 92, p. 129.
"A Quadrina for Your Wedding" (for Chris Mooney). [Footwork] 92, p. 129.
3062. JENKINS, Cathleen E.
"The Next Time." [Art&Und] (1:4) Jl-Ag 92, p. 6.
3063. JENKINS, Louis
"Spring Break-Up." [GettyR] (5:2) Spr 92, p. 344.
3064. JENKINS, Mike
"Peculiar Pagans" (for Dave and Kim). [CharR] (18:1) Spr 92, p. 83-84.

3065. JENKINS, Miriam B.
"Epithalamion after the Fact." [Kalliope] (14:1) 92, p. 69.
"Fantasy." [Kalliope] (14:1) 92, p. 70.
3066. JENKS, Deneen
"The Drowning." [CimR] (100) Jl 92, p. 108.
3067. JENNERMAN, Donald L.
"While Reading Latin Poetry in a Public Library." [Hellas] (3:1) Spr 92, p. 21.
3068. JENNINGS, Lane
"Reviewing Vermont." [Vis] (39) 92, p. 42.
3069. JENSEN, Laura
"The Autumn Sky." [Field] (46) Spr 92, p. 59.
"Clever Skata." [Field] (46) Spr 92, p. 61.
"Green Chevy." [Field] (46) Spr 92, p. 60.
3070. JEROME, Judson
"74." [Sparrow] (59) S 92, p. 23.
"Adolescence." [Sparrow] (59) S 92, p. 23.
"The Nap" (In Memoriam, 1927-1991). [Bogg] (65) 92, p. 10.
"The Sinew of Survival." [Sparrow] (59) S 92, p. 24.
3071. JEROZAL, Gregory
"Another View." [PoetL] (87:1) Spr 92, p. 12.
"A Farewell." [InterPR] (18:1) Spr 92, p. 56.
"To Buy a Bed." [HampSPR] Wint 92, p. 40-41.
3072. JESS (San Francisco)
"An Ouzel Plainting of a Stale-Loaf" [sic]. [PoetryUSA] (24) 92, p. 18.
JESSEAU, Ardessa Nica
See NICA-JESSEAU, Ardessa
JEW, Shalin Hai
See HAI-JEW, Shalin
3073. JEWELL, D.
"It's a sharkdance in the summertime animal lust." [BlackBR] (15) Spr-Sum 92, p. 47.
3074. JEWELL, Terri (Terri L.)
"Beneath All the Fighting." [EvergreenC] (7:2) Sum-Fall 92, p. 38.
"Harriet's Power." [AfAmRev] (26:2) Sum 92, p. 228.
"Moving In." [SinW] (47) Sum-Fall 92, p. 111-112.
"Reasons and Strange Rejections." [SinW] (46) Spr 92, p. 9.
JIAN, Yu
See YU, Jian
3075. JIANU, Angela
"Sports Poem" (tr. of Denisa Comanescu, w. Adam Sorkin). [Vis] (38) 92, p. 34.
3076. JIMÉNEZ, Ydilia
"A Reinaldo Arenas" (In Memoriam). [Nuez] (4:12) 92, p. 4.
3077. JIMENEZ CORRETJER, Zoe
"Cronicas Interplanetarias" (2 selections). [Luz] (1) My 92, p. 27-29.
3078. JIN, Ha
"If You Had Not Thrown Me Away." [TriQ] (86) Wint 92-93, p. 27.
JINI, Hwang
See HWANG, Jini
3079. JOBE, Carey
"Mount Mitchell." [Poem] (67) My 92, p. 14.
"A Riverside Burial Mound." [Poem] (67) My 92, p. 15.
JOCOBOWITZ, Judah
See JACOBOWITZ, Judah
3080. JOE, Reyna
"Sinta Mira." [LitR] (35:4) Sum 92, p. 615.
"Sit 'n See" (tr. by Richinel Ansano and Joceline Clemencia). [LitR] (35:4) Sum 92, p. 576.
3081. JOENSEN, Leyvoy
"Ghosts" (tr. of Joanes Nielsen). [Vis] (38) 92, p. 46.
3082. JOH, Elizabeth
"Arrangements." [PaintedB] (47) 92, p. 50.
"Web." [PaintedB] (47) 92, p. 51.
3083. JOHLER, Walt
"On the Roof." [Bogg] (65) 92, p. 59.
3084. JOHNSON, Barbara
"Temperature 32° F." [Writer] (105:6) Je 92, p. 25.

3085. JOHNSON, Bob
"Choices." [Noctiluca] (1:2) Wint 92 [on cover: Wint 93], p. 19.
3086. JOHNSON, Bradley
"Maybe I'll Give Them One More Day." [SlipS] (12) 92, p. 93.
"Why the Fear?" [SlipS] (12) 92, p. 90-92.
3087. JOHNSON, Brian
"The Sea, My Well, My Mirror." [RagMag] (10:2) 92, p. 99.
3088. JOHNSON, Dan
"Sky Lore." [LullwaterR] (3:2) Spr 92, p. 68.
"A Wedding One Year." [LullwaterR] (3:2) Spr 92, p. 14.
3089. JOHNSON, Frank
"Ferns." [Caliban] (11) 92, p. 145.
"Where Your Town Ends." [Caliban] (11) 92, p. 146.
3090. JOHNSON, Frankie Rolfe
"Potting Soil." [Obs] (7:1/2) Spr-Sum 92, p. 89-90.
3091. JOHNSON, Gillian
"Val." [PraF] (13:4, #61) Wint 92-93, p. 54-57.
3092. JOHNSON, Greg
"Convalescing." [PraS] (66:1) Spr 92, p. 36-37.
3093. JOHNSON, Jean Youell
"Creative energy." [Bogg] (65) 92, p. 37.
3094. JOHNSON, Judith
"In Jane's Red Room." [Chelsea] (53) 92, p. 43.
"Surrounded by Jerks" (South Africa and elsewhere). [Chelsea] (53) 92, p. 42-43.
JOHNSON, Linda Monacelli
See MONACELLI-JOHNSON, Linda
3095. JOHNSON, Marael
"Common Blah Marriage." [ChironR] (11:3) Aut 92, p. 6.
"My Rhymes / His Reason." [ChironR] (11:3) Aut 92, p. 6.
"Truth Decay." [ChironR] (11:3) Aut 92, p. 6.
"Waiting Games." [ChironR] (11:3) Aut 92, p. 6.
3096. JOHNSON, Mark Allan
"Credo." [BellArk] (8:2) Mr-Ap 92, p. 25.
"Go Fly a Kite." [BellArk] (8:4) Jl-Ag 92, p. 23.
"I've Got a Secret." [BellArk] (8:5) S-O 92, p. 4.
"Orientation." [BellArk] (8:2) Mr-Ap 92, p. 25.
"Persistence." [BellArk] (8:5) S-O 92, p. 4.
"Resistance." [BellArk] (8:5) S-O 92, p. 4.
"Rule of Gold." [BellArk] (8:5) S-O 92, p. 4.
"Safety Last." [BellArk] (8:4) Jl-Ag 92, p. 23.
"A Separate Rhythm." [BellArk] (8:2) Mr-Ap 92, p. 25.
"Shadow and Light." [BellArk] (8:5) S-O 92, p. 4.
"To Buy or Rent." [BellArk] (8:4) Jl-Ag 92, p. 24.
"Touch Became Electric." [BellArk] (8:5) S-O 92, p. 4.
3097. JOHNSON, Michael (Michael L.)
"Advice about Blue Grass." [PaintedHR] (6) Spr 92, p. 33.
"Brook." [Wind] (22:71) 92, p. 37.
"De Senectute Grammatici." [Amelia] (7:1, #20) 92, p. 159.
"The Death of a Debutante." [Amelia] (7:1, #20) 92, p. 160.
"A Dry Spell." [Parting] (5:1) Sum 92, p. 10.
"Farewell to Cynthia" (tr. of Propertius, Elegies, III, 25). [Parting] (5:2) Wint 92-93, p. 28-29.
"Frederick Remington." [ManhatPR] (14) [92?], p. 27.
"In Mid-1890 a Reporter for the Medicine Lodge *Cresset* Updates Readers on the Condition of Charley Shuneman . . . ." [Parting] (5:1) Sum 92, p. 11.
"Meditation" (tr. of Carlos Sahagún). [WebR] (16) Fall 92, p. 15.
"Old Folks' Home." [Wind] (22:71) 92, p. 26.
"Onece [sic] Johnson Explains the Habit of Eating Dirt." [CoalC] (5) My 92, p. 4.
"Oscar Wilde in Paris" (tr. of Guillermo Carnero). [WebR] (16) Fall 92, p. 14.
"Poet to Poet" (For Li-Young Lee). [Amelia] (7:1, #20) 92, p. 155.
"The Prehistoric Man from the Hauslab Pass." [Nimrod] (35:2) Spr-Sum 92, p. 100.
"A Requiem for Leonard Bernstein." [CapeR] (27:1) Spr 92, p. 49.
"Skinny-Dipping at Midnight." [LitR] (35:3) Spr 92, p. 384.
"Summer Still." [ManhatPR] (14) [92?], p. 27.
"Ultrasound" (for Kathleen). [Amelia] (7:1, #20) 92, p. 159.
"The Word" (tr. of Carlos Sahagún). [WebR] (16) Fall 92, p. 16.

3098. JOHNSON, Nancy
"Pastoral in a Paper Swamp." [ColEng] (53:5) S 91, p. 537.
3099. JOHNSON, Pyke, Jr.
"The Blacksmith Plover" (On Safari, Botswana). [Light] (2) Sum 92, p. 26.
"Unicorn in Winter." [Light] (4) Wint 92-93, p. 20.
3100. JOHNSON, Robert K.
"First Sign of Spring." [Wind] (22:71) 92, p. 5.
"In My Fifties." [ConnPR] (11:1) 92, p. 26.
"While On a Summer Stroll." [Wind] (22:71) 92, p. 5.
3101. JOHNSON, Sam F.
"Eye Rising." [Poetry] (159:4) Ja 92, p. 205.
3102. JOHNSON, Sheila Golburgh
"Myself in Love." [NegC] (12:1/2) 92, p. 188-189.
3103. JOHNSON, Shirley Golburgh
"The Smew." [Writer] (105:3) Mr 92, p. 24.
3104. JOHNSON, Sören
"At Epidauros." [Poem] (68) N 92, p. 63.
"Comic Book Heroes." [Poem] (68) N 92, p. 65.
"Las Cruces." [AnotherCM] (24) Fall 92, p. 95.
"The Fall of the Temple." [Poem] (68) N 92, p. 64.
"Fragment." [CarolQ] (44:2) Wint 92, p. 73.
"In Los Arcos." [CumbPR] (11:2) Spr 92, p. 20.
"Seven Degrees." [CarolQ] (44:2) Wint 92, p. 72.
3105. JOHNSON, Susan
"My Mother's Vacuum." [Kalliope] (15:1) 92, p. 11.
"Of Mist Nets and Mis-Identities." [BelPoJ] (43:2) Wint 92-93, p. 32-33.
"What She Knows." [Kalliope] (15:1) 92, p. 12.
3106. JOHNSON, Susie Paul
"Loretto Says." [GeoR] (46:4) Wint 92, p. 752-753.
"Sex in a Dress." [NegC] (12:1/2) 92, p. 66.
3107. JOHNSON, Tyler Miller
"The Boat Builders." [CarolQ] (45:1) Fall 92, p. 47-48.
3108. JOHNSON, William
"Winter Carrots." [HiramPoR] (51/52) Fall 91-Sum 92, p. 44-45.
3109. JOHNSTON, Agnes N.
"Cycles." [HolCrit] (29:1) F 92, p. 19.
3110. JOHNSTON, Allan
"7:30." [BlackBR] (16) Wint-Spr 92-93, p. 6.
3111. JOHNSTON, Brian
"Monument to the Five Greatest Words in English Literature" (Concrete Poem, by Jo-Ann Bonnett and brian j(o(h)n)ston). [WestCL] (26:3, #9) Wint 92-93, p. 74.
3112. JOHNSTON, Fred
"In the Library." [CreamCR] (16:2) Fall 92, p. 61.
"Lorca." [RiverS] (36) 92, p. 77-81.
"Making Weapons." [Grain] (20:2) Sum 92, p. 43.
3113. JOHNSTON, George
"I Am No Flower" (tr. of Steinbjorn Jacobsen). [Vis] (38) 92, p. 47.
3114. JOHNSTON, Marilyn E.
"In Plain View." [SmPd] (29:2, #85) Spr 92, p. 16.
"The September Thistle." [SmPd] (29:2, #85) Spr 92, p. 15.
"To Work in Frozen Haste." [SmPd] (29:2, #85) Spr 92, p. 16.
3115. JOHNSTON, Mark
"Never to the Present: War Poem." [PoetL] (87:2) Sum 92, p. 45-46.
"The Seven Deadly Sins of My Teenage Years." [WebR] (16) Fall 92, p. 42.
"Truck Pile-Up." [WebR] (16) Fall 92, p. 43.
3116. JOHNSTON, Stella
"Telling Stories." [WestHR] (46:3) Fall 92 [i.e. (46:4) Wint 92], p. 387-389.
3117. JOHNSTON, Sue Ann
"To Serve." [CanLit] (133) Sum 92, p. 127-128.
3118. JOHNSTONE, Megan Morwen
"Blackberry Wars." [Blueline] (13) 92, p. 39.
3119. JOLICOEUR, Marie-Ange
"Mon Ile." [LitR] (35:4) Sum 92, p. 601-602.
"My Island" (tr. by Betty Wilson). [LitR] (35:4) Sum 92, p. 511.

3120. JOLLIFF, William
"Another Reason Not to Give Your Son Your Name." [WebR] (16) Fall 92, p. 112.
"Fishing the Breeches." [PaintedB] (47) 92, p. 40-41.
"A History of Gardening." [PaintedB] (47) 92, p. 39.
"Jericho." [SycamoreR] (4:1) Wint 92, p. 48.
"Loving God From Behind." [LullwaterR] (3:3) Sum 92, p. 8.
"Loving Is the Worst of Christian Weather." [CinPR] (23) Wint 91-92, p. 55.
"Outside St. Peters Home at Lakeside." [CapeR] (27:1) Spr 92, p. 38.
"The Passover." [SycamoreR] (4:1) Wint 92, p. 47.
"Seedtime." [CutB] (37) Wint 92, p. 97-98.
"Sometimes Something Soft." [MidwQ] (33:2) Wint 92, p. 200.
"Threshers' Knives." [CapeR] (27:1) Spr 92, p. 39.
"Visiting the Homeplace: Fulton Creek, Ghosts, Bare Feet." [BellR] (15:2) Fall 92, p. 13.
"Walking Late With My Son." [SpoonRQ] (17:1/2) Wint-Spr 92, p. 10-11.
3121. JONES, Alice
"Absence." [GettyR] (5:1) Wint 92, p. 162-163.
"Balance Point." [GettyR] (5:1) Wint 92, p. 164-166.
"Brother and Sister." [Poetry] (159:5) F 92, p. 279-280.
"The Cadaver." [NewEngR] (14:3) Sum 92, p. 35-46.
"The Feast." [BelPoJ] (43:1) Fall 92, p. 37.
"Home." [BelPoJ] (43:1) Fall 92, p. 36.
"The Pool." [CreamCR] (16:1) Spr 92, p. 111.
"The Senescent Ovary." [BelPoJ] (42:3) Spr 92, p. 44.
3122. JONES, Arlene
"Once I Went to Evora." [GreenMR] (NS 5:2) Spr-Sum 92, p. 41.
"Piazza Navona in Summer." [PraS] (66:1) Spr 92, p. 62-63.
"Saints' Relics at the Museo Civico, in San Sepolcro" (From: In Search of Piero Della Francesca, 1420-1492). [GreenMR] (NS 5:2) Spr-Sum 92, p. 40.
3123. JONES, Benjamin
"Sugar." [LullwaterR] (4:1) Fall 92, p. 48-49.
3124. JONES, Bhala
"Lament." [Gypsy] (18) 92, p. 110-111.
3125. JONES, Bill
"Drawing Venus." [Footwork] 92, p. 125.
"Freedom." [Footwork] 92, p. 125.
JONES, Charlene Diehl
See DIEHL-JONES, Charlene
3126. JONES, D. G.
"Fin de Siècle Springtime Ramble" (2nd prize, Grain Prose Poem contest). [Grain] (20:4) Wint 92, p. 12-13.
3127. JONES, F.
"Tenement." [Verse] (9:3) Wint 92, p. 152.
3128. JONES, Jean
"The Angel of Death." [Pembroke] (24) 92, p. 151.
3129. JONES, Jill
"Around Here." [Vis] (40) 92, p. 36.
"Old Hotels Sing." [Vis] (40) 92, p. 23.
3130. JONES, John
"At the Metropolitan." [HangL] (61) 92, p. 46.
"Medium Infraction." [HangL] (61) 92, p. 45.
"Mexican Journey, with Atheist, Aesthete and Queer" (for Larry Johnson, "promoter of joy," dead of AIDS). [HangL] (61) 92, p. 47.
"Poem: The whisky is sulfur." [HangL] (61) 92, p. 46.
JONES, LeRoi
See BARAKA, Amiri
3131. JONES, Patricia Spears
"The Usual Suspect" (from the "Billie Holiday Chronicles"). [AmerV] (26) Spr 92, p. 97-98.
3132. JONES, Richard
"The Black Hat." [TriQ] (86) Wint 92-93, p. 98-99.
"Dancing." [TriQ] (86) Wint 92-93, p. 101-102.
"Lanterns." [Poetry] (161:1) O 92, p. 30-31.
"Leaving Los Angeles at Last." [OnTheBus] (4:2/5:1, #10/11) 92, p. 115-116.
"Scars." [Poetry] (161:1) O 92, p. 28-29.
"The Siesta." [TriQ] (86) Wint 92-93, p. 100.

3133. JONES, Robert C.
"If Mr. Wallace Stevens Instead of Mrs. Elizabeth Barrett Browning Had Written Sonnet #43 from the Portuguese." [EngJ] (80:6) O 91, p. 103.
3134. JONES, Rodney
"Apocalyptic Narrative." [NewEngR] (14:3) Sum 92, p. 5-8.
"Driving into Town." [CutB] (38) Sum 92, p. 1-2.
"Enough." [IndR] (15:2) Fall 92, p. 125.
"Eternity." [CutB] (38) Sum 92, p. 3-4.
"Familiars." [IndR] (15:2) Fall 92, p. 126.
"For the New Nihilists." [SouthernR] (28:4) Aut, O 92, p. 865-867.
"Grand Projection." [NewEngR] (14:4) Fall 92, p. 233-234.
"My Persona." [NewEngR] (14:4) Fall 92, p. 235.
"New Material." [AmerPoR] (21:3) My-Je 92, p. 56.
"The Privacy of Women." [ParisR] (34:122) Spr 92, p. 152-159.
"Second Nature." [NewEngR] (14:4) Fall 92, p. 236.
"Speaking Up." [NewEngR] (14:4) Fall 92, p. 237-238.
"A Story of the Great War." [SouthernR] (28:4) Aut, O 92, p. 864-865.
"Thirty-One Flavors of Houses." [NewEngR] (14:4) Fall 92, p. 238-239.
"White Mexicans." [SouthernR] (28:4) Aut, O 92, p. 861-863.
3135. JONES, Roger (*See also* JONES, Roger Allen)
"Original Sin." [TexasR] (13:1/2) Spr-Sum 92, p. 94.
"Smoke." [CimR] (101) O 92, p. 107.
"Sooner or Later." [CimR] (101) O 92, p. 107-108.
3136. JONES, Roger Allen (*See also* JONES, Roger)
"Honey Can You Call My Boy/Friend, Jimmy, Be/Cause, I Can't, Be/Cause, He Marry & Be/Cause, I Want to Know What Happen." [PaintedB] (48) 92, p. 38-39.
3137. JONES, Seaborn
"Pro Patria." [NewYorkQ] (47) 92, p. 79.
3138. JONES, Tom
"Easter." [ManhatPR] (14) [92?], p. 36.
3139. JONES, Willie M.
"Aunts." [AfAmRev] (26:2) Sum 92, p. 258-259.
JONES TALSARNAU, Ieuan
See TALSARNAU, Ieuan Jones
JONG, Daphne de
See De JONG, Daphne
3140. JORDAN, Barbara
"Dragonfly Reserve." [NewYorker] (68:14) 25 My 92, p. 36.
"Threshold." [Atlantic] (269:3) Mr 92, p. 83.
3141. JORDAN, June
"Letter to Haruko from Decorah, Iowa, U.S.A." [KenR] (NS 14:1) Wint 92, p. 128 - 129.
3142. JORDAN, Martha B.
"Deep Waters" (Selections: 7, 15-17, tr. of Francisco Hernández). [Manoa] (4:2) Fall 92, p. 23-24.
3143. JORDAN, Richard
"Dead Line." [Obs] (7:1/2) Spr-Sum 92, p. 93.
"The Dole." [Obs] (7:1/2) Spr-Sum 92, p. 92.
"Hagar's Trail." [Obs] (7:1/2) Spr-Sum 92, p. 94.
"A Husker's Way." [Obs] (7:1/2) Spr-Sum 92, p. 94-95.
"Indigo Fog." [Obs] (7:1/2) Spr-Sum 92, p. 91-92.
3144. JORIS, Pierre
"Flight" (tr. of Kurt Schwitters, w. Jerome Rothenberg). [Boulevard] (7:2/3, #20/21) Fall 92, p. 168-170.
"Threadsuns" (Selections: 18 poems, being the complete fourth cycle, tr. of Paul Celan). [Sulfur] (12:1, #30) Spr 92, p. 36-45.
3145. JORON, Andrew
"Nightdawn." [PoetryUSA] (24) 92, p. 21.
3146. JOSELOW, Beth
"Blacker Pacific." [Shiny] (7/8) 92, p. 115.
3147. JOSEPH, Allison
"Composition." [Parting] (5:1) Sum 92, p. 1-2.
"Dialogue: For White Women Poets." [PaintedHR] (5) Wint 92, p. 24-25.
"Film Noir." [Plain] (12:3) Spr 92, p. 30-31.
"Genealogy." [Crazy] (42) Spr 92, p. 40-44.

"The Good Parting." [PoetC] (24:1) Fall 92, p. 8.
"The New Bride." [Journal] (16:2) Fall-Wint 92, p. 83-85.
"Nice Work If You Can Get It." [Journal] (16:2) Fall-Wint 92, p. 86-88.

3148. JOSEPH, Lawrence
"About This." [MichQR] (31:2) Spr 92, p. 179-180.
"A Particular Examination of Conscience." [Boulevard] (7:2/3, #20/21) Fall 92, p. 128-129.
"Sentimental Education." [MichQR] (31:1) Wint 92, p. 111-113.

3149. JOSLIN, Ann
"Wedding Song: For W.H.A." [Plain] (13:1) Fall 92, p. 13.

JOTEI, Kashiwagi
See KASHIWAGI, Jotei

JOURNOUD, Claude Royet
See ROYET-JOURNOUD, Claude

3150. JOZSEF, Attila
"Without Hope" (tr. by Edwin Morgan). [Trans] (26) Spr 92, p. 36-37.

3151. JUARROZ, Roberto
"Eleventh IV.20" (for Eduardo Acevedo, tr. by Mary Crow). [Pequod] (34) 92, p. 52.
"Eleventh 11.15" (tr. by Mary Crow). [AnotherCM] (23) Spr 92, p. 103.

3152. JUHL, Timothy J.
"Laguna Night." [ChironR] (11:4) Wint 92, p. 47.

3153. JULIA, Lucie
"Fleurs de Sacrifices." [LitR] (35:4) Sum 92, p. 610.
"Recherche." [LitR] (35:4) Sum 92, p. 610.
"Sacrificial Flowers" (tr. by Betty Wilson). [LitR] (35:4) Sum 92, p. 527-528.
"Searching" (tr. by Betty Wilson). [LitR] (35:4) Sum 92, p. 5j28.

JUNICHIRO, Tanizaki
See TANIZAKI, Junichiro

3154. JUNKINS, Donald
"Pamplona: The Iron Balconies above the Running Bulls." [NoDaQ] (60:2) Spr 92, p. 279.
"Sunday Morning in February with Coffee Cup in Hand." [ConnPR] (11:1) 92, p. 12-13.

3155. JURAGA, Dubravka
"Parting at Kalemegdan" (tr. of Milos Crnjanski, w. David Sanders). [NewOR] (19:3/4) Fall-Wint 92, p. 108.

3156. JURGENSEN, Manfred
"Southern Suburbs, Brisbane" (for Kerry Montero). [Footwork] 92, p. 137.

3157. JUSTICE, Donald
"1980 — December 12." [SenR] (21:2) 91, p. 95.
"The Ballad of Charles Starkweather" (w. Robert Mezey). [Verse] (8:3/9:1) Wint - Spr 92, p. 31-32.
"The Grandfathers." [Verse] (8:3/9:1) Wint-Spr 92, p. 57.
"Seawind: A Song." [AntR] (50:1/2) Wint-Spr 92, p. 413.
"Song of the Hours." [SenR] (21:2) 91, p. 93-94.
"Song of the State Troopers." [SenR] (21:2) 91, p. 93.

3158. KABIR
"Five Ecstatic Songs" (tr. by Andrew McCord). [GrandS] (11:3 #43) 92, p. 82-84.

3159. KABOTIE, Mike
"Transistor Windows." [Jacaranda] (6:1/2) Wint-Spr 92, p. 80-81.

3160. KADERLI, Dan
"Driving Interpretation." [Hellas] (3:1) Spr 92, p. 44.
"Her Hungry Hollers." [Bogg] (65) 92, p. 6.
"Lifelines." [NegC] (12:1/2) 92, p. 68.
"The Road to Wizdom." [NegC] (12:1/2) 92, p. 67.

3161. KADMON, Leiv
"Under the Tree." [Caliban] (11) 92, p. 151.

3162. KAHF, Mohja
"Lateefa." [Vis] (38) 92, p. 7-10.

3163. KAHN, Wilma
"In Memoriam" (For Eric, August 26, 1992). [Art&Und] (1:5) S-O 92, p. 12.

3164. KAIBARA, Fusae
"In the grain's beard." [Amelia] (6:4, #19) 92, p. 87.

3165. KAKMI, D'metri
"Intimacy." [Vis] (40) 92, p. 29.

3166. KALAMARAS, George
"The Black Rose on My Forehead." [Contact] (10:62/63/64) Fall 91-Spr 92, p. 57.
"I Am a Suburb of Chicago." [Contact] (10:62/63/64) Fall 91-Spr 92, p. 58-59.
"I Could Drift Toward Dissolve." [Caliban] (11) 92, p. 79.
"Once I Could Force an Orange." [Talisman] (9) Fall 92, p. 219-220.
"The Raw and the Cooked." [Asylum] (7:3/4) 92, p. 64.
"They Don't Know How Lucky They Are." [Contact] (10:62/63/64) Fall 91-Spr 92, p. 56.
3167. KALDAS, Pauline
"Bird Lessons." [MichQR] (31:4) Fall 92, p. 549-550.
3168. KALENDEK, Julie
"Same Island." [Epoch] (41:3) 92, p. 392-394.
3169. KALINSKI, Todd
"2 Insomniacs & the Cat." [WormR] (32:4 #128) 92, p. 140.
"The Bunker." [RagMag] (10:1) 92, p. 67.
"The House of the Holy." [CoalC] (5) My 92, p. 13.
"Rooms with the Poor." [BlackBR] (16) Wint-Spr 92-93, p. 20.
"The Set Up." [WormR] (32:4 #128) 92, p. 141.
"Train Thunder." [RagMag] (10:1) 92, p. 66.
3170. KALZ, Jill
"Roadside Coons." [CreamCR] (16:2) Fall 92, p. 19.
3171. KAMAL, Daud
"Dedication" (tr. of Faiz Ahman Faiz). [Vis] (38) 92, p. 47.
"For Those Who Hate the Moon." [Vis] (38) 92, p. 44.
3172. KAMAU, H. B.
"Ancestors." [ChangingM] (24) Sum-Fall 92, p. 23.
"Summer Noise." [ChangingM] (24) Sum-Fall 92, p. 23.
3173. KAMIENSKA, Anna
"Small Things" (tr. by Tomasz P. Krzeszowski and Desmond Graham). [Verse] (8:3/9:1) Wint-Spr 92, p. 110.
3174. KAMINSKI, Helena
"At the End of the Twentieth Century, the Barbary Rim." [Agni] (36) 92, p. 67-68.
3175. KAMRAN, Gilani
"World's Garden: The First Stage" (Our Time Speaks with the Time to Come. The first section of the long poem, "Bagh-i Dunya/World's Garden," 1987, tr. by Alamgir Hashmi). [Elf] (2:2) Sum 92, p. 32-33.
3176. KANE, Paul
"Shadows." [WestHR] (46:2) Sum 92, p. 161.
3177. KANGAS, J. R.
"If Wishes Are Forces." [ChironR] (11:4) Wint 92, p. 43.
"Kaffir Lily." [PaintedHR] (5) Wint 92, p. 23.
"Three Stabs at a Definition." [ChironR] (11:4) Wint 92, p. 42.
3178. KANTCHEV, Nikolai
"Miracle" (tr. by Lisa Sapinkopf and Georgi Belev). [Vis] (39) 92, p. 20.
"White Moments" (tr. by B. R. Strahan, w. Pamela Perry). [Confr] (48/49) Spr-Sum 92, p. 218.
3179. KANTOLA, Kevin S.
"Building." [ChamLR] (10/11) Spr-Fall 92, p. 118-119.
3180. KANTOR, Péter
"On Liberty" (tr. by László Baránszky). [Agni] (35) 92, p. 270-271.
3181. KANYADI, Sándor
"On That Evening" (tr. by Len Roberts). [NowestR] (30:3) 92, p. 45.
3182. KAPECZ, Zsuzsa
"The Monster" (tr. by Nicholas Kolumban). [OnTheBus] (4:2/5:1, #10/11) 92, p. 264-265.
3183. KAPLAN, Cheryl
"The Big Jane Fence." [NewYorkQ] (49) 92, p. 103.
"File In!" [Pequod] (34) 92, p. 119-121.
3184. KAPLAN, Joy
"Giraffes." [HangL] (60) 92, p. 91.
"The two girls are behind the house." [HangL] (60) 92, p. 90-91.
3185. KAPLAN, Susan
"The Perfect Thing." [AnotherCM] (24) Fall 92, p. 96-97.
3186. KAPOOR, Suman K.
"The Blacksmith's Son." [Elf] (2:1) Spr 92, p. 22-23.
"Makeshift Cradle." [Elf] (2:1) Spr 92, p. 24.

"The Sculptor's Wife." [OnTheBus] (4:2/5:1, #10/11) 92, p. 117-118.

3187. KAPPATOS, Rigas
"Carta" (tr. of Alejandro Baras, w. Carlos Montemayor). [Nuez] (4:12) 92, p. 24.
"Pasan los Asiáticos" (tr. of Alejandro Baras, w. Carlos Montemayor). [Nuez] (4:12) 92, p. 24.

3188. KAPSALIS, Adamandia
"A Telling Silence." [Lactuca] (15) Mr 92, p. 54.

3189. KARANDIKAR, Vinda
"Himayoga" (A Meditation on Snow, Chicago, 1967-68, tr. by Vinay Dharwadker). [ChiR] (38:1/2) 92, p. 212-217.

3190. KARÉNINE, Vincent-Marc
"Hatteras Night" (tr. by Louis Oivier). [CharR] (18:1) Spr 92, p. 95-96.

3191. KARETNICK, Jen
"Blossoms." [SpoonRQ] (17:3/4) Sum-Fall 92, p. 12-13.
"Duckie Takes a Dive." [SpoonRQ] (17:3/4) Sum-Fall 92, p. 14.
"Warm Tuna Milkshake." [SpoonRQ] (17:3/4) Sum-Fall 92, p. 15.

3192. KARPOWICZ, Dean
"Remigration." [CoalC] (5) My 92, p. 10.

3193. KARR, Mary
"Don Giovanni's Confessor." [Poetry] (159:5) F 92, p. 258-259.
"Donna Giovanna's Failure." [WillowS] (30) Sum 92, p. 11-13.
"Getting Ready for the Garbage Man." [WillowS] (30) Sum 92, p. 10.
"The Legion." [TriQ] (84) Spr-Sum 92, p. 116-117.

3194. KARR, Muriel
"At Iris's Wedding in the Woods." [BellArk] (8:3) My-Je 92, p. 22.
"Bowls So Empty." [BellArk] (8:5) S-O 92, p. 12.
"Bowls So Empty." [BellArk] (8:6) N-D 92, p. 7.
"Church." [BellArk] (8:5) S-O 92, p. 21.
"Clearly Not." [BellArk] (8:2) Mr-Ap 92, p. 21.
"Cold Fusion." [BellArk] (8:3) My-Je 92, p. 22.
"Despite the Web." [BellArk] (8:2) Mr-Ap 92, p. 21.
"Elevate to Affection." [BellArk] (8:6) N-D 92, p. 7.
"The Ex-Wife Attends the Wedding Wearing White." [PaintedB] (45) 92, p. 10.
"Oh, Paul — Let's Not Ask for the Moon — We Have the Stars." [BellArk] (8:2) Mr-Ap 92, p. 21.
"Princess en Route to Marry an Unknown King." [SmPd] (29:1, #84) Wint 92, p. 31.
"Rind." [BellArk] (8:2) Mr-Ap 92, p. 13.
"Rind." [BellArk] (8:2) Mr-Ap 92, p. 21.
"Sing the Hope." [BellArk] (8:5) S-O 92, p. 12.
"Sing the Hope." [BellArk] (8:6) N-D 92, p. 7.
"That Summer." [BellArk] (8:2) Mr-Ap 92, p. 9.
"Till Praise." [BellArk] (8:5) S-O 92, p. 13.
"Till Praise." [BellArk] (8:6) N-D 92, p. 7.
"We Link." [BellArk] (8:1) Ja-F 92, p. 13.
"Why Muriel?" [BellArk] (8:5) S-O 92, p. 21.
"Why Muriel?" [BellArk] (8:6) N-D 92, p. 7.

3195. KARRER, Pearl
"The Revelers" (wall painting, Tomb of the Leopards, Tarquinia, Italy, circa 470 B.C.). [Vis] (39) 92, p. 43.

3196. KASCHNITZ, Marie Luise
"Nicht Gesagt." [AntigR] (90) Sum 92, p. 88.
"Silent" (tr. by Colin O'Connell and Uta Doerr). [AntigR] (90) Sum 92, p. 89.

3197. KASDORF, Julia
"At the Acme Bar & Grill." [NewYorker] (68:4) 16 Mr 92, p. 38.
"A Family History." [NewYorker] (68:25) 10 Ag 92, p. 36.
"Freundschaft." [NewYorker] (68:16) 8 Je 92, p. 42.
"Prospect Park, Holy Week." [NewYorker] (68:9) 20 Ap 92, p. 44.
"What I Learned from my Mother." [WestB] (30) 92, p. 42.

3198. KASHIWAGI, Jotei (1763-1819)
"In Yoshiwara" (tr. by Graeme Wilson). [Jacaranda] (6:1/2) Wint-Spr 92, p. 151.

3199. KASHNER, Sam
"Appointment at the Louvre." [HangL] (61) 92, p. 49-50.
"As a Bee Leaves the Flower." [HangL] (61) 92, p. 51.
"At the Plinth." [HangL] (60) 92, p. 27.
"Cat." [HangL] (60) 92, p. 30.
"The Crocodile." [HangL] (60) 92, p. 29.

"In Memoriam to the One Addressed As You." [HangL] (61) 92, p. 50.
"Independent Study." [HangL] (61) 92, p. 48.
"The Lion." [HangL] (60) 92, p. 29.
"An Old Puzzle." [HangL] (60) 92, p. 28.
"The Owl." [HangL] (60) 92, p. 30.
"Pigeons." [HangL] (60) 92, p. 30.
"The Recruit." [HangL] (60) 92, p. 26-27.
"The Turtle." [HangL] (60) 92, p. 29.

3200. KASISCHKE, Laura
"Arms." [Jacaranda] (6:1/2) Wint-Spr 92, p. 34-35.
"The Edge of the Husband." [NewDeltaR] (8:2) Spr-Sum 91, p. 45-46.

3201. KASPER, M.
"Celebrations" (tr. of Piotr Sommer, w. the author). [NewYorker] (68:45) 28 D 92-4 Ja 93, p. 126.

3202. KASZUBA, Sophia
"White Shirt." [AntigR] (90) Sum 92, p. 7.

3203. KATES, J.
"Joseph." [DenQ] (26:4) Spr 92, p. 38.
"Nothing Nothing" (tr. of Tatyana Shcherbina). [KenR] (NS 14:4) Fall 92, p. 119 - 121.
"Rest 8.6.8.8.6." [FloridaR] (18:1) Spr-Sum 92, p. 69.
"To Lucy" (female, aged ?). [FloridaR] (18:1) Spr-Sum 92, p. 68.
"Untitled: Bound by the heart to the ignorant" (tr. of Olga Popova). [PaintedB] (45) 92, p. 26-27.
"Untitled: His wife is a suicide" (tr. of Alexandra Sozonova). [PaintedB] (45) 92, p. 28-29.

3204. KATROVAS, Richard
"Black English." [SouthernR] (28:4) Aut, O 92, p. 868-869.
"Cold Front." [NoAmR] (277:2) Mr-Ap 92, p. 23.
"If I could" (tr. of Svetlana Burianová, w. Dominika Winterová). [NewOR] (19:3/4) Fall-Wint 92, p. 25.
"Midnight" (tr. of Jan Rejzek, w. Dominika Winterová). [NewOR] (19:3/4) Fall - Wint 92, p. 24.
"Night at the Singles Dorm" (tr. of Jirí Zácek, w. Dominika Winterová). [NewOR] (19:3/4) Fall-Wint 92, p. 29.
"Prague Fisherman" (tr. of Josef Simon, w. Dominika Winterová). [NewOR] (19:3/4) Fall-Wint 92, p. 27.
"The Swans of Prague" (tr. of Zdena Bratrsovská, w. Dominika Winterová). [NewOR] (19:3/4) Fall-Wint 92, p. 26.
"Troja at Eight in the Evening" (tr. of Karel Sys, w. Dominika Winterová). [NewOR] (19:3/4) Fall-Wint 92, p. 28.
"A Walk Around the Brewery" (tr. of Ivan Wernisch, w. Dominika Winterová). [NewOR] (19:3/4) Fall-Wint 92, p. 30.

3205. KATZ, Bobbi
"In Sam's Garden." [EngJ] (81:4) Ap 92, p. 94.

3206. KATZ, David M.
"The Consolation of Philosophy" (Homage to Salman Rushdie). [NewRep] (205:30 [sic, i.e. 206:3]) 20 Ja 92, p. 44.

3207. KATZ, Steven B.
"Waking into History" (After Ingmar Bergman's "The Serpent's Egg" — for my son). [SouthernPR] (32:1) Spr 92, p. 7-8.

3208. KATZ, Susan A.
"Retreat." [NegC] (12:1/2) 92, p. 69.

3209. KATZ-LEVINE, Judy
"Elegy for Sam." [Noctiluca] (1:2) Wint 92 [on cover: Wint 93], p. 16.
"Ghazal for Sappho." [Noctiluca] (1:2) Wint 92 [on cover: Wint 93], p. 17.
"Healing Skin." [Noctiluca] (1:1) Spr 92, p. 32.
"Legends on My Birthday" (2.25.91). [Noctiluca] (1:1) Spr 92, p. 31.
"Lush Ghazal" (for Jenny Barber). [Noctiluca] (1:2) Wint 92 [on cover: Wint 93], p. 18.
"Our Wedding." [Noctiluca] (1:1) Spr 92, p. 30-31.
"Supermarket." [US1] (26/27) 92, p. 34.
"The Umpire." [Sun] (197) Ap 92, p. 13.
"We Were Young." [Noctiluca] (1:1) Spr 92, p. 29.

3210. KAUFFMAN, Janet
"Poem 1." [Caliban] (11) 92, p. 8.

"Poem 2." [Caliban] (11) 92, p. 8.
"Poem 3." [Caliban] (11) 92, p. 9.
"Poem 4." [Caliban] (11) 92, p. 9.

3211. KAUFMAN, Andrew
"The Cinnamon Bay Sonnets" (Excerpt). [CreamCR] (16:2) Fall 92, p. 57.

3212. KAUFMAN, Debra
"Fever." [CarolQ] (44:3) Spr-Sum 92, p. 83.
"The Roy Rogers Show." [VirQR] (68:4) Aut 92, p. 700-701.
"Something Quiet." [VirQR] (68:4) Aut 92, p. 697-700.

3213. KAUFMAN, Shirley
"Forever After." [Manoa] (4:2) Fall 92, p. 111-112.
" *Hamsin* Breaking After Five Days." [SnailPR] (2:2) Fall-Wint 92, p. 30.
"Riding the Elephant." [Manoa] (4:2) Fall 92, p. 110-111.
"Waiting." [Iowa] (22:1) Wint 92, p. 85-87.

3214. KAUSS, St-John
"Ma Femme aux Yeux de Brocart" (extraits, pour Guedlie Lafayette). [Callaloo] (15:3) Sum 92, p. 703-704.
"My Wife with the Brocade Eyes" (excerpts, for Guedlie Lafayette, tr. by Carrol F. Coates). [Callaloo] (15:3) Sum 92, p. 701-702.

3215. KAUSS, St-Valentin
"The Charm of the Bitter Dream" (tr. by Carrol F. Coates). [Callaloo] (15:3) Sum 92, p. 699.
"Charmes de l'Amer Songe." [Callaloo] (15:3) Sum 92, p. 700.
"O dans l'Ignorance de Toute Frayeur." [Callaloo] (15:3) Sum 92, p. 696.
"Oh in the Absence of All Fear" (tr. by Carrol F. Coates). [Callaloo] (15:3) Sum 92, p. 695.

3216. KAVEN, Bob
"Hysteria." [Noctiluca] (1:1) Spr 92, p. 6-7.
"Little Metaphysical Poem." [Noctiluca] (1:1) Spr 92, p. 5.

3217. KAY, John
"My New Life." [WindO] (56) Fall-Wint 92, p. 25-26.
"Spring." [WindO] (56) Fall-Wint 92, p. 26.

3218. KAZENBROOT, Nelly
"Little Bird." [Grain] (20:2) Sum 92, p. 66.

3219. KAZUK, A. R.
"Flesh Floating into Dream." [YellowS] (39) Spr-Sum 92, p. 15.

KAZUKO, Shiraishi
See SHIRAISHI, Kazuko

KEATING, Helane Levine
See LEVINE-KEATING, Helane

3220. KEAY, Robert
"Who Loves Ya, Baby?" [Amelia] (7:1, #20) 92, p. 117.

3221. KEEFER, Janice Kulyk
"All the Beautiful Naked Women Take Up Their Beds and Walk Out of the Picture." [MalR] (100) Fall 92, p. 139-140.
"Canada." [PraF] (13:3, #60) Aut 92, p. 67-68.
"Cherries" (for Branko Gorjup). [MalR] (100) Fall 92, p. 136.
"Elizabeth Smart, aetatis 70." [MalR] (100) Fall 92, p. 150-151.
"Emilie Flöge." [MalR] (100) Fall 92, p. 143-145.
"For Branko." [PoetryC] (12:3/4) Jl 92, p. 17.
"Homecoming." [PraF] (13:3, #60) Aut 92, p. 69.
"In Praise of Gravity." [MalR] (100) Fall 92, p. 137-138.
"Journey." [PraF] (13:3, #60) Aut 92, p. 68.
"Le Long du Lac" (for Bronwen Wallace, 1945-1989). [PoetryC] (12:3/4) Jl 92, p. 17.
"Pierre Bonnard Nu à Contre-Jour." [PoetryC] (12:3/4) Jl 92, p. 17.
"Plat de Nuit." [MalR] (100) Fall 92, p. 141-142.
"Reading" (for Connie). [MalR] (100) Fall 92, p. 146-147.
"Sacra Conversazione" (for Jane Magrath). [MalR] (100) Fall 92, p. 148-149.
"Thérèse / Balthus." [MalR] (100) Fall 92, p. 134-135.
"Two Letters." [PraF] (13:3, #60) Aut 92, p. 70-72.

3222. KEEGAN, Linda
"Reading into Love." [HawaiiR] (16:2, #35) Spr 92, p. 30.
"Remembering Danelions." [CapeR] (27:1) Spr 92, p. 6.
"A Variation of the Witch Story." [Bogg] (65) 92, p. 39.

3223. KEELAN, Claudia
"Fallout." [AntR] (50:3) Sum 92, p. 511.
"Incest." [Sulfur] (12:1, #30) Spr 92, p. 70.
"Parable 6." [NewAW] (10) Fall 92, p. 82-83.
"The Queen of Tragedy, Awake from the Basement." [Sulfur] (12:1, #30) Spr 92, p. 69-70.
"To My Teacher" (#1). [Agni] (35) 92, p. 226.
3224. KEELEY, Carol
"The Chase." [NewAW] (10) Fall 92, p. 91-92.
"Wild Fissure." [NewAW] (10) Fall 92, p. 93.
3225. KEELEY, Edmund
"The End of Donona, I and II" (tr. of Yannis Ritsos). [Trans] (26) Spr 92, p. 8-10.
3226. KEEN, Suzanne
"Possessions" (for Bill Bennett. Winner, Annual Free Verse Contest, 1991). [AnthNEW] (4) 92, p. 10.
3227. KEENAN, Deborah
"Architecture." [Shen] (42:4) Wint 92, p. 97.
3228. KEENAN, Gary
"Myrddin's Bodhran." [BrooklynR] (9) 92, p. 72.
3229. KEENER, Christopher
"Another Breakfast." [Outbr] (23) 92, p. 24-25.
3230. KEENER, LuAnn
"Color Documentary." [CapeR] (27:1) Spr 92, p. 43.
"Elephants." [QW] (35) Sum-Fall 92, p. 100-101.
"Marine Iguana." [CapeR] (27:1) Spr 92, p. 42.
"Sweet Briar Colony, the Lovers." [QW] (35) Sum-Fall 92, p. 102.
"The Woman Who Paints Demons" (for Miriam Beerman). [NegC] (12:3) 92, p. 89 - 90.
3231. KEINEG, Paol
"Eight Poems: A, B, C, D, E, F, G, H" (tr. by C. D. Wright). [ParisR] (34:122) Spr 92, p. 201-205.
3232. KEITA, Nzadi
"After Prayer Meetin'." [Footwork] 92, p. 71.
"Back Road." [Footwork] 92, p. 71.
"Sermonette." [Footwork] 92, p. 71.
"Short Letter, 1943." [Footwork] 92, p. 71.
3233. KEITH, Bill
"African Design." [RagMag] (10:2) 92, p. 85.
"Harlequinode." [RagMag] (10:2) 92, p. 74.
"Poem." [RagMag] (10:2) 92, p. 49.
"Sfumato: Homage to Leonardo da Vinci." [RagMag] (10:2) 92, p. 25.
"Snakes." [RagMag] (10:2) 92, p. 102.
3234. KEITH, W. J.
"Chickadees." [AntigR] (89) Spr 92, p. 8.
"Country Cemetery." [AntigR] (89) Spr 92, p. 9.
"For Douglas Lochhead." [AntigR] (89) Spr 92, p. 7.
3235. KELEN, S. K.
"Directions." [PoetryC] (12:3/4) Jl 92, p. 33.
"Gondwanaland." [PoetryC] (12:3/4) Jl 92, p. 33.
"Hyperion." [PoetryC] (12:3/4) Jl 92, p. 33.
"Joe Wilson Goes to Town." [PoetryC] (12:3/4) Jl 92, p. 33.
3236. KELL, Richard
"The Victims." [Stand] (33:3) Sum 92, p. 54-57.
3237. KELLER, David
"At the Player Piano Again." [Footwork] 92, p. 63.
"The Best Wishes." [Footwork] 92, p. 64.
"The Best Wishes." [LaurelR] (26:1) Wint 92, p. 54.
"The Buzzards." [PoetryNW] (33:3) Aut 92, p. 7.
"Comedy." [LaurelR] (26:1) Wint 92, p. 55.
"Friends, Outside, Night." [ThRiPo] (39/40) 92-93, p. 130.
"The Future." [PoetryNW] (33:3) Aut 92, p. 5.
"Hunting for Magic." [Footwork] 92, p. 63.
"In the Middle of the Journey." [ThRiPo] (39/40) 92-93, p. 129.
"Joining a Choir." [US1] (26/27) 92, p. 45.
"Mussels." [ThRiPo] (39/40) 92-93, p. 128-129.
"A New Day." [LaurelR] (26:1) Wint 92, p. 56.

"Saying the Right Thing." [Footwork] 92, p. 63.
"Silver." [PoetryNW] (33:3) Aut 92, p. 3-4.
"Spring Snow." [PoetryNW] (33:3) Aut 92, p. 6.

3238. KELLER, Pat
"Soldiers." [SouthernPR] (32:1) Spr 92, p. 15-16.

3239. KELLER, Tsipi
"Last Poems" (tr. of Dan Pagis). [QRL] (Poetry Series 11: vol. 31) 92, 61 p.

3240. KELLEY, Janine Soucie
"Milk Carton." [Kalliope] (14:1) 92, p. 51.

3241. KELLEY, Karen
"Map of Heaven (Letter to Justin)." [Sulfur] (12:1, #30) Spr 92, p. 71-76.
"Raceway: Indian Version (Virtual Reality No. 4)." [Avec] (5:1) 92, p. 29.
"The Strategy of Appearance" (Virtual Reality No. 10). [PaintedB] (46) 92, p. 18 - 20.

3242. KELLEY, Steven
"Arch." [ChatR] (13:1) Fall 92, p. 19-26.

3243. KELLEY, Tina (*See also* KELLY, Tina)
"Grow You Back." [LitR] (35:3) Spr 92, p. 346.

3244. KELLMAN, Anthony
"Ballad of the Limestone." [GrahamHR] (16) Fall 92, p. 52-53.
"Graves of the Sea." [GrahamHR] (16) Fall 92, p. 51.
"Summer Heat." [Obs] (7:1/2) Spr-Sum 92, p. 96-97.

3245. KELLMAN, Stephen G. (Steven G.)
"Chanson." [Light] (1) Spr 92, p. 16.
"I Never Saw a Moor." [Light] (4) Wint 92-93, p. 16.
"Parity." [Light] (3) Aut 92, p. 16.

3246. KELLOGG, David
"Aranmore." [PraS] (66:1) Spr 92, p. 59-61.
"Triptych." [SycamoreR] (4:1) Wint 92, p. 55.

3247. KELLY, Anne
"The Day Mt. St. Helen's Erupted." [Event] (21:1) Spr 92, p. 60-61.

3248. KELLY, Brigit Pegeen
"Boticelli's St. Sebastian." [SycamoreR] (4:2) Sum 92, p. 17.
"The Column of Mercury Recording the Temperature of Night." [Journal] (16:2) Fall-Wint 92, p. 10-11.
"Distraction of Fish and Flowers in the Kill." [Journal] (16:2) Fall-Wint 92, p. 12 - 13.
"A Green Wood." [SpoonRQ] (17:3/4) Sum-Fall 92, p. 49-50.
"The Music Lesson." [AmerV] (26) Spr 92, p. 95-96.
"The White Pilgrim: Old Christian Cemetery." [GettyR] (5:1) Wint 92, p. 86-89.

3249. KELLY, Patrick
"Emtpy Can, Empty Words." [PaintedB] (48) 92, p. 34-35.

3250. KELLY, Patt
"Weight." [SinW] (46) Spr 92, p. 62.

3251. KELLY, Robert
"Mapping." [GrandS] (11:3 #43) 92, p. 53-57.

3252. KELLY, Robert A.
"From Purgatory Mary Flannery Reflects on Writing." [AntigR] (91) Fall 92, p. 83.
"From Purgatory Mary Flannery Tells Elizabeth Bishop." [AntigR] (91) Fall 92, p. 81-82.
"Papère." [AntigR] (91) Fall 92, p. 84-85.

3253. KELLY, Timothy P.
"Will This Change?" (from "Articulation." Finalist, The Pablo Neruda Prize for Poetry). [Nimrod] (36:1) Fall-Wint 92, p. 55.

3254. KELLY, Tina (*See also* KELLEY, Tina)
"From the New York Times, a 19-Year-Old Photographer Doused and Burned Under Pinochet." [BelPoJ] (43:2) Wint 92-93, p. 9.
"Looking Only for 'Yes'" (courtesy of Suraphong Kanchananaga's Practical Thai). [BelPoJ] (43:2) Wint 92-93, p. 8-9.
"The Pornography of Recent Times." [BelPoJ] (43:2) Wint 92-93, p. 10.

3255. KELLY, Tom
"At Her Feet." [Stand] (33:2) Spr 92, p. 61.

3256. KELLY-DeWITT, Susan
"House of Childhood." [PraS] (66:1) Spr 92, p. 67.
"The Presidio, 1947." [PraS] (66:1) Spr 92, p. 63-65.
"San Francisco, 1949." [PraS] (66:1) Spr 92, p. 65-67.

3257. KEMP, Penn
"An Ounce of Essential." [Arc] (29) Aut 92, p. 46.
3258. KEMPHER, Ruth Moon
"November Poems, Resurrected for Haunting RA." [Jacaranda] (6:1/2) Wint-Spr 92, p. 32-33.
"She Attends the MLA Convention, Falters, Finds the Wrong Door and Tells Noted Author Where to Go." [Bogg] (65) 92, p. 35.
"Toenail Poem." [Kalliope] (14:3) 92, p. 6-7.
3259. KEMPNER, Bob
"Near a Wabash River levee raunchy clergymen abound." [Light] (2) Sum 92, p. 29.
3260. KEMPTON, Karl
"A Facet of Crow." [Noctiluca] (1:2) Wint 92 [on cover: Wint 93], p. 7.
3261. KENDALL, Robert
"Cashing In on a Moment of Understanding." [ManhatPR] (14) [92?], p. 10.
3262. KENDIG, Diane
"Crossing the Ohio After Seeing Mapplethorpe's 'Perfect Moment'." [ChangingM] (24) Sum-Fall 92, p. 7.
"I Am Going to Speak of My Women" (tr. of Daisy Zamora). [SingHM] (20) 92, p. 27-29.
3263. KENISTON, Ann
"Goodbye to My Parents." [LitR] (35:3) Spr 92, p. 360.
"Hunger." [PoetL] (87:3) Fall 92, p. 31-32.
"Nine Rules for Living Alone." [NewYorkQ] (49) 92, p. 45-47.
"Persephone Lying in Bed." [Crazy] (42) Spr 92, p. 72.
"Sestina." [Crazy] (42) Spr 92, p. 70-71.
3264. KENNEDY, Anne
"In the Garden." [SouthernHR] (26:3) Sum 92, p. 212-213.
"Two Poems from Buck Mountain." [SouthernHR] (26:3) Sum 92, p. 214.
3265. KENNEDY, Chris
"The Devil's Workshop." [NoDaQ] (60:3) Sum 92, p. 127-128.
"Legacy." [OnTheBus] (4:2/5:1, #10/11) 92, p. 119.
3266. KENNEDY, John
"Cowboy Love." [TarRP] (31:2) Spr 92, p. 35.
3267. KENNEDY, X. J.
"Ancient Catastrophes Revisited." [Light] (3) Aut 92, p. 3.
"Apocrypha." [Light] (3) Aut 92, p. 4.
"Ballad Shard." [SewanR] (100:2) Spr 92, p. 271.
"Black Velvet Art." [SewanR] (100:3) Sum 92, p. 375.
"Cowhand Song." [Light] (3) Aut 92, p. 4.
"The Cow's Revenge." [Light] (1) Spr 92, p. 12.
"A Culinary Surprise." [Light] (3) Aut 92, p. 3.
"Dancing with the Poets at Piggy's" (for Alan Dugan). [LaurelR] (26:1) Wint 92, p. 68-69.
"Defending the Canon." [Light] (2) Sum 92, p. 10.
"Drat These Brats!" [Light] (3) Aut 92, p. 6.
"Elizabethan Theater: A Suspicion." [Light] (3) Aut 92, p. 5.
"Empty House Singing to Itself." [Nat] (254:14) 13 Ap 92, p. 498.
"Enlightenment (Song for Ancient Voices)." [NewYorkQ] (48) 92, p. 50.
"Four Literati." [NewYorkQ] (47) 92, p. 36.
"Ghastly Brats." [Light] (3) Aut 92, p. 5.
"History of Strong Drink." [Light] (3) Aut 92, p. 5.
"Medical Types of Personality." [Light] (3) Aut 92, p. 4.
"Naval Intelligence." [Light] (3) Aut 92, p. 5.
"A Penitent Giuseppe Belli Enters Heaven" (for Miller Williams). [Sparrow] (59) S 92, p. 27.
"Postscript to an Apocalypse." [Light] (3) Aut 92, p. 5.
"Reflection on Far Eastern Cuisine." [Light] (3) Aut 92, p. 3.
"Sensual Music." [NewYorkQ] (49) 92, p. 37.
"Snug." [SewanR] (100:3) Sum 92, p. 376.
"Sonnet with Immortality Written All Over It." [Sparrow] (59) S 92, p. 28.
"Spooky Doings." [Light] (3) Aut 92, p. 4.
"Suffering Ungladly." [Light] (3) Aut 92, p. 3.
"Summer Children." [FourQ] (6:1) Spr 92, p. 12.
"Summer Children." [TexasR] (13:3/4) Fall-Wint 92, p. 109.
"A Visit from St. Sigmund." [Light] (4) Wint 92-93, p. 20.
"Wild Death Purveyor." [Light] (3) Aut 92, p. 3.

3268. KENNELL, Galway
"Divinity." [YellowS] (39) Spr-Sum 92, p. 5.
"Flower of Five Blossoms." [YellowS] (39) Spr-Sum 92, p. 7-9.
"Last Gods." [YellowS] (39) Spr-Sum 92, p. 6.
3269. KENNING, Janet
"Estrella Mountains." [Ploughs] (18:1) Spr 92, p. 224.
"Notes on Arrogance." [Ploughs] (18:1) Spr 92, p. 225.
3270. KENNY, Maurice
"Manhattan" (I think this is New York City, January 7, 1985). [AnotherCM] (24) Fall 92, p. 98.
"El Paso del Norte, March 8, 1984" (While observing two soldiers kiss good-bye in the Alamagordo, N.M. bus station). [JamesWR] (9:2) Wint 92, p. 16.
"Sunflower." [AmerV] (26) Spr 92, p. 11.
3271. KENSETH, Arnold
"Uneasy Rider." [Agni] (35) 92, p. 235.
3272. KENYON, Jane
"Biscuit." [VirQR] (68:4) Aut 92, p. 706.
"Gettysburg: July 1, 1863." [NewYorker] (68:21) 13 Jl 92, p. 38.
"Having It Out with Melancholy." [Poetry] (161:2) N 92, p. 86-89.
"History: Hamden, Connecticut." [VirQR] (68:4) Aut 92, p. 704-705.
"Not Writing." [VirQR] (68:4) Aut 92, p. 706.
"Pharaoh." [NewYorker] (68:38) 9 N 92, p. 100.
"The Secret." [VirQR] (68:4) Aut 92, p. 705.
"Three Small Oranges." [VirQR] (68:4) Aut 92, p. 704.
3273. KEON, Wayne
"At Allison Pass." [Arc] (29) Aut 92, p. 41.
"Rainy Days." [Dandel] (19:2) 92, p. 21-22.
"Silver and Rain." [CanLit] (134) Aut 92, p. 41.
3274. KEPLER, Tom
"Silence Heard Twice." [Wind] (22:71) 92, p. 33.
3275. KERALIS, Spence
"Delivery" (Elbert County, Colorado, Easter 1989). [Event] (21:2) Sum 92, p. 56.
3276. KERKHOVEN, John
"Gnossiennes" (an interpretation of the music by Erik Satie). [CapilR] (2:9) Fall 92, p. 58-62.
"No Restrictions." [CapilR] (2:9) Fall 92, p. 63-65.
3277. KERLEY, Gary
"Emerson's Labels." [SouthernPR] (32:1) Spr 92, p. 50.
3278. KERLIKOWSKE, Elizabeth
"Holiday." [Parting] (5:2) Wint 92-93, p. 40-41.
"Manz and Womanz." [Parting] (5:1) Sum 92, p. 31-33.
"Rock Scissors Paper." [Parting] (5:2) Wint 92-93, p. 42-43.
"Soldiers." [Parting] (5:1) Sum 92, p. 5-7.
3279. KEROUAC, Jack
"Something Serious for Al Gelpi." [Talisman] (8) Spr 92, p. 19.
3280. KERR, Diane
"Laura G. I Love You and Always Will." [Kalliope] (15:1) 92, p. 33.
3281. KERR, Don
"Auto Didactic" (Selections: 21, 25). [Arc] (28) Spr 92, p. 17-18.
"Auto Didactic" (Selections: 32, 39). [Quarry] (41:2) Spr 92, p. 45-46.
"If Pablo Neruda Returned to Earth As a Canadian." [Grain] (20:1) Spr 92, p. 124 - 125.
"Returning to the Prairies from the Old World." [Grain] (20:1) Spr 92, p. 123-124.
3282. KERR, Walter H.
"Meeting a Poet Just Starting Out and Being Asked to Act the Clapper." [Light] (3) Aut 92, p. 7.
3283. KERSHNER, Brandon
"Marriage." [ChatR] (12:3) Spr 92, p. 12.
3284. KERWIN, Bill
"Breaking the Falls." [Hellas] (3:1) Spr 92, p. 18.
3285. KESSLER, Jascha
"1937" (tr. of Ottó Orbán, w. Maria Körösy). [Jacaranda] (6:1/2) Wint-Spr 92, p. 142.
"Light?" (tr. of Milan Richter). [Jacaranda] (6:1/2) Wint-Spr 92, p. 140-141.
"Mother Tongues" (tr. of Kirsti Simonsuuri, w. the author). [Nimrod] (35:2) Spr - Sum 92, p. 52.

"The Names of the Idols" (tr. of József Tornai). [Nimrod] (35:2) Spr-Sum 92, p. 32.
"Never at the Horse at Two" (tr. of Milan Richter, w. the author). [LitR] (25:2) Wint 92, p. 182.
"On a Cart" (from "Our Bearings at Sea": A Novel-in-Poems, tr. of Ottó Orbán, w. Mária Körösy). [Nimrod] (35:2) Spr-Sum 92, p. 34.
"Opus" (tr. of Kirsti Simonsuuri, w. the author). [Nimrod] (35:2) Spr-Sum 92, p. 52.
"Solar Eclipse" (tr. of József Tornai). [Nimrod] (35:2) Spr-Sum 92, p. 33.
"What You've Written" (tr. of Milan Richter, w. the author). [LitR] (25:2) Wint 92, p. 181.

3286. KESSLER, Milton
"Riding First Car: *Learning the Boxes*." [Sulfur] (12:2, #31) Fall 92, p. 167-174.

3287. KESSLER, Sydney
"In the Garden." [LitR] (35:3) Spr 92, p. 422.
"One for 1936." [Parting] (5:2) Wint 92-93, p. 7.
"Smith and Halperin" (December 1944). [Parting] (5:2) Wint 92-93, p. 7.

3288. KESTENBAUM, Stuart
"I Am Fishing for God." [BelPoJ] (43:1) Fall 92, p. 12-13.

3289. KETCHEK, Michael
"Charlie Said." [ChironR] (11:3) Aut 92, p. 30.
"A man might have." [Spitball] (42) Fall 92, p. 7.
"Untitled: There are these dangerous positions." [ChironR] (11:3) Aut 92, p. 29.
"Untitled: You see I belive." [ChironR] (11:2) Sum 92, p. 29.

3290. KEYES, Scott
"Balloon with Fireflies." [Light] (1) Spr 92, p. 23.

3291. KEYS, Kerry Shawn
"14. Transcendence is the costume of the buzzard." [Iowa] (22:2) Spr-Sum 92, p. 163.
"64. The parakeets are packed into cages." [Iowa] (22:2) Spr-Sum 92, p. 164.
"The Crab" (tr. of Lêdo Ivo). [NowestR] (30:2) 92, p. 50.
"Santa Leopoldina Asylum" (tr. of Lêdo Ivo). [NowestR] (30:2) 92, p. 49.
"To the Gnawers" (tr. of Lêdo Ivo). [NowestR] (30:2) 92, p. 51-52.

3292. KEYWORTH, Suzanne
"For My Neighbor, Henry." [Kalliope] (15:1) 92, p. 6-7.
"Hansel and Gretel." [Shen] (42:3) Fall 92, p. 110.
"Retrieval." [ChatR] (13:1) Fall 92, p. 63.

3293. KHARPERTIAN, Theodore
"Happy Marriage." [Talisman] (9) Fall 92, p. 174.

3294. KHOURY-GHATA, Vénus
"Disguised under our skin" (tr. by Lisa Holbrook). [SpoonRQ] (17:3/4) Sum-Fall 92, p. 42.
"If there were not these men enslaved to the sun" (tr. by Lisa Holbrook). [SpoonRQ] (17:3/4) Sum-Fall 92, p. 43.
"Stained by prayers and fears" (tr. by Lisa Holbrook). [SpoonRQ] (17:3/4) Sum-Fall 92, p. 44.

3295. KHRAMOV, Evgeny
"And so, one day, my country did rise up" (tr. by F. D. Reeve). [SenR] (22:1) Spr 92, p. 39.
"My love, a letter, a letter from me to you" (tr. by F. D. Reeve). [SenR] (22:1) Spr 92, p. 38.

3296. KI no TOMONORI
"Each spring sets out the same" (Kokinshu 57, in Japanese and English, tr. by Emily Nguyen). [Archae] (4) late 92-early 93, p. 17.

3297. KI no TSURAYUKI (ca. 872-945)
"Plum fragrance" (Kokinshu 336, in Japanese and English, tr. by Emily Nguyen). [Archae] (4) late 92-early 93, p. 14.

3298. KIDMAN, Fiona
"Wakeful Nights." [MalR] (99) Sum 92, p. 49-54.

3299. KIEFER, Rita
"About Mortification." [InterPR] (18:2) Fall 92, p. 72-73.
"The King of Fourth Street Road" (for Marianne). [Interim] (11:1) Spr-Sum 92, p. 7.

3300. KIERNAN, Phyllis
"Home Land." [MidAR] (13:2) 92, p. 156.

3301. KIJNER, Janine
"Farmhouse." [Kalliope] (14:1) 92, p. 38-39.

3302. KIKEL, Rudy
"Erogenous Zones" (4 selections). [KenR] (NS 14:1) Wint 92, p. 100-104.

3303. KILLIAN, Kevin
"White Shadows of the South Seas" (for Leslie Scalapino). [Talisman] (8) Spr 92, p. 174.
3304. KILLIAN, Sean
"Having Gone to Pick It Up." [PaintedB] (46) 92, p. 23-24.
"Thrust into a Tenancy." [DenQ] (26:4) Spr 92, p. 39-40.
"Witchnurse." [Talisman] (9) Fall 92, p. 175.
3305. KILMER NICHOLAS
"Zigzag." [Pequod] (34) 92, p. 160-162.
3306. KIM, Sandee
"The Old Guitarist." [WillowR] (19) Spr 92, p. 23.
3307. KIM, Yong U.
"Buying New Shoes in Berlin, NJ." [Boulevard] (7:2/3, #20/21) Fall 92, p. 132-133.
"Eight Months." [Ploughs] (18:1) Spr 92, p. 61-62.
"Kissing *Lycanthrope*." [Ploughs] (18:1) Spr 92, p. 63-64.
3308. KIM, Yoon Sik
"L'Impression de Degas." [NewYorkQ] (47) 92, p. 78.
"A Letter of Recommendation." [NewYorkQ] (49) 92, p. 76.
3309. KIMBALL, Cristen
"Blue-Eyed Gretel in a Car Wash." [ChatR] (13:1) Fall 92, p. 62.
"Cape Cod Evening" (after Edward Hopper). [WilliamMR] (30) 92, p. 81.
3310. KIMBALL, Michael
"A Coke and a Smile." [WormR] (32:3, #127) 92, p. 94.
"My Girlfriend's Father." [WormR] (32:3, #127) 92, p. 95.
"Three English Women." [NewYorkQ] (48) 92, p. 58.
"To Russell Edson." [AnotherCM] (23) Spr 92, p. 104.
3311. KIMMEL, Larry
"The Pearl." [WebR] (16) Fall 92, p. 104.
3312. KINCAID, Joan Payne
"Ball." [Parting] (5:1) Sum 92, p. 8.
"A Case of Too Many." [Epiphany] (3:2) Ap (Spr) 92, p. 93-94.
"Discord." [Epiphany] (3:2) Ap (Spr) 92, p. 94.
"Her Membranes Are." [Archae] (4) late 92-early 93, p. 46-47.
"Out of the Mist." [Parting] (5:1) Sum 92, p. 30.
"The President Blows It Away." [Parting] (5:1) Sum 92, p. 29-30.
"Short History of Six Centuries." [Archae] (4) late 92-early 93, p. 48.
"Sous." [Archae] (4) late 92-early 93, p. 49.
3313. KING, J. J.
"Come Clean." [NewYorkQ] (47) 92, p. 85.
3314. KING, Jane
"Cliches for an Unfaithful Husband." [LitR] (35:4) Sum 92, p. 539.
"The Father." [LitR] (35:4) Sum 92, p. 538.
"Fellow Traveller." [LitR] (35:4) Sum 92, p. 540.
"For Fergus." [LitR] (35:4) Sum 92, p. 539.
"Irresponsibility." [LitR] (35:4) Sum 92, p. 537.
"Pure Light." [LitR] (35:4) Sum 92, p. 538.
"Teaching Experience." [LitR] (35:4) Sum 92, p. 539.
KING, Janeen Werner
See WERNER-KING, Janeen
KING, Julie Dlugi
See DLUGI-KING, Julie
3315. KING, June W.
"The Collector." [Kalliope] (14:2) 92, p. 15.
3316. KING, Kenneth
"Play Danny Boy." [JamesWR] (9:3) Spr 92, p. 7.
3317. KING, Lyn
"Belfast Cemetery." [PoetryC] (12:2) Ap 92, p. 20.
"Eclipse." [PoetryC] (12:2) Ap 92, p. 20.
"Timing." [PoetryC] (12:2) Ap 92, p. 20.
"Uncelebrated." [PoetryC] (12:2) Ap 92, p. 21.
"A White Porcelain Jug." [PoetryC] (12:2) Ap 92, p. 21.
3318. KING, Martha
"Spill." [NewAW] (10) Fall 92, p. 100.
3319. KING, R. D.
"Purpose." [NowestR] (30:2) 92, p. 46.
"Vibrational." [NowestR] (30:2) 92, p. 45.

3320. KING, Rima
"Accidents Will Happen." [MassR] (23:1) Spr 92, p. 148.
3321. KING, Robert
"Birds & Fish: Through a Needle's Eye." [BellArk] (8:3) My-Je 92, p. 8-13.
3322. KING, Robert (*See also* KING, Robert S.)
"Open Range." [BellArk] (8:5) S-O 92, p. 10-11.
3323. KING, Robert S. (*See also* KING, Robert)
"Communion." [Amelia] (7:1, #20) 92, p. 134.
"Desire and Peace." [BlackBR] (16) Wint-Spr 92-93, p. 42.
"Men." [Amelia] (7:1, #20) 92, p. 135-136.
"Moving to the City." [BlackBR] (16) Wint-Spr 92-93, p. 41.
"Soldier Ants." [BlackBR] (16) Wint-Spr 92-93, p. 41.
"Song of My Other Self." [Amelia] (7:1, #20) 92, p. 134-135.
3324. KING, Willie James
"In the Cradle." [Obs] (7:1/2) Spr-Sum 92, p. 98-99.
3325. KINGA, Fabó
"A Szó Színeváltozása." [Os] (35) Fall 92, p. 18.
"The Word's Color Change" (tr. by Zsuzsanna Ozsváth and Martha Satz). [Os] (35) Fall 92, p. 19.
3326. KINNELL, Galway
"Hitchhiker." [NewYorker] (68:36) 26 O 92, p. 66.
"I Explain a Few Things" (tr. of Pablo Neruda). [Trans] (26) Spr 92, p. 30-32.
3327. KINOSHITA, Choshoshi (1569-1649)
"Watching the Moon" (tr. by Graeme Wilson). [Jacaranda] (6:1/2) Wint-Spr 92, p. 151.
3328. KINSALLA, John
"On Kenneth Noland's *Magic Box* 1959." [DogRR] (11:2, #22) Fall-Wint 92, p. 34-35.
"Strobe: The Road from Toodyay to New Norcia." [DogRR] (11:2, #22) Fall-Wint 92, p. 35.
3329. KINSER, Michael R.
"Opportunities." [Spitball] (42) Fall 92, p. 48.
3330. KINZIE, Mary
"Fear the Season." [Atlantic] (269:3) Mr 92, p. 82.
"Impromptu." [ThRiPo] (39/40) 92-93, p. 133.
"Xenophilia." [ThRiPo] (39/40) 92-93, p. 131-132.
3331. KIPP, Karen
"Air" (for Lynda Schrausnagel). [Crazy] (43) Wint 92, p. 22-23.
"Pink." [Crazy] (43) Wint 92, p. 24-25.
3332. KIRBY, David
"Flaco Jimenez, King of the Conjunto Accordion." [ArtfulD] (22/23) 92, p. 110-111.
"Eine Götterdämmerung in Mudville." [GettyR] (5:3) Sum 92, p. 405.
3333. KIRBY, Mark
"Autumn: Evening Tennis." [Comm] (119:20) 20 N 92, p. 21.
3334. KIRCHDORFER, Ulf
"If You Can't Say Anything Bad Don't Say It." [NewYorkQ] (48) 92, p. 58.
"Squirrels with Soul." [SoDakR] (30:2) Sum 92, p. 105.
3335. KIRCHER, Pamela
"Alba." [OhioR] (48) 92, p. 53.
"Looking at the Sea." [OhioR] (48) 92, p. 51-52.
3336. KIRCHWEY, Karl
"Between Roscoe and Absarokee." [LitR] (36:1) Fall 92, p. 28-29.
"Liberators." [ParisR] (34:122) Spr 92, p. 194-195.
"Memnon." [YaleR] (80:3) Jl 92, p. 132-134.
"Saint Rock (The Cloisters)." [NewRep] (207:19) 2 N 92, p. 28.
"The Snow Sphinx." [WestHR] (46:3) Fall 92, p. 244-245.
"Two Studies of Lesbos (after Thucydides)" (to Henri Cole). [WestHR] (46:3) Fall 92, p. 273-275.
3337. KIRK, Joe E.
"A very Knowing student." [Wind] (22:71) 92, p. 14.
3338. KIRK, Laurie
"Potter's Field." [SlipS] (12) 92, p. 88.
3339. KIRK, Lee Crawley
"Crow in November." [WormR] (32:3, #127) 92, p. 85.
"Roof Food." [WormR] (32:3, #127) 92, p. 85.

3340. KIRK, Norman Andrew
"Morning." [NegC] (12:1/2) 92, p. 70.
3341. KIRK, Raymond
"Three Teachers." [ChatR] (12:2) Wint 92, p. 94.
3342. KIRKPATRICK, Robert
"Cotman's *Devil's Elbow, Rokeby Park.*" [CarolQ] (45:1) Fall 92, p. 52.
"Doing Push-ups on a Sumaq Rug." [CarolQ] (45:1) Fall 92, p. 51.
3343. KIRKPATRICK, Stephen Hale
"The New Jerusalem's Thanksgiving, 1676/1989." [NewYorkQ] (49) 92, p. 105.
3344. KIRKUP, James
"Cemetery of Sinera" (Selections: I-V, tr. of Salvador Espriu). [Stand] (33:4) Aut 92, p. 151-152.
"Dark Sorrow" (tr. of Margherita Guidacci). [Stand] (33:4) Aut 92, p. 106-107.
"Easy Prey" (tr. of Salvador Espriu). [Stand] (33:4) Aut 92, p. 151.
"The Flock of Sheep" (tr. of Umberto Saba). [Stand] (33:4) Aut 92, p. 105.
"For a Canticle in the Temple" (tr. of Salvador Espriu). [Stand] (33:4) Aut 92, p. 151.
"For My People of Sépharad" (tr. of Salvador Espriu). [Stand] (33:4) Aut 92, p. 150.
"If One Cry Is Added to Another" (tr. of Pier Paolo Pasolini). [Stand] (33:4) Aut 92, p. 110.
"Prometheus" (tr. of Salvador Espriu). [Stand] (33:4) Aut 92, p. 150.
"Shorthand Account of a Massacre" (Egypticus Sculpture, Stanga, Gotland, tr. of Kris Tanzberg). [Stand] (33:4) Aut 92, p. 85.
"Thomas More" (tr. of Kris Tanzberg). [Stand] (33:4) Aut 92, p. 84.
3345. KIRSCHENBAUM, Blossom S.
"Das Kapital." [Light] (2) Sum 92, p. 18-19.
3346. KIRSCHNER, Elizabeth
"The Blueness of Stars." [ThRiPo] (39/40) 92-93, p. 135-136.
"The Dinosaur's Bone." [NoDaQ] (60:1) Wint 92, p. 293-294.
"The Fall of Light." [ThRiPo] (39/40) 92-93, p. 137.
"Monstrous Mistakes." [TarRP] (32:1) Fall 92, p. 39.
"Tipping Back." [LitR] (35:3) Spr 92, p. 325.
"Two Blue Swans." [ThRiPo] (39/40) 92-93, p. 134.
3347. KIRSTEN-MARTIN, Diane
"Changing the Weather." [Zyzzyva] (8:3) Fall 92, p. 84-85.
3348. KISSANE, Andy
"Bat Crush." [Vis] (40) 92, p. 24-25.
"Fancy Footwork." [Vis] (40) 92, p. 23.
"Inside the Bottle." [Vis] (38) 92, p. 40-41.
3349. KITSON, Herb
"Farting in a Restaurant." [NewYorkQ] (47) 92, p. 56.
"Who Do You Think You Are?" [NewYorkQ] (49) 92, p. 36.
3350. KITUAI, Kathy
"An Ill Wind." [Footwork] 92, p. 137.
"Somewhere Around the Block." [Footwork] 92, p. 137.
3351. KIYOOKA, Roy
"Phyllis." [WestCL] (25:3, #6) Wint 91-92, p. 150.
3352. KLANG, Gary
"Natif Natal" (Excerpt from "Ex-Ile"). [Callaloo] (15:3) Sum 92, p. 596.
"Native Natal" (Excerpt from "Ex-Ile," tr. by Carrol F. Coates). [Callaloo] (15:3) Sum 92, p. 595.
"O Mere des Sept Douleurs" (Excerpt from "Ex-Ile"). [Callaloo] (15:3) Sum 92, p. 600.
"Oh Mother of the Seven Sorrows" (Excerpt from "Ex-Ile," tr. by Carrol F. Coates). [Callaloo] (15:3) Sum 92, p. 599.
"Orphan of My Island" (Excerpt from "Ex-Ile," tr. by Carrol F. Coates). [Callaloo] (15:3) Sum 92, p. 597.
"Orphelin de Mon Ile" (Excerpt from "Ex-Ile"). [Callaloo] (15:3) Sum 92, p. 598.
3353. KLAPPERT, Peter
"The Old Dead Grandmother Line." [Light] (4) Wint 92-93, p. 8.
3354. KLAR, Barbara
"The Parting Gift" (3rd prize, Grain Prose Poem contest). [Grain] (20:4) Wint 92, p. 13.
3355. KLASS, Stephen
"Chalcidice" (tr. of Johannes Edfelt). [Hellas] (3:1) Spr 92, p. 44.

3356. KLASSEN, Sarah
"Arbat Street" (August, 1991). [Arc] (29) Aut 92, p. 9.
"Diorama." [Arc] (29) Aut 92, p. 10-11.
"Heimatlied" (from the series "The Old Woman Sings"). [PraF] (13:3, #60) Aut 92, p. 73.
"Learning to Swim" (from the series "The Old Woman Sings"). [PraF] (13:3, #60) Aut 92, p. 74.
"A Partial Guide to the Pushkin Galleries." [Arc] (29) Aut 92, p. 5-8.
"Summer Stories: Exile." [Grain] (20:1) Spr 92, p. 126.
"Time Travel" (from the series "The Old Woman Sings"). [PraF] (13:3, #60) Aut 92, p. 75-76.
"Two Simone Weil Poems." [Event] (21:1) Spr 92, p. 29-35.
"Vital Signs." [Grain] (20:1) Spr 92, p. 127.
3357. KLEIN, Michael
"The Contribution" (for Marie Howe). [KenR] (NS 14:1) Wint 92, p. 113.
"The Government." [LitR] (36:1) Fall 92, p. 47.
"Letters from the Front." [LitR] (36:1) Fall 92, p. 46-47.
"The Music of Craving." [Ploughs] (18:4) Wint 92-93, p. 46.
"Prayer: Subway." [NewMyths] (1:2/2:1) 92, p. 14.
"Removes." [KenR] (NS 14:1) Wint 92, p. 112.
"The Tides." [Ploughs] (18:4) Wint 92-93, p. 48-49.
"We Are Not Alone." [Ploughs] (18:4) Wint 92-93, p. 47.
3358. KLEINER, Gregg
"China." [Lactuca] (15) Mr 92, p. 23.
"Dry." [Lactuca] (15) Mr 92, p. 23.
"Their Isthmus." [Lactuca] (15) Mr 92, p. 24.
3359. KLEINSCHMIDT, Edward
"Autograph." [DenQ] (26:3) Wint 92, p. 31-32.
"Father Death." [OnTheBus] (4:2/5:1, #10/11) 92, p. 120.
"I Believe That Yes." [Boulevard] (7:2/3, #20/21) Fall 92, p. 89-90.
"Logophobia" (for R. H. W. Dillard). [ColEng] (53:6) O 91, p. 664.
"Motive." [KenR] (NS 14:3) Sum 92, p. 31-32.
"Sotto Voce." [Zyzzyva] (8:3) Fall 92, p. 99-100.
"Still Life." [WillowS] (30) Sum 92, p. 81.
"Syllable." [MassR] (23:1) Spr 92, p. 159.
"Time Frame." [Boulevard] (7:2/3, #20/21) Fall 92, p. 91-92.
"Vice Versa." [MassR] (23:1) Spr 92, p. 160.
3360. KLEINZAHLER, August
"Flynn's End." [ParisR] (34:122) Spr 92, p. 268-269.
"Follain's Paris" (adapted from the French, w. Deborah Treisman). [Thrpny] (50) Sum 92, p. 4.
"Song." [ParisR] (34:122) Spr 92, p. 266.
"Spring Trances." [NewYorker] (68:13) 18 My 92, p. 34.
"A Valentine." [ParisR] (34:122) Spr 92, p. 267.
"Winter Ball." [NewYorker] (68:3) 9 Mr 92, p. 32.
3361. KLIPSCHUTZ
"The Bunkport Chronicles." [FreeL] (9) Wint 92, p. 24.
"Ghazal of the Distant Present." [LitR] (35:3) Spr 92, p. 407.
"Little Knell." [PoetC] (23:2) Wint 92, p. 8.
"Streets and Gardens." [PoetC] (23:2) Wint 92, p. 6-7.
3362. KLOEFKORN, William
"A City Waking Up." [TarRP] (32:1) Fall 92, p. 26-27.
"Cures." [SoDakR] (30:4) Wint 92, p. 58-59.
"Just in Case." [CimR] (99) Ap 92, p. 37-38.
"A Man and a Boy Fishing." [CimR] (99) Ap 92, p. 38.
"Sycamore." [CreamCR] (16:2) Fall 92, p. 42.
"That Summer." [SoDakR] (30:4) Wint 92, p. 56-57.
"Treehouse." [NoDaQ] (60:1) Wint 92, p. 310-311.
"Walking Home, Late October." [NoDaQ] (60:1) Wint 92, p. 309-310.
3363. KLUTTS, Randy
"Commuter's Dilemma." [SlipS] (12) 92, p. 58.
3364. KLUZNIK, Michael
"Runaway Truck Ramp." [Grain] (20:3) Fall 92, p. 153-154.
"Up Jumped the Devil." [Grain] (20:1) Spr 92, p. 236-237.
3365. KNIGHT, Arthur Winfield
"Buffalo Bill Cody: Honors." [NewYorkQ] (47) 92, p. 40.

"Jim Younger: Cider." [PaintedHR] (6) Spr 92, p. 19.
"Jim Younger: Silence." [PoetL] (87:1) Spr 92, p. 19.
"Laura Bullion: Magic." [PoetL] (87:1) Spr 92, p. 18.
"Paulita Jaramillo: Nursing." [LullwaterR] (3:3) Sum 92, p. 17.
"The Pause That Refreshes." [MoodySI] (27) Spr 92, p. 42.

3366. KNIGHT, Joan
"I Don't Do Black Poetry" (Eve of Saint Agnes Contest winner). [NegC] (12:3) 92, p. 5.

3367. KNIGHT, Lynne
"All We Intended." [CreamCR] (16:2) Fall 92, p. 113-114.
"And Afterwards, the Longing." [PoetryNW] (33:1) Spr 92, p. 44.
"The Bodies of Lovers." [PoetryE] (33) Spr 92, p. 61.
"Empty Arms." [PoetryE] (33) Spr 92, p. 64.
"Lilies." [PoetryE] (33) Spr 92, p. 62.
" *Still Life* as an Inexact Translation." [NoDaQ] (60:4) Fall 92, p. 70-71.
"There, in My Grandfather's Old Green Buick." [PoetryE] (33) Spr 92, p. 63.

3368. KNIGHT, Stephen
"The Bottle of Smoke." [Verse] (9:3) Wint 92, p. 138.

3369. KNIGHT, William
"This Was Your Garden." [Quarry] (41:1) Wint 92, p. 40.
"Waiting at River's Bend for You." [Quarry] (41:1) Wint 92, p. 40.

3370. KNIGHTEN, Merrell
"Petitioner." [ChironR] (11:1) Spr 92, p. 27.

3371. KNOBLOCH, Marta
"Lacio Drom" (tr. of Roman Bled, w. Dino Tebaldi). [Vis] (38) 92, p. 16.

3372. KNOEPFLE, John
"Four Corners and the Little White Pea." [SpoonRQ] (17:1/2) Wint-Spr 92, p. 27 - 36.
"Poems for Hard-Toed Boots." [SouthernR] (28:1) Wint, Ja 92, p. 95-97.
"Untitled: Are you in there?" [Farm] (9:2) Fall-Wint 92-93, p. 30-33.

3373. KNOTT, Bill
"Today's Story (Oh, Synesthesia! #12)." [PoetC] (24:1) Fall 92, p. 25-26.
"Unredeemed." [PoetC] (24:1) Fall 92, p. 22-24.

3374. KNOX, Ann B.
"Begin." [CumbPR] (12:1) Fall 92, p. 8.
"Biker's Girl" (Second Prize, Robert Penn Warren Poetry Prize). [CumbPR] (12:1) Fall 92, p. 6.
"Circles." [Poetry] (159:5) F 92, p. 254.
"Preparing to Go" (Honorable Mention, Robert Penn Warren Poetry Prize). [CumbPR] (12:1) Fall 92, p. 7.
"Singing Man" (Bronze figure by Ernst Barlach). [Sparrow] (59) S 92, p. 19.

3375. KNOX, Caroline
"Chicago 1985." [ParisR] (34:125) Wint 92, p. 120-121.
"Nashotah." [ParisR] (34:125) Wint 92, p. 123.
"Sleepers Wake." [ParisR] (34:125) Wint 92, p. 121-122.

3376. KNUTTGEN, Carol
"A Day of Substitute Teaching (Southern Calif. 1970's)." [NewYorkQ] (49) 92, p. 106.

3377. KO, Chang Soo
"Polishing hte Porcelain Lamp" (tr. of Jae-Chun Park). [WebR] (16) Fall 92, p. 29.
"Scarecrow's Song No. 2" (tr. of Jae-Chun Park). [WebR] (16) Fall 92, p. 29.

3378. KOBYLARZ, Philip
"Summer, I Blindly Loved the Fair Girl." [PacificR] (11) 92-93, p. 59.

3379. KOCH, Kenneth
"The First Step." [GrandS] (11:1, #41) 92, p. 82-93.
"Poems by Ships at Sea." [NewYorker] (68:21) 13 Jl 92, p. 32.
"Talking to Patrizia." [Poetry] (160:4) Jl 92, p. 204-207.

3380. KOCH, Timothy D.
"Maxwell Timothy G." [EngJ] (81:6) O 92, p. 92.

3381. KOCHER, Ruth Ellen
"Black White Arms." [AfAmRev] (26:2) Sum 92, p. 283.
"Ending in Fire." [PraS] (66:2) Sum 92, p. 79-80.
"Ghost." [PraS] (66:2) Sum 92, p. 78-79.
"Storm." [PraS] (66:2) Sum 92, p. 80-81.

3382. KOEHN, David
"Coil." [CutB] (37) Wint 92, p. 35.

3383. KOERNER, Edgar
"The Good Boy." [Confr] (48/49) Spr-Sum 92, p. 213.
3384. KOERTGE, Ron
"5:00." [OnTheBus] (4:2/5:1, #10/11) 92, p. 121.
"Beautiful Eyes for a Boy." [LindLM] (11:3) S 92, p. 18.
"Fundamentalist Group Rejects Nudist Campsite." [OnTheBus] (4:2/5:1, #10/11) 92, p. 121-122.
"Is that why there is no swan on this menu?" [LindLM] (11:3) S 92, p. 18.
"Local Clergy Target Porn Shop." [OnTheBus] (4:2/5:1, #10/11) 92, p. 122.
"The New Docent Practices in Her Own Apartment." [LindLM] (11:3) S 92, p. 18.
"Sweaters." [BrooklynR] (9) 92, p. 5.
3385. KOESTENBAUM, Phyllis
"More Later" (in memory of James Schuyler). [BrooklynR] (9) 92, p. 6.
"Women Artists Sestina." [PoetL] (87:4) Wint 92-93, p. 9-10.
3386. KOESTER, Rohn
"Searching for Pinecones in Springtime." [CoalC] (5) My 92, p. 14.
"Walter and Bob." [CoalC] (5) My 92, p. 11.
3387. KOHLER, Sandra
"Bread." [WestB] (30) 92, p. 111.
"Craving." [WestB] (30) 92, p. 110.
"Vessel" (from "Ars Poetica Feminae"). [Calyx] (14:2) Wint 92-93, p. 5.
KOKI, Francisco Alvarez
See ALVAREZ-KOKI, Francisco
3388. *KOKINSHU*
"Translations from the 10th century Japanese *Kokinshu*" (by Sam Hamill). [AnotherCM] (23) Spr 92, p. 90-91.
3389. KOLATKAR, Arun
"Snapshot" (tr. by Vinay Dharwadker). [ChiR] (38:1/2) 92, p. 44.
3390. KOLBE, Uwe
"Early Dawn" (tr. by John Epstein). [Shiny] (7/8) 92, p. 141.
"To Live" (tr. by John Epstein). [Shiny] (7/8) 92, p. 140.
3391. KOLIAS, Helen
"Blessed Events" (tr. of Jenny Mastoraki, w. Mary Gilliland). [Nimrod] (35:2) Spr - Sum 92, p. 68-69.
"Classics Illustrated" (tr. of Jenny Mastoraki, w. Mary Gilliland). [Nimrod] (35:2) Spr-Sum 92, p. 70-71.
3392. KOLLAR, Mary E.
"To Bronson Alcott from His Daughter, Louisa." [EngJ] (80:8) D 91, p. 99.
3393. KOLODINSKY, Alison
"Absence." [FloridaR] (18:2) Fall-Wint 92, p. 74-75.
"Adoption." [Poetry] (160:3) Je 92, p. 151.
"Body Art Poses Risk of Infection" (Headline: Daytona Beach News Journal, March '90). [Kalliope] (14:3) 92, p. 12-13.
"Poem for My Widowed Neighbor" (for Danna). [CreamCR] (16:2) Fall 92, p. 79.
3394. KOLUMBAN, Nicholas
"At the Albanian Bakery" (tr. of Otto Tolnai). [OnTheBus] (4:2/5:1, #10/11) 92, p. 263.
"A Chance   Crumbling River Banks" (tr. of Zsuzsa Takacs). [OnTheBus] (4:2/5:1, #10/11) 92, p. 268-269.
"A Close Friend of Words" (tr. of Sándor Csoóri). [AntigR] (90) Sum 92, p. 55.
"Far" (tr. of Jenö Dsida). [CharR] (18:2) Fall 92, p. 115.
"Go, Journey Inside" (from Romania, tr. of Béla Markó). [SilverFR] (23) Wint 92, p. 34-35.
"I Missed Their *Panzerfausts*" (Germany 1945). [AnotherCM] (23) Spr 92, p. 136.
"I'm Resurrected." [WebR] (16) Fall 92, p. 35.
"In Another Country (1966)" (tr. of János Oláh). [OnTheBus] (4:2/5:1, #10/11) 92, p. 267.
"In Honor of a Fisherman" (tr. of Imre Oravecz). [ArtfulD] (22/23) 92, p. 35.
"Meditation" (tr. of János Oláh). [OnTheBus] (4:2/5:1, #10/11) 92, p. 266.
"The Monster" (tr. of Zsuzsa Kapecz). [OnTheBus] (4:2/5:1, #10/11) 92, p. 264-265.
"My Room" (tr. of Iren Negyesy). [WebR] (16) Fall 92, p. 35.
"On the Porch" (tr. of Jenö Dsida). [ArtfulD] (22/23) 92, p. 37.
"One Liners" (tr. of Sandor Weöres). [Pequod] (34) 92, p. 112.
"Residents of the Mountain" (tr. of Jenö Dsida). [ArtfulD] (22/23) 92, p. 36.
"A Traveler in the Soviet Union" (tr. of János Oláh). [SilverFR] (23) Wint 92, p. 36.
"Two Women." [SilverFR] (23) Wint 92, p. 25.

3395. KOMESHOK, Stephen
"On Being Catholic." [Footwork] 92, p. 87.
"Why Must the Common Man Be — So Common?" [Footwork] 92, p. 87.

3396. KOMUNYAKAA, Yusef
"Balance." [Iowa] (22:3) Fall 92, p. 68.
"Basilique." [AfAmRev] (26:2) Sum 92, p. 214-215.
"Because I Didn't Die." [NewEngR] (14:2) Spr 92, p. 31.
"Butterfly-Towed Shoes." [AfAmRev] (26:2) Sum 92, p. 213-214.
"A Call from the Terrace." [SouthernR] (28:1) Wint, Ja 92, p. 32.
"The Cooling Board." [NewEngR] (14:2) Spr 92, p. 32.
"The Curator of Kosinski's Masks." [Caliban] (11) 92, p. 74.
"Epithalamium." [PoetryE] (33) Spr 92, p. 75.
"Euphony." [Iowa] (22:3) Fall 92, p. 66.
"Genet." [Caliban] (11) 92, p. 75.
"Glory." [SouthernR] (28:1) Wint, Ja 92, p. 32-33.
"Gristmill." [KenR] (NS 14:1) Wint 92, p. 59.
"Immigrants." [KenR] (NS 14:1) Wint 92, p. 60-61.
"In Love with the Nightstalker." [Agni] (35) 92, p. 94.
"Kosmos." [MassR] (23:1) Spr 92, p. 87-89.
"Meditations on a Smoothing Iron." [Agni] (35) 92, p. 93.
"Mercy." [Agni] (35) 92, p. 95.
"Modern Medea." [AfAmRev] (26:2) Sum 92, p. 214.
"Moonshine." [NewEngR] (14:2) Spr 92, p. 33.
"Nocturne (Blue Trains)." [SouthernR] (28:1) Wint, Ja 92, p. 34-35.
"Nude Tango." [NewEngR] (14:2) Spr 92, p. 36-37.
"Ode to the Maggot." [Thrpny] (49) Spr 92, p. 31.
"Playthings." [KenR] (NS 14:1) Wint 92, p. 63-66.
"Praising Dark Places." [SouthernR] (28:1) Wint, Ja 92, p. 35.
"Sex, Magnolias, & Speed." [NewEngR] (14:2) Spr 92, p. 34.
"Shotguns." [Iowa] (22:3) Fall 92, p. 67.
"Springtime Jitterbug." [Iowa] (22:3) Fall 92, p. 65-66.
"Touch." [NewEngR] (14:2) Spr 92, p. 35.
"A Trailer at the Edge of a Forest." [NewEngR] (14:2) Spr 92, p. 36.
"Trap." [Field] (46) Spr 92, p. 21.
"Triangles." [Field] (46) Spr 92, p. 20.
"Work." [Iowa] (22:3) Fall 92, p. 64-65.
"Yellow Dog Café." [KenR] (NS 14:1) Wint 92, p. 61-62.

3397. KONCEL, Mary A.
"Blue Chicken in a Foreign Country." [MinnR] (39) Fall-Wint 92-93, p. 14.

3398. KONO, Juliet S.
"By Heart." [SycamoreR] (4:2) Sum 92, p. 53.

KOON, Woon
See WOON, Koon

3399. KOONS, Barbara
"Getting It All Together." [HopewellR] (4) 92, p. 13.

3400. KOONTZ, Haven
"Heartland." [SycamoreR] (4:2) Sum 92, p. 24-25.

3401. KOOSER, Ted
"The Afterlife." [ThRiPo] (39/40) 92-93, p. 139-140.
"The Back Door." [Hudson] (44:4) Wint 92, p. 621-622.
"Ditch-Burning in February." [AntR] (50:3) Sum 92, p. 516.
"A Finding." [ThRiPo] (39/40) 92-93, p. 139.
"Fireflies." [CreamCR] (16:1) Spr 92, p. 73.
"The Gilbert Stuart Portrait of Washington." [ThRiPo] (39/40) 92-93, p. 137-138.
"A Goodbye Handshake." [NoDaQ] (60:1) Wint 92, p. 317.
"Nocturne." [CreamCR] (16:1) Spr 92, p. 71.
"Pasture Trees." [CreamCR] (16:1) Spr 92, p. 72.
"Snake Skin." [Hudson] (44:4) Wint 92, p. 621.
"Sparklers." [NoDaQ] (60:1) Wint 92, p. 319.
"A Statue of the Unknown Soldier." [NoDaQ] (60:1) Wint 92, p. 320-321.
"A Stoneware Crock." [NoDaQ] (60:1) Wint 92, p. 318.

3402. KOPLAND, Rutger
"Still-Life with Sunflowers" (tr. by James Brockway). [Stand] (33:4) Aut 92, p. 115.

3403. KOPLITZ, Bill
"Bonefish." [Writer] (105:6) Je 92, p. 25.

3404. KÖRÖSY, Mária
"1937" (tr. of Ottó Orbán, w. Jascha Kessler). [Jacaranda] (6:1/2) Wint-Spr 92, p. 142.
"The Angel of Traffic" (Los Angeles, tr. of Ottó Orbán, w. Bruce Berlind). [KenR] (NS 14:1) Wint 92, p. 83.
"The Dazzling Disparity in Size" (Minnesota Public Radio, metro area traffic report, tr. of Ottó Orbán, w. Bruce Berlind). [KenR] (NS 14:1) Wint 92, p. 84.
"The Dream of H. Bosch" (tr. of Imre Oravecz, w. Bruce Berlind). [PoetryE] (33) Spr 92, p. 167.
"The End of Adventures" (A KSTP TV Publication: "AIDS — What to know about It?", tr. of Ottó Orbán, w. Bruce Berlind). [Nimrod] (35:2) Spr-Sum 92, p. 35.
"The Four-Wheeled Man" (tr. of Ottó Orbán, w. Bruce Berlind). [KenR] (NS 14:1) Wint 92, p. 82.
"From a Philosopher's Insights" (tr. of Gyula Illyé, w. Bruce Berlind). [SilverFR] (23) Wint 92, p. 33.
"In a Blacksmith's House on the Puszta" (tr. of Gyula Illyés, w. Bruce Berlind). [TexasR] (13:3/4) Fall-Wint 92, p. 87-88.
"The Journey of Barbarus" (tr. of Ottó Orbán, w. Bruce Berlind). [ParisR] (34:123) Sum 92, p. 134.
"Mr. E. Veryman, President of Whatever Works Works" (tr. of Ottó Orbán, w. Bruce Berlind). [Nimrod] (35:2) Spr-Sum 92, p. 36.
"A Nest for Seasons in the Concrete Jungle" (tr. of Gyula Illyé, w. Bruce Berlind). [SilverFR] (23) Wint 92, p. 29.
"Oklahoma Summer" (tr. of Ottó Orbán, w. Bruce Berlind). [Nimrod] (35:2) Spr - Sum 92, p. 37.
"Old Fiddlers' Picnic" (tr. of Ottó Orbán, w. Bruce Berlind). [Nimrod] (35:2) Spr - Sum 92, p. 35.
"On a Cart" (from "Our Bearings at Sea": A Novel-in-Poems, tr. of Ottó Orbán, w. Jascha Kessler). [Nimrod] (35:2) Spr-Sum 92, p. 34.
"Once Again" (tr. of Imre Oravecz, w. Bruce Berlind). [LitR] (25:2) Wint 92, p. 176.
"Phoenix" (tr. of Gyula Illyés, w. Bruce Berlind). [TexasR] (13:3/4) Fall-Wint 92, p. 89-91.
"The Sun Is Shining" (tr. of Imre Oravecz, w. Bruce Berlind). [LitR] (25:2) Wint 92, p. 177.
"Supper" (tr. of Imre Oravecz, w. Bruce Berlind). [ArtfulD] (22/23) 92, p. 33.
"Uncle Gábor" (tr. of Imre Oravecz, w. Bruce Berlind). [WebR] (16) Fall 92, p. 33 - 34.
"Water" (tr. of Imré Oravecz, w. Bruce Berlind). [PartR] (59:2) Spr 92, p. 266-267.
"Why Wouldn't I Live in America?" (tr. of Ottó Orbán, w. Bruce Berlind). [LitR] (25:2) Wint 92, p. 173-175.
"With a Stranger" (tr. of Gyula Illyé, w. Bruce Berlind). [SilverFR] (23) Wint 92, p. 31.
"World-Order" (tr. of Gyula Illyé, w. Bruce Berlind). [SilverFR] (23) Wint 92, p. 30.
"You Could Have Spotted Me" (tr. of Gyula Illyé, w. Bruce Berlind). [SilverFR] (23) Wint 92, p. 32.

3405. KORT, Ellen
"Counter-Clockwise." [Nimrod] (36:1) Fall-Wint 92, p. 14.
"For Goldilocks: The Husband Speaks" (First Prize, The Pablo Neruda Prize for Poetry). [Nimrod] (36:1) Fall-Wint 92, p. 10-11.
"A Meditation of Bees." [Nimrod] (36:1) Fall-Wint 92, p. 12.
"Moving Slightly Left from Center." [Nimrod] (36:1) Fall-Wint 92, p. 13.

3406. KORT, Susanne
"In the Black." [Gypsy] (19) 92, p. 29.
"Lillian." [AntR] (50:3) Sum 92, p. 524.
"Lullaby." [GrahamHR] (16) Fall 92, p. 17.
"Married Nights." [GrahamHR] (16) Fall 92, p. 19-20.
"Pan American — Flight 44." [GrahamHR] (16) Fall 92, p. 18.

3407. KOSTELANETZ, Richard
"Couplets & Triplets II: Poems & Stories." [WritersF] (18) 92, p. 74.
"Destitution. Unresolved conflict. Strike. Hello. Pervade. Dead on Sunday." [Parting] (5:1) Sum 92, p. 37.
"From (Complete) Shorter Stories." [CrabCR] (8:1) Sum-Fall 92, p. 6.
"Increments" (w. Kathie Antrim). [ChironR] (11:2) Sum 92, p. 11.

"Intelligence of Rhyming: Poems & Stories — VIII." [SmPd] (29:3, #86) Fall 92, p. 28-30.
"Lovings Three: A Collection of Stories" (Excerpt). [WorldL] (3) 92, p. 34-36.
"Minimal Fictions" (Conception by Richard Kostelanetz, Translations/Calligraphy by Shao Kuan Sng). [Nimrod] (36:1) Fall-Wint 92, p. 80-81.
"Openings 1988a." [WestHR] (46:3) Fall 92, p. 280-283.
"Openings (1992)." [TampaR] (5) Fall 92, p. 66.
"Solos, Duets, Trios, & Choruses (Membrane/Future)" (with preface). [Archae] (3) early 92, p. 26-35.
"Triplets: Poems & Stories." [Footwork] 92, p. 44-45.
"Update" (whose paragraphs may be read backward, as well as forward). [ChamLR] (10/11) Spr-Fall 92, p. 113-117.

3408. KOSTER, Kim
"Anna, Starting Her Last Quilt." [Calyx] (14:1) Sum 92, p. 10-11.

3409. KOSTOLEFSKY, Joseph
"After Williams." [Epiphany] (3:1) Ja (Wint) 92, p. 20.
"Buy American." [Epiphany] (3:1) Ja (Wint) 92, p. 17-18.
"A Night with Radio X E R B." [Epiphany] (3:1) Ja (Wint) 92, p. 19-20.

3410. KOSTOPULOS-COOPERMAN, C. (Celeste)
"Buenos Aires" (tr. of Marjorie Agosín). [Harp] (284:1703) Ap 92, p. 34.
"To Jose Daniel" (tr. of Marjorie Agosin). [AmerV] (26) Spr 92, p. 210-22.

3411. KOTAMRAJU, Mala
"Isn't She Not a Bird" (tr. of Nina Iskrenko, w. Forrest Gander). [Agni] (35) 92, p. 166-167.

3412. KOTT, Michael
"According to Steinhaus" (tr. of Agnieszka Osiecka). [ParisR]] (34:124) Fall 92, p. 134-135.
"Thank God for This Little Reverie" (tr. of Agnieszka Osiecka). [ParisR]] (34:124) Fall 92, p. 135.

3413. KOTZIN, Miriam N.
"Checkout Line." [PaintedB] (48) 92, p. 33.
"Clairvoyant." [Confr] (50) Fall 92, p. 271.
"The Pond." [Boulevard] (7:1, #19) Spr 92, p. 133-135.
"Shards." [Confr] (50) Fall 92, p. 270.
"Sunflower." [SouthernHR] (26:4) Fall 92, p. 352-353.

3414. KOUMJIAN, Vaughn
"Adieu." [Light] (4) Wint 92-93, p. 14.
"On Forever Looking at Bobby Thomson's Homer." [Light] (1) Spr 92, p. 26.

3415. KOUROUS, Sharon
"Stalagma." [Poem] (67) My 92, p. 28.

3416. KOVACIK, Karen
"As My Husband Translates from the Polish." [Confr] (48/49) Spr-Sum 92, p. 236.
"German Gothic" (tr. of Katarzyna Borún). [GrahamHR] (16) Fall 92, p. 50.
"Her" (tr. of Katarzyna Borún). [GrahamHR] (16) Fall 92, p. 48.
"Penelomedea" (tr. of Katarzyna Borún). [GrahamHR] (16) Fall 92, p. 49.

3417. KOVACS, Edna
"Aria." [BellArk] (8:2) Mr-Ap 92, p. 20.
"For Grass Valley, Oregon." [BellArk] (8:3) My-Je 92, p. 7.
"Frescoes." [BellArk] (8:4) Jl-Ag 92, p. 25.
"Harvest." [BellArk] (8:3) My-Je 92, p. 21.
"Harvest." [BellArk] (8:3) My-Je 92, p. 23.
"Moon Talk: First Mammogram." [BellArk] (8:1) Ja-F 92, p. 28.
"Pastorale." [BellArk] (8:2) Mr-Ap 92, p. 25.
"Spirit Quest." [BellArk] (8:4) Jl-Ag 92, p. 21.

3418. KOVACS, Quincy
"Drunk." [Vis] (40) 92, p. 27.
"Tracy." [Vis] (40) 92, p. 25-26.

3419. KOWIT, Steve
"The Erased." [OnTheBus] (4:2/5:1, #10/11) 92, p. 123-124.
"Rain." [NewYorkQ] (49) 92, p. 77.
"Sweet Sixteen." [OnTheBus] (4:2/5:1, #10/11) 92, p. 124.

3420. KOWNACKI, Mary Lou
"Mercy." [ChrC] (109:34) 18-25 N 92, p. 1064.

3421. KOZER, José
"Enfermo en Su Pabellón." [Nuez] (4:12) 92, p. 25.

3422. KRAEFT, Norman
"Morning After." [Bogg] (65) 92, p. 55.
3423. KRAFT, Eugene
"Esu's Itch." [AfAmRev] (26:2) Sum 92, p. 284.
"When the Rains Come." [AfAmRev] (26:2) Sum 92, p. 284-285.
3424. KRAJKOVICH, Joseph C.
"Say Deeply She Falls Shallow." [JlNJPo] (14:1) Spr 92, p. 27.
3425. KRAMER, Aaron
"Before Night" (tr. of Avrom Sutzkever). [Vis] (38) 92, p. 34.
"In the Vilna Ghetto: July 1943" (tr. of Avrom Sutzkever). [Vis] (38) 92, p. 33.
3426. KRAMER, Janice
"Let the Ones Without Skeletons Open the First Closets or Those Who Have Not Stoned Cast the First Sin" (by/though Janice/Janus Aurah Karmah/Kramer). [PoetryUSA] (24) 92, p. 8.
3427. KRAMER, Larry
"The Public Monuments." [Poetry] (159:4) Ja 92, p. 207-208.
3428. KRAPF, Norbert
"The Greyhound at the Bryant Homestead" (for Richard Wilbur). [NegC] (12:1/2) 92, p. 71-72.
"Supper in the Village." [Contact] (10:62/63/64) Fall 91-Spr 92, p. 47.
3429. KRASZEWSKI, Charles S.
"Rovigo" (tr. of Zbigniew Herbert). [Antaeus] (69) Aut 92, p. 61-62.
3430. KRAUS, Jim
"Comrade." [ChamLR] (10/11) Spr-Fall 92, p. 127-128.
"Public Acts / Private Acts." [ChamLR] (10/11) Spr-Fall 92, p. 131-132.
"Reading Old Newspapers." [ChamLR] (10/11) Spr-Fall 92, p. 129-130.
3431. KRAUS, Sharon
"Asthma." [PraS] (66:1) Spr 92, p. 115-117.
"The Struggle." [PraS] (66:1) Spr 92, p. 117-118.
"What If." [PraS] (66:1) Spr 92, p. 118-120.
"When They Named Me." [PraS] (66:1) Spr 92, p. 114-115.
3432. KRAUSE, Olga
"Untitled: What was your pink nipple" (in Russian and English, tr. by Sonja Franeta). [SinW] (46) Spr 92, p. 18.
3433. KRAUSHAAR, Mark
"The Neighbors." [PoetryNW] (33:2) Sum 92, p. 4.
"Regret." [CumbPR] (12:1) Fall 92, p. 39.
3434. KRAUSS, Janet
"Provocation on My Granddaughter's Entering Kindergarten." [PaintedHR] (6) Spr 92, p. 25.
3435. KRAVANJA, Sonja
"Again the streets are silent, the stillness dark" (tr. of Tomaz Salamun). [Descant] (23:3, #78) Fall 92, p. 86.
"Andraz" (tr. of Tomaz Salamun). [Nimrod] (35:2) Spr-Sum 92, p. 57.
"Andraz" (tr. of Tomaz Salamun). [Verse] (8:3/9:1) Wint-Spr 92, p. 126.
"Biography of Dreamtime" (Selections: 1, 5-6, tr. of Ales Debeljak). [Nimrod] (35:2) Spr-Sum 92, p. 58-59.
"Clumsy Guys" (tr. of Tomaz Salamun). [WillowS] (29) Wint 92, p. 19.
"The Hunter" (tr. of Tomaz Salamun). [Nimrod] (35:2) Spr-Sum 92, p. 55.
"National that forget their story-telling" (tr. of Tomaz Salamun). [Nimrod] (35:2) Spr-Sum 92, p. 53.
"Responsibility" (tr. of Tomaz Salamun). [Verse] (8:3/9:1) Wint-Spr 92, p. 126.
"Things, VII" (tr. of Tomaz Salamun). [PartR] (59:2) Spr 92, p. 269.
"The White Ithaca" (tr. of Tomaz Salamun). [Nimrod] (35:2) Spr-Sum 92, p. 56.
"White Ithaca" (tr. of Tomaz Salamun). [WillowS] (29) Wint 92, p. 18.
"Without Anesthesia" (Selections: 1, 3, 7, tr. of Ales Debeljak). [Nimrod] (35:2) Spr-Sum 92, p. 60-61.
"Without Anesthesia VI" (tr. of Ales Debeljak). [Vis] (39) 92, p. 32.
3436. KRAWCZYK, Carl-Michal
"The Coathanger." [OxfordM] (8:2) Fall-Wint 92, p. 10.
3437. KRECHEL, Ursula
"Hymn to Urban Middle Class Women" (tr. by Jo Tudor). [Stand] (33:4) Aut 92, p. 63-64.
"To Mainz!" (tr. by Jo Tudor). [Stand] (33:4) Aut 92, p. 62-63.
3438. KREITER-FORONDA, Carolyn
"The Rosetta Stone." [Vis] (39) 92, p. 38.

3439. KRETZ, Thomas
"Admitting Nothing." [RagMag] (10:2) 92, p. 73.
"College Prom in Ogleby Park." [ConnPR] (11:1) 92, p. 34.
"Hawaiian Interlude." [ChamLR] (10/11) Spr-Fall 92, p. 76.
"Many and No One." [FourQ] (6:1) Spr 92, p. 20.
"Qumran Community." [Quarry] (41:4) Fall 92, p. 70.
"Tycoon Till the End." [DogRR] (11:1) Spr-Sum 92, p. 31.
"When the Weather's Right." [ChrC] (109:17) 13 My 92, p. 516.
3440. KRISS, Barbara
"Full Circle." [NewYorkQ] (48) 92, p. 103.
3441. KROEKER, G. W.
"At Fifty." [Pearl] (16) Fall 92, p. 59.
"Green Extravagance." [Pearl] (16) Fall 92, p. 59.
3442. KROK, Peter
"Second Shift." [MidwQ] (33:4) Sum 92, p. 410.
3443. KROLL, Ernest
"At Houlihan's." [Light] (3) Aut 92, p. 25.
"Baldpate." [Light] (4) Wint 92-93, p. 21.
"Crossing the Colorado" (Needles). [MidwQ] (33:4) Sum 92, p. 411.
"The Offering" (1492-1992). [MidwQ] (34:1) Aut 92, p. 69.
"Routines." [WebR] (16) Fall 92, p. 85.
"Rummage Sale." [HolCrit] (29:5) D 92, p. 17.
"Sherwood Anderson." [NewYorkQ] (47) 92, p. 86.
"The Wedding." [SmPd] (29:1, #84) Wint 92, p. 20.
3444. KROLOW, Karl
"Artist" (tr. by Stuart Friebert). [TarRP] (32:1) Fall 92, p. 29.
"Daring" (tr. by Stuart Friebert). [Field] (46) Spr 92, p. 53.
"Earlier" (tr. by Stuart Friebert). [Field] (46) Spr 92, p. 52.
"A Feeble Affair" (tr. by Stuart Friebert). [ChamLR] (10/11) Spr-Fall 92, p. 165.
"Gemeinsamer Frühling." [TarRP] (32:1) Fall 92, p. 30.
"Künstler." [TarRP] (32:1) Fall 92, p. 28.
"The Landscape Where Illusion Begins" (Translation Chapbook Series, No. 18, in German and English, tr. by Stuart Friebert). [MidAR] (12:2) 92, p. 59-87.
"Nice" (tr. by Stuart Friebert). [Field] (46) Spr 92, p. 54.
"Pomological Poems" (7 poems, tr. by Stuart Friebert). [WebR] (16) Fall 92, p. 5-9.
"Shared Spring" (tr. by Stuart Friebert). [TarRP] (32:1) Fall 92, p. 31.
"Supper" (tr. by Stuart Friebert). [ChamLR] (10/11) Spr-Fall 92, p. 166.
"Waking Dream" (tr. by Stuart Friebert). [Field] (46) Spr 92, p. 55.
"Way Down" (tr. by Stuart Friebert). [ArtfulD] (22/23) 92, p. 32.
"When It Was Time" (tr. by Stuart Friebert). [ChamLR] (10/11) Spr-Fall 92, p. 164.
3445. KROMAN, Deborah
"San Francisco Mountain." [SoCoast] (13) Je 93 [i.e. 92], p. 32.
"West Texas Mountain." [SoCoast] (13) Je 93 [i.e. 92], p. 33.
3446. KRONEN, Steve
"The Fishermen Pull Their Boats In." [YellowS] (41) Fall-Wint 92-93, p. 6.
"The Lepers Who Tend the Hothouse Flowers." [Shen] (42:4) Wint 92, p. 78-79.
"London, 1943." [Poetry] (161:3) D 92, p. 153.
"Married Woman." [SouthernR] (28:4) Aut, O 92, p. 871.
"Near and Far" (St. Agnes' Eve, Loxahatchee Orange Groves." [SouthernR] (28:4) Aut, O 92, p. 870-871.
"A Short History of Christianity." [SouthernR] (28:4) Aut, O 92, p. 872.
"The World's Deserts" (For Ivonne on the occasion of our wedding). [Poetry] (161:3) D 92, p. 154-155.
3447. KRONENFELD, Judy
"Ego Answers." [PassN] (13:1) Sum 92, p. 32.
"Short Dream of Old Terror." [Light] (4) Wint 92-93, p. 18.
"Snowblindness" (for my one and only daughter). [ManhatPR] (14) [92?], p. 39.
"When You Listen to Me." [ManhatPR] (14) [92?], p. 39.
3448. KRÜGER, Michael
"The End of Art" (tr. by Lauren Hahn). [WebR] (16) Fall 92, p. 12.
"A Garden for Keith Jarrett" (tr. by Michael Hamburger). [Stand] (33:4) Aut 92, p. 66-67.
"On Hope" (tr. by Lauren Hahn). [WebR] (16) Fall 92, p. 12.
3449. KRUSOE, Jim
"The Arrival of the Surrealists in Allegheny, Pennsylvania." [DenQ] (26:4) Spr 92, p. 41-42.

3450. KRYSL, Marilyn
"The Blessing." [ChiR] (37:4) 92, p. 84.
3451. KRZESZOWSKI, Tomasz P.
"Small Things" (tr. of Anna Kamienska, w. Desmond Graham). [Verse] (8:3/9:1) Wint-Spr 92, p. 110.
3452. KUBICEK, J. L.
"The 'Uncertainty' Principle." [ChamLR] (10/11) Spr-Fall 92, p. 163.
3453. KUBY, Lolette
"How It Was." [Farm] (9:2) Fall-Wint 92-93, p. 28-29.
3454. KUCHINSKY, Walter
"School." [RagMag] (10:1) 92, p. 61.
3455. KUDERKO, Lynne (Lynne M.)
"Distances." [SpoonRQ] (17:3/4) Sum-Fall 92, p. 104-107.
"Driving Back from a Writers' Conference, Florida." [PoetryNW] (33:4) Wint 92 - 93, p. 39.
"Geometry of Loss." [PoetryNW] (33:4) Wint 92-93, p. 40-41.
"Letter to a Poet Whose Country Is at War" (for Nejc Bernard, Ljubljana, Slovenia). [NegC] (12:3) 92, p. 91-92.
"What to Make of Dreams." [PoetryNW] (33:4) Wint 92-93, p. 41.
3456. KUFFEL, Frances
"The First Choir: Seraphim." [GeoR] (46:1) Spr 92, p. 53-54.
3457. KUHN, Jessie
"Angry the Old People" (tr. of Homero Aridjis). [AmerPoR] (21:6) N-D 92, p. 36.
"Rain in the Night" (tr. of Homero Aridjis). [AmerPoR] (21:6) N-D 92, p. 36.
"Teotihuacán" (tr. of Homero Aridjis). [AmerPoR] (21:6) N-D 92, p. 36.
"Words Don't Tell" (tr. of Homero Aridjis). [AmerPoR] (21:6) N-D 92, p. 36.
3458. KULAK, Lorne
"Digging Potatoes." [Grain] (20:3) Fall 92, p. 155.
"The Hemmies." [Grain] (20:1) Spr 92, p. 239-240.
"How Ramona Lost a Finger." [Grain] (20:3) Fall 92, p. 156.
"The Meatmarket." [Grain] (20:3) Fall 92, p. 156.
"Mining by the Book." [Grain] (20:1) Spr 92, p. 238-239.
"Mother Loses It." [Grain] (20:3) Fall 92, p. 155.
"Ramona's Father." [Grain] (20:3) Fall 92, p. 154.
"Ramona's Mother." [Grain] (20:3) Fall 92, p. 154.
3459. KULIK, William
"Anecdote" (tr. of Tristan Tzara). [AmerPoR] (21:4) Jl-Ag 92, p. 5.
"Bifurcation" (tr. of Tristan Tzara). [AmerPoR] (21:4) Jl-Ag 92, p. 4.
"Casting Off" (tr. of Tristan Tzara). [AmerPoR] (21:4) Jl-Ag 92, p. 4.
"Complete Circuit of Moon and Color" (tr. of Tristan Tzara). [AmerPoR] (21:4) Jl - Ag 92, p. 3.
"The Death of Guillaume Apollinaire" (tr. of Tristan Tzara). [AmerPoR] (21:4) Jl - Ag 92, p. 4.
"Easier Said Than Done" (tr. of Tristan Tzara). [AmerPoR] (21:4) Jl-Ag 92, p. 5.
"Epidermis of the Night Growth" (tr. of Tristan Tzara). [AmerPoR] (21:4) Jl-Ag 92, p. 3.
"For Robert Desnos" (tr. of Tristan Tzara). [AmerPoR] (21:4) Jl-Ag 92, p. 5.
"Forbidden Fire" (Selections: II, IX, XI, tr. of Tristan Tzara). [AmerPoR] (21:4) Jl - Ag 92, p. 4.
"The Horse" (tr. of Tristan Tzara). [AmerPoR] (21:4) Jl-Ag 92, p. 6.
"Hotel Light" (tr. of Tristan Tzara). [AmerPoR] (21:4) Jl-Ag 92, p. 6.
"Optimism Unveiled" (tr. of Tristan Tzara). [AmerPoR] (21:4) Jl-Ag 92, p. 3.
"Ox on the Tongue" (Selections: XIV, XV, tr. of Tristan Tzara). [AmerPoR] (21:4) Jl-Ag 92, p. 5.
"Undiscoverable Past" (tr. of Tristan Tzara). [AmerPoR] (21:4) Jl-Ag 92, p. 6.
"The Wave" (tr. of Tristan Tzara). [AmerPoR] (21:4) Jl-Ag 92, p. 5.
3460. KUMIN, Maxine
"Anniversary." [AmerPoR] (21:1) Ja-F 92, p. 43.
"The Chambermaids in the Marriott in Mid-morning." [AmerPoR] (21:1) Ja-F 92, p. 43.
"Hay." [AmerPoR] (21:1) Ja-F 92, p. 44-45.
"Indian Summer." [AmerPoR] (21:1) Ja-F 92, p. 43.
"The Nuns of Childhood: Two Views." [Atlantic] (269:2) F 92, p. 80.
"October, Yellowstone Park." [Ploughs] (18:1) Spr 92, p. 215-217.
"Spring Training." [Witness] (6:2) 92, p. 9.
"The Succession." [AmerPoR] (21:1) Ja-F 92, p. 44.

3461. KUNERT, Guenter (Günter)
"Biography" (tr. by Agnes Stein). [Verse] (9:2) Sum 92, p. 93.
"Ephesus" (tr. by Agnes Stein). [Verse] (9:2) Sum 92, p. 93.
"Garden at Breitenfelde" (tr. by Reinhold Grimm). [Pembroke] (24) 92, p. 45.
"Guests of Summer" (tr. by Reinhold Grimm). [Pembroke] (24) 92, p. 48.
"Perspective" (tr. by Reinhold Grimm). [Pembroke] (24) 92, p. 49.
"Taking Leave" (tr. by Reinhold Grimm). [Pembroke] (24) 92, p. 47.
"The Transformation" (tr. by Reinhold Grimm). [Pembroke] (24) 92, p. 46.
3462. KUNITZ, Stanley
"Chariot" (for Varujan Boghosian). [GettyR] (5:2) Spr 92, p. 210.
"In the Dark House." [Atlantic] (270:4) O 92, p. 69.
3463. KUNZE, Reiner
"Advance Guard Here" (tr. by Thomas S. Edwards). [NewOR] (19:2) Sum 92, p. 69.
"Bittgedanke, Dir zu Füssen." [NewOR] (19:2) Sum 92, p. 72.
"Den Literaturbetrieb Fliehend." [NewOR] (19:2) Sum 92, p. 70.
"Diary Page 75" (Karlsbad, Thomayer Sanitarium, tr. by Lori M. Fisher). [Trans] (26) Spr 92, p. 41.
"Fleeing the Literary Business" (tr. by Thomas S. Edwards). [NewOR] (19:2) Sum 92, p. 70.
"In Der Provence." [NewOR] (19:2) Sum 92, p. 74.
"In the Provence" (tr. by Thomas S. Edwards). [NewOR] (19:2) Sum 92, p. 74.
"Nachtfahrt." [NewOR] (19:2) Sum 92, p. 71.
"Night Journey" (tr. by Thomas S. Edwards). [NewOR] (19:2) Sum 92, p. 71.
"Plea at Your Feet" (tr. by Thomas S. Edwards). [NewOR] (19:2) Sum 92, p. 72.
"Refuge Behind Refuge" (for Peter Huchel, tr. by Robin Fulton). [Stand] (33:4) Aut 92, p. 71.
"Under Dying Trees" (tr. by Thomas S. Edwards). [NewOR] (19:2) Sum 92, p. 73.
"Unter Sterbenden Baumen." [NewOR] (19:2) Sum 92, p. 73.
"Vortrupps Hier." [NewOR] (19:2) Sum 92, p. 69.
3464. KUPCHIK, Seth
"I Always Believed I Was a Saint." [Jacaranda] (6:1/2) Wint-Spr 92, p. 129.
3465. KUPFER, Gabi
"Soil" (For my brother, Zachariah). [Kaleid] (25) Sum-Fall 92, p. 34.
3466. KUPPNER, Frank
"First General Druidical Service." [Verse] (9:3) Wint 92, p. 60-65.
3467. KURZ, Egon
"Benny Sniffed Me." [SoCoast] (13) Je 93 [i.e. 92], p. 47.
"In Other Words." [Light] (1) Spr 92, p. 8.
3468. KUSHNER, Aleksandr
"As Catullus Wrote" (from "Apollo in the Snow," tr. by Paul Graves and Carol Ueland). [Arion] 3d series (1:2) Spr 91, p. 128.
3469. KUSHNER, Tony
"The Second Month of Mourning." [Thrpny] (49) Spr 92, p. 13.
3470. KUSTERS, Wiel
"Ballad of the Salamander" (tr. by Scott Rollins). [Trans] (26) Spr 92, p. 11-12.
3471. KUTCHINS, Laurie
"Full Circle." [WestB] (30) 92, p. 58-59.
"The Same Road." [PaintedB] (45) 92, p. 12.
"Settling." [TarRP] (32:1) Fall 92, p. 41.
3472. KUTLAR, Onat
"War and Peace" (tr. by Talat Sait Halman). [Trans] (26) Spr 92, p. 38.
3473. KUUSISTO, Stephen
"Apocryphal Story." [SenR] (22:2) Fall 92, p. 68.
"Biography." [SenR] (22:2) Fall 92, p. 67.
"The King's Sorrow" (tr. of Edith Södergran). [SenR] (22:2) Fall 92, p. 61.
"Longing for Colors" (tr. of Edith Södergran). [SenR] (22:2) Fall 92, p. 62.
"Memento" (tr. of Jarkko Laine). [PoetryE] (33) Spr 92, p. 165.
"Necessary Angels" (poets in their youth). [SenR] (22:2) Fall 92, p. 66.
"No Name for It." [SenR] (22:2) Fall 92, p. 63.
"Talking Books." [SenR] (22:2) Fall 92, p. 64-65.
3474. KUZMA, Greg
"Lunch Break at Vien Dong." [NoDaQ] (60:4) Fall 92, p. 82.
3475. KWA, Lydia
"Translating Fortune" (a long poem based on actual fortune cookie sayings). [Grain] (20:1) Spr 92, p. 178-183.

3476. KWASNY, Melissa
"Aspen." [PoetryNW] (33:4) Wint 92-93, p. 28.
"Shade." [PoetryNW] (33:4) Wint 92-93, p. 27-28.
"Songbirds." [PoetryNW] (33:4) Wint 92-93, p. 26-27.
"Tree." [PoetryNW] (33:4) Wint 92-93, p. 29.
3477. KWIATEK, JoEllen
"August." [IndR] (15:2) Fall 92, p. 26.
"Nearer God, Nearer Realite" (— Gwen John). [IndR] (15:2) Fall 92, p. 25.
KYOKO, Mori
See MORI, Kyoko
La . . .
See also names beginning with "La" without the following space, filed below in their alphabetic positions, e.g., LaSALLE.
La BRUNO, Carmen Michael
See LaBRUNO, Michael (Carmen Michael)
La BRUNO, Michael
See LaBRUNO, Michael (Carmen Michael)
3478. La LOCA
"Leda, Broken, Winged." [Thrpny] (48) Wint 92, p. 11.
La MERS, Joyce
See LaMERS, Joyce
3479. La ROCCA, Lynda
"Journey." [NewYorkQ] (47) 92, p. 84.
"The Statues" (Winner, Annual Free Verse Contest, 1991). [AnthNEW] (4) 92, p. 29.
3480. La RUE, Mark
"Where You Are Is Where." [AmerPoR] (21:6) N-D 92, p. 56.
3481. La SARRE, Zulu
"Cuentos desde la Eternidad" (Selection: "La Palabra"). [Luz] (1) My 92, p. 51.
"El Dictador" (a Mickey Kaplan). [Luz] (1) My 92, p. 67.
"The Dictator" (to Mickey Kaplan). [Luz] (1) My 92, p. 66.
"El Libro de los Perdidos" (2 selections). [Luz] (1) My 92, p. 43-46.
"La Palabra." [Luz] (1) My 92, p. 34.
3482. LaBONTÉ, Karen
"The Reasonable." [CimR] (99) Ap 92, p. 52.
LABRA, Carilda Oliver
See OLIVER LABRA, Carilda
3483. LaBRUNO, Michael (Carmen Michael)
"Blessings." [Footwork] 92, p. 73.
"Book Rejection." [Footwork] 92, p. 73.
"Epiphany / Nadine's Poem" (Bimini / 1978). [NegC] (12:3) 92, p. 93-95.
"New Brunswick / Spread Skies Beckon." [Footwork] 92, p. 72.
"Of Innocence or Guilt." [Footwork] 92, p. 72.
"A Stolen Poem." [Footwork] 92, p. 73.
"War." [NegC] (12:1/2) 92, p. 73.
3484. LACKEY, Joe
"Hurling Jonson at Speeding Trucks." [NegC] (12:1/2) 92, p. 74-75.
"In Memory of E.E. Cummings." [NegC] (12:1/2) 92, p. 76-77.
3485. LaFEMINA, Gerry
"Pastoral." [SouthernPR] (32:1) Spr 92, p. 24-25.
"Waking Up in the Afternoon After Falling Asleep Listening to Charlie Parker." [SenR] (22:1) Spr 92, p. 66.
3486. LAGIER, Jennifer
"Bypassed Roadside Icon." [Lactuca] (15) Mr 92, p. 17.
"Evicted Farmer's Museum." [Lactuca] (15) Mr 92, p. 18.
"Hometown Reunion." [Lactuca] (15) Mr 92, p. 17.
"Library Service." [SlipS] (12) 92, p. 95.
3487. LAHTI, Will
"Cook High School." [WormR] (32:4 #128) 92, p. 146.
"Ecochauvinism." [WormR] (32:4 #128) 92, p. 146.
3488. LAI, Larissa
"Calling Home." [WestCL] (26:2, #8) Fall 92, p. 104-105.
"The Escape." [WestCL] (26:2, #8) Fall 92, p. 100-103.
3489. LAIN, Sheryl
"Autumn Baptism." [ChrC] (109:28) 7 O 92, p. 863.

3490. LAINE, Jarkko
"Memento" (tr. by Stephen Kuusisto). [PoetryE] (33) Spr 92, p. 165.
3491. LAINO, E. J. Miller
"Lost and Found." [Kalliope] (14:3) 92, p. 15.
3492. LAKE, Kathleen
"The Cure." [Sun] (199) Je-Jl 92, p. 21.
"In the Absence." [Sun] (199) Je-Jl 92, p. 20.
"The Kitchen." [Sun] (199) Je-Jl 92, p. 21.
3493. LAKE, Whitney
"A Short Novel." [US1] (26/27) 92, p. 47.
LALIGA, Lourdes Rensoli
See RENSOLI LALIGA, Lourdes
3494. LALLY, Michael
"Having It All." [Shiny] (7/8) 92, p. 47-51.
3495. LAMANTIA, Philip
"Egypt" (In honor of R. A. Schwaller de Lubicz. From a visit on the Nile (Hapy), Autumn, 1989). [CityLR] (5) 92, p. 74-76.
3496. LAMARQUE, Vivan
"The Gentleman of the Footprints" (tr. by Renata Treitel). [NewOR] (19:3/4) Fall - Wint 92, p. 153.
3497. LAMB, Elizabeth Searle
"Five Haiku." [Noctiluca] (1:2) Wint 92 [on cover: Wint 93], p. 32.
"For Lafcadio Hearn." [Noctiluca] (1:2) Wint 92 [on cover: Wint 93], p. 33.
3498. LAMB, Jessica
"Bodies of Water." [CarolQ] (44:2) Wint 92, p. 79.
3499. LAMBERT, Jane
"Sprung Rhythm." [Confr] (48/49) Spr-Sum 92, p. 222.
3500. LAMBERT, Nancy
"All My Best Friends Together I'd Kill them." [OnTheBus] (4:2/5:1, #10/11) 92, p. 125.
3501. LAMBERTON, Dan
"All-Girl Rodeo, 1959." [PoetryNW] (33:2) Sum 92, p. 36-37.
"A Slaughter." [PoetryNW] (33:2) Sum 92, p. 37-38.
"Under the House." [PoetryNW] (33:2) Sum 92, p. 38-39.
3502. LaMERS, Joyce
"Baize Ballade." [Light] (1) Spr 92, p. 27.
"Dogged Duo." [Light] (1) Spr 92, p. 30.
"Geography Lesson." [Light] (3) Aut 92, p. 13.
"Goose Bonnet Sonnet." [Light] (1) Spr 92, p. 12.
"Is there a monster in Loch Ness?" [Light] (3) Aut 92, p. 29.
"Over Thirty." [Light] (3) Aut 92, p. 22.
"Stopped at Tahoe for inspection." [Light] (4) Wint 92-93, p. 29.
"A Theological Discussion." [Light] (4) Wint 92-93, p. 26.
3503. LAMPORT, Felicia
"Mom's the Word." [Light] (4) Wint 92-93, p. 17.
"Pasta? Basta!: A Minority Report." [Light] (1) Spr 92, p. 10.
"S&Lementary Principles." [Light] (2) Sum 92, p. 18.
3504. LAMSTEIN, Sarah
"Dead of Winter." [Noctiluca] (1:2) Wint 92 [on cover: Wint 93], p. 7.
3505. LANCASTER, John
"For the Secret." [Verse] (9:3) Wint 92, p. 102.
"The Queer." [Verse] (9:3) Wint 92, p. 103.
3506. LAND, Thomas
"Clarity." [Amelia] (7:1, #20) 92, p. 150.
"The Drunkard." [Amelia] (6:4, #19) 92, p. 130.
"Eve's Harden [i.e., Garden?]." [Amelia] (7:1, #20) 92, p. 150.
"Solomon's Footprint" (In memoriam Szilagyi Geza). [Amelia] (7:1, #20) 92, p. 150.
"The Three Bricklayers." [Amelia] (6:4, #19) 92, p. 130.
3507. LANDAU, Julie
"Tieh Lüan Hua" (tr. of Su Shih). [Trans] (26) Spr 92, p. 103.
3508. LANDECKER, Hannah
"Polychaos." [CapilR] (2:9) Fall 92, p. 45-47.
3509. LANDGRAF, Susan
"Finding: Curtis Smith's 'Ancestral Voices' with Color Illustration by Richard Williams." [Nimrod] (36:1) Fall-Wint 92, p. 36.

"If You Were Glass I Could See Inside. If I Were Wiser I'd Mend the Break." [Kalliope] (14:1) 92, p. 50.
"Learn to Be Receptive to What Befalls" (Taoist Book of Days). [Vis] (39) 92, p. 18.
"My Father, After Magritte's Pipe Paintings." [Nimrod] (36:1) Fall-Wint 92, p. 33.
"Newborn." [Amelia] (7:1, #20) 92, p. 147.
"On This Hallowed Eve's Night." [Nimrod] (36:1) Fall-Wint 92, p. 34-35.
"We Are All Aliens Here." [Nimrod] (36:1) Fall-Wint 92, p. 38-39.
"What's Buried Changes the Ground" (from *What's Buried Changes the Ground*. First Honorable Mention, The Pablo Neruda Prize for Poetry). [Nimrod] (36:1) Fall-Wint 92, p. 32.
"With His Hands." [Nimrod] (36:1) Fall-Wint 92, p. 37.

3510. LANDIS, Maxine
"Kissing the Frog" (for Helen). [OnTheBus] (4:2/5:1, #10/11) 92, p. 128.
"My Olive Tree." [OnTheBus] (4:2/5:1, #10/11) 92, p. 126.
"Stories My Husband Tells at Dinner." [OnTheBus] (4:2/5:1, #10/11) 92, p. 126 - 127.

3511. LANE, Donna
"Dear Chet C. Smith." [NewYorkQ] (48) 92, p. 91.

3512. LANE, Joel
"The Other Side." [JamesWR] (9:3) Spr 92, p. 6.

3513. LANE, M. Travis
"Come Up and Be Dead!" (for Jenny Wren). [SouthernR] (28:2) Spr, Ap 92, p. 262 - 263.
"Fall-Winter 1990-1991." [AntigR] (90) Sum 92, p. 63-68.
"Half Past." [SouthernR] (28:2) Spr, Ap 92, p. 261-262.

3514. LANE, Patrick
"Father." [SouthernR] (28:2) Spr, Ap 92, p. 294-295.

3515. LANE, S. Susan (Sigrun Susan)
"Bells at Wadenhoe." [MalR] (101) Wint92, p. 108.
"Father's Story III." [CrabCR] (8:1) Sum-Fall 92, p. 4.
"Legger, Harecastle Tunnel." [SingHM] (20) 92, p. 9-10.
"Post War." [MalR] (101) Wint92, p. 109.

3516. LANE, William
"The Accident." [HangL] (60) 92, p. 31.
"Praise for the Forest of Your Hair." [HangL] (60) 92, p. 31.

3517. LANGAGNE, Eduardo
"Discoveries" (tr. by Reginald Gibbons). [TriQ] (85) Fall 92, p. 218.

3518. LANGE, Aimee
"People You May Encounter, Here." [HangL] (61) 92, p. 97-98.
"Soozie Floozie." [HangL] (61) 92, p. 98.

3519. LANGFORD, Martin
"Upstream From Halvorsen's." [Footwork] 92, p. 101.

3520. LANGHORNE, Henry
"Geometry" (Plato, Gorgias, 508a). [NegC] (12:3) 92, p. 96.
"Touring the Metropolitan Museum One December Afternoon." [NegC] (12:1/2) 92, p. 78.

3521. LANGLAS, James
"Connections" (For Jack). [Poetry] (160:3) Je 92, p. 150.
"A Loss of Memory." [Poetry] (160:1) Ap 92, p. 3-4.
"Raising Children." [CutB] (37) Wint 92, p. 95-96.
"Sickness." [Poetry] (160:1) Ap 92, p. 4.

3522. LANGTON, Charles
"River Festival." [CimR] (99) Ap 92, p. 53.

3523. LANGTON, Daniel J.
"June Twentieth." [NoAmR] (277:2) Mr-Ap 92, p. 23.
"Michael." [SenR] (22:2) Fall 92, p. 97.
"One Tallus: A Letter." [Light] (1) Spr 92, p. 21.
"A Village." [Light] (1) Spr 92, p. 7.

3524. LANOUE, David
"Something Small." [NewOR] (19:1) Spr 92, p. 98.

3525. LANSDOWN, Andrew
"The Visitor" (for Nicholas). [Verse] (9:3) Wint 92, p. 127.

3526. LANSING, Gerrit
"In the Grip of the Octopus." [Sulfur] (12:2, #31) Fall 92, p. 161.

3527. LANTZ, Sarah
"Spring Migration in Fars" (From Chatwin's Notebooks). [Calyx] (14:1) Sum 92, p. 6.
"Traveling, South of Juba." [DenQ] (26:3) Wint 92, p. 33.
3528. LAO, Linette
"Black Susans." [Caliban] (11) 92, p. 49-50.
"Evolution." [Caliban] (11) 92, p. 51.
"Rules and Etiquette." [Caliban] (11) 92, p. 52.
"Untitled: It wears a pyramid of needles walking through you." [Caliban] (11) 92, p. 50.
"Untitled: The neutral angel sends me a postcard from the city." [Caliban] (11) 92, p. 51.
3529. LAPIDUS, Jacqueline
"Hidden in Beach Grass." [Hellas] (3:2) Fall 92, p. 90.
3530. LARDNER, Ted
"Eating Magic Mushrooms at Wayne's House." [Caliban] (11) 92, p. 126-127.
3531. LAREW, Hiram
"Anxious or Wise" (winner of the 1992 Louisiana Literature Prize for Poetry). [LouisL] (9:1) Spr 92, p. 57-58.
LaROCCA, Lynda
See La ROCCA, Lynda
3532. LARSEN, Barbara
"3:00 A.M. at the Grand Terminus Hotel." [RagMag] (10:2) 92, p. 61.
"Lincoln's Birthday." [RagMag] (10:2) 92, p. 59.
"New Beginnings." [RagMag] (10:2) 92, p. 59.
"Sara Vaughn, 1924-1990." [RagMag] (10:2) 92, p. 60.
"Trip Home." [RagMag] (10:2) 92, p. 58.
3533. LARSEN, Jeanne
"Correspondence in April." [NewEngR] (14:2) Spr 92, p. 102-103.
"In Brown Creek Valley, Thinking of War." [NewEngR] (14:2) Spr 92, p. 104-105.
3534. LARSEN, Lance
"A Missionary Considers His Converts" (Pichelemu, Chile 1981). [PoetryE] (33) Spr 92, p. 76-77.
"Walking Around." [NewRep] (206:8) 24 F 92, p. 36.
3535. LARSON, Allen
"Requiem." [ChiR] (37:4) 92, p. 61-62.
3536. LARSON, Rustin
"The Paternal Side." [NewYorker] (68:31) 21 S 92, p. 52.
"Poem Without Eyelids." [PassN] (13:2) Wint 92, p. 9.
LaRUE, Mark La
See La RUE, Mark
3537. LARVERGNE, Alfredo
"Y en la Radio, Mario Cantaba." [Nuez] (4:12) 92, p. 21.
3538. LaSALLE, Peter
"Amtrak." [SoDakR] (30:4) Wint 92, p. 113.
"The Beach Club in Winter." [SoDakR] (30:4) Wint 92, p. 112.
"Bums Sweetly Dreaming." [PoetL] (87:3) Fall 92, p. 35.
"Ciudad Acuña." [HampSPR] Wint 92, p. 35.
"The Dream Buses of Southern India." [AnotherCM] (24) Fall 92, p. 99.
"I Go Back to Eliot." [ConnPR] (11:1) 92, p. 6.
"Manifesto." [MinnR] (39) Fall-Wint 92-93, p. 3.
"Mirrors in Winter." [ColEng] (54:4) Ap 92, p. 422.
LASCURAIN, Ignacio García
See GARCIA LASCURAIN, Ignacio
3539. LASDUN, James
"The Calling of the Apostle Matthew." [ParisR]] (34:124) Fall 92, p. 50-51.
3540. LASHER, Susan
"The American Philosopher." [PartR] (59:1) Wint 92, p. 98-101.
3541. LASKE, Otto
"Härte." [Os] (34) Spr 92, p. 24.
"Irdische Landschaft." [Os] (34) Spr 92, p. 25.
"Mistral." [Os] (35) Fall 92, p. 15.
"Morgen." [Os] (35) Fall 92, p. 14.
3542. LASKER-SCHÜLER, Else
"Hagar and Ishmael" (tr. by Betty Falkenberg). [Boulevard] (7:2/3, #20/21) Fall 92, p. 240.

"Jacob and Esau" (tr. by Betty Falkenberg). [Boulevard] (7:2/3, #20/21) Fall 92, p. 241.

3543. LASKEY, Michael
"Clock Work." [Verse] (8:3/9:1) Wint-Spr 92, p. 78.
"Sleep-Talking." [Verse] (8:3/9:1) Wint-Spr 92, p. 79.

3544. LASSELL, Michael
"At the Memorial Service for Richard Royal (1949-1990)" (For Eve Ensler). [Art&Und] (1:3) Spr 92, p. 13.
"Brady Street, San Francisco" (For Roberto Muñoz). [Art&Und] (1:1) Fall 91, p. 9.
"Christmas." [Amelia] (6:4, #19) 92, p. 51-54.
"Diva" (For Alexander Zubak). [ChironR] (11:4) Wint 92, p. 23.
"Dressing for Work." [Art&Und] (1:5) S-O 92, p. 9.
"Imagining a Peach." [ChironR] (11:4) Wint 92, p. 23.
"L. A. Times." [Amelia] (7:1, #20) 92, p. 161.
"Leaving L.A." [Art&Und] (1:5) S-O 92, p. 9.
"Prism" (For Kenny — again, two years gone). [Amelia] (6:4, #19) 92, p. 76-77.
"Running into Ramon." [ChironR] (11:4) Wint 92, p. 23.

3545. LaTERRE, David C.
"Border Domesticate." [RagMag] (10:2) 92, p. 83.

3546. LAU, Evelyn
"City of Men." [CapilR] (2:8) Spr 92, p. 38-39.
"Cold Shower." [Grain] (20:4) Wint 92, p. 78.
"Coming Home." [TampaR] (5) Fall 92, p. 37.
"It's Boxing Day." [CapilR] (2:8) Spr 92, p. 40-41.
"Mexico, Second-hand." [Grain] (20:4) Wint 92, p. 81.
"The Photographer." [Grain] (20:4) Wint 92, p. 79-80.
"Safe Trips." [CapilR] (2:8) Spr 92, p. 36-37.

3547. LAUCHLAN, Michael
"Scars." [NewEngR] (14:2) Spr 92, p. 150.

3548. LAUGHLIN, J. (James) (*See also* LAUGHLIN, Jim)
"Agatha." [Interim] (11:1) Spr-Sum 92, p. 24.
"Are You Still Alone." [Interim] (11:1) Spr-Sum 92, p. 22.
"An Attestation." [Conjunc] (18) 92, p. 175.
"Before I Die." [Interim] (11:1) Spr-Sum 92, p. 23.
"The Church Ladies." [NewYorkQ] (49) 92, p. 38.
"The Country Road." [NewYorker] (68:43) 14 D 92, p. 80.
"The Death of the Village Post Office." [Agni] (35) 92, p. 305.
"Don't Try to Explain." [ParisR] (34:125) Wint 92, p. 243.
"The Enchanted Birchtree." [Conjunc] (18) 92, p. 177.
"The English Governess." [Light] (2) Sum 92, p. 20.
"The Figure in the Stone." [ParisR] (34:125) Wint 92, p. 242.
"In My Imagination." [Agni] (35) 92, p. 304.
"The Inscription." [Conjunc] (18) 92, p. 176.
"The Intruder." [Interim] (11:1) Spr-Sum 92, p. 22.
"Little Bits of Paper" (An Ars Poetica). [Poetry] (160:2) My 92, p. 74-75.
"Long & Languorous." [ParisR] (34:125) Wint 92, p. 244-245.
"The Moths" (Remembering Nabokov). [ParisR] (34:123) Sum 92, p. 35-36.
"Odi et Amo." [ParisR] (34:125) Wint 92, p. 243-244.
"The Old Indian" (for Gary Snyder). [Conjunc] (18) 92, p. 175.
"A Problem of Semantics." [NewAW] (10) Fall 92, p. 27.
"The Rodent." [Light] (3) Aut 92, p. 18.
"The Shameful Profession." [Poetry] (160:2) My 92, p. 76-77.
"The Story of Rhodope." [Conjunc] (19) 92, p. 297.
"Story of the Fool and the Cakes" (Adapted from the Tawney/Penzer translation of Somadeva's "Katha Sarit Sagara," Sanskrit, 3rd c. A.D.). [Conjunc] (18) 92, p. 174.
"Story of the Snake Who Told His Secret to a Woman" (Adapted from the Tawney/Penzer translation of Somadeva's "Katha Sarit Sagara," Sanskrit, 3rd c. A.D.). [Conjunc] (18) 92, p. 173.
"The Stranger." [Conjunc] (19) 92, p. 296-297.
"The Sultan's Justice." [Conjunc] (18) 92, p. 176.
"To Mistress Kate Gill." [Light] (1) Spr 92, p. 16.
"The Transformation" (Koran, xxi, via Burton). [Conjunc] (18) 92, p. 174.
"La Tristesse." [NewYorker] (68:16) 8 Je 92, p. 36.
"Two Scenes from the Literary Scene & a Letter." [NewAW] (10) Fall 92, p. 28-29.

3549. LAUGHLIN, Jim (*See also* LAUGHLIN, J. (James))
"Living Between." [FloridaR] (18:2) Fall-Wint 92, p. 70-71.
3550. LAUREL, Hya
"Speedy Knew." [Bogg] (65) 92, p. 53.
3551. LAUTERMILCH, Steven
"To a Young Maiden: Dakota Skull, Mask, Song without Words." [ColR] (9:1) Spr - Sum 92, p. 89-93.
3552. LAUX, Dorianne
"China." [AmerPoR] (21:4) Jl-Ag 92, p. 38.
"Dust." [Agni] (36) 92, p. 56.
"Twelve." [YellowS] (Ten Years [i.e. 40]) Sum-Fall 92, p. 40.
"What We Carry" (for D.M.). [Zyzzyva] (8:2) Sum 92, p. 66-67.
3553. LAUZON, Mary Elizabeth
"The Price of Grain." [AntigR] (91) Fall 92, p. 146.
3554. LAVIERA, Tato
"Bochinche Bilingüe." [Americas] (20:3/4) Fall-Wint 92, p. 208.
"Latero Story." [Americas] (20:3/4) Fall-Wint 92, p. 203-204.
"Melao." [Americas] (20:3/4) Fall-Wint 92, p. 207.
"Viejo." [Americas] (20:3/4) Fall-Wint 92, p. 205-206.
3555. LAVIERI, Jon
"Waiting for the Pitch." [NewYorkQ] (47) 92, p. 49.
3556. LAWLER, Patrick
"Dead Woman Works Miracles." [NewDeltaR] (8:1) Fall 90-Wint 91, p. 68-69.
"(Food)." [CentralP] (21) Spr 92, p. 8-17.
"Human Head Transplant Successful." [NewDeltaR] (8:1) Fall 90-Wint 91, p. 70.
3557. LAWLOR, William
"The Right to Bear Arms." [SoCoast] (13) Je 93 [i.e. 92], p. 22-23.
3558. LAWNER, Lynn
"For Kavafy." [SouthernPR] (32:2) Fall 92, p. 33-35.
3559. LAWRENCE, Anthony
"Brown Glass." [SenR] (22:2) Fall 92, p. 95-96.
3560. LAWRENCE, Patricia
"Sea Turtle" (Winner, Annual Free Verse Contest, 1991). [AnthNEW] (4) 92, p. 25.
3561. LAWRY, Mercedes
"Blind Joy." [RiverC] (12:2) Spr 92, p. 49.
"The Laundress." [PoetL] (87:1) Spr 92, p. 51.
3562. LAWSON, Scott L.
"The Mechanistic Ballade." [NegC] (12:1/2) 92, p. 190.
3563. LAWTON, Harry
"After the War: A Retrospect" (For Vance Bourjailly). [Caliban] (11) 92, p. 15-32.
"Anacapa Island." [PacificR] (11) 92-93, p. 22-23.
"The Granada Express" (For Lisa Conyers). [PacificR] (11) 92-93, p. 24-26.
"Mount Rainier." [CharR] (18:2) Fall 92, p. 103.
3564. LAYTON, Peter
"Brown Hues." [JINJPo] (14:1) Spr 92, p. 26.
"Cute Fuzzy Animals, Garfield." [FreeL] (10) Sum 92, p. 20.
"Toeing, Camber." [DogRR] (11:2, #22) Fall-Wint 92, p. 3.
3565. LAZARD, Naomi
"Love's Captives" (tr. of Faiz Ahmed Faiz). [Trans] (26) Spr 92, p. 95.
"Prison Meeting" (tr. of Faiz Ahmed Faiz). [Trans] (26) Spr 92, p. 39-40.
"When Autumn Came" (tr. of Faiz Ahmed Faiz). [Trans] (26) Spr 92, p. 5.
3566. LAZARUS, Emma
"The New Colossus." [YaleR] (80:3) Jl 92, p. 118.
3567. LAZZERONI, Elaine
"The Day the Eland Almost Ate My Hand." [NegC] (12:3) 92, p. 97.
Le . . .
See also names beginning with "Le" without the following space, filed below in their alphabetic positions, e.g., LeFEVRE.
3568. Le DRESSAY, Anne
"Blood from Stone." [Arc] (29) Aut 92, p. 51.
"The Desert." [PoetryC] (12:3/4) Jl 92, p. 43.
"I Am No Longer Close Enough." [AntigR] (90) Sum 92, p. 56.
"A Perfect Hatred." [PoetryC] (12:3/4) Jl 92, p. 43.
"To Break the Silence" (for Gwen and Linda and Tom and Vaden). [PraF] (13:4, #61) Wint 92-93, p. 60.

3569. Le GUIN, Ursula K.
"Fragments from the Women's Writing." [BelPoJ] (43:1) Fall 92, p. 9-11.
3570. Le LYS, Éli
"Second Coming" (for Christopher Carey). [PoetryUSA] (24) 92, p. 24.
3571. LEA, Sydney
"Beautiful Miles." [NewYorker] (67:48) 20 Ja 92, p. 30-31.
"Valedictions" (for Erika, and for George). [GeoR] (46:2) Sum 92, p. 238-239.
LEADY, Dave
See LEEDY, Dave
3572. LEAS, Patricia
"Oklahoma, 1934." [EngJ] (80:7) N 91, p. 99.
3573. LEASE, Joseph
"Petition." [Agni] (36) 92, p. 125.
"The Room." [GrandS] (11:3 #43) 92, p. 133-137.
3574. LeBLANC, René
"Motion Picture." [Poem] (68) N 92, p. 4.
3575. LEBOW, David
"Talking." [Poem] (67) My 92, p. 34.
"The Wolf's Story." [Poem] (67) My 92, p. 35.
3576. LEBRON, Lolita
"Alone" (tr. by Gloria F. Waldman). [LitR] (35:4) Sum 92, p. 519.
"I Have Seen You" (tr. by Gloria F. Waldman). [LitR] (35:4) Sum 92, p. 520.
"Sola." [LitR] (35:4) Sum 92, p. 606.
"Te He Mirado." [LitR] (35:4) Sum 92, p. 606-607.
3577. LECHAY, Dan
"Last Night." [Agni] (36) 92, p. 171.
3578. LECKIE, Ross
"On the Death of a Cat." [US1] (26/27) 92, p. 18.
3579. LECKNER, Carole H.
"The New Whaler." [Descant] (23:4/24:1, #78/79) Wint-Spr 92-93, p. 90-91.
3580. LeCOMPTE, Kendall
"The Bird in Flight." [Comm] (119:4) 28 F 92, p. 12.
3581. LECONTE de LISLE, Charles-René Marie
"Venus de Milo" (in French and English). [YaleR] (80:3) Jl 92, p. 109-111.
3582. LECUYER, Tess
"Mr Potato Head Consorts with Your Childhood Memories." [13thMoon] (10:1/2) 92, p. 47-48.
3583. LEDBETTER, J. T.
"After the Rains." [Nimrod] (36:1) Fall-Wint 92, p. 117.
"Brother Ross." [Lactuca] (15) Mr 92, p. 14-15.
"Letting Our Dreams Touch" (L.A. soup kitchen). [Lactuca] (15) Mr 92, p. 8-13.
"The River" (honorable mention, Eve of Saint Agnes Contest). [NegC] (12:3) 92, p. 14-15.
"Some Memory." [Lactuca] (15) Mr 92, p. 13.
"Turley's Woods." [Lactuca] (15) Mr 92, p. 16.
"When Grandmother Sleeps." [PaintedHR] (6) Spr 92, p. 36.
LeDRESSAY, Anne
See Le DRESSAY, Anne
3584. LEE, C. Allyson
"Recipe." [WestCL] (26:2, #8) Fall 92, p. 13-17.
3585. LEE, Candace
"The Song of Cane." [Vis] (39) 92, p. 33.
3586. LEE, David
"Doc." [Ploughs] (18:1) Spr 92, p. 89-94.
"Ugly." [RiverS] (36) 92, p. 38-42.
3587. LEE, Gregory B.
"I'm Reading" (tr. of Duoduo). [ManhatR] (6:2) Fall 92, p. 9.
"I've Always Delighted in a Shaft of Light in the Depth of Night" (tr. of Duoduo). [ManhatR] (6:2) Fall 92, p. 8.
"Morning" (tr. of Duoduo). [ManhatR] (6:2) Fall 92, p. 11-12.
"The Rivers of Amsterdam" (tr. of Duoduo). [ManhatR] (6:2) Fall 92, p. 5.
"There Is No" (tr. of Duoduo). [ManhatR] (6:2) Fall 92, p. 10.
"Watching the Sea" (tr. of Duoduo). [ManhatR] (6:2) Fall 92, p. 6-7.
"Windmill" (tr. of Duoduo). [ManhatR] (6:2) Fall 92, p. 4.
3588. LEE, John B.
"I Liked to Shuck Peas." [Dandel] (19:2) 92, p. 12.

"I Was Raspberry Picking with My Cousins When Puberty Struck." [Dandel] (19:2) 92, p. 11.

3589. LEE, Nancy
"Turret Lathe." [SingHM] (20) 92, p. 55-56.

3590. LEE, Pete
"A Different Tack" (after Lao Tzu). [Plain] (13:1) Fall 92, p. 14.
"Hiking In." [DogRR] (11:2, #22) Fall-Wint 92, p. 16.
"Once Bitten." [CoalC] (5) My 92, p. 4.
"Ravens Are the Smartest." [DogRR] (11:2, #22) Fall-Wint 92, p. 17.
"Riverbank." [ChamLR] (10/11) Spr-Fall 92, p. 16.

3591. LEE, Stellasue
"Escape." [OnTheBus] (4:2/5:1, #10/11) 92, p. 129.
"A Walk Through the Woods on Hood Canal." [OnTheBus] (4:2/5:1, #10/11) 92, p. 130.

3592. LEE, Yay Seok
"Cabbage moths furling." [Amelia] (7:1, #20) 92, p. 7.

3593. LEEDY, David
"Mother and Child" (for Jim Rosen). [Comm] (119:12) 19 Je 92, p. 23.

3594. LEER, Norman
"My Father's Earthquake." [DogRR] (11:2, #22) Fall-Wint 92, p. 48.

3595. LEFCOURT, Peter
"Lust Among the Melons." [HawaiiR] (16:2, #35) Spr 92, p. 64.
"The Rest of My Life." [HawaiiR] (16:2, #35) Spr 92, p. 63.

3596. LEFFLER, Merrill
"Metaphor." [PoetL] (87:1) Spr 92, p. 16.
"Passion." [PoetL] (87:1) Spr 92, p. 17.

3597. LEGAGNEUR, Serge
"Urinaires" (extrait). [Callaloo] (15:3) Sum 92, p. 708-710.
"Urinary" (excerpt, tr. by Carrol F. Coates). [Callaloo] (15:3) Sum 92, p. 705-707.

3598. LeGARDEUR, Lili
"One Theory." [AmerPoR] (21:2) Mr-Ap 92, p. 48.
"Spinsters." [QW] (34) Wint-Spr 92, p. 69.
"What's New?" [AmerPoR] (21:5) S-O 92, p. 29.

3599. LEGGO, Carl
"Anthony's Nose." [AntigR] (90) Sum 92, p. 106-107.
"Diaries." [AntigR] (90) Sum 92, p. 108.
"Diaries." [Dandel] (19:1) 92, p. 10.
"Fuses and Roses." [Dandel] (19:1) 92, p. 9.
"Going Down the Road." [AntigR] (90) Sum 92, p. 105.
"Growing Up Perpendicular on the Side of a Hill." [Grain] (20:3) Fall 92, p. 115 - 118.
"My Grandmother and Knowlton Nash." [CanLit] (134) Aut 92, p. 58-59.
"Where Do Babies Come From?" [Dandel] (19:1) 92, p. 11.

LeGUIN, Ursula K.
See Le GUIN, Ursula K.

3600. LEHBERT, Margitt
"After school with blondes into the basin" (tr. of Rainer Schedlinski). [Shiny] (7/8) 92, p. 143.
"Blue (II)" (tr. of Sabine Techel). [Shiny] (7/8) 92, p. 142.
"Breath Less" (for Klaus Hensel, tr. of Ernest Wichner). [Shiny] (7/8) 92, p. 145.
"Breaths shallow as a meadow" (tr. of Rainer Schedlinski). [Shiny] (7/8) 92, p. 143.
"Like Joyce in Triest" (tr. of Hans-Ullrich Treichel). [Shiny] (7/8) 92, p. 137.
"Luckily II" (tr. of Walter Thümler). [Shiny] (7/8) 92, p. 144.
"Proceedings" (Part I, tr. of Ernest Wichner). [Shiny] (7/8) 92, p. 145-146.
"Prometheus" (tr. of Hans-Ullrich Treichel). [Shiny] (7/8) 92, p. 137.
"Rip Full Moon" (tr. of Sabine Techel). [Shiny] (7/8) 92, p. 142.
"The Roller-Skaters" (tr. of Richard Wagner). [Shiny] (7/8) 92, p. 134.
"Such Green" (tr. of Walter Thümler). [Shiny] (7/8) 92, p. 144.
"Unter den Linden" (tr. of Steffen Mensching). [Shiny] (7/8) 92, p. 136.
"What Is Normal" (tr. of Richard Wagner). [Shiny] (7/8) 92, p. 134-135.
"Without an Echo" (tr. of Steffen Mensching). [Shiny] (7/8) 92, p. 136.

3601. LEHMAN, David
"The Assignment." [BrooklynR] (9) 92, p. 53.
"Dark Passage." [NewRep] (207:20) 9 N 92, p. 48.
"The Drowning." [VirQR] (68:2) Spr 92, p. 306-307.
"First Lines." [AntR] (50:3) Sum 92, p. 508.

"Guilt Trip." [AntR] (50:3) Sum 92, p. 509.
"The Interruption." [WestHR] (46:2) Sum 92, p. 200-201.
"Last Words." [NewRep] (206:15) 13 Ap 92, p. 40.
"Second Thoughts." [VirQR] (68:2) Spr 92, p. 306.
"The Visit." [NewAW] (10) Fall 92, p. 84.
"The Vocalist" (Selection: 2, w. Ron Horning). [DenQ] (26:3) Wint 92, p. 28-29.

3602. LEIDER, Emily W.
"Always This Black-and-White." [ChiR] (38:3) 92, p. 56-57.

3603. LEIGH-LOOHUIZEN, Ria
"Aesthetics" (tr. of Luuk Gruwez). [SouthernR] (28:2) Spr, Ap 92, p. 331.
"Fat People" (tr. of Luuk Gruwez). [SouthernR] (28:2) Spr, Ap 92, p. 330-331.
"Hell under a Skirt" (tr. of Luuk Gruwez). [SouthernR] (28:2) Spr, Ap 92, p. 329.
"Shipwreck" (tr. of Adriaan Morriën). [Trans] (26) Spr 92, p. 97-98.
"Years Later" (tr. of Luuk Gruwez). [SouthernR] (28:2) Spr, Ap 92, p. 332.

3604. LEIPER, Esther M.
"The Forest Feel." [Amelia] (7:1, #20) 92, p. 124.
"Grasping at Straws." [Amelia] (7:1, #20) 92, p. 18.
"Mount Washington Rescue." [Amelia] (7:1, #20) 92, p. 96.
"A Raw Deal." [Amelia] (7:1, #20) 92, p. 18.
"The Wars of Faery" (for C.S. Lewis. Book II, Canto VII-VIII). [Amelia] (6:4, #19) 92, p. 89-98.
"The Wars of Faery" (For C.S. Lewis. Book II, Cantos IX-X). [Amelia] (7:1, #20) 92, p. 99-108.

3605. LELAND, Natasha
"Postcard form Paradise." [HarvardA] (127:1) Fall 92, p. 19.

3606. LELOS, Cynthia
"The Closet." [WormR] (32:4 #128) 92, p. 134-135.
"Dressing Maria." [WormR] (32:4 #128) 92, p. 135-136.
"Untitled: 'You're right my dear,' Carmen said, 'I was once a model.'" [WormR] (32:4 #128) 92, p. 133-134.

LeLYS, Éli
See Le LYS, Éli

3607. LEMMON, Amy
"December Groceries." [CinPR] (23) Wint 91-92, p. 11.
"Feeding a New Void." [ChatR] (12:4) Sum 92, p. 48-49.

LENDECH, René Téllez
See TELLEZ LENDECH, René

3608. LENHART, Michael
"14. The witch rules like Caesar in her chocolate house." [Asylum] (7:3/4) 92, p. 30.

3609. LENIHAN, Dan
"The Home Video." [Bogg] (65) 92, p. 34.

3610. LENNON, Frank
"No More Poems." [PoetC] (23:3) Spr 92, p. 36.

3611. LENNON, Joan
"47 Words for Snow." [Dandel] (19:1) 92, p. 17.
"The Small Grammarian." [Dandel] (19:1) 92, p. 16.

3612. LENTINI, Javier
"La Cenicienta." [Inti] (36) Otoño 92, p. 149-150.
"Petra Pan." [Inti] (36) Otoño 92, p. 151.
"Rompecabezas." [Nuez] (4:12) 92, p. 23.
"The Rothko Chapel." [Nuez] (4:12) 92, p. 23.

3613. LEON, Dave
"An Ortega Chile Sickness." [Pearl] (16) Fall 92, p. 30.
"Whorehouse Document #3 for Julie from Spud Land." [Pearl] (16) Fall 92, p. 30.

3614. LEON, Peter
"A Yellow Flower." [LitR] (35:3) Spr 92, p. 380-382.

3615. LEONHARDT, Kenneth
"Beeing There." [Light] (3) Aut 92, p. 16.
"Butt Talks." [Light] (3) Aut 92, p. 7.
"Gloria in Excelsis Deo Light." [Light] (1) Spr 92, p. 7.
"Letting Fame Go to My 'Ed." [Light] (2) Sum 92, p. 7.
"Love in Bloom." [Light] (4) Wint 92-93, p. 16.
"The More Things Change." [Light] (2) Sum 92, p. 16.
"The Mystique of Miss Teaks." [Light] (1) Spr 92, p. 9.
"Underground Inform-Ants?" [Light] (1) Spr 92, p. 21.
"Untitled: This poem's title is Untitled." [Light] (1) Spr 92, p. 26.

"What Excite Meant." [Light] (4) Wint 92-93, p. 7.
3616. LEPKOWSKI, Frank J.
"Lake Erie Serenade." [SycamoreR] (4:2) Sum 92, p. 18-19.
"Thinking Seriously About Life." [SycamoreR] (4:2) Sum 92, p. 20.
3617. LEPORE, Dominick
"The Day Begins." [Footwork] 92, p. 75.
"Today." [Footwork] 92, p. 75.
3618. LEPSON, Ruth
"For the Dead" (after Adrienne Rich's "For the Dead"). [Agni] (36) 92, p. 170.
"It's about the same amount of pain." [Parting] (5:1) Sum 92, p. 9.
"Why not take pictures of ordinary days, for instance" (For Lisa). [Parting] (5:1) Sum 92, p. 9.
3619. LERCHER, Ruth
"Mouse Head." [OnTheBus] (4:2/5:1, #10/11) 92, p. 131.
3620. LERNER, Laurence
"For Mali." [AmerS] (61:2) Spr 92, p. 256.
3621. LERNER, Linda
"City Rain." [NewYorkQ] (48) 92, p. 68.
"Riding, Subway Natives Riding." [NewYorkQ] (47) 92, p. 50-51.
3622. LERNER, Viviane
"Letting Go." [PoetryUSA] (24) 92, p. 22.
LEROY, Félix Morisseau
See MORISSEAU-LEROY, Félix
3623. LESCOËT, Henri de
"En las Sendas de Mi Huerto" (a Rafael Bordao). [Nuez] (4:12) 92, p. 16.
"Soy el Extranjero." [Nuez] (4:12) 92, p. 16.
3624. LESLIE, Naton
"Mercy." [CimR] (100) Jl 92, p. 117-118.
"Obeah." [SnailPR] (2:1) Spr-Sum 92, p. 22-23.
"Union." [InterPR] (18:1) Spr 92, p. 79-80.
3625. LESSER, Rika
"Black Stones: IX." [Art&Und] (1:2) Wint 92, p. 9.
"Love." [PartR] (59:1) Wint 92, p. 102-103.
"The Other Life." [SouthwR] (77:1) Wint 92, p. 96-100.
3626. LESSING, Karin
"The Year Zero." [Sulfur] (12:2, #31) Fall 92, p. 187-190.
3627. LESTER-MASSMAN, Gordon
"Numbers" (21, 85, 20). [YellowS] (39) Spr-Sum 92, p. 38-41.
3628. LETELIER-RUZ, Elias
"Abandon." [PoetryC] (12:3/4) Jl 92, p. 22.
"The House of Dario." [PoetryC] (12:3/4) Jl 92, p. 22.
"The Statue." [PoetryC] (12:3/4) Jl 92, p. 22.
3629. LETO, D. Nico (Denise Nico)
"It Is This Way for Us." [Footwork] 92, p. 78.
"Mrs. Eliot's Eyes." [Footwork] 92, p. 78.
"My Lover's Mouth." [ChironR] (11:4) Wint 92, p. 41.
"Of All the Blue Expanse." [EvergreenC] (7:2) Sum-Fall 92, p. 21.
"Tonight the Moon." [ChironR] (11:4) Wint 92, p. 41.
3630. LEUNG, Ping-Kwan
"Refurnishing" (tr. by Gordon T. Osing and the author). [CrabCR] (8:1) Sum-Fall 92, p. 19.
LEV, Dina Ben
See BEN-LEV, Dina
3631. LEV, Donald
"Summer Ode." [NewYorkQ] (49) 92, p. 40.
3632. LEVANT, Jonathan
"Half Needing Half Wanting Like a." [ChamLR] (10/11) Spr-Fall 92, p. 121.
3633. LEVASSEUR, Jeanne
"Appetite." [Nimrod] (36:1) Fall-Wint 92, p. 46-47.
"Donkey." [Nimrod] (36:1) Fall-Wint 92, p. 48.
"Moonjumpers" (Honorable Mention, The Pablo Neruda Prize for Poetry). [Nimrod] (36:1) Fall-Wint 92, p. 45.
3634. LEVELOCK, Yann
"I Don't Know Yet" (tr. of Hélène Dorion). [Stand] (33:2) Spr 92, p. 136-139.
3635. LEVENSON, Christopher
"Travelling Light" (for Anne and Michael Hamburger). [Arc] (29) Aut 92, p. 21.

3636. LEVENTHAL, Ann Z.
"Born Once." [GeoR] (46:3) Fall 92, p. 452.
3637. LEVERTOV, Denise
"Against Intrusion." [AmerPoR] (21:4) Jl-Ag 92, p. 39.
"The Composition" (*Woman at the Harpsichord*, by Emmanuel de Witte, 1617-1692, Musée des Beaux Arts, Montréal). [AmerPoR] (21:4) Jl-Ag 92, p. 39.
"Contrasting Gestures." [AmerPoR] (21:4) Jl-Ag 92, p. 40.
"Dream Instruction." [Zyzzyva] (8:3) Fall 92, p. 81-82.
"Idyll." [AmerPoR] (21:4) Jl-Ag 92, p. 40.
"In California During the Gulf War." [AmerPoR] (21:4) Jl-Ag 92, p. 40.
"Joie de Vivre." [AntR] (50:1/2) Wint-Spr 92, p. 193.
"Letter to a Friend." [NewAW] (10) Fall 92, p. 25-26.
"Mysterious Disappearance of May's Past Perfect." [NewAW] (10) Fall 92, p. 24.
"Namings." [AmerPoR] (21:4) Jl-Ag 92, p. 40.
3638. LEVEY, Robin
"The Peace Child." [ManhatPR] (14) [92?], p. 42.
3639. LEVI, Steven C.
"The Wreck of the *Tordenskjold*." [Amelia] (6:4, #19) 92, p. 28-32.
3640. LEVI, Tikva
"Purim Sequence" (tr. by Ammiel Alcalay). [PaintedB] (47) 92, p. 16-25.
3641. LEVI, Toni Mergentime
"Her Last Gift" (On Georgia O'Keeffe). [ManhatPR] (14) [92?], p. 23.
3642. LEVIN, Dana
"The Weatherman." [Ploughs] (18:1) Spr 92, p. 105-106.
3643. LEVIN, Leonid
"At the Crossing" (Chernobyl Poems, tr. of Lyubov Sirota, w. Elisavietta Ritchie). [Calyx] (14:2) Wint 92-93, p. 70-72.
"Burden" (Chernobyl Poems, tr. of Lyubov Sirota, w. Elisavietta Ritchie). [Calyx] (14:2) Wint 92-93, p. 66-67.
"Fate" (Triptych. Chernobyl Poems, tr. of Lyubov Sirota, w. Elisavietta Ritchie). [Calyx] (14:2) Wint 92-93, p. 73-75.
"Radiophobia" (Chernobyl Poems, tr. of Lyubov Sirota, w. Elisavietta Ritchie). [Calyx] (14:2) Wint 92-93, p. 68-69.
"To Pripyat" (Chernobyl Poems, tr. of Lyubov Sirota, w. Elisavietta Ritchie). [Calyx] (14:2) Wint 92-93, p. 64-65.
"Your Glance Will Trip on My Shadow" (Chernobyl Poems, tr. of Lyubov Sirota, w. Elisavietta Ritchie). [Calyx] (14:2) Wint 92-93, p. 63.
"Your glance will trip on my shadow" ("Chernobyl Poems," tr. of Liubov Sirota, w. Elisavietta Ritchie). [NewYorkQ] (48) 92, p. 109.
3644. LEVINE, Anne-Marie
"Brown Study." [Ploughs] (18:4) Wint 92-93, p. 157.
"Novena." [Ploughs] (18:4) Wint 92-93, p. 155-156.
LEVINE, Judy Katz
See KATZ-LEVINE, Judy
3645. LEVINE, Mark
"The Message." [NewYorker] (68:15) 1 Je 92, p. 32.
3646. LEVINE, Miriam
"The Fight." [Noctiluca] (1:1) Spr 92, p. 20.
3647. LEVINE, Philip
"Autumn Begins" (tr. of Antonio Machado, w. José Elgorriago). [NewEngR] (14:4) Fall 92, p. 43.
"Blue and Blue." [Hudson] (45:3) Aut 92, p. 396-398.
"Fields of Soria" (tr. of Antonio Machado, w. José Elgorriago). [NewEngR] (14:4) Fall 92, p. 39-42.
"Francisco, I'll Bring You Red Carnations." [NewEngR] (14:2) Spr 92, p. 17-19.
"Getting There." [Hudson] (45:3) Aut 92, p. 393-395.
"The House So Dear" (tr. of Antonio Machado, w. José Elgorriago). [NewEngR] (14:4) Fall 92, p. 43.
"I Go on Dreaming" (tr. of Antonio Machado, w. José Elgorriago). [NewEngR] (14:4) Fall 92, p. 44.
"In the Center of the Square" (tr. of Antonio Machado, w. José Elgorriago). [NewEngR] (14:4) Fall 92, p. 45.
"In the Dark." [Hudson] (45:3) Aut 92, p. 395-396.
"Letter to the Capitol." [AntR] (50:1/2) Wint-Spr 92, p. 131.
"My Sister's Voice." [NewYorker] (68:17) 15 Je 92, p. 36.
"The Old Testament." [Hudson] (45:3) Aut 92, p. 398-399.

"On the Meeting of Garcia Lorca and Hart Crane." [NewYorker] (68:35) 19 O 92, p. 79.
"The Rebellion of Bread." [QW] (36) Wint 92-93, p. 116.
"This World." [GeoR] (46:3) Fall 92, p. 418.
"The Trade." [GeoR] (46:3) Fall 92, p. 419-420.
"Triage." [NewRep] (205:28/29 [sic, i.e. 206:1/2]) 6-13 Ja 92, p. 40.

3648. LEVINE, Rachel
"Bird Prayer." [AnotherCM] (23) Spr 92, p. 137-139.

3649. LEVINE, Rosalind
"Under Montana Stars." [OnTheBus] (4:2/5:1, #10/11) 92, p. 132-133.

3650. LEVINE, Suzanne Jill
"In This Warm Dark Mosque" (tr. of Coral Bracho). [TriQ] (85) Fall 92, p. 382-384.
"Refracted in Your Life Like an Enigma" (tr. of Coral Bracho). [TriQ] (85) Fall 92, p. 385-386.

3651. LEVINE-KEATING, Helane
"Definition." [Rohwedder] (7) Spr-Sum 92, p. 7.

3652. LEVINSON, James H. (James Heller)
"Epistrophy for T. Monk." [FreeL] (10) Sum 92, p. 22.
"Epistrophy for T. Monk." [SpoonRQ] (17:1/2) Wint-Spr 92, p. 85.
"Red Dress." [ChironR] (11:1) Spr 92, p. 27.
"Remember in the Dark." [SpoonRQ] (17:1/2) Wint-Spr 92, p. 86-88.
"To Fill, to Empty." [SmPd] (29:1, #84) Wint 92, p. 8.
"Tripping." [SmPd] (29:1, #84) Wint 92, p. 9.

3653. LEVIS, Larry
"The Cocoon." [ThRiPo] (39/40) 92-93, p. 143.
"For Zbigniew Herbert, Summer, 1971, Los Angeles." [ThRiPo] (39/40) 92-93, p. 140-141.
"Idle Companion" (for Eric Walker and Abby Wolf). [QW] (36) Wint 92-93, p. 131 - 133.
"Magnolia." [ThRiPo] (39/40) 92-93, p. 141-142.
"Story." [ThRiPo] (39/40) 92-93, p. 143-144.
"Though His Name Is Infinite, My Father Is Asleep." [AntR] (50:1/2) Wint-Spr 92, p. 302-304.

3654. LEVITIN, Alexis
"Animals" (tr. of Eugénio de Andrade). [Trans] (26) Spr 92, p. 90.
"Another Madrigal" (tr. of Eugénio de Andrade). [Os] (34) Spr 92, p. 5.
"Arima" (tr. of Eugénio de Andrade). [TexasR] (13:3/4) Fall-Wint 92, p. 72.
"Dedikation #5" (tr. of Egito Gonçalves). [Agni] (36) 92, p. 132.
"Do Not Ask" (tr. of Eugénio de Andrade). [Os] (34) Spr 92, p. 7.
"Home" (tr. of Eugénio de Andrade). [Trans] (26) Spr 92, p. 22.
"Litany with Your Face" (tr. of Eugénio de Andrade). [InterPR] (18:2) Fall 92, p. 17.
"Madrigal" (tr. of Eugénio de Andrade). [Os] (34) Spr 92, p. 5.
"Peaches" (tr. of Eugénio de Andrade). [Trans] (26) Spr 92, p. 23.
"Solar Matter" (Selections: 28, 37, tr. of Eugénio de Andrade). [SnailPR] (2:1) Spr - Sum 92, p. 20-21.
"Song" (tr. of Eugénio de Andrade). [InterPR] (18:2) Fall 92, p. 15.
"Song Written in the Sands of Laga" (tr. of Eugénio de Andrade). [TexasR] (13:3/4) Fall-Wint 92, p. 73.
"Still on Purity" (tr. of Eugénio de Andrade). [Trans] (26) Spr 92, p. 23.
"To Follow Still Those Signs" (tr. of Eugénio de Andrade). [Trans] (26) Spr 92, p. 22.
"To My Enemies" (tr. of Eugénio de Andrade). [GrahamHR] (16) Fall 92, p. 75.
"Where To" (tr. of Eugénio de Andrade). [GrahamHR] (16) Fall 92, p. 76.

3655. LEVITT, Peter
"Death Miniatures" (Excertps)." [OnTheBus] (4:2/5:1, #10/11) 92, p. 134-135.
"Las Piedras del Cielo (Sky Stones" (Selections: XXX, VI, tr. of Pablo Neruda). [OnTheBus] (4:2/5:1, #10/11) 92, p. 278-279.

3656. LEVY, Andrew
"Babbleology" (2 selections). [NewAW] (10) Fall 92, p. 57-59.
"Fields of Leisure." [Talisman] (8) Spr 92, p. 91-96.

3657. LEVY, Howard
"The Vibrant Archipelagos." [GettyR] (5:4) Aut 92, p. 610-612.

3658. LEVY, Kathryn
"Railroad Crossing." [ManhatPR] (14) [92?], p. 40.

3659. LEVY, Robert (Robert J.)
"Kinship." [GeoR] (46:1) Spr 92, p. 27.
"New Age." [ParisR] (34:122) Spr 92, p. 196.
3660. LEWIS, Adrian
"Because." [Jacaranda] (6:1/2) Wint-Spr 92, p. 82.
3661. LEWIS, Graham
"Lester's Tales." [Epiphany] (3:4) O (Fall) 92, p. 261-262.
"Serpentina Reconsiders." [Epiphany] (3:4) O (Fall) 92, p. 263-265.
"Toby the Half-Boy." [Epiphany] (3:4) O (Fall) 92, p. 266.
3662. LEWIS, J. Patrick
"The Falling." [LaurelR] (26:1) Wint 92, p. 70-71.
"Knowledge, Ltd." [Light] (2) Sum 92, p. 15.
"A Monumental Bore." [Light] (4) Wint 92-93, p. 9.
"Précis on Reaganism." [Light] (1) Spr 92, p. 23.
"A Russian Samovar of Impressive Pedigree." [SpoonRQ] (17:3/4) Sum-Fall 92, p. 26.
"Rust." [ChironR] (11:2) Sum 92, p. 26.
"To the Kiev Station." [LaurelR] (26:1) Wint 92, p. 71.
"Yuppy Love." [Light] (1) Spr 92, p. 14.
3663. LEWIS, Jim
"Sanctuaries." [SouthernR] (28:1) Wint, Ja 92, p. 79-82.
3664. LEWIS, Joel
"Alba." [Contact] (10:62/63/64) Fall 91-Spr 92, p. 46.
"Blue Comedy." [NewAW] (10) Fall 92, p. 68.
"Buying Heaven on Credit" (3 selections). [Talisman] (9) Fall 92, p. 181-182.
"Cold Water Street" (homage to Philip Whalen). [NewAW] (10) Fall 92, p. 69.
"For Lu Yu." [Contact] (10:62/63/64) Fall 91-Spr 92, p. 46.
"Puddles of Wisdom." [NewAW] (10) Fall 92, p. 70.
"Rhapsody Spaniel." [NewYorkQ] (47) 92, p. 52.
3665. LEWIS, Kate
"The Dowry." [OxfordM] (8:2) Fall-Wint 92, p. 19.
3666. LEWIS, Lisa
"Genesis." [PoetryE] (33) Spr 92, p. 78-79.
"Quadriplegics." [PoetryE] (33) Spr 92, p. 83-84.
"The Ride to the Airport." [ArtfulD] (22/23) 92, p. 151-153.
"The Urinating Man." [PoetryE] (33) Spr 92, p. 80-82.
3667. LEWIS, Melvin E.
"Doors 21" (For Charles A. Fullenwider). [Obs] (7:1/2) Spr-Sum 92, p. 100-102.
"Doors 22." [Obs] (7:1/2) Spr-Sum 92, p. 102-104.
3668. LEZAMA LIMA, José
"Thoughts in Havana" (tr. by James Irby). [Sulfur] (12:2, #31) Fall 92, p. 70-79.
3669. LI, He
"Ballad of the Old Jade Hunter at Indigo River" (tr. by Jodi Varon). [ColR] (9:1) Spr-Sum 92, p. 114.
3670. LI, Min Hua (*See also* CREW, Louie)
"Preserved." [OnTheBus] (4:2/5:1, #10/11) 92, p. 114.
3671. LI, Po
"Mounting the Yellow Crane Tower" (in Chinese and English, tr. by Gail Ghai and Tracy Xie). [Epiphany] (3:1) Ja (Wint) 92, p. 28.
"Parched Grasses" (in Chinese and English, tr. by Gail Ghai and Tracy Xie). [Epiphany] (3:1) Ja (Wint) 92, p. 29.
"Quiet Night Thoughts" (in Chinese and English, tr. by Gail Ghai and Tracy Xie). [Epiphany] (3:1) Ja (Wint) 92, p. 30.
3672. LI, Qing-Zhao
"Drinking Joy" (To the Tune of Rumengling, tr. by Gordon T. Osing, Min Xiao - Hong, and Huang Hai-Peng). [CrabCR] (8:1) Sum-Fall 92, p. 18.
"In Praise of Lotus" (To the Tune of Yuanwangsun, tr. by Gordon T. Osing, Min Xiao-Hong, and Huang Hai-Peng). [CrabCR] (8:1) Sum-Fall 92, p. 18.
LIAN, Yang
See YANG, Lian
3673. LIATSOS, Sandra
"At the Cemetery." [CapeR] (27:1) Spr 92, p. 23.
3674. LIBBEY, Elizabeth
"Come Into the Night Grove." [ThRiPo] (39/40) 92-93, p. 145-147.
"Juana Bautista Lucero, Circa 1926, to Her Photographer." [ThRiPo] (39/40) 92-93, p. 147-148.

"Spring And." [ThRiPo] (39/40) 92-93, p. 144-145.

3675. LIDDY, James
"Jack's Sermon for James Mayer." [CreamCR] (16:2) Fall 92, p. 37.
"Richard, Oremus." [CreamCR] (16:2) Fall 92, p. 35-36.

3676. LIEBERMAN, Laurence
"The Ballad of Garfield John" (for Dave Smith). [NewEngR] (14:3) Sum 92, p. 200 - 208.
"Brangwen: Witness from Frankfurt." [SouthernR] (28:2) Spr, Ap 92, p. 238-243.
"Bulwark." [NewEngR] (14:3) Sum 92, p. 197-199.
"Saviour of Assassins." [Nat] (254:4) 3 F 92, p. 139.
"Shirma: Witness from Carriacou." [SouthernR] (28:2) Spr, Ap 92, p. 229-234.
"Stubby Carrot." [SouthernR] (28:2) Spr, Ap 92, p. 235-238.
"Tartine, Strumming Her Opera." [CharR] (18:2) Fall 92, p. 59-60.
"Tartine's Banishment." [SouthwR] (77:2/3) Spr-Sum 92, p. 167-169.

3677. LIEBERMAN, Michael
"I Know This." [HighP] (7:2) Fall 92, p. 64.
"In Her Mind." [Sonora] (22/23) Spr 92, p. 16.
"Listening for Aphrodite." [Sonora] (22/23) Spr 92, p. 17.

3678. LIEBLER, M. L.
"Assassination." [SlipS] (12) 92, p. 55.

3679. LIECHTY, J. (John)
"New Mexico." [BellArk] (8:1) Ja-F 92, p. 7.
"The Room at Rabat." [BellArk] (8:1) Ja-F 92, p. 23.
"Proposal for Life after Death." [BellArk] (8:4) Jl-Ag 92, p. 24.

3680. LIEN, Barbara
"Notes on Count Dracula." [Parting] (5:2) Wint 92-93, p. 34.

3681. LIER, Susan
"Grackles" (Winner, Annual Free Verse Contest, 1991). [AnthNEW] (4) 92, p. 13.
"Walking Bonnevale Road." [PassN] (13:1) Sum 92, p. 3.

3682. LIES, Betty
"Ice Fishing." [US1] (26/27) 92, p. 43.

3683. LIETZ, Robert
"At Railroad and Sugar." [SenR] (22:2) Fall 92, p. 71-72.
"Persephone's First Born in Ohio." [AntR] (50:4) Fall 92, p. 716-717.
"Returning Home." [Blueline] (13) 92, p. 18-19.

3684. LIFSHIN, Lyn
"After Crystal Night." [HampSPR] Wint 92, p. 15.
"Ankle." [WindO] (56) Fall-Wint 92, p. 19-20.
"Another Ratso Rizzo Dream." [ColEng] (54:7) N 92, p. 829.
"Art Dealer Takes Fifth in Murder Trial." [SlipS] (12) 92, p. 34.
"Basil." [MidwQ] (33:4) Sum 92, p. 413.
"Being Jewish in a Small Town." [HampSPR] Wint 92, p. 14.
"Burn Patients Given Life or Death Choice . . . ." [ChironR] (11:2) Sum 92, p. 10.
"Charlie." [ChironR] (11:3) Aut 92, p. 15.
"Coffee Madonna." [WormR] (32:1, #125) 92, p. 16.
"Cover Your Mouth When You Cough." [Parting] (5:1) Sum 92, p. 23-24.
"Daughter of the Mass Murderer." [NewYorkQ] (49) 92, p. 48.
"December Monday." [LullwaterR] (4:1) Fall 92, p. 28.
"Did You Know I Love You." [SouthernPR] (32:1) Spr 92, p. 12-13.
"Dried Red Roses." [Caliban] (11) 92, p. 122.
"Driving Back." [Footwork] 92, p. 15.
"Earl." [Caliban] (11) 92, p. 121-122.
"Even That October." [ChironR] (11:2) Sum 92, p. 10.
"Four Years After Chernoble." [BlackBR] (15) Spr-Sum 92, p. 28.
"Hearing You Say You Know Where Your Blue USA News T Shirt Is." [RagMag] (10:1) 92, p. 15.
"High Blood Pressure Madonna." [WormR] (32:1, #125) 92, p. 16.
"Hollyhocks Near the Pueblo." [ChironR] (11:2) Sum 92, p. 10.
"Hurricane Madonna, 1." [WormR] (32:1, #125) 92, p. 16.
"Hurricane Madonna, 2." [WormR] (32:1, #125) 92, p. 16.
"I Was Four in Dotted." [GreensboroR] (52) Sum 92, p. 134.
"In Downtown Schenectady." [Caliban] (11) 92, p. 124-125.
"It Comes Back." [Parting] (5:1) Sum 92, p. 26.
"It Does Bother Me, the Slut Image." [WormR] (32:1, #125) 92, p. 15.
"It Was Like." [DogRR] (11:2, #22) Fall-Wint 92, p. 29.
"It Was the Edges She Saw." [DogRR] (11:2, #22) Fall-Wint 92, p. 28-29.

"It's Easier, Classical Music." [ColEng] (54:7) N 92, p. 831.
"Jack the Ripper." [CapeR] (27:1) Spr 92, p. 22.
"Jack the Ripper Goes to Price Chopper." [NewYorkQ] (48) 92, p. 54.
"July Dark Enough." [Epoch] (41:2) 92, p. 262-263.
"Kent State, May 1970." [WormR] (32:1, #125) 92, p. 15.
"Let Me Make French Toast For You." [ChironR] (11:2) Sum 92, p. 10.
"The Mad Girl Sees How Women Stay with Lovers Who Beat Them." [NewYorkQ] (47) 92, p. 36.
"The Mad Girl Takes All the Pain." [BlackBR] (15) Spr-Sum 92, p. 28.
"The Mad Girl Walks into the Mirror." [Pearl] (16) Fall 92, p. 14.
"The Mad Girl Wishes She'd Seen He Was." [ChironR] (11:2) Sum 92, p. 10.
"Madonna Loves What He Ways." [WormR] (32:1, #125) 92, p. 16.
"Madonna of the Enablers." [WindO] (56) Fall-Wint 92, p. 20.
"Madonna Who Puts Her Man on a Pedestal." [WormR] (32:1, #125) 92, p. 14.
"Madonna Who's Had It with Him." [WormR] (32:1, #125) 92, p. 16.
"Main Squeeze Madonna." [WormR] (32:1, #125) 92, p. 16.
"My Last Manuscript." [Footwork] 92, p. 15.
"My Mother and the Matches." [SenR] (22:1) Spr 92, p. 64-65.
"My Mother and the Stocks." [WormR] (32:1, #125) 92, p. 15.
"My Mother and the Stove and a Washer, Dryer." [Footwork] 92, p. 15.
"My Mother, Dying." [FreeL] (10) Sum 92, p. 7.
"My Mother, High on Demerol." [OxfordM] (8:2) Fall-Wint 92, p. 26-27.
"My Mother on the Couch." [CreamCR] (16:1) Spr 92, p. 120.
"My Mother Says She Is Glad She Doesn't Remember." [FreeL] (10) Sum 92, p. 6.
"My Mother's Address Book." [NewDeltaR] (9:2) Spr-Sum 92, p. 42.
"My Mother's Wrinkled Skin." [ColEng] (54:7) N 92, p. 832.
"My Uncle Sells the Store." [Blueline] (13) 92, p. 40-41.
"New Hampshire." [MidwQ] (33:4) Sum 92, p. 412.
"Pavorotti and Mehta on TV." [Kalliope] (15:1) 92, p. 43.
"The Pearls." [InterPR] (18:2) Fall 92, p. 74-75.
"Photographs of Mothers and Daughters." [CarolQ] (44:3) Spr-Sum 92, p. 104.
"Photographs of Mothers and Daughters." [Interim] (11:1) Spr-Sum 92, p. 6.
"Plymouth Women." [InterPR] (18:2) Fall 92, p. 76-77.
"Reading Madonna." [WormR] (32:1, #125) 92, p. 16.
"Refrigerator Madonna." [WormR] (32:1, #125) 92, p. 16.
"Rubbing My Mother's Back." [OxfordM] (8:2) Fall-Wint 92, p. 30.
"The She Loved Me Mantra." [RagMag] (10:1) 92, p. 16.
"She Said Reading the Memoirs There's Something About These Women." [Parting] (5:2) Wint 92-93, p. 38.
"Sometimes It Seems Like Before." [CoalC] (5) My 92, p. 12.
"Staying in My Mother's Apartment the First Time Without Her." [Grain] (20:4) Wint 92, p. 96.
"Staying in the Apartment." [FloridaR] (18:1) Spr-Sum 92, p. 108-109.
"Unease." [WormR] (32:1, #125) 92, p. 15.
"Unease" (Two poems). [Amelia] (6:4, #19) 92, p. 49.
"The Visit." [Parting] (5:2) Wint 92-93, p. 25.
"Waitress Madonna." [WormR] (32:1, #125) 92, p. 16.
"Washing My Mother's Hands." [OxfordM] (8:2) Fall-Wint 92, p. 28-29.
"Wearing the White Sneakers, Mama, That Were Too Big." [InterPR] (18:1) Spr 92, p. 81-82.
"When I First Saw Myself in a Mirror." [ChironR] (11:2) Sum 92, p. 14.
"When Someone Is Dying." [Parting] (5:2) Wint 92-93, p. 26.
"When These Hot Nights." [RagMag] (10:1) 92, p. 17.
"With You Lying There on the Other Side of the Bed." [Sun] (196) Mr 92, p. 23.
"The Yarzeit Light." [ColEng] (54:7) N 92, p. 830-831.
"You Take For Granted." [WilliamMR] (30) 92, p. 18-19.
"The Zuni Bracelet Split in Two, the Silver Even Ragged." [Caliban] (11) 92, p. 123.

3685. LIKEN, Lisa
"Wish Upon a Star." [Gypsy] (19) 92, p. 34-35.
"Wish Upon a Star." [Pearl] (16) Fall 92, p. 14.

3686. LILBURN, Tim
"Batchawana Bay." [Quarry] (41:2) Spr 92, p. 58-60.

3687. LILJA, Claes
"Oh Yes, It Hurts" (tr. of Karin Boye). [NewYorkQ] (49) 92, p. 75.

3688. LILLEY, Susan
"County Fair." [FloridaR] (18:2) Fall-Wint 92, p. 32.
3689. LILLY, Rebecca
"Seasonal" (after Charles Wright). [LullwaterR] (4:1) Fall 92, p. 8.
"Snow." [Verse] (8:3/9:1) Wint-Spr 92, p. 117.
"The Wind in the Trees." [Verse] (8:3/9:1) Wint-Spr 92, p. 118.
3690. LIM, Ma. Fatima V.
"Anniversary." [SycamoreR] (4:2) Sum 92, p. 31.
"Luzviminda." [Manoa] (4:1) Spr 92, p. 40-41.
"Sledgehammer." [CumbPR] (11:2) Spr 92, p. 37-38.
"Unheeding the Warnings." [Manoa] (4:1) Spr 92, p. 40.
3691. LIMA, Chely
"Poem in Which I Celebrate" (tr. by AnneMaria Bankay). [LitR] (35:4) Sum 92, p. 451.
"Poema en el Que Celebro." [LitR] (35:4) Sum 92, p. 591.
LIMA, José Lezama
See LEZAMA LIMA, José
3692. LIMAN, Claude
"After His Reading at Chateau Ste. Michelle Winery, William Stafford Drives Home Alone." [CrabCR] (8:1) Sum-Fall 92, p. 9.
"A Dome Car Diptych" (for Richard Hugo). [CrabCR] (8:1) Sum-Fall 92, p. 7-8.
3693. LIN, Tan
"Love, Being, In." [NewAW] (10) Fall 92, p. 77-78.
3694. LINDBERG, Judy
"After Identifying a Body." [HiramPoR] (51/52) Fall 91-Sum 92, p. 46.
"Every Fourth of July." [Northeast] (5:6) Spr 92, p. 14.
"For Dean." [SpoonRQ] (17:1/2) Wint-Spr 92, p. 22-23.
"Observer." [Northeast] (5:6) Spr 92, p. 13.
"On Hatteras Pier." [SouthernPR] (32:1) Spr 92, p. 60.
"On Moving into an Old Farmhouse." [SpoonRQ] (17:1/2) Wint-Spr 92, p. 21.
"Pier Fishing" (Honorable Mention, New Letters Poetry Award). [NewL] (58:2) Wint 92, p. 78-79.
"Two Paintings by Vilhelm Hammershoi." [SpoonRQ] (17:1/2) Wint-Spr 92, p. 24-25.
3695. LINDGARD, Susan
"Shopping." [Amelia] (6:4, #19) 92, p. 59.
3696. LINDGREN, Esten
"Harpoon." [PoetryUSA] (24) 92, p. 33.
3697. LINDGREN, John
"Dialogue with a Corpse." [PoetryNW] (33:1) Spr 92, p. 18-19.
"The Ferns." [Nimrod] (36:1) Fall-Wint 92, p. 120.
"The Fortress." [SewanR] (100:1) Wint 92, p. 63.
"History" (tr. of Juan Gelman). [Vis] (39) 92, p. 14.
"Octopus" (Monterey Bay Aquarium). [NewYorker] (68:23) 27 Jl 92, p. 44.
"The Way It Happens" (tr. of Juan Gelman). [Vis] (39) 92, p. 14.
3698. LINDHOLM, Trish
"Oh Those Curves." [Spitball] (42) Fall 92, p. 2.
3699. LINDNER, April
"Condom." [PraS] (66:3) Fall 92, p. 78-79.
"Inoculation." [PraS] (66:3) Fall 92, p. 80.
3700. LINDNER, Carl
"The Administrator and the Back Burner Stove." [FourQ] (6:2) Fall 92, p. 8.
"The Door." [Poetry] (160:1) Ap 92, p. 2.
"Exercise Bike." [Northeast] (5:7) Wint 92-93, p. 15.
"Finding a Quarter in My Garden." [FloridaR] (18:1) Spr-Sum 92, p. 65.
"Guilt Trip." [LitR] (35:3) Spr 92, p. 359.
"Skin." [LitR] (25:2) Wint 92, p. 276.
"The Warrior: Boundaries." [LitR] (35:3) Spr 92, p. 358.
3701. LINDOW, Sandra
"The Darkness Behind the Door in the Wall." [Kaleid] (25) Sum-Fall 92, p. 56.
"Her Story" (for Michael H. Brown). [Kaleid] (25) Sum-Fall 92, p. 56.
3702. LINDQUIST, Kristen
"Infinity at Otter Creek." [OxfordM] (8:2) Fall-Wint 92, p. 59.
"Sea Voices." [OxfordM] (8:2) Fall-Wint 92, p. 58.
3703. LINDSAY, Frannie
"All of the Chairs Are Monuments." [DenQ] (26:3) Wint 92, p. 34-35.

3704. LINDSAY, Maurice
"Highland Waterfall." [Interim] (11:1) Spr-Sum 92, p. 24.
3705. LINEBARGER, Jim
"Academic Scene." [WormR] (32:1, #125) 92, p. 4.
"Doxology." [WormR] (32:1, #125) 92, p. 5.
"Essay Question." [WormR] (32:1, #125) 92, p. 3-4.
"Experienced Teacher Longs for Halcyon Days." [WormR] (32:1, #125) 92, p. 5.
3706. LINEBERGER, James
"Childhood's End." [PraS] (66:2) Sum 92, p. 81-84.
"I Will Not Let Thee Go, Except Thou Bless Me." [HangL] (61) 92, p. 53-54.
"It Is This Way with Collectors." [HayF] (11) Fall-Wint 92, p. 78.
"Jarrell." [OntR] (37) Fall-Wint 92-93, p. 83-84.
"Nighttown." [RagMag] (10:2) 92, p. 21-24.
"To the Lighthouse, with No Direction Home." [RagMag] (10:2) 92, p. 16-20.
3707. LINEHAN, Susan
"No Seaweed I." [FourQ] (6:2) Fall 92, p. 10.
"Po Valley, 1963." [FourQ] (6:2) Fall 92, p. 9.
3708. LINETT, Deena
"Notes from a Bicycle Trip with Marianne Moore in Rock Springs, Wyoming (April-August 1990)." [NegC] (12:3) 92, p. 98-100.
3709. LING, Greg
"The Farmer Around Dawn." [HiramPoR] (51/52) Fall 91-Sum 92, p. 47.
3710. LINMARK, Rinehardt Z.
"Day I: A Portrait of the Poet, Small-kid Time." [WillowS] (29) Wint 92, p. 35-39.
3711. LINTON, David
"Empty in the Night." [Light] (4) Wint 92-93, p. 8.
"Uncle's Jack." [SoCarR] (24:2) Spr 92, p. 126.
3712. LIOTTA, P. H.
"Epitaph" (tr. of Branko Miljkovic). [Nimrod] (35:2) Spr-Sum 92, p. 62-63.
"In Transylvania" (Brasov, Day of the Dead). [Vis] (39) 92, p. 12.
"Requiem" (Selection: VIII, tr. of Branko Miljkovic). [Nimrod] (35:2) Spr-Sum 92, p. 62-63.
"To Timisoara." [Vis] (39) 92, p. 13.
3713. LIPPMAN, Matthew
"Afternoon in the Jungle Shop." [Iowa] (22:2) Spr-Sum 92, p. 131.
"Children's Book." [Iowa] (22:2) Spr-Sum 92, p. 130.
"Valentine's Day 1991." [SenR] (22:1) Spr 92, p. 67-68.
3714. LIPSITZ, Lou
"Car Fucking Poem" (for Johannes Muntzing). [CarolQ] (44:3) Spr-Sum 92, p. 122 - 123.
"Inner Family." [SouthernPR] (32:2) Fall 92, p. 67-68.
3715. LISHAN, Stuart
"Dreaming the Colony: Six Days." [OnTheBus] (4:2/5:1, #10/11) 92, p. 136.
"Dreaming the Colony: Six Days" (Selection: Day 3). [AntR] (50:3) Sum 92, p. 505.
"Three Soundings of January Snow." [Boulevard] (7:1, #19) Spr 92, p. 62.
3716. LISKER, Roy
"XI." [MinnR] (39) Fall-Wint 92-93, back cover.
LISLE, Charles-René Marie Leconte de
See LECONTE de LISLE, Charles-René Marie
3717. LISOWSKI, Joseph
"Doldrums." [Amelia] (7:1, #20) 92, p. 80.
"In the Green Stream." [Epiphany] (3:1) Ja (Wint) 92, p. 27.
"Mt. Chung-Nan." [Epiphany] (3:1) Ja (Wint) 92, p. 26.
"On the Holy Mountain." [Epiphany] (3:1) Ja (Wint) 92, p. 25.
"Seeing a Friend Off." [Epiphany] (3:1) Ja (Wint) 92, p. 24.
3718. LITT, Iris
"What I Wanted to Say." [Lactuca] (15) Mr 92, p. 18.
3719. LITTAURER, Andrew
"Antipodes." [SewanR] (100:4) Fall 92, p. 553.
"Whitman's Return." [SewanR] (100:4) Fall 92, p. 554.
3720. LITTLE, Geraldine C.
"Flags." [US1] (26/27) 92, p. 32.
"Poem About Heartbreak." [WestHR] (46:3) Fall 92 [i.e. (46:4) Wint 92], p. 421.
3721. LITTLE, Jack
"Bible Story." [Light] (4) Wint 92-93, p. 25.
"Father Unknown." [Light] (4) Wint 92-93, p. 18.

"Natural History Mystery." [Light] (3) Aut 92, p. 18.
"Thrift Shift." [Light] (3) Aut 92, p. 19.

3722. LITTLETON, Mark R.
"Blue." [ChrC] (109:32) 4 N 92, p. 991.

3723. LIU, Newton
"Mountain Stream Spilling from a Dream" (From "The Wild Moon" series, tr. of Tang Yaping, w. Tony Barnstone). [LitR] (35:3) Spr 92, p. 384.

3724. LIU, Timothy
"911." [KenR] (NS 14:2) Spr 92, p. 126.
"Eros Apteros." [WestHR] (46:2) Sum 92, p. 144.
"More Than Half the Leaves Already Down." [SouthwR] (77:2/3) Spr-Sum 92, p. 208.
"On a Hill at Night in a Chair Under Stars." [Caliban] (11) 92, p. 96.
"Patience." [Caliban] (11) 92, p. 96.
"Pornography." [KenR] (NS 14:2) Spr 92, p. 127.
"Sodom and Gomorrah." [Caliban] (11) 92, p. 97.
"The Storm." [WestHR] (46:2) Sum 92, p. 145.
"Walking in a World Where We Are Sometimes Loved." [WestHR] (46:2) Sum 92, p. 146.

3725. LLAURADO, Armando A.
"Consummatus Sum." [Nuez] (4:10/11) 92, p. 21.

3726. LLEWELLYN, C.
"Written by Himself" (After Frederick Douglass). [Nat] (255:20) 14 D 92, p. 751.

LLOSA, Ricardo Pau
See PAU-LLOSA, Ricardo

3727. LLOYD, D. H.
"Crystals." [ChironR] (11:2) Sum 92, p. 29.

3728. LLOYD, Margaret
"What Keeps Me Here." [MinnR] (39) Fall-Wint 92-93, p. 19.
"What She Wants." [MinnR] (39) Fall-Wint 92-93, p. 20.

3729. LOBA
"I reach in slithering wrist." [SinW] (47) Sum-Fall 92, p. 76.

LOCA, La
See La LOCA

3730. LOCKE, Duane
"One Submits to Avoid Disagreeable Consequences." [Gypsy] (19) 92, p. 10.
"Texte de Jouissance 32." [Archae] (4) late 92-early 93, p. 44.
"Texte de Jouissance 33." [Archae] (4) late 92-early 93, p. 43.

3731. LOCKE, Mona M.
"Jersey Cows at Midnight." [NegC] (12:1/2) 92, p. 191.

3732. LOCKLIN, Gerald
"All They Are Saying Is *Give Peace a Chance*." [Pearl] (15) Spr-Sum 92, p. 8.
"And the Gray Matter Per Capita of the Judges?" [WormR] (32:3, #127) 92, p. 119.
"Are We Having a Good Timex Yet?" [WormR] (32:3, #127) 92, p. 121.
"Cats Hate Me Because I Don't Fall for Their Bullshit." [WormR] (32:3, #127) 92, p. 122.
"The Color Is Not Purple." [ChironR] (11:2) Sum 92, p. 6.
"A Different Drummer." [WormR] (32:1, #125) 92, p. 35.
"Dionysus, God of Wine and Poetry." [SlipS] (12) 92, p. 12-13.
"Election '92: Family Values." [WormR] (32:4 #128) 92, p. 170.
"Flirting with Disaster." [WormR] (32:4 #128) 92, p. 169-170.
"Gerald Does Some Serious Self-Flagellation." [WormR] (32:3, #127) 92, p. 122.
"Getting Their Brains Beat Out." [SlipS] (12) 92, p. 11-12.
"I Could Definitely Use One." [Pearl] (15) Spr-Sum 92, p. 9.
"I Should Have Tied a String Around My Elbow." [WormR] (32:1, #125) 92, p. 35.
"An Immortal in the Flesh." [WormR] (32:3, #127) 92, p. 120-121.
"In the Free Blue — Wassily Kandinsky." [ChironR] (11:2) Sum 92, p. 6.
"Just Yesterday, in Fact." [OnTheBus] (4:2/5:1, #10/11) 92, p. 137-138.
"Mending the Agenda." [WormR] (32:3, #127) 92, p. 119.
"My Bedroom at Arles." [Pearl] (15) Spr-Sum 92, p. 8.
"My Wife's Two Toads." [WormR] (32:4 #128) 92, p. 168-169.
"Ogre Roosting." [WormR] (32:3, #127) 92, p. 119.
"Old Nassau's Black Sheep." [WormR] (32:4 #128) 92, p. 168.
"Only in Frisco." [WormR] (32:4 #128) 92, p. 169.
"Paradise Remembered." [WormR] (32:4 #128) 92, p. 170.
"A Red Ribbon Week." [WormR] (32:1, #125) 92, p. 36.

"Slamming the Ol' Size 13 Back Between the Dentures." [WormR] (32:3, #127) 92, p. 119.
"So What Is *Our* Excuse?" [WormR] (32:3, #127) 92, p. 121.
"The Spider's Other Orifice." [Pearl] (15) Spr-Sum 92, p. 9.
"Tat for Tit." [SlipS] (12) 92, p. 11.
"Toadlogic." [WormR] (32:1, #125) 92, p. 35.
"We'll Be Racing to Loot the Joint Savings Account." [Pearl] (16) Fall 92, p. 29.
"What No One Ever Tells the Just-Divorced Husband." [WormR] (32:3, #127) 92, p. 122.
"What the Psychologists Call Self-Expression the Priests Called Self-Abuse." [Pearl] (16) Fall 92, p. 29.
"You Say You've Always Been Above Such Thinking." [ChironR] (11:2) Sum 92, p. 6.

3733. LOCKWOOD, Virginia
"Spring Priorities." [US1] (26/27) 92, p. 32.

3734. LODEIZEN, Hans
"When Shall I Have the Courage" (tr. by James Brockway). [Stand] (33:4) Aut 92, p. 114.

3735. LODEN, Rachel
"Archaeology (As If the Present Mattered)." [MidwQ] (34:1) Aut 92, p. 69-70.
"Blue Car." [YellowS] (41) Fall-Wint 92-93, p. 33.
"Desperate Measures." [GreenMR] (NS 5:2) Spr-Sum 92, p. 84.
"The Killer Instinct." [NewAW] (10) Fall 92, p. 95.
"You Will Enter History." [NewAW] (10) Fall 92, p. 94.

3736. LOGAN, Kelli A.
"Proposal." [HawaiiR] (16:2, #35) Spr 92, p. 62.

3737. LOGAN, Sally
"Confronting Compulsions." [Crucible] (28) Fall 92, p. 24.

3738. LOGAN, William
"Florida in January." [SouthwR] (77:2/3) Spr-Sum 92, p. 264.
"Flower, of Zimbabwe." [Pequod] (33) 92, p. 50.
"Iowa." [NewYorker] (68:35) 19 O 92, p. 120.
"The Lesser Depths." [WestHR] (46:3) Fall 92, p. 219.
"Lux et Veritas." [Pequod] (33) 92, p. 48.
"Marx." [Verse] (9:2) Sum 92, p. 94.
"Masses and Motels." [Pequod] (33) 92, p. 49.
"Miss Lonelyhearts." [SewanR] (100:1) Wint 92, p. 64-65.
"The Presence of Evil in Ancient Texts." [Thrpny] (48) Wint 92, p. 4.
"Weeds." [Nat] (254:12) 30 Mr 92, p. 424.

3739. LOGGHE, Joan
"Sophia's Gone." [Noctiluca] (1:2) Wint 92 [on cover: Wint 93], p. 31.
"The Sugar Orchids." [HayF] (10) Spr-Sum 92, p. 88-89.

3740. LOMKE, Evander
"Two Views in Mexico." [Confr] (50) Fall 92, p. 280-281.

LONERGAN, Janet Gill
See GILL-LONERGAN, Janet

3741. LONG, Barbara Meetze
"Leaving the River." [CapeR] (27:2) Fall 92, p. 48.

3742. LONG, Doughtry 'Doc'
"Stormy Monday." [JlNJPo] (14:1) Spr 92, p. 25.

3743. LONG, Joel
"As We Drove Through Sheridan." [Poem] (67) My 92, p. 70-71.
"The Train." [Poem] (67) My 92, p. 69.

3744. LONG, Laura Marteney
"Speeding through Nebraska." [Kalliope] (15:1) 92, p. 28-29.

3745. LONG, Lisa
"Breaking the Silence." [ChironR] (11:4) Wint 92, p. 24.
"Life Begins Here." [ChironR] (11:4) Wint 92, p. 24.
"Sobriety." [ChironR] (11:4) Wint 92, p. 24.
"Thanksgiving." [ChironR] (11:4) Wint 92, p. 24.

3746. LONG, Priscilla
"Black Diamonds." [CinPR] (23) Wint 91-92, p. 30.
"Woman at 47." [BellR] (15:2) Fall 92, p. 44.

3747. LONG, Richard
"Parade." [NewYorkQ] (47) 92, p. 53.

3748. LONG, Robert (Robert Hill)
"The Beam." [KenR] (NS 14:4) Fall 92, p. 19-20.
"The City." [Poetry] (159:6) Mr 92, p. 321-322.
"Concentrate on the Rake." [GreenMR] (NS 5:2) Spr-Sum 92, p. 61-62.
"Return to Nowheresville." [Poetry] (159:6) Mr 92, p. 320.
3749. LONGACRE, R. Barton
"Anthropology B.S." [SpoonRQ] (17:3/4) Sum-Fall 92, p. 66.
3750. LONGLAND, Jean R.
"Breyten Breytenbach" (tr. of Mário Cesariny). [Stand] (33:4) Aut 92, p. 136-140.
3751. LONGLEY, Judy
"Blue Snow." [SouthernR] (28:4) Aut, O 92, p. 874.
"Outer Banks." [SouthernR] (28:4) Aut, O 92, p. 873.
"Winter Landscape with a Glory of Angels" (after a painting by Brueghel and Rottenhammer — for John). [SouthernPR] (32:1) Spr 92, p. 30.
3752. LONGLEY, Michael
"Autumn Lady's Tresses." [Verse] (9:3) Wint 92, p. 3.
"Couplet." [Verse] (9:3) Wint 92, p. 4.
"Form." [Verse] (9:3) Wint 92, p. 3.
"A Gift of Boxes." [Verse] (9:3) Wint 92, p. 4.
"A Grain of Rice." [Verse] (9:3) Wint 92, p. 4.
"The Ship of the Wind" (after the Dutch). [Verse] (9:3) Wint 92, p. 5.
"A Shiso Leaf." [Verse] (9:3) Wint 92, p. 3.
"The Stone Garden." [Verse] (9:3) Wint 92, p. 4.
LONKHUYZEN, Harold V. van
See Van LONKHUYZEN, Harold V.
3753. LOO, Jeffrey
"A Year Without Sky." [HayF] (11) Fall-Wint 92, p. 92.
LOOHUIZEN, Ria Leigh
See LEIGH-LOOHUIZEN, Ria
3754. LOOKINGBILL, Colleen
"Incognita" (Selection: I). [Avec] (5:1) 92, p. 95-99.
3755. LOOMIS, Jon
"The Epileptic." [OhioR] (48) 92, p. 88-89.
"News from Planet Earth." [OhioR] (48) 92, p. 90.
3756. LOONEY, George
"Fallen from Grace." [OxfordM] (6:2) Fall-Wint 90, p. 34.
"The Language of Angels." [HighP] (7:1) Spr 92, p. 54-61.
"Local Anesthesia." [LitR] (25:2) Wint 92, p. 224-225.
"A Small Space So Filled with Grief" (for June Sylvester). [TarRP] (31:2) Spr 92, p. 18-19.
"The Worst We Can Do." [LitR] (25:2) Wint 92, p. 223.
LOOS, Eileen A. Schrottke
See SCHROTTKE LOOS, Eileen A.
3757. LOOTS, Barbara
"Brother Dog, Sister Cat" (w. Gail White). [Light] (1) Spr 92, p. 13.
3758. LOOTS, Barbara K.
"Shelter" (for Gene). [CapeR] (27:2) Fall 92, p. 3.
3759. LOPES, Damian
"Dull Reflection." [WestCL] (26:1, #7) Spr 92, p. 61.
"Un Pays Bilingual." [WestCL] (26:1, #7) Spr 92, p. 61.
3760. LOPEZ, Danilo
"Norwick." [HayF] (11) Fall-Wint 92, p. 103.
3761. LOPEZ, L. Luis
"Encounter with La Llorona." [Americas] (20:2) Sum 92, p. 60-62.
"For Old Men." [Americas] (20:2) Sum 92, p. 63.
3762. LOPEZ ADORNO, Pedro
"Bodywriting." [Americas] (20:1) Spr 92, p. 45.
"On Becoming Calibans" (for City Island's palmipeds, in loving tribute). [Americas] (20:1) Spr 92, p. 48.
"On Becoming Calibans" (for City Island's palmipeds, in loving tribute). [Callaloo] (15:4) Fall 92, p. 943-944.
"Skirmish." [Americas] (20:1) Spr 92, p. 46.
"Unfinished Journey." [Americas] (20:1) Spr 92, p. 47.
"Voyage." [Callaloo] (15:4) Fall 92, p. 945.
"Within the Mist." [Americas] (20:1) Spr 92, p. 49.

3763. LOPEZ BILBAO, Manuel
"Venturesome Sedition" (tr. of Tino Villanueva). [InterPR] (18:1) Spr 92, p. 37, 39.
3764. LOPEZ FERNANDEZ, Alberto
"LLevan Flores a la Virgen." [Nuez] (4:10/11) 92, p. 4.
LORANT, Laurie Robertson
See ROBERTSON-LORANT, Laurie
LORCA, Federico García
See GARCIA LORCA, Federico
3765. LORD, Ted
"Oh, for the Life of a Window Box" (Christian Cemetery, Rome). [NegC] (12:1/2) 92, p. 80.
"Poem of My Mother's Memory." [PassN] (13:2) Wint 92, p. 19.
3766. LORENZEN, Karl
"An Ear in Each Hand." [NewYorkQ] (47) 92, p. 55.
3767. LORTS, Jack e
"Empty Trees." [EngJ] (80:8) D 91, p. 98.
3768. LOTT, Clarinda Harris
"Rock'n'Roll." [Vis] (39) 92, p. 40.
3769. LOTT, Joyce Greenberg
"Black-Clothed Women" (Dedicated to Janis Gay). [EngJ] (80:6) O 91, p. 102.
3770. LOTT, Rick
"Lullaby for a Child of Water." [Crazy] (42) Spr 92, p. 45-46.
"Monuments." [QW] (35) Sum-Fall 92, p. 106-107.
"My Father Trying Doors." [SoCarR] (25:1) Fall 92, p. 90.
LOTTO, Jeffrey de
See DeLOTTO, Jeffrey
3771. LOTU, Denize
"Vèvè" (in English). [Callaloo] (15:3) Sum 92, p. 641-642.
"Vèvè" (in Haitian Creole). [Callaloo] (15:3) Sum 92, p. 639-640.
3772. LOUDIN, Robert
"Lover's Moon." [NegC] (12:1/2) 92, p. 79.
3773. LOUIS, Adrian C.
"Dust World." [ChironR] (11:2) Sum 92, p. 2.
"Indian Giver." [Caliban] (11) 92, p. 159.
"Indian Giver." [NoDaQ] (60:3) Sum 92, p. 162.
"Tumbleweed Sex Prayer." [ChiR] (37:4) 92, p. 19.
"Verdell's Red-Blooded Blues." [Caliban] (11) 92, p. 158.
"Verdell's View of Crazy Horse." [Caliban] (11) 92, p. 157.
"A Visit to My Mother's Grave." [ChironR] (11:2) Sum 92, p. 2.
3774. LOUIS, Barbra Anna
"Nobody Ever Told Me." [Footwork] 92, p. 101.
LOUIS, Janine Tavernier
See TAVERNIER-LOUIS, Janine
3775. LOURIE, Dick
"Lyric Sonnet." [Noctiluca] (1:1) Spr 92, p. 25.
LOUTARD, Jean-Baptiste Tati
See TATI-LOUTARD, Jean-Baptiste
3776. LOUYS, Pierre
"Hymn to the Night" (from "Epigrammes dans l'Ile de Chypre, la Chanson de Bilitis," tr. by Frederick Lowe). [YellowS] (Ten Years [i.e. 40]) Sum-Fall 92, p. 37.
"Pan's Flute" (from "Bucoliques en Pamphylie, la Chanson de Bilitis," tr. by Frederick Lowe). [YellowS] (Ten Years [i.e. 40]) Sum-Fall 92, p. 36.
3777. LOVELACE, Skyler
"Egyptologist's Morning Stretch." [DenQ] (26:4) Spr 92, p. 43.
3778. LOVELADY, Wendy
"Backyard." [Crucible] (28) Fall 92, p. 59.
3779. LOVELOCK, Yann
"Earth in tare" (tr. of Albert Maquet). [Os] (34) Spr 92, p. 9.
"Polar Season" (Selection: 3). [Os] (35) Fall 92, p. 4.
"Ravels" (tr. of Robert Grafé). [Stand] (33:4) Aut 92, p. 5.
"Stone on stone" (tr. of Albert Maquet). [Os] (34) Spr 92, p. 8.
"Under" (Selection: 4). [Os] (35) Fall 92, p. 5.
"Where is it" (tr. of Albert Maquet). [Os] (34) Spr 92, p. 10.
LOW, Jackson Mac
See Mac LOW, Jackson

3780. LOWE, Frederick
"Hymn to the Night" (from "Epigrammes dans l'Ile de Chypre, la Chanson de Bilitis," tr. of Pierre Louys). [YellowS] (Ten Years [i.e. 40]) Sum-Fall 92, p. 37.
"Pan's Flute" (from "Bucoliques en Pamphylie, la Chanson de Bilitis," tr. of Pierre Louys). [YellowS] (Ten Years [i.e. 40]) Sum-Fall 92, p. 36.
"A Rhapsodic Note." [YellowS] (41) Fall-Wint 92-93, p. 36.
3781. LOWE, Justin
"Hourglass." [Vis] (38) 92, p. 41.
"Waiting." [Vis] (40) 92, p. 34.
3782. LOWE, Zachary
"The Shed." [ChironR] (11:4) Wint 92, p. 28.
"The Suicide Speaks." [ChironR] (11:2) Sum 92, p. 17.
3783. LOWENSTEIN, Robert
"The Best Way to Go." [DogRR] (11:1) Spr-Sum 92, p. 25.
"Surprise." [HiramPoR] (51/52) Fall 91-Sum 92, p. 48.
3784. LOWENTHAL, Bennett
"Eleven Places." [CimR] (100) Jl 92, p. 44-45.
3785. LOWERY, Joanne
"Beautiful Barn Morning." [PacificR] (11) 92-93, p. 62.
"The Booming of Nighthawks." [SoDakR] (30:4) Wint 92, p. 119.
"Crossing to Capernaum." [Comm] (119:2) 31 Ja 92, p. 30.
"Do Not Remove This Tag." [SpoonRQ] (17:3/4) Sum-Fall 92, p. 101.
"Faraway Places." [SmPd] (29:2, #85) Spr 92, p. 20.
"Heart." [PoetL] (87:2) Sum 92, p. 18.
"Metaphor and Wings." [SmPd] (29:2, #85) Spr 92, p. 17.
"Poems Where the Deer Sleep." [WillowS] (30) Sum 92, p. 54-55.
"The Reason a Barn Burns." [SmPd] (29:2, #85) Spr 92, p. 19.
"Sighs." [SmPd] (29:2, #85) Spr 92, p. 18.
"Summer, Illinois, Sometime." [SoDakR] (30:4) Wint 92, p. 120.
"We Meet and Drive to the South Side of Chicago." [SpoonRQ] (17:3/4) Sum-Fall 92, p. 102.
3786. LOWERY, Malcolm
"After Publication of Under the Volcano." [MoodySI] (27) Spr 92, p. 30.
3787. LOWITZ, Leza
"Ah, women" (tr. of Ei Akitsu, w. Akemi Tomioka). [Harp] (285:1706) Jl 92, p. 26.
"A ball of flesh" (tr. of Ei Akitsu, w. Akemi Tomioka). [Harp] (285:1706) Jl 92, p. 26.
"Eros & Thanatos." [Noctiluca] (1:1) Spr 92, p. 42.
"Haiku" (3 poems, tr. of Sonoko Nakamura, w. Miyuki Aoyama). [Noctiluca] (1:2) Wint 92 [on cover: Wint 93], p. 3.
"Leaving my house" (tr. of Ei Akitsu, w. Akemi Tomioka). [Harp] (285:1706) Jl 92, p. 26.
"Sorting out" (tr. of Ei Akitsu, w. Akemi Tomioka). [Harp] (285:1706) Jl 92, p. 26.
"Tokyo: Setsubun." [Noctiluca] (1:1) Spr 92, p. 40-41.
"Why was I given breasts" (tr. of Ei Akitsu, w. Akemi Tomioka). [Harp] (285:1706) Jl 92, p. 26.
3788. LOWMAN, Anthony W.
"Daydreams of a Bloody Grunt." [ChironR] (11:1) Spr 92, p. 24.
3789. LOWY, Stephen
"I Love the Weather." [WestCL] (26:1, #7) Spr 92, p. 44-47.
"Thinking of the 70s." [WestCL] (26:1, #7) Spr 92, p. 48-50.
3790. LOYNAZ, Dulce Maria
"Acuarium." [LitR] (35:4) Sum 92, p. 593.
"Aquarium" (tr. by Betty Wilson, w. Pam Mordecai). [LitR] (35:4) Sum 92, p. 454.
"Compra." [LitR] (35:4) Sum 92, p. 592.
"The Horseman" (tr. by Betty Wilson). [LitR] (35:4) Sum 92, p. 453.
"Imperfect Poem" (tr. by AnneMaria Bankay). [LitR] (35:4) Sum 92, p. 452.
"El Jinete." [LitR] (35:4) Sum 92, p. 592.
"Poema Imperfecto." [LitR] (35:4) Sum 92, p. 591-592.
"Purchase" (tr. by Betty Wilson, w. Pam Mordecai). [LitR] (35:4) Sum 92, p. 453.
3791. LOZYNSKY, Artem
"Indolent yellow." [Amelia] (7:1, #20) 92, p. 109.
3792. LUBIANO, Wahneema
"Acts of Courage." [AfAmRev] (26:2) Sum 92, p. 229-230.
"The Language of Necessity." [AfAmRev] (26:2) Sum 92, p. 230-231.

3793. LUBY, Barry J.
"Island of Childhood" (tr. of Olga Ramirez de Arelano Nolla). [LitR] (35:4) Sum 92, p. 521.
3794. LUCE, Gregory
"Directive." [CimR] (101) O 92, p. 109.
"Night Driving." [CimR] (101) O 92, p. 110.
3795. LUCERO, Anthony
"After the Storm." [ChironR] (11:3) Aut 92, p. 29.
"The Living Party." [ChironR] (11:2) Sum 92, p. 17.
3796. LUCIA, Joe
"Another." [BellR] (15:1) Spr 92, p. 49.
"Going for Beer on the Evening of the First Leaves." [BellR] (15:1) Spr 92, p. 48.
3797. LUCZAK, Raymond
"The Purpose of Astronomy" (for Sam Edwards. Selection from "The Singing Bridge: A National AIDS Poetry Archive"). [Art&Und] (1:1) Fall 91, p. 15.
3798. LUDOWESE, Egon
"The Graceville Poems" (9 poems. Dedicated to Lucy Ludowese). [RagMag] (10:1) 92, p. 35-46.
3799. LUDVIGSON, Susan
"Etiam Peccata." [SouthernPR] (32:2) Fall 92, p. 7-18.
"Gabriel's Story." [MissR] (20:3) Spr 92, p. 100-101.
"Grace." [OhioR] (48) 92, p. 50.
"Innocence." [SouthernR] (28:4) Aut, O 92, p. 876-877.
"Inventing My Parents" (after Edward Hopper's "Nighthawks," 1942). [SouthernR] (28:4) Aut, O 92, p. 875-876.
"The Owl Snake." [MissR] (20:3) Spr 92, p. 102-103.
"The Pal Lunch" (after Edward Hopper's "Nighthawks," 1942). [KenR] (NS 14:3) Sum 92, p. 81-82.
"Rainy Morning in Puivert." [GeoR] (46:1) Spr 92, p. 74-76.
"The Visitation." [AmerV] (26) Spr 92, p. 99.
"What If." [Nat] (255:17) 23 N 92, p. 643.
3800. LUDWIG, Sidura Chaiya
"A Free Fly." Sparks! Writing by High School Students (1:1), a supplement to [PraF] (13:4, #61) Wint 92-93, p. 11.
"Kindling in the Forest." Sparks! Writing by High School Students (1:1), a supplement to [PraF] (13:4, #61) Wint 92-93, p. 12.
3801. LUDWIN, Peter
"The Inheritance." [MidwQ] (34:1) Aut 92, p. 70-73.
3802. LUISI, David
"Terminal Scene." [CapeR] (27:2) Fall 92, p. 44.
3803. LUMSDEN, D. M.
"Shopping." [Vis] (40) 92, p. 20-22.
LUNA ROBLES, Margarita
See ROBLES, Margarita Luna
3804. LUNDAY, Robert
"On Lake Kivu." [NewMyths] (1:2/2:1) 92, p. 121.
"The World Is Mine." [NewMyths] (1:2/2:1) 92, p. 119-120.
3805. LUNDBERG, Carol (Carol Wade)
"Rune." [CumbPR] (12:1) Fall 92, p. 48.
"Under a Thin Film of Ice." [CumbPR] (11:2) Spr 92, p. 39.
3806. LUNDE, David
"In Response to Vice-Magistrate Chang" (tr. of Wang Wei). [HampSPR] Wint 92, p. 11.
"Seeing Yuan Second Off to An Hsi" (tr. of Wang Wei). [HampSPR] Wint 92, p. 11.
3807. LUNDE, Diane
"Womanlaugh." [13thMoon] (10:1/2) 92, p. 49.
3808. LUSCHEI, Glenna
"Galaxy." [Confr] (48/49) Spr-Sum 92, p. 201.
"Unnamed." [Confr] (48/49) Spr-Sum 92, p. 201.
3809. LUSH, Laura
"Barn." [Grain] (20:3) Fall 92, p. 92.
"Broken Heels." [Dandel] (19:1) 92, p. 27.
"Dolly and Rose." [Dandel] (19:1) 92, p. 26.
"The Dry." [Grain] (20:3) Fall 92, p. 92.
"First Born." [Arc] (29) Aut 92, p. 54.

"Fish." [Arc] (29) Aut 92, p. 53.
"For My Mother Ironing." [PoetryC] (12:3/4) Jl 92, p. 44.
"Garden." [Dandel] (19:1) 92, p. 29.
"Hunter." [PoetryC] (12:3/4) Jl 92, p. 44.
"Piano." [PoetryC] (12:3/4) Jl 92, p. 44.
"Pigs." [Grain] (20:3) Fall 92, p. 91.
"Snakes." [Arc] (29) Aut 92, p. 52.
"Softly in German." [Dandel] (19:1) 92, p. 28.
"Winter." [PoetryC] (12:3/4) Jl 92, p. 44.

3810. LUSK, Daniel
"Beholder." [HayF] (11) Fall-Wint 92, p. 61.
"Bird on His Head." [US1] (26/27) 92, p. 38.
"Codes." [HayF] (11) Fall-Wint 92, p. 60.
"Dream of Grinding Corn." [TarRP] (30:2) Spr 91, p. 26-27.
"Drinking the Farm." [CutB] (38) Sum 92, p. 36-37.
"Footprint of the Ballerina." [Vis] (38) 92, p. 23-24.
"North Iowa Pachyderms: A Geography." [LaurelR] (26:1) Wint 92, p. 6-13.
"Visiting the Folks." [NoAmR] (277:1) Ja-F 92, p. 25.

3811. LUTERMAN, Alison
"That Lazy Old Alligator Mr. Time." [Sun] (202) O 92, p. 34-35.

3812. LUX, Thomas
"Amiel's Leg." [ThRiPo] (39/40) 92-93, p. 149-150.
"Autobiographical." [TriQ] (86) Wint 92-93, p. 57-58.
"Barn Fire." [ThRiPo] (39/40) 92-93, p. 151.
"Edgar Allen Poe Meets Sarah Hale (author of 'Mary Had a Little Lamb')." [VirQR] (68:2) Spr 92, p. 299.
"Emily's Mom" (Emily Norcross Dickinson, 1804-1882, mother of Emily Elizabeth Dickinson, 1830-1886). [TriQ] (86) Wint 92-93, p. 54-55.
"Endive." [VirQR] (68:2) Spr 92, p. 300.
"Gold on Mule." [ThRiPo] (39/40) 92-93, p. 150.
"Grim Town in a Steep Valley." [Field] (46) Spr 92, p. 64.
"An Horatian Notion." [TriQ] (86) Wint 92-93, p. 56.
"I Love You Sweatheart." [TriQ] (86) Wint 92-93, p. 53.
"A Large Branch Splintered Off a Tree in a Storm." [Field] (46) Spr 92, p. 65.
"Proscribed." [AmerV] (26) Spr 92, p. 37.
"Shaving the Graveyard." [VirQR] (68:2) Spr 92, p. 298-299.
"Solo Native." [ThRiPo] (39/40) 92-93, p. 148-149.
"Virgule." [Atlantic] (269:1) Ja 92, p. 89.
"Walt Whitman's Brain Dropped on Laboratory Floor" (from "The Drowned River"). [MassR] (23:1) Spr 92, p. 91.

3813. LUZI, Mario
"Mother and Son" (tr. by Ned Condini). [Trans] (26) Spr 92, p. 65.
"Nighttime Washes the Mind" (tr. by Ned Condini). [MidAR] (12:2) 92, p. 23.

3814. LUZZARO, Susan
"Halcyon." [QW] (34) Wint-Spr 92, p. 87-88.

3815. LUZZI, Joyce K.
"Barn for Sale." [LitR] (35:3) Spr 92, p. 376.
"Ready or Not, Columbus." [MidwQ] (34:1) Aut 92, p. 73-74.
"Saturday at the Art Museum." [CumbPR] (11:2) Spr 92, p. 24.

LYFSHIN, Lyn
See LIFSHIN, Lyn

3816. LYKIARD, Alexis
"Persistence of the Species." [SoCoast] (12) Ja 92, p. 55.

3817. LYLE, K. Curtis
"Abide with Me." [Eyeball] (1) 92, p. 3.
"Love Is the Law." [Eyeball] (1) 92, p. 4-5.

3818. LYLES, Peggy Willis
"Haiku" (4 poems). [Northeast] (5:6) Spr 92, p. 10.

3819. LYNCH, Janice
"Left Behind." [GreenMR] (NS 5:2) Spr-Sum 92, p. 42.
"Myth of First Lovers." [GreenMR] (NS 5:2) Spr-Sum 92, p. 43.

3820. LYNCH, John
"Tantalus." [Shen] (42:1) Spr 92, p. 30.

3821. LYNCH, Thomas
"At the Opening of Oak Grove Cemetery Bridge." [Witness] (5:1) 91, p. 136-138.
"Casablanca." [Witness] (5:1) 91, p. 133.

"Custody." [Witness] (5:1) 91, p. 134.
"Grimalkin." [ParisR] (34:122) Spr 92, p. 160-161.
"The Lives of Women." [Witness] (5:1) 91, p. 132.
"A Rhetoric Upon Brother Michael's Rhetoric Upon the Window." [Witness] (5:1) 91, p. 134-135.
"Veni Creator Spiritus." [Witness] (5:1) 91, p. 133.

3822. LYNE, Sandford
"Praise." [VirQR] (68:3) Sum 92, p. 489.

3823. LYNN, Catherine
"The Cleaning People." [SlipS] (12) 92, p. 100-103.
"Credibility." [WormR] (32:1, #125) 92, p. 25-26.
"Ed." [Pearl] (15) Spr-Sum 92, p. 28.
"Full-cycle." [WormR] (32:1, #125) 92, p. 22-23.
"The Life You Save." [WormR] (32:1, #125) 92, p. 29-30.
"Natural Selection." [WormR] (32:1, #125) 92, p. 27-28.
"A Nice Place to Visit, But You Wouldn't Want to Live There." [WormR] (32:1, #125) 92, p. 31-32.
"The Novice." [WormR] (32:1, #125) 92, p. 30-31.
"Outlet." [Gypsy] (18) 92, p. 88-89.
"Prediction." [Pearl] (16) Fall 92, p. 31.
"The Scientific Mind." [WormR] (32:1, #125) 92, p. 32.
"Sometimes Being Manic Is an Asset." [WormR] (32:1, #125) 92, p. 28-29.
"Super Woman." [WormR] (32:1, #125) 92, p. 23-25.
"To Reach the Common Folk." [WormR] (32:1, #125) 92, p. 26-27.
"Why?" [ChironR] (11:3) Aut 92, p. 32.

LYNN, Elizabeth Cook
See COOK-LYNN, Elizabeth

3824. LYNN-ALLYN, Adeline
"River Town." [BellR] (15:2) Fall 92, p. 5.

3825. LYNSKEY, Edward (Edward C.)
"1903: Motor-Flight Across America." [ChatR] (12:4) Sum 92, p. 46.
"The Courtship of Mary Todd Lincoln" (To Mercy Ann Levering, Springfield, December 1840). [ChiR] (38:3) 92, p. 22.
"Mrs. Lincoln's Sack Cloth" (to Elizabeth Keckley, 1868). [ChiR] (38:3) 92, p. 23.
"Ole Jos. Johnston's Waltz." [HampSPR] Wint 92, p. 30.
"The Tree Surgeon's Ladder." [ManhatPR] (14) [92?], p. 20.
"The Tree Surgeon's Mural Painted of Youth." [HampSPR] Wint 92, p. 31.

3826. LYON, Hillary
"Sought, Unsought." [MidwQ] (34:1) Aut 92, p. 74.

3827. LYONS, Kimberly
"Ecru." [BrooklynR] (9) 92, p. 92.
"Garnet." [WestCL] (26:2, #8) Fall 92, p. 58-60.
"Okra." [WestCL] (26:2, #8) Fall 92, p. 61.
"Olives." [WestCL] (26:2, #8) Fall 92, p. 61.
"Rayographs." [WestCL] (26:2, #8) Fall 92, p. 62.

3828. LYONS, Richard
"As Long as We Are Here." [OhioR] (48) 92, p. 48-49.
"The Battle of Carnival & Lent." [AmerV] (26) Spr 92, p. 107-109.

3829. LYONS, Robert
"Camping Out." [BellArk] (8:6) N-D 92, p. 20.
"A Walk in the Woods." [BellArk] (8:6) N-D 92, p. 20.

LYS, Éli le
See Le LYS, Éli

3830. LYSENKO, Myron
"Easily Pleased." [WormR] (32:1, #125) 92, p. 5.
"Lost & Found." [WormR] (32:1, #125) 92, p. 5.
"The Peril of Take-Away." [WormR] (32:1, #125) 92, p. 6.
"Typewriter in Control." [WormR] (32:1, #125) 92, p. 6.

3831. LYTHGOE, Michael H.
"Fighter Pilot in Firefly Night." [Elf] (2:2) Sum 92, p. 28.
"The Sounds of Geese in Vietnam." [LullwaterR] (3:3) Sum 92, p. 20.
"Summer Sits as a Foreigner Dressed for the Wrong Season." [LullwaterR] (3:3) Sum 92, p. 10-11.

3832. LYTLE, Leslie
"A Call for It." [LitR] (35:3) Spr 92, p. 324.

Mac . . .
See also names beginning with Mc . . .
3833. Mac LOW, Jackson
"100-Line Poem" (for Gino Di Maggio). [Avec] (5:1) 92, p. 132-134.
"Ancients" (for Annie). [Sulfur] (12:2, #31) Fall 92, p. 163-165.
"Carcinogen." [WestCL] (26:2, #8) Fall 92, p. 65-68.
"Coelentertain Megalomaniasis." [Avec] (5:1) 92, p. 129.
"A Curious Occasion" (a poem for John Cage after his 79th birthday). [Sulfur] (12:2, #31) Fall 92, p. 162-163.
"Forties" (9). [Talisman] (9) Fall 92, p. 115-116.
"Forties" (Four Poems). [Shiny] (7/8) 92, p. 53-60.
"Giant Philosophical Otters." [WestCL] (26:2, #8) Fall 92, p. 63-64.
"Hop Tempestuous" (a poem for Mei-mei Berssenbrugge). [Talisman] (9) Fall 92, p. 117-118.
"Interred Stirps." [Avec] (5:1) 92, p. 131.
"Panchatantra Quest." [Avec] (5:1) 92, p. 130.
"Rebus Effort Remove Government" (a poem for John Cage's 79th birthday). [Talisman] (8) Spr 92, p. 10.
"Retreated Degree." [Avec] (5:1) 92, p. 129.
3834. MacBETH, George
"The Stepfather." [Stand] (33:2) Spr 92, p. 8.
3835. MacBRYDE, Brendon
"Here." [WilliamMR] (30) 92, p. 56.
"Love Poem." [WilliamMR] (30) 92, p. 7.
"Women, When Expressing Sincere." [LullwaterR] (3:2) Spr 92, p. 72.
3836. MacCORMAIC, Eoghan
"Acquaintance Renewed." [SenR] (22:1) Spr 92, p. 88.
"A Good Visit." [SenR] (22:1) Spr 92, p. 87.
"Multitone Monotone." [SenR] (22:1) Spr 92, p. 86.
"No News, Good News." [SenR] (22:1) Spr 92, p. 89.
"Point Number Three." [SenR] (22:1) Spr 92, p. 84.
"A Reflection Across the Yard." [SenR] (22:1) Spr 92, p. 85.
3837. MacDIARMID, Hugh
"In the Slums of Glasgow." [PoetryUSA] (24) 92, p. 11.
3838. MacDONALD, C. G.
"The Makings." [PoetL] (87:3) Fall 92, p. 36.
"Phillip Larkin." [SoDakR] (30:4) Wint 92, p. 60.
"Riddles from the Postmodern." [PoetL] (87:3) Fall 92, p. 37.
3839. MacDONALD, Walter
"Leaving the Middle Years." [CarolQ] (44:3) Spr-Sum 92, p. 31.
3840. MacDONNELL, Justin
"Blood on Snow." [Footwork] 92, p. 133.
"Grand." [Footwork] 92, p. 133.
"Tides." [Footwork] 92, p. 133.
3841. MacFADYEN, Janet
"The Expanding Universe." [MalR] (98) Spr 92, p. 92.
"The Sleeping Gypsy." [MalR] (98) Spr 92, p. 91.
3842. MacGREGOR, Terri (Terry)
"Morality Is Visceral." [Nimrod] (36:1) Fall-Wint 92, p. 121.
"Polyopia." [LaurelR] (26:2) Sum 92, p. 20.
"Present Sense." [Nimrod] (36:1) Fall-Wint 92, p. 122.
"The Starry Night." [LaurelR] (26:2) Sum 92, p. 21.
3843. MacGUIRE, James P.
"End of the Year: NYC." [ManhatPR] (14) [92?], p. 49.
3844. MACH, Jean
"Giuseppe." [SlipS] (12) 92, p. 75-77.
3845. MACHADO, Antonio
"Autumn Begins" (tr. by José Elgorriago and Philip Levine). [NewEngR] (14:4) Fall 92, p. 43.
"Fields of Soria" (tr. by José Elgorriago and Philip Levine). [NewEngR] (14:4) Fall 92, p. 39-42.
"The House So Dear" (tr. by José Elgorriago and Philip Levine). [NewEngR] (14:4) Fall 92, p. 43.
"I Go on Dreaming" (tr. by José Elgorriago and Philip Levine). [NewEngR] (14:4) Fall 92, p. 44.

"In the Center of the Square" (tr. by José Elgorriago and Philip Levine). [NewEngR] (14:4) Fall 92, p. 45.

3846. MACHADO, Gladys
"Cuentas Claras" (4 selections). [Luz] (2) S 92, p. 7-12.
"Ourselves" (tr. by Veronica Miranda). [Luz] (2) S 92, p. 9.
"Ven Federiquito." [Luz] (2) S 92, p. 45-46.

3847. MACHAN, Katharyn Howd
"Adultery." [WestB] (30) 92, p. 109.
"At the Abortion Clinic" (For my daughter Nora). [US1] (26/27) 92, p. 31.
"Closing Your Eyes." [Footwork] 92, p. 18.
"Evening Silk." [Footwork] 92, p. 18.
"In the Place Where War Begins." [Footwork] 92, p. 18.
"Negative." [Gypsy] (18) 92, p. 79-80.
"Playing at Forever." [Footwork] 92, p. 18.
"Teaching." [SlipS] (12) 92, p. 24.
"Touch." [ArtfulD] (22/23) 92, p. 149.

3848. MACIAS, Elva
"For Aries" (tr. by Cynthia Steele). [TriQ] (85) Fall 92, p. 115.
"On Capricorn" (tr. by Cynthia Steele). [TriQ] (85) Fall 92, p. 113-114.
"Open House" (to Roger Brindis, tr. by Cynthia Steele). [TriQ] (85) Fall 92, p. 116.
"Tulijá River" (tr. by Cynthia Steele). [TriQ] (85) Fall 92, p. 117.

3849. MacINNES, Judi
"Finch." [CapilR] (2:9) Fall 92, p. 92-96.
"Form Single Line." [CapilR] (2:9) Fall 92, p. 84-91.
"Wide Open Legs in Onion Sheets." [CapilR] (2:9) Fall 92, p. 83.

3850. MacINNES, Mairi
"Ten at Night." [Stand] (33:2) Spr 92, p. 9.

3851. MACIOCI, R. Nikolas
"Cafes of Childhood." [Pearl] (15) Spr-Sum 92, p. 53.
"Clay Crocodile." [SoCoast] (12) Ja 92, p. 27.
"A Good Kill." [Plain] (12:3) Spr 92, p. 17.

3852. MacKAY-BROOK, Kimball
"Seeing Art on 'A Day Without Art'." [Journal] (16:2) Fall-Wint 92, p. 17-20.

3853. MacKAYE, Katherine
"October Seventh" (For Jeff G. Selection from "The Singing Bridge: A National AIDS Poetry Archive"). [Art&Und] (1:2) Wint 92, p. 17.

3854. MacKENZIE, Ginny
"Academic Dreamlife." [ArtfulD] (22/23) 92, p. 16-17.
"After the Air-Raid" (tr. of Gu Cheng, w. Wei Guo). [ArtfulD] (22/23) 92, p. 20.
"Dream Garden" (tr. of Gu Cheng, w. Wei Guo). [ArtfulD] (22/23) 92, p. 19.
"The Green Window" (tr. of Gu Cheng, w. Wei Guo). [ArtfulD] (22/23) 92, p. 18.
"Undercover" (tr. of Gu Cheng, w. Wei Guo). [Pequod] (34) 92, p. 124.
"What Is There" (tr. of Shu Ting, w. Wei Guo). [Pequod] (34) 92, p. 122-123.
"When the Dog Wakes Up." [LitR] (35:3) Spr 92, p. 312-313.

3855. MacKENZIE, John
"Lust Poem." [PraF] (13:4, #61) Wint 92-93, p. 63.
"The Sequential Moon." [PraF] (13:4, #61) Wint 92-93, p. 62.
"Tote 'em" (for Watson Lake, YT). [PraF] (13:4, #61) Wint 92-93, p. 61.

3856. MacKENZIE, Rob
"Off Ardglas." [Verse] (8:3/9:1) Wint-Spr 92, p. 101.

3857. MACKEY, Mary
"Wrestling with Angels." [YellowS] (Ten Years [i.e. 40]) Sum-Fall 92, p. 15.

3858. MacKINNON, Brian
"By the Eternal Waters." [PraF] (13:4, #61) Wint 92-93, p. 64.

3859. MacKINNON, Margaret
"Border Storm." [QW] (34) Wint-Spr 92, p. 72-73.
"Gingko Leaves." [HayF] (11) Fall-Wint 92, p. 93.
"Insect Singers." [QW] (34) Wint-Spr 92, p. 74.

3860. MACKLIN, Elizabeth
"Billboard" (tr. of Alexis Gomez Rosa). [Nimrod] (36:1) Fall-Wint 92, p. 76.
"Fall Back." [NewYorker] (68:38) 9 N 92, p. 92.
"Great Distance Between Two Walls" (tr. of Alexis Gomez Rosa). [Nimrod] (36:1) Fall-Wint 92, p. 77.
"The Lazy Girl Was Never Scolded." [NewYorker] (68:31) 21 S 92, p. 36.
"The Nearsighted." [NewYorker] (67:47) 13 Ja 92, p. 28-29.
"The Season." [NewYorker] (68:14) 25 My 92, p. 42.

"Two Bear." [Thrpny] (48) Wint 92, p. 16.
"The Watches." [NewYorker] (68:4) 16 Mr 92, p. 46-47.

3861. MacLEAN, Pam Calabrese
"Fat Kid." [AntigR] (90) Sum 92, p. 126.
"My Father." [AntigR] (90) Sum 92, p. 127.

3862. MacLEOD, Sue
"Who Is She?" [AntigR] (89) Spr 92, p. 47-48.

MacLOW, Jackson
See Mac LOW, Jackson

3863. MacMANUS, Mariquita
"Sunday Afternoon." [PoetL] (87:4) Wint 92-93, p. 19.

3864. MacNEACAIL, Aonghas
"A Dream in Poznan." [Stand] (33:4) Aut 92, p. 142.

3865. MacPHERSON, Jennifer B.
"Naming." [Kalliope] (14:1) 92, p. 71.

3866. MacPHERSON, Mary
"Judgement." [Vis] (40) 92, p. 43.

3867. MacPHERSON, Sandra
"Women and Vision." [KenR] (NS 14:3) Sum 92, p. 154-156.

3868. MACRAE, Douglas
"Photographs: A Statement." [Dandel] (19:3) 92, p. 31.

3869. MADARIAGA, Marcela
"Cuando las hojas trazan." [Nuez] (4:10/11) 92, p. 7.

3870. MADDEN, Mary Kay
"My Tits." [Kalliope] (14:3) 92, p. 38.

3871. MADDOX, Marjorie
"After Learning of Our Own Deaths." [PaintedB] (47) 92, p. 43.
"Almanac." [CapeR] (27:1) Spr 92, p. 5.
"Aqueous / Vitreous." [CapeR] (27:1) Spr 92, p. 4.
"Just When I Think I Am Comfortable, the Doorbell Rings." [CutB] (37) Wint 92, p. 22-23.
"The Minister Preaches His Wife's Funeral at Night." [PaintedB] (47) 92, p. 44.
"Premonition and Light." [PaintedB] (47) 92, p. 42.

3872. MADDUX, Carolyn
"Cache Valley Wedding" (for Steve and Karen). [BellArk] (8:6) N-D 92, p. 3.
"Grove Street Locusts." [BellArk] (8:1) Ja-F 92, p. 11.
"I Walked Out in an April Morning." [BellArk] (8:3) My-Je 92, p. 25.
"Married." [BellArk] (8:4) Jl-Ag 92, p. 25.
"El Nino." [BellArk] (8:5) S-O 92, p. 1.
"Saving Your Poems" (for K. W.). [BellArk] (8:3) My-Je 92, p. 25.
"Whalewatching." [BellArk] (8:3) My-Je 92, p. 25.
"Wishkah." [BellArk] (8:4) Jl-Ag 92, p. 25.
"Words for an Apple." [BellArk] (8:2) Mr-Ap 92, p. 14.

3873. MADIGAN, Rick
"Straight into Darkness." [NoAmR] (277:5) S-O 92, p. 5.

3874. MADONICK, Michael David
"The Sardine Can." [NewEngR] (14:3) Sum 92, p. 47.
"Settled In." [NewEngR] (14:3) Sum 92, p. 48-49.

3875. MADSEN, Janet
"The Room of Falling Maps" (for my brother). [Quarry] (41:4) Fall 92, p. 51-53.
"Seeking Asylum." [Quarry] (41:4) Fall 92, p. 54-55.

3876. MADSON, Arthur
"Left Hand." [Crucible] (28) Fall 92, p. 49.

3877. MADUEÑO, Amalio
"Agua." [Americas] (20:2) Sum 92, p. 37.
"Agua." [PraS] (66:2) Sum 92, p. 47.
"Alambristas." [Americas] (20:2) Sum 92, p. 42.
"Alambristas." [Americas] (20:3/4) Fall-Wint 92, p. 255.
"Arroyo." [Americas] (20:2) Sum 92, p. 44.
"The Bato Prepares for Winter." [Americas] (20:2) Sum 92, p. 45.
"The Bato Prepares for Winter." [Americas] (20:3/4) Fall-Wint 92, p. 256.
"Border Crossing." [Americas] (20:2) Sum 92, p. 36.
"Chimayo." [PraS] (66:2) Sum 92, p. 48.
"Tio Nico." [Americas] (20:2) Sum 92, p. 38-41.
"Where is L.A." [Americas] (20:2) Sum 92, p. 43.
"Where Is L.A." [PraS] (66:2) Sum 92, p. 45-46.

3878. MAEHWA
"My Thoughts of Him" (tr. by Constantine Contogenis and Wolhee Choe). [Pequod] (34) 92, p. 117.
3879. MAGEE, John
"Trench Veteran." [CapeR] (27:1) Spr 92, p. 27.
3880. MAGEE, Kevin
"Caytive Tongue" (Excerpts). [Talisman] (8) Spr 92, p. 130-132.
"Happy Face" (Selection: 1). [DenQ] (27:1) Sum 92, p. 126-129.
3881. MAGELLAN, Martha Elizabeth
"Somebody Husband." [LindLM] (11:3) S 92, p. 10.
MAGGIO, Jill di
See DIMAGGIO, Jill
3882. MAGGIO, Mike
"Killing a Jew." [BlackBR] (16) Wint-Spr 92-93, p. 35.
3883. MAGIERA, Mark
"The Ice Cream Man." [Amelia] (7:1, #20) 92, p. 83.
"Save the Barking Dog." [Amelia] (7:1, #20) 92, p. 83.
3884. MAGINNES, Al
"Fairy Rings." [GeoR] (46:2) Sum 92, p. 344.
"Jobs." [Poetry] (160:3) Je 92, p. 145-146.
"Koufax." [Pembroke] (24) 92, p. 94.
"Lake." [SouthernPR] (32:1) Spr 92, p. 61-63.
"A Light for the Spider." [NegC] (12:1/2) 92, p. 83-84.
"Playing Catch." [LouisL] (9:1) Spr 92, p. 80-81.
"The World Drowning." [TarRP] (31:2) Spr 92, p. 13.
3885. MAGORIAN, James
"Borderland." [MidwQ] (34:1) Aut 92, p. 75.
"My Father's Clock." [ChironR] (11:3) Aut 92, p. 27.
3886. MAHAPATRA, Anuradha
"About My Little Sister" (tr. by Paramita Banerjee and Carolyne Wright). [KenR] (NS 14:2) Spr 92, p. 75.
"Cow and Grandmother" (tr. by Paramita Banerjee and Carolyne Wright). [KenR] (NS 14:2) Spr 92, p. 75-76.
"Household Snake" (tr. by Jyotirmoy Datta and Carolyne Wright). [KenR] (NS 14:2) Spr 92, p. 76-77.
"A Little Folktale" (tr. by Paramita Banerjee and Carolyne Wright). [KenR] (NS 14:2) Spr 92, p. 74.
3887. MAHAPATRA, Jayanta
"Bone of Time." [ChiR] (38:1/2) 92, p. 77.
"The Hollow Mouth." [RiverS] (36) 92, p. 61.
"Possessions." [KenR] (NS 14:2) Spr 92, p. 158-159.
"The Shadow of Day." [SewanR] (100:2) Spr 92, p. 273.
"Sickles." [KenR] (NS 14:2) Spr 92, p. 157.
"Wandering into Each Other." [SewanR] (100:2) Spr 92, p. 272.
3888. MAHAPATRA, Sitakanta
"Winter Morning, Mist" (tr. by B. K. Das). [ChiR] (38:1/2) 92, p. 73.
3889. MAHON, Derek
"Dawn at St. Patrick's." [AmerPoR] (21:4) Jl-Ag 92, p. 14.
"Night Drive" (tr. of Rainer Maria Rilke). [Trans] (26) Spr 92, p. 21.
"The Yaddo Letter" (for Rory and Katie). [AmerPoR] (21:4) Jl-Ag 92, p. 15-16.
3890. MAHON, Jeanne
"Dark Lady." [WestB] (30) 92, p. 86.
"When God Finally Appeared." [WestB] (30) 92, p. 85.
3891. MAHON, Robert Lee
"Icarus Falls on I-44." [WebR] (16) Fall 92, p. 108.
"The Specialist." [Comm] (119:6) 27 Mr 92, p. 23.
3892. MAHONEY, Lisa
"Noon Recess." [FloridaR] (18:2) Fall-Wint 92, p. 111.
3893. MAHONEY, MaryJo
"Our Bodies, Ourselves." [Nat] (254:8) 2 Mr 92, p. 283.
3894. MAIER, Carol
"Angel Dust" (2 selections, tr. of Carlota Caulfield). [Luz] (2) S 92, p. 20-24.
3895. MAILMAN, Douglas
"Home Pond." [Amelia] (6:4, #19) 92, p. 15.
3896. MAINHARD, Hermine
"April 11, 1989." [Sonora] (22/23) Spr 92, p. 98.

"Web." [Sonora] (22/23) Spr 92, p. 97.

3897. MAIO, Samuel
"Dream Life." [SoDakR] (30:4) Wint 92, p. 63-65.
"From the Notebooks of Count Galeazzo Ciano" (October 1942). [CharR] (18:2) Fall 92, p. 70.
"In Memoriam." [CharR] (18:2) Fall 92, p. 72.
"Making Connections: Since the Close of the Allen Mine." [SoDakR] (30:4) Wint 92, p. 61-62.
"Nude." [CharR] (18:2) Fall 92, p. 71-72.

3898. MAJ, Bronislaw
"At Night" (tr. by Daniel Bourne). [Salm] (93) Wint 92, p. 187.
"No one will ever claim the age we live in" (tr. by Daniel Bourne). [GrahamHR] (16) Fall 92, p. 81.
"Probably he can only see" (tr. by Daniel Bourne). [GrahamHR] (16) Fall 92, p. 80.

3899. MAJOR, Alice
"Aubade." [PoetryC] (13:1) N 92, p. 16.
"Intimations of Mortality." [PoetryC] (13:1) N 92, p. 16.
"Safe Keeping." [PoetryC] (13:1) N 92, p. 16.
"We Were Young Together." [PoetryC] (13:1) N 92, p. 16.

3900. MAJOR, Clarence
"Chelsea Snow as a Plot Against Humanity." [NewMyths] (1:2/2:1) 92, p. 130.
"Fix." [NewMyths] (1:2/2:1) 92, p. 129.
"Honey Dripper" (Lexington, Georgia, 1902). [MichQR] (31:2) Spr 92, p. 244.
"Perspective on Noise." [NewMyths] (1:2/2:1) 92, p. 131.
"Present Tense." [Epoch] (41:2) 92, p. 260.

3901. MAKEEVER, Ann T.
"Behold." [Caliban] (11) 92, p. 141.

3902. MAKOFSKE, Mary
"After the Cold War." [PoetC] (23:3) Spr 92, p. 9.
"The Facts." [PoetC] (23:3) Spr 92, p. 8.

3903. MAKSIMOVIC, Desanka
"For Those Who Trip Over the Doorstep" (tr. by Nina Zivancevic). [Talisman] (8) Spr 92, p. 145.

3904. MAKUCK, Peter
"Day of the Warbler" (for Ron Hoag). [CimR] (98) Ja 92, p. 80-81.

3905. MALCOLM, Bruce
"Beggars Changing Places." [PassN] (13:2) Wint 92, p. 5.
"In the Arms of Mercy." [PassN] (13:2) Wint 92, p. 5.
"Lilith." [DenQ] (26:4) Spr 92, p. 44-45.
"One Good Window." [AmerPoR] (21:2) Mr-Ap 92, p. 21.

3906. MALDONADO, Jesús María
"Hay Compadres" (Para mi compadre, Alvaro Tijerina de Toppenish, Washington). [BilingR] (17:2) My-Ag 92, p. 164.
"Ines Perez, el Little General de Corpus." [BilingR] (17:2) My-Ag 92, p. 162-163.

3907. MALDONADO-REYES, Vilma
"Sunday Papers" (Selection: #34). [Callaloo] (15:4) Fall 92, p. 963.

3908. MALI, Taylor McDowell
"I Wash Dishes." [TampaR] (5) Fall 92, p. 24.

3909. MALINOWITZ, Michael
"L.A. Is" (for M.A.L.S.). [Boulevard] (7:1, #19) Spr 92, p. 191.

3910. MALONE, Jacquelyn
"Four Seasons of Summer." [SycamoreR] (4:1) Wint 92, p. 34-36.
"Saxophone in Summer." [SycamoreR] (4:1) Wint 92, p. 33.
"Time and the Tight Wire Walker" (Third Prize, Robert Penn Warren Poetry Prize). [CumbPR] (12:1) Fall 92, p. 9.

3911. MALONE, Joe L.
"Avacelette Fox." [Hellas] (3:1) Spr 92, p. 19.

3912. MALPEZZI, Frances M.
"Kalypso's Aubade." [NegC] (12:1/2) 92, p. 100.

3913. MAMET, David
"Hotel Atlantic." [GrandS] (11:1, #41) 92, p. 145-147.

3914. MANCHESTER, Susan A.
"I Haven't Seen Your Mother in Five Years." [NegC] (12:1/2) 92, p. 85-86.
"My Mother's Voices." [GeoR] (46:1) Spr 92, p. 28.

3915. MANDEL, Charlotte
"Birthday Chorus." [US1] (26/27) 92, p. 47.

"The Children's Science Museum." [Footwork] 92, p. 60.
"Painting the Sea." [Footwork] 92, p. 60.
"Turnover Begins in Room 10." [Footwork] 92, p. 60.
"Walking on Sand." [Footwork] 92, p. 60.

3916. MANDEL, Peter
"The Desk-Maker." [PoetryNW] (33:1) Spr 92, p. 15-16.
"The Farmer and His Wife." [PoetryNW] (33:1) Spr 92, p. 14-15.
"The Night Laundry." [PoetryNW] (33:1) Spr 92, p. 16.

3917. MANDEL, Tom
"The Cave." [Talisman] (9) Fall 92, p. 82-97.
"Does He Know?" [Avec] (5:1) 92, p. 93.
"Semahot." [Avec] (5:1) 92, p. 94.

3918. MANDELL, Chris
"Thin Hope." [Kalliope] (14:3) 92, p. 68.

3919. MANDRAKE, Jill
"The Alligator People." [Event] (21:1) Spr 92, p. 83.
"Brenda M." [Event] (21:1) Spr 92, p. 84.

3920. MANER, John
"Witching Season." [MidAR] (12:2) 92, p. 47.

3921. MANERA, Matthew
"Taking Leave." [CanLit] (134) Aut 92, p. 8.

3922. MANESIOTIS, Joy
"The Lesson." [PraS] (66:3) Fall 92, p. 111.
"Molly." [PraS] (66:3) Fall 92, p. 110.
"On Your Birthday, Four Months After Your Death." [Thrpny] (49) Spr 92, p. 14.

3923. MANGAN, Kathy
"Inscription in an 1896 Edition of Shakespeare's Sonnets." [MissR] (20:3) Spr 92, p. 111.
"Making the Fire, Thinking of My Father" (Ireland). [Shen] (42:2) Sum 92, p. 62 - 63.
"Suspended Moments at the State Park" (for JTW). [Shen] (42:2) Sum 92, p. 61.

3924. MANGAN, Pat
"The Bear." [Iowa] (22:1) Wint 92, p. 181-182.
"Dandelions." [Iowa] (22:1) Wint 92, p. 182.
"The Harness." [Iowa] (22:1) Wint 92, p. 181.

3925. MANGLITZ, Lawrence W.
"A Stray Slide from Ibiza, 1962." [JamesWR] (9:2) Wint 92, p. 16.

3926. MANKIEWICZ, Angela C. (Angela Consolo)
"The Poet's Quest" (or, Silly Sestina). [Amelia] (7:1, #20) 92, p. 114-115.
"Tyrant." [Amelia] (6:4, #19) 92, p. 85.

3927. MANN, Barbara
"Ezekiel's Daughter." [Confr] (50) Fall 92, p. 284.

3928. MANN, Chris
"In Memoriam: Alfred Blose." [Stand] (33:3) Sum 92, p. 30-31.

3929. MANNER, Eeva-Liisa
"The Cambrian Series: II (Shells)" (tr. by Ritva Poom). [ManhatR] (6:2) Fall 92, p. 22-23.

3930. MANNING, Linda
"She Dreamed the Prairie." [Quarry] (41:4) Fall 92, p. 29-30.

3931. MANRIQUE, Jaime
"The Nat King Cole Years." [BrooklynR] (9) 92, p. 2-4.

3932. MANRIQUEZ MONTOYA, Lucía
"Lontananza." [Nuez] (4:10/11) 92, p. 10.
"Virgins" (tr. by Reginald Gibbons). [TriQ] (85) Fall 92, p. 169.

3933. MANROE, Candace Ord
"Sensory Deprivation." [TexasR] (13:3/4) Fall-Wint 92, p. 92.

3934. MANSELL, Chris
"The Cat Machine." [AntigR] (90) Sum 92, p. 128.

3935. MANSFIELD, Michelle
"Daddy's Dust." [OnTheBus] (4:2/5:1, #10/11) 92, p. 141-142.
"First Kiss" (dedicated to Tess Gallagher). [OnTheBus] (4:2/5:1, #10/11) 92, p. 139 - 140.
"Spoonfulls." [OnTheBus] (4:2/5:1, #10/11) 92, p. 140-141.

3936. MANSON, Jeff
"Poem Written on Toilet Paper" (Dedicated to Jack Kerouac). [MoodySI] (27) Spr 92, p. 36.

3937. MANSOUR, Joyce
"Breastplate" (tr. by Molly Bendall). [Field] (46) Spr 92, p. 46.
"Light as a Shuttle Desire" (tr. by Molly Bendall). [Field] (46) Spr 92, p. 47-48.
3938. MANSOUR, Mónica
"The street doesn't understand what I say" (tr. by Reginald Gibbons). [TriQ] (85) Fall 92, p. 118.
"There are lovers who appear" (tr. by Reginald Gibbons). [TriQ] (85) Fall 92, p. 118-119.
"Women — for example, three women" (tr. by Reginald Gibbons). [TriQ] (85) Fall 92, p. 119.
3939. MANYARROWS, Victoria Lena
"Making Magic." [SinW] (47) Sum-Fall 92, p. 109.
"Touch." [Elf] (2:2) Sum 92, p. 38.
3940. MANYÉ i MARTI, Lourdes
"II. There is also the housewife in seventeen" (tr. of Miquel Martí i Pol, w. Wayne Cox). [Stand] (33:4) Aut 92, p. 145.
"III. The leaves and also the rustle of the leaves" (tr. of Miquel Martí i Pol, w. Wayne Cox). [Stand] (33:4) Aut 92, p. 145.
"IV. There are dull afternoons and exciting afternoons" (tr. of Miquel Martí i Pol, w. Wayne Cox). [Stand] (33:4) Aut 92, p. 146.
"V. I bid you good-bye with leaves. I will return next year." (tr. of Miquel Martí i Pol, w. Wayne Cox). [Stand] (33:4) Aut 92, p. 147.
"The Dark Drum" (tr. of Miquel Martí i Pol, w. Wayne Cox). [Chelsea] (53) 92, p. 78-79.
"Not to Cry" (tr. of Miquel Martí i Pol, w. Wayne Cox). [Chelsea] (53) 92, p. 77.
"Water Wheel" (tr. of Miquel Martí i Pol, w. Wayne Cox). [Chelsea] (53) 92, p. 76.
3941. MAPANJE, Jack
"Scrubbing the Furious Walls of Mikuyu Prison." [Stand] (33:3) Sum 92, p. 6.
"The Streak-Tease at Mikuyu Prison, 25th Sept, 1987." [Stand] (33:3) Sum 92, p. 4 - 5.
"Tethered Border Fugitive Upon Release" (For Mercy & the children). [Stand] (33:3) Sum 92, p. 7.
3942. MAPP, Erica
"The Bouquet" (Van Gogh, 1887, Paris). [Comm] (119:22) 18 D 92, p. 11.
3943. MAPSON, Jo-Ann
"Elegy for Dog Whistle." [KenR] (NS 14:2) Spr 92, p. 90.
3944. MAQUET, Albert
"Earth in tare" (tr. by Yann Lovelock). [Os] (34) Spr 92, p. 9.
"Où-ce." [Os] (34) Spr 92, p. 10.
"Pîre so pîre." [Os] (34) Spr 92, p. 8.
"Stone on stone" (tr. by Yann Lovelock). [Os] (34) Spr 92, p. 8.
"Têre èwale." [Os] (34) Spr 92, p. 9.
"Where is it" (tr. by Yann Lovelock). [Os] (34) Spr 92, p. 10.
3945. MARAINI, Dacia
"Far" (tr. by Corrado Federici). [PoetryC] (13:1) N 92, p. 23.
3946. MARAULT, Geneviève
"Ex." [Parting] (5:2) Wint 92-93, p. 6.
3947. MARCELLO, Leo Luke
"The Last Visit" (Elegy for the friend who confronting another AIDS death said, "Happiness is the only option I have left"). [Art&Und] (1:4) Jl-Ag 92, p. 6.
3948. MARCHAND, Blaine
"Baby Mice" (corrected reprint from 12:4). [PraF] (13:2, #59) Sum 92, p. 88-89.
3949. MARCHANT, Fred (Frederick J.)
"Bristlecone." [GettyR] (5:2) Spr 92, p. 239.
"Eyes Shut, Walden Pond." [Ploughs] (18:4) Wint 92-93, p. 198.
"Lazarus." [Ploughs] (18:4) Wint 92-93, p. 196.
"Memo to Stafford." [Amelia] (7:1, #20) 92, p. 63.
"State Lines." [ConnPR] (11:1) 92, p. 8.
"Stillness in South Carolina." [Ploughs] (18:4) Wint 92-93, p. 197.
"Sunday, After a Storm." [NegC] (12:3) 92, p. 101.
"Tamarisk." [Amelia] (7:1, #20) 92, p. 53.
3950. MARCHENA-GEERMAN, Lydia
"Poem B." [LitR] (35:4) Sum 92, p. 577.
"Poem B" (in Papiamentu). [LitR] (35:4) Sum 92, p. 615.
3951. MARCHITTI, Elizabeth
"May Thunderstorm." [Footwork] 92, p. 77.

"The Trees and the Roses Remember." [Footwork] 92, p. 77.
3952. MARCINIAK, Virginia Volini
"Pain, you are my oldest friend." [Comm] (119:18) 23 O 92, p. 12.
3953. MARCOU, Daniel
"Quilt of Marsh." [Northeast] (5:6) Spr 92, p. 40.
3954. MARCUS, Ben
"Canibalism, Common Term for Evasion." [Avec] (5:1) 92, p. 83.
"Jumping, System or Technique for Detecting." [Avec] (5:1) 92, p. 84.
"Old Person, Sudden Drop in a Stream." [Avec] (5:1) 92, p. 83.
3955. MARCUS, Jacqueline
"On Turning Thirty." [OhioR] (48) 92, p. 82.
3956. MARCUS, Mordecai
"1930: Mastoid Operation" (For Joseph Irving Berlin, M.D., 1883-1964). [JINJPo] (14:1) Spr 92, p. 24.
"Entrancements" (A Plainsongs Award Poem). [Plain] (12:3) Spr 92, p. 4.
"From the Tree of Knowledge." [WebR] (16) Fall 92, p. 109-110.
"A Moment of Song." [TarRP] (31:2) Spr 92, p. 20.
"Psychopompous." [WebR] (16) Fall 92, p. 110.
"Renewed Report." [PoetC] (23:3) Spr 92, p. 14.
"Uncertain Changes." [SnailPR] (2:1) Spr-Sum 92, p. 18-19.
3957. MARCUS, Peter
"In the Pain of Your Garden." [YellowS] (41) Fall-Wint 92-93, p. 18.
"My Sister's Girlfriend." [GreenMR] (NS 5:2) Spr-Sum 92, p. 108.
"Song for My Mother's Miscarriages." [NegC] (12:1/2) 92, p. 87.
"Statue of Eros without Wings." [Poetry] (160:4) Jl 92, p. 208.
"Swans, Penguins, Whales, & Us." [NoAmR] (277:2) Mr-Ap 92, p. 25.
"Tunnels." [GreenMR] (NS 5:2) Spr-Sum 92, p. 109.
3958. MARDIS, James
"Fear." [AfAmRev] (26:2) Sum 92, p. 238.
"For Dexter Gordon." [AfAmRev] (26:2) Sum 92, p. 239.
3959. MARGOSHES, Dave
"Strikes Often." [CanLit] (134) Aut 92, p. 97-98.
3960. MARGRAFF, Ruth
"Dinosaur with All Drawers Shut." [Footwork] 92, p. 113.
"Earl's House." [Footwork] 92, p. 113.
"Hole in My Lap to Sit In." [Footwork] 92, p. 113.
"Shortcake." [Footwork] 92, p. 112.
"Sweeping the Church." [Footwork] 92, p. 113.
3961. MARGUERITTE
"They Have Seen Granite Move." [Talisman] (9) Fall 92, p. 184.
3962. MARIANI, Paul
"The Bombings" (for John). [NewEngR] (14:4) Fall 92, p. 61-62.
"Manhattan" (for Robert Creeley). [NewEngR] (14:4) Fall 92, p. 60-61.
"Music As Desire." [QW] (36) Wint 92-93, p. 98-99.
"Saying Goodbye." [QW] (36) Wint 92-93, p. 100.
"Shadow Portrait." [NewEngR] (14:4) Fall 92, p. 59-60.
3963. MARIE, Tydal
"Dwayne." [NegC] (12:1/2) 92, p. 88.
3964. MARIELS, Coni
"Hosanna for Hyenas." [Zyzzyva] (8:2) Sum 92, p. 32-35.
3965. MARINELLI, Joanne
"Electromagnetic Western Omelets When Custer on Pyramid Power Tours the 21st Century in a Flying Gondola." [OxfordM] (8:1) Spr-Sum 92, p. 80-82.
3966. MARINER, Jo
"After a Bad Night of Sleep and Hurricane Warnings." [MidwQ] (33:3) Spr 92, p. 316.
3967. MARKKO, Kathleen
"Science." [NewAW] (10) Fall 92, p. 110.
3968. MARKO, Béla
"Forróság / Torrid Heat" (in Hungarian and English, tr. by Sylva Csiffary). [Nimrod] (35:2) Spr-Sum 92, p. 40.
"Go, Journey Inside" (from Romania, tr. by Nicholas Kolumban). [SilverFR] (23) Wint 92, p. 34-35.
3969. MARKOS, Don
"Dionysus Old." [Northeast] (5:7) Wint 92-93, p. 8.

3970. MARKOTIC, Nicole
"Hockey in South Africa." [WestCL] (26:3, #9) Wint 92-93, p. 26-30.
3971. MARKS, Gigi
"Afternoon Comfort." [Farm] (9:1) Spr-Sum 92, p. 38.
3972. MARKS, Nina Christina Marie
"Picture on the Wall" (November 1991). [NewAW] (10) Fall 92, p. 112.
"This Poem Does What I Want." [NewAW] (10) Fall 92, p. 111.
3973. MARKS, S. J.
"Before the End of Summer." [AmerPoR] (21:4) Jl-Ag 92, p. 36.
"Cherries." [AmerPoR] (21:4) Jl-Ag 92, p. 36.
3974. MARLATT, Daphne
"The Proper Response to a Poem Is Another Poem" (— Phyllis "Webb). [WestCL] (25:3, #6) Wint 91-92, p. 42.
3975. MARLIS, Stefanie
"All of a Sudden." [YellowS] (41) Fall-Wint 92-93, p. 35.
"The Cat." [ArtfulD] (22/23) 92, p. 140.
"Coincidence." [Manoa] (4:1) Spr 92, p. 137.
"Desire." [YellowS] (41) Fall-Wint 92-93, p. 35.
"Hail and Gravel." [YellowS] (41) Fall-Wint 92-93, p. 34.
"The Hole." [Manoa] (4:1) Spr 92, p. 137.
"Knock at the Door." [Manoa] (4:1) Spr 92, p. 137.
"Repair." [PoetryE] (33) Spr 92, p. 85.
"This Spring It Seems the Rain Will Not Stop." [YellowS] (41) Fall-Wint 92-93, p. 34.
3976. MARPLE, Vivian
"List of Things She Brought, or When My Grandmother Arrived in Spirit River . . . ." [Arc] (29) Aut 92, p. 45.
"The name Amelia is on my tongue." [Arc] (29) Aut 92, p. 43.
"Potion for the First Garden." [PraF] (13:4, #61) Wint 92-93, p. 65.
"Salad for Disaffection." [PraF] (13:4, #61) Wint 92-93, p. 68.
"Second Love Story." [Event] (21:2) Sum 92, p. 42.
"She wipes her hands on her apron." [Arc] (29) Aut 92, p. 44.
"What Has Not Been Said About the Garden." [PraF] (13:4, #61) Wint 92-93, p. 66-67.
3977. MARQUART, Debra
"Motorcade." [CumbPR] (12:1) Fall 92, p. 60-61.
3978. MARSHALL, Dan
"Spirits Above and Below Me." [RagMag] (10:2) 92, p. 77.
3979. MARSHALL, Ernest
"To the Girl in the Porno Magazine." [Crucible] (28) Fall 92, p. 28.
3980. MARSHALL, Ian
"Living with the Famous Poet." [SpiritSH] (57) Spr-Sum 92, p. 57-58.
3981. MARSHALL, Jack
"Field and Wave, Body and Book." [Talisman] (9) Fall 92, p. 12-15.
3982. MARSHALL, John
"Borderline." [PraF] (13:4, #61) Wint 92-93, p. 64.
"Found Poem." [CanLit] (135) Wint 92, p. 78.
"Natural Dream Lexicon." [CanLit] (135) Wint 92, p. 31-32.
3983. MARSHALL, Michael
"Sex Education." [EvergreenC] (7:2) Sum-Fall 92, p. 40.
3984. MARSHALL, Tod
"Breakfast." [BellArk] (8:3) My-Je 92, p. 7.
"Carpenter's Song." [BellArk] (8:4) Jl-Ag 92, p. 24.
"I See a Blind Couple in the Park." [BellArk] (8:3) My-Je 92, p. 7.
"Illuminatiuon." [BellArk] (8:6) N-D 92, p. 1.
"Time Zones." [BellArk] (8:6) N-D 92, p. 1.
"What I'll Tell the Judge at the Adoption Hearing." [BellArk] (8:6) N-D 92, p. 1.
3985. MARSHBURN, Sandra
"Watching the Weather Channel." [CinPR] (23) Wint 91-92, p. 20.
3986. MARSTON, Jane
"It's Who You Are That Counts." [SouthernHR] (26:2) Spr 92, p. 144.
3987. MARTEAU, Robert
"Les Muses de la Mer." [Os] (35) Fall 92, p. 20-21.
3988. MARTEL, Rafael Román
"Del Papel y el Fuego." [Nuez] (4:10/11) 92, p. 25.

3989. MARTENS, Caroline Rowe
"Haiku: After a storm tide." [Amelia] (7:1, #20) 92, p. 154.
3990. MARTENS, Oscar
"The Floodgates." [PraF] (13:4, #61) Wint 92-93, p. 69-71.
MARTHA CHRISTINA
See CHRISTINA, Martha
MARTHA ELIZABETH
See ELIZABETH, Martha
MARTI, Lourdes Manyé i
See MANYÉ i MARTI, Lourdes
3991. MARTI i POL, Miquel
"II. There is also the housewife in seventeen" (tr. by Wayne Cox and Lourdes Manyé i Martí). [Stand] (33:4) Aut 92, p. 145.
"III. The leaves and also the rustle of the leaves" (tr. by Wayne Cox and Lourdes Manyé i Martí). [Stand] (33:4) Aut 92, p. 145.
"IV. There are dull afternoons and exciting afternoons" (tr. by Wayne Cox and Lourdes Manyé i Martí). [Stand] (33:4) Aut 92, p. 146.
"V. I bid you good-bye with leaves. I will return next year." (tr. by Wayne Cox and Lourdes Manyé i Martí). [Stand] (33:4) Aut 92, p. 147.
"The Dark Drum" (tr. by Wayne Cox and Lourdes Manyé i Martí). [Chelsea] (53) 92, p. 78-79.
"Not to Cry" (tr. by Wayne Cox and Lourdes Manyé i Martí). [Chelsea] (53) 92, p. 77.
"Water Wheel" (tr. by Wayne Cox and Lourdes Manyé i Martí). [Chelsea] (53) 92, p. 76.
3992. MARTIA, Dominic
"Kerouac's Road, a Remembrance." [MoodySI] (27) Spr 92, p. 15.
3993. MARTIAL
"Epigrams" (8 selections, tr. by William Matthews). [AntR] (50:4) Fall 92, p. 714 - 715.
"Epigrams" (Selections: III.lxi, V.xlvii, IX.iv, X.xlix, X.xci, XI.xiv, XI.xxiv, XII.xiii, XII.xx, XII.xxx, tr. by William Matthews). [Pequod] (34) 92, p. 68-72.
3994. MARTIEN, Jerry
"Aftershocks." [Zyzzyva] (8:4) Wint 92, p. 85-86.
3995. MARTIN, Daniel
"Blue Sun Country." [BellArk] (8:4) Jl-Ag 92, p. 23.
"City: Driving." [BellArk] (8:4) Jl-Ag 92, p. 19.
3996. MARTIN, Doug
"Kicking Up Tongues of Snow." [JamesWR] (10:1) Fall 92, p. 9.
3997. MARTIN, E. B.
"The International Year of Tibet." [Crucible] (28) Fall 92, p. 53-54.
3998. MARTIN, Herbert Woodward
"Final W." [GrandS] (11:1, #41) 92, p. 175.
3999. MARTIN, Joseph
"Antiquarian." [Poem] (68) N 92, p. 22.
"Country Antiques." [Poem] (68) N 92, p. 21.
"On Joseph Vernet's *Coast Scene: Evening, 1751*." [Poem] (68) N 92, p. 20.
4000. MARTIN, Kathleen
"Ballad of the Bard" (or, Will Hath-Not-a-Way with Anne). [Light] (1) Spr 92, p. 22.
4001. MARTIN, Lynn
"Burn Me." [WillowR] (19) Spr 92, p. 25.
"Dead Oak." [WillowR] (19) Spr 92, p. 24.
"A Sense of Artistry." [Outbr] (23) 92, p. 70.
MARTIN, Martha Rogers
See ROGERS-MARTIN, Martha
4002. MARTIN, Richard
"The Good Old Days." [ChironR] (11:2) Sum 92, p. 14.
"The Student." [ChironR] (11:1) Spr 92, p. 23.
4003. MARTIN, W.
"The Gloves from the Camp" (tr. of Nico Graf). [Stand] (33:4) Aut 92, p. 113.
4004. MARTINEZ, Dionisio (Dionisio D.)
"The Affairs of Disaster" (Translation Chapbook Series, No. 20, tr. of Angel Cuadra, w. Silvia Curbelo). [MidAR] (13:2) 92, p. 43-67.
"All We Really Know About Darkness." [Journal] (16:2) Fall-Wint 92, p. 24.

"Avant-Dernières Pensées." [SenR] (22:2) Fall 92, p. 37-38.
"Beat." [Journal] (16:2) Fall-Wint 92, p. 23.
"Burden." [IndR] (15:1) Spr 92, p. 64-65.
"Chez Mondrian, Paris, 1926." [KenR] (NS 14:1) Wint 92, p. 126-127.
"Complacency." [VirQR] (68:3) Sum 92, p. 493-494.
"The End of August." [CarolQ] (44:2) Wint 92, p. 84-85.
"Fascination." [VirQR] (68:3) Sum 92, p. 494-495.
"Flood" (after paintings by Humberto Calzada). [Iowa] (22:2) Spr-Sum 92, p. 159 - 162.
"Ghost." [Ploughs] (18:1) Spr 92, p. 175-176.
"Gnossiennes." [SenR] (22:2) Fall 92, p. 34-35.
"Hesperia." [Ploughs] (18:1) Spr 92, p. 174.
"How to Read a Trout Stream." [Witness] (6:2) 92, p. 133-134.
"Hysteria." [Witness] (6:2) 92, p. 132-133.
"Impractical Solutions." [PraS] (66:3) Fall 92, p. 36.
"In the Unlikely Event." [NowestR] (30:2) 92, p. 81.
"Inclined Plane." [GreenMR] (NS 5:2) Spr-Sum 92, p. 87-89.
"Incomplete Combustion." [Ploughs] (18:1) Spr 92, p. 170-173.
"Je Te Veux." [SenR] (22:2) Fall 92, p. 36.
"A Necessary Story." [KenR] (NS 14:1) Wint 92, p. 125-126.
"Nocturnes." [SenR] (22:2) Fall 92, p. 39-40.
"The Risk of Being on the Safe Side" (for Adrian). [Witness] (6:2) 92, p. 135.
"Take a Card, Any Card." [PraS] (66:3) Fall 92, p. 37.
"Tenderness." [GreenMR] (NS 5:2) Spr-Sum 92, p. 85-86.
"There Are No Sundays in Romania." [IndR] (15:1) Spr 92, p. 63.
"What Fails Us." [Ploughs] (18:1) Spr 92, p. 177-178.
"What Your Mother Will Not Sing." [PraS] (66:3) Fall 92, p. 34-35.
"When Sound Is Diffused, Some of It Breaks." [Journal] (16:2) Fall-Wint 92, p. 25.

MARTINEZ, Manuel Díaz
See DIAZ MARTINEZ, Manuel

4005. MARTINEZ, Ruben Gerard
"In the Park." [Gypsy] (19) 92, p. 54.
"Morning." [OxfordM] (8:1) Spr-Sum 92, p. 13.

4006. MARTINEZ, Victoriano
"Mistakes." [HighP] (7:3) Wint 92, p. 115-116.

4007. MARTINEZ RIVAS
"Carcass." [LindLM] (11:1) Mr 92, p. 9.
"In Memoriam Luisita Ramirez Mercado, 11 April 1989." [LindLM] (11:1) Mr 92, p. 9.
"Un Sueño." [LindLM] (11:1) Mr 92, p. 9.
"Un Toulouse-Lautrec en Pancasan de Granada." [LindLM] (11:1) Mr 92, p. 9.

MARTINO, Marjorie de
See DeMARTINO, Marjorie

4008. MARTONE, John
"Bed's made." [Northeast] (5:7) Wint 92-93, p. 21.
"Bouquet." [Northeast] (5:7) Wint 92-93, p. 21.
"Per Hour." [AnotherCM] (23) Spr 92, p. 140.
"Seating." [Northeast] (5:7) Wint 92-93, p. 21.
"September 3." [ShadowP] (3) 92, p. 15-22.
"Tokonoma / Project." [AnotherCM] (23) Spr 92, p. 141.
"The War, the Age Was Just Beginning." [AnotherCM] (23) Spr 92, p. 142.

4009. MARVIN, Jay
"Edge City." [BlackBR] (15) Spr-Sum 92, p. 45-46.
"My American Dream." [Gypsy] (19) 92, p. 67.

4010. MARVIN, John
"Wind Flutes of the Sonora." [Elf] (2:4) Wint 92, p. 40-41.

4011. MARX, Anne
"Morning After." [Amelia] (7:1, #20) 92, p. 125.

4012. MARX, Paul
"Morningside Heights." [LitR] (25:2) Wint 92, p. 269.

4013. MARZAN, Julio
"Call Out My Number" (tr. of Julia de Burgos). [LitR] (35:4) Sum 92, p. 518.
"Glenn Miller's Music Is a Trunk" (tr. of Carmen Valle). [LitR] (35:4) Sum 92, p. 524.
"I Travel in the Braid of Time" (extract from an untitled selection in the anthology "Inventing a Word," tr. of Etnairis Rivera). [LitR] (35:4) Sum 92, p. 522.

"I'm Going to Break Out" (tr. of Carmen Valle). [LitR] (35:4) Sum 92, p. 523.
"Poem with the Final Tune" (tr. of Julia de Burgos). [LitR] (35:4) Sum 92, p. 517.
"What Is Lived" (tr. of Carmen Valle). [LitR] (35:4) Sum 92, p. 523-524.

4014. MASARIK, Al
"Free to Walk." [NewYorkQ] (48) 92, p. 98.
"Indian Cemetery." [HighP] (7:2) Fall 92, p. 19-20.
"Kimball Friday Night." [HighP] (7:2) Fall 92, p. 16.
"Preparing for Prison Workshop." [OnTheBus] (4:2/5:1, #10/11) 92, p. 143.
"Truck Stop Cafe." [HighP] (7:2) Fall 92, p. 17-18.

4015. MASON, Clif
"From the Dead Before." [PoetL] (87:1) Spr 92, p. 21-22.
"A Rwandan Shield." [Plain] (13:1) Fall 92, p. 17.

4016. MASON, David
"The Body of Anaxagoras" (tr. of Yiorgos Chouliaras, w. the author). [NoDaQ] (60:4) Fall 92, p. 12.
"The Day Arrives" (tr. of Yiorgos Chouliaras, w. the poet). [PoetL] (87:4) Wint 92-93, p. 47.
"The Dream of Phernazes" (tr. of Yiorgos Chouliaras, w. the author). [GrandS] (11:2, #42) 92, p. 147-149.
"The Family of Greeks" (tr. of Yiorgos Chouliaras, w. the author). [GrandS] (11:2, #42) 92, p. 150.
"Thus" (tr. of Yiorgos Chouliaras, w. the poet). [PoetL] (87:4) Wint 92-93, p. 46.

4017. MASON, Janet
"Newborn Rhythms" (for Barbara). [ChironR] (11:4) Wint 92, p. 45.

4018. MASON, Julian
"The Crane." [SoCarR] (24:2) Spr 92, p. 48.
"Markings." [SouthernPR] (32:2) Fall 92, p. 70-71.

4019. MASON, Keith Antar
"Moving Target." [Zyzzyva] (8:4) Wint 92, p. 59-63.

4020. MASON, Kenneth C.
"Puck's Song." [Amelia] (7:1, #20) 92, p. 149-150.
"Sestina: Into the Pleistocene" (At Mammoth Site, Hot Springs, South Dakota, with mother and son). [Amelia] (7:1, #20) 92, p. 148-149.

4021. MASSARO, M. A.
"Father and Son." [Plain] (13:1) Fall 92, p. 15.

4022. MASSER, Jim J.
"The Levee Mermaid." [CapeR] (27:2) Fall 92, p. 24.

MASSMAN, Gordon Lester
See LESTER-MASSMAN, Gordon

4023. MASTERSON, Dan
"Ballooning." [GettyR] (5:4) Aut 92, p. 626-627.
"The Mandy Poem." [OntR] (37) Fall-Wint 92-93, p. 62-64.

4024. MASTERSON, Ray
"Battle Hymn of the Poor!" [PoetryUSA] (24) 92, p. 28.

4025. MASTORAKI, Jenny
"Blessed Events" (in Greek and English, tr. by Mary Gilliland and Helen Kolias). [Nimrod] (35:2) Spr-Sum 92, p. 68-69.
"Classics Illustrated" (tr. by Mary Gilliland and Helen Kolias). [Nimrod] (35:2) Spr-Sum 92, p. 70-71.

4026. MASTURZO, Don
"Debris." [Confr] (50) Fall 92, p. 287.
"He Who Works the Hollow Hill." [Chelsea] (53) 92, p. 48.
"Washing Up." [Chelsea] (53) 92, p. 49.

4027. MATANLE, Stephen
"Errand." [Poetry] (159:4) Ja 92, p. 213.

4028. MATHEWS, Harry
"Sestina with Inteview" (tr. of Oskar Pastior). [ParisR] (34:123) Sum 92, p. 37-38.

4029. MATHUR, Ashok
"S.A.A." [CanLit] (132) Spr 92, p. 155.
"Thumbs" (three excerpts from a poemnovel-in-progress). [CanLit] (132) Spr 92, p. 56-58.

4030. MATOS, Edwin
"Fue Ayer." [LindLM] (11:1) Mr 92, p. 17.
"Las Horas Muertas." [Nuez] (4:10/11) 92, p. 24.
"Noche de Inspiracion." [LindLM] (11:1) Mr 92, p. 17.

4031. MATOVICH, Judy J.
"Caning." [TarRP] (30:2) Spr 91, p. 18.
4032. MATSON, Jeff
"The Settlement." [JamesWR] (9:2) Wint 92, p. 8.
4033. MATSON, Suzanne
"Greek." [Shen] (42:2) Sum 92, p. 85.
4034. MATTAWA, Khaled
"Growing Up with a Sears Catalog in Benghazi, Libya." [MichQR] (31:4) Fall 92, p. 516-517.
"Let Us Believe Again." [MichQR] (31:4) Fall 92, p. 518-519.
"Maryam." [PoetryE] (33) Spr 92, p. 86-90.
"Ramadan." [MissR] (20:3) Spr 92, p. 104-105.
4035. MATTERN, Grace
"Rebuilding." [HangL] (60) 92, p. 42.
4036. MATTFIELD, Mary
"Don't Be Surprised" (tr. of Maria Banus). [PoetryE] (33) Spr 92, p. 164.
"Monstril / Monsters" (tr. of Maria Banus). [Nimrod] (35:2) Spr-Sum 92, p. 41.
4037. MATTHEW, Antonia
"Lament." [Nimrod] (36:1) Fall-Wint 92, p. 95-96.
4038. MATTHEWS, David
"Pablo's Blues." [WindO] (56) Fall-Wint 92, p. 13.
"She's Gone." [WindO] (56) Fall-Wint 92, p. 14.
4039. MATTHEWS, Jack
"The Cheerleaders." [ThRiPo] (39/40) 92-93, p. 152-153.
"Gravity's the Villain in This Piece." [ThRiPo] (39/40) 92-93, p. 153-154.
"Paradigm of a Hero." [ThRiPo] (39/40) 92-93, p. 152.
"The People in These Houses." [ThRiPo] (39/40) 92-93, p. 153.
4040. MATTHEWS, William
"?" [PassN] (13:1) Sum 92, p. 12.
"The Bear at the Dump." [Atlantic] (269:4) Ap 92, p. 76.
"A Citizen." [SouthwR] (77:2/3) Spr-Sum 92, p. 405.
"Crowd Control." [Light] (2) Sum 92, p. 11.
"Epigrams" (8 selections, tr. of Martial). [AntR] (50:4) Fall 92, p. 714-715.
"Epigrams" (Selections: III.lxi, V.xlvii, IX.iv, X.xlix, X.xci, XI.xiv, XI.xxiv, XII.xiii, XII.xx, XII.xxx, tr. of Martial). [Pequod] (34) 92, p. 68-72.
"Fireworks." [NewYorker] (68:20) 6 Jl 92, p. 30.
"His Muse." [Light] (1) Spr 92, p. 7.
"Lost Time for Sale." [GettyR] (5:3) Sum 92, p. 423.
"Mardi Gras, New Orleans, a Recent Year." [GrahamHR] (16) Fall 92, p. 34.
"Money." [PassN] (13:1) Sum 92, p. 13.
"Note Left for Gerald Stern in an Office I Borrowed, and He Would Next, at a Summer Writers' Conference." [NewEngR] (14:4) Fall 92, p. 53-54.
"Our Town." [PassN] (13:1) Sum 92, p. 12.
"The Party." [GrahamHR] (16) Fall 92, p. 35.
"A Postcard from Mt. Etna." [GrahamHR] (16) Fall 92, p. 33.
"Private Eye." [PassN] (13:1) Sum 92, p. 12.
"The Rented House in Maine." [OhioR] (48) 92, p. 19-20.
"The Rookery at Hawthornden." [Shen] (42:3) Fall 92, p. 44-45.
"Self-Help." [Crazy] (42) Spr 92, p. 35-36.
"Sentence." [NewEngR] (14:4) Fall 92, p. 52.
"The Shades." [NewEngR] (14:4) Fall 92, p. 55.
"The Shadow Knows." [GrahamHR] (16) Fall 92, p. 31-32.
"Smart Money." [OhioR] (48) 92, p. 21.
"The Spokesman." [Shen] (42:3) Fall 92, p. 45.
"This Spud's For You." [NewEngR] (14:4) Fall 92, p. 56-57.
4041. MATTHIAS, John
"Inventory of a Poem" (for Vasco Popa, tr. of Branko Miljkovic, w. Vladeta Vuckovic). [TriQ] (86) Wint 92-93, p. 39.
"An Orphic Legacy" (tr. of Branko Miljkovic, w. Vladeta Vuckovic). [TriQ] (86) Wint 92-93, p. 41.
"While You Are Singing" (tr. of Branko Miljkovic, w. Vladeta Vuckovic). [TriQ] (86) Wint 92-93, p. 40.
MATTIA, Sally de
See De MATTIA, Sally

4042. MAUNICK, Edouard
"Exposed to Sun" (tr. by Brian Evenson and David Beus). [CentralP] (21) Spr 92, p. 134-138.

4043. MAURER, Bonnie
"Death Sits on the Radiator." [HopewellR] (4) 92, p. 34.

4044. MAURER-ALVAREZ, Pansy
"The Glassblower." [CimR] (100) Jl 92, p. 59.
"The Way Things Will Go." [CimR] (100) Jl 92, p. 60.

4045. MAURIN-GOTIN, Renée
"Canoe Race" (tr. by Betty Wilson). [LitR] (35:4) Sum 92, p. 530.
"Course de Yoles." [LitR] (35:4) Sum 92, p. 611.
"King Carnival Done" (tr. by Betty Wilson). [LitR] (35:4) Sum 92, p. 529.
"Vaval Mò." [LitR] (35:4) Sum 92, p. 610-611.

4046. MAVIGLIA, Joseph
"Congas." [Descant] (23:3, #78) Fall 92, p. 34-35.
"Corrido" (Mexican Folk Song). [Descant] (23:3, #78) Fall 92, p. 32.
"A Filament of Prayer." [Descant] (23:3, #78) Fall 92, p. 36.
"Night Without Echo." [Descant] (23:3, #78) Fall 92, p. 33.

4047. MAX, Lin
"The Piemaker." [Calyx] (14:1) Sum 92, p. 34.
"This Part of Your Body" (to Annie at 12, beginning the menses). [Calyx] (14:1) Sum 92, p. 35.
"With a Whip Going Up His Ass" (Robert Mapplethorpe's Self Portrait 1978). [Calyx] (14:1) Sum 92, p. 33.

4048. MAXSON, H. A.
"Among Cattails." [CimR] (100) Jl 92, p. 111-113.

4049. MAXWELL, Glyn
"Beast's Good Dream." [Verse] (8:3/9:1) Wint-Spr 92, p. 76-77.
"Rumpelstiltskin." [Atlantic] (269:1) Ja 92, p. 89.
"Star the Lad." [Verse] (8:3/9:1) Wint-Spr 92, p. 77.

4050. MAXWELL, Margo
"Pastorals" (4 poems). [Farm] (9:1) Spr-Sum 92, p. 17-24.

4051. MAXWELL, Marina Ama Omowale
"For Women Going Under" (For Malechi, the mother who burnt herself in Trinidad, and for all the others. 1977/78). [LitR] (35:4) Sum 92, p. 565.

4052. MAY, Eleanor Rodman
"For One Like Zelda." [Crucible] (28) Fall 92, p. 5-6.

4053. MAY, Michael
"Before She Comes Home." [Bogg] (65) 92, p. 52.

4054. MAY, Paul
"Light Opera." [Verse] (9:2) Sum 92, p. 6.

MAYANS, Fernando Sanchez
See SANCHEZ MAYANS, Fernando

4055. MAYER, Barbara J.
"The Horse on the Drapes." [Crucible] (28) Fall 92, p. 37-38.

4056. MAYER, Bernadette
"Ethics of Sleep" (Excerpt). [WestCL] (26:2, #8) Fall 92, p. 69-71.
"Noun Pileup of Travel on M15 Bus." [Talisman] (8) Spr 92, p. 177-179.

4057. MAYERS, Florence Cassen
"Design: Marrakesh." [CreamCR] (16:2) Fall 92, p. 108-109.
"Steph." [MichQR] (31:1) Wint 92, p. 109-110.

4058. MAYERS, T. R.
"The Streetlamps at the Edge of Reality." [MoodySI] (27) Spr 92, p. 27.

4059. MAYES, Frances
"Good Friday, Driving Home." [Iowa] (22:2) Spr-Sum 92, p. 49-50.
"Green Thoughts." [NewAW] (10) Fall 92, p. 72-75.
"When Rain Pulls the Wind Off the Arno at Night." [Iowa] (22:2) Spr-Sum 92, p. 50-51.

4060. MAYHALL, Jane
"Calliope." [NegC] (12:1/2) 92, p. 81.
"Can You Love Somebody for Fifty Years?" [NewYorkQ] (47) 92, p. 37.
"Sounds of Heavy Metal." [NegC] (12:1/2) 92, p. 82.

4061. MAYNE, Robert L.
"Body Language." [PoetL] (87:3) Fall 92, p. 33-34.

4062. MAYO, Jeanette
"Creation." [NegC] (12:3) 92, p. 102.

4063. MAYR, Suzette
"For U. M." [WestCL] (26:3, #9) Wint 92-93, p. 31-32.
"Maidens." [WestCL] (26:3, #9) Wint 92-93, p. 34.
"Water Sports." [WestCL] (26:3, #9) Wint 92-93, p. 33-34.
4064. MAYRÖCKER, Friederike
"Heiligenanstalt" (tr. by Rosmarie Waldrop). [GrandS] (11:2, #42) 92, p. 49-56.
MAYTORENA, Manuel Antonio Serna
See SERNA-MAYTORENA, Manuel Antonio
4065. MAZUR, Gail
"Blue." [ParisR] (34:125) Wint 92, p. 55-56.
"Desire." [AmerV] (26) Spr 92, p. 4-5.
"I Wish I Want I need." [WestHR] (46:3) Fall 92 [i.e. (46:4) Wint 92], p. 403 - 405.
"I'm a Stranger Here Myself." [Agni] (35) 92, p. 91-92.
"In Houston." [Boulevard] (7:2/3, #20/21) Fall 92, p. 270-271.
"Snake in the Grass." [ParisR] (34:125) Wint 92, p. 54-55.
"Why You Travel." [AmerV] (26) Spr 92, p. 3.
4066. MAZZOCCO, Robert
"Cook's Tour." [NewYorker] (68:10) 27 Ap 92, p. 44.
"Good Times." [NewYorker] (68:2) 2 Mr 92, p. 38.
Mc . . .
See also names beginning with Mac . . .
4067. Mc CRARY, Jim
"Untitled: July 19, 1991." [Avec] (5:1) 92, p. 121-122.
"Untitled: July 20, 1991." [Avec] (5:1) 92, p. 123.
4068. McADAMS, Janet
"A Child's Geography." [WebR] (16) Fall 92, p. 99.
4069. McALPINE, Cam
"Symbols." [CapilR] (2:9) Fall 92, p. 42-44.
4070. McALPINE, Katherine
"Combat Fatigue." [Sparrow] (59) S 92, p. 9.
"I Begin Life on My Own Account, and Don't Like It." [SlipS] (12) 92, p. 98.
"The Legendary Ms. Nin." [Light] (4) Wint 92-93, p. 15.
"Plus Ç'Est la Même Chose" (lines written upon chaperoning the seventh grade dance. Winner of Discovery — The Nation '92). [Nat] (254:19) 18 My 92, p. 671.
"The Rooster and the Owl." [Light] (1) Spr 92, p. 13.
"Scenes of '64." [Sparrow] (59) S 92, p. 8.
"Sonnet Stew" (from *The Sonnet: An Anthology*, Index of First Lines). [Sparrow] (59) S 92, p. 9.
"Stranger at the Party." [Sparrow] (59) S 92, p. 8.
"Waiting for Winter in La Sardina Loca" (winner of Discovery — The Nation '92). [Nat] (254:19) 18 My 92, p. 671.
4071. McARTHUR, Mac
"Da Cunha." [JamesWR] (9:2) Wint 92, p. 10.
"Final Past My Arms." [Arc] (29) Aut 92, p. 47-48.
"The Rock and the Giraffe." [JamesWR] (9:4) Sum 92, p. 6.
"This Afternoon Is Family." [JamesWR] (9:3) Spr 92, p. 20.
4072. McAULEY, James J.
"The Aviaries of Doctor Harbinger." [PoetryNW] (33:2) Sum 92, p. 18-19.
"Samarkand." [PoetryNW] (33:2) Sum 92, p. 17.
"Self-Portrait, with Masks" (after Rembrandt). [Shen] (42:4) Wint 92, p. 60.
"Sunday in Miami" (for Donald Justice). [Shen] (42:4) Wint 92, p. 58-59.
4073. McBREEN, Joan
"The Terminology of Love." [Verse] (9:3) Wint 92, p. 10.
"A Walled Garden in Moylough." [Grain] (20:3) Fall 92, p. 53.
4074. McBRIDE, Mekeel
"The Going Away." [Conscience] (13:3) Aut 92, p. 9.
"The Going Under of the Evening Land." [ThRiPo] (39/40) 92-93, p. 144-145.
"Loneliness." [ThRiPo] (39/40) 92-93, p. 154-155.
"The Miraculous Shrine of the Stairway Dime." [Nat] (254:9) 9 Mr 92, p. 316.
"Red Letters." [ThRiPo] (39/40) 92-93, p. 156-157.
"Weather Report." [Conscience] (13:3) Aut 92, p. 25.
"Window." [SouthwR] (77:2/3) Spr-Sum 92, p. 229.
4075. McBRIDE, Regina
"Beauty and the Beast." [AntR] (50:3) Sum 92, p. 498.

4076. McCABE, Victoria
"Affinities for Russians" (for B.Z. Niditch). [HolCrit] (29:2) Ap 92, p. 18.
"Editor's Salutations, Fairly Typical" (for William Packard and Paul Dilsaver). [NewYorkQ] (48) 92, p. 94.
"Help." [NewYorkQ] (49) 92, p. 57.
"Outline for a *Life* of Balzac." [Poetry] (159:6) Mr 92, p. 331-336.
"Rat Metaphor." [SouthernPR] (32:1) Spr 92, p. 59-60.
"Self Portrait in Oddish Syllabics." [NewYorkQ] (47) 92, p. 41.
4077. McCAIN, Gillian
"Breathlessly for a Few Seconds." [PaintedB] (48) 92, p. 61.
4078. McCALLISTER, Andy
"Poetry Hah." [ChironR] (11:2) Sum 92, p. 12.
4079. McCANN, Janet
"Skating" (for P.C.). [JINJPo] (14:2) Aut 92, p. 10-12.
"Thank You, Scientific American" (1st Honorable Mention, 6th Annual Contest). [SoCoast] (13) Je 93 [i.e. 92], p. 45.
4080. McCANN, Kathleen M.
"Wait for Me." [MidwQ] (33:2) Wint 92, p. 201.
4081. McCARTHY, Eugene
"Courage at Sixty." [HampSPR] Wint 92, p. 54.
4082. McCARTHY, Kevin
"Spread Release." [YellowS] (41) Fall-Wint 92-93, p. 37.
4083. McCARTHY, Ted
"Prospecting." [Vis] (38) 92, p. 25.
4084. McCARTHY, Tim
"Faith in Roots." [ChatR] (13:1) Fall 92, p. 46.
4085. McCARTIN, Jim
"Do You Think I Care?" [Footwork] 92, p. 95.
"Finding Happiness." [Footwork] 92, p. 95.
"Geraniums." [Footwork] 92, p. 95.
"Images." [Footwork] 92, p. 95.
"John Lennon (1940-1980)." [Footwork] 92, p. 95.
4086. McCARTY, Neil J.
"Jo Ann." [RagMag] (10:2) 92, p. 66.
"Memories Return." [RagMag] (10:2) 92, p. 69.
"Rafting the McKenzie." [RagMag] (10:2) 92, p. 68-69.
"Virgin Pines." [RagMag] (10:2) 92, p. 67.
4087. McCASLIN, Susan
"The Wisdom Poems." [BellArk] (8:2) Mr-Ap 92, p. 4-6.
4088. McCAUGHEY, Kevin
"Telescope." [WebR] (16) Fall 92, p. 78-79.
4089. McCLANAHAN, Rebecca
"Pardon." [GeoR] (46:2) Sum 92, p. 275.
"Salvage" (for a dead sister). [IndR] (15:1) Spr 92, p. 58.
"X." [GeoR] (46:2) Sum 92, p. 276-277.
4090. McCLATCHY, J. D.
"Chott." [ParisR]] (34:124) Fall 92, p. 44-46.
"Proust in Bed." [ParisR] (34:125) Wint 92, p. 246-248.
"Taking Leave." [ParisR]] (34:124) Fall 92, p. 46.
4091. McCLELLAN, Jane
"At the Edges." [CumbPR] (11:2) Spr 92, p. 26.
"Aubade, or Morning Lovesong." [MidwQ] (33:2) Wint 92, p. 202.
"Close Companions." [Crucible] (28) Fall 92, p. 47-48.
4092. McCLURE, Michael
"Field 4." [PoetryUSA] (24) 92, p. 12.
"Field 5." [PoetryUSA] (24) 92, p. 13.
"Fields" (Selections: 1-3). [Talisman] (9) Fall 92, p. 4-10.
4093. McCLUSKEY, Sally
"Grandfather Hears That It's Finally Finished and Speaks of How Delmer Lived and Delmer Died." [Epiphany] (3:4) O (Fall) 92, p. 307.
"Old Man Fishing on Muddy Water." [Epiphany] (3:4) O (Fall) 92, p. 305.
"On the Morning Her Lover Died at War, She Dreamt." [Epiphany] (3:4) O (Fall) 92, p. 306.
4094. McCOMBS, Davis
"Ernest Hemingway *Faena*" (First Prize, poetry contest). [HarvardA] (126:3) Spr 92, p. 24.

4095. McCOMBS, Judith
"Opening." [RiverS] (36) 92, p. 19.
4096. McCORD, Andrew
"An Apology" (tr. of Faiz Ahmed Faiz). [Agni] (36) 92, p. 20.
"Five Ecstatic Songs" (tr. of Kabir). [GrandS] (11:3 #43) 92, p. 82-84.
"Last Days" (tr. of Faiz Ahmed Faiz). [Agni] (35) 92, p. 234.
"Lincoln in Richmond." [Agni] (36) 92, p. 53.
4097. McCORD, Katherine
"Carnival." [ChamLR] (10/11) Spr-Fall 92, p. 31-32.
4098. McCORD, Sandy
"Daylight Savings." [HiramPoR] (51/52) Fall 91-Sum 92, p. 49.
"Speakeasy." [Bogg] (65) 92, p. 34.
"This Last." [CapeR] (27:2) Fall 92, p. 28.
4099. McCORKLE, James
"Junonia." [Boulevard] (7:2/3, #20/21) Fall 92, p. 280-281.
4100. McCORMICK, Brian
"Bat in Fridge." [Descant] (23:3, #78) Fall 92, p. 67-68.
"The Ice Capades, an Elegy for Ice." [Descant] (23:3, #78) Fall 92, p. 72-74.
"Objects Closer Than They Appear and Lost for Words Besides." [Descant] (23:3, #78) Fall 92, p. 69-71.
4101. McCORMICK, Jen
"Mabel." [CumbPR] (12:1) Fall 92, p. 54-55.
"Rails." [CumbPR] (12:1) Fall 92, p. 56-57.
McCRARY, Jim
See Mc CRARY, Jim
4102. McCRORY, John
"Local Customs." [ArtfulD] (22/23) 92, p. 54.
"The Solace." [ArtfulD] (22/23) 92, p. 55.
"Symptoms of Earthly Decay." [ArtfulD] (22/23) 92, p. 56-57.
4103. McCUE, Duncan
"The Last Real Indian." [MalR] (100) Fall 92, p. 120-123.
"Nishnawbe at Kentucky Fried." [MalR] (100) Fall 92, p. 124.
4104. McCULLOUGH, L. E.
"Buddy Lee Perriman Reflects on the Persian Gulf Crisis, Day 15." [CoalC] (5) My 92, p. 13.
"Buddy Lee Perriman Reflects on the Persian Gulf Crisis, Day 15." [Comm] (119:2) 31 Ja 92, p. 24.
"Buddy Lee Perriman Reflects on the Persian Gulf Crisis, Day 15." [WestB] (30) 92, p. 108.
"Club Lido, Kansas City, 1044" [i.e. 1944]. [RagMag] (10:2) 92, p. 100.
"Club Lido, Kansas City, 1944." [ChamLR] (10/11) Spr-Fall 92, p. 41.
"Club Lido, Kansas City, 1944." [Outbr] (23) 92, p. 64.
"Hey You Sitting There Looking at This." [Gypsy] (19) 92, p. 48.
"Hey You Sitting There Looking at This." [RagMag] (10:2) 92, p. 101.
"Strays." [ChamLR] (10/11) Spr-Fall 92, p. 42-43.
4105. McCULLOUGH, Lisa J.
"Woman at a Writing Table" (detail from a Japanese six-fold screen, ink and color on silk, late Heian period). [CumbPR] (12:1) Fall 92, p. 76.
4106. McCURDY, Harold
"The Haul." [ChrC] (109:14) 22 Ap 92, p. 428.
"Stillness." [ChrC] (109:4) 29 Ja 92, p. 84.
4107. McDADE, Thomas Michael
"Tangles." [CoalC] (5) My 92, p. 1.
4108. McDANIEL, Jeffrey
"Following Her to Sleep." [Ploughs] (18:4) Wint 92-93, p. 92-93.
"Technology." [Ploughs] (18:4) Wint 92-93, p. 94.
4109. McDANIEL, Mary (Mary Catherine)
"Family Crossing." [FloridaR] (18:1) Spr-Sum 92, p. 91-93.
"Top This." [Farm] (9:2) Fall-Wint 92-93, p. 76.
"The Woman at the Window." [Farm] (9:2) Fall-Wint 92-93, p. 77.
4110. McDANIEL, Wilma Elizabeth
"Family Connections." [HangL] (61) 92, p. 55.
"Holiday Accommodations." [HangL] (61) 92, p. 56.
"Incident Before Visiting Professor's Lecture." [HangL] (61) 92, p. 56.
4111. McDONALD, Christopher
"Poem for My Sleeping Father." [BrooklynR] (9) 92, p. 65.

McDONALD, Hazel Simmons
See SIMMONS-McDONALD, Hazel
4112. McDONALD, Irene B.
"Cat, Spider, Hummingbird." [NegC] (12:1/2) 92, p. 90-91.
4113. McDONALD, Paul
"The Crab Hunters." [CoalC] (5) My 92, p. 12.
4114. McDONALD, Walter
"After Eden." [Agni] (35) 92, p. 124.
"Boys with Chihuahua Dogs." [FloridaR] (18:1) Spr-Sum 92, p. 94-95.
"Crops, Pumps, All Rotting Posts." [CinPR] (23) Wint 91-92, p. 13.
"The Digs in Escondido Canyon." [Poetry] (160:4) Jl 92, p. 188.
"The Dust of Father's Barn." [Manoa] (4:2) Fall 92, p. 152.
"Faith Is a Radical Master." [NoDaQ] (60:4) Fall 92, p. 149.
"First View of the Enemy." [Poem] (67) My 92, p. 66.
"For Friends Missing in Action." [ArtfulD] (22/23) 92, p. 72.
"Grace and the Blood of Goats." [ColEng] (54:7) N 92, p. 827.
"The Hairpin Curve at Durango." [AmerS] (61:1) Wint 92, p. 107-108.
"Hawks in the World They Own." [ColEng] (54:7) N 92, p. 826.
"Heirlooms." [Atlantic] (270:5) N 92, p. 108.
"Learning to Live with Sandstorms." [NoDaQ] (60:4) Fall 92, p. 150.
"Leaving the Middle Years." [Agni] (35) 92, p. 125.
"Leaving the Middle Years." [SouthernPR] (32:1) Spr 92, p. 49.
"Living on Open Plains." [ArtfulD] (22/23) 92, p. 71.
"Living on Open Plains." [ConnPR] (11:1) 92, p. 5.
"Living on Open Plains." [Manoa] (4:2) Fall 92, p. 151-152.
"Luck of the Draw on Hardscrabble." [HiramPoR] (51/52) Fall 91-Sum 92, p. 50.
"Mending the Fence on Hardscrabble." [LaurelR] (26:1) Wint 92, p. 93.
"Mending the Fence on Hardscrabble." [NoDaQ] (60:4) Fall 92, p. 151.
"The Middle Years." [Poem] (67) My 92, p. 67.
"The Middle Years." [SycamoreR] (4:1) Wint 92, p. 20-21.
"Quarrels and the Laws of Mercy." [MichQR] (31:2) Spr 92, p. 226-227.
"Releasing the Hawk in August." [OxfordM] (7:1) Spr-Sum 91, p. 52.
"Riding on Hardscrabble." [ColEng] (53:8) D 91, p. 909.
"Slick When Wet." [Poem] (67) My 92, p. 68.
"Soaring at Lubbock." [OxfordM] (7:1) Spr-Sum 91, p. 53.
"The Summer Before the War." [Manoa] (4:2) Fall 92, p. 151.
"The Winter Before the War." [ColEng] (53:8) D 91, p. 908.
"Wishing for More Than Thunder." [Poetry] (160:4) Jl 92, p. 187.
4115. McDONOUGH, Deirdre
"Ikebana." [AntR] (50:3) Sum 92, p. 528.
4116. McDOUGALL, Jo
"My Father, Who Wants to Discover America." [MidwQ] (34:1) Aut 92, p. 75-76.
4117. McDOUGLE, Tom
"A Blue-Tailed Lizard on the Porch of Alabama's Oldest Wood-Framed House" (Mooresville, 11 August 1991." [Elf] (2:2) Sum 92, p. 37.
"Pompes Funebres Bigot at 8 Rue du Cloitre Notre Dame" (name and address of the funeral home in Paris that prepared the body of the late Jim Morrison). [NegC] (12:1/2) 92, p. 92.
4118. McDOWELL, Robert
"All the Broken Boys and Girls." [Hudson] (45:2) Sum 92, p. 238-241.
"My Corporate Life." [Hudson] (45:2) Sum 92, p. 234-238.
"October." [Boulevard] (7:1, #19) Spr 92, p. 194.
"Their Fathers and Mothers Were Drinkers." [Hudson] (45:2) Sum 92, p. 241-242.
"The Travelers." [Hudson] (45:2) Sum 92, p. 242.
4119. McELROY, Colleen J.
"Drawing in the Dark — A Jazz Monochrome" (for Miles Davis). [MassR] (23:3) Fall 92, p. 356-357.
"In the Blind Eye of Love's Shiny Moon." [MassR] (23:3) Fall 92, p. 355-356.
"The Moon and Malaysia." [KenR] (NS 14:4) Fall 92, p. 124-133.
4120. McEWAN, Angela
"Daring of the Brief Suns" (2 selections, tr. of Lydia Velez-Roman). [Luz] (2) S 92, p. 13-19.
"Meditation" (tr. of Francisco Alvarez-Koki). [Luz] (1) My 92, p. 17, 19.
"Tramp" (tr. of Ester de Izaguirre). [Luz] (1) My 92, p. 11.

4121. McFADDEN, David
"Gold" (After Hilda Doolittle's "End in Torment: A Memoir of Ezra Pound"). [MalR] (98) Spr 92, p. 82-83.
"Kalamazoo: The Big Picture." [MalR] (98) Spr 92, p. 78.
"Lady Lazarus." [MalR] (98) Spr 92, p. 79.
"Parenthood." [MalR] (98) Spr 92, p. 77.
"Susan's Dream." [MalR] (98) Spr 92, p. 80-81.
4122. McFADDEN, Tomás
"El Poeta de las Calles." [Nuez] (4:12) 92, p. 25.
4123. McFARLAND, Ron
"Burning the Bad Nuns." [LullwaterR] (3:2) Spr 92, p. 53.
"Cleaning Up Our Act." [HampSPR] Wint 92, p. 16-17.
"Sky Walk" (2nd Honorable Mention, 6th Annual Contest). [SoCoast] (13) Je 93 [i.e. 92], p. 38-39.
4124. McFARLANE, Scott
"Haiku Gene, Hakujiin." [WestCL] (26:3, #9) Wint 92-93, p. 75-77.
"Marlatt's Steveston." [CanLit] (135) Wint 92, p. 11-14.
"Slo Can Crossroads." [WestCL] (26:3, #9) Wint 92-93, p. 78-79.
4125. McFEE, Michael
"Buzzard." [Atlantic] (270:5) N 92, p. 109.
"Forbidden." [Light] (2) Sum 92, p. 23.
"Linville Caverns." [GreensboroR] (53) Wint 92-93, p. 98.
"Paradise." [TarRP] (32:1) Fall 92, p. 40.
"Politics." [KenR] (NS 14:4) Fall 92, p. 169-170.
"The Roof Men." [KenR] (NS 14:4) Fall 92, p. 169.
"Triolet." [Light] (4) Wint 92-93, p. 18.
4126. McFERREN, Martha
"Dog Suicide." [LouisL] (9:1) Spr 92, p. 59-61.
"Knees and Necks / New Orleans." [PoetryNW] (33:1) Spr 92, p. 42-43.
"Puremouth." [LouisL] (9:1) Spr 92, p. 61-62.
4127. McFERRIN, Linda Watanabe
"Kylos." [SouthernPR] (32:1) Spr 92, p. 57-58.
4128. McGEE, Lynn
"Brick." [OntR] (36) Spr-Sum 92, p. 80.
"How He Got There." [OntR] (36) Spr-Sum 92, p. 77-79.
"Waking." [ManhatPR] (14) [92?], p. 41.
4129. McGEEVER, Kathey
"Sine Wave." [Amelia] (6:4, #19) 92, p. 80.
4130. McGLYNN, Bryan
"Tradition." [NewYorkQ] (47) 92, p. 49.
4131. McGLYNN, Paul D.
"Magical Regression." [RagMag] (10:2) 92, p. 84.
4132. McGOVERN, Martin
"To Chanteuse in Summer." [OhioR] (48) 92, p. 36.
4133. McGOVERN, Robert
"The Case for Civilization." [Epiphany] (3:2) Ap (Spr) 92, p. 92.
"First Bean Sprout, 29 May." [Epiphany] (3:2) Ap (Spr) 92, p. 92.
"For Nick" (at 16). [Epiphany] (3:2) Ap (Spr) 92, p. 91.
4134. McGRAIL, John
"On the Thirteenth Day." [Hellas] (3:1) Spr 92, p. 46.
"To a Mermaid." [Hellas] (3:1) Spr 92, p. 46.
4135. McGRATH, Campbell
"Dawn." [OhioR] (48) 92, p. 67-68.
"Music Box." [NewAW] (10) Fall 92, p. 76.
"Night Travellers." [NewYorker] (68:40) 23 N 92, p. 102.
"Ode to the Wild Horses of Caineville, Utah." [TriQ] (84) Spr-Sum 92, p. 108-112.
"Sunset, Route 90, Brewster County, Texas." [OhioR] (48) 92, p. 69.
"Wild Thing." [AnotherCM] (24) Fall 92, p. 100-102.
4136. McGRATH, Chris
"Sushi." [OnTheBus] (4:2/5:1, #10/11) 92, p. 144.
4137. McGRATH, Donald
"The Box." [AntigR] (89) Spr 92, p. 76-77.
"The Fathers." [PoetryC] (12:2) Ap 92, p. 5.
"Fatima High." [PoetryC] (12:2) Ap 92, p. 5.
"Outside Looking In." [AntigR] (89) Spr 92, p. 75.
"The Porch." [PoetryC] (12:2) Ap 92, p. 5.

"The Stable." [Grain] (20:3) Fall 92, p. 90.
"Sunday Afternoon." [PoetryC] (12:2) Ap 92, p. 5.

4138. McGUINN, Rex
"Looking for Real Toads." [Os] (34) Spr 92, p. 28.
"Notes for Crispin." [SouthernPR] (32:1) Spr 92, p. 58-59.

4139. McGUIRE, Catherine
"Weed." [CapeR] (27:2) Fall 92, p. 40.

4140. McGUIRE, Shannon Marquez
"Poem of Summer, 1990." [CapeR] (27:2) Fall 92, p. 36-37.

4141. McHUGH, Heather
"Coming." [AmerV] (26) Spr 92, p. 23-24.
"Connubial." [Iowa] (22:1) Wint 92, p. 44-45.
"Hurricane." [AmerV] (26) Spr 92, p. 25.
"In Light of Time." [ThRiPo] (39/40) 92-93, p. 157-158.
"Nightlight: Eye of the Owl" (tr. of Blaga Dimitrova, w. Nikolai Popov). [Trans] (26) Spr 92, p. 53-54.
"Numberless." [Iowa] (22:1) Wint 92, p. 41-42.
"Untitled: There is much unsaid." [VirQR] (68:1) Wint 92, p. 73-74.
"White Mind and Roses." [VirQR] (68:1) Wint 92, p. 70-71.
"Window: Thing As Participle." [VirQR] (68:1) Wint 92, p. 72-73.
"The Woman Who Laughed on Calvary." [Iowa] (22:1) Wint 92, p. 42-44.

4142. McINNIS, Nadine
"Insemination." [Grain] (20:3) Fall 92, p. 75-76.

4143. McINTOSH, Joan
"Artist in a Nursing Home." [HopewellR] (4) 92, p. 32.

4144. McINTOSH, Michael
"How These Things Happen." [NewYorkQ] (47) 92, p. 48.

4145. McKAY, Don
"Meditation on Antique Glass." [PottPort] (14:1) Spr-Sum 92, p. 71.
"Pen in Hand." [PottPort] (14:1) Spr-Sum 92, p. 70.
"Song for the Varied Thrush." [PottPort] (14:1) Spr-Sum 92, p. 71.

4146. McKEAN, James
"Concert" (Honorable Mention, The Pablo Neruda Prize for Poetry). [Nimrod] (36:1) Fall-Wint 92, p. 49.
"Quarry." [Nimrod] (36:1) Fall-Wint 92, p. 52.
"Snow Angel." [Nimrod] (36:1) Fall-Wint 92, p. 50-51.

4147. McKEE, Louis
"Air Guitar." [Pearl] (16) Fall 92, p. 35.
"In Her Dream." [ChironR] (11:3) Aut 92, p. 29.
"The Soldier." [PaintedB] (48) 92, p. 70-71.

4148. McKEITHEN, Anne
"The Blue Returns." [Pembroke] (24) 92, p. 117.

4149. MCKELVEY, Barbara R.
"History." [PraF] (13:3, #60) Aut 92, p. 109.
"To You." [PraF] (13:3, #60) Aut 92, p. 110-111.

4150. McKENTY, Bob
"The Bobcat." [Light] (2) Sum 92, p. 24.
"Déjà Vu." [Light] (3) Aut 92, p. 19.
"Election-Year Anni-Verse." [Light] (3) Aut 92, p. 19.
"The Lion." [Light] (1) Spr 92, p. 13.
"Loose Lips Sink Ships." [Light] (3) Aut 92, p. 19.
"The Orang Utan." [Light] (3) Aut 92, p. 16.
"Penguins." [Light] (4) Wint 92-93, p. 10.
"Pensive." [Light] (4) Wint 92-93, p. 21.
"Peter walked on Galilee." [Light] (3) Aut 92, p. 29.
"To Peas." [Light] (4) Wint 92-93, p. 23.
"Woe, Be Gone!" [Light] (3) Aut 92, p. 19.

4151. McKENZIE, Alex
"Tracking." [Poetry] (161:1) O 92, p. 21.

4152. McKENZIE, Jeffrey
"Hurricanes." [SycamoreR] (4:1) Wint 92, p. 40.

4153. McKENZIE, Lee
"Texas at Three." [PraS] (66:3) Fall 92, p. 51.
"The Thorne Rooms at the Chicago Institute." [PraS] (66:3) Fall 92, p. 48-49.
"Where the Gladiola Grow" (After reading Gerald Stern's "For Night to Come"). [PraS] (66:3) Fall 92, p. 49-50.

4154. McKENZIE, Rusty
"Even If." [RagMag] (10:1) 92, p. 9.
"Words." [RagMag] (10:1) 92, p. 8.
4155. McKERNAN, John
"I Have Always Wanted to Stay Eleven Years Old." [PoetryE] (33) Spr 92, p. 91.
"James Dean in Nebraska." [ColEng] (54:7) N 92, p. 828.
"Ode to Elvis Presley." [NewYorkQ] (47) 92, p. 61-62.
"The Size of Death." [CumbPR] (11:2) Spr 92, p. 6.
4156. McKETHAN, Joanna Allred
"Book Club Meeting" (in a Small Southern Town). [Crucible] (28) Fall 92, p. 9.
4157. McKIBBAN, Teri
"Grade School Retribution." [PacificR] (11) 92-93, p. 48.
4158. McKINNEY, Joshua
"Out of Work." [CreamCR] (16:2) Fall 92, p. 45.
"Unmaking the Manes." [CreamCR] (16:2) Fall 92, p. 44.
4159. McKINNON, Patrick (Pat)
"How I Got to Work Yesterday." [SlipS] (12) 92, p. 43-44.
"The Michaletti Poem." [Lactuca] (15) Mr 92, p. 52.
"Poem for Devin." [Lactuca] (15) Mr 92, p. 54.
"The Quitting Poem." [SlipS] (12) 92, p. 44-46.
"Straddling the Boney Death." [Lactuca] (15) Mr 92, p. 53.
4160. McLAUGHLIN-CARRUTH, J.
"Do Not Disturb" (For H.). [SouthernHR] (26:3) Sum 92, p. 240.
"Percussion" (For Jeff Barr). [GrahamHR] (16) Fall 92, p. 94.
4161. McLAURIN, Tim
"David." [Pembroke] (24) 92, p. 100-101.
"Julia." [Pembroke] (24) 92, p. 97-99.
4162. McLEAN, Dirk
"The House on Hermitage Road" (Selections: 4 poems). [WestCL] (26:2, #8) Fall 92, p. 93-99.
4163. McLEAN, Sammy
"Disgust" (tr. of Helga M. Novak). [SnailPR] (2:2) Fall-Wint 92, p. 28.
"Dismal Place" (tr. of Helga M. Novak). [SnailPR] (2:2) Fall-Wint 92, p. 28.
"March Through" (tr. of Helga M. Novak). [Vis] (39) 92, p. 35.
"The Stranger" (tr. of Rainer Brambach). [Vis] (39) 92, p. 34.
"Summer" (tr. of Georg Trakl). [SnailPR] (2:2) Fall-Wint 92, p. 29.
4164. McLEAN, Susan
"Plane Geometry for Lovers." [Kalliope] (14:2) 92, p. 12.
4165. McLEOD, Milt
"Morning-Glories and Children." [TarRP] (31:2) Spr 92, p. 7.
"What the Leica Saw" (for John Howard Griffin, 1920-1980). [TarRP] (31:2) Spr 92, p. 6.
4166. McMAHON, Lynne
"Bedtime." [Shen] (42:2) Sum 92, p. 64-65.
"My South." [OxfordM] (7:1) Spr-Sum 91, p. 84.
"Reading Virgil." [Field] (46) Spr 92, p. 51.
"Slammed Door." [OxfordM] (7:1) Spr-Sum 91, p. 87.
"Spring Fever." [Atlantic] (269:3) Mr 92, p. 82.
"The Toy Box." [OxfordM] (7:1) Spr-Sum 91, p. 85-86.
4167. McMANUS, James
"Purple Ritual." [AnotherCM] (24) Fall 92, p. 103-105.
4168. McMILLAN, James A.
"Letter from the Reservoir." [OxfordM] (8:1) Spr-Sum 92, p. 79.
4169. McMILLAN, Peter
"Another Greek Gift" (Homage to Dobson). [Light] (2) Sum 92, p. 22.
4170. McMILLIAN, Jeff
"Vision" (for Herman Melville). [JamesWR] (10:1) Fall 92, p. 16.
4171. McMURRAY, Earl
"Lyric." [Poem] (67) My 92, p. 24.
"A Man in a Boat." [Poem] (67) My 92, p. 23.
4172. McNAIR, Wesley
"The Before People." [ThRiPo] (39/40) 92-93, p. 159.
"Coming for Brad Newcomb." [PoetryNW] (33:4) Wint 92-93, p. 8-10.
"Francis Bound." [PoetryNW] (33:4) Wint 92-93, p. 6-7.
"House in Spring." [ThRiPo] (39/40) 92-93, p. 158.
"Making Things Clean." [SewanR] (100:3) Sum 92, p. 379.

"My Brother Inside the Revolving Doors." [ThRiPo] (39/40) 92-93, p. 159-160.
"The One Who Will Save You." [PoetryNW] (33:4) Wint 92-93, p. 3-4.
"The Secret." [PoetryNW] (33:4) Wint 92-93, p. 5-6.
"When the Trees Came for Her." [SewanR] (100:3) Sum 92, p. 377-378.

4173. McNALL, Sally Allen
"Among Schoolchildren" (against W. B. Y.). [SingHM] (20) 92, p. 43-44.
"Different from What Anyone Supposed" (Whitman, "Song of Myself," 6). [PraS] (66:1) Spr 92, p. 111-112.
"The Dinosaur We Didn't See." [MidwQ] (33:3) Spr 92, p. 317.
"The Source of Knowledge" (for Denise Low). [PraS] (66:1) Spr 92, p. 113.

4174. McNALLY, John
"Equal Vessels." [Talisman] (9) Fall 92, p. 209.
"In Lieu and Despotic." [Talisman] (9) Fall 92, p. 208-209.

4175. McNALLY, Stephen
"Sentenced." [ColEng] (54:6) O 92, p. 718-719.

4176. McNAMARA, Katherine
"Old Woman Scraping Skin." [AmerV] (27) 92, p. 87-93.

4177. McNAMEE, John
"Inclusion as a Form of Gratitude" (In Memoriam, Gerard Manley Hopkins, The Centenary of His Death, 1989). [PaintedB] (47) 92, p. 57-59.
"Traffic Light." [PaintedB] (47) 92, p. 60.
"Winter Solstice." [PaintedB] (47) 92, p. 55.

4178. McNEIL, Christine
"Weather People." [Verse] (8:3/9:1) Wint-Spr 92, p. 132.

4179. McNEIL, Elizabeth
"Cityscape." [ChironR] (11:3) Aut 92, p. 28.
"Hohokam." [CreamCR] (16:1) Spr 92, p. 84-85.
"Of Wild Things." [ChamLR] (10/11) Spr-Fall 92, p. 190.

4180. McNEIL, Jean
"Exodus Charlie and His Jazz Ensemble." [AntigR] (90) Sum 92, p. 8-10.

4181. McNULTY, Ted
"Doolin." [Verse] (8:3/9:1) Wint-Spr 92, p. 134.

4182. McPHERSON, James L.
"Palimpsest." [Vis] (39) 92, p. 24.

4183. McPHERSON, Michael
"The Anarchist Recants." [ChamLR] (10/11) Spr-Fall 92, p. 125.
"Legacy." [Manoa] (4:1) Spr 92, p. 112.
"Pacific Blue." [ChamLR] (10/11) Spr-Fall 92, p. 126.
"Quiet Title." [Manoa] (4:1) Spr 92, p. 113.
"Water." [Manoa] (4:1) Spr 92, p. 112-113.

4184. McPHERSON, Sandra
"Bedrooms." [NewYorker] (67:48) 20 Ja 92, p. 36.
"Bluegum: On the Curving Paths of Golden Gate Park." [TriQ] (86) Wint 92-93, p. 50-52.
"Coastscape and Mr. Begley." [YaleR] (80:1/2) Apr 92, p. 81-84.
"Landscape Painter, Salmon Creek, July." [Field] (47) Fall 92, p. 64.
"Landscape with Master Class, Northern Oregon Coast." [SouthernR] (28:2) Spr, Ap 92, p. 226-228.
"Ode to Baron Samedi and Other Guédés." [Field] (47) Fall 92, p. 65-67.
"Spirit Writings." [Field] (47) Fall 92, p. 68-69.
"Two Men Trading Dance Movements at Tabby's Blues Box and Heritage Hall, Baton Rouge." [ParisR]] (34:124) Fall 92, p. 52-55.

4185. McQUILKIN, Rennie
"Another System." [MalR] (101) Wint92, p. 125.
"Archibald and the Mockingbird." [CinPR] (23) Wint 91-92, p. 69.
"Archibald Commits Himself to Foxhollow." [CinPR] (23) Wint 91-92, p. 68.
"Company." [PraS] (66:1) Spr 92, p. 35-36.
"Going Under." [Poetry] (160:3) Je 92, p. 147.
"Last Minute" (after Winslow Homer). [PraS] (66:1) Spr 92, p. 34-35.
"The Mugging." [MalR] (101) Wint92, p. 126.
"Playing Crab." [CumbPR] (11:2) Spr 92, p. 42.
"Self-Portrait at Fourteen." [MalR] (101) Wint92, p. 127.
"Too Much Mourning." [LitR] (35:3) Spr 92, p. 406.
"The Tracking." [Poetry] (161:3) D 92, p. 141-142.
"Whistler: Arrangements in Blue and Gold." [MalR] (101) Wint92, p. 128-130.
"Wyckoff, 1935." [CumbPR] (11:2) Spr 92, p. 43.

4186. McRAY, Paul
"Floaters." [CutB] (38) Sum 92, p. 38-39.
4187. McSEVENEY, Angela
"Repotting a Plant." [Verse] (8:3/9:1) Wint-Spr 92, p. 97.
"Reviewed." [Verse] (8:3/9:1) Wint-Spr 92, p. 96.
4188. McTAVISH, Sandra
"The Aborter." [ChrC] (109:15) 29 Ap 92, p. 444.
4189. MEAD, Jane
"The Case of the Misplaced Caption." [Ploughs] (18:4) Wint 92-93, p. 88-91.
"Fall." [BostonR] (17:1) F 92, p. 20.
"If." [BostonR] (17:1) F 92, p. 20.
"The Lord and the General Din of the World." [VirQR] (68:3) Sum 92, p. 484-485.
"The Man in the Poetry Lounge." [VirQR] (68:3) Sum 92, p. 486-488.
"Point of Departure" (108th at the Hudson). [Pequod] (34) 92, p. 49-50.
"Sparrow, My Sparrow." [BostonR] (17:1) F 92, p. 20.
"Tired." [BostonR] (17:1) F 92, p. 20.
"To Vincent Van Gogh of the House He Painted in 1890, the Year of His Death." [NoDaQ] (60:4) Fall 92, p. 46-47.
4190. MEAD, S. E.
"Dreamland U.S.A." [Comm] (119:12) 19 Je 92, p. 23.
"You." [EvergreenC] (7:1) Wint-Spr 92, p. 39.
4191. MEADE, Mary Ann
"Lovers: Chauffeur and Charwoman." [CreamCR] (16:1) Spr 92, p. 129.
4192. MEADOWS, Patrick
"Westbygod." [NewL] (58:3) Spr 92, p. 69-71.
4193. MECKLEM, Todd
"Dinner at Mel's" (w. Denise Dumars). [Pearl] (15) Spr-Sum 92, p. 62.
"Surfaces." [Asylum] (7:3/4) 92, p. 46.
4194. MEDEIROS, John T.
"Dust." [ChironR] (11:4) Wint 92, p. 27.
"Serendipity." [ChironR] (11:4) Wint 92, p. 27.
4195. MEDINA, Pablo
"The Apostate." [Americas] (20:3/4) Fall-Wint 92, p. 232.
"Cuba." [LindLM] (11:2) Je 92, p. 5.
"Everyone Will Have to Listen" (tr. of Tania Diaz Castro, w. Carolina Hospital). [AmerV] (29) 92, p. 18.
"Madame America." [Americas] (20:3/4) Fall-Wint 92, p. 229-231.
4196. MEDINA, Rubén
"Poets Don't Go to Paris Anymore" (for José Peguero, tr. by Reginald Gibbons). [TriQ] (85) Fall 92, p. 166-167.
"Priam" (tr. by Reginald Gibbons). [TriQ] (85) Fall 92, p. 163-165.
4197. MEE, Mike
"Georgetown for Drinks." [MinnR] (38) Spr-Sum 92, p. 52-55.
4198. MEEDS, Bridget
"Battleground." [Gypsy] (18) 92, p. 77-78.
4199. MEEK, Jay
"Behind Schedule." [Grain] (20:1) Spr 92, p. 216.
"The Night Café." [Grain] (20:1) Spr 92, p. 215.
"Story." [Grain] (20:1) Spr 92, p. 214-215.
"Vienna in the Rain." [ThRiPo] (39/40) 92-93, p. 161-162.
"A Walk Around the Lake." [ThRiPo] (39/40) 92-93, p. 162-163.
"Walls." [ThRiPo] (39/40) 92-93, p. 163-164.
"The Week the Dirigible Came." [ThRiPo] (39/40) 92-93, p. 160-161.
4200. MEENAKSHI, R.
"If Hot Flowers Come to the Street" (tr. by Martha Ann Selby and K. Paramasivam). [ChiR] (38:1/2) 92, p. 32-33.
MEER, Arnela Ten
See Ten MEER, Arnela
4201. MEGAW, Neill
"Birdbaby." [SoCoast] (12) Ja 92, p. 8-9.
"Extraterrestrials Discover Earth." [SoCoast] (13) Je 93 [i.e. 92], p. 34.
"How the Other Half Lives." [Light] (3) Aut 92, p. 12.
"In the Midi" (Untitled lithograph by Claude Grosperrin). [NegC] (12:1/2) 92, p. 93.
"Just Missed, Again." [Hellas] (3:1) Spr 92, p. 57.
"Last Words of Methuselah" (The genealogies in Genesis . . .). [NegC] (12:1/2) 92, p. 94.

"The Linen Chest and the Laundry Hamper." [SoCoast] (12) Ja 92, p. 44.
"Out of the Hand of Babes and Sucklings." [Hellas] (3:1) Spr 92, p. 56.
"Pale Cast of Thought." [Hellas] (3:1) Spr 92, p. 57.
"Siobhan." [SoCoast] (13) Je 93 [i.e. 92], p. 8.
"Song for a Shakespearean Fool." [Light] (4) Wint 92-93, p. 7.
"The Suitor's Farewell: Song for Pennywhistle." [SoCoast] (13) Je 93 [i.e. 92], p. 17.
"The Way It Ought to Be." [Outbr] (23) 92, p. 38-39.

4202. MEHNERT, David
"Wiljan" (Dutch Barge Wiljan, moored at St. Mary's Church, Battersea). [WestHR] (46:2) Sum 92, p. 147.

4203. MEHR, Rochelle Hope
"At the Poetry Reading." [Bogg] (65) 92, p. 35.

4204. MEHRHOFF, Charlie
"As Far As the Eye." [DogRR] (11:2, #22) Fall-Wint 92, p. 39.
"For $4.00." [DogRR] (11:1) Spr-Sum 92, p. 15.
"Notes on Poetic Forms." [DogRR] (11:1) Spr-Sum 92, p. 15.
"The Pan Indian Movement / Beginning." [DogRR] (11:1) Spr-Sum 92, p. 14-15.

4205. MEIER, Kay
"Forty Years After Their Deaths, I Invite My Parents to Diner." [WillowR] (19) Spr 92, p. 29-30.
"Night Rooms." [SpoonRQ] (17:1/2) Wint-Spr 92, p. 109.

MEIGS, James Hawley
See HAWLEY-MEIGS, James

4206. MEINBRESSE, Tim
"Listen To." [RagMag] (10:2) 92, p. 98.

4207. MEINHOFF, Michael
"Waikiki." [ChamLR] (10/11) Spr-Fall 92, p. 133.

4208. MEINKE, Peter
"Black Holes & Einstein." [TampaR] (5) Fall 92, p. 25.
"Liquid Paper." [Writer] (105:2) F 92, p. 24.
"Scars." [Atlantic] (269:5) My 92, p. 104.
"Soldiers with Green Leggings" (Villa Schifanoia, 1987). [Writer] (105:2) F 92, p. 26.

4209. MEISSNER, William (Bill)
"After Going Off the Road During the Snowstorm." [ThRiPo] (39/40) 92-93, p. 165 - 166.
"Hitting into the Wind: Judging Fly Balls Hit by My Father, 1957." [Turnstile] (3:2) 92, p. 56-57.
"Summer of 1963: The Orbit of the Wiffle Ball." [MidAR] (12:2) 92, p. 45-46.
"Twisters." [ThRiPo] (39/40) 92-93, p. 166-167.

4210. MEISTER, Shirley Vogler
"Getting the Hang of It." [Light] (2) Sum 92, p. 11.
"Non-Runner's Lament." [Light] (1) Spr 92, p. 30.

4211. MEKULA, Janice (Janice A.)
"Memory." [EngJ] (81:8) D 92, p. 85.
"Things to Do Around a Lake" (after Gary Snyder). [EngJ] (81:7) N 92, p. 99.

4212. MELCHER, Michael
"Bright Waves Spoke." [Wind] (22:71) 92, p. 23.

4213. MELNYCZUK, Askold
"God Is With Us" (tr. of Bohdan Boychuk). [PartR] (59:2) Spr 92, p. 272.
"The Grapes of Generation" (tr. of Bohdan Boychuk). [PartR] (59:2) Spr 92, p. 273 - 274.
"Open My Lips" (tr. of Bohdan Boychuk). [PartR] (59:2) Spr 92, p. 273.
"Your Plenitude" (tr. of Bohdan Boychuk). [PartR] (59:2) Spr 92, p. 271-272.

4214. MELNYK, George
"On Eating a Mars Bar in the Palace of the Popes." [PraF] (13:3, #60) Aut 92, p. 124.
"Sand" (for Julia). [PraF] (13:3, #60) Aut 92, p. 126.
"Teahouse." [PraF] (13:3, #60) Aut 92, p. 125.

MELO NETO, João Cabral de
See NETO, João Cabral de Melo

4215. MELTZ, Daniel
"Lesterville." [AmerPoR] (21:1) Ja-F 92, p. 36.
"Nell's Villa." [AmerPoR] (21:1) Ja-F 92, p. 36.

4216. MEMMER, Philip
"The Fishing Poets" (for James Seay). [CarolQ] (45:1) Fall 92, p. 31.

4217. MENDEZ, Estrellita
"Changing the Sheets." [OnTheBus] (4:2/5:1, #10/11) 92, p. 145-146.
4218. MENDIOLA, Víctor Manuel
"Like the Ocean" (tr. by Reginald Gibbons). [TriQ] (85) Fall 92, p. 202.
"The Room" (tr. by Reginald Gibbons). [TriQ] (85) Fall 92, p. 201.
4219. MENEBROKER, Ann
"Commuting." [Bogg] (65) 92, p. 13-14.
"Downtown Hotel 9-29-91." [Bogg] (65) 92, p. 11.
"Stand-Up Comic." [Bogg] (65) 92, p. 11-12.
4220. MENEFEE, Sarah
"A Curb-by-the-Fender Life." [AmerPoR] (21:5) S-O 92, p. 19.
4221. MENEMENCIOGLU, Nermin
"Avalanche" (tr. of Metin Altiok). [Trans] (26) Spr 92, p. 89.
MENOZZI, Wallis Wilde
See WILDE-MENOZZI, Wallis
4222. MENSCHING, Steffen
"Unter den Linden" (tr. by Margitt Lehbert). [Shiny] (7/8) 92, p. 136.
"Without an Echo" (tr. by Margitt Lehbert). [Shiny] (7/8) 92, p. 136.
4223. MENZIES, Ian
"Dead Cow in Heatwave." [Grain] (20:3) Fall 92, p. 94.
"South Wind." [Grain] (20:3) Fall 92, p. 107.
4224. MERCER, Lianne Elizabeth
"At the Fence." [Kalliope] (15:1) 92, p. 31-32.
4225. MERCK, Bryan E.
"Abomination" (for Sylvia Plath). [HiramPoR] (51/52) Fall 91-Sum 92, p. 51-52.
4226. MERCURIO, Katherine M.
"Remembering Thoreau." [Elf] (2:4) Wint 92, p. 34.
4227. MERRIAM, Eve
"The Great Chain of Being." [FreeL] (9) Wint 92, p. 14-15.
"Playing with Paper Clips in the Singles Bar." [Light] (1) Spr 92, p. 15.
"Red." [FreeL] (10) Sum 92, p. 5.
4228. MERRILL, Christopher
"Lines on the Winter Solstice." [NewOR] (19:3/4) Fall-Wint 92, p. 68.
4229. MERRILL, James
"A Downward Look." [NewRep] (207:26) 21 D 92, p. 42.
"Pearl." [Nat] (254:12) 30 Mr 92, p. 421.
"Self-Portrait in Tyvek(TM) Windbreaker." [NewYorker] (68:1) 24 F 92, p. 38-39.
4230. MERRILL, Karen
"Bordertown, 1987." [DenQ] (26:4) Spr 92, p. 46-48.
4231. MERRIN, Jeredith
"Fourth and Main." [KenR] (NS 14:4) Fall 92, p. 69-70.
4232. MERRITT, Constance
"Etude for Memory and Guitar." [QW] (35) Sum-Fall 92, p. 112-114.
MERS, Joyce la
See LaMERS, Joyce
4233. MERTON, Andrew
"The Penitent." [Conscience] (13:1) Spr 92, p. 28.
"The Right-to-Life Booth at the County Fair." [Conscience] (13:1) Spr 92, p. 8.
"Vasectomy." [Conscience] (13:4) Wint 92-93, p. 38.
"A Young Mother (1960)." [Conscience] (13:3) Aut 92, p. 35.
4234. MERWIN, W. S.
"After the Spring." [Poetry] (160:3) Je 92, p. 125.
"Fox Sleep." [Poetry] (161:1) O 92, p. 5-8.
"Gododdin" (Excerpt, tr. of Aneirin). [GrandS] (11:2, #42) 92, p. 174-181.
"The Hummingbird" (From a Brazilian legend recounted by Ernesto Morales). [Poetry] (161:1) O 92, p. 4.
"Mirage." [Poetry] (160:3) Je 92, p. 127.
"Missing." [Atlantic] (269:4) Ap 92, p. 82.
"Net." [NewYorker] (68:30) 14 S 92, p. 74.
"Panes." [Poetry] (160:3) Je 92, p. 128-130.
"Present." [NewYorker] (68:26) 17 Ag 92, p. 36.
"The Real World of Manuel Córdova." [AmerPoR] (21:5) S-O 92, p. 3-6.
"The Ring of Fire." [YaleR] (80:4) O 92, p. 62-69.
"Search Party." [Poetry] (159:5) F 92, p. 251-252.
"The Stranger" (After a Guarani legend recorded by Ernesto Morales). [Poetry] (161:1) O 92, p. 1-3.

"A Summer Night." [Poetry] (160:3) Je 92, p. 126.

4235. MESCUDI, Robbie
"Of Poisoned Sleep." [Rohwedder] (7) Spr-Sum 92, p. 31-33.

4236. MESSER, Sarah
"The Amazons." [Witness] (6:1) 92, p. 31.
"The Woman Almost Blows Up." [Witness] (6:1) 92, p. 32-33.

4237. MESSERLI, Douglas
"Order." [WashR] (18:4) D 92-Ja 93, p. 15.

4238. MÉTELLUS, Jean
"Anacaona" (Selections from the 4 act play). [Callaloo] (15:2) Spr 92, p. 328-337.

4239. METODIEV, Ivan
"Garden of Questions" (tr. by Lisa Sapinkopf, w. Georgi Belev). [CrabCR] (8:1) Sum-Fall 92, p. 15.

4240. METRAS, Gary
"Idyll." [Os] (35) Fall 92, p. 7.

4241. METZGER, Deena
"Finding a Sabbath Among the Ruins." [OnTheBus] (4:2/5:1, #10/11) 92, p. 147 - 148.

4242. METZGER, Wendell
"Bad One." [MoodySI] (27) Spr 92, p. 22.
"Travel Is Good for You." [MoodySI] (27) Spr 92, p. 22.

4243. MEUEL, David
"Freshly Cut Roses." [BellArk] (8:4) Jl-Ag 92, p. 23.
"Personality." [Pearl] (15) Spr-Sum 92, p. 59.

4244. MEYER, David C.
"Clay" (for Paul and Alta Mae Hessert." [CapeR] (27:2) Fall 92, p. 2.
"Legacy." [Elf] (2:2) Sum 92, p. 36-37.
"Love Comes in a Red Cap." [CapeR] (27:2) Fall 92, p. 1.

4245. MEYER, Thomas
"Eternity." [JamesWR] (9:4) Sum 92, p. 10.

4246. MEYER, W. M., Jr.
"On Writing for Friends." [HolCrit] (29:2) Ap 92, p. 19.

4247. MEYERS, Linda Curtis
"Peace for All Living Things on Earth" (from a child's drawing). [PoetryNW] (33:4) Wint 92-93, p. 24.

4248. MEYERS, Susan
"At Your Doorstep." [Crucible] (28) Fall 92, p. 42.

4249. MEZEI, Balázs
"Stuttering to Rainer, in Darkness" (tr. by Gregory S. d'Elia). [Agni] (35) 92, p. 257 - 258.

4250. MEZEY, Robert
"1929" (tr. of Jorge Luis Borges). [WestHR] (46:2) Sum 92, p. 122-123.
"Alexandria, 641 A.D." (tr. of Jorge Luis Borges). [Iowa] (22:3) Fall 92, p. 70-71.
"Another Version of Proteus" (tr. of Jorge Luis Borges). [Iowa] (22:3) Fall 92, p. 69-70.
"Ash" (tr. of Jorge Luis Borges). [Iowa] (22:3) Fall 92, p. 73.
"The Ballad of Charles Starkweather" (w. Donald Justice). [Verse] (8:3/9:1) Wint - Spr 92, p. 31-32.
"Caesar" (tr. of Jorge Luis Borges). [Raritan] (12:2) Fall 92, p. 22.
"Camden, 1892" (tr. of Jorge Luis Borges). [NewYRB] (39:10) 28 My 92, p. 5.
"Chess" (tr. of Jorge Luis Borges). [Raritan] (12:2) Fall 92, p. 26-27.
"The Clepsydra" (tr. of Jorge Luis Borges). [Raritan] (12:2) Fall 92, p. 24.
"Clouds" (tr. of Jorge Luis Borges, w. Richard Barnes). [Iowa] (22:3) Fall 92, p. 72.
"Everness" (tr. of Jorge Luis Borges, w. Dick Barnes). [SoCoast] (12) Ja 92, p. 37.
"Ewigkeit" (tr. of Jorge Luis Borges, w. Dick Barnes). [SoCoast] (12) Ja 92, p. 35.
"The Exile" (1977, tr. of Jorge Luis Borges). [SoCoast] (12) Ja 92, p. 33.
"Fifteen Coins" (tr. of Jorge Luis Borges). [WestHR] (46:2) Sum 92, p. 124-126.
"For a Version of the I Ching" (tr. of Jorge Luis Borges). [NewYRB] (39:11) 11 Je 92, p. 25.
"Fourteen-Syllable Lines" (tr. of Jorge Luis Borges, w. Dick Barnes). [ArtfulD] (22/23) 92, p. 27.
"General Quiroga Rides to His Death in a Carriage" (tr. of Jorge Luis Borges, w. Richard Barnes). [Iowa] (22:3) Fall 92, p. 71-72.
"Heraclitus" (East Lansing, 1976, tr. of Jorge Luis Borges). [Raritan] (12:2) Fall 92, p. 25.
"In Praise of Darkness" (tr. of Jorge Luis Borges). [Poetry] (161:1) O 92, p. 11-12.

"The Inquisitor" (tr. of Jorge Luis Borges, w. Dick Barnes). [ParisR] (34:125) Wint 92, p. 233.
"Last Evening" (tr. of Jorge Luis Borges, w. Dick Barnes). [ParisR] (34:125) Wint 92, p. 229.
"Lines I Might Have Written and Lost Around 1922" (tr. of Jorge Luis Borges). [ArtfulD] (22/23) 92, p. 29.
"The Lost" (tr. of Jorge Luis Borges). [ArtfulD] (22/23) 92, p. 28.
"Manuel Peyrou" (tr. of Jorge Luis Borges). [Field] (47) Fall 92, p. 103.
"Manuscript Found in a Conrad Novel" (tr. of Jorge Luis Borges). [Field] (47) Fall 92, p. 102.
"May 20, 1928" (tr. of Jorge Luis Borges). [Poetry] (161:1) O 92, p. 10.
"Milonga of the Stranger" (tr. of Jorge Luis Borges, w. Dick Barnes). [ParisR] (34:125) Wint 92, p. 229-230.
"The Moon" (tr. of Jorge Luis Borges, w. Dick Barnes). [ParisR] (34:125) Wint 92, p. 232.
"Music Box" (tr. of Jorge Luis Borges). [GrandS] (11:3 #43) 92, p. 184.
"My Books" (tr. of Jorge Luis Borges). [Harp] (284:1700) Ja 92, p. 42.
"The Nightmare" (tr. of Jorge Luis Borges, w. Richard Barnes). [GrandS] (11:3 #43) 92, p. 185.
"Proteus" (tr. of Jorge Luis Borges). [Iowa] (22:3) Fall 92, p. 69.
"Tea Dance at the Nautilus Hotel (1925)" (On a painting by Donald Justice). [Verse] (8:3/9:1) Wint-Spr 92, p. 34.
"The Thing I Am" (tr. of Jorge Luis Borges, w. Dick Barnes). [ParisR] (34:125) Wint 92, p. 231-232.
"The Things" (tr. of Jorge Luis Borges). [Raritan] (12:2) Fall 92, p. 23.
"To a Minor Poet of 1899" (tr. of Jorge Luis Borges). [Raritan] (12:2) Fall 92, p. 23.
"To My Father" (tr. of Jorge Luis Borges). [SoCoast] (12) Ja 92, p. 39.
"A Wolf" (tr. of Jorge Luis Borges). [Poetry] (161:1) O 92, p. 9.

4251. MICHAUD, Michael Gregg
"June 23, 1991." [ChironR] (11:4) Wint 92, p. 28.
"June 25, 1974." [ChironR] (11:4) Wint 92, p. 28.
"May 17, 1990." [ChironR] (11:4) Wint 92, p. 28.
"Sept. 4, 1974." [ChironR] (11:4) Wint 92, p. 28.

4252. MICHELINE, Jack
"It Is Not Here on Earth What I Am Seeking." [ChironR] (11:1) Spr 92, p. 6.
"My City." [ChironR] (11:1) Spr 92, p. 6.
"Poem: Genius is a ragged lion." [ChironR] (11:1) Spr 92, p. 6.

4253. MICUS, Edward
"Boy in a Rice Paddy, Head Shot." [SpoonRQ] (17:1/2) Wint-Spr 92, p. 107.
"Sin City, An Khe." [SpoonRQ] (17:1/2) Wint-Spr 92, p. 106.
"Things Moving." [CutB] (37) Wint 92, p. 63-64.
"Viet Nam Memorial." [SpoonRQ] (17:1/2) Wint-Spr 92, p. 108.

4254. MIDDLETON, David
"Thoreau's Farewell to Concord." [SewanR] (100:4) Fall 92, p. 555-556.

4255. MIECZKOWSKI, Rondo
"The AIDS Dance" (Sections. Selection from "The Singing Bridge: A National AIDS Poetry Archive"). [Art&Und] (1:2) Wint 92, p. 15.

4256. MIKESELL, Janice H.
"Straight Brown Hair." [Kalliope] (14:3) 92, p. 43.

4257. MIKITA, Nancy
"Be Merry and Dead." [Asylum] (7:3/4) 92, p. 52.

4258. MIKOFSKY, Bernard S.
"Violin Lessons." [Talisman] (9) Fall 92, p. 183.

4259. MIKOLEY, Jim
"Great Writers, #49." [NewYorkQ] (49) 92, p. 37.

4260. MIKULEC, Patrick B.
"Carp." [ChamLR] (10/11) Spr-Fall 92, p. 145.
"Fly Paper." [ChamLR] (10/11) Spr-Fall 92, p. 144.
"The Send-Off." [ChamLR] (10/11) Spr-Fall 92, p. 146.

4261. MILANÉS, Pablo
"Cuando Te Encontré" (w. Silvio Rodríguez). [Areíto] (3:10/11) Abril 92, inside front cover.
"De un Pájaro, las Dos Alas." [Areíto] (3:10/11) Abril 92, p. 80.
"La Vida No Vale Nada." [Areíto] (3:10/11) Abril 92, p. 80.

4263. MILES, Asa
"The Dead in Christ Shall Rise." [LullwaterR] (3:2) Spr 92, p. 48-49.

"On the Bridge to Georgia I Watch the Death of My Travelling Companion, a Mantis I Named Chester." [LullwaterR] (4:1) Fall 92, p. 47.

4264. MILES, Jeff
"Buffalo." [InterPR] (18:2) Fall 92, p. 69.
"Divination." [SouthernPR] (32:2) Fall 92, p. 21-22.
"Full Moon." [InterPR] (18:2) Fall 92, p. 68.

4265. MILES, Judi Kiefer
"At Eleven." [US1] (26/27) 92, p. 38.
"Divorce Can Be So Easy." [JINJPo] (14:1) Spr 92, p. 23.

4266. MILES, Margaret
"Butcher-Sculptor, County Sligo, Ireland." [HolCrit] (29:4) O 92, p. 16.

4267. MILES, Steve
"After 2:00 am." [HawaiiR] (16:2, #35) Spr 92, p. 79-80.
"Breaking the Skin." [HawaiiR] (16:2, #35) Spr 92, p. 78-79.

4268. MILJKOVIC, Branko
"Epitaph" (in Serbo-Croatian and English, tr. by P. H. Liotta). [Nimrod] (35:2) Spr - Sum 92, p. 62-63.
"Inventory of a Poem" (for Vasco Popa, tr. by John Matthias and Vladeta Vuckovic). [TriQ] (86) Wint 92-93, p. 39.
"An Orphic Legacy" (tr. by John Matthias and Vladeta Vuckovic). [TriQ] (86) Wint 92-93, p. 41.
"Requiem" (Selection: VIII, in Serbo-Croatian and English, tr. by P. H. Liotta). [Nimrod] (35:2) Spr-Sum 92, p. 62-63.
"While You Are Singing" (tr. by John Matthias and Vladeta Vuckovic). [TriQ] (86) Wint 92-93, p. 40.

4269. MILLEN, Ivan
"The Singing." [AntigR] (90) Sum 92, p. 116.

4270. MILLER, A. McA.
"Accordion Post-Card, for Sharon" (Variations on a Theme by Wright of Derby). [BelPoJ] (43:1) Fall 92, p. 40-41.
"Transcript." [BelPoJ] (43:1) Fall 92, p. 38-39.

4271. MILLER, Arthur M.
"February Harvest." [Vis] (39) 92, p. 28-29.

4272. MILLER, Carol (Carol E.)
"Hawthorne Makes Himself a Woman" (a response to that "damned mob of scribbling women" who steal the reading public). [MinnR] (38) Spr-Sum 92, p. 28.
"In Her Dream." [MinnR] (39) Fall-Wint 92-93, p. 2.
"Mary in Drag." [CreamCR] (16:1) Spr 92, p. 100.
" *Woman's Head*, Joan Miro, 1938." [CreamCR] (16:1) Spr 92, p. 101.

4273. MILLER, Carolyn
"Elegy for a Poet" (for Tom McAfee). [NewYorkQ] (47) 92, p. 57.

4274. MILLER, Craig
"Busride." [MoodySI] (27) Spr 92, p. 43-44.

4275. MILLER, D. D.
"Gandy-Dancer." [Amelia] (6:4, #19) 92, p. 72.

4276. MILLER, Derek
"After Viewing Some 20th Century American Etchings." [HangL] (61) 92, p. 57.

4277. MILLER, E. Ethelbert
"Carmen and the Fire Across Town." [AmerV] (26) Spr 92, p. 85.

4278. MILLER, Elizabeth Gamble
"The Gaze That Nothing Owns" (Translation Chapbook Series, No. 19, tr. of Claudio Rodríguez). [MidAR] (13:1) 92, p. 173-205.
"Sunflower" (tr. of Claudio Rodríguez). [NewOR] (19:3/4) Fall-Wint 92, p. 38.

4279. MILLER, Errol
"Asylum." [Elf] (2:4) Wint 92, p. 26-27.
"In the Art-Park." [WindO] (56) Fall-Wint 92, p. 10.
"In the Brownwater Bars of Delta." [BellR] (15:2) Fall 92, p. 24.
"Last Light over Dixie." [Crucible] (28) Fall 92, p. 33-34.
"The Last Line." [FreeL] (10) Sum 92, p. 11.
"The New Age in Dixie." [Plain] (13:1) Fall 92, p. 16-17.
"Star City Concerto." [Northeast] (5:7) Wint 92-93, p. 14.
"Towards the James River." [Parting] (5:1) Sum 92, p. 38.
"Unemployed in Sterlington, La." [SlipS] (12) 92, p. 69.
"Where the Delta Ends." [ChatR] (12:3) Spr 92, p. 43.

4280. MILLER, Greg
"From the Museum." [ParisR] (34:123) Sum 92, p. 125.
4281. MILLER, Heather Ross
"Brown Turkey Figs, a Temptation." [SouthernR] (28:4) Aut, O 92, p. 878.
"Telling Lies." [SouthernR] (28:4) Aut, O 92, p. 879.
4282. MILLER, Hugh
"Notes Toward Sketches for a Chef d'Oeuvre: Law, Liberal Arts, Medicine. Canons of Evidence" (for Verna Andersen Miller and Deborah Spurrier Hoffman). [AntigR] (89) Spr 92, p. 57-58.
"St. Jerome" (In memory of Fr. R.J. MacSween, 1915-1990). [AntigR] (89) Spr 92, p. 59.
"Streptococci and Stroke" (for Nadine Margaret Spurrier). [AntigR] (89) Spr 92, p. 60.
4283. MILLER, Jane
"Caliente." [SenR] (21:2) 91, p. 146-147.
"Coupling." [AmerV] (26) Spr 92, p. 70-73.
"Wyoming Gospel." [GreenMR] (NS 5:2) Spr-Sum 92, p. 44.
4284. MILLER, Jeanette
"La Mujer" (From "Fórmulas para combatir el miedo"). [LitR] (35:4) Sum 92, p. 602-603.
"My Casa." [LitR] (35:4) Sum 92, p. 602.
"My House" (tr. by Catherine Guzmán). [LitR] (35:4) Sum 92, p. 512.
"Parallax." [PraS] (66:2) Sum 92, p. 35-36.
"Sextant." [PraS] (66:2) Sum 92, p. 35.
"Woman" (tr. by Catherine Guzmán). [LitR] (35:4) Sum 92, p. 513.
4285. MILLER, John M.
"No More Experiments." [NegC] (12:1/2) 92, p. 89.
4286. MILLER, John N.
"Sunday Afternoon on Grande Jatte Island" (Art Institute of Chicago). [TarRP] (30:2) Spr 91, p. 21.
4287. MILLER, Kevin
"After Harlan's Recurring Dream of Magpies." [NegC] (12:1/2) 92, p. 99.
"For Three." [NegC] (12:1/2) 92, p. 95-96.
"Take More Than Pictures" (Grenå, Denmark). [NegC] (12:1/2) 92, p. 97-98.
4288. MILLER, Kim
"La Abuela." [CreamCR] (16:1) Spr 92, p. 126-127.
4289. MILLER, Leslie Adrienne
"My Students Catch Me Dancing." [ThRiPo] (39/40) 92-93, p. 167-168.
"The Substitute." [ThRiPo] (39/40) 92-93, p. 169-171.
"Swimming with Horses." [AmerV] (26) Spr 92, p. 47-49.
"Temporary Services." [KenR] (NS 14:3) Sum 92, p. 6-9.
"The Weather of Invention." [ThRiPo] (39/40) 92-93, p. 168-169.
4290. MILLER, Linda
"Ideal of Neil." [MoodySI] (27) Spr 92, p. 48.
4291. MILLER, Lisa
"Keeping Apart." [Conscience] (13:1) Spr 92, p. 17.
4292. MILLER, Mark
"Along Back Forest Road." [Amelia] (7:1, #20) 92, p. 81.
"Friesian, Outside Pyree Dairy." [Amelia] (7:1, #20) 92, p. 82.
"Shoalhaven River." [Amelia] (7:1, #20) 92, p. 81-82.
4293. MILLER, Philip
"As the Day Is Long." [LitR] (35:3) Spr 92, p. 357.
"God!" [Poetry] (160:6) S 92, p. 317.
"He Dreamed of Water." [Poem] (68) N 92, p. 29.
"The Long and the Short of It." [Poetry] (160:6) S 92, p. 318.
"The Morning Star." [Poem] (68) N 92, p. 28.
"Our Elders." [LitR] (35:3) Spr 92, p. 356.
"What the Child Says." [TarRP] (30:2) Spr 91, p. 10.
4294. MILLER, Stephen Paul
"Ralph Kramden Emerson *Tonight.*" [Talisman] (8) Spr 92, p. 182-184.
4295. MILLER, Timothy
"The Tides of Heaven" (for Robert Brady). [Hellas] (3:1) Spr 92, p. 53.
4296. MILLER, William
"Infant CPR." [TarRP] (30:2) Spr 91, p. 8-9.
MILLER LAINO, E. J.
See LAINO, E. J. Miller

4297. MILLETT, John
"Autumn Lights from a Colonial Parlour." [Footwork] 92, p. 123.
"Catfish." [Footwork] 92, p. 124.
"Come into the shadow of the church." [Vis] (40) 92, p. 19.
"Domenikos - Theotokopoulos - El Greco." [Footwork] 92, p. 123.
"Etienne." [Footwork] 92, p. 124.
"Face in Belmore Park." [Amelia] (6:4, #19) 92, p. 70-71.
"Hillscape with Horses and Black Swans." [Footwork] 92, p. 123.
"Jean in the Shadow of a Night Hunter (Sydney)." [Footwork] 92, p. 118.
"Kaddish for Shulamite" (Poem for five voices). [Footwork] 92, p. 120.
"Lake Poem — Slag Heap in Foreground." [Footwork] 92, p. 118.
"Letter to an Unknown Woman." [Footwork] 92, p. 119.
"The Man from Dunbarton Steel Inc." [Amelia] (6:4, #19) 92, p. 69-70.
"Miniature Battle Scene — War Museum." [Footwork] 92, p. 121-123.
"Poem to a Woman from Groningen." [Footwork] 92, p. 120.
"The Princess in a Butcher's Shop." [Amelia] (6:4, #19) 92, p. 68-69.
"Silver Dory." [Footwork] 92, p. 124.
"Snake at Callaghan's Farm." [Footwork] 92, p. 119.
"Song of the Night." [Footwork] 92, p. 124.
"Sunday gathers in the wild motor-bike boys." [Vis] (40) 92, p. 19.
"Water Diviner." [Footwork] 92, p. 124.

4298. MILLIGAN, Paula
"Ancient Poets." [BellArk] (8:1) Ja-F 92, p. 12.
"Contact." [BellArk] (8:1) Ja-F 92, p. 13.
"If Truth Is Dreamed of Before Waking." [BellArk] (8:2) Mr-Ap 92, p. 14.
"Spectrum." [BellArk] (8:3) My-Je 92, p. 5.

4299. MILLIS, Christopher
"One Sense." [SenR] (22:2) Fall 92, p. 80.
"The Writer at the Trident Cafe." [SenR] (22:2) Fall 92, p. 79.

4300. MILLS, Jess
"Size." [Kalliope] (14:3) 92, p. 62.

4301. MILLS, Laurel
"After the Hysterectomy." [Calyx] (14:1) Sum 92, p. 44.
"Choosing Love." [RagMag] (10:2) 92, p. 28.
"Inventing Our Lives." [Kalliope] (14:2) 92, p. 4.
"Say It Is Ragged Need." [RagMag] (10:2) 92, p. 27.
"This Summer." [RagMag] (10:2) 92, p. 26.

4302. MILLS, Mark
"US 1." [Obs] (7:1/2) Spr-Sum 92, p. 105-106.

4303. MILLS, Paul
"Hurricane in the Gulf of Campeche." [Verse] (8:3/9:1) Wint-Spr 92, p. 127.

4304. MILLS, Ralph J., Jr.
"Crocus / Flicker." [Northeast] (5:7) Wint 92-93, p. 7.
"Their Lines / Drawn." [Northeast] (5:7) Wint 92-93, p. 6.

4305. MILLS, Todd Easton
"Tuesday Night." [OnTheBus] (4:2/5:1, #10/11) 92, p. 155.
"Upwind." [OnTheBus] (4:2/5:1, #10/11) 92, p. 151-155.
"The Vincent Franchise." [OnTheBus] (4:2/5:1, #10/11) 92, p. 149.
"Wretchedness So Pure." [OnTheBus] (4:2/5:1, #10/11) 92, p. 150-151.

4306. MILLS, W. H. (Wilmer Hastings)
"Journal of a Deer Hunter." [TarRP] (31:2) Spr 92, p. 33-34.
"The Last Castrato" (d. 1924). [PoetC] (23:3) Spr 92, p. 17-18.
"Pampau." [HolCrit] (29:5) D 92, p. 18.
"Testimony of an Orphan." [LullwaterR] (3:3) Sum 92, p. 18-19.

4307. MILNER, Mark
"In Memory of Miles Davis." [Dandel] (19:2) 92, p. 17.
"Untitled: Although it is winter, and the skeletons." [Dandel] (19:2) 92, p. 18.

4308. MILOSZ, Czeslaw
"Capri" (tr. by the author and Robert Hass). [NewYorker] (68:41) 30 N 92, p. 157.
"A Lecture" (tr. by the author and Robert Hass). [NewYorker] (68:18) 22 Je 92, p. 32.
"Why?" (tr. by the author and Robert Hass). [NewRep] (206:24) 15 Je 92, p. 44.

4309. MILTNER, Robert
"Love's Silences." [NewYorkQ] (47) 92, p. 59.
"Pushing Buttons." [NewYorkQ] (48) 92, p. 95-96.

4310. MIMNERMOS
"The Brainsex Paintings" (tr. by Anne Carson). [Raritan] (11:3) Wint 92, p. 3-5.
4311. MIN, Xiao-Hong
"Drinking Joy" (To the Tune of Rumengling, tr. of Qing-Zhao Li, w. Gordon T. Osing and Huang Hai-Peng). [CrabCR] (8:1) Sum-Fall 92, p. 18.
"In Praise of Lotus" (To the Tune of Yuanwangsun, tr. of Qing-Zhao Li, w. Gordon T. Osing and Huang Hai-Peng). [CrabCR] (8:1) Sum-Fall 92, p. 18.
4312. MINANEL, S.
"Take a Gander at This Source!" [Light] (2) Sum 92, p. 15.
4313. MINDOCK, Gloria
"Denied Emotion." [Noctiluca] (1:1) Spr 92, p. 16.
4314. MINEHAN, Mike
"Prodigal." [Vis] (40) 92, p. 42-43.
4315. MINOT, Leslie
"After the Rain Has Ended" (tr. of Ketaki Kushari Dyson, w. Satadru Sen). [ChiR] (38:1/2) 92, p. 188.
4316. MINTON, Helena
"Liane Reads Her Unmailed Letter Aloud." [ConnPR] (11:1) 92, p. 24-25.
"The Rooster That Wakes Me in Mexico." [WestB] (30) 92, p. 55.
"Walls in Mexico." [PoetC] (23:2) Wint 92, p. 15.
4317. MINTZ, Florinda
"About the Poet" (tr. of Pablo Antonio Cuadra, w. Paul Vangelisti). [OnTheBus] (4:2/5:1, #10/11) 92, p. 272.
"De Rerum Natura" (tr. of David Escobar Galindo, w. Paul Vangelisti). [OnTheBus] (4:2/5:1, #10/11) 92, p. 274.
"Exiles" (Dedicated to Stefan Baciu, tr. of Pablo Antonio Cuadra, w. Paul Vangelisti). [OnTheBus] (4:2/5:1, #10/11) 92, p. 273.
"Letter with Roses" (tr. of David Escobar Galindo, w. Paul Vangelisti). [OnTheBus] (4:2/5:1, #10/11) 92, p. 275.
4318. MINTZER, Elaine
"The Actor" (for Jack, of course). [OnTheBus] (4:2/5:1, #10/11) 92, p. 156.
"Free or Fee." [Rohwedder] (7) Spr-Sum 92, p. 12.
"Medusa." [OnTheBus] (4:2/5:1, #10/11) 92, p. 156.
"Not Yet Extinct." [Pearl] (15) Spr-Sum 92, p. 52.
"The Way to Break Wild Daughters." [OnTheBus] (4:2/5:1, #10/11) 92, p. 157.
4319. MINUS, Ed
"Ponte Vedra." [NewDeltaR] (8:2) Spr-Sum 91, p. 12.
"Questions for Mrs. America at Myrtle Beach." [NewDeltaR] (8:2) Spr-Sum 91, p. 13.
4320. MIODRAG, Alfi
"Pebbles, Cobbles, Bubbles" (tr. by the author). [ChangingM] (24) Sum-Fall 92, p. 30.
4321. MIRANDA, Josie
"Uno a Uno." [SinW] (47) Sum-Fall 92, p. 69.
4322. MIRANDA, S. Jacqueline
"Caribbean Waters." [SinW] (47) Sum-Fall 92, p. 138.
4323. MIRANDA, Verónica
"La Guerra" (tr. of Jessica Rutberg). [Luz] (2) S 92, p. 47.
"Ourselves" (tr. of Gladys Machado). [Luz] (2) S 92, p. 9.
4324. MIRRIAM-GOLDBERG, Caryn
"Subway." [TarRP] (30:2) Spr 91, p. 13.
"The Woman Who Cannot Feel." [TarRP] (30:2) Spr 91, p. 12.
4325. MIRSKIN, Jerry
"Joe, 2 a.m." [NewMyths] (1:2/2:1) 92, p. 186.
4326. MISANCHUK, Melanie
"Airplane." [Dandel] (19:3) 92, p. 18.
"CKS." [Dandel] (19:3) 92, p. 25.
"Cool." [Dandel] (19:3) 92, p. 24.
"Cows." [Dandel] (19:3) 92, p. 22.
"Cut." [Dandel] (19:3) 92, p. 17.
"I Can't Rhyme." [Dandel] (19:3) 92, p. 19.
"Jimmy Chair." [Dandel] (19:3) 92, p. 26.
"St. Vitus's Dance, Amsterdam." [Dandel] (19:3) 92, p. 21.
"Wheelborrow." [Dandel] (19:3) 92, p. 23.
"You Said You'd Call." [Dandel] (19:3) 92, p. 20.

4327. MISENTI, Neva
"Donna's Out Today." [SingHM] (20) 92, p. 75.
4328. MISRA, Kalidas
"Possession." [FourQ] (6:2) Fall 92, p. 16.
4329. MITCHELL, Elaine
"In Memoriam." [Light] (1) Spr 92, p. 7.
"One Thing Leads to Another." [Light] (4) Wint 92-93, p. 9.
"Vantage Point." [Light] (1) Spr 92, p. 24.
4330. MITCHELL, Gwendolyn
"House of Women." [PraS] (66:3) Fall 92, p. 52-53.
4331. MITCHELL, Homer
"A Fish Story" (for David). [SouthernR] (28:3) Sum, Jl 92, p. 617-618.
"The Mundane." [SouthernR] (28:3) Sum, Jl 92, p. 618.
"Once Again." [SouthernR] (28:3) Sum, Jl 92, p. 619.
4332. MITCHELL, John
"A Day in the Life of a Housewife." [Footwork] 92, p. 134.
"First Day." [Footwork] 92, p. 134.
4333. MITCHELL, Mark
"Audrey's Tea and Bath." [SpoonRQ] (17:1/2) Wint-Spr 92, p. 20.
"The Six Trees." [SpoonRQ] (17:3/4) Sum-Fall 92, p. 118.
4334. MITCHELL, Rick
"Fathers, Sons, and Remembrance." [ChironR] (11:3) Aut 92, p. 27.
4335. MITCHELL, Roger
"Bare Branches, One Crow." [SpoonRQ] (17:3/4) Sum-Fall 92, p. 97.
"Captious Will." [NewAW] (10) Fall 92, p. 104.
"The Glass on the Table." [SpoonRQ] (17:3/4) Sum-Fall 92, p. 99.
"Last Poem." [SpoonRQ] (17:3/4) Sum-Fall 92, p. 100.
"Scaly Flank." [PoetryNW] (33:3) Aut 92, p. 46-47.
"We Interrupt This Poem." [SpoonRQ] (17:3/4) Sum-Fall 92, p. 98.
"White Winged Swarming." [GreenMR] (NS 5:2) Spr-Sum 92, p. 68-74.
4336. MITCHELL, Susan
"Rainbow." [AmerPoR] (21:4) Jl-Ag 92, p. 44-45.
"Self Portrait with Two Faces." [AmerPoR] (21:4) Jl-Ag 92, p. 43-44.
4337. MITCHELL, Wendy
"Four Hands." [Amelia] (6:4, #19) 92, p. 32.
4338. MITCHNER, Gary
"Antonio's Laments." [WestHR] (46:1) Spr 92, p. 7-9.
"Leaving Hilton Head Island" (from the Morgan Series). [ParisR] (34:125) Wint 92, p. 158.
"Morgan on Larkin." [WestHR] (46:1) Spr 92, p. 10-11.
"Morgan Watches *Now, Voyager*" (from the Morgan Series). [ParisR] (34:125) Wint 92, p. 156.
"Morgan's Degradation." [WestHR] (46:1) Spr 92, p. 12-13.
"A Victim of Personality" (from the Morgan Series). [ParisR] (34:125) Wint 92, p. 159.
"Worrying About Shoes" (from the Morgan Series). [ParisR] (34:125) Wint 92, p. 1 57.
4339. MITRE, Eduardo
"Itea" (tr. by Maria Herrera Sobek). [OnTheBus] (4:2/5:1, #10/11) 92, p. 277.
"To an Image" (In memoriam, Jaime Saenz, tr. by Maria Herrera Sobek). [OnTheBus] (4:2/5:1, #10/11) 92, p. 276.
4340. MITTERMANN, Lauren
"Four Russians Held Briefly for Stealing at K-Mart Store." [RagMag] (10:2) 92, p. 62-63.
"Washing a Green Bowl." [RagMag] (10:2) 92, p. 64-65.
MIYUKI, Aoyama
See AOYAMA, Miyuki
4341. MIZEJEWSKI, Linda
"Anaerobics: Elaine Powers, Wheeling, West Virginia." [ThRiPo] (39/40) 92-93, p. 172-173.
"Parents Sleeping." [ThRiPo] (39/40) 92-93, p. 171-172.
4342. MIZER, Ray
"Autumns Long Past." [BellArk] (8:1) Ja-F 92, p. 3.
"Autumns Long Past." [BellArk] (8:1) Ja-F 92, p. 27.
"Light Switch." [BellArk] (8:2) Mr-Ap 92, p. 6.
"Light Switch" (corrected reprint). [BellArk] (8:3) My-Je 92, p. 25.

"Parable in Jivetime." [WebR] (16) Fall 92, p. 102.

4343. MOBILIA, Mary Lynch
"An Excellent H ^{2}O." [Light] (4) Wint 92-93, p. 24.
"His Father's Eyes." [Light] (4) Wint 92-93, p. 23.
"Hot Air: Cold Comfort." [Light] (1) Spr 92, p. 23.

4344. MOBLEY, Carla
"Mother-In-Law." [PraF] (13:4, #61) Wint 92-93, p. 72.
"Vows." [PraF] (13:4, #61) Wint 92-93, p. 73.

4345. MOCARSKI, Tim
"Drought." [EngJ] (80:5) S 91, p. 93.

4346. MOCK, Jeff
"The Bucher's Man at His Favorite Stop, 1927." [PassN] (13:1) Sum 92, p. 14.
"Landscape with Mute and Oak." [ArtfulD] (22/23) 92, p. 112-113.
"Natural Habitats" (Greensboro Review Literary Award Poem). [GreensboroR] (53) Wint 92-93, p. 65-67.
"Peach Trees, February." [ChiR] (37:4) 92, p. 80-83.
"Saint Thomas." [HolCrit] (29:3) Je 92, p. 13.
"Where the World Begins." [BelPoJ] (42:4) Sum 92, p. 34.

4347. MOE, Frederick
"Awake Past Midnight." [DogRR] (11:2, #22) Fall-Wint 92, p. 42.

4348. MOES, Christopher
"Maine Sleeps." [EvergreenC] (7:1) Wint-Spr 92, p. 45.
"Mr. Sugar Packet." [EvergreenC] (7:1) Wint-Spr 92, p. 46.

4349. MOFFATT, Deborah
"A Desolation As of War." [Verse] (8:3/9:1) Wint-Spr 92, p. 98-99.
"Far from Home." [Verse] (8:3/9:1) Wint-Spr 92, p. 98.

4350. MOFFEIT, Tony
"Talking with Ghosts." [MoodySI] (27) Spr 92, p. 41.

4351. MOFFETT, Judith
"Forsythia" (for Ted). [KenR] (NS 14:1) Wint 92, p. 20-22.
"Ragged Sonnet." [KenR] (NS 14:1) Wint 92, p. 20.

4352. MOHR, Bill
"The Soul's Bright O." [OnTheBus] (4:2/5:1, #10/11) 92, p. 158.

4353. MOHR, Marilyn
"March 1990." [Noctiluca] (1:2) Wint 92 [on cover: Wint 93], p. 8.

4354. MOHYLNY, Attila
"Beatles (A Cycle)" (tr. by Virlana Tkacz and Wanda Phipps). [Agni] (36) 92, p. 249-252.

4355. MOIR, James M.
"The Reality of My Head." [Event] (21:1) Spr 92, p. 28.

4356. MOLDAW, Carol
"Beads of Rain." [NewYorker] (68:41) 30 N 92, p. 108.
"Menses." [Noctiluca] (1:2) Wint 92 [on cover: Wint 93], p. 38.
"Reb Shmerl and the Water Spirit: A Hassidic Tale." [KenR] (NS 14:1) Wint 92, p. 55-58.
"Waking." [Noctiluca] (1:2) Wint 92 [on cover: Wint 93], p. 37.

MOLEN, Robert vander
See VanderMOLEN, Robert

4357. MOLINA, Josefa
"Mestiza." [SinW] (47) Sum-Fall 92, p. 71.

4358. MOLINA CABALLERO, José
"La Costumbre de Vivir." [Nuez] (4:10/11) 92, p. 38.
"Lecho de Salitre" (Del libro inédito "Menú para dos"). [Nuez] (4:10/11) 92, p. 38.
"La Llamada del Deseo." [Nuez] (4:10/11) 92, p. 38.

4359. MOLINO, Anthony
"Passi Passaggi" (Selection: poem, tr. of Antonio Porta). [Trans] (26) Spr 92, p. 6-7.

4360. MOLNAR, Judit
"Forgotten Fires" (from "Elfelejtett Tüzek," tr. of Károly Bari). [PoetryC] (12:2) Ap 92, p. 24.
"Gypsy-Row" (from "Elfelejtett Tüzek," tr. of Károly Bari). [PoetryC] (12:2) Ap 92, p. 24.
"Pvt. János Vajda's Confession in Front of Sándor Petöfi's Immortal Soul" (tr. of Károly Bari). [PoetryC] (12:2) Ap 92, p. 24.

4361. MOMADAY, N. Scott
"Earth and I Gave You Turquoise." [Jacaranda] (6:1/2) Wint-Spr 92, p. 83.

4362. MONACELLI-JOHNSON, Linda
"Hammock Songs" (for Carol Bess). [Pembroke] (24) 92, p. 93.
4363. MONACO, Cory
"Annette's Czech Accent." [WormR] (32:4 #128) 92, p. 138.
"Cold." [WormR] (32:4 #128) 92, p. 138.
"The Hill." [WormR] (32:4 #128) 92, p. 138.
"How I Live." [WormR] (32:4 #128) 92, p. 138.
"No Night Birds." [WormR] (32:4 #128) 92, p. 140.
"Scissor-Like." [WormR] (32:4 #128) 92, p. 139.
"Symmetry of Vodkation." [WormR] (32:4 #128) 92, p. 139.
4364. MONAHAN, Jean
"April Melancholy." [CumbPR] (12:1) Fall 92, p. 78-79.
4365. MONEY, Peter
"To the Lady in Pink Standing on Top of the Bridge." [Lactuca] (15) Mr 92, p. 2-4.
4366. MONROE, Melissa
"Below the Surface." [SenR] (22:1) Spr 92, p. 75.
"The Dream" (tr. of Ernst Herbeck). [GrandS] (11:1, #41) 92, p. 221.
"Homesickness" (tr. of Ernst Herbeck). [GrandS] (11:1, #41) 92, p. 219.
"Morning" (tr. of Ernst Herbeck). [GrandS] (11:1, #41) 92, p. 219.
"The Squirrel" (tr. of Ernst Herbeck). [GrandS] (11:1, #41) 92, p. 223.
4367. MONTAG, Tom
"A 4th of July & Wedding Celebration" (for Ed Duarte). [Northeast] (5:6) Spr 92, p. 27.
"The Last Punishment" (for my mother). [Northeast] (5:6) Spr 92, p. 26.
"Poem: Words — just words." [Northeast] (5:6) Spr 92, p. 28.
4368. MONTALE, Eugenio
"After a Flight" (tr. by William Arrowsmith). [AmerPoR] (21:3) My-Je 92, p. 33-34.
"All Souls' Day" (from the "Quaderno di quattro anni," tr. by William Arrowsmith). [AmerPoR] (21:3) My-Je 92, p. 35.
"Aspasia" (tr. by William Arrowsmith). [ParisR] (34:122) Spr 92, p. 98.
"The Chiming Pendulum Clock" (tr. by William Arrowsmith). [Boulevard] (7:2/3, #20/21) Fall 92, p. 123.
"The Dead" (tr. by William Arrowsmith). [PartR] (59:2) Spr 92, p. 259-260.
"El Desdichado" (tr. by William Arrowsmith). [WestHR] (46:3) Fall 92, p. 228.
"Early or Late" (tr. by William Arrowsmith). [AmerPoR] (21:3) My-Je 92, p. 35.
"L'Élan Vital" (tr. by William Arrowsmith). [WestHR] (46:3) Fall 92, p. 229.
"Fanfare" (tr. by William Arrowsmith). [Pequod] (33) 92, p. 160-162.
"Intermezzo" (tr. by William Arrowsmith). [Trans] (26) Spr 92, p. 29.
"Lac D'Annecy" (tr. by William Arrowsmith). [Boulevard] (7:2/3, #20/21) Fall 92, p. 124.
"The Lemon Trees" (tr. by William Arrowsmith). [AmerPoR] (21:3) My-Je 92, p. 35.
"The Lord of the Revels" (tr. by William Arrowsmith). [WestHR] (46:3) Fall 92, p. 230.
"Motets" (tr. by Jonathan Galassi). [GrandS] (11:1, #41) 92, p. 24-33.
"North Wind" (tr. by Antony Oldknow). [WebR] (16) Fall 92, p. 28.
"Piròpo, in Conclusion" (tr. by William Arrowsmith). [AmerPoR] (21:3) My-Je 92, p. 34.
"Reading Cavafy" (tr. by William Arrowsmith). [ParisR] (34:122) Spr 92, p. 97.
"Sorapis, Forty Years Ago" (tr. by William Arrowsmith). [ParisR] (34:122) Spr 92, p. 94.
"To Pio Rajna" (tr. by William Arrowsmith). [ParisR] (34:122) Spr 92, p. 95.
"Transvestisms" (tr. by William Arrowsmith). [ParisR] (34:122) Spr 92, p. 96.
4369. MONTALVO, Berta G.
"Grito" (A Reinaldo Arenas). [Nuez] (4:12) 92, p. 10.
4370. MONTEMAYOR, Carlos
"Carta" (tr. of Alejandro Baras, w. Rigas Kappatos). [Nuez] (4:12) 92, p. 24.
"The Memory of Silver" (tr. by Russell M. Cluff and L. Howard Quackenbush). [TriQ] (85) Fall 92, p. 203-204.
"Pasan los Asiáticos" (tr. of Alejandro Baras, w. Rigas Kappatos). [Nuez] (4:12) 92, p. 24.
4371. MONTEOÑATE, Libia
"El Tronco." [Nuez] (4:12) 92, p. 16.
4372. MONTES HUIDOBRO, Matías
"El Canto del Atomo." [Ometeca] (2:2) 91 [published 92], p. 20-21.
"La Voz de la Furia." [Ometeca] (2:2) 91 [published 92], p. 22-23.

4373. MONTGOMERY, M. S.
"The Golden Age of Gay Literature." [Art&Und] (1:5) S-O 92, p. 12.
"Sapphics on Ejaculation" (for Father's Day). [ChangingM] (24) Sum-Fall 92, p. 23.
4374. MONTGOMERY, Missy Marie
"Some Kind of Blues." [CutB] (38) Sum 92, p. 44.
4375. MONTGOMERY, Nan
"At Suppertime." [RagMag] (10:1) 92, p. 56.
"Common Blue." [RagMag] (10:1) 92, p. 54-55.
"The Hopi Potter Nampeyo." [RagMag] (10:1) 92, p. 57.
MONTOYA, Lucía Manríquez
See MANRIQUEZ MONTOYA, Lucía
4376. MOODY, Shirley
"Arcimboldo's Spell" (Giuseppe Arcimboldo, Italian Painter, 1527-1593). [Crucible] (28) Fall 92, p. 51-52.
4377. MOOERS, Vernon
"Down in the Mines." [Dandel] (19:2) 92, p. 7.
"The Hanging Tree." [AntigR] (89) Spr 92, p. 98.
"Lilliput Lane." [AntigR] (89) Spr 92, p. 97.
"Outport School." [Dandel] (19:2) 92, p. 6.
4378. MOOLMAN, Kobus
"The Boy Who Went Out Too Far." [Stand] (33:3) Sum 92, p. 59.
"On the Death of Ugogo." [Stand] (33:3) Sum 92, p. 59.
"To My Obstinate Muse." [Stand] (33:3) Sum 92, p. 58.
4379. MOOLTEN, David
"1968." [SouthernPR] (32:1) Spr 92, p. 17-19.
"Chemistry Set." [Boulevard] (7:1, #19) Spr 92, p. 192-193.
"Freight." [SouthernPR] (32:1) Spr 92, p. 16-17.
"The Night." [GeoR] (46:1) Spr 92, p. 142-143.
"Pinocchio." [PoetryNW] (33:3) Aut 92, p. 39-40.
4380. MOONEY, Sharon
"Hy.ster.i.cal, [Gk, hysterikos, of the womb], uncontrollable emotions." [Rohwedder] (7) Spr-Sum 92, p. 17.
4381. MOOR, Tony
"Straight from the Streets." [AfAmRev] (26:2) Sum 92, p. 282.
4382. MOORE, Abd al-Hayy
"Message to the Tyrant." [Nat] (255:5) 17-24 Ag 92, p. 184.
4383. MOORE, Barbara
"I Would Like To." [BelPoJ] (43:2) Wint 92-93, p. 26-27.
"Ode to Wood." [MidAR] (13:2) 92, p. 160-162.
"What We Want." [BelPoJ] (43:2) Wint 92-93, p. 28-30.
4384. MOORE, Cynthia
"Walking on a Frozen Lake." [SoDakR] (30:2) Sum 92, p. 113.
4385. MOORE, Ed (Edward)
"House of a Thousand Windows." [NewAW] (10) Fall 92, p. 114-116.
"Open Ground." [AnotherCM] (23) Spr 92, p. 143-144.
4386. MOORE, Ellen E.
"Mary Finishes Her Last Growing Spurt." [Pearl] (15) Spr-Sum 92, p. 27.
4387. MOORE, Eugenia
"Winter Path." [Amelia] (6:4, #19) 92, p. 77.
4388. MOORE, George B.
"Apocrypha." [MinnR] (39) Fall-Wint 92-93, p. 17-18.
"Housekeeping." [MinnR] (39) Fall-Wint 92-93, p. 15-16.
"The Transformation of Nature." [Poetry] (160:2) My 92, p. 88-89.
4389. MOORE, Honor
"Sitting for Inge Morath." [Hellas] (3:2) Fall 92, p. 95.
4390. MOORE, Janice Townley
"Gentsy Avenue." [PaintedHR] (6) Spr 92, p. 17.
"Julia Child's Duck." [Light] (2) Sum 92, p. 13.
4391. MOORE, Jim
"After My Father's Death." [AntR] (50:3) Sum 92, p. 506.
"Here, There" (January 1, 1990). [ColR] (9:1) Spr-Sum 92, p. 47-48.
"In Romania." [PoetryE] (33) Spr 92, p. 93.
"Queen Elizabeth on TV." [PoetryE] (33) Spr 92, p. 92.
"Think of the World as a Week Alone." [ColR] (9:1) Spr-Sum 92, p. 45-46.
4392. MOORE, Lenard D.
"After Desert Storm." [Crucible] (28) Fall 92, p. 40.

"Driving to the Wedding Rehearsal." [Crucible] (28) Fall 92, p. 41.
"Haiku." [Wind] (22:71) 92, p. 25.
"Heavenbird." [AfAmRev] (26:2) Sum 92, p. 267.
"Letter from Kuwait." [Crucible] (28) Fall 92, p. 39.
"My Mother Speaks of a Ball of Fire, 1967." [Obs] (7:1/2) Spr-Sum 92, p. 107-108.
"The Near Miss." [Obs] (7:1/2) Spr-Sum 92, p. 108.

4393. MOORE, Leslie S.
"To a Garden Spider: Black-and-Yellow Argiope." [EngJ] (81:4) Ap 92, p. 94.

4394. MOORE, Mary
"Mater Mother" (Oak, Boulder, Slope). [Field] (46) Spr 92, p. 45.
"Yellow" (from "Alpha." Finalist, The Pablo Neruda Prize for Poetry). [Nimrod] (36:1) Fall-Wint 92, p. 54.

4395. MOORE, Miles David
"Prologue: Fatslug Hears the Philosopher." [NewYorkQ] (47) 92, p. 60.

4396. MOORE, Richard (*See also* MOORE, Richard O.)
"Cultural Transplant." [Light] (2) Sum 92, p. 12.
"Floral." [Light] (3) Aut 92, p. 21.
"For a Cultured Child Weeping." [Amelia] (6:4, #19) 92, p. 131.
"For the Cold Night." [Sparrow] (59) S 92, p. 18.
"Peach." [CumbPR] (11:2) Spr 92, p. 44.
"The Poem: A Farewell to My Students." [Iowa] (22:1) Wint 92, p. 186-187.
"Sonnet: To get drunk on a summer." [Sparrow] (59) S 92, p. 18.
"Squirrels." [Iowa] (22:1) Wint 92, p. 188.
"Suburb Song." [Light] (4) Wint 92-93, p. 22.
"This Moment" (for Gertrude Moore, 1892-1980). [CumbPR] (12:1) Fall 92, p. 47.
"What's in a Name?" [Light] (2) Sum 92, p. 11.

4397. MOORE, Richard O. (*See also* MOORE, Richard)
"Eulogy" (for Lewis Hill). [Talisman] (8) Spr 92, p. 28.

4398. MOORE, Todd
"He'd Buried." [ChironR] (11:3) Aut 92, p. 29.
"I Was W/Latigo." [Bogg] (65) 92, p. 6.
"When the Taylor." [EngJ] (81:2) F 92, p. 97.

4399. MOORHEAD, Andrea
"Cat Mountain." [Os] (35) Fall 92, p. 23-31.
"Letter to a Lost Land." [Rohwedder] (7) Spr-Sum 92, p. 39.
"The Night Around the Heart." [Os] (34) Spr 92, p. 18-19.
"Resurrection." [MidwQ] (33:2) Wint 92, p. 204.
"This Grave I Carry Within." [Os] (34) Spr 92, p. 22-23.
"Washing of Snow." [Confr] (48/49) Spr-Sum 92, p. 211.
"Where Light Has Touched." [MidwQ] (33:2) Wint 92, p. 203.

4400. MOOSE, Ruth
"Grass." [SouthernPR] (32:2) Fall 92, p. 69-70.
"My Brother, the Tree." [NewDeltaR] (8:2) Spr-Sum 91, p. 88-89.
"On the Road to Damascus." [Crucible] (28) Fall 92, p. 18.
"Sorrow." [NewDeltaR] (8:2) Spr-Sum 91, p. 90-91.
"The Tortoise." [EngJ] (81:8) D 92, p. 84.

4401. MORA, Pat
"1992" (Canon del Sumidero, Mexico). [IndR] (15:1) Spr 92, p. 81-82.
"Bailando." [Americas] (20:3/4) Fall-Wint 92, p. 175.
"Elena." [Americas] (20:3/4) Fall-Wint 92, p. 176.

4402. MORABITO, Fabio
"The Last of the Tribe" (tr. by Reginald Gibbons). [TriQ] (85) Fall 92, p. 92-95.
"Vacant Lots" (2 selections, tr. by Judith Infante). [Manoa] (4:2) Fall 92, p. 183-190.

4403. MORALES, Harry
"Choosing My Landscape" (tr. of Mario Benedetti). [Nimrod] (36:1) Fall-Wint 92, p. 79.
"Colibrí" (para Tess, tr. of Raymond Carver). [Nuez] (4:10/11) 92, p. 24.
"However" (from "Only in the Meantime: Poems 1948-1950," tr. of Mario Benedetti). [Nimrod] (36:1) Fall-Wint 92, p. 78.
"Nocturnal" (tr. of Mario Benedetti). [InterPR] (18:2) Fall 92, p. 29, 31.
"Typist" (tr. of Mario Benedetti). [AmerV] (26) Spr 92, p. 91-92.

4404. MORALES, Rosario
"If I Was to Start My Life Over Again." [Callaloo] (15:4) Fall 92, p. 961-962.

4405. MORAMARCO, Fred
"Irreconcilable Differences." [LitR] (35:3) Spr 92, p. 353.
"Novel." [Pearl] (15) Spr-Sum 92, p. 64-65.

4406. MORAN, Duncan
"Where There Is No Other." [Sun] (199) Je-Jl 92, p. 38.
4407. MORAN, Kevin
"Guts." [SlipS] (12) 92, p. 104-105.
4408. MORAN, Ronald
"A Change in Barometric Pressure." [SmPd] (29:1, #84) Wint 92, p. 10.
"Uncle Curly and Aunt Edna." [ChironR] (11:3) Aut 92, p. 26.
4409. MORAN, William L.
"Prayer to the Gods of the Night" (literal tr. of an Old Babylonian poem, re - translated by David Ferry). [Arion] 3d series (1:1) Wint 90, p. 186.
4410. MORDECAI, Pam (Pamela C.)
"Aquarium" (tr. of Dulce Maria Loynaz, w. Betty Wilson). [LitR] (35:4) Sum 92, p. 454.
"Declaration of Love" (tr. of Carilda Oliver Labra, w. Betty Wilson). [LitR] (35:4) Sum 92, p. 461.
"Elegy" (tr. of Carilda Oliver Labra, w. Betty Wilson). [LitR] (35:4) Sum 92, p. 462.
"Expect It" (for Jellicoe Taylor." [CinPR] (23) Wint 91-92, p. 44.
"More on My Sister." [CinPR] (23) Wint 91-92, p. 43.
"More on My Sister." [LitR] (35:4) Sum 92, p. 494.
"My Sister." [CinPR] (23) Wint 91-92, p. 42.
"My Sister." [LitR] (35:4) Sum 92, p. 493-494.
"My Sister Takes Over." [LitR] (35:4) Sum 92, p. 495-496.
"Purchase" (tr. of Dulce Maria Loynaz, w. Betty Wilson). [LitR] (35:4) Sum 92, p. 453.
"Rebirth" (tr. of Nancy Morejon, w. Kathleen Weaver). [LitR] (35:4) Sum 92, p. 460.
"Rondel" (tr. of Carilda Oliver Labra, w. Betty Wilson). [LitR] (35:4) Sum 92, p. 462.
"Wednesday Chronicle." [CinPR] (23) Wint 91-92, p. 41.
4411. MOREJON, Nancy
"Black Man" (tr. by J. R. Pereira). [LitR] (35:4) Sum 92, p. 459.
"Church Spire Against the Sky" (tr. by J. R. Pereira). [LitR] (35:4) Sum 92, p. 457.
"Farewell" (in Spanish). [LitR] (35:4) Sum 92, p. 593.
"Farewell" (tr. by J. R. Pereira). [LitR] (35:4) Sum 92, p. 455.
"Hilandera." [LitR] (35:4) Sum 92, p. 594-595.
"Looking Within" (tr. by J. R. Pereira). [LitR] (35:4) Sum 92, p. 457.
"Mirar Adentro." [LitR] (35:4) Sum 92, p. 593.
"Negro." [LitR] (35:4) Sum 92, p. 595.
"Rebirth" (tr. by Kathleen Weaver, w. Pam Mordecai). [LitR] (35:4) Sum 92, p. 460.
"Renacimiento." [LitR] (35:4) Sum 92, p. 593-594.
"Soldado y Yo." [LitR] (35:4) Sum 92, p. 596.
"Soldier and I" (tr. by Kathleen Weaver). [LitR] (35:4) Sum 92, p. 460.
"Spinning Woman" (tr. by J. R. Pereira). [LitR] (35:4) Sum 92, p. 458.
"Torre de Iglesia Contra Cielo." [LitR] (35:4) Sum 92, p. 594.
4412. MORELAND, Nancy
"4 A.M. Feeding." [Amelia] (7:1, #20) 92, p. 55.
MORELOS TORRES
See TORRES, Morelos
4413. MORENO, Gean
"Wild Horses." [MidwQ] (34:1) Aut 92, p. 76-77.
4414. MORGAN, Edwin
"A Memorial." [JamesWR] (9:4) Sum 92, p. 7.
"Without Hope" (tr. of Attila József). [Trans] (26) Spr 92, p. 36-37.
4415. MORGAN, Elizabeth Seydel
"Solon and Sappho As Statues." [Shen] (42:3) Fall 92, p. 85.
"The Virginia Capitol." [Shen] (42:3) Fall 92, p. 82-83.
"What Turns the Wheel of Fortune." [Shen] (42:3) Fall 92, p. 84.
4416. MORGAN, Frederick
"Flora." [SewanR] (100:4) Fall 92, p. 559.
"Primer." [SewanR] (100:4) Fall 92, p. 557-558.
4417. MORGAN, Robert
"Fever Wit." [MichQR] (31:2) Spr 92, p. 264.
"Kraut Crock." [SouthernR] (28:4) Aut, O 92, p. 882.
"Laying By." [SenR] (22:1) Spr 92, p. 6.
"Meadow Mole." [SouthernR] (28:4) Aut, O 92, p. 882-883.
"Open Fires." [SouthernR] (28:4) Aut, O 92, p. 881-882.

"Orphan Tongue." [SouthernR] (28:4) Aut, O 92, p. 880.
"Outbuildings." [SouthernR] (28:4) Aut, O 92, p. 880-881.
"Thrush Doctor." [MichQR] (31:2) Spr 92, p. 263.

4418. MORGAN, Veronica
"Still Life." [ThRiPo] (39/40) 92-93, p. 174-175.
"Within the Greenhouse Effect." [ThRiPo] (39/40) 92-93, p. 173-174.

4419. MORGANSTEIN, Linda
"The Elements of Mourning" (A poem in five stages. Honorable mention, Eve of Saint Agnes Contest). [NegC] (12:3) 92, p. 16-37.

4420. MORI, Kyoko
"Fallout" (Editors' Prize Winner). [MissouriR] (15:1) 92, p. 24-26.

4421. MORIARTY, Laura
"The Midnight Man" (Selection: "12 O'Clock High). [Avec] (5:1) 92, p. 6.
"Symmetry" (Selections). [Avec] (5:1) 92, p. 7-8.

4422. MORIARTY, Michael
"Catechism." [NewYorkQ] (48) 92, p. 51.
"Gift to My Son." [NewYorkQ] (48) 92, p. 51.
"A Law." [NewYorkQ] (48) 92, p. 52.
"My Epitaph." [NewYorkQ] (48) 92, p. 51.
"Performing." [NewYorkQ] (48) 92, p. 52.
"Show Business." [NewYorkQ] (48) 92, p. 51.
"Writing." [NewYorkQ] (47) 92, p. 35.

4423. MORINSKI, Olwyn
"Flight Lines" (Poems about Amelia Earhart: 12 selections). [MalR] (99) Sum 92, p. 26-38.

4424. MORISSEAU, Roland
"La Chanson de Roland" (extraits). [Callaloo] (15:3) Sum 92, p. 645-646.
"Poemes de Reconnaissance" (Excerpts, tr. by Carrol F. Coates). [Callaloo] (15:3) Sum 92, p. 647-648.
"Poemes de Reconnaissance" (extraits). [Callaloo] (15:3) Sum 92, p. 649-650.
"La Promeneuse au Jardin" (Excerpts, tr. by Carrol F. Coates). [Callaloo] (15:3) Sum 92, p. 651-656.
"La Promeneuse au Jardin" (extraits). [Callaloo] (15:3) Sum 92, p. 652-658.
"Songs from Roland" (Excerpts, tr. by Carrol F. Coates). [Callaloo] (15:3) Sum 92, p. 643-644.

4425. MORISSEAU-LEROY, Félix
"Dyakout 1, 2, 3, 4" (Selections). [Callaloo] (15:3) Sum 92, p. 672-678.
"Dyakout 1, 2, 3, 4" (Selections, tr. by Carrol F. Coates). [Callaloo] (15:3) Sum 92, p. 671-677.

4426. MORITS, Yunna
"Kittens" (tr. by Daniel Weissbort). [Stand] (33:2) Spr 92, p. 94.
"My Apple-Tree Land" (tr. by Daniel Weissbort). [Stand] (33:2) Spr 92, p. 95.
"Pulling Aside the Curtain on the Other World" (tr. by Daniel Weissbort). [Stand] (33:2) Spr 92, p. 95.

4427. MORITZ, A. F.
"April Fool's Day, Mount Pleasant Cemetery." [SpoonRQ] (17:1/2) Wint-Spr 92, p. 26.
"The Car." [Comm] (119:19) 6 N 92, p. 24.
"The Famous Works." [AntigR] (89) Spr 92, p. 114-115.
"Hymn of Praise." [AmerPoR] (21:5) S-O 92, p. 10.
"Imaginative Purity." [Quarry] (41:1) Wint 92, p. 55.
"In Puerto Rico." [Comm] (119:19) 6 N 92, p. 24.
"Industry." [PoetryC] (12:3/4) Jl 92, p. 42.
"Outdoor Crucifix and Clock Radio." [AmerPoR] (21:5) S-O 92, p. 10.
"The Source." [PoetryC] (12:3/4) Jl 92, p. 42.
"Streetcar." [Comm] (119:19) 6 N 92, p. 24.
"The Tulip." [PoetryE] (33) Spr 92, p. 94.
"Wings." [Journal] (16:2) Fall-Wint 92, p. 22.

4428. MORLEY, Hilda
"For John Cage's Etudes Australes" (as played by Greta Sultan). [GrandS] (11:3 #43) 92, p. 31.
"For Pierre Matisse 1900-1989." [NewAW] (10) Fall 92, p. 18-19.
"A Presence, Wild." [NewAW] (10) Fall 92, p. 17.

MORLEY, Liz Abrams
See ABRAMS-MORLEY, Liz

4429. MÖRLING, Malena
"Constellations." [NewEngR] (14:4) Fall 92, p. 63.
"For F.M. Who Did Not Get Killed Yesterday on 57th Street." [NewEngR] (14:4) Fall 92, p. 64.
"For Joseph Cornell." [Ploughs] (18:4) Wint 92-93, p. 95.
"Standing on the Earth Among the Cows" (for Elena). [Ploughs] (18:4) Wint 92-93, p. 96.
"We Are Here." [Ploughs] (18:4) Wint 92-93, p. 97.
4430. MOROUNEY, Bob
"I Scoff a Lot." [AntigR] (91) Fall 92, p. 145.
"Typical." [AntigR] (91) Fall 92, p. 144.
4431. MORRIËN, Adriaan
"Shipwreck" (tr. by Ria Leigh-Loohuizen). [Trans] (26) Spr 92, p. 97-98.
4432. MORRILL, Donald
"The Ascent." [ChatR] (12:4) Sum 92, p. 47.
"Father and Son and." [LaurelR] (26:2) Sum 92, p. 40-41.
"Ichetucknee." [HighP] (7:2) Fall 92, p. 28.
"Produce." [HighP] (7:2) Fall 92, p. 29-30.
"Singles' Guide to Marrieds." [GreensboroR] (53) Wint 92-93, p. 110.
"Travels of Rusticiano of Pisa." [PoetL] (87:4) Wint 92-93, p. 21-22.
4433. MORRIS, Bernard E.
"Crustacean Harmony." [HiramPoR] (51/52) Fall 91-Sum 92, p. 54-55.
"The Fall of Features." [Plain] (13:1) Fall 92, p. 21.
"The Recluse." [Interim] (11:1) Spr-Sum 92, p. 10-11.
"You Promise Nothing." [HiramPoR] (51/52) Fall 91-Sum 92, p. 53.
4434. MORRIS, Carol
"Pardon Me Ma'am." [SlipS] (12) 92, p. 97.
4435. MORRIS, Daniel
"Bryce Passage." [WestHR] (46:3) Fall 92, p. 285-287.
4436. MORRIS, Herbert
"Grimm" (For David Wojahn). [DenQ] (27:1) Sum 92, p. 5-12.
"Soldiers." [Crazy] (43) Wint 92, p. 55-62.
4437. MORRIS, John T.
"Beyond the Hills" (A Double Shakespearian Sonnet). [NegC] (12:1/2) 92, p. 101.
"Lenten Limerick." [NegC] (12:1/2) 92, p. 220.
"Moronic License." [NegC] (12:1/2) 92, p. 220.
"Shorted Stop." [NegC] (12:1/2) 92, p. 220.
4438. MORRIS, Kathryn
"Bacon Poems." [Quarry] (41:4) Fall 92, p. 26.
"Fugitive." [Quarry] (41:4) Fall 92, p. 28.
"Gala." [Quarry] (41:4) Fall 92, p. 25.
"Until the Streetlights Come On." [Quarry] (41:4) Fall 92, p. 27.
"Watering Ban." [Quarry] (41:4) Fall 92, p. 27.
4439. MORRIS, Mervyn
"Mariners." [CinPR] (23) Wint 91-92, p. 46.
"Meeting." [CinPR] (23) Wint 91-92, p. 47.
"Nursery." [CinPR] (23) Wint 91-92, p. 45.
"Walk Good." [CinPR] (23) Wint 91-92, p. 45.
4440. MORRIS, Peter
"Numerator." [ChironR] (11:3) Aut 92, p. 16.
MORRISON, C. Dean
See DEAN-MORRISON, C.
4441. MORRISON, Kathi
"Amnesiac's Paradise" (after Paul Gaugin's *Landscape in Brittany*). [RiverC] (12:2) Spr 92, p. 66.
"Disappearance." [RiverC] (12:2) Spr 92, p. 67.
"Plea to Apollo." [NewYorkQ] (49) 92, p. 73.
4442. MORRISON, Lillian
"At Bay." [Light] (2) Sum 92, p. 12.
"Lineage." [Light] (4) Wint 92-93, p. 9.
"Seaside Conversation." [Light] (3) Aut 92, p. 14.
4443. MORRISON, R. H.
"All That Is Done, Done, Done Forever" (tr. of Alexander Blok). [LitR] (35:3) Spr 92, p. 383.
"Bird-Fancier's Street Cry" (tr. of Joaquín Antonio Peñalosa). [AntigR] (91) Fall 92, p. 103.

"Child of Night" (tr. of Joaquín Antonio Peñalosa). [AntigR] (91) Fall 92, p. 101.
"Hymn to Work" (tr. of Joaquín Antonio Peñalosa). [AntigR] (91) Fall 92, p. 99.
"Ice-Cube" (tr. of Joaquín Antonio Peñalosa). [AntigR] (91) Fall 92, p. 105.
"In Praise of Madness" (tr. of Joaquín Antonio Peñalosa). [AntigR] (91) Fall 92, p. 97.

4444. MORRISON, Rhonda
"The Leaves." [SouthernPR] (32:1) Spr 92, p. 35-36.

4445. MORRISON, Richard
"Another Metaphor for Fear" (For F. S.). [Art&Und] (1:4) Jl-Ag 92, p. 12.

4446. MORRISON, Rusane
"St. Jarlath's Church & Elementary School, 1964." [HiramPoR] (51/52) Fall 91-Sum 92, p. 56.

4447. MORRISSETTE, George
"Going to Yorkton." [PraF] (13:3, #60) Aut 92, p. 141.
"Invited to the CFL" (for Sig Laser). [PraF] (13:3, #60) Aut 92, p. 139-140.

4448. MORROW, M. E.
"Fathers and Sons." [AmerS] (61:3) Sum 92, p. 435.

4449. MORSE, Cheryl
"Dear Dr. Freud." [CapeR] (27:2) Fall 92, p. 38.

4450. MORTEN, Eric
"Suicide Note: A Work in Progress." [CapilR] (2:9) Fall 92, p. 7-16.

MORTIZ, A. F.
See MORITZ, A. F.

4451. MORTON, Colleen
"Bestial." [PoetL] (87:4) Wint 92-93, p. 37.
"Signals from First." [PoetL] (87:4) Wint 92-93, p. 36.

4452. MOSCONA, Myriam
"Naturalization Papers" (tr. by Cynthia Steele). [TriQ] (85) Fall 92, p. 347.
"The Transients" (2 selections, tr. by Teresa Anderson). [Manoa] (4:2) Fall 92, p. 21-22.

4453. MOSELEY, J.
"Same Profile." [Vis] (39) 92, p. 17.

4454. MOSEMAN, Jolene
"Catching the Wind." [Plain] (13:1) Fall 92, p. 7.

4455. MOSES, Daniel David
"Hotel Centrale, Rotterdam." [CanLit] (134) Aut 92, p. 74-75.

4456. MOSLEY, Walter
"Window Next to the Killer's House." [Thrpny] (50) Sum 92, p. 16.

4457. MOSS, Howard
"It." [AntR] (50:1/2) Wint-Spr 92, p. 354.

4458. MOSS, Jackie
"The Following." [Confr] (50) Fall 92, p. 277.

4459. MOSS, Thylias
"Approaching Venus's-Flytrap During a Hungarian Film: A Subtitle." [Antaeus] (69) Aut 92, p. 107-108.
"The Magicians." [OnTheBus] (4:2/5:1, #10/11) 92, p. 159-160.

MOTT, Robert de
See DeMOTT, Robert

MOUNTAIN, Mary Tall
See TALLMOUNTAIN, Mary

4460. MOURÉ, Erin
"4 Dreams of the Adriatic Sea." [Quarry] (41:2) Spr 92, p. 11-13.
"A Grassy Knoll." [PraF] (13:4, #61) Wint 92-93, p. 83-91.
"Hope Stories." [Descant] (23:4/24:1, #78/79) Wint-Spr 92-93, p. 30-41.
"Oars." [CanLit] (133) Sum 92, p. 76-77.
"Ships." [CanLit] (133) Sum 92, p. 143.
"These Drugs." [CanLit] (133) Sum 92, p. 126-127.
"What Was Said." [Quarry] (41:2) Spr 92, p. 14-16.

4461. MROUE, Haas H.
"Beirut Survivors Anonymous." [MichQR] (31:4) Fall 92, p. 637-638.

4462. MUDIMBE, V. Y.
"The Order of Drift" (tr. by Eric Sellin). [Trans] (26) Spr 92, p. 13.

4463. MUELLER, John
"Alive at Last" (Excerpt). [PoetryUSA] (24) 92, p. 17.

4464. MUELLER, Lisel
"1990." [PoetryE] (33) Spr 92, p. 98.

"American Literature." [PoetryE] (33) Spr 92, p. 99.
"Eyes and Ears." [ColR] (9:1) Spr-Sum 92, p. 32-33.
"Field Recording." [ColR] (9:1) Spr-Sum 92, p. 34-35.
"Imaginary Paintings." [ParisR]] (34:124) Fall 92, p. 167-168.
"Immortality." [Poetry] (161:2) N 92, p. 97.
"The Late-Born Daughters." [WillowR] (19) Spr 92, p. 34.
"Midwinter Notes." [GeoR] (46:4) Wint 92, p. 625-626.
"Mirrors." [ParisR]] (34:124) Fall 92, p. 169.
"On Foot." [ColR] (9:1) Spr-Sum 92, p. 36.
"Photograph." [IndR] (15:2) Fall 92, p. 124.
"Popular Music." [IndR] (15:2) Fall 92, p. 123.
"Time and Place." [PoetryE] (33) Spr 92, p. 95-97.
"Tradeoff." [ColR] (9:1) Spr-Sum 92, p. 38.
"Who am I to speak for the homeless." [SenR] (21:2) 91, p. 159-160.
"Why I Need the Birds." [IndR] (15:2) Fall 92, p. 122.

4465. MUELLER, Veronica
"Lot's Wife." [ChrC] (109:35) 2 D 92, p. 1105.

4466. MUHLHAUSEN, Linda
"Knotweed." [Writer] (105:6) Je 92, p. 24.

4467. MUKHERJEE, Kanchan Kuntala
"Along the Railroad Track" (tr. by Paramita Banerjee and Arlene Zide). [ChiR] (38:1/2) 92, p. 122-123.

4468. MULCAHY, Barbara
"The Kibbutz Searchlight." [PoetryC] (13:1) N 92, p. 17.
"Muskeg." [PoetryC] (13:1) N 92, p. 17.
"Night Round of the Multipara." [Grain] (20:1) Spr 92, p. 184.
"There Is Something Too Revealing About Houses." [AntigR] (91) Fall 92, p. 115.
"This Morning I Want to Forget." [PraF] (13:4, #61) Wint 92-93, p. 57.
"When We Were Flying to Peace River a Hunter Told Me This Story About When He Went to Alaska." [Grain] (20:1) Spr 92, p. 185.

4469. MULKERN, Terence
"Notice to Mariners." [NewEngR] (14:2) Spr 92, p. 157.
"Tapioca." [NewEngR] (14:2) Spr 92, p. 158.

4470. MULKEY, Richard
"Revolution Begins in Persia, 1779." [NoDaQ] (60:3) Sum 92, p. 125-126.

4471. MULLEN, Laura
"Appearances." [Antaeus] (69) Aut 92, p. 112-114.
"Secrets." [Agni] (36) 92, p. 93-94.

4472. MULLIGAN, John
"Trying to Remember." [Sun] (196) Mr 92, p. 34.

4473. MULLINS, Cecil J.
"Big Foot." [Hellas] (3:2) Fall 92, p. 54.
"Spring Freeze." [Hellas] (3:1) Spr 92, p. 58.
"Willows and Oaks." [CapeR] (27:1) Spr 92, p. 24.

4474. MULRANE, Scott
"Two Horses." [CreamCR] (16:1) Spr 92, p. 94.

4475. MULROONEY, C.
"I Hear the Beaches There Are Black" (tr. of André Breton). [PacificR] (11) 92-93, p. 43.

4476. MUNDELL, William
"Finding Light." [NewYorkQ] (48) 92, p. 72.

4477. MUNDLAY, Asha
"Night has come to an end, the woman starts her grinding" (tr. of Aruna Dhere, w. Arlene Zide). [ChiR] (38:1/2) 92, p. 103.

4478. MUNHYANG
"All Right Then" (tr. by Constantine Contogenis and Wolhee Choe). [Pequod] (34) 92, p. 115.

4479. MUNRO, Jane
"Animal Lives." [Event] (21:2) Sum 92, p. 57.
"A Dream of Margaret Atwood." [PoetryC] (12:3/4) Jl 92, p. 9.
"Nursery Rhyme." [PoetryC] (12:3/4) Jl 92, p. 9.
"Shelburne Farms." [PoetryC] (12:3/4) Jl 92, p. 9.

4480. MURA, David
"The Blueness of the Day." [NewEngR] (14:3) Sum 92, p. 66-77.

4481. MURATORI, Fred
"Unstable Companions." [DenQ] (26:4) Spr 92, p. 49.

4482. MURAWSKI, Elisabeth
"Proof." [LitR] (25:2) Wint 92, p. 255.
4483. MURCIANO, Carlos
"The Mirror" (tr. by Louis Bourne). [Stand] (33:4) Aut 92, p. 148-149.
4484. MURPHY, Bruce
"Requiem." [Thrpny] (49) Spr 92, p. 20.
4485. MURPHY, Erin
"Itinerary." [GeoR] (46:1) Spr 92, p. 114-115.
4486. MURPHY, Kay
"Forced Returns." [SpoonRQ] (17:3/4) Sum-Fall 92, p. 19-21.
"Petrarchan Light in Illinois." [SpoonRQ] (17:3/4) Sum-Fall 92, p. 16-18.
4487. MURPHY, Mary-Lynn
"Fall." [Dandel] (19:2) 92, p. 10.
4488. MURPHY, Peter E.
"The Healing" (for Amanda). [JlNJPo] (14:1) Spr 92, p. 22.
"The Neighborhood." [JlNJPo] (14:1) Spr 92, p. 21.
"Sobriety." [US1] (26/27) 92, p. 46.
"The Tuning." [Comm] (119:13) 17 Jl 92, p. 16.
4489. MURPHY, Sheila (Sheila E.)
"Choreography." [AnotherCM] (23) Spr 92, p. 147.
"A Little Narration." [NewYorkQ] (47) 92, p. 59.
"Politics equals sex that does not quite occur." [WashR] (18:3) O-N 92, p. 27.
"She drops irregularly sliced segments of language." [Talisman] (9) Fall 92, p. 187.
"Steep Phases of Guitar Strokes." [AnotherCM] (23) Spr 92, p. 145.
"The Weight and Feel of Harps." [AnotherCM] (23) Spr 92, p. 146.
"What about her ego frosts." [WashR] (18:3) O-N 92, p. 27.
"What to anticipate." [WashR] (18:3) O-N 92, p. 27.
4490. MURPHY, Stan
"Kerouac." [MoodySI] (27) Spr 92, p. 12.
4491. MURPHY, Susan
"A Change in Luck." [DenQ] (26:4) Spr 92, p. 50-51.
4492. MURRAY, Barbara
"Our House." [Bogg] (65) 92, p. 51.
4493. MURRAY, Charmaine
"Morning Call." [Writer] (105:3) Mr 92, p. 21.
4494. MURRAY, G. E.
"Notes from a Druid Passing Through New York." [CharR] (18:2) Fall 92, p. 95-96.
"The Rainy Season Arrives in Southern Kyushu." [PacificR] (11) 92-93, p. 85.
4495. MURRAY, Les
"The Ballad of the Barbed Wire Ocean." [PartR] (59:1) Wint 92, p. 97-98.
"Equinoctial Gales at Hawthornden Castle." [Verse] (9:2) Sum 92, p. 3.
"Incorrigible Grace." [Comm] (119:10) 22 My 92, p. 12.
"Poetry and Religion." [Comm] (119:10) 22 My 92, p. 11.
4496. MURREY, Matthew
"Ammit, Devourer of Hearts." [PoetryE] (33) Spr 92, p. 100.
"Behind the Jewel." [PoetryE] (33) Spr 92, p. 101.
"Dead Cow Farm" (Inspired by a Robert Graves poem which bears the same title). [MidwQ] (33:4) Sum 92, p. 414.
4497. MUSE, Charlotte
"Song Line Through My House." [Vis] (38) 92, p. 12.
4498. MUSIAL, Grzegorz
"Looking at Photographs" (for R., tr. by Lia Purpura, w. the author). [SenR] (22:2) Fall 92, p. 54-55.
"Only a Shadow" (to my mother, tr. by Lia Purpura, w. the author). [SenR] (22:2) Fall 92, p. 52-53.
4499. MUSKAT, Timothy
"The Dreaming Dog." [Poem] (68) N 92, p. 3.
"Plumb Lines." [Poem] (68) N 92, p. 1.
"The Proximity of Waking." [Poem] (68) N 92, p. 2.
4500. MUSKE, Carol
"Last Take." [Field] (47) Fall 92, p. 104-105.
"Little L.A. Villanelle." [Poetry] (161:3) D 92, p. 133.
"Prague: Two Journals." [Field] (47) Fall 92, p. 106-111.
"Unsent Letter 3" (Retro Vivo). [AmerV] (26) Spr 92, p. 117-118.
4501. MUTH, Parke
"An Exchange of Gifts." [ManhatPR] (14) [92?], p. 50-52.

4502. MUTHIEN, Marcellus J.
"Of Change" (for I.M.). [JamesWR] (9:3) Spr 92, p. 7.
4503. MUTIS, Alvaro
"Every Poem" (tr. by Jim Normington). [Talisman] (8) Spr 92, p. 142.
4504. MUTTON, Paul
"Adjectives." [Quarry] (41:1) Wint 92, p. 16.
"Investigating a Possibility." [WestCL] (26:1, #7) Spr 92, p. 64.
"The Preliminaries." [WestCL] (26:1, #7) Spr 92, p. 63.
4505. MYCUE, Edward
"Let's See If We Can't Unbottom Some Quiet Compassion Here." [Caliban] (11) 92, p. 93.
"Torn Topping with Sky Bleeding Through." [LindLM] (11:3) S 92, p. 18.
"Total Man." [LindLM] (11:3) S 92, p. 18.
4506. MYERS, Douglas
"Lost Paths at Canyon de Chelly." [DogRR] (11:1) Spr-Sum 92, p. 22-23.
"Madison Buffalo Jump." [DogRR] (11:1) Spr-Sum 92, p. 24.
4507. MYERS, Jack
"Double Overtime, Sudden Death." [Witness] (6:2) 92, p. 160-161.
4508. MYERS, Joan Rohr
"After Easter." [ChrC] (109:15) 29 Ap 92, p. 453.
"In Lent" (for one who does not swim). [ChrC] (109:9) 11 Mr 92, p. 268.
"Women's Studies." [Comm] (119:10) 22 My 92, p. 16.
4509. MYERS, Neil
"Creator Spirit." [CharR] (18:1) Spr 92, p. 91.
"Gateless Gate." [OhioR] (48) 92, p. 98-100.
4510. MYLES, Eileen
"Closing Up Shop." [KenR] (NS 14:1) Wint 92, p. 108-109.
"Goodbye." [HangL] (60) 92, p. 37.
"Jumble." [NewEngR] (14:4) Fall 92, p. 209-210.
"Memorial." [HangL] (60) 92, p. 34-35.
"New Poem." [HangL] (60) 92, p. 38-39.
"The New True Blackness." [HangL] (60) 92, p. 33.
"PV." [NewEngR] (14:4) Fall 92, p. 210-212.
"Rut." [KenR] (NS 14:1) Wint 92, p. 105-107.
"Sleepless." [HangL] (60) 92, p. 40-41.
"Tell Me." [HangL] (60) 92, p. 36-37.
"To the Maiden of Choice." [Art&Und] (1:3) Spr 92, p. 14-15.
"Untitled: I always put my pussy." [KenR] (NS 14:1) Wint 92, p. 107-108.
"Waterfall." [NewEngR] (14:4) Fall 92, p. 213-215.
4511. MYONGOK
"Don't Tell Me the Face" (tr. by Constantine Contogenis and Wolhee Choe). [Pequod] (34) 92, p. 116.
4512. MYRVAAGNES, Naomi
"Claim." [Noctiluca] (1:1) Spr 92, p. 4.
4513. NADELMAN, Cynthia
"In the American Paintings Room." [NewAW] (10) Fall 92, p. 101-102.
4514. NAGEL, Lorachina
"Amazing Grace." [CapeR] (27:2) Fall 92, p. 32.
4515. NAGLER, Robert
"After a Painting, "Girls Running: Walberswick Pier" c. 1910." [GreenMR] (NS 5:2) Spr-Sum 92, p. 63.
"After a Picture Called *The Tempest* by Giorgione." [MidAR] (12:2) 92, p. 50.
"Glass." [Gypsy] (19) 92, p. 43.
"The Innocent" (Guadalajara Cathedral). [PoetL] (87:3) Fall 92, p. 38.
"Mme. Hellu Is 94." [OxfordM] (8:1) Spr-Sum 92, p. 32-33.
"On a Painting, 'Bus Stop Stabbing,' by John Valdez (1984)." [Gypsy] (19) 92, p. 44.
"Riot." [ArtfulD] (22/23) 92, p. 114.
"The Sacred." [DogRR] (11:2, #22) Fall-Wint 92, p. 5.
4516. NAIR, Rukmini Bhaya
"Genderole." [ChiR] (38:1/2) 92, p. 71.
"Hundru Falls, Ranchi." [ChiR] (38:1/2) 92, p. 72.
"The Hyoid Bone." [ChiR] (38:1/2) 92, p. 68-69.
4517. NAJERA, Francisco
"Despertando de una Pesadilla." [Luz] (2) S 92, p. 54.
"Te recostaste una vez más." [Luz] (2) S 92, p. 53.
"Y Cae." [Nuez] (4:12) 92, p. 26.

4518. NAKAMURA, Sonoko
"Haiku" (3 poems, tr. by Miyuki Aoyama and Leza Lowitz). [Noctiluca] (1:2) Wint 92 [on cover: Wint 93], p. 3.
4519. NAMJOSHI, Suniti
"Failed Prayers" (from "St. Suniti and the Dragon"). [CanLit] (132) Spr 92, p. 31.
4520. NANDKUMAR, Pratibha
"Poem: When I was groping for a new poem" (tr. by A. K. Ramanujan). [ChiR] (38:1/2) 92, p. 9-10.
4521. NAPIER, Alan
"Fishing in the Deep Seeing." [OxfordM] (6:2) Fall-Wint 90, p. 32-33.
"Two Cocks Die." [MidAR] (12:2) 92, p. 29-31.
4522. NARA
"White Paper" (tr. by Narayana Rao). [ChiR] (38:1/2) 92, p. 150.
4523. NARAYAN, Kunwar
"Preparations of War" (tr. by Vinay Dharwadker and Aparna Dharwadker). [ChiR] (38:1/2) 92, p. 149.
4524. NASDOR, Marc
"Returning Vultures" (Selections: Part 2, 2/15, 2/16). [Talisman] (8) Spr 92, p. 169.
4525. NASH, Mildred J.
"The First Fairy Tale." [Light] (2) Sum 92, p. 23.
4526. NASH, Roger
"Still Life: Iced Water and an Orange at Jericho." [AntigR] (90) Sum 92, p. 136.
NATALE, Nanci Roth
See ROTH-NATALE, Nanci
4527. NATHAN, Doug
"Come Little Mousie Let Us Dine Together." [OnTheBus] (4:2/5:1, #10/11) 92, p. 161.
4528. NATHAN, Leonard
"Alchemist." [NewYorker] (68:16) 8 Je 92, p. 68.
"Attentions." [PoetL] (87:3) Fall 92, p. 13.
"Commentary." [Salm] (96) Fall 92, p. 168.
"In the Woods." [NewYorker] (68:26) 17 Ag 92, p. 48.
"Many Kinds." [Chelsea] (53) 92, p. 41.
"The Old Poet." [Salm] (96) Fall 92, p. 169.
"Out on the Flats." [Zyzzyva] (8:3) Fall 92, p. 107.
"Potato Eaters." [NewYorker] (68:10) 27 Ap 92, p. 58.
"The Silents." [PoetL] (87:3) Fall 92, p. 12.
"Truth" (for Jamie Nathan, my grandson). [Zyzzyva] (8:3) Fall 92, p. 111.
4529. NATHAN, Norman
"Love Song in Black." [SpiritSH] (57) Spr-Sum 92, p. 56.
4530. NATHANIEL, Isabel
"The Coast of Texas." [Ploughs] (18:1) Spr 92, p. 107-108.
"Peacocks." [SouthernPR] (32:2) Fall 92, p. 45-46.
4531. NATT, Gregory
"Death As a Friend" (from a woodcut by Alfred Rethel, 1851). [Vis] (38) 92, p. 35.
"Nighthawks. Baby, Please Don't Leave Me." [JlNJPo] (14:2) Aut 92, p. 15-16.
4532. NAUGHTON, James
"And They Come, the Guests Awaiting Liquor" (tr. of Sylva Fischerová). [PraS] (66:4) Wint 92, p. 110-111.
"Black Tiger" (tr. of Sylva Fischerová). [PraS] (66:4) Wint 92, p. 109-110.
"Drinking Coffee" (tr. of Sylva Fischerová). [PraS] (66:4) Wint 92, p. 103.
"The Garden" (tr. of Sylva Fischerová). [PraS] (66:4) Wint 92, p. 104-106.
"Lovers in the Sand" (tr. of Sylva Fischerová). [PraS] (66:4) Wint 92, p. 104.
"Necessary" (tr. of Sylva Fischerová). [PraS] (66:4) Wint 92, p. 106-108.
"The Stones Speak Czech" (tr. of Sylva Fischerová). [PraS] (66:4) Wint 92, p. 108.
4533. NAUGHTON, Lara
"Wine's Turn." [PaintedB] (47) 92, p. 52.
4534. NAYDAN, Michael (Michael M.)
"After Russia (1928)" (2 selections, tr. of Marina Tsvetaeva). [Confr] (48/49) Spr - Sum 92, p. 216-217.
"A Definition of Poetry" (tr. of Oksana Zabuzhko). [Agni] (36) 92, p. 9-10.
4535. NEBORAK, Victor
"Genesis" (from the forthcoming collection, "Alter-ego," tr. by Jars Balan). [PraF] (13:3, #60) Aut 92, p. 142-144.
"Supper" (from the forthcoming collection, "Alter-ego," tr. by Jars Balan). [PraF] (13:3, #60) Aut 92, p. 146.

"There are mirrors and doors" (from the forthcoming collection, "Alter-ego," tr. by Jars Balan). [PraF] (13:3, #60) Aut 92, p. 145.
"What kind of a beast" (from the forthcoming collection, "Alter-ego," tr. by Jars Balan). [PraF] (13:3, #60) Aut 92, p. 144.

4536. NEEDELL, Claire
"In the Home: A Sequence." [Talisman] (9) Fall 92, p. 160-166.

4537. NEELON, Ann
"World Series." [GettyR] (5:3) Sum 92, p. 460-461.

4538. NEGYESY, Iren
"My Room" (tr. by Nicholas Kolumban). [WebR] (16) Fall 92, p. 35.

4539. NEILSON, Melanie
"Erosion Finally" (Excerpts, after Berenice Abbott, Walker Evans and Thomas More). [Talisman] (9) Fall 92, p. 130-131.
"Erosion Finally" (Selections). [Shiny] (7/8) 92, p. 119-124.
Four graphic poems. [WestCL] (26:2, #8) Fall 92, p. 72-73.

4540. NEILSON, Sylvia D.
"Paging Charon." [Light] (4) Wint 92-93, p. 26.
"Turtle Hurdle." [Light] (3) Aut 92, p. 18.

4541. NeJAME, Adele
"A Ryder Nocturne and *The Temple of the Mind*." [Ploughs] (18:1) Spr 92, p. 113-114.

NEJAT, Murat Nemet
See NEMET-NEJAT, Murat

4542. NELMS, Sheryl (Sheryl L.)
"Bag Lady." [Lactuca] (15) Mr 92, p. 58.
"Sack Man." [ChrC] (109:14) 22 Ap 92, p. 431.
"Wild Grapes." [NegC] (12:1/2) 92, p. 102.

4543. NELSON, Bonnie
"The Band Quits Playing at 3 a.m. in Waikiki." [BellArk] (8:6) N-D 92, p. 5.

4544. NELSON, Eric
"Boys and Nature" (for David Graham). [SouthernR] (28:3) Sum, Jl 92, p. 610-611.
"The Family in the River." [SouthernR] (28:3) Sum, Jl 92, p. 608-610.

4545. NELSON, Gale
"In Accuracies." [Talisman] (9) Fall 92, p. 157-159.

4546. NELSON, George
"From Green Note Book." [NewAW] (10) Fall 92, p. 119.

4547. NELSON, Melanie Hope
"The Weaver." [SinW] (47) Sum-Fall 92, p. 110.

4548. NELSON, Michael
"The Alchemy of Time." [JamesWR] (9:4) Sum 92, p. 6.

4549. NELSON, Paul
"Returning the Box." [WillowS] (30) Sum 92, p. 74-75.

4550. NELSON, Sandra
"Fishing the Black Branch." [NewOR] (19:3/4) Fall-Wint 92, p. 76.
"Flies." [LouisL] (9:1) Spr 92, p. 78-79.
"For My Venus of Willendorf." [Kalliope] (14:3) 92, p. 56.
"Outside the Moon Sat Smoking." [IndR] (15:2) Fall 92, p. 121.
"Seeing You in Lace." [BelPoJ] (42:4) Sum 92, p. 29.
"Seurat's *Model Seated*." [PassN] (13:1) Sum 92, p. 3.
"Trompe L'Oeil Love." [LaurelR] (26:2) Sum 92, p. 43.
"What It's Like When You're a Finn." [SingHM] (20) 92, p. 12-13.

4551. NEMET-NEJAT, Murat
"Statue of Lions" (tr. of Cemal Süreya). [Trans] (26) Spr 92, p. 108-109.
"Turkish Voices" (Selections: 3 poems). [Talisman] (8) Spr 92, p. 146-147.

4552. NERSESIAN, Arthur
"Milk and Bananas." [Art&Und] (1:3) Spr 92, p. 10.

4553. NERUDA, Pablo
"The Book of Questions" (Selections: XVII, XIII, V, VII, XXVIII, LIX, tr. by William O'Daly). [PoetryE] (33) Spr 92, p. 168-173.
"I Explain a Few Things" (tr. by Galway Kinnell). [Trans] (26) Spr 92, p. 30-32.
"Ode to Federico García Lorca" (tr. by Greg Simon and Steven F. White). [NowestR] (30:1) 92, p. 65-68.
"Las Piedras del Cielo (Sky Stones" (Selections: XXX, VI, tr. by Peter Levitt). [OnTheBus] (4:2/5:1, #10/11) 92, p. 278-279.

4554. NESBIT, William N.
"Cycle." [Parting] (5:1) Sum 92, p. 13-14.

4555. NESTER, Richard
"Homestead." [ChatR] (13:1) Fall 92, p. 60.
"My Son, Contrary to Medical Expectations, Is Born Laughing." [SenR] (22:1) Spr 92, p. 60.
"Poem with Cattle." [CutB] (37) Wint 92, p. 93-94.
4556. NESTOR, Jack
"Song of Rahway." [JlNJPo] (14:1) Spr 92, p. 18-20.
4557. NETO, Agostinho
"Beyond Poetry" (tr. by Victor di Suvero). [Nimrod] (36:1) Fall-Wint 92, p. 92.
"Night" (tr. by Victor di Suvero). [Nimrod] (36:1) Fall-Wint 92, p. 91.
"Pause" (tr. by Victor di Suvero). [Nimrod] (36:1) Fall-Wint 92, p. 90.
4558. NETO, João Cabral de Melo
"Cemetery in Pernambuco" (tr. by Richard Zenith). [Trans] (26) Spr 92, p. 42.
4559. NETTELBECK, F. A.
"Reciting a litany of horrors." [PaintedB] (48) 92, p. 13-16.
4560. NEUMANN, Kurt
"Autumn Ecology." [PoetryE] (33) Spr 92, p. 105.
"Methodist Prayer List." [PoetryE] (33) Spr 92, p. 103-104.
"Travelling with Presents." [PoetryE] (33) Spr 92, p. 102.
4561. NEUTZE, Diana
"Here and Now." [Kalliope] (15:1) 92, p. 9.
4562. NEVILL, Sue
"Elizabeth Brown" (died December 24, 1991). [Dandel] (19:2) 92, p. 24.
4563. NEVILLE, Tam Lin
"I Write in a Diary for Kathy." [MidAR] (12:2) 92, p. 127-128.
4564. NEVIN, Kathryn L.
"After So Much Adjusting." [Ometeca] (2:2) 91 [published 92], p. 31.
4565. NEWCOMB, Richard
"The Poster I Had on the Back of My Front Door Said This." [BellArk] (8:4) Jl-Ag 92, p. 19.
"Sonnet: A Line for Every Summer I've Come to the Town Where You Used to Live." [BellArk] (8:4) Jl-Ag 92, p. 19.
4566. NEWEY, Robert
"In Forests." Sparks! Writing by High School Students (1:1), a supplement to [PraF] (13:4, #61) Wint 92-93, p. 15.
"Me and the Indian." Sparks! Writing by High School Students (1:1), a supplement to [PraF] (13:4, #61) Wint 92-93, p. 14.
"Momma." Sparks! Writing by High School Students (1:1), a supplement to [PraF] (13:4, #61) Wint 92-93, p. 13.
"Windows." Sparks! Writing by High School Students (1:1), a supplement to [PraF] (13:4, #61) Wint 92-93, p. 16.
4567. NEWLAND, Emily
"Cleavage." [Light] (1) Spr 92, p. 16.
"I Had a Small Evangelist." [Light] (1) Spr 92, p. 31.
4568. NEWLING, Bruce E.
"Have Crate, Will Travel." [Light] (1) Spr 92, p. 13.
"I Left My Heart in Ouagadougou." [Light] (3) Aut 92, p. 13.
4569. NEWLOVE, John
"Autobiography" (2 poems). [Grain] (20:1) Spr 92, p. 277.
"No Song." [Grain] (20:1) Spr 92, p. 277.
4570. NEWMAN, P. B.
"A Certain Slant of Light." [TarRP] (31:2) Spr 92, p. 22.
"Underwater." [SoCarR] (25:1) Fall 92, p. 70.
4571. NEWMAN, Wade
"In Memoriam" (Roger Hecht 1926-1990). [HolCrit] (29:2) Ap 92, p. 16.
"Politician." [Light] (3) Aut 92, p. 19.
4572. NEWMANN, Joan
"One to Rot and One to Grow, One for Pigeon One for Crow." [Verse] (9:3) Wint 92, p. 8.
4573. NEWSOM, Vera
"De Mortuis." [Footwork] 92, p. 145.
"Dinner in the Garden." [Footwork] 92, p. 145.
"The Lane." [Footwork] 92, p. 145.
"Not Ready Yet." [Footwork] 92, p. 146.
"The Red Hole" (for Robert Gray). [Footwork] 92, p. 146.

4574. NEWTH, Rebecca
"Photograph of Ray Charles by James Kriegsmann." [Epiphany] (3:4) O (Fall) 92, p. 243.
4575. NEWTON, Monty R.
"Open Well." [Plain] (12:3) Spr 92, p. 18.
4576. NEWTON-RIOS, Alexandra
"Argentina." [Callaloo] (15:4) Fall 92, p. 931.
"Argentine Light" (Honorable Mention, New Letters Poetry Award). [NewL] (58:2) Wint 92, p. 80-81.
"Plaza Independencia." [Callaloo] (15:4) Fall 92, p. 929-930.
4577. NGUEDAM, Christophe
"Fruits" (for Marie-Anne, tr. by Julia Older). [Nimrod] (35:2) Spr-Sum 92, p. 123.
"Hope" (tr. by Julia Older). [Nimrod] (35:2) Spr-Sum 92, p. 123.
4578. NGUYEN, Emily
"Each spring sets out the same" (Kokinshu 57, tr. of Ki no Tomonori). [Archae] (4) late 92-early 93, p. 17.
"Frost one thread" (Kokinshu 291, tr. of Fujiwara no Sekio). [Archae] (4) late 92 - early 93, p. 15.
"How he cries out" (Kokinshu 109, tr. of Priest Sosei). [Archae] (4) late 92-early 93, p. 16.
"October." [Archae] (4) late 92-early 93, p. 11.
"Plum fragrance" (Kokinshu 336, tr. of Ki no Tsurayuki). [Archae] (4) late 92-early 93, p. 14.
"Poems, in the Style of the *Kokinshu*." [Archae] (4) late 92-early 93, p. 13.
"Solid Ground." [Archae] (4) late 92-early 93, p. 12.
4579. NGUYEN, Phuong D.
"The Tears." Sparks! Writing by High School Students (1:1), a supplement to [PraF] (13:4, #61) Wint 92-93, p. 21.
4580. NICA-JESSEAU, Ardessa
"I Got the Orange Throb." [CapilR] (2:9) Fall 92, p. 51-52.
"I'm Trying to Understand Your Heroin, Heroin Baby." [CapilR] (2:9) Fall 92, p. 49-50.
"Torpedo Rash." [CapilR] (2:9) Fall 92, p. 53-54.
4581. NICCOLAI, Guilia
"Syntactic and Verbal" (tr. by Corrado Federici). [PoetryC] (13:1) N 92, p. 23.
4582. NICCUM, Terri
"Funeral." [OnTheBus] (4:2/5:1, #10/11) 92, p. 162-163.
"Sketches." [OnTheBus] (4:2/5:1, #10/11) 92, p. 163-164.
4583. NICHOLAS, Douglas
"The Shout." [CumbPR] (12:1) Fall 92, p. 80-81.
"The Singer Major Wiley." [CumbPR] (12:1) Fall 92, p. 82-83.
4584. NICHOLS, Janet
"Brother-in-Law." [Lactuca] (15) Mr 92, p. 19.
"Denial." [Lactuca] (15) Mr 92, p. 19.
"Last List." [Lactuca] (15) Mr 92, p. 20.
"Radiation." [Lactuca] (15) Mr 92, p. 20.
"Seven Cartons." [Lactuca] (15) Mr 92, p. 20.
"Waiting." [Lactuca] (15) Mr 92, p. 19.
4585. NICK, Dagmar
"Flushing the Game" (tr. by Jim Barnes). [ArtfulD] (22/23) 92, p. 15.
"Twilight" (tr. by Jim Barnes). [Trans] (26) Spr 92, p. 80.
4586. NICKERSON, Sheila
"Because She Likes Small Architecture." [DogRR] (11:1) Spr-Sum 92, p. 16.
"In the Kitchen, January." [DogRR] (11:1) Spr-Sum 92, p. 17.
NICOLA, Deborah de
See De NICOLA, Deborah
4587. NICOLA, Noel
"María del Carmen." [Areíto] (3:10/11) Abril 92, p. 81.
4588. NICOSIA, Gerald
"Going Out of Business." [MoodySI] (27) Spr 92, p. 45.
4589. NIDITCH, B. Z.
"1944." [SpiritSH] (57) Spr-Sum 92, p. 35.
"1944: Mid Europa." [AnotherCM] (24) Fall 92, p. 108-110.
"Boston: A View of the Nineties." [SpiritSH] (57) Spr-Sum 92, p. 28.
"Budapest." [SpiritSH] (57) Spr-Sum 92, p. 34.
"Consume America." [FreeL] (9) Wint 92, p. 28.

"Gulag, Once Removed." [SpiritSH] (57) Spr-Sum 92, p. 33.
"James Schuyler" (In Memoriam). [ChironR] (11:4) Wint 92, p. 47.
"Katyn Forest." [SpiritSH] (57) Spr-Sum 92, p. 31.
"Lenin." [BlackBR] (15) Spr-Sum 92, p. 29-20.
"Lenin." [SpiritSH] (57) Spr-Sum 92, p. 36.
"On Realizing My Vocation." [SpiritSH] (57) Spr-Sum 92, p. 38.
"Prague." [SpiritSH] (57) Spr-Sum 92, p. 32.
"Sandor Woeres." [SpiritSH] (57) Spr-Sum 92, p. 26.
"Solidarity." [SpiritSH] (57) Spr-Sum 92, p. 27.
"St. Petersburg." [SpiritSH] (57) Spr-Sum 92, p. 29.
"Summer House, Winter House." [SpiritSH] (57) Spr-Sum 92, p. 30.
"Summerthing." [Amelia] (7:1, #20) 92, p. 146.
"Thom Gunn." [Amelia] (6:4, #19) 92, p. 121.
"Twenty Centuries For This." [DogRR] (11:2, #22) Fall-Wint 92, p. 7a.
"Vienna's Last Waltz." [NegC] (12:3) 92, p. 103-107.
"Vilnius." [SpiritSH] (57) Spr-Sum 92, p. 37.
"Want Ad." [Asylum] (7:3/4) 92, p. 7.
"Weimarian." [FreeL] (9) Wint 92, p. 29.

4590. NIEDECKER, Lorine
"Beyond What." [WestCL] (26:1, #7) Spr 92, p. 84.
"Canvass." [WestCL] (26:1, #7) Spr 92, p. 82-83.
"I Heard." [WestCL] (26:1, #7) Spr 92, p. 84.
"Lake Superior." [Raritan] (12:2) Fall 92, p. 67-70.
"Memorial Day." [WestCL] (26:1, #7) Spr 92, p. 84-85.
"The 'New Goose' Manuscript." [WestCL] (26:1, #7) Spr 92, p. 99-107.
"Promise of a Brilliant Funeral." [WestCL] (26:1, #7) Spr 92, p. 79-80.
"When Ecstasy Is Inconvenient." [WestCL] (26:1, #7) Spr 92, p. 77-78.

4591. NIEDELMAN, Hilda L.
"'A Loaf of Bread,' The Walrus Said, 'Is What We Chiefly Need'." [Confr] (48/49) Spr-Sum 92, p. 232-233.

4592. NIELSEN, Dan
"Don't Be Ridiculous." [Pearl] (16) Fall 92, p. 9.
"I Don't Know." [Pearl] (16) Fall 92, p. 9.
"The Last Scout Meeting." [Pearl] (16) Fall 92, p. 9.
"When He No Longer Found Hair in His Soup." [Pearl] (16) Fall 92, p. 9.

4593. NIELSEN, Daryl
"Passenger Seat." [HawaiiR] (16:2, #35) Spr 92, p. 65.

4594. NIELSEN, Joanes
"Ghosts" (tr. by Leyvoy Joensen). [Vis] (38) 92, p. 46.

4595. NIELSEN, Kristy
"Watching a Man Work." [MidAR] (13:2) 92, p. 168-169.

4596. NIETO, Margarita
"Latin and Jazz" (tr. of Gonzalo Rojas). [OnTheBus] (4:2/5:1, #10/11) 92, p. 281.
"Made by Everyone: Poetry" (tr. of Juan Gustavo Cobo Borda). [OnTheBus] (4:2/5:1, #10/11) 92, p. 271.
"Portraits" (tr. of Juan Gustavo Cobo Borda). [OnTheBus] (4:2/5:1, #10/11) 92, p. 270.
"What Do You Do When You Love?" (tr. of Gonzalo Rojas). [OnTheBus] (4:2/5:1, #10/11) 92, p. 280.

4597. NIKOLAEVA, Olesia
"A Party on Women's Day" (tr. by Paul Graves and Carol Ueland). [KenR] (NS 14:4) Fall 92, p. 117-118.
"Seven Beginnings" (tr. by Paul Graves and Carol Ueland). [KenR] (NS 14:4) Fall 92, p. 115-116.
"Untitled: Here, everything gets eaten: drippings, marinade" (tr. by Paul Graves and Carol Ueland). [KenR] (NS 14:4) Fall 92, p. 117.

4598. NIMMO, Kurt
"Business As Usual." [SlipS] (12) 92, p. 7-10.
"Gorilla Game." [SlipS] (12) 92, p. 5-7.

4599. NIMNICHT, Nona
"The Beggar at Chartres." [CapeR] (27:1) Spr 92, p. 36-37.

4600. NIMS, John Frederick
"The Hearings on TV." [Light] (3) Aut 92, p. 19.
"Hymn." [Light] (4) Wint 92-93, p. 25.
"A Memory of Places." [SewanR] (100:4) Fall 92, p. 560.
"Now That You're Here." [Sparrow] (59) S 92, p. 31.

"On Her Seventy-fith." [Light] (1) Spr 92, p. 29.
"The Powers of Heaven and Earth." [Hudson] (44:4) Wint 92, p. 603-606.
"Read My Lips." [Light] (3) Aut 92, p. 19.
"The Sloth." [Light] (4) Wint 92-93, p. 21.
"Three Simple Sonnets." [Nimrod] (35:2) Spr-Sum 92, p. 3-4.
"Worth in the World." [SewanR] (100:4) Fall 92, p. 561.

4601. NINNIS, Jennifer
"Basketweavers." [Vis] (39) 92, p. 31-32.

NIORD, Chard de
See DeNIORD, Chard

4602. NISTLER, Tod
"Daddy's Boy." [EvergreenC] (7:2) Sum-Fall 92, p. 39.

4603. NIWA, Maureen
"The Branding." [Grain] (20:3) Fall 92, p. 59.
"Prairie Boys." [Grain] (20:3) Fall 92, p. 60.

4604. NIXON, John, Jr.
"In Purple Ink." [Comm] (119:21) 4 D 92, p. 12.
"Lunar Lines." [ChrC] (109:23) 29 Jl-5 Ag 92, p. 714.
"Night Storm." [Hellas] (3:1) Spr 92, p. 43.
"October Butterfly." [ChrC] (109:28) 7 O 92, p. 872.
"Second Primer." [Comm] (119:16) 25 S 92, p. 21.
"Undertakers." [Sparrow] (59) S 92, p. 28.

4605. NOBLES, Edward
"Daily Dilemma." [Agni] (35) 92, p. 272-273.
"Inside Plastic." [DenQ] (26:4) Spr 92, p. 52.

4606. NOGUERE, Suzanne
"Soma." [LullwaterR] (3:3) Sum 92, p. 40-41.

4607. NOHR, Brian
"Amniotic Apple." [FreeL] (10) Sum 92, p. 19.

4608. NOHRNBERG, Peter
"Fuse." [HarvardA] (127:4 [i.e. 126:4?]) Sum 92, p. 29.

4609. NOLAN, Pat
"Stupid Face Renku" (w. Keith Abbott and Michael Sowl). [HangL] (60) 92, p. 6 - 11.

4610. NOLLA, Olga Ramirez de Arelano
"Island of Childhood" (tr. by Barry J. Luby). [LitR] (35:4) Sum 92, p. 521.

NOORD, Barbara van
See Van NOORD, Barbara

4611. NORBERG, Viktoria
"Mermaids." [PacificR] (11) 92-93, p. 104-107.
"Poem Written About Photograph Taken (Chariton, Iowa: 1953)." [PacificR] (11) 92-93, p. 102-103.
"Sans Serif." [PacificR] (11) 92-93, p. 100-101.

NORD, Chard de
See DeNIORD, Chard

4612. NORD, Gennie
"Tripoli." [WillowR] (19) Spr 92, p. 22.

4613. NORDBRANDT, Henrik
"Aegina" (tr. by the author and Alex Taylor). [Vis] (38) 92, p. 15.
"China Observed through Greek Rain in Turkish Coffee" (tr. by Anne Born). [Stand] (33:4) Aut 92, p. 7-8.
"I Have Squandered My Money on Roses" (tr. by Alex Taylor). [Vis] (39) 92, p. 40.
"Our Love Is Like Byzantium" (tr. by Anne Born). [Stand] (33:4) Aut 92, p. 6-7.
"The Water Mirror" (tr. by Anne Born). [Stand] (33:4) Aut 92, p. 8.

4614. NORDFORS, Douglas
"Animal Behavior." [CreamCR] (16:1) Spr 92, p. 130-131.
"Long Pause." [HampSPR] Wint 92, p. 50.
"September 23, 1988." [CreamCR] (16:1) Spr 92, p. 132.
"Shelter." [HampSPR] Wint 92, p. 51.

4615. NORDHAUS, Jean
"Arroyo Seco: A House at the Crossroads." [PraS] (66:2) Sum 92, p. 112-113.

4616. NORDLING, Gayle
"Life Here & Hereafter, a Phototropism" (for Linda Simmons). [RagMag] (10:2) 92, p. 31.
"Sucking Noise from Emptiness." [RagMag] (10:2) 92, p. 30-31.

4617. NORDSTROM, Tracy
"Contract." [RagMag] (10:1) 92, p. 51.
"Gift." [RagMag] (10:1) 92, p. 53.
"Snapshots." [RagMag] (10:1) 92, p. 52.
4618. NORMAN, Chad
"Blue Comes the Jay" (for Patricia Young). [PoetryC] (12:3/4) Jl 92, p. 26.
"Fog in the Steadfast Fir" (for Jen). [PoetryC] (12:3/4) Jl 92, p. 26.
"In the Sky a Streelight Plays the Moon." [PoetryC] (12:3/4) Jl 92, p. 26.
"March of the Cedars" (for Jen). [PoetryC] (12:3/4) Jl 92, p. 26.
"Starlings" (for Patricia Young). [Event] (21:1) Spr 92, p. 59.
"Tame Geese." [Dandel] (19:2) 92, p. 33.
4619. NORMAN, Glenn
"Creation Is At Hand." [DogRR] (11:1) Spr-Sum 92, p. 26.
4620. NORMINGTON, Jim
"Alabama in Bloom" (for Paul Robeson, tr. of Efraín Huerta). [Talisman] (8) Spr 92, p. 143.
"Every Poem" (tr. of Alvaro Mutis). [Talisman] (8) Spr 92, p. 142.
4621. NORRIS, David
"Konnichi Wa Sakura." [CharR] (18:2) Fall 92, p. 78.
"Photograph of Peace Park, Nagasaki." [CharR] (18:2) Fall 92, p. 79.
"Sakura." [CharR] (18:2) Fall 92, p. 79.
"Where the Walls Meet." [CharR] (18:2) Fall 92, p. 80.
4622. NORRIS, Ken
"Cold." [PraF] (13:4, #61) Wint 92-93, p. 92.
"To the Bastard Who Crippled Me." [PraF] (13:4, #61) Wint 92-93, p. 92.
4623. NORRIS, Leslie
"A Grain of Sand." [TarRP] (32:1) Fall 92, p. 32-34.
"In Cefn Cemetery." [TarRP] (32:1) Fall 92, p. 34-35.
"Owen Sullivan and the Horse." [TarRP] (32:1) Fall 92, p. 35-36.
4624. NORSE, Harold
"The Italian Notebook" (Excerpt). [PoetryUSA] (24) 92, p. 23.
4625. NORTH, William
"Two Infinities." [ChrC] (109:37) 16 D 92, p. 1166.
4626. NORTH SUN, Nila
"Moving Camp Too Far." [Jacaranda] (6:1/2) Wint-Spr 92, p. 84.
4627. NORTHROP, Michael
"Death of a Circus Animal." [Asylum] (7:3/4) 92, p. 40.
4628. NORTHUP, Harry
"My Favorites Begin." [OnTheBus] (4:2/5:1, #10/11) 92, p. 165.
4629. NOSOW, Robert
"Dialogue / Canyon." [MidAR] (12:2) 92, p. 24.
4630. NOSTRAND, Jennifer
"Luxembourg Gardens." [GreensboroR] (52) Sum 92, p. 3.
4631. NOTLEY, Alice
"Red Zinnias." [Talisman] (8) Spr 92, p. 163-168.
4632. NOVAK, Boris
"Kronanje / Coronation" (1 selection in Slovenian, 4 in English, tr. by the author). [Nimrod] (35:2) Spr-Sum 92, p. 5-7.
"Magistrale" (tr. by the author). [Nimrod] (35:2) Spr-Sum 92, p. 7.
4633. NOVAK, Helga M.
"Disgust" (tr. by Sammy McLean). [SnailPR] (2:2) Fall-Wint 92, p. 28.
"Dismal Place" (tr. by Sammy McLean). [SnailPR] (2:2) Fall-Wint 92, p. 28.
"March Through" (tr. by Sammy McLean). [Vis] (39) 92, p. 35.
4634. NOVAK, Katherine Bush
"During and Immediately After: Challenger: or What Television Further Explodes." [SmPd] (29:3, #86) Fall 92, p. 36.
4635. NOWAK, Nancy
"Because Some Desire." [SouthernPR] (32:1) Spr 92, p. 9-10.
4636. NOYES, H. F.
"Haiku" (two poems). [Amelia] (7:1, #20) 92, p. 44.
"Oil-soaked, smoke-choked." [Amelia] (6:4, #19) 92, p. 64.
4637. NUCKOLS, Carrie
"My First and Fatal Date." [PoetryUSA] (24) 92, p. 32.
4638. NUÑEZ, Ana Rosa
"Postor del Aire" (Para Berta Randin, pintora de Ana Rosa Núñez). [Nuez] (4:10/11) 92, p. 16.

4639. NURKSE, D.
"The Checkpoints." [HangL] (60) 92, p. 43-44.
"The Debt." [HangL] (60) 92, p. 45.
"Evergreen in Summer." [YellowS] (Ten Years [i.e. 40]) Sum-Fall 92, p. 32.
"Late May at Little Rapids." [YellowS] (41) Fall-Wint 92-93, p. 32.
"Newborn." [HangL] (60) 92, p. 45.
"Theories of Limited War." [FreeL] (9) Wint 92, p. 4.
"Venus in the First House." [YellowS] (41) Fall-Wint 92-93, p. 32.
"Visiting Rights." [ManhatPR] (14) [92?], p. 47.
4640. NUSSBAUM, Elaine
"Stacking Wood Beside the Sculptures." [DogRR] (11:1) Spr-Sum 92, p. 37.
"The Teapot." [DogRR] (11:1) Spr-Sum 92, p. 36.
4641. NUSSBAUM, Emily S.
"The Trap." [CapeR] (27:2) Fall 92, p. 50.
4642. NYE, Naomi Shihab
"Broken Clock." [MichQR] (31:4) Fall 92, p. 458.
"Escape." [CreamCR] (16:2) Fall 92, p. 30.
"Flashbulb." [MichQR] (31:4) Fall 92, p. 459.
"Pins." [MichQR] (31:4) Fall 92, p. 460-461.
"Speaking Arabic." [MichQR] (31:4) Fall 92, p. 462.
"What She Was Doing at Home." [CreamCR] (16:2) Fall 92, p. 31.
"White Coals." [MichQR] (31:4) Fall 92, p. 457.
"Yeast." [CreamCR] (16:2) Fall 92, p. 29.
4643. NYHART, Al
"Oilfields." [CapeR] (27:1) Spr 92, p. 2.
4644. NYSTROM, Karen
"Leave Her Out." [DenQ] (26:3) Wint 92, p. 39-40.
"Poem in Voices." [AnotherCM] (24) Fall 92, p. 113-114.
"Varied Suits." [AnotherCM] (24) Fall 92, p. 111-112.
4645. NYTE, Gregory
"Flight." [CanLit] (135) Wint 92, p. 123.
"Loss of a Daughter." [Event] (21:3) Fall 92, p. 76.
"On Dying." [CapilR] (2:9) Fall 92, p. 78.
"To My Daughter." [CanLit] (135) Wint 92, p. 122.
4646. O RIORDAIN, Seán
"Claustrophobia" (tr. by James Gleasure). [Trans] (26) Spr 92, p. 63.
"Fever" (tr. by Richard Ryan). [Trans] (26) Spr 92, p. 64.
4647. O TUAMA, Seán
"A Gaeltacht Rousseau" (tr. from the Irish by the author). [Trans] (26) Spr 92, p. 82.
"Love-Game" (tr. from the Irish by the author). [Trans] (26) Spr 92, p. 81.
4648. OAKLEY, Evan
"Broken Hearing Aids." [Jacaranda] (6:1/2) Wint-Spr 92, p. 143.
4649. OATES, Joyce Carol
"Frequent Flier." [Boulevard] (7:1, #19) Spr 92, p. 59.
"Frequent Flier." [NewRep] (207:18) 26 O 92, p. 44.
"He Was Talking About His Friend." [Boulevard] (7:2/3, #20/21) Fall 92, p. 278.
"Locking-Through" (from "The Time Travelers," 1989). [Elf] (2:4) Wint 92, p. 24 - 25.
"Mantua Sportsmen's Club, 1957." [NewMyths] (1:2/2:1) 92, p. 207.
"Old Concord Cemetery." [Boulevard] (7:1, #19) Spr 92, p. 60.
"Piano Tuner, in His Thirties, Pony-Tailed." [NewMyths] (1:2/2:1) 92, p. 206.
"Summer Squall." [Boulevard] (7:1, #19) Spr 92, p. 61.
4650. OBA, Ryan
"Obon." [Jacaranda] (6:1/2) Wint-Spr 92, p. 36-37.
4651. OBBINK, Laura Apol
"Errant." [EngJ] (81:8) D 92, p. 85.
4652. OBEJAS, Achy
"Kimberle." [Americas] (20:3/4) Fall-Wint 92, p. 158.
"Sugarcane." [Americas] (20:3/4) Fall-Wint 92, p. 159-160.
4653. OBERST, Terrance
"Once Upon a Time." [Plain] (12:3) Spr 92, p. 14.
4654. O'BRIEN, Barbara
"The Prophet Explains Religion." [Sun] (195) F 92, p. 12-13.
4655. O'BRIEN, Geoffrey
"Ancients" (Selections: 2 poems). [Talisman] (8) Spr 92, p. 135-136.
"Ionized Cloud." [NewAW] (10) Fall 92, p. 50.

"Marginalia." [NewAW] (10) Fall 92, p. 47.
"Virgilian Herb." [NewAW] (10) Fall 92, p. 48-49.

4656. O'BRIEN, Jean
"Unlearning You." [Interim] (11:2) Fall-Wint 92-93, p. 7.

4657. O'BRIEN, Judith Tate
"Olfaction: One Way of Knowing." [SouthernPR] (32:1) Spr 92, p. 33-34.

4658. O'BRIEN, Laurie
"Flood Tide" (Second Place, The Paintbrush Award, Poetry). [PaintedHR] (7) Fall 92, p. 10.
"Go to Sleep in Poems" (Second Place, The Paintbrush Award, Poetry). [PaintedHR] (7) Fall 92, p. 11.
"How the Tenor Sings" (Second Place, The Paintbrush Award, Poetry). [PaintedHR] (7) Fall 92, p. 9.
"In Maine" (Second Place, The Paintbrush Award, Poetry). [PaintedHR] (7) Fall 92, p. 8-9.
"Light Has Always Attracted Them." [NegC] (12:1/2) 92, p. 103.
"Swimming After Birds." [PaintedHR] (5) Wint 92, p. 31.
"The Whale Watcher at Home." [SouthernR] (28:2) Spr, Ap 92, p. 319.

4659. O'BRIEN, Lawrence F.
"Sunstroke." [Hellas] (3:1) Spr 92, p. 47.

4660. O'BRIEN, Mark
"Breathing." [Sun] (203) N 92, p. 27.
"Karen." [Sun] (203) N 92, p. 26-27.

4661. O'BRIEN, Maureen
"Hear(t) Be(at)." [Kalliope] (14:3) 92, p. 52.

4662. O'BRIEN, Michael
"Odalisque." [LitR] (35:3) Spr 92, p. 345.

4663. O'BRIEN, Sean
"Special Train." [Verse] (9:2) Sum 92, p. 48-49.

4664. O'CALLAGHAN, Conor
"Three Villanelles in California." [Verse] (9:3) Wint 92, p. 14-15.

4665. O'CALLAGHAN, T. Colm
"An Inheritance." [Parting] (5:1) Sum 92, p. 28.

4666. OCAMPO, Silvina
"The Pines" (tr. by Jason Weiss). [Trans] (26) Spr 92, p. 24.
"A Tiger Speaks" (tr. by Greg Geleta). [Asylum] (7:3/4) 92, p. 38-39.

4667. OCAMPO, Victor R.
"The Old Homestead." [Wind] (22:71) 92, p. 22.

4668. OCHESTER, Ed
"The Canaries in Uncle Arthur's Basement." [ThRiPo] (39/40) 92-93, p. 177.
"New Day." [ThRiPo] (39/40) 92-93, p. 177-178.
"The Relatives." [ThRiPo] (39/40) 92-93, p. 175-177.

4669. O'CONNELL, Colin
"Silent" (tr. of Marie Luise Kaschnitz, w. Uta Doerr). [AntigR] (90) Sum 92, p. 89.

4670. O'CONNELL, Richard
"F. Scott Fitzgerald." [Light] (4) Wint 92-93, p. 16.
"Ode Upon the Completion of the Second Year of Jack's Reign." [Light] (3) Aut 92, p. 20.

4671. O'CONNOR, Deirdre
"An English Introduction to Japanese Poetry." [NoDaQ] (60:3) Sum 92, p. 44.
"Poem Ending in Desire." [WestB] (30) 92, p. 40.
"Snow as a Vanishing That Reappears Down Here." [NoDaQ] (60:3) Sum 92, p. 43.
"Soup." [WestB] (30) 92, p. 41.

4672. O'DALY, William
"The Book of Questions" (Selections: XVII, XIII, V, VII, XXVIII, LIX, tr. of Pablo Neruda). [PoetryE] (33) Spr 92, p. 168-173.

4673. ODAM, Joyce
"Grievances." [Parting] (5:1) Sum 92, p. 14.
"The Importance of Old Snapshots." [ChamLR] (10/11) Spr-Fall 92, p. 40.
"A Night Reflection." [BellR] (15:2) Fall 92, p. 41.
"Self Containment." [ChamLR] (10/11) Spr-Fall 92, p. 39.
"Skit." [Bogg] (65) 92, p. 39.
"The Suicide's Children." [BellR] (15:2) Fall 92, p. 40.

4674. ODLIN, Reno
"Back to Beaucaire." [AntigR] (90) Sum 92, p. 117.

4675. O'DONNELL, Kathleen
"For Thelma and Louise." [SinW] (48) Wint 92-93, p. 29-30.
4676. O'DONNELL, Mark
"Brain, Heart, and Hand." [NewRep] (207:21) 16 N 92, p. 42.
"Pandora Then Heard a Small Voice" (a friend has been diagnosed with AIDS). [Art&Und] (1:1) Fall 91, p. 20.
4677. O'DRISCOLL, Dennis
"Couples." [Verse] (9:3) Wint 92, p. 10-11.
4678. O'DWYER, Kieran P.
"Facing Death." [Plain] (13:1) Fall 92, p. 11.
4679. O'DWYER, Tess
"The Empire of Dreams" (3 excerpts, tr. of Giannina Braschi, w. José Vázquez - Amaral). [Luz] (1) My 92, p. 20-26.
"Pastoral" (Excerpt, tr. of Giannina Braschi). [Sonora] (22/23) Spr 92, p. 116.
4680. OESTREICHER, Joy
"Momjob." [FreeL] (10) Sum 92, p. 21.
4681. OFFEN, Ron
"Another and Another Plea." [CoalC] (5) My 92, p. 9.
"Hour Song." [CoalC] (5) My 92, p. 5.
"Punker." [Pearl] (15) Spr-Sum 92, p. 17.
4682. OGDEN, Hugh
"Above Salmon Brook, the Darkness" (for Annette). [HiramPoR] (51/52) Fall 91 - Sum 92, p. 57.
"The Balcony at Dusk." [TarRP] (32:1) Fall 92, p. 45-46.
"The Birches, the Old Railroad Bed" (for Annette). [MalR] (101) Wint92, p. 86-87.
"The Island" (for Annette). [LullwaterR] (3:3) Sum 92, p. 9.
"Oquossoc, by the Window" (for Annette). [MalR] (101) Wint92, p. 88-89.
4683. O'GRADY, Jennifer
"Moths." [Poetry] (160:5) Ag 92, p. 259.
"Singular Constructions." [SenR] (22:2) Fall 92, p. 76-77.
4684. O'HALLORAN, Jamie
"Fortune Teller." [BellArk] (8:3) My-Je 92, p. 21.
"In Praise of Hopkins and Birds." [BellArk] (8:3) My-Je 92, p. 23.
4685. O'HARA, Frank
"For Grace, After a Party." [NewEngR] (14:4) Fall 92, p. 232.
4686. O'HARA, Kathleen
"In Memory of John Steptoe" (who died 25 July 1863 of wounds received at Gettysburg. A Plainsongs Award Poem). [Plain] (12:3) Spr 92, p. 20-21.
4687. O'HARA, Mark
"Listening to Water." [Epiphany] (3:3) Jl (Sum) 92, p. 177-178.
"Prokofiev and the Bear." [Epiphany] (3:3) Jl (Sum) 92, p. 180.
"Saint Pelagia the Fisherwoman." [Epiphany] (3:3) Jl (Sum) 92, p. 179.
4688. O'HAY, Charles
"Through the Leaking Glass." [Lactuca] (16) Ag 92, p. 9.
4689. O'HEHIR, Diana
"Coming Forth by Day" (Selections: Spell 163, Spell 149). [KenR] (NS 14:4) Fall 92, p. 62-64.
4690. O'HERN, James
"Endless Time." [OnTheBus] (4:2/5:1, #10/11) 92, p. 166-167.
"Maiden Voyage." [OnTheBus] (4:2/5:1, #10/11) 92, p. 166.
4691. OJAIDE, Tanure
"The Abibiman Saga." [Stand] (33:3) Sum 92, p. 33-35.
"Cannons for the Brave" (For Irherhe). [Stand] (33:3) Sum 92, p. 32.
"Homage: To Idiagbon." [Stand] (33:3) Sum 92, p. 36.
"Mbira." [HayF] (11) Fall-Wint 92, p. 113-114.
4692. OKAMURA, Tricia M.
"Tamiko's Dream." [ChamLR] (10/11) Spr-Fall 92, p. 54-56.
4693. OKSON
"Do They Say" (tr. by Constantine Contogenis and Wolhee Choe). [Pequod] (34) 92, p. 118.
4694. OLAH, János
"In Another Country (1966)" (tr. by Nicholas Kolumban). [OnTheBus] (4:2/5:1, #10/11) 92, p. 267.
"Meditation" (tr. by Nicholas Kolumban). [OnTheBus] (4:2/5:1, #10/11) 92, p. 266.
"A Traveler in the Soviet Union" (tr. by Nicholas Kolumban). [SilverFR] (23) Wint 92, p. 36.

4695. OLDER, Julia
"Fruits" (for Marie-Anne, tr. of Christophe Nguedam). [Nimrod] (35:2) Spr-Sum 92, p. 123.
"Hope" (tr. of Christophe Nguedam). [Nimrod] (35:2) Spr-Sum 92, p. 123.
"Tattoo" (from "Hermaphroditus in America"). [Nimrod] (35:2) Spr-Sum 92, p. 105.
"Two Worlds" (Spoleto, Italy, 1966). [Nimrod] (35:2) Spr-Sum 92, p. 103-104.
4696. OLDKNOW, Antony
"Eye Music." [CreamCR] (16:1) Spr 92, p. 119.
"Horses." [LitR] (35:3) Spr 92, p. 373.
"Imagine." [Vis] (38) 92, p. 28.
"Lovers." [Asylum] (7:3/4) 92, p. 65.
"North Wind" (tr. of Eugenio Montale). [WebR] (16) Fall 92, p. 28.
"People on a Bridge." [AmerPoR] (21:6) N-D 92, p. 41.
"Possible Love." [MinnR] (38) Spr-Sum 92, p. 29.
4697. OLDS, Jennifer
"Eating Mathilda." [Pearl] (16) Fall 92, p. 10-11.
4698. OLDS, Sharon
"19." [TriQ] (84) Spr-Sum 92, p. 19." [TriQ] (84) Spr-Sum 92, p. 99-100.
"The Day They Tied Me Up." [Verse] (8:3/9:1) Wint-Spr 92, p. 120.
"Death." [BostonR] (17:2) Mr-Ap 92, p. 8.
"The Elopement." [Field] (47) Fall 92, p. 85-86.
"The Falls." [Field] (47) Fall 92, p. 83-84.
"His Smell." [Salm] (93) Wint 92, p. 79-80.
"I Wanted to Be There When My Father Died." [AmerPoR] (21:1) Ja-F 92, p. 29.
"Last Words." [Thrpny] (49) Spr 92, p. 21.
"The Look." [AmerPoR] (21:1) Ja-F 92, p. 28.
"Love in Blood Time." [YellowS] (39) Spr-Sum 92, p. 16.
"The Moment the Two Worlds Meet." [YellowS] (39) Spr-Sum 92, p. 17.
"My Father Speaks to Me From the Dead." [AmerPoR] (21:1) Ja-F 92, p. 29.
"The Native." [TriQ] (84) Spr-Sum 92, p. 101-102.
"Parent Visiting Day." [Salm] (93) Wint 92, p. 78.
"The Request." [AmerPoR] (21:1) Ja-F 92, p. 28.
"The Sighting." [Nat] (255:1) 6 Jl 92, p. 30.
"The Struggle." [AmerPoR] (21:1) Ja-F 92, p. 28.
"To My Father." [Salm] (93) Wint 92, p. 81.
"The Urn." [Salm] (93) Wint 92, p. 80-81.
"Warrior: 5th Grade." [TriQ] (84) Spr-Sum 92, p. 97-98.
"What I Liked About It." [TriQ] (84) Spr-Sum 92, p. 95-96.
"When the Dead Ask My Father About Me." [Thrpny] (49) Spr 92, p. 21.
4699. OLEAF, Jerry
"Anger." [Footwork] 92, p. 68.
"The Deaf Man." [Footwork] 92, p. 68.
4700. OLINKA, Sharon
"American Fragments." [NewDeltaR] (8:2) Spr-Sum 91, p. 15-18.
"Cremations." [AmerV] (28) 92, p. 20-23.
4701. OLIVE, Harry
"Banners Yield No Peace." [Amelia] (7:1, #20) 92, p. 133.
"Banquet." [Plain] (12:3) Spr 92, p. 19.
4702. OLIVEIRA, Carlos de
"Childhood" (tr. by William Jay Smith). [Trans] (26) Spr 92, p. 58.
4703. OLIVER, Douglas
"Navasutra" (Selection: II). [Talisman] (8) Spr 92, p. 137-141.
"Pine." [Archae] (3) early 92, p. 5.
4704. OLIVER, Mary
"At Blackwater Pond." [ThRiPo] (39/40) 92-93, p. 179.
"At Old Whorehouse." [ThRiPo] (39/40) 92-93, p. 180-181.
"Blackberries." [NewEngR] (14:4) Fall 92, p. 227.
"Dancers at Banstead." [AntR] (50:1/2) Wint-Spr 92, p. 162.
"Death and the Dealer of Death." [ParisR]] (34:124) Fall 92, p. 178-179.
"Hummingbirds." [Poetry] (160:4) Jl 92, p. 209-210.
"Morning at Great Pond." [ThRiPo] (39/40) 92-93, p. 179-180.
"Pink Moon — the Pond." [NewEngR] (14:4) Fall 92, p. 227-228.
"Poppies." [KenR] (NS 14:2) Spr 92, p. 94-95.
"The Rabbit." [ThRiPo] (39/40) 92-93, p. 181.
"The Swan." [ParisR]] (34:124) Fall 92, p. 179.
"White Flowers." [Atlantic] (269:3) Mr 92, p. 83.

"White Flowers." [YellowS] (41) Fall-Wint 92-93, p. 4.

4705. OLIVER LABRA, Carilda

"Declaración de Amor." [LitR] (35:4) Sum 92, p. 596.

"Declaration of Love" (tr. by Betty Wilson, w. Pam Mordecai). [LitR] (35:4) Sum 92, p. 461.

"Elegia." [LitR] (35:4) Sum 92, p. 597.

"Elegy" (tr. by Betty Wilson, w. Pam Mordecai). [LitR] (35:4) Sum 92, p. 462.

"Ovillejo." [LitR] (35:4) Sum 92, p. 597.

"Rondel" (tr. by Betty Wilson, w. Pam Mordecai). [LitR] (35:4) Sum 92, p. 462.

4706. OLIVIER, Louis

"Hatteras Night" (tr. of Vincent-Marc Karénine). [CharR] (18:1) Spr 92, p. 95-96.

4707. OLLÉ, Carmen

"Nights of Adrenalin" (Selections: xxv-xxvi, in Spanish). [AnotherCM] (23) Spr 92, p. 148-152.

"Nights of Adrenalin" (Selections: xxv-xxvi, tr. by Anne Archer). [AnotherCM] (23) Spr 92, p. 149-153.

4708. OLSEN, Jackie

"Five Minutes Fast." [Epiphany] (3:4) O (Fall) 92, p. 286.

"Pearl." [Epiphany] (3:4) O (Fall) 92, p. 287-291.

4709. OLSEN, William

"After Chartres." [GettyR] (5:2) Spr 92, p. 300-302.

"And the Snow." [IndR] (15:2) Fall 92, p. 46-48.

"At the Bus Stop." [IndR] (15:2) Fall 92, p. 49.

"Bottomland." [IndR] (15:2) Fall 92, p. 43-45.

"Burning Houses." [NewEngR] (14:3) Sum 92, p. 122-123.

"The Human Brain." [PoetryNW] (33:1) Spr 92, p. 3-5.

"Natural History." [PoetryNW] (33:1) Spr 92, p. 6-7.

"Raptors." [PoetryNW] (33:1) Spr 92, p. 7-8.

"Schoolyard with Jay." [Sonora] (22/23) Spr 92, p. 33-34.

"The Suicides." [NewEngR] (14:3) Sum 92, p. 124-126.

4710. OLSON, Kirby

"Afternoons of Gambling." [Asylum] (7:3/4) 92, p. 31.

"Evolution." [Light] (3) Aut 92, p. 24.

4711. OLSON, Sandra

"Devolution." [Kalliope] (14:3) 92, p. 61.

4712. OMANSON, Bradley

"Her Father's War." [SewanR] (100:1) Wint 92, p. 66-67.

"Last Stand." [SewanR] (100:1) Wint 92, p. 68.

4713. OMAYE, Gabriel

"Resonancia." [Nuez] (4:10/11) 92, p. 9.

4714. O'NEILL, Brian

"Clones." [Agni] (35) 92, p. 175.

4715. ONESCHUK, Kate

"Advice to Winter's Child." [ChiR] (37:4) 92, p. 15.

4716. ONESS, Chad

"Pre-Inspection." [Stand] (33:2) Spr 92, p. 16.

ONG J-SON, Wooi-chin

See WOOI-CHIN, J-son

ONOFRIO, Lisa d'

See D'ONOFRIO, Lisa

4717. OPENGART, Bea

"Not Sleeping." [Journal] (16:2) Fall-Wint 92, p. 90.

"Small Plane Overhead." [Journal] (16:2) Fall-Wint 92, p. 91.

4718. ORAC, Vera

"Lazarus, White Holly Berries" (tr. of Sylva Fischerová, w. Stuart Friebert and the author). [PraS] (66:4) Wint 92, p. 89-90.

"Moravia" (tr. of Sylva Fischerová, w. Stuart Friebert and the author). [PraS] (66:4) Wint 92, p. 86-87.

"Pax Vobiscum" (tr. of Sylva Fischerová, w. Stuart Friebert and the author). [PraS] (66:4) Wint 92, p. 87-88.

"Who Knows Something about Women?" (tr. of Sylva Fischerová, w. Stuart Friebert and the author). [PraS] (66:4) Wint 92, p. 85-86.

"X X X: and what remained, a desire for destiny" (tr. of Sylva Fischerová, w. Stuart Friebert and the author). [PraS] (66:4) Wint 92, p. 84-85.

"X X X: Give me ashes, earth, and my dead" (tr. of Sylva Fischerová, w. Stuart Friebert and the author). [PraS] (66:4) Wint 92, p. 88-89.

4719. ORAVECZ, Imré
"Afterwards You Came Out" (tr. by Bruce Berlind). [Sonora] (22/23) Spr 92, p. 127.
"As You Recall" (tr. by Bruce Berlind). [Sonora] (22/23) Spr 92, p. 129.
"At First It Was Easy" (tr. by Bruce Berlind). [PoetL] (87:4) Wint 92-93, p. 43.
"The Dream of H. Bosch" (tr. by Bruce Berlind and Maria Körösy). [PoetryE] (33) Spr 92, p. 167.
"I Confess, I'm Still" (tr. by Bruce Berlind). [GrahamHR] (16) Fall 92, p. 14.
"I Loved Someone Before You" (tr. by Bruce Berlind). [GrahamHR] (16) Fall 92, p. 13.
"In Honor of a Fisherman" (tr. by Nicholas Kolumban). [ArtfulD] (22/23) 92, p. 35.
"Last Night" (tr. by Bruce Berlind). [Sonora] (22/23) Spr 92, p. 128.
"Once Again" (tr. by Bruce Berlind, w. Mária Körösy). [LitR] (25:2) Wint 92, p. 176.
"The Sun Is Shining" (tr. by Bruce Berlind, w. Mária Körösy). [LitR] (25:2) Wint 92, p. 177.
"Supper" (tr. by Bruce Berlind. w. Mária Körösy). [ArtfulD] (22/23) 92, p. 33.
"Then I Picked Up That Woman" (tr. by Bruce Berlind). [GrahamHR] (16) Fall 92, p. 16.
"Tonight, Around Eleven" (tr. by Bruce Berlind). [GrahamHR] (16) Fall 92, p. 15.
"Uncle Gábor" (tr. by Bruce Berlind and Mária Korösy). [WebR] (16) Fall 92, p. 33 - 34.
"Water" (tr. by Bruce Berlind, w. Mária Körösy). [PartR] (59:2) Spr 92, p. 266-267.
"You Ask" (tr. by Bruce Berlind). [PoetL] (87:4) Wint 92-93, p. 41.
"You Don't Love Me Anymore" (tr. by Bruce Berlind). [PoetL] (87:4) Wint 92-93, p. 42.
4720. ORBAN, Ottó
"1937" (tr. by Jascha Kessler and Maria Körösy). [Jacaranda] (6:1/2) Wint-Spr 92, p. 142.
"The Angel of Traffic" (Los Angeles, tr. by Bruce Berlind, w. Mária Körösy). [KenR] (NS 14:1) Wint 92, p. 83.
"The Dazzling Disparity in Size" (Minnesota Public Radio, metro area traffic report, tr. by Bruce Berlind, w. Mária Körösy). [KenR] (NS 14:1) Wint 92, p. 84.
"The End of Adventures" (A KSTP TV Publication: "AIDS — What to know about It?", tr. by Bruce Berlind, w. Mária Körösy). [Nimrod] (35:2) Spr-Sum 92, p. 35.
"The Four-Wheeled Man" (tr. by Bruce Berlind, w. Mária Körösy). [KenR] (NS 14:1) Wint 92, p. 82.
"The Journey of Barbarus" (tr. by Bruce Berlind, w. Maria Körösy). [ParisR] (34:123) Sum 92, p. 134.
"Mr. E. Veryman, President of Whatever Works Works" (tr. by Bruce Berlind, w. Mária Körösy). [Nimrod] (35:2) Spr-Sum 92, p. 36.
"Oklahoma Summer" (tr. by Bruce Berlind, w. Mária Körösy). [Nimrod] (35:2) Spr - Sum 92, p. 37.
"Old Fiddlers' Picnic" (tr. by Bruce Berlind, w. Mária Körösy). [Nimrod] (35:2) Spr - Sum 92, p. 35.
"On a Cart" (from "Our Bearings at Sea": A Novel-in-Poems, tr. by Jascha Kessler, w. Mária Körösy). [Nimrod] (35:2) Spr-Sum 92, p. 34.
"Why Wouldn't I Live in America?" (tr. by Bruce Berlind and Mária Körösy). [LitR] (25:2) Wint 92, p. 173-175.
ORDONEZ ARGUELLO, Alberto
See ARGUELLO, Alberto Ordonez
ORIOL, Robert Berrouët
See BERROUËT-ORIOL, Robert
ORIORDAIN, Seán
See O RIORDAIN, Seán
4721. ORLEN, Steve
"Plaza Real, Barcelona" (for Casper le Fèvre, tr. of Esther Jansma, w. the author). [Agni] (35) 92, p. 173.
"Transportation" (tr. of Esther Jansma, w. the author). [Agni] (35) 92, p. 174.
4722. ORLOWSKY, D. (Dzvinia)
"Burying Dolls." [BelPoJ] (42:3) Spr 92, p. 5.
"Our Grotto." [SycamoreR] (4:2) Sum 92, p. 52.
4723. ORMSBY, Eric
"Adages of a Grandmother." [NewYorker] (68:39) 16 N 92, p. 91.
"Grackle." [NewYorker] (68:33) 5 O 92, p. 118.
"Highway Grasses." [Blueline] (13) 92, p. 3.

"Mullein." [Blueline] (13) 92, p. 1-2.

4724. ORMSHAW, Peter
"Learning the Land." [PraF] (13:3, #60) Aut 92, p. 148.
"Pickling." [PraF] (13:3, #60) Aut 92, p. 147.
"Used Book" (for Peter J. Semko). [PraF] (13:3, #60) Aut 92, p. 149.

4725. ORNATOWSKI, Cesar
"When I uncorked the bottle" (tr. of Edward Stachura). [InterPR] (18:2) Fall 92, p. 39, 41.

4726. O'ROURKE, Charlene No Bears
"Crossing Over." [SinW] (47) Sum-Fall 92, p. 139.
"Sun Dance, AIM, and Wolves came dancing." [SinW] (47) Sum-Fall 92, p. 121.
"We walk, We fall." [SinW] (47) Sum-Fall 92, p. 28.

4727. O'ROURKE, Donny
"For James Schuyler." [Verse] (8:3/9:1) Wint-Spr 92, p. 100.
"Robbie." [Verse] (9:3) Wint 92, p. 139.

4728. OROZCO, Olga
"The Deaths" (tr. by Mary Crow). [InterPR] (18:2) Fall 92, p. 25.
"El Extranjero." [InterPR] (18:2) Fall 92, p. 22.
"The Foreigner" (tr. by Mary Crow). [InterPR] (18:2) Fall 92, p. 23.
"Las Muertes." [InterPR] (18:2) Fall 92, p. 24.
"Olga Orozco" (in Spanish and English, tr. by Mary Crow). [InterPR] (18:2) Fall 92, p. 18-21.

4729. ORR, Ed
"City 1 Parking Booth, June 8, 1990." [YellowS] (Ten Years [i.e. 40]) Sum-Fall 92, p. 32.

4730. ORR, Gregory
"The Abortion." [DenQ] (26:4) Spr 92, p. 54.
"Aubade: Leaving for Work." [HampSPR] Wint 92, p. 20.
"The Cliff." [DenQ] (26:4) Spr 92, p. 53.
"Father's Song." [Poetry] (160:3) Je 92, p. 152.
"Rising at 5." [HampSPR] Wint 92, p. 20.

4731. ORR, Priscilla
"At the Vet Cemetery." [Footwork] 92, p. 39.
"Prayer Basket." [Footwork] 92, p. 39.
"Shoreline in the Late Afternoon" (for Joan). [Footwork] 92, p. 39.

4732. ORR, Thomas Alan
"Cattle Magnet." [HopewellR] (4) 92, p. 7.
"Rabbit Light." [HopewellR] (4) 92, p. 23.

4733. ORSINI, Georgianna
"The Perfect Lover." [Boulevard] (7:1, #19) Spr 92, p. 184.
"Praise." [Boulevard] (7:1, #19) Spr 92, p. 185.

4734. ORT, Daniel
"The Widow Cory." [TexasR] (13:3/4) Fall-Wint 92, p. 93.

4735. ORTEGA, Frank
"Waiting for Sunset." [SenR] (22:1) Spr 92, p. 69-70.

4736. ORTEGA, Julio
"Trilce" (Selections: XXXII, XXXVI, XXXVIII, tr. of César Vallejo, w. Clayton Eshleman). [GrandS] (11:1, #41) 92, p. 57-61.
"Trilce" (Selections: LXXI-LXXIII, tr. of César Vallejo, w. Clayton Eshleman). [WorldL] (3) 92, p. 1-3.

4737. ORTIZ, Simon J.
"And the Land Is Just As Dry" (line from a song by Peter LaFarge). [Jacaranda] (6:1/2) Wint-Spr 92, p. 86-87.

ORTIZ COFER, Judith
See COFER, Judith Ortiz

4738. ORVINO, Jennie
"Lips. Lips against spicy, fragrant cheek." [NewYorkQ] (48) 92, p. 101.

4739. OSADCHAYA, Irina
"Untitled: A man comes in, his suit is crumpled" (tr. of Sergei Timofeyev, w. Lyn Hejinian). [Avec] (5:1) 92, p. 39.
"White Heart" (tr. of Sergei Timofeyev, w. Lyn Hejinian). [Avec] (5:1) 92, p. 39.

4740. OSBEY, Brenda Marie
"Expeditus." [AmerPoR] (21:3) My-Je 92, p. 8-9.
"Moses Goes Home to Soweto." [AmerV] (26) Spr 92, p. 112-114.

4741. OSERS, Ewald
"Hope" (tr. of Milan Richter). [PraS] (66:4) Wint 92, p. 149-152.

"I Don't Believe" (tr. of Zdenek Vanícek). [PraS] (66:4) Wint 92, p. 163-164.
"Light?" (Mehr Licht — Goethe, tr. of Milan Richter). [PraS] (66:4) Wint 92, p. 152-153.
"The Old Jewish Quarter in Prague" (for Ivan Jelínek, tr. of Zdenek Vanícek). [PraS] (66:4) Wint 92, p. 165.
"Open Letter" (tr. of Ivana Bozdechová). [PraS] (66:4) Wint 92, p. 35.
"What You Have Written" (tr. of Milan Richter). [PraS] (66:4) Wint 92, p. 148-149.

4742. OSHEROW, Jacqueline
"Fornacette, 1990, Spring." [ParisR] (34:122) Spr 92, p. 162-165.
"Relocation." [NewRep] (207:17) 19 O 92, p. 42.
"What We'd Do, Emily, If You Came Home." [NewRep] (206:10) 9 Mr 92, p. 43.
"What We'd Say If We Explained Ourselves to Trees." [NewEngR] (14:4) Fall 92, p. 190.

4743. O'SIADHAIL, Michael
"The Sergeants' Sons." [Stand] (33:4) Aut 92, p. 13.

4744. OSIECKA, Agnieszka
"According to Steinhaus" (tr. by Michael Kott). [ParisR]] (34:124) Fall 92, p. 134 - 135.
"Thank God for This Little Reverie" (tr. by Michael Kott). [ParisR]] (34:124) Fall 92, p. 135.

4745. OSING, Gordon T.
"Ah, Mama" (tr. of Shu Ting, w. De-an Wu Swihart). [CrabCR] (8:1) Sum-Fall 92, p. 20.
"Drinking Joy" (To the Tune of Rumengling, tr. of Qing-Zhao Li, w. Min Xiao - Hong and Huang Hai-Peng). [CrabCR] (8:1) Sum-Fall 92, p. 18.
"In Praise of Lotus" (To the Tune of Yuanwangsun, tr. of Qing-Zhao Li, w. Min Xiao-Hong and Huang Hai-Peng). [CrabCR] (8:1) Sum-Fall 92, p. 18.
"Refurnishing" (tr. of Ping-Kwan Leung, w. the author). [CrabCR] (8:1) Sum-Fall 92, p. 19.
"Two, Maybe Three Different Memories" (tr. of Shu Ting, w. De-an Wu Swihart). [CrabCR] (8:1) Sum-Fall 92, p. 21.

4746. OSMER, James
"Carnivore Spiel." [Pearl] (15) Spr-Sum 92, p. 45.
"Learning How to Mop." [SlipS] (12) 92, p. 107.
"Residue." [WormR] (32:4 #128) 92, p. 146.
"Selling the Land, Selling the Sun." [DogRR] (11:1) Spr-Sum 92, p. 8.
"Simplicity Is Salvation." [WormR] (32:4 #128) 92, p. 146.
"Smudged Dali." [DogRR] (11:1) Spr-Sum 92, p. 8.

4747. OSTERHAUS, Joe
"Pepper." [AntR] (50:3) Sum 92, p. 520-521.

4748. OSTRIKER, Alicia
"The Antithesis." [PoetryE] (33) Spr 92, p. 106-107.
"Appearance and Reality" (in memory of May Swenson). [Nat] (254:12) 30 Mr 92, p. 423.
"Belt." [Epiphany] (3:4) O (Fall) 92, p. 228.
"Jonah's Gourd Vine." [Nat] (255:16) 16 N 92, p. 576.
"Locker-Room Conversation." [Atlantic] (269:3) Mr 92, p. 92.
"Middle-Aged Woman at a Pond." [OntR] (36) Spr-Sum 92, p. 31.
"Migrant." [US1] (26/27) 92, p. 34.
"A reading and lecture trip to Oregon, Berkeley, and San Diego." [SenR] (21:2) 91, p. 178-179.
"Still Life: A Glassful of Zinnias on My Daughter's Kitchen Table." [AmerPoR] (21:3) My-Je 92, p. 36.
"Triptych" (Walker Art Center, Minneapolis). [Epiphany] (3:4) O (Fall) 92, p. 227.
"What I Want." [Poetry] (159:4) Ja 92, p. 203-204.

4749. OSTROM, Hans
"Sierra Nevada: Cold Work Moment." [Ploughs] (18:1) Spr 92, p. 16-17.

4750. OSUNDARE, Niyi
"The Word Is an Egg." [Stand] (33:3) Sum 92, p. 29.

4751. OTERO, Blas de
"The Fatal" (tr. by Louis Bourne). [AmerPoR] (21:6) N-D 92, p. 46.
"I Between Poplars and Rivers?" (tr. by Louis Bourne). [AmerPoR] (21:6) N-D 92, p. 48.
"Man in Disgrace" (tr. by Louis Bourne). [AmerPoR] (21:6) N-D 92, p. 47.
"Mortal and Alive" (tr. by Louis Bourne). [AmerPoR] (21:6) N-D 92, p. 46.
"Sun Round Alone" (tr. by Louis Bourne). [AmerPoR] (21:6) N-D 92, p. 47.

"Then and Moreover" (tr. by Louis Bourne). [AmerPoR] (21:6) N-D 92, p. 47.

4752. OTT, Gil
"Straight back sitting." [PaintedB] (48) 92, p. 52-53.

4753. OTTEN, Charlotte F.
"For the Record." [ManhatPR] (14) [92?], p. 38.

4754. OTTERY, Jim
"Where There Is Water." [Vis] (38) 92, p. 38.

OTUAMA, Seán
See O TUAMA, Seán

4755. OULLETTE, Connie
"Calgary." [Lactuca] (15) Mr 92, p. 33.
"The Nameless Lost." [Lactuca] (15) Mr 92, p. 31.
"Next of Kin." [Lactuca] (15) Mr 92, p. 32.
"The Woman Who Doesn't Exist." [Lactuca] (15) Mr 92, p. 28-30.

4756. OVERTON, Ron
"Barracuda." [HangL] (60) 92, p. 47.
"Goodbye, Pork Pie Hat." [HangL] (60) 92, p. 48.
"La Nevada" (from a series of poems based on the titles of Gil Evans songs). [HangL] (60) 92, p. 46.

4757. OWEN, Sue
"Fire and Brimstone." [Poetry] (160:1) Ap 92, p. 31.
"I Think about Ink." [DenQ] (26:4) Spr 92, p. 55.

4758. OWENBEY, Brian
"Isabella." [ChironR] (11:3) Aut 92, p. 30.

4759. OWENS, David
"I Write the Absence of You." [WindO] (56) Fall-Wint 92, p. 22.
"The Man-Made Pond." [WindO] (56) Fall-Wint 92, p. 21.

4760. OWENS, James
"When We All Lived in the Forest." [Wind] (22:71) 92, p. 24.

4761. OWENS, June
"And Philadelphus." [Plain] (12:3) Spr 92, p. 22-23.

4762. OWENS, Scott
"Breakings." [PoetC] (23:2) Wint 92, p. 11-12.
"Cedar Waxwings." [Crucible] (28) Fall 92, p. 21.
"Creek Walking." [CimR] (100) Jl 92, p. 109.
"Keeping House." [PoetC] (23:2) Wint 92, p. 13-14.
"Norman Dreams He Is a Puppet." [ChatR] (13:1) Fall 92, p. 59.
"R Is My Favorite Letter." [CimR] (100) Jl 92, p. 110.
"Sisyphus' Wife." [BellR] (15:2) Fall 92, p. 26-27.
"Trailing Their Darkness Behind Them." [CreamCR] (16:2) Fall 92, p. 40-41.

4763. OWENS, Suzanne
"Beauty." [OntR] (37) Fall-Wint 92-93, p. 122-123.
"Kneeling Here Beside Your Trunk." [OntR] (37) Fall-Wint 92-93, p. 121-122.
"Thirst." [Ploughs] (18:4) Wint 92-93, p. 70-71.
"The Toy Box." [Ploughs] (18:4) Wint 92-93, p. 72.
"Virtually Spotless." [Ploughs] (18:4) Wint 92-93, p. 73-74.

4764. OWER, John
"Adding It Up." [SoCarR] (25:1) Fall 92, p. 112.

4765. OWNBEY, Brian
"Dear Mary." [Caliban] (11) 92, p. 171.
"Fire Parade." [Caliban] (11) 92, p. 170.

4766. OXLEY, Kathleen Horan
"Woman Conquers Bridges." [US1] (26/27) 92, p. 18.

4767. OZSVATH, Zsuzsanna
"The Tree of Pleasure" (tr. of Dárday István, w. Martha Satz). [Os] (35) Fall 92, p. 17.
"The Word's Color Change" (tr. of Fabó Kinga, w. Martha Satz). [Os] (35) Fall 92, p. 19.

4768. PACE, Rosalind
"This Is English and I Am Speaking It No Matter What." [ThRiPo] (39/40) 92-93, p. 183.
"Tingel-Tangel" (from a Handcoloured lithograph, 1895, by Edvard Munch). [ThRiPo] (39/40) 92-93, p. 182.

4769. PACERNICK, Gary
"Enigma." [PoetryE] (33) Spr 92, p. 111.
"Here I Am." [PoetryE] (33) Spr 92, p. 108.

"Query." [PoetryE] (33) Spr 92, p. 109.
"The Roofer." [PoetryE] (33) Spr 92, p. 110.

4770. PACKARD, William
"Acting Class." [NewYorkQ] (49) 92, p. 51.
"Jury Duty." [NewYorkQ] (47) 92, p. 46.
"The Seducer" (tr. of Herman Hesse). [NewYorkQ] (48) 92, p. 82.
"The Teacher of Poetry." [NewYorkQ] (47) 92, p. 10.

4771. PADDOCK, Nancy
"Buffalo Burgers, or How the West Was Won." [Grain] (20:1) Spr 92, p. 37.

4772. PADEL, Ruth
"History of a Therapist." [Poetry] (160:1) Ap 92, p. 6.

4773. PADGETT, Ron
"Light Reading." [RiverS] (36) 92, p. 92.

4774. PADHI, Bibhu
"Letter to My Wife." [PoetL] (87:3) Fall 92, p. 14.

4775. PADILLA, Lizbeth
"A Pesar de la Fiebre." [Nuez] (4:10/11) 92, p. 7.

4776. PADILLA, Mario René
"My Cousin Charles." [ChironR] (11:1) Spr 92, p. 10.
"El Pobrecito." [NegC] (12:1/2) 92, p. 192-193.

4777. PAGANO, Eva
"Muse." [NewYorkQ] (47) 92, p. 83.

4778. PAGE, Carolyn
"Home Free." [Pembroke] (24) 92, p. 74-76.

4779. PAGE, P. K.
"After Hearing *Satyagraha*, an Opera, by Philip Glass." [MalR] (100) Fall 92, p. 35-37.
"The Hologram." [MalR] (100) Fall 92, p. 40-41.
"A Part." [MalR] (100) Fall 92, p. 39.
"The Trick." [MalR] (100) Fall 92, p. 38.

4780. PAGE, William
"Alliance." [SouthernPR] (32:1) Spr 92, p. 64.
"This Is Not." [MissR] (20:3) Spr 92, p. 106-107.

4781. PAGIS, Dan
"Last Poems" (tr. by Tsipi Keller). [QRL] (Poetry Series 11: vol. 31) 92, 61 p.

4782. PAGLIARANI, Elio
"Hypothesis on What Is Ours" (tr. by Corrado Federici). [PoetryC] (13:1) N 92, p. 21.

4783. PAGNUCCI, Gianfranco
"Other." [MidwQ] (33:2) Wint 92, p. 205.

4784. PAINO, Frankie
"Halloween." [KenR] (NS 14:3) Sum 92, p. 40-41.
"Indian Summer." [IndR] (15:2) Fall 92, p. 67-68.
"Pentecost: Collingwood School Fire, Cleveland, 1908." [QW] (36) Wint 92-93, p. 124-126.
"The Phantom's Sonnets." [AntR] (50:4) Fall 92, p. 731.
"Sometimes the Dead." [KenR] (NS 14:3) Sum 92, p. 41-43.

4785. PAINO, Gerrie
"Blessing." [GreenMR] (NS 5:2) Spr-Sum 92, p. 45-46.
"What I Want to Tell You." [GreenMR] (NS 5:2) Spr-Sum 92, p. 47-48.

4786. PALADINO, Thomas
"Mimmo Paladino's Earthly Paradiso." [InterPR] (18:2) Fall 92, p. 66-67.

4787. PALANA, Jim
"Joe Medwick — 1934." [Spitball] (41) Sum 92, p. 19.

4788. PALENCIA, Elaine Fowler
"The Classics." [SpoonRQ] (17:1/2) Wint-Spr 92, p. 37.
"Mother Says." [SpoonRQ] (17:1/2) Wint-Spr 92, p. 38.
"Today at the Gynecologist's." [SpoonRQ] (17:1/2) Wint-Spr 92, p. 39-40.

4789. PALMA, Lisa
"Abortion." [NewYorkQ] (48) 92, p. 81.
"The Tree." [NewYorkQ] (49) 92, p. 69.

4790. PALMA, Mary
"Sligo in the Summer." [LullwaterR] (3:2) Spr 92, p. 50.

PALMA, Ray di
See DiPALMA, Ray

4791. PALMER, Leigh
"She Tries to Narrow Down His Doubts." [GreensboroR] (52) Sum 92, p. 53-54.
4792. PALMER, Michael
"Cities." [Sulfur] (12:1, #30) Spr 92, p. 154-159.
"Money" (tr. of Aleksei Parshchikov, w. Darlene Reddaway). [Conjunc] (19) 92, p. 79-82.
"Three Russian Songs." [Epoch] (41:1) 92, p. 106-109.
4793. PALMER, William (Wm.)
"This? This?" [NewDeltaR] (9:2) Spr-Sum 92, p. 1.
4794. PALMER, Winthrop
"Bodies of Thirst." [Confr] (50) Fall 92, p. 261.
"Braque — La Route au Chateau." [Confr] (50) Fall 92, p. 261.
"Commercial." [Confr] (50) Fall 92, p. 262.
"Resort." [Confr] (50) Fall 92, p. 262.
"Shore Village." [Confr] (50) Fall 92, p. 262.
4795. PALMQUIST, Tira
"As If Only the Imperfect Leaves Us." [GreensboroR] (53) Wint 92-93, p. 3.
4796. PALUMBO, Maria
"The day father got on the train." [NewYorkQ] (48) 92, p. 79.
"Every week, one can hear the screams." [NewYorkQ] (49) 92, p. 54.
"Kaplmeier marches around." [NewYorkQ] (47) 92, p. 47.
4797. PANDE, Mrinal
"The Girl's Desire Moves among the Bangles" (tr. of Gagan Gill, w. Arlene Zide). [ChiR] (38:1/2) 92, p. 106-107.
"Two Women Knitting" (tr. by Arlene Zide and the author). [ChiR] (38:1/2) 92, p. 96.
4798. PANKEY, Eric
"Bric-a-Brac." [Poetry] (160:2) My 92, p. 93.
"The Colonialist on the Island." [NewL] (58:4) 92, p. 59.
"For Clare." [CinPR] (23) Wint 91-92, p. 26-27.
"The Holly and the Ivy" (WFP 1926-1989). [DenQ] (26:3) Wint 92, p. 42.
"Nearsighted." [SouthwR] (77:1) Wint 92, p. 137-138.
"The Plum on the Sill." [DenQ] (26:3) Wint 92, p. 41.
4799. PAOLA, Suzanne
"Death Which Is Natural & Not to Be Lamented, Feared Nor Longed For." [NewEngR] (14:3) Sum 92, p. 134-136.
"In the Cathedral of the Company of Death." [Ploughs] (18:4) Wint 92-93, p. 173 - 175.
"Rain." [Boulevard] (7:2/3, #20/21) Fall 92, p. 266-267.
"The Two." [PartR] (59:1) Wint 92, p. 104-105.
4800. PAPA, Jim
"California." [ColEng] (54:8) D 92, p. 942.
4801. PAPA, Marco
"The Women Work" (tr. by John Satriano). [ConnPR] (11:1) 92, p. 21-22.
4802. PAPE, Greg
"The Big One." [MidAR] (12:2) 92, p. 153-154.
"In the Bluemist Motel." [MidAR] (12:2) 92, p. 151-152.
4803. PAPE, Kristin
"We Escape." [WestB] (30) 92, p. 38.
"What I Can Say About Uncles." [WestB] (30) 92, p. 39.
4804. PAPE, Ronald
"The Paint on the House." [OnTheBus] (4:2/5:1, #10/11) 92, p. 168.
PAPPAS, Rita Signorelli
See SIGNORELLI-PAPPAS, Rita
4805. PAPPAS, Theresa
"The Desert Art" (a postcard from the Desert of Maine). [OxfordM] (8:2) Fall-Wint 92, p. 60.
"Sand Bed" (a postcard from the Desert of Maine). [OxfordM] (8:2) Fall-Wint 92, p. 61.
4806. PARADIS, Philip
"Brown Trout in a Pool, Holding." [CimR] (101) O 92, p. 130.
"Morning in the Heartland: Milk Truck, Elms." [CimR] (101) O 92, p. 129-130.
"Visitor." [SouthernHR] (26:2) Spr 92, p. 132.
4807. PARAMASIVAM, K.
"Avatars" (tr. of V. Indira Bhavani, w. Martha Ann Selby). [ChiR] (38:1/2) 92, p. 189-191.

"If Hot Flowers Come to the Street" (tr. of R. Meenakshi, w. Martha Ann Selby). [ChiR] (38:1/2) 92, p. 32-33.
"Wanted: A Broom" (tr. of Cantirakanti, w. Martha Ann Selby). [ChiR] (38:1/2) 92, p. 31.

4808. PARAMESWARAN, Uma
"Demeter I Miss You." [CanLit] (132) Spr 92, p. 107.
"A Wedding Song." [CanLit] (132) Spr 92, p. 145.

4809. PARCERISAS, Francesc
"Variation on a Poem by Lawrence Durrell" (tr. by Hardie St. Martin). [Trans] (26) Spr 92, p. 94.

4810. PARDES, Joan Rudel
"License Plates Become Her Talisman." [SoCarR] (24:2) Spr 92, p. 153.

4811. PARHAM, Robert
"Cleaning behind the Cattle." [LullwaterR] (4:1) Fall 92, p. 46.
"Two Lives." [NegC] (12:1/2) 92, p. 104-105.
"The Will to Be Amazed." [WilliamMR] (30) 92, p. 95.

4812. PARIENTI, Jessica Rachel
"Trees" (honorable mention, Eve of Saint Agnes Contest). [NegC] (12:3) 92, p. 38 - 39.

4813. PARISH, Barbara Shirk
"Shells." [Plain] (12:3) Spr 92, p. 31.

4814. PARK, Jae-Chun
"Polishing hte Porcelain Lamp" (tr. by Chang Soo Ko). [WebR] (16) Fall 92, p. 29.
"Scarecrow's Song No. 2" (tr. by Chang Soo Ko). [WebR] (16) Fall 92, p. 29.

4815. PARK, Joon
"Magritte's Lost Jockey." [CarolQ] (44:2) Wint 92, p. 88.

4816. PARK, William
"Keeping Still." [Verse] (8:3/9:1) Wint-Spr 92, p. 134.

4817. PARKE, Nancy
"Sister Mary Harmonica in Transit." [Comm] (119:7) 10 Ap 92, p. 12-13.

4818. PARKER, Alan Michael
"The Copper Beech" (for Alec). [WestHR] (46:2) Sum 92, p. 121.
"Flash Fire, Los Alamos." [DenQ] (26:4) Spr 92, p. 56.
"The Meniscus." [ParisR] (34:122) Spr 92, p. 276-277.
"Reading *Antony and Cleopatra* Aloud on Summer Vacation." [WestHR] (46:2) Sum 92, p. 120.
"Studio Art." [Salm] (94/95) Spr-Sum 92, p. 84.
"The Year of the Snake." [Salm] (94/95) Spr-Sum 92, p. 83-84.

PARKER, Michael Alan
See PARKER, Alan Michael

4819. PARKER, Pam A.
"Brooklyn Crossing." [ParisR] (34:125) Wint 92, p. 236.
"Coup de Foudre." [ParisR] (34:125) Wint 92, p. 237.
"History" (Munich, December 6, 1919). [ParisR] (34:125) Wint 92, p. 238.

4820. PARKIN, Barbara
"By Scent." [PraF] (13:2, #59) Sum 92, p. 58-59.

4821. PARKINSON, Chrysa
"Black Jenny, or When Father Died." [PoetryUSA] (24) 92, p. 14.

4822. PARKINSON, Tom
"Berkeley 1947" (In Memorium, from "Homage to Jack Spicer"). [PoetryUSA] (24) 92, p. 14.
"Homage to a Tom-Cat" (In Memorium). [PoetryUSA] (24) 92, p. 14.
"My Father's Death" (In Memorium). [PoetryUSA] (24) 92, p. 14.

4823. PARKS, Ian
"Fire Escape." [ChironR] (11:2) Sum 92, p. 13.

4824. PARKS-SATTERFIELD, Deb (Deborah)
"Trumpet Call of the 7th Angel." [EvergreenC] (7:1) Wint-Spr 92, p. 73.

4825. PAROLINI, Joe R.
"Brother Climber." [Wind] (22:71) 92, p. 25.

4826. PARRA, Nicanor
"The Imaginary Man" (tr. by Claudia Quiroz). [Antaeus] (69) Aut 92, p. 63.
"The Pope's Poems" (tr. by Claudia Quiroz). [Antaeus] (69) Aut 92, p. 64-65.
"Rest in Peace" (tr. by Edith Grossman). [Trans] (26) Spr 92, p. 55-56.

4827. PARRAN, Robert J.
"To Jack Kerouac" (Gratitude from a Masculine Poet). [NegC] (12:1/2) 92, p. 106.

4828. PARSHCHIKOV, Aleksei
"Money" (tr. by Darlene Reddaway, w. Michael Palmer). [Conjunc] (19) 92, p. 79 - 82.
4829. PARSLEY, Jamie Allen
"Beneath a Moth's Gray Wing." [EvergreenC] (7:2) Sum-Fall 92, p. 85.
"A Poem on the Anniversary of V. Woof's Cremation." [EvergreenC] (7:2) Sum-Fall 92, p. 84.
4830. PARTHASARATHY, R.
"The Attar of Tamil." [ChiR] (38:1/2) 92, p. 59.
"Kannaki." [ChiR] (38:1/2) 92, p. 58.
"Snow Country." [Salm] (93) Wint 92, p. 178-182.
4831. PARTRIDGE, Dixie
"Bonedrift: Year of Loss." [Kalliope] (14:1) 92, p. 10.
"Lost Lake" (With my Daughter, 15). [Blueline] (13) 92, p. 27.
"A Shedding of Summers." [SouthernPR] (32:1) Spr 92, p. 48-49.
"Song for Yellow." [Blueline] (13) 92, p. 4.
"Winter Loss" (for B. R., after her husband's death of cancer). [HolCrit] (29:3) Je 92, p. 19.
4832. PASOLINI, Pier Paolo
"If One Cry Is Added to Another" (tr. by James Kirkup). [Stand] (33:4) Aut 92, p. 110.
PASQUALE, Emanuel di
See Di PASQUALE, Emanuel
4833. PASS, John
"And Ghostly Possibility (Threat 'For the letter killeth'." [Event] (21:1) Spr 92, p. 38-39.
"And Promise) of Rejuvenation 'but the spirit giveth life'." [Event] (21:1) Spr 92, p. 40-41.
"But Not Begotten, Dead." [Event] (21:1) Spr 92, p. 42-43.
"Of the Human to the Last Word." [MalR] (99) Sum 92, p. 90.
"Of the Least and Loneliest — Father." [MalR] (99) Sum 92, p. 89.
PASSAGE, Mary du
See Du PASSAGE, Mary
4834. PASSARELLA, Lee
"Europa and the Bull." [Poem] (68) N 92, p. 66.
"The Geometry of Loneliness at Brigantine Island." [JlNJPo] (14:1) Spr 92, p. 16 - 17.
"MIA." [LullwaterR] (4:1) Fall 92, p. 12.
4835. PASSER, Jay
"Evolution." [Caliban] (11) 92, p. 99.
"The Starved." [Caliban] (11) 92, p. 98.
4836. PASSERA, William E.
"Flash Powder." [Epiphany] (3:2) Ap (Spr) 92, p. 113.
"Grandfather's Fortune." [Epiphany] (3:2) Ap (Spr) 92, p. 112.
"Springfield." [Epiphany] (3:2) Ap (Spr) 92, p. 114.
4837. PASTAN, Linda
"Almost an Elegy." [Poetry] (160:3) Je 92, p. 136-138.
"The Arithmetic of Alternation." [GettyR] (5:4) Aut 92, p. 665.
"At Home." [ThRiPo] (39/40) 92-93, p. 184-185.
"At Indian River Inlet." [GettyR] (5:4) Aut 92, p. 666-667.
"Baseball." [GettyR] (5:3) Sum 92, p. 389.
"Beall Mountain Seasonal." [SouthernR] (28:1) Wint, Ja 92, p. 73-74.
"Because." [ThRiPo] (39/40) 92-93, p. 184.
"The Birds." [CreamCR] (16:1) Spr 92, p. 108.
"Espaliered Pear Trees." [Poetry] (160:3) Je 92, p. 139.
"Flowers." [GeoR] (46:1) Spr 92, p. 63.
"Foreshadowing." [IndR] (15:1) Spr 92, p. 80.
"Ghosts." [SouthernR] (28:1) Wint, Ja 92, p. 72.
"The Hat Lady." [ConnPR] (11:1) 92, p. 39.
"Ideal City" (Oil on panel, central Italy, c. 1500). [ParisR] (34:123) Sum 92, p. 133.
"Leaves." [GettyR] (5:4) Aut 92, p. 668-669.
"An Old Song." [Writer] (105:10) O 92, p. 15.
"Only Child." [Writer] (105:10) O 92, p. 16.
"PM/AM" (Selection: "AM"). [Writer] (105:10) O 92, p. 18.

4838. PASTERNAK, Boris
"Spring Rainstorm" (tr. by Mark Rudman, w. Bohdan Boychuk). [NewYRB] (39:21) 17 D 92, p. 10.
4839. PASTIOR, Oskar
"Sestina with Inteview" (tr. by Harry Mathews). [ParisR] (34:123) Sum 92, p. 37 - 38.
4840. PASTOR, Ned
"Haute on the Hog." [Amelia] (7:1, #20) 92, p. 35.
"Inveigled by the Bagel." [Light] (1) Spr 92, p. 11.
"One Upmanship a la Carte." [Amelia] (7:1, #20) 92, p. 132.
"The only connection I see." [Amelia] (6:4, #19) 92, p. 129.
"Sage Distinction." [Light] (2) Sum 92, p. 12.
"Someone for Everyone." [Light] (3) Aut 92,.p. 15.
4841. PATCHEN, Kenneth
"What Is the Beautiful?" [FreeL] (9) Wint 92, p. 33-36.
4842. PATEL, Gieve
"You Too." [ChiR] (38:1/2) 92, p. 60.
4843. PATERSON, Don
"The Alexandrian Library." [Verse] (9:3) Wint 92, p. 53-59.
"Curtains." [Verse] (9:2) Sum 92, p. 4.
"The Electric Brae." [Verse] (9:2) Sum 92, p. 3.
"Sunset, Visingsö" (after Kjell-Ake Geissler). [Verse] (9:2) Sum 92, p. 4.
4844. PATILIS, Yannis
"It takes a lot of yourself" (tr. by Gary Sea). [Nimrod] (35:2) Spr-Sum 92, p. 73.
4845. PATRICK, Kathleen
"Toll Bridge." [SingHM] (20) 92, p. 57.
4846. PATRICK, William B.
"In Comstock Prison." [NoDaQ] (60:4) Fall 92, p. 44-45.
4847. PATTAY, Ricq
"Destination." [MidAR] (13:2) 92, p. 73-74.
"Snow Over Michigan" (for K.). [MidAR] (13:2) 92, p. 71-72.
4848. PATTEN, Karl
"Flying Over the Sand Hills of Nebraska." [CinPR] (23) Wint 91-92, p. 62-63.
"In the Pen." [FourQ] (6:1) Spr 92, p. 14.
4849. PATTERSON, Veronica
"A Charm Against the Language of Politics." [Sun] (203) N 92, p. 15.
"Combing." [Sun] (204) D 92, p. 24.
"The Debt." [MidAR] (12:2) 92, p. 8-9.
"How I Created the Universe" (for Evan). [MidAR] (12:2) 92, p. 6-7.
4850. PATTON, Patti
"Anchoring Off Molokini." [MidAR] (12:2) 92, p. 116-117.
"Because We Surfaced." [MidAR] (12:2) 92, p. 118.
"In the Meadow of Grownups." [MidAR] (12:2) 92, p. 119.
4851. PATTON, Rena
"A Canticle for the Kidney, Beginning at the 11th Rib." [SouthernPR] (32:1) Spr 92, p. 56.
"Hawk Down." [SouthernPR] (32:2) Fall 92, p. 46-47.
"Lamentation for Newtonian Physics." [Poem] (68) N 92, p. 43.
"Lila's Open Heart." [Poem] (68) N 92, p. 42.
"A Woman's Song." [Kalliope] (14:3) 92, p. 39.
4852. PAU-LLOSA, Ricardo (Richard)
"Adriano Lambe's Florida." [MidwQ] (34:1) Aut 92, p. 78-79.
"Ambiguities." [Manoa] (4:1) Spr 92, p. 15-16.
"Amelia Pelaez." [OnTheBus] (4:2/5:1, #10/11) 92, p. 169.
"Analogies." [MidwQ] (34:1) Aut 92, p. 77-78.
"Barroco." [Shen] (42:1) Spr 92, p. 73-74.
"Batista." [HayF] (11) Fall-Wint 92, p. 42.
"Cedro y Caoba." [LitR] (36:1) Fall 92, p. 15.
"Cemeterio Colón." [BostonR] (17:3/4) My-Jl 92, p. 4.
"Chocolate" (for Gabriel Warren). [QW] (34) Wint-Spr 92, p. 67-68.
"Conscience." [HayF] (11) Fall-Wint 92, p. 43.
"The Daughter." [MidwQ] (34:1) Aut 92, p. 79-80.
"Divided Forest" (after the painting by Sebastian Spreng). [IndR] (15:1) Spr 92, p. 59-60.
"Dominos." [PraS] (66:1) Spr 92, p. 88-89.
"Frutas." [ThRiPo] (39/40) 92-93, p. 186-187.

"Ganaderia." [ThRiPo] (39/40) 92-93, p. 187.
"La Hora de los Mameyes." [Manoa] (4:1) Spr 92, p. 13-15.
"The Island of Mirrors." [ThRiPo] (39/40) 92-93, p. 188.
"The Map." [Boulevard] (7:2/3, #20/21) Fall 92, p. 272-274.
"Las Meninas." [Shen] (42:1) Spr 92, p. 75.
"Minas de Cobre." [LitR] (36:1) Fall 92, p. 16.
"Ostiones y Cangrejos Moros." [ThRiPo] (39/40) 92-93, p. 185-186.
"Pesca de Esponjas." [MinnR] (39) Fall-Wint 92-93, p. 4.
"Playa de Varadero." [MinnR] (39) Fall-Wint 92-93, p. 5.
"Plazas." [MichQR] (31:2) Spr 92, p. 265-266.
"Rafael Soriano" (After his painting, "La Espera"). [PraS] (66:1) Spr 92, p. 87-88.
"Sierra Maestra." [SycamoreR] (4:1) Wint 92, p. 32.
"Trauma." [Chelsea] (53) 92, p. 50-51.
"Trinidad, Ciudad Colonial." [MidwQ] (34:1) Aut 92, p. 80.
"Virgilio Piñera." [ColR] (9:1) Spr-Sum 92, p. 112.
"Wilfredo Lam." [Journal] (16:2) Fall-Wint 92, p. 73-74.

4853. PAUL, Charles
"The God-like Flash" (tr. of Uli Becker). [ParisR] (34:123) Sum 92, p. 41-42.

4854. PAULHUS, Greg J.
"Impossible Things Before Breakfast." [CanLit] (133) Sum 92, p. 15.

4855. PAVESE, Cesare
"Alter Ego" (tr. by Scott Davison). [CharR] (18:1) Spr 92, p. 97.
"Awakening" (tr. by Scott Davison). [CimR] (100) Jl 92, p. 102.
"The Boy Who Was in Me" (tr. by Scott Davison). [CimR] (100) Jl 92, p. 101-102.
"La Casa." [ChiR] (38:3) 92, p. 68.
"Creation" (tr. by Scott Davison). [CimR] (100) Jl 92, p. 105.
"Earth and Death" (tr. by Scott Davison). [Paint] (19:37) Spr 92, p. 48-53.
"End of the Fantasy" (tr. by Scott Davison). [CharR] (18:1) Spr 92, p. 98.
"The Friend Who Sleeps" (tr. by Scott Davison). [CimR] (100) Jl 92, p. 104.
"Habits" (tr. by Scott Davison). [CimR] (100) Jl 92, p. 103.
"The House" (tr. by Scott Davison). [ChiR] (38:3) 92, p. 69.
"I Will Pass Through Piazza di Spagna" (tr. by Scott Davison). [ChiR] (38:3) 92, p. 75.
"Indifference" (tr. by Scott Davison). [CimR] (100) Jl 92, p. 104-105.
"Landlords" (tr. by Scott Davison). [ChiR] (38:3) 92, p. 72-73.
"Passerò per Piazza di Spagna." [ChiR] (38:3) 92, p. 74.
"The Peace That Reigns" (tr. by Scott Davison). [Poetry] (161:1) O 92, p. 13-14.
"Proprietari." [ChiR] (38:3) 92, p. 70-71.
"Sad Wine" (tr. by Scott Davison). [QW] (35) Sum-Fall 92, p. 118.
"Song" (tr. by Scott Davison). [CharR] (18:1) Spr 92, p. 96.
"Street Song" (tr. by Scott Davison). [Poetry] (161:1) O 92, p. 14-15.

4856. PAVLICH, Walter
"Awareness." [Poetry] (160:5) Ag 92, p. 253.
"The Blessing of the Animals." [Comm] (119:5) 13 Mr 92, p. 19.
"Carefulness." [AntR] (50:4) Fall 92, p. 718.
"The Cast of *Freaks*." [LaurelR] (26:1) Wint 92, p. 72-73.
"The Closest Thing to Church, Other Than Church." [Manoa] (4:2) Fall 92, p. 154 - 155.
"Epiphany on the Dominion of Water." [Manoa] (4:1) Spr 92, p. 104.
"The Fifth Season." [Manoa] (4:2) Fall 92, p. 155-156.
"The Flower Meaning Woe." [Manoa] (4:1) Spr 92, p. 107-108.
"If God Were an Electric Fence." [ColR] (9:1) Spr-Sum 92, p. 148.
"The Man at Cape Lookout." [CinPR] (23) Wint 91-92, p. 58.
"Night Fire Outside Bakersfield." [Manoa] (4:2) Fall 92, p. 153-154.
"Overlooking the Pacific, Family Reunion, Celebrating My Brother's Child, Ecola State Park." [Manoa] (4:1) Spr 92, p. 105-107.
"Road with Five Waterfalls." [Poetry] (160:5) Ag 92, p. 252.
"Robot Dreams." [Shen] (42:1) Spr 92, p. 47-48.
"A Run for John." [Shen] (42:1) Spr 92, p. 48-49.
"Street Pile." [Poetry] (161:2) N 92, p. 94.

4857. PAVLOV, Konstantin
"Pastoral" (tr. by Ludmilla Popova-Wightman). [LitR] (25:2) Wint 92, p. 178.
"Prelude — The Spiders" (tr. by Ludmilla Popova-Wightman). [LitR] (25:2) Wint 92, p. 178.

4858. PAWLAK, Mark
"Dress Well and Succeed" (— Men's garters ad, c. 1928). [Noctiluca] (1:1) Spr 92, p. 22.
"Electroliers." [SmPd] (29:1, #84) Wint 92, p. 21-22.
"Indian Life in the 60's, Trading Cards c. 1910" (Selections: 2, 5, for Ron Overton). [Noctiluca] (1:1) Spr 92, p. 21.
4859. PAWLOWSKI, Robert
"Study: At Sixty" (Chateau de la Napoule, Cote d'Azur, 1990). [Vis] (38) 92, p. 24.
4860. PAYACK, Peter
"Concrete Poem" (Sidewalk Poetry Festival, 1976. Photo). [Noctiluca] (1:1) Spr 92, p. 1.
"The White Line." [Noctiluca] (1:2) Wint 92 [on cover: Wint 93], p. 27.
4861. PAYNE, Bill
"Private Smiles." [Vis] (40) 92, p. 41.
4862. PAYNE, Craig
"Tree on the Overhang." [Confr] (50) Fall 92, p. 288.
4863. PEABODY, Rick
"Off Base" (2 selections). [WashR] (17:6) Ap-My 92, p. 13.
4864. PEACE, Kathleen
"September." [Writer] (105:6) Je 92, p. 25.
4865. PEACH, Hilary
"Gloompoem." [CapilR] (2:9) Fall 92, p. 40-41.
"This Is the Picture Which Will be Repeated." [CapilR] (2:9) Fall 92, p. 36-39.
4866. PEACOCK, Molly
"Cancelled Elegy." [HampSPR] Wint 92, p. 19.
"Good Girl." [Hellas] (3:2) Fall 92, p. 96.
"Prairie Prayer." [SouthwR] (77:2/3) Spr-Sum 92, p. 287.
4867. PEATTIE, Noel
"Sphinx." [Contact] (10:62/63/64) Fall 91-Spr 92, p. 62.
4868. PECK, Barbara
"A Place to Hide." [Rohwedder] (7) Spr-Sum 92, p. 12.
4869. PECK, Gail J.
"The Last Time I Saw Morris Happy." [MalR] (101) Wint92, p. 51.
"Navels." [MalR] (101) Wint92, p. 52.
"When My Uncle Came Home." [CarolQ] (44:3) Spr-Sum 92, p. 82.
4870. PECK, Steve
"Algonquin Physics." [BellArk] (8:5) S-O 92, p. 21.
"The Golden Bough Brakes and Down Comes Baby, Cradle and All." [BellArk] (8:6) N-D 92, p. 20.
4871. PEELER, Tim
"Extra Innings." [Spitball] (40) Spr 92, p. 51-52.
"The Fall I Bet My Lunch Money for a Week on the Cards in the Series." [Spitball] (41) Sum 92, p. 26-27.
"When Dizzy." [Spitball] (41) Sum 92, p. 25.
PEENEN, H. J. van
See Van PEENEN, H. J.
4872. PEIRCE, Kathleen
"Him." [Field] (46) Spr 92, p. 102-103.
"Need Increasing Itself by Rounds." [Field] (46) Spr 92, p. 107.
4873. PELENSKY, Olga
"A Smell of Salting" (For V. Bokov, tr. of Yevgeny Yevtushenko). [Vis] (39) 92, p. 34.
4874. PELLETIER, Andrew T.
"Night Game at Damaschke Field." [Spitball] (42) Fall 92, p. 46-47.
4875. PELLETIER, Gus
"Adam and Eve in *The Paradise*." [CumbPR] (12:1) Fall 92, p. 71-72.
"Turning Around in a Country Town." [CumbPR] (12:1) Fall 92, p. 69-70.
4876. PELLETIERE, Marcia
"Betrothal." [HiramPoR] (51/52) Fall 91-Sum 92, p. 58.
"Her Hands." [QW] (35) Sum-Fall 92, p. 105.
4877. PEMBER, John
"Heels." [Footwork] 92, p. 31.
"Honest Fear." [Footwork] 92, p. 31.
"Running on Full." [Footwork] 92, p. 31.
4878. PEÑALOSA, Joaquín Antonio
"Bird-Fancier's Street Cry" (tr. by R. H. Morrison). [AntigR] (91) Fall 92, p. 103.

"Child of Night" (tr. by R. H. Morrison). [AntigR] (91) Fall 92, p. 101.
"Cubo de Hielo." [AntigR] (91) Fall 92, p. 104.
"Elogio de la Locura." [AntigR] (91) Fall 92, p. 96.
"Hijo de la Noche." [AntigR] (91) Fall 92, p. 100.
"Himno al Trabajo." [AntigR] (91) Fall 92, p. 98.
"Hymn to Work" (tr. by R. H. Morrison). [AntigR] (91) Fall 92, p. 99.
"Ice-Cube" (tr. by R. H. Morrison). [AntigR] (91) Fall 92, p. 105.
"In Praise of Madness" (tr. by R. H. Morrison). [AntigR] (91) Fall 92, p. 97.
"Pregón del Pajarero." [AntigR] (91) Fall 92, p. 102.

4879. PENDARVIS, E. D.
"Lauscaux." [SmPd] (29:2, #85) Spr 92, p. 21.

4880. PENDER, Stephen
"The Birds of Tarshish." [Quarry] (41:2) Spr 92, p. 55-57.

4881. PENFOLD, Maia
"Grand Canyon." [Sun] (202) O 92, p. 22-23.

4882. PENFOLD, Nita
"The Woman with the Wild-Grown Hair Relaxes After Another Long Day." [SlipS] (12) 92, p. 106-107.

PENG, Wang Tai
See WANG, Tai Peng

4883. PENHA, James W.
"Party's Over." [Gypsy] (19) 92, p. 53.

4884. PENN, Robert E.
"Community." [Art&Und] (1:1) Fall 91, p. 13.
"Hecklers' Fear." [Art&Und] (1:1) Fall 91, p. 13.
"Others' Comfort." [Art&Und] (1:3) Spr 92, p. 12.

4885. PENNANT, Edmund
"Bare Facts." [NewYorkQ] (49) 92, p. 49.
"Vincent's Ear." [Confr] (48/49) Spr-Sum 92, p. 208.
"Visitor's Day" (Lewisburg Penitentiary). [NewYorkQ] (49) 92, p. 50.

4886. PENNEY, Scott
"New Haven." [Amelia] (6:4, #19) 92, p. 66.

4887. PENNY, Michael
"Ampersand (Autumn) (#1)." [Quarry] (41:1) Wint 92, p. 26.
"Ampersand (Spring) (#1)." [Quarry] (41:1) Wint 92, p. 25.
"Ampersand (Summer) (#1)." [Quarry] (41:1) Wint 92, p. 24.
"Ampersand (Sutures) (#1)." [Grain] (20:1) Spr 92, p. 224.

4888. PERCHAN, Robert J
"Children's Book." [WormR] (32:3, #127) 92, p. 96.
"Nails." [WormR] (32:3, #127) 92, p. 95-96.

4889. PERCHIK, Simon
"135. A death mask : the bird." [NewL] (58:3) Spr 92, p. 99.
"370. The sun must crave fruit." [Caliban] (11) 92, p. 136.
"379. Dug out block by block :the arch." [Caliban] (11) 92, p. 137.
"457. Straight from Ringling, bowlegged." [NewYorkQ] (48) 92, p. 73.
"Ancient boats have always wept and the sea." [SnailPR] (2:2) Fall-Wint 92, p. 5.
"And though these shelves are cooled." [NowestR] (30:2) 92, p. 47.
"And wet your thumb on your finger." [SnailPR] (2:1) Spr-Sum 92, p. 7.
"A death mask: the bird." [PoetC] (24:1) Fall 92, p. 12.
"Each step closer, your coffin." [PoetC] (24:1) Fall 92, p. 11.
"It's easier to change your name." [JlNJPo] (14:1) Spr 92, p. 15.
"Not until these stars began to cluster." [PraS] (66:3) Fall 92, p. 86-87.
"The same *Krupp?* this coffee-mill." [PraS] (66:3) Fall 92, p. 85-86.
"Still alone — so many rings." [CoalC] (5) My 92, p. 9.
"Still alone — so many rings." [RagMag] (10:2) 92, p. 29.
"Stone, stone, stone, not a drop." [Boulevard] (7:1, #19) Spr 92, p. 99.
"— to be the darkness just forming." [BlackWR] (18:2) Spr-Sum 92, p. 19.
"Untitled: To keep you from rotting." [HighP] (7:1) Spr 92, p. 97.
"Untying my shoe :I wave." [InterPR] (18:1) Spr 92, p. 68-69.
"Using both hands now, this bulb." [PoetL] (87:2) Sum 92, p. 19-20.

PEREDNIK, Jorge Santiago
See SANTIAGO PEREDNIK, Jorge

4890. PEREIRA, J. R.
"Black Man" (tr. of Nancy Morejon). [LitR] (35:4) Sum 92, p. 459.
"Church Spire Against the Sky" (tr. of Nancy Morejon). [LitR] (35:4) Sum 92, p. 457.

"Farewell" (tr. of Nancy Morejon). [LitR] (35:4) Sum 92, p. 455.
"Looking Within" (tr. of Nancy Morejon). [LitR] (35:4) Sum 92, p. 457.
"Spinning Woman" (tr. of Nancy Morejon). [LitR] (35:4) Sum 92, p. 458.

4891. PEREIRA, Peter
"Angel of Death." [JamesWR] (9:4) Sum 92, p. 6.
"Chambered Nautilus." [EvergreenC] (7:2) Sum-Fall 92, p. 73-74.
"On Hearing a Newly Discovered Recording Believed to Be of Walt Whitman Reading 'America'." [ChironR] (11:4) Wint 92, p. 44.
"Revolving Restaurant" (for Dean Allan). [EvergreenC] (7:2) Sum-Fall 92, p. 72.

4892. PEREIRA, Sam
"A Choice." [CreamCR] (16:1) Spr 92, p. 99.
"From Saucers." [Manoa] (4:2) Fall 92, p. 10-11.
"Norge." [CreamCR] (16:1) Spr 92, p. 98.
"October 20, 1985" (for John). [Manoa] (4:2) Fall 92, p. 11-12.

4893. PEREIRA, Teresinka
"Hambre." [LindLM] (11:1) Mr 92, p. 22.
"Nube." [LindLM] (11:1) Mr 92, p. 22.
"Nuestro Amor." [LindLM] (11:1) Mr 92, p. 22.

4894. PERELMAN, Bob
"Laptop." [PaintedB] (46) 92, p. 6-7.
"Pastures New." [PaintedB] (48) 92, p. 44-45.
"Repetition / Revelation." [PaintedB] (46) 92, p. 8-10.
"Virtual Reality." [Sulfur] (12:1, #30) Spr 92, p. 151-153.

4895. PERETZ, Maya
"Ode to the Hands" (tr. of Halina Poswiatowska). [SnailPR] (2:1) Spr-Sum 92, p. 5.
"The Peasant Woman" (tr. of Anna Swirszczynska). [SnailPR] (2:1) Spr-Sum 92, p. 4.

4896. PEREZ, Michelle
"The Hill." [BlackBR] (16) Wint-Spr 92-93, p. 17-18.
"My Sister's Anatomy Book." [NewYorkQ] (49) 92, p. 71.
"Promotions." [SingHM] (20) 92, p. 72.

4897. PEREZ, Moira
"Birthday Poem" (tr. of Ana Maria Fagundo, w. Steven Ford Brown). [SenR] (22:1) Spr 92, p. 49.
"Dawn in the Monastery of the Olive Trees" (for Julia Gonzalez, tr. of Ana Maria Fagundo, w. Steven Ford Brown). [SenR] (22:1) Spr 92, p. 51-52.
"The Sower" (tr. of Ana Maria Fagundo, w. Steven Ford Brown). [SenR] (22:1) Spr 92, p. 50.

4898. PEREZ, Nola
"De Haan." [Kalliope] (14:1) 92, p. 5.

4899. PÉREZ-BUSTILLO, Camilo
"Cuando los Cantos Se Vuelven Aga" (para *Diario Latino*, El Salvador, 1991, tr. of Martín Espada). [PaintedB] (48) 92, p. 10-11.
"Now I Take My Leave" (tr. of Juan Antonio Corretjer, w. Martín Espada). [Callaloo] (15:4) Fall 92, p. 951.

4900. PÉREZ FIRMAT, Gustavo
"Ars Amandi." [BilingR] (17:1) Ja-Ap 92, p. 78.
"Evita y Gustavito (Composite)." [Americas] (20:1) Spr 92, p. 40.
"Lime Cure." [Americas] (20:1) Spr 92, p. 38.
"Lime Cure." [Americas] (20:3/4) Fall-Wint 92, p. 253.
"On Whether My Father Deserves a Poem." [Americas] (20:1) Spr 92, p. 39.
"The Operation." [Americas] (20:1) Spr 92, p. 44.
"The Operation." [BilingR] (17:1) Ja-Ap 92, p. 77.
"The Poet Discusses the Opposite Sex." [BilingR] (17:1) Ja-Ap 92, p. 77-78.
"The Poet's Mother Gives Him a Birthday Present." [Americas] (20:1) Spr 92, p. 42.
"The Poet's Mother Gives Him a Birthday Present." [Americas] (20:3/4) Fall-Wint 92, p. 254.
"Quiet Time." [Americas] (20:1) Spr 92, p. 41.
"What's Wrong with Me." [Americas] (20:1) Spr 92, p. 43.

4901. PÉREZ GUTIERREZ, Amparo
"Genesis (III)." [LindLM] (11:2) Je 92, p. 8.

4902. PERI ROSSI, Cristina
"The Age of the Sea" (tr. by Judith Barrington). [Trans] (26) Spr 92, p. 28.
"Babel Bárbara" (for Federica, tr. by Diana P. Decker). [QRL] (Poetry Series 11: vol. 31) 92, 52 p.

4903. PERILLO, Lucia Maria
"An Amplified Gesture." [Zyzzyva] (8:3) Fall 92, p. 39.
"The Body Mutinies." [NowestR] (30:2) 92, p. 76.
"Dressage." [PoetryE] (33) Spr 92, p. 112.
"Elephant." [NowestR] (30:2) 92, p. 77-78.
"The Evolution of Landscapes." [QW] (36) Wint 92-93, p. 128.
"For the Female Serial Killers." [OntR] (36) Spr-Sum 92, p. 34.
"Limits" (1991 John Williams Andrews Prize Winner). [PoetL] (87:1) Spr 92, p. 8-11.
"Occupation." [PoetryE] (33) Spr 92, p. 113.
"The Rise of Western Underwear in Japan." [NowestR] (30:2) 92, p. 75.
"Skin." [OntR] (36) Spr-Sum 92, p. 32-33.
"Testament (Genesis 22:7)" (for Hedda Nussbaum). [PoetryE] (33) Spr 92, p. 114.
"What One Loves Are Things That Fade." [Zyzzyva] (8:3) Fall 92, p. 41.
4904. PERKINS, James Ashbrook
"Hot Air Balloons." [Footwork] 92, p. 38.
"I Too Know a Woman." [Footwork] 92, p. 38.
"Iron Stars." [US1] (26/27) 92, p. 25.
"A Poem About a Goose" (for Jane). [Footwork] 92, p. 38.
"Sled Poem" (for Jimbo and Brook). [Footwork] 92, p. 38.
"Waterloo 1990." [Footwork] 92, p. 38.
4905. PERKINS, Leialoha Apo
"Ends" (Response to Anne Bradstreet's "Contemplations"). [ChamLR] (10/11) Spr-Fall 92, p. 19-20.
4906. PERKINS, Leslie D.
"As I was paddling down the Po." [Light] (3) Aut 92, p. 29.
4907. PERKINS, S. D.
"Cymone, before Le Club Glamoure." [MoodySI] (27) Spr 92, p. 10.
4908. PERLBERG, Mark
"The Color of the Spirit." [Hudson] (45:2) Sum 92, p. 276.
"The Last News from *Voyager*." [Hudson] (45:2) Sum 92, p. 276.
"Love Letters." [WillowR] (19) Spr 92, p. 14.
4909. PERLMAN, Anne S.
"At Fifty in the Crystal-Dead Eye of the Center." [ThRiPo] (39/40) 92-93, p. 190.
"Family Reunion." [ThRiPo] (39/40) 92-93, p. 191.
"Summer Adjustments." [ThRiPo] (39/40) 92-93, p. 189.
"Survival." [ThRiPo] (39/40) 92-93, p. 190.
4910. PERLMAN, John
"At Rockland Lake." [Noctiluca] (1:2) Wint 92 [on cover: Wint 93], p. 28.
"Legion Their Numbers." [Talisman] (8) Spr 92, p. 107-112.
"A resonant notion." [ShadowP] (3) 92, p. 4.
"Vamping on the Itinerary's Antiphon." [ShadowP] (3) 92, p. 5-6.
4911. PERONARD, Kai
"Another Time." [Lactuca] (16) Ag 92, p. 14.
"First Light." [Lactuca] (16) Ag 92, p. 13.
"I Woke Up." [Lactuca] (16) Ag 92, p. 13.
"Nighttime." [Lactuca] (16) Ag 92, p. 14.
4912. PERRAULT, John
"Ethiopia." [Comm] (119:14) 14 Ag 92, p. 15.
"Palace of Justice." [Comm] (119:9) 8 My 92, p. 20.
4913. PERRINE, Laurence
"Advice for Preachers." [Light] (4) Wint 92-93, p. 25.
"Hypochondriac." [Light] (4) Wint 92-93, p. 12.
"In this Erie competition, rival poets." [Light] (3) Aut 92, p. 29.
"The Liffey sleeps." [Light] (4) Wint 92-93, p. 29.
"Limerick: Have you ever been near a giraffe." [Light] (3) Aut 92, p. 18.
"Would there be any dark tarn of Auber." [Light] (2) Sum 92, p. 29.
4914. PERRY, Aaren Yeatts
"Abortion # -1." [PaintedB] (48) 92, p. 47-48.
4915. PERRY, Elizabeth
"Prospero's Correlative." [SouthernPR] (32:2) Fall 92, p. 30.
4916. PERRY, Greg
"Greenfields." [PoetL] (87:3) Fall 92, p. 11.
4917. PERRY, Pamela
"White Moments" (tr. of Nikolai Kantchev, w. B. R. Strahan). [Confr] (48/49) Spr-Sum 92, p. 218.

4918. PERRY, Stephen
"Cowbells from India with Two Tones." [TarRP] (30:2) Spr 91, p. 30-31.
"Excavation." [KenR] (NS 14:2) Spr 92, p. 25-26.
"Fishing Nights for Raccoons." [MidwQ] (33:2) Wint 92, p. 206.
"Kat." [PoetryE] (33) Spr 92, p. 115-116.
"Thief's Perfume." [YellowS] (Ten Years [i.e. 40]) Sum-Fall 92, p. 34.
4919. PERSINGER, Christopher
"Ciudad Juárez." [PacificR] (11) 92-93, p. 88.
4920. PERSUN, Terry L.
"Teaching Death." [Lactuca] (16) Ag 92, p. 69.
4921. PESEROFF, Joyce
"Adolescent." [ThRiPo] (39/40) 92-93, p. 193-194.
"Bluebird." [ThRiPo] (39/40) 92-93, p. 192.
"Camptown Races." [AmerV] (29) 92, p. 50-51.
"A Dog in the Lifeboat." [ThRiPo] (39/40) 92-93, p. 194-195.
"A Revelation" (after a story by Flannery O'Connor). [MassR] (23:3) Fall 92, p. 335-336.
4922. PESICH, Robert
"My Mother Continues to Stuff Bell Peppers for Dinner" (for Jagoda). [CutB] (38) Sum 92, p. 126-127.
4923. PESSOA, Fernando (Alberto Caeiro)
"The Keeper of Sheep" (Excerpt, tr. by Edwin Honig and Susan M. Brown). [Trans] (26) Spr 92, p. 14-15.
4924. PESSOLANO, Linda
"Elegy for Sandy." [Noctiluca] (1:1) Spr 92, p. 34.
"Roadtrip." [Noctiluca] (1:1) Spr 92, p. 33.
4925. PESTANA, Emily
"Airship." [Parting] (5:2) Wint 92-93, p. 30.
"Entering." [Parting] (5:2) Wint 92-93, p. 11.
4926. PETACCIA, Mario
"Jealousy." [NewYorkQ] (47) 92, p. 58.
4927. PETERNEL, Joan
"Hollowed Precinct" (3rd Honorable Mention, 6th Annual Contest). [SoCoast] (13) Je 93 [i.e. 92], p. 52-53.
4928. PETERS, Christine D.
"The Night Parade." [SenR] (22:2) Fall 92, p. 21.
4929. PETERS, Darrell J.
"January Road." [LullwaterR] (3:2) Spr 92, p. 46-47.
4930. PETERS, Patrick
"Expectations." [PoetryE] (33) Spr 92, p. 117.
4931. PETERS, Robert
"Boy on the Beach" (from "Snapshots for a Serial Killer"). [FreeL] (9) Wint 92, p. 22.
"Cat with Nasturtiums" (from "Snapshots for a Serial Killer"). [FreeL] (9) Wint 92, p. 23.
"Cruising Coast Highway at Night." [OnTheBus] (4:2/5:1, #10/11) 92, p. 171.
"Devotions." [OnTheBus] (4:2/5:1, #10/11) 92, p. 170-171.
"Inside Mitchum." [ChironR] (11:4) Wint 92, p. 19.
"Mitchum As fish-Slayer." [ChironR] (11:4) Wint 92, p. 19.
"New Lover." (from "Snapshots for a Serial Killer"). [GreenMR] (NS 5:2) Spr-Sum 92, p. 65.
"School Friend." [OnTheBus] (4:2/5:1, #10/11) 92, p. 170.
"Snapshots for a Serial Killer: A Fiction" (14 poems). [Pearl] (15) Spr-Sum 92, p. 29-43.
"Suburbanite Washing His Car" (from "Snapshots for a Serial Killer"). [GreenMR] (NS 5:2) Spr-Sum 92, p. 64.
"Thanksgiving Day, 1989." [Archae] (3) early 92, p. 21-24.
"Torso." [Pearl] (16) Fall 92, p. 66.
"Wild Strawberries." [ChironR] (11:4) Wint 92, p. 19.
4932. PETERS, Susan
"Return Engagement." [EngJ] (80:6) O 91, p. 102.
4933. PETERSEN, Keith
"I cannot see him now, but know he's there." [NewYorkQ] (49) 92, p. 70.
4934. PETERSON, Allan
"Alarm." [ChatR] (13:1) Fall 92, p. 44.
"Dangerous Help." [WillowS] (30) Sum 92, p. 14.

"Discourse." [ChatR] (13:1) Fall 92, p. 43.
"Five Violins." [RiverC] (12:2) Spr 92, p. 21.
"Floods." [RiverC] (12:2) Spr 92, p. 22.
"Game of Hands." [GreensboroR] (52) Sum 92, p. 153.
"Knife in the Sand." [BlackBR] (15) Spr-Sum 92, p. 41.
"Lifeline." [SpoonRQ] (17:1/2) Wint-Spr 92, p. 18.
"Lips Like That." [NewDeltaR] (8:2) Spr-Sum 91, p. 47.
"Lullaby." [ArtfulD] (22/23) 92, p. 91.
"Monogram." [NewDeltaR] (9:2) Spr-Sum 92, p. 22.
"Nightshirt." [ArtfulD] (22/23) 92, p. 92.
"A Spell of Assurance." [NegC] (12:3) 92, p. 108.
"Theory to Match the Facts." [RiverC] (12:2) Spr 92, p. 23.
"Those Whales." [GreensboroR] (52) Sum 92, p. 154.
"Trouble with Illusion: The Great Zelmo in the E. R." [WillowS] (30) Sum 92, p. 15.

4935. PETERSON, Jim
"Let Me Find It." [CharR] (18:1) Spr 92, p. 93-94.
"The Man in the Green Truck." [TarRP] (30:2) Spr 91, p. 2-3.
"Now Leasing." [TarRP] (30:2) Spr 91, p. 1-2.
"Opening Night." [GeoR] (46:3) Fall 92, p. 522-523.

4936. PETERSON, William M.
"October Mountain." [Confr] (48/49) Spr-Sum 92, p. 207.

4937. PETIT, Michael
"One Thousand Cranes." [Atlantic] (270:1) Jl 92, p. 67.

4938. PETREMAN, David A.
"Father Petek of the Wind." [CarolQ] (44:2) Wint 92, p. 86.

4939. PETRIE, Paul
"Caryle and the Roosters." [NegC] (12:1/2) 92, p. 107.
"Games at Dusk" (For Jim Marshall). [LitR] (35:3) Spr 92, p. 323.
"The Question." [NegC] (12:1/2) 92, p. 108.

4940. PETROSKY, Anthony
"Rituals." [OhioR] (48) 92, p. 86-87.

4941. PETTIGREW, C. J.
"Koyukon Riddle" (honourable mention, Grain Prose Poem contest). [Grain] (20:4) Wint 92, p. 19.

4942. PETTIT, Carolyn
"Messages from Underground, the French Lop." [NegC] (12:1/2) 92, p. 109.

4943. PETTIT, Michael
"7 Beef Cows." [PoetL] (87:3) Fall 92, p. 5-6.
"Abandoned Drive-In." [SouthernR] (28:4) Aut, O 92, p. 884-885.
"Employment Alternatives." [PraS] (66:3) Fall 92, p. 114-115.
"Kentucky Barber College." [PraS] (66:3) Fall 92, p. 116-117.
"Puritan Shoes." [SouthernR] (28:4) Aut, O 92, p. 885-886.
"Watson's Barroom Geometry." [PraS] (66:3) Fall 92, p. 115.

4944. PFEIFER, Michael
"Good Night, Mr. Durante." [LaurelR] (26:1) Wint 92, p. 32.

4945. PFLUM, Richard
"Inventing a Ruin." [HopewellR] (4) 92, p. 8.

4946. PHELPS, Anthony
"Black Orchid" (Excerpt, tr. by Carrol F. Coates). [Callaloo] (15:2) Spr 92, p. 371 - 375.
"Carib Father" (To Franck Fouché, tr. by Carrol F. Coates). [Callaloo] (15:2) Spr 92, p. 347-351.
"Even the Sun Is Naked" (Selections: II-III, tr. by Gregory Hall). [Callaloo] (15:2) Spr 92, p. 357-363.
"Meme le Soleil Est Nu" (Selections: II-III). [Callaloo] (15:2) Spr 92, p. 364-370.
"Orchidee Negre" (Excerpt). [Callaloo] (15:2) Spr 92, p. 376-380.
"Pere Caraibe" (à Franck Fouché). [Callaloo] (15:2) Spr 92, p. 352-356.

4947. PHILBRICK, Stephen
"What You Won't Say." [Talisman] (8) Spr 92, p. 185.

4948. PHILLIPS, Adora
"Photograph & Story in the Press: The Mother Whose Children Burned to Death." [ThRiPo] (39/40) 92-93, p. 196.
"The Summer My Mother Fell in Love and Wanted to Leave My Father." [ThRiPo] (39/40) 92-93, p. 195-196.

4949. PHILLIPS, Carl
"Fra Lippo Lippi and the Vision of Henley." [ParisR] (34:122) Spr 92, p. 207.
"In the Blood, Winnowing." [KenR] (NS 14:2) Spr 92, p. 119-121.
"Lullabye for the Wounded Eros." [PoetryNW] (33:3) Aut 92, p. 21-22.
"Memories of the Revival." [KenR] (NS 14:2) Spr 92, p. 121-122.
"Romance." [PoetryNW] (33:3) Aut 92, p. 22-23.
4950. PHILLIPS, James-L
"The Violet Air." [Amelia] (7:1, #20) 92, p. 61.
4951. PHILLIPS, Louis
"Bureaucracy at the Center of Modern Life." [SoCoast] (13) Je 93 [i.e. 92], p. 46.
"Chaucerian Sonnet: A Tale of the Clark of Kent." [Light] (3) Aut 92, p. 8.
"The Difference." [Confr] (50) Fall 92, p. 279.
"Fire on the Lake." [Footwork] 92, p. 19.
"How does President Polk." [Light] (2) Sum 92, p. 17.
"Johnny Inkslinger Goes to Work for the WPA to Write a Travel-Guide to America's Inner Cities." [Footwork] 92, p. 19.
"Johnny Inkslinger Runs White Lighting on the Back Roads of Tennessee." [Wind] (22:71) 92, p. 26.
"The Krazy Kat Rag" (In memory of George Herriman, for Paul & Jean Frame. Selections: "L'Argument," 1-4). [Light] (2) Sum 92, p. 27-29.
"The Krazy Kat Rag" (Selections: 5-7). [Light] (3) Aut 92, p. 27-28.
"The Krazy Kat Rag" (Selections: 8-11). [Light] (4) Wint 92-93, p. 27-28.
"Listening to Brahms' Piano Concerto No. 3 in C Minor with the Hope of Becoming Inspired with a New Idea." [Footwork] 92, p. 19.
"More Academic Graffiti." [Light] (1) Spr 92, p. 21.
"On the Perils of Non-Free Verse." [Light] (4) Wint 92-93, p. 7.
"The Revolt of the Tuba Players." [Light] (1) Spr 92, p. 8.
4952. PHILLIPS, Michael L. (Michael Lee)
"Butcher Shop in Sligo, Ireland" (for Michael Quirke). [LitR] (35:3) Spr 92, p. 405.
"Faces Sing, and Louder Sing, at the Reunion." [NewYorkQ] (47) 92, p. 82-83.
"The Nymphomaniac." [CimR] (99) Ap 92, p. 54-55.
"The Tongue and the Blonde." [SouthernPR] (32:1) Spr 92, p. 21.
4953. PHILLIPS, Robert
"Baltimore & Ohio R. R." (for and after Stephen Dobyns). [Hudson] (44:4) Wint 92, p. 615-616.
"On a Drawing by Glen Baxter." [ParisR] (34:125) Wint 92, p. 112-113.
"Whereabouts." [WestHR] (46:1) Spr 92, p. 93.
4954. PHILLIPS, Timothy R.
"Tribal Passages." [MidwQ] (34:1) Aut 92, p. 81.
4955. PHILLIPS, Walt
"Adobe." [Amelia] (7:1, #20) 92, p. 137.
"Adversaries." [SlipS] (12) 92, p. 20.
"Biography." [Amelia] (7:1, #20) 92, p. 137.
"Coombs Down in Plant 11." [SlipS] (12) 92, p. 21.
"Lobotomy Paul." [ChironR] (11:2) Sum 92, p. 13.
"Oil Smoke Renegade." [SlipS] (12) 92, p. 20.
"Salute to the Drab." [SlipS] (12) 92, p. 20.
"Voice of a Stranger." [Amelia] (7:1, #20) 92, p. 137.
4956. PHILOCTÈTE, René
"A Collage for Servant Children" (tr. by Cheryl Thomas and Carrol F. Coates). [Callaloo] (15:3) Sum 92, p. 619-620.
"Collage pour Enfants de Masion." [Callaloo] (15:3) Sum 92, p. 621-622.
"La Misere au Soleil." [Callaloo] (15:3) Sum 92, p. 618.
"Misery by Sunlight" (tr. by Cheryl Thomas and Carrol F. Coates). [Callaloo] (15:3) Sum 92, p. 617.
4957. PHILPOT, Tracy
"The Sheltering Temptation." [Caliban] (11) 92, p. 152.
"The Sliding Scale of Censorship." [DenQ] (26:3) Wint 92, p. 43.
4958. PHIPPS, Wanda
"Beatles (A Cycle)" (tr. of Attila Mohylny, w. Virlana Tkacz). [Agni] (36) 92, p. 249-252.
4959. PICABIA, Francis
"Purring Poetry" (Excerpt, tr. by Geoffrey Young). [Avec] (5:1) 92, p. 89-92.
4960. PICAZO, Juan Pablo
"Canción del Inconforme Nocturno." [Nuez] (4:10/11) 92, p. 7.

4961. PICCIONE, Anthony
"If Some Had Been Dreaming of Women." [ColR] (9:1) Spr-Sum 92, p. 41.
"It Was a Silence Settling on the Cabin." [ColR] (9:1) Spr-Sum 92, p. 39.
"When My Wife Is Away Time Fills the Cabin and Nothing Happens." [ColR] (9:1) Spr-Sum 92, p. 40.
4962. PIERCE, Deborah
"The Right Painter." [CumbPR] (11:2) Spr 92, p. 25.
4963. PIERCY, Marge
"Art for Art's Sake." [ChironR] (11:1) Spr 92, p. 3.
"Belly Good." [Kalliope] (14:3) 92, p. 8-9.
"Do Not Erect the Wall Before Yourselves" (for Carolyn Forche and Harry Mattison). [Vis] (38) 92, p. 36-38.
"A Little Monument." [SoCoast] (13) Je 93 [i.e. 92], p. 42-43.
"My Rich Uncle, Whom I Only Met Three Times." [ChironR] (11:1) Spr 92, p. 3.
"The Mystery of the Flies." [ChironR] (11:1) Spr 92, p. 3.
"Salt in the Afternoon." [YellowS] (Ten Years [i.e. 40]) Sum-Fall 92, p. 4.
"Season of Breakage." [SoCoast] (13) Je 93 [i.e. 92], p. 48-49.
4964. PIERMAN, Carol J.
"Eight Cows." [ThRiPo] (39/40) 92-93, p. 199-200.
"How We Learned About Friction." [ThRiPo] (39/40) 92-93, p. 197.
"Hunter's Moon." [SycamoreR] (4:1) Wint 92, p. 22-23.
"Pilgrims." [ThRiPo] (39/40) 92-93, p. 198-199.
"Sweet." [SycamoreR] (4:1) Wint 92, p. 24-25.
PIERO, W. S. di
See Di PIERO, W. S.
4965. PIERRE, Charles
"Tambourine." [SmPd] (29:3, #86) Fall 92, p. 32.
4966. PIERRO, Albino
"Perhaps You Want Me" (tr. by Luigi Bonaffini). [Vis] (39) 92, p. 39.
"Yesterday" (tr. by Luigi Bonaffini). [Vis] (39) 92, p. 39.
4967. PIGNOTTI, Lamberto
"Infinite Forms of Entertainment" (tr. by Corrado Federici). [PoetryC] (13:1) N 92, p. 21.
4968. PILIBOSIAN, Helene
"To My Daughter." [Plain] (13:1) Fall 92, p. 18-19.
4969. PILINSZKY, János
"Four-Liner" (tr. by Emery George). [SouthernHR] (26:1) Wint 92, p. 26.
"The Henchman's Room" (tr. by Emery George). [SouthernHR] (26:1) Wint 92, p. 25.
"A Hóhér Szobája." [SouthernHR] (26:1) Wint 92, p. 25.
"Holy Thief" (for Mari Töröcsik, tr. by Emery George). [PartR] (59:2) Spr 92, p. 268.
"Meetings" (for Júlia Szilágyi, tr. by Emery George). [Nimrod] (35:2) Spr-Sum 92, p. 31.
"Négysoros." [SouthernHR] (26:1) Wint 92, p. 26.
"Örökmozgó." [SouthernHR] (26:1) Wint 92, p. 24.
"Perpetuum Mobile" (tr. by Emery George). [SouthernHR] (26:1) Wint 92, p. 24.
"Találkozások" (Szilágyi Júliának). [Nimrod] (35:2) Spr-Sum 92, p. 31.
4970. PILKINGTON, Ace G.
"The Pulse of Light." [WeberS] (9:2) Spr-Sum 92, p. 48.
4971. PILKINGTON, Kevin
"Watching the Day from the Twenty-Fifth Floor." [Confr] (50) Fall 92, p. 285-286.
"When Iowa Was Washed Away with Milk" (for my sister). [Iowa] (22:2) Spr-Sum 92, p. 166.
4972. PILLER, John
"Like This." [CreamCR] (16:1) Spr 92, p. 124.
"On Chesapeake Bay." [CreamCR] (16:1) Spr 92, p. 122-123.
4973. PILLING, Marilyn (Marilyn Gear)
"Going to Work." [Event] (21:2) Sum 92, p. 62.
"One Missing, Three Out for the Day from the Nursing Home." [AntigR] (90) Sum 92, p. 135.
4974. PIÑA ZENTELLA, Marta
"La Madre del Hombre Muere." [Nuez] (4:10/11) 92, p. 4.
4975. PINARD, Mary
"Augury: January 16, 1991." [IndR] (15:2) Fall 92, p. 21-22.
"Du Pont's Black Powder Mills: Self-Guided Tour." [IndR] (15:2) Fall 92, p. 23-24.

4976. PINCKNEY, Diana
"The Company of Goats" (Second Prize, 1992 Literary Contest). [Crucible] (28) Fall 92, p. 3.
"Grand Strand Reunion." [ChatR] (13:1) Fall 92, p. 29-30.
4977. PINDAR, Stephanie
"Taking the Pip." [Bogg] (65) 92, p. 42.
4978. PINE/CHRISTY, Ana
"That Summer." [MoodySI] (27) Spr 92, p. 16.
"Vegas." [MoodySI] (27) Spr 92, p. 16.
4979. PINES, James M.
"A Farewell to Blurbs." [AmerS] (61:2) Spr 92, p. 275-276.
4980. PING, Chin Woon
"In My Mother's Dream." [KenR] (NS 14:1) Wint 92, p. 135-136.
PING, Chou
See CHOU, Ping
4981. PING, Wang
"Between Dreams." [WestCL] (26:2, #8) Fall 92, p. 78.
"Educational Trip." [WestCL] (26:2, #8) Fall 92, p. 77.
"Of Flesh and Spirit." [WestCL] (26:2, #8) Fall 92, p. 74-75.
"She Is That Reed." [WestCL] (26:2, #8) Fall 92, p. 76.
PING-KWAN, Leung
See LEUNG, Ping-Kwan
4982. PINGARRON, Michael
"After an Eclipse" (for my father). [LindLM] (11:1) Mr 92, p. 15.
"Bitter Prayer" (after César Vallejo). [LindLM] (11:1) Mr 92, p. 15.
"Estoy Cansado de Ser un Camino." [LindLM] (11:1) Mr 92, p. 15.
"Recalling a Kansan Night." [LindLM] (11:1) Mr 92, p. 15.
4983. PINKARD, Ron
"If the Tollund Man Toured the United States." [Lactuca] (16) Ag 92, p. 15-16.
4984. PINKWATER, Susan
"Praying Mantis." [NewYorkQ] (49) 92, p. 72.
4985. PINO, José Manuel del
"Ajhjfiefoeklxiuwe" (tr. by G. J. Racz). [SenR] (22:1) Spr 92, p. 47-48.
"Chambord Castle" (tr. by G. J. Racz). [SenR] (22:1) Spr 92, p. 44-46.
PIÑON, Evangelina Vigil
See VIGIL-PIÑON, Evangelina
4986. PINSKY, Robert
"Inferno: Canto XXVIII" (tr. of Dante Alighieri). [ParisR] (34:123) Sum 92, p. 110 - 115.
4987. PINSON, Hermine
"Marvin Gaye's Lament." [AfAmRev] (26:2) Sum 92, p. 260-261.
"What Can You Do with a Fan." [AfAmRev] (26:2) Sum 92, p. 262-263.
PINTO, John di
See Di PINTO, John
4988. PIOMBINO, Nick
"The Broken Angel." [CentralP] (21) Spr 92, p. 173-174.
"Light Street." [Avec] (5:1) 92, p. 50-54.
"Semblance." [OnTheBus] (4:2/5:1, #10/11) 92, p. 172.
4989. PIONTEK, Heinz
"Man at Ninety" (tr. by Ken Fontenot). [NewOR] (19:1) Spr 92, p. 23.
4990. PIORKOWSKI, Krystyna
"Over a Glass of Wine" (tr. of Wislawa Szymborska). [Trans] (26) Spr 92, p. 61-62.
4991. PIR, Karamshi
"Crow" (tr. of Kamal Vora). [ChiR] (38:1/2) 92, p. 205.
4992. PIRANI, Ayaz
"East African Studies" (1992 AWP Intro Award Winner). [IndR] (15:2) Fall 92, p. 145-146.
4993. PISTOLAS, Androula Savvas
"The High Rock." [Pearl] (15) Spr-Sum 92, p. 22.
"Visiting Joseph." [Pearl] (15) Spr-Sum 92, p. 22.
4994. PITKIN, Anne
"Winter Ghazals." [Poetry] (161:3) D 92, p. 132.
4995. PITZER, N. Andrea
"Sacrifice." [PoetL] (87:1) Spr 92, p. 13-14.

4996. PLA BENITO, Juan Luis
"Poemas" (Para "La Nuez": I. "Quiero que en mi verso," II. "Por qué mi poema es como esta mano"). [Nuez] (4:12) 92, p. 28.
4997. PLANTOS, Ted
"Canadian Club." [Arc] (29) Aut 92, p. 22-23.
"The Newfy Girl." [Dandel] (19:1) 92, p. 8.
4998. PLATER, Lynda
"The Humber Light." [Verse] (9:3) Wint 92, p. 152.
4999. PLATH, Sylvia
"Black Rook in Rainy Weather." [AntR] (50:1/2) Wint-Spr 92, p. 150-151.
5000. PLATT, Donald
"Along Magnolia St." [PoetryNW] (33:3) Aut 92, p. 13-15.
"Fresh Peaches, Fireworks, & Guns" (winner of Discovery — The Nation '92). [Nat] (254:19) 18 My 92, p. 670-671.
"Untitled: Why does this abstract." [PoetryNW] (33:3) Aut 92, p. 11-12.
5001. PLETCHER, Bob
"Cecelia's Complaint." [AntigR] (89) Spr 92, p. 146.
5002. PLEVIN, Arlene
"Malcolm X Park, Washington, D.C." [WashR] (17:6) Ap-My 92, p. 14.
5003. PLUMB, Hudson
"Packing." [WebR] (16) Fall 92, p. 44.
5004. PLUMB, Vivienne
"Frida's Spell for Strong Hearts." [Vis] (40) 92, p. 52.
5005. PLUMLY, Stanley
"Armistice Poppies." [Sonora] (22/23) Spr 92, p. 172.
"Complaint Against the Arsonist." [VirQR] (68:3) Sum 92, p. 481-482.
5006. PLYMELL, Charles
"San Francisco Ward" (for Bill MacNeil, painter, San Francisco). [JamesWR] (10:1) Fall 92, p. 9.
PO, Li
See LI, Po
5007. POBO, Kenneth
"Aaron Hobnobs." [Amelia] (6:4, #19) 92, p. 119.
"Aaron's in Love Again." [Amelia] (6:4, #19) 92, p. 119-120.
"Begonia Comfort." [Interim] (11:1) Spr-Sum 92, p. 4.
"Holding." [ChironR] (11:4) Wint 92, p. 25.
"Hustler." [SlipS] (12) 92, p. 36.
"Jennifer's Bone Trilliums." [Poem] (67) My 92, p. 29.
"Mary Alice Stung." [Poem] (67) My 92, p. 30.
"Purple Sill." [Grain] (20:3) Fall 92, p. 29.
"Queer Bashed." [JamesWR] (10:1) Fall 92, p. 16.
"Rethinking a Moan." [ChironR] (11:4) Wint 92, p. 25.
"Rudy Tashkenheld." [JamesWR] (9:2) Wint 92, p. 8.
"Travis on Willy." [JamesWR] (9:4) Sum 92, p. 12.
"Trina Hears Felicia Chirp." [Farm] (9:2) Fall-Wint 92-93, p. 34.
"Waiting." [Poem] (67) My 92, p. 31.
"Waupaca, Wisconsin." [Grain] (20:3) Fall 92, p. 28.
5008. POCH, John E.
"The Recompense." [MidAR] (12:2) 92, p. 27-28.
POL, Miquel Marti i
See MARTI i POL, Miquel
5009. POLAK, Maralyn Lois
"Transformation" (for Roger Armstrong). [PaintedB] (48) 92, p. 28-29.
5010. POLKINHORN, Christa
"Crossings." [OnTheBus] (4:2/5:1, #10/11) 92, p. 173-174.
5011. POLLARD, J. A.
"Comma." [Amelia] (6:4, #19) 92, p. 43.
5012. POLLARD, Velma
"The Best Philosophers I Know Can't Read and Write" (for the Lady of Mandahl Peak). [LitR] (35:4) Sum 92, p. 499-501.
"Conversation (again?)." [LitR] (35:4) Sum 92, p. 497-498.
"Fly." [CinPR] (23) Wint 91-92, p. 50-51.
"My Daughter Resembles Harry Belafonte's Daughter." [CinPR] (23) Wint 91-92, p. 52.
"Screws Loose." [CinPR] (23) Wint 91-92, p. 53.

"Woman in Goteborg (with a Basket on Her Bicycle)." [CinPR] (23) Wint 91-92, p. 48-49.

5013. POLLENTIER, Nicole
"Between the Birdbath and the Garden." [HangL] (61) 92, p. 99-100.
"Farm Road 11." [HangL] (61) 92, p. 101.

5014. POLLET, Sylvester
"Talk American" (For MaJo, 1990). [NewYorkQ] (48) 92, p. 74.

5015. POLLITT, Katha
"Wisdom of the Desert Fathers." [NewYorker] (68:19) 29 Je 92, p. 32.

5016. POMEROY, Mark
"I Don't Know." [OnTheBus] (4:2/5:1, #10/11) 92, p. 175.

PONCE, Gabriela Eguía-Lis
See EGUIA-LIS PONCE, Gabriela

5017. PONGE, Francis
"The Wasp" (to Jean Paul Sartre and Simone de Beauvoir, tr. by Ann Glenn). [AmerPoR] (21:6) N-D 92, p. 43-44.

5018. PONIEWAZ, Jeff
"Dahmer's Inferno." [ChironR] (11:4) Wint 92, p. 16.
"How to Make a Wino Stop Bothering You in Pere Marquette Park." [NewYorkQ] (48) 92, p. 80.
"I'm Going to Let My Balls Hang Out." [ChironR] (11:4) Wint 92, p. 16.
"Lament for Bob's Cock." [ChironR] (11:4) Wint 92, p. 16.
"Liberace Picked Me." [JamesWR] (10:1) Fall 92, p. 9.
"Why Young Men Wore Their Hair Long in the Sixties." [NewYorkQ] (47) 92, p. 38-39.

5019. PONSOT, Marie
"Beautiful Theory" (At the Getty). [KenR] (NS 14:4) Fall 92, p. 15-17.
"Even." [Comm] (119:8) 24 Ap 92, p. 12.
"Even." [NewYorker] (68:23) 27 Jl 92, p. 36.
"Pourriture Noble" (a moral tale, for: Sauternes, the fungus *cenaria*, and the wild old). [KenR] (NS 14:4) Fall 92, p. 17-18.

PONT, Kathryn Cullen du
See CULLEN-DuPONT, Kathryn

5020. POOLE, Joan Lauri
"Guardians." [NewYorkQ] (49) 92, p. 68.
"In the Language of Orchids." [BrooklynR] (9) 92, p. 71.
"Love-Charm Song." [NewYorkQ] (47) 92, p. 67.

5021. POOLE, Richard
"Silence." [WebR] (16) Fall 92, p. 82.
"The Woman at Endor." [WebR] (16) Fall 92, p. 80-81.

5022. POOM, Ritva
"The Cambrian Series: II (Shells)" (tr. of Eeva-Liisa Manner). [ManhatR] (6:2) Fall 92, p. 22-23.

5023. POPE, Deborah
"Accident." [TarRP] (32:1) Fall 92, p. 23.
"Beginning." [TarRP] (32:1) Fall 92, p. 24.
"Equinox." [SouthernR] (28:4) Aut, O 92, p. 889-890.
"Leaving." [PraS] (66:3) Fall 92, p. 108-109.
"The Summer I Was Pregnant." [SouthernR] (28:4) Aut, O 92, p. 887-888.
"Les Voyeurs." [SouthernPR] (32:2) Fall 92, p. 18-19.
"What Is Last." [PoetryNW] (33:2) Sum 92, p. 3.

5024. POPE, Deidre
"Biopsy." [TarRP] (30:2) Spr 91, p. 4.
"Changes" (for Robyn). [Kalliope] (14:2) 92, p. 14.
"Good Touch, Bad Touch." [BelPoJ] (42:3) Spr 92, p. 37-39.
"Straight Talk." [BelPoJ] (42:3) Spr 92, p. 40-41.

5025. POPOV, Nikolai
"Nightlight: Eye of the Owl" (tr. of Blaga Dimitrova, w. Heather McHugh). [Trans] (26) Spr 92, p. 53-54.

5026. POPOVA, Olga
"Untitled: Bound by the heart to the ignorant" (in Russian and English, tr. by J. Kates). [PaintedB] (45) 92, p. 26-27.

5027. POPOVA-WIGHTMAN, Ludmilla
"Amnesia in Reverse" (tr. of Blaga Dimitrova). [LitR] (25:2) Wint 92, p. 180.
"Forbidden Sea" (tr. of Blaga Dimitrova, w. Elizabeth Anne Socolow). [US1] (26/27) 92, p. 26.

"Pastoral" (tr. of Konstantin Pavlov). [LitR] (25:2) Wint 92, p. 178.
"Prelude — The Spiders" (tr. of Konstantin Pavlov). [LitR] (25:2) Wint 92, p. 178.
"The Shadows of the Trees" (tr. of Blaga Dimitrova). [LitR] (25:2) Wint 92, p. 179 - 180.

5028. PORDZIK, Ralph
"The Secret Life of Kaspar Hauser." [Stand] (33:4) Aut 92, p. 78-80.

5029. PORNOFF, Horrah
"Derision." [GrandS] (11:3 #43) 92, p. 101.

5030. PORTA, Antonio
"Passi Passaggi" (Selection: poem, tr. by Anthony Molino). [Trans] (26) Spr 92, p. 6-7.

5031. PORTER, Anne
"Autumn Crocus." [Comm] (119:17) 9 O 92, p. 23.

5032. PORTER, Burt
"Modesty." [Hellas] (3:1) Spr 92, p. 26.

5033. PORTER, Helen Fogwill
"Wild People." [Grain] (20:2) Sum 92, p. 151-152.

5034. PORTERFIELD, Laurel
"Jump Rope Song." [Kalliope] (14:1) 92, p. 42.
"Left Turn." [Kalliope] (14:1) 92, p. 42.
"Small Prayer." [Kalliope] (14:1) 92, p. 42.

5035. PORTERFIELD, Susan
"Bird." [MidAR] (13:2) 92, p. 158-159.

5036. PORTWOOD, Pamela
"In Hollow Bone." [Outbr] (23) 92, p. 48.
"Tea Leaves and Crow's Feet." [Outbr] (23) 92, p. 47.
"Words." [Vis] (38) 92, p. 42-43.

5037. POSTER, Carol
"Basic Rockcraft." [Outbr] (23) 92, p. 26.

5038. POSWIATOWSKA, Halina
"Ode to the Hands" (tr. by Maya Peretz). [SnailPR] (2:1) Spr-Sum 92, p. 5.

5039. POTOKAR, Jure
"Persons" (tr. by Michael Biggins). [GrandS] (11:3 #43) 92, p. 186.
"Touching" (tr. by Michael Biggins). [GrandS] (11:3 #43) 92, p. 187.

5040. POUND, Omar
"Baghdad: On a Bus to the Front." [NewMyths] (1:2/2:1) 92, p. 134.
"Princeton Honors Bush (1991)." [AntigR] (89) Spr 92, p. 81.
"Speaker's Corner: London." [NewMyths] (1:2/2:1) 92, p. 132-133.

5041. POUNTHIOUN, Diallo
"Ndar." [Os] (35) Fall 92, p. 36-37.
"Septembre à Dakar." [Os] (35) Fall 92, p. 38.

5042. POVERNY, Rick
"Delivery." [Footwork] 92, p. 23.
"My Mother Refuses to Have Cataract Surgery." [Footwork] 92, p. 23.

5043. POWELL, Dannye Romine
"At Morrow Mountain." [SycamoreR] (4:1) Wint 92, p. 51.
"Mary Lamb: The Murder." [BelPoJ] (43:2) Wint 92-93, p. 6-7.
"My Mother, Becoming a Widow." [GeoR] (46:2) Sum 92, p. 356.
"Sorrow, Looking Like Abraham Lincoln, Keeps Knocking on My Back Door." [NowestR] (30:3) 92, p. 39-41.
"Two High-Strung Sisters and the Wizardry of Their Basket of Words." [LaurelR] (26:2) Sum 92, p. 50.
"Why Didn't the Caged Bird Sing?" [Northeast] (5:6) Spr 92, p. 20.

5044. POWELL, Douglas A.
"Always Returning: Holidays and Burials. Not Every." [JamesWR] (9:4) Sum 92, p. 7.
"Going Past the Long Faces. Of Houses Adjusted." [ChironR] (11:2) Sum 92, p. 9.
"He Imitates His Wife: No Young Drop from the Gap." [ChironR] (11:2) Sum 92, p. 9.
"The Mind Is a Shapely Genital. Faces: Elaborate." [ChironR] (11:2) Sum 92, p. 9.
"Of All the Modern Divisions You Are." [ChironR] (11:2) Sum 92, p. 9.
"Sounding the Depths: She Slides in the Bath." [ChironR] (11:2) Sum 92, p. 9.

5045. POWELL, Jim
"Beauty & the Cripple." [Conjunc] (19) 92, p. 248-257.
"Sappho: A Garland" (tr. of Sappho). [TriQ] (86) Wint 92-93, p. 224-243.

5046. POWELL, Kevin
"Harlem: Neo-image." [Obs] (7:1/2) Spr-Sum 92, p. 111.
"Love / a Many Splintered Thing" (for Karla). [Obs] (7:1/2) Spr-Sum 92, p. 111 - 112.
"She Has Many Ancestors" (for Lisa Teasley). [Obs] (7:1/2) Spr-Sum 92, p. 109.
"Soul Interlude." [Obs] (7:1/2) Spr-Sum 92, p. 110-111.
5047. POWELL, Lynn
"Strategy." [US1] (26/27) 92, p. 35.
5048. POWELL, Marcy S.
"Betting on the Nags." [Light] (3) Aut 92, p. 16.
"Horse Sense." [Light] (4) Wint 92-93, p. 10.
"Nightly." [Light] (2) Sum 92, p. 23.
"Seafaring." [Light] (3) Aut 92, p. 14.
"Those Smart Sardines." [Light] (1) Spr 92, p. 13.
"Whistler and Mother." [Light] (1) Spr 92, p. 25.
5049. POWER, Marjorie
"During a Humid Spell." [Kalliope] (14:2) 92, p. 27-28.
"The Shutter Goes Click." [CreamCR] (16:2) Fall 92, p. 81.
5050. POWERS, Dan
"Aching Hands." [NewYorkQ] (47) 92, p. 69.
"Lover." [Pearl] (15) Spr-Sum 92, p. 15.
"Moonslide Mystic." [Pearl] (15) Spr-Sum 92, p. 15.
"So Much for the Other Senses." [Pearl] (15) Spr-Sum 92, p. 15.
5051. POWERS, Kathleen
"Specifics." [NewYorkQ] (47) 92, p. 84.
5052. POWERS, Michael
"I Believe in Jesus and John the Baptist." [JamesWR] (10:1) Fall 92, p. 13.
"Question." [JamesWR] (10:1) Fall 92, p. 13.
5053. POWLEY, William H.
"A Crate of Letters." [TarRP] (31:2) Spr 92, p. 41.
5054. POYNER, Ken
"Kepler's Discovery of Elliptical Orbits." [Iowa] (22:2) Spr-Sum 92, p. 165.
5055. PRADO, Holly
"Ave Maria." [ColR] (9:1) Spr-Sum 92, p. 111.
"Chillier Weather." [Chelsea] (53) 92, p. 85.
"Married in This House of Particular Windows." [Pearl] (15) Spr-Sum 92, p. 23.
"Refuses Those Houses Already Built." [Chelsea] (53) 92, p. 86.
"The Solstice Calendar." [Pearl] (15) Spr-Sum 92, p. 23.
"This Close." [Chelsea] (53) 92, p. 87.
"The Young Woman in Autumn, When Persephone Returns to Her Husband." [ColR] (9:1) Spr-Sum 92, p. 109-110.
5056. PRAED, Winthrop Mackworth
"One More Quadrille." [Light] (1) Spr 92, p. 32.
5057. PRAEGER, Frank C.
"Out Walking on the Heights Overlooking Portage Lake." [ChamLR] (10/11) Spr - Fall 92, p. 170.
5058. PRAHLAD, Sw. Anand (Dennis Folly)
"The Claremont." [Obs] (7:1/2) Spr-Sum 92, p. 114-115.
"Insomnia." [Obs] (7:1/2) Spr-Sum 92, p. 115.
"Prayer to Granny." [Obs] (7:1/2) Spr-Sum 92, p. 113-114.
5059. PRAISNER, Wanda S.
"The Clipping" (For Tom). [US1] (26/27) 92, p. 44.
5060. PRATIKAKIS, Manolis
"Clay Jug" (tr. by Parina Stiakaki). [Stand] (33:4) Aut 92, p. 98.
5061. PRATT, Charles W.
"La Diva." [Light] (2) Sum 92, p. 21.
"The Diva." [Light] (2) Sum 92, p. 21.
5062. PRAY, Bethany
"Conception." [VirQR] (68:1) Wint 92, p. 82-83.
"Island Honeymoon." [VirQR] (68:1) Wint 92, p. 81-82.
5063. PREFONTAINE, Jay R.
"The Muse." [ChatR] (13:1) Fall 92, p. 27.
5064. PRELUTSKY, Jack
"A Great Unexpected Dilemma." [Light] (2) Sum 92, p. 19.
"The Vegetarian." [Light] (4) Wint 92-93, p. 24.

5065. PRESNELL, Barbara
"Norman in the Broccoli." [Crucible] (28) Fall 92, p. 35-36.
5066. PRESSER, Scott
"The Mother." [PaintedB] (48) 92, p. 74.
5067. PRICE, Caroline
"The Heart of the Country." [Stand] (33:2) Spr 92, p. 15.
"Slow Movement." [Stand] (33:2) Spr 92, p. 14.
5068. PRICE, V. B.
"Chaco Elegies." [SoDakR] (30:1) Spr 92, p. 137-145.
5069. PRIDGEN, Charlotte
"The Difference Between Women & Men" (or, What REALLY Goes on in the Executive Washroom. 1992 AWP Intro Award Winner). [IndR] (15:2) Fall 92, p. 148-149.
5070. PRIDMORE, Saxby
"The Boys' Own Annual." [Vis] (40) 92, p. 33.
PRIEST, Travis du
See DuPRIEST, Travis
5071. PRINCIPE, Concetta
"Silent Cantos." [MalR] (99) Sum 92, p. 87-88.
5072. PRINZMETAL, Donna
"Poem for Spring." [Rohwedder] (7) Spr-Sum 92, p. 21.
5073. PRITAM, Amrita
"Pariah Dog" (tr. by Arlene Zide and the author). [ChiR] (38:1/2) 92, p. 132-133.
5074. PRITCHARD, Selwyn
"Heart Attack." [GreenMR] (NS 5:2) Spr-Sum 92, p. 27.
"Suppressing the Welsh." [LaurelR] (26:1) Wint 92, p. 94.
5075. PRIVETT, Katharine
"Attila József: an Obituary." [Poem] (67) My 92, p. 18-19.
"Flesh is Venus's-flytrap." [Poem] (67) My 92, p. 22.
"I Know Better." [Poem] (67) My 92, p. 20.
"Quiescent, Every Surface, Dormant, Every Sound." [Poem] (67) My 92, p. 21.
5076. PROPER, Stan
"Dress." [SmPd] (29:3, #86) Fall 92, p. 32.
"A fire engine screams." [Pearl] (16) Fall 92, p. 34.
"Gladiators." [Lactuca] (16) Ag 92, p. 38.
"Heart." [SmPd] (29:1, #84) Wint 92, p. 13.
"In sunlight." [Amelia] (6:4, #19) 92, p. 120.
"Just a Phase." [Lactuca] (16) Ag 92, p. 38.
"Just the Facts." [Lactuca] (16) Ag 92, p. 38.
"Laundro-mat." [BlackBR] (16) Wint-Spr 92-93, p. 23.
"Louisa." [Pearl] (16) Fall 92, p. 8.
"Red Socks." [Pearl] (16) Fall 92, p. 12.
"Right Arm." [Lactuca] (16) Ag 92, p. 39.
"Taxidermist." [BlackBR] (15) Spr-Sum 92, p. 32.
"Wall Flowers" (1st Prize, 6th Annual Contest). [SoCoast] (12) Ja 92, p. 46-47.
"Werewolf." [Lactuca] (16) Ag 92, p. 39.
5077. PROPERTIUS
"Dream" (Propertius II.26A, tr. by Diane Arnson Svarlien). [Arion] 3d series (1:1) Wint 90, p. 184.
"Farewell to Cynthia" (Elegies, III, 25, in Latin and English, tr. by Michael L. Johnson). [Parting] (5:2) Wint 92-93, p. 28-29.
5078. PROPP, Karen
"The Roseate Terns." [RiverC] (12:2) Spr 92, p. 48.
5079. PROSNITZ, Howard
"Love Wanders." [Footwork] 92, p. 97.
5080. PROULX, Bev
"It Begins with Fire's Smell." [RagMag] (10:2) 92, p. 82.
5081. PRUCHA, Christine Berg
"Borrowed Evening." [SoCoast] (12) Ja 92, p. 24-25.
5082. PRUFER, Kevin
"Sestina" (for my sister, where she is). [CumbPR] (12:1) Fall 92, p. 50-51.
"The Third Rail" (For Doris, who's seen more exciting times). [CimR] (99) Ap 92, p. 48-49.
"Ways of Seeing" (a letter to the artist). [CumbPR] (12:1) Fall 92, p. 49.
5083. PRUITT, Patricia
"Drawing Point" (Excerpts). [Talisman] (9) Fall 92, p. 210-213.

5084. PRUNTY, Wyatt
"The Angel and the Beast." [NewEngR] (14:4) Fall 92, p. 208.
"Distances." [SouthernR] (28:4) Aut, O 92, p. 891-892.
"Haying." [SouthernR] (28:4) Aut, O 92, p. 892-894.
"Returning." [Boulevard] (7:1, #19) Spr 92, p. 168.
"Suburban Note." [Verse] (9:2) Sum 92, p. 8.
"Taxi Dance, Montana 1937." [SouthernR] (28:4) Aut, O 92, p. 894-895.
"The Water Slide along the Beach." [SouthernR] (28:4) Aut, O 92, p. 895-896.
5085. PUCHALA, Vlado
"Cemeteries" (tr. by the author and James Sutherland-Smith). [PraS] (66:4) Wint 92, p. 147.
"So Deeply Do I Love You" (tr. by the author and James Sutherland-Smith). [PraS] (66:4) Wint 92, p. 148.
"The Teacher's Wake" (tr. by the author and James Sutherland-Smith). [PraS] (66:4) Wint 92, p. 147.
5086. PULLEY, Nancy
"Security Light." [HopewellR] (4) 92, p. 8.
5087. PUMAREGA, Emilynn J.
"Overlooked." [NegC] (12:1/2) 92, p. 110.
5088. PUNYI, Christopher
"The Jungle Lady of Siberia." [Gypsy] (19) 92, p. 58.
5089. PURDY, Al
"The Freezing Music." [WorldL] (3) 92, p. 18-19.
5090. PURPURA, Lia
"Looking at Photographs" (for R., tr. of Grzegorz Musial, w. the author). [SenR] (22:2) Fall 92, p. 54-55.
"Only a Shadow" (to my mother, tr. of Grzegorz Musial, w. the author). [SenR] (22:2) Fall 92, p. 52-53.
5091. PURSIFULL, Carmen (Carmen M.)
"The Bed." [Americas] (19:2) Sum 91, p. 47-49.
"The Boji Stones." [CoalC] (5) My 92, p. 18.
"Mourning in a Parallel Universe." [Americas] (19:2) Sum 91, p. 54-56.
"Nineteen Sixty Nine in Jacksonville Beach." [Americas] (19:2) Sum 91, p. 50-53.
"To You on Wave #Negative 4." [Americas] (19:2) Sum 91, p. 57-59.
"Tourist." [Americas] (19:2) Sum 91, p. 42-46.
5092. PURYEAR, Paul
"Night Watch." [Amelia] (6:4, #19) 92, p. 39-42.
5093. PYE, Virginia
"Your Leather Sofa" (For Tom Black). [Art&Und] (1:4) Jl-Ag 92, p. 9.
5094. PYRCZ, Heather
"Gazelles." [WestCL] (25:3, #6) Wint 91-92, p. 141.
"Spider Webb." [WestCL] (25:3, #6) Wint 91-92, p. 141.
5095. PYTKO, J. F.
"Ad Lib." [BlackBR] (16) Wint-Spr 92-93, p. 30.
QASSIM, Samih al-
See Al-QASSIM, Samih
QING, Ai
See AI, Qing
QING-ZHAO, Li
See LI, Qing-Zhao
5096. QIU, Xiaolong
"A Jing Dynastry Goat." [NewL] (58:4) 92, p. 151-152.
"Li Shangying's English Version." [NewL] (58:4) 92, p. 150.
5097. QUACKENBUSH, L. Howard
"The Memory of Silver" (tr. of Carlos Montemayor, w. Russell M. Cluff). [TriQ] (85) Fall 92, p. 203-204.
5098. QUAGLIANO, Tony
"Between a Rock and Mahatma Gandhi." [NewYorkQ] (48) 92, p. 84-85.
"Ezra's ABC's, and Deeds." [NewYorkQ] (49) 92, p. 52.
"Making Light" (On three works in "The Honolulu Paper"). [HawaiiR] (16:2, #35) Spr 92, p. 104-105.
"Raymond Chandler." [ChamLR] (10/11) Spr-Fall 92, p. 194-196.
5099. QUATTLEBAUM, Mary
"Cassandra." [Conscience] (13:2) Sum 92, p. 13.
5100. QUENNEVILLE, Freda
"Juke-Box Kali." [ChatR] (13:1) Fall 92, p. 31-34.

"Odysseus and Einstein." [ChatR] (13:1) Fall 92, p. 35.
5101. QUESENBERRY, Mattie F.
"Leaving Lost Creek." [Wind] (22:71) 92, p. 27.
5102. QUINN, Bernetta
"As to a Fire." [Pembroke] (24) 92, p. 22.
5103. QUINN, Fran
"The Prepositions of You." [HopewellR] (4) 92, p. 32.
"Story." [HopewellR] (4) 92, p. 28.
5104. QUINN, John (*See also* QUINN, John Robert)
"Better Bamboo." [Interim] (11:1) Spr-Sum 92, p. 18.
5105. QUINN, John Robert (*See also* QUINN, John)
"Snow." [ChrC] (109:3) 22 Ja 92, p. 70.
5106. QUINTANA, Leroy V.
"Grandmother, How Quickly the Days Pass." [MinnR] (38) Spr-Sum 92, p. 24-25.
5107. QUINTERO, Alfredo E.
"Otros Días." [Nuez] (4:10/11) 92, p. 10.
5108. QUINTILIUS
"A Fragment from Quintilius: Empedocles said" (tr. by Peter Russell). [JlNJPo] (14:1) Spr 92, p. 12.
"A Fragment from Quintilius: That jackass Polybius, who taught that History depends on facts" (tr. by Peter Russell). [JlNJPo] (14:1) Spr 92, p. 11.
5109. QUIRARTE, Vicente
"A Woman and a Man" (tr. by Reginald Gibbons). [TriQ] (85) Fall 92, p. 160-161.
5110. QUIROZ, Claudia (Claudia R.)
"The Imaginary Man" (tr. of Nicanor Parra). [Antaeus] (69) Aut 92, p. 63.
"Plaza Murillo, La Paz: 35 Years Later" (for my mother). [RiverS] (36) 92, p. 32.
"The Pope's Poems" (tr. of Nicanor Parra). [Antaeus] (69) Aut 92, p. 64-65.
"Upon Your Return to Peru" (for Jose-Luis). [RiverS] (36) 92, p. 33-34.
5111. RAAB, Lawrence
"For You" (for Judy). [ThRiPo] (39/40) 92-93, p. 202.
"The Garden." [Nat] (254:9) 9 Mr 92, p. 314.
"Looking at a Book of Pictures by Caspar David Friedrich." [Shen] (42:2) Sum 92, p. 82-83.
"The Lost Things." [Poetry] (160:3) Je 92, p. 144.
"Magic Problems." [Shen] (42:2) Sum 92, p. 83-84.
"On the Island." [ThRiPo] (39/40) 92-93, p. 203-204.
"The Peonies on My Desk." [Poetry] (160:3) Je 92, p. 143.
"The Room." [ThRiPo] (39/40) 92-93, p. 200-201.
"What He Thought About the Party." [Poetry] (160:5) Ag 92, p. 270-271.
"The Witch's Story." [ThRiPo] (39/40) 92-93, p. 201-202.
5112. RABBITT, Thomas
"For Those Who Will Live Forever." [ThRiPo] (39/40) 92-93, p. 206.
"My Father's Watch." [ThRiPo] (39/40) 92-93, p. 204-205.
"Pig, a Biography." [OhioR] (48) 92, p. 34.
"The Protestant Ethic & the Museum at Moundville." [OhioR] (48) 92, p. 35.
"Tortoise." [ThRiPo] (39/40) 92-93, p. 205.
5113. RABINOWITZ, Anna
"Art-Crazy Old Man." [Confr] (50) Fall 92, p. 266.
"Auld Lang Syne." [HampSPR] Wint 92, p. 38.
"The Crossing." [CumbPR] (12:1) Fall 92, p. 58-59.
"Deep Hems." [HampSPR] Wint 92, p. 39.
"In the Regard of Elephants." [LullwaterR] (3:3) Sum 92, p. 12.
"Limited Visibility." [DenQ] (26:4) Spr 92, p. 57-58.
"Syllables." [Epoch] (41:3) 92, p. 397.
"Without." [Epoch] (41:3) 92, p. 396.
5114. RABINOWITZ, Sima
"Against Gravity." [ChironR] (11:4) Wint 92, p. 44.
"Spellcheck." [EvergreenC] (7:2) Sum-Fall 92, p. 54-55.
"Table Talk." [EvergreenC] (7:2) Sum-Fall 92, p. 52-53.
5115. RACHEL, Naomi
"Round of Ground, or Air or Ought." [HampSPR] Wint 92, p. 48-49.
5116. RACHLIN, Ellen
"Lemons." [Confr] (50) Fall 92, p. 269.
"Lost Pelicans." [Confr] (50) Fall 92, p. 268.
5117. RACZ, G. J.
"Ajhjfiefoeklxiuwe" (tr. of José Manuel del Pino). [SenR] (22:1) Spr 92, p. 47-48.

"Chambord Castle" (tr. of José Manuel del Pino). [SenR] (22:1) Spr 92, p. 44-46.
5118. RADAVICH, David
"Abe Lincoln on Donahue." [WillowR] (19) Spr 92, p. 26.
"Auto-Righteousness." [Light] (1) Spr 92, p. 20.
5119. RADER, Judith
"Corn Maiden." [SpiritSH] (57) Spr-Sum 92, p. 41.
"Dogs in the Sheep." [SpiritSH] (57) Spr-Sum 92, p. 39.
"Green Father." [SpiritSH] (57) Spr-Sum 92, p. 40.
5120. RADIGAN, John
"The Frost Giants." [Blueline] (13) 92, p. 76.
5121. RADIN, Doris
"Journey." [Vis] (38) 92, p. 22.
5122. RADJKOEMAR, Asha
"Poem: Je baadde naast de put." [LitR] (35:4) Sum 92, p. 618.
"Poem: you were bathing" (tr. from the Dutch). [LitR] (35:4) Sum 92, p. 589.
5123. RADNER, Rebecca
"The Flight." [Iowa] (22:1) Wint 92, p. 183.
5124. RADNOTI, Miklós
"Fragment" (tr. by Emery George). [Nimrod] (35:2) Spr-Sum 92, p. 30.
"I Cannot Know" (tr. by Emery George). [Nimrod] (35:2) Spr-Sum 92, p. 29.
"Nem Tudhatom." [Nimrod] (35:2) Spr-Sum 92, p. 28.
5125. RAE, Mary
"Caruso (1873-1921)." [Hellas] (3:1) Spr 92, p. 43.
5126. RAFFA, Elissa
"Three Rages." [EvergreenC] (7:2) Sum-Fall 92, p. 68-71.
5127. RAFFEL, Burton
"A Hard Mortality to Handle." [LitR] (35:3) Spr 92, p. 324.
5128. RAFFERTY, Charles
"The Bog Shack." [WestB] (30) 92, p. 57.
"Christmas Lights." [Outbr] (23) 92, p. 49.
"Courtship." [Vis] (39) 92, p. 37-38.
"Finding Her." [Parting] (5:2) Wint 92-93, p. 2.
"First Kiss." [Vis] (39) 92, p. 37.
"The Great Blue Heron." [RagMag] (10:2) 92, p. 34.
"Hooky." [Outbr] (23) 92, p. 50-51.
"The Mammoth." [RagMag] (10:2) 92, p. 35.
"Putting the Bed Together." [RagMag] (10:2) 92, p. 32-33.
"Understanding the Pond." [WestB] (30) 92, p. 56.
5129. RAFTERY, Julie
"Summer." [OnTheBus] (4:2/5:1, #10/11) 92, p. 176.
"Untitled: Frying eggs stick in the center of my brain." [OnTheBus] (4:2/5:1, #10/11) 92, p. 176.
5130. RAGAN, James
"August 19, 1991." [NewL] (58:4) 92, p. 148-149.
"The Birth of God (from an Early Photograph)." [Nimrod] (35:2) Spr-Sum 92, p. 85-86.
"The Dogs of China." [NewL] (58:4) 92, p. 147.
"Dreaming a Flood of Conscience." [Nimrod] (35:2) Spr-Sum 92, p. 87.
5131. RAHIM, Jennifer
"Meditations Upon the Word." [LitR] (35:4) Sum 92, p. 563-564.
"Rules for Initiating a Citizen." [LitR] (35:4) Sum 92, p. 561-562.
"Sight." [LitR] (35:4) Sum 92, p. 560.
5132. RAINE, Craig
"In Modern Dress." [AntR] (50:1/2) Wint-Spr 92, p. 352-353.
"A Martian Sends a Postcard Home." [Jacaranda] (6:1/2) Wint-Spr 92, p. 4-5.
"Muse." [Jacaranda] (6:1/2) Wint-Spr 92, p. 2-3.
"Watching From the Wings." [Jacaranda] (6:1/2) Wint-Spr 92, p. 1.
5133. RAISON, Philip
"Demolition of the Delaware County Courthouse." [CapeR] (27:1) Spr 92, p. 41.
5134. RAIZISS, Sonia
"Cocktail Aquarium." [Poetry] (159:4) Ja 92, p. 214-215.
5135. RAJEC, Elizabeth Molnar
"Muteness" (tr. of Joli Gadanyi). [Confr] (48/49) Spr-Sum 92, p. 219.
5136. RAJEEVAN, Savitri
"The Slant" (tr. by Ayyappa Paniker and Arlene Zide). [ChiR] (38:1/2) 92, p. 164-165.

5137. RAKOSI, Carl
"Americana." [Zyzzyva] (8:3) Fall 92, p. 49.
"Annotations." [NewAW] (10) Fall 92, p. 21.
"Drunkard's Alley." [Sulfur] (12:2, #31) Fall 92, p. 200-201.
"Epitaph on the Short Form." [NewAW] (10) Fall 92, p. 23.
"In the Poet's Eye." [Sulfur] (12:2, #31) Fall 92, p. 200.
"Little People Sailing on Words." [NewAW] (10) Fall 92, p. 20.
"Meditation." [Conjunc] (19) 92, p. 121.
"Minimal Village." [Sulfur] (12:2, #31) Fall 92, p. 201.
"Museum of Historical Objects: New Acquisition." [Thrpny] (51) Fall 92, p. 34.
"Narrative of the Image." [Conjunc] (19) 92, p. 119-120.
"The New World." [Conjunc] (19) 92, p. 120.
"Observation." [Talisman] (9) Fall 92, p. 11.
"Ode to a Nightingale." [Talisman] (9) Fall 92, p. 11.
"The Realists." [NewAW] (10) Fall 92, p. 22.
"Shakespearian Street." [Talisman] (8) Spr 92, p. 4.
5138. RALSTON, Jim
"Balancing on the Wind." [Sun] (197) Ap 92, p. 19.
5139. RAMANUJAN, A. K.
"American Tourist" (tr. of B. C. Ramachandra Sharma, using the author's English version). [ChiR] (38:1/2) 92, p. 67.
"Butcher's Tao." [ChiR] (38:1/2) 92, p. 208-209.
"Elegy." [ChiR] (38:1/2) 92, p. 206-207.
"Poem: When I was groping for a new poem" (tr. of Pratibha Nandkumar). [ChiR] (38:1/2) 92, p. 9-10.
"To Mother" (tr. of S. Usha). [ChiR] (38:1/2) 92, p. 162-163.
5140. RAMER, Maura
"The Turtles of Kahalu'u Bay." [ChamLR] (10/11) Spr-Fall 92, p. 72.
RAMEY, Debra El
See El RAMEY, Debra
RAMIREZ de ARELANO NOLLA, Olga
See NOLLA, Olga Ramirez de Arelano
5141. RAMKE, Bin
"An Algebra of Innocence." [NewAW] (10) Fall 92, p. 103.
"The Consolations of Grammar." [Shen] (42:3) Fall 92, p. 65.
"Tricks." [SouthernR] (28:4) Aut, O 92, p. 897-898.
"The Uses of Enchantment — Bruno Bettelheim." [AmerV] (26) Spr 92, p. 104.
5142. RAMMELKAMP, Charles
"Confessions of a Rapist." [Pearl] (16) Fall 92, p. 8.
5143. RAMNATH, S.
"After the Victory Parade." [Gypsy] (18) 92, p. 149-150.
"Death of a Traitor." [Lactuca] (16) Ag 92, p. 37.
"A Different Life." [Epiphany] (3:3) Jl (Sum) 92, p. 184.
"Of One Good Woman." [Epiphany] (3:3) Jl (Sum) 92, p. 185.
"Opening a Window." [Epiphany] (3:3) Jl (Sum) 92, p. 186.
"Sestina." [Lactuca] (16) Ag 92, p. 36-37.
"Soon Wind Will Sway." [ChironR] (11:1) Spr 92, p. 22.
RAMOS ROSA, António
See ROSA, António Ramos
5144. RAMSEY, Martha
"Now." [Boulevard] (7:1, #19) Spr 92, p. 188.
5145. RAMSEY, Paul
"Bicycling Sequence." [ManhatPR] (14) [92?], p. 26.
"The Clock on the Beach." [FourQ] (6:2) Fall 92, p. 29.
"Fuel." [FourQ] (6:1) Spr 92, p. 37.
"In Memory of Howard Nemerov." [PoetC] (23:3) Spr 92, p. 25.
"Lute Song, After a Parting: A Sonnet." [Sparrow] (59) S 92, p. 29.
"Postcard." [PoetC] (23:3) Spr 92, p. 25.
"A Riddle." [Light] (2) Sum 92, p. 7.
5146. RAMSEY,William
"The Death of Gérard de Nerval." [Hellas] (3:1) Spr 92, p. 52.
"Monsieur Transitive." [Hellas] (3:1) Spr 92, p. 51.
5147. RAND, Harry
"Concerning Men and Women." [AmerPoR] (21:5) S-O 92, p. 47.
"Nazi Poem." [AmerPoR] (21:5) S-O 92, p. 47.
"Omit nothing." [AmerPoR] (21:5) S-O 92, p. 47.

5148. RANDALL, D'Arcy
"Giverny." [QW] (34) Wint-Spr 92, p. 89.
"Portraits of Mary Cassatt." [MalR] (101) Wint92, p. 53-63.
5149. RANDALL, Deborah
"The Peat Cutter." [Verse] (8:3/9:1) Wint-Spr 92, p. 102.
5150. RANDALL, Margaret
"I Also Sing of Myself" (tr. of Soleida Ríos). [LitR] (35:4) Sum 92, p. 464.
"I Want the Words Back" (for Ruth Salvaggio). [Calyx] (14:2) Wint 92-93, p. 6-9.
"Of the Sierra" (tr. of Soleida Ríos). [LitR] (35:4) Sum 92, p. 463.
5151. RANDOLPH, Robert (Robert M.)
"Old Stove Dance Hall, Circa 1967." [MidAR] (12:2) 92, p. 41-43.
"R. Cory in Winter." [Poetry] (161:3) D 92, p. 151.
"Today's Poet" (tr. of Eero Suvilehto, w. the author). [Nimrod] (35:2) Spr-Sum 92, p. 51.
"A Woman." [LullwaterR] (4:1) Fall 92, p. 39.
5152. RANDOLPH, Sarah
"Distance." [Iowa] (22:3) Fall 92, p. 114.
"Interior." [Iowa] (22:3) Fall 92, p. 114.
5153. RANKIN, Paula
"Bedtime Story." [ThRiPo] (39/40) 92-93, p. 208.
"Fifteen." [ThRiPo] (39/40) 92-93, p. 207.
"For the Obese." [ThRiPo] (39/40) 92-93, p. 209-210.
"To the House Ghost." [ThRiPo] (39/40) 92-93, p. 206.
"Two Lovers on Bridge in Winter." [ThRiPo] (39/40) 92-93, p. 208-209.
5154. RANKIN, Rush
"Wise Men." [PoetL] (87:1) Spr 92, p. 27.
"The Women of Maine." [ThRiPo] (39/40) 92-93, p. 210-213.
5155. RANKOVIC, Catherine
"Sonnet #3." [13thMoon] (10:1/2) 92, p. 50.
5156. RANNEY, Michael
"Negative Dreamer." [Zyzzyva] (8:4) Wint 92, p. 123-124.
5157. RANVILLE, Kevin
"Behind the Veil of Dreams." Sparks! Writing by High School Students (1:1), a supplement to [PraF] (13:4, #61) Wint 92-93, p. 26.
5158. RANZONI, Pat
"Housekeeping of a Kind." [SpoonRQ] (17:1/2) Wint-Spr 92, p. 17.
5159. RAO, Narayana
"White Paper" (tr. of Nara). [ChiR] (38:1/2) 92, p. 150.
5160. RAO, R. Raj
"Only Connect." [JamesWR] (9:3) Spr 92, p. 1.
5161. RAO, Velcheru Narayana
"For the Lord of the Animals" (Excerpt, tr. of Dhurjati, w. Hank Heifetz). [Trans] (26) Spr 92, p. 119-120.
5162. RAPANT, Larry
"To Kill a Very Small Bug in January." [PassN] (13:1) Sum 92, p. 30.
5163. RAPP, John
"The Man Leaned." [SouthernPR] (32:1) Spr 92, p. 25.
5164. RAPPLEYE, Greg
"The Salmon Factory Sestina." [Parting] (5:1) Sum 92, p. 35-36.
5165. RAS, Barbara
"Low Planes." [MassR] (23:1) Spr 92, p. 133-134.
5166. RASH, Ron
"The Barn." [SoCarR] (25:1) Fall 92, p. 32.
"Stanley Fish in the Afterlife." [SoCarR] (24:2) Spr 92, p. 116.
5167. RASHID, Ian Iqbal
"A Pass to India." [CanLit] (132) Spr 92, p. 7.
5168. RATCLIFFE, Eric
"Deafness Is a Handicap." [SoCoast] (12) Ja 92, p. 54.
5169. RATCLIFFE, Stephen
"Paris, Friday." [Talisman] (9) Fall 92, p. 188.
"Poem in Prose" (Excerpts). [Avec] (5:1) 92, p. 135-136.
"Shortly After 21." [Talisman] (9) Fall 92, p. 188.
5170. RATH, Ramakanta
"A Love Poem" (tr. by the author). [ChiR] (38:1/2) 92, p. 76.
"A Poem for Sriradha" (tr. by the author). [ChiR] (38:1/2) 92, p. 74-75.

RATOLLO, A. de
See DeRATOLLO, A.
5171. RATZLAFF, Keith
"My Students Against the Cemetery Pines." [PoetryNW] (33:4) Wint 92-93, p. 18 - 19.
5172. RAVEN, Arlene
"Colored." [LitR] (36:1) Fall 92, p. 31-34.
5173. RAWKINREC, Iam
"Do Chimpanzees See the Universe." [ChironR] (11:1) Spr 92, p. 25.
"Getting Well Altitude." [NewYorkQ] (49) 92, p. 63.
"Silo of Seed." [NewYorkQ] (48) 92, p. 61.
"Things I Wanted to Do." [NewYorkQ] (47) 92, p. 68.
5174. RAWLINGS, Jane B.
"1,000,000,000,000,000,000,000." [US1] (26/27) 92, p. 17.
"Colophon." [JlNJPo] (14:1) Spr 92, p. 14.
"Directions." [JlNJPo] (14:1) Spr 92, p. 13.
5175. RAWLINS, Susan
"Letting Go and Holding." [PoetC] (23:2) Wint 92, p. 19-20.
"Way to Go." [PoetC] (23:2) Wint 92, p. 21-22.
5176. RAWORTH, Tom
"Survival." [WestCL] (26:1, #7) Spr 92, p. 7-14.
5177. RAWSON, Eric
"Man with a Gun at the Palmer Club." [CreamCR] (16:2) Fall 92, p. 60.
"Nude Finally Unfinished" (in the spirit of Marcel Duchamp). [CreamCR] (16:2) Fall 92, p. 58-59.
5178. RAWSON, Joanna
"Moment's Notice." [AmerPoR] (21:1) Ja-F 92, p. 31.
"Samaritan." [AmerPoR] (21:1) Ja-F 92, p. 32.
"Self-portraits by Frida Kahlo." [AmerPoR] (21:1) Ja-F 92, p. 31.
5179. RAY, David
"After Whitman." [FreeL] (9) Wint 92, p. 32.
"Holladay's Sin." [Amelia] (6:4, #19) 92, p. 16-17.
"Instead of Roses." [ColEng] (53:6) O 91, p. 665.
"The Picture Taken by the Lover None of Her Friends Ever Met." [PoetC] (23:3) Spr 92, p. 12-13.
"Spies." [NewL] (58:4) 92, p. 128-130.
"Suite for Ray and Tess." [Footwork] 92, p. 13-14.
"Toward the Smile" (for Brian Turner). [ArtfulD] (22/23) 92, p. 73.
"World War II" (for Maurice Gee, New Zealand novelist). [NewL] (58:4) 92, p. 130-131.
5180. RAY, Judy
"Deep Eddy" (Austin, Texas). [Footwork] 92, p. 43.
5181. RAY, Sunil B.
"Another Country" (tr. of Nabaneeta Dev Sen, w. Carolyne Wright and the author). [Agni] (36) 92, p. 214.
"Room" (tr. of Nabaneeta Dev Sen, w. Carolyne Wright). [ChiR] (38:1/2) 92, p. 17.
"So Many Crazy Blue Hills" (tr. of Nabaneeta Dev Sen, w. Carolyne Wright). [ChiR] (38:1/2) 92, p. 18-19.
5182. RAYMOND, Clarinda Harriss
"The Year Nears Monopause." [Kalliope] (15:1) 92, p. 4.
5183. READING, Peter
"Perduta Gente" (Excerpts). [Conjunc] (19) 92, p. 9-14.
5184. REAGLER, Robin
"The Drowners." [SouthernPR] (32:2) Fall 92, p. 41.
"Nocturne." [ChironR] (11:4) Wint 92, p. 42.
"Red Rhythms." [ChironR] (11:4) Wint 92, p. 44.
5185. REAMS, James
"Para Siempre de Puntillas" (tr. by Carlos García). [Nuez] (4:10/11) 92, p. 25.
5186. RECIPUTI, Natalie
"From His Daughter." [BellArk] (8:2) Mr-Ap 92, p. 3.
"Here Again Is Blue Spring." [BellArk] (8:1) Ja-F 92, p. 21.
"Old Poem Refinished." [BellArk] (8:1) Ja-F 92, p. 21.
"Recalling Helen." [BellArk] (8:1) Ja-F 92, p. 21.
"Recalling Helen" (corrected reprint). [BellArk] (8:2) Mr-Ap 92, p. 3.
"Sheba on the Stoop." [BellArk] (8:3) My-Je 92, p. 22.
"Snapshot." [BellArk] (8:1) Ja-F 92, p. 21.

5187. RECTOR, Liam
"Working Wrong." [Agni] (36) 92, p. 14-19.
RED, Rockin'
See ROCKIN' RED
5188. RED HAWK
"2 Ways of Crossing the Creek." [OnTheBus] (4:2/5:1, #10/11) 92, p. 177-178.
"The Art of Dying." [OnTheBus] (4:2/5:1, #10/11) 92, p. 177.
"Master, Master, Lord of the Dance." [Atlantic] (269:3) Mr 92, p. 81.
5189. REDDAWAY, Darlene
"Money" (tr. of Aleksei Parshchikov, w. Michael Palmer). [Conjunc] (19) 92, p. 79 - 82.
5190. REDEKOP, Fred
"Rivers." [SouthernPR] (32:1) Spr 92, p. 65-66.
5191. REDGROVE, Peter
"At the Butterfly Farm." [ManhatR] (6:2) Fall 92, p. 31.
"Blake and Smells." [PoetryUSA] (24) 92, p. 36.
"Climax Forest." [GrandS] (11:2, #42) 92, p. 190-191.
"Eve's Apple." [ParisR] (34:122) Spr 92, p. 91-93.
"Getting the Tree Ready." [PoetryUSA] (24) 92, p. 36.
"His Idea of Glory." [ManhatR] (6:2) Fall 92, p. 30.
"His Upbringing." [PoetryUSA] (24) 92, p. 37.
"Ironing Ancestors." [PoetryUSA] (24) 92, p. 34.
"Lecheries." [Stand] (33:2) Spr 92, p. 59.
"Lofty & Sally." [Stand] (33:2) Spr 92, p. 58.
"The Monster-Scent" (War Surplus Battleship Sold to Frankenstein for Laboratory). [ManhatR] (6:2) Fall 92, p. 25-29.
"Not Herself Eve." [PoetryUSA] (24) 92, p. 37.
"Orphelia." [PoetryUSA] (24) 92, p. 36.
"A Passing Cloud." [ManhatR] (6:2) Fall 92, p. 32-33.
"The Priestesses." [PoetryUSA] (24) 92, p. 35.
"Sniffing Tom." [PoetryUSA] (24) 92, p. 37.
"Tree." [ParisR] (34:122) Spr 92, p. 90-91.
"The Witch." [PoetryUSA] (24) 92, p. 37.
5192. REDGROVE, Zoë
"Haiku." [PoetryUSA] (24) 92, p. 33.
5193. REDHILL, Michael
"Deck Building." [PoetryC] (12:3/4) Jl 92, p. 40.
"Harvest." [PoetryC] (12:3/4) Jl 92, p. 40.
5194. REDMOND, Eugene B.
"Face to Face with the Blues." [Eyeball] (1) 92, p. 10-11.
5195. REECE, Spencer
"Autumn Song." [RagMag] (10:1) 92, p. 25.
"Stars." [RagMag] (10:1) 92, p. 24.
REED, Alison T. (Alison Touster)
See TOUSTER-REED, Alison
5196. REED, Jeremy
"Seven Admissions." [ParisR]] (34:124) Fall 92, p. 173-174.
"Taxi to the End of the World." [ParisR]] (34:124) Fall 92, p. 174-175.
"Underground." [KenR] (NS 14:3) Sum 92, p. 147.
"You Were Wearing Black." [KenR] (NS 14:3) Sum 92, p. 146.
5197. REED, John R.
"Huron Night." [CentR] (36:3) Fall 92, p. 537.
"Walking at Night by the Lake." [CentR] (36:3) Fall 92, p. 536.
"Woman Combing Her Hair." [ManhatPR] (14) [92?], p. 53.
5198. REEDER, Kathryn
"Giacometti's Woman." [Confr] (50) Fall 92, p. 275.
5199. REES, Elizabeth (Elizabeth Rose)
"Hanina, After Lebanon." [Turnstile] (3:2) 92, p. 23-24.
"Landscape with Snow." [LouisL] (9:1) Spr 92, p. 67-68.
"Ohm Poem." [ChatR] (12:2) Wint 92, p. 65-66.
"Running to the Grocery with Mark." [Pequod] (34) 92, p. 51.
5200. REESE, Steven
"Dream House." [PoetryNW] (33:1) Spr 92, p. 32-33.
"If You Lived Here." [WestB] (30) 92, p. 21.
"One Hallow's Even." [PoetryNW] (33:1) Spr 92, p. 31-32.
"The Thick of It" (GRC, 1918-1991). [WestB] (30) 92, p. 20.

"A Twenty." [PoetryNW] (33:1) Spr 92, p. 33-34.

5201. REEVE, Dave
"He Didn't Blink." [ChironR] (11:3) Aut 92, p. 9.
"Kit's Bar." [ChironR] (11:3) Aut 92, p. 9.
"Nearing Draft Induction, 1966." [ChironR] (11:3) Aut 92, p. 9.

5202. REEVE, F. D.
"And so, one day, my country did rise up" (tr. of Evgeny Khramov). [SenR] (22:1) Spr 92, p. 39.
"Catching Up." [AmerPoR] (21:6) N-D 92, p. 32.
"Five Drops of Sky" (tr. of Andrei Voznesensky). [AmerPoR] (21:1) Ja-F 92, p. 48.
"Goldfish at Sunrise." [AmerPoR] (21:6) N-D 92, p. 32.
"Moscow, Tatyana's Day." [AmerPoR] (21:6) N-D 92, p. 32.
"My love, a letter, a letter from me to you" (tr. of Evgeny Khramov). [SenR] (22:1) Spr 92, p. 38.
"Salt Ash." [NoDaQ] (60:1) Wint 92, p. 69-70.

5203. REEVES, Elena
"Collage" (Excerpts, tr. of Jaime Sabines). [InterPR] (18:1) Spr 92, p. 11-15.

5204. REEVES, Ramona
"Firstborn." [ManhatPR] (14) [92?], p. 11.

5205. REFFE, Candice
"Again in the Round Room." [Ploughs] (18:4) Wint 92-93, p. 41.
"Indian Summer." [Ploughs] (18:4) Wint 92-93, p. 42.
"Provincetown: Invocation." [Agni] (35) 92, p. 247-248.
"Salamander." [Agni] (35) 92, p. 249.
"What Glows." [Ploughs] (18:4) Wint 92-93, p. 43.

5206. REGE, P. S.
"Questions" (tr. by Vinay Dharwadker). [ChiR] (38:1/2) 92, p. 42-43.

5207. REHM, Pam
"A Man Sets Sail with the Fair Wind of Hope." [Sulfur] (12:1, #30) Spr 92, p. 122 - 125.

5208. REIBETANZ, John
"Earth Cellar." [CanLit] (134) Aut 92, p. 98.
"Gibraltar Point" (4 selections). [Quarry] (41:2) Spr 92, p. 35-44.
"Treasure Islands." [AntigR] (91) Fall 92, p. 135-136.

5209. REICHARD, William
"Cost of Living." [ChironR] (11:4) Wint 92, p. 42.
"For Natalie." [BellArk] (8:3) My-Je 92, p. 20.
"Fort Collins, Colorado." [BellArk] (8:3) My-Je 92, p. 20.
"Oragami." [JamesWR] (9:2) Wint 92, p. 11.
"What We Step Across." [BellArk] (8:3) My-Je 92, p. 20.

5210. REID, Alastair
"Near-Sighted" (tr. of Louise van Santen). [Trans] (26) Spr 92, p. 45.

5211. REID, Catherine
"Cold Cure." [GreenMR] (NS 5:2) Spr-Sum 92, p. 96-97.

5212. REID, Jamie
"The Awakening." [WestCL] (26:3, #9) Wint 92-93, p. 63-64.
"Cairo." [WestCL] (26:3, #9) Wint 92-93, p. 66.
"Glass Town." [WestCL] (26:3, #9) Wint 92-93, p. 65.
"The Man Whose Path Was on Fire 1." [WestCL] (26:3, #9) Wint 92-93, p. 59-60.
"One says I am." [WestCL] (26:3, #9) Wint 92-93, p. 61-62.

5213. REID, Joan
"January Umbrage." [MoodySI] (27) Spr 92, p. 34.

5214. REID, Monty
"Writing-On-Stone." [WestCL] (26:2, #8) Fall 92, p. 23-30.

5215. REIDEL, James
"Cicadas." [NewYorker] (68:21) 13 Jl 92, p. 58.
"The year is like a year a thousand years ago" (from "Under the Iron of the Moon," tr. of Thomas Bernhard). [ArtfulD] (22/23) 92, p. 30.

5216. REIFF, Sandra
"Never Nowhere." [LitR] (25:2) Wint 92, p. 281.
"One of Them." [LitR] (25:2) Wint 92, p. 280.

5217. REIMER, David
"Blaze King of Montana." [CutB] (38) Sum 92, p. 96-97.

5218. REINER, Christopher
"Doing Good." [Avec] (5:1) 92, p. 103-105.

5219. REIS, Donna
"Gail Exploits Liver Paté." [NewYorkQ] (49) 92, p. 64.
5220. REISS, James
"Carnegie Hill." [Pequod] (33) 92, p. 192.
"Game." [Nat] (255:12) 19 O 92, p. 448.
5221. REITER, David (David P.)
"Getting Away" (for Bob Pinter). [AntigR] (89) Spr 92, p. 140.
"Making the Bed." [Dandel] (19:1) 92, p. 23.
"Sea Gypsies." [Stand] (33:2) Spr 92, p. 140-141.
"Stanley Park Seawalk." [Amelia] (7:1, #20) 92, p. 156-157.
"Sunset at Point Grey." [Amelia] (7:1, #20) 92, p. 157-158.
5222. REITER, Jendi
"Burnt Norite" (or, If T.S. Eliot had been a chemist). [HangL] (61) 92, p. 58-59.
5223. REITER, Thomas
"High Plains Photography." [PoetryNW] (33:4) Wint 92-93, p. 20-21.
"The Landloper." [SouthernHR] (26:2) Spr 92, p. 142-143.
"Rant Findlay and the Floating Town." [GettyR] (5:4) Aut 92, p. 686-688.
"Serials." [PoetryNW] (33:4) Wint 92-93, p. 19-20.
"Tick." [Ascent] (17:1) Fall 92, p. 27.
5224. REJZEK, Jan
"Midnight" (tr. by Dominika Winterová and Richard Katrovas). [NewOR] (19:3/4) Fall-Wint 92, p. 24.
5225. REMINGTON, Rebekah
"A Garden of Pathos." [Iowa] (22:3) Fall 92, p. 180-181.
"The Passing of Barbed Wire." [MichQR] (31:3) Sum 92, p. 323.
5226. REMOTO, Danton
"Candles" (Sto. Domingo Church, 1984). [Manoa] (4:1) Spr 92, p. 71.
"To Carlos Orchida." [Manoa] (4:1) Spr 92, p. 72.
5227. REMPLE, Margaret
"George Bush Returns From Hell to Live and Work in a Prosthesis Factory." [MidAR] (12:2) 92, p. 48-49.
5228. REMSKI, Matthew
"Canadian Poem." [PoetryC] (12:3/4) Jl 92, p. 29.
"Deducant Te Angeli" (for Luciano, in memory of his father). [Quarry] (41:4) Fall 92, p. 24.
"Good Friday." [Quarry] (41:4) Fall 92, p. 23.
"Nocturne." [PoetryC] (12:3/4) Jl 92, p. 29.
"The Singing That Wakes Me." [PoetryC] (12:3/4) Jl 92, p. 29.
"Thanksgiving Hymn." [PoetryC] (12:3/4) Jl 92, p. 29.
5229. REMY, Philippe
"Au Jeu" (Excerpt, tr. by Michele Brondy). [Vis] (39) 92, p. 18.
"In Stain" (tr. by Michele Brondy). [Vis] (38) 92, p. 39.
5230. RENDLEMAN, Danny
"Family, Easter Portrait, 1952." [CutB] (37) Wint 92, p. 91-92.
5231. RENDON, José
"Bad Memory." [Americas] (19:2) Sum 91, p. 67-68.
"Letter from Laredo." [Americas] (19:2) Sum 91, p. 71-72.
"To Maribel on Her Engagement to a Long Time Boyfriend." [Americas] (19:2) Sum 91, p. 69-70.
5232. RENDRICK, Bernice
"Amazing Relief." [Lactuca] (15) Mr 92, p. 43.
"Reconciliation." [Lactuca] (15) Mr 92, p. 43-44.
5233. RENIKER, Sherry
"Cherry-Falling-Moon Maze" (tr. of Tsuneko Yoshikawa). [Noctiluca] (1:1) Spr 92, p. 50-51.
"Etude en Janvier." [Noctiluca] (1:2) Wint 92 [on cover: Wint 93], p. 23.
"Japan Moment (#888)" (Kawasaki, Spring '91). [Noctiluca] (1:1) Spr 92, p. 49.
"Town of Complete Strangers" (tr. of Yoshikawa Tsuneko). [Noctiluca] (1:2) Wint 92 [on cover: Wint 93], p. 21-23.
5234. RENKL, Margaret
"Vespers" (for my brother). [ManhatPR] (14) [92?], p. 37.
5235. RENNERT-CARTER, Roberta
"The Fruit That Falls." [Calyx] (14:1) Sum 92, p. 48-49.
"The Hair, the Harmony & the Handout." [OnTheBus] (4:2/5:1, #10/11) 92, p. 179.

5236. RENSOLI LALIGA, Lourdes
"Vuelco de la Ficción y de la Bruma" (A Carlos Miguel, a Jacobo Machover, a Felipe Lázaro, a Pancho Vives, a José Mario). [Nuez] (4:12) 92, p. 20.
"Woodstock" (A los nacidos entre 1945 y 1956 incluyendo a los renegados). [LindLM] (11:4) D 92, p. 27.
5237. REPP, John
"Five Dollars." [Journal] (16:2) Fall-Wint 92, p. 75-76.
"Wedding." [LitR] (35:3) Spr 92, p. 395.
5238. RESNICOW, Herbert
"If Money Makes the Mare — Go!" [Light] (4) Wint 92-93, p. 17.
"Mutterings Over a Kitchen Sink." [Light] (3) Aut 92, p. 22.
5239. RESS, Lisa
"Crossing the Lawn, the Stars." [SycamoreR] (4:1) Wint 92, p. 38-39.
"Sod Busting." [SpoonRQ] (17:1/2) Wint-Spr 92, p. 53.
"With Kafka." [ColR] (9:1) Spr-Sum 92, p. 149.
5240. RETALLACK, Joan
"After Rimages" (Excerpt). [PaintedB] (46) 92, p. 25.
"Afterimages" (Selection: "Journal of a Lunar Eclipse"). [Avec] (5:1) 92, p. 16-21.
RETAMAR, Roberto Fernández
See FERNANDEZ RETAMAR, Roberto
5241. RETSOV, Samuel
"Blue Sweater." [Talisman] (9) Fall 92, p. 172.
"He Likes to Read." [Talisman] (9) Fall 92, p. 173.
"In Your Words." [PoetryUSA] (24) 92, p. 24.
"Salt." [Talisman] (9) Fall 92, p. 172.
"Wheel of Fortune." [Talisman] (8) Spr 92, p. 116-117.
5242. REVARD, Carter
"Driving in Oklahoma." [Jacaranda] (6:1/2) Wint-Spr 92, p. 85.
5243. REVELL, Donald
"The Hotel Sander." [ThRiPo] (39/40) 92-93, p. 213-214.
"In Company." [ParisR] (34:123) Sum 92, p. 86-92.
"The Lame One." [Boulevard] (7:1, #19) Spr 92, p. 169-170.
"The Other the Wings." [ThRiPo] (39/40) 92-93, p. 214-215.
"Polygamy." [AmerPoR] (21:3) My-Je 92, p. 47.
"The Secessions on Loan." [Agni] (36) 92, p. 128-129.
"Stilling." [Agni] (36) 92, p. 130.
"Why and Why Now." [NewAW] (10) Fall 92, p. 81.
5244. REVERDY, Pierre
"On the Other Side" (tr. by Brent Duffin and Catherine Berg). [Vis] (38) 92, p. 19.
REVUELTA, Gutierrez
See GUTIERREZ REVUELTA, Pedro
REVUELTA, Pedro Gutierrez
See GUTIERREZ REVUELTA, Pedro
5245. REWAK, William J.
"The Hardest." [WritersF] (18) 92, p. 117.
"This Sad Raccoon." [WritersF] (18) 92, p. 116.
REYES, Vilma Maldonado
See MALDONADO-REYES, Vilma
REYK, Paul van
See Van REYK, Paul
5246. REYNOLDS, Craig A.
"In Hospital." [Art&Und] (1:4) Jl-Ag 92, p. 9.
5247. RHETT, Kathryn
"Arc." [GrandS] (11:2, #42) 92, p. 79.
"I Am the Elder." [GrandS] (11:2, #42) 92, p. 80.
5248. RHOADES, Lisa
"Fill." [OxfordM] (8:2) Fall-Wint 92, p. 43.
"Like Rain to Loosen." [OxfordM] (8:2) Fall-Wint 92, p. 44.
"Winter Apples." [PoetryE] (33) Spr 92, p. 118.
5249. RHODENBAUGH, Suzanne
"My America That Divides." [CimR] (98) Ja 92, p. 77.
5250. RHODES, Martha
"All the Soups." [VirQR] (68:4) Aut 92, p. 701-702.
"Possession." [Ploughs] (18:4) Wint 92-93, p. 180.
"Recurrent Fever." [VirQR] (68:1) Wint 92, p. 77.
"Soft Rag." [VirQR] (68:4) Aut 92, p. 703.

"Song." [VirQR] (68:4) Aut 92, p. 702.
"Sweeping the Floor." [VirQR] (68:4) Aut 92, p. 703-704.
"Without Gloves." [Ploughs] (18:4) Wint 92-93, p. 181.

5251. RIACH, Alan
"Late Spring Morning." [Verse] (9:2) Sum 92, p. 95.
"A Poem About Four Feet." [Verse] (8:3/9:1) Wint-Spr 92, p. 99.
"A Promise." [Verse] (9:2) Sum 92, p. 86.

5252. RICE, Paul
"Drinking Father." [Crazy] (42) Spr 92, p. 62-63.
"Herbs" (for Lois Baldwin McConeghey). [Crazy] (42) Spr 92, p. 60-61.
"Spring Arts Festival — Horry County, South Carolina." [Crazy] (42) Spr 92, p. 64 - 65.
"Wanting Stone." [Crucible] (28) Fall 92, p. 22-23.

5253. RICE, R. Hugh
"My Shadow." [Writer] (105:3) Mr 92, p. 23.

5254. RICH, Adrienne
"1948: Jews." [Nat] (255:18) 30 N 92, p. 674.
"An Atlas of the Difficult World" (Selection from Part I). [Nat] (255:18) 30 N 92, p. 674.
"In Those Years." [YaleR] (80:1/2) Apr 92, p. 77.
"Not Somewhere Else, But Here." [SouthwR] (77:2/3) Spr-Sum 92, p. 210-212.
"Rachel." [YaleR] (80:1/2) Apr 92, p. 78.
"Tattered Kaddish." [Nat] (255:18) 30 N 92, p. 674.
"Two Arts." [Nat] (255:18) 30 N 92, p. 674.

5255. RICH, Mark
"Body Counts." [Poem] (67) My 92, p. 65.

5256. RICH, Susanna
"The Buck" (4th Honorable Mention, 6th Annual Contest). [SoCoast] (13) Je 93 [i.e. 92], p. 26-27.

5257. RICHARD, Brad
"The Death of Little Red Cap." [NoAmR] (277:6) N-D 92, p. 50.
"Motion Series No. 10: Flight." [Asylum] (7:3/4) 92, p. 63.

5258. RICHARDS, Marilee
"Colors." [WestB] (30) 92, p. 78-79.
"Coming Apart." [HampSPR] Wint 92, p. 26.
"Gathering Material." [SpoonRQ] (17:1/2) Wint-Spr 92, p. 52.
"Lingerie Drawer." [LitR] (25:2) Wint 92, p. 282.
"Meeting the Movie Star." [CimR] (98) Ja 92, p. 83-84.
"Vagrant." [HampSPR] Wint 92, p. 27.

5259. RICHARDSON, Amy
"Be Still" (Winner, Annual Free Verse Contest, 1991). [AnthNEW] (4) 92, p. 19.

5260. RICHARDSON, Barbara
"Gansey." [Epiphany] (3:4) O (Fall) 92, p. 245.
"Palouse." [Epiphany] (3:4) O (Fall) 92, p. 244.

5261. RICHARDSON, Francis L.
"O Rrose [sic], Thou Art Sick" (for, and against, Marcel Duchamp). [WestHR] (46:1) Spr 92, p. 14-15.
"The Prodigal Son." [WestHR] (46:1) Spr 92, p. 16.

5262. RICHARDSON, James
"Anyway." [Boulevard] (7:1, #19) Spr 92, p. 167.
"Post-Romantic." [Poetry] (159:6) Mr 92, p. 337.

5263. RICHARDSON, Peter
"At the Picnic Table." [MalR] (99) Sum 92, p. 96-97.

5264. RICHARDSON, Tiffany
"A Fisherman and His Wife." [AmerV] (26) Spr 92, p. 102-103.
"Why Organize a Universe This Way?" [AmerV] (26) Spr 92, p. 100-101.

5265. RICHETTI, Peter
"After Hours." [Witness] (6:1) 92, p. 150-151.

5266. RICHEY, Joseph
"Receta para Preparar un Pueblo." [Nuez] (4:12) 92, p. 33.

5267. RICHMAN, Elliot
"A Billion Scuds Bursting Over Arles." [WindO] (56) Fall-Wint 92, p. 6.
"The Burning Cities of Desire." [CoalC] (5) My 92, p. 15.
"Give Us This Day Our Daily Bread." [SlipS] (12) 92, p. 27.
"The Informer." [SlipS] (12) 92, p. 27-28.
"Last Ferry Crossing." [HiramPoR] (51/52) Fall 91-Sum 92, p. 59.

"The Phoenix." [CoalC] (5) My 92, p. 18.
"The Sunflowers of Sullivan Ballou." [CoalC] (5) My 92, p. 15.
"The Tap of Drum for Drill and Dress Parade." [WindO] (56) Fall-Wint 92, p. 7-8.
"Victory." [WindO] (56) Fall-Wint 92, p. 5.

5268. RICHMAN, Jan
"Drug Stories." [Caliban] (11) 92, p. 128.

5269. RICHMAN, Liliane
"Budapest Vignettes, 1989." [BlackBR] (15) Spr-Sum 92, p. 10.

5270. RICHMAN, Robert
"Fall Fair, Pageant of Balloons." [YaleR] (80:4) O 92, p. 75.
"Possession." [Poetry] (159:5) F 92, p. 257.
"The Townhouse." [Salm] (96) Fall 92, p. 176.

5271. RICHMAN, Steven
"The Curator." [Poem] (68) N 92, p. 26-27.
"The Fifth Watch of a Holocaust." [Poem] (68) N 92, p. 25.
"Teddy's." [Footwork] 92, p. 50.

5272. RICHMOND, Don
"Some Stayed." [Plain] (12:3) Spr 92, p. 24.

5273. RICHMOND, Steve
"The Terrible Fact." [ChironR] (11:1) Spr 92, p. 26.

5274. RICHSTONE, Mary
"Harvest." [Light] (4) Wint 92-93, p. 12.

5275. RICHSTONE, May
"Chameleon." [Light] (2) Sum 92, p. 23.
"Chameleon." [Light] (4) Wint 92-93, p. 21.
"Food Pyramid." [Light] (4) Wint 92-93, p. 23.
"Miles Apart." [Light] (1) Spr 92, p. 27.

5276. RICHTER, Jennifer
"The Only Word We Have in Common Is *No*." [PoetL] (87:4) Wint 92-93, p. 35.

5277. RICHTER, Milan
"Hope" (tr. by Ewald Osers). [PraS] (66:4) Wint 92, p. 149-152.
"Light?" (Mehr Licht — Goethe, tr. by Ewald Osers). [PraS] (66:4) Wint 92, p. 152-153.
"Light?" (tr. by Jascha Kessler). [Jacaranda] (6:1/2) Wint-Spr 92, p. 140-141.
"Never at the Horse at Two" (tr. by Jascha Kessler and the author). [LitR] (25:2) Wint 92, p. 182.
"What You Have Written" (tr. by Ewald Osers). [PraS] (66:4) Wint 92, p. 148-149.
"What You've Written" (tr. by Jascha Kessler and the author). [LitR] (25:2) Wint 92, p. 181.

5278. RIDL, Jack
"First Cut." [PoetryE] (33) Spr 92, p. 119-120.
"Hearing the Landscape Tell the Story" (from a line by James Wright). [PassN] (13:1) Sum 92, p. 14.
"Homage to the Same Place." [FreeL] (10) Sum 92, p. 13.
"Jazz Dance for a Missing Daughter." [DenQ] (26:4) Spr 92, p. 59-61.
"Now, in Fall." [WebR] (16) Fall 92, p. 84.
"Turnpike Crossing." [WebR] (16) Fall 92, p. 83.
"Waiting for the Sculpture to Stop Breathing" (For David). [FreeL] (10) Sum 92, p. 12.

5279. RIDLAND, John
"Flutter of Laughter." [Light] (2) Sum 92, p. 20.
"Not This One." [Light] (4) Wint 92-93, p. 15.
"Some Days." [Light] (3) Aut 92, p. 24.

5280. RIEGEL, Katherine
"Walnuts." [Plain] (13:1) Fall 92, p. 30.

5281. RIEL, Steven
"The Day After Your Funeral." [JamesWR] (9:4) Sum 92, p. 7.
"Just Before" (from Triptych Within a Snapshot, 1967). [EvergreenC] (7:1) Wint-Spr 92, p. 59.

5282. RIELLY, Edward J.
"Iowa or Heaven." [Spitball] (40) Spr 92, p. 2.

5283. RIENSTRA, Debra
"Sidewalk Apocalypse." [ChrC] (109:14) 22 Ap 92, p. 421.

5284. RIFENBURGH, Daniel
"Donald Justice Before a Soft-Drink Vending Machine." [NewRep] (206:11) 16 Mr 92, p. 36.

5285. RIGG, Sharon
"Verbless Frank." [CapeR] (27:2) Fall 92, p. 43.
5286. RIGSBEE, David
"Almost You." [WillowS] (29) Wint 92, p. 82.
"La Bohème." [SouthernR] (28:3) Sum, Jl 92, p. 612.
"Differential." [Pembroke] (24) 92, p. 116.
"Heat." [NewOR] (19:1) Spr 92, p. 17-18.
"Intruder." [WilliamMR] (30) 92, p. 66-67.
"A New Business." [LitR] (35:3) Spr 92, p. 344.
"Turner's Mists." [SouthernR] (28:3) Sum, Jl 92, p. 613-614.
5287. RILEY, Joanne M.
"Finger Hymns." [Footwork] 92, p. 69.
"The Plum Tree Tenant." [Footwork] 92, p. 70.
"The Sin of the Good Thief." [Footwork] 92, p. 69.
"Winter: Sleeping in the Cathedral." [Footwork] 92, p. 70.
5288. RILEY, Michael D.
"Groundhog." [CumbPR] (11:2) Spr 92, p. 8-9.
"The Offices of Lust." [Vis] (38) 92, p. 26.
"Snow Man." [Poetry] (161:3) D 92, p. 145-146.
"Those Who Go Gently." [Farm] (9:2) Fall-Wint 92-93, p. 88.
5289. RILEY, Tom
"Artificial Intelligence." [Light] (4) Wint 92-93, p. 14.
"Changing the Earth." [Light] (1) Spr 92, p. 23.
"Solid All the Same." [Light] (2) Sum 92, p. 15.
"The Straight and Narrow." [Light] (2) Sum 92, p. 17.
5290. RILKE, Rainer Maria
"1. Again and again, never mind we know love's landscape" (tr. by Stuart Friebert). [CentR] (36:3) Fall 92, p. 534.
"2. I want to speak up, no more the worried" (tr. by Stuart Friebert). [CentR] (36:3) Fall 92, p. 534.
"The Archaic Torso of Apollo" (adaption by James Bland). [WindO] (56) Fall-Wint 92, p. 29.
"Archäischer Torso Apollos." [WindO] (56) Fall-Wint 92, p. 30.
"Blacknose Shark" (tr. by Stuart Friebert). [CentR] (36:3) Fall 92, p. 535.
"Night Drive" (tr. by Derek Mahon). [Trans] (26) Spr 92, p. 21.
5291. RINALDI, Nicholas
"The Bombing of Basra." [CapeR] (27:1) Spr 92, p. 14.
"The Bombing of Basra." [ConnPR] (11:1) 92, p. 11.
"Colonel Mahumd [i.e., Mahmud?] Naquib." [CapeR] (27:1) Spr 92, p. 15.
"Old Beggar By the Gate of Tekrit." [CarolQ] (44:3) Spr-Sum 92, p. 58.
5292. RIND, Sherry
"Among the Chosen." [PoetryNW] (33:1) Spr 92, p. 26-27.
5293. RING, Kevin
"The Kerouac and Cassady Late Show." [MoodySI] (27) Spr 92, p. 17.
5294. RINGER, Darby
"Sacraments." [BellArk] (8:2) Mr-Ap 92, p. 14.
5295. RINGER, Marinelle
"Sestina." [CimR] (101) O 92, p. 131-132.
RIORDAIN, Seán O
See O RIORDAIN, Seán
5296. RIORDAN, Maurice
"Last Call." [Verse] (9:3) Wint 92, p. 33.
5297. RIOS, Alberto
"Five Indiscretions, or." [Americas] (20:3/4) Fall-Wint 92, p. 182-186.
"On January 5, 1984, El Santo the Wrestler Died, Possibly." [Americas] (20:3/4) Fall-Wint 92, p. 187-188.
RIOS, Alexandra Newton
See NEWTON-RIOS, Alexandra
5298. RIOS, Francisco A.
"A Caín" (Plegaria y maldición en memoria de Santos Rodríguez, asesinado en Dallas, Texas, julio, 1973). [Americas] (19:2) Sum 91, p. 62-63.
"El Aborto." [Americas] (19:2) Sum 91, p. 60-61.
5299. RIOS, Soleida
"De la Sierra." [LitR] (35:4) Sum 92, p. 597-598.
"I Also Sing of Myself" (tr. by Margaret Randall). [LitR] (35:4) Sum 92, p. 464.
"Of the Sierra" (tr. by Margaret Randall). [LitR] (35:4) Sum 92, p. 463.

"Tambien Me Canto." [LitR] (35:4) Sum 92, p. 598.

RIPER, Craig van
See Van RIPER, Craig

5300. RIPTON, J. (John)
"Early Wind." [LindLM] (11:1) Mr 92, p. 8.
"Ice Moon." [LindLM] (11:1) Mr 92, p. 8.
"In Tenochtitlán*" (*Mexico City). [LitR] (35:3) Spr 92, p. 392-395.
"Up Pond." [Footwork] 92, p. 108-110.

5301. RISDON, Adrian
"Fritz" (from "The Book of Rejections"). [JamesWR] (9:3) Spr 92, p. 1.

5302. RISSEEUW-WINKEL, Ilse
"Full Moon." [LitR] (35:4) Sum 92, p. 578-579.

5303. RISTAU, Harland
"Autumn Walk." [Northeast] (5:7) Wint 92-93, p. 9.

5304. RITCHIE, Elisavietta
"Afterthought." [NewYorkQ] (48) 92, p. 86.
"At the Crossing" (Chernobyl Poems, tr. of Lyubov Sirota, w. Leonid Levin). [Calyx] (14:2) Wint 92-93, p. 70-72.
"Bedtime Stories." [AmerS] (61:1) Wint 92, p. 79-80.
"Benedictus Omnia." [NewYorkQ] (49) 92, p. 65-66.
"Burden" (Chernobyl Poems, tr. of Lyubov Sirota, w. Leonid Levin). [Calyx] (14:2) Wint 92-93, p. 66-67.
"Fate" (Triptych. Chernobyl Poems, tr. of Lyubov Sirota, w. Leonid Levin). [Calyx] (14:2) Wint 92-93, p. 73-75.
"Overflying Russia." [AmerS] (61:2) Spr 92, p. 210-212.
"Radiophobia" (Chernobyl Poems, tr. of Lyubov Sirota, w. Leonid Levin). [Calyx] (14:2) Wint 92-93, p. 68-69.
"Teatime in Leningrad." [AmerS] (61:4) Aut 92, p. 530-532.
"To Pripyat" (Chernobyl Poems, tr. of Lyubov Sirota, w. Leonid Levin). [Calyx] (14:2) Wint 92-93, p. 64-65.
"Wedding Ring Waltz." [NewYorkQ] (47) 92, p. 89.
"Your Glance Will Trip on My Shadow" (Chernobyl Poems, tr. of Lyubov Sirota, w. Leonid Levin). [Calyx] (14:2) Wint 92-93, p. 63.
"Your glance will trip on my shadow" ("Chernobyl Poems," tr. of Liubov Sirota, w. Leonid Levin). [NewYorkQ] (48) 92, p. 109.
"Zurab." [Amelia] (7:1, #20) 92, p. 36-39.

5305. RITCHINGS, Joan Drew
"Carrier." [Light] (2) Sum 92, p. 19.
"Japanese Beetle." [Light] (2) Sum 92, p. 24.
"Net." [Light] (1) Spr 92, p. 23.

5306. RITKES, Daniel
"My Glass." [OnTheBus] (4:2/5:1, #10/11) 92, p. 181.

5307. RITSOS, Yannis
"Calculated Behavior" (tr. by Minas Savvas). [Elf] (2:1) Spr 92, p. 20.
"Damp your sandals" (tr. by Amanda Baltatzi and Jose Garcia). [Vis] (39) 92, p. 39.
"The End of Donona, I and II" (tr. by Edmund Keeley). [Trans] (26) Spr 92, p. 8-10.
"Farm Woman" (tr. by Stratis Haviaras). [Trans] (26) Spr 92, p. 77-78.
"Self Sympathy" (tr. by Minas Savvas). [Elf] (2:1) Spr 92, p. 21.
"Third Series" (Selections: 10, 23, 27, 42, 48, tr. by José García and Adamantia Baltatzi). [PaintedHR] (5) Wint 92, p. 5.
"The Wood-Cutter" (tr. by Minas Savvas). [CarolQ] (44:2) Wint 92, p. 76.

5308. RITTENHOUSE, Wayne
"Neighborhood Bars." [NewYorkQ] (49) 92, p. 67.

5309. RIVARD, David
"Against Recovery." [NewEngR] (14:4) Fall 92, p. 146-147.
"Change My Evil Ways." [NewEngR] (14:4) Fall 92, p. 147-149.

5310. RIVAS, José Luis
"A Season of Paradise" (tr. by Reginald Gibbons). [TriQ] (85) Fall 92, p. 407-412.

5311. RIVERA, Diana
"Learning to Speak." [Americas] (20:3/4) Fall-Wint 92, p. 225-228.

5312. RIVERA, Etnairis
"I Travel in the Braid of Time" (extract from an untitled selection in the anthology "Inventing a Word," tr. by Julio Marzán). [LitR] (35:4) Sum 92, p. 522.
"Viajo en la Trenza del Tiempo" (A fragment from "Inventing a word"). [LitR] (35:4) Sum 92, p. 607.

RIVERA, Juan Coronel
See CORONEL RIVERA, Juan
5313. RIVERA, Silvia Tomasa
"Es la hora de las brujas." [InterPR] (18:1) Spr 92, p. 36.
"I Saw You in the Park" (tr. by Cynthia Steele). [TriQ] (85) Fall 92, p. 400.
"It is the witches' hour" (tr. by Margo Bender). [InterPR] (18:1) Spr 92, p. 47.
"What I Wouldn't Give to Know" (tr. by Cynthia Steele). [TriQ] (85) Fall 92, p. 401.
5314. RIVERO, Mario
"Lights" (tr. by Elizabeth B. Clark). [Pequod] (34) 92, p. 181.
"Smooth" (tr. by Elizabeth B. Clark). [Pequod] (34) 92, p. 180.
5315. RIVERS, Ann
"Fragile: Handle with Care." [Crucible] (28) Fall 92, p. 31-32.
5316. RIZO, Félix
"Todas las Noches." [Nuez] (4:10/11) 92, p. 37.
5317. RNO, Sung J.
"The Mounds." [ChamLR] (10/11) Spr-Fall 92, p. 51-53.
"Night." [Caliban] (11) 92, p. 92.
"Window." [Caliban] (11) 92, p. 91.
5318. ROBBINS, Anthony
"Living Is Easy." [Chelsea] (53) 92, p. 88-90.
"Many Happy Returns." [Chelsea] (53) 92, p. 91.
"Pedagogy." [NoDaQ] (60:3) Sum 92, p. 5.
"South Southwest." [Agni] (35) 92, p. 274.
5319. ROBBINS, Doren
"Myself, Strandorf, and the Beggar from the Underworld." [OnTheBus] (4:2/5:1, #10/11) 92, p. 182-184.
5320. ROBBINS, Martin
"Bottle Collector." [CimR] (99) Ap 92, p. 39-40.
"In Our Home Movies." [CimR] (99) Ap 92, p. 39.
5321. ROBBINS, Mary Susannah
"Spring, the Present." [Outbr] (23) 92, p. 37.
5322. ROBBINS, Richard
"Cul-de-Sac." [Pearl] (15) Spr-Sum 92, p. 19.
5323. ROBBINS, Tim
"Children's Bible." [HangL] (60) 92, p. 50.
"Coming In." [HangL] (60) 92, p. 49.
"Lao Tse's Butterfly." [HangL] (61) 92, p. 60.
"Progeny." [HangL] (61) 92, p. 61-62.
"Resurrection." [HangL] (60) 92, p. 51.
"You Have a Way." [HangL] (61) 92, p. 63-64.
5324. ROBERGE, Richard
"In What Was Not the North Sea." [YellowS] (41) Fall-Wint 92-93, p. 9.
5325. ROBERSON, Ed
"Aerialist Narratives" (Excerpts). [Epoch] (41:3) 92, p. 398-401.
"Ask for 'How High the Moon'" (for Nathaniel Mackey — from "Aerialist Narratives"). [Talisman] (9) Fall 92, p. 74-78.
5326. ROBERTS, Andy
"Onward Christian Soldiers." [Gypsy] (19) 92, p. 6.
"Passion." [RagMag] (10:2) 92, p. 50.
"Smiley." [BlackBR] (15) Spr-Sum 92, p. 44.
"Victorious." [HiramPoR] (51/52) Fall 91-Sum 92, p. 60.
5327. ROBERTS, Bertha
"Snow White: The Sequel." [Sun] (199) Je-Jl 92, p. 19.
5328. ROBERTS, Beth K.
"Ode to Horseshoe Crab." [BlackWR] (18:2) Spr-Sum 92, p. 104.
"Poem: He entered, saw me sitting at the table watching my wrinkled." [Poem] (67) My 92, p. 25.
"Rib Cage." [Poem] (67) My 92, p. 27.
"Thé Après Midi, Ménage à Trois." [Poem] (67) My 92, p. 26.
5329. ROBERTS, Cynthia
"Separation * Persons." [PaintedB] (46) 92, p. 32-38.
5330. ROBERTS, Jack
"Kenneth, What's the Frequency." [Boulevard] (7:2/3, #20/21) Fall 92, p. 185-187.
5331. ROBERTS, Joshua
"The Sparrow and the Winter's Nest of Snow" (w. Len Roberts). [ChiR] (38:3) 92, p. 50-51.

5332. ROBERTS, Katrina
"Troy's Baby." [NegC] (12:3) 92, p. 109-110.
5333. ROBERTS, Kevin
"The Chair." [CanLit] (134) Aut 92, p. 96-97.
"Chimo — Lion's Gate." [Descant] (23:1/2, #76/77) Spr-Sum 92, p. 108.
"Cobalt 3." [Descant] (23:1/2, #76/77) Spr-Sum 92, p. 106-107.
"No Plath Please." [Descant] (23:1/2, #76/77) Spr-Sum 92, p. 109.
5334. ROBERTS, Len
"Checking the Underwear." [HolCrit] (29:2) Ap 92, p. 17-18.
"The Distant Breath" (tr. of Géza Szöcs, w. Maria Szende). [Field] (46) Spr 92, p. 23.
"I Wanted to Arrange" (tr. of Sandor Csoori). [IndR] (15:2) Fall 92, p. 72.
"Learning about the Heart" (17 poems. Winner of the 1991 Gerald Cable Poetry Chapbook Competition). [SilverFR] (22) 92, 32 p.
"Learning Animals and Insects in Third Grade." [BostonR] (17:2) Mr-Ap 92, p. 19.
"Learning the Angels." [MichQR] (31:1) Wint 92, p. 34-35.
"Learning the Leaves." [SouthernR] (28:2) Spr, Ap 92, p. 264-266.
"Letter to the American Poet Gregory Corso" (tr. of Sándor Csoóri, w. László Vértes). [Agni] (36) 92, p. 253-255.
"The Nine Choirs." [Iowa] (22:2) Spr-Sum 92, p. 128-129.
"No Kin of Yours, Just a Friend" (tr. of Sándor Csoóri, w. Laszlo Vertes). [KenR] (NS 14:1) Wint 92, p. 86-87.
"On That Evening" (tr. of Sándor Kányádi). [NowestR] (30:3) 92, p. 45.
"The Power of Numbers." [NewEngR] (14:3) Sum 92, p. 190-191.
"Returning Home from the Flight After the War" (tr. of Sándor Csoóri). [Field] (46) Spr 92, p. 22.
"Somebody Consoles Me with a Poem" (tr. of Sándor Csoóri, w. Laszlo Vertes). [KenR] (NS 14:1) Wint 92, p. 85-86.
"The Sparrow and the Winter's Nest of Snow" (w. Joshua Roberts). [ChiR] (38:3) 92, p. 50-51.
"This and That." [QW] (35) Sum-Fall 92, p. 103-104.
"The Time Has Come" (tr. of Sandor Csoori). [PoetryE] (33) Spr 92, p. 163.
"While the Tractor Idled." [SouthernR] (28:2) Spr, Ap 92, p. 266-267.
5335. ROBERTS, Stephen R.
"Muddy Sky." [HopewellR] (4) 92, p. 27.
"Perfect Figure-Eights." [Blueline] (13) 92, p. 17.
5336. ROBERTS, Teresa Noelle
"Harvesting Basil." [BellArk] (8:1) Ja-F 92, p. 3.
"Newborn." [BellArk] (8:5) S-O 92, p. 13.
"Thaw." [BellArk] (8:1) Ja-F 92, p. 3.
"Turning the Garden." [BellArk] (8:1) Ja-F 92, p. 3.
"What the River Said, Wildflower Gorge." [BellArk] (8:1) Ja-F 92, p. 23.
"The Year's Wheel." [BellArk] (8:5) S-O 92, p. 13.
5337. ROBERTS, Tony
"The Testament of Elizabeth Elles" (1756). [Stand] (33:2) Spr 92, p. 135.
5338. ROBERTSON, Louise
"Pygmalion's Statue." [LullwaterR] (3:3) Sum 92, p. 22-23.
5339. ROBERTSON, Robin
"Affair of Kites." [SouthernR] (28:2) Spr, Ap 92, p. 304.
"The Bulls" (after Leconte de Lisle). [SouthernR] (28:2) Spr, Ap 92, p. 301.
"Fledging." [SouthernR] (28:2) Spr, Ap 92, p. 303.
"Sleeper in the Valley" (after Rimbaud). [SouthernR] (28:2) Spr, Ap 92, p. 302.
"Storm." [SouthernR] (28:2) Spr, Ap 92, p. 302-303.
5340. ROBERTSON, William
"Farm Wife." [Grain] (20:3) Fall 92, p. 113.
"Hotel Fire." [Descant] (23:3, #78) Fall 92, p. 151.
"A New BMW Is Good to Talk About." [Descant] (23:3, #78) Fall 92, p. 152.
"One Explanation." [Descant] (23:3, #78) Fall 92, p. 155.
"Something I Tell My Son." [Descant] (23:3, #78) Fall 92, p. 150.
"Somewhere Else." [Grain] (20:3) Fall 92, p. 114.
"Strategies." [Descant] (23:3, #78) Fall 92, p. 153-154.
5341. ROBERTSON-LORANT, Laurie
"Summer Symposium." [SoCoast] (12) Ja 92, p. 41.
5342. ROBINS, Corinne
"Dying for It." [AnotherCM] (24) Fall 92, p. 129.

5343. ROBINSON, Elizabeth
"The Aperture" (for Jim Stipe). [Epoch] (41:1) 92, p. 111.
"Call." [Epoch] (41:1) 92, p. 110.
"Collapsed Wall." [Caliban] (11) 92, p. 10.
"Oil." [Shiny] (7/8) 92, p. 110.
"Sao Bento." [Epoch] (41:1) 92, p. 112-113.
"Scapulimancy." [Caliban] (11) 92, p. 12.
"Scent." [Shiny] (7/8) 92, p. 109.
"The Shirt." [Caliban] (11) 92, p. 11.
5344. ROBINSON, James Miller
"Take This Stone." [BellR] (15:1) Spr 92, p. 34.
5345. ROBINSON, Kit
"Counter Meditation" (Selections: 31-38). [Shiny] (7/8) 92, p. 41-45.
"Visceral Reluctance." [GrandS] (11:1, #41) 92, p. 102-103.
5346. ROBISON, Margaret
"How We Stopped Playing Tackle Football with the Boys." [Wind] (22:71) 92, p. 28-29.
"Implications." [HayF] (11) Fall-Wint 92, p. 45.
"Lancaster Prison, 1986." [HayF] (11) Fall-Wint 92, p. 44.
5347. ROBLES, Margarita Luna
"Entre la Luna y Nosotros" (title of a relief print by Emmanuel Catarino Montoya — for Juana Alicia, Luna llena de septiembre, 1985). [InterPR] (18:1) Spr 92, p. 83.
5348. ROBNOLT, J'laine
"Keeper of the Flame." [Elf] (2:1) Spr 92, p. 40.
"Sanctuary." [Elf] (2:1) Spr 92, p. 41.
ROBYN SARAH
See SARAH, Robyn
5349. ROCA, Daniel Jácome (Daniel Jacomé)
"Espectaculo Acuatico." [LindLM] (11:1) Mr 92, p. 6.
"El Sangre-azul." [Nuez] (4:12) 92, p. 21.
5350. ROCA, John
"Foreboding on a Warm Winter Night in Toledo." [Spitball] (40) Spr 92, p. 20-21.
5351. ROCA, Juan Manuel
"Tailor's Monologue" (tr. by Don Share). [Noctiluca] (1:2) Wint 92 [on cover: Wint 93], p. 15.
ROCCA, Lynda La
See La ROCCA, Lynda
5352. ROCEWICZ, Tadeusz
"In the beginning" (tr. by Jeanne DeWeese). [NowestR] (30:3) 92, p. 47.
"It's high time" (to the memory of Konstanty Puzyna, tr. by Jeanne DeWeese). [NowestR] (30:3) 92, p. 48.
5353. ROCHE, Judith
"Dendrites." [Rohwedder] (7) Spr-Sum 92, p. 20.
"Helen: When They Called Her Witch." [Rohwedder] (7) Spr-Sum 92, p. 18-19.
5354. ROCKIN' RED
"A Leak in the Attic." [Light] (3) Aut 92, p. 7.
5355. ROCKWELL, Tom
"1938." [MassR] (23:3) Fall 92, p. 358-360.
"Casanova could not satisfy his hunger." [NewYorkQ] (49) 92, p. 53-54.
"De Terre." [NewYorkQ] (47) 92, p. 43-45.
"Seduction." [NewYorkQ] (48) 92, p. 75-79.
5356. RODEFER, Stephen
"Spurwhang Filch." [GrandS] (11:3 #43) 92, p. 173.
5357. RODEMAN, Juliet
"Histories." [WebR] (16) Fall 92, p. 105-106.
"Rumors of History." [AntR] (50:4) Fall 92, p. 736.
5358. RODENKO, Paul
"Poem: Trunk of flames, patience" (tr. by Arie Staal). [Vis] (38) 92, p. 44.
5359. RODERICK, John M.
"The Reservoir." [EngJ] (81:4) Ap 92, p. 95.
5360. RODITI, Edouard
"The Dark Ages" (revision of a poem which appeared originally in *Poems, 1928-1948*). [WorldL] (3) 92, p. 25.
"Hertza" (tr. of Benjamin Fondane, w. Franz Hodjak). [Pequod] (34) 92, p. 76-77.
"In Praise of Democracy." [WorldL] (3) 92, p. 24.

"Meditation on 'The Discourses' of Machiavelli." [Talisman] (8) Spr 92, p. 14-15.
"Tonight the Stars Are in Tatters" (tr. of Fouad El-Etr). [Caliban] (11) 92, p. 37.

5361. RODRIGUEZ, Claudio
"The Gaze That Nothing Owns" (Translation Chapbook Series, No. 19, in Spanish and English, tr. by Elizabeth Gamble Miller). [MidAR] (13:1) 92, p. 173-205.
"Sunflower" (tr. by Elizabeth Gamble Miller). [NewOR] (19:3/4) Fall-Wint 92, p. 38.

5362. RODRIGUEZ, Luis J.
"They Come to Dance." [ChironR] (11:3) Aut 92, p. 17.

5363. RODRIGUEZ, Pilar
"Autodefinición." [Americas] (19:2) Sum 91, p. 64-65.
"Triángulo Prohibido." [Americas] (19:2) Sum 91, p. 66.

5364. RODRIGUEZ, Rafael H.
"Otro Nocturno de los Angeles." [LindLM] (11:4) D 92, p. 17.

5365. RODRIGUEZ, Reina Maria
"Como un Extraño Pájaro Que Viene del Sur." [LitR] (35:4) Sum 92, p. 598-599.
"Like a Strange Bird from the South" (tr. by AnneMaria Bankay). [LitR] (35:4) Sum 92, p. 465.
"Soñar los Trenes." [LitR] (35:4) Sum 92, p. 599.
"Train Dreams" (tr. by AnneMaria Bankay). [LitR] (35:4) Sum 92, p. 466.

5366. RODRIGUEZ, Silvio
"Cuando Te Encontré" (w. Pablo Milanés). [Areíto] (3:10/11) Abril 92, inside front cover.
"Leyenda." [Areíto] (3:10/11) Abril 92, p. 79.
"El Necio." [Areíto] (3:10/11) Abril 92, p. inside back cover.

5367. RODRIGUEZ, W. R.
"The Great Cockfight Bust." [Turnstile] (3:2) 92, p. 25-26.

5368. ROE, Margie McCreless
"Threads." [ChrC] (109:25) 26 Ag-2 S 92, p. 774.

5369. ROESKE, Paulette
"The Ecstasy of St. Teresa" (After Bernini). [WillowS] (29) Wint 92, p. 10-11.

5370. ROFFMAN, Rosaly DeMaios
"Coming Back." [OxfordM] (6:2) Fall-Wint 90, p. 74.

5371. ROGACZEWSKI, Frank
"It Could Be Worse." [AnotherCM] (23) Spr 92, p. 159-160.

5372. ROGAL, Stan
"Blue Rose" (for Baudelaire). [Quarry] (41:1) Wint 92, p. 27.

5373. ROGERS, Bertha
"Blue Sky." [MidwQ] (33:2) Wint 92, p. 207.
"New Year's Day." [SmPd] (29:1, #84) Wint 92, p. 24.
"Vultures." [Crucible] (28) Fall 92, p. 7.
"Widow." [NegC] (12:3) 92, p. 111-112.

5374. ROGERS, Charles
"Prison Visit" (Winner, Annual Free Verse Contest, 1991). [AnthNEW] (4) 92, p. 22.

5375. ROGERS, Daryl
"Before Work." [SlipS] (12) 92, p. 38.
"Dress Up." [SlipS] (12) 92, p. 37.

5376. ROGERS, Pattiann
"Are Some Sins Hosannas?" [PoetryNW] (33:3) Aut 92, p. 27-28.
"Crux." [SoCarR] (25:1) Fall 92, p. 12-13.
"Goddamn Theology." [TriQ] (86) Wint 92-93, p. 32-33.
"Infanticide." [PoetryNW] (33:3) Aut 92, p. 26-27.
"Life History and the Plain Facts." [SoCarR] (25:1) Fall 92, p. 14-15.
"Rocking and Resurrection." [IndR] (15:1) Spr 92, p. 56-57.
"Winter Camping." [SoCarR] (25:1) Fall 92, p. 13-14.
"Winter Fishing." [IndR] (15:1) Spr 92, p. 55.

5377. ROGERS, Shannon
"Blue Velvet." [PacificR] (11) 92-93, p. 41.
"Sharing Flesh." [PacificR] (11) 92-93, p. 42.

5378. ROGERS-MARTIN, Martha
"The First Supper." [PoetryUSA] (24) 92, p. 25.

5379. ROGOFF, Jay
"The Cutoff" (3 selections). [KenR] (NS 14:3) Sum 92, p. 1-5.
"Everything But Everything." [Salm] (93) Wint 92, p. 183-185.
"Life Sentence." [Agni] (35) 92, p. 288-289.

5380. ROGOW, Zack
"A Note on the Type." [NewDeltaR] (9:2) Spr-Sum 92, p. 94.
5381. ROHWER, Lee Orcutt
"Healing Ritual." [Footwork] 92, p. 104.
"Heritage Mothers." [Footwork] 92, p. 104.
5382. ROJAS, Gonzalo
"Latin and Jazz" (tr. by Margarita Nieto). [OnTheBus] (4:2/5:1, #10/11) 92, p. 281.
"What Do You Do When You Love?" (tr. by Margarita Nieto). [OnTheBus] (4:2/5:1, #10/11) 92, p. 280.
5383. ROJO, Daniel
"Trades." [Americas] (20:1) Spr 92, p. 50-51.
"Trades." [ChangingM] (24) Sum-Fall 92, p. 30.
5384. ROLANDS, Tim
"Augury." [Paint] (19:37) Spr 92, p. 15.
"Memory." [Paint] (19:37) Spr 92, p. 14.
5385. ROLLINGS, Alane
"Differences in the Frequency of Weeping." [DenQ] (26:4) Spr 92, p. 64-67.
"Evolution and the Adequacy of Goodness of Heart." [TampaR] (5) Fall 92, p. 12 - 13.
"The Heat That Colors Need." [GettyR] (5:4) Aut 92, p. 642-643.
"Living on Kindness." [CimR] (98) Ja 92, p. 78-79.
"Precious Little." [SouthernR] (28:4) Aut, O 92, p. 899-900.
"To Love to Distraction." [DenQ] (26:4) Spr 92, p. 62-63.
"To the Infinite Power." [NoDaQ] (60:1) Wint 92, p. 283-284.
5386. ROLLINS, Scott
"Ballad of the Salamander" (tr. of Wiel Kusters). [Trans] (26) Spr 92, p. 11-12.
5387. ROMAN, Joseph
"Campcraft." [SoDakR] (30:2) Sum 92, p. 107.
"Montreal." [SoDakR] (30:2) Sum 92, p. 106.
ROMAN, Lydia Velez
See VELEZ-ROMAN, Lydia
5388. ROMANO, Mercedes
"Nací de pie sobre un pez durante el sueño de Dios." [Nuez] (4:10/11) 92, p. 8.
5389. ROMANO, Rose
"Basta." [Footwork] 92, p. 59.
"Broadway and Fillmore." [SlipS] (12) 92, p. 85.
"The Bucket." [Footwork] 92, p. 56.
"Call It Macaroni." [Footwork] 92, p. 59.
"Dago Street." [Footwork] 92, p. 57-58.
"Maledizione." [Footwork] 92, p. 57.
"Not to Be Trusted." [Footwork] 92, p. 56.
"The Pasta Poems." [Footwork] 92, p. 58.
"Wop Talk." [Footwork] 92, p. 53-55.
5390. ROMANOS, Maryse
"Drumbeat of Life" (tr. by Betty Wilson). [LitR] (35:4) Sum 92, p. 531-532.
"Tam Tam de Vie." [LitR] (35:4) Sum 92, p. 611-612.
5391. ROMERO, Leo
"Diane's Knocking." [Americas] (20:3/4) Fall-Wint 92, p. 244.
"How Did I Land Up in This City." [Americas] (20:3/4) Fall-Wint 92, p. 240.
"I Bring Twins Over to Meet Pito." [Americas] (20:3/4) Fall-Wint 92, p. 238-239.
"Pito Had a Dream That." [Americas] (20:3/4) Fall-Wint 92, p. 241-243.
"The Road to Waldo." [BilingR] (17:1) Ja-Ap 92, p. 75-76.
"There's the House." [BilingR] (17:1) Ja-Ap 92, p. 76.
"When Pito Tried to Kill." [Americas] (20:3/4) Fall-Wint 92, p. 245-247.
ROMINE-POWELL, Dannye
See POWELL, Dannye Romine
5392. ROMOND, Edwin
"At Jayne Mansfield's Grave." [Sun] (203) N 92, p. 21.
"Home Fire" (for Mary). [Sun] (203) N 92, p. 23.
"The Moment Before My Mother Died." [Sun] (203) N 92, p. 22.
"Something I Could Tell You About Love." [Sun] (203) N 92, p. 20.
"Spring at 40." [Sun] (203) N 92, p. 20.
"This Year's May." [Sun] (203) N 92, p. 22.
5393. ROMTVEDT, David
"Eating Dinner at My Sister's." [CrabCR] (8:1) Sum-Fall 92, p. 14.
"For Small Towns." [CharR] (18:1) Spr 92, p. 85-86.

"My Art." [Event] (21:1) Spr 92, p. 36.
"The Rose Bushes." [Event] (21:1) Spr 92, p. 37.
"This Year's Wood." [CutB] (37) Wint 92, p. 13.

5394. RONAN, John
"At the Prolapse Fat Pageant." [Interim] (11:1) Spr-Sum 92, p. 17.
"Interstate 91." [Interim] (11:1) Spr-Sum 92, p. 16.

5395. RONK, Martha
"Eye Closed." [Talisman] (9) Fall 92, p. 189.
"The History of Gender." [DenQ] (27:1) Sum 92, p. 20.
"Imagination." [DenQ] (27:1) Sum 92, p. 21.

ROOKE, Katerina Angelaki
See ANGELAKI-ROOKE, Katerina

5396. ROONEY, Mary Schooler
"1946-1986." [Poem] (68) N 92, p. 34.
"Mushrooming." [Poem] (68) N 92, p. 35.

5397. ROOT, Judith
"Naming the Shells." [ThRiPo] (39/40) 92-93, p. 216-217.
"Small Differences." [ThRiPo] (39/40) 92-93, p. 215-216.
"Snail Winter." [ThRiPo] (39/40) 92-93, p. 217-218.

5398. ROOT, Larry Joe
"Bridge People." [Pearl] (15) Spr-Sum 92, p. 50.
"The Race for Space." [Pearl] (15) Spr-Sum 92, p. 50.

5399. ROOT, William Pitt
"For a Russian Poet Who Has Fallen Silent." [Nimrod] (35:2) Spr-Sum 92, p. 81-82.
"In the Well of Twilight." [Nimrod] (35:2) Spr-Sum 92, p. 83.

5400. ROPPEL, Katherine
"Sunday Morning Off Blue Ridge Parkway" (Winner, Annual Free Verse Contest, 1991). [AnthNEW] (4) 92, p. 18.

5401. ROQUÉ, Rosa Ma
"Lies." [Sonora] (22/23) Spr 92, p. 102.
"That Father's House." [Sonora] (22/23) Spr 92, p. 103.

5402. RORIPAUGH, Lee Ann
"Carpe Diem." [PoetL] (87:1) Spr 92, p. 32.

ROSA, Alexis Gomez
See GOMEZ ROSA, Alexis

5403. ROSA, António Ramos
"Knowing No Secrets Having No Visions" (tr. by Richard Zenith). [Stand] (33:4) Aut 92, p. 141.
"To Start Out from Minerals from Steep Sides" (tr. by Richard Zenith). [NewOR] (19:2) Sum 92, p. 18.

5404. ROSBERG, Rose
"Ejaculations." [Plain] (12:3) Spr 92, p. 25.

5405. ROSE, Carol
"Body Images" (for Joan Turner). [PraF] (13:4, #61) Wint 92-93, p. 94.
"The Call." [Dandel] (19:3) 92, p. 30.
"For Chrystos." [Dandel] (19:3) 92, p. 29.
"Gifts" (for neal). [PraF] (13:4, #61) Wint 92-93, p. 93.
"Growing Pains." [PraF] (13:4, #61) Wint 92-93, p. 95.
"Kitchens of My Childhood." [Dandel] (19:3) 92, p. 27.
"New Day in Jerusalem." [Dandel] (19:3) 92, p. 28.

5406. ROSE, Dorothy (Dorothy L.)
"Naval Reserve Nurse." [Gypsy] (18) 92, p. 15-16.
"Slinging Hash." [SlipS] (12) 92, p. 70-71.

5407. ROSE, Karen
"Memory During Antidepressant Treatment." [NewYorker] (67:52) 17 F 92, p. 36.

5408. ROSE, Tony
"My Civil War." [OnTheBus] (4:2/5:1, #10/11) 92, p. 185.
"The Poets." [OnTheBus] (4:2/5:1, #10/11) 92, p. 186.
"Sacrifice." [OnTheBus] (4:2/5:1, #10/11) 92, p. 186.

5409. ROSE, Wendy
"The Endangered Roots of a Person." [Jacaranda] (6:1/2) Wint-Spr 92, p. 88-89.

5410. ROSE, Wilga
"Black Swan to Currawong." [Footwork] 92, p. 142.
"Blowfly." [Footwork] 92, p. 144.
"Canowindra." [Footwork] 92, p. 144.
"Clinical Psychology." [Footwork] 92, p. 142.

"Dead Leaves." [Footwork] 92, p. 142.
"Evening." [Footwork] 92, p. 143.
"Ferry Passing." [Footwork] 92, p. 142.
"Gull." [Footwork] 92, p. 143.
"Images at the Gallery." [Footwork] 92, p. 144.
"In the Garden at Varuna." [Vis] (40) 92, p. 37.
"Kite." [Bogg] (65) 92, p. 58.
"Old Gum." [Footwork] 92, p. 143.
"Picking Wild Lilies." [Footwork] 92, p. 144.
"Prisoner." [Footwork] 92, p. 142.
"Recessional." [Footwork] 92, p. 143.
"Tai Chi." [Footwork] 92, p. 142.
"Tai Chi." [Vis] (40) 92, p. 34.
"Trespassers Prosecuted." [Vis] (40) 92, p. 37-38.

5411. ROSEBERRY, Brenda
"A Woman Waiting for the Bus." [Amelia] (7:1, #20) 92, p. 124.

5412. ROSEN, Deborah Nodler
"The Stone." [WillowR] (19) Spr 92, p. 20.

5413. ROSEN, Kenneth
"Dürer's Four Witches." [ParisR] (34:125) Wint 92, p. 239-241.
"Rainbow Head." [VirQR] (68:2) Spr 92, p. 304-305.
"Red Twilight." [MassR] (23:3) Fall 92, p. 352-254.

5414. ROSEN, Michael J.
"The Golden Goat." [WestHR] (46:3) Fall 92, p. 306-307.
"The Growing Conditions." [YaleR] (80:4) O 92, p. 76-77.
"The New Neighbors Who Rent Next Door, Their Laundry." [Thrpny] (48) Wint 92, p. 25.

5415. ROSENBAUM, Kirk
"An American Tragedy." [ChironR] (11:1) Spr 92, p. 21.

5416. ROSENBERG, Liz
"Admiring the Enemy." [AmerPoR] (21:6) N-D 92, p. 8.
"After Hours." [AmerPoR] (21:6) N-D 92, p. 8.
"The Birthday Party." [AmerPoR] (21:6) N-D 92, p. 7.
"The Black Shoe." [AmerPoR] (21:6) N-D 92, p. 8.
"The Dark Side." [NewEngR] (14:2) Spr 92, p. 84.
"Dying." [Poetry] (160:2) My 92, p. 87.
"Fairy Tales." [Nat] (255:4) 3-10 Ag 92, p. 151.
"If Love Is Like the Rain." [AmerPoR] (21:6) N-D 92, p. 7.
"A Lesson in Anatomy." [AmerPoR] (21:6) N-D 92, p. 7.
"The Silence of Women." [TriQ] (86) Wint 92-93, p. 69.
"Third First Snow." [NewEngR] (14:2) Spr 92, p. 85.
"When They Sleep All the Time." [AmerPoR] (21:6) N-D 92, p. 8.

5417. ROSENBERG, Martin
"Hard-Boiled." [Light] (1) Spr 92, p. 11.

5418. ROSENFIELD, Kim
"Advice." [Shiny] (7/8) 92, p. 91.
"Marriott Times Square 1991." [Shiny] (7/8) 92, p. 92.

5419. ROSENSTOCK, Gabriel
"To My Husband Who Labours on the Great Wall" (tr. by the author). [WebR] (16) Fall 92, p. 36-37.

5420. ROSENTHAL, David (Dave) (*See also* ROSENTHAL, David H.)
"Easier Test." [PaintedB] (46) 92, p. 29.
"Mind." [WashR] (18:1) Je-Jl 92, p. 6.
"One Way Out." [PaintedB] (48) 92, p. 49.

5421. ROSENTHAL, David H. (*See also* ROSENTHAL, David (Dave))
"Memory of Venice: Winter." [Pequod] (34) 92, p. 143.
"Stalking the Elusive Present." [Pequod] (34) 92, p. 144.
"The Visitor." [Pequod] (34) 92, p. 142.

5422. ROSENTHAL, Irv
"Bring." [SoCoast] (13) Je 93 [i.e. 92], p. 19.

5423. ROSENTHAL, Laura
"The Mom Thing." [HangL] (61) 92, p. 64.
"Steel Trout." [NewAW] (10) Fall 92, p. 71.

5424. ROSENTHAL, M. L.
"Awake and Remember!" [SouthernR] (28:3) Sum, Jl 92, p. 626-628.

5425. ROSENZWEIG, Geri
"After Her Heart Attack I Give Her a Bubble Bath." [RiverC] (12:2) Spr 92, p. 73 - 74.
5426. ROSKOS, David
"January 2nd / 1990 / 10:55 a.m." [Lactuca] (15) Mr 92, p. 69.
"True Sounds of Liberty." [NewYorkQ] (47) 92, p. 88.
5427. ROSS, David
"Code." [BellArk] (8:3) My-Je 92, p. 1.
"Paradigm." [BellArk] (8:3) My-Je 92, p. 1.
"Turn." [BellArk] (8:3) My-Je 92, p. 1.
5428. ROSS, Linwood (Linwood M.)
"Terminal Moves." [Lactuca] (16) Ag 92, p. 31-32.
"A Useless Poem" (For Huey Newton). [FreeL] (9) Wint 92, p. 30-31.
5429. ROSSELLI, Amelia
"Arranged" (tr. by Corrado Federici). [PoetryC] (13:1) N 92, p. 23.
5430. ROSSER, J. Allyn
"April Again." [PassN] (13:2) Wint 92, p. 18.
"Beckett Dead Imagine" (for Jan Jonson). [GeoR] (46:2) Sum 92, p. 272-274.
"Buffalo Bayou." [Poetry] (161:1) O 92, p. 16-18.
"Deep Pond at Dusk in Heavy Rain Against Pines." [Poetry] (161:1) O 92, p. 18-19.
"Heart to India" (Volume 14, Encyclopedia Americana). [GeoR] (46:2) Sum 92, p. 271.
"Portrait." [PassN] (13:2) Wint 92, p. 18.
"Raven." [Poetry] (161:1) O 92, p. 20.
ROSSI, Cristina Peri
See PERI ROSSI, Cristina
5431. ROSSI, Lee
"The Butcher's Son." [Jacaranda] (6:1/2) Wint-Spr 92, p. 148.
"Confessions." [Jacaranda] (6:1/2) Wint-Spr 92, p. 149-150.
"Swamp Lives." [Jacaranda] (6:1/2) Wint-Spr 92, p. 146-147.
5432. ROSSINI, Frank
"After Reading *The Tao of Physics*." [ChironR] (11:2) Sum 92, p. 8.
"This for That." [ChironR] (11:2) Sum 92, p. 8.
"The Threat of Organized Labor." [ChironR] (11:2) Sum 92, p. 8.
5433. ROSSMAN, Ed
"Raccoons." [ChironR] (11:3) Aut 92, p. 32.
5434. ROSU, Dona
"Creation" (tr. of Marin Sorescu, w. W. D. Snograss and Luciana Costea). [Poetry] (159:4) Ja 92, p. 191.
"I Bound Up the Trees' Eyes" (tr. of Marin Sorescu, w. W. D. Snograss and Luciana Costea). [Poetry] (159:4) Ja 92, p. 194.
"Solemnly" (tr. of Marin Sorescu, w. W. D. Snograss and Luciana Costea). [Poetry] (159:4) Ja 92, p. 192.
"Thieves" (tr. of Marin Sorescu, w. W. D. Snograss and Luciana Costea). [Poetry] (159:4) Ja 92, p. 193.
5435. ROTELLA, Alexis
"Dirt." [ChironR] (11:3) Aut 92, p. 32.
"Knees." [ChironR] (11:3) Aut 92, p. 28.
5436. ROTH, Ron
"Over the Hard Fields." [SoDakR] (30:4) Wint 92, p. 114.
5437. ROTH, Susan Harned
"Curfew." [Footwork] 92, p. 107.
"Portrait of His Family." [Footwork] 92, p. 107.
5438. ROTH-NATALE, Nanci
"Jason-Brendan-Justin." [BellArk] (8:3) My-Je 92, p. 20.
"The Quiet Season." [BellArk] (8:1) Ja-F 92, p. 3.
5439. ROTHENBERG, Jerome
"Flight" (tr. of Kurt Schwitters, w. Pierre Joris). [Boulevard] (7:2/3, #20/21) Fall 92, p. 168-170.
"Four Bear Songs" (tr. of Kurt Schwitters). [Conjunc] (18) 92, p. 138-139.
"Improvisation No. 2" (Spring. The Mother). [PoetryUSA] (24) 92, p. 21.
"The Lorca Variations: 'Lunar Grapefruits'." [Conjunc] (18) 92, p. 198-202.
5440. ROTHMAN, David J.
"A Life." [Journal] (16:2) Fall-Wint 92, p. 21.
"The Maple." [TarRP] (30:2) Spr 91, p. 15.

"Postepithalamium" (for Jimmy and Elena Butler and their daughter Devon). [ManhatPR] (14) [92?], p. 6.
5441. ROTHMAN, Susan Noe
"Forest of Anger." [Pearl] (16) Fall 92, p. 33.
"Just Another August Day." [SlipS] (12) 92, p. 68.
5442. ROUSE, Anne
"Country Pursuits." [Atlantic] (269:3) Mr 92, p. 82.
5443. ROUSSEAU, Ann
"Barefoot." [EngJ] (81:4) Ap 92, p. 95.
5444. ROUX, Claire-Sara
"Captives among the stalks" (tr. by Jim Barnes). [ArtfulD] (22/23) 92, p. 14.
"The song is choked" (tr. by Jim Barnes). [ArtfulD] (22/23) 92, p. 13.
5445. ROVETTI, Doris
"Waiting for Pathology." [NegC] (12:3) 92, p. 113.
5446. ROWE, Ellen
"Legacy of Brownstone Mountain." [Footwork] 92, p. 102.
5447. ROWE, Kelly
"Love Poem for the Other Woman." [ChatR] (12:4) Sum 92, p. 58-59.
5448. ROWE, Michael
"Untitled: You scan the cloudless skies" (March 27th, 1989). [JamesWR] (9:2) Wint 92, p. 8.
5449. ROXMAN, Susanna
"The Peat-Bog." [OxfordM] (8:2) Fall-Wint 92, p. 12.
"The Salt Lick." [OxfordM] (8:2) Fall-Wint 92, p. 11.
5450. ROY, Camille
"The soft light over the LA hills seemed rubbed with an eraser." [BrooklynR] (9) 92, p. 11-12.
"When I was small the world started at my stomach." [BrooklynR] (9) 92, p. 10.
"An XY Story" (Excerpts). [BrooklynR] (9) 92, p. 8-9.
5451. ROY, Lucinda
"Caracole." [NewOR] (19:3/4) Fall-Wint 92, p. 58-59.
5452. ROYET-JOURNOUD, Claude
"i.e." (Selections: 7-8, tr. by Keith Waldrop). [Avec] (5:1) 92, p. 55-56.
5453. ROZEWICZ, Tadeusz
"In the beginning" (tr. by Jeanne DeWeese). [Descant] (23:3, #78) Fall 92, p. 144.
"In the Middle of Life" (tr. by Ioanna-Veronika Warwick). [SenR] (22:2) Fall 92, p. 50-51.
"It's high time" (to the memory of Konstanty Puzyna, tr. by Jeanne DeWeese). [Descant] (23:3, #78) Fall 92, p. 147.
"Old Women" (tr. by Ioanna-Veronika Warwick). [SenR] (22:2) Fall 92, p. 49.
"Poetry not always takes the shape of verse" (tr. by Jeanne DeWeese). [Descant] (23:3, #78) Fall 92, p. 148.
"Something Like That" (tr. by Jeanne DeWeese). [Descant] (23:3, #78) Fall 92, p. 149.
"'Success' and Requests" (tr. by Jeanne DeWeese). [Descant] (23:3, #78) Fall 92, p. 145-146.
5454. RUARK, Gibbons
"Late December." [NewRep] (207:14) 28 S 92, p. 34.
5455. RUBIN, Anele
"Pa." [Footwork] 92, p. 79.
"Rose Mary." [Footwork] 92, p. 79.
5456. RUBIN, Larry
"The Bachelor, As Poet: 40th High School Reunion." [NegC] (12:3) 92, p. 114.
5457. RUBIN, Mordecai
"Soneto a Mi Madre." [Nuez] (4:10/11) 92, p. 31.
"Soneto a Mi Padre." [Nuez] (4:10/11) 92, p. 31.
5458. RUBIN, Stan Sanvel
"Australia" (for Karla). [TarRP] (32:1) Fall 92, p. 22.
"Halloween." [RiverC] (12:2) Spr 92, p. 17.
"The Islands." [RiverC] (12:2) Spr 92, p. 18-20.
5459. RUCHTE, Susan
"Danse a la Ville." [NewMyths] (1:2/2:1) 92, p. 87.
5460. RUCKER, Trish
"I Dream About Snakes." [CarolQ] (44:2) Wint 92, p. 77.
"The Morning After We Broke Things Off." [TarRP] (32:1) Fall 92, p. 25.
"Painting of a Summer Sky." [CarolQ] (44:2) Wint 92, p. 78.

"Swallow Creek." [ThRiPo] (39/40) 92-93, p. 219.
"The Swallows of Capistrano." [ThRiPo] (39/40) 92-93, p. 219-220.
"Wedding." [BellR] (15:2) Fall 92, p. 21.

5461. RUCKERT, Jan
"I Always Get Away." [OnTheBus] (4:2/5:1, #10/11) 92, p. 188-189.
"War Wounds." [OnTheBus] (4:2/5:1, #10/11) 92, p. 187-188.

5462. RUCKMAN, Kim
"Broken Bow, Nebraska — 1897." [Plain] (12:3) Spr 92, p. 26.
"What I Used to Know." [Plain] (13:1) Fall 92, p. 31.

5463. RUDD, Dawn
"The Enemy." [SinW] (47) Sum-Fall 92, p. 57-58.
"The Enemy" (corrected reprint from #47). [SinW] (48) Wint 92-93, p. 95-96.

5464. RUDE, Don
"On Saturdays" (3rd Prize, 6th Annual Contest). [SoCoast] (12) Ja 92, p. 45.

5465. RUDMAN, Mark
"Double Vision." [Agni] (35) 92, p. 290-298.
"Dreams of Cities: (February, 1991)." [Boulevard] (7:2/3, #20/21) Fall 92, p. 162 - 166.
"Elsewhere" (for Chris Benfey). [Ploughs] (18:1) Spr 92, p. 179-180.
"More Fire." [KenR] (NS 14:3) Sum 92, p. 86-87.
"Notes on Atonement." [TriQ] (86) Wint 92-93, p. 70-80.
"Robe." [KenR] (NS 14:3) Sum 92, p. 85-86.
"The Sorgue" (Song for Yvonne, tr. of Rene Char). [Pequod] (34) 92, p. 185.
"Spring Rainstorm" (tr. of Boris Pasternak, w. Bohdan Boychuk). [NewYRB] (39:21) 17 D 92, p. 10.

5466. RUDOLF, Anthony
"XIX. The trees remember more clearly than us" (tr. of Philippe Delaveau). [Stand] (33:4) Aut 92, p. 47.
"Bell" (tr. of Edmond Jabès). [Stand] (33:4) Aut 92, p. 38.
"Deep Waters" (tr. of Edmond Jabès). [Stand] (33:4) Aut 92, p. 32-37.
"Dog" (tr. of Edmond Jabès). [Stand] (33:4) Aut 92, p. 38.
"Mirror" (tr. of Edmond Jabès). [Stand] (33:4) Aut 92, p. 38.
"Sometimes" (tr. of Benjamin Fondane). [Stand] (33:4) Aut 92, p. 39.
"Song for Three Dead Men, Astonished" (tr. of Edmond Jabès). [Stand] (33:4) Aut 92, p. 37.

5467. RUDOLPH, Nancy
"They Lead Themselves" (with photographs). [Callaloo] (15:2) Spr 92, p. 495-497.

RUE, Mark La
See La RUE, Mark

5468. RUEFLE, Mary
"Continua." [BostonR] (17:6) N-D 92, p. 21.
"Depicted on a Screen." [BostonR] (17:6) N-D 92, p. 21.
"Ecce Homo." [BostonR] (17:6) N-D 92, p. 21.
"Funny Story." [BostonR] (17:6) N-D 92, p. 21.
"Timberland." [BostonR] (17:6) N-D 92, p. 21.

5469. RUFF, John
"Today, During the President's Address" (for J.P. and gin). [RiverC] (12:2) Spr 92, p. 1-2.
"What I Have Learned from the Gutter" (For Robert Ruff 1922-1987). [RiverC] (12:2) Spr 92, p. 3-5.

5470. RUFFIN, Paul
"Llano Estacado: The Naming." [MidwQ] (34:1) Aut 92, p. 82.

5471. RUGGIERI, Helen
"Art in the Park: Selling Potpourri on Sunday." [SingHM] (20) 92, p. 59-60.
"The Groundhog." [Blueline] (13) 92, p. 96.
"Naiad of the Pickup Truck." [Blueline] (13) 92, p. 55.
"Newport Jazz Festival 1958." [Poem] (67) My 92, p. 60.
"Out of the Blue." [NewYorkQ] (47) 92, p. 70.
"Speaking in Tongues." [Poem] (67) My 92, p. 59.

5472. RUGO, Marieve
"Victory" (May 8th and 9th, 1945). [NoDaQ] (60:4) Fall 92, p. 72.

5473. RUIZ, Jean Marie
"Afterthoughts." [Jacaranda] (6:1/2) Wint-Spr 92, p. 28-29.
"Expectations." [Jacaranda] (6:1/2) Wint-Spr 92, p. 25.
"Listening." [Jacaranda] (6:1/2) Wint-Spr 92, p. 26.
"La Rubia." [Jacaranda] (6:1/2) Wint-Spr 92, p. 27.

"The Year of the Ram." [Jacaranda] (6:1/2) Wint-Spr 92, p. 30-31.
5474. RUIZ, Judy
"The Aubade to Oatmeal." [Epiphany] (3:4) O (Fall) 92, p. 276.
"By Any Other Name." [Epiphany] (3:4) O (Fall) 92, p. 270.
"The Constant Tumble." [Epiphany] (3:4) O (Fall) 92, p. 274.
"Digging a Hole in the Sea." [Epiphany] (3:4) O (Fall) 92, p. 273.
"Evolute." [Epiphany] (3:4) O (Fall) 92, p. 268.
"How You Will Know." [Epiphany] (3:4) O (Fall) 92, p. 271.
"Not Me." [Epiphany] (3:4) O (Fall) 92, p. 269.
"The Sweet of How." [Epiphany] (3:4) O (Fall) 92, p. 275.
"The Town." [Epiphany] (3:4) O (Fall) 92, p. 272.
5475. RUIZ DE TORRES, Juan
"Cerrar los Ojos." [Nuez] (4:10/11) 92, p. 24.
5476. RULLMAN, Craig
"The Harvest." [Interim] (11:1) Spr-Sum 92, p. 21.
5477. RUNCIMAN, Lex
"Glass." [ColEng] (54:8) D 92, p. 939-940.
5478. RUNYAN, Tana Williams
"Amtrak Pioneer." [Grain] (20:2) Sum 92, p. 88.
"My Cutting Board." [Grain] (20:2) Sum 92, p. 87.
5479. RUSS, Don
"Jacob, Dying in Egypt." [Poem] (67) My 92, p. 12-13.
"Pictures." [PoetL] (87:2) Sum 92, p. 32.
"Resurrection Man" (Grandison Harris, 1811?-1911, Medical College of Georgia, Augusta). [SouthernHR] (26:4) Fall 92, p. 350-351.
"Vampire Rules." [ChatR] (13:1) Fall 92, p. 47.
"Winter Place." [Poem] (67) My 92, p. 11.
5480. RUSSELL, Dale
"The Bottom." [MoodySI] (27) Spr 92, p. 27.
5481. RUSSELL, Frazier
"How We Are Spared: For My Grandfather." [AmerV] (26) Spr 92, p. 6.
5482. RUSSELL, Gillian Harding
"The Cost of Living or Sharing a Bath with My Daughter." [Dandel] (19:2) 92, p. 8 - 9.
5483. RUSSELL, Peter
"A Fragment from Quintilius: Empedocles said." [JlNJPo] (14:1) Spr 92, p. 12.
"A Fragment from Quintilius: That jackass Polybius, who taught that History depends on facts." [JlNJPo] (14:1) Spr 92, p. 11.
5484. RUSSELL, Thomas
"To a Child Born Dead." [LouisL] (9:1) Spr 92, p. 65.
5485. RUSSO, Albert
"Out of Reach, Out of Touch." [Amelia] (6:4, #19) 92, p. 84-85.
5486. RUSSO, Gianna
"Keeping the Light" (for Granddaddy). [PoetL] (87:2) Sum 92, p. 33-34.
5487. RUSSO, John Paul
"Al Poco Giorno" (tr. of Dante). [HarvardA] (125th Anniversary Issue) F 92, p. 9.
5488. RUSSO, Linda V.
"Of Finding Things." [Kalliope] (14:1) 92, p. 40.
5489. RUTBERG, Jessica
"La Guerra" (tr. by Verónica Miranda). [Luz] (2) S 92, p. 47.
"The War." [Luz] (2) S 92, p. 46.
5490. RUTKOWSKI, Thaddeus
"Equal Opportunity." [Parting] (5:2) Wint 92-93, p. 33.
"Voicemail Seance." [ChironR] (11:3) Aut 92, p. 30.
5491. RUTSALA, Vern
"American Dream." [ThRiPo] (39/40) 92-93, p. 221-222.
"Becoming American." [Poetry] (160:3) Je 92, p. 131-132.
"Ghosts." [LitR] (35:3) Spr 92, p. 341.
"Moon Driving." [ColEng] (54:3) Mr 92, p. 287.
"The Shack Outside Boise." [ThRiPo] (39/40) 92-93, p. 220-221.
"Skaters." [ThRiPo] (39/40) 92-93, p. 222-223.
"Writing to the Past." [ColEng] (54:3) Mr 92, p. 288.
5492. RUTTER, Mark
"Communion." [Bogg] (65) 92, p. 7.
"I Open the Stove Door." [PottPort] (14:2) Fall-Wint 92, p. 67.
"Under Blows of the Axe." [PottPort] (14:2) Fall-Wint 92, p. 68.

5493. RUWE, Donelle
"The Brace." [MidAR] (12:2) 92, p. 157-158.
"What I Explain About My Nightmare." [MidAR] (12:2) 92, p. 159.
RUZ, Elias Letelier
See LETELIER-RUZ, Elias
5494. RUZESKY, Jay
"Gambler at the Great Canadian Casino." [Event] (21:2) Sum 92, p. 53.
"Groundhog Day." [MalR] (100) Fall 92, p. 182-183.
"Painting the Yellow House Blue." [MalR] (100) Fall 92, p. 185-186.
"Petroglyphs." [Event] (21:2) Sum 92, p. 52.
"Sergei Krikalev on the Space Station Mir." [MalR] (100) Fall 92, p. 179-181.
5495. RYAN, Carla
"Damn the Birds." [FourQ] (6:2) Fall 92, p. 17.
5496. RYAN, Gregory A.
"The Allurement." [GreenMR] (NS 5:2) Spr-Sum 92, p. 98.
5497. RYAN, Kay
"Turtle." [NewRep] (206:25) 22 Je 92, p. 36.
5498. RYAN, R. M.
"Light Works." [Light] (4) Wint 92-93, p. 7.
5499. RYAN, Richard
"Fever" (tr. of Seán O Riordain). [Trans] (26) Spr 92, p. 64.
5500. RYBICKI, John
"Against Light." [Caliban] (11) 92, p. 173.
"Gravity." [Caliban] (11) 92, p. 172.
5501. RYLANDER, Edith
"Find the Balance Point." [SingHM] (20) 92, p. 100-101.
5502. RYOKAN
"Kanshi" (Selection: 2 poems, tr. by Burton Watson). [Trans] (26) Spr 92, p. 18.
"Waka" (7 selections, tr. by Burton Watson). [Trans] (26) Spr 92, p. 19.
SABA, Elias Abu
See ABU SABA, Elias
5503. SABA, Umberto
"The Flock of Sheep" (tr. by James Kirkup). [Stand] (33:4) Aut 92, p. 105.
"The Goat" (tr. by Keith Bosley). [Stand] (33:4) Aut 92, p. 105.
5504. SABASU, Irare
"Sustenance." [SinW] (47) Sum-Fall 92, p. 59-60.
5505. SABINES, Jaime
"Collage" (Excerpts, in Spanish and English, tr. by Elena Reeves). [InterPR] (18:1) Spr 92, p. 10-15.
SACHIKO, Yoshihara
See YOSHIHARA, Sachiko
5506. SACHS, Paul Morris — for Nelly
"The Alphabet" (tr. of Horst Bienek). [Trans] (26) Spr 92, p. 79.
5507. SAENZ, Benjamin Alire
"The Altars of May" (New Mexico, 1959). [NewL] (58:3) Spr 92, p. 24-25.
5508. SAFE, Natasha
"L'Oustau de Baumanière" (Les Baux de Provence). [AmerV] (28) 92, p. 99-100.
5509. SAFFORD, Charles
"L'Arrivée du Bûcher." [SouthernHR] (26:1) Wint 92, p. 66.
"Blizzard." [SouthernHR] (26:4) Fall 92, p. 354.
"Coming to Seed." [SpoonRQ] (17:1/2) Wint-Spr 92, p. 89.
"The Ice Riders." [SpoonRQ] (17:1/2) Wint-Spr 92, p. 92.
"Living with Cannibals." [PoetL] (87:2) Sum 92, p. 14.
"Nightcap." [SycamoreR] (4:1) Wint 92, p. 49.
"Somebody in My Bed." [Plain] (13:1) Fall 92, p. 34.
"Somebody in My Bed." [SpoonRQ] (17:1/2) Wint-Spr 92, p. 90.
"Tornado Watch." [Plain] (12:3) Spr 92, p. 27.
"Uncle Ray's Party." [NewDeltaR] (9:1) Fall 91-Wint 92, p. 53.
"Vigil." [SpoonRQ] (17:1/2) Wint-Spr 92, p. 91.
5510. SAFIR, Natalie
"Ancestry." [Rohwedder] (7) Spr-Sum 92, p. 11.
"Tribute to Henry Moore." [Rohwedder] (7) Spr-Sum 92, p. 11.
5511. SAGAN, Miriam
"An Alphabet of Angels." [Noctiluca] (1:2) Wint 92 [on cover: Wint 93], p. 35-36.
"Black Grapes." [Bogg] (65) 92, p. 47.
"Blue Dress." [Noctiluca] (1:1) Spr 92, p. 11.

"The Lonesome Death of Federico Garcia Lorca." [Asylum] (7:3/4) 92, p. 43-44.
"Pecos Wilderness." [Noctiluca] (1:1) Spr 92, p. 12.
"Sacajawea." [HayF] (10) Spr-Sum 92, p. 54.
"Shell in the Desert" (Rebecca Salsbury James, 1891-1968). [Noctiluca] (1:2) Wint 92 [on cover: Wint 93], p. 34.
"Skunk Cabbage." [Noctiluca] (1:1) Spr 92, p. 13-15.
"Wise Men." [Noctiluca] (1:1) Spr 92, p. 15.
"Za/zen." [Noctiluca] (1:2) Wint 92 [on cover: Wint 93], p. 37.

5512. SAGASER, Elizabeth Harris
"The Eve of Conception (I)." [ChiR] (38:3) 92, p. 65.
"The Eve of Conception (II)." [ChiR] (38:3) 92, p. 66-67.

5513. SAGER, Bruce
"Riddle." [Elf] (2:3) Fall 92, p. 32.

5514. SAGOFF, Maurice
"Clerihew: Mark Twain." [Light] (3) Aut 92, p. 11.
"Norman Rockwell." [Light] (1) Spr 92, p. 25.
"'Pithecanthropus,' said Mrs. Erectus." [Light] (2) Sum 92, p. 12.

5515. SAHAGUN, Carlos
"Meditation" (tr. by Michael L. Johnson). [WebR] (16) Fall 92, p. 15.
"The Word" (tr. by Michael L. Johnson). [WebR] (16) Fall 92, p. 16.

5516. SAHAY, Raghuvir
"The Battle of Man and Fish" (tr. by Harish Trivedi). [ChiR] (38:1/2) 92, p. 144 - 145.
"Fear" (tr. by Vinay Dharwadker). [ChiR] (38:1/2) 92, p. 148.
"The Handicapped Caught in a Camera" (tr. by Harish Trivedi). [ChiR] (38:1/2) 92, p. 146-147.

5517. SAIL, Lawrence
"Woodlouse" (i.m. Paul Klee). [Stand] (33:3) Sum 92, p. 27.

SAINT
See also ST. (filed as spelled)

5518. SAINT-GRÉGOIRE, Erma
"Elle Etait Venue d'Aubes Lointaines" (pour Marie). [Callaloo] (15:2) Spr 92, p. 469.
"I Understood, But Too Late" (tr. by Carrol F. Coates). [Callaloo] (15:2) Spr 92, p. 476.
"J'ai Compris Mais Trop Tard." [Callaloo] (15:2) Spr 92, p. 477.
"La Ou S'Impriment." [Callaloo] (15:2) Spr 92, p. 471.
"Sereine, in Situ . . . pour les Morts." [Callaloo] (15:2) Spr 92, p. 474-475.
"Serene, in Situ . . . for the Dead" (tr. by Carrol F. Coates). [Callaloo] (15:2) Spr 92, p. 472-473.
"She Had Come from Faraway Dawns" (for Marie, tr. by Carrol F. Coates). [Callaloo] (15:2) Spr 92, p. 468.
"Where the Cinders Are Imprinted" (tr. by Carrol F. Coates). [Callaloo] (15:2) Spr 92, p. 470.

5519. SAJE, Natasha
"Chocolates." [Antaeus] (69) Aut 92, p. 111.
"Rampion." [Antaeus] (69) Aut 92, p. 110.
"Reeling." [Chelsea] (53) 92, p. 108-109.

5520. SAKNUSSEMM, Kristopher
"Away Games." [Amelia] (7:1, #20) 92, p. 24-25.
"In the Devil's Cornfield." [Amelia] (7:1, #20) 92, p. 23.
"Mad Mouse." [Amelia] (7:1, #20) 92, p. 22-23.
"Second Honeymoon." [FreeL] (10) Sum 92, p. 25.
"Sky Class." [SoCarR] (24:2) Spr 92, p. 74.
"Soldier in the Egg." [Amelia] (7:1, #20) 92, p. 21-22.

5521. SALA, Jerome
"The Individuals Club (A Proposal)." [OnTheBus] (4:2/5:1, #10/11) 92, p. 190-191.

5522. SALAAM, Kalamu ya
"Bahian beauty." [Amelia] (6:4, #19) 92, p. 23.

5523. SALADYGA, M.
"Ganson Street." [MoodySI] (27) Spr 92, p. 47.

5524. SALAMONE, Karen
"The Institution of Yellow." [BellArk] (8:3) My-Je 92, p. 21.
"New Season." [BellArk] (8:3) My-Je 92, p. 21.
"Thoughts in a Pallid Season." [BellArk] (8:3) My-Je 92, p. 21.

5525. SALAMUN, Tomaz
"Again the streets are silent, the stillness dark" (tr. by Sonja Kravanja). [Descant] (23:3, #78) Fall 92, p. 86.
"All these are gifts" (tr. by the author and Anselm Hollo). [AmerPoR] (21:4) Jl-Ag 92, p. 41.
"Andraz" (tr. by Sonja Kravanja). [Nimrod] (35:2) Spr-Sum 92, p. 57.
"Andraz" (tr. by Sonja Kravanja). [Verse] (8:3/9:1) Wint-Spr 92, p. 126.
"The Cantina in Queretaro" (tr. by Michael Biggins). [Descant] (23:3, #78) Fall 92, p. 83.
"Clumsy Guys" (tr. by Sonja Kravanja). [WillowS] (29) Wint 92, p. 19.
"Hear me out" (tr. by Michael Biggins). [AmerPoR] (21:4) Jl-Ag 92, p. 42.
"The Hunter" (tr. by Michael Biggins). [ParisR] (34:122) Spr 92, p. 89.
"The Hunter" (tr. by Sonja Kravanja). [Nimrod] (35:2) Spr-Sum 92, p. 55.
"I Love You" (tr. by Michael Biggins). [Descant] (23:3, #78) Fall 92, p. 84-85.
"In Central Europe" (tr. by Michael Biggins). [AmerPoR] (21:4) Jl-Ag 92, p. 41.
"Man and Boy" (tr. by Michael Biggins). [AmerPoR] (21:4) Jl-Ag 92, p. 42.
"Narodi, ki nehajo pripovedovati storijo" (Excerpt). [Nimrod] (35:2) Spr-Sum 92, p. 53.
"Nations that forget their story-telling" (tr. by Sonja Kravanja). [Nimrod] (35:2) Spr-Sum 92, p. 53.
"Responsibility" (tr. by Sonja Kravanja). [Verse] (8:3/9:1) Wint-Spr 92, p. 126.
"Things: VII" (tr. by Sonja Kravanja). [PartR] (59:2) Spr 92, p. 269.
"To Read: To Love" (tr. by Michael Biggins). [AmerPoR] (21:4) Jl-Ag 92, p. 42.
"A Tribe" (tr. by the author and Anselm Hollo). [AmerPoR] (21:4) Jl-Ag 92, p. 41.
"The White Ithaca" (tr. by Sonja Kravanja). [Nimrod] (35:2) Spr-Sum 92, p. 56.
"White Ithaca" (tr. by Sonja Kravanja). [WillowS] (29) Wint 92, p. 18.

5526. SALAS, Floyd
"The Politics of Poetry" (dedicated to Stephen Arkin and the Bay Guardian). [PoetryUSA] (24) 92, p. 20.

5527. SALEH, Dennis
"The Say." [Pearl] (15) Spr-Sum 92, p. 60.

5528. SALEMI, Joseph S.
"Miss Crespo's Halloween." [Amelia] (6:4, #19) 92, p. 103.

5529. SALERNO, Joe
"In the Heaven of Obscurity." [PoetC] (23:3) Spr 92, p. 30-31.

5530. SALGADO, Dante
"Balandra" (fragmentos). [Nuez] (4:10/11) 92, p. 10.

5531. SALINAS, Luis Omar
"Cancer." [Americas] (20:1) Spr 92, p. 32-33.
"Middle Age." [Americas] (20:3/4) Fall-Wint 92, p. 197.
"Nights in Fresno." [Americas] (20:3/4) Fall-Wint 92, p. 195.
"Poem for Ernesto Trejo" (In Memory). [Americas] (20:1) Spr 92, p. 37.
"Poem for Ernesto Trejo" (In Memory). [Americas] (20:3/4) Fall-Wint 92, p. 199.
"Poem: Swans darkened on a passage East." [Americas] (20:1) Spr 92, p. 34.
"Sweeet Drama." [Americas] (20:1) Spr 92, p. 36.
"Sweet Drama." [Americas] (20:3/4) Fall-Wint 92, p. 198.
"What Is My Name?" [Americas] (20:3/4) Fall-Wint 92, p. 194.
"When the Evening Is Quiet." [Americas] (20:3/4) Fall-Wint 92, p. 196.
"Women in My Youth." [Americas] (20:1) Spr 92, p. 35.

5532. SALINAS, Pedro
"Numbers" (tr. by David Garrison). [ColR] (9:1) Spr-Sum 92, p. 113.
"Yes" (tr. by Joe Bolton). [NewOR] (19:3/4) Fall-Wint 92, p. 161.

SALLE, Peter la
See LaSALLE, Peter

5533. SALLI, Donna
"To My Liver." [Hellas] (3:1) Spr 92, p. 48.

5534. SALOM, Philip
"Day of the Waterspouts." [TampaR] (5) Fall 92, p. 52.
"The Gap." [TampaR] (5) Fall 92, p. 53.
"Listening to Paul Robeson." [NewL] (58:4) 92, p. 60-61.

5535. SALTER, A. Bryan
"At the Flying A Service." [SlipS] (12) 92, p. 35-36.
"June Harvest." [SlipS] (12) 92, p. 35.

5536. SALTER, Mary Jo
"Argument." [NewYorker] (68:42) 7 D 92, p. 126.
"A Rough Night." [NewYorker] (68:18) 22 Je 92, p. 44.

5537. SALTMAN, Benjamin
"Bodhisattva in Anger." [PoetL] (87:2) Sum 92, p. 17.
"Downtown Time." [Asylum] (7:3/4) 92, p. 61.
"Leaving My Father." [NegC] (12:1/2) 92, p. 196.
"Myself As a House." [NegC] (12:1/2) 92, p. 194-195.
5538. SALZMAN, Eva
"Boreal Owl." [NewYorker] (68:44) 21 D 92, p. 100.
"Chamois." [Verse] (9:2) Sum 92, p. 95.
"Hatred." [Verse] (8:3/9:1) Wint-Spr 92, p. 119.
"Lucky Strikes." [NewYorker] (68:33) 5 O 92, p. 92.
"Taste." [Verse] (8:3/9:1) Wint-Spr 92, p. 119.
5539. SAMARAS, Nicholas
"The Answers." [Poetry] (160:2) My 92, p. 82-84.
"Autobiography." [Chelsea] (53) 92, p. 53-54.
"Fasting." [ParisR] (34:123) Sum 92, p. 80-83.
"Forged Documents." [Chelsea] (53) 92, p. 52.
"The Last Weekend in May." [Gypsy] (18) 92, p. 154-157.
"Metanoia." [IndR] (15:1) Spr 92, p. 53.
"Nuclear Winter." [NoAmR] (277:2) Mr-Ap 92, p. 47.
"The Vocabulary We Could Not Use." [ParisR] (34:123) Sum 92, p. 78-79.
5540. SAMFORD, T. C.
"Undertow." [SoDakR] (30:2) Sum 92, p. 111.
5541. SAMMONS, Toni
"Coffee at Macy's" (for DKY). [Epoch] (41:1) 92, p. 120-121.
"Redemption." [Epoch] (41:1) 92, p. 114-119.
5542. SAMPLE, Kevin
"The Lesson." [TexasR] (13:3/4) Fall-Wint 92, p. 94-95.
5543. SAMPSON, Dennis
"For Your Arrival" (To Sandra McPherson). [OhioR] (48) 92, p. 25-26.
5544. SANCHEZ, Carol Lee
"Conversations from the Nightmare." [Jacaranda] (6:1/2) Wint-Spr 92, p. 90.
5545. SANCHEZ, Ricardo
"En-Ojitos: Canto a Piñero" (recuerdos dejan huellas en las humosas palabras, El Paso — 10 Nov. 88). [Americas] (20:3/4) Fall-Wint 92, p. 213-214.
"Notas a Federico García Lorca (con Disculpas y Festejos)." [Americas] (20:3/4) Fall-Wint 92, p. 215-222.
5546. SANCHEZ MAYANS, Fernando
"Poema XV. Podríamos conocernos alguna vez del tiempo." [LindLM] (11:4) D 92, p. 17.
"Poema XVI. Día a día nuestra arcáica delgadez se purifica." [LindLM] (11:4) D 92, p. 17.
5547. SANDERS, Bonny Barry
"Reasons for Going On to Something New." [Plain] (13:1) Fall 92, p. 22.
"Until the Valley Circles Under Us." [Plain] (12:3) Spr 92, p. 38.
5548. SANDERS, David
"The Alternates" (for Margaret). [HiramPoR] (51/52) Fall 91-Sum 92, p. 63-64.
"The Observatory." [HiramPoR] (51/52) Fall 91-Sum 92, p. 61-62.
"Parting at Kalemegdan" (tr. of Milos Crnjanski, w. Dubravka Juraga). [NewOR] (19:3/4) Fall-Wint 92, p. 108.
5549. SANDERS, Ed
"Melville's Father." [Sulfur] (12:2, #31) Fall 92, p. 104-117.
5550. SANDERS, Kristine
"To the Man Who Gave Me Blue Eyes, a Pointy Nose, and a Stuttering Problem at the Age of 2." [Pearl] (16) Fall 92, p. 11.
5551. SANDERS, Lori
"E Ticket." [ChironR] (11:3) Aut 92, p. 26.
"Love on the Playground" (Or Jim's Got the Cooties). [Pearl] (16) Fall 92, p. 12.
5552. SANDERS, Mark
"Another Kind of War." [AntigR] (90) Sum 92, p. 118.
"How to Sing, How to Dance." [Plain] (13:1) Fall 92, p. 32-33.
"In the Company of Pagans." [Northeast] (5:6) Spr 92, p. 23-24.
"The Moments" (for Jerra). [OxfordM] (8:1) Spr-Sum 92, p. 8-9.
"The Other Two." [OxfordM] (8:1) Spr-Sum 92, p. 10-11.
5553. SANDERS, Tony
"Cul-de-sac" (after Robbe-Grillet). [NewRep] (206:9) 2 Mr 92, p. 40.
"Other Music." [OhioR] (48) 92, p. 76-77.

"Partial Eclipse." [OhioR] (48) 92, p. 75.
"Rote of Spring." [WestHR] (46:1) Spr 92, p. 17.
"To Hugo von Hofmannsthal." [WestHR] (46:1) Spr 92, p. 19.
"Trakl's Hat." [WestHR] (46:1) Spr 92, p. 18.
"Wendy's Scarf." [PraS] (66:2) Sum 92, p. 113-114.
"Words to Penelope" (Amherst, Massachusetts, 1886). [WestHR] (46:3) Fall 92, p. 272.

5554. SANDSTROEM, Yvonne L.
"Austin, Texas" (tr. of Lars Gustafsson). [NewYorker] (68:27) 24 Ag 92, p. 36.
"Itemized Expenses" (August Strindberg, 1849-1912, tr. of Lars Gustafsson). [NewYorker] (68:7) 6 Ap 92, p. 30.

5555. SANDY, Stephen
"A Bamboo Brushpot." [NewRep] (207:13) 21 S 92, p. 44.
"Beachcomber." [AmerPoR] (21:3) My-Je 92, p. 17.
"Fort Burial." [Salm] (96) Fall 92, p. 172-173.
"Gulf Memo." [Atlantic] (270:3) S 92, p. 56.
"The Tack." [MichQR] (31:1) Wint 92, p. 73-77.

5556. SANER, Reg
"Dandelion." [LaurelR] (26:2) Sum 92, p. 84.
"North Rim Esplanade Sundown." [Poetry] (160:5) Ag 92, p. 249.
"The Red Poppy." [Poetry] (160:5) Ag 92, p. 250.
"Spring Song." [Poetry] (160:5) Ag 92, p. 250.
"What Wilderness Tells You." [Poetry] (160:5) Ag 92, p. 251.

5557. SANGER, Peter
"Black Rain." [AntigR] (89) Spr 92, p. 78.
"Newscast." [AntigR] (89) Spr 92, p. 79.
"Windfalls." [AntigR] (89) Spr 92, p. 80.

5558. SANGER, Richard
"Colonial Incident." [AntigR] (91) Fall 92, p. 116.
"Family Romance." [AntigR] (89) Spr 92, p. 108.
"Travels with My Aunt." [AntigR] (89) Spr 92, p. 106-107.

5559. SANGUINETI, Edoardo
"In the Beginning Was Calculation" (tr. by Corrado Federici). [PoetryC] (13:1) N 92, p. 20.

5560. SANSOM, Peter
"Of the Masses." [Verse] (9:3) Wint 92, p. 106.

5561. SANTEN, Louise van
"Near-Sighted" (tr. by Alastair Reid). [Trans] (26) Spr 92, p. 45.

5562. SANTIAGO, Jo
"She Swelled." [Interim] (11:2) Fall-Wint 92-93, p. 15-17.

5563. SANTIAGO-BACA, Jimmy
"Martín III." [Americas] (20:3/4) Fall-Wint 92, p. 189-193.

5564. SANTIAGO PEREDNIK, Jorge
"The Shock of the Lenders" (Main Fragment, tr. by Molly Weigel). [Sulfur] (12:2, #31) Fall 92, p. 43-50.

5565. SANTOS, Sherod
"Portrait of a Couple on an Evening Late in the 20th Century." [Nat] (254:3) 27 Ja 92, p. 103.

5566. SANTOS SILVA, Loreina
"XIX. The witches are skirting the coastline" (tr. by Anthony Hunt). [Nimrod] (36:1) Fall-Wint 92, p. 73.
"Apocryphal Children" (from "Metalepsis," tr. by Anthony Hunt). [Nimrod] (36:1) Fall-Wint 92, p. 71-72.

5567. SAPIA, Yvonne
"Aquí." [Americas] (20:3/4) Fall-Wint 92, p. 174.
"Defining the Grateful Gesture." [Americas] (20:3/4) Fall-Wint 92, p. 172-173.
"Del Medio del Sueño." [Americas] (20:3/4) Fall-Wint 92, p. 169.
"La Desconocida." [Americas] (20:3/4) Fall-Wint 92, p. 171.
"Emergency Stopping Only." [ChatR] (12:3) Spr 92, p. 47.
"The Figure Emerging." [CinPR] (23) Wint 91-92, p. 7.
"La Mujer, Her Back to the Spectator." [Americas] (20:3/4) Fall-Wint 92, p. 170.

5568. SAPINKOPF, Lisa
"The All, the Nothing" (From "Beginning and End of Snow," 1991, tr. of Yves Bonnefoy). [Confr] (50) Fall 92, p. 296-297.
"And When the Winter Wind" (tr. of Georgi Borisov, w. Georgi Belev). [CrabCR] (8:1) Sum-Fall 92, p. 17.

"At Night" (tr. of Boris Hristov). [ConnPR] (11:1) 92, p. 33.
"Beginning and End of Snow" (tr. of Yves Bonnefoy). [QRL] (Poetry Series 11: vol. 31) 92, 37 p.
"Between Two Shopfronts" (tr. of Georgi Belev, w. the author). [Vis] (39) 92, p. 19 - 20.
"A Cry" (tr. of Georgi Belev). [MidAR] (13:2) 92, p. 78.
"The Curved Mirror" (From "Ce qui fut sans lumière" (1987), tr. of Yves Bonnefoy). [Verse] (9:3) Wint 92, p. 51.
"Debut en Fin de la Neige" (Excerpt, tr. of Yves Bonnefoy). [QW] (35) Sum-Fall 92, p. 117.
"Dove" (tr. of Georgi Belev, w. the author). [WebR] (16) Fall 92, p. 13.
"The Dream's Restlessness" (tr. of Yves Bonnefoy). [Agni] (35) 92, p. 58-62.
"Garden of Questions" (tr. of Ivan Metodiev, w. Georgi Belev). [CrabCR] (8:1) Sum-Fall 92, p. 15.
"Give the snow a good interrogation!" (tr. of Georgi Belev, w. the author). [Confr] (50) Fall 92, p. 299.
"Hopkins Forest" (tr. of Yves Bonnefoy). [Pequod] (34) 92, p. 110-111.
"Love" (tr. of Georgi Belev, w. the author). [HolCrit] (29:2) Ap 92, p. 16.
"Memory" (A cycle of fifteen poems. Selection: II, tr. of Marin Georgiev, w. Georgi Belev). [Agni] (36) 92, p. 164-165.
"Miracle" (tr. of Nikolai Kantchev, w. Georgi Belev). [Vis] (39) 92, p. 20.
"Monastery" (tr. of Ivan Davidkov, w. Georgi Belev). [Nimrod] (35:2) Spr-Sum 92, p. 25.
"Moth" (tr. of Georgi Belev). [Nimrod] (35:2) Spr-Sum 92, p. 27.
"Night Storm" (tr. of Georgi Belev, w. the author). [ArtfulD] (22/23) 92, p. 38.
"The Old City" (tr. of Ivan Teofilov, w. Georgi Belev). [Nimrod] (35:2) Spr-Sum 92, p. 24.
"On Snow-Laden Branches" (tr. of Yves Bonnefoy). [NewOR] (19:3/4) Fall-Wint 92, p. 82-83.
"The Only Rose" (tr. of Yves Bonnefoy). [SpoonRQ] (17:3/4) Sum-Fall 92, p. 46 - 48.
"Passing the Fire" (tr. of Yves Bonnefoy). [Salm] (96) Fall 92, p. 170-171.
"Rock on the Seashore" (tr. of Georgi Belev). [Boulevard] (7:1, #19) Spr 92, p. 210.
"Romance" (tr. of Georgi Belev). [Nimrod] (35:2) Spr-Sum 92, p. 26.
"A Scene" (tr. of Ani Ilkov, w. Georgi Belev). [Agni] (36) 92, p. 162-163.
"Sealed Garden" (tr. of Georgi Belev). [PartR] (59:2) Spr 92, p. 270.
"A Sign from Heaven" (tr. of Boris Hristov, w. Georgi Belev). [CrabCR] (8:1) Sum - Fall 92, p. 16.
"Spaces" (tr. of Georgi Belev). [PartR] (59:2) Spr 92, p. 270-271.
"The Sparrow Hawk" (tr. of Yves Bonnefoy). [Stand] (33:4) Aut 92, p. 46.
"A Stone" (tr. of Yves Bonnefoy). [Stand] (33:4) Aut 92, p. 45.
"The Trees" (From "Ce qui fut sans lumière" (1987), tr. of Yves Bonnefoy). [Verse] (9:3) Wint 92, p. 52.
"Untitled: Should you wish someone dead" (tr. of Georgi Belev). [Boulevard] (7:1, #19) Spr 92, p. 211-212.
"The Voice Resumed" (tr. of Yves Bonnefoy). [NewOR] (19:3/4) Fall-Wint 92, p. 81.

5569. SAPPHIRE
"American Dreams." [CityLR] (5) 92, p. 130-136.
"Boys Love Baseball (or a Quarter Buys a Lot in 1952)." [BrooklynR] (9) 92, p. 32 - 34.
"Poem for Jennifer, Marla, Tawana & Me." [SinW] (47) Sum-Fall 92, p. 100-105.

5570. SAPPHO
"Evening Star" (tr. by Diana Der-Hovanessian). [13thMoon] (10:1/2) 92, p. 36.
"I Loved You Athis" (tr. by Diana Der-Hovanessian). [13thMoon] (10:1/2) 92, p. 36.
"Mother, I Cannot Weave" (tr. by Diana Der-Hovanessian). [13thMoon] (10:1/2) 92, p. 35.
"My Mother" (tr. by Diana Der-Hovanessian). [13thMoon] (10:1/2) 92, p. 36.
"Sappho: A Garland" (tr. by Jim Powell). [TriQ] (86) Wint 92-93, p. 224-243.
"To Aphrodite" (tr. by Diana Der-Hovanessian). [13thMoon] (10:1/2) 92, p. 35.
"Yearning" (tr. by Diana Der-Hovanessian). [13thMoon] (10:1/2) 92, p. 35.

5571. SARACENO, Stephen
"Green with Envy." [Pearl] (16) Fall 92, p. 51.

5572. SARAH, Robyn
"Ad Lib for Bone Flute." [MalR] (98) Spr 92, p. 66-69.

"Hommage à Roget" (for Jack Hannan). [CanLit] (133) Sum 92, p. 90-91.
"Letter." [PoetryC] (12:2) Ap 92, p. 6.
"Nisi." [PoetryC] (12:2) Ap 92, p. 6.
"Once, Desire." [PoetryC] (12:2) Ap 92, p. 6.
"Partita." [CanLit] (133) Sum 92, p. 108.

5573. SARANG, Vilas
"Deciphering a Stone Inscription" (tr. of Vasant Abaji Dahake). [ChiR] (38:1/2) 92, p. 97.

5574. SARGENT, Robert
"Mr. Buddy Bishop of Salem, Virginia." [HampSPR] Wint 92, p. 13.
"The Piano Seat Cover." [Pembroke] (24) 92, p. 149.
"What She Said." [PoetL] (87:3) Fall 92, p. 40.

SARRE, Zulu la
See La SARRE, Zulu

5575. SARTON, May
"After the Long Enduring" (For Charles). [Poetry] (161:3) D 92, p. 128.
"Bliss." [Poetry] (161:3) D 92, p. 130.
"Coming into Eighty." [ParisR] (34:123) Sum 92, p. 33.
"The Cosset Lamb" (with three work sheets). [WeberS] (9:2) Spr-Sum 92, p. 33-36.
"The Ender, the Beginner." [ParisR] (34:123) Sum 92, p. 31.
"A Handful of Thyme." [Poetry] (161:3) D 92, p. 129.
"Lunch in the Garden." [Poetry] (161:3) D 92, p. 126.
"The O's of November." [Poetry] (161:3) D 92, p. 125.
"Rinsing the Eye." [ParisR] (34:123) Sum 92, p. 32.
"The Teacher." [Poetry] (161:3) D 92, p. 127.

5576. SASANOV, Catherine
"Cathedral." [MidAR] (13:2) 92, p. 15-16.
"Sugar Bones, Sugar Tears: Oaxaca, Mexico" (For Harold Grosowsky, 1919-1981). [MidAR] (13:2) 92, p. 13-14.

5577. SASSER, Albert
"My ears, sensitized" (Excerpt). [PoetryUSA] (24) 92, p. 27.
"Untitled: No one truly understands the depth of wounds." [PoetryUSA] (24) 92, p. 27.
"With Reason to Doubt Everything." [PoetryUSA] (24) 92, p. 26.

5578. SATRIANO, John
"The Women Work" (tr. of Marco Papa). [ConnPR] (11:1) 92, p. 21-22.

5579. SATTERFIELD, Ben
"Spelling." [Light] (1) Spr 92, p. 9.

SATTERFIELD, Deb (Deborah) Parks
See PARKS-SATTERFIELD, Deb (Deborah)

5580. SATTERFIELD, Jane
"History." [CarolQ] (45:1) Fall 92, p. 53.
"The Moon in the Cup of the Mind." [QW] (36) Wint 92-93, p. 120.
"A Small Life." [NoAmR] (277:4) Jl-Ag 92, p. 37.
"Sonata." [SouthernPR] (32:1) Spr 92, p. 47.

5581. SATZ, Martha
"The Tree of Pleasure" (tr. of Dárday István, w. Zsuzsanna Ozsváth). [Os] (35) Fall 92, p. 17.
"The Word's Color Change" (tr. of Fabó Kinga, w. Zsuzsanna Ozsváth). [Os] (35) Fall 92, p. 19.

5582. SAVAGE, Tom
"Hallelujah, We're a Bum Again." [Talisman] (8) Spr 92, p. 172.

5583. SAVAGEAU, Cheryl
"French Girls Are Fast." [BostonR] (17:5) S-O 92, p. 18.

5584. SAVARD, Jeannine
"The Bishop Dreams He Was a Brunette in Paris in 1860" (for Brian). [Iowa] (22:3) Fall 92, p. 111-112.
"A Carnival Figure of Guatemalan Clay." [ThRiPo] (39/40) 92-93, p. 225.
"The Chase." [VirQR] (68:3) Sum 92, p. 483.
"The Daughter's Brooch." [ThRiPo] (39/40) 92-93, p. 223-224.
"The Descent of Fire." [ThRiPo] (39/40) 92-93, p. 225-226.
"Exposure: Two Women." [Manoa] (4:1) Spr 92, p. 19-20.
"The Fall." [ThRiPo] (39/40) 92-93, p. 224-225.
"The Good Order" (for my husband). [Manoa] (4:1) Spr 92, p. 18-19.
"Gravitational Masses in the Dream Way." [Iowa] (22:3) Fall 92, p. 112-113.
"Heat's Elect." [Ploughs] (18:1) Spr 92, p. 223.

"The Little Mouthfuls." [VirQR] (68:3) Sum 92, p. 483-484.
"No Wall, No Moon." [VirQR] (68:3) Sum 92, p. 482.
"The Rain in Five Places Over Chino Valley." [Ploughs] (18:1) Spr 92, p. 222.
"The Turning Sky." [Manoa] (4:1) Spr 92, p. 20.

5585. SAVARESE, Ralph (Ralph D.)
"By Story's End: A Poem for Three Readers." [BelPoJ] (42:4) Sum 92, p. 24-28.
"Memorial Day" (On America's Failed Free Verse Invasion of the Underworld, "So That Men Might Die and Be Remembered"). [AmerPoR] (21:2) Mr-Ap 92, p. 25.

5586. SAVERY, Pancho
"1969." [HangL] (60) 92, p. 53.
"Anything." [HangL] (60) 92, p. 53.
"The Hospital." [HangL] (60) 92, p. 53.
"The Joys of Fatherhood (VII)." [HangL] (60) 92, p. 52.
"New England." [HangL] (60) 92, p. 52.
"Reconstructing Harvard Square" (for Robert Creeley). [HangL] (60) 92, p. 52.
"The Shadow." [HangL] (60) 92, p. 54.
"Thelonious." [HangL] (60) 92, p. 54.

5587. SAVITT, Lynne
"A T & T Connection." [ChironR] (11:1) Spr 92, p. 20.
"After the Rape" (for my son, Matthew). [NewYorkQ] (48) 92, p. 66.
"Marriage Haze." [NewYorkQ] (49) 92, p. 56.

5588. SAVOIE, Terry
"Mingus / Imagination." [Sonora] (22/23) Spr 92, p. 130-131.
"Mr. Henry." [AnotherCM] (24) Fall 92, p. 151-152.
"Nags." [NoAmR] (277:2) Mr-Ap 92, p. 24.
"Playing Basketball." [Farm] (9:1) Spr-Sum 92, p. 49.
"Unrequited Love." [Elf] (2:4) Wint 92, p. 28.

5589. SAVORY, Elaine
"Flame Tree Time." [LitR] (35:4) Sum 92, p. 555.
"For My Father (Now I Can Feel Words in a Poem)." [LitR] (35:4) Sum 92, p. 553.
"For the Lady Concerned That Poets Reveal Intimacies." [LitR] (35:4) Sum 92, p. 551.
"Moonsong of Sister Rabbit." [LitR] (35:4) Sum 92, p. 554.
"Witch Talk." [LitR] (35:4) Sum 92, p. 552.

5590. SAVVAS, Minas
"Calculated Behavior" (tr. of Yannis Ritsos). [Elf] (2:1) Spr 92, p. 20.
"Self Sympathy" (tr. of Yannis Ritsos). [Elf] (2:1) Spr 92, p. 21.
"The Wood-Cutter" (tr. of Yannis Ritsos). [CarolQ] (44:2) Wint 92, p. 76.

5591. SAYA, Tom
"I saw an assassin." [WormR] (32:1, #125) 92, p. 7.
"The Princess and the Animals (2)." [Asylum] (7:3/4) 92, p. 23.
"The Princess and the Animals (3)." [Asylum] (7:3/4) 92, p. 24-25.
"Wasp." [GreensboroR] (53) Wint 92-93, p. 96.

5592. SAYYED, Yasmin A.
"Breaths on My Mirror." [SinW] (47) Sum-Fall 92, p. 19-24.

5593. SCALAPINO, Leslie
"Defoe" (Excerpt). [ColR] (9:2) Fall 92, p. 56-63.
"Walking Life" (Excerpts). [AmerPoR] (21:2) Mr-Ap 92, p. 42-45.

5594. SCAMAHORN, Mark
"A Fall." [OnTheBus] (4:2/5:1, #10/11) 92, p. 192.
"God Is Everywhere." [OnTheBus] (4:2/5:1, #10/11) 92, p. 192.

5595. SCAMMACCA, Nat
"My Madness Chasing Itself." [Footwork] 92, p. 12.

5596. SCAMMELL, Michael
"Wind" (tr. of Veno Taufer). [Vis] (38) 92, p. 43.

5597. SCAMMELL, William
"Inventions" (In Memoriam Norman Nicholson, 1914-1987). [KenR] (NS 14:2) Spr 92, p. 34-35.
"On the Approach to My 49th Birthday." [KenR] (NS 14:2) Spr 92, p. 33.

5598. SCANNELL, Joseph
"South Beach." [MinnR] (39) Fall-Wint 92-93, p. 11-12.

5599. SCARBOROUGH, Jessica
"Untitled: There is no vacancy in this house" (from "About Time III," William James Association's Prison Arts Project, 1987). [PoetryUSA] (24) 92, p. 26.

5600. SCARBROUGH, George
"The Train." [SouthernR] (28:4) Aut, O 92, p. 901.
5601. SCATES, Maxine
"August." [Crazy] (42) Spr 92, p. 56-57.
"Fear." [AmerPoR] (21:2) Mr-Ap 92, p. 27.
"Grief." [Crazy] (42) Spr 92, p. 58-59.
5602. SCHAACK, F. J.
"I See You Peeking." [EngJ] (81:3) Mr 92, p. 93.
5603. SCHAD, Janice D.
"Mute the Singer, Withering the Tree." [Elf] (2:4) Wint 92, p. 30.
5604. SCHAEDLER, Brad
"An Old Cemetery Far from the Main Road." [Plain] (13:1) Fall 92, p. 23.
5605. SCHAEFER, Eileen Blas
"Deified." [EngJ] (81:7) N 92, p. 98.
5606. SCHAFFER, Amanda
"August" (Second Prize, poetry contest). [HarvardA] (126:3) Spr 92, p. 15.
"The Rival" (After Sylvia Plath). [HarvardA] (127:1) Fall 92, p. 8.
"Through Her Glass Eye" (Third Prize, poetry contest). [HarvardA] (126:3) Spr 92, p. 33.
5607. SCHAFFER, Teya
"Jackie." [SinW] (46) Spr 92, p. 19.
5608. SCHAFFNER, M. A.
"Ms. Muffet." [CumbPR] (12:1) Fall 92, p. 26.
5609. SCHAIN, Eliot
"Jersey Teens." [JlNJPo] (14:2) Aut 92, p. 41.
5610. SCHAPIRO, Jane
"Alignment." [AmerS] (61:3) Sum 92, p. 436.
"Moonrock." [WebR] (16) Fall 92, p. 73-74.
"The Pessimist." [GettyR] (5:1) Wint 92, p. 79.
5611. SCHAUM, D. C.
"The Raising of American Motors." [CreamCR] (16:2) Fall 92, p. 18.
5612. SCHEDLER, Gilbert
"Zen and the American Economy." [ChrC] (109:12) 8 Ap 92, p. 366.
5613. SCHEDLINSKI, Rainer
"After school with blondes into the basin" (tr. by Margitt Lehbert). [Shiny] (7/8) 92, p. 143.
"Breaths shallow as a meadow" (tr. by Margitt Lehbert). [Shiny] (7/8) 92, p. 143.
5614. SCHEELE, Roy
"Avatars." [Northeast] (5:7) Wint 92-93, p. 4.
"White Poppies." [Northeast] (5:7) Wint 92-93, p. 3.
5615. SCHEIBLI, Silvia
"Frijole Beach." [MidwQ] (33:4) Sum 92, p. 415.
"Purisima Creek." [MidwQ] (33:4) Sum 92, p. 415.
5616. SCHEIER, Libby
"Lines." [PoetryC] (13:1) N 92, p. 5.
"Solving Death." [PoetryC] (13:1) N 92, p. 5.
"Sound." [PoetryC] (13:1) N 92, p. 5.
5617. SCHELLER, Linda
"The Examination." [PoetryE] (33) Spr 92, p. 121.
5618. SCHELLING, Andrew
"After Kshemendra and Hakim Bey." [Talisman] (8) Spr 92, p. 12-13.
"Dug into earth's crust" (tr. of Bhartrihari). [Sulfur] (12:1, #30) Spr 92, p. 160.
"Grieve, brother" (tr. of Bhartrihari). [Sulfur] (12:1, #30) Spr 92, p. 160-161.
"Philip Whalen." [Sulfur] (12:2, #31) Fall 92, p. 51-52.
"The Translation." [Sulfur] (12:2, #31) Fall 92, p. 52-53.
5619. SCHENDEL, Christopher
"When We Were Poor." [Pearl] (16) Fall 92, p. 57-58.
5620. SCHENKER, Donald
"August Thirty First, Nineteen Eighty Nine" (for Kerouac). [OnTheBus] (4:2/5:1, #10/11) 92, p. 193-194.
"Field Throwing Birds at a Sky." [NewYorkQ] (47) 92, p. 103.
5621. SCHIFF, Laura
"Snowline" (tr. of Éva Tóth). [RiverS] (36) 92, p. 89.
"Teiresias' Lament" (tr. of Éva Tóth). [RiverS] (36) 92, p. 88.
5622. SCHILPP, Margot
"Balconies." [QW] (36) Wint 92-93, p. 101-102.

5623. SCHIMEL, Lawrence
"There is a bridge I know of." [Writer] (105:3) Mr 92, p. 23.

5624. SCHIMKE, Lee
"The Night." [HangL] (61) 92, p. 102.

5625. SCHINDEL, Andrew
"Bart's Pleasure in Rain." [US1] (26/27) 92, p. 44.

5626. SCHLOSS, David
"Mapplethorpe on Trial, 1990." [WestHR] (46:3) Fall 92 [i.e. (46:4) Wint 92], p. 390.

5627. SCHLOSSMAN, Lin
"Tourists in Rouen." [Poem] (67) My 92, p. 16-17.

5628. SCHMIDT, Margo A.
"From Cumbria." [MidwQ] (33:4) Sum 92, p. 416.
"The Vigil." [MidwQ] (33:4) Sum 92, p. 417.

5629. SCHMIDT, Paulette
"Another Time" (tr. of Philippe Soupault). [CharR] (18:2) Fall 92, p. 111.
"Autumn Eternal" (tr. of Philippe Soupault). [CharR] (18:2) Fall 92, p. 114.
"Calendar" (tr. of Philippe Soupault). [CharR] (18:2) Fall 92, p. 110.
"Comrade" (tr. of Philippe Soupault). [CharR] (18:2) Fall 92, p. 112-113.
"With Clasped Hands" (tr. of Philippe Soupault). [CharR] (18:2) Fall 92, p. 109-110.

5630. SCHMITT, Peter
"At a 13th-Birthday Party." [SouthernR] (28:3) Sum, Jl 92, p. 603-604.
"Elegy for Christopher Bright (1956-1984)." [SouthernR] (28:3) Sum, Jl 92, p. 598 - 601.
"My Classmate, Elvis Presley." [SouthernR] (28:3) Sum, Jl 92, p. 602-603.
"The Parking Lots of Summer." [SouthernR] (28:3) Sum, Jl 92, p. 601-602.
"Under Desks." [Nat] (255:5) 17-24 Ag 92, p. 188.

5631. SCHMITZ, Dennis
"The Ladder: Roger Vail's Photo of a Rockface in the Carrara (Italy) Marble Quarries." [Field] (47) Fall 92, p. 96-97.
"Roger Vail's Photo of a Worked-Out Mountain in the Carrara (Italy) Marble Quarries." [Field] (47) Fall 92, p. 98-99.

5632. SCHNACKENBERG, Gjertrud
"Angels Grieving over the Dead Christ" (The epitaphios of Thessaloniki). [YaleR] (80:1/2) Apr 92, p. 169-173.
"A Gilded Lapse of Time" (Ravenna). [NewYorker] (68:17) 15 Je 92, p. 44-45.
"A Monument in Utopia" (Osip Mandelstam). [NewYorker] (68:37) 2 N 92, p. 95 - 96.
"The Resurrection" (Piero della Francesca). [NewYorker] (68:31) 21 S 92, p. 42-43.
"Tiberius Learns of the Resurrection" (Eusebius, History of the Church, I.ii). [YaleR] (80:1/2) Apr 92, p. 174-180.

5633. SCHNEIDER, Pat
"The Old Woman." [Parting] (5:1) Sum 92, p. 12.

5634. SCHNEIDERS, Jay
"Sinai." [HayF] (10) Spr-Sum 92, p. 31.

5635. SCHOEBERLEIN, Marion
"Emily Dickinson." [HolCrit] (29:4) O 92, p. 14.

5636. SCHOENBERGER, Nancy
"Four for Theodore Roethke." [NewEngR] (14:3) Sum 92, p. 106-109.
"The Wood Corpse." [NewEngR] (14:3) Sum 92, p. 105-106.

5637. SCHOFIELD, Don
"Lesson in Waking." [OxfordM] (6:2) Fall-Wint 90, p. 30.
"Snapshot." [OxfordM] (6:2) Fall-Wint 90, p. 31.

5638. SCHOMER, Jeremy
"Poetically Incorrect." [Hellas] (3:1) Spr 92, p. 45.

5639. SCHONBRUN, Adam
"Fighting: A New York Poem." [Noctiluca] (1:2) Wint 92 [on cover: Wint 93], p. 11.
"Midsummer Dream" (Clearfield, PA 7/91). [Noctiluca] (1:2) Wint 92 [on cover: Wint 93], p. 9.
"Visions of Reb Dovid." [Noctiluca] (1:2) Wint 92 [on cover: Wint 93], p. 10-11.

5640. SCHÖNMAIER, Eleonore
"Flight into Puppetry." [AntigR] (89) Spr 92, p. 126.
"Play Box Collection." [AntigR] (89) Spr 92, p. 125.
"Treading Fast Rivers." [Quarry] (41:4) Fall 92, p. 47-50.

5641. SCHOONOVER, Amy Jo
"Threnody in the Style of a Rondo." [CapeR] (27:1) Spr 92, p. 40.
5642. SCHORB, E. M.
"An Antiquary of the Future." [CinPR] (23) Wint 91-92, p. 54.
"Come a Cropper." [ColEng] (54:6) O 92, p. 717-718.
"Come a Cropper." [WebR] (16) Fall 92, p. 86-87.
"The Honey House." [ChiR] (38:3) 92, p. 52-53.
"Houdini and the Dying Swan." [SewanR] (100:3) Sum 92, p. o380-381.
"Incognito." [ChatR] (12:4) Sum 92, p. 30-31.
"The Letter, 1942." [TarRP] (30:2) Spr 91, p. 28-30.
"Poetry in Motion." [ColEng] (54:6) O 92, p. 716.
"Poetry in Motion." [WritersF] (18) 92, p. 115.
"A Reply." [WebR] (16) Fall 92, p. 87.
"The Secret Agent." [JINJPo] (14:1) Spr 92, p. 10.
5643. SCHORR, Laurie
"Amusement." [ThRiPo] (39/40) 92-93, p. 226-227.
5644. SCHOTT, Lynn Rigney
"Small Potatoes." [CutB] (38) Sum 92, p. 93.
5645. SCHOTT, Penelope Scambly
"Argument with My Feet: The Feet Win." [SouthernPR] (32:2) Fall 92, p. 71-72.
"For My Mother Turning Seventy-One." [US1] (26/27) 92, p. 32.
"Ledgers of the Borderless Self" (Derby Wharf, Salem, Massachusetts, 1990). [AmerV] (26) Spr 92, p. 52-54.
5646. SCHOULTZ, Solveig von
"Inland" (tr. by Vera Vance). [Vis] (38) 92, p. 45.
5647. SCHRAMM, Darrell G. H.
"Bravado, or the Grocer from Palestine." [FreeL] (9) Wint 92, p. 16-17.
"The Terminated." [FreeL] (9) Wint 92, p. 17.
5648. SCHREIBER, Ron
"Dreams (2)." [HangL] (61) 92, p. 67.
"Even the Birds." [HangL] (61) 92, p. 68.
"Finches" (Selection from "The Singing Bridge: A National AIDS Poetry Archive"). [Art&Und] (1:2) Wint 92, p. 17.
"Lighting Candles (11-5-87)." [Wind] (22:71) 92, p. 7.
"Little White Jones." [HangL] (61) 92, p. 66.
5649. SCHREINER, Steven
"Imposing Presence." [WebR] (16) Fall 92, p. 71-72.
"The Monster in Me." [WebR] (16) Fall 92, p. 70-71.
5650. SCHROEDER, Ruth
"Creek." [Event] (21:2) Sum 92, p. 60-61.
5651. SCHROTTKE LOOS, Eileen A.
"Onions" (for Jeanne Voege). [Confr] (50) Fall 92, p. 293.
SCHÜLER, Else Lasker
See LASKER-SCHÜLER, Else
5652. SCHULMAN, Grace
"For That Day Only" (New York, June 11, 1883). [KenR] (NS 14:3) Sum 92, p. 121-123.
5653. SCHULS, Reneé A.
"A Special Silence." [Elf] (2:1) Spr 92, p. 36.
5654. SCHULTE, Jane H.
"The Figures of Farrtown." [WillowR] (19) Spr 92, p. 7.
5655. SCHULTZ, Robert
"Black Velvet." [Hudson] (45:1) Spr 92, p. 82-83.
"Vietnam War Memorial, Night." [Hudson] (45:1) Spr 92, p. 81-82.
"Winter in Eden." [Hudson] (45:1) Spr 92, p. 83-84.
5656. SCHULTZ, Susan M.
"Descriptions with Place." [ChamLR] (10/11) Spr-Fall 92, p. 17-18.
"Lost Cities." [Verse] (8:3/9:1) Wint-Spr 92, p. 107-108.
5657. SCHURING, Amy
"A Child Asleep in Its Own Life." [SenR] (22:1) Spr 92, p. 81.
5658. SCHUSTER, Marc
"Boots." [SpiritSH] (57) Spr-Sum 92, p. 54.
"Old Summer." [SpiritSH] (57) Spr-Sum 92, p. 54.
"Temptation." [SpiritSH] (57) Spr-Sum 92, p. 55.
5659. SCHUYLER, James
"Light from Canada." [AmerPoR] (21:1) Ja-F 92, p. 39.

5660. SCHWARTZ, Deborah
"After the Movies of Treblinka." [SinW] (46) Spr 92, p. 41.
5661. SCHWARTZ, Hillel
"Drift." [MissR] (20:3) Spr 92, p. 108-110.
"First Word" (for ALR at year's end). [BelPoJ] (42:4) Sum 92, p. 32-33.
"The Greenhouse Effect." [CentR] (36:1) Wint 92, p. 129.
"Monterey Jack." [PoetL] (87:1) Spr 92, p. 31.
"The Pasha, for Sherbets and Fine Ices." [Lactuca] (15) Mr 92, p. 44.
"Walking with Heidi Among the Haida." [CanLit] (135) Wint 92, p. 95-96.
5662. SCHWARTZ, Howard
"Lailah" (for Laya Firestone-Seghi). [RiverS] (36) 92, p. 36.
"The Scribe." [RiverS] (36) 92, p. 35.
5663. SCHWARTZ, Leonard
"Gnostic Blessing I." [Agni] (35) 92, p. 275-276.
"Poet and Shadow" (tr. of Benjamin Fondane). [Pequod] (34) 92, p. 96.
"Ulysses" (Excerpt, tr. of Benjamin Fondane). [Pequod] (34) 92, p. 97-98.
5664. SCHWARTZ, Lloyd
"The Two Churches (A Dream)." [Boulevard] (7:2/3, #20/21) Fall 92, p. 188-192.
5665. SCHWARTZ, Lynne Sharon
"In Solitary." [LitR] (36:1) Fall 92, p. 55-58.
"Urban Insomnia." [PraS] (66:2) Sum 92, p. 49-51.
5666. SCHWARTZ, Naomi
"Three Poems of Old-World Antiques" (First Runner Up, New Letters Poetry Award). [NewL] (58:2) Wint 92, p. 37-40.
5667. SCHWARTZ, Ruth L.
"In Guatemala" (for Lynda and Ned. First Place, New Letters Poetry Award). [NewL] (58:2) Wint 92, p. 6.
"Near Us, a New House" (First Place, New Letters Poetry Award). [NewL] (58:2) Wint 92, p. 5.
"Possible" (First Place, New Letters Poetry Award). [NewL] (58:2) Wint 92, p. 7.
5668. SCHWEIK, Joanne L.
"Not to Have Missed It." [Blueline] (13) 92, p. 5.
5669. SCHWERER, Eric
"Choked with Joy." [ArtfulD] (22/23) 92, p. 136.
5670. SCHWERNER, Armand
"Dreamer's Transport" (New Year's Readings, St. Mark's Church 1/1/90). [Talisman] (8) Spr 92, p. 16-18.
"The Lot Pit." [ColR] (9:2) Fall 92, p. 64-76.
5671. SCHWITTERS, Kurt
"Flight" (tr. by Jerome Rothenberg and Pierre Joris). [Boulevard] (7:2/3, #20/21) Fall 92, p. 168-170.
"Four Bear Songs" (tr. by Jerome Rothenberg). [Conjunc] (18) 92, p. 138-139.
5672. SCOFIELD, James
"Eden." [BellArk] (8:6) N-D 92, p. 12.
"The Garden." [BellArk] (8:2) Mr-Ap 92, p. 8.
"Ne Plus Ultra." [MidwQ] (34:1) Aut 92, p. 83.
5673. SCOTELLARO, Rocco
"Like This, My Papa in America" (tr. by Ruth Feldman and Brian Swann). [Stand] (33:4) Aut 92, p. 108.
5674. SCOTT, Caitlin
"Two Girls at Parochial School." [Thrpny] (48) Wint 92, p. 24.
5675. SCOTT, Carlos
"Thinking of You!." Sparks! Writing by High School Students (1:1), a supplement to [PraF] (13:4, #61) Wint 92-93, p. 32.
5676. SCOTT, Charlie
"'The Magic Mirror' by Jackson Pollock" (after showing it to some fourth-graders). [WestHR] (46:3) Fall 92 [i.e. (46:4) Wint 92], p. 422-423.
5677. SCOTT, David
"Garden, 1954." [Grain] (20:2) Sum 92, p. 150.
"Wood Well, 1951." [Grain] (20:2) Sum 92, p. 149.
5678. SCOTT, F. R.
"Landscape Estranged" (tr. of Roland Giguère). [Trans] (26) Spr 92, p. 27.
5679. SCOTT, Georgia
"Going to Bermuda." [NewDeltaR] (9:2) Spr-Sum 92, p. 43.
5680. SCOTT, Giles
"Ernestine Anderson, Born Houston, 1928." [HawaiiR] (16:2, #35) Spr 92, p. 67.

"Japanese Rock-Gardens." [HawaiiR] (16:2, #35) Spr 92, p. 66.

5681. SCOTT, Mark
"Drosophila." [WestHR] (46:2) Sum 92, p. 194.

5682. SCOTT, Martin
"The Mechanical Billboard." [WillowS] (29) Wint 92, p. 48-49.

5683. SCOTT, Peter Dale
"The Spirit of Chancery." [Witness] (6:1) 92, p. 100-104.

5684. SCOTT, Whitney
"Jello Helps." [Art&Und] (1:2) Wint 92, p. 8.

5685. SCOVILLE, Shelagh
"Counterpunch." [Light] (1) Spr 92, p. 18.

5686. SCRIMGEOUR, James R.
"Human Brain: Figure 11.1." [CapeR] (27:2) Fall 92, p. 6.

5687. SCRIVENER, Mark
"Evening Comes Softly." [Footwork] 92, p. 125.
"Late Winter, Sunday Morning." [Footwork] 92, p. 125.
"This Lunar Night." [Footwork] 92, p. 125.

5688. SCRIVNER, Jay
"Dear." [PoetryNW] (33:3) Aut 92, p. 16.
"The House of Redeeming Love." [PoetryNW] (33:3) Aut 92, p. 16-17.

5689. SCRUGGS, Patricia L.
"Preparation." [OnTheBus] (4:2/5:1, #10/11) 92, p. 195.

5690. SCRUTON, James
"The Art of Skipping Stones." [Farm] (9:1) Spr-Sum 92, p. 50-51.
"The Dream of Young Achilles." [HayF] (11) Fall-Wint 92, p. 46.
"A Game of Marbles." [Farm] (9:1) Spr-Sum 92, p. 52.
"Objects in Mirror Are Closer Than They Appear." [PoetL] (87:4) Wint 92-93, p. 45.

5691. SEA, Gary
"An Autistic Child Dreams Inside a Box." [WebR] (16) Fall 92, p. 111-112.
"The First Sonnet" (tr. of Jesse Thoor). [Nimrod] (35:2) Spr-Sum 92, p. 9.
"It takes a lot of yourself" (tr. of Yannis Patlilis). [Nimrod] (35:2) Spr-Sum 92, p. 73.
"Sixth Postscript" (tr. of Jesse Thoor). [Nimrod] (35:2) Spr-Sum 92, p. 10.
"Sonnet of the Man Who Lay Sick Along the Way" (he was traveling from Jerusalem to Jericho, tr. of Jesse Thoor). [Nimrod] (35:2) Spr-Sum 92, p. 11.

5692. SEAMAN, Barbara
"Myology of a Poem." [Kaleid] (25) Sum-Fall 92, p. 35.
"Plant Beans Right Side Up." [Kaleid] (25) Sum-Fall 92, p. 35.

5693. SEARLES, G. J.
"La Fantasía." [Light] (1) Spr 92, p. 14.
"Sighting." [Light] (2) Sum 92, p. 12.

5694. SEARS, Donald
"The Cheer Leading Squad." [NegC] (12:1/2) 92, p. 197.

5695. SEARS, Peter
"Oregon Rain." [PoetC] (23:2) Wint 92, p. 30.
"Slip Away." [AntR] (50:3) Sum 92, p. 510.
"Standing Water." [PoetC] (23:2) Wint 92, p. 29.

5696. SEATON, Maureen
"Baby Boomer Dreams of Drowning in a Strange Bathtub." [WestB] (30) 92, p. 36 - 37.
"Candles." [KenR] (NS 14:1) Wint 92, p. 97.
"Chalice." [LaurelR] (26:1) Wint 92, p. 88.
"Ecofeminism in the Year 2000" (w. Denise Duhamel). [MidAR] (13:2) 92, p. 125 - 129.
"A Flicker of Apocalypse." [ParisR] (34:125) Wint 92, p. 162.
"I'm Not Black But I Dreamed This Poem." [KenR] (NS 14:1) Wint 92, p. 98-99.
"The Little King's Mom." [LaurelR] (26:1) Wint 92, p. 88.
"Pulse." [KenR] (NS 14:1) Wint 92, p. 97-98.
"Sing Sing." [ParisR] (34:125) Wint 92, p. 160-161.
"Slow Dance." [ParisR] (34:125) Wint 92, p. 160.
"Woman Circling Lake." [ParisR] (34:125) Wint 92, p. 161.
"The Zen of Crime." [Atlantic] (270:5) N 92, p. 81.

5697. SEBASTIAN, Robert M.
"The Game of the Name." [Light] (3) Aut 92, p. 15.
"Stazione Termini — Roma." [Light] (4) Wint 92-93, p. 16.

5698. SECOR, Nanette
"Complimentary Carnations." [SingHM] (20) 92, p. 68-69.
"Lover: *Labor*." [13thMoon] (10:1/2) 92, p. 51.
5699. SEFFINGA, Jeff
"Young Cattle in Spring." [Grain] (20:3) Fall 92, p. 93.
5700. SEGAL, J. L.
"Before you venture into this tunnel of love you must know simply this." Sparks! Writing by High School Students (1:1), a supplement to [PraF] (13:4, #61) Wint 92-93, p. 28.
"Crack." Sparks! Writing by High School Students (1:1), a supplement to [PraF] (13:4, #61) Wint 92-93, p. 27-28.
"Undying Wishes." Sparks! Writing by High School Students (1:1), a supplement to [PraF] (13:4, #61) Wint 92-93, p. 28.
5701. SEGALEN, Victor
"Tablet of Wisdom" (tr. by Dorothy Aspinwall). [WebR] (16) Fall 92, p. 31.
5702. SEGALL, Pearl Bloch
"The High Cost of Fortune Cookies." [Light] (2) Sum 92, p. 12.
5703. SEIBLES, Timothy (Tim)
"After All." [KenR] (NS 14:3) Sum 92, p. 159-160.
"Like This." [Callaloo] (15:4) Fall 92, p. 912-913.
"The Motion." [SpoonRQ] (17:1/2) Wint-Spr 92, p. 93.
"Natasha in a Mellow Mood" (apologies to Bullwinkle and Rocky). [IndR] (15:2) Fall 92, p. 169-170.
"Prelude." [Callaloo] (15:4) Fall 92, p. 914.
"Slow Dance." [IndR] (15:2) Fall 92, p. 165-168.
"What It Comes Down To" (for James Mardis)." [KenR] (NS 14:3) Sum 92, p. 157 - 158.
5704. SEIDENSTICKER, Edward G.
"In Praise of Shadows" (tr. of Junichiro Tanizaki, w. Thomas J. Harper). [Trans] (26) Spr 92, p. 66.
5705. SEIDMAN, Hugh
"Ball Game." [Sulfur] (12:2, #31) Fall 92, p. 103.
"Child." [Sulfur] (12:2, #31) Fall 92, p. 103.
"Icon." [Pequod] (34) 92, p. 140-141.
"Jim Wright & Larry." [Pequod] (34) 92, p. 138-139.
"My Little Parents." [Sulfur] (12:2, #31) Fall 92, p. 102.
"One Threatened." [Sulfur] (12:2, #31) Fall 92, p. 102-103.
5706. SEIFERLE, Rebecca
"Third-Degree Burns." [CutB] (37) Wint 92, p. 36-37.
"Trilce" (Selections: xxxiii, xxxv, tr. of César Vallejo). [NewOR] (19:1) Spr 92, p. 36-37.
5707. SEIGEL, Shizue
"Too Long in the Same Bed." [NegC] (12:1/2) 92, p. 201-202.
5708. SEILER, Barry
"Dion and the Belmonts." [HangL] (60) 92, p. 56.
"The Golden Thread." [Footwork] 92, p. 96.
"Incidental Music." [HangL] (60) 92, p. 57.
"New Shoes." [HangL] (60) 92, p. 56.
5709. SEITZER, Carol
"Yams." [Confr] (48/49) Spr-Sum 92, p. 227-228.
SEKIO, FUJIWARA no
See FUJIWARA no SEKIO
5710. SELAWSKY, John (John T.)
"Giulietta." [SoDakR] (30:4) Wint 92, p. 116.
"The Grebe." [SoDakR] (30:4) Wint 92, p. 117.
"The Pike" (for my father). [Blueline] (13) 92, p. 39.
"The Red Efts." [DogRR] (11:1) Spr-Sum 92, p. 6.
"Summer Dusk, New Jersey." [DogRR] (11:1) Spr-Sum 92, p. 7.
5711. SELBY, Joan
"A State of Holy Matrimony." [PoetL] (87:3) Fall 92, p. 39.
5712. SELBY, Martha Ann
"Avatars" (tr. of V. Indira Bhavani, w. K. Paramasivam). [ChiR] (38:1/2) 92, p. 189 - 191.
"If Hot Flowers Come to the Street" (tr. of R. Meenakshi, w. K. Paramasivam). [ChiR] (38:1/2) 92, p. 32-33.

"Wanted: A Broom" (tr. of Cantirakanti, w. K. Paramasivam). [ChiR] (38:1/2) 92, p. 31.

5713. SELBY, Spencer
"Collapse Body Text." [PaintedB] (46) 92, p. 21-22.
"The Long Default." [BlackWR] (18:2) Spr-Sum 92, p. 7-9.
"Material." [Talisman] (9) Fall 92, p. 200.
"Message in a Bottle." [Sulfur] (12:2, #31) Fall 92, p. 202-203.

5714. SELCH, A. H.
"Return to Kitchawan." [Calyx] (14:2) Wint 92-93, p. 45-47.

5715. SELLERS, Heather
"Orlando, 1964." [SoCarR] (24:2) Spr 92, p. 154.

5716. SELLIN, Eric
"On the Congo River" (tr. of Jean-Baptiste Tati-Loutard). [Trans] (26) Spr 92, p. 51.
"The Order of Drift" (tr. of V. Y. Mudimbe). [Trans] (26) Spr 92, p. 13.
"Sugar" (tr. of Sony Labou Tansi). [Trans] (26) Spr 92, p. 57.

5717. SELMAN, Robyn
"Descent." [WestHR] (46:3) Fall 92 [i.e. (46:4) Wint 92], p. 406-407.
"Directions to My House." [WestHR] (46:3) Fall 92 [i.e. (46:4) Wint 92], p. 408.
"New Language This Meaning." [KenR] (NS 14:4) Fall 92, p. 74-75.
"Story." [KenR] (NS 14:4) Fall 92, p. 73-74.

5718. SELTZER, Joanne
"A Collection of Maps." [Kalliope] (14:3) 92, p. 41.

5719. SELTZER, Michael
"Hard Water." [BelPoJ] (42:4) Sum 92, p. 30-31.
"Out of the Petri Dish." [Light] (2) Sum 92, p. 11.

5720. SELVING, Jan
"For the Quiet Fat Man at Little Carnegie." [AntR] (50:4) Fall 92, p. 708-709.

5721. SEMANSKY, C. (Chris)
"Accidental." [LullwaterR] (3:2) Spr 92, p. 30.
"Dear John." [JlNJPo] (14:2) Aut 92, p. 42.
"How the Rain Fell." [NoDaQ] (60:3) Sum 92, p. 41-42.
"Self Portrait with Possible Future Problems." [BellR] (15:2) Fall 92, p. 38.

5722. SEMENOVICH, Joseph
"Fear Poem." [DogRR] (11:2, #22) Fall-Wint 92, p. 15.

5723. SEMONES, Charles
"Elegy for a Moment in a Summer." [CapeR] (27:2) Fall 92, p. 29.
"Fallsong" (for R. W.). [LullwaterR] (3:3) Sum 92, p. 46.
"Fugitive from Jericho" (for W. H.). [LullwaterR] (3:2) Spr 92, p. 11-13.

SEN, Nabaneeta Dev
See DEV SEN, Nabaneeta

5724. SEN, Satadru
"After the Rain Has Ended" (tr. of Ketaki Kushari Dyson, w. Leslie Minot). [ChiR] (38:1/2) 92, p. 188.

SENA, Laura Hennessey de
See HENNESSEY-DeSENA, Laura

5725. SENECA
"Hercules in Frenzy" (Selection: Chorus, Act One, tr. by Dana Gioia). [Sparrow] (59) S 92, p. 32-34.
"On Cithaeron" (tr. by David R. Slavitt). [GrandS] (11:1, #41) 92, p. 105-115.

5726. SENECHAL, Diana
"Another" (tr. of Bella Akhmadulina). [Trans] (26) Spr 92, p. 106.
"Don't Devote Much Time to Me" (tr. of Bella Akhmadulina). [Trans] (26) Spr 92, p. 105.
"A New Notebook" (tr. of Bella Akhmadulina). [Trans] (26) Spr 92, p. 107.
"Untruth" (tr. of Tomas Venclova). [Confr] (50) Fall 92, p. 298.
"Who Knows If I May Roam the Earth" (tr. of Bella Akhmadulina). [Trans] (26) Spr 92, p. 106.

5727. SENIOR, Olive
"Meditation on Yellow." [LitR] (35:4) Sum 92, p. 502-507.
"Moonshine Dolly." [LitR] (35:4) Sum 92, p. 508.

5728. SENS, Jean-Marc
"La Route aux Hommes" (after Jean Dubuffet). [InterPR] (18:2) Fall 92, p. 78.

SEOK, Lee Yay
See LEE, Yay Seok

5729. SEQUEIRA, José
"La Noche Se Va." [Nuez] (4:12) 92, p. 20.

5730. SERAFINO, Allan
"My Father's Body." [Event] (21:1) Spr 92, p. 53.
5731. SERNA-MAYTORENA, Manuel Antonio
"El Borrador." [InterPR] (18:1) Spr 92, p. 24.
"Creación." [InterPR] (18:1) Spr 92, p. 26.
"Creation" (tr. by Margo Bender). [InterPR] (18:1) Spr 92, p. 27.
"Echos" (tr. by Margo Bender). [InterPR] (18:1) Spr 92, p. 29.
"Ecos." [InterPR] (18:1) Spr 92, p. 28.
"The Eraser" (tr. by Margo Bender). [InterPR] (18:1) Spr 92, p. 25.
"Offering" (in Spanish and English, tr. by Margo Bender). [InterPR] (18:1) Spr 92, p. 32-35.
"Prelude" (tr. by Margo Bender). [InterPR] (18:1) Spr 92, p. 31, 33.
"Preludio." [InterPR] (18:1) Spr 92, p. 30, 32.
5732. SERPAS, Martha R.
"Before Ash Wednesday." [Kalliope] (14:1) 92, p. 9.
5733. SERRANO, Francisco
"Voces" (fragmentos: 2, 7, 9). [Nuez] (4:10/11) 92, p. 7.
5734. SERRAO, Achille
"That Year" (tr. by Luigi Bonaffini). [Vis] (39) 92, p. 22.
5735. SESHADRI, Vijay
"Divination in the Park." [NewYorker] (68:12) 11 My 92, p. 36.
"The Reappeared." [NewYorker] (68:29) 7 S 92, p. 38.
"Street Scene." [Thrpny] (51) Fall 92, p. 4.
"The Testimonies of Ramon Fernandez." [Agni] (36) 92, p. 243-246.
"A Werewolf in Brooklyn." [Thrpny] (50) Sum 92, p. 13.
5736. SETTLE, Judith Holmes
"The Writing Lesson." [Crucible] (28) Fall 92, p. 56.
5737. SETTLE, Martin (Marty)
"15 Penises on the Sistine Chapel." [SouthernPR] (32:1) Spr 92, p. 53-55.
"Half Hour Workout." [SpoonRQ] (17:1/2) Wint-Spr 92, p. 43-44.
"Man at the Falls." [SpoonRQ] (17:1/2) Wint-Spr 92, p. 41-42.
"Poem to Percival and All Knights of a Second Marriage." [SouthernPR] (32:2) Fall 92, p. 50-55.
5738. SEVERNA, Maia
"Paihia Honeymoon." [Vis] (40) 92, p. 44.
5739. SEXTON, Anne
"My Friend, My Friend" (For M.W.K. who hesitates each time she sees a young girl wearing The Cross). [AntR] (50:1/2) Wint-Spr 92, p. 152.
5740. SEXTON, Rae
"Horace Trenerry" (South Australian Artist, 1901-1958). [Footwork] 92, p. 147.
"The Stone Mason." [Footwork] 92, p. 147.
5741. SEXTON, Tom
"Homecoming." [ParisR] (34:123) Sum 92, p. 135.
5742. SHADOIAN, Jack
"Square Deals." [BellR] (15:2) Fall 92, p. 42.
SHAHID ALI, Agha
See ALI, Agha Shahid
5743. SHAND-ALLFREY, Phyllis
"The Child's Return" (For Jean Rhys). [LitR] (35:4) Sum 92, p. 535.
"Colonial Committee." [LitR] (35:4) Sum 92, p. 536.
"Expatriates" (from :Palm and Oak"). [LitR] (35:4) Sum 92, p. 534-535.
"The Gypsy to Her Baby" (For Phina). [LitR] (35:4) Sum 92, p. 533.
"Love for an Island." [LitR] (35:4) Sum 92, p. 534.
5744. SHANGE, Ntozake
"MESL (Male English As a Second Language): In Defense of Bilingualism." [YellowS] (Ten Years [i.e. 40]) Sum-Fall 92, p. 28-29.
"A Third Generation Geechee Myth for Yr Birthday" (For John Purcell). [YellowS] (39) Spr-Sum 92, p. 28-29.
5745. SHANNON, Mike
"The Al Hrabosky Case." [Spitball] (41) Sum 92, p. 2.
SHAO, Kuan Sng
See SNG,Shao Kuan
5746. SHAPCOTT, Jo
"The Mad Cow on Tour: The Alps." [Verse] (8:3/9:1) Wint-Spr 92, p. 80-82.
"The Room." [SouthernR] (28:2) Spr, Ap 92, p. 291.
"Tom and Jerry Visit England." [SouthernR] (28:2) Spr, Ap 92, p. 289-290.

"Vegetable Love." [SouthernR] (28:2) Spr, Ap 92, p. 291-293.
5747. SHAPIRO, David
"Dido to Aeneas." [Conjunc] (19) 92, p. 311-312.
"A Dream" (Fairfield Porter, 1907-1975). [Boulevard] (7:2/3, #20/21) Fall 92, p. 269.
"An Evening Without Criticism." [Shiny] (7/8) 92, p. 63.
"A Lost Poem" ("poems of Jesus" — E. Pagels). [Shiny] (7/8) 92, p. 64.
"A Note and Poem by Joe Ceravolo in a Dream." [Shiny] (7/8) 92, p. 61-62.
"Sentences." [PaintedB] (46) 92, p. 30.
"You are the You." [Boulevard] (7:2/3, #20/21) Fall 92, p. 268.
5748. SHAPIRO, Gregg (Greg)
"Diet of Strange Men." [ChironR] (11:4) Wint 92, p. 44.
"Night Laundry." [SoCoast] (13) Je 93 [i.e. 92], p. 55.
"Teacher's Pet." [WillowR] (19) Spr 92, p. 31.
"We." [Asylum] (7:3/4) 92, p. 22.
5749. SHAPIRO, Harvey
"Another Story." [PoetryE] (33) Spr 92, p. 123.
"The Encounter." [PoetryE] (33) Spr 92, p. 122.
"Shoppers." [Boulevard] (7:1, #19) Spr 92, p. 206.
5750. SHAPIRO, Lara
"And only the non-Russian name is not yet strewn" (tr. of Natalya Gorbanevskaya). [GrahamHR] (16) Fall 92, p. 10.
"In the far away long ago far" (tr. of Natalya Gorbanevskaya). [GrahamHR] (16) Fall 92, p. 11.
"In the far away long ago far" (tr. of Natalya Gorbanevskaya). [Vis] (38) 92, p. 29.
"The soul of this love no longer even breathes" (tr. of Natalya Gorbanevskaya). [GrahamHR] (16) Fall 92, p. 12.
SHARAT CHANDRA, G. S.
See CHANDRA, G. S. Sharat
5751. SHARE, Don
"The Fair Hills of Ireland." [Witness] (6:1) 92, p. 49.
"First Song" (tr. of Miguel Hernández). [Noctiluca] (1:2) Wint 92 [on cover: Wint 93], p. 14.
"In the Depths of Man" (tr. of Miguel Hernández). [Noctiluca] (1:2) Wint 92 [on cover: Wint 93], p. 13.
"Tailor's Monologue" (tr. of Juan Manuel Roca). [Noctiluca] (1:2) Wint 92 [on cover: Wint 93], p. 15.
5752. SHARETT, Deirdre
"Hunger." [Footwork] 92, p. 91.
5753. SHARFMAN, Bern
"Athletes' Feat." [Light] (4) Wint 92-93, p. 11.
"Communication Gap." [Light] (3) Aut 92, p. 21.
5754. SHARKEY, David
"Eyewitness." [Wind] (22:71) 92, p. 30.
5755. SHARKEY, Lee
"Clients of the State." [Kaleid] (24) Wint-Spr 92, p. 22.
"Queen Marie." [Jacaranda] (6:1/2) Wint-Spr 92, p. 130-131.
5756. SHARMA, B. C. Ramachandra
"American Tourist" (tr. by A. K. Ramanujan, using the author's English version). [ChiR] (38:1/2) 92, p. 67.
5757. SHAW, Brenda
"Marbles." [Bogg] (65) 92, p. 58.
5758. SHAW, Catherine
"Adipose Ode." [ChrC] (109:26) 9-16 S 92, p. 806.
"The Marginal Way." [Elf] (2:1) Spr 92, p. 28.
"Preparation for the Dance." [Elf] (2:1) Spr 92, p. 25.
"Warts and All." [Elf] (2:1) Spr 92, p. 26-27.
5759. SHAW, Jeanne Osborne
"Washing the Car" (Winner, Annual Free Verse Contest, 1991). [AnthNEW] (4) 92, p. 11.
5760. SHAW, Luci
"At the Nursing Home" (for my mother). [SoCoast] (12) Ja 92, p. 20.
"Diamonds That Leap." [ChrC] (109:3) 22 Ja 92, p. 68.
"Golden Delicious." [SoCoast] (12) Ja 92, p. 19.
"When Your Last Parent Dies." [SoCoast] (12) Ja 92, p. 21.

5761. SHAW, Nancy
"Scoptocratic" (2 selections). [Avec] (5:1) 92, p. 22-24.
5762. SHAW, Robert B.
"An Aspen Grove." [NewRep] (207:7) 10 Ag 92, p. 38.
"Last Days in Camden." [Poetry] (159:6) Mr 92, p. 325-330.
"The Pupil." [SouthwR] (77:4) Aut 92, p. 532-533.
5763. SHAW, Stephen I.
"Sketch from a Train Window." [CumbPR] (12:1) Fall 92, p. 74-75.
5764. SHCHERBINA, Tatyana
"Nothing Nothing" (tr. by J. Kates). [KenR] (NS 14:4) Fall 92, p. 119-121.
5765. SHEARD, Norma Voorhees
"X. We Close the Door Now" (June 1990, From "Bondstone"). [Footwork] 92, p. 80.
"XI. Angel." [Footwork] 92, p. 80.
"Brighton Beach." [Footwork] 92, p. 80.
"Sciurus." [Footwork] 92, p. 80.
"Snow Deer." [NewYorkQ] (47) 92, p. 96.
"Water" (for Ann and Joe). [US1] (26/27) 92, p. 33.
5766. SHEBELSKI, R. C.
"Effective Deterrent." [Light] (4) Wint 92-93, p. 12.
"Meet Meal." [Light] (3) Aut 92, p. 11.
5767. SHECK, Laurie
"At the End of September" (after Peter Levi). [Agni] (35) 92, p. 178-179.
"The Book of Persephone." [Agni] (35) 92, p. 176-177.
"Filming Jocasta." [ParisR] (34:122) Spr 92, p. 189-190.
5768. SHECTMAN, Robin
"Mattie at the Opera." [BelPoJ] (43:2) Wint 92-93, p. 25.
"Mattie Translates the Seaside Flowers of Chile." [BelPoJ] (43:2) Wint 92-93, p. 24.
"Morning Among the Gardeners." [LitR] (25:2) Wint 92, p. 261.
5769. SHEEHAN, Marc J.
"Before Dawn on the Picket Line." [SlipS] (12) 92, p. 56.
5770. SHEEHAN, T. (Tom)
"Breaking Windows in Jack's House." [SpoonRQ] (17:3/4) Sum-Fall 92, p. 67-69.
"John Maciag." [HiramPoR] (51/52) Fall 91-Sum 92, p. 65.
"Those Who Eye the Young (2), Sam Mitt Parker: Coach/Judge/Scout 1899-1988." [Spitball] (40) Spr 92, p. 18-19.
5771. SHEEHAN, Timothy J.
"Solart." [LitR] (25:2) Wint 92, p. 283.
5772. SHEFFER, Roger
"Gothics." [Blueline] (13) 92, p. 62.
"Minnesota Crimes." [PoetC] (24:1) Fall 92, p. 27.
"Not Wanted." [SycamoreR] (4:2) Sum 92, p. 39.
"Seen Walking Between Here and Janesville." [CutB] (38) Sum 92, p. 6.
5773. SHEFFER, Susannah
"Art Class." [SingHM] (20) 92, p. 97.
SHEKERJIAN, Regina deCormier
See DeCORMIER-SHEKERJIAN, Regina
5774. SHELBY, Spencer
"Anxiety" (from "Combat Without Weapons"). [WashR] (17:5) F-Mr 92, p. 14.
"Hemisphere" (from "Combat Without Weapons"). [WashR] (17:5) F-Mr 92, p. 14.
5775. SHELDON, Anne
"Catherine of Valois Remembers Her First Husband, 1435." [PoetL] (87:2) Sum 92, p. 11-13.
"Seneca Forest." [Vis] (38) 92, p. 14.
5776. SHELDON, Glenn
"Lenny's Rented Swan." [ChironR] (11:4) Wint 92, p. 47.
"One Man's Biography, One Man's Autobiography." [EvergreenC] (7:1) Wint-Spr 92, p. 9-11.
"With Mariah, in the Valley of the Moon." [JamesWR] (10:1) Fall 92, p. 16.
5777. SHELNUTT, Eve
"Amalie, 1846." [OxfordM] (6:2) Fall-Wint 90, p. 3.
"At the Mass Graveyard." [ThRiPo] (39/40) 92-93, p. 228-229.
"The Author Exiled." [WeberS] (9:1) Wint 92, p. 44.
"Cuba to Think About." [ChatR] (12:4) Sum 92, p. 44-45.
"The Day of Consuelo Gonzales." [OxfordM] (6:2) Fall-Wint 90, p. 4.
"Family." [ThRiPo] (39/40) 92-93, p. 227.

"A Little Story." [WeberS] (9:1) Wint 92, p. 47.
"Love." [WeberS] (9:1) Wint 92, p. 48.
"Memory." [ThRiPo] (39/40) 92-93, p. 227.
"Memory." [WeberS] (9:1) Wint 92, p. 46.
"O Hero." [ThRiPo] (39/40) 92-93, p. 229-230.
"The Poet's Wife." [WeberS] (9:1) Wint 92, p. 45.
"The Triumph of Children." [ThRiPo] (39/40) 92-93, p. 228.
"We Have Drowned Our Passion Like Kittens." [WeberS] (9:1) Wint 92, p. 45.

5778. SHEPARD, Miriam
"Anoitment." [Confr] (48/49) Spr-Sum 92, p. 231.

5779. SHEPARD, Neil
"Mid-winter Thaw, Vermont: A Visit from My Wife." [PoetryE] (33) Spr 92, p. 124.

5780. SHEPARD, Roy
"Sabbath Coffee." [ChrC] (109:18) 20-27 My 92, p. 547.

5781. SHEPHERD, Gail
"Hard Freeze in Frostproof." [PassN] (13:1) Sum 92, p. 31.
"Mother Sleeping." [PassN] (13:1) Sum 92, p. 31.
"The Prodigal's Return." [PraS] (66:2) Sum 92, p. 119-120.
"Tropic." [PraS] (66:2) Sum 92, p. 118-119.

5782. SHEPHERD, J. Barrie
"Ashes to Ashes." [ChrC] (109:8) 4 Mr 92, p. 244.
"Defining Holy Thursday." [ChrC] (109:13) 15 Ap 92, p. 401.
"Drought." [ChrC] (109:7) 26 F 92, p. 220.
"King." [ChrC] (109:37) 16 D 92, p. 1162.
"On the Eleventh Day of Christmas." [ChrC] (109:38) 23-30 D 92, p. 1190.
"Surgical Reminders: Advent." [ChrC] (109:36) 9 D 92, p. 1133.

5783. SHEPHERD, Reginald
"All of This and Nothing." [JamesWR] (9:2) Wint 92, p. 10.
"The Friend." [Poetry] (161:2) N 92, p. 80.
"Kindertotenlieder." [Poetry] (161:2) N 92, p. 79.
"Narcissus Explains." [PoetryNW] (33:4) Wint 92-93, p. 38.
"Paradise." [KenR] (NS 14:4) Fall 92, p. 77-78.
"The Slave Dream." [JamesWR] (9:2) Wint 92, p. 11.
"Slaves." [KenR] (NS 14:4) Fall 92, p. 76.
"What Cannot Be Kept." [KenR] (NS 14:4) Fall 92, p. 77.
"Whatever Wants to Be Seen Must Be Touched." [WestHR] (46:3) Fall 92, p. 242-243.

5784. SHEPPARD, Simon
"Ivy League" (Selection from "The Singing Bridge: A National AIDS Poetry Archive"). [Art&Und] (1:2) Wint 92, p. 17.

5785. SHEPPARD, Susan
"Abandoned House" (Winner of the "In Pittsburgh" award for 1990). [ChironR] (11:1) Spr 92, p. 9.
"Poem of Forgiveness." [ChironR] (11:1) Spr 92, p. 9.

5786. SHEPPERSON, Janet
"Reclaimed Land." [SouthernR] (28:1) Wint, Ja 92, p. 77-78.
"This Room Is Closing Now." [SouthernR] (28:1) Wint, Ja 92, p. 76-77.

5787. SHERER, Ray J.
"Daughter's Poem." [Footwork] 92, p. 100.

5788. SHERLOCK, Francis (Francis G.)
"The Digger." [HawaiiR] (16:2, #35) Spr 92, p. 90.
"An Escape." [BlackBR] (15) Spr-Sum 92, p. 43.
"Knotted to the Drafthorse." [HawaiiR] (16:2, #35) Spr 92, p. 91.
"Mind Country." [BlackBR] (15) Spr-Sum 92, p. 42.

5789. SHERLOCK, Karl J.
"Slaves." [JamesWR] (9:4) Sum 92, p. 10.

5790. SHERMAN, Alana
"Subject to Change." [OxfordM] (6:2) Fall-Wint 90, p. 5.

5791. SHERMAN, Jean L.
"My Father." [OnTheBus] (4:2/5:1, #10/11) 92, p. 196-198.
"Two-Colored World." [OnTheBus] (4:2/5:1, #10/11) 92, p. 196.

5792. SHERMAN, Kenneth
"Asian Cities." [Descant] (23:4/24:1, #78/79) Wint-Spr 92-93, p. 179-183.
"The Eschatology of Bees." [Grain] (20:2) Sum 92, p. 126.
"Fat Black Bird." [PoetryC] (12:3/4) Jl 92, p. 18.
"Fish Cart." [Grain] (20:2) Sum 92, p. 125.

"Hollowe'en Pumpkin." [Grain] (20:2) Sum 92, p. 127.
"Mahabalipuram: Dravidian Ruins." [PoetryC] (12:3/4) Jl 92, p. 18.
"Travelling Carnival." [Descant] (23:3, #78) Fall 92, p. 139-141.
"Treasure of the Sierra Madre." [PoetryC] (12:3/4) Jl 92, p. 18.
"Visiting Eli Mandel." [Descant] (23:3, #78) Fall 92, p. 142-143.

5793. SHERMAN, Maurina S.
"Arroyo Burro Trail Santa Ynez River to Camino Cielo" (for Drew). [QW] (36) Wint 92-93, p. 122-123.

5794. SHERMAN, Nancy
"The Art of Penmanship." [MassR] (23:1) Spr 92, p. 17-18.
"If Everything Is a Subject." [MassR] (23:1) Spr 92, p. 16.

5795. SHERMAN, Susan
"Albuquerque Summer '89." [Contact] (10:62/63/64) Fall 91-Spr 92, p. 39.
"Grandmother." [Contact] (10:62/63/64) Fall 91-Spr 92, p. 37.
"It Was Easier Then." [Contact] (10:62/63/64) Fall 91-Spr 92, p. 35.
"Phoenix." [Contact] (10:62/63/64) Fall 91-Spr 92, p. 38.
"Rituals / A Turning Back." [Contact] (10:62/63/64) Fall 91-Spr 92, p. 36-37.
"Taking Leave." [Contact] (10:62/63/64) Fall 91-Spr 92, p. 40.

5796. SHERRILL, Jan-Mitchell
"Home Care" (For Allen Barnett). [Art&Und] (1:3) Spr 92, p. 10.
"John's Death" (For Randy Pumphrey). [Art&Und] (1:1) Fall 91, p. 9.

5797. SHEVIN, David
"Why East and West Don't Understand One Another." [CutB] (38) Sum 92, p. 11 - 12.

SHI-ZHENG, Chen
See CHEN, Shi-Zheng

5798. SHIELDS, Bill
"A 1978 Ghost Poem." [Pearl] (16) Fall 92, p. 34.
"Ghost Poems." [FreeL] (9) Wint 92, p. 6-7.
"I Brought the War Home to You" (for Kathleen). [NewYorkQ] (49) 92, p. 47.
"Nam Nightmares." [NewYorkQ] (48) 92, p. 68.
"White Trash." [SnailPR] (2:2) Fall-Wint 92, p. 11.
"Winners & Other Losers." [NewYorkQ] (47) 92, p. 93.
"Years." [NewYorkQ] (47) 92, p. 93.

5799. SHIELDS, Carol
"Fall." [NoDaQ] (60:1) Wint 92, p. 59.

5800. SHIFFRIN, Nancy
"The Man Who Sees Combat." [OnTheBus] (4:2/5:1, #10/11) 92, p. 199.

SHIH, Su
See SU, Shih

5801. SHIKATANI, Gerry
"Points of View: The Garden." [WestCL] (26:2, #8) Fall 92, p. 31-33.

5802. SHINDER, Jason
"Crime." [Agni] (35) 92, p. 236-237.
"Exterior Street, New York City — Night." [Ploughs] (18:4) Wint 92-93, p. 147.
"King's Highway." [Ploughs] (18:4) Wint 92-93, p. 148.
"Work" (for Stanley Kunitz). [Ploughs] (18:4) Wint 92-93, p. 145-146.
"X." [Agni] (35) 92, p. 238.

5803. SHIPP, Adriana
"Boca Oficial." [Americas] (19:3/4) Wint 91, p. 53-54.
"La Chanteuse de Jazz." [Americas] (19:3/4) Wint 91, p. 51.
"La Pachanga" (Para el equipo de KXLU — Alma del Barrio). [Americas] (19:3/4) Wint 91, p. 52.

5804. SHIPP, R. D.
"Industry." [Sulfur] (12:1, #30) Spr 92, p. 79-80.
"S&M." [Sulfur] (12:1, #30) Spr 92, p. 79.
"Twin Cousins to the Martyr." [Sulfur] (12:1, #30) Spr 92, p. 77-78.

5805. SHIPPY, Peter (Peter Jay)
"This State of Grace Is Consuming Me." [AnotherCM] (24) Fall 92, p. 158.
"Walking the North Shore, Summer, with Beatrice Smith." [DenQ] (26:4) Spr 92, p. 68.

5806. SHIRAISHI, Kazuko
"Al's Inside His Sax and Won't Come Out" (tr. by Sally Ito). [WestCL] (26:3, #9) Wint 92-93, p. 83.
"The Ostrich Is Short Tempered Because" (tr. by Sally Ito). [WestCL] (26:3, #9) Wint 92-93, p. 82.

"Penguin Cafe" (tr. by Sally Ito). [WestCL] (26:3, #9) Wint 92-93, p. 80-82.
"The Way Birds Laugh" (tr. by Sally Ito). [WestCL] (26:3, #9) Wint 92-93, p. 83.

5807. SHIRLEY, Aleda
"The Curve of Forgetting." [SouthernR] (28:4) Aut, O 92, p. 902-903.
"Late Night Radio." [DenQ] (26:3) Wint 92, p. 44-45.
"Texas." [SouthernR] (28:4) Aut, O 92, p. 903-905.

5808. SHOAF, Diann Blakely
"First Fall: Eve." [SouthernHR] (26:2) Spr 92, p. 152.
"The Man Under the Bed." [NewOR] (19:2) Sum 92, p. 8.
"Staying Home." [TarRP] (32:1) Fall 92, p. 42.

5809. SHOEMAKER, Lynn
"Old Woman Selling a Fish." [MinnR] (38) Spr-Sum 92, p. 36-37.

5810. SHOMER, Enid
"Articulos Religiosos." [Field] (47) Fall 92, p. 92-93.
"The Candidate from Indio: Jacqueline Cochran's Congressional Campaign." [CinPR] (23) Wint 91-92, p. 22-25.
"Pope Joan" (Being Documents Found on the Body of Pope John VIII). [Poetry] (159:6) Mr 92, p. 340-345.
"Pope Joan" (corrected printing of section II. "After Love", stanzas 1-2, Mr 92 issue). [Poetry] (160:3) Je 92, p. 174.
"Table for Four." [MassR] (23:3) Fall 92, p. 444-446.
"Thistles." [Field] (47) Fall 92, p. 94-95.
"Wanting His Child." [ParisR] (34:123) Sum 92, p. 126.

5811. SHOPTAW, John
"Three Tenors." [NewAW] (10) Fall 92, p. 96.

5812. SHORB, Michael
"At the Samoan Cookhouse." [Vis] (39) 92, p. 4-5.

5813. SHORT, Gary
"The Design of Pain." [PoetryE] (33) Spr 92, p. 125-126.
"Field of Vision." [WritersF] (18) 92, p. 107.
"Grace." [CimR] (99) Ap 92, p. 58.
"Out of Night." [CimR] (99) Ap 92, p. 57.
"Sophal Niem and the Moon in the Bucket." [PoetryE] (33) Spr 92, p. 127-128.

5814. SHORT, Steve
"Psalm 18, in Uplands" (an adaptation). [Stand] (33:2) Spr 92, p. 142-144.

5815. SHOT, Danny
"The Living Legend." [PaintedB] (48) 92, p. 36-37.

5816. SHU, Ting
"Ah, Mama" (tr. by De-an Wu Swihart and Gordon T. Osing). [CrabCR] (8:1) Sum - Fall 92, p. 20.
"Two, Maybe Three Different Memories" (tr. by De-an Wu Swihart and Gordon T. Osing). [CrabCR] (8:1) Sum-Fall 92, p. 21.
"What Is There" (tr. by Ginny MacKenzie and Wei Guo). [Pequod] (34) 92, p. 122 - 123.

5817. SHUGRUE, Jim
"In a Motel Room in Nebraska." [PoetryE] (33) Spr 92, p. 129.

5818. SHUKLA, Prayag
"Wayside Station" (tr. by Harish Trivedi). [ChiR] (38:1/2) 92, p. 143.

5819. SHUMAKER, Peggy
"Milagros." [WillowS] (29) Wint 92, p. 83.
"Strong Stars." [Ploughs] (18:1) Spr 92, p. 193.
"Young Boy Dancing at Playa los Muertos." [Ploughs] (18:1) Spr 92, p. 194-195.

5820. SHUNNEY, Kate
"He Gave Me the Gift." [BellArk] (8:4) Jl-Ag 92, p. 1.
"Knowing Our Work." [BellArk] (8:4) Jl-Ag 92, p. 1.
"What My Dreams Would Bring." [BellArk] (8:4) Jl-Ag 92, p. 1.

5821. SHURIN, Aaron
"Her Own." [Talisman] (8) Spr 92, p. 118-122.
"One More Step." [CentralP] (21) Spr 92, p. 163.
"Told." [CentralP] (21) Spr 92, p. 164.

5822. SHUTTLE, Penelope
"Cold One." [PoetryUSA] (24) 92, p. 36.
"Icon of the Divine Yoni." [ManhatR] (6:2) Fall 92, p. 37.
"Into the Solar" (from The Solar, Trerice Manor, Cornwall, U.K.). [ManhatR] (6:2) Fall 92, p. 34-35.
"Night." [ManhatR] (6:2) Fall 92, p. 36.

"Taxing the Rain." [Verse] (8:3/9:1) Wint-Spr 92, p. 109.
"Trick Horse." [Stand] (33:2) Spr 92, p. 92-93.

5823. SHUTTLEWORTH, Red
"Outfielder." [WestB] (30) 92, p. 62-63.

5824. SICOLI, Dan
"Hancock." [SlipS] (12) 92, p. 110.

5825. SIDNEY, Joan Seliger
"The Healer Within, the Healer Without." [NewYorkQ] (48) 92, p. 107.

5826. SIEGAL, Lauri
"This Great Stone" (3rd place winner, Chiron Review 1992 Poetry Contest). [ChironR] (11:3) Aut 92, p. 15.

5827. SIEGEL, Garret
"The Year His Father Died." [AnthNEW] (4) 92, p. (Winner, Annual Free Verse Contest, 1991). [AnthNEW] (4) 92, p. 14.

5828. SIEGEL, Holli
"Selfish." [JINJPo] (14:1) Spr 92, p. 9.

5829. SIEGEL, Joan I.
"The Cruelty of Glass." [Northeast] (5:7) Wint 92-93, p. 5.
"Doors" (for Marian Clarke). [OxfordM] (6:2) Fall-Wint 90, p. 92.
"Unveiling." [Kalliope] (15:1) 92, p. 42.

5830. SIEGEL, June
"The Slug." [Light] (1) Spr 92, p. 12.

5831. SIEGENTHALER, Peter
"From here and now and you." [Os] (34) Spr 92, p. 3.
"War Journal" (Selections: January 13-14, 24, 28, March 3, Easter 1991). [Os] (34) Spr 92, p. 13-15.

5832. SIEVERS, Kelly
"Regal Copper" (Ixtapa, Mexico). [HayF] (11) Fall-Wint 92, p. 73-74.

5833. SIGNORELLI-PAPPAS, Rita
"Black Coat." [ColEng] (54:8) D 92, p. 938.
"A Child's Blindness." [Interim] (11:2) Fall-Wint 92-93, p. 20.
"Jane Austen at Forty." [Calyx] (14:1) Sum 92, p. 46-47.
"Manzoni's Dead Daughters." [NewOR] (19:3/4) Fall-Wint 92, p. 60.
"Shelley's Heart." [PoetL] (87:3) Fall 92, p. 7.
"Swans." [CumbPR] (11:2) Spr 92, p. 12.

5834. SIKORSKY, Christina
"Babstia's House." [PraF] (13:3, #60) Aut 92, p. 167.
"Dear Nina." [PraF] (13:3, #60) Aut 92, p. 168.

5835. SIKTANC, Karel
"Dance of Death" (Excerpt, tr. by Daniela Drazanová and Karel Drazan). [PraS] (66:4) Wint 92, p. 171-172.

5836. SILBERG, Richard
"Door." [OnTheBus] (4:2/5:1, #10/11) 92, p. 200-201.

5837. SILESKY, Barry
"Do-It-Yourself." [FreeL] (10) Sum 92, p. 30.
"The New Design." [FreeL] (10) Sum 92, p. 30.
"The New Design." [NewAW] (10) Fall 92, p. 105-106.
"Oktoberfest." [Boulevard] (7:2/3, #20/21) Fall 92, p. 279.
"Thor's Helper." [SouthernPR] (32:1) Spr 92, p. 44-46.
"Ultrasound." [OnTheBus] (4:2/5:1, #10/11) 92, p. 202.

5838. SILEX, Edgar
"Laughter." [ChironR] (11:3) Aut 92, p. 11.
"Swastika." [ChironR] (11:3) Aut 92, p. 11.

5839. SILKIN, Jon
"Apparition." [Iowa] (22:1) Wint 92, p. 82-83.
"Fathers." [AmerPoR] (21:4) Jl-Ag 92, p. 34.
"Fathers." [Stand] (33:2) Spr 92, p. 51.
"Four Related Poems" (Selections: 3 poems, for Ed Kessler, Richard McCann and Henry Taylor). [AmerPoR] (21:4) Jl-Ag 92, p. 34.
"Honouring the Father." [MissR] (20:3) Spr 92, p. 99.
"Intimacy." [Iowa] (22:1) Wint 92, p. 84.
"Psalmists." [Bogg] (65) 92, p. 31-32.
"Tenderness." [Stand] (33:2) Spr 92, p. 50.
"Through Leaves and Fragmented Light" (for Margaret and Michael Mott). [Iowa] (22:1) Wint 92, p. 83.
"Trying to Hide Treblinka." [Iowa] (22:1) Wint 92, p. 81.

5840. SILKO, Leslie
"Story from Bear Country." [Jacaranda] (6:1/2) Wint-Spr 92, p. 91-93.
5841. SILLIMAN, Ron
"Non" (Excerpt, for Jackson Mac Low). [Talisman] (9) Fall 92, p. 110-114.
5842. SILLITOE, Linda
"Composite Pictures." [WeberS] (9:2) Spr-Sum 92, p. 62.
"Nightwalk." [WeberS] (9:2) Spr-Sum 92, p. 61.
"October Shoot." [WeberS] (9:2) Spr-Sum 92, p. 62.
5843. SILVA, Eddie
"The Fathers We Dream." [LullwaterR] (3:2) Spr 92, p. 8-9.
5844. SILVA, Fernando
"Diarrhea" (tr. by Chuck Wachtel). [HangL] (60) 92, p. 58-61.
"Epigram" (tr. by Chuck Wachtel). [HangL] (60) 92, p. 62.
"La Salud del Niño" (Selection: Foreword, tr. by Chuck Wachtel). [HangL] (60) 92, p. 62.
SILVA, Loreina Santos
See SANTOS SILVA, Loreina
5845. SILVA, Sam
"In Memory of Jack Kerouac." [DogRR] (11:2, #22) Fall-Wint 92, p. 22.
"Publishing the Dog." [DogRR] (11:2, #22) Fall-Wint 92, p. 2.
"Saturday, in These Weekends." [DogRR] (11:2, #22) Fall-Wint 92, p. 22.
5846. SILVERMAN, Herschel
"To Construct a Blues for Moe My Best Man in Jersey City." [MoodySI] (27) Spr 92, p. 3-5.
5847. SILVERMARIE, Sue
"In the Moon Lodge." [ChironR] (11:4) Wint 92, p. 6.
"Under the Sun." [ChironR] (11:4) Wint 92, p. 6.
5848. SILVERSTEIN, David
"Dreaming of Fire, Waking with Burns." [Noctiluca] (1:2) Wint 92 [on cover: Wint 93], p. 1.
"The Electric Blue Worm" (Unyu Tenzan Onsen). [Noctiluca] (1:1) Spr 92, p. 48.
"Smoke" (from the chapbook "Apparitions"). [Noctiluca] (1:2) Wint 92 [on cover: Wint 93], p. 2.
"Walking Ferocity to the Door." [Noctiluca] (1:1) Spr 92, p. 48.
5849. SIMAR, Sue Ann
"Easter." [BlackBR] (15) Spr-Sum 92, p. 18.
"Saddam." [BlackBR] (15) Spr-Sum 92, p. 31.
5850. SIMIC, Charles
"At the Hairdresser" (phantasmagoria, tr. of Novica Tadic). [Field] (46) Spr 92, p. 17.
"Cornell Notebooks" (Selections). [Epoch] (41:2) 92, p. 201-232.
"The Dead." [NewYorker] (68:9) 20 Ap 92, p. 90.
"A Feather Plucked from the Tail of the Fiery Hen" (tr. of Novica Tadic). [Field] (46) Spr 92, p. 13-14.
"Haunted Mind." [PartR] (59:1) Wint 92, p. 96-97.
"Little Picture Catalogue" (tr. of Novica Tadic). [Field] (46) Spr 92, p. 16.
"My Night Labors" (tr. of Novica Tadic). [Field] (47) Fall 92, p. 114.
"The Night Game of the Maker of Faces" (tr. of Novica Tadic). [Field] (47) Fall 92, p. 113.
"Night Sonnet" (tr. of Novica Tadic). [Field] (47) Fall 92, p. 112.
"Nobody" (tr. of Novica Tadic). [Field] (46) Spr 92, p. 12.
"The Oldest Child." [NewYorker] (68:33) 5 O 92, p. 128.
"On a Side Street." [NewYorker] (68:39) 16 N 92, p. 80.
"The Prodigal." [NewYorker] (68:1) 24 F 92, p. 70.
"Romantic Sonnet." [PartR] (59:1) Wint 92, p. 96.
"A Sentimental Voyage around My Room" (tr. of Jovan Hristic). [ParisR]] (34:124) Fall 92, p. 143.
"Song to the Lamb" (tr. of Novica Tadic). [Field] (46) Spr 92, p. 15.
"Text, Silk" (tr. of Novica Tadic). [Field] (46) Spr 92, p. 11.
"That Night They All Gathered on the Highest Tower" (tr. of Jovan Hristic). [ParisR]] (34:124) Fall 92, p. 143.
"This Morning." [NewYorker] (68:25) 10 Ag 92, p. 30.
"Three Photographs." [NewYorker] (68:17) 15 Je 92, p. 78.
"To a Marksman" (tr. of Novica Tadic). [Field] (47) Fall 92, p. 115.
"Toys, Dream" (tr. of Novica Tadic). [Field] (46) Spr 92, p. 10.

5851. SIMMERMAN, Jim
"For Everything We Can't Put Down." [NewEngR] (14:3) Sum 92, p. 169-175.
"Money." [Journal] (16:2) Fall-Wint 92, p. 77-78.
"Vesperal." [AntR] (50:4) Fall 92, p. 707.
5852. SIMMONS-McDONALD, Hazel
"Drought." [LitR] (35:4) Sum 92, p. 543.
"Interlude." [LitR] (35:4) Sum 92, p. 541.
"Strange Wheat." [LitR] (35:4) Sum 92, p. 544.
"Ted." [LitR] (35:4) Sum 92, p. 542.
5853. SIMON, Anne
"The Lure." [BellArk] (8:6) N-D 92, p. 25.
"Mapping." [BellArk] (8:6) N-D 92, p. 25.
5854. SIMON, Beth
"Before Typhoid." [Northeast] (5:7) Wint 92-93, p. 12.
"How Angels Leave Dubuque." [ChironR] (11:2) Sum 92, p. 30.
"Noon in the North." [Northeast] (5:7) Wint 92-93, p. 13.
5855. SIMON, Greg
"Ode to Federico García Lorca" (tr. of Pablo Neruda, w. Steven F. White). [NowestR] (30:1) 92, p. 65-68.
5856. SIMON, John Oliver
"Con Permiso" (for Donald Schenker). [OnTheBus] (4:2/5:1, #10/11) 92, p. 203.
5857. SIMON, Josef
"Prague Fisherman" (tr. by Dominika Winterová and Richard Katrovas). [NewOR] (19:3/4) Fall-Wint 92, p. 27.
5858. SIMON, Maurya
"Epiphany." [GettyR] (5:1) Wint 92, p. 78.
"Madrigal." [GettyR] (5:1) Wint 92, p. 76-77.
"On Our Twentieth Anniversary." [GeoR] (46:2) Sum 92, p. 355.
"Penelope and Delilah." [GettyR] (5:1) Wint 92, p. 74-75.
"Rapture." [GettyR] (5:1) Wint 92, p. 73.
5859. SIMONE, Roberta
"A Clerihew Couple." [Light] (1) Spr 92, p. 22.
"More Clerihew Couples." [Light] (4) Wint 92-93, p. 16.
5860. SIMONS, Louise
"August 29 in Elkins Park." [PaintedB] (48) 92, p. 60.
5861. SIMONSUURI, Kirsti
"Mother Tongues" (tr. by Jascha Kessler and the author). [Nimrod] (35:2) Spr-Sum 92, p. 52.
"Opus" (tr. by Jascha Kessler and the author). [Nimrod] (35:2) Spr-Sum 92, p. 52.
5862. SIMPSON, Anne
"Demeter." [Dandel] (19:3) 92, p. 7.
"The Great Maya, Mother of Buddha." [Dandel] (19:3) 92, p. 11-12.
"Jocasta." [Dandel] (19:3) 92, p. 5.
"Julian of Norwich." [Dandel] (19:3) 92, p. 16.
"Mary." [Dandel] (19:3) 92, p. 8-9.
"Rhea." [Dandel] (19:3) 92, p. 6.
"Sarah." [Dandel] (19:3) 92, p. 10.
"Wealhtheow." [Dandel] (19:3) 92, p. 13-14.
"The Wife of Eadwacer." [Dandel] (19:3) 92, p. 15.
5863. SIMPSON, Bertha B.
"Nine Times Out of Ten." [Light] (2) Sum 92, p. 23.
5864. SIMPSON, Grace
"Veronese's 'Wedding at Cana'." [HampSPR] Wint 92, p. 18.
5865. SIMPSON, Louis
"August." [Hudson] (45:1) Spr 92, p. 67-69.
"The Believer." [Hudson] (45:1) Spr 92, p. 69-70.
"Berkeley in the Sixties." [Hudson] (45:1) Spr 92, p. 70-71.
"Her Weekend in the Country." [Hudson] (45:1) Spr 92, p. 72.
"Outward Forms." [SouthernR] (28:3) Sum, Jl 92, p. 622-625.
"Patsy." [Hudson] (45:1) Spr 92, p. 71.
"Stairs." [Hudson] (45:1) Spr 92, p. 72-73.
"Suddenly." [Hudson] (45:1) Spr 92, p. 73-74.
"West End Avenue." [Hudson] (45:1) Spr 92, p. 75.
5866. SIMPSON, Nancy
"Morning." [SenR] (22:2) Fall 92, p. 78.

5867. SIMS, Roberta Laulicht
"The Bookbinder." [TarRP] (31:2) Spr 92, p. 36-37.
"Chores." [HampSPR] Wint 92, p. 29.
"Obsession." [HampSPR] Wint 92, p. 28.
"Skins." [PoetryE] (33) Spr 92, p. 130.
5868. SINE, Georgia
"Tornado Warning." [ThRiPo] (39/40) 92-93, p. 230.
5869. SINGER, Davida
"Scorpio." [SinW] (46) Spr 92, p. 72.
5870. SINGH, Kedarnath
"Blank Page" (tr. by Vinay Dharwadker). [ChiR] (38:1/2) 92, p. 46-47.
"Language of Communication" (tr. by Vinay Dharwadker). [ChiR] (38:1/2) 92, p. 45.
5871. SINK, Susan
"Coda: Summer on the Dig." [Poetry] (160:4) Jl 92, p. 189.
"Obsessive Memory Sestina." [MinnR] (39) Fall-Wint 92-93, p. 21-22.
5872. SINROSTRO, Rodrigo
"De Brevitate Vitae II." [Nuez] (4:10/11) 92, p. 5.
5873. SIROTA, Liubov (Lyubov)
"At the Crossing" (Chernobyl Poems, tr. by Leonid Levin and Elisavietta Ritchie). [Calyx] (14:2) Wint 92-93, p. 70-72.
"Burden" (Chernobyl Poems, tr. by Leonid Levin and Elisavietta Ritchie). [Calyx] (14:2) Wint 92-93, p. 66-67.
"Fate" (Triptych. Chernobyl Poems, tr. by Leonid Levin and Elisavietta Ritchie). [Calyx] (14:2) Wint 92-93, p. 73-75.
"Radiophobia" (Chernobyl Poems, tr. by Leonid Levin and Elisavietta Ritchie). [Calyx] (14:2) Wint 92-93, p. 68-69.
"To Pripyat" (Chernobyl Poems, tr. by Leonid Levin and Elisavietta Ritchie). [Calyx] (14:2) Wint 92-93, p. 64-65.
"Your Glance Will Trip on My Shadow" (Chernobyl Poems, tr. by Leonid Levin and Elisavietta Ritchie). [Calyx] (14:2) Wint 92-93, p. 63.
"Your glance will trip on my shadow" ("Chernobyl Poems," tr. by Leonid Levin and Elisavietta Ritchie). [NewYorkQ] (48) 92, p. 109.
5874. SIROWITZ, Hal
"Deformed Finger." [HangL] (61) 92, p. 74.
5875. SIZEMORE, Aaron
"Poetry & Razorblades." [MoodySI] (27) Spr 92, p. 30.
5876. SKAU, Michael
"After the Bomb" (Selections: XXVI-XXVIII, XXX). [CumbPR] (11:2) Spr 92, p. 30-33.
5877. SKELLEY, Jack
"Green Goddess." [BrooklynR] (9) 92, p. 38.
5878. SKELTON, Robin
"Lament for Ignacio Sanchez Majias" (Excerpt, tr. of Federico Garcia Lorca). [Arc] (28) Spr 92, p. 63.
"Samhain" (for Allison). [PottPort] (14:2) Fall-Wint 92, p. 62.
"Silly Song" (tr. of Federico Garcia Lorca). [Arc] (28) Spr 92, p. 60.
"The Spell of Form" (5 poems). [Arc] (28) Spr 92, p. 37-53.
"Street of the Mutes" (tr. of Federico Garcia Lorca). [Arc] (28) Spr 92, p. 60.
"Tree, Tree" (tr. of Federico Garcia Lorca). [Arc] (28) Spr 92, p. 64-65.
5879. SKENE, K. V.
"Calliope" (epic poetry). [Dandel] (19:2) 92, p. 16.
"Clio" (history). [Dandel] (19:2) 92, p. 15.
"Erato" (lyric poetry). [Dandel] (19:2) 92, p. 13.
"Fire Water." [CanLit] (134) Aut 92, p. 76.
"Melpomene" (tragedy). [Dandel] (19:2) 92, p. 14.
5880. SKILLING, Keith A. F.
"Holocaust." [Crucible] (28) Fall 92, p. 25.
5881. SKILLINGS, R. D.
"Song for the Three Sisters." [VirQR] (68:4) Aut 92, p. 708.
5882. SKILLMAN, Judith
"Amnesia." [NowestR] (30:3) 92, p. 35.
"The Knitting Bag." [SilverFR] (23) Wint 92, p. 16-17.
"The Night Nurse." [LaurelR] (26:2) Sum 92, p. 24-25.
"Nine Years without Music." [SilverFR] (23) Wint 92, p. 14-15.
"The Problem of a Horse Without Water." [NowestR] (30:3) 92, p. 33-34.

"This Could Be Zayde's Birthday." [NowestR] (30:3) 92, p. 31-32.
"Where It Leads." [SilverFR] (23) Wint 92, p. 18.

5883. SKINNER, Knute
"A Fragment." [NewYorkQ] (49) 92, p. 38.
"Friday Evening." [OnTheBus] (4:2/5:1, #10/11) 92, p. 204.

5884. SKLAREW, Myra
"Homage to Siena." [Confr] (48/49) Spr-Sum 92, p. 188-189.

5885. SKLOOT, Floyd
"Barrelfire Harmony." [Journal] (16:2) Fall-Wint 92, p. 79-80.
"Cannon Beach." [Gypsy] (18) 92, p. 44-45.
"Evenings." [WritersF] (18) 92, p. 51.
"Object Assembly." [NewEngR] (14:4) Fall 92, p. 144-145.
"Ravel at Swim." [PoetryNW] (33:3) Aut 92, p. 8-9.

5886. SKOVRON, Alex
"Don Giovanni's Prayer." [Vis] (40) 92, p. 17.
"Faking It." [Vis] (40) 92, p. 18.
"The Jester." [Vis] (40) 92, p. 16.
"The Note." [Vis] (40) 92, p. 17.
"Oasis." [Vis] (40) 92, p. 16.

5887. SKOYLES, John
"Good Cheer." [ThRiPo] (39/40) 92-93, p. 231-232.
"The Head of Tasso." [ThRiPo] (39/40) 92-93, p. 232-233.
"In Memoriam." [ThRiPo] (39/40) 92-93, p. 233-234.

5888. SKRANDE, Eva
"Lies." [AmerV] (29) 92, p. 67.

5889. SKRUPSKELIS, Viktoria
"Orpheus and Eurydice" (tr. of Judith Vaiciunaite, w. Stuart Friebert). [Confr] (50) Fall 92, p. 300-303.
"Pastorals" (tr. of Judita Vaiciunaite, w. Stuart Friebert). [HayF] (10) Spr-Sum 92, p. 51.
"The Rebel" (tr. of Judita Vaiciunaite, w. Stuart Friebert). [HayF] (10) Spr-Sum 92, p. 50.

5890. SKVARLA, Jeanne
"After the Election." [ColEng] (54:5) S 92, p. 592-593.
"Neither Here Nor There." [ColEng] (54:5) S 92, p. 591.
"Nightwatch." [ColEng] (54:5) S 92, p. 594.
"Poem: Because it's supposed to be spring." [ColEng] (54:5) S 92, p. 591.
"Poem: When I came to." [ColEng] (54:5) S 92, p. 593.

5891. SKYRIE, David
"Rosemary." [Bogg] (65) 92, p. 40.

5892. SLAPIKAS, C. (Carolyn)
"Have you had me." [NewYorkQ] (48) 92, p. 52.
"Late News." [NewYorkQ] (47) 92, p. 92.
"Oh Joints." [NewYorkQ] (49) 92, p. 64.

5893. SLATTERY, Phillip
"Faust." [HolCrit] (29:1) F 92, p. 19.

5894. SLATTERY, Susan
"In Medias Res." [ColR] (9:1) Spr-Sum 92, p. 140.
"Night Hitchhiker." [ColR] (9:1) Spr-Sum 92, p. 138-139.

5895. SLATTERY, William
"Ripple Effect." [Amelia] (7:1, #20) 92, p. 150.

5896. SLAUGHTER, William
"China Poem with Birds and Clocks." [NewYorkQ] (47) 92, p. 87.

5897. SLAVITT, David R.
"Museum of Science: Discovery Room" (for Hannah and Isaac). [Light] (1) Spr 92, p. 24.
"On Cithaeron" (tr. of Seneca). [GrandS] (11:1, #41) 92, p. 105-115.

5898. SLAYMAKER, Bob
"De-Evolution." [SlipS] (12) 92, p. 104.
"Vegetable Seller, Nairobi." [SlipS] (12) 92, p. 103-104.

5899. SLESINGER, Warren
"Anhedonia." [Iowa] (22:1) Wint 92, p. 119.
"Garden." [Iowa] (22:1) Wint 92, p. 119.
"Wave." [Iowa] (22:1) Wint 92, p. 120.

5900. SLICER, Deborah
"Outside of Richmond, Virginia, Sunday." [TarRP] (30:2) Spr 91, p. 43.

"Snow." [TarRP] (30:2) Spr 91, p. 42.
5901. SLOAN, Bob
"Rowan County, 1937" (The Chain Carrier). [Wind] (22:71) 92, p. 31-33.
5902. SLOAN, Margy
"Infiltration." [Talisman] (8) Spr 92, p. 75-79.
5903. SLOBODZIAN, George
"Pysanka: The Written Egg." [PraF] (13:3, #60) Aut 92, p. 170.
"Radisson Slough." [PraF] (13:3, #60) Aut 92, p. 171-172.
5904. SLONE, G. Tod
"Slingshot *Échappatoire*." [MoodySI] (27) Spr 92, p. 40.
5905. SLOWINSKI, Stephanie
"The Immigrant." [Calyx] (14:1) Sum 92, p. 16.
"Tattoo Woman." [MidAR] (13:2) 92, p. 7-8.
5906. SLYMAN, Ernest
"Giraffe." [Light] (1) Spr 92, p. 12.
"Postage Stamps." [Light] (2) Sum 92, p. 19.
5907. SMALDONE, Jerry
"Ain't It the Truth." [SlipS] (12) 92, p. 72.
5908. SMALL, Abbott
"The Dead Lady." [RagMag] (10:1) 92, p. 58.
"Poem from Miami Beach." [Wind] (22:71) 92, p. 2.
"Three Eggs." [RagMag] (10:1) 92, p. 59.
5909. SMALL, Jean
"A Sun Song." [LitR] (35:4) Sum 92, p. 586.
5910. SMALLFIELD, Edward
"Self-Portrait with Thorn Necklace and Hummingbirds." [Caliban] (11) 92, p. 76.
"Stain." [Caliban] (11) 92, p. 77-78.
5911. SMEE, Sonia
"Mmmmmmmmmmmmmmmmmmmmmmmm." [WestCL] (26:3, #9) Wint 92-93, p. 37.
"Sons." [WestCL] (26:3, #9) Wint 92-93, p. 36-37.
"Triangle." [WestCL] (26:3, #9) Wint 92-93, p. 35.
5912. SMITH, Alan
"Burning Four Days as Kennel Assistant at Hopewell Veterinary Hospital." [Lactuca] (16) Ag 92, p. 43-44.
5913. SMITH, Anthony
"An Attempt at Leaving the 20th Century." [Pearl] (15) Spr-Sum 92, p. 20.
5914. SMITH, Arthur
"After Dinner with a Beautiful Woman, I Wade into the Rolling Tennessee." [Crazy] (42) Spr 92, p. 28.
"Bad Bells." [Crazy] (43) Wint 92, p. 9.
"Because There Is." [Crazy] (43) Wint 92, p. 14-15.
"Grace." [Crazy] (43) Wint 92, p. 12-13.
"Heaven." [Crazy] (43) Wint 92, p. 10-11.
"Isle of Palms." [Crazy] (43) Wint 92, p. 16-17.
"A Late Walk on the World's Fair Site." [Crazy] (42) Spr 92, p. 29.
"Lucky." [Crazy] (43) Wint 92, p. 7-8.
"The Sea of Blessings Is Beyond Measure." [Crazy] (42) Spr 92, p. 26-27.
"Whatever Light." [Crazy] (42) Spr 92, p. 24-25.
5915. SMITH, Barbara F.
"Her Petting on a Sunday Afternoon." [SoCoast] (12) Ja 92, p. 26.
"Protest." [Lactuca] (16) Ag 92, p. 40.
5916. SMITH, Beatrice
"Embroideries." [US1] (26/27) 92, p. 43.
5917. SMITH, Bruce
"Against the Maker." [Agni] (36) 92, p. 35-36.
"Mercy Seat" (for Billie Holiday). [GrandS] (11:1, #41) 92, p. 116-117.
"Self-Portrait as Foreign Policy." [Agni] (36) 92, p. 37.
5918. SMITH, C. E.
"Electrotherapy." [RagMag] (10:1) 92, p. 71.
"My Last Warning." [RagMag] (10:1) 92, p. 70.
5919. SMITH, C. O.
"Clockpunch Badge" (for Kyle). [PacificR] (11) 92-93, p. 16-17.
"Denial." [PacificR] (11) 92-93, p. 20-21.
"Obituaries." [PacificR] (11) 92-93, p. 18-19.

5920. SMITH, Cassandra F.
"I Would Miss." [Obs] (7:1/2) Spr-Sum 92, p. 116-117.
5921. SMITH, Charlie
"At the Bright Mouth." [Crazy] (42) Spr 92, p. 75.
"The Fiddler." [GeoR] (46:3) Fall 92, p. 513.
"Ice." [NewYorker] (67:46) 6 Ja 92, p. 32.
"Money." [NewYorker] (68:35) 19 O 92, p. 70.
"Mother at Eighty." [NewYorker] (68:27) 24 Ag 92, p. 56.
"The Palms." [Thrpny] (51) Fall 92, p. 38.
"The Plum-Shaped Heart." [ParisR] (34:123) Sum 92, p. 96-97.
"Sunday Morning." [Sonora] (22/23) Spr 92, p. 113.
"White Shining Sea." [NewYorker] (67:52) 17 F 92, p. 32.
"Winter Door." [Nat] (255:6) 31 Ag-7 S 92, p. 224.
5922. SMITH, Dave (*See also* SMITH, David James & SMITH, David Marshall)
"Bunny's Restaurant." [NewEngR] (14:4) Fall 92, p. 123-133.
"The Fisherman's Whore." [ThRiPo] (39/40) 92-93, p. 234-235.
"Hollis Summers." [ColEng] (53:7) N 91, p. 794-795.
"March Storm, Poquoson, Virginia, 1963." [ThRiPo] (39/40) 92-93, p. 235-236.
"Near the Docks." [ThRiPo] (39/40) 92-93, p. 236-237.
"Wreckage at Lake Pontchartrain." [NewYorker] (68:5) 23 Mr 92, p. 42.
5923. SMITH, David James (*See also* SMITH, Dave & SMITH, David Marshall)
"Above Treeline." [SoDakR] (30:2) Sum 92, p. 108.
"The Ditch." [FloridaR] (18:2) Fall-Wint 92, p. 114-115.
"Faith." [LaurelR] (26:2) Sum 92, p. 70.
"Near Treeline." [MinnR] (38) Spr-Sum 92, p. 34-35.
"The Quiet Ambition of Grass." [MidAR] (12:2) 92, p. 2.
"What Is Necessary." [SoDakR] (30:2) Sum 92, p. 109.
5924. SMITH, David Marshall (*See also* SMITH, Dave & SMITH, David James)
"Biographed." [BelPoJ] (43:2) Wint 92-93, p. 36-37.
5925. SMITH, Dean
"Obsession." [PoetryE] (33) Spr 92, p. 131.
5926. SMITH, Douglas Burnet
"P.S." [Event] (21:2) Sum 92, p. 54-55.
5927. SMITH, Ellen
"His Five-Thirty Funk." [OxfordM] (8:2) Fall-Wint 92, p. 1.
5928. SMITH, Ethridge E.
"Flying." [OnTheBus] (4:2/5:1, #10/11) 92, p. 206.
"Night Seed Rituals." [OnTheBus] (4:2/5:1, #10/11) 92, p. 205-206.
5929. SMITH, Francis J.
"Quiet in the Trees, Please!" [Light] (1) Spr 92, p. 16.
5930. SMITH, Grace Haynes
"Sleeping Dolphins" (Winner, Annual Free Verse Contest, 1991). [AnthNEW] (4) 92, p. 20.
5931. SMITH, Hal
"Final Scene." [Vis] (40) 92, p. 53.
5932. SMITH, J. D.
"After Saint Martin." [ChrC] (109:34) 18-25 N 92, p. 1054.
"Little Bucharest." [Vis] (38) 92, p. 6.
SMITH, James Sutherland
See SUTHERLAND-SMITH, James
5933. SMITH, Jane Bowman
"In the Patient Rain." [SouthernPR] (32:2) Fall 92, p. 38-39.
5934. SMITH, Jennifer E.
"2 a.m." (a blues song for poets). [AfAmRev] (26:2) Sum 92, p. 264-265.
5935. SMITH, Joan Jobe
"The 1992 L.A. Riots Bring Back Memories." [WormR] (32:4 #128) 92, p. 145.
"And Lots of Wavy Hair Like Liberace." [WormR] (32:4 #128) 92, p. 141.
"Before the Ice in the Tea Melts." [WormR] (32:4 #128) 92, p. 142.
"Boredome." [WormR] (32:4 #128) 92, p. 144-145.
"The Coolest Car in School." [WormR] (32:4 #128) 92, p. 142-143.
"The Hollow Cost." [ChironR] (11:3) Aut 92, p. 4.
"Hot Tamales." [Calyx] (14:2) Wint 92-93, p. 56-57.
"Me and My Mother's Morphine." [ChironR] (11:3) Aut 92, p. 4.
"Mute Force." [WormR] (32:4 #128) 92, p. 143-144.
"On the Way to Disneyland." [SlipS] (12) 92, p. 18-19.

5936. SMITH, John
"Ice Storm." [US1] (26/27) 92, p. 37.
"Jugtown Mountain" (For pd). [LitR] (35:3) Spr 92, p. 374.
"Lived Like a Saint." [JlNJPo] (14:2) Aut 92, p. 24.
"Skinny Dipping." [JlNJPo] (14:2) Aut 92, p. 23.
5937. SMITH, Jonathan
"Ars Filosofia." [QW] (34) Wint-Spr 92, p. 90.
5938. SMITH, Jordan
"Gingerbread." [SouthernR] (28:2) Spr, Ap 92, p. 320-325.
"Job." [NewEngR] (14:4) Fall 92, p. 83-84.
"Lilac." [NewEngR] (14:4) Fall 92, p. 84.
"With a White Dog in Night Snow." [WestHR] (46:2) Sum 92, p. 202-203.
5939. SMITH, Karen H.
"Scene from Voyages on Chicago Elevator Trains." [Amelia] (7:1, #20) 92, p. 155.
"Wandering Men." [Amelia] (7:1, #20) 92, p. 155.
5940. SMITH, Ken
"Doing the Accounts." [Stand] (33:2) Spr 92, p. 96.
5941. SMITH, Kevin J.
"Heigh Ho Heigh Ho." [SlipS] (12) 92, p. 77.
5942. SMITH, Kirsten (Kirsten M.)
"The Chess Game." [Nimrod] (36:1) Fall-Wint 92, p. 29.
"The Clutch of Angels" (Second Prize, The Pablo Neruda Prize for Poetry). [Nimrod] (36:1) Fall-Wint 92, p. 27-28.
"The Hand of Kentucky." [Shen] (42:4) Wint 92, p. 29.
"The Movie Buffs." [Nimrod] (36:1) Fall-Wint 92, p. 30.
5943. SMITH, Kurt
"Blowing Up the Lab." [Writer] (105:3) Mr 92, p. 22.
5944. SMITH, Larry
"The Reconciling." [ArtfulD] (22/23) 92, p. 148.
5945. SMITH, Linda Wasmer
"Above Cotton" (for Lois Lark Wasmer, 1902-1928). [SnailPR] (2:1) Spr-Sum 92, p. 11.
"The Good Wife." [SingHM] (20) 92, p. 11.
"Let Them Eat Roast Tom Turkey or Honey Glazed Ham and a Choice of Three Accompaniments." [SnailPR] (2:2) Fall-Wint 92, p. 9.
"Pencil Points." [Light] (1) Spr 92, p. 21.
"Political Platforms." [Kalliope] (14:3) 92, p. 40.
5946. SMITH, Margaret
"One Old Care." [NewYorkQ] (47) 92, p. 77.
5947. SMITH, Michael S.
"Battle Dressing." [Plain] (12:3) Spr 92, p. 28.
"The Crumbling Plinth." [Elf] (2:4) Wint 92, p. 31.
"Flowers from Our Garden." [Plain] (12:3) Spr 92, p. 29.
"Here's the Poem You Asked For." [PoetL] (87:2) Sum 92, p. 7.
"Still a Wilting Wallflower by." [Hellas] (3:1) Spr 92, p. 42.
"Twilight Farewell." [WritersF] (18) 92, p. 40.
5948. SMITH, Pat (*See also* SMITH, Patricia)
"Grief Sounds" (for D.R.). [SpoonRQ] (17:1/2) Wint-Spr 92, p. 7.
"There Are Women." [SpoonRQ] (17:1/2) Wint-Spr 92, p. 8.
5949. SMITH, Patricia (*See also* SMITH, Pat)
"Always in the Head." [ParisR]] (34:124) Fall 92, p. 130-131.
"Annie Pearl Smith Discovers Moonlight." [Agni] (36) 92, p. 47-49.
"If I Cannot Dance" (Marketplace, Tangier, 1990). [Noctiluca] (1:2) Wint 92 [on cover: Wint 93], p. 4-5.
"Nickel Wine and Deep Kisses" (Cabrini Green Housing Project, Chicago, 1982). [Agni] (36) 92, p. 44-46.
"Skinhead." [Agni] (36) 92, p. 41-43.
"Speaking Out the Stars" (for Michael and Brother Blue). [Noctiluca] (1:2) Wint 92 [on cover: Wint 93], p. 6.
5950. SMITH, Paul Andrew E.
"Carom." [WillowR] (19) Spr 92, p. 5-6.
"Steam" (for Annie). [HawaiiR] (16:2, #35) Spr 92, p. 117.
"Wicker." [WillowR] (19) Spr 92, p. 2-4.
5951. SMITH, Paul Douglas
"Camels in a Hard Pack." [Plain] (12:3) Spr 92, p. 13.

5952. SMITH, R. T.
"Angels." [GettyR] (5:2) Spr 92, p. 215.
"Apple Voyage." [ChatR] (12:2) Wint 92, p. 20-21.
"Birds, in the Vigor of Memory." [NoDaQ] (60:3) Sum 92, p. 3-4.
"The Convert." [SouthernPR] (32:2) Fall 92, p. 63-65.
"Conviction." [GettyR] (5:2) Spr 92, p. 214.
"Gnaw." [Farm] (9:1) Spr-Sum 92, p. 36-37.
"Gristle in the Cellar." [FreeL] (10) Sum 92, p. 9.
"Gristle Teazel, Gristle Bear." [SouthernPR] (32:2) Fall 92, p. 65-66.
"Halcion" (for Hayden Carruth). [Journal] (16:2) Fall-Wint 92, p. 94-95.
"The History of Ukiyo-e, Red Fuji." [Poem] (68) N 92, p. 7.
"If Insomnia Is Not a Dry Seed." [Journal] (16:2) Fall-Wint 92, p. 96-97.
"It Is a Hunger." [Journal] (16:2) Fall-Wint 92, p. 98-101.
"Loss Song." [FreeL] (10) Sum 92, p. 8.
"Perfect" (for Jerome Ward). [SouthernPR] (32:2) Fall 92, p. 66-67.
"Possum." [EngJ] (80:5) S 91, p. 92.
"Sect" (New Lebanon). [Poetry] (161:3) D 92, p. 136-137.
"The Sewing" (For Salman Rushdie). [PoetL] (87:2) Sum 92, p. 28.
"She Said, Can't We Just Be Friends." [Sun] (201) S 92, p. 37.
"Translation." [Poem] (68) N 92, p. 5.
"Water Hawk." [Farm] (9:1) Spr-Sum 92, p. 35.
"When Emerson." [Poem] (68) N 92, p. 6.
"The Would-Be Renaissance Man Waxes Anacreonic" (To D.M.). [LitR] (25:2) Wint 92, p. 226.
5953. SMITH, Robert Lavett
"The Bo Tree" (for John and Madhavi). [DogRR] (11:1) Spr-Sum 92, p. 3.
"Sand Dollars." [TarRP] (30:2) Spr 91, p. 35.
"The Slow Loris." [TarRP] (30:2) Spr 91, p. 34.
5954. SMITH, Russell
"Diana." [AntigR] (89) Spr 92, p. 139.
5955. SMITH, Samuel Random
"Old Ethan Remembers Wyoming." [CreamCR] (16:2) Fall 92, p. 65.
5956. SMITH, Serena
"Adolescence." [CreamCR] (16:1) Spr 92, p. 88.
"Shell Island." [CreamCR] (16:1) Spr 92, p. 89.
5957. SMITH, Shannon Mark
"Elegy: On Going to Bed." [Stand] (33:2) Spr 92, p. 19.
5958. SMITH, Sheila K.
"Bolu's Dream: Ololufe Mi." [RiverS] (36) 92, p. 37.
5959. SMITH, Stephen
"The Mosquito Country." [Verse] (9:3) Wint 92, p. 136.
SMITH, Thomas H.
See SPLAKE, T. Kilgore [pen name]
5960. SMITH, Todd
"Crossing." [LullwaterR] (4:1) Fall 92, p. 26.
5961. SMITH, Tom
"Some Kisses Wake the Dead." [CumbPR] (12:1) Fall 92, p. 77.
5962. SMITH, William D.
"Salt and Pepper." [JlNJPo] (14:2) Aut 92, p. 8.
"Visions from Inner Space." [JlNJPo] (14:1) Spr 92, p. 8.
5963. SMITH, William Jay
"Childhood" (tr. of Carlos de Oliveira). [Trans] (26) Spr 92, p. 58.
"The Dog from Next Door Still Comes Over" (tr. of Sándor Csoóri). [Trans] (26) Spr 92, p. 104.
"A World in Crystal" (tr. of Gyula Illyés). [Trans] (26) Spr 92, p. 25-26.
5964. SMITH, Willie
"Special Forces Pet of the Month." [Asylum] (7:3/4) 92, p. 72.
5965. SMITH-SOTO, Mark
"Cave Canem" (tr. of María Victoria Atencia). [InterPR] (18:1) Spr 92, p. 19.
"The Frontier" (tr. of María Victoria Atencia). [InterPR] (18:1) Spr 92, p. 17.
"Mozart, Concerto No. 20" (tr. of Clara Janés). [InterPR] (18:1) Spr 92, p. 9.
"November" (tr. of Pureza Canelo). [InterPR] (18:1) Spr 92, p. 21, 23.
"Scaffolding of Wind" (to Mexican dance, tr. of Iliana Godoy). [InterPR] (18:2) Fall 92, p. 49.
"Star of twilight among the trees" (tr. of Clara Janés). [InterPR] (18:1) Spr 92, p. 7.

5966. SMITHER, Elizabeth
"Amateur Athletic Meeting." [Verse] (9:2) Sum 92, p. 8.
"The Ha-Ha." [Verse] (9:2) Sum 92, p. 7.
"Jennifer's Wedding." [Vis] (40) 92, p. 45.
"Kept Awake by a Party." [Vis] (40) 92, p. 45.
"A Little Town, at Night, from the Air." [Verse] (9:2) Sum 92, p. 7.
5967. SMITS, Ronald F.
"Sunday on the South Side." [SouthernR] (28:2) Spr, Ap 92, p. 252-253.
"The Watercolors of East Carson Street." [SouthernR] (28:2) Spr, Ap 92, p. 253.
5968. SMOCK, Frederick
"An Angel Approaches Theophilus, Secretary to the Judge Who Condemned Dorothea" (martyred 303). [GreenMR] (NS 5:2) Spr-Sum 92, p. 39.
"Angels." [Poetry] (160:1) Ap 92, p. 28.
"St. Columba, et Ursa Syriacus, Sens, Gaul" (martyred 304). [GreenMR] (NS 5:2) Spr-Sum 92, p. 38.
"St. Leocadia Appears to Alban Butler, Busy Compiling His *Lives*" (martyred 304?). [GreenMR] (NS 5:2) Spr-Sum 92, p. 37.
5969. SMOKEWOOD, Elaine
"I Dream My Grandmother Dreaming." [PoetryNW] (33:3) Aut 92, p. 30-31.
"The Lost Handbag." [PoetryNW] (33:3) Aut 92, p. 29.
"On My Sister's Painting of Our Grandmother at Ninety, Dressed in Red." [PoetryNW] (33:3) Aut 92, p. 29-30.
5970. SMUKLER, Linda
"Lawns." [AmerV] (28) 92, p. 28-29.
5971. SMYTH, Edward Martin
"The Stonemason's Haunts." [Hellas] (3:2) Fall 92, p. 35-36.
5972. SMYTH, Richard
"What Milk Knows." [SouthernPR] (32:1) Spr 92, p. 46-47.
5973. SNELLING, Kenneth
"Deposed Royalty." [SoCoast] (12) Ja 92, p. 7.
"Lament of a Very Senior Citizen." [SoCoast] (12) Ja 92, p. 6.
"On Being Born." [HolCrit] (29:4) O 92, p. 19.
5974. SNEYD, Steve
"First Burn the Code Book." [CoalC] (5) My 92, p. 17.
"Night Owl Long Ago." [CoalC] (5) My 92, p. 17.
"October Company." [CoalC] (5) My 92, p. 17.
"A Variety to Name for His Wife." [CoalC] (5) My 92, p. 17.
"The Vikings Did It." [CoalC] (5) My 92, p. 16.
"The Worm of Wharncliffe." [CoalC] (5) My 92, p. 16.
5975. SNG, Shao Kuan
"Minimal Fictions" (Conception by Richard Kostelanetz, Translations/Calligraphy by Shao Kuan Sng). [Nimrod] (36:1) Fall-Wint 92, p. 80-81.
5976. SNIDER, Clifton
"Bush War, the Gulf." [Pearl] (15) Spr-Sum 92, p. 49.
"The Great Pretenders" (for Klaus Nomi, Sylvester, and Freddie Mercury). [ChironR] (11:4) Wint 92, p. 11.
"Hanging On." [ChironR] (11:4) Wint 92, p. 11.
"I Hear a Symphony" (for Adam Bushman). [ChironR] (11:4) Wint 92, p. 11.
"L.A. Is Burning." [Pearl] (16) Fall 92, p. 25.
"My Buddha, My Baby, My Pet." [ChironR] (11:2) Sum 92, p. 32.
5977. SNIDER, Kat
"Writing Poems." [NewYorkQ] (48) 92, p. 104.
5978. SNIVELY, Susan
"The Speed of the Drift" (VI, VIII-IX). [MassR] (23:2) Sum 92, p. 258-260.
5979. SNODGRASS, Ann
"Anzio." [Agni] (35) 92, p. 277.
5980. SNODGRASS, W. D.
"Creation" (tr. of Marin Sorescu, w. Dona Rosu and Luciana Costea). [Poetry] (159:4) Ja 92, p. 191.
"Dance Suite: Hip Hop." [Light] (3) Aut 92, p. 10.
"Elena Ceauçescu's Bed" (Romania, 1991). [Nat] (255:16) 16 N 92, p. 570.
"I Bound Up the Trees' Eyes" (tr. of Marin Sorescu, w. Dona Rosu and Luciana Costea). [Poetry] (159:4) Ja 92, p. 194.
"Snow Songs." [KenR] (NS 14:4) Fall 92, p. 156-160.
"Solemnly" (tr. of Marin Sorescu, w. Dona Rosu and Luciana Costea). [Poetry] (159:4) Ja 92, p. 192.

"Thieves" (tr. of Marin Sorescu, w. Dona Rosu and Luciana Costea). [Poetry] (159:4) Ja 92, p. 193.
"W. D.'s Midnight Carnival: Dumbbell Rhymes." [Light] (2) Sum 92, p. 8.

5981. SNOEK, Paul
"Poem for Beginners" (tr. by Claire Nicolas White). [Trans] (26) Spr 92, p. 83.
"Poem for the Day After Tomorrow" (tr. by Claire Nicolas White). [Trans] (26) Spr 92, p. 84.

5982. SNOW, Barbara
"Midwinter Spring." [Kalliope] (14:1) 92, p. 6.

5983. SNOW, Karen
"Hare." [BelPoJ] (42:3) Spr 92, p. 6-8.

5984. SNYDER, Emile
"Who, if I cried out, would hear me among the angels" (— Rilke's "Duino Elegies 1"). [NewYorkQ] (48) 92, p. 68.

5985. SNYDER, Gary
"Earrings Dangling and Miles of Desert." [YaleR] (80:1/2) Apr 92, p. 49-51.
"Ripples on the Surface." [GrandS] (11:2, #42) 92, p. 21.

5986. SNYDER, Jena
"For Baba, August 18, 1990" (In memory of Maria Muzyka, January 7, 1901 - August 17, 1990). [PraF] (13:3, #60) Aut 92, p. 173-174.
"Plums." [PraF] (13:3, #60) Aut 92, p. 174-175.

5987. SNYDER, Jennifer
"Fish Poems." [Iowa] (22:3) Fall 92, p. 183-184.
"Texas." [Iowa] (22:3) Fall 92, p. 184-188.

SNYDER, Kaye Bache
See BACHE-SNYDER, Kaye

5988. SNYDER, Margery
"Seismogramme." [OnTheBus] (4:2/5:1, #10/11) 92, p. 207.

5989. SOBEK, Maria Herrera
"Itea" (tr. of Eduardo Mitre). [OnTheBus] (4:2/5:1, #10/11) 92, p. 277.
"To an Image" (In memoriam, Jaime Saenz, tr. of Eduardo Mitre). [OnTheBus] (4:2/5:1, #10/11) 92, p. 276.

5990. SOBEL, Carolyn
"Friends." [ManhatPR] (14) [92?], p. 31.
"Instrument." [ManhatPR] (14) [92?], p. 32.
"October Wind." [ManhatPR] (14) [92?], p. 32.
"Parking Lot at Three O'Clock." [ManhatPR] (14) [92?], p. 30-31.
"Playscript." [ManhatPR] (14) [92?], p. 30.
"To Live on Fire." [ManhatPR] (14) [92?], p. 32.

5991. SOBIN, Gustaf
"Tracing a Thirst" (for E.F.). [Talisman] (9) Fall 92, p. 16-17.
"Transparent Itineraries, 1991." [Sulfur] (12:1, #30) Spr 92, p. 59-63.
"The Villas of Andrea Palladio." [Sulfur] (12:1, #30) Spr 92, p. 63-65.

SOCAS, Olga Torres
See TORRES SOCAS, Olga

5992. SOCOLOW, Elizabeth (Elizabeth Anne)
"Forbidden Sea" (tr. of Blaga Dimitrova, w. Ludmilla Popova-Wightman). [US1] (26/27) 92, p. 26.
"Moving House." [US1] (26/27) 92, p. 37.

5993. SÖDERGRAN, Edith
"The King's Sorrow" (tr. by Stephen Kuusisto). [SenR] (22:2) Fall 92, p. 61.
"Longing for Colors" (tr. by Stephen Kuusisto). [SenR] (22:2) Fall 92, p. 62.

5994. SOFIELD, David
"Aubade" (On a "Talking Pyramid" Clock). [NewRep] (206:19) 11 My 92, p. 38.

5995. SOIFER, Mark
"The City of Wires" (Excerpt). [Parting] (5:2) Wint 92-93, p. 32.

5996. SOKENU, Julius Olusola
"The Bride of Rain." [Nimrod] (35:2) Spr-Sum 92, p. 116-117.
"Dios." [Nimrod] (35:2) Spr-Sum 92, p. 115.

5997. SOLANO, Enrique
"El Poeta Me Miraba Mustio." [Nuez] (4:10/11) 92, p. 37.

5998. SOLARCZYK, Bart
"Standing Eight Count." [SlipS] (12) 92, p. 87.

5999. SOLDOFSKY, Alan
"The Beginning of Summer." [GrandS] (11:2, #42) 92, p. 115-117.
"Chin Music." [GettyR] (5:3) Sum 92, p. 539.

6000. SOLJAK, Katie
"Old Wooden Radio." [Pearl] (16) Fall 92, p. 54-55.
6001. SOLLNER, Patricia
"And on my forehead" (tr. of Marina Tsvetaeva). [SenR] (22:1) Spr 92, p. 35.
"I burned a handful of hair" (tr. of Marina Tsvetaeva). [SenR] (22:1) Spr 92, p. 34.
"I'll tell you the story" (tr. of Marina Tsvetaeva). [SenR] (22:1) Spr 92, p. 33.
"I've come home" (tr. of Marina Tsvetaeva). [SenR] (22:1) Spr 92, p. 37.
"Neither stanzas nor stars will be my salvation" (tr. of Marina Tsvetaeva). [SenR] (22:1) Spr 92, p. 36.
6002. SOLOMON, Marvin
"Los Arboles de Aranjuez." [PassN] (13:2) Wint 92, p. 21.
"Genealogy." [WormR] (32:3, #127) 92, p. 96.
"The Headache That Wasn't There, Isn't There." [Poetry] (159:6) Mr 92, p. 318.
"Lear and Seurat, Walking." [WormR] (32:3, #127) 92, p. 97.
"Ravel's Botero." [PassN] (13:2) Wint 92, p. 21.
6003. SOLOMON, Sandy
"Drawing from the Evidence" (for my father). [AntR] (50:3) Sum 92, p. 507.
"For Ernesto Cardenal Who Wrestles with a Question About Turning the Other Cheek." [PoetryE] (33) Spr 92, p. 132-133.
"In Deepest February." [PoetryE] (33) Spr 92, p. 134.
"Petit Mal." [GettyR] (5:1) Wint 92, p. 126-127.
"Political Refugee, One Month On." [Thrpny] (51) Fall 92, p. 19.
"Progressive." [GettyR] (5:1) Wint 92, p. 128-129.
"A Rescue." [Thrpny] (49) Spr 92, p. 34.
"Silent Poem." [PoetryE] (33) Spr 92, p. 135.
6004. SOLONCHE, J. R.
"My Father's Death." [HampSPR] Wint 92, p. 8.
"Schopenhauer at the Englischer Hof: A Monologue." [AmerS] (61:4) Aut 92, p. 602-603.
"Terra Cotta." [HampSPR] Wint 92, p. 7.
6005. SOMECK, Roni
"Embroidered Rag: Poem on Umm Kulthum" (tr. by Ammiel Alcalay). [Paint] (19:37) Spr 92, p. 44.
"Jasmine: Poem on Sandpaper" (tr. by Ammiel Alcalay). [Paint] (19:37) Spr 92, p. 43.
6006. SOMMER, Jason
"Meyer Tsits and the Children." [RiverS] (36) 92, p. 69-71.
6007. SOMMER, Piotr
"Celebrations" (tr. by the author and M. Kasper). [NewYorker] (68:45) 28 D 92-4 Ja 93, p. 126.
6008. SONDE, Susan
"If Freedom Were a Large Pearl." [AnotherCM] (24) Fall 92, p. 169.
"Scattered Thoughts, Sacred Thoughts." [LullwaterR] (3:3) Sum 92, p. 42-43.
"These Sad Ruins." [CreamCR] (16:2) Fall 92, p. 38-39.
6009. SONG, Cathy
"Adagio." [Poetry] (160:6) S 92, p. 323-325.
"Chinese Checkers." [PraS] (66:1) Spr 92, p. 100-101.
"The Devoted" (for Keiko). [Shen] (42:1) Spr 92, p. 22-23.
"The Hand That Feeds." [Ploughs] (18:1) Spr 92, p. 59-60.
"The Hotel by the Lake." [Poetry] (160:6) S 92, p. 322-323.
"Killing Time." [PraS] (66:1) Spr 92, p. 97-98.
"Late August." [CreamCR] (16:1) Spr 92, p. 78-82.
"Leaf" (for my sister). [Shen] (42:1) Spr 92, p. 24.
"The Man in the Moon." [CreamCR] (16:1) Spr 92, p. 76-77.
"Mooring." [CreamCR] (16:1) Spr 92, p. 74-75.
"Square Mile." [Poetry] (160:6) S 92, p. 325-326.
"Tangerines and Rain." [PraS] (66:1) Spr 92, p. 98-100.
6010. SONGDAECHUN
"An Urban Butterfly" (tr. by Constantine Contogenis and Wolhee Choe). [Pequod] (34) 92, p. 114.
6011. SONGI
"Has the Silver River above risen further" (a Kisang Poem in Korean and English, tr. by Constantine Contogenis and Wolhee Choe). [GrandS] (11:3 #43) 92, p. 174-175.

6012. SONIAT, Katherine (Kathryn)
"Approaching New Orleans: A Summer Scene." [FloridaR] (18:2) Fall-Wint 92, p. 72-73.
"Balboa in Spring." [NewOR] (19:3/4) Fall-Wint 92, p. 61.
"The Blue Book." [ColEng] (54:1) Ja 92, p. 35.
"Bronze John." [SouthernR] (28:3) Sum, Jl 92, p. 629-631.
"Coming into the River Parishes." [SouthernPR] (32:2) Fall 92, p. 42-43.
"Crivelli's Pièta Angel." [LitR] (35:3) Spr 92, p. 354-355.
"A Far Latitude of North." [SouthernPR] (32:1) Spr 92, p. 30-31.
"Gens de Couleur Libres: Ladies and Men." [BelPoJ] (43:1) Fall 92, p. 14-16.
"The House at 1140 Royal Street." [SouthernR] (28:3) Sum, Jl 92, p. 632-634.
"In Time." [SouthernHR] (26:3) Sum 92, p. 229.
"Mount View Pure." [AmerV] (26) Spr 92, p. 105-106.
"A Scrap of What the Yellow Fever Orphan Had to Say." [SouthernR] (28:3) Sum, Jl 92, p. 631.
"Some Broomstick Shades" (from a sequence of poems on New Orleans, "Coming into the River Parishes"). [LaurelR] (26:2) Sum 92, p. 82.

6013. SONNEBORN, C. L. (Carrie Louise)
"Afterwords." [Footwork] 92, p. 131.
"Answering Machine." [Footwork] 92, p. 131.
"City Weather Report." [Footwork] 92, p. 131.
"Coffee Break." [Footwork] 92, p. 130.
"Dream." [Footwork] 92, p. 130.
"Idle Promises." [Vis] (40) 92, p. 28-29.
"Propaganda" (for George). [Footwork] 92, p. 132.
"Shades of Green." [Footwork] 92, p. 130.
"Women Walks." [Footwork] 92, p. 132.

6014. SONNENBERG, Ben
"Fragment" (for Anne Carson). [Raritan] (11:3) Wint 92, p. 16.

SONOKO, Nakamura
See NAKAMURA, Sonoko

6015. SOOPKIAN, Touba
"Which One Do You Mean." [Pearl] (15) Spr-Sum 92, p. 61.

6016. SOPHOCLES
"The Cure at Troy" (Choruses, from "Philoctetes," tr. by Seamus Heaney). [Arion] 3d series (1:2) Spr 91, p. 131-138.

6017. SORBY, Angela
"Antarctica" (Written upon the signing of a 1991 U.N.-sponsored treaty designed to preserve Antarctica as an "unclaimed continent"). [SycamoreR] (4:1) Wint 92, p. 31.
"Distance Learning." [SycamoreR] (4:1) Wint 92, p. 30.
"Uma." [SpoonRQ] (17:3/4) Sum-Fall 92, p. 127.
"Uses of Enchantment." [SpoonRQ] (17:3/4) Sum-Fall 92, p. 128.

6018. SORENSEN, Sally Jo
"Enmity." [PoetC] (23:3) Spr 92, p. 10.
"Stomping the Snakes." [WestB] (30) 92, p. 24.

6019. SORESCU, Marin
"Creation" (tr. by W. D. Snograss, w. Dona Rosu and Luciana Costea). [Poetry] (159:4) Ja 92, p. 191.
"I Bound Up the Trees' Eyes" (tr. by W. D. Snograss, w. Dona Rosu and Luciana Costea). [Poetry] (159:4) Ja 92, p. 194.
"Solemnly" (tr. by W. D. Snograss, w. Dona Rosu and Luciana Costea). [Poetry] (159:4) Ja 92, p. 192.
"Thieves" (tr. by W. D. Snograss, w. Dona Rosu and Luciana Costea). [Poetry] (159:4) Ja 92, p. 193.

6020. SORESTAD, Glen
"The Houndkeeper." [Grain] (20:1) Spr 92, p. 133.
"In Memoriam" (for Don Polson 1934-1988). [Dandel] (19:1) 92, p. 18.
"Waiting for the Deer." [Dandel] (19:1) 92, p. 19.

6021. SORKIN, Adam (Adam J.)
"Anatomy of a December Night" (tr. of Liliana Ursu). [PassN] (13:2) Wint 92, p. 13.
"Bait" (tr. of Liliana Ursu). [PassN] (13:2) Wint 92, p. 13.
"Blind Above the Words" (tr. of Cezar Baltag, w. the poet). [PoetL] (87:4) Wint 92 - 93, p. 38.
"Cats of the Vatican" (tr. of Mircea Dinescu, w. Sergiu Celac). [ArtfulD] (22/23) 92, p. 39.

"The Discovery of Romania" (tr. of Mihai Ursachi, w. Magda Teodorescu). [Nimrod] (35:2) Spr-Sum 92, p. 42.
"The Gray Squirrel" (tr. of Cezar Baltag, w. the poet). [PoetL] (87:4) Wint 92-93, p. 38.
"Meditation in Frenchman's Gulf" (tr. of Mihai Ursachi, w. Magda Teodorescu). [Nimrod] (35:2) Spr-Sum 92, p. 43-44.
"Seascape" (tr. of Liliana Ursu). [PassN] (13:2) Wint 92, p. 13.
"Sports Poem" (tr. of Denisa Comanescu, w. Angela Jianu). [Vis] (38) 92, p. 34.
"You Haven't a Face" (tr. of Liliana Ursu). [PassN] (13:2) Wint 92, p. 13.

6022. SORNBERGER, Judith
"Judith of Bethulia Holds Off a Mob at the Abortion Clinic." [PraS] (66:3) Fall 92, p. 53-54.
"Leaving *King Lear*." [TarRP] (31:2) Spr 92, p. 4.
"Lunar Eclipse: Take Back the Night." [PraS] (66:3) Fall 92, p. 54-55.
"A Voice for Others" (for Joanne, Folklorist). [Kalliope] (14:2) 92, p. 16-17.
"Your Gleaming Eye" (for Dolores). [SingHM] (20) 92, p. 102-103.

6023. SOSEI, Priest
"How he cries out" (Kokinshu 109, in Japanese and English, tr. by Emily Nguyen). [Archae] (4) late 92-early 93, p. 16.

6024. SOSNOFF, Granate
"Mrs. Matsuda." [SinW] (47) Sum-Fall 92, p. 31.
"Mrs. Matsuda" (number two). [SinW] (47) Sum-Fall 92, p. 32-33.

6025. SOSSAMAN, Stephen
"Cu Chi Tunnel Rat." [SoCoast] (13) Je 93 [i.e. 92], p. 24.

6026. SOTERES, Peter
"Telling Land." [SouthernHR] (26:4) Fall 92, p. 312.

6027. SOTO, Gary
"College Car." [Ploughs] (18:1) Spr 92, p. 97-98.
"First Love." [CreamCR] (16:1) Spr 92, p. 83.
"Magazine Advice." [Ploughs] (18:1) Spr 92, p. 99.
"Making Up Time" (In memory of Ernesto Trejo). [Poetry] (160:4) Jl 92, p. 198 - 199.
"Not Knowing." [Ploughs] (18:1) Spr 92, p. 95-96.

6028. SOTO VERGÉS, Rafael
"Escudo de Dulzura, Hojaldre Tierno" (Dylan Thomas). [InterPR] (18:1) Spr 92, p. 44.
"Sweet Shield, Delicate Pastry" (Dylan Thomas, tr. by Carmen Sotomayor). [InterPR] (18:1) Spr 92, p. 45.

6029. SOTOMAYOR, Carmen
"Intact Fire" (Elegy for Vicente Aleixandre, tr. of Concha Zardoya). [InterPR] (18:1) Spr 92, p. 41, 43.
"Sweet Shield, Delicate Pastry" (Dylan Thomas, tr. of Rafael Soto Vergés). [InterPR] (18:1) Spr 92, p. 45.

6030. SOULAR, James
"Letter to Billy." [SpoonRQ] (17:3/4) Sum-Fall 92, p. 115.
"Numbah One." [SpoonRQ] (17:3/4) Sum-Fall 92, p. 116.
"Zippo Raid." [SpoonRQ] (17:3/4) Sum-Fall 92, p. 117.

6031. SOUPAULT, Philippe
"Another Time" (tr. by Paulette Schmidt). [CharR] (18:2) Fall 92, p. 111.
"Autumn Eternal" (tr. by Paulette Schmidt). [CharR] (18:2) Fall 92, p. 114.
"Calendar" (tr. by Paulette Schmidt). [CharR] (18:2) Fall 92, p. 110.
"Comrade" (tr. by Paulette Schmidt). [CharR] (18:2) Fall 92, p. 112-113.
"Hands That Pray" (tr. by Gregg Ellis). [PoetryE] (33) Spr 92, p. 161-162.
"With Clasped Hands" (tr. by Paulette Schmidt). [CharR] (18:2) Fall 92, p. 109-110.

6032. SOUSA, Dian
"Sometimes I Sleep with a Stone on My Heart to Keep It from Moving Through the Moon and Stars." [ChironR] (11:3) Aut 92, p. 13.

6033. SOUTHWICK, Marcia
"Horse on the Wall." [ThRiPo] (39/40) 92-93, p. 239-240.
"The Ruins." [ThRiPo] (39/40) 92-93, p. 238.
"The Sun Speaks." [ThRiPo] (39/40) 92-93, p. 239.

6034. SOWL, Michael
"Stupid Face Renku" (w. Keith Abbott and Pat Nolan). [HangL] (60) 92, p. 6-11.

6035. SOZONOVA, Alexandra
"Untitled: His wife is a suicide" (in Russian and English, tr. by J. Kates). [PaintedB] (45) 92, p. 28-29.

6036. SPACKS, Barry
"Alba." [NewOR] (19:3/4) Fall-Wint 92, p. 16.
"Final Page." [CimR] (100) Jl 92, p. 119.
"Fourteen." [Witness] (6:2) 92, p. 41.
"Lovers Meditating." [SewanR] (100:2) Spr 92, p. 275.
"Lovers on an Elephant" (after a Jaina Miniature). [SewanR] (100:2) Spr 92, p. 274.
"The Practice." [Poetry] (160:5) Ag 92, p. 283.
"PraiserBird." [Interim] (11:2) Fall-Wint 92-93, p. 8.
6037. SPADY, Susan
"The Ark in Flames." [CimR] (99) Ap 92, p. 42-43.
"Fever." [PraS] (66:2) Sum 92, p. 120-121.
"First Home." [PraS] (66:2) Sum 92, p. 121-122.
"I Practice This Ending." [CimR] (99) Ap 92, p. 41.
"Tending Flowers" (for Carol). [Calyx] (14:1) Sum 92, p. 42.
"Two." [Calyx] (14:1) Sum 92, p. 43.
6038. SPAGNUOLO, Peter
"The Gnostic Decoding of Lee Harvey Oswald." [Thrpny] (50) Sum 92, p. 8.
SPANCKEREN, Kathryn van
See Van SPANCKEREN, Kathryn
6039. SPARROW
"Atlas." [Sun] (201) S 92, p. 24.
"Euripides." [Sun] (194) Ja 92, p. 23.
"Fists." [Sun] (201) S 92, p. 25.
"Poem: The baby my wife had yesterday, Sylvia Mae." [Sun] (201) S 92, p. 22.
"The Presidency." [Sun] (201) S 92, p. 21.
6040. SPARSHOTT, Francis
"Local News." [AntigR] (91) Fall 92, p. 27.
"The Way We Were." [AntigR] (91) Fall 92, p. 28.
"Winds." [AntigR] (91) Fall 92, p. 29-30.
6041. SPASSER, Constance Corzilius
"Saved." [Calyx] (14:1) Sum 92, p. 40-41.
6042. SPAULDING, John
"Afternoon Raid" (from Nineteenth-Century Photographs). [PraS] (66:2) Sum 92, p. 89-90.
"Bohemia" (from Nineteenth-Century Photographs). [PraS] (66:2) Sum 92, p. 90.
"In the Hotel Pavilion" (from Nineteenth-Century Photographs). [PraS] (66:2) Sum 92, p. 90.
"Sleep." [PoetryE] (33) Spr 92, p. 136.
"Walking on Water: The Cathedral at Wells" (from Nineteenth-Century Photographs). [PraS] (66:2) Sum 92, p. 89.
6043. SPAZIANI, Maria Luisa
"The Cancer of Civilization" (tr. by Corrado Federici). [PoetryC] (13:1) N 92, p. 22.
6044. SPEAKES, Richard
"A Blues." [PoetryE] (33) Spr 92, p. 137.
"Colleague." [TarRP] (30:2) Spr 91, p. 14.
"I Beseech Thee, and Thy Mercy." [Poetry] (160:2) My 92, p. 91.
"Pussy." [PassN] (13:2) Wint 92, p. 17.
"Veteran." [PassN] (13:2) Wint 92, p. 17.
6045. SPEARMAN, Glenn
"MUSA — Physics" (Excerpt). [PoetryUSA] (24) 92, p. 23.
6046. SPECTOR, Donna
"Each Night, Coming to Your Room." [HiramPoR] (51/52) Fall 91-Sum 92, p. 66-67.
6047. SPEER, Laurel
"Bad Girl." [CoalC] (5) My 92, p. 7.
"Crab & Man." [Elf] (2:2) Sum 92, p. 40.
"Crew." [CoalC] (5) My 92, p. 7.
"Eating Cherries in Athens." [OnTheBus] (4:2/5:1, #10/11) 92, p. 210.
"Emily, Emily Come Into the Garden." [ChironR] (11:4) Wint 92, p. 8.
"Evil." [SnailPR] (2:2) Fall-Wint 92, p. 6.
"How Careless the Destruction of Lions in Our Midst." [Footwork] 92, p. 92.
"I'm the horse. I am cold, collar and traces." [SlipS] (12) 92, p. 65.
"Love Poem for 52." [ChironR] (11:4) Wint 92, p. 8.
"Mutter / Mother." [CrabCR] (8:1) Sum-Fall 92, p. 3.
"One of the Great Mysteries of All Time." [CrabCR] (8:1) Sum-Fall 92, p. 3.
"Passchendaele at Home." [SnailPR] (2:2) Fall-Wint 92, p. 7.

"The Poem Elizabeth Forgot at Wimpole Street." [ChironR] (11:4) Wint 92, p. 8.
"Porter in the Paddock." [ChironR] (11:4) Wint 92, p. 8.
"Stevie Smith Visits the Queen." [Paint] (19:37) Spr 92, p. 21.
"You Can't Sell a Black and White Film. Life Is in Color" (— James Salter, "The Cinema"). [ManhatPR] (14) [92?], p. 12.
"Zsa Zsa Gabor tittle-tootled out in her Rolls-Royce." [Kalliope] (14:3) 92, p. 32.

6048. SPEES, Benjamin
"Father Song." [BellArk] (8:1) Ja-F 92, p. 27.
"Writing Desk." [BellArk] (8:1) Ja-F 92, p. 23.

6049. SPEISER, E. A.
"Gilgamesh: Tables X and XI" (literal tr. of the Babylonian epic, re-translated by David Ferry). [Arion] 3d series (1:3) Fall 91, p. 92-116.
"Ishtar & Gilgamesh" (from Tablet VI of *The Gilgamesh Epic*, based on the literal of E. A. Speiser, version by David Ferry). [PartR] (59:2) Spr 92, p. 260-263.

6050. SPENCE, Michael
"Be a Man." [SycamoreR] (4:1) Wint 92, p. 52-54.
"Running in a Country of Rain." [BostonR] (17:6) N-D 92, p. 11.
"To Whistle" (or [i.e., for?] Sharon Hashimoto). [CharR] (18:2) Fall 92, p. 94.
"Watersong." [NewOR] (19:3/4) Fall-Wint 92, p. 117.

6051. SPERA, Gabriel
"Mr. Daly." [Poetry] (160:1) Ap 92, p. 5.
"My Ex-Husband." [Poetry] (159:5) F 92, p. 260-261.
"The One That Almost Got Way." [NewEngR] (14:2) Spr 92, p. 159.

6052. SPERANZA, Anthony
"The Poem of the Hired Driver." [Plain] (12:3) Spr 92, p. 35.

6053. SPHERES, Duane (Duane R.)
"Grandpa Russ and the Saturday Night Fight: The Hammer vs. the Maul." [BellArk] (8:6) N-D 92, p. 21.
"Shenyman." [BellArk] (8:4) Jl-Ag 92, p. 21.
"Strawberries." [BellArk] (8:6) N-D 92, p. 12.

6054. SPICEHANDLER, Daniel
"Mutation." [Amelia] (7:1, #20) 92, p. 58.

6055. SPIGLE, Naomi
"Everything's Going to Be All Right." [Kalliope] (14:1) 92, p. 49.

6056. SPINELLI, Eileen
"Spring — Again." [Footwork] 92, p. 84.
"Trapped." [Footwork] 92, p. 84.

6057. SPINNER, A. E.
"Ebbing tide whistles." [Amelia] (6:4, #19) 92, p. 9.

6058. SPINNER, Bettye T.
"How to Sauté a Poem." [EngJ] (81:6) O 92, p. 93.

6059. SPIRENG, Matthew J.
"Compass Points." [Poem] (68) N 92, p. 46.
"Fish on Land." [CarolQ] (45:1) Fall 92, p. 49.
"In Candlelight." [OxfordM] (7:1) Spr-Sum 91, p. 107.
"Indian Artifact" (In memory of Leonard Eisenberg, b. 17 July 1943, d. 10 July 1992). [HolCrit] (29:5) D 92, p. 18-19.
"The Line of Air and Water." [TarRP] (30:2) Spr 91, p. 24-25.
"Older Kids." [CapeR] (27:1) Spr 92, p. 50.
"Queen Anne's Lace." [Blueline] (13) 92, p. 5.
"Some Old Men." [PoetL] (87:4) Wint 92-93, p. 26.

6060. SPIRES, Elizabeth
"An Anniversary." [Boulevard] (7:1, #19) Spr 92, p. 207.
"Letter in July." [Poetry] (160:4) Jl 92, p. 218.

6061. SPIRO, Peter
"Closing the Lid on My Grandmother's Coffin." [NegC] (12:3) 92, p. 115-116.
"Day Off." [Parting] (5:1) Sum 92, p. 34.
"Naming the World" (for the students in room 516). [Journal] (16:2) Fall-Wint 92, p. 104-105.
"Tone Deaf." [Journal] (16:2) Fall-Wint 92, p. 102-103.
"Tone Deaf." [OxfordM] (8:1) Spr-Sum 92, p. 47.
"The Toughest Guy in Brooklyn" (For J.J., 1952-1971). [Footwork] 92, p. 34.
"Trees & Flowers." [OxfordM] (8:1) Spr-Sum 92, p. 45.
"What the Cat Perceives." [Outbr] (23) 92, p. 61.
"When Class Goes Really Well." [OxfordM] (8:1) Spr-Sum 92, p. 46.
"When Someone From the Block Gets Out." [Footwork] 92, p. 35.

"Why I Will Not Get My Hair Styled" (For Frank and Rocco, and for the red & white pole, that it spin well into the next century). [Footwork] 92, p. 34.
"A Young Girl, Drawing" (Class 3-4, P.S. 194, Brooklyn, New York). [Footwork] 92, p. 35.

6062. SPIVACK, Kathleen
"Blue Shirt." [Amelia] (6:4, #19) 92, p. 42.

6063. SPIVACK, Susan Fantl
"Falling Leaves." [Calyx] (14:1) Sum 92, p. 8-9.
"The Life of the Mind." [YellowS] (41) Fall-Wint 92-93, p. 33.

6064. SPLAKE (*See also* SPLAKE, T. Kilgore)
"And, It Never Rains in Sunny California." [MoodySI] (27) Spr 92, p. 28.

6065. SPLAKE, T. Kilgore (*See also* SPLAKE)
"Day Five." [Bogg] (65) 92, p. 16.
"Growing Smaller." [Pearl] (16) Fall 92, p. 32.

6066. SPRING, Justin
"Fighters." [AmerPoR] (21:2) Mr-Ap 92, p. 26.
"Returning to Port: Manatee River." [BellR] (15:1) Spr 92, p. 43.
"Unrequited Love." [AmerPoR] (21:2) Mr-Ap 92, p. 26.

6067. SPRINGER, Tom
"Old Buildings." [Writer] (105:12) D 92, p. 18.

6068. SQUIRES, Radcliffe
"The Envoy." [Iowa] (22:2) Spr-Sum 92, p. 77.
"Journey Five." [Iowa] (22:2) Spr-Sum 92, p. 71-72.
"Journey Four." [Iowa] (22:2) Spr-Sum 92, p. 71.
"Journey One." [Iowa] (22:2) Spr-Sum 92, p. 69.
"Journey Seven." [Iowa] (22:2) Spr-Sum 92, p. 73-74.
"Journey Six." [Iowa] (22:2) Spr-Sum 92, p. 72-73.
"Journey Three." [Iowa] (22:2) Spr-Sum 92, p. 70.
"Journey Two." [Iowa] (22:2) Spr-Sum 92, p. 70.
"The Nice Children." [Iowa] (22:2) Spr-Sum 92, p. 75.
"Pollution." [Iowa] (22:2) Spr-Sum 92, p. 76.
"Small Yellow Wasps." [Iowa] (22:2) Spr-Sum 92, p. 74.

6069. SRIVASTAVA, Satyendra
"The Noble Torturer." [Verse] (9:3) Wint 92, p. 135.
"The Tiger." [Verse] (9:3) Wint 92, p. 135-136.

ST. . . .
See also Saint . . .

6070. ST. ANDREWS, B. A.
"The Anniversary Waltz." [ChamLR] (10/11) Spr-Fall 92, p. 169.
"Burying the Cat." [BellR] (15:2) Fall 92, p. 18.

6071. ST. CLAIR, Donald D.
"6 East, Line 100." [EngJ] (81:1) Ja 92, p. 97.

6072. ST. GERMAIN, Sheryl
"Hoping for Disaster." [HighP] (7:1) Spr 92, p. 77-78.
"Looking for Fossils." [HighP] (7:1) Spr 92, p. 79-80.
"Street Market, Otavalo." [NewL] (58:3) Spr 92, p. 20-23.

6073. ST. JACQUES, Elizabeth
"The harpist's fingernails." [Amelia] (6:4, #19) 92, p. 140.

6074. ST. JOHN, David
"Celeste in the Rain." [HayF] (11) Fall-Wint 92, p. 24.
"Christmas in Taos." [Ploughs] (18:1) Spr 92, p. 212-213.
"A Distant Tune" (in memory of Robinson Jeffers). [Ploughs] (18:1) Spr 92, p. 214.
"A Fortunate Man." [HayF] (11) Fall-Wint 92, p. 21-22.
"A Message for Monique." [HayF] (11) Fall-Wint 92, p. 23.
"The Mist." [HayF] (11) Fall-Wint 92, p. 25.
"My Grandfather's Cap." [GettyR] (5:3) Sum 92, p. 478-479.
"A Sense of Things." [AntR] (50:1/2) Wint-Spr 92, p. 254.
"Sleepers Naked under Moonlight." [MassR] (23:1) Spr 92, p. 105.

6075. ST. JOHN, Primus
"Carnival." [ThRiPo] (39/40) 92-93, p. 244-245.
"Reading a Story to My Child." [ThRiPo] (39/40) 92-93, p. 241-244.

6076. ST. MARTIN, Hardie
"Impression of Exile" (tr. of Luis Cernuda). [Trans] (26) Spr 92, p. 43-44.
"Variation on a Poem by Lawrence Durrell" (tr. of Francesc Parcerisas). [Trans] (26) Spr 92, p. 94.

6077. STAAL, Arie
"Poem: Trunk of flames, patience" (tr. of Paul Rodenko). [Vis] (38) 92, p. 44.
6078. STACHENFELD, Mari Elaine
"Dreaming Elaine." [Rohwedder] (7) Spr-Sum 92, p. 40.
6079. STACHURA, Edward
"Kiedy odkorkowalem butelke." [InterPR] (18:2) Fall 92, p. 38, 40.
"When I uncorked the bottle" (tr. by Cesar Ornatowski). [InterPR] (18:2) Fall 92, p. 39, 41.
6080. STACY, Barbara
"Buttoning Back." [Nimrod] (35:2) Spr-Sum 92, p. 101.
"Preview." [Nimrod] (35:2) Spr-Sum 92, p. 102.
6081. STAFFORD, Charles
"A Death in the Family." [BellR] (15:1) Spr 92, p. 37.
"Family Party." [BellR] (15:1) Spr 92, p. 36.
6082. STAFFORD, Kim R.
"Feather Bag, Stick Bag." [ThRiPo] (39/40) 92-93, p. 247.
"Opening the Book." [ThRiPo] (39/40) 92-93, p. 246.
"Walking to the Mailbox." [ThRiPo] (39/40) 92-93, p. 245-246.
6083. STAFFORD, William
"Annals of *T'ai Chi:* 'Push Hands'." [Poetry] (160:6) S 92, p. 320.
"Both Ways." [ThRiPo] (39/40) 92-93, p. 248.
"For Alexis Christa von Hartmann: Proved Not Guilty." [ThRiPo] (39/40) 92-93, p. 248.
"Grace Abounding." [CharR] (18:1) Spr 92, p. 76.
"How It Goes." [CharR] (18:1) Spr 92, p. 75.
"Impasse." [Field] (47) Fall 92, p. 120.
"Left for the Back Pages." [Field] (47) Fall 92, p. 121.
"The Magic Mountain." [Poetry] (160:6) S 92, p. 321.
"Nine." [Light] (1) Spr 92, p. 8.
"Nor Marble Nor the Gilded Monuments." [NewMyths] (1:2/2:1) 92, p. 203.
"Not in the Headlines." [NewMyths] (1:2/2:1) 92, p. 204-205.
"One Sudden Indian." [Footwork] 92, p. 11.
"Opening an Imperfectly Sealed Time Capsule." [Light] (4) Wint 92-93, p. 14.
"Preservation." [ThRiPo] (39/40) 92-93, p. 249.
"Thinking About the Natives." [Footwork] 92, p. 11.
"Third Street." [Poetry] (160:6) S 92, p. 319-320.
"Twelfth Birthday." [ThRiPo] (39/40) 92-93, p. 149.
"What It All Means." [CharR] (18:1) Spr 92, p. 75.
"Writing." [Light] (2) Sum 92, p. 10.
6084. STAHLECKER, Beth
"Field of Sky." [SenR] (22:2) Fall 92, p. 86-88.
6085. STAINER, Pauline
"Thomas Traherne in the Orient." [Verse] (9:2) Sum 92, p. 97.
6086. STALLINGS, A. E.
"Apollo Takes Charge of His Muses." [BelPoJ] (43:2) Wint 92-93, p. 5.
6087. STALLONE, Barbara
"In the Earth Cellar." [MidwQ] (34:1) Aut 92, p. 84-86.
"Supernumerary." [Amelia] (7:1, #20) 92, p. 28.
6088. STANDING, Sue
"Bagatelles." [AmerV] (26) Spr 92, p. 77-78.
"La Blanchisseuse (Toulouse-Lautrec)." [SouthernR] (28:1) Wint, Ja 92, p. 98.
"Coeur D'Alene." [Agni] (35) 92, p. 46.
"Jack Dracula." [NewDeltaR] (9:1) Fall 91-Wint 92, p. 56.
"Men" (after Ritsos). [AmerV] (26) Spr 92, p. 79.
"Yusuf Abdulla Jaffer & Co. (Perfumers)" (for Donna Kerner). [Agni] (35) 92, p. 43-45.
6089. STANFORD, Ann Folwell
"October Like Caged Birds: Four Rains." [HolCrit] (29:5) D 92, p. 19.
6090. STANIZZI, John L.
"Wind Shift" (for chuck conkling). [SpoonRQ] (17:1/2) Wint-Spr 92, p. 9.
6091. STANKO, Mary Rudbeck
"Calling Down the Moon." [Archae] (4) late 92-early 93, p. 20.
"Centerfold." [Archae] (4) late 92-early 93, p. 18.
"Otherwise Indisposed." [Crucible] (28) Fall 92, p. 20.
"Wayfarer." [Archae] (4) late 92-early 93, p. 19.

6092. STANNARD, J. E.
"The Jacket." [Verse] (9:3) Wint 92, p. 129.
"The Sea, the Sea." [Verse] (9:3) Wint 92, p. 129.
"Tamed, Tamed." [Verse] (9:3) Wint 92, p. 129.
6093. STANSBERGER, Richard
"The King of the Mountain." [CinPR] (23) Wint 91-92, p. 59.
6094. STANTON, Joseph
"Edward Hopper's Solitude." [ChamLR] (10/11) Spr-Fall 92, p. 199.
"Toads." [ChamLR] (10/11) Spr-Fall 92, p. 200-201.
6095. STANTON, Maura
"Biography." [ThRiPo] (39/40) 92-93, p. 252.
"Brise Marine" (after Mallarmé). [NoDaQ] (60:4) Fall 92, p. 9.
"Childhood." [ThRiPo] (39/40) 92-93, p. 250.
"Cleo." [NoDaQ] (60:4) Fall 92, p. 10-11.
"Ice Storm on the Pennsylvania Turnpike." [GreenMR] (NS 5:2) Spr-Sum 92, p. 5.
"The Isle of Kokomo." [HopewellR] (4) 92, p. 13.
"Ivory Tower." [GreenMR] (NS 5:2) Spr-Sum 92, p. 6-7.
"Relax." [HopewellR] (4) 92, p. 28.
"Shoplifters." [ThRiPo] (39/40) 92-93, p. 251-252.
"Sunday Graveyard." [ThRiPo] (39/40) 92-93, p. 252-253.
"Three Red Pears." [NoDaQ] (60:4) Fall 92, p. 7-8.
6096. STARCK, Clemens
"Reading the Gospels in the Lee Hotel." [Event] (21:2) Sum 92, p. 68-69.
6097. STARK, Susan Verelon
"Blue Vase." [Epiphany] (3:1) Ja (Wint) 92, p. 5-6.
"Fallen Leaf" (For D. S.). [Epiphany] (3:1) Ja (Wint) 92, p. 2.
"Guardian." [Epiphany] (3:1) Ja (Wint) 92, p. 3.
"Waterfall." [Epiphany] (3:1) Ja (Wint) 92, p. 4.
6098. STARKE, Anthony
"I Fear My Own Forgetting." [Chelsea] (53) 92, p. 120-121.
6099. STARKEY, David
"Eminent Domain." [Hellas] (3:1) Spr 92, p. 50.
"Illegal Alien." [PaintedHR] (6) Spr 92, p. 18.
"In Heavy Fog Outside of Bishopville, South Carolina." [CharR] (18:1) Spr 92, p. 87.
"Interview." [BelPoJ] (43:1) Fall 92, p. 26-33.
"Koan Americana." [Pearl] (16) Fall 92, p. 24.
"Miscarriage." [CharR] (18:1) Spr 92, p. 88.
"Stopping at the Overheated Vehicles Exit South of Grapevine." [NewDeltaR] (9:1) Fall 91-Wint 92, p. 54-55.
"To an Astronomer." [TarRP] (31:2) Spr 92, p. 24.
"Tools." [Poem] (67) My 92, p. 61.
"The Unbearable." [LaurelR] (26:2) Sum 92, p. 19.
6100. STARNES, Sofia M.
"Breathe Deeply Now" (for tio Felix, 1921-1990). [SmPd] (29:3, #86) Fall 92, p. 34.
6101. STARRETT, Virginia
"Adventure on the High Sneeze." [Light] (2) Sum 92, p. 23.
"Grandma's Dish." [NegC] (12:1/2) 92, p. 198.
6102. STARZEC, Larry
"How It Is." [WillowR] (19) Spr 92, p. 28.
6103. STATIA, Ini
"Black Woman" (tr. from the Dutch). [LitR] (35:4) Sum 92, p. 580-581.
"Zwarte Vrouw." [LitR] (35:4) Sum 92, p. 616.
6104. STAUDT, David
"Asthma." [PaintedB] (47) 92, p. 46.
"Bake Oven Knob." [PaintedB] (47) 92, p. 48.
"Bless These." [CapeR] (27:1) Spr 92, p. 9.
"A Good Date." [ChatR] (12:4) Sum 92, p. 55.
"Northeast Extension." [PaintedB] (47) 92, p. 49.
"Packerton." [PaintedB] (45) 92, p. 14-15.
"Spike." [PaintedB] (47) 92, p. 47.
"Temporary." [GreensboroR] (53) Wint 92-93, p. 28-29.
"White Acre" (Sea of Japan, Winter 1989). [CapeR] (27:1) Spr 92, p. 8.
6105. STEARNS, Laura
"Passage." [SouthernPR] (32:1) Spr 92, p. 14-15.

6106. STECKO, Boris Victor
"Passages." [SmPd] (29:1, #84) Wint 92, p. 34.
6107. STEDINGH, R. W.
"Cherry Tree." [CapilR] (2:8) Spr 92, p. 33.
"Coho Salmon." [CapilR] (2:8) Spr 92, p. 31.
"Easter Lily" (for Anne). [CapilR] (2:8) Spr 92, p. 32.
"Rock Dove." [CapilR] (2:8) Spr 92, p. 34.
"Salmonberry." [CapilR] (2:8) Spr 92, p. 35.
6108. STEDMAN, Judy
"KV #137." [Bogg] (65) 92, p. 30.
"MC ^{2}." [Bogg] (65) 92, p. 30.
"Remembering the Sixties." [Bogg] (65) 92, p. 30.
6109. STEEGE, Kristin
"Bread" (First Place, The Paintbrush Award, Poetry). [PaintedHR] (7) Fall 92, p. 6 - 7.
"A Dream About Omnipotence." [HiramPoR] (51/52) Fall 91-Sum 92, p. 68-69.
"We Are Going to Eat My Mother" (First Place, The Paintbrush Award, Poetry). [PaintedHR] (7) Fall 92, p. 5-6.
6110. STEELE, Charlotte Musial
"July Early Morning in Big Pond." [PottPort] (14:2) Fall-Wint 92, p. 85-86.
"Variations on a Dream." [PottPort] (14:2) Fall-Wint 92, p. 86-87.
"Woman in the Moon." [PottPort] (14:2) Fall-Wint 92, p. 84.
6111. STEELE, Cynthia
"The Cenote at Zac-quí" (tr. of Elsa Cross). [TriQ] (85) Fall 92, p. 248-250.
"For Aries" (tr. of Elva Macías). [TriQ] (85) Fall 92, p. 115.
"I Saw You in the Park" (tr. of Silvia Tomasa Rivera). [TriQ] (85) Fall 92, p. 400.
"Letter to the Wolf" (tr. of Carmen Boullosa). [TriQ] (85) Fall 92, p. 84-86.
"Naturalization Papers" (tr. of Myriam Moscona). [TriQ] (85) Fall 92, p. 347.
"On Capricorn" (tr. of Elva Macías). [TriQ] (85) Fall 92, p. 113-114.
"Open House" (to Roger Brindis, tr. of Elva Macías). [TriQ] (85) Fall 92, p. 116.
"Tulijá River" (tr. of Elva Macías). [TriQ] (85) Fall 92, p. 117.
"What I Wouldn't Give to Know" (tr. of Silvia Tomasa Rivera). [TriQ] (85) Fall 92, p. 401.
6112. STEELE, Frank
"The Salesman" (March, 1987. To the Memory of My Father, 1903-1987). [PoetryE] (33) Spr 92, p. 138-147.
6113. STEELE, Holly
"Dad." Sparks! Writing by High School Students (1:1), a supplement to [PraF] (13:4, #61) Wint 92-93, p. 29.
6114. STEELE, Lenora Jean
"Spring Cleaning." [PottPort] (14:1) Spr-Sum 92, p. 27.
6115. STEELE, Patricia
"Reduction." [EngJ] (80:8) D 91, p. 99.
6116. STEELE, Rory
"Fevers." [Footwork] 92, p. 146.
"Oral Histories." [Footwork] 92, p. 146.
6117. STEELE, Timothy
"December in Los Angeles." [Poetry] (161:3) D 92, p. 134.
"Hortulus." [Poetry] (161:3) D 92, p. 135.
"In Passing." [SouthwR] (77:1) Wint 92, p. 56.
"Just as Well." [Hellas] (3:2) Fall 92, p. 52.
"Luck." [Hellas] (3:2) Fall 92, p. 50-51.
6118. STEELE, Will
"Assurance." [SenR] (22:1) Spr 92, p. 83.
"Sleeping on a Mountain." [SenR] (22:1) Spr 92, p. 82.
6119. STEFAN, Marina
"The Photographer in His Garden." [WestHR] (46:3) Fall 92, p. 224-225.
"To a Harpsichord Player." [WestHR] (46:3) Fall 92, p. 226-227.
6120. STEFANILE, Felix
"You, Ciampol, taking long looks at that crone" ("Two Views of Courtly Love," tr. of Cecco Angiolieri). [Sparrow] (59) S 92, p. 15.
"You, who through my eyes reached to my heart" ("Two Views of Courtly Love," tr. of Guido Cavalcanti). [Sparrow] (59) S 92, p. 15.
STEFANO, Darin de
See DeSTEFANO, Darin

STEFANO, John de
See De STEFANO, John
6121. STEFFEY, Neil S.
"No Laurel." [SycamoreR] (4:1) Wint 92, p. 27-29.
"Turbulence." [PaintedB] (45) 92, p. 13.
6122. STEFFLER, John
"Alban Berg." [PoetryC] (12:3/4) Jl 92, p. 30-31.
"The Breeze Itself." [PoetryC] (12:3/4) Jl 92, p. 31.
"On a Lawn Chair at Night." [PoetryC] (12:3/4) Jl 92, p. 31.
"Tell Me I'm Not Making This Up." [PoetryC] (12:3/4) Jl 92, p. 30.
6123. STEIN, Agnes
"Biography" (tr. of Gunter Kunert). [Verse] (9:2) Sum 92, p. 93.
"Ephesus" (tr. of Gunter Kunert). [Verse] (9:2) Sum 92, p. 93.
6124. STEIN, Alice (*See also* STEIN, Alice P.)
"A Difference of Tastes." [Light] (2) Sum 92, p. 24.
6125. STEIN, Alice P. (*See also* STEIN, Alice)
"Retirement Thought." [Light] (3) Aut 92, p. 22.
"To an Innkeeper." [Light] (1) Spr 92, p. 22.
"Toast." [Light] (3) Aut 92, p. 14.
6126. STEIN, Charles
"They Take the Car Away" (from "theforestforthetrees"). [Conjunc] (19) 92, p. 290 - 292.
6127. STEIN, Deborah
"Figure a Flower." [SingHM] (20) 92, p. 61.
6128. STEIN, Dona Luongo
"Winter, Villa Montalvo." [SycamoreR] (4:1) Wint 92, p. 45-46.
"Winter (Villa Montalvo)" (corrected reprint from 4:1). [SycamoreR] (4:2) Sum 92, p. 43-44.
6129. STEIN, Jill
"Sharing an Omelette at La Groceria." [US1] (26/27) 92, p. 25.
6130. STEIN, Joyce
"It's Time Now!" [OnTheBus] (4:2/5:1, #10/11) 92, p. 211.
6131. STEIN, Kevin
"Anatomy Display" (Woman and Horse, Dickson Mounds Museum). [Shen] (42:1) Spr 92, p. 50-51.
"Awaiting My Daughter's Suitor." [MissouriR] (15:1) 92, p. 94-95.
"Baseball Arrives in Richmond, Indiana, 1869." [IndR] (15:2) Fall 92, p. 142.
"Benefit Picnic, Cigar Makers' Strike, August 1884." [MissouriR] (15:1) 92, p. 92 - 93.
"Black Bread." [MissouriR] (15:1) 92, p. 86-88.
"Fathers." [QW] (36) Wint 92-93, p. 113-115.
"Human Commerce." [IndR] (15:2) Fall 92, p. 139-141.
"It Didn't Begin with Horned Owls Hooting at Noon." [DenQ] (26:4) Spr 92, p. 69.
"Night Shift, after Drinking Dinner, Container Corporation of America, 1972." [NoAmR] (277:4) Jl-Ag 92, p. 33.
"The Presence of God in Our Lives." [PoetryNW] (33:2) Sum 92, p. 32-33.
"Rooster Saved from the Soup Pan." [PoetryNW] (33:2) Sum 92, p. 33-34.
"St. Andrew's Catholic Men's Choir, After Practice, at Blickwedels's Tavern and Grocery." [MissouriR] (15:1) 92, p. 89-91.
"Two Hungers." [MissouriR] (15:1) 92, p. 84-85.
6132. STEIN, Michael
"Route Four." [HighP] (7:2) Fall 92, p. 21-22.
"Venice, California." [Salm] (94/95) Spr-Sum 92, p. 82.
6133. STEINEM, Robert
"Listening to You Sleep." [Elf] (2:3) Fall 92, p. 35.
6134. STEINGESSER, Martin
"Testimony, April 14, 1986." [BelPoJ] (43:2) Wint 92-93, p. 16-17.
6135. STEINKE, René
"The Ruined Abbey, March." [CumbPR] (11:2) Spr 92, p. 27.
6136. STEINMAN, Lisa M.
"Narrative/Lyric." [QW] (36) Wint 92-93, p. 117.
6137. STEKERT, Ellen J.
"Elliot's Sunset" (tr. of Luz María Umpierre). [Americas] (19:3/4) Wint 91, p. 48-50.
6138. STELIGA, Heather S. J.
"City of the Dead Poets" (tr. of Lian Yang, w. Shi-Zheng Chen). [GrahamHR] (16) Fall 92, p. 100.

"Games of Lies" (tr. of Lian Yang, w. Shi-Zheng Chen). [GrahamHR] (16) Fall 92, p. 98-99.
"War Museum" (tr. of Lian Yang, w. Shi-Zheng Chen). [GrahamHR] (16) Fall 92, p. 101-102.
"Winter Garden" (tr. of Lian Yang, w. Shi-Zheng Chen). [GrahamHR] (16) Fall 92, p. 95-97.

6139. STELMACH, Marjorie
"Doorways." [MalR] (101) Wint92, p. 25-46.
"If I Get It Wrong." [SouthernPR] (32:1) Spr 92, p. 5-6.

6140. STENSON, Sharon
"Perspective I: Still Life w/ Alley Gate" (Terre Haute — 1952). [13thMoon] (10:1/2) 92, p. 52-54.

6141. STEPANCHEV, Stephen
"Homeless." [Poetry] (161:2) N 92, p. 96.
"Thinking About Tu Fu." [Poetry] (161:3) D 92, p. 147.

6142. STEPHENS, Christine
"Unfolding My Sister." [CapeR] (27:1) Spr 92, p. 30-31.

6143. STEPHENS, S. A.
"Three, Breathing" (Excerpt). [Iowa] (22:3) Fall 92, p. 101-110.

6144. STEPHENSON, Debora
"Defense." [Ometeca] (2:2) 91 [published 92], p. 32-33.

6145. STEPHENSON, Gregory
"The Lacunae." [CimR] (100) Jl 92, p. 46.

6146. STEPHENSON, Shelby
"A Parable of the Miracle Mile." [Light] (4) Wint 92-93, p. 23.

6147. STEPHENSON, Victoria
"In Order To." [ManhatPR] (14) [92?], p. 8.
"Instrumental Arrangements." [ManhatPR] (14) [92?], p. 8.
"Merton." [ManhatPR] (14) [92?], p. 9.

6148. STEPP, Dianne Williams
"Married at Midlife: The First Six Months." [BellArk] (8:6) N-D 92, p. 13.

6149. STEPTO, Gabriel
"Crazeology." [KenR] (NS 14:3) Sum 92, p. 24.

6150. STEPTOE, Lamont B.
"Oppressed, We Are One." [PaintedB] (47) 92, p. 27.
"Short Circuited." [PaintedB] (48) 92, p. 69.
"Such Belief." [Eyeball] (1) 92, p. 12.
"To the Father of Me." [Eyeball] (1) 92, p. 12.

6151. STERLING, Phillip
"The Communion of Saints." [OxfordM] (6:2) Fall-Wint 90, p. 56.
"Learning to Sing with Our Hands." [OxfordM] (6:2) Fall-Wint 90, p. 57.
"This Night." [CapeR] (27:1) Spr 92, p. 35.
"The Voice Discovers Elegy" (R.J.S. 1939-1991). [SenR] (22:1) Spr 92, p. 62-63.

6152. STERN, Gerald
"I Hate My Moaning." [ThRiPo] (39/40) 92-93, p. 255.
"If the Lark Had Thorns." [AmerPoR] (21:3) My-Je 92, p. 41.
"Nobody Else Living." [ThRiPo] (39/40) 92-93, p. 254.
"Peddler's Village." [ThRiPo] (39/40) 92-93, p. 253-254.
"Red with Pink" (Poetry Chapbook: 6 poems). [BlackWR] (18:2) Spr-Sum 92, p. 75-86.
"Sending Back the Gloom." [Boulevard] (7:1, #19) Spr 92, p. 118-119.
"The Smell of Death." [AmerPoR] (21:3) My-Je 92, p. 42-43.
"Someone Will Do It for Me." [Boulevard] (7:1, #19) Spr 92, p. 116-117.
"Sylvia." [Field] (46) Spr 92, p. 8-9.
"The Thought of Heaven." [AmerPoR] (21:3) My-Je 92, p. 42.
"Two Daws." [GettyR] (5:2) Spr 92, p. 211-213.

6153. STERN, Gerd
"From Z to A" (for them). [Archae] (4) late 92-early 93, p. 45.

6154. STERN, Joan
"July 8, 1983." [Confr] (50) Fall 92, p. 294.

6155. STERN, Robert
"Cathedral." [AntigR] (90) Sum 92, p. 91.
"Muse." [AntigR] (90) Sum 92, p. 90.
"Stones." [AntigR] (90) Sum 92, p. 92.

6156. STERNLIEB, Barry
"Drawing the Line." [MidwQ] (34:1) Aut 92, p. 86-87.

"Lady Ch'eng." [QW] (35) Sum-Fall 92, p. 115.
"North Coast." [ManhatPR] (14) [92?], p. 22.

6157. STEVENS, Allen
"Homing." [Verse] (9:3) Wint 92, p. 137.

6158. STEVENS, Geoff
"Kerouac's Town." [CoalC] (5) My 92, p. 13.

6159. STEVENS, Jim
"All These Miles and Years." [RagMag] (10:2) 92, p. 96.
"Goodbye and Thanks." [RagMag] (10:2) 92, p. 97.
"Last Reel." [SoDakR] (30:2) Sum 92, p. 110.
"The Roads Around Santiago." [Arc] (29) Aut 92, p. 19-20.
"Schizophrenia." [Light] (1) Spr 92, p. 26.

6160. STEVENS, May
"Kate's Poem's (Purloined)." [LitR] (36:1) Fall 92, p. 91.

6161. STEVENS, Tina
"Feast of the Dead." [LaurelR] (26:1) Wint 92, p. 74-77.

6162. STEVENSON, Anne
"Negatives." [Stand] (33:2) Spr 92, p. 146-147.
"Painting It In" (Mist in North Wales). [NewEngR] (14:4) Fall 92, p. 188-189.
"Salter's Gate" (for Peter). [PartR] (59:3) Sum 92, p. 474-475.
"Trinity at Low Tide." [NewEngR] (14:4) Fall 92, p. 189.

6163. STEVENSON, Terry B.
"Eclipse, Kona, Hawaii, July 11, 1991." [OnTheBus] (4:2/5:1, #10/11) 92, p. 213.
"The Tick of Each Clock." [OnTheBus] (4:2/5:1, #10/11) 92, p. 212.

6164. STEVENSON, Warren
"Miss Claycorn." [AntigR] (91) Fall 92, p. 137-138.

6165. STEVER, Edward W. (Edward William)
"Carnivores." [SlipS] (12) 92, p. 26.
"Profit Sharing." [SlipS] (12) 92, p. 26-27.
"Revising Myself" (3rd place winner, Chiron Review 1992 Poetry Contest). [ChironR] (11:3) Aut 92, p. 15.

6166. STEVER, Margo
"The Cello." [HarvardA] (125th Anniversary Issue) F 92, p. 14.

6167. STEVICK, Mark
"Chewing Gum." [SpoonRQ] (17:3/4) Sum-Fall 92, p. 70.
"In Passing." [Hellas] (3:1) Spr 92, p. 42.
"What Matters." [CapeR] (27:2) Fall 92, p. 46-47.

6168. STEWARD, D. E.
"Main Line." [JlNJPo] (14:1) Spr 92, p. 7.
"North." [JlNJPo] (14:2) Aut 92, p. 37.

6169. STEWART, Dolores
"Avebury." [ChiR] (37:4) 92, p. 57-60.
"Letter to Burpee Seed Co." [Confr] (50) Fall 92, p. 267.
"Object Lesson." [Kalliope] (15:1) 92, p. 5.
" *Os*, the Letter A, Rune of Mouth, Breath, Messages, and Inspiration." [BelPoJ] (42:3) Spr 92, p. 1.
"Out of Bounds." [SouthernPR] (32:2) Fall 92, p. 39.

6170. STEWART, Frank
"'Ama'u." [Ploughs] (18:1) Spr 92, p. 219.
"Angels of the Mission of the Southern Cross." [Ploughs] (18:1) Spr 92, p. 221.
"Kamuela." [Ploughs] (18:1) Spr 92, p. 220.
"Mauna Loa at 7,000 Feet." [Ploughs] (18:1) Spr 92, p. 218.

6171. STEWART, Jack
"Handkerchief" (for Lu Stone). [Poem] (68) N 92, p. 17.
"Sid-Mar's, Lake Pontchartrain." [Poem] (68) N 92, p. 19.
"Shooting Pool at the Famous" (for Elliot Wasserman). [Poem] (68) N 92, p. 18.

6172. STEWART, Kate
"I'm Turning into a Museum." [ChamLR] (10/11) Spr-Fall 92, p. 33-35.

6173. STEWART, Pamela
"A Beautiful Town in Vermont." [HighP] (7:1) Spr 92, p. 76.

6174. STEWART, Robert
"Hero." [DenQ] (26:3) Wint 92, p. 46-47.
"Palm Sunday." [Stand] (33:2) Spr 92, p. 106.

6175. STEWART, Shannon
"Travels." [Event] (21:3) Fall 92, p. 66-67.

6176. STEWART, Susan
"The Forest." [TriQ] (86) Wint 92-93, p. 34-36.
"The Meadow." [TriQ] (86) Wint 92-93, p. 37-38.
"Medusa Anthology." [ColR] (9:2) Fall 92, p. 77-88.
6177. STEWART, W. Gregory
"Dillo." [Amelia] (7:1, #20) 92, p. 67.
"My Neighborhood Was So Tough." [Amelia] (7:1, #20) 92, p. 57.
6178. STIAKAKI, Parina
"Clay Jug" (tr. of Manolis Pratikakis). [Stand] (33:4) Aut 92, p. 98.
6179. STICKNEY, John
"Drill: What I Want." [Caliban] (11) 92, p. 89.
"Important Points to Notice." [Caliban] (11) 92, p. 88.
"Much Later" (after Elena Stefoi). [Caliban] (11) 92, p. 90.
6180. STICKNEY, Trumbull
"Mnemosyne." [Sparrow] (59) S 92, p. 41.
6181. STILES, Cheryl
"Execution Rocks." [Amelia] (6:4, #19) 92, p. 107.
"The New Physician." [Amelia] (6:4, #19) 92, p. 107-109.
"Shrimper's Wife." [Amelia] (6:4, #19) 92, p. 109.
6182. STILL, Gloria
"Two Blue Dresses." [HopewellR] (4) 92, p. 17.
6183. STILL, James
"Of Concern." [AmerV] (27) 92, p. 3.
6184. STILLWELL, Marie
"Pavane for Old Lovers." [WebR] (16) Fall 92, p. 66.
6185. STINSON, Don
"Circus of the Stars." [CapeR] (27:1) Spr 92, p. 10.
6186. STINSON, Susan
"The Line." [KenR] (NS 14:2) Spr 92, p. 124-125.
"Nannie on the Carpet." [KenR] (NS 14:2) Spr 92, p. 123.
6187. STOLOFF, Carolyn
"Anticipating the End of Distance." [SouthernR] (28:3) Sum, Jl 92, p. 620-621.
"Offering." [Paint] (19:37) Spr 92, p. 11-12.
"Picking Up Stitches." [Paint] (19:37) Spr 92, p. 13.
6188. STOLTZFUS, Dawn
"A Proper Burial." [LullwaterR] (3:3) Sum 92, p. 55.
6189. STONE, Alison
"The Body's Small Pleasures." [Poetry] (160:3) Je 92, p. 156.
"Heritage." [Poetry] (160:3) Je 92, p. 154-155.
"Just Like Sister Ray Said." [NewYorkQ] (48) 92, p. 67.
"Lower East Side Halloween." [Confr] (48/49) Spr-Sum 92, p. 210-211.
"The Ninety-Ninth Percentile." [NewYorkQ] (47) 92, p. 94.
"Not Finding Tranquility by the Lake." [Poetry] (160:6) S 92, p. 338.
"Persephone's First Season in Hell." [Poetry] (161:1) O 92, p. 22.
"Sex Talk Among Women." [NewYorkQ] (49) 92, p. 55.
"Since '81." [Witness] (6:1) 92, p. 169.
6190. STONE, Carole
"Edward Hopper's *Corn Hill, Truro* (1930)." [US1] (26/27) 92, p. 35.
6191. STONE, Ken
"The Coyote Anxiously Howls." [BlackBR] (15) Spr-Sum 92, p. 30.
6192. STONE, Myrna J.
"Sisters in the Flesh." [BostonR] (17:1) F 92, p. 30.
6193. STONE, Reynold
"Miklòs Radnóti (1909-1944)." [AntigR] (89) Spr 92, p. 36.
6194. STONE, Ruth
"It Follows." [AmerPoR] (21:5) S-O 92, p. 32.
"Leaving New York with Harry." [AmerPoR] (21:5) S-O 92, p. 34.
"Living Space." [Footwork] 92, p. 12.
"The Lost World." [Boulevard] (7:2/3, #20/21) Fall 92, p. 127.
"Metamorphosis." [AmerV] (27) 92, p. 4.
"On the Outer Banks." [Boulevard] (7:2/3, #20/21) Fall 92, p. 126.
"Otherwise." [Boulevard] (7:2/3, #20/21) Fall 92, p. 125.
"Resonance." [AmerPoR] (21:5) S-O 92, p. 32.
"Simplicity." [NewMyths] (1:2/2:1) 92, p. 17.
"The System." [AmerPoR] (21:5) S-O 92, p. 34.
"Talking to the Dead." [NewMyths] (1:2/2:1) 92, p. 16.

"That Winter." [AmerPoR] (21:5) S-O 92, p. 33.
"A Very Stretched Sennet." [AmerPoR] (21:5) S-O 92, p. 33.

6195. STONEY, Leland
"The Draft." [Chelsea] (53) 92, p. 110-113.
"Not Quite Courting Morgana." [SoCoast] (13) Je 93 [i.e. 92], p. 9.
"Time Piece." [Asylum] (7:3/4) 92, p. 62.

6196. STORTONI, Laura Anna
"Broken Spears" (Freely adapted from a Nahuatl account, written in 1528 by anonymous authors in Tlatelolco). [MidwQ] (34:1) Aut 92, p. 88-89.
"Montezuma Sends His Messengers to Cortés" (Freely adapted from Aztec documents in Nahuatl reported by Fray Bernardino de Sahagun). [MidwQ] (34:1) Aut 92, p. 87-88.

6197. STOUT, Robert Joe
"At the Start of a New Journey." [WebR] (16) Fall 92, p. 45.
"Not-Quite Divorce." [ChrC] (109:21) 1-8 Jl 92, p. 646.

6198. STRAHAN, B. R. (Bradley R.)
"White Moments" (tr. of Nikolai Kantchev, w. Pamela Perry). [Confr] (48/49) Spr - Sum 92, p. 218.

6199. STRAND, Mark
"After Our Planet." [ParisR] (34:125) Wint 92, p. 108-111.
"Coming to This." [NewEngR] (14:4) Fall 92, p. 226.
"Dark Harbor" (Selections: I-III). [WeberS] (9:3) Fall 92, p. 5-7.
"Dark Harbor" (Selections: I-V). [Antaeus] (69) Aut 92, p. 29-33.
"From the Academy of Revelations." [NewRep] (207:6) 3 Ag 92, p. 35.
"Here." [NewYorker] (67:49) 27 Ja 92, p. 46.
"In the Night Without End." [NewYorker] (68:29) 7 S 92, p. 30-31.
"Labrador." [NewYorker] (68:11) 4 My 92, p. 42-43.
"Our Masterpiece Is the Private Life." [NewYorker] (68:37) 2 N 92, p. 66.
"Shooting Whales" (for Judith and Leon Major). [AntR] (50:1/2) Wint-Spr 92, p. 285-287.
"A Suite of Appearances" (To Octavio Mariejo Paz). [Boulevard] (7:1, #19) Spr 92, p. 19-21.
"Under the Glass Bell" (tr. of Maja Herman, w. the author). [ParisR] (34:123) Sum 92, p. 34.
"What Will Happen." [YaleR] (80:3) Jl 92, p. 50-52.

6200. STRANGE, Jason
"Voice Lessons." [WillowS] (29) Wint 92, p. 34.

6201. STRANGE, Sharan
"Grandmother's Clothes." [Agni] (36) 92, p. 64-65.
"Jimmy's First Cigarette." [Agni] (36) 92, p. 66.

6202. STRATIDAKIS, Eileen
"Other Stations." [CapeR] (27:2) Fall 92, p. 18.
"Park." [SycamoreR] (4:2) Sum 92, p. 26.

6203. STRAUS, Doris (Doris May)
"Drouth." [Amelia] (7:1, #20) 92, p. 125.
"Pepperdine." [Amelia] (7:1, #20) 92, p. 51.

6204. STRAUS, Marc J.
"An Elephant Crossed the Road." [Field] (46) Spr 92, p. 66-69.
"Lecture to Second-Year Medical Students" (for Peter Russo). [TriQ] (86) Wint 92 - 93, p. 84-86.
"The Log of Pi." [TriQ] (86) Wint 92-93, p. 87.
"One Word." [Ploughs] (18:4) Wint 92-93, p. 103.
"St. Maarten Vacation." [TriQ] (86) Wint 92-93, p. 88-90.
"What I Heard on the Radio Today." [Ploughs] (18:4) Wint 92-93, p. 104-105.

6205. STRAUSS, Gwen
"Pyromancy." [ManhatPR] (14) [92?], p. 25.

6206. STRECKFUS, Katherine
"Good Night." [SoCoast] (13) Je 93 [i.e. 92], p. 16.

6207. STRELOW, Michael
"Flowers." [SilverFR] (23) Wint 92, p. 21.
"Salmon." [SilverFR] (23) Wint 92, p. 20.

6208. STREPPONI, Blanca
"Ars Moriendi." [Inti] (36) Otoño 92, p. 157.
"Azteca." [Inti] (36) Otoño 92, p. 158-159.
"El Jardin del Verdugo." [Inti] (36) Otoño 92, p. 160-162.
"Palabras de Gregorio Magno (590)." [Inti] (36) Otoño 92, p. 159.

"Sueño." [Inti] (36) Otoño 92, p. 158.
6209. STREVER, Jan
"A Mechanical Solution to an Unmanageable Life." [DenQ] (26:4) Spr 92, p. 70-71.
6210. STRICKER, Meredith
"Man in a White Suit" (From a First Language). [Rohwedder] (7) Spr-Sum 92, p. 26-29.
"Red Willow" (From a First Language). [Rohwedder] (7) Spr-Sum 92, p. 24-25.
6211. STRINGHAM, Mike
"Dry Season." [CapeR] (27:2) Fall 92, p. 49.
6212. STROFFOLINO, Chris
"Better Known As a Blur." [Shiny] (7/8) 92, p. 117-118.
"Like a Laugh That Never Happened (a Fragment)" (for Susan Stroffolino 6/18/42 - 5/13/92). [PaintedB] (48) 92, p. 56-57.
"Nature Tampered Ego Berating Beauty" (for Spencer Selby). [WashR] (18:1) Je-Jl 92, p. 16.
6213. STROUD, D. M.
"House Against the Wind." [Noctiluca] (1:1) Spr 92, p. 44.
"To the One Crippled by Polio" (from the book "Lines Drawn Towards"). [Noctiluca] (1:1) Spr 92, p. 43.
6214. STRUTHERS, Ann
"February." [PoetC] (23:2) Wint 92, p. 27.
"Old Aunts." [PoetC] (23:2) Wint 92, p. 28.
6215. STRYK, Dan
"Job." [HolCrit] (29:1) F 92, p. 16.
"Stones." [SoDakR] (30:4) Wint 92, p. 118.
"Symbol." [CharR] (18:2) Fall 92, p. 97-98.
6216. STUART, Dabney
"Bi-Lingual." [Light] (4) Wint 92-93, p. 5.
"Coming To." [FourQ] (6:2) Fall 92, p. 30-31.
"Convenience." [Light] (4) Wint 92-93, p. 3.
"Country Music." [Light] (4) Wint 92-93, p. 3.
"Décolleté." [Light] (4) Wint 92-93, p. 5.
"Dedication for a Book of My Poems." [Light] (4) Wint 92-93, p. 3.
"Double Exposures." [MassR] (23:1) Spr 92, p. 135-140.
"Environmental." [Light] (1) Spr 92, p. 25.
"Foreplay." [NoAmR] (277:2) Mr-Ap 92, p. 27.
"Gull" (Cathedral Square, Christchurch, New Zealand). [PraS] (66:3) Fall 92, p. 73 - 75.
"High Culture." [Light] (4) Wint 92-93, p. 3.
"Intellectual History." [Light] (4) Wint 92-93, p. 5.
"Laud." [Light] (4) Wint 92-93, p. 3.
"Leavetaking." [Chelsea] (53) 92, p. 114-115.
"Long Gone." [Turnstile] (3:2) 92, p. 87-92.
"Open the Gates." [Light] (4) Wint 92-93, p. 4.
"Percussion." [TriQ] (86) Wint 92-93, p. 45-46.
"Punchy" (for the Whithams). [Light] (4) Wint 92-93, p. 6.
"Regular Guy." [Light] (4) Wint 92-93, p. 3.
"Rilke Applies for Tenure." [PoetC] (24:1) Fall 92, p. 20-21.
"Sagas of the Newborn" (Selection: "Feeding"). [Light] (4) Wint 92-93, p. 5.
"Sandbox" (for Ellen). [Light] (4) Wint 92-93, p. 4.
"The Writing Machine." [SouthernR] (28:1) Wint, Ja 92, p. 75.
6217. STUBBS, Andrew
"Trivial Pursuit." [AntigR] (89) Spr 92, p. 145.
STUBBS, John Heath
See HEATH-STUBBS, John
6218. STUCKI, Marcia V.
"The Mare One Morning." [Northeast] (5:7) Wint 92-93, p. 16.
6219. STUDER, Constance
"Frida Kahlo: What the Water Gave Me." [SingHM] (20) 92, p. 95-96.
6220. STULL, Richard
"Impudent Baggage." [NewAW] (10) Fall 92, p. 85.
"Long Distance." [Pequod] (34) 92, p. 61-63.
6221. STURGEON, Shawn
"Misreading Our Lives." [NewRep] (206:14) 6 Ap 92, p. 39.
"A Tramp Explains His Presence in the Suburbs to a Police Officer." [Pearl] (15) Spr-Sum 92, p. 14.

6222. SU, Dong-Po
"Ding Feng Bo (Calming the Wind and Waves)" (tr. by Yun Wang). [WillowS] (30) Sum 92, p. 16.
"Qian Diao (The Front Tune)" (tr. by Yun Wang). [WillowS] (30) Sum 92, p. 17.
6223. SU, Shih
"Tieh Lüan Hua" (tr. by Julie Landau). [Trans] (26) Spr 92, p. 103.
6224. SUBACH, Karen
"Mysteries: A Meditation" (2 selections). [Kalliope] (14:2) 92, p. 18.
"Termites." [Kalliope] (14:3) 92, p. 65-67.
6225. SUBRAMAN, Belinda
"A Celibate Life." [Parting] (5:1) Sum 92, p. 11.
"Crash Course for Goodie-Two-Shoes." [Amelia] (6:4, #19) 92, p. 124.
"Don't You Love the Lingo?" [Gypsy] (18) 92, p. 43.
"He's a Clock." [Parting] (5:1) Sum 92, p. 10.
"Hitchcock's Lost Notes for 'Bozo's Accidental Revenge'." [Epiphany] (3:4) O (Fall) 92, p. 241.
"Meddling Woman." [Pearl] (16) Fall 92, p. 34.
"She'll Show You Hers If You'll Show Her Yours." [Epiphany] (3:4) O (Fall) 92, p. 242.
6226. SUK, Julie
"Beyond the Hill." [Poetry] (159:5) F 92, p. 268.
"In Eterno." [SouthernHR] (26:2) Spr 92, p. 130-131.
"Playing Against Sleep." [Poetry] (159:5) F 92, p. 267.
"Quicksilver." [Poetry] (159:5) F 92, p. 269.
"Remembering the Plot." [Poetry] (159:5) F 92, p. 266.
"La Tempesta." [Poetry] (159:5) F 92, p. 270-271.
"Underworld." [RiverC] (12:2) Spr 92, p. 24-25.
6227. SUKNASKI, Andrew
"Divining for Aunt Amelja's Origins" (in memory of mike suknaski). [PraF] (13:3, #60) Aut 92, p. 176-178.
6228. SULLIVAN, Gary
"Two Poems for Marta." [Talisman] (8) Spr 92, p. 11.
6229. SULLIVAN, John
"Bright Skin of My Mother, O America." [BlackBR] (15) Spr-Sum 92, p. 20-22.
"Bright Skin of My Mother, O America" (slightly different version from printed in #15). [BlackBR] (16) Wint-Spr 92-93, p. 10-12.
"She." [CoalC] (5) My 92, p. 4.
"True Emergency." [HayF] (11) Fall-Wint 92, p. 101-102.
6230. SULLIVAN, Katherine
"There Were Bald Eagles Here." [HayF] (10) Spr-Sum 92, p. 73.
6231. SULLIVAN, Kathleen
"Sleep." [OxfordM] (7:1) Spr-Sum 91, p. 97.
6232. SULLIVAN, Sally
"The Abused Child, Like the Letter O." [Pembroke] (24) 92, p. 95.
6233. SULTAN, Linda
"Cal I For Nia." [Light] (1) Spr 92, p. 19.
"The Weather Forecast." [Light] (3) Aut 92, p. 12.
6234. SUMMER, David
"Fleeing Cuba." [PoetL] (87:1) Spr 92, p. 29.
6235. SUMMERFELDT, Vicki
"Might I But Moor — Tonight — in Thee." [Grain] (20:2) Sum 92, p. 105.
6236. SUMNER, David
"After." [BellR] (15:1) Spr 92, p. 38.
"Aspects of Death." [CumbPR] (11:2) Spr 92, p. 4.
"Below." [Footwork] 92, p. 138.
"Landscapes." [WeberS] (9:1) Wint 92, p. 67.
"Language." [SoCoast] (13) Je 93 [i.e. 92], p. 28-29.
"Left Behind." [AntigR] (90) Sum 92, p. 142.
"The Visitor." [LaurelR] (26:2) Sum 92, p. 69.
SUN, Nila North
See NORTH SUN, Nila
6237. SUNDAHL, Daniel James
"Aubade for the Last Performing Tattooed Lady." [WritersF] (18) 92, p. 36.
"Four French Children Lying on the Grass" (c. 1942). [Blueline] (13) 92, p. 96.
"Hiroshima Maiden: an Imaginary Translation from the Japanese" (Selection: 5). [AntigR] (89) Spr 92, p. 19-20.

"Hiroshima Maidens: Imaginary Translations from the Japanese" (Selections: 6, 10). [DogRR] (11:1) Spr-Sum 92, p. 18-20.
"In the Veteran's Hospital, the Woman Doctor Has a Vision of God" (circa 1947). [Footwork] 92, p. 98.
"Interjection #10: Entelechy." [WindO] (56) Fall-Wint 92, p. 9.
"Ismene in a Traveling Hat" (circa 400 B.C.). [WritersF] (18) 92, p. 37.

6238. SUNDVALL, Herbert
"Chi Kung Practice, Camp Indralaya — Orcas Island" (9/15/91). [BellArk] (8:1) Ja - F 92, p. 13.

6239. SUNICO, Ramón C.
"The Sad Art of Making Paper." [Manoa] (4:1) Spr 92, p. 69-70.

6240. SUPERVIELLE, Jules
"Without Walls" (tr. by Geoffrey Gardner). [PartR] (59:1) Wint 92, p. 106-107.

6241. SUPRANER, Robyn
"Butter and Eggs" (for K.N.B.). [Confr] (50) Fall 92, p. 291-292.

6242. SÜREYA, Cemal
"Statue of Lions" (tr. by Murat Nemet-Nejat). [Trans] (26) Spr 92, p. 108-109.

6243. SURRATT, Jerl
"A Flight of Angels." [KenR] (NS 14:4) Fall 92, p. 71-72.

6244. SUTHERILL, Colin
"Southpaw." [ChironR] (11:2) Sum 92, p. 13.

6245. SUTHERLAND, Fraser
"Turning Toward." [PoetryC] (12:2) Ap 92, p. 12-13.

6246. SUTHERLAND-SMITH, James
"Cemeteries" (tr. of Vlado Puchala, w. the author). [PraS] (66:4) Wint 92, p. 147.
"Psychics." [ManhatPR] (14) [92?], p. 55.
"So Deeply Do I Love You" (tr. of Vlado Puchala, w. the author). [PraS] (66:4) Wint 92, p. 148.
"The Teacher's Wake" (tr. of Vlado Puchala, w. the author). [PraS] (66:4) Wint 92, p. 147.

6247. SUTPHEN, Joyce
"Reading Sylvia Plath in London." [CapeR] (27:1) Spr 92, p. 46.
"Somewhere, Close to Dover Beach." [CapeR] (27:1) Spr 92, p. 47.

6248. SUTTON, Catherine
"The Devil at the Library." [AmerV] (27) 92, p. 94.

6249. SUTTON, Dorothy
"It Is Good." [Pembroke] (24) 92, p. 81.

6250. SUTTON, Pamela
"Smart Rocks, Brilliant Pebbles." [AntR] (50:3) Sum 92, p. 499.

6251. SUTTON, Walt
"The Secret." [OnTheBus] (4:2/5:1, #10/11) 92, p. 214-216.

6252. SUTZKEVER, Avrom
"Before Night" (tr. by Aaron Kramer). [Vis] (38) 92, p. 34.
"In the Vilna Ghetto: July 1943" (tr. by Aaron Kramer). [Vis] (38) 92, p. 33.

SUVERO, Victor Di
See Di SUVERO, Victor

6253. SUVILEHTO, Eero
"Päivän Runo." [Nimrod] (35:2) Spr-Sum 92, p. 50.
"Today's Poet" (tr. by Robert M. Randolph and the author). [Nimrod] (35:2) Spr - Sum 92, p. 51.

6254. SUZANNE
"Don't Say Grace — A Movement." [SinW] (47) Sum-Fall 92, p. 106-107.

6255. SVARLIEN, Diane Arnson
"Dream" (Propertius II.26A, tr. of Propertius). [Arion] 3d series (1:1) Wint 90, p. 184.
"Pyrrha" (after Horace, Odes I.5). [Arion] 3d series (1:1) Wint 90, p. 185.

6256. SVENONIUS, Elaine
"As a Voice." [OnTheBus] (4:2/5:1, #10/11) 92, p. 217.

6257. SVOBODA, Terese
"Brassieres: Prison or Showcase." [AmerPoR] (21:1) Ja-F 92, p. 47.
"A Few Drops of Blood or Grenadine." [Agni] (35) 92, p. 281-282.

6258. SWAIM, Alice Mackenzie
"With Beauty in Each Stitch." [Amelia] (7:1, #20) 92, p. 109.

6259. SWAN, Diane
"Crazy." [BostonR] (17:5) S-O 92, p. 22.
"Garden." [BostonR] (17:5) S-O 92, p. 22.

"Ice Fishing." [BostonR] (17:5) S-O 92, p. 22.
"Legs." [BostonR] (17:5) S-O 92, p. 22.
"Saving the Best for Last." [BostonR] (17:5) S-O 92, p. 22.

6260. SWAN, Marc
"An apple a day." [WormR] (32:3, #127) 92, p. 89.
"Dream Paths." [WormR] (32:3, #127) 92, p. 90.
"The Form That Shaped the Clay." [WormR] (32:3, #127) 92, p. 90.
"If It Were Only This Easy." [WormR] (32:3, #127) 92, p. 89.
"One Way Ride." [WormR] (32:3, #127) 92, p. 91.
"Standing Tall." [WormR] (32:3, #127) 92, p. 91.

6261. SWANDER, Mary
"Amish Phone Booth." [KenR] (NS 14:4) Fall 92, p. 161-162.
"Early Frost." [WillowS] (30) Sum 92, p. 51.

6262. SWANEY, George
"Aunt Mary Catherine Bids the World Adieu." [PoetryE] (33) Spr 92, p. 148.
"Feel My Goodness." [Gypsy] (19) 92, p. 54.

6263. SWANN, Brian
"Counterpoint." [Agni] (35) 92, p. 253.
"Fibre" (tr. of Bartolo Cattafi, w. Ruth Feldman). [Stand] (33:4) Aut 92, p. 111.
"Like This, My Papa in America" (tr. of Rocco Scotellaro, w. Ruth Feldman). [Stand] (33:4) Aut 92, p. 108.
"Taking the Sun in a Carpark Beside the East River." [Agni] (35) 92, p. 252.
"Variations on the First Elegy." [ColEng] (54:8) D 92, p. 940-941.

6264. SWANNELL, Anne
"The Catacombs." [Dandel] (19:1) 92, p. 24-25.
"Ellie and the Bronze Man." [PraF] (13:4, #61) Wint 92-93, p. 96.

6265. SWANSON, Catherine
"Hurricane." [HopewellR] (4) 92, p. 18.
"Saxophone." [Grain] (20:2) Sum 92, p. 89.
"To Emily." [Grain] (20:2) Sum 92, p. 90.

6266. SWANSON, Suzanne (Suzanne M.)
"About My People." [Grain] (20:3) Fall 92, p. 27.
"Where the Fracture Lies." [Kalliope] (15:1) 92, p. 38-39.

6267. SWARTWOUT, Susan
"Orpheus: The First Time." [CapeR] (27:1) Spr 92, p. 1.
"Our Bodies Speak Their Lines" (to my son. Honorable mention, Eve of Saint Agnes Contest). [NegC] (12:3) 92, p. 40-41.

6268. SWEENEY, Blair
"Moment." [BrooklynR] (9) 92, p. 31.

6269. SWEENEY, Matthew
"Banknotes." [Verse] (9:3) Wint 92, p. 33.

6270. SWEENEY, Patrick
"After the flood." [BlackBR] (16) Wint-Spr 92-93, p. 29.
"City daffodils." [BlackBR] (16) Wint-Spr 92-93, p. 29.
"Eleven Senryu." [WindO] (56) Fall-Wint 92, p. 3-4.
"In this Storm." [BlackBR] (16) Wint-Spr 92-93, p. 29.

6271. SWEET, John
"Four Rooms." [ChamLR] (10/11) Spr-Fall 92, p. 161-162.

6272. SWENSEN, Cole (*See also* SWENSON, Cole)
"Address." [Avec] (5:1) 92, p. 61.
"The Backs of Things." [Avec] (5:1) 92, p. 57.
"Ghazal Photographing Fire." [Avec] (5:1) 92, p. 60.
"An Insomniac Ghazal Walking Through Hallways." [Avec] (5:1) 92, p. 58.
"Last." [Avec] (5:1) 92, p. 62.
"Or Volant." [Avec] (5:1) 92, p. 59.

6273. SWENSON, Cole (*See also* SWENSEN, Cole)
"Tourism." [AnotherCM] (24) Fall 92, p. 161.
"Without Number." [AnotherCM] (24) Fall 92, p. 160.

6274. SWENSON, Karen
"The Guide." [Pequod] (34) 92, p. 163.

6275. SWENSON, May
"Advice to the Sexes." [Light] (3) Aut 92, p. 21.

6276. SWIFT, Doug
"Hunter." [HiramPoR] (51/52) Fall 91-Sum 92, p. 70.

6277. SWIFT, Joan
"Bright Night Rain." [PoetryNW] (33:2) Sum 92, p. 31.

"Nightjar" (Nepal). [PoetryNW] (33:2) Sum 92, p. 30-31.
6278. SWIFT, Matthew
"At the Moment I Become Words" (for Biard). [CarolQ] (45:1) Fall 92, p. 46.
6279. SWIHART, De-an Wu
"Ah, Mama" (tr. of Shu Ting, w. Gordon T. Osing). [CrabCR] (8:1) Sum-Fall 92, p. 20.
"Two, Maybe Three Different Memories" (tr. of Shu Ting, w. Gordon T. Osing). [CrabCR] (8:1) Sum-Fall 92, p. 21.
6280. SWIRSZCZYNSKA, Anna
"The Peasant Woman" (tr. by Maya Peretz). [SnailPR] (2:1) Spr-Sum 92, p. 4.
6281. SWIST, Wally
"The Bookdealer's Breakdown." [PoetryE] (33) Spr 92, p. 149.
"Shamisen" (from "Heartbeat: the Children of the Drum"). [Os] (34) Spr 92, p. 27.
6282. SYLTE, Karen
"Camp Robbers." [HawaiiR] (16:2, #35) Spr 92, p. 118.
6283. SYLVAIN, Patrick
"Adieu Miles." [AfAmRev] (26:2) Sum 92, p. 280.
"Démon de la Trompette." [Agni] (36) 92, p. 211-213.
"Gerald." [Agni] (36) 92, p. 209-210.
6284. SYLVESTER, Janet
"The Falls." [MichQR] (31:1) Wint 92, p. 78-79.
"The Mark of Flesh." [TriQ] (86) Wint 92-93, p. 30-31.
6285. SYLVESTER, June
"In Avon" (for Mary Gray Sylvester, 1928-1984). [TarRP] (30:2) Spr 91, p. 6-7.
6286. SYLVESTER, Michael Andre
"The Contents of This Story May Have Settled During Shipping." [Asylum] (7:3/4) 92, p. 80-82.
6287. SYS, Karel
"Troja at Eight in the Evening" (tr. by Dominika Winterová and Richard Katrovas). [NewOR] (19:3/4) Fall-Wint 92, p. 28.
6288. SYVERTSEN, Paul
"Iceland." [ManhatPR] (14) [92?], p. 34.
6289. SZAFRANSKI, Bernadette
"Sometimes." [EngJ] (80:7) N 91, p. 98.
6290. SZE, Arthur
"Archipelago." [ParisR] (34:123) Sum 92, p. 116-124.
"The Flower Path." [Manoa] (4:2) Fall 92, p. 103-104.
"The Los Alamos Museum." [Caliban] (11) 92, p. 13.
"Mushroom Hunting in the Jemez Mountains." [Manoa] (4:2) Fall 92, p. 104.
"Original Memory." [Manoa] (4:2) Fall 92, p. 104-106.
"The Shapes of Leaves." [Ometeca] (2:2) 91 [published 92], p. 24.
6291. SZEMAN, Sherri
"Unframed Daguerreotype." [KenR] (NS 14:2) Spr 92, p. 136-138.
6292. SZENDE, Maria
"The Distant Breath" (tr. of Géza Szöcs, w. Len Roberts). [Field] (46) Spr 92, p. 23.
6293. SZÖCS, Géza
"The Distant Breath" (tr. by Len Roberts and Maria Szende). [Field] (46) Spr 92, p. 23.
6294. SZPORLUK, Larissa
"Armorial Bearings." [PassN] (13:1) Sum 92, p. 4.
"French Union." [PassN] (13:1) Sum 92, p. 4.
"Look, Lilies." [Kalliope] (14:1) 92, p. 4.
"Remotion." [GreenMR] (NS 5:2) Spr-Sum 92, p. 60.
"Sleigh." [GreenMR] (NS 5:2) Spr-Sum 92, p. 59.
"Wandering Ice." [MidwQ] (33:3) Spr 92, p. 318.
"Whirligig." [Asylum] (7:3/4) 92, p. 9.
6295. SZUMIGALSKI, Anne
"The Thin Pale Man." [PraF] (13:1, #58) Spr 92, p. 126-133.
6296. SZUMOWSKI, Margaret C.
"Czechek's Stamps." [Agni] (35) 92, p. 283-284.
6297. SZYMBORSKA, Wislawa
"Census" (tr. by Ioanna-Veronika Warwick). [SenR] (22:2) Fall 92, p. 47-48.
"Gratitude" (tr. by Ioanna-Veronika Warwick). [SenR] (22:2) Fall 92, p. 43-44.
"Lot's Wife" (tr. by Ioanna-Veronika Warwick). [SenR] (22:2) Fall 92, p. 45-46.
"Maybe All This" (tr. by Stanislaw Baranczak and Clare Cavanagh). [NewYorker] (68:43) 14 D 92, p. 94.

"One Version of Events" (tr. by Stanislaw Baranczak and Clare Cavanagh). [ManhatR] (6:2) Fall 92, p. 43-46.
"Over a Glass of Wine" (tr. by Krystyna Piorkowski). [Trans] (26) Spr 92, p. 61-62.
"Still Life with a Toy Balloon" (tr. by Ioanna-Veronika Warwick). [SenR] (22:2) Fall 92, p. 41-42.

6298. TACIUCH, Dean
"Next." [Confr] (50) Fall 92, p. 273.
"Tongueless Blue." [Confr] (50) Fall 92, p. 272.

6299. TADIC, Novica
"At the Hairdresser" (phantasmagoria, tr. by Charles Simic). [Field] (46) Spr 92, p. 17.
"A Feather Plucked from the Tail of the Fiery Hen" (tr. by Charles Simic). [Field] (46) Spr 92, p. 13-14.
"Little Picture Catalogue" (tr. by Charles Simic). [Field] (46) Spr 92, p. 16.
"My Night Labors" (tr. by Charles Simic). [Field] (47) Fall 92, p. 114.
"The Night Game of the Maker of Faces" (tr. by Charles Simic). [Field] (47) Fall 92, p. 113.
"Night Sonnet" (tr. by Charles Simic). [Field] (47) Fall 92, p. 112.
"Nobody" (tr. by Charles Simic). [Field] (46) Spr 92, p. 12.
"Song to the Lamb" (tr. by Charles Simic). [Field] (46) Spr 92, p. 15.
"Text, Silk" (tr. by Charles Simic). [Field] (46) Spr 92, p. 11.
"To a Marksman" (tr. by Charles Simic). [Field] (47) Fall 92, p. 115.
"Toys, Dream" (tr. by Charles Simic). [Field] (46) Spr 92, p. 10.

6300. TAGER, David
"Moses, in Exile." [Poem] (68) N 92, p. 60-62.

6301. TAGG, John
"Things Left Undone." [OxfordM] (6:2) Fall-Wint 90, p. 18-19.

6302. TAGGART, John
"Sainte-Chapell" (in memory of Oliver Messiaen). [Sulfur] (12:2, #31) Fall 92, p. 166.
"What She Heard." [NowestR] (30:1) 92, p. 18-23.

6303. TAGLIABUE, John
"Breathing, Well-Being." [Chelsea] (53) 92, p. 47.
"Changes in the Atmosphere." [Elf] (2:3) Fall 92, p. 29.
"Lyrical Spirits Not Altogether Dampened." [Chelsea] (53) 92, p. 46.
"Redbreasts and Panoply Aplenty." [Elf] (2:3) Fall 92, p. 28.
"Though You Were Expecting It You Were Surpised." [NewYorkQ] (49) 92, p. 58.
"Untitled: Beautiful means land and sky are making love." [Elf] (2:3) Fall 92, p. 28.
"Well Supplied with Fancies and Desires." [Elf] (2:3) Fall 92, p. 30.
"Whitman and I and Others, and the Language Experiment." [Elf] (2:3) Fall 92, p. 31.

6304. TAI, Kin Man Young
"The Butterfly Is Alive in Sunny Trinidad." [GrahamHR] (16) Fall 92, p. 68-69.
"Life Under a Tin Roof." [GrahamHR] (16) Fall 92, p. 72-73.
"Shakespeare and Trinidad Mas." [GrahamHR] (16) Fall 92, p. 70-71.

6305. TAKACS, Nancy
"The Beginning of Spring." [WeberS] (9:1) Wint 92, p. 14.
"First Snow." [WeberS] (9:1) Wint 92, p. 11-12.
"The House Where the Music Began." [WeberS] (9:1) Wint 92, p. 12-13.
"Quitting." [ColR] (9:1) Spr-Sum 92, p. 150-151.
"Waterings." [WeberS] (9:1) Wint 92, p. 15.

6306. TAKACS, Zsuzsa
"A Chance   Crumbling River Banks" (tr. by Nicholas Kolumban). [OnTheBus] (4:2/5:1, #10/11) 92, p. 268-269.

6307. TAKARA, Kathryn
"Moonlight at Malaekahana." [ChamLR] (10/11) Spr-Fall 92, p. 83.

6308. TAKSA, Mark
"Thrift." [NewDeltaR] (8:1) Fall 90-Wint 91, p. 107-108.

TAL, Vicki Clark de
See DeTAL, Vicki Clark

6309. TALCOTT, William
"Scattered Showers." [NewAW] (10) Fall 92, p. 109.

6310. TALL, Deborah
"The Balloons." [Nat] (254:5) 10 F 92, p. 175.
"The Rule of Berries" (for Wendy). [Nat] (254:18) 11 My 92, p. 642.

TALL BEAR, Kimberly
See TALLBEAR, Kimberly
TALL MOUNTAIN, Mary
See TALLMOUNTAIN, Mary
6311. TALLBEAR, Kimberly
"Baby's Poem." [Archae] (3) early 92, p. 54.
"White Feet." [Archae] (3) early 92, p. 52-53.
6312. TALLEY, Doug
"April in the Wind." [Hellas] (3:2) Fall 92, p. 46.
"A Hope of Children." [Hellas] (3:2) Fall 92, p. 33-34.
6313. TALLMOUNTAIN, Mary
"The Last Wolf." [Jacaranda] (6:1/2) Wint-Spr 92, p. 98.
6314. TALSARNAU, Ieuan Jones
"May" (tr. by Keith Bosley). [Stand] (33:4) Aut 92, p. 153.
6315. TAMARKIN, Molly
"An Introduction to Field Theory." [Jacaranda] (6:1/2) Wint-Spr 92, p. 133.
6316. TAMEN, Pedro
"Delphi, Opus 12" (Selections: 1, 4, tr. by Richard Zenith). [LitR] (25:2) Wint 92, p. 218.
"The Hated Dice That Leave My Hand" (tr. by Richard Zenith). [LitR] (25:2) Wint 92, p. 219.
TAN, Lin
See LIN, Tan
6317. TANELLI, Orazio
"The Bells of the Town." [Footwork] 92, p. 43.
6318. TANG, Ya Ping
"Mountain Stream Spilling from a Dream" (From "The Wild Moon" series, tr. by Tony Barnstone and Newton Liu). [LitR] (35:3) Spr 92, p. 384.
TANG, Yaping
See TANG, Ya Ping
6319. TANIZAKI, Junichiro
"In Praise of Shadows" (tr. by Thomas J. Harper and Edward G. Seidensticker). [Trans] (26) Spr 92, p. 66.
6320. TANNER, Anita
"Dreams We Seldom Visit." [HolCrit] (29:4) O 92, p. 14.
6321. TANSI, Sony Labou
"Sugar" (tr. by Eric Sellin). [Trans] (26) Spr 92, p. 57.
6322. TANZBERG, Kris
"Shorthand Account of a Massacre" (Egypticus Sculpture, Stanga, Gotland, tr. by James Kirkup). [Stand] (33:4) Aut 92, p. 85.
"Thomas More" (tr. by James Kirkup). [Stand] (33:4) Aut 92, p. 84.
6323. TAPAHONSO, Luci
"Hills Brothers Coffee." [Jacaranda] (6:1/2) Wint-Spr 92, p. 94-95.
6324. TARAKHEL, Massuillah
"I Remember." Sparks! Writing by High School Students (1:1), a supplement to [PraF] (13:4, #61) Wint 92-93, p. 30.
"Past & Present." Sparks! Writing by High School Students (1:1), a supplement to [PraF] (13:4, #61) Wint 92-93, p. 30.
6325. TARDOS, Anne
"Un bon beginner immer inner well reformed." [CentralP] (21) Spr 92, p. 40.
"I say 'hommage'." [CentralP] (21) Spr 92, p. 54.
6326. TARLOW, Steven
"Psalms and Eggs." [ConnPR] (11:1) 92, p. 7.
6327. TARN, Natasha
"Multitude of One" (Selections: 17-23). [ColR] (9:2) Fall 92, p. 89-102.
6328. TARN, Nathaniel
"Angel, with Sword." [AnotherCM] (23) Spr 92, p. 167-168.
"Hawk's Place, Lobo Canyon, New Mexico." [AnotherCM] (23) Spr 92, p. 169-170.
6329. TARNAWSKY, Yuriy
"Children" (Selection: 4). [Agni] (35) 92, p. 134.
"I Forgot Her Blue Ice." [Agni] (35) 92, p. 132.
"Two Crucifixions." [Agni] (35) 92, p. 133.
6330. TARPLEY, Natasha
"Parting the Waters or Sinking" (for Till and all of us who have parted the waters). [AfAmRev] (26:2) Sum 92, p. 270.
"Slow Dance." [Callaloo] (15:4) Fall 92, p. 928.

"To Alabama" (for my grandaddy and my daddy). [AfAmRev] (26:2) Sum 92, p. 270-271.

6331. TARTIVITA, Carmelo
"Come Tonight." [SpiritSH] (57) Spr-Sum 92, p. 47.
"Lemon Trees." [SpiritSH] (57) Spr-Sum 92, p. 48.

6332. TARTT, Peggy Ann
"Origin." [AfAmRev] (26:2) Sum 92, p. 290.

6333. TASHJIAN, Janet
"For Cesar Vallejo." [Kalliope] (15:1) 92, p. 22.
"Kitchen." [Rohwedder] (7) Spr-Sum 92, p. 13.
"White." [Rohwedder] (7) Spr-Sum 92, p. 15.

6334. TATE, James
"50 Views of Tokyo." [Field] (47) Fall 92, p. 62-63.
"Autosuggestion: USS North Carolina." [Field] (47) Fall 92, p. 59-60.
"Contagion." [ThRiPo] (39/40) 92-93, p. 257-258.
"Deaf Girl Playing." [ThRiPo] (39/40) 92-93, p. 256-257.
"Epithalamion for Tyler." [AmerPoR] (21:3) My-Je 92, p. 45.
"In My Own Backyard." [AmerPoR] (21:2) Mr-Ap 92, p. 60.
"A Jangling Yarn." [Field] (46) Spr 92, p. 82-83.
"More Later, Less the Same." [NewYorker] (68:30) 14 S 92, p. 38.
"My Great Great Etc. Uncle Patrick Henry." [ThRiPo] (39/40) 92-93, p. 257.
"On the Subject of Doctors." [Field] (46) Spr 92, p. 80.
"Poem: Language was almost impossible in those days." [Field] (46) Spr 92, p. 81-82.
"Rustin Steel Is Driving the Crew to the River." [ThRiPo] (39/40) 92-93, p. 258.
"Sensitive Ears." [Field] (46) Spr 92, p. 76-77.
"Teaching the Ape to Write Poems." [ThRiPo] (39/40) 92-93, p. 255.
"A Voyage from Stockholm to Take Advantage of Lower Prices on the Finnish Island of Aland." [Field] (46) Spr 92, p. 78-79.
"What a Patient Does." [Field] (47) Fall 92, p. 61.

6335. TATI-LOUTARD, Jean-Baptiste
"On the Congo River" (tr. by Eric Sellin). [Trans] (26) Spr 92, p. 51.

6336. TATTER, Federico
"Añoranza." [Nuez] (4:12) 92, p. 28.
"La Ciudad Desierta." [Nuez] (4:12) 92, p. 28.
"Nocturno." [Nuez] (4:12) 92, p. 28.

6337. TAUFER, Veno
"Wind" (tr. by Michael Scammell). [Vis] (38) 92, p. 43.

6338. TAUS, Roger
"Bird, Poem @ 06/11/90." [OnTheBus] (4:2/5:1, #10/11) 92, p. 218.
"Running the Ridge." [OnTheBus] (4:2/5:1, #10/11) 92, p. 218.

6339. TAVERNIER-LOUIS, Janine
"Liqueurs Fortes." [LitR] (35:4) Sum 92, p. 600-601.
"Liqueurs from My Homeland" (Extract from "Splendeur," tr. by Betty Wilson). [LitR] (35:4) Sum 92, p. 510.

6340. TAVES, J. Rebecca
"Love and Dogs." Sparks! Writing by High School Students (1:1), a supplement to [PraF] (13:4, #61) Wint 92-93, p. 31-32.

6341. TAYLOR, Alexander (Alex)
"Aegina" (tr. of Henrik Nordbrandt, w. the author). [Vis] (38) 92, p. 15.
"Eyewitness." [Footwork] 92, p. 27.
"I Have Squandered My Money on Roses" (tr. of Henrik Nordbrandt). [Vis] (39) 92, p. 40.
"Once in Esteli." [Footwork] 92, p. 27.
"Voices in the Park." [Footwork] 92, p. 24-26.
"Walking." [Footwork] 92, p. 26.

6342. TAYLOR, Alvin Constantine
"Cornelia." [AfAmRev] (26:2) Sum 92, p. 232.
"The Tourists." [AfAmRev] (26:2) Sum 92, p. 232-233.

6343. TAYLOR, Bruce
"The Artist" (tr. of Han Yong-Woon). [Trans] (26) Spr 92, p. 110.
"Cinnamon Moon" (tr. of Han Yong-Woon). [Trans] (26) Spr 92, p. 111.
"Starcrossed." [SoCoast] (13) Je 93 [i.e. 92], p. 14-15.

6344. TAYLOR, Effie MacIsaac
"To My Cousin: Dead at Forty" (honourable mention, Grain Prose Poem contest). [Grain] (20:4) Wint 92, p. 20.

6345. TAYLOR, Eleanor Ross
"The Shaker Abecedarius." [SewanR] (100:4) Fall 92, p. 562-564.
"The Sky Watcher." [SouthernR] (28:4) Aut, O 92, p. 906-907.
6346. TAYLOR, Jane Vincent
"Precious Metal." [NegC] (12:3) 92, p. 117-118.
6347. TAYLOR, Jonathan
"Mr. John Heraclitus Smith Tries to Hang on to the Reality of Things during a Visit to Swanage" (reprinted to correct error in the Spr 91 issue). [CumbPR] (11:2) Spr 92, p. 45-46.
6348. TAYLOR, Judith
"Dinner Time." [OnTheBus] (4:2/5:1, #10/11) 92, p. 220.
"The Rowboat, The Water." [Kalliope] (15:1) 92, p. 8.
"Velvet Drips." [OnTheBus] (4:2/5:1, #10/11) 92, p. 219.
6349. TAYLOR, Kate
"Love Hangs on the Line." [SinW] (46) Spr 92, p. 88.
6350. TAYLOR, Keith
"Hockey: An Apology." [Witness] (6:2) 92, p. 93.
6351. TAYLOR, Nancy Ellis
"My Summer Solstice Change." [Writer] (105:6) Je 92, p. 26.
6352. TAYLOR, R. J.
"Andamooka Moon." [Footwork] 92, p. 126.
"Night Bus Ride." [Footwork] 92, p. 126.
"Somnambulist." [Footwork] 92, p. 126.
6353. TAYLOR, Thomas
"Dialogue with a Mirror" (Selections: 18, 41, 66, 88). [DogRR] (11:1) Spr-Sum 92, p. 28-29.
6354. TAYLOR, Wanda
"Good Morning, McDonald's" (from "With the Wind at My Back and Ink in My Blood," a collection of poems by Chicago's homeless). [PoetryUSA] (24) 92, p. 29.
TAYLOR-GRAHAM
See GRAHAM, Taylor
6355. TAYSON, Richard
"The End." [Art&Und] (1:4) Jl-Ag 92, p. 12.
6356. TEASLEY, Lisa
"Untitled: Moving in the room." [Eyeball] (1) 92, p. 27.
6357. TEBALDI, Dino
"Lacio Drom" (tr. of Roman Bled, w. Marta Knobloch). [Vis] (38) 92, p. 16.
6358. TECHEL, Sabine
"Blue (II)" (tr. by Margitt Lehbert). [Shiny] (7/8) 92, p. 142.
"Rip Full Moon" (tr. by Margitt Lehbert). [Shiny] (7/8) 92, p. 142.
6359. TEDESCO, Cynthia
"Bridge Crossings" (for Yolanda Lugo, 4/91). [Outbr] (23) 92, p. 73-74.
6360. TEICHMANN, Sandra Gail
"Classical Tape #G457F." [ColEng] (54:8) D 92, p. 941-942.
6361. TEILLIER, Jorge
"Afternoon" (tr. by Carolyne Wright). [TampaR] (5) Fall 92, p. 59.
"Poema de Invierno." [InterPR] (18:2) Fall 92, p. 26.
"Winter Poem" (tr. by Mary Crow). [InterPR] (18:2) Fall 92, p. 27.
"Wooden Mill" (tr. by Carolyne Wright). [TampaR] (5) Fall 92, p. 60.
6362. TELLEZ LENDECH, René
"Capto Mariposas." [Nuez] (4:10/11) 92, p. 10.
6363. TEMPLE, Charles
"Tirateo" (Santiago de los Caballeros, R.D, 3 de febrero de 1991). [SenR] (22:1) Spr 92, p. 71-73.
6364. TEMPLETON, Ardis Possanza
"For My Daughter at Eighteen." [Footwork] 92, p. 99.
"Jessup Girl." [Footwork] 92, p. 99.
TEMPSKI, Stanislaw Esden
See ESDEN-TEMPSKI, Stanislaw
6365. Ten MEER, Arnela
"Gossip" (tr. by Richinel Ansano and Joceline Clemencia). [LitR] (35:4) Sum 92, p. 582.
"Redu." [LitR] (35:4) Sum 92, p. 617.

6366. TENENBAUM, Molly
"The Hundred-Year Floods Could Come Every Year." [PoetryNW] (33:1) Spr 92, p. 17.
"The Tulip Problem." [PoetryNW] (33:3) Aut 92, p. 42-45.
"Why I Like to Go Outside on Windy Afternoons." [PoetryNW] (33:4) Wint 92-93, p. 42-43.
6367. TEODORESCU, Magda
"The Discovery of Romania" (tr. of Mihai Ursachi, w. Adam Sorkin). [Nimrod] (35:2) Spr-Sum 92, p. 42.
"Meditation in Frenchman's Gulf" (tr. of Mihai Ursachi, w. Adam Sorkin). [Nimrod] (35:2) Spr-Sum 92, p. 43-44.
6368. TEOFILOV, Ivan
"The Old City" (tr. by Lisa Sapinkopf, w. Georgi Belev). [Nimrod] (35:2) Spr-Sum 92, p. 24.
6369. TEPEXCUINTLE, Alice
"Brush with the Law." [CapilR] (2:9) Fall 92, p. 26-27.
"Ive Seen You on All These Highways." [CapilR] (2:9) Fall 92, p. 23-25.
"The orange trucks road thru yer heartland." [CapilR] (2:9) Fall 92, p. 21-22.
"Real Life Drama." [CapilR] (2:9) Fall 92, p. 28.
"Slid from yr stirrups bold." [CapilR] (2:9) Fall 92, p. 17-20.
6370. TERENCE, Susan
"Tricking the Air" (honorable mention, Eve of Saint Agnes Contest). [NegC] (12:3) 92, p. 42-43.
6371. TERMAN, Philip
"In Cather Country." [NoAmR] (277:2) Mr-Ap 92, p. 24.
"The Schwitz." [NewEngR] (14:2) Spr 92, p. 62-63.
6372. TERRANOVA, Elaine
"10 Years Old." [SycamoreR] (4:2) Sum 92, p. 32-33.
"Black Narcissus, the Movie." [AmerPoR] (21:6) N-D 92, p. 19.
"In the Bindery." [SlipS] (12) 92, p. 89-90.
"The Line." [Boulevard] (7:1, #19) Spr 92, p. 189-190.
"The Mad School." [AmerPoR] (21:6) N-D 92, p. 20.
"Phobia." [AmerPoR] (21:6) N-D 92, p. 19.
TERRE, David C. la
See LaTERRE, David C.
6373. TERRILL, Richard
"The Heaven of Saxophones." [PassN] (13:2) Wint 92, p. 25.
6374. TERRIS, Susan
"Semper Fi." [CapeR] (27:2) Fall 92, p. 14.
"Washrag." [Calyx] (14:1) Sum 92, p. 45.
6375. TERRY, Patricia
"Frequency" (tr. of Rene Char, w. Mary Ann Caws). [Pequod] (34) 92, p. 183.
"In Love" (tr. of Rene Char, w. Mary Ann Caws). [Pequod] (34) 92, p. 182.
"With a Free Scythe" (tr. of Rene Char, w. Mary Ann Caws). [Pequod] (34) 92, p. 184.
6376. TESSIER, Jacqulin
"But I Didn't Cry." [Gypsy] (18) 92, p. 145-146.
6377. TETI, Zona
"Poem: Gone was the silence called 'flower,' called 'trying'." [Verse] (8:3/9:1) Wint - Spr 92, p. 118.
6378. THACKER, Doug
"A Little Latin." [ChangingM] (24) Sum-Fall 92, p. 23.
"To a Lover: The Mask and Voice of Decay." [ChangingM] (24) Sum-Fall 92, p. 23.
6379. THACKREY, Susan
"Part IV: No." [Talisman] (9) Fall 92, p. 132-138.
6380. THARP, Peg
"Keeper of Color and Light." [SycamoreR] (4:2) Sum 92, p. 21-22.
6381. THATCHER, Timothy E.
"Sailing." [AmerS] (61:3) Sum 92, p. 420-423.
6382. THAXTON, Terry Ann
"Wallpaper." [FloridaR] (18:1) Spr-Sum 92, p. 66-67.
6383. THEODOROU, Victoria
"The Voice of the Watchman" (tr. by Eleni Fourtouni). [PoetryC] (12:3/4) Jl 92, p. 32.
6384. THEROUX, Alexander
"Padre Todopoderoso." [GrahamHR] (16) Fall 92, p. 63.

"Vinyl Junkie." [PoetryE] (33) Spr 92, p. 151.
"Wittgenstein's Proposal." [PoetryE] (33) Spr 92, p. 150.

6385. THESEN, Sharon
"13 Views, a Pastorale" (for Phyllis Webb). [MalR] (100) Fall 92, p. 81-93.
"What?" [WestCL] (25:3, #6) Wint 91-92, p. 149.

6386. THIBODEAUX, Raymond
"Crabbing." [LouisL] (9:1) Spr 92, p. 73.
"The Troubled Logic of Narcissus." [CreamCR] (16:1) Spr 92, p. 114-115.

6387. THIERS, Naomi
"Capital: Voices." [WashR] (17:6) Ap-My 92, p. 15.
"Still." [WashR] (17:6) Ap-My 92, p. 15.
"The Visit." [VirQR] (68:3) Sum 92, p. 489-490.

6388. THOMAS, Bart
"Doppelgangers." [OnTheBus] (4:2/5:1, #10/11) 92, p. 221-224.

6389. THOMAS, Cheryl
"A Collage for Servant Children" (tr. of René Philoctète, w. Carrol F. Coates). [Callaloo] (15:3) Sum 92, p. 619-620.
"Misery by Sunlight" (tr. of René Philoctète, w. Carrol F. Coates). [Callaloo] (15:3) Sum 92, p. 617.

6390. THOMAS, Christopher
"At 15 I Discover St. Mark's Cathedral." [ChironR] (11:4) Wint 92, p. 20.
"On Being Gay." [EvergreenC] (7:1) Wint-Spr 92, p. 5.
"Supervising the Camp Showers." [ChironR] (11:4) Wint 92, p. 20.

6391. THOMAS, Denise
"Bedtime Story." [Manoa] (4:2) Fall 92, p. 9.
"How We Beome the Trees." [HighP] (7:1) Spr 92, p. 81.
"Love at the End of America." [Manoa] (4:2) Fall 92, p. 8.
"Notes from the Interior." [NoDaQ] (60:3) Sum 92, p. 45.
"One Evening We Discuss the Future." [Manoa] (4:2) Fall 92, p. 7-8.

6392. THOMAS, Don
"Water Tower." [HighP] (7:3) Wint 92, p. 91.

6393. THOMAS, Elizabeth
"Mexican Landscape with Idea." [ColEng] (54:1) Ja 92, p. 31-32.
"Wild Pines." [ColEng] (54:1) Ja 92, p. 33.

6394. THOMAS, F. Richard
"Letter to My Ex on Her New Book of Poems." [ChironR] (11:3) Aut 92, p. 13.

6395. THOMAS, Julia
"Play of Time." [BellArk] (8:2) Mr-Ap 92, p. 25.

6396. THOMAS, Laurence W.
"Aubade." [AntR] (50:4) Fall 92, p. 721.

6397. THOMAS, Lorenzo
"L'Argent." [AfAmRev] (26:2) Sum 92, p. 269.
"The Audie Murphy Game." [AfAmRev] (26:2) Sum 92, p. 269.
"How You Can Worry." [AfAmRev] (26:2) Sum 92, p. 268.

6398. THOMAS, M. A.
"Domino." [BellR] (15:2) Fall 92, p. 25.

6399. THOMAS, P. L.
"Don't Let Your Legs." [Amelia] (7:1, #20) 92, p. 158.

6400. THOMAS, Peter
"The Scholar and the Cowboy." [NegC] (12:1/2) 92, p. 111-113.

6401. THOMAS, Randolph
"A Blessing." [PoetL] (87:4) Wint 92-93, p. 16.
"Confinement." [ChatR] (13:1) Fall 92, p. 36.
"My Brother, the Girl from West Virginia, and the Man with Anybody's Face." [SenR] (22:2) Fall 92, p. 89-90.
"One Way Out." [LaurelR] (26:2) Sum 92, p. 22.
"Revenant." [QW] (35) Sum-Fall 92, p. 110-111.

THOMAS, Roxana Elvridge
See ELVRIDGE-THOMAS, Roxana

6402. THOMAS, Sally
"Child in Trunk." [WillowS] (29) Wint 92, p. 59-60.
"Subway." [WillowS] (29) Wint 92, p. 61-63.

6403. THOMAS, Scott
"Imagination." [Confr] (48/49) Spr-Sum 92, p. 187.

6404. THOMAS, Terry
"Dollars Damn Me" (A Plainsongs Award Poem). [Plain] (13:1) Fall 92, p. 5.

"Fortunato: a Post." [Plain] (12:3) Spr 92, p. 9.
"Prufrock Is a Drip." [Plain] (12:3) Spr 92, p. 8.
"Scorpion Pressed in Paper." [Plain] (13:1) Fall 92, p. 28.
"Unraveling Through the Park." [HampSPR] Wint 92, p. 34.

6405. THOMATOS, Elena
"Childhood & Education." [HangL] (60) 92, p. 66.

6406. THOMPSON, Craig
"This Bear Does Not Go Under." [BlackBR] (15) Spr-Sum 92, p. 24.

6407. THOMPSON, Dorothy Perry
"Tour, Creswell, NC, 1989." [AfAmRev] (26:2) Sum 92, p. 220.

6408. THOMPSON, Edgar H.
"Homecoming." [Wind] (22:71) 92, p. 19.

6409. THOMPSON, Ray
"Sixth Street" (In Memoriam, died homeless 1990, San Francisco). [PoetryUSA] (24) 92, p. 28.

6410. THOMPSON, Rebecca
"Tribute to Harold Pinter." [NewYorkQ] (49) 92, p. 62.

6411. THOMPSON, Ricki
"After the Divorce." [Shen] (42:4) Wint 92, p. 35.
"Daniel in the Lions' Dean" (a painting by Peter Paul Rubens). [Shen] (42:4) Wint 92, p. 34.
"The Escape." [Kalliope] (14:2) 92, p. 29.
"Learning Lutheran Sex." [Thrpny] (50) Sum 92, p. 14.
"Marriage." [Thrpny] (51) Fall 92, p. 15.

6412. THOMPSON, Tom
"Heal Cry." [JlNJPo] (14:2) Aut 92, p. 13-14.

6413. THOMSON, Derick
"Climbing Rocks." [Stand] (33:4) Aut 92, p. 143.

6414. THOOR, Jesse
"Das Erste Sonett." [Nimrod] (35:2) Spr-Sum 92, p. 8.
"The First Sonnet" (tr. by Gary Sea). [Nimrod] (35:2) Spr-Sum 92, p. 9.
"Sixth Postscript" (tr. by Gary Sea). [Nimrod] (35:2) Spr-Sum 92, p. 10.
"Sonnet of the Man Who Lay Sick Along the Way" (he was traveling from Jerusalem to Jericho, tr. by Gary Sea). [Nimrod] (35:2) Spr-Sum 92, p. 11.

6415. THORBURN, Alexander
"The School." [SouthwR] (77:2/3) Spr-Sum 92, p. 284-285.

6416. THORBURN, Russell
"If Jesus Wasn't Murdered." [Northeast] (5:7) Wint 92-93, p. 22.
"The Second Meeting of the Judas Fan Club." [Parting] (5:2) Wint 92-93, p. 3.

6417. THORNDALE, David
"Deep in the cave." [Amelia] (6:4, #19) 92, p. 20.

6418. THORNTON, Carol
"Packing Wood." [Grain] (20:1) Spr 92, p. 256.

6419. THORNTON, Laura
"Languor" (After the painting "Indolence" by Jean-Baptiste Greuze). [Field] (46) Spr 92, p. 49-50.

6420. THORNTON, Thomas E.
"Whose Woods These Are I Think I Know" (by Robert Trump). [EngJ] (80:6) O 91, p. 103.

6421. THORPE, Allison
"As I Listen to Hatchell Tell Snake Stories." [Poem] (68) N 92, p. 10.
"The Moving of Mugwort" (For B). [Poem] (68) N 92, p. 11.
"While Pulling Weeds, She Contemplates the Chinese Poet and the Fine Edge of Dark" (For J D Marion). [Poem] (68) N 92, p. 12.

6422. THORPE, Ronald
"Moon Bath." [Footwork] 92, p. 48.

6423. THORSON, Ian
"Sweet Mother." [HangL] (60) 92, p. 92.

6424. THÜMLER, Walter
"Luckily II" (tr. by Margitt Lehbert). [Shiny] (7/8) 92, p. 144.
"Such Green" (tr. by Margitt Lehbert). [Shiny] (7/8) 92, p. 144.

6425. THURMAN, Alexandra
"Assume Then." [OxfordM] (8:1) Spr-Sum 92, p. 22-23.

6426. THURSTON, Michael
"Infidelity." [CoalC] (5) My 92, p. 9.

6427. THYME, Lauren O.
"Rabbits Are Fragile." [NegC] (12:1/2) 92, p. 200.
6428. TIAN, Huigang
"City Dawn." [CrabCR] (8:1) Sum-Fall 92, p. 22.
6429. TIBBETTS, Frederick
"An Eclogue." [Ploughs] (18:4) Wint 92-93, p. 176-177.
"From Horace." [WestHR] (46:2) Sum 92, p. 192.
"Lemurs." [WestHR] (46:2) Sum 92, p. 193.
"To Miranda." [Ploughs] (18:4) Wint 92-93, p. 178-179.
"Topmost Rooms." [SouthwR] (77:4) Aut 92, p. 572.
"View of a Waterfall." [NewMyths] (1:2/2:1) 92, p. 122.
"The Yard Before Your House Is Built." [US1] (26/27) 92, p. 18.
6430. TIBULLUS
"Three from Tibullus" (1.2, 1.6, 1.10, tr. by Rachel Hadas). [Arion] 3d series (2:1) Wint 92, p. 148-156.
6431. TICHY, Susan
"Muly Deer." [HighP] (7:1) Spr 92, p. 62-63.
6432. TICKNOR, Kerrie
"Poland's Ghosts." [Amelia] (6:4, #19) 92, p. 65.
6433. TIEBER, Linda
"Once again he is here." [NewYorkQ] (48) 92, p. 110.
6434. TIEMAN, John Samuel
"Prayer for Marilyn Monroe" (tr. of Ernesto Cardenal). [RiverS] (36) 92, p. 67-68.
6435. TIFFANY, Daniel
"Delicatessen." [AntR] (50:3) Sum 92, p. 504.
6436. TIGAN, Joseph Redden
"Untitled: Even during summer it stood and slumbered." [HighP] (7:3) Wint 92, p. 92.
6437. TIGER, Madeline
"The Back Yard." [Footwork] 92, p. 159.
"I Made You Into a Prayer." [Footwork] 92, p. 159.
"La Madonna con Bambino" (by Neroccio di Bartolomeo Landi, 1447-1500, Siena - Pinacoteca). [OxfordM] (6:2) Fall-Wint 90, p. 58-59.
"The Practical Reinvention of God." [Footwork] 92, p. 158.
"Two Birds." [Footwork] 92, p. 159.
6438. TILLINGHAST, Richard
"Aubade." [ParisR]] (34:124) Fall 92, p. 166.
"A Backward Glance at Galway." [NewEngR] (14:4) Fall 92, p. 184-185.
"First Morning Home Again." [CumbPR] (12:1) Fall 92, p. 73.
"A History of Windows." [SouthernPR] (32:2) Fall 92, p. 20-21.
"The Night of Displacement" (from the Turkish of Sezai Karakoc). [NewEngR] (14:4) Fall 92, p. 185-186.
"A Quiet Pint in Kinvara." [Shen] (42:3) Fall 92, p. 24-25.
"Southbound Pullman, 1945." [NewEngR] (14:4) Fall 92, p. 186-187.
"Table" (tr. of Edip Cansever). [Atlantic] (270:6) D 92, p. 81.
6439. TIMM, Steve
"The Night." [RagMag] (10:2) 92, p. 80.
"One of Those Days in Early March." [RagMag] (10:2) 92, p. 81.
"The Tactician." [RagMag] (10:2) 92, p. 80.
6440. TIMOFEYEV, Sergei
"Untitled: A man comes in, his suit is crumpled" (tr. by Irina Osadchaya, w. Lyn Hejinian). [Avec] (5:1) 92, p. 39.
"White Heart" (tr. by Irina Osadchaya, w. Lyn Hejinian). [Avec] (5:1) 92, p. 39.
TING, Shu
See SHU, Ting
6441. TINLEY, Bill
"Toronto Nocturne" (for Joe Leyden). [Stand] (33:4) Aut 92, p. 10-12.
6442. TISHMAN, Art
"Nature Study: The Cluster Fly." [LaurelR] (26:2) Sum 92, p. 47.
6443. TJIN-a-SIE, Yvone Mechtelli
"Poem: A black I am" (Anonymous translation from the Dutch). [LitR] (35:4) Sum 92, p. 587-588.
"Poem: Een neger ben ik." [LitR] (35:4) Sum 92, p. 617-618.
6444. TKACZ, Virlana
"Beatles (A Cycle)" (tr. of Attila Mohylny, w. Wanda Phipps). [Agni] (36) 92, p. 249-252.

6445. TOBIN, Daniel
"American Legion." [LitR] (25:2) Wint 92, p. 257-259.
"Blues." [NewDeltaR] (8:2) Spr-Sum 91, p. 75.
"Galilee" (A seaport town in Connecticut). [AmerS] (61:4) Aut 92, p. 565-566.
"Hanging Curtains." [TarRP] (31:2) Spr 92, p. 8.
6446. TOBIN, Jim
"Iron Mist & Starch." [WritersF] (18) 92, p. 54.
6447. TOBOLA, Deborah
"Dear Abby: From the FBI" (a found poem). [Rohwedder] (7) Spr-Sum 92, p. 22-23.
TODD, Nita Hooper
See HOOPER-TODD, Nita
6448. TODD, Patrick
"The Wonder of Silver." [CutB] (38) Sum 92, p. 5.
6449. TOFER, Merle, II
"As a Poet I Remember Every Man That I Fuck." [ChironR] (11:4) Wint 92, p. 15.
"Hunger." [ChironR] (11:4) Wint 92, p. 15.
6450. TOKARCZYK, Michelle M.
"Driving in America." [ColEng] (54:6) O 92, p. 719-720.
"What He Has to Say." [Vis] (39) 92, p. 21.
6451. TOKUNO, Ken
"Angels." [BellArk] (8:1) Ja-F 92, p. 7.
"Clarity." [BellArk] (8:4) Jl-Ag 92, p. 21.
"The End of Vanilla." [BellArk] (8:4) Jl-Ag 92, p. 23.
"Jii" (April 3, 1989). [CrabCR] (8:1) Sum-Fall 92, p. 29.
"Lava Dust: An Elegy." [BellArk] (8:1) Ja-F 92, p. 7.
"A Note to My Wife on Our Daughters' Second Birthday." [BellArk] (8:4) Jl-Ag 92, p. 24.
"Remembrances of Songs Past." [BellArk] (8:4) Jl-Ag 92, p. 25.
6452. TOLAN, James
"Blood Sport" (1992 AWP Intro Award Winner). [IndR] (15:2) Fall 92, p. 150.
"State of the Union." [BlackBR] (16) Wint-Spr 92-93, p. 8-9.
6453. TOLEK
"Fill." [Gypsy] (19) 92, p. 25.
6454. TOLNAI, Otto
"At the Albanian Bakery" (tr. by Nicholas Kolumban). [OnTheBus] (4:2/5:1, #10/11) 92, p. 263.
6455. TOM, Karen
"Untitled: Morning came and I found myself driving in this car." [ChironR] (11:1) Spr 92, p. 23.
6456. TOMIOKA, Akemi
"Ah, women" (tr. of Ei Akitsu, w. Leza Lowitz). [Harp] (285:1706) Jl 92, p. 26.
"A ball of flesh" (tr. of Ei Akitsu, w. Leza Lowitz). [Harp] (285:1706) Jl 92, p. 26.
"Leaving my house" (tr. of Ei Akitsu, w. Leza Lowitz). [Harp] (285:1706) Jl 92, p. 26.
"Sorting out" (tr. of Ei Akitsu, w. Leza Lowitz). [Harp] (285:1706) Jl 92, p. 26.
"Why was I given breasts" (tr. of Ei Akitsu, w. Leza Lowitz). [Harp] (285:1706) Jl 92, p. 26.
6457. TOMLINSON, Charles
"At Twilight." [Nimrod] (35:2) Spr-Sum 92, p. 2.
"Blaubeuren." [Hudson] (45:1) Spr 92, p. 77-78.
"Crossing the Moor" (To Paula and Fred). [Stand] (33:2) Spr 92, p. 98.
"February." [Nimrod] (35:2) Spr-Sum 92, p. 1.
"Giverny." [Nimrod] (35:2) Spr-Sum 92, p. 1.
"The House on the Susquehanna." [GettyR] (5:2) Spr 92, p. 318.
"Looking Down" (for Attilio Bertolucci on his first flight). [Hudson] (45:1) Spr 92, p. 80.
"The Morning Moon." [Stand] (33:2) Spr 92, p. 98.
"Picking Mushrooms by Moonlight." [Hudson] (45:1) Spr 92, p. 79.
"Response to Hopkins." [Hudson] (45:1) Spr 92, p. 78-79.
"Sea Poem." [AmerPoR] (21:6) N-D 92, p. 29.
"Upstate." [Hudson] (45:1) Spr 92, p. 76-77.
6458. TOMLINSON, Rawdon
"Grief at 4 A.M." [WritersF] (18) 92, p. 37-38.
"How the Dead Come Back" (for Walter Hall). [WritersF] (18) 92, p. 38-39.
"Letter in Middle Age to My Ex-Wife, Not Mailed." [PoetC] (24:1) Fall 92, p. 5.
"Lightning-Struck Boy." [MinnR] (38) Spr-Sum 92, p. 26-27.

"Night Wind." [LaurelR] (26:2) Sum 92, p. 42.
"Pain Fugue." [PoetC] (24:1) Fall 92, p. 6-7.

TOMONORI, Ki no
See KI no TOMONORI

6459. TOMPKINS, Leslie Crutchfield
"Crossing." [Northeast] (5:6) Spr 92, p. 18.
"Don't Leave Your Dreams with Me." [Northeast] (5:6) Spr 92, p. 17.

6460. TONKS, Tatiana
"A Stranger Home" (Selection: 27). [Quarry] (41:4) Fall 92, p. 71.

6461. TONSAS, A.
"A Story." [WritersF] (18) 92, p. 144.

6462. TOPP, Mike
"Dicks." [BrooklynR] (9) 92, p. 36.
"A Fjord." [Talisman] (9) Fall 92, p. 221.
"The Four Basic Food Groups." [BrooklynR] (9) 92, p. 36.
"Some of the Movies Around Here." [BrooklynR] (9) 92, p. 36.
"Totem Pole." [BrooklynR] (9) 92, p. 37.

6463. TORNAI, József
"The Names of the Idols" (tr. by Jascha Kessler). [Nimrod] (35:2) Spr-Sum 92, p. 32.
"Solar Eclipse" (tr. by Jascha Kessler). [Nimrod] (35:2) Spr-Sum 92, p. 33.

6464. TORNEO, Dave
"Night Portents." [ManhatPR] (14) [92?], p. 44.

6465. TORRA, Joseph
"After the Revolution." [Noctiluca] (1:2) Wint 92 [on cover: Wint 93], p. 16.
"Landscape." [Talisman] (8) Spr 92, p. 104.
"Reading Spicer's *After Lorca* Thinking About Jonas and Wieners." [Agni] (35) 92, p. 233.
"The Road to the City." [Talisman] (8) Spr 92, p. 104.
"Thin White Light." [Agni] (35) 92, p. 230-232.

6466. TORRES, Fernando
"The Christ-Bearer." [PoetryUSA] (24) 92, p. 15.

TORRES, Juan Ruiz de
See RUIZ DE TORRES, Juan

6467. TORRES, Morelos
"Perpetuum Mobile." [Nuez] (4:10/11) 92, p. 6.

6468. TORRES, O.
"Silencio." [Nuez] (4:12) 92, p. 21.

6469. TORRES-GUZMAN, Esteban
"Corn." [Americas] (20:2) Sum 92, p. 50-52.
"Cosmogony." [Americas] (20:2) Sum 92, p. 48-49.
"Texcalapan (at the Stream Surrounded by Rocks)." [Americas] (20:2) Sum 92, p. 46-47.

6470. TORRES SOCAS, Olga
"Gloria." [LindLM] (11:1) Mr 92, p. 20.
"La Mar." [LindLM] (11:1) Mr 92, p. 20.
"Las Ratas." [LindLM] (11:1) Mr 92, p. 20.

6471. TORRESON, Rodney
"Backboard and Hoop." [Northeast] (5:6) Spr 92, p. 15.
"Maris of the Cards." [Spitball] (41) Sum 92, p. 34-35.
"The Trade." [Spitball] (40) Spr 92, p. 24-25.
"When Father Castrated Hogs." [Northeast] (5:6) Spr 92, p. 16.

6472. TORREVILLAS, Rowena
"At Chong's." [Manoa] (4:1) Spr 92, p. 44-45.
"Fly-over Country." [Manoa] (4:1) Spr 92, p. 42-43.
"Photographs of Calamity." [Manoa] (4:1) Spr 92, p. 43-44.

6473. TOSTESON, Heather
"Jars" (winner of Discovery — The Nation '92). [Nat] (254:19) 18 My 92, p. 672.

6474. TOTH, Éva
"Discussion and Confession" (tr. by Peter Jay). [Trans] (26) Spr 92, p. 85-86.
"Genesis" (tr. by Peter Jay). [Trans] (26) Spr 92, p. 115.
"Snowline" (tr. by Laura Schiff). [RiverS] (36) 92, p. 89.
"Teiresias' Lament" (tr. by Laura Schiff). [RiverS] (36) 92, p. 88.
"Thursday Night" (tr. by D. A. Demers). [Trans] (26) Spr 92, p. 87.

6475. TOTTEN, B. R.
"Kingdom" (for William Davis). [BellArk] (8:1) Ja-F 92, p. 4-6.

6476. TOTTY, Janis A.
"String." [EvergreenC] (7:1) Wint-Spr 92, p. 60-63.
6477. TOUSTER-REED, Alison
"The Family Circle." [Event] (21:3) Fall 92, p. 70-71.
"The Gorstein Family" (to Laurence Lerner and his merman poem). [AntigR] (90) Sum 92, p. 73-77.
"The Lever of Love." [Poem] (67) My 92, p. 39.
"Past Prayer." [Poem] (67) My 92, p. 42.
"Remembering Grandmother." [Footwork] 92, p. 81.
"The Threads of Love." [Poem] (67) My 92, p. 40-41.
"Waterfall" (for Linda). [Footwork] 92, p. 81.
6478. TOWLE, Andrew
"Hard Evidence." [Ploughs] (18:4) Wint 92-93, p. 124.
"In Consideration: The White Pitcher." [Ploughs] (18:4) Wint 92-93, p. 125.
"Sea Migration." [Ploughs] (18:4) Wint 92-93, p. 126-127.
6479. TOWLE, Parker
"Book Cover Blurb" (Winner, Annual Free Verse Contest, 1991). [AnthNEW] (4) 92, p. 12.
6480. TOWNLEY, Roderick
"Star Cemetery." [NoAmR] (277:2) Mr-Ap 92, p. 27.
6481. TOWNSEND, Alison
"The Blue Dress." [PraS] (66:2) Sum 92, p. 115-116.
"Raising Water." [SingHM] (20) 92, p. 98-99.
6482. TOWNSEND, Ann
"After the End." [Crazy] (42) Spr 92, p. 21-22.
"As Children Love to Spin Themselves." [IndR] (15:2) Fall 92, p. 85-86.
"Crown of Glory." [Crazy] (42) Spr 92, p. 23.
"Early Autumn, Hedgeapples." [CharR] (18:2) Fall 92, p. 101.
"Frog Pond." [CharR] (18:2) Fall 92, p. 102.
"The Gift." [AntR] (50:3) Sum 92, p. 497.
"The Language of Diplomacy: Adult Comp." [NewEngR] (14:2) Spr 92, p. 91-92.
"Local Merchant." [SouthernR] (28:2) Spr, Ap 92, p. 278.
"Mid-February, White Light." [SouthernR] (28:2) Spr, Ap 92, p. 279.
"Modern Love." [NewEngR] (14:2) Spr 92, p. 92-93.
"Rouge." [KenR] (NS 14:2) Spr 92, p. 91-92.
"A Trick of the Eye." [KenR] (NS 14:2) Spr 92, p. 92-93.
"While I Bathed." [Crazy] (42) Spr 92, p. 19-20.
6483. TOWNSEND, Cheryl (Cheryl A.)
"I Can't Help It That." [ChironR] (11:3) Aut 92, p. 28.
"Seduction Almost." [Pearl] (16) Fall 92, p. 15.
"Smart Ass Blonde." [ChironR] (11:1) Spr 92, p. 20.
6484. TOWNSEND, Melissa
"He's there in the shadow of your little girl's dream." [Conjunc] (19) 92, p. 138.
"I Spent Two Years Trying to Perfect His Pained Look." [Conjunc] (19) 92, p. 136.
"It's Not Just the Sweet & Sour Sauce under Your Clothing." [Conjunc] (19) 92, p. 137.
6485. TRACHTENBERG, Paul
"Mad Stephens' Espresso Party in Huntington Beach: A Gay Fairy Tale" (Excerpt). [JamesWR] (10:1) Fall 92, p. 6.
"Sir Robert." [ChironR] (11:4) Wint 92, p. 19.
6486. TRAIL, B. D.
"Die(t)ing." [Lactuca] (16) Ag 92, p. 44.
"Formation." [NewYorkQ] (49) 92, p. 43.
"Golf." [ChironR] (11:3) Aut 92, p. 28.
"Highway Losers." [Lactuca] (16) Ag 92, p. 44.
"Viet Haikus." [NewYorkQ] (47) 92, p. 91.
6487. TRAKL, Georg
"At the Fringe" (tr. by L. D. Davidson and Christopher Hewitt). [PassN] (13:1) Sum 92, p. 31.
"Summer" (tr. by Sammy McLean). [SnailPR] (2:2) Fall-Wint 92, p. 29.
"Summer" (tr. by Steven Frattali). [WebR] (16) Fall 92, p. 11.
6488. TRAN, Barbara
"Fairy Tale." [SouthernPR] (32:2) Fall 92, p. 26-27.
"Thu Duc." [SouthernPR] (32:2) Fall 92, p. 25-26.
6489. TRANTER, John
"Backyard." [Harp] (284:1704) My 92, p. 42.

"Dark Harvest." [ParisR] (34:123) Sum 92, p. 127-132.
"Opus Dei." [Verse] (8:3/9:1) Wint-Spr 92, p. 73-75.
"The Other Side of the Bay." [NewAW] (10) Fall 92, p. 37-39.

6490. TRASK, Haunani-Kay
"Hawai'i." [ChamLR] (10/11) Spr-Fall 92, p. 89-94.

6491. TRAUB, Tom
"Everyone Gets a Cut of Our Love." [CapeR] (27:1) Spr 92, p. 3.

6492. TRAUNSTEIN, Russ
"Blue Bandit." [Light] (1) Spr 92, p. 13.

6493. TRAXLER, Patricia
"The Lesson." [Agni] (36) 92, p. 50-51.
"The Promise" (for C.C.). [Agni] (36) 92, p. 52-53.
"The Rules of Joy." [Agni] (35) 92, p. 41-42.
"The Wife Talks in Her Sleep." [AmerV] (26) Spr 92, p. 86-88.

6494. TREBY, Ivor C.
"Apollonicon." [JamesWR] (9:3) Spr 92, p. 1.

6495. TREFETHEN, Florence
"The Cells Sestina." [BellR] (15:2) Fall 92, p. 22-23.

6496. TREICHEL, Hans-Ullrich
"Like Joyce in Triest" (tr. by Margitt Lehbert). [Shiny] (7/8) 92, p. 137.
"Prometheus" (tr. by Margitt Lehbert). [Shiny] (7/8) 92, p. 137.

6497. TREISMAN, Deborah
"Follain's Paris" (adapted from the French, w. August Kleinzahler). [Thrpny] (50) Sum 92, p. 4.

6498. TREITEL, Renata
"Daisy." [InterPR] (18:1) Spr 92, p. 65.
"The Gentleman of the Footprints" (tr. of Vivan Lamarque). [NewOR] (19:3/4) Fall - Wint 92, p. 153.
"Lineage of Poets." [InterPR] (18:1) Spr 92, p. 66.

6499. TREMMEL, Robert
"Common Ground" (To the Memory of Charles Tremel, b. Germany, d. Roselle Township, Carrol Co., Iowa, "Last of October," 1875). [MidwQ] (34:1) Aut 92, p. 89-90.

6500. TRENT, Tina
"Every Father Wants His Son to." [LullwaterR] (4:1) Fall 92, p. 50.
"Technology Gives Life." [LullwaterR] (4:1) Fall 92, p. 40-41.

6501. TRETHEWEY, Eric
"Neighbors." [LitR] (25:2) Wint 92, p. 252-253.
"Old Sycamores." [HolCrit] (29:4) O 92, p. 16.

TREVIÑO, Gloria Velásquez
See VELASQUEZ TREVIÑO, Gloria

6502. TRILLIN, Calvin
"Adieu, Bush's Men." [Nat] (255:20) 14 D 92, p. 725.
"Adieu to You, J. Danforth Quayle." [Nat] (255:22) 28 D 92, p. 797.
"Baker, Baker, Miracle Maker (A Campaign Nursery Rhyme)." [Nat] (255:8) 21 S 92, p. 268.
"Baker, Baker, Miracle Maker (Reprise)." [Nat] (255:15) 9 N 92, p. 529.
"Bush and Iran/ *Contra*." [Nat] (255:13) 26 O 92, p. 457.
"A California Poll." [Nat] (254:22) 8 Je 92, p. 773.
"Chariot of Embers." [Nat] (254:2) 20 Ja 92, p. 41.
"Clarkclifford" (A cautionary air, sung to the tune of "Titwillow"). [Nat] (255:21) 21 D 92, p. 761.
"Clinton and Gore: A Cheer for Moderates." [Nat] (255:4) 3-10 Ag 92, p. 125.
"Comforting Thoughts for Bush Campaign Re Clinton-Like Questions." [Nat] (254:17) 4 My 92, p. 581.
"Dingbat Re-evaluated." [Nat] (254:4) 3 F 92, p. 113.
"The Eighties Re-examined." [Nat] (254:12) 30 Mr 92, p. 401.
"Far Eastern Travel." [Nat] (254:3) 27 Ja 92, p. 77.
"A Father's Role." [Nat] (254:23) 15 Je 92, p. 809.
"George Bush at the Martin Luther King Jr. Center for Nonviolent Social Change, January 17, 1992." [Nat] (254:5) 10 F 92, p. 150.
"Gorbachev's Reward." [Nat] (254:1) 6-13 Ja 92, p. 5.
"How Presidents Are Remembered." [Nat] (254:7) 24 F 92, p. 221.
"Insurmountable Obstacle." [Nat] (254:14) 13 Ap 92, p. 473.
"Jack Kemp (A White-Guy Rap)." [Nat] (254:21) 1 Je 92, p. 737.

"My Heart Belongs to You and Capital Gains (A Country Song for Republicans)." [Nat] (255:7) 14 S 92, p. 233.
"The New Jerry Brown." [Nat] (254:15) 20 Ap 92, p. 509.
"The New World Order — Central European Division." [Nat] (254:9) 9 Mr 92, p. 293.
"On Force Used by Police in an Arrest for a Traffic Violation." [Nat] (254:20) 25 My 92, p. 689.
"On the European Treaty Vote." [Nat] (255:11) 12 O 92, p. 385.
"On the Modern Olympics." [Nat] (255:6) 31 Ag-7 S 92, p. 197.
"On the Privacy of Passport Files." [Nat] (255:16) 16 N 92, p. 566.
"On the Publication of *Sex*." [Nat] (255:17) 23 N 92, p. 617.
"On the Reappearance of Ross Perot." [Nat] (255:12) 19 O 92, p. 421.
"Perot Begins." [Nat] (254:19) 18 My 92, p. 653.
"Perot Ends." [Nat] (255:5) 17-24 Ag 92, p. 161.
"Perot, Snooping." [Nat] (255:2) 13 Jl 92, p. 41.
"Presidential Purity Test." [Nat] (254:18) 11 My 92, p. 617.
"Prevailing Presidential Standards." [Nat] (254:11) 23 Mr 92, p. 365.
"The Primaries Are Over." [Nat] (254:24) 22 Je 92, p. 845.
"A Republican Canvasser Discusses Clinton's Draft Problems with a Prospective Voter." [Nat] (255:10) 5 O 92, p. 349.
"The Ross Perot Guide to Answering Embarrassing Questions." [Nat] (254:25) 29 Je 92, p. 881.
"Second-Guessing." [Nat] (254:13) 6 Ap 92, p. 437.
"So Far." [Nat] (255:19) 7 D 92, p. 689.
"Some Advice for the President." [Nat] (254:10) 16 Mr 92, p. 329.
"The Squabbles of Europe." [Nat] (255:14) 2 N 92, p. 493.
"Texas Remake for the Campaign." [Nat] (254:8) 2 Mr 92, p. 257.
"To Bill Clinton — A Word of Warning." [Nat] (255:18) 30 N 92, p. 653.
"The Troubles of Princess Di." [Nat] (255:3) 20-27 Jl 92, p. 77.
"The Voters' Mood After Three Months of Intense Exposure to the Democratic Process." [Nat] (254:16) 27 Ap 92, p. 545.
"Weak Dollar Blues." [Nat] (255:9) 28 S 92, p. 313.
"What Buchanan Is Saying." [Nat] (254:6) 27 F 92, p. 185.
"Whatever Happened to Clinton?" [Nat] (255:1) 6 Jl 92, p. 5.

6503. TRIMMER, Greg
"On the Note of the New Terror." [Iowa] (22:3) Fall 92, p. 182.

6504. TRINIDAD, David
"The Bomb Shelter" (for Henry Flesh). [Shiny] (7/8) 92, p. 107-108.
"Last Night." [NewDeltaR] (8:2) Spr-Sum 91, p. 69.
"Wednesday Morning." [ChironR] (11:4) Wint 92, p. 42.
"What Debbie & Cameron Lost in New York." [NewDeltaR] (8:2) Spr-Sum 91, p. 68.
"Yvette Mimieux in Hit Lady." [NewDeltaR] (8:2) Spr-Sum 91, p. 70.

6505. TRIPATHY, Sunanda
"The Tryst" (tr. by J. P. Das and Arlene Zide). [ChiR] (38:1/2) 92, p. 211.

6506. TRIPLETT, Pimone
"Snapshots with Wide Apertures Shown on the Road." [HangL] (61) 92, p. 76-77.

6507. TRITICA, John
"Elaborations." [Talisman] (9) Fall 92, p. 198-199.

6508. TRITTO, Michael
"The Reception." [CumbPR] (12:1) Fall 92, p. 67-68.

6509. TRIVEDI, Harish
"The Battle of Man and Fish" (tr. of Raghuvir Sahay). [ChiR] (38:1/2) 92, p. 144-145.
"The Handicapped Caught in a Camera" (tr. of Raghuvir Sahay). [ChiR] (38:1/2) 92, p. 146-147.
"Wayside Station" (tr. of Prayag Shukla). [ChiR] (38:1/2) 92, p. 143.

6510. TRIVELPIECE, Laurel
"Bringing in the Cows." [Poetry] (160:3) Je 92, p. 141-142.
"Outside the Garden." [Poetry] (160:3) Je 92, p. 140.
"The Turkish Bee." [Poetry] (160:5) Ag 92, p. 260.

6511. TROTMAN, Annette
"Barbados." [LitR] (35:4) Sum 92, p. 556-557.

6512. TROUPE, Quincy
"Las Cruces, New Mexico" (For Keith Wilson, Donna Epps Ramsey, Andrew Wall, Charles Thomas, Thomas Hocksema & the Indian who told me much of this). [Pequod] (33) 92, p. 181-183.
"Falling Down Roads of Sleep." [Pequod] (33) 92, p. 180.
6513. TROWBRIDGE, William
"Faith, as Boeing 747." [Light] (1) Spr 92, p. 31.
"Flashbacks." [GettyR] (5:4) Aut 92, p. 656.
"Slug." [SpoonRQ] (17:1/2) Wint-Spr 92, p. 110.
"Urn Burial." [Journal] (16:2) Fall-Wint 92, p. 93.
6514. TROYANOVITCH, Steve
"Dream Dealer" (for Philip Whalen). [MoodySI] (27) Spr 92, p. 17.
"Mexican Sunset" (for Jack Kerouac). [MoodySI] (27) Spr 92, p. 17.
6515. TRUDELL, John
"To God." [Jacaranda] (6:1/2) Wint-Spr 92, p. 96-97.
TRUJILLO, César A. González
See GONZALEZ-T., César A.
6516. TRULOCK, Steven A.
"The Cabin at White Rock." [CapeR] (27:2) Fall 92, p. 41.
6517. TRUSCOTT, Robert Blake
"A. G. Bell Considers the Sea" (from a photo of the inventor). [Epiphany] (3:3) Jl (Sum) 92, p. 174-176.
"Bridging" (from a photograph by Feininger — Brooklyn Bridge). [Epiphany] (3:3) Jl (Sum) 92, p. 168-173.
TSUNEKO, Yoshikawa
See YOSHIKAWA, Tsuneko
TSURAYUKI, Ki no
See KI no TSURAYUKI (ca. 872-945)
6518. TSVETAEVA, Marina
"After Russia (1928)" (2 selections, tr. by Michael Naydan). [Confr] (48/49) Spr - Sum 92, p. 216-217.
"And on my forehead" (tr. by Patricia Sollner). [SenR] (22:1) Spr 92, p. 35.
"I burned a handful of hair" (tr. by Patricia Sollner). [SenR] (22:1) Spr 92, p. 34.
"I'll tell you the story" (tr. by Patricia Sollner). [SenR] (22:1) Spr 92, p. 33.
"I've come home" (tr. by Patricia Sollner). [SenR] (22:1) Spr 92, p. 37.
"Neither stanzas nor stars will be my salvation" (tr. by Patricia Sollner). [SenR] (22:1) Spr 92, p. 36.
"Untitled: I like it that you're sick, but not for me" (tr. by Gwenan Wilbur). [TriQ] (86) Wint 92-93, p. 29.
TUAMA, Seán O
See O TUAMA, Seán
6519. TUCKER, Memye Curtis
"For Mumtaz." [CumbPR] (12:1) Fall 92, p. 52.
"Return." [CumbPR] (12:1) Fall 92, p. 53.
6520. TUDOR, Jo
"Hymn to Urban Middle Class Women" (tr. of Ursula Krechel). [Stand] (33:4) Aut 92, p. 63-64.
"To Mainz!" (tr. of Ursula Krechel). [Stand] (33:4) Aut 92, p. 62-63.
6521. TUENI, Nadia
"Through colors" (tr. by Lisa Holbrook). [SpoonRQ] (17:3/4) Sum-Fall 92, p. 45.
6522. TUFTS, Carol
"Thirty Years Later." [Pearl] (15) Spr-Sum 92, p. 26.
6523. TULLIS, Rod
"At the Water's Edge" (to Sara). [PoetryNW] (33:1) Spr 92, p. 22-23.
"Dogwood." [SpoonRQ] (17:3/4) Sum-Fall 92, p. 27.
"Lake Carlos at Sunset." [PoetryNW] (33:1) Spr 92, p. 20-22.
"My Father in an Orchard." [SpoonRQ] (17:3/4) Sum-Fall 92, p. 28-29.
"This Could Easily Be a Lie." [SycamoreR] (4:1) Wint 92, p. 17-19.
6524. TULLOCH, Meg
"Rosseau's Sleeping Gypsy." [CreamCR] (16:2) Fall 92, p. 90.
6525. TULLOSS, Rod
"Blood." [Archae] (3) early 92, p. 12.
"Buzzard Raiser." [Archae] (4) late 92-early 93, p. 50.
"Flight 806." [US1] (26/27) 92, p. 36.
"The Girl Who Invented Rilke." [Archae] (3) early 92, p. 6.
"Names." [Archae] (3) early 92, p. 7-10.

"A Narrow Garden in Heemsteede." [Archae] (3) early 92, p. 11.
"Stillie." [US1] (26/27) 92, p. 36.

6526. TUMBLESON, Ray
"The Farnsworth Room." [Bogg] (65) 92, p. 5.
"Frankenstein." [HolCrit] (29:2) Ap 92, p. 15.

6527. TUNISIA, Kristina
"Song of Autumn." [Caliban] (11) 92, p. 174.

6528. TURCO, Lewis
"Amathophobia: The Fear of Dust." [NewYorkQ] (49) 92, p. 59.
"Letter to Mother." [Confr] (48/49) Spr-Sum 92, p. 192-193.
"The Migration." [NewYorkQ] (48) 92, p. 69.
"A Serenade of Youth, an Envoy in Middle Age." [Confr] (48/49) Spr-Sum 92, p. 194-195.

6529. TURCZYN, Amahl
"Mushroom and Eve." [PoetL] (87:1) Spr 92, p. 28.

6530. TURCZYN, Christine
"Awakening." [Footwork] 92, p. 165.
"Dream." [Footwork] 92, p. 165.

6531. TURKLE, Ann
"Summer Feeding." [HiramPoR] (51/52) Fall 91-Sum 92, p. 71.

6532. TURLOW, Steven
"The Musicians." [CreamCR] (16:2) Fall 92, p. 84-85.

6533. TURNER, Alberta
"Anyone, Lifting." [ThRiPo] (39/40) 92-93, p. 258-259.
"Elm Street." [ThRiPo] (39/40) 92-93, p. 259.
"Meditation Upon Ought." [ThRiPo] (39/40) 92-93, p. 259.

6534. TURNER, Brian
"Euphemistically." [NewL] (58:4) 92, p. 153.

6535. TURNER, Ken
"Pearls." [JlNJPo] (14:2) Aut 92, p. 7.
"Watching the Gulf War on TV." [JlNJPo] (14:1) Spr 92, p. 6.

6536. TURNER, Marjorie L.
"Like Lonely Runaways." [Writer] (105:12) D 92, p. 19.

6537. TURNER, Michael B.
"Colony" (for Andre Gide). [Amelia] (6:4, #19) 92, p. 118.

6538. TURNER, Steph
"'How You Feelin'?' Is Obviously Rhetorical." [SmPd] (29:3, #86) Fall 92, p. 35.

6539. TURNER, T. N.
"The Ancient Philosophers." [Epiphany] (3:2) Ap (Spr) 92, p. 111.
"Cats and Their Things." [Epiphany] (3:2) Ap (Spr) 92, p. 110-111.

6540. TURPIN, Mark
"Before Groundbreak." [Ploughs] (18:4) Wint 92-93, p. 40.
"Photograph from Antietam." [Ploughs] (18:4) Wint 92-93, p. 38-39.

6541. TUTWILER, Mary
"Kayla's House." [LouisL] (9:2) Fall 92, p. 42-45.

6542. TWICHELL, Chase
"Bad Movie, Bad Audience." [ParisR]] (34:124) Fall 92, p. 163.
"Ghost Birches." [SouthernR] (28:2) Spr, Ap 92, p. 283-284.
"A Seduction." [ParisR]] (34:124) Fall 92, p. 164-165.
"The Whirlpool." [Nat] (255:22) 28 D 92, p. 823.

6543. TZAGOLOFF, Helen
"A Few Pointers on Preparing for a Job Interview." [SingHM] (20) 92, p. 73.

6544. TZARA, Tristan
"Anecdote" (tr. by William Kulik). [AmerPoR] (21:4) Jl-Ag 92, p. 5.
"Bifurcation" (tr. by William Kulik). [AmerPoR] (21:4) Jl-Ag 92, p. 4.
"Casting Off" (tr. by William Kulik). [AmerPoR] (21:4) Jl-Ag 92, p. 4.
"Complete Circuit of Moon and Color" (tr. by William Kulik). [AmerPoR] (21:4) Jl-Ag 92, p. 3.
"The Death of Guillaume Apollinaire" (tr. by William Kulik). [AmerPoR] (21:4) Jl-Ag 92, p. 4.
"Easier Said Than Done" (tr. by William Kulik). [AmerPoR] (21:4) Jl-Ag 92, p. 5.
"Epidermis of the Night Growth" (tr. by William Kulik). [AmerPoR] (21:4) Jl-Ag 92, p. 3.
"For Robert Desnos" (tr. by William Kulik). [AmerPoR] (21:4) Jl-Ag 92, p. 5.
"Forbidden Fire" (Selections: II, IX, XI, tr. by William Kulik). [AmerPoR] (21:4) Jl-Ag 92, p. 4.

"The Horse" (tr. by William Kulik). [AmerPoR] (21:4) Jl-Ag 92, p. 6.
"Hotel Light" (tr. by William Kulik). [AmerPoR] (21:4) Jl-Ag 92, p. 6.
"Optimism Unveiled" (tr. by William Kulik). [AmerPoR] (21:4) Jl-Ag 92, p. 3.
"Ox on the Tongue" (Selections: XIV, XV, tr. by William Kulik). [AmerPoR] (21:4) Jl-Ag 92, p. 5.
"Undiscoverable Past" (tr. by William Kulik). [AmerPoR] (21:4) Jl-Ag 92, p. 6.
"The Wave" (tr. by William Kulik). [AmerPoR] (21:4) Jl-Ag 92, p. 5.

6545. UBA, George
"Dawn in the Internment Camp at Heart Mountain" (Wyoming, 1943). [Ploughs] (18:1) Spr 92, p. 9.
"Master Oki, Keeper of Days." [Ploughs] (18:1) Spr 92, p. 10-11.
"The Sanity of Tomatoes." [Ploughs] (18:1) Spr 92, p. 12-13.

UDHARI, Abdullah al-
See Al-UDHARI, Abdullah

6546. UELAND, Carol
"As Catullus Wrote" (from "Apollo in the Snow," tr. of Aleksandr Kushner, w. Paul Graves). [Arion] 3d series (1:2) Spr 91, p. 128.
"A Party on Women's Day" (tr. of Olesia Nikolaeva, w. Paul Graves). [KenR] (NS 14:4) Fall 92, p. 117-118.
"Seven Beginnings" (tr. of Olesia Nikolaeva, w. Paul Graves). [KenR] (NS 14:4) Fall 92, p. 115-116.
"Untitled: Here, everything gets eaten: drippings, marinade" (tr. of Olesia Nikolaeva, w. Paul Graves). [KenR] (NS 14:4) Fall 92, p. 117.

UEMA, Marck L. Beggs
See BEGGS, Marck (Marck L.)

6547. UGUAY, Marie
"L'Otre Vie (Beyond Life)" (Excerpts, tr. by Annabelle Honza). [GrahamHR] (16) Fall 92, p. 86-93.

6548. UHLICH, Richard
"Final Instructions." [LitR] (25:2) Wint 92, p. 277.

6549. ULACIA, Manuel
"The Stone at the Bottom" (tr. by Reginald Gibbons). [TriQ] (85) Fall 92, p. 78-83.

6550. ULKU, A. K.
"Bad Thoughts, Mixed Messages." [MalR] (101) Wint92, p. 76.

6551. ULLMAN, Leslie
"Courage." [AmerV] (26) Spr 92, p. 67-68.
"One Side of Me Writes to the Other." [KenR] (NS 14:1) Wint 92, p. 1-3.
"Running Horse." [Poetry] (160:6) S 92, p. 339-340.

6552. ULMER, James
"The Art of Poetry." [Crazy] (42) Spr 92, p. 73-74.
"Ladderback at Morning." [PraS] (66:3) Fall 92, p. 77-78.

6553. UMPHREY, Michael
"Summer Softball." [CutB] (37) Wint 92, p. 14-17.

6554. UMPIERRE, Luz María
"Bella Ilusión Que Fugaz." [Americas] (19:3/4) Wint 91, p. 39-40.
"Elliot's Sunset" (tr. by Ellen J. Stekert). [Americas] (19:3/4) Wint 91, p. 48-50.
"For Ellen" (tr. by Patsy Boyer). [Americas] (19:3/4) Wint 91, p. 44.
"Para Ellen." [Americas] (19:3/4) Wint 91, p. 43.
"Poema para Elliot Gilbert." [Americas] (19:3/4) Wint 91, p. 45-47.
"To a Beautiful Illusion, Fleeting" (tr. by Patsy Boyer). [Americas] (19:3/4) Wint 91, p. 41-42.

6555. UNGER, Barbara
"Chava." [TarRP] (30:2) Spr 91, p. 53-54.
"Immies." [TarRP] (30:2) Spr 91, p. 55.
"Pioneer Women." [SingHM] (20) 92, p. 8.

6556. UNGER, David
"The Angel of Jealousy" (tr. of Isaac Goldemberg). [RiverS] (36) 92, p. 73.
"El Chino Lihn" (1929-1988). [Nuez] (4:10/11) 92, p. 19.
"The Race" (for Isaac Goldemberg). [RiverS] (36) 92, p. 72.

6557. UNGRIA, Ricardo M. de
"Angel Radio." [Manoa] (4:1) Spr 92, p. 36-38.

6558. UPDIKE, John
"Ancient Optics." [NewRep] (206:20) 18 My 92, p. 42.
"Back from Vacation." [Poetry] (160:4) Jl 92, p. 202.
"Burning Trash." [NewYorker] (68:42) 7 D 92, p. 92.
"Celery." [NewRep] (207:23) 30 N 92, p. 32.

"Elderly Sex." [Poetry] (160:4) Jl 92, p. 203.
"Fall." [AmerPoR] (21:2) Mr-Ap 92, p. 35.
"In Malaysia." [Poetry] (160:4) Jl 92, p. 211-212.
"July." [NewYorker] (68:22) 20 Jl 92, p. 30.
"Literary Dublin." [Light] (1) Spr 92, p. 20.
"Miami." [HarvardA] (125th Anniversary Issue) F 92, p. 29.
"Neoteny." [OntR] (37) Fall-Wint 92-93, p. 100-101.
"Rio de Janeiro." [NewYorker] (68:34) 12 O 92, p. 68.
"To a Former Mistress, Now Dead." [Poetry] (160:4) Jl 92, p. 201.
"Working Outdoors in Winter." [AmerPoR] (21:2) Mr-Ap 92, p. 35.

6559. UPTON, Lee
"A Daughter." [ThRiPo] (39/40) 92-93, p. 261-262.
"The Debt." [ThRiPo] (39/40) 92-93, p. 260-261.
"Lost Child." [ThRiPo] (39/40) 92-93, p. 260.
"Recitative." [AmerV] (26) Spr 92, p. 83-84.
"Relentless Experiment." [AmerV] (26) Spr 92, p. 81-82.
"Water Lily as Creation." [LaurelR] (26:2) Sum 92, p. 17.
"Women's Labors." [MassR] (23:1) Spr 92, p. 48-49.

6560. URBAIN, John
"Lunch." [Lactuca] (16) Ag 92, p. 11-12.

6561. URDANG, Constance
"The River-Keeper's Song." [TriQ] (86) Wint 92-93, p. 68.
"Transcendence." [Poetry] (160:2) My 92, p. 90.

6562. URDANG, Elliott
"Amber" (tr. of Ana Blandiana, w. Marguerite Dorian). [MidAR] (13:2) 92, p. 9.
"Mother" (tr. of Ana Blandiana, w. Marguerite Dorian). [MidAR] (13:2) 92, p. 10.
"Piéta" (tr. of Ana Blandiana, w. Marguerite Dorian). [MidAR] (13:2) 92, p. 11-12.

6563. URQUHART, Alan
"3. Pinke Zinke." [Footwork] 92, p. 147.
"Bloodshot." [Vis] (40) 92, p. 8.
"In Praise of Monuments." [Vis] (40) 92, p. 7.

6564. URREA, Luis
"I Tried to Write a Poem About This Once a Year for Thirteen Years." [Agni] (35) 92, p. 63-65.

6565. URROZ, Eloy
"El Agua en su albedrío." [Nuez] (4:10/11) 92, p. 9.

6566. URSACHI, Mihai
"The Discovery of Romania" (tr. by Adam Sorkin and Magda Teodorescu). [Nimrod] (35:2) Spr-Sum 92, p. 42.
"Meditation in Frenchman's Gulf" (tr. by Adam Sorkin and Magda Teodorescu). [Nimrod] (35:2) Spr-Sum 92, p. 43-44.

6567. URSU, Liliana
"Anatomy of a December Night" (tr. by Adam J. Sorkin). [PassN] (13:2) Wint 92, p. 13.
"Bait" (tr. by Adam J. Sorkin). [PassN] (13:2) Wint 92, p. 13.
"Herbstmanöver" (from "Zoná de Protectie," tr. by Fleur Adcock). [13thMoon] (10:1/2) 92, p. 8.
"Port Angeles" (tr. by Tess Gallagher, w. the author). [PassN] (13:2) Wint 92, p. 12.
"Seascape" (tr. by Adam J. Sorkin). [PassN] (13:2) Wint 92, p. 13.
"Vieux Jeu" (from "Piata Aurarilor," tr. by Fleur Adcock). [13thMoon] (10:1/2) 92, p. 7.
"You Haven't a Face" (tr. by Adam J. Sorkin). [PassN] (13:2) Wint 92, p. 13.

6568. USCHUK, Pamela
"Autumn Eclipse." [Calyx] (14:2) Wint 92-93, p. 14-15.
"Hunter's Moon, Fire Moon." [MidAR] (12:2) 92, p. 21-22.

6569. USHA, S.
"To Mother" (tr. by A. K. Ramanujan). [ChiR] (38:1/2) 92, p. 162-163.

6570. VAETH, Kim
"The Bath." [KenR] (NS 14:1) Wint 92, p. 111.
"Here." [KenR] (NS 14:1) Wint 92, p. 110.

6571. VAICIUNAITE, Judita (Judith)
"Orpheus and Eurydice" (tr. by Viktoria Skrupskelis and Stuart Friebert). [Confr] (50) Fall 92, p. 300-303.
"Pastorals" (tr. by Viktoria Skrupskelis and Stuart Friebert). [HayF] (10) Spr-Sum 92, p. 51.

"The Rebel" (tr. by Viktoria Skrupskelis and Stuart Friebert). [HayF] (10) Spr-Sum 92, p. 50.

6572. VAIL, Desire
"Summer's Dray." [Blueline] (13) 92, p. 19.

6573. VAILE, Jonathan
"Blue Cowboy" (After Trakl's "De Profundis"). [PoetL] (87:2) Sum 92, p. 5.
"The Victory Parade: June 8, 1991." [BlackBR] (15) Spr-Sum 92, p. 16-18.

6574. VALDÉS, Grisel
"En Octubre Primavera." [LindLM] (11:4) D 92, p. 21.

VALDÉS, Jorge Vélez
See VÉLEZ VALDÉS, Jorge

6575. VALENTINE, Jean
"At My Mother's Grave." [Field] (46) Spr 92, p. 5.
"At the Door." [HayF] (10) Spr-Sum 92, p. 78.
"Butane." [HayF] (10) Spr-Sum 92, p. 30.
"The First Angel." [Field] (46) Spr 92, p. 6.
"Flower." [BrooklynR] (9) 92, p. 99.
"My Mother's Body, My Professor, My Bower." [HayF] (10) Spr-Sum 92, p. 79.
"Sick, Away from Home." [NewYorker] (68:24) 3 Ag 92, p. 48.
"Still Life, for Matisse." [AmerV] (26) Spr 92, p. 74.
"To Plath, to Sexton." [LitR] (36:1) Fall 92, p. 38.
"Yield Everything, Force Nothing." [Field] (46) Spr 92, p. 7.

6576. VALENTINE, William
"A Sorrowful Mystery." [NewYorkQ] (47) 92, p. 89.

6577. VALÉRY, Paul
"The Maritime Graveyard" (tr. by Gerald Burns). [AnotherCM] (23) Spr 92, p. 173 - 175.

6578. VALINOTTI, Nick
"Magnolia." [BrooklynR] (9) 92, p. 60.

6579. VALLARINO, Roberto
"Dogs" (tr. by Reginald Gibbons). [TriQ] (85) Fall 92, p. 206.

6580. VALLE, Carmen
"Glenn Miller's Music Is a Trunk" (tr. by Julio Marzán). [LitR] (35:4) Sum 92, p. 524.
"I'm Going to Break Out" (tr. by Julio Marzán). [LitR] (35:4) Sum 92, p. 523.
"Lo Vivido." [LitR] (35:4) Sum 92, p. 608.
"La Música de Glenn Miller." [LitR] (35:4) Sum 92, p. 608-609.
"What Is Lived" (tr. by Julio Marzán). [LitR] (35:4) Sum 92, p. 523-524.
"Yo Me Voy a Largar." [LitR] (35:4) Sum 92, p. 607-608.

6581. VALLEJO, César
"Considerando en frío, imparcialmente." [Inti] (36) Otoño 92, p. 81-82.
"Hoy me gusta la vida mucho menos." [Inti] (36) Otoño 92, p. 75-76.
"Parado en una piedra." [Inti] (36) Otoño 92, p. 89-90.
"Quedéme a calentar la tinta en que me ahogo." [Inti] (36) Otoño 92, p. 97-98.
"Quisiera hoy ser feliz de buena gana." [Inti] (36) Otoño 92, p. 105-106.
"Trilce" (Selections: XXXII, XXXVI, XXXVIII, in Spanish). [GrandS] (11:1, #41) 92, p. 56-60.
"Trilce" (Selections: XXXII, XXXVI, XXXVIII, tr. by Clayton Eshleman, w. Julio Ortega). [GrandS] (11:1, #41) 92, p. 57-61.
"Trilce" (Selections: xxxiii, xxxv, tr. by Rebecca Seiferle). [NewOR] (19:1) Spr 92, p. 36-37.
"Trilce" (Selections: LXXI-LXXIII, tr. by Clayton Eshleman and Julio Ortega). [WorldL] (3) 92, p. 1-3.

6582. VALLICELLA, Philip
"Living in the World." [RagMag] (10:1) 92, p. 64.
"One Door." [RagMag] (10:1) 92, p. 65.

6583. VALVERDE, Maya C.
"Pipe Carriers." [SinW] (47) Sum-Fall 92, p. 43.

Van . . .
See also names beginning with "Van" without the following space, filed below in their alphabetic positions.

6584. Van ARSDALE, Sarah
"Accidents." [OxfordM] (6:2) Fall-Wint 90, p. 85-86.
"Dear Peggy." [ChironR] (11:4) Wint 92, p. 17.
"Kiss." [ChironR] (11:4) Wint 92, p. 17.
"Lake Effect." [PassN] (13:2) Wint 92, p. 23.

"Pepper." [ChironR] (11:4) Wint 92, p. 17.
6585. Van BEEK, Edith
"Wanting the Light." [Quarry] (41:4) Fall 92, p. 69.
6586. Van BRUNT, Lloyd
"Judgment Day." [JamesWR] (10:1) Fall 92, p. 16.
"Rattlesnake Cove." [Confr] (48/49) Spr-Sum 92, p. 197-198.
"Rembrandt's Horses" (for S.). [HampSPR] Wint 92, p. 53-54.
"Untitled: I want the stillness of snow in woods." [AmerPoR] (21:1) Ja-F 92, p. 46.
6587. Van BUREN, David
"Someone Else." [HiramPoR] (51/52) Fall 91-Sum 92, p. 72.
"Women in Chairs" (Four paintings by Edward Hopper). [CutB] (37) Wint 92, p. 88-90.
6588. Van den BEUKEL, Karlien
"The Observatory Graveyard Demolished." [Stand] (33:3) Sum 92, p. 12.
6589. Van DUYN, Mona
"At the Mall." [NewRep] (207:3/4) 13-20 Jl 92, p. 48.
"A Certain Age" (minimalist sonnet). [PoetryNW] (33:1) Spr 92, p. 13.
"The Choice" (minimalist sonnet). [PoetryNW] (33:1) Spr 92, p. 13.
"The Delivery." [NewYorker] (68:2) 2 Mr 92, p. 32-33.
"Emergency Room" (Turnpike, Anywhere, U.S.A.). [Nat] (254:23) 15 Je 92, p. 832.
"Endings." [YaleR] (80:1/2) Apr 92, p. 79-80.
"Extra Time." [Poetry] (160:2) My 92, p. 69-70.
"Fallen Angel" (For Ray, Sandy, Sondra, May, Leanna, Mary, Tom H. — Death's six-month harvest). [CreamCR] (16:2) Fall 92, p. 16-17.
"From the Mantel." [NoAmR] (277:3) My-Je 92, p. 33.
"Have You Seen Me?" (Lost Children Ads). [NoAmR] (277:3) My-Je 92, p. 33.
"Long Stretch Minimalist Sonnet" (For Howard). [Poetry] (160:2) My 92, p. 63.
"Minimalist Sonnets." [Poetry] (160:2) My 92, p. 64-65.
"Miranda Grows Up" (minimalist sonnet). [PoetryNW] (33:1) Spr 92, p. 13.
"Mr. and Mrs. Jack Sprat in the Kitchen" (Extended minimalist sonnet). [Poetry] (160:2) My 92, p. 66.
"One Strategy for Loving the World." [NoAmR] (277:3) My-Je 92, p. 33.
"Passing Thought." [Poetry] (160:2) My 92, p. 67-68.
"Rascasse." [NewYorker] (68:44) 21 D 92, p. 92-93.
6590. Van GERVEN, Claudia
"Nut Contemplates Motherhood." [SingHM] (20) 92, p. 41-42.
6591. Van GUNDY, Douglas
"Nostalgia." [BellArk] (8:3) My-Je 92, p. 20.
"You and I Hear Music in the Falling of Acorns." [BellArk] (8:3) My-Je 92, p. 20.
6592. Van HERK, Aritha
"And Silence Is Also a Nakedness" (an inter-text to *Naked Poems*). [WestCL] (25:3, #6) Wint 91-92, p. 175-184.
"Belly, Belly." [Grain] (20:1) Spr 92, p. 212-213.
6593. Van HORN, Stephanie
"Arithmetic." [Calyx] (14:2) Wint 92-93, p. 54-55.
"Creation." [PaintedHR] (5) Wint 92, p. 6-7.
6594. Van LONKHUYZEN, Harold V.
"My Vocation." [ChrC] (109:11) 1 Ap 92, p. 340.
6595. Van NOORD, Barbara
"Freud Experiences a Metaphor." [Kalliope] (14:1) 92, p. 36-37.
"January Thaw." [GreensboroR] (52) Sum 92, p. 155.
"Red Carnations" (for my father, d. 12/21/64). [CapeR] (27:1) Spr 92, p. 7.
6596. Van PEENEN, H. J.
"Bumper Stickers." [BellArk] (8:3) My-Je 92, p. 21.
"Henry River Swingbridge" (St. James Walkway, South Island, New Zealand). [BellArk] (8:3) My-Je 92, p. 21.
"A Sulfur Bath" (Hammer Springs, South Island, New Zealand). [BellArk] (8:3) My-Je 92, p. 20.
6597. Van REYK, Paul
"Scheherazade." [JamesWR] (9:3) Spr 92, p. 12.
"Vertigo." [JamesWR] (9:3) Spr 92, p. 12.
6598. Van RIPER, Craig
"Christmastime, 1990." [Epiphany] (3:3) Jl (Sum) 92, p. 192.
"Everything Must Go." [OnTheBus] (4:2/5:1, #10/11) 92, p. 180.
"Here in Balboa Park a Bag." [OnTheBus] (4:2/5:1, #10/11) 92, p. 180.
"Love Poem." [Epiphany] (3:3) Jl (Sum) 92, p. 192.

"A Reason to Give." [Epiphany] (3:3) Jl (Sum) 92, p. 193.
Van SANTEN, Louise
See SANTEN, Louise van
6599. Van SPANCKEREN, Kathryn
"The Generations" (Excerpt). [Ploughs] (18:1) Spr 92, p. 14-15.
6600. Van WALLEGHEN, Michael
"Album Epilepticus" (for Jim). [Crazy] (43) Wint 92, p. 50-54.
"The Awards Banquet." [Hudson] (45:2) Sum 92, p. 255-259.
"The Brave Adventure" (for Paul Friedman). [PraS] (66:1) Spr 92, p. 91-93.
"The Broken Jars." [PraS] (66:1) Spr 92, p. 89-91.
"Catch Him!" [PraS] (66:1) Spr 92, p. 95-96.
"The Hunk" (Florida, 1988). [Crazy] (43) Wint 92, p. 46-47.
"In the Chariot Drawn by Dragons." [Hudson] (45:2) Sum 92, p. 259-260.
"Missed Connections" (January 1, 1990). [PraS] (66:1) Spr 92, p. 93-95.
"Uncle Jerry." [Crazy] (43) Wint 92, p. 48-49.
6601. Van WERT, William (William F.)
"Against Monogramy" (for Joseph McElroy). [PaintedB] (46) 92, p. 45-46.
"Grief Stages." [PaintedB] (46) 92, p. 44.
"In Duras." [PaintedB] (48) 92, p. 27.
6602. Van WINCKEL, Nance
"After Hiking All Day." [AntR] (50:3) Sum 92, p. 518.
"Bourgeois Blues." [AmerV] (26) Spr 92, p. 63-64.
"Continental Divide." [PoetryNW] (33:4) Wint 92-93, p. 13-15.
"Double Negative." [IndR] (15:1) Spr 92, p. 61-62.
"The Hounds of Heaven." [Ascent] (17:1) Fall 92, p. 37.
"The Old Men of the Wilderness Club." [GettyR] (5:4) Aut 92, p. 685.
"Our Mother Is from the Old Country." [Ascent] (17:1) Fall 92, p. 38.
"Repercussion" (Laramie Rodeo, 1976). [NewEngR] (14:4) Fall 92, p. 181.
"Restaurant with Four Minus One." [AmerPoR] (21:4) Jl-Ag 92, p. 31.
"Two Rains." [NewEngR] (14:4) Fall 92, p. 182-183.
"Under an Imposter's Hat." [AmerPoR] (21:4) Jl-Ag 92, p. 31.
VanBEEK, Edith
See Van BEEK, Edith
VanBRUNT, Lloyd
See Van BRUNT, Lloyd
6603. VANCE, Bob
"Drunk Together." [SmPd] (29:2, #85) Spr 92, p. 25.
6604. VANCE, Christine
"In Dick's Trailer Town." [PoetryE] (33) Spr 92, p. 152.
6605. VANCE, Richard
"Relief." [LitR] (25:2) Wint 92, p. 277.
6606. VANCE, Vera
"Inland" (tr. of Solveig von Schoultz). [Vis] (38) 92, p. 45.
6607. Vanden EYNDEN, Keith
"Skeletal Trees." [CinPR] (23) Wint 91-92, p. 63.
6608. VANDENBURGH, Jane
"Elements of Risk." [Thrpny] (51) Fall 92, p. 16.
Vander . . .
See also names beginning with "Vander" without the following space, filed below in their alphabetic positions, e.g. VanderMOLEN.
6609. Vander WAL, Jane Aaron
"The Author." [AntigR] (89) Spr 92, p. 116.
6610. VANDERLIP, Brian
"Dangling Affirmations from a Flat Church Roof." [PoetryC] (12:2) Ap 92, p. 7.
6611. VanderMOLEN, Robert
"Countryside." [ArtfulD] (22/23) 92, p. 64.
"Deer Camp." [ArtfulD] (22/23) 92, p. 65.
"Flies." [Caliban] (11) 92, p. 112.
"History." [NewAW] (10) Fall 92, p. 107-108.
"Saturday." [ArtfulD] (22/23) 92, p. 66.
VanderWAL, Jane Aaron
See Vander WAL, Jane Aaron
6612. VANDO, Gloria
"Fire." [KenR] (NS 14:3) Sum 92, p. 112-114.
VanDUYN, Mona
See Van DUYN, Mona

6613. VANGELISTI, Paul
"About the Poet" (tr. of Pablo Antonio Cuadra, w. Florinda Mintz). [OnTheBus] (4:2/5:1, #10/11) 92, p. 272.
"De Rerum Natura" (tr. of David Escobar Galindo, w. Florinda Mintz). [OnTheBus] (4:2/5:1, #10/11) 92, p. 274.
"Exiles" (Dedicated to Stefan Baciu, tr. of Pablo Antonio Cuadra, w. Florinda Mintz). [OnTheBus] (4:2/5:1, #10/11) 92, p. 273.
"Letter with Roses" (tr. of David Escobar Galindo, w. Florinda Mintz). [OnTheBus] (4:2/5:1, #10/11) 92, p. 275.
VanGERVEN, Claudia
See Van GERVEN, Claudia
6614. VANICEK, Zdenek
"I Don't Believe" (tr. by Ewald Osers). [PraS] (66:4) Wint 92, p. 163-164.
"The Old Jewish Quarter in Prague" (for Ivan Jelínek, tr. by Ewald Osers). [PraS] (66:4) Wint 92, p. 165.
VanSPANCKEREN, Kathryn
See Van SPANCKEREN, Kathryn
6615. VANTOMME, Dianne
"Coastlands." [OnTheBus] (4:2/5:1, #10/11) 92, p. 225.
"Potter's Place." [OnTheBus] (4:2/5:1, #10/11) 92, p. 225-226.
VanWALLEGHEN, Michael
See Van WALLEGHEN, Michael
VanWINCKEL, Nance
See Van WINCKEL, Nance
6616. VARELA, Blanca
"Ejercicios Materiales." [LindLM] (11:3) S 92, p. 3.
"Village Song" (tr. by Stephanie Anderson). [Field] (47) Fall 92, p. 70-71.
6617. VARGAS, Juan Carlos
"De Orbe Novo." [ChiR] (38:3) 92, p. 5-16.
6618. VARLEY, Jane
"Midwest Religion." [Iowa] (22:1) Wint 92, p. 179-180.
6619. VARON, Jodi
"Ballad of the Old Jade Hunter at Indigo River" (tr. of Li He). [ColR] (9:1) Spr-Sum 92, p. 114.
6620. VASCONCELLOS, Cherry Jean
"No One Could See What I Saw in the Guy." [Pearl] (16) Fall 92, p. 15.
"Norman Vincent Peale." [Pearl] (15) Spr-Sum 92, p. 55.
6621. VASSILAKIS, Nico
"Light Devours Sound." [CentralP] (21) Spr 92, p. 63-69.
"To Prove Ground." [Caliban] (11) 92, p. 163-167.
6622. VAUGHN, R. M.
"Looking at Mr. Goodbar." [PottPort] (14:1) Spr-Sum 92, p. 24-25.
6623. VAULTONBURG, Thomas L.
"The Hollow Bone." [Caliban] (11) 92, p. 155.
"Mad Breakfast." [Caliban] (11) 92, p. 156.
"Returning to the Heart" (For Emily). [ChironR] (11:3) Aut 92, p. 7.
"Starting From Bucharest." [ChironR] (11:3) Aut 92, p. 7.
6624. VAYENAS, Nasos
"The Birth of Aphrodite" (tr. by John Chioles). [Trans] (26) Spr 92, p. 96.
6625. VAZIRANI, Reetika
"Amma's Ruby." [AmerV] (26) Spr 92, p. 123.
"Devi." [KenR] (NS 14:2) Spr 92, p. 72.
"Lobster." [KenR] (NS 14:2) Spr 92, p. 72.
"Mica." [KenR] (NS 14:2) Spr 92, p. 71.
"Mrs. Biswas." [Callaloo] (15:4) Fall 92, p. 903-905.
"On the Fast Train." [KenR] (NS 14:2) Spr 92, p. 73.
"White Elephants." [LitR] (36:1) Fall 92, p. 99.
6626. VAZQUEZ, Lourdes
"La Duna." [LindLM] (11:1) Mr 92, p. 16.
"El Ronroneo de las Palomas." [LindLM] (11:1) Mr 92, p. 16.
6627. VAZQUEZ-AMARAL, José
"The Empire of Dreams" (3 excerpts, tr. of Giannina Braschi, w. Tess O'Dwyer). [Luz] (1) My 92, p. 20-26.
6628. VEAZEY, Mary
"Conundrums." [Light] (4) Wint 92-93, p. 8.

6629. VECCHIO, M. J.
"In Monet's *Pool of Water Lilies*." [PoetL] (87:4) Wint 92-93, p. 13.
"Letter from Chang-Kan" (After Fenollosa's translation of Li Po). [PoetL] (87:4) Wint 92-93, p. 11-12.
6630. VEGA, Eduardo
"Strawberry Hill 1982." [Caliban] (11) 92, p. 148.
6631. VEGA, Janine Pommy
"Fox Song" (Condormarca, Callejón de Huaylas, Perú, September 1990). [RiverS] (36) 92, p. 29.
"Hiroshima Day." [RiverS] (36) 92, p. 26-27.
"Hualcapampa" (Hualcapampa, Marcará, Perú, September, 1990). [RiverS] (36) 92, p. 28.
"Postcard from Slovakia." [Archae] (3) early 92, p. 13-14.
6632. VELASQUEZ TREVIÑO, Gloria
"Un Amante Hindu." [BilingR] (17:2) My-Ag 92, p. 166-167.
"Arturo" (for Arturo Islas). [BilingR] (17:2) My-Ag 92, p. 168.
"Frida y Yo." [BilingR] (17:2) My-Ag 92, p. 167-168.
"Old Black Shoes." [BilingR] (17:2) My-Ag 92, p. 169.
"La Pobreza." [BilingR] (17:2) My-Ag 92, p. 165.
"Recuerdos." [BilingR] (17:2) My-Ag 92, p. 165-166.
"Self-Portrait 1991." [BilingR] (17:2) My-Ag 92, p. 170.
"Superwoman." [BilingR] (17:2) My-Ag 92, p. 166.
6633. VÉLEZ, Gonzalo
"Historia." [Nuez] (4:12) 92, p. 27.
6634. VELEZ-ROMAN, Lydia
"Daring of the Brief Suns" (2 selections, tr. by Angela McEwan). [Luz] (2) S 92, p. 13-19.
"Osadia de los Soles Truncos / Daring of the Brief Suns" (2 selections). [Luz] (2) S 92, p. 13-19.
6635. VÉLEZ VALDÉS, Jorge
"Herejia." [LindLM] (11:4) D 92, p. 17.
6636. VENCLOVA, Tomas
"Untruth" (tr. by Diana Senechal). [Confr] (50) Fall 92, p. 298.
6637. VENKATESHAMURTHY, H. S.
"Electric Lights Come to Puttalli" (tr. by A. K. Ramanujan). [ChiR] (38:1/2) 92, p. 120-121.
6638. VENZKE, Philip
"Making a Briquette Chimney." [EngJ] (80:5) S 91, p. 93.
6639. VERÄNDERUNG, Orts
"An Architexture of Its Own." [Archae] (3) early 92, p. 56.
"Lies As Historical Reference Points" (Selections: Lie #7, Lie #2). [Archae] (3) early 92, p. 57-58.
6640. VERDECIA, Carlos
"El Coleccionista." [LindLM] (11:2) Je 92, p. 15.
"El Profeta" (Al toti, pájaro de buen agüero). [LindLM] (11:2) Je 92, p. 15.
"Quiromancia" (A Joseíto, sabio teósofo). [LindLM] (11:2) Je 92, p. 15.
"Stella by Starlight." [LindLM] (11:2) Je 92, p. 15.
VERGÉS, Rafael Soto
See SOTO VERGÉS, Rafael
6641. VERNER, Dan
"Most Eager for Fame." [EngJ] (80:5) S 91, p. 92.
6642. VERNON, William (William J.)
"Arriving at Boot Camp." [Lactuca] (15) Mr 92, p. 45.
"Friday Nights After Cleaning Up *The Western Star* Complex." [Lactuca] (15) Mr 92, p. 46.
"Man with Roots." [HiramPoR] (51/52) Fall 91-Sum 92, p. 73-74.
"When We Went Home Again." [Lactuca] (15) Mr 92, p. 45.
6643. VERSTEEG, Tom
"A Brief History of Desire." [MidAR] (13:2) 92, p. 31-32.
6644. VERSTEGEN, Peter
"Little Litany for the Third World" (tr. by James Brockway). [Stand] (33:4) Aut 92, p. 116.
6645. VÉRTES, László
"Letter to the American Poet Gregory Corso" (tr. of Sándor Csoóri, w. Len Roberts). [Agni] (36) 92, p. 253-255.

"No Kin of Yours, Just a Friend" (tr. of Sándor Csoóri, w. Len Roberts). [KenR] (NS 14:1) Wint 92, p. 86-87.
"Somebody Consoles Me with a Poem" (tr. of Sándor Csoóri, w. Len Roberts). [KenR] (NS 14:1) Wint 92, p. 85-86.

6646. VERTREACE, Martha M.
"The Crossing." [Elf] (2:3) Fall 92, p. 22-27.
"Dickson Mounds" (for Jim Plath). [SpoonRQ] (17:3/4) Sum-Fall 92, p. 119-120.
"Elmhurst-Chicago Stone Company." [Farm] (9:2) Fall-Wint 92-93, p. 60-61.
"Hurricane Hazel." [Epiphany] (3:4) O (Fall) 92, p. 253.
"Trimming Woodwork." [Epiphany] (3:4) O (Fall) 92, p. 252.

6647. VETOCK, Jeff
"Passage" (Selections: 3 poems). [WashR] (18:3) O-N 92, p. 11.

VIDAL, Carlos Adolfo Gutierrez
See GUTIERREZ VIDAL, Carlos Adolfo

6648. VIDLER, John
"Dangerous." [Bogg] (65) 92, p. 33.

6649. VIERECK, Peter
"Games." [Salm] (94/95) Spr-Sum 92, p. 137.
"Looking Around." [AmerPoR] (21:4) Jl-Ag 92, p. 6.
"Tide." [Boulevard] (7:2/3, #20/21) Fall 92, p. 29-69.

6650. VIGIL, Mary Black
"Shapechanger: The Muse." [NegC] (12:1/2) 92, p. 199.

6651. VIGIL-PIÑON, Evangelina
"The Bridge People." [Americas] (20:3/4) Fall-Wint 92, p. 161-162.
"Dumb Broad!" [Americas] (20:3/4) Fall-Wint 92, p. 163-165.
"Telephone Line." [Americas] (20:3/4) Fall-Wint 92, p. 166-168.

6652. VILCHIS, Jaime B.
"Bolero." [Ometeca] (2:2) 91 [published 92], p. 28-30.

6653. VILLALONGO, José A., Sr.
"Witness for a Marriage Certificate, Paterson Board of Health July 20, 1991." [Footwork] 92, p. 75.

6654. VILLANO, Nancy
"In the Waiting Room." [Footwork] 92, p. 100.

6655. VILLANUEVA, Alma
"The Continuance." [SinW] (47) Sum-Fall 92, p. 140-141.

6656. VILLANUEVA, Tino
"Alliance of the Kingdoms" (Selections from Part II. Flocks: 1-2, 5-6, tr. of Jorge Esquinca). [Manoa] (4:2) Fall 92, p. 128-130.
"La Aventuranza de la Sedición." [InterPR] (18:1) Spr 92, p. 36, 38.
"Convocation of Words" (tr. by James Hoggard). [TriQ] (86) Wint 92-93, p. 96-97.
"Promised Lands" (tr. by James Hoggard). [TriQ] (86) Wint 92-93, p. 93-95.
"Venturesome Sedition" (tr. by Manuel López Bilbao). [InterPR] (18:1) Spr 92, p. 37, 39.
"You, If No One Else" (tr. by James Hoggard). [TriQ] (86) Wint 92-93, p. 91-92.

VILLARD, Denis
See DAVERTIGE (Denis Villard)

6657. VILLAURRUTIA, Xavier
"Nocturne in Which Death Speaks" (tr. by Felix Jimenez). [Thrpny] (49) Spr 92, p. 16.
"Nostalgia for Death" (1938, 2 selections, tr. by Eliot Weinberger). [Sulfur] (12:2, #31) Fall 92, p. 54-57.

6658. VINOGRAD, Julia
"Growing Up Without Religion." [ChironR] (11:1) Spr 92, p. 12.
"Safe Sex." [Art&Und] (1:2) Wint 92, p. 8.
"Summer" (from "Eye Contact Is a Confession"). [PoetryUSA] (24) 92, p. 25.
"T.V. Coverage." [ChironR] (11:1) Spr 92, p. 12.
"Why I'm Against the Death Penalty" (for Robert Harris). [ChironR] (11:1) Spr 92, p. 12.

6659. VINZ, Mark
"The Lesson" (for the poetry class). [HayF] (11) Fall-Wint 92, p. 90.
"Reckonings" (near Minneota, Minnesota, for Bill Holm). [HighP] (7:3) Wint 92, p. 93.

6660. VIOLI, Paul
"Narrative Drift." [Talisman] (8) Spr 92, p. 180-181.
"Sideshow." [Sulfur] (12:2, #31) Fall 92, p. 58-66.

6661. VISCUSI, Robert
"Advice from Heroes." [Footwork] 92, p. 66.
"Catechism." [Footwork] 92, p. 66.
"The Doctor Who Came from Italy." [Footwork] 92, p. 66.
"The Fat Parade." [Footwork] 92, p. 66.
6662. VITEK, Jack
"Correspondence." [Amelia] (6:4, #19) 92, p. 67.
"Paco." [Amelia] (7:1, #20) 92, p. 77.
6663. VITIELLO, Christopher
"Residue." [Verse] (9:2) Sum 92, p. 96.
6664. VITIELLO, Justin
"I Grew Up As Turnpikes." [Footwork] 92, p. 50.
"Russian Roulette." [Footwork] 92, p. 49.
VITO, E. B. de
See De VITO, E. B.
6665. VIVES, Pancho
"Este Miedo." [LindLM] (11:1) Mr 92, p. 19.
"Los Grandes Arboles Que Vi en la Tarde." [LindLM] (11:1) Mr 92, p. 19.
6666. VIVIAN, Pat
"Holding" (Selection from "The Singing Bridge: A National AIDS Poetry Archive"). [Art&Und] (1:1) Fall 91, p. 15.
6667. VLASOPOLOS, Anca
"Colossal Dream." [SpoonRQ] (17:1/2) Wint-Spr 92, p. 94-96.
"Life in the Country." [CumbPR] (12:1) Fall 92, p. 25.
6668. VNUCAK, Ann
"Almost." [PassN] (13:2) Wint 92, p. 7.
"Excerpts From My Father's War Journal." [PassN] (13:2) Wint 92, p. 6.
"An Unmailed Letter to a Dead Kid Brother" (129th Construction Battalion, Lingayen Gulf, 1944). [LullwaterR] (3:3) Sum 92, p. 44-45.
6669. VOGEL, Angela
"Breaking Bread Outside the Museum Cafe." [CapeR] (27:2) Fall 92, p. 20.
6670. VOGEL, Constance
"The Borrower." [WillowR] (19) Spr 92, p. 27.
"Lily Glow." [Elf] (2:3) Fall 92, p. 39.
"Sisters." [EngJ] (81:1) Ja 92, p. 96.
6671. VOGEL, Frank
"A Bladder Matter." [Light] (4) Wint 92-93, p. 21.
"Unflurried" (Thanksgiving, 1991). [Hellas] (3:2) Fall 92, p. 32.
6672. VOGELSANG, Arthur
"40 Watts." [Pequod] (33) 92, p. 136.
"2215 Spruce." [ColR] (9:1) Spr-Sum 92, p. 43.
"The Alps." [Pequod] (33) 92, p. 134-135.
"Double Bind." [ColR] (9:1) Spr-Sum 92, p. 44.
"The Face." [Pequod] (33) 92, p. 137.
"The Future." [DenQ] (26:3) Wint 92, p. 48-49.
"Kisser." [Pequod] (33) 92, p. 138.
"Philadelphia." [DenQ] (26:3) Wint 92, p. 50.
"Slipping Around." [AmerV] (26) Spr 92, p. 80.
"Two Monkeys." [ColR] (9:1) Spr-Sum 92, p. 42.
"Two Problems." [Pequod] (33) 92, p. 139-140.
"A Video Unit and Its Destination in Eastern Europe." [Pequod] (33) 92, p. 141-142.
6673. VOIGT, Ellen Bryant
"At the Piano: Variations." [TriQ] (84) Spr-Sum 92, p. 120-122.
"Effort at Speech" (for William Meredith). [SouthernR] (28:4) Aut, O 92, p. 908 - 909.
"First Song." [TriQ] (84) Spr-Sum 92, p. 118-119.
"Fish." [SouthernR] (28:4) Aut, O 92, p. 909-910.
"Gobelins." [VirQR] (68:3) Sum 92, p. 495-496.
"The Harness." [SouthernR] (28:4) Aut, O 92, p. 912-913.
"Herzenlied." [SouthernR] (28:4) Aut, O 92, p. 910-911.
"The Pond." [SouthernR] (28:4) Aut, O 92, p. 911-912.
"Self-Portrait at Laguardia." [SenR] (22:1) Spr 92, p. 5.
"Song and Story." [Atlantic] (269:5) My 92, p. 113.
"The Soothsayer." [Thrpny] (50) Sum 92, p. 11.
"Thorn-Apple." [NewEngR] (14:3) Sum 92, p. 219.
"Thorn-Apple: Variations." [NewEngR] (14:3) Sum 92, p. 220-222.

"Variations: The Innocents." [AmerPoR] (21:5) S-O 92, p. 41-42.
6674. VOLBORTH, Judith
"Native Winter" (for Brenda). [Jacaranda] (6:1/2) Wint-Spr 92, p. 99.
6675. VOLDSETH, Beverly
"I Wash the Bodies." [SingHM] (20) 92, p. 45-46.
"Spring Poem." [RagMag] (10:1) 92, p. 75.
"Still Life with Apple." [RagMag] (10:2) 92, p. 103.
6676. VOLKMAN, Karen
"Awards Night." [SouthernR] (28:4) Aut, O 92, p. 914-915.
"Evening." [TarRP] (31:2) Spr 92, p. 23.
"The Late Show." [QW] (34) Wint-Spr 92, p. 81-82.
"Over Coffee." [PraS] (66:1) Spr 92, p. 27.
"The Pregnant Lady Playing Tennis." [PraS] (66:1) Spr 92, p. 26.
"Wings, Mouth, Range." [PraS] (66:1) Spr 92, p. 28-29.
6677. VOLKOW, Verónica
"The Beginning" (Selections: 1, 9, tr. by Iona Wishaw). [TriQ] (85) Fall 92, p. 342-344.
"The House" (tr. by Iona Whishaw). [LitR] (25:2) Wint 92, p. 215.
"In the Valley of Zapata" (tr. by Iona Whishaw). [LitR] (25:2) Wint 92, p. 216-217.
"Popocatépetl" (tr. by Reginald Gibbons). [TriQ] (85) Fall 92, p. 345.
"Quito" (tr. by Reginald Gibbons). [TriQ] (85) Fall 92, p. 346.
"The Star" (tr. by Iona Whishaw). [LitR] (25:2) Wint 92, p. 216.
Von SCHOULTZ, Solveig
See SCHOULTZ, Solveig von
6678. VOPAT, Carole
"You Open the Door" (for Michael Guard, July 22, 1954-April 8, 1992). [JamesWR] (9:4) Sum 92, p. 15.
"Your Armani Smile" (for Peter Austin Weber, April 28, 1953-June 7, 1991). [JamesWR] (9:4) Sum 92, p. 15.
6679. VORA, Kamal
"Crow" (tr. by Karamshi Pir). [ChiR] (38:1/2) 92, p. 205.
6680. VOSE, Devon
"Bed and Breakfast." [BellArk] (8:1) Ja-F 92, p. 7.
"Bellevue Evening." [BellArk] (8:6) N-D 92, p. 25.
"Breaking Ground." [BellArk] (8:6) N-D 92, p. 25.
"Dancing Balloons." [BellArk] (8:1) Ja-F 92, p. 6.
"Lake." [BellArk] (8:3) My-Je 92, p. 23.
"Single Daffodil." [BellArk] (8:4) Jl-Ag 92, p. 23.
"Small Rain." [BellArk] (8:4) Jl-Ag 92, p. 21.
"Spring Break." [BellArk] (8:4) Jl-Ag 92, p. 21.
"This Deck." [BellArk] (8:6) N-D 92, p. 25.
VOSS, Dale de
See DeVOSS, Dale
6681. VOSS, Fred
"Apples and Oranges." [SlipS] (12) 92, p. 62.
"Attacking the Problem" (Special Section: 39 poems). [WormR] (32:4 #128) 92, p. 147-166.
"Bad." [Pearl] (16) Fall 92, p. 26.
"Get a Job." [SlipS] (12) 92, p. 61.
"God Bless America." [SlipS] (12) 92, p. 63.
"Good Customer." [Pearl] (15) Spr-Sum 92, p. 11.
"Great Potential." [Pearl] (15) Spr-Sum 92, p. 10.
"Hierarchy." [SlipS] (12) 92, p. 59-60.
"Institutions." [SlipS] (12) 92, p. 60-61.
"Malpractice." [Pearl] (15) Spr-Sum 92, p. 10.
"Men of Steel." [SlipS] (12) 92, p. 59.
"On Their Own." [Pearl] (16) Fall 92, p. 26.
"Praying to Be Recalled." [SlipS] (12) 92, p. 62-63.
"Safety Valve." [SlipS] (12) 92, p. 63-64.
"Splurging." [SlipS] (12) 92, p. 58.
"Thanks a Lot." [SlipS] (12) 92, p. 64.
"Wasting Time." [SlipS] (12) 92, p. 60.
6682. VOZNESENSKY, Andrei
"Five Drops of Sky" (tr. by F. D. Reeve). [AmerPoR] (21:1) Ja-F 92, p. 48.
6683. VRETTAKOS, Nikiphoros
"The Speech of Hands" (tr. by Thomas Doulis). [Nimrod] (35:2) Spr-Sum 92, p. 72.

6684. VUCKOVIC, Vladeta
"Inventory of a Poem" (for Vasco Popa, tr. of Branko Miljkovic, w. John Matthias). [TriQ] (86) Wint 92-93, p. 39.
"An Orphic Legacy" (tr. of Branko Miljkovic, w. John Matthias). [TriQ] (86) Wint 92-93, p. 41.
"While You Are Singing" (tr. of Branko Miljkovic, w. John Matthias). [TriQ] (86) Wint 92-93, p. 40.
6685. W. T. K.
"Mirage." [GreensboroR] (52) Sum 92, p. 18.
6686. WACHTEL, Chuck
"Diarrhea" (tr. of Fernando Silva). [HangL] (60) 92, p. 58-61.
"Epigram" (tr. of Fernando Silva). [HangL] (60) 92, p. 62.
"La Salud del Niño" (Selection: Foreword, tr. of Fernando Silva). [HangL] (60) 92, p. 62.
6687. WACKETT, Jim
"Liturgy." [CreamCR] (16:2) Fall 92, p. 80.
6688. WADELL, Chuck
"I Have No Words." [RagMag] (10:2) 92, p. 75.
6689. WAGNER, Anneliese
"Heinz Jost's Birthday: September 19, 1941." [KenR] (NS 14:2) Spr 92, p. 139-140.
"Vienna, 1938" (for Muriel Gardiner, the model for Julia). [NegC] (12:3) 92, p. 119.
6690. WAGNER, Chuck
"Blimps." [HopewellR] (4) 92, p. 8.
"The Ships of the British Navy." [HopewellR] (4) 92, p. 12.
6691. WAGNER, Mark
"A Fine Cold." [Agni] (36) 92, p. 87-88.
"The Horn of Hard Water." [Agni] (36) 92, p. 85-86.
6692. WAGNER, Mary Michael
"Bedtime Story." [SpoonRQ] (17:3/4) Sum-Fall 92, p. 33-35.
"Mother." [SpoonRQ] (17:3/4) Sum-Fall 92, p. 31-32.
6693. WAGNER, Maryfrances
"What We Become." [MidwQ] (33:2) Wint 92, p. 208.
6694. WAGNER, Richard
"The Roller-Skaters" (tr. by Margitt Lehbert). [Shiny] (7/8) 92, p. 134.
"What Is Normal" (tr. by Margitt Lehbert). [Shiny] (7/8) 92, p. 134-135.
6695. WAGNER, Robert
"The Corner Store." [SmPd] (29:2, #85) Spr 92, p. 23.
"The Dresser." [SmPd] (29:3, #86) Fall 92, p. 7.
"Extended Epode to an Olive." [Light] (1) Spr 92, p. 11.
"Shine, Sir?" [SmPd] (29:2, #85) Spr 92, p. 22.
"Wonders Never Cease." [Light] (4) Wint 92-93, p. 25.
6696. WAGNER, Shari
"The Dog That Disappeared in a Storm and Never Came Back." [HopewellR] (4) 92, p. 33.
"The Farm Wife Sees the Shadows of Great Ships." [HopewellR] (4) 92, p. 12.
6697. WAGNER, Shelly
"For Ashley." [OnTheBus] (4:2/5:1, #10/11) 92, p. 228.
"Shoes." [OnTheBus] (4:2/5:1, #10/11) 92, p. 227-228.
6698. WAH, Fred
"Music at the Heart of Thinking" (5 selections). [WestCL] (25:3, #6) Wint 91-92, p. 185-187.
6699. WAHLE, F. Keith
"Meditation on Mortality." [CinPR] (23) Wint 91-92, p. 66-67.
6700. WAHLERT, Donna
"Explaining to My Children." [Kalliope] (15:1) 92, p. 41.
6701. WAID, Mark
"Monochromat." [Talisman] (9) Fall 92, p. 196-197.
6702. WAIDTLOW, Donna
"After the Flight of the Tern." [BellArk] (8:1) Ja-F 92, p. 7.
6703. WAKOSKI, Diane
"Blue Suede Shoes." [CreamCR] (16:2) Fall 92, p. 103-105.
"Emeralds." [Paint] (19:37) Spr 92, p. 24.
"His Bedroom Voice." [CreamCR] (16:2) Fall 92, p. 106-107.
"Jason the Sailor" (A section, volume II, "The Archaeology of Movies and Books"). [Manoa] (4:2) Fall 92, p. 57-67.
"On the Terrace of Point Dume." [Paint] (19:37) Spr 92, p. 22-23.

WAL, Jane Aaron Vander
See Vander WAL, Jane Aaron

6704. WALD, Diane
"More to Say." [ColEng] (53:8) D 91, p. 905-907.

6705. WALDECKI, Michael E.
"Before the Mill-Rats Got Laid-Off." [SlipS] (12) 92, p. 78.
"Lost Somewhere in Old-Timers Cafe." [SlipS] (12) 92, p. 78.
"Quality Control." [SlipS] (12) 92, p. 78.

6706. WALDEN, William
"Feeble Resolve." [Light] (4) Wint 92-93, p. 12.

6707. WALDERS, Davi
"Jephtha's Daughter." [SenR] (22:1) Spr 92, p. 58-59.

6708. WALDMAN, Gloria F.
"Alone" (tr. of Lolita Lebron). [LitR] (35:4) Sum 92, p. 519.
"I Have Seen You" (tr. of Lolita Lebron). [LitR] (35:4) Sum 92, p. 520.

6709. WALDMAN, Ken
"Big Moose Hits Truck." [Manoa] (4:1) Spr 92, p. 110-111.
"Indian Summer at the Salvage Yard: A Flywheel Cover." [SycamoreR] (4:1) Wint 92, p. 50.
"Washing Dishes on My 33rd Birthday." [Manoa] (4:1) Spr 92, p. 109-110.
"Wesley." [Pearl] (15) Spr-Sum 92, p. 52.

6710. WALDROP, Keith
"i.e." (Selections: 7-8, tr. of Claude Royet-Journoud). [Avec] (5:1) 92, p. 55-56.
"Potential Random" (Excerpts). [Avec] (5:1) 92, p. 40-42.

6711. WALDROP, Rosmarie
"Heiligenanstalt" (tr. of Friederike Mayröcker). [GrandS] (11:2, #42) 92, p. 49-56.
"A Key into the Language of America." [Avec] (5:1) 92, p. 47-49.
"A Wanderer's Phrase Buch" (tr. of Tom Ahern for German travelers). [Avec] (5:1) 92, p. 25-27.

6712. WALKER, Alice
"Right to Life: What Can the White Man Say to the Black Woman?" [Conscience] (13:2) Sum 92, p. 26.

6713. WALKER, Anne
"I Didn't Think These Places Existed." [AntigR] (89) Spr 92, p. 132.

6714. WALKER, David
"Bakersfield Winters." [Amelia] (6:4, #19) 92, p. 106.

6715. WALKER, Jeanne Cowan
"Overheard." [OxfordM] (8:2) Fall-Wint 92, p. 70.

6716. WALKER, Jeanne Murray
"The Accident." [Shen] (42:2) Sum 92, p. 104-106.
"The Immigrants Stranded." [Shen] (42:1) Spr 92, p. 85-86.
"Immigrating from Russia, 1909." [Shen] (42:1) Spr 92, p. 84-85.
"Stranger Than Fiction: The Notes & Queries of a *Daily Exposé* Reporter — A Poem in Voices" (for Molly). [QRL] (Poetry Series 11: vol. 31) 92, 79 p.

6717. WALKER, John
"Forever Blue (Ode to Chet Baker)." [MoodySI] (27) Spr 92, p. 11.
"Jack (1)." [MoodySI] (27) Spr 92, p. 11.

6718. WALKER, Larry
"Designs of Skin, Religion, and Trade." [SpoonRQ] (17:3/4) Sum-Fall 92, p. 108 - 109.
"Giving Thanks on a Salmon Boat Off the Port of Kenosha." [BellArk] (8:1) Ja-F 92, p. 6.

6719. WALKER, Lynne
"The Apple." [WormR] (32:3, #127) 92, p. 93.
"Memorial Day (1990)." [WormR] (32:3, #127) 92, p. 94.

6720. WALKER, Sue
"Peahens and Flannery O'Connor." [Kalliope] (14:3) 92, p. 31.

6721. WALLACE, Anne C.
"Arlene." [Footwork] 92, p. 61.
"Cold in the House." [Footwork] 92, p. 62.
"Ernest." [Footwork] 92, p. 61.

6722. WALLACE, Bonnie Jeanne
"Waiting to Bleed." [Conscience] (13:3) Aut 92, p. 21.

6723. WALLACE, D. M.
"Looking for Someone." [SilverFR] (23) Wint 92, p. 19.

6724. WALLACE, Jan
"The Ladies of the Club." [PoetryNW] (33:1) Spr 92, p. 47.
"Ornithology Lesson." [PoetryNW] (33:1) Spr 92, p. 46-47.
"The Passion of Doctor Dixie." [PoetryNW] (33:1) Spr 92, p. 45.
"Surrender" (for Gray Lambert, 1958-1991). [Field] (46) Spr 92, p. 44.
"Under" (for pk). [Field] (46) Spr 92, p. 43.
6725. WALLACE, Lili
"My Grandmother's House." [Kalliope] (15:1) 92, p. 44.
6726. WALLACE, Naomi
"Ode to Blood." [Salm] (93) Wint 92, p. 186.
6727. WALLACE, Robert
"Ars Celare Artem." [Light] (3) Aut 92, p. 9.
"Cellular." [Light] (4) Wint 92-93, p. 14.
"The Double Play." [ThRiPo] (39/40) 92-93, p. 264-265.
"Driving By." [ThRiPo] (39/40) 92-93, p. 263.
"A Fresco of Swans and Bears." [ThRiPo] (39/40) 92-93, p. 263.
"In a Spring Still Not Written Of." [ThRiPo] (39/40) 92-93, p. 265-266.
"Per Aspera ad Astra." [Light] (3) Aut 92, p. 24.
"Riding in a Stranger's Funeral." [ThRiPo] (39/40) 92-93, p. 264.
6728. WALLACE, Ronald
"1959." [ArtfulD] (22/23) 92, p. 139.
"The Bad Carpenter." [Poem] (67) My 92, p. 62.
"Earthly Pleasures." [AmerS] (61:4) Aut 92, p. 563-564.
"February 14." [Poetry] (159:5) F 92, p. 281.
"The Furnace Men." [Poetry] (161:3) D 92, p. 152.
"Pantoum: The Sturdy of Worry." [PoetryNW] (33:2) Sum 92, p. 29.
"The Sitting Place." [Poem] (67) My 92, p. 64.
"Sweetcorn." [ArtfulD] (22/23) 92, p. 138.
"War and Peace." [Poem] (67) My 92, p. 63.
"A Word in the Face." [TarRP] (31:2) Spr 92, p. 42.
6729. WALLACE, T. H. S.
"But I, I, Telemachus." [ChironR] (11:2) Sum 92, p. 28.
"Summa." [ChironR] (11:3) Aut 92, p. 28.
6730. WALLACE-CRABBE, Chris
"Paperboy Time." [Verse] (9:3) Wint 92, p. 149.
WALLEGHEN, Michael van
See Van WALLEGHEN, Michael
6731. WALLENSTEIN, Barry
"Bliss/L." [OxfordM] (7:1) Spr-Sum 91, p. 96.
"The Comedy Show." [Confr] (50) Fall 92, p. 264.
6732. WALLS, Doyle Wesley
"Burning Poems." [Interim] (11:2) Fall-Wint 92-93, p. 17-19.
"Settling In." [BelPoJ] (43:2) Wint 92-93, p. 38.
6733. WALSH, Joy
"Driver Meets Leo Kirby in Vermont." [SlipS] (12) 92, p. 40-41.
6734. WALSH, Marnie
"Emmet-Kills Warrior, Turtle Mountain Reservation." [Jacaranda] (6:1/2) Wint-Spr 92, p. 100-101.
6735. WALSH, Marty
"The Battle of San Romano." [Poem] (68) N 92, p. 24.
"Buddha and the Moose." [BelPoJ] (42:4) Sum 92, p. 15.
"The Secret of Flying." [Plain] (13:1) Fall 92, p. 29.
"Under Brennock Hill." [Poem] (68) N 92, p. 23.
6736. WALSH, Sara K.
"The Mandarin's Clothes." [US1] (26/27) 92, p. 44.
6737. WALSH, William
"The Dream Team." [Spitball] (42) Fall 92, p. 8-9.
6738. WALTER, Eugene
"Dailyness." [NegC] (12:1/2) 92, p. 117.
"Late One Night." [NegC] (12:1/2) 92, p. 116.
"The Poet on His Seventieth Birthday." [NegC] (12:1/2) 92, p. 114-115.
6739. WALTER, Victor
"I'll Get a Horse." [ChamLR] (10/11) Spr-Fall 92, p. 160.
6740. WALTERS, Berylene
"Fishing Loreto." [BellR] (15:2) Fall 92, p. 16-17.

6741. WALZER, Kevin
"Road Deconstruction." [PoetC] (23:3) Spr 92, p. 35.
6742. WANEK, Connie
"Ski Tracks." [VirQR] (68:4) Aut 92, p. 706-707.
6743. WANG, Lenore Baeli
"Grandma's Player Piano." [Footwork] 92, p. 91.
"On Killing Insects" (for Sue Hettmansperger). [SinW] (48) Wint 92-93, p. 79-80.
WANG, Ping
See PING, Wang
6744. WANG, Tai Peng
"Timeless Faces of Beijing Opera." [Gypsy] (19) 92, p. 57-58.
6745. WANG, Wei
"Deep South Mountain" (tr. by Tony Barnstone, Willis Barnstone and Xu Haixin). [LitR] (25:2) Wint 92, p. 220.
"For Someone Far Away" (tr. by Tony Barnstone, Willis Barnstone and Xu Haixin). [LitR] (25:2) Wint 92, p. 220.
"In Response to Vice-Magistrate Chang" (tr. by David Lunde). [HampSPR] Wint 92, p. 11.
"In the Mountains" (tr. by Tony Barnstone, Willis Barnstone and Xu Haixin). [LitR] (25:2) Wint 92, p. 221.
"Lakeside Pavilion" (tr. by Tony Barnstone, Willis Barnstone and Xu Haixin). [LitR] (25:2) Wint 92, p. 221.
"Night Over the Huai River" (tr. by Tony Barnstone, Willis Barnstone and Xu Haixin). [LitR] (25:2) Wint 92, p. 220.
"Seeing Yuan Second Off to An Hsi" (tr. by David Lunde). [HampSPR] Wint 92, p. 11.
"Winter Night, Writing About My Emotion" (tr. by Tony Barnstone, Willis Barnstone and Xu Haixin). [LitR] (25:2) Wint 92, p. 221.
6746. WANG, Yun
"Ding Feng Bo (Calming the Wind and Waves)" (tr. of Dong-Po Su). [WillowS] (30) Sum 92, p. 16.
"Discord." [Vis] (38) 92, p. 45.
"Qian Diao (The Front Tune)" (tr. of Dong-Po Su). [WillowS] (30) Sum 92, p. 17.
"A Tree in 'Cultural Revolution'." [PoetL] (87:4) Wint 92-93, p. 17-18.
6747. WANIEK, Marilyn (Marilyn Nelson)
"Abba Jacob and the Angel" (homage to Henri Cartier-Bresson). [SouthernR] (28:1) Wint, Ja 92, p. 100.
"Abba Jacob at Bat." [SouthernR] (28:1) Wint, Ja 92, p. 99.
"Diverne's Waltz." [Hellas] (3:2) Fall 92, p. 89.
"Epithalamium and Shivaree" (for Linda and Debbie). [Obs] (7:1/2) Spr-Sum 92, p. 119.
"The Sacrament of Poverty" (for Judy Maines, in memory of David LaMarre). [Obs] (7:1/2) Spr-Sum 92, p. 118.
"Solitude in Soweto." [SouthernR] (28:1) Wint, Ja 92, p. 100.
6748. WANLESS, Norma
"Bordado o Picadero." [Nuez] (4:12) 92, p. 14.
"Felino Entorno." [Nuez] (4:12) 92, p. 14.
"Murciélago." [Nuez] (4:12) 92, p. 14.
6749. WAPNER, Kenneth
"My Friend the Buddhist Priest." [Archae] (4) late 92-early 93, p. 35.
"Pale Threads." [Archae] (4) late 92-early 93, p. 37.
"Red Bean Ice Cream." [Archae] (4) late 92-early 93, p. 38.
"The Temple Harlot and the Old Straw Mat." [Archae] (4) late 92-early 93, p. 36.
6750. WARAT, Ruth
"Inquisitors, Dead and in Power. Their Use of Torture is Abominable, ..." [Chelsea] (53) 92, p. 116-117.
"Love and Hunt in the Dark Room" (After photographs by Emmet Gowin). [Chelsea] (53) 92, p. 118-119.
"Reunion. Class of 1966." [AntigR] (89) Spr 92, p. 61-62.
6751. WARD, B. J.
"Bleeding Jesus." [HiramPoR] (51/52) Fall 91-Sum 92, p. 75-76.
"Dancing with the Teacher" (for Maureen Kosa). [HiramPoR] (51/52) Fall 91-Sum 92, p. 77-78.
"Drunk Again, I Stumble Home on Euclid and Cut Across Thornden Park Baseball Field." [Sun] (201) S 92, p. 38.
"Hometown: Alliance, New Jersey." [Sun] (201) S 92, p. 38.

6752. WARD, David
"Something Like a Symphony" (Excerpts). [Bogg] (65) 92, p. 17.
6753. WARD, Hazel
"The Long Look Back." [Sparrow] (59) S 92, p. 20.
"Paul Klee." [Sparrow] (59) S 92, p. 20.
6754. WARD, Herman M.
"The Old Dance." [Footwork] 92, p. 96.
6755. WARD, Robert (*See also* WARD, Robert R.)
"A Butcher Explains to His Children the Significance of His Father's Stroke" (from "Seven Views of a Nursing Home"). [Jacaranda] (6:1/2) Wint-Spr 92, p. 144-145.
"Winter Fields, 1962." [SilverFR] (23) Wint 92, p. 7-9.
6756. WARD, Robert R. (*See also* WARD, Robert)
"Even Little Words Make Boxes That Are Hard to Get Out Of" (A Plainsongs Award Poem). [Plain] (13:1) Fall 92, p. 38.
"Hawk, Heron, Her." [RagMag] (10:2) 92, p. 86-89.
6757. WARD, Scott
"Abandoned Convalescent Home at Blount Springs, Alabama." [HiramPoR] (51/52) Fall 91-Sum 92, p. 79-80.
"The Last Night." [HiramPoR] (51/52) Fall 91-Sum 92, p. 81-82.
"The O-H Bond." [OnTheBus] (4:2/5:1, #10/11) 92, p. 229-230.
6758. WARD, Thomas
"Degrees of Absence West of Rainier." [Spitball] (40) Spr 92, p. 22-23.
6759. WARDEN, Marine Robert
"For Ora." [Asylum] (7:3/4) 92, p. 54.
WARHAFT, Gail Holst
See HOLST-WARHAFT, Gail
6760. WARING, Richard
"For Mount Desert Island" (Excerpt). [Noctiluca] (1:2) Wint 92 [on cover: Wint 93], p. 8.
6761. WARR, Michael
"Searching for Hair in Stockholm." [NewAW] (10) Fall 92, p. 113.
6762. WARREN, Gerry
"You're Being Paged." [WritersF] (18) 92, p. 162.
6763. WARREN, Hans
"Sometimes" (tr. by James Brockway). [Stand] (33:4) Aut 92, p. 115.
6764. WARREN, Rebecca
"Boston Museum: Ch'in Terra Cottas." [Pembroke] (24) 92, p. 140.
"The True History of the World." [Pembroke] (24) 92, p. 139.
6765. WARREN, Rosanna
"The Broken Pot." [SenR] (22:2) Fall 92, p. 11-13.
"The Farm." [Boulevard] (7:2/3, #20/21) Fall 92, p. 119.
"A Garland from Alcman" (tr. of Alcman). [Arion] 3d series (1:1) Wint 90, p. 179.
"Hagar." [SenR] (22:2) Fall 92, p. 16-17.
"In Creve Coeur, Missouri." [AnthNEW] (4) 92, p. 8.
"Lena's House: Watercolor" (for ECW, with apologies to Sir Philip Sidney). [SenR] (22:2) Fall 92, p. 14-15.
"An Old Cubist" (Reverdy photographed by Brassai, Paris, 1947). [SenR] (22:2) Fall 92, p. 18-19.
"The Twelfth Day." [YaleR] (80:4) O 92, p. 40-42.
"Two Days Before." [GeoR] (46:2) Sum 92, p. 357.
"Umbilical" (for Katherine, age 8). [Boulevard] (7:2/3, #20/21) Fall 92, p. 120-122.
6766. WARREN, Shirley
"The Night Gardener." [SingHM] (20) 92, p. 58.
6767. WARRINGTON, Neil
"The Wall at Visnar." [Verse] (8:3/9:1) Wint-Spr 92, p. 101.
6768. WARROCK, Anna M.
"Demeter's Daughters." [CumbPR] (12:1) Fall 92, p. 4-5.
"Family Fights." [CapeR] (27:1) Spr 92, p. 25.
"Vermeer" (First Prize, Robert Penn Warren Poetry Prize). [CumbPR] (12:1) Fall 92, p. 2-3.
6769. WARSH, Lewis
"Elective Surgery." [Shiny] (7/8) 92, p. 101-105.
"Travelogue." [AmerPoR] (21:4) Jl-Ag 92, p. 48.
6770. WARWICK, Ioanna-Veronika
"After." [PaintedB] (47) 92, p. 38.

"Bird Milk." [SouthernPR] (32:2) Fall 92, p. 62-63.
"Blood Soup" (Honorable Mention, The Paintbrush Award, Poetry). [PaintedHR] (7) Fall 92, p. 14-15.
"Census" (tr. of Wislawa Szymborska). [SenR] (22:2) Fall 92, p. 47-48.
"The Class Photograph." [MinnR] (38) Spr-Sum 92, p. 19-20.
"The Cleaning Woman." [MinnR] (38) Spr-Sum 92, p. 18-19.
"The Cleaning Woman." [SoCoast] (12) Ja 92, p. 42-43.
"The Dumb Supper." [SpoonRQ] (17:1/2) Wint-Spr 92, p. 12-13.
"Factories in Lodz." [SpoonRQ] (17:1/2) Wint-Spr 92, p. 16.
"Grand Canyon." [Parting] (5:2) Wint 92-93, p. 37.
"Gratitude" (tr. of Wislawa Szymborska). [SenR] (22:2) Fall 92, p. 43-44.
"The High Diver" (First Prize, 1992 Literary Contest). [Crucible] (28) Fall 92, p. 1 - 2.
"Holofernes." [PaintedB] (47) 92, p. 34-35.
"Hurricane Ridge." [MidwQ] (33:4) Sum 92, p. 418.
"In the Middle of Life" (tr. of Tadeusz Rózewicz). [SenR] (22:2) Fall 92, p. 50-51.
"Laundry: A Historical Document." [PaintedB] (47) 92, p. 36-37.
"Lot's Wife" (tr. of Wislawa Szymborska). [SenR] (22:2) Fall 92, p. 45-46.
"Member of the Church." [SpoonRQ] (17:1/2) Wint-Spr 92, p. 14-15.
"Old Women" (tr. of Tadeusz Rózewicz). [SenR] (22:2) Fall 92, p. 49.
"Orpheus." [CapeR] (27:1) Spr 92, p. 26.
"Patriotism." [NoDaQ] (60:1) Wint 92, p. 291-292.
"Scars" (for Charles). [PaintedHR] (6) Spr 92, p. 34-35.
"Still Life with a Toy Balloon" (tr. of Wislawa Szymborska). [SenR] (22:2) Fall 92, p. 41-42.
"To an Unknown Lover." [Parting] (5:2) Wint 92-93, p. 5.
"Wheat" (for the people of the village of Ponikla). [NewOR] (19:1) Spr 92, p. 9.

6771. WASHINGTON, Gene
"San Donato di Torre, 17 March 1394." [Light] (2) Sum 92, p. 25-26.

6772. WATADA, Terry
"Whistling Past the Graveyard." [GreensboroR] (52) Sum 92, p. 138-139.

6773. WATERHOUSE, Philip A.
"Internal Bleeding." [Gypsy] (19) 92, p. 28.

6774. WATERMAN, Diane
"Jack Kerouac's Cat." [MoodySI] (27) Spr 92, p. 2.

6775. WATERS, Chocolate
"My Personal Wants to Get Personal With You" (SWF seeks SWM or BJM or DJM or MWM or M&M's). [HolCrit] (29:2) Ap 92, p. 17.

6776. WATERS, Mary Ann
"Father of Turtles" (In the voice of Nicolas Pat Kab, Quintana Roo, Mexico). [SenR] (22:2) Fall 92, p. 91-92.
"Humpty Dumpty." [GettyR] (5:1) Wint 92, p. 178.
"Humpty Dumpty." [Harp] (284:1705) Je 92, p. 40.
"Ping-Pong Doubles Match." [Witness] (6:2) 92, p. 142-143.
"Señor Tristeza." [GettyR] (5:1) Wint 92, p. 177.

6777. WATERS, Michael
"Fifth Alarm." [NoDaQ] (60:3) Sum 92, p. 86.
"Gridlock." [CimR] (98) Ja 92, p. 86.
"Keats' Lips." [ThRiPo] (39/40) 92-93, p. 266-268.
"Miles Weeping" (Koh Samui, Thailand). [ThRiPo] (39/40) 92-93, p. 268-269.
"The Mystery of the Caves." [ThRiPo] (39/40) 92-93, p. 270-271.
"Not Love" (For KH). [Poetry] (160:4) Jl 92, p. 194.
"Wasps" (for my father). [CimR] (98) Ja 92, p. 85.

6778. WATKINS, William John
"Acrostic Sonnet for Sandra." [SoCoast] (13) Je 93 [i.e. 92], p. 18.
"Marine Thermodynamics." [JlNJPo] (14:2) Aut 92, p. 18.
"Momentary Quavers." [SoCoast] (13) Je 93 [i.e. 92], p. 44.
"Paternoster for Poets Failing at Failing." [WritersF] (18) 92, p. 34.
"Talent and Other Parasites." [WritersF] (18) 92, p. 35.

6779. WATSON, Anna
"Merry-Go-Round" (tr. of Sachiko Yoshihara). [Vis] (38) 92, p. 21.

6780. WATSON, Anthony
"Redemption." [US1] (26/27) 92, p. 31.

6781. WATSON, Burton
"Kanshi" (Selection: 2 poems, tr. of Ryokan). [Trans] (26) Spr 92, p. 18.
"Waka" (7 selection, tr. of Ryokan). [Trans] (26) Spr 92, p. 19.

6782. WATSON, Lawrence
"End of Summer, Lake of the Woods, Minnesota." [WindO] (56) Fall-Wint 92, p. 23.
"Everything That Is Wrong with America." [HighP] (7:3) Wint 92, p. 113-114.
"Out-of-Body Experience." [CimR] (99) Ap 92, p. 46-47.
"Winter Light." [LaurelR] (26:2) Sum 92, p. 80-81.
"Writing Poems." [WindO] (56) Fall-Wint 92, p. 24.
6783. WATSON, Randall
"From the Treatment Center." [Shen] (42:4) Wint 92, p. 32-33.
6784. WATSON, Robert
"A Balloon Rises." [SoCarR] (25:1) Fall 92, p. 208.
6785. WATSON, Stephen
"Today." [Stand] (33:3) Sum 92, p. 70.
6786. WATT, Glenn
"The Wound." [PassN] (13:2) Wint 92, p. 22.
6787. WATTERSON, William Collins
"To a Young Museum Guard." [Poetry] (159:4) Ja 92, p. 222.
6788. WATTISON, Meredith
"Edvard Munch's Shoes." [Vis] (40) 92, p. 15.
"Green Almonds?" [Vis] (38) 92, p. 31.
6789. WATTS, David
"Little League Tryouts." [GettyR] (5:3) Sum 92, p. 547.
6790. WATTS, Margaret
"Fish Broth at a School in Rio Claro" (with thanks to Rabindranath). [LitR] (35:4) Sum 92, p. 568-570.
"The Lost Indian." [LitR] (35:4) Sum 92, p. 567.
"To a Correspondent Who Thought Before Seeing Me I Was Black." [LitR] (35:4) Sum 92, p. 568.
"To My Grandmother and Her Late Guffaw." [LitR] (35:4) Sum 92, p. 570.
6791. WAUGHTEL, Michele
"In Susie's Closet." [NewYorkQ] (49) 92, p. 94.
6792. WAYBRANT, Linda
"Connections." [PoetryC] (12:2) Ap 92, p. 16.
"I Have Ridden the Subway While It Rained Torrents." [PoetryC] (12:2) Ap 92, p. 16.
"In the Dark." [PoetryC] (12:2) Ap 92, p. 16.
6793. WAYMAN, Tom
"Billy on Industrial Progress." [PoetryNW] (33:1) Spr 92, p. 30-31.
"The Creeks of Richards Creek." [Caliban] (11) 92, p. 149.
"Dark Mirror." [Event] (21:3) Fall 92, p. 64-65.
"Headlands." [Event] (21:1) Spr 92, p. 52.
"The Houséd Heart." [Event] (21:1) Spr 92, p. 50-51.
"The Iceberg, the Shadow." [TriQ] (86) Wint 92-93, p. 42-44.
"In the Spirit." [Caliban] (11) 92, p. 150.
"The Loves of the Penis." [Event] (21:1) Spr 92, p. 48-49.
"The Man Who Logged the West Ridge." [OntR] (36) Spr-Sum 92, p. 84-85.
"The Politics of the House: Alarm Clock." [MalR] (101) Wint92, p. 79-80.
"The Politics of the House: Beds." [CanLit] (133) Sum 92, p. 54.
"The Politics of the House: Counters." [CanLit] (133) Sum 92, p. 55.
"The Politics of the House: The Elements." [MalR] (101) Wint92, p. 81-85.
"Thicket." [NoDaQ] (60:4) Fall 92, p. 135-136.
6794. WAYNE, Jane O.
"Intensive Care." [Poetry] (161:2) N 92, p. 83.
"On the Heart List." [Poetry] (161:2) N 92, p. 84.
"Waiting Room." [Poetry] (161:2) N 92, p. 82.
"Waking Up." [Poetry] (161:2) N 92, p. 85.
6795. WEATHERFORD, Carole Boston
"The Upper Hand." [Obs] (7:1/2) Spr-Sum 92, p. 120-123.
6796. WEAVER, Kathleen
"Rebirth" (tr. of Nancy Morejon, w. Pam Mordecai). [LitR] (35:4) Sum 92, p. 460.
"Soldier and I" (tr. of Nancy Morejon). [LitR] (35:4) Sum 92, p. 460.
6797. WEAVER, Michael (Michael S.)
"Ascensions and Disruptions" (for George H. Bass. Providence Journal VII). [AfAmRev] (26:2) Sum 92, p. 257.
"Hamilton Place." [Obs] (7:1/2) Spr-Sum 92, p. 124-125.
"Never a World But Lingering" (for Chris & Katie). [PaintedB] (46) 92, p. 26-28.

"The Philadelphian" (for Sallye Warr). [PaintedB] (48) 92, p. 67-68.
"Richmond Roller." [Obs] (7:1/2) Spr-Sum 92, p. 125-126.
"Sidney Bechet." [HampSPR] Wint 92, p. 47.

6798. WEAVER, Roger
"When Church Is Not Enough." [DogRR] (11:1) Spr-Sum 92, p. 13.

6799. WEBB, Charles
"At Supper Time" (for Russell Edson). [ChironR] (11:1) Spr 92, p. 11.
"The Death of Santa Claus." [FloridaR] (18:2) Fall-Wint 92, p. 116-117.
"The Death of Yiddish." [PoetL] (87:4) Wint 92-93, p. 8.
"Disclaimer." [WormR] (32:3, #127) 92, p. 83-84.
"Earrings." [NewYorkQ] (49) 92, p. 60-61.
"Flossing His Teeth." [ChironR] (11:1) Spr 92, p. 11.
"Hard-Boiled Eggs." [WormR] (32:3, #127) 92, p. 82.
"His Life in Baseball." [ChironR] (11:1) Spr 92, p. 11.
"An Honest Man." [WormR] (32:4 #128) 92, p. 132-133.
"How I Acquired My Taste in Women." [OnTheBus] (4:2/5:1, #10/11) 92, p. 231.
"I Want to Make One Thing Perfectly Clear." [WormR] (32:4 #128) 92, p. 129-130.
"Marriage of Weeb." [WormR] (32:3, #127) 92, p. 81.
"Poem for the Future." [PassN] (13:2) Wint 92, p. 19.
"Reading the Water" (3rd place winner, Chiron Review 1992 Poetry Contest). [ChironR] (11:3) Aut 92, p. 14.
"Scams" (With thanks to Joe Williams). [WormR] (32:4 #128) 92, p. 130-132.
"Symptoms: A Translation." [Pearl] (16) Fall 92, p. 52.
"Vikings." [Pearl] (15) Spr-Sum 92, p. 54.

6800. WEBB, Robert T.
"Coexistence." [BlackBR] (15) Spr-Sum 92, p. 38.
"In the Boneyard of Our Dead Mothers." [BlackBR] (15) Spr-Sum 92, p. 4-5.
"My Life in the Beak of *La Gazza Ladra*." [LullwaterR] (3:2) Spr 92, p. 26.
"Stations of the Cross: An AIDS Poem." [AmerV] (27) 92, p. 43-57.

6801. WEBB, Simon
"Bonaparte's Bar." [Lactuca] (15) Mr 92, p. 50-51.
"House Guests." [Lactuca] (15) Mr 92, p. 51.

6802. WEBER, Mark
"Above It All." [Pearl] (16) Fall 92, p. 27.
"Ah, to Be a Writer." [WormR] (32:3, #127) 92, p. 87.
"Battle of the Scullery." [WormR] (32:1, #125) 92, p. 34.
"Burritos & Bach." [WormR] (32:3, #127) 92, p. 86.
"Conveyance." [WormR] (32:1, #125) 92, p. 33.
"The English." [WormR] (32:3, #127) 92, p. 86.
"In the Living Room." [WormR] (32:3, #127) 92, p. 87.
"IQ." [SlipS] (12) 92, p. 24.
"Like a Character from Bruegel." [WormR] (32:1, #125) 92, p. 33.
"My Girlfriend." [WormR] (32:1, #125) 92, p. 34.
"Nolo Contendre." [Pearl] (16) Fall 92, p. 27.
"Notes Toward Resume." [SlipS] (12) 92, p. 22.
"Of Calliopes and Banjos." [WormR] (32:1, #125) 92, p. 34.
"A Question of Immediacy." [WormR] (32:3, #127) 92, p. 86.
"Ready to Go." [WormR] (32:3, #127) 92, p. 87.
"Shitfaced at the Silver Dollar Saloon." [Pearl] (15) Spr-Sum 92, p. 12.
"T.L. Kryss Hugged Me on 9th Street Today." [WormR] (32:3, #127) 92, p. 88.
"Ten Cents of Coffee." [WormR] (32:3, #127) 92, p. 85.
"Wirk." [SlipS] (12) 92, p. 23.

6803. WEBSTER, Catherine
"Child." [BellArk] (8:5) S-O 92, p. 8-9.
"Elvis's Prophecy." [BellArk] (8:6) N-D 92, p. 8-11.
"Fig Tree on Messick Road." [Zyzzyva] (8:4) Wint 92, p. 114-115.
"I'm Tireless, I Hear and Behold God in Every Blade of Field Corn." [BellArk] (8:6) N-D 92, p. 11.
"I'm Wind Poppy, Inhaling My Own Filaments, Pollen. Stem Erect, Poppyhead, Open." [BellArk] (8:5) S-O 92, p. 9.
"Leppy Calf's Hide." [BellArk] (8:5) S-O 92, p. 6.
"Song for Making Hay." [BellArk] (8:5) S-O 92, p. 7.

6804. WEBSTER, Diane
"Buddha statue." [DogRR] (11:1) Spr-Sum 92, p. 38.
"Look over the dam." [DogRR] (11:1) Spr-Sum 92, p. 25.
"Tuft of cat hair." [DogRR] (11:1) Spr-Sum 92, p. 38.

"Wyoming desert." [DogRR] (11:1) Spr-Sum 92, p. 25.

6805. WEBSTER, Ed
"Last Night I Dreamt You Were Raising an Aviary." [CinPR] (23) Wint 91-92, p. 56.
"Logomachy." [PaintedB] (46) 92, p. 43.

6806. WEDDLE, Jeff
"Freud Visits the Tropics." [ChironR] (11:1) Spr 92, p. 14.
"Patchen Things Up." [ChironR] (11:1) Spr 92, p. 14.
"Picasso the Great Haircut." [ChironR] (11:1) Spr 92, p. 14.
"Pilgrimage." [MoodySI] (27) Spr 92, p. 48.
"Where Were You?" [ChironR] (11:1) Spr 92, p. 14.

6807. WEDEL, Steven E.
"Life on the Clock." [Writer] (105:3) Mr 92, p. 1.

6808. WEEKS, Daniel
"Clarissa Among the Bovines." [CimR] (100) Jl 92, p. 114-115.

6809. WEEKS, Robert Lewis
"Green Like the Trees of Summer." [NegC] (12:1/2) 92, p. 119.
"Renewal of Sunrise Space." [RiverC] (12:2) Spr 92, p. 71-72.
"Sitting in the Middle of Violets." [HampSPR] Wint 92, p. 25.
"Smoke." [HampSPR] Wint 92, p. 24.

WEESE, Jeanne de
See DeWEESE, Jeanne

WEI, Guo
See GUO, Wei

WEI, Wang
See WANG, Wei

6810. WEIDMAN, Phil
"A Little Edge" (A Wormwoood Chapbook: 110 poems). [WormR] (32:2, #126) 92, p. 41-80.

6811. WEIGEL, Molly
"The Shock of the Lenders" (Main Fragment, tr. of Jorge Santiago Perednik). [Sulfur] (12:2, #31) Fall 92, p. 43-50.

6812. WEIGL, Bruce
"The Biography of Fatty's Bar and Grille." [AmerPoR] (21:2) Mr-Ap 92, p. 4.
"Blues at the Equinox." [TriQ] (84) Spr-Sum 92, p. 5.
"Blues in the Afterworld." [AmerPoR] (21:2) Mr-Ap 92, p. 4.
"For the Woman in the Trees." [AmerPoR] (21:2) Mr-Ap 92, p. 5.
"The Forms of 11th Avenue." [AmerPoR] (21:2) Mr-Ap 92, p. 4.
"Lines Written in Fever." [AmerPoR] (21:2) Mr-Ap 92, p. 4.
"Rapture." [AmerPoR] (21:2) Mr-Ap 92, p. 5.
"Shelter." [AmerPoR] (21:2) Mr-Ap 92, p. 3.
"Why We Are Forgiven." [AmerPoR] (21:2) Mr-Ap 92, p. 3.

6813. WEIL, James L.
"Menhirs at Carnac." [ShadowP] (3) 92, p. 7.

6814. WEIL, Joe
"Poem Arrived at While Eating Cauliflower." [JlNJPo] (14:1) Spr 92, p. 3-4.
"Snapper." [JlNJPo] (14:1) Spr 92, p. 5.

6815. WEIMER, Dana
"The Angel of the Waters" (Bethesda Fountain Terrace, 72nd Street, Central Park). [HayF] (11) Fall-Wint 92, p. 98.
"Inertia." [HayF] (11) Fall-Wint 92, p. 97.

6816. WEIN, Terren Llana
"Bowls and Spoons." [BellArk] (8:5) S-O 92, p. 5.
"Ivy and Apples." [BellArk] (8:5) S-O 92, p. 5.

6817. WEINBERG, Viola
"May Day for Rickey." [EngJ] (81:2) F 92, p. 96.

6818. WEINBERGER, Eliot
"Nostalgia for Death" (1938, 2 selections, tr. of Xavier Villaurrutia). [Sulfur] (12:2, #31) Fall 92, p. 54-57.

6819. WEINBERGER, Florence
"The Nun." [Rohwedder] (7) Spr-Sum 92, p. 45.
"Poems on the Mountain, in a House Full of Women." [Rohwedder] (7) Spr-Sum 92, p. 43-45.
"The River Women of Thailand." [ManhatPR] (14) [92?], p. 33.

6820. WEINGARTEN, Roger
"Amber." [WestHR] (46:3) Fall 92 [i.e. (46:4) Wint 92], p. 362-363.

"Ghost Wrestling." [WestHR] (46:3) Fall 92 [i.e. (46:4) Wint 92], p. 359-361.
"In the Cloud Chamber." [AmerPoR] (21:5) S-O 92, p. 47.

6821. WEINMAN, Paul
"New Age Love." [FreeL] (9) Wint 92, p. 31.

6822. WEINRAUB, Richard
"Haiku: Hurricane Hugo." [SoCarR] (25:1) Fall 92, p. 170.
"John Robinson: Sermon on Klok-steeg, Leyden, 1620." [Confr] (48/49) Spr-Sum 92, p. 223-224.
"Samuel Fuller: Leech, Leyden, 1620." [Confr] (48/49) Spr-Sum 92, p. 225.
"William Brewster: Dream Upon Leaving Leyden." [Confr] (48/49) Spr-Sum 92, p. 226.

6823. WEINRICH, Dan
"Checks and Balances." [FreeL] (9) Wint 92, p. 5.

6824. WEINSTEIN, Debra
"Twilight." [BrooklynR] (9) 92, p. 40.

6825. WEINSTEIN, Muriel
"The Visit." [Outbr] (23) 92, p. 76-77.

6826. WEINTRAUB, J.
"On Viewing 'The Old Shepherd's Chief Mourner'." [Outbr] (23) 92, p. 72.

6827. WEIR, Anthony
"Time and the Record." [JamesWR] (9:3) Spr 92, p. 1.

6828. WEIS, Lyle
"On a Distant Shelf." [Dandel] (19:2) 92, p. 19.

6829. WEIS, Miriam L.
"Carta Póstuma a Reinaldo Arenas." [Nuez] (4:12) 92, p. 4.

6830. WEIS, Robert
"Reinaldo Arenas." [Nuez] (4:12) 92, p. 4.

6831. WEISS, David
"I Wanted to Write a Poem of Great, at Least Come, Public Significance." [NoAmR] (277:4) Jl-Ag 92, p. 20.

6832. WEISS, Irving
"Bent Nails." [Archae] (3) early 92, p. 18-20.

6833. WEISS, Jason
"The Pines" (tr. of Silvina Ocampo). [Trans] (26) Spr 92, p. 24.

6834. WEISS, Marta
"1945." [HangL] (60) 92, p. 93.
"M4 at 4 P.M." [HangL] (60) 92, p. 93.
"Painted-Perfect Lemons" (for Allan). [HangL] (60) 92, p. 94.
"Pomegranate." [HangL] (60) 92, p. 94.

6835. WEISS, Sigmund
"On Observing a Painting of a Train Passing into the Horizon." [Lactuca] (16) Ag 92, p. 23.
"Where Is the Station-Master." [Lactuca] (16) Ag 92, p. 22.

6836. WEISS, Theodore
"Flypaper" (after a drawing by Hokusai). [AmerPoR] (21:1) Ja-F 92, p. 30.
"Shorthand." [AmerPoR] (21:1) Ja-F 92, p. 30.
"Through Our Hands." [AmerPoR] (21:1) Ja-F 92, p. 30.

6837. WEISSBORT, Daniel
"Kittens" (tr. of Yunna Morits). [Stand] (33:2) Spr 92, p. 94.
"My Apple-Tree Land" (tr. of Yunna Morits). [Stand] (33:2) Spr 92, p. 95.
"Pulling Aside the Curtain on the Other World" (tr. of Yunna Morits). [Stand] (33:2) Spr 92, p. 95.

6838. WEISSERMAN, Gary
"The Prnciple of Uncertainty." [LullwaterR] (3:3) Sum 92, p. 56-57.

6839. WEISSLITZ, E. F.
"Baldpate Pond, Summer." [SpoonRQ] (17:1/2) Wint-Spr 92, p. 45-47.

6840. WEISSMAN, Benjamin
"Squash." [BrooklynR] (9) 92, p. 62.

6841. WEITZMAN, Sarah Brown
"The Sculptor of Eve." [YellowS] (Ten Years [i.e. 40]) Sum-Fall 92, p. 18.

6842. WELBOURN, Cynthia
"Don." [Amelia] (6:4, #19) 92, p. 131.

6843. WELCH, Don
"The Aspirations of Bronze" (on looking at the sculpture Athleta). [Nimrod] (35:2) Spr-Sum 92, p. 107.
"The Brown Grouse." [CharR] (18:2) Fall 92, p. 105.

"Hemingway in Idaho." [CharR] (18:2) Fall 92, p. 104.
"White Cranes in Spring." [Nimrod] (35:2) Spr-Sum 92, p. 106.

6844. WELCH, James
"In My Lifetime." [Jacaranda] (6:1/2) Wint-Spr 92, p. 106.

6845. WELDON, Maureen
"Unbroken." [CoalC] (5) My 92, p. 12.

6846. WELISH, Marjorie
"Casting Sequences." [Sulfur] (12:1, #30) Spr 92, p. 22-23.
"Grace's Tree, I." [Conjunc] (19) 92, p. 258.
"Twenty-Three Modern Stories." [Sulfur] (12:1, #30) Spr 92, p. 23-24.

6847. WELLS, Kellie
"Hell." [Gypsy] (19) 92, p. 24-25.

6848. WELLS, Shanna
"Big Blue." [Amelia] (7:1, #20) 92, p. 69.
"Watching David Sleep." [Amelia] (6:4, #19) 92, p. 134.

6849. WELLS, Susan
"Dream 3." [Calyx] (14:1) Sum 92, p. 38-39.
"In My Daughter's Old Room." [Calyx] (14:1) Sum 92, p. 36-37.

6850. WENDELL, Julia
"The Undertaker's Wife." [PraS] (66:2) Sum 92, p. 116-118.

6851. WENTHE, William
"Fictions." [TriQ] (86) Wint 92-93, p. 23-24.
"Trope." [Poetry] (159:6) Mr 92, p. 338-339.

6852. WEÖRES, Sandor
"One Liners" (tr. by Nicholas Kolumban). [Pequod] (34) 92, p. 112.

6853. WERNER, Charles T.
"Primogenital." [DogRR] (11:1) Spr-Sum 92, p. 30.

6854. WERNER-KING, Janeen
"The Grandfather" (Tumbling Glacier). [Dandel] (19:2) 92, p. 28.
"The Grandmother" (Mist Glacier). [Dandel] (19:2) 92, p. 27.
"The Old Ones." [Dandel] (19:2) 92, p. 26.

6855. WERNISCH, Ivan
"A Walk Around the Brewery" (tr. by Dominika Winterová and Richard Katrovas). [NewOR] (19:3/4) Fall-Wint 92, p. 30.

WERT, William (William F.) van
See VAN WERT, William (William F.)

6856. WESLEY, Constance
"Dolly's Baby." [Dandel] (19:2) 92, p. 25.

6857. WESLOWSKI, Dieter
"Because We Cannot See the Wind." [ManhatPR] (14) [92?], p. 35.
"Constellation." [Caliban] (11) 92, p. 40.
"Let Me Close My Eyes." [Caliban] (11) 92, p. 41.
"A Loose Epistle to Paul Celan." [Nimrod] (36:1) Fall-Wint 92, p. 119.
"Miracle." [MalR] (101) Wint92, p. 92.
"Now It's the Barn Angel." [Caliban] (11) 92, p. 41.
"Reclamation." [Caliban] (11) 92, p. 40.
"Sign." [Nimrod] (36:1) Fall-Wint 92, p. 119.
"The Sixth Hour." [Nimrod] (36:1) Fall-Wint 92, p. 118.
"Walking through My Father." [MalR] (101) Wint92, p. 93.

6858. WEST, Allen C.
"Beethoven's *Sixth* on Ohio 661." [RagMag] (10:2) 92, p. 46-47.
"Dark Things." [RagMag] (10:2) 92, p. 45.
"Ring of Truth." [RagMag] (10:2) 92, p. 44.

6859. WEST, Charles
"What to Do with an Artichoke." [Light] (2) Sum 92, p. 14.

6860. WEST, David
"Cleaning Doves with My Second Cousin." [SouthernPR] (32:1) Spr 92, p. 20-21.

6861. WEST, Jean
"The Sower in Pennsylvania." [LullwaterR] (4:1) Fall 92, p. 52-57.

6862. WEST, John Foster
"Retiree." [Crucible] (28) Fall 92, p. 43.

6863. WEST, Richard M.
"Ms. Lonelyhearts & Mr. Feelgood." [WormR] (32:3, #127) 92, p. 115-117.
"The Pope Has Spoken." [WormR] (32:3, #127) 92, p. 117-118.
"Turkish Delight." [WormR] (32:3, #127) 92, p. 18.

6864. WEST, Thomas A., Jr.
"Catacombs." [OxfordM] (6:2) Fall-Wint 90, p. 20.
6865. WESTERFIELD, Nancy (Nancy G.)
"Calling with Christmas Dinner." [ChrC] (109:37) 16 D 92, p. 1162.
"Campus Cat." [EngJ] (81:8) D 92, p. 84.
"Feeding the Birds." [Plain] (12:3) Spr 92, p. 33.
"The Geode." [Farm] (9:2) Fall-Wint 92-93, p. 62.
"Go Dancing." [Comm] (119:21) 4 D 92, p. 14.
"The Hour of the Lilies." [EngJ] (80:5) S 91, p. 93.
"Institutional Lawn Chairs." [ChrC] (109:29) 14 O 92, p. 905.
"Motion Sickness." [Comm] (119:21) 4 D 92, p. 14.
"Student in My Front Row." [ChrC] (109:33) 11 N 92, p. 1031.
"Wars in the Family." [FourQ] (6:1) Spr 92, p. 61.
"The Way the Poet Read." [Plain] (13:1) Fall 92, p. 24.
"What the Tree Knows." [Plain] (12:3) Spr 92, p. 33.
"A Woman's Handbag." [ChrC] (109:6) 19 F 92, p. 180.
6866. WESTFALL, Marilyn
"A City Lake in West Texas." [Lactuca] (16) Ag 92, p. 28.
"Clarissa." [Lactuca] (16) Ag 92, p. 27-28.
"Neighbor." [Lactuca] (16) Ag 92, p. 28.
6867. WESTON, Joanna M.
"Coatetelco." [Dandel] (19:1) 92, p. 5.
6868. WETZSTEON, Rachel
"Song." [SouthwR] (77:1) Wint 92, p. 59-60.
"The Wanderer's New Life." [NewRep] (206:5) 3 F 92, p. 35.
6869. WEXELBLATT, Robert
"Divine Wind, Or the Final Solution in the Suburbs." [CrabCR] (8:1) Sum-Fall 92, p. 12.
"Greenhouse." [ChatR] (12:3) Spr 92, p. 15-17.
"Vita Brevis." [MidwQ] (34:1) Aut 92, p. 91-92.
"What Do You Need?" [HiramPoR] (51/52) Fall 91-Sum 92, p. 83.
6870. WEXLER, Evelyn
"The Persistence of Memory Bytes." [LitR] (35:3) Spr 92, p. 375.
6871. WEXLER, Joan
"The Tuba City Truck Stop." [Outbr] (23) 92, p. 75.
6872. WHALEN, John
"The Radical Politics of Light." [YellowS] (41) Fall-Wint 92-93, p. 20-21.
"To You with Toes in the Lake and Stars in Your Teeth." [YellowS] (41) Fall-Wint 92-93, p. 21.
6873. WHALEN, Tom
"Again and Again There Is a Spasm in the Looking Glass." [Chelsea] (53) 92, p. 92.
"The Master Says His Prayers at Night." [Chelsea] (53) 92, p. 93.
"Reckoning." [Hellas] (3:1) Spr 92, p. 23.
6874. WHALLEY, Karen
"After My Son's Surgery." [BellArk] (8:2) Mr-Ap 92, p. 25.
"Assignment for a Lit Class." [BellArk] (8:5) S-O 92, p. 5.
"Becoming What You Love." [BellArk] (8:1) Ja-F 92, p. 6.
"A Burden Lifting from Her." [BellArk] (8:2) Mr-Ap 92, p. 14.
"Walking Among the Animals." [BellArk] (8:1) Ja-F 92, p. 13.
6875. WHARTON, Edith
"Mona Lisa." [YaleR] (80:3) Jl 92, p. 103.
6876. WHEATLEY, Patience
"Anniversaries." [Descant] (23:4/24:1, #78/79) Wint-Spr 92-93, p. 158.
"The Astrologer's Daughter." [Descant] (23:4/24:1, #78/79) Wint-Spr 92-93, p. 155.
"Reflections." [Descant] (23:4/24:1, #78/79) Wint-Spr 92-93, p. 156-157.
6877. WHEELER, Charles B.
"Hawk, Cars, Vole, Runner." [TarRP] (30:2) Spr 91, p. 40-41.
"Overpass." [TarRP] (30:2) Spr 91, p. 39-40.
6878. WHEELER, Sue (*See also* WHEELER, Susan)
"10¢ a Slice." [Grain] (20:2) Sum 92, p. 64.
"Moving." [Grain] (20:2) Sum 92, p. 64-65.
"Soft-Bodied." [Grain] (20:2) Sum 92, p. 65.
"Spring: Certainties." [BellR] (15:2) Fall 92, p. 46.
"Their Futures Drift Like Ash Across the City" (Triangle Shirtwaist Factory, 1911). [Arc] (29) Aut 92, p. 24.
"To My Husband Who Died." [BellR] (15:2) Fall 92, p. 45.

6879. WHEELER, Susan (*See also* WHEELER, Sue)
"Debates." [ParisR]] (34:124) Fall 92, p. 141-142.
"The Fiercest." [NewAW] (10) Fall 92, p. 35-36.
"Knowledge, Say." [Talisman] (9) Fall 92, p. 203-204.
"The Source of Distress." [Witness] (5:1) 91, p. 36.
"The Stable Earth, the Deep Salt Sea." [BrooklynR] (9) 92, p. 7.
"Stud Muffin." [Witness] (5:1) 91, p. 37.
6880. WHEELOCK, C. Webster
"Another Dozen Reasons." [Light] (2) Sum 92, p. 12.
"Gargano, Italia." [Sparrow] (59) S 92, p. 30.
"Paper Ladies." [Hellas] (3:1) Spr 92, p. 59.
"Post-Mortems." [Sparrow] (59) S 92, p. 30.
"Venice in Winter." [Hellas] (3:1) Spr 92, p. 60.
6881. WHISHAW, Iona
"The House" (tr. of Veronica Volkow). [LitR] (25:2) Wint 92, p. 215.
"In the Valley of Zapata" (tr. of Veronica Volkow). [LitR] (25:2) Wint 92, p. 216 - 217.
"The Star" (tr. of Veronica Volkow). [LitR] (25:2) Wint 92, p. 216.
6882. WHITE, Calvin
"1956, Armstrong, B.C." [AntigR] (91) Fall 92, p. 106.
6883. WHITE, Claire Nicolas
"Ars Poetica" (tr. of Philippe Delaveau). [Footwork] 92, p. 90.
"Eucharis" (tr. of Philippe Delaveau). [Footwork] 92, p. 90.
"I N R I." [Footwork] 92, p. 105.
"Poem for Beginners" (tr. of Paul Snoek). [Trans] (26) Spr 92, p. 83.
"Poem for the Day After Tomorrow" (tr. of Paul Snoek). [Trans] (26) Spr 92, p. 84.
"Riding at Anchor." [Confr] (48/49) Spr-Sum 92, p. 202-204.
"Talking to God." [Footwork] 92, p. 105.
6884. WHITE, Danny
"At the Conference." [BellR] (15:2) Fall 92, p. 34.
6885. WHITE, Fred D.
"At the Rodin Museum, Stanford." [CapeR] (27:2) Fall 92, p. 7.
"My Father's Bust of Me, Age 4." [CapeR] (27:2) Fall 92, p. 8.
6886. WHITE, Gail
"Advice to the Lioness." [Light] (4) Wint 92-93, p. 10.
"Brother Dog, Sister Cat" (w. Barbara Loots). [Light] (1) Spr 92, p. 13.
"Epitaph on a Realtor." [Light] (4) Wint 92-93, p. 21.
"My Personal Recollections of Not Being Asked to the Prom." [Sparrow] (59) S 92, p. 29.
"Old Woman and 25 Cats." [MidwQ] (33:2) Wint 92, p. 209.
"The Penniless Poet Invokes the Muse." [Light] (3) Aut 92, p. 9.
"Wetbacks cross the Rio Grande." [Light] (3) Aut 92, p. 29.
"Wetbacks cross the Rio Grande." [Light] (4) Wint 92-93, p. 29.
6887. WHITE, J. P.
"Cold Cup of Coffee." [Crazy] (43) Wint 92, p. 26-28.
"Degas." [Poetry] (159:4) Ja 92, p. 216.
"Essay on History and Eternity." [NoAmR] (277:6) N-D 92, p. 39.
"The Horse Thief." [Pequod] (33) 92, p. 176-179.
"Reading Tu Fu, China's Greatest Poet, 1244 Years After He Failed to Secure an Official Scholar's Post." [GettyR] (5:4) Aut 92, p. 715.
"The Red Camellia." [GreenMR] (NS 5:2) Spr-Sum 92, p. 36.
"The Salt Hour." [GreenMR] (NS 5:2) Spr-Sum 92, p. 33-35.
6888. WHITE, Marsha
"The Farm" (for Dorcas Watters). [GrahamHR] (16) Fall 92, p. 61-62.
6889. WHITE, Melissa
"Woman's Body Hides Secret-Telling Spy" (3 selections). [Noctiluca] (1:1) Spr 92, p. 47.
6890. WHITE, Michael
"The Solving Memory of Things." [WestHR] (46:1) Spr 92, p. 86-87.
6891. WHITE, Nancy
"The Air They Breathe." [MassR] (23:2) Sum 92, p. 199.
"Eve's Garden." [Field] (47) Fall 92, p. 89-91.
"Father on Black Ice." [Ploughs] (18:4) Wint 92-93, p. 119-121.
"Man." [Ploughs] (18:4) Wint 92-93, p. 122.
"To My Sins." [MassR] (23:2) Sum 92, p. 200.
"When You Unloose." [Ploughs] (18:4) Wint 92-93, p. 123.

6892. WHITE, Philip
"Solitaire." [PoetL] (87:1) Spr 92, p. 15.
6893. WHITE, Raisa
"Habitación vs Habitación." [LitR] (35:4) Sum 92, p. 599-600.
"Room vs. Room" (tr. by AnneMaria Bankay). [LitR] (35:4) Sum 92, p. 467.
6894. WHITE, Steven F.
"Ode to Federico García Lorca" (tr. of Pablo Neruda, w. Greg Simon). [NowestR] (30:1) 92, p. 65-68.
6895. WHITE, Sylvia
"Blue Angel." [OnTheBus] (4:2/5:1, #10/11) 92, p. 232.
"Dry Places." [OnTheBus] (4:2/5:1, #10/11) 92, p. 233.
6896. WHITE, Tama Hood
"Robes of Wind, Wings of Fire." [SouthernHR] (26:1) Wint 92, p. 18.
6897. WHITEHEAD, James
"After Years of Family a Local Man's Last Words." [LaurelR] (26:1) Wint 92, p. 90.
"Coldstream Taggart — the College Textbook Salesman — Proposes to His Long - Time Friend Doctor Annie While Listening to Music." [LaurelR] (26:2) Sum 92, p. 102.
"Coldstream Taggart, the College Traveler, Introduces His Country Doctor Friend." [LaurelR] (26:2) Sum 92, p. 98.
"Coldstream, the College Traveler, Tells of Meeting Toulouse Bergeron, Doctor Annie's Rich and Famous Estranged Husband." [LaurelR] (26:2) Sum 92, p. 99-102.
"A Poem for My Humerus." [LaurelR] (26:1) Wint 92, p. 90-92.
"That Mobile Lawyer's Life of Desire." [LaurelR] (26:1) Wint 92, p. 92.
6898. WHITEHEAD, Thomas
"Designing for Dumpsters." [Light] (1) Spr 92, p. 24.
"Friends Say I'm a Lot More Loyal Now." [Light] (3) Aut 92, p. 16.
"The Perpetual Death of My Uncle." [Hellas] (3:1) Spr 92, p. 21.
"Waiter, What's This Chat du Jour?" [Light] (3) Aut 92, p. 10.
6899. WHITEHORN, Laura
"After the Confiscation of GCN #2" (Lexington, 1992). [SinW] (48) Wint 92-93, p. 60.
"Fourteen Days, Loss of Privileges" (DC Jail). [SinW] (48) Wint 92-93, p. 60.
6900. WHITEMAN, Roberta Hill
"Patterns." [Jacaranda] (6:1/2) Wint-Spr 92, p. 102-103.
6901. WHITEMAN, Walt
"Live Oak with Moss." [AmerPoR] (21:2) Mr-Ap 92, p. 57-59.
6902. WHITING, Nathan
"The Cricket in Red." [OxfordM] (8:1) Spr-Sum 92, p. 31.
"Prayer for Hostility." [GrahamHR] (16) Fall 92, p. 83.
"Sun on Faces." [GrahamHR] (16) Fall 92, p. 82.
6903. WHITLEDGE, Jane
"Requesting a Tree." [SoCoast] (13) Je 93 [i.e. 92], p. 20.
6904. WHITLOW, Carolyn Beard
"Book of Routh." [KenR] (NS 14:2) Spr 92, p. 152-153.
6905. WHITMAN, Ruth
"Exile: Jerusalem." [AmerV] (28) 92, p. 80.
"Hatshepsut: Conversation with a Pharaoh" (Selections: 7, 49). [RiverS] (36) 92, p. 49-50.
"Hatshepsut, Speak to Me" (Selections: 4 poems). [13thMoon] (10:1/2) 92, p. 55-59.
"Statistics" (honorable mention, Eve of Saint Agnes Contest). [NegC] (12:3) 92, p. 44.
6906. WHITMAN, Walt
"Poem of the Propositions of Nakedness." [Sulfur] (12:2, #31) Fall 92, p. 4-7.
6907. WHITMORE, Susan M.
"Eve." [NewYorkQ] (47) 92, p. 90.
6908. WHITNEY, J. Stephen
"Cemetery Ride." [AfAmRev] (26:2) Sum 92, p. 272.
"Gumbo Dance." [AfAmRev] (26:2) Sum 92, p. 272.
"Miles." [AfAmRev] (26:2) Sum 92, p. 273.
6909. WHITNEY, Rondalyn Varney
"Finally, Isis!" [Kalliope] (14:3) 92, p. 20.
6910. WHITNEY, Ross R.
"Bonneville, on Blocks, in a Red Barn." [PoetryNW] (33:3) Aut 92, p. 23.
"Departure." [BelPoJ] (42:4) Sum 92, p. 22.

"Finis." [Amelia] (6:4, #19) 92, p. 122.
"Horseman." [BelPoJ] (42:4) Sum 92, p. 23.
"A Nickel in Your Hand." [TarRP] (30:2) Spr 91, p. 11.
"Tribute." [FreeL] (9) Wint 92, p. 28.
"Witness." [Amelia] (6:4, #19) 92, p. 102.

6911. WHITTEMORE, Reed
"A Difference." [Light] (4) Wint 92-93, p. 18.

6912. WHITTEN, Kathleen
"Invitation au Voyage." [YellowS] (41) Fall-Wint 92-93, p. 21.

6913. WHITTIER, John Greenleaf
"The Bartholdi Statue." [YaleR] (80:3) Jl 92, p. 121.

6914. WHITTINGHAM, Brian
"The Black Squad." [Verse] (9:3) Wint 92, p. 150.

6915. WICHNER, Ernest
"Breath Less" (for Klaus Hensel, tr. by Margitt Lehbert). [Shiny] (7/8) 92, p. 145.
"Proceedings" (Part I, tr. by Margitt Lehbert). [Shiny] (7/8) 92, p. 145-146.

6916. WICKELHAUS, Martha
"Bad Luck Penny." [ColEng] (54:4) Ap 92, p. 418.
"Cheshire Moon." [ColEng] (54:4) Ap 92, p. 420.
"Happily Married." [ColEng] (54:4) Ap 92, p. 419.
"High Fly." [ColEng] (54:4) Ap 92, p. 421.

6917. WICKLIFFE, Warren B.
"Leaf-Touching." [ChironR] (11:4) Wint 92, p. 45.

6918. WIDERKEHR, Richard
"The Hallway." [CrabCR] (8:1) Sum-Fall 92, p. 11-12.
"Out There." [CrabCR] (8:1) Sum-Fall 92, p. 10.
"Red Curtains." [CrabCR] (8:1) Sum-Fall 92, p. 10-11.

6919. WIDUP, David
"Love Song #5." [OnTheBus] (4:2/5:1, #10/11) 92, p. 234.
"Patches." [AnotherCM] (24) Fall 92, p. 162-166.

6920. WIENEKE, Connie
"Loretta Gets Toreador Pants." [CutB] (37) Wint 92, p. 65-66.

6921. WIENERS, John
"707 Scott Street: A Journal for Billie Holiday" (includes poems). [Conjunc] (19) 92, p. 83-98.

6922. WIER, Dara
"Barely There." [ThRiPo] (39/40) 92-93, p. 272-273.
"Closed Shop, Closed for Repairs." [NoAmR] (277:3) My-Je 92, p. 45.
"Daytrip to Paradox." [ThRiPo] (39/40) 92-93, p. 274-275.
"The Innate Deception of Unspoiled Beauty." [ThRiPo] (39/40) 92-93, p. 271.
"Lucille and Ernie's Master Bedroom." [ThRiPo] (39/40) 92-93, p. 273-274.
"Lucille's Kumquat Colored Kimono." [ThRiPo] (39/40) 92-93, p. 272.

6923. WIEWEL, Chris
"Planting." [RiverS] (36) 92, p. 47-48.

6924. WIGGS, Terry
"Derby Day, Nuevo Laredo." [Lactuca] (15) Mr 92, p. 38-40.
"Horse Latitudes." [Lactuca] (15) Mr 92, p. 36-38.
"Imagining Little Rock." [Lactuca] (15) Mr 92, p. 35-36.

6925. WIGHT, Ernest A., Jr.
"A Morning Drive Home." [MidwQ] (33:4) Sum 92, p. 419.

WIGHTMAN, Ludmilla Popova
See POPOVA-WIGHTMAN, Ludmilla

6926. WIGUTOW, Warren
"Sonnet: The Three Disgraces." [Blueline] (13) 92, p. 83.

6927. WILBUR, Gwenan
"Untitled: I like it that you're sick, but not for me" (tr. of Marina Tsvetaeva). [TriQ] (86) Wint 92-93, p. 29.

6928. WILBUR, Richard
"For the Student Strikers." [AntR] (50:1/2) Wint-Spr 92, p. 194.
"Inferno" (Selection: Canto XXV, tr. of Dante). [Antaeus] (69) Aut 92, p. 21-28.
"Lines on a Postcard, in Response to the Poem on the Left." [Light] (1) Spr 92, p. 13.

6929. WILCOX, Brad
"Where to Go on a Sunday Morning." [SmPd] (29:2, #85) Spr 92, p. 13.

6930. WILCOX, Patricia
"Bear After Dancing." [SpiritSH] (57) Spr-Sum 92, p. 18.

"Flood." [SpiritSH] (57) Spr-Sum 92, p. 19.
"Influences." [SpiritSH] (57) Spr-Sum 92, p. 20.
"International Folk Song." [SpiritSH] (57) Spr-Sum 92, p. 19.

6931. WILD, Gerald
"Blues Sonata in Spring Flat." [Elf] (2:1) Spr 92, p. 32.
"Schools End." [Elf] (2:1) Spr 92, p. 30-31.
"Untitled: In north Orleans County." [Elf] (2:1) Spr 92, p. 31.

6932. WILD, Peter
"Ducks." [ConnPR] (11:1) 92, p. 23.
"Husbands." [PoetL] (87:4) Wint 92-93, p. 20.
"Marching Bands." [LaurelR] (26:1) Wint 92, p. 89.
"Pioneers." [AnotherCM] (24) Fall 92, p. 167.
"Real Work." [Wind] (22:71) 92, p. 34-35.
"Schubert's Mother." [Wind] (22:71) 92, p. 34.
"Why Popes Don't Write Books." [HiramPoR] (51/52) Fall 91-Sum 92, p. 84.
"The Women of Lands' End." [HiramPoR] (51/52) Fall 91-Sum 92, p. 85.

6933. WILDE-MENOZZI, Wallis
"Cactus." [CimR] (100) Jl 92, p. 53-54.
"Large Doors." [CreamCR] (16:1) Spr 92, p. 103-107.
"Nearing Anne Frank." [Agni] (35) 92, p. 278-280.
"Talking with Jehanne Marchesi, Translator." [SpoonRQ] (17:3/4) Sum-Fall 92, p. 103.
"To Primo Levi, April 11, 1987." [SouthernR] (28:3) Sum, Jl 92, p. 615-616.
"Words." [MissR] (20:3) Spr 92, p. 112-113.

6934. WILDER, Dwain
"The Dancing Bones of the Sea." [ShadowP] (3) 92, p. 3.
"On Loma Garden." [ShadowP] (3) 92, p. 1-2.

6935. WILDER, Rex
"Cows, Bounded on Three Sides by Impenetrable Oak." [SouthwR] (77:1) Wint 92, p. 73.
"Parc Floral des Moutiers." [AntR] (50:4) Fall 92, p. 737.
"René Underground." [Poetry] (160:1) Ap 92, p. 29-30.
"Sounding Aboard the Rafaella." [Nat] (255:13) 26 O 92, p. 484.

6936. WILDMAN, Ed
"The Toughest." [AntigR] (91) Fall 92, p. 114.

6937. WILER, Jack
"Meditations on Natural Man." [PaintedB] (48) 92, p. 40-41.

6938. WILKIE, Pamela
"On Killing a Hornet with a Flat-Iron." [CumbPR] (12:1) Fall 92, p. 28.
"Peregrination." [CumbPR] (12:1) Fall 92, p. 29.

6939. WILKINSON, Claude
"Fall Song." [Poem] (67) My 92, p. 50.
"A Simpler Optimism." [Poem] (67) My 92, p. 49.

6940. WILLARD, Nancy
"At the Optometrist's." [NewYorker] (68:29) 7 S 92, p. 50.
"The Exodus of Peaches." [NewYorker] (68:23) 27 Jl 92, p. 30.
"Guesthouse, Union City, Michigan." [NewYorker] (68:12) 11 My 92, p. 60.
"A Member of the Wedding." [Field] (47) Fall 92, p. 123.
"A Very Still Life." [Field] (47) Fall 92, p. 122.

6941. WILLARD, Nathan
"Smoking Crayons." [CoalC] (5) My 92, p. 5.

6942. WILLCOCKSON, Sharon Godbey
"Delayed Condolence." [NewYorkQ] (49) 92, p. 91.

6943. WILLCOX, Steve
"Feeding the Grass." [Parting] (5:2) Wint 92-93, p. 39.

6944. WILLERTON, Chris
"Landscape with Reservoir." [LitR] (25:2) Wint 92, p. 254-255.

6945. WILLEY, Edward
"A.E. Housman in Afterlife." [Light] (1) Spr 92, p. 20.

6946. WILLIAMS, C. K.
"A Dream of Mind" (3 selections). [KenR] (NS 14:1) Wint 92, p. 131-134.
"A Dream of Mind: The Gap." [Thrpny] (49) Spr 92, p. 23.
"Helen." [AmerPoR] (21:1) Ja-F 92, p. 3-5.
"Incorporeal Ruler" (tr. of Adam Zagajewski, w. Renata Gorczynski and Benjamin Ivry). [Thrpny] (48) Wint 92, p. 4.
"The Insult." [NewYorker] (68:9) 20 Ap 92, p. 38.

"Scar." [KenR] (NS 14:1) Wint 92, p. 130-131.
6947. WILLIAMS, David (*See also* WILLIAMS, David Earl)
"Almost One." [MichQR] (31:4) Fall 92, p. 605-606.
6948. WILLIAMS, David Earl (*See also* WILLIAMS, David)
"Physics." [RagMag] (10:1) 92, p. 30.
"Sudden: A Poem for the Woman in the Next Room." [RagMag] (10:1) 92, p. 29.
6949. WILLIAMS, Diane
"Before Love at the Festival (from the Open a Vein Series)." [ChironR] (11:4) Wint 92, p. 18.
"The Big Bang Theory." [ChironR] (11:4) Wint 92, p. 18.
6950. WILLIAMS, Gerald
"Ignorance." [NegC] (12:1/2) 92, p. 118.
6951. WILLIAMS, Jonathan
"Cobwebbery." [NegC] (12:1/2) 92, p. 167-168.
"Night Landscape in Nelson County, Kentucky." [NegC] (12:1/2) 92, p. 166.
"Three Sayings from Highlands, North Carolina." [NegC] (12:1/2) 92, p. 164-165.
6952. WILLIAMS, Loretta Ann
"Lake Sevier's a playa." [Amelia] (6:4, #19) 92, p. 54.
"Lunch Hour." [Amelia] (7:1, #20) 92, p. 143.
6953. WILLIAMS, Miller
"Closing the House." [KenR] (NS 14:1) Wint 92, p. 25.
"A Day in the Death." [KenR] (NS 14:1) Wint 92, p. 24-25.
"The Groom Kisses the Bride and the Mind of the Young Preacher Wanders Again." [NewEngR] (14:2) Spr 92, p. 112.
"Home from the Grave to News of War and Madness." [LaurelR] (26:1) Wint 92, p. 78.
"I Can Only Stay for Fifteen Minutes." [KenR] (NS 14:1) Wint 92, p. 23-24.
"ICU: Space/Time in the Waiting Room." [LaurelR] (26:1) Wint 92, p. 79.
"Learning Russian." [KenR] (NS 14:1) Wint 92, p. 23.
"Mise en Scène." [Light] (1) Spr 92, p. 27.
"Pulling Back." [LaurelR] (26:1) Wint 92, p. 78.
"RSVP." [Sparrow] (59) S 92, p. 31.
"The Shrinking Lonesome Sestina Starting with Long Lines." [NewEngR] (14:2) Spr 92, p. 113-114.
"Sum, Es, Est." [LaurelR] (26:1) Wint 92, p. 79.
6954. WILLIAMS, Mo
"Solitude." [Noctiluca] (1:2) Wint 92 [on cover: Wint 93], p. 40.
"Stone in Riot." [Noctiluca] (1:2) Wint 92 [on cover: Wint 93], p. 40.
"This Long Room." [Noctiluca] (1:2) Wint 92 [on cover: Wint 93], p. 41.
6955. WILLIAMS, Rynn
"Carnivores." [BrooklynR] (9) 92, p. 67.
"The Final Repast." [BellR] (15:2) Fall 92, p. 33.
"I Get Off in the Woods." [BrooklynR] (9) 92, p. 66.
"In Colombia." [SouthernPR] (32:1) Spr 92, p. 67-70.
"Photosynthesis." [SouthernPR] (32:1) Spr 92, p. 71.
6956. WILLIAMSON, Greg
"The Carpenters." [WestHR] (46:3) Fall 92 [i.e. (46:4) Wint 92], p. 358.
"An Economic Proposal." [NewRep] (207:15) 5 O 92, p. 42.
"Eye Strains." [SouthwR] (77:4) Aut 92, p. 534.
"A Small Junkyard." [WestHR] (46:2) Sum 92, p. 189-191.
6957. WILLIS, Dawn Diez
"John Eight." [Zyzzyva] (8:4) Wint 92, p. 39.
6958. WILLIS, Elizabeth
"A Maiden" (Excerpts). [Epoch] (41:3) 92, p. 402-405.
"UNDER THE ARC / of Disaster." [PaintedB] (48) 92, p. 58-59.
6959. WILLIS, Mary (*See also* WILLIS, Mary-Sherman)
"Black Hole." [CanLit] (133) Sum 92, p. 142.
6960. WILLIS, Mary-Sherman (*See also* WILLIS, Mary)
"Three Sonnets on Form." [NewRep] (207:30 [sic, i.e. 207:5]) 27 Jl 92, p. 63.
6961. WILLIS, Paul
"Annunciation." [SoCoast] (12) Ja 92, p. 3.
"A Firm Prediction." [SoCoast] (12) Ja 92, p. 4-5.
6962. WILLOW, Morgan Grayce
"Scylla and Charybdis" (thank you June Jordan & Laurie Anderson). [SinW] (46) Spr 92, p. 103-105.

6963. WILLS, Jackie
"Out of Bounds." [Verse] (9:3) Wint 92, p. 148.
6964. WILLSON, John
"The Son We Had." [NowestR] (30:2) 92, p. 79-80.
6965. WILNER, Eleanor
"Being As I Was, How Could I Help." [Boulevard] (7:1, #19) Spr 92, p. 53-54.
"Generic Vision, 1991." [Boulevard] (7:1, #19) Spr 92, p. 51-52.
6966. WILOCH, Thomas
"Words Our Parents Say." [Bogg] (65) 92, p. 10.
6967. WILSON, Alan R.
"Perseus the Champion." [ChiR] (37:4) 92, p. 17.
"Triangulum Australe the Southern Triangle." [ChiR] (37:4) 92, p. 18.
6968. WILSON, Barbara Hurd
"The Russian Water Grandfather." [PraS] (66:2) Sum 92, p. 51-52.
6969. WILSON, Betty
"Aquarium" (tr. of Dulce Maria Loynaz, w. Pam Mordecai). [LitR] (35:4) Sum 92, p. 454.
"Canoe Race" (tr. of Renee Maurin-Gotin). [LitR] (35:4) Sum 92, p. 530.
"Danger Zone" (tr. of Cira Andres). [LitR] (35:4) Sum 92, p. 449.
"Declaration of Love" (tr. of Carilda Oliver Labra, w. Pam Mordecai). [LitR] (35:4) Sum 92, p. 461.
"Drumbeat of Life" (tr. of Maryse Romanos). [LitR] (35:4) Sum 92, p. 531-532.
"Elegy" (tr. of Carilda Oliver Labra, w. Pam Mordecai). [LitR] (35:4) Sum 92, p. 462.
"Encounter" (tr. of Marie-Therese Colimon). [LitR] (35:4) Sum 92, p. 509.
"The Horseman" (tr. of Dulce Maria Loynaz). [LitR] (35:4) Sum 92, p. 453.
"King Carnival Done" (tr. of Renee Maurin-Gotin). [LitR] (35:4) Sum 92, p. 529.
"Liqueurs from My Homeland" (Extract from "Splendeur," tr. of Janine Tavernier - Louis). [LitR] (35:4) Sum 92, p. 510.
"My Island" (tr. of Marie-Ange Jolicoeur). [LitR] (35:4) Sum 92, p. 511.
"Purchase" (tr. of Dulce Maria Loynaz, w. Pam Mordecai). [LitR] (35:4) Sum 92, p. 453.
"Reflections" (tr. of Georgina Herrera Cárdenas). [LitR] (35:4) Sum 92, p. 450.
"Rondel" (tr. of Carilda Oliver Labra, w. Pam Mordecai). [LitR] (35:4) Sum 92, p. 462.
"Sacrificial Flowers" (tr. of Lucie Julia). [LitR] (35:4) Sum 92, p. 527-528.
"Searching" (tr. of Lucie Julia). [LitR] (35:4) Sum 92, p. 5j28.
6970. WILSON, David
"Leg It." [Bogg] (65) 92, p. 40.
6971. WILSON, Don D.
"Spring" (tr. of Petya Dubarova). [SenR] (22:2) Fall 92, p. 57.
"Summer has run off, like singing water" (tr. of Petya Dubarova). [SenR] (22:2) Fall 92, p. 58.
"There in the clouds, somewhere in crazy vines" (tr. of Petya Dubarova). [SenR] (22:2) Fall 92, p. 59-60.
"To Fifteen-Year-Olds" (tr. of Petya Dubarova). [SenR] (22:2) Fall 92, p. 56.
6972. WILSON, Fiona
"Aliyah" (For David). [Verse] (9:2) Sum 92, p. 86.
6973. WILSON, Graeme
"In Yoshiwara" (tr. of Kashiwagi Jotei, 1763-1819). [Jacaranda] (6:1/2) Wint-Spr 92, p. 151.
"Lightning" (tr. of Emperor Fushimi, 1265-1317). [Jacaranda] (6:1/2) Wint-Spr 92, p. 151.
"Watching the Moon" (tr. of Kinoshita Choshoshi, 1569-1649). [Jacaranda] (6:1/2) Wint-Spr 92, p. 151.
6974. WILSON, Hannah
"Where the Ends of Bone Meet." [Turnstile] (3:2) 92, p. 6.
6975. WILSON, John
"My Mother, Understanding Her Father." [CoalC] (5) My 92, p. 2-3.
6976. WILSON, Miles
"Body." [Poetry] (160:1) Ap 92, p. 8-9.
6977. WILSON, Ralph
"Cows with Windows" (Kansas State Experimental Farm). [Journal] (16:2) Fall - Wint 92, p. 30.
"Deep Kansas." [Journal] (16:2) Fall-Wint 92, p. 28-29.

6978. WILSON, Reuel K.
"Dance" (for Maria Kuncewiczowa, tr. of Jola Barylanka). [Trans] (26) Spr 92, p. 102.
6979. WILSON, Steve
"The New World." [MidwQ] (34:1) Aut 92, p. 92.
6980. WIMAN, Christian
"Sweet Dreams." [Shen] (42:3) Fall 92, p. 61.
"Threshold." [Shen] (42:3) Fall 92, p. 62-64.
6981. WIMP, Jet
"The Discovery of Infinity." [Boulevard] (7:1, #19) Spr 92, p. 208-209.
6982. WINCH, Terence
"Material Bones." [BrooklynR] (9) 92, p. 95.
WINCKEL, Nance van
See Van WINCKEL, Nance
6983. WINFIELD, William
"History." [InterPR] (18:2) Fall 92, p. 70-71.
WINKEL, Ilse Risseeuw
See RISSEEUW-WINKEL, Ilse
6984. WINSLOW, Ethel
"Festival." [HopewellR] (4) 92, p. 13.
6985. WINTER, Jonah
"Sleep." [ChiR] (37:4) 92, p. 16.
6986. WINTER, Levi
"Blue Balls and the 'A' Train." [ChironR] (11:4) Wint 92, p. 48.
6987. WINTEROVA, Dominika
"If I could" (tr. of Svetlana Burianová, w. Richard Katrovas). [NewOR] (19:3/4) Fall-Wint 92, p. 25.
"Midnight" (tr. of Jan Rejzek, w. Richard Katrovas). [NewOR] (19:3/4) Fall-Wint 92, p. 24.
"Night at the Singles Dorm" (tr. of Jirí Zácek, w. Richard Katrovas). [NewOR] (19:3/4) Fall-Wint 92, p. 29.
"Prague Fisherman" (tr. of Josef Simon, w. Richard Katrovas). [NewOR] (19:3/4) Fall-Wint 92, p. 27.
"The Swans of Prague" (tr. of Zdena Bratrsovská, w. Richard Katrovas). [NewOR] (19:3/4) Fall-Wint 92, p. 26.
"Troja at Eight in the Evening" (tr. of Karel Sys, w. Richard Katrovas). [NewOR] (19:3/4) Fall-Wint 92, p. 28.
"A Walk Around the Brewery" (tr. of Ivan Wernisch, w. Richard Katrovas). [NewOR] (19:3/4) Fall-Wint 92, p. 30.
6988. WINTERS, Bayla
"Like a Second Skin, a Third Eye." [Lactuca] (15) Mr 92, p. 49-50.
"The Nuclear Winter of Our Discontent." [Lactuca] (15) Mr 92, p. 49.
6989. WINTERS, Mary
"Dead Animals." [ChamLR] (10/11) Spr-Fall 92, p. 120.
6990. WINTZ, Anita
"Out in the Tyrrhenian Sea." [Light] (3) Aut 92, p. 29.
6991. WINWOOD, David
"Night and." [WritersF] (18) 92, p. 164.
"Village Tale." [Verse] (9:3) Wint 92, p. 11.
"Village Tale." [WritersF] (18) 92, p. 163.
6992. WISCOMBE, Samuel, Jr.
"Relict." [SmPd] (29:3, #86) Fall 92, p. 37.
"Spectacles." [SmPd] (29:3, #86) Fall 92, p. 38.
6993. WISDOM, Michael
"The waves, below." [WillowR] (19) Spr 92, p. 31.
6994. WISE, Katherine
"Chattanooga Lookouts Vs. New York Yankees, April 2, 1931" (Virne Beatrice (Jackie) Mitchell 1914-1978). [BelPoJ] (43:1) Fall 92, p. 5.
6995. WISEMAN, Christopher
"At the Door." [Event] (21:3) Fall 92, p. 74-75.
"Bedside Manners." [Trans] (26) Spr 92, p. 101.
"Contract Not Renewed (Max Jaffa d. 1991)." [Arc] (29) Aut 92, p. 28.
"Grandfather, the Somme, an Invoice." [Quarry] (41:4) Fall 92, p. 84-90.
"Postcard (August 22, 1911)." [Arc] (29) Aut 92, p. 27.
"Tea Dances, My Father's Motorbike." [Arc] (29) Aut 92, p. 25-26.
"Thinking About AIDS." [Trans] (26) Spr 92, p. 100.

6996. WISEMAN, Jonathan
"Clandestine Sestina." [Dandel] (19:2) 92, p. 30-31.
"My Father's Study." [Dandel] (19:2) 92, p. 29.
6997. WISHAW, Iona
"The Beginning" (Selections: 1, 9, tr. of Verónica Volkow). [TriQ] (85) Fall 92, p. 342-344.
WIT, Johan de
See De WIT, Johan
6998. WITEK, Terri
"Sonnet in Which We Are Summoned to Compare Your Habits." [OhioR] (48) 92, p. 81.
"When My Daughter Leaves I Take Her Room." [OhioR] (48) 92, p. 79-80.
6999. WITHERS, Garland A.
"Untitled: Today I am thirsty for black tea with ice." [EvergreenC] (7:2) Sum-Fall 92, p. 22-23.
7000. WITT, Harold
"American Lit" (3 selections). [BellArk] (8:6) N-D 92, p. 24.
"American Lit" (4 selections). [BellArk] (8:3) My-Je 92, p. 19.
"The Art of Poetry." [Wind] (22:71) 92, p. 36.
"Artemis." [NewYorkQ] (48) 92, p. 63.
"At Washoe County Library." [CharR] (18:1) Spr 92, p. 80.
"A Bird of Morning." [MidwQ] (33:3) Spr 92, p. 319.
"Bury the Dead" (American Lit). [Sparrow] (59) S 92, p. 21.
"City Lights." [CharR] (18:2) Fall 92, p. 75.
"Delmore Schwartz." [CharR] (18:1) Spr 92, p. 81.
"Dirt." [PoetL] (87:4) Wint 92-93, p. 29-30.
"Elizabeth Bishop?" [CharR] (18:2) Fall 92, p. 75.
"Galway" (American Lit). [NewYorkQ] (47) 92, p. 42.
"Gentle Instead." [LitR] (35:3) Spr 92, p. 355.
"The Good Earth." [CharR] (18:2) Fall 92, p. 73.
"Grass" (American Lit). [PoetC] (23:3) Spr 92, p. 26.
"Humboldt's Gift." [CharR] (18:1) Spr 92, p. 82.
"I Do, They Will." [BellArk] (8:1) Ja-F 92, p. 27.
"I Studied Shelley." [Light] (4) Wint 92-93, p. 15.
"In 1492." [MidwQ] (34:1) Aut 92, p. 93.
"Josh Lutz." [BellArk] (8:5) S-O 92, p. 12.
"Leonard Said." [BellArk] (8:2) Mr-Ap 92, p. 7.
"Lolita." [CharR] (18:1) Spr 92, p. 81.
"Mark Strand Complains" (American Lit). [Sparrow] (59) S 92, p. 21.
"Miniver Cheevy." [CharR] (18:2) Fall 92, p. 73.
"Pantheon: A Pindaric Ode." [BellArk] (8:6) N-D 92, p. 13.
"Playboy." [CharR] (18:2) Fall 92, p. 74.
"A Streetcar Named Desire." [Wind] (22:71) 92, p. 36.
"To a God Unknown." [BellArk] (8:2) Mr-Ap 92, p. 7.
"A Tree Grows in Brooklyn." [CharR] (18:2) Fall 92, p. 74.
"Waiting for Lefty." [CharR] (18:1) Spr 92, p. 80.
"William Stafford" (American Lit). [PoetC] (23:3) Spr 92, p. 27.
WITT, Jim de
See DeWITT, Jim
7001. WITT, Sandra
"First Snow, Iowa." [ManhatPR] (14) [92?], p. 13.
WITT, Susan Kelly de
See KELLY-DeWITT, Susan
7002. WITTE, Francine
"Kong." [PoetC] (23:3) Spr 92, p. 15.
"My Cousin's Hands." [PoetC] (23:3) Spr 92, p. 16.
"Rosebud." [Outbr] (23) 92, p. 66.
"Trio." [TarRP] (31:2) Spr 92, p. 21.
"Your Mother's Lover." [Confr] (48/49) Spr-Sum 92, p. 205.
7003. WITTE, George
"1890s, After a Storm" (a photograph in Wilson Library, Chapel Hill, North Carolina). [Shen] (42:1) Spr 92, p. 87-88.
"The Hive." [SenR] (22:2) Fall 92, p. 81-83.
"October Rose." [PraS] (66:3) Fall 92, p. 89-90.
"The Ticket." [PraS] (66:3) Fall 92, p. 88.
"Yours Truly." [PraS] (66:3) Fall 92, p. 89.

7004. WOESSNER, Warren
"Old Southampton Burial Ground." [Bogg] (65) 92, p. 9.
7005. WOHLFELD, Valerie
"A Prayer of Baritoned and Salted Air." [WestHR] (46:3) Fall 92, p. 311-313.
"Rain." [IndR] (15:1) Spr 92, p. 70.
"Sea Change." [IndR] (15:1) Spr 92, p. 71-74.
7006. WOIKOW, Igor
"For Frankie Edith Kerouac Parker." [MoodySI] (27) Spr 92, p. 29.
7007. WOJAHN, David
"Diptych." [AmerV] (26) Spr 92, p. 75-76.
"The First Six Seals." [PoetryNW] (33:2) Sum 92, p. 5-7.
"Videotape of Fighting Swans, Boston Public Gardens." [PoetryNW] (33:2) Sum 92, p. 8.
"Workmen Photographed inside the Reactor: Chernobyl." [SouthernR] (28:2) Spr, Ap 92, p. 305-306.
7008. WOLF, David
"Love Letter from Michigan." [HampSPR] Wint 92, p. 10.
"Random Gales." [HampSPR] Wint 92, p. 9.
7009. WOLF, Michele
"Astigmatism." [SouthernPR] (32:1) Spr 92, p. 19-20.
7010. WOLFF, Daniel
"Approaching the Peak of a Hill at Sixty." [Thrpny] (51) Fall 92, p. 6.
"Lines from Inside an Empire." [ParisR] (34:122) Spr 92, p. 206.
WOLHEE, Choe
See CHOE, Wolhee
7011. WOLMAN, Kenneth
"Historiography." [Footwork] 92, p. 48.
7012. WONG, Doris
"A Suicide Note." [Plain] (13:1) Fall 92, p. 20.
7013. WOO, David
"Empty Room." [NewYorker] (68:8) 13 Ap 92, p. 38.
"Expatriates." [Zyzzyva] (8:2) Sum 92, p. 69.
"Grandfather Writes His Will." [NewYorker] (68:30) 14 S 92, p. 30.
"Singularities." [SouthwR] (77:2/3) Spr-Sum 92, p. 349.
7014. WOOD, Eve (Eve E. M.)
"The Envelope." [GrahamHR] (16) Fall 92, p. 74.
"The Largess" (For Jo). [MidwQ] (33:3) Spr 92, p. 320.
7015. WOOD, Harriett
"Love-Letters Lost in the Mail." [Amelia] (6:4, #19) 92, p. 129.
7016. WOOD, Peter
"The Silent Child." [US1] (26/27) 92, p. 36.
7017. WOOD, Renate
"Blood." [ThRiPo] (39/40) 92-93, p. 275-276.
"Cabbages." [ThRiPo] (39/40) 92-93, p. 277-278.
"The Pilot." [ThRiPo] (39/40) 92-93, p. 276.
7018. WOOD, Susan
"Not the First Love Poem." [SouthernR] (28:4) Aut, O 92, p. 916-917.
7019. WOODCOCK, George
"As I Please." [CanLit] (133) Sum 92, p. 9.
"Silence in Emptiness" (On "The Red Room" by Peter Ilsted, 1915). [CanLit] (133) Sum 92, p. 16.
"Tolstoy at Yasnaya Polyana." [SewanR] (100:2) Spr 92, p. 276-282.
7020. WOODFORD, Keisha Lynette
"Paterson." [Footwork] 92, p. 74.
"Paterson 2." [Footwork] 92, p. 74.
"Word." [Footwork] 92, p. 74.
7021. WOODMAN, Christopher
"Connemara Trousers" (Selections: I-V, for the men in western Ireland who as boys wore skirts "to disguise them from the faeries." And for J.T. and other lovers). [KenR] (NS 14:3) Sum 92, p. 148-153.
7022. WOODRING, Robert G.
"Crayola" (For Bill Stafford). [HawaiiR] (16:2, #35) Spr 92, p. 51.
"Darktime Ritual." [HawaiiR] (16:2, #35) Spr 92, p. 52.
7023. WOODRUFF, William
"Apples ripe in green leaves." [WormR] (32:1, #125) 92, p. 8.
"In the desert soldiers." [WormR] (32:1, #125) 92, p. 8.

"Jammed into an unearthed." [WormR] (32:1, #125) 92, p. 8.
"Old churches ringing" (corrected reprint from No. 124). [WormR] (32:1, #125) 92, p. 8.
"A remembrance of your legs." [WormR] (32:1, #125) 92, p. 8.
"That moving queue." [WormR] (32:1, #125) 92, p. 8.
"Through hills." [WormR] (32:1, #125) 92, p. 8.
"Under crushing feet." [WormR] (32:1, #125) 92, p. 8.

7024. WOODS, Alison
"'Raptivist' on The Morning News Program." [OnTheBus] (4:2/5:1, #10/11) 92, p. 235.

7025. WOODS, Christopher
"Ghost." [ChamLR] (10/11) Spr-Fall 92, p. 168.
"If I See Her Again." [ChamLR] (10/11) Spr-Fall 92, p. 167.

7026. WOODS, Gregory
"Napoli" (from "Urban Encounters"). [JamesWR] (9:3) Spr 92, p. 13.
"Nottingham" (from "Urban Encounters"). [JamesWR] (9:3) Spr 92, p. 12.

7027. WOODS, Linda
"It was summer & all around the Delta." [Bogg] (65) 92, p. 15.

7028. WOODSON, Rose Maria
"Mandela." [AfAmRev] (26:2) Sum 92, p. 281.

7029. WOODSUM, Douglas
"The Frigid Lover and the Elephant of Hope." [AntR] (50:4) Fall 92, p. 728.

7030. WOODWARD, Jeffrey
"For Twelfth Night." [ChrC] (109:1) 1-8 Ja 92, p. 13.

7031. WOOI-CHIN, J-son
"A Night with Ann Sexton." [Vis] (39) 92, p. 15-17.
"Rantau Abang." [Nimrod] (36:1) Fall-Wint 92, p. 82-83.

7032. WOOLF, Geoffrey
"1978." [Spitball] (40) Spr 92, p. 17.
"From the Alternate Lives of the Great Detectives." [PoetL] (87:4) Wint 92-93, p. 7.
"Situation Comedy." [PoetL] (87:4) Wint 92-93, p. 6.

7033. WOOLLEN, Ian
"November 2." [SmPd] (29:1, #84) Wint 92, p. 32.

7034. WOOLLEY, David
"Time & Emotion Study." [CoalC] (5) My 92, p. 15.

7035. WOOLSEY, Linda Mills
"The Weaver Sits in on a Poetry Workshop." [LullwaterR] (4:1) Fall 92, p. 60-61.

7036. WOON, Koon
"The Book of Changes." [BellArk] (8:3) My-Je 92, p. 24.
"In This Town No Bird Finds Me Fancy." [BellArk] (8:2) Mr-Ap 92, p. 13.
"Often a Man." [BellArk] (8:3) My-Je 92, p. 24.
"Poem for S.H.J." [BellArk] (8:2) Mr-Ap 92, p. 11.
"The Preference of Pinball Machines." [BellArk] (8:3) My-Je 92, p. 24.
"The Universe Asserts Itself Over Time." [BellArk] (8:3) My-Je 92, p. 24.
"Why Poets Are Often Insane" (after Donald Justice). [BellArk] (8:4) Jl-Ag 92, p. 19.

7037. WORLEY, James
"By Heart." [ChrC] (109:37) 16 D 92, p. 1164.
"Grain Silos." [ChrC] (109:16) 6 My 92, p. 487.
"Knowing My Better." [ChrC] (109:3) 22 Ja 92, p. 60.

7038. WORLEY, Jeff
"Beginnings." [LitR] (25:2) Wint 92, p. 222.
"Duck Poem." [CumbPR] (11:2) Spr 92, p. 10-11.
"Face-Off." [WritersF] (18) 92, p. 186.
"For the Kid in the Louisville Bar Wearing a Tie-dyed T-shirt." [SpoonRQ] (17:3/4) Sum-Fall 92, p. 122-123.
"Fortune." [ChiR] (37:4) 92, p. 55-56.
"I Like Reading Critics." [SpoonRQ] (17:3/4) Sum-Fall 92, p. 124-125.
"Letter From My Mother." [CreamCR] (16:2) Fall 92, p. 112.
"Never So Easy." [SpoonRQ] (17:3/4) Sum-Fall 92, p. 121.
"On My Deathbed" (a love poem). [GeoR] (46:3) Fall 92, p. 514-515.
"Parable of the Prematurely Miserable." [CreamCR] (16:2) Fall 92, p. 110-111.
"Subvocalization." [PoetryNW] (33:3) Aut 92, p. 41.
"Wednesday's." [WritersF] (18) 92, p. 185.

7039. WORMSER, Baron
"1978." [ManhatR] (6:2) Fall 92, p. 41-42.

"Millenarians" (after Zbigniew Herbert). [RiverS] (36) 92, p. 74-75.
"On the Bus to Houston." [ParisR] (34:122) Spr 92, p. 274-275.
"Rudinsky's, 1953." [ManhatR] (6:2) Fall 92, p. 39-40.
"Somerset County." [ParisR] (34:122) Spr 92, p. 273-274.
"Sonnet: When the troops don't find the trade union." [RiverS] (36) 92, p. 76.

7040. WOROZBYT, Theodore, Jr.
"An Entire Body of Reasons." [PraS] (66:1) Spr 92, p. 121-122.
"Horoscope" (For Marie). [Poetry] (161:3) D 92, p. 156-158.
"It." [PoetL] (87:4) Wint 92-93, p. 27-28.
"A Particle Physicist Picks Up the Muse in Mel's Deli." [Poetry] (160:1) Ap 92, p. 13-14.
"Taking." [PoetC] (24:1) Fall 92, p. 9-10.
"Two Real Fingers, Sharpened But Soft." [IndR] (15:2) Fall 92, p. 87-88.

7041. WOS, Joanna H.
"And When Your Mother Dies" (in memory of Dah-Lah-Hewn-Go). [Contact] (10:62/63/64) Fall 91-Spr 92, p. 60.

7042. WRANOVIX, Ann Marie
"Flash Flood." [FourQ] (6:1) Spr 92, p. 56.
"For a Daughter." [FourQ] (6:1) Spr 92, p. 55.

7043. WREGGITT, Andrew
"Home Movie." [Grain] (20:1) Spr 92, p. 278-279.
"Rain." [Quarry] (41:1) Wint 92, p. 39.
"Safe." [Quarry] (41:1) Wint 92, p. 38-39.
"Satellites." [Grain] (20:1) Spr 92, p. 280.

7044. WRIGHT, A. J.
"At Night." [GreensboroR] (53) Wint 92-93, p. 118.

7045. WRIGHT, C. D.
"Eight Poems: A, B, C, D, E, F, G, H" (tr. of Paol Keineg). [ParisR] (34:122) Spr 92, p. 201-205.
"Hotels." [ThRiPo] (39/40) 92-93, p. 280.
"The Lesson." [ThRiPo] (39/40) 92-93, p. 279-280.
"Morning Star." [AmerPoR] (21:5) S-O 92, p. 34.
"One Summer." [ThRiPo] (39/40) 92-93, p. 281.
"Scratch Music." [ThRiPo] (39/40) 92-93, p. 278-279.
"A Series of Actions." [AmerPoR] (21:5) S-O 92, p. 34.
"This Couple." [ThRiPo] (39/40) 92-93, p. 280-281.

7046. WRIGHT, Carolyne
"About My Little Sister" (tr. of Anuradha Mahapatra, w. Paramita Banerjee). [KenR] (NS 14:2) Spr 92, p. 75.
"After the Explosion of Mount St. Helens, the Retiring Grade-School Teacher Goes for a Long Walk Through the Wheatlands" (Odessa, Washington: May, 1980. For George P. Elliott, 1918-1980). [Ploughs] (18:1) Spr 92, p. 162-163.
"Afternoon" (tr. of Jorge Teillier). [TampaR] (5) Fall 92, p. 59.
"Another Country" (tr. of Nabaneeta Dev Sen, w. Sunil B. Ray and the author). [Agni] (36) 92, p. 214.
"Cow and Grandmother" (tr. of Anuradha Mahapatra, w. Paramita Banerjee). [KenR] (NS 14:2) Spr 92, p. 75-76.
"Eulene at Khajuraho." [MichQR] (31:2) Spr 92, p. 241-243.
"Harumi." [NegC] (12:3) 92, p. 120-122.
"Household Snake" (tr. of Anuradha Mahapatra, w. Jyotirmoy Datta). [KenR] (NS 14:2) Spr 92, p. 76-77.
"A Little Folktale" (tr. of Anuradha Mahapatra, w. Paramita Banerjee). [KenR] (NS 14:2) Spr 92, p. 74.
"Notes on the Author's Last Journey to the Town of His Birth" (To Stefan Baciu in Hawaii, and to Vasile Igna, my unknown cousin in Cluj, Transylvania). [CreamCR] (16:2) Fall 92, p. 70-75.
"The Ritual of *Sati*" (tr. of Gita Chattopadhyay, w. Paramita Banerjee). [ChiR] (38:1/2) 92, p. 93.
"Room" (tr. of Nabaneeta Dev Sen, w. Sunil B. Ray). [ChiR] (38:1/2) 92, p. 17.
"So Many Crazy Blue Hills" (tr. of Nabaneeta Dev Sen, w. Sunil B. Ray). [ChiR] (38:1/2) 92, p. 18-19.
"Survivor's Story" (For Istvan). [CreamCR] (16:2) Fall 92, p. 68-69.
"Wooden Mill" (tr. of Jorge Teillier). [TampaR] (5) Fall 92, p. 60.

7047. WRIGHT, Charles
"Absence inside an Absence." [SouthernR] (28:4) Aut, O 92, p. 919.

"As Our Bodies Rise, Our Names Turn into Light." [MichQR] (31:3) Sum 92, p. 362.
"East of the Blue Ridge, Our Tombs Are in the Dove's Throat." [SouthwR] (77:2/3) Spr-Sum 92, p. 231.
"Miles Davis and Elizabeth Bishop Fake the Break." [Poetry] (160:6) S 92, p. 311.
"Not Everyone Can See the Truth, But He Can Be It." [MichQR] (31:3) Sum 92, p. 361.
"Peccatology." [Poetry] (160:6) S 92, p. 312.
"Still Life with Spring and Time to Burn." [SouthernR] (28:4) Aut, O 92, p. 918.
"There Is No Shelter." [ParisR] (34:125) Wint 92, p. 228.
"To the Egyptian Mummy in the Etruscan Museum at Cortona." [ParisR] (34:125) Wint 92, p. 227.
"With Eddie and Nancy in Arezzo at the Caffe Grande." [Field] (47) Fall 92, p. 100.
"With Simic and Marinetti at the Giubbe Rosse." [Field] (47) Fall 92, p. 101.

7048. WRIGHT, Franz
"Entry in an Unknown Hand." [ThRiPo] (39/40) 92-93, p. 283-285.
"Joseph Come Back As the Dusk (1950-1982)." [ThRiPo] (39/40) 92-93, p. 283.
"The Needle: For a Friend Who Disappeared." [ThRiPo] (39/40) 92-93, p. 281-282.
"Pawtucket Postcards." [ThRiPo] (39/40) 92-93, p. 282-283.
"Planes." [Field] (47) Fall 92, p. 116-117.
"Untitled: The unanswering cold, like a stepfather." [Field] (47) Fall 92, p. 119.
"The Weeping." [Field] (47) Fall 92, p. 118.

7049. WRIGHT, Howard
"After Rain." [Verse] (9:3) Wint 92, p. 12.
"The Bachelor's Walk." [Verse] (8:3/9:1) Wint-Spr 92, p. 135.
"Pennies." [Verse] (9:3) Wint 92, p. 13.
"Second Front." [Bogg] (65) 92, p. 9.
"To a Stiltwalker." [Verse] (9:3) Wint 92, p. 12.

7050. WRIGHT, Kirby
"The Mark of the Ass." [ArtfulD] (22/23) 92, p. 93.

7051. WRIGHT, Nancy Means
"Aunt Jo Refuses Physical Therapy." [SmPd] (29:3, #86) Fall 92, p. 12.
"Changing Direction" (for Alice). [SmPd] (29:3, #86) Fall 92, p. 10-11.
"Opportunist." [Outbr] (23) 92, p. 19-20.
"Passing Place." [SmPd] (29:3, #86) Fall 92, p. 8-9.

7052. WRIGHT, Oscar L.
"I Read in the Newspaper Today That." [Epiphany] (3:1) Ja (Wint) 92, p. 8-9.
"Thanatopsis." [Epiphany] (3:1) Ja (Wint) 92, p. 10.
"There Is a Special Place." [Epiphany] (3:1) Ja (Wint) 92, p. 7.

7053. WRIGHT, Terry
"Art Studio." [Epiphany] (3:3) Jl (Sum) 92, p. 165.
"Chapel." [Epiphany] (3:3) Jl (Sum) 92, p. 166.
"Eclipse." [Epiphany] (3:3) Jl (Sum) 92, p. 167.
"Play Rehearsal." [Epiphany] (3:3) Jl (Sum) 92, p. 164.
"Portrait." [Epiphany] (3:3) Jl (Sum) 92, p. 163.

7054. WRIGHT, Tom
"Beat Time." [HawaiiR] (16:2, #35) Spr 92, p. 93.

7055. WRIGLEY, Robert
"Confession." [PoetryNW] (33:4) Wint 92-93, p. 22.
"Cosmography" (for Jordan). [IndR] (15:1) Spr 92, p. 75.
"Hal's Bells." [PoetryNW] (33:4) Wint 92-93, p. 23.
"The New World." [IndR] (15:1) Spr 92, p. 76-77.
"Some Dream of Us." [YellowS] (41) Fall-Wint 92-93, p. 29.

WTK
See W. T. K.

7056. WUNDHEILER, Luitgard N.
"At the white phylacteries" (tr. of Paul Celan). [PartR] (59:2) Spr 92, p. 265.
"Corroded by the undreamed" (tr. of Paul Celan). [PartR] (59:2) Spr 92, p. 264.
"Flower" (tr. of Paul Celan). [PartR] (59:2) Spr 92, p. 263.
"Pale filaments of suns" (tr. of Paul Celan). [PartR] (59:2) Spr 92, p. 264.
"With their masts singing earthwards" (tr. of Paul Celan). [PartR] (59:2) Spr 92, p. 264.

7057. WURSTER, Michael
"Discipline." [PoetL] (87:2) Sum 92, p. 10.

7058. WYATT, Charles
"Advice to the Flute Player." [BelPoJ] (42:4) Sum 92, p. 16-21.

"The Day Is Made of Rain." [BellR] (15:2) Fall 92, p. 39.
"Journey to Bethesda." [NegC] (12:3) 92, p. 123-128.
"Translations of Dreams." [Nimrod] (36:1) Fall-Wint 92, p. 125-128.
"Translations of Dreams II." [Nimrod] (36:1) Fall-Wint 92, p. 129-131.
"Translations of Dreams III." [Nimrod] (36:1) Fall-Wint 92, p. 132-134.
"Translations of Dreams IV." [Nimrod] (36:1) Fall-Wint 92, p. 135-138.

7059. WYATT, Thomas
"They Flee from Me." [CimR] (98) Ja 92, p. 101.

7060. WYMAN, Linda
"Planting Forsythia on April 4" (for G. G., 1879-1984). [CapeR] (27:2) Fall 92, p. 39.

7061. WYNAND, Derk
"Kingdoms of Absence." [PraF] (13:4, #61) Wint 92-93, p. 97.
"Little Spring Songs." [AntigR] (89) Spr 92, p. 33-34.
"My Narcissus." [AntigR] (89) Spr 92, p. 35.
"Sombre." [MalR] (100) Fall 92, p. 114.
"Starlings One August." [MalR] (100) Fall 92, p. 111-112.
"This Morning, Hanging by a Thread." [AntigR] (90) Sum 92, p. 21.
"The Uncommon Flowers." [MalR] (100) Fall 92, p. 113.
"Winter Structures." [AntigR] (90) Sum 92, p. 20.
"Wintry Light." [AntigR] (90) Sum 92, p. 19.

7062. WYNNE, Warrick
"20 Thousand Leagues Under the Sea" (for Isabelle). [Vis] (40) 92, p. 15.

7063. WYNNYCKYJ, Andrij
"Mingus from Lviv." [PraF] (13:3, #60) Aut 92, p. 188.
"This Time." [PraF] (13:3, #60) Aut 92, p. 189.

XIAO-HONG, Min
See MIN, Xiao-Hong

XIAOLONG, Qiu
See QIU, Xiaolong

7064. XIE, Tracy
"Mounting the Yellow Crane Tower" (tr. of Li Po, w. Gail Ghai). [Epiphany] (3:1) Ja (Wint) 92, p. 28.
"Parched Grasses" (tr. of Li Po, w. Gail Ghai). [Epiphany] (3:1) Ja (Wint) 92, p. 29.
"Quiet Night Thoughts" (tr. of Li Po, w. Gail Ghai). [Epiphany] (3:1) Ja (Wint) 92, p. 30.

7065. XU, Haixin
"Deep South Mountain" (tr. of Wei Wang, w. Tony Barnstone and Willis Barnstone). [LitR] (25:2) Wint 92, p. 220.
"For Someone Far Away" (tr. of Wei Wang, w. Tony Barnstone and Willis Barnstone). [LitR] (25:2) Wint 92, p. 220.
"In the Mountains" (tr. of Wei Wang, w. Tony Barnstone and Willis Barnstone). [LitR] (25:2) Wint 92, p. 221.
"Lakeside Pavilion" (tr. of Wei Wang, w. Tony Barnstone and Willis Barnstone). [LitR] (25:2) Wint 92, p. 221.
"Night Over the Huai River" (tr. of Wei Wang, w. Tony Barnstone and Willis Barnstone). [LitR] (25:2) Wint 92, p. 220.
"Winter Night, Writing About My Emotion" (tr. of Wei Wang, w. Tony Barnstone and Willis Barnstone). [LitR] (25:2) Wint 92, p. 221.

XUELIANG, Chen
See CHEN, Xueliang

7066. YALIM, Özcan
"Those Women" (tr. by Talat Sait Halman). [Trans] (26) Spr 92, p. 88.

7067. YAMADA, Leona
"Breaking Steps." [HawaiiR] (16:2, #35) Spr 92, p. 75-76.

7068. YAMANAKA, Lois-Ann
"Girlie and Asi Frenz4-Eva." [HawaiiR] (16:2, #35) Spr 92, p. 9-10.
"Prince PoPo, Prince JiJi." [Zyzzyva] (8:4) Wint 92, p. 118-120.

7069. YAMRUS, John
"He Had One Eye." [Bogg] (65) 92, p. 50.

7070. YANCY, Keith
"Death Flight." [Obs] (7:1/2) Spr-Sum 92, p. 132-133.
"Doing the Daddy Thing." [Obs] (7:1/2) Spr-Sum 92, p. 127-128.
"Dumb Shit." [Obs] (7:1/2) Spr-Sum 92, p. 128-129.
"A Good Day in a Bad Neighborhood." [Obs] (7:1/2) Spr-Sum 92, p. 130-131.
"Green." [Obs] (7:1/2) Spr-Sum 92, p. 133-134.

"The Legend." [AfAmRev] (26:2) Sum 92, p. 240.
"The Legend." [Obs] (7:1/2) Spr-Sum 92, p. 131-132.
"Old Black Men That Done Made It." [Obs] (7:1/2) Spr-Sum 92, p. 129-130.

7071. YANDOW, Andrea
"For Adrienne Rich, On Language" (erratum: title has "Andrienne" instead of "Adrienne"). [GreenMR] (NS 5:2) Spr-Sum 92, p. 110-112.

7072. YANEZ, Mirta
"Chronology." [LitR] (35:4) Sum 92, p. 468-469.
"The Duties of Womanhood." [LitR] (35:4) Sum 92, p. 469.

7073. YANG, Lian
"City of the Dead Poets" (tr. by Heather S. J. Steliga. w. Shi-Zheng Chen). [GrahamHR] (16) Fall 92, p. 100.
"Games of Lies" (tr. by Heather S. J. Steliga. w. Shi-Zheng Chen). [GrahamHR] (16) Fall 92, p. 98-99.
"War Museum" (tr. by Heather S. J. Steliga. w. Shi-Zheng Chen). [GrahamHR] (16) Fall 92, p. 101-102.
"Winter Garden" (tr. by Heather S. J. Steliga. w. Shi-Zheng Chen). [GrahamHR] (16) Fall 92, p. 95-97.

7074. YANNONE, Sandra
"Bess Houdini Remembers Night Before the Modern World." [Ploughs] (18:4) Wint 92-93, p. 195.

7075. YANOFF, J. M.
"D." [DenQ] (26:4) Spr 92, p. 72.

YAPING, Tang
See TANG, Ya Ping

7076. YARBROUGH, R. Scott
"While She Is In Michigan." [CreamCR] (16:2) Fall 92, p. 11.

7077. YARBROUGH, Roberta Zybach
"In Coping Mode." [Kaleid] (25) Sum-Fall 92, p. 39.
"Monthly Visit to the Clinic." [Kaleid] (25) Sum-Fall 92, p. 39.

7078. YAU, John
"Angel Atrapado VI." [AmerPoR] (21:6) N-D 92, p. 4.
"Angel Atrapado XV." [AmerPoR] (21:6) N-D 92, p. 4-5.
"Angel Atrapado XVII." [AmerPoR] (21:6) N-D 92, p. 5.
"Avila." [AmerPoR] (21:6) N-D 92, p. 4.
"Avila 2." [AmerPoR] (21:6) N-D 92, p. 4.
"Avila 3." [AmerPoR] (21:6) N-D 92, p. 4.
"Chinese Landscape Above Caracas." [AmerPoR] (21:6) N-D 92, p. 3.
"Diptych." [AmerPoR] (21:6) N-D 92, p. 6.
"Each Other 1." [AmerPoR] (21:6) N-D 92, p. 5.
"Each Other 2." [AmerPoR] (21:6) N-D 92, p. 5.
"Each Other 3." [AmerPoR] (21:6) N-D 92, p. 5.
"Each Other 4." [AmerPoR] (21:6) N-D 92, p. 5.
"Each Other 5." [AmerPoR] (21:6) N-D 92, p. 6.
"Each Other 6." [AmerPoR] (21:6) N-D 92, p. 6.
"The Painter Asks" (for Brice Marden). [AmerPoR] (21:6) N-D 92, p. 3.
"Second Diptych." [PaintedB] (46) 92, p. 31.

7079. YAVUZ, Hilmi
"Mystery" (tr. by Feyyaz Fergar). [Trans] (26) Spr 92, p. 16-17.

7080. YEASTING, J. E.
"Idolatry." [Kalliope] (14:1) 92, p. 8.

7081. YEATS, George
"Poem of Lancelot Switchback." [SouthernR] (28:3) Sum, Jl 92, p. 497-498.

7082. YEN, Linda
"Breaking Away." [Gypsy] (19) 92, p. 23.

7083. YENSER, Stephen
"A Table of Greene Fields" (For Willard Yenser). [PartR] (59:3) Sum 92, p. 476.

7084. YERPE, Dale G.
"Conversation about Sex with My Father on the Way Home from Little League, Pulled Over by the Gas Station." [CumbPR] (11:2) Spr 92, p. 40.
"Marriage Vow: The Mother of the Groom." [CumbPR] (11:2) Spr 92, p. 41.

7085. YEVTUSHENKO, Yevgeny
"A Smell of Salting" (For V. Bokov, tr. by Olga Pelensky). [Vis] (39) 92, p. 34.

YISRAEL, Shulamith Bat
See BAT-YISRAEL, Shulamith

7086. YODER, Cynthia F.
"In Your House" (To my grandmother on her 80th birthday). [Elf] (2:3) Fall 92, p. 37.
7087. YOHANCE, L.
"The Death Poem." [Obs] (7:1/2) Spr-Sum 92, p. 135-136.
YONG-WOON, Han
See HAN, Yong-Woon
YOON, Sik Kim
See KIM, Yoon Sik
7088. YOPP, Julie Brinson
"Downtown II: Lucky St." [MoodySI] (27) Spr 92, p. 46.
7089. YORK, Maggie
"The Longest Day." [Verse] (9:3) Wint 92, p. 147.
"Mars." [Verse] (9:3) Wint 92, p. 147.
7090. YOSHIHARA, Sachiko
"Merry-Go-Round" (tr. by Anna Watson). [Vis] (38) 92, p. 21.
7091. YOSHIKAWA, Tsuneko
"Cherry-Falling-Moon Maze" (tr. by Sherry Reniker). [Noctiluca] (1:1) Spr 92, p. 50-51.
"Town of Complete Strangers" (tr. by Sherry Reniker). [Noctiluca] (1:2) Wint 92 [on cover: Wint 93], p. 21-23.
7092. YOUNG, Brian
"City Meat." [AnotherCM] (23) Spr 92, p. 178-179.
"Prometheus in the Alcoholic Rain." [Ploughs] (18:1) Spr 92, p. 102.
"Public Television." [AnotherCM] (23) Spr 92, p. 176-177.
"Snowing Desert." [Ploughs] (18:1) Spr 92, p. 101.
"Valarie." [Ploughs] (18:1) Spr 92, p. 100.
7093. YOUNG, David
"About the Brain" (tr. of Miroslav Holub, w. Dana Hábová). [GrahamHR] (16) Fall 92, p. 38-39.
"Imagination" (tr. of Miroslav Holub, w. Dana Hábová). [GrahamHR] (16) Fall 92, p. 36-37.
"My Mother Learns Spanish" (tr. of Miroslav Holub, w. Dana Hábová). [Field] (47) Fall 92, p. 76-77.
"Spinal Cord" (tr. of Miroslav Holub, w. Dana Hábová). [Field] (47) Fall 92, p. 75.
"The Third Language" (tr. of Miroslav Holub, w. Dana Hábová). [GrahamHR] (16) Fall 92, p. 40-41.
7094. YOUNG, Dean
"The Business of Love Is Cruelty." [PoetryE] (33) Spr 92, p. 153-154.
"Note to Tony Enclosed with My Old Jean Jacket." [IndR] (15:2) Fall 92, p. 3-5.
"On Being Asked by a Student If He Should Ask Out a Certain Girl." [Thrpny] (48) Wint 92, p. 18.
"Storms." [AmerPoR] (21:2) Mr-Ap 92, p. 14.
"While You Were at the Doctor's." [IndR] (15:2) Fall 92, p. 6-7.
7095. YOUNG, Ellen Roberts
"Worship." [ChrC] (109:18) 20-27 My 92, p. 549.
7096. YOUNG, Geoffrey
"Purring Poetry" (Excerpt, tr. of Francis Picabia). [Avec] (5:1) 92, p. 89-92.
7097. YOUNG, George
"A Fine and Wondrous Fire." [LitR] (25:2) Wint 92, p. 225.
7098. YOUNG, Jim
"Lovey-Dovey." [Light] (4) Wint 92-93, p. 11.
"Thanksgiving." [Wind] (22:71) 92, p. 37.
7099. YOUNG, Karl
"Milestones, Set 2" (Selections). [Noctiluca] (1:1) Spr 92, p. 23-24.
7100. YOUNG, Kevin
"Degrees." [GrahamHR] (16) Fall 92, p. 29.
"Whitewash." [GrahamHR] (16) Fall 92, p. 28.
7101. YOUNG, Michael T.
"The Curious Little Girl" (A painting by Camille Corot). [HiramPoR] (51/52) Fall 91-Sum 92, p. 86.
7102. YOUNG, Patricia
"Among the Yellow Lilies." [MalR] (100) Fall 92, p. 165.
"Another Tangerine." [MalR] (100) Fall 92, p. 168.
"Blue Salt and Silence." [Footwork] 92, p. 30.
"Boyfriends." [Grain] (20:4) Wint 92, p. 135-136.

"Carpeted Silence." [Footwork] 92, p. 28.
"Choosing an Image to Live With." [Quarry] (41:2) Spr 92, p. 63-64.
"Fantastic Revenge." [Grain] (20:4) Wint 92, p. 136-137.
"The Gift." [MalR] (100) Fall 92, p. 171-172.
"Invisible Among Us." [Footwork] 92, p. 28.
"It Used to Be." [Footwork] 92, p. 28.
"Merry-Go-Round." [Event] (21:2) Sum 92, p. 48-49.
"Movie Star Kisses." [PraF] (13:4, #61) Wint 92-93, p. 99.
"The Octopus Dines Out." [PraF] (13:4, #61) Wint 92-93, p. 98.
"Raking the Moon." [MalR] (100) Fall 92, p. 166-167.
"Repair Van." [Footwork] 92, p. 29.
"Scrap!" [Footwork] 92, p. 29.
"Sick Child." [Event] (21:2) Sum 92, p. 50.
"Speeding Down the Coast." [Footwork] 92, p. 29.
"Track and Field Day." [Footwork] 92, p. 30.
"A Treeless Country." [MalR] (100) Fall 92, p. 169-170.
"Verbascum." [Quarry] (41:2) Spr 92, p. 64-65.

7103. YOUNG, Ree
"What Counts." [EngJ] (81:2) F 92, p. 97.

7104. YOUNG BEAR, Ray (Ray A.)
"Coming Back Home." [Jacaranda] (6:1/2) Wint-Spr 92, p. 104-105.
"In the First Place of My Life" (Excerpts from "Black Eagle Child: The Facepaint Narratives"). [GeoR] (46:1) Spr 92, p. 116-125.

7105. YOUNGBLOM, Tracy
"Growing Big." [Shen] (42:4) Wint 92, p. 99.
"O Earthly Zion." [Shen] (42:4) Wint 92, p. 98.

7106. YOUNGS, Anne Ohman
"Landscapes on Fourth Street." [Elf] (2:4) Wint 92, p. 32.
"A Reason for Distance." [MidwQ] (33:3) Spr 92, p. 321.

7107. YU, Jian
"Fish" (tr. by the Beloit/Fudan Translation Workshop). [ManhatR] (6:2) Fall 92, p. 20-21.

7108. YUAN, Chen
"The Slumming-Place" (version by Michael Benedikt). [Light] (2) Sum 92, p. 18.
"The Summer Palace" (tr. by Witter Bynner). [Light] (2) Sum 92, p. 18.

YUN, Wang
See WANG, Yun

7109. YUNGKANS, Jonathan
"Frederick's, Hollywood Blvd." [Pearl] (15) Spr-Sum 92, p. 59.
"What Goes Around Comes Around." [Pearl] (16) Fall 92, p. 28.

7110. YURKIEVICH, Saúl
"Cockcrow from Afar" (tr. by Cola Franzen). [WorldL] (3) 92, p. 9.
"The park shrunk to its wintry marrow" (tr. by Cola Franzen). [WorldL] (3) 92, p. 8.
"Quiet" (tr. by Cola Franzen). [NewOR] (19:3/4) Fall-Wint 92, p. 125.
"Winnowing" (tr. by Cola Franzen). [WorldL] (3) 92, p. 10-12.

7111. YURMAN, R.
"Polyp." [Parting] (5:2) Wint 92-93, p. 27.

7112. ZABIELSKI, Laverne
"Caste." [Sun] (200) Ag 92, p. 16.

7113. ZABLE, Jeffrey
"For a Split Second." [NewYorkQ] (48) 92, p. 115.
"In Appreciation." [Lactuca] (15) Mr 92, p. 4.

7114. ZABOROWSKI, K. Copeland
"Nuclear Pregnancy." [JINJPo] (14:1) Spr 92, p. 1-2.

7115. ZABRANSKY, Richard
"Isis and Osiris." [WillowR] (19) Spr 92, p. 9.
"I've Been Told I Take Things Too Seriously." [SpoonRQ] (17:3/4) Sum-Fall 92, p. 24-25.
"My Wife Sends Us to Adoption Class." [SpoonRQ] (17:3/4) Sum-Fall 92, p. 22-23.
"Prayer Flags at 18,000 Feet." [WillowR] (19) Spr 92, p. 10-11.

7116. ZABUZHKO, Oksana
"A Definition of Poetry" (tr. by Michael M. Naydan). [Agni] (36) 92, p. 9-10.
"Night Tram" (in Ukrainian and English, tr. by James Brasfield). [InterPR] (18:2) Fall 92, p. 10-11.
"Sweetness of words" (in Ukrainian and English, tr. by James Brasfield). [InterPR] (18:2) Fall 92, p. 12-13.

"Throw on a flagrant cape" (in Ukrainian and English, tr. by James Brasfield). [InterPR] (18:2) Fall 92, p. 8-9.

7117. ZACEK, Jirí
"Night at the Singles Dorm" (tr. by Dominika Winterová and Richard Katrovas). [NewOR] (19:3/4) Fall-Wint 92, p. 29.

7118. ZAGAJEWSKI, Adam
"Incorporeal Ruler" (tr. by Renata Gorczynski, Benjamin Ivry, and C. K. Williams). [Thrpny] (48) Wint 92, p. 4.

7119. ZALLER, Robert
"The Howling" (tr. of Lili Bita). [InterPR] (18:2) Fall 92, p. 5, 7.

7120. ZALUSKI, John
"Manhattan Elegy" (Selection from "The Singing Bridge: A National AIDS Poetry Archive"). [Art&Und] (1:2) Wint 92, p. 16.

7121. ZAMORA, Daisy
"I Am Going to Speak of My Women" (tr. by Diane Kendig). [SingHM] (20) 92, p. 27-29.

7122. ZANDVAKILI, Katayoon
"The Green." [MassR] (23:3) Fall 92, p. 462.
"Untitled: Now, love at twenty-four." [MassR] (23:3) Fall 92, p. 463.

ZANT, Frank Van
See Van ZANT, Frank

7123. ZANZOTTO, Andrea
"Horizons" (tr. by Corrado Federici). [PoetryC] (13:1) N 92, p. 21.
"Idiom (Idioma)" (8 selections, tr. by Beverly Allen). [Sulfur] (12:2, #31) Fall 92, p. 220-228.

7124. ZARDOYA, Concha
"Fuego Intacto" (Elegía a Vicente Aleixandre). [InterPR] (18:1) Spr 92, p. 40, 42.
"Intact Fire" (Elegy for Vicente Aleixandre, tr. by Carmen Sotomayor). [InterPR] (18:1) Spr 92, p. 41, 43.

7125. ZARIN, Cynthia
"The Anthill." [NewYorker] (68:38) 9 N 92, p. 88.
"Fire Lyric." [YaleR] (80:3) Jl 92, p. 135-136.
"The Mechanical Arm." [NewRep] (207:25) 14 D 92, p. 32.
"The Pamet Puma." [ParisR] (34:122) Spr 92, p. 270-271.
"Recollection." [ParisR] (34:122) Spr 92, p. 272.
"Ruby at Auction" (for Vickie Karp). [NewRep] (206:23) 8 Je 92, p. 48.
"White Violets in South Hadley." [NewYorker] (68:34) 12 O 92, p. 88.

7126. ZAROU-ZOUZOUNIS, Lorene
"Her Heart Is a Rose Petal and Her Skin Is Granite." [CityLR] (5) 92, p. 182-183.

7127. ZARUCCHI, Roy
"Dear Bud." [Pembroke] (24) 92, p. 77.

7128. ZARZAR, Nancy Craig
"Burial." [SouthernPR] (32:1) Spr 92, p. 38-40.
"Journal Entry, August 26, 1965." [SouthernPR] (32:1) Spr 92, p. 41-42.

7129. ZARZYSKI, Paul
"Hurley High." [CreamCR] (16:1) Spr 92, p. 93.
"Salt Water Love." [CreamCR] (16:1) Spr 92, p. 90-92.

7130. ZAWINSKI, Andrena
"First Kiss" (W. Va., Autumn). [Elf] (2:2) Sum 92, p. 39.
"Moving Day, 4th of July." [Kalliope] (15:1) 92, p. 10.

7131. ZAYAS, Coral
"Desde la Ventana de un Banco, 8th Street." [Nuez] (4:10/11) 92, p. 24.

7132. ZEALAND, Karen
"At the Borderline." [HayF] (11) Fall-Wint 92, p. 62.
"Passion at the Chat 'n Chew Diner." [ThRiPo] (39/40) 92-93, p. 285-286.
"The Primitives Knew How Defenseless." [ThRiPo] (39/40) 92-93, p. 286-287.
"A Still Life, Untitled." [ThRiPo] (39/40) 92-93, p. 286.

7133. ZECK, Greg
"Auroral." [Bogg] (65) 92, p. 57.

7134. ZEIDNER, Lisa
"Bach." [ThRiPo] (39/40) 92-93, p. 288-289.
"Kafka Poem." [ThRiPo] (39/40) 92-93, p. 290.
"Transvestite." [ThRiPo] (39/40) 92-93, p. 287-288.

7135. ZEIGER, David
"Brazil's Disposable Children." [FreeL] (9) Wint 92, p. 9.

7136. ZEIGER, Gene
"The Box." [PassN] (13:2) Wint 92, p. 9.
7137. ZEIGER, Lila
"Some Famous Artist Clerihews." [Light] (1) Spr 92, p. 25.
7138. ZEIGLER, Geraldine
"Happy Birthday." [SmPd] (29:1, #84) Wint 92, p. 8.
7139. ZEISER, Linda
"Fearless Lady, Fearful Times" (For My Jan). [ChironR] (11:4) Wint 92, p. 14.
"Notes From a Jewess." [ChironR] (11:4) Wint 92, p. 14.
"Waxing the Moon on Sundays." [ChironR] (11:4) Wint 92, p. 14.
7140. ZELCER, Brook
"Anything But Amish." [WormR] (32:4 #128) 92, p. 167.
"Morning Marriage." [WormR] (32:4 #128) 92, p. 167.
"Perhaps a Marigold." [WormR] (32:4 #128) 92, p. 167.
"Popular in Greenland." [WormR] (32:4 #128) 92, p. 167.
"Three-Piece Dinner with Fries." [WormR] (32:4 #128) 92, p. 168.
7141. ZELESKO, Friederike
"Federico Garcia Lorca" (Rosita stays single or the language of flowers — in different gardens, tr. by Renata Cinti). [Vis] (38) 92, p. 18.
7142. ZELL, Ann
"Water Rites." [Verse] (9:3) Wint 92, p. 9.
7143. ZELLER, Muriel
"Spring Naked Night." [BellArk] (8:6) N-D 92, p. 25.
7144. ZELTZER, Joel
"1910" (an interlude, new york, august 1929, tr. of Federico Garcia Lorca). [NewYorkQ] (47) 92, p. 97.
"Death" (tr. of Federico Garcia Lorca). [ChironR] (11:2) Sum 92, p. 4.
"Gypsy Nun" (tr. of Federico Garcia Lorca). [ChironR] (11:2) Sum 92, p. 4.
"Song of Neztahualcoyotl 1" (tr. of Alberto Ordonez Arguello). [NewYorkQ] (49) 92, p. 101.
7145. ZENITH, Richard
"Cemetery in Pernambuco" (tr. of João Cabral de Melo Neto). [Trans] (26) Spr 92, p. 42.
"Delphi, Opus 12" (Selections: 1, 4, tr. of Pedro Tamen). [LitR] (25:2) Wint 92, p. 218.
"The Hated Dice That Leave My Hand" (tr. of Pedro Tamen). [LitR] (25:2) Wint 92, p. 219.
"Knowing No Secrets Having No Visions" (tr. of António Ramos Rosa). [Stand] (33:4) Aut 92, p. 141.
"The Lover Transforms" (tr. of Herberto Helder). [Stand] (33:4) Aut 92, p. 130.
"Seated Theory — II" (tr. of Herberto Helder). [Stand] (33:4) Aut 92, p. 131.
"To Start Out from Minerals from Steep Sides" (tr. of António Ramos Rosa). [NewOR] (19:2) Sum 92, p. 18.
ZENTELLA, Marta Piña
See PIÑA ZENTELLA, Marta
ZENTNER, Robert Gurry
See GURRY-ZENTNER, Robert
7146. ZEPPA, Mary
"Bible Stories." [OxfordM] (6:2) Fall-Wint 90, p. 1-2.
"The Cat and I, Glenn Gould and Bach." [OxfordM] (8:1) Spr-Sum 92, p. 68.
"Prayer." [OxfordM] (8:1) Spr-Sum 92, p. 71-72.
"Witness." [OxfordM] (8:1) Spr-Sum 92, p. 69-70.
7147. ZERDEN, D. L.
"An Edward Hopper Album." [SouthernPR] (32:1) Spr 92, p. 5153.
7148. ZETTELMEYER, Carl
"Heading for Eszterhom." [FloridaR] (18:2) Fall-Wint 92, p. 31.
"Ritual." [FloridaR] (18:2) Fall-Wint 92, p. 30.
7149. ZHDANOV, Ivan
"On New Year's Day" (tr. by John High, w. Julie Gesin). [Avec] (5:1) 92, p. 124.
"Untitled: ('Stone')" (tr. by John High, w. Julie Gesin). [Avec] (5:1) 92, p. 124.
7150. ZIDE, Arlene
"Along the Railroad Track" (tr. of Kanchan Kuntala Mukherjee, w. Paramita Banerjee). [ChiR] (38:1/2) 92, p. 122-123.
"The Girl's Desire Moves among the Bangles" (tr. of Gagan Gill, w. Mrinal Pande). [ChiR] (38:1/2) 92, p. 106-107.

"The Husband Speaks" (tr. of Popati Hiranandani, w. the author). [ChiR] (38:1/2) 92, p. 180-181.
"Night has come to an end, the woman starts her grinding" (tr. of Aruna Dhere, w. Asha Mundlay). [ChiR] (38:1/2) 92, p. 103.
"Pariah Dog" (tr. of Amrita Pritam, w. the author). [ChiR] (38:1/2) 92, p. 132-133.
"The Tryst" (tr. of Sunanda Tripathy, w. J. P. Das). [ChiR] (38:1/2) 92, p. 211.
"Two Women Knitting" (tr. of Mrinal Pande, w. the author). [ChiR] (38:1/2) 92, p. 96.

7151. ZIEMBA, Elizabeth
"Flight Pattern." [CoalC] (5) My 92, p. 6.
"Rose." [CoalC] (5) My 92, p. 6.
"Untitled: She unwinds the coil." [CoalC] (5) My 92, p. 6.

7152. ZIMMER, Paul (Paul J.)
"The Brain of the Spider." [DenQ] (26:3) Wint 92, p. 51.
"The Day I Became a Poet." [Crazy] (43) Wint 92, p. 30.
"Easter 1991." [Crazy] (43) Wint 92, p. 29.
"The Failings." [ThRiPo] (39/40) 92-93, p. 292-294.
"Father Animus and Zimmer." [ThRiPo] (39/40) 92-93, p. 291-292.
"Intimations of Fatherhood: Operation Desert Rock, 1955." [NewL] (58:3) Spr 92, p. 72.
"Leaves of Zimmer" (from "The Zimmer Poems"). [MassR] (23:1) Spr 92, p. 106.
"The Light." [PraS] (66:3) Fall 92, p. 117-118.
"Omens in Southwest Wisconsin." [LaurelR] (26:2) Sum 92, p. 62-63.
"The Persistence of Fatherhood." [MassR] (23:3) Fall 92, p. 454.
"The Queen." [ThRiPo] (39/40) 92-93, p. 294-295.
"Raw and Absolute." [GettyR] (5:3) Sum 92, p. 390.
"Remembering Power Hitters." [GettyR] (5:3) Sum 92, p. 391.
"Shadows Flooding." [PoetryNW] (33:2) Sum 92, p. 40-41.
"Song of the Black Dog." [PoetryNW] (33:2) Sum 92, p. 40.
"What I Know About Owls." [Crazy] (43) Wint 92, p. 31.

7153. ZIMMERMAN, Ken
"Death." [PoetryE] (33) Spr 92, p. 156.
"Her Hands." [PoetryE] (33) Spr 92, p. 157.
"The Room." [PoetryE] (33) Spr 92, p. 155.

7154. ZIMMERMAN, Lisa Horton
"Persian Gulf, January 25, 1991." [BlackBR] (15) Spr-Sum 92, p. 14.

7155. ZIMMERMAN, Mark
"What Happened to Hitler's Moustache." [CreamCR] (16:1) Spr 92, p. 109.

7156. ZINNES, Harriet
"Aftermath." [DenQ] (26:4) Spr 92, p. 73-75.
"All Things Have Their Center in Their Dying." [RiverS] (36) 92, p. 30-31.
"Fishing." [Agni] (35) 92, p. 250-251.

7157. ZIOLKOWSKI, Heidi
"For Dennis Jurgens, Battered by His Adoptive Mother Until He Finally Died at the Age of 3." [ChironR] (11:2) Sum 92, p. 27-28.

7158. ZIRLIN, Larry
"Counting." [HangL] (61) 92, p. 89.

7159. ZIVANCEVIC, Nina
"Artificial Limb" (tr. of Gordana Cirjanic). [Talisman] (8) Spr 92, p. 144.
"European Show" (tr. of Liljana Djurdjic). [Talisman] (8) Spr 92, p. 144.
"For Those Who Trip Over the Doorstep" (tr. of Desanka Maksimovic). [Talisman] (8) Spr 92, p. 145.

7160. ZOLA, Jim
"Forecasting." [ChatR] (12:2) Wint 92, p. 5.
"The Long Winter." [ChatR] (12:2) Wint 92, p. 2.
"Matins." [ChatR] (12:2) Wint 92, p. 4.
"The Old Time Drummer." [ChatR] (12:2) Wint 92, p. 3.
"Phalaenopsis." [ChatR] (12:2) Wint 92, p. 1.

7161. ZOLLER, James A.
"A Finger of Ground." [OxfordM] (7:1) Spr-Sum 91, p. 2-3.
"Touring Moss Lake." [OxfordM] (7:1) Spr-Sum 91, p. 1.

7162. ZORDANI, Bob
"After the Divorce Hearing, I Confess My Sins." [SpoonRQ] (17:3/4) Sum-Fall 92, p. 126.
"A Fish Story." [YellowS] (41) Fall-Wint 92-93, p. 7-9.

7163. ZOUMÉ, Baubé
"The Sacrificial Cock." [Nimrod] (35:2) Spr-Sum 92, p. 121-122.

ZOUZOUNIS, Lorene Zarou
See ZAROU-ZOUZOUNIS, Lorene

7164. ZUBER, Isabel
"Marginalia." [AmerV] (29) 92, p. 72.

7165. ZUCKER, David
"Caught" (tr. of Gyula Illyés, w. Emoke B'racz). [WebR] (16) Fall 92, p. 31.
"Housebound." [ChatR] (12:2) Wint 92, p. 24-26.
"Moriah" (To Dennis Silk). [Thrpny] (48) Wint 92, p. 31.
"New Faces." [WebR] (16) Fall 92, p. 32.

7166. ZULAUF, Sander
"Life Is Short." [NegC] (12:3) 92, p. 129.

7167. ZWEIG, Martha
"For Peter." [ChironR] (11:2) Sum 92, p. 28.
"Two Merriments." [AnotherCM] (24) Fall 92, p. 168.

7168. ZWICKY, Jan
"Five Songs for Relinquishing the Earth." [PoetryC] (12:2) Ap 92, p. 23.
"Passing Sangudo." [PoetryC] (12:2) Ap 92, p. 23.

7169. ZYDEK, Fredrick
"Everything I Am." [Event] (21:1) Spr 92, p. 44.
"Eye of the Storm." [Footwork] 92, p. 65.
"Learning to Pray II." [ChrC] (109:23) 29 Jl-5 Ag 92, p. 713.
"Letter to Eccles at Winlock." [PraF] (13:2, #59) Sum 92, p. 45.
"Letter to Wagoner from Decatur Street." [Amelia] (6:4, #19) 92, p. 127-128.
"Omaha" (for S. J. Holmes). [Elf] (2:4) Wint 92, p. 42.
"Second Storm." [Footwork] 92, p. 65.

Title Index

Titles are arranged alphanumerically, with numerals filed in numerical order before letters. Each title is followed by one or more author entry numbers, which refer to the numbered entries in the first part of the volume. Entry numbers are preceded by a space colon space (:). Any numeral which preceeds the space colon space (:) is part of the title, not an entry number. Poems with "Untitled" in the title position are entered under "Untitled" followed by the first line of the poem and also directly under the first line. Numbered titles are entered under the number and also under the part following the number.

About the Authors

RAFAEL CATALA (B.A., M.A., Ph.D., New York University) is president of The Ometeca Institute and editor-in-chief of *The Ometeca Journal*, both dedicated to the study and encouragement of relations between the sciences and the humanities. He was born in Las Tunas, Cuba in 1942 and came to the United States in 1961. His books of poetry and literary criticism, as well as many essays and poems, have been published in the United States, Canada, Latin America, and Europe. He has taught Latin American Literature at NYU, Lafayette College, and Seton Hall University. In 1993-94 he was visiting professor at the University of Costa Rica. Catalá is a major proponent and practitioner of *cienciapoesía* (sciencepoetry), an embodiment of the integration of aesthetics, ethics, and the sciences. A new book of critical essays about Catalá's poetry and literary work will be published in 1994: *Rafael Catalá: del Círculo cuadrado a la cienciapoesía — Hacia una nueva poética latinoamericana* (Ed. by Luis A. Jiménez. Kent, WA: Ventura One).

JAMES D. ANDERSON (B.A., Harvard College, M.S.L.S., D.L.S., Columbia University) is associate dean and professor of the School of Communication, Information, and Library Studies, at Rutgers–The State University of New Jersey. His library career included service at Sheldon Jackson College, Sitka, Alaska, and the Portland (Oregon) Public Library. He taught at Columbia, St. John's, and the City University of New York before coming to Rutgers in 1977, where he specializes in the design of textual databases for information retrieval. Major projects have included the international bibliography and database of the Modern Language Association of America and the bilingual (French & English) *Bibliography of the History of Art*, sponsored by the J. Paul Getty Trust and the French Centre National de la Recherche Scientifique in Paris. At Rutgers he also chairs the President's Select Committee for Lesbian and Gay Concerns, and for the Presbyterian Church (U.S.A.), he edits and publishes the monthly journal *More Light Update*, on lesbian and gay issues within that denomination.